CRC
Standard
Mathematical
Tables

28th Edition

Editor of Mathematics and Statistics

William H. Beyer, Ph.D.
Chairman
Department of Mathematical Sciences
University of Akron
Akron, Ohio

CRC Press, Inc.
Boca Raton, Florida

Direct all inquiries to CRC Press, Inc., 2000 Corporate Blvd., N.W., Boca Raton, Florida, 33431.

© 1987 by CRC Press, Inc.
Second Printing, 1987

©1974, 1975, 1976, 1978, 1981 by CRC Press, Inc.
©1964, 1965, 1967, 1968, 1969, 1970, 1971, 1972, 1973 by The Chemical Rubber Co.

All Rights Reserved
Library of Congress Card No. 30-4052
International Standard Book No. 0-8493-0628-0

PREFACE

It has long been the estblished policy of CRC Press, Inc. to publish, in handbook form, the most up-to-date, authoritative, logically arranged, and readily usable reference material available. Prior to the preparation of this 28th Edition of the *CRC Standard Math Tables*, the contents of predecessor editions were carefully examined to determine if certain tables or reference materials should be altered, expanded, or deleted. The net result is that this 28th Edition has been prepared to provide an adequately broad spectrum of traditional and modern mathematical sciences data necessary for today's world. The *Handbook* provides an important aid to the teaching profession, to the student, and to the many other users who require the table or fact for investigating or creating answers to today's challenging problems.

The same successful format which characterized the 25th, 26th, and 27th Editions of the *Handbook* has been retained. Material is presented in a multi-sectional format, with each section containing a valuable collection of fundamental reference material — both tabular and expository. Several desirable additions — powers of numbers, partial differential equations, mathematical symbols and abbreviations — are to be noted throughout this new edition. The customary reference data contained in earlier editions is repeated. It is hoped that the changes will prove beneficial to the users of the *Handbook*. It is suggested that if the user desires more extensive and/or additional reference mateial than is provided in this *Handbook*, he or she refer to other CRC publications such as the *CRC Handbook of Mathematical Sciences*, the *CRC Handbook of Tables for Probability and Statistics*, etc.

The Editor gratefully acknowledges the services rendered by Paul Gottehrer, Editor, for the handling of the detail work which is so essential in the final production of this edition.

All errors called to our attention have, to the best of the Editor's knowledge, been corrected. As in the past, CRC Press, Inc. and the Editor invite and welcome constructive comments from the many users of the *Handbook*. These comments are a most effective means for keeping the editions of the *CRC Standard Math Tables* updated and abreast of the times.

William H. Beyer, Editor

TABLE OF CONTENTS

GREEK ALPHABET

Greek letter	Greek name	English equivalent	Greek letter	Greek name	English equivalent
A α	Alpha	a	N ν	Nu	n
B β	Beta	b	Ξ ξ	Xi	x
Γ γ	Gamma	g	O o	Omicron	ŏ
Δ δ	Delta	d	Π π	Pi	p
E ε	Epsilon	ĕ	P ρ	Rho	r
Z ζ	Zeta	z	Σ σ ς	Sigma	s
H η	Eta	ē	T τ	Tau	t
Θ θ ϑ	Theta	th	Υ υ	Upsilon	u
I ι	Iota	i	Φ φ φ	Phi	ph
K κ	Kappa	k	X χ	Chi	ch
Λ λ	Lambda	l	Ψ ψ	Psi	ps
M μ	Mu	m	Ω ω	Omega	ō

THE NUMBER OF EACH DAY OF THE YEAR

Day of Mo.	Jan.	Feb.	Mar.	Apr.	May	Jun.	Jul.	Aug.	Sep.	Oct.	Nov.	Dec.	Day of Mo.
1	1	32	60	91	121	152	182	213	244	274	305	335	1
2	2	33	61	92	122	153	183	214	245	275	306	336	2
3	3	34	62	93	123	154	184	215	246	276	307	337	3
4	4	35	63	94	124	155	185	216	247	277	308	338	4
5	5	36	64	95	125	156	186	217	248	278	309	339	5
6	6	37	65	96	126	157	187	218	249	279	310	340	6
7	7	38	66	97	127	158	188	219	250	280	311	341	7
8	8	39	67	98	128	159	189	220	251	281	312	342	8
9	9	40	68	99	129	160	190	221	252	282	313	343	9
10	10	41	69	100	130	161	191	222	253	283	314	344	10
11	11	42	70	101	131	162	192	223	254	284	315	345	11
12	12	43	71	102	132	163	193	224	255	285	316	346	12
13	13	44	72	103	133	164	194	225	256	286	317	347	13
14	14	45	73	104	134	165	195	226	257	287	318	348	14
15	15	46	74	105	135	166	196	227	258	288	319	349	15
16	16	47	75	106	136	167	197	228	259	289	320	350	16
17	17	48	76	107	137	168	198	229	260	290	321	351	17
18	18	49	77	108	138	169	199	230	261	291	352	352	18
19	19	50	78	109	139	170	200	231	262	292	323	353	19
20	20	51	79	110	140	171	201	232	263	293	324	354	20
21	21	52	80	111	141	172	202	233	264	294	325	355	21
22	22	53	81	112	142	173	203	234	265	295	326	356	22
23	23	54	82	113	143	174	204	235	266	296	327	357	23
24	24	55	83	114	144	175	205	236	267	297	328	358	24
25	25	56	84	115	145	176	206	237	268	298	329	359	25
26	26	57	85	116	146	177	207	238	269	299	330	360	26
27	27	58	86	117	147	178	208	239	270	300	331	361	27
28	28	59	87	118	148	179	209	240	271	301	332	362	28
29	29	*	88	119	149	180	210	241	272	302	333	363	29
30	30		89	120	150	181	211	242	273	303	334	364	30
31	31		90		151		212	243		304		365	31

* In leap years, after February 28, add 1 to the tabulated number.

SI SYSTEM OF MEASUREMENT

SI, which is the abbreviation of the French words "Système Internationale d'Unites," is the accepted abbreviation for the International Metric System, which has seven base units, as shown below.

UNITS FOR A SYSTEM OF MEASURES AS USED INTERNATIONALLY

Quantity measured	Unit	Abbreviation
Length	meter	m
Mass	kilogram	kg
Time	second	s
Electric current	ampere	A
Temperature	degree Kelvin	K
Luminous intensity	candela	cd
Amount of substance	mole	mol

RECOMMENDED DECIMAL MULTIPLES AND SUBMULTIPLES

Multiples and submultiples	Prefixes	Symbols
10^{18}	exa	E
10^{15}	peca	P
10^{12}	tera	T
10^{9}	giga	G
10^{6}	mega	M
10^{3}	kilo	k
10^{2}	hecto	h
10	deca	da
10^{-1}	deci	d
10^{-2}	centi	c
10^{-3}	milli	m
10^{-6}	micro	μ (greek mu)
10^{-9}	nano	n
10^{-12}	pico	p
10^{-15}	femto	f
10^{-18}	atto	a

Conversion Factors – Metric to English

To obtain	Multiply	By
Inches	Centimeters	0.3937007874
Feet	Meters	3.280839895
Yards	Meters	1.093613298
Miles	Kilometers	0.6213711922
Ounces	Grams	$3.527396195 \times 10^{-2}$
Pounds	Kilograms	2.204622622
Gallons(U.S. Liquid)	Liters	0.2641720524
Fluid ounces	Milliliters (cc)	$3.381402270 \times 10^{-2}$
Square inches	Square centimeters	0.1550003100
Square feet	Square meters	10.76391042
Square yards	Square meters	1.195990046
Cubic inches	Milliliters (cc)	$6.102374409 \times 10^{-2}$
Cubic feet	Cubic meters	35.31466672
Cubic yards	Cubic meters	1.307950619

Conversion Factors – English to Metric*

To obtain	Multiply	By
Microns	Mils	**25.4**
Centimeters	Inches	**2.54**
Meters	Feet	**0.3048**
Meters	Yards	**0.9144**
Kilometers	Miles	**1.609344**
Grams	Ounces	28.34952313
Kilograms	Pounds	0.45359237
Liters	Gallons (U.S. Liquid)	3.785411784
Milliliters (cc)	Fluid ounces	29.57352956
Square centimeters	Square inches	**6.4516**
Square meters	Square feet	**0.09290304**
Square meters	Square yards	**0.83612736**
Milliliters (cc)	Cubic inches	**16.387064**
Cubic meters	Cubic feet	$2.831684659 \times 10^{-2}$
Cubic meters	Cubic yards	0.764554858

Conversion Factors – General*

To obtain	Multiply	By
Atmospheres	Feet of water @ 4°C	2.950×10^{-2}
Atmospheres	Inches of mercury @ 0°C	3.342×10^{-2}
Atmospheres	Pounds per square inch	6.804×10^{-2}
BTU	Foot-pounds	1.285×10^{-3}
BTU	Joules	9.480×10^{-4}
Cubic feet	Cords	**128**

*Boldface numbers are exact; others are given to ten significant figures where so indicated by the multiplier factor.

Conversion Factors – General (Continued)

To obtain	Multiply	By
Degree (angle)	Radians	57.2958
Ergs	Foot-pounds	1.356×10^7
Feet	Miles	**5280**
Feet of water @ 4°C	Atmospheres	33.90
Foot-pounds	Horsepower-hours	1.98×10^6
Foot-pounds	Kilowatt-hours	2.655×10^6
Food-pounds per min	Horsepower	3.3×10^4
Horsepower	Foot-pounds per sec	1.818×10^{-3}
Inches of mercury @ 0°C	Pounds per square inch	2.036
Joules	BTU	1054.8
Joules	Foot-pounds	1.35582
Kilowatts	BTU per min	1.758×10^{-2}
Kilowatts	Foot-pounds per min	2.26×10^{-5}
Kilowatts	Horsepower	0.745712
Knots	Miles per hour	0.86897624
Miles	Feet	1.894×10^{-4}
Nautical miles	Miles	0.86897624
Radians	Degrees	1.745×10^{-2}
Square feet	Acres	**43560**
Watts	BTU per min	17.5796

Temperature Factors

$$°F = 9/5 \, (°C) + 32$$

Fahrenheit temperature = 1.8 (temperature in kelvins) -459.67

$$°C = 5/9 \, [(°F) - 32]$$

Celsius temperature = temperature in kelvins -273.15

Fahrenheit temperature = 1.8 (Celsius temperature) $+32$

DECIMAL EQUIVALENTS OF FRACTIONS OF AN INCH

```
          1/64 =  0.015 625         11/32 22/64 = 0.343 75                      43/64 = 0.671 875
   1/32   2/64 =   .031 25                23/64 =  .359 375   11/16 22/32 44/64 =  .687 5
          3/64 =   .046 875   3/8   12/32 24/64 =  .375                         45/64 =  .703 125
1/16 2/32 4/64 =   .062 5                 25/64 =  .390 625            23/32 46/64 =  .718 75
          5/64 =   .078 125         13/32 26/64 =  .406 25                      47/64 =  .734 375
   3/32   6/64 =   .093 75                27/64 =  .421 875   3/4 24/32 48/64 =  .75
          7/64 =   .109 375   7/16 14/32 28/64 =  .437 5                       49/64 =  .765 625
1/8  4/32 8/64 =   .125                   29/64 =  .453 125            25/32 50/64 =  .781 25
          9/64 =   .140 625         15/32 30/64 =  .468 75                      51/64 =  .796 875
   5/32  10/64 =   .156 25                31/64 =  .484 375   13/16 26/32 52/64 =  .812 5
         11/64 =   .171 875   1/2   16/32 32/64 =  .50                          53/64 =  .828 125
3/16 6/32 12/64 =  .187 5                 33/64 =  .515 625            27/32 54/64 =  .843 75
         13/64 =   .203 125         17/32 34/64 =  .531 25                      55/64 =  .859 375
   7/32  14/64 =   .218 75                35/64 =  .546 875   7/8 28/32 56/64 =  .875
         15/64 =   .234 375   9/16 18/32 36/64 =  .562 5                        57/64 =  .890 625
1/4  8/32 16/64 =  .25                    37/64 =  .578 125            29/32 58/64 =  .906 25
         17/64 =   .265 625         19/32 38/64 =  .593 75                      59/64 =  .921 875
   9/32  18/64 =   .281 25                39/64 =  .609 375   15/16 30/32 60/64 =  .937 5
         19/64 =   .296 875   5/8   20/32 40/64 =  .625                         61/64 =  .953 125
5/16 10/32 20/64 =  .312 5                41/64 =  .640 625            31/32 62/64 =  .968 75
         21/64 =   .328 125         21/32 42/64 =  .656 25                      63/64 =  .984 375
```

PHYSICAL CONSTANTS

Equatorial radius of the earth = 6378.388 km = 3963.34 miles (statute).
Polar radius of the earth, 6356.912 km = 3949.99 miles (statute).
1 degree of latitude at $40°$ = 69 miles.
1 international nautical mile = 1.15078 miles (statute) = 1852 m = 6076.115 ft.
Mean density of the earth = 5.522 g/cm^3 = 344.7 lb/ft^3.
Constant of gravitation, $(6.673 ± 0.003) × 10^{-8} cm^3 gm^{-1} s^{-2}$.
Acceleration due to gravity at sea level, latitude $45°=980.6194 cm/s^2$ = 32.1726 ft/sec^2.
Length of seconds pendulum at sea level, latitude $45°$ = 99.3575 cm = 39.1171 in.
1 knot (international) = 101.269 ft/min = 1.6878 ft/sec = 1.1508 miles (statute)/hr.
1 micron = 10^{-4} cm.
1 angstrom = 10^{-8} cm.
Mass of hydrogen atom = $(1.67339 ± 0.0031) × 10^{-24}$ g.
Density of mercury at $0°C$ = 13.5955 g/ml.
Density of water at $3.98°C$ = 1.000000 g/ml.
Density, maximum, of water, at $3.98°C$ = 0.999973 g/cm^3.
Density of dry air at $0°C$, 760 mm = 1.2929 g/liter.
Velocity of sound in dry air at $0°C$ = 331.36 m/s - 1087.1 ft/sec.
Velocity of light in vacuum = $(2.997925 ± 0.000002) × 10^{10}$ cm/s.
Heat of fusion of water $0°C$ = 79.71 cal/g.
Heat of vaporization of water $100°C$ = 539.55 cal/g.
Electrochemical equivalent of silver 0.001118 g/sec international amp.
Absolute wave length of red cadmium light in air at $15°C$, 760 mm pressure = 6438.4696 A.
Wave length of orange-red line of krypton 86 = 6057.802 A.

π CONSTANTS

$$\pi = 3.14159\ 26535\ 89793\ 23846\ 26433\ 83279\ 50288\ 41971\ 69399\ 37511$$
$$1/\pi = 0.31830\ 98861\ 83790\ 67153\ 77675\ 26745\ 02872\ 40689\ 19291\ 48091$$
$$\pi^2 = 9.8690\ 44010\ 89358\ 61883\ 44909\ 99876\ 15113\ 53136\ 99407\ 24079$$
$$\log_e \pi = 1.14472\ 98858\ 49400\ 17414\ 34273\ 51353\ 05871\ 16472\ 94812\ 91531$$
$$\log_{10}\pi = 0.49714\ 98726\ 94133\ 85435\ 12682\ 88290\ 89887\ 36516\ 78324\ 38044$$
$$\log_{10}\sqrt{2\pi} = 0.39908\ 99341\ 79057\ 52478\ 25035\ 91507\ 69595\ 02099\ 34102\ 92128$$

CONSTANTS INVOLVING e

$$e = 2.71828\ 18284\ 59045\ 23536\ 02874\ 71352\ 66249\ 77572\ 47093\ 69996$$
$$1/e = 0.36787\ 94411\ 71442\ 32159\ 55237\ 70161\ 46086\ 74458\ 11131\ 03177$$
$$e^2 = 7.38905\ 60989\ 30650\ 22723\ 04274\ 60575\ 00781\ 31803\ 15570\ 55185$$
$$M = \log_{10}e = 0.43429\ 44819\ 03251\ 82765\ 11289\ 18916\ 60508\ 22943\ 97005\ 80367$$
$$1/M = \log_e 10 = 2.30258\ 50929\ 94045\ 68401\ 79914\ 54684\ 36420\ 76011\ 01488\ 62877$$
$$\log_{10}M = 9.63778\ 43113\ 00536\ 78912\ 29674\ 98645 - 10$$

π' AND e^n CONSTANTS

$$\pi' = 22.45915\ 77183\ 61045\ 47342\ 71522$$
$$e^n = 23.14069\ 26327\ 79269\ 00572\ 90864$$
$$e^{-n} = 0.04321\ 39182\ 63772\ 24977\ 44177$$
$$e^{1/2\,n} = 4.81047\ 73809\ 65351\ 65547\ 30357$$
$$= e^{-1/2\,n} = 0.20787\ 95763\ 50761\ 90854\ 69556$$

NUMERICAL CONSTANTS

$$\sqrt{2} = 1.41421\ 35623\ 73095\ 04880\ 16887\ 24209\ 69807\ 85696\ 71875\ 37695$$
$$\sqrt[3]{2} = 1.25992\ 10498\ 94873\ 16476\ 72106\ 07278\ 22835\ 05702\ 51464\ 70151$$
$$\log_e 2 = 0.69314\ 71805\ 59945\ 30941\ 72321\ 21458\ 17656\ 80755\ 00134\ 36026$$
$$\log_{10}2 = 0.30102\ 99956\ 63981\ 19521\ 37388\ 94724\ 49302\ 67881\ 89881\ 46211$$
$$\sqrt{3} = 1.73205\ 08075\ 68877\ 29352\ 74463\ 41505\ 87236\ 69428\ 05253\ 81039$$
$$\sqrt[3]{3} = 1.44224\ 95703\ 07408\ 38232\ 16383\ 10780\ 10958\ 83918\ 69253\ 49935$$
$$\log_e 3 = 1.09861\ 22886\ 68109\ 69139\ 52452\ 36922\ 52570\ 46474\ 90557\ 82275$$
$$\log_{10}3 = 0.47712\ 12547\ 19662\ 43729\ 50279\ 03255\ 11530\ 92001\ 28864\ 19070$$

OTHER CONSTANTS

$$\text{Euler's Constant } \gamma = 0.57721\ 56649\ 01532\ 86061$$
$$\log_e \gamma = -0.54953\ 93129\ 81644\ 82234$$
$$\text{Golden Ratio } \phi = 1.61803\ 39887\ 49894\ 84820\ 45868\ 34365\ 63811\ 77203\ 09180$$

NUMBERS CONTAINING π

	Number	Logarithm		Number	Logarithm
π	3.1415 927	0.4971 499	$2\pi^2$	19.7392 088	1.2953 297
2π	6.2831 853	0.7981 799	$\pi/180$	0.0174 533	8.2418 774 − 10
3π	9.4247 780	0.9742 711	$180/\pi$	57.2957 795	1.7581 226
4π	12.5663 706	1.0992 099	$4\pi^2$	39.4784 176	1.5963 597
8π	25.1327 412	1.4002 399	$1/\pi^2$	0.1013 212	9.0057 003 − 10
$\pi/2$	1.5707 963	0.1961 199	$1/(2\pi^2)$	0.0506 606	8.7046 703 − 10
$\pi/3$	1.0471 976	0.0200 286	$1/(4\pi^2)$	0.0253 303	8.4036 403 − 10
$\pi/4$	0.7853 982	9.8950 899 − 10	$\sqrt{\pi}$	1.7724 539	0.2485 749
$\pi/6$	0.5235 988	9.7189 986 − 10	$\dfrac{\sqrt{\pi}}{2}$	0.8862 269	9.9475 449 − 10
$\pi/8$	0.3926 991	9.5940 599 − 10	$\dfrac{\sqrt{\pi}}{4}$	0.4431 135	9.6465 149 − 10
$2\pi/3$	2.0943 951	0.3210 586	$\sqrt{\dfrac{\pi}{2}}$	1.2533 141	0.0980 599
$4\pi/3$	4.1887 902	0.6220 886	$\sqrt{\dfrac{2}{\pi}}$	0.7978 846	9.9019 401 − 10
$1/\pi$	0.3183 099	9.5028 501 − 10	π^3	31.0062 767	1.4914 496
$2/\pi$	0.6366 198	9.8038 801 − 10	$\sqrt[3]{\pi}$	1.4645 919	0.1657 166
$4/\pi$	1.2732 395	0.1049 101	$1/\sqrt[3]{\pi}$	0.6827 841	9.8342 834 − 10
$1/(2\pi)$	0.1591 549	9.2018 201 − 10	$\sqrt[3]{\pi^2}$	2.1450 294	0.3314 332
$1/(4\pi)$	0.0795 775	8.9007 901 − 10	$1/\sqrt{\pi}$	0.5641 896	9.7514 251 − 10
$1/(6\pi)$	0.0530 516	8.7246 989 − 10	$1/\sqrt{2\pi}$	0.3989 423	9.6009 101 − 10
$1/(8\pi)$	0.0397 887	8.5997 601 − 10	$2/\sqrt{\pi}$	1.1283 792	0.0524 551
π^2	9.8696 044	0.9942 997			

MULTIPLES OF $\dfrac{\pi}{2}$

n	$n\dfrac{\pi}{2}$	n	$n\dfrac{\pi}{2}$	n	$n\dfrac{\pi}{2}$	n	$n\dfrac{\pi}{2}$
1	1.57079 63268	26	40.84070 44967	51	80.11061 26665	76	119.38502 08364
2	3.14159 26536	27	42.41150 08235	52	81.68140 89933	77	120.95131 71632
3	4.71238 89804	28	43.98229 71503	53	83.25220 53201	78	122.52211 34900
4	6.28318 53072	29	45.55309 34771	54	84.82300 16469	79	124.09290 98168
5	7.85398 16340	30	47.12388 98038	55	86.39379 79737	80	125.66370 61436
6	9.42477 79608	31	48.69468 61306	56	87.96459 43005	81	127.23450 24704
7	10.99557 42876	32	50.26548 24574	57	89.53539 06273	82	128.80529 87972
8	12.56637 06144	33	51.83627 87842	58	91.10618 69541	83	130.37609 51240
9	14.13716 69412	34	53.40707 51110	59	92.67698 32809	84	131.94689 14508
10	15.70796 32679	35	54.97787 14378	60	94.24777 96077	85	133.51768 77776
11	17.27875 95947	36	56.54866 77646	61	95.81857 59345	86	135.08848 41044
12	18.84955 59215	37	58.11946 40914	62	97.38937 22613	87	136.65928 04312
13	20.42035 22483	38	59.69026 04182	63	98.96016 85881	88	138.23007 67580
14	21.99114 85751	39	61.26105 67450	64	100.53096 49149	89	139.80087 30847
15	23.56194 49019	40	62.83185 30718	65	102.10176 12417	90	141.37166 94115
16	25.13274 12287	41	64.40264 93986	66	103.67255 75685	91	142.94246 57383
17	26.70533 75555	42	65.97344 57254	67	105.24335 38953	92	144.51326 20651
18	28.27433 38823	43	67.54424 20522	68	106.81415 02221	93	146.08405 83919
19	29.84513 02091	44	69.11503 83790	69	108.38494 65488	94	147.65485 47187
20	31.41592 65359	45	70.68583 47058	70	109.95574 28765	95	149.22565 10455
21	32.98672 28627	46	72.25663 10326	71	111.52653 92024	96	150.79644 73723
22	34.55751 91895	47	73.82742 73594	72	113.09733 55292	97	152.36724 36991
23	36.12831 55163	48	75.39822 36862	73	114.66813 18560	98	153.93804 00259
24	37.69911 18431	49	76.96902 00129	74	116.23892 81828	99	155.50883 63527
25	39.26990 81699	50	78.53981 63397	75	117.80972 45096	100	157.07963 26795

II. ALGEBRA

FACTORS AND EXPANSIONS

$(a \pm b)^2 = a^2 \pm 2ab + b^2$.

$(a \pm b)^3 = a^3 \pm 3a^2 b + 3ab^2 \pm b^3$.

$(a \pm b)^4 = a^4 \pm 4a^3 b + 6a^2 b^2 \pm 4ab^3 + b^4$.

$a^2 - b^2 = (a - b)(a + b)$.

$a^2 + b^2 = (a + b\sqrt{-1})(a - b\sqrt{-1})$.

$a^3 - b^3 = (a - b)(a^2 + ab + b^2)$.

$a^3 + b^3 = (a + b)(a^2 - ab + b^2)$.

$a^4 + b^4 = (a^2 + ab\sqrt{2} + b^2)(a^2 - ab\sqrt{2} + b^2)$.

$a^n - b^n = (a - b)(a^{n-1} + a^{n-2} b + \ldots + b^{n-1})$.

$a^n - b^n = (a + b)(a^{n-1} - a^{n-2} b + \ldots - b^{n-1})$.

$\qquad\qquad$ for even values of n.

$a^n + b^n = (a + b)(a^{n-1} - a^{n-2} b + \ldots + b^{n-1})$,

$\qquad\qquad$ for odd values of n.

$a^4 + a^2 b^2 + b^4 = (a^2 + ab + b^2)(a^2 - ab + b^2)$.

$(a + b + c)^2 = a^2 + b^2 + c^2 + 2ab + 2ac + 2bc$.

$(a + b + c)^3 = a^3 + b^3 + c^3 + 3a^2(b + c) + 3b^2(a + c) +$

$\qquad\qquad\qquad 3c^2(a + b) + 6abc$.

$(a + b + c + d + \ldots)^2 = a^2 + b^2 + c^2 + d^2 + \ldots +$

$2a(b + c + d + \ldots) + 2b(c + d + \ldots) + 2c(d + \ldots) + \ldots$

See also under Series.

POWERS AND ROOTS

$a^x \times a^y = a^{(x + y)}$.

$a^0 = 1$ [if $a \neq 0$]

$(ab)^x = a^x b^x$.

$\dfrac{a^x}{a^y} = a^{(x - y)}$.

$a^{-x} = \dfrac{1}{a^x}$.

$\left(\dfrac{a}{b}\right)^x = \dfrac{a^x}{b^x}$.

$(a^x)^y = a^{xy}$.

$a^{\frac{1}{x}} = \sqrt[x]{a}$.

$\sqrt[x]{ab} = \sqrt[x]{a}\,\sqrt[x]{b}$.

$\sqrt[x]{\sqrt[y]{a}} = \sqrt[xy]{a}$.

$a^{\frac{x}{y}} = \sqrt[y]{a^x}$.

$\sqrt[x]{\dfrac{a}{b}} = \dfrac{\sqrt[x]{a}}{\sqrt[x]{b}}$.

PROPORTION

If $\dfrac{a}{b} = \dfrac{c}{d}$, $\qquad$ then $\qquad$ $\dfrac{a + b}{b} = \dfrac{c + d}{d}$,

$$\dfrac{a - b}{b} = \dfrac{c - d}{d}, \qquad\qquad \dfrac{a - b}{a + b} = \dfrac{c - d}{c + d}.$$

ARITHMETIC PROGRESSION*

An arithmetic progression is a sequence of numbers such that each number differs from the previous number by a constant amount, called the *common difference*.

If a_1 is the first term; a_n the nth term; d the common difference; n the number of terms; and s_n the sum of n terms —

$$a_n = a_1 + (n - 1)d, \quad s_n = \frac{n}{2}\,[a_1 + a_n].$$

$$s_n = \frac{n}{2}\,[2a_1 + (n - 1)d].$$

The arithmetic mean between a and b is given by $\dfrac{a + b}{2}$.

GEOMETRIC PROGRESSION*

A geometric progression is a sequence of numbers such that each number bears a constant ratio, called the *common ratio*, to the previous number.

If a_1 is the first term; a_n the nth term; r the common ratio; n the number of terms; and s_n the sum of n terms

$$a_n = a_1 r^{n-1}; \; s_n = a_1\,\frac{1 - r^n}{1 - r}$$

$$= a_1\,\frac{r^n - 1}{r - 1}, \quad r \neq 1.$$

$$= \frac{a_1 - ra_n}{1 - r}$$

$$= \frac{ra_n - a_1}{r - 1}$$

If $|r| < 1$, then the sum of an infinite geometrical progression converges to the limiting value

$$\frac{a_1}{1 - r}, \quad \left[s_\infty = \lim_{n \to \infty} \frac{a_1(1 - r^n)}{1 - r} = \frac{a_1}{1 - r}\right]$$

The geometric mean between a and b is given by $\sqrt{ab}$.

*It is customary to represent a_n by l in a finite progression and refer to it as the last term.

HARMONIC PROGRESSION

A sequence of numbers whose reciprocals form an arithmetic progression is called an harmonic progression. Thus

$$\frac{1}{a_1}, \quad \frac{1}{a_1 + d}, \quad \frac{1}{a_1 + 2d}, \cdots, \frac{1}{a_1 + (n - 1)d}, \cdots,$$

where

$$\frac{1}{a_n} = \frac{1}{a_1 + (n - 1)d}$$

forms an harmonic progression. The harmonic mean between a and b is given by $\dfrac{2ab}{a + b}$.

If A, G, H respectively represent the arithmetic mean, geometric mean, and harmonic mean between a and b, then $G^2 = AH$.

QUADRATIC EQUATIONS

Any quadratic equation may be reduced to the form,—

$$ax^2 + bx + c = 0$$

Then

$$x = \frac{-b \pm \sqrt{b^2 - 4ac}}{2a}$$

If a, b, and c are real then:

If $b^2 - 4ac$ is positive, the roots are real and unequal;

If $b^2 - 4ac$ is zero, the roots are real and equal;

If $b^2 - 4ac$ is negative, the roots are imaginary and unequal.

CUBIC EQUATIONS

A cubic equation, $y^3 + py^2 + qy + r = 0$ may be reduced to the form,—

$$x^3 + ax + b = 0$$

by substituting for y the value, $x - \dfrac{p}{3}$. Here

$$a = \tfrac{1}{3}(3q - p^2) \text{ and } b = \tfrac{1}{27}(2p^3 - 9pq + 27r).$$

For solution let,—

$$A = \sqrt[3]{-\frac{b}{2} + \sqrt{\frac{b^2}{4} + \frac{a^3}{27}}}, \qquad B = -\sqrt[3]{+\frac{b}{2} + \sqrt{\frac{b^2}{4} + \frac{a^3}{27}}},$$

then the values of x will be given by,

$$x = A + B, \quad -\frac{A + B}{2} + \frac{A - B}{2}\sqrt{-3}, \quad -\frac{A + B}{2} - \frac{A - B}{2}\sqrt{-3}.$$

If p, q, r are real, then:

If $\dfrac{b^2}{4} + \dfrac{a^3}{27} > 0$, there will be one real root and two conjugate complex roots;

If $\dfrac{b^2}{4} + \dfrac{a^3}{27} = 0$, there will be three real roots of which at least two are equal;

If $\dfrac{b^2}{4} + \dfrac{a^3}{27} < 0$, there will be three real and unequal roots.

Trigonometric Solution of the Cubic Equation

The form $x^3 + ax + b = 0$ with $ab \neq 0$ can always be solved by transforming it to the trigonometric identity

$$4 \cos^3 \theta - 3 \cos \theta - \cos (3\theta) \equiv 0.$$

Let $x = m \cos \theta$, then

$$x^3 + ax + b \equiv m^3 \cos^3 \theta + am \cos \theta + b \equiv 4 \cos^3 \theta - 3 \cos \theta - \cos (3\theta) \equiv 0.$$

Hence

$$\frac{4}{m^3} = -\frac{3}{am} = \frac{-\cos(3\theta)}{b},$$

from which follows that

$$m = 2 \sqrt{-\frac{a}{3}}, \quad \cos (3\theta) = \frac{3b}{am}.$$

Any solution θ_1 which satisfies $\cos (3\theta) = \dfrac{3b}{am}$, will also have the solutions

$$\theta_1 + \frac{2\pi}{3} \quad \text{and} \quad \theta_1 + \frac{4\pi}{3}.$$

The roots of the cubic $x^3 + ax + b = 0$ are

$$2 \sqrt{-\frac{a}{3}} \cos \theta_1, \quad 2 \sqrt{-\frac{a}{3}} \cos \left(\theta_1 + \frac{2\pi}{3} \right), \quad 2 \sqrt{-\frac{a}{3}} \cos \left(\theta_1 + \frac{4\pi}{3} \right).$$

Example where hyperbolic functions are necessary for solution with latter procedure

The roots of the equation $x^3 - x + 2 = 0$ may be found as follows:

Here

$$a = -1, \quad b = 2, \quad m = 2 \sqrt{\tfrac{1}{3}} = 1.155$$

$$\cos (3\theta) = \frac{6}{-1.155} = -5.196$$

$$\cos (3\theta) = -\cos (3\theta - \pi) = -\cosh [i(3\theta - \pi)] = -5.196.$$

Using hyperbolic function tables for cosh $[i(3\theta - \pi)] = 5.196$, it is found that

$$i(3\theta - \pi) = 2.332.$$

Thus

$$3\theta - \pi = -i(2.332).$$
$$3\theta = \pi - i(2.332)$$
$$\theta_1 = \frac{\pi}{3} - i(0.777)$$
$$\theta_1 + \frac{2\pi}{3} = \pi - i(0.777)$$
$$\theta_1 + \frac{4\pi}{3} = \frac{5\pi}{3} - i(0.777)$$

$$\cos \theta_1 = \cos \left[\frac{\pi}{3} - i(0.777) \right]$$

$$= \left(\cos \frac{\pi}{3} \right) [\cos i(0.777)] + \left(\sin \frac{\pi}{3} \right) [\sin i(0.777)]$$

$$= \left(\cos \frac{\pi}{3} \right) (\cosh 0.777) + i \left(\sin \frac{\pi}{3} \right) (\sinh 0.777)$$

$$= (0.5)(1.317) + i(0.866)(0.858) = 0.659 + i(0.743).$$

Note that

$$\cos \mu = \cosh (i\mu) \quad \text{and} \quad \sin \mu = -i \sinh (i\mu).$$

Similarly

$$\cos \left(\theta_1 + \frac{2\pi}{3} \right) = \cos [\pi - i(0.777)]$$

$$= (\cos \pi)(\cosh 0.777) + i(\sin \pi)(\sinh 0.777)$$

$$= -1.317,$$

and

$$\cos \left(\theta_1 + \frac{4\pi}{3} \right) = \cos \left[\frac{5\pi}{3} - i(0.777) \right]$$

$$= \left(\cos \frac{5\pi}{3} \right) (\cosh 0.777) + i \left(\sin \frac{5\pi}{3} \right) (\sinh 0.777)$$

$$= (0.5)(1.317) - i(0.866)(0.858) = 0.659 - i(0.743).$$

The required roots are

$$1.155[0.659 + i(0.743)] = 0.760 + i(0.858)$$
$$(1.155)(-1.317) = -1.520$$
$$(1.155)[0.659 - i(0.743)] = 0.760 - i(0.858).$$

QUARTIC OR BIQUADRATIC EQUATION

A quartic equation,

$$x^4 + ax^3 + bx^2 + cx + d = 0,$$

has the *resolvent cubic equation*

$$y^3 - by^2 + (ac - 4d)y - a^2d + 4bd - c^2 = 0.$$

Let y be any root of this equation, and

$$R = \sqrt{\frac{a^2}{4} - b + y}.$$

If $R \neq 0$, then let

$$D = \sqrt{\frac{3a^2}{4} - R^2 - 2b + \frac{4ab - 8c - a^3}{4R}}$$

and

$$E = \sqrt{\frac{3a^2}{4} - R^2 - 2b - \frac{4ab - 8c - a^3}{4R}}$$

If $R = 0$, then let

$$D = \sqrt{\frac{3a^2}{4} - 2b + 2\sqrt{y^2 - 4d}}$$

and

$$E = \sqrt{\frac{3a^2}{4} - 2b - 2\sqrt{y^2 - 4d}}.$$

Then the four roots of the original equation are given by

$$x = -\frac{a}{4} + \frac{R}{2} \pm \frac{D}{2}$$

and

$$x = -\frac{a}{4} - \frac{R}{2} \pm \frac{E}{2}.$$

EQUATION $x^n = c$

Using DeMoivre's theorem:

$$(\cos \theta + i \sin \theta)^n = \cos n\theta + i \sin n\theta; \quad i = \sqrt{-1},$$

the equation $x^n = c$ has n roots given by

$$x = \sqrt[n]{c} \left(\cos \frac{2m\pi}{n} + i \sin \frac{2m\pi}{n} \right) \text{if } c > 0,$$

or

$$x = \sqrt[n]{-c} \left(\cos \frac{(2m+1)\pi}{n} + i \sin \frac{(2m+1)\pi}{n} \right) \text{ if } c < 0,$$

where m takes the n values $0, 1, 2, \ldots (n-1)$ giving n roots.

PARTIAL FRACTIONS

This section applies only to rational algebraic fractions with numerator of lower degree than the denominator. Improper fractions can be reduced to proper fractions by long division.

Every fraction may be expressed as the sum of component fractions whose denominators are factors of the denominator of the original fraction.

Let $N(x)$ = numerator, a polynomial of the form

$$n_0 + n_1 x + n_2 x^2 + \cdots + n_i x^i$$

I. *Non-repeated Linear Factors*

$$\frac{N(x)}{(x-a)G(x)} = \frac{A}{x-a} + \frac{F(x)}{G(x)}$$

$$A = \left[\frac{N(x)}{G(x)}\right]_{x-a}$$

$F(x)$ determined by methods discussed in the following sections.

Example:

$$\frac{x^2 + 3}{x(x-2)(x^2 + 2x + 4)} = \frac{A}{x} + \frac{B}{x-2} + \frac{F(x)}{x^2 + 2x + 4}$$

$$A = \left[\frac{x^2 + 3}{(x-2)(x^2 + 2x + 4)}\right]_{x-0} = -\frac{3}{8}$$

$$B = \left[\frac{x^2 + 3}{x(x^2 + 2x + 4)}\right]_{x-2} = \frac{4 + 3}{2(4 + 4 + 4)} = \frac{7}{24}$$

II. *Repeated Linear Factors*

$$\frac{N(x)}{x^m G(x)} = \frac{A_0}{x^m} + \frac{A_1}{x^{m-1}} + \cdots + \frac{A_{m-1}}{x} + \frac{F(x)}{G(x)}$$

$$F(x) = f_0 + f_1 x + f_2 x^2 + \cdots, \quad G(x) = g_0 + g_1 x + g_2 x^2 + \cdots$$

$$A_0 = \frac{n_0}{g_0}, \quad A_1 = \frac{n_1 - A_0 g_1}{g_0}, \quad A_2 = \frac{n_2 - A_0 g_2 - A_1 g_1}{g_0}$$

General term:

$$A_k = \frac{1}{g_0}\left[n_k - \sum_{i=0}^{k-1} A_i g_{k-i}\right]$$

$$*m = 1 \begin{cases} f_0 = n_1 - A_0 g_1 \\ f_1 = n_2 - A_0 g_2 \\ f_j = n_{j+1} - A_0 g_{j+1} \end{cases}$$

$$m = 2 \begin{cases} f_0 = n_2 - A_0 g_2 - A_1 g_1 \\ f_1 = n_3 - A_0 g_3 - A_1 g_2 \\ f_j = n_{j+2} - [A_0 g_{j+2} + A_1 g_{j+1}] \end{cases}$$

$$m = 3 \begin{cases} f_0 = n_3 - A_0 g_3 - A_1 g_2 - A_2 g_1 \\ f_1 = n_4 - A_0 g_4 - A_1 g_3 - A_2 g_2 \\ f_j = n_{j+3} - [A_0 g_{j+3} + A_1 g_{j+2} + A_2 g_{j+1}] \end{cases}$$

$$\text{any } m: \quad f_j = n_{m+j} - \sum_{i=0}^{m-1} A_i g_{m+j-i}$$

Example:

$$\frac{x^2 + 1}{x^3(x^2 - 3x + 6)} = \frac{A_0}{x^3} + \frac{A_1}{x^2} + \frac{A_2}{x} + \frac{f_1 x + f_0}{x^2 - 3x + 6}$$

$$A_0 = \frac{1}{6}, \quad A_1 = \frac{0 - (\frac{1}{6})(-3)}{6} = \frac{1}{12},$$

$$A_2 = \frac{1 - (\frac{1}{6})(1) - (\frac{1}{12})(-3)}{6} = \frac{13}{72},$$

$$m = 3 \begin{cases} f_0 = 0 - \frac{1}{6}(0) + \frac{1}{12}(1) - \frac{13}{72}(-3) = \frac{11}{24} \\ f_1 = 0 - \frac{1}{6}(0) - \frac{1}{12}(0) - \frac{13}{72}(1) = -\frac{13}{72} \end{cases}$$

*Note: If $G(x)$ contains linear factors, $F(x)$ may be determined by previous section I.

III. *Repeated Linear Factors*

$$\frac{N(x)}{(x - a)^m G(x)} = \frac{A_0}{(x - a)^m} + \frac{A_1}{(x - a)^{m-1}} + \cdots + \frac{A_{m-1}}{(x - a)} + \frac{F(x)}{G(x)}$$

Change to form $\dfrac{N'(y)}{y^m G'(y)}$ by substitution of $x = y + a$. Resolve into partial fractions in terms of y as described in Section II. Then express in terms of x by substitution $y = x - a$.

Example:

$$\frac{x - 3}{(x - 2)^2(x^2 + x + 1)}$$

Let $x - 2 = y$, $x = y + 2$

$$\frac{(y + 2) - 3}{y^2[(y + 2)^2 + (y + 2) + 1]} = \frac{y - 1}{y^2(y^2 + 5y + 7)} = \frac{A_0}{y^2} + \frac{A_1}{y} + \frac{f_1 y + f_0}{y^2 + 5y + 7}$$

$$A_0 = -\frac{1}{7}, \quad A_1 = \frac{1 - (-\frac{1}{7})(5)}{7} = \frac{12}{49},$$

$$m = 2 \begin{cases} f_0 = 0 - (-\frac{1}{7})(1) - (\frac{12}{49})(5) = -\frac{53}{49} \\ f_1 = 0 - (-\frac{1}{7})(0) - (\frac{12}{49})(1) = -\frac{12}{49} \end{cases}$$

$$\therefore \quad \frac{y - 1}{y^2(y^2 + 5y + 7)} = \frac{-\frac{1}{7}}{y^2} + \frac{\frac{12}{49}}{y} + \frac{-\frac{12}{49}y - \frac{53}{49}}{y^2 + 5y + 7}$$

Let $y = x - 2$, then

$$\frac{x - 3}{(x - 2)^2(x^2 + x + 1)} = \frac{-\frac{1}{7}}{(x - 2)^2} + \frac{\frac{12}{35}}{(x - 2)} + \frac{-\frac{12}{49}(x - 2) - \frac{53}{49}}{x^2 + x + 1}$$

$$= -\frac{1}{7(x - 2)^2} + \frac{12}{35(x - 2)} + \frac{-12x - 29}{49(x^2 + x + 1)}$$

IV. *Repeated Linear Factors*

Alternative method of determining coefficients:

$$\frac{N(x)}{(x - a)^m G(x)} = \frac{A_0}{(x - a)^m} + \cdots + \frac{A_k}{(x - a)^{m-k}} + \cdots + \frac{A_{m-1}}{x - a} + \frac{F(x)}{G(x)}$$

$$A_k = \frac{1}{k!} \left\{ D_x^k \left[\frac{N(x)}{G(x)} \right] \right\}_{x=a}$$

where D_x^k is the differentiating operator, and the derivative of zero order is defined as:

$$D_x^0 u = u.$$

V. *Factors of Higher Degree*

Factors of higher degree have the corresponding numerators indicated.

$$\frac{N(x)}{(x^2 + h_1 x + h_0) G(x)} = \frac{a_1 x + a_0}{x^2 + h_1 x + h_0} + \frac{F(x)}{G(x)}$$

$$\frac{N(x)}{(x^2 + h_1 x + h_0)^2 G(x)} = \frac{a_1 x + a_0}{(x^2 + h_1 x + h_0)^2} + \frac{b_1 x + b_0}{(x^2 + h_1 x + h_0)} + \frac{F(x)}{G(x)}$$

$$\frac{N(x)}{(x^3 + h_2 x^2 + h_1 x + h_0) G(x)} = \frac{a_2 x^2 + a_1 x + a_0}{x^3 + h_2 x^2 + h_1 x + h_0} + \frac{F(x)}{G(x)}$$

etc.

Problems of this type are determined first by solving for the coefficients due to linear factors as shown above, and then determining the remaining coefficients by the general methods given below.

VI. *General Methods for Evaluating Coefficients*

1.　　　$$\frac{N(x)}{D(x)} = \frac{N(x)}{G(x) H(x) L(x)} = \frac{A(x)}{G(x)} + \frac{B(x)}{H(x)} + \frac{C(x)}{L(x)} + \cdots$$

Multiply both sides of equation by $D(x)$ to clear fractions. Then collect terms, equate like powers of x, and solve the resulting simultaneous equations for the unknown coefficients.

2. Clear fractions as above. Then let x assume certain convenient values ($x = 1, 0, -1, \ldots$). Solve the resulting equations for the unknown coefficients.

3.　　　$$\frac{N(x)}{G(x) H(x)} = \frac{A(x)}{G(x)} + \frac{B(x)}{H(x)}$$

Then

$$\frac{N(x)}{G(x) H(x)} - \frac{A(x)}{G(x)} = \frac{B(x)}{H(x)}$$

If $A(x)$ can be determined, such as by Method I, then $B(x)$ can be found as above.

BASIC CONCEPTS IN ALGEBRA

Dr. W. E. Deskins

I. ALGEBRA OF SETS

1. Intuitively a set is a collection of objects called the elements of the set. Set and set membership are generally accepted as basic, undefined terms used to define and construct mathematical systems.

   The notation $a \in A$ indicates that a is an element of the set A. The notation $a \notin A$ means that a is not a member of A.

   A set is sometimes specified by listing its elements within a set of braces: $\{a\}$ is the set containing only the element a.

2. Set A is a subset of set B provided $a \in A$ implies $a \in B$. This is denoted by $A \subseteq B$. Every set has as a subset the empty or null set, denoted by ϕ, which has no elements.

3. Set A equals set B, written $A = B$, if and only if $A \subseteq B$ and $B \subseteq A$. A is a proper subset of B, sometimes indicated by $A \subset B$, if and only if $A \subseteq B$ and $A \neq B$; then B has at least one element which does not belong to A.

4. The Cartesian product of sets A and B, denoted by $A \times B$, is the set of all ordered pairs (a, b) where $a \in A$ and $b \in B$. A subset R of $A \times A$ is a binary relation on A, and this is an equivalence relation on A provided (i) $(a, a) \in R$ for every $a \in A$, (ii) $(a, b) \in R$ implies $(b, a) \in R$, and (iii) $(a, b) \in R$ and $(b, c) \in R$ imply $(a, c) \in R$. Ordinary equality of numbers, equality of sets, and congruence of plane figures are examples of equivalence relations.

5. A subset F of $A \times B$ is a *function* from A to B provided each element of A appears exactly once as the first element of a pair in F. A function F from A to B is *onto* provided each element of B appears at least once as the second element of a pair in F. It is *one-to-one* provided each element of B appears at most once as the second element of a pair in F. A function from $A \times A$ to A is a *binary operation* on A. Addition and multiplication of ordinary numbers are examples of binary operations.

6. If consideration is restricted to elements and subsets of a particular set I, then I is the universal set.

7. Common binary operations on subsets of I are: $A \cup B$, the union or join of sets A and B, is the set of all elements of I which belong to either A or B or both A and B.

   $A \cap B$, the intersection or meet of sets A and B, is the set of all elements of I which belong to both A and B.

   $A \setminus B$, the difference of sets A and B, is the set of elements of I which belong to A but not B.

   The difference $I \setminus A$ is denoted by A' and called the complement of A (relative to I). Except in dealing with the concept of complementation the use of a universal set is not essential to the above ideas.

8. Some theorems basic to the Algebra of Sets:

   Let A, B, and C be arbitrary subsets of a universal set I.

   (a) (Commutativity) $A \cup B = B \cup A$ and $A \cap B = B \cap A$.

   (b) (Associativity) $(A \cup B) \cup C = A \cup (B \cup C)$ and
   $(A \cap B) \cap C = A \cap (B \cap C)$.

(c) (Distributivity) $A \cap (B \cup C) = (A \cap B) \cup (A \cap C)$ and
$A \cup (B \cap C) = (A \cup B) \cap (A \cup C)$.

(d) (Idempotency) $A \cup A = A \cap A = A$.

(e) Properties of I and ϕ: $A \cap I = A \cup \phi = A$,
$A \cup I = I$, and
$A \cap \phi = \phi$.

(f) $(A \cap B) \cup (A \backslash B) = A$.

(g) $(A \backslash B) \cup B = A \cup B$.

(h) $A \subseteq A \cup B$.

(i) $A \cap B \subseteq A$.

(j) $A \cup B = A$ if and only if $B \subseteq A$.

(k) $A \cap B = A$ if and only if $A \subseteq B$.

(m) $A \backslash B = A \backslash (A \cap B)$.

(n) (DeMorgan's Theorem) $(A \backslash B) \cap (A \backslash C) = A \backslash (B \cup C)$ and
$(A \backslash B) \cup (A \backslash C) = A \backslash (B \cap C)$.

(o) $(A \cup B)' = A' \cap B'$ and $(A \cap B)' = A' \cup B'$.

(p) $A \cup A' = I$ and $A \cap A' = \phi$.

9. A mathematical system S is a set $S = \{E, O, A\}$ where E is a nonempty set of elements, O is a set of relations and operations on E, and A is a set of axioms, postulates, or assumptions concerning the elements of E and O.

10. The Algebra of Sets provides an example of a mathematical system called a Boolean Algebra (or Boolean Ring) which is defined as:

Set E of elements $a, b, c, \ldots$;

Set O of 2 binary operations $\oplus$ and $\otimes$; (Here $a \oplus b$ denotes the image of (a, b) under the binary operation.)

Set A of axioms for all a, b, c of E:

A_1. The binary operations are commutative; i.e.,

$$a \oplus b = b \oplus a \quad \text{and} \quad a \otimes b = b \otimes a.$$

A_2. Each binary operation is distributive over the other; i.e.,

$$a \oplus (b \otimes c) = (a \oplus b) \otimes (a \oplus c) \quad \text{and} \quad a \otimes (b \oplus c) = (a \otimes b) + (a \otimes c).$$

A_3. There exist elements e and z in E such that for each $a \in E$, $a \oplus z = a$ and $a \otimes e = a$.

A_4. For each $a \in E$ there exists an element $a' \in E$ such that $a \otimes a' = e$ and $a \oplus a' = z$.

In the algebra of subsets of a (universal) set I, ϕ plays the role of z, I that of e, $\cup$ that of $\oplus$, and $\cap$ that of $\otimes$.

11. A Boolean Algebra has the Principle of Duality: If the interchanges of $\begin{Bmatrix} \oplus \text{ and } \otimes \\ e \text{ and } z \end{Bmatrix}$ are made in a correct statement, then the result is also a correct statement.

12. In addition to the Algrebra of Sets which is a Boolean Algebra, other representations of Boolean Algebra that are interesting of themselves and valuable for their applications are:

(a) The Algebra of Symbolic Logic

(b) The Algebra of Switching Currents

Algebra of Sets	Binary Operator	Symbolic Logic	Binary Operator	Switching Circuits	Binary Operator
Union of 2 sets	$\cup$	Disjunction of 2 propositions	$\vee$	2 switches in $\parallel$	$+$
Intersection of 2 sets	$\cap$	Conjunction of 2 propositions	$\wedge$	2 switches in series	$\times$
Complement of a set A		Negation of a proposition T, F	$\sim$	on-off, or 1, 0	1 or $^{-}$

Both in symbolic logic and in switching circuits, we can consider "0" and "1" as the elements, in the former representing "False" and "True"; in the latter, "Off" and "On", satisfying the following "rules":

$$\left. \begin{array}{l} 0 + 0 = 0 \\ 1 + 1 = 1 \end{array} \right\} \text{ i.e. } a + a = a$$

$$\left. \begin{array}{l} 0 \times 0 = 0 \\ 1 \times 1 = 1 \end{array} \right\} \text{ i.e. } a \times a = a$$

$$0' = 1$$

$$1' = 0$$

$$\left. \begin{array}{l} 0 + 0' = 0 + 1 = 1 \\ 1 + 1' = 1 + 0 = 1 \end{array} \right\} \text{ i.e. } a + a' = 1$$

$$\left. \begin{array}{l} 0 \times 0' = 0 \times 1 = 0 \\ 1 \times 1' = 1 \times 0 = 0 \end{array} \right\} a \times a' = 0$$

In switching circuits:

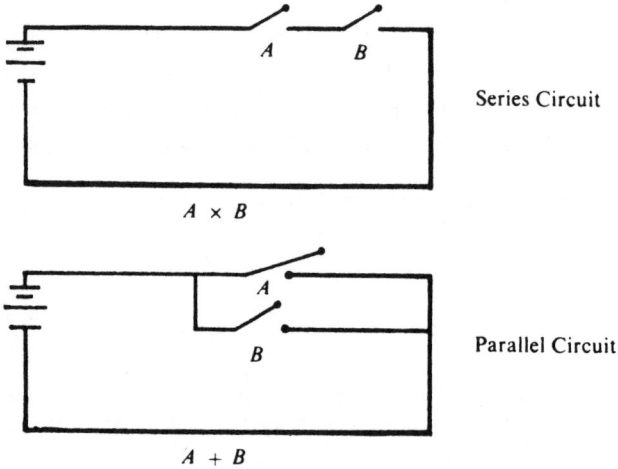

Series Circuit

$A \times B$

Parallel Circuit

$A + B$

here, "0" represents an open circuit: $A = 0$ and "1"

a closed circuit: $A = 1$

In the Algebra of Symbolic Logic, we use *Truth Tables* to define the operations $\wedge$, $\vee$, $\sim$ as follows:

					Other Operators Used	
p	q	$p \wedge q$	$p \vee q$	$\sim p$	$p \rightarrow q$	$p \leftrightarrow q$
T	T	T	T	F	T	T
T	F	F	T	F	F	F
F	T	F	T	T	T	F
F	F	F	F	T	T	T

13. In order to re-emphasize the use of switching circuits and their relation to truth tables the following is included. Conventionally a "1" represents "True" and a "0" represents "False." The switching circuit symbols are $-$, $\cdot$, $+$, $\rightarrow$, $\equiv$ representing "Not," "And," "Or," "Implies," "Equivalent" respectively and their Truth Table Definitions are

p	q	$p \cdot q$	$p + q$	$-p$	$p \rightarrow q$	$p \equiv q$
0	0	0	0	1	1	1
0	1	0	1	1	1	0
1	0	0	1	0	0	0
1	1	1	1	0	1	1

The comparison with the Algebra of Symbolic Logic being obvious. The "rules" for these circuits are as follows:

$$0 + 0 = 0$$
$$1 + 1 = 1$$
$$1 + 0 = 0 + 1 = 1$$
$$0 \cdot 0 = 0$$
$$1 \cdot 1 = 1$$
$$0 \cdot 1 = 1 \cdot 0 = 0$$
$$\bar{0} = 1$$
$$\bar{1} = 0$$

Mechanical switches or relays are represented by

———— p ————   or   ———— $\bar{p}$ ————

the former indicating that the circuit is closed, i.e. the switch is made, when $p = 1$ and the latter indicating the converse namely that the circuit is closed when $\bar{p} = 1$ or, what amounts to the same thing, when $p = 0$.

Electronic switches or gates are represented by more complex symbols—four in all, three of which are independent and can stand alone

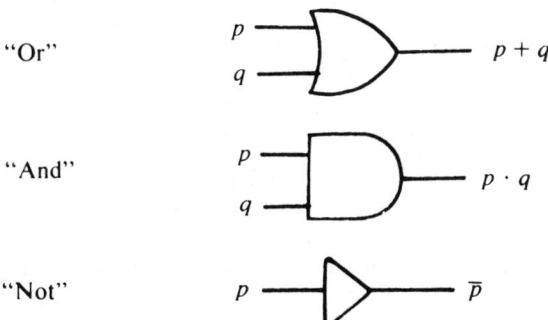

"Or"

"And"

"Not"

and one which represents the negation of an input or an output and is used with one of the above

"Not"

An example of its use on an input line is

$\overline{p} + q$

or on an output is

$\overline{p \cdot q}$

and on both

$\overline{\overline{p} \cdot q} \ (= p + \overline{q})$

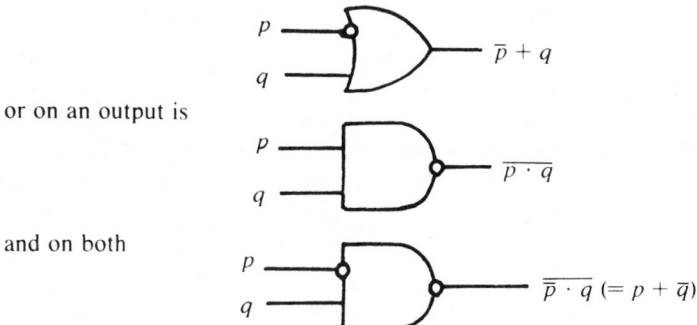

The basic functions obtained from the two types of switching circuits are

$1 \longrightarrow p \longrightarrow p$ $\qquad$ $p \longrightarrow p$

$1 \longrightarrow \overline{p} \longrightarrow \overline{p}$ $\qquad$ $p \longrightarrow \overline{p}$

$1 \longrightarrow p \longrightarrow q \longrightarrow p \cdot q$ $\qquad$ $\begin{matrix} p \\ q \end{matrix} \longrightarrow p \cdot q$

$1 \longrightarrow \begin{matrix} p \\ q \end{matrix} \longrightarrow p + q$ $\qquad$ $\begin{matrix} p \\ q \end{matrix} \longrightarrow p + q$

$1 \longrightarrow \begin{matrix} \overline{p} \\ q \end{matrix} \longrightarrow p \rightarrow q$ $\qquad$ $\begin{matrix} p \\ q \end{matrix} \longrightarrow p \rightarrow q$

$1 \longrightarrow \begin{matrix} p - q \\ \overline{p} - q \end{matrix} \longrightarrow p \equiv q$ $\qquad$ $\begin{matrix} p \\ q \\ p \\ q \end{matrix} \longrightarrow p \equiv q$

All the above electronic circuits can be negated by simply adding a negating circle to the output as for example in

Alternative circuits however, which are direct analogues of their relay switching counterparts, are

The operation + is sometimes referred to as the "Inclusive Or" and ≢ as the "Exclusive Or", the former having the value "True" when both the inputs are "True"— see the truth table.   Note that $p \not\equiv q$ is a shorthand for $\overline{p \equiv q}$.

14. Two sets A and B are equivalent (have same cardinal) if and only if there exists a one-to-one correspondence between the elements of the two sets.   This is an equivalence relation on the collection of subsets of set I.

A set is infinite if and only if it is equivalent with a proper subset of itself.

A set is called countably (denumerably) infinite if it is equivalent with the set of all positive integers.   The set of all rational numbers is countably infinite but the set of all real numbers is noncountably infinite.   The cardinal of the set of all rational numbers is denoted by (aleph null); the cardinal of the set of reals is denoted by (aleph).

II. ABSTRACT ALGEBRAIC SYSTEMS

1. *Semigroup.*   A semigroup is a system $\{S, \theta, A\}$; S is a nonempty set $\{a, b, c, \ldots\}$, θ consists of one binary operation on S, denoted by $*$, and A consists of the axiom

   A_1.   Associativity: $a * (b * c) = (a * b) * c$ for all $a, b, c \in S$.

   Basic Theorem.   *(Generalized Associativity).*   If $a_1, a_2, \ldots, a_n$ are elements of S then all associations of the n elements yield the same "product". (For example,

   $$a * ((b * c) * d) = a * (b * (c * d)) = (a * b) * (c * d), \text{etc.})$$

2. *Group.*   A group is a system $\{G, \theta, A\}$; G is a nonempty set $\{a, b, c, \ldots\}$, θ consists of one binary operation denoted by $\circ$, and A consists of the axioms:

   A_1.   Associativity: $a \circ (b \circ c) = (a \circ b) \circ c$ for all $a, b, c \in G$.

   A_2.   Identity Element: G contains an element e having the property, $a \circ e = e \circ a = a$ for every $a \in G$.

   A_3.   Inverse Element: For each $a \in G$ there is an element $a' \in G$ with the property, $a \circ a' = a' \circ a = e$.

   If the following additional axiom belongs to A,

   A_4.   Commutativity: $a \circ b = b \circ a$ for all $a, b \in G$. Then the group is called Abelian (after Niels Henrik Abel). Some basic theorems:

   (a) The element e (Axiom A_2) is unique. Then e is *the* identity element of G.

   (b) The element a' (Axiom A_3) is unique for each $a \in G$.   Then a' is *the* inverse of a in G.

   (c) The equation $a \circ x = b$ has a unique solution in G, viz., $x = a' \circ b$.

   (d) $(a')' = a$ and $(a \circ b)' = b' \circ a'$.

   (e) $a \circ b = a \circ c$ if and only if $b = c$.

   If a nonempty subset H of G satisfies the two conditions:

   H_1. $a \circ b \in H$ whenever $a, b \in H$.   (Closure)

   H_2. $a \in H$ if and only if $a' \in H$.

   then H is a *subgroup* of G.

   (Lagrange).   If G is a finite set then the number of elements in H divides the number of elements in G.

Example of group.   Let G be the set of all one-to-one functions from a nonempty S onto itself.   For any $f, g \in G$, define the function $f \circ g$ as the function which maps s onto $f(g(s))$, for each $s \in S$.   Relative to this binary operation G is a group, the *symmetric group* of all permutations on S.

Each group is essentially a subgroup of the symmetric group of some set S.

3. *Ring.*   A ring is a system $\{R, \theta, A\}$; R is a nonempty set $\{a, b, c, \ldots\}$, θ consists of two binary operations denoted by $+$ and $\times$, and A consists of the axioms:

A_0.   Relative to addition (i.e., $+$) R is an Abelian group in which the identity element is denoted by z and the inverse of a is denoted by $-a$.

M_0.   Relative to multiplication (i.e., $\times$) R is a semigroup.

D_1.   Left distributive: $a \times (b + c) = (a \times b) + (a \times c)$, all $a, b, c \in R$.

D_2.   Right distributive: $(b + c)a = (b \times a) + (c \times a)$, all $a, b, c \in R$.

EXAMPLE 1.   The set of all integers (whole numbers) and ordinary addition and multiplication.

EXAMPLE 2.   The set of all real functions continuous on the interval $0 \leq y \leq 1$, with addition and multiplication defined by $(f + g)(y) = f(y) + g(y)$, sum of real numbers, and $(f \times g)(y) = f(y) \times g(y)$, product of real numbers.

Special types of rings have been studied extensively.

3.1   *Integral Domain.*   An integral domain is a ring R in which multiplication ($\times$) satisfies the additional assumptions:

M_1.   Commutativity: $a \times b = b \times a$ for all a and b in R.

M_2.   Multiplicative identity: R contains an element $e \neq z$ with the property $a \times e = e \times a = a$ for all a in R.

M_3.   Cancellation: $a \times b = a \times c$ if and only if $b = c$.

An element u of integral domain R is a *unit* provided R contains v such that $u \times v = e$.

An element p of integral domain R is a *prime* (irreducible element) provided $p = a \times b$ implies that exactly one of the elements a or b is a unit.

The elements of integral domain R which differ from z and are neither units nor primes are *composites*.

In some integral domains (such as the ring of integers) each composite can be factored uniquely (up to unit factors) as the product of a finite set of primes. However in the integral domain of all entire functions this is not true.

3.2   *Field.*   A field is an integral domain in which every element except z is a unit. In other words, the non-z elements form an Abelian group relative to multiplication ($\times$).

EXAMPLE 1.   The rational field consisting of ordinary fractions, addition, and multiplication.

EXAMPLE 2.   The set of all real numbers $a + b\sqrt{2}$, a and b rational.   Then

$$(a + b\sqrt{2}) + (c + d\sqrt{2}) = (a + c) + (b + d)\sqrt{2} \text{ and}$$
$$(a + b\sqrt{2}) \times (c + d\sqrt{2}) = (ac + 2bd) + (ad + bc)\sqrt{2}.$$

Besides these well-known examples there exist finite fields (sometimes called Galois fields).

EXAMPLE 3.   Let p be a prime integer.   Denote by $GF(p)$ the p integers $0, 1, \ldots,$
$p - 1$.   Define addition($\oplus$) of two of these elements a and b as the
remainder of $a + b$ (ordinary addition) after division by p.   (Thus
$1 \oplus (p - 1) = 0$.)

Define $a \otimes b$, the product, to be the remainder of ab (ordinary multiplication) after division by p.   (Thus, when $p = 3$, $2 \otimes 2 = 1$.)   The
resulting system $\{GF(p), \oplus, \otimes\}$ is the (modular) field of integers modulo p.

3.3   *Skew Field or Division Ring.*   A skew field is a ring in which the non-z elements
form a group relative to multiplication ($\times$).

The classical example of a skew field is the ring of real *quaternions*, first described by W. R. Hamilton.   A quaternion is expressible in the form $ae + bi +$
$cj + dk$ where a, b, c, and d are real numbers and e, i, j, and k are elements which
commute with all real numbers and multiply as follows:

$$e \times e = e, \quad e \times i = i \times e = i, \quad e \times j = j \times e = j, \quad e \times k = k \times e = k;$$
$$i \times i = -e, \quad i \times j = k, \quad j \times i = -k, \quad i \times k = -j, \quad k \times i = j,$$
$$j \times j = -e, \quad j \times k = i, \quad k \times j = -i, \quad k \times k = -e.$$

These elements distribute over addition. e is generally identified with and written
as the real number 1.

3.4   *Matric Ring.*   The matric ring $M_n(R)$ over the ring R, where n is a positive
integer, consists of all doubly-ordered sets of n^2 elements of R, written as an
array

$$\begin{pmatrix} a_{1,1} & a_{1,2} \cdots a_{1,n} \\ a_{2,1} & a_{2,2} \cdots a_{2,n} \\ \vdots \\ a_{n,1} & \cdots \quad\quad a_{n,n} \end{pmatrix} = (a_{i,j})$$

with addition and multiplication defined as follows:

$$(a_{i,j}) + (b_{i,j}) = (a_{i,j} + b_{i,j})$$
$$(a_{i,j}) \times (b_{i,j}) = (c_{i,j})$$

where

$$c_{i,j} = \sum_{k-1}^{n} a_{i,k} b_{k,j}, \quad i = 1, \ldots, n \quad \text{and} \quad j = 1, \ldots, n.$$

If $n > 1$, then multiplication is noncommutative in general; i.e., $(a_{i,j}) \times (b_{i,j})$
can differ from $(b_{i,j}) \times (a_{i,j})$.   Moreover, the product of two nonzero matrices can
be the zero matrix (which consists of only the element z in all n^2 positions).

A similar useful method for forming a new ring from a known ring utilizes
sequences.

3.5   *Power Series and Polynomial Ring.*   Let R be a ring in which multiplication ($\times$) is
commutative.   The set $PS(R)$ of all sequences $(a_0, a_1, \ldots)$ with $a_i \in R$ is the
power series ring of R, with addition and multiplication defined as

$$(a_0, a_1, \ldots) \oplus (b_0, b_1, \ldots) = (a_0 + b_0, \quad a_1 + b_1, \ldots) \text{ and}$$
$$(a_0, a_1, \ldots) \oplus (b_0, b_1, \ldots) = (c_0, c_1, \ldots)$$

where

$$c_0 = a_0 \times b_0, \quad c_1 = a_0 \times b_1 + a_1 \times b_0, \ldots, \text{ and,}$$

generally,

$$c_n = a_0 \times b_n + a_1 \times b_{n-1} + \cdots + a_n \times b_0.$$

The subset $P(R)$ of $PS(R)$ consisting of those sequences $(a_0, a_1, \ldots)$ in which at
most only finitely many of the a_i differ from z, form a ring relative to the addition

and multiplication just defined. This ring $\{P(R),\oplus,\otimes\}$, is the polynomial ring of R.

Some theorems for rings, fields, etc.

(a) In a ring R, if $a = b$ and $c = d$, then $a + c = b + d$ and $a \times c = b \times d$.

(b) In a ring R, $-(-a) = a$; $(-a) \times b = a \times (-b) = -(a \times b)$; and $(-a) \times (-b) = a \times b$, for all $a,b \in R$.

(c) In a ring R, $a \times z = z \times a = z$, for all $a \in R$.

(d) In a ring R the equation $a + x = b$ has a unique solution, viz., $x = -a + b$.

(f) In a field, skew field, or integral domain, $a \times b = z$ if and only if a and/or b equals z.

(g) A finite integral domain is a field.

(h) The polynomial ring of an integral domain is also an integral domain.

(i) The power series ring of an integral domain is also an integral domain.

(j) A ring is a field provided it is both an integral domain and a skew field.

(k) If R is a (skew) field, then the equation $a \times y = b$, $a \neq z$, has a unique solution $y = a' \times b$.

(l) The polynomial ring and the power series ring of a field are unique factorization domains.

4. *Vector Space.* A vector space $V(F)$ over a field F consists of a nonempty set V (the vectors), a binary operation $(\oplus)$ on V, a function (called *scalar multiplication*) from the product set $F \times V$ onto V with the image of (a,ν) denoted by $a \circ \nu$, and the following axioms:

A_0. Relative to addition $(\oplus)$ V is an Abelian group in which the identity element (vector) is denoted by z and the inverse of ν is denoted by $-\nu$.

M_1. $a \circ (b \circ \nu) = (ab) \circ \nu$ for all $a,b \in F$ and $\nu \in F$. (Here ab denotes the product of a and b in F.)

M_2. $1 \circ \nu = \nu$ for all $\nu \in V$. (Here 1 denotes the multiplicative indentity element of F.)

D_1. $a \circ (\mu \oplus \nu) = (a \circ \mu) \oplus (a \circ \nu)$ for all $a \in F$, $\mu, \nu \in V$.

D_2. $(a + b) \circ \nu \doteq (a \circ \nu) \oplus (b \circ \nu)$ for all $a,b \in F$, $\nu \in V$. (Here $+$ denotes addition in the field F.)

The elements of F are referred to as *scalars*.

EXAMPLE 1.   The polynomial ring $P(F)$ of a field F is a vector space over F. In this example scalar multiplication is a special case of the multiplication defined for $P(F)$.

EXAMPLE 2.   Denote by $C_n(F)$ the set of all n-tuples, $(a_1,a_2,\ldots,a_n)$, n a positive integer, with all $a_i \in F$. Define

$$(a_1,\ldots,a_n) \oplus (b_1,\ldots,b_n) = (a_1 + b_1,\ldots,a_n + b_n) \quad \text{and}$$
$$c \circ (a_1,\ldots,a_n) = (c \times a_1,\ldots,c \times a_n),$$

where $+$ and $\times$ denote the addition and multiplication, respectively, of the field F. Relative to $\oplus$ and $\circ$, $C_n(F)$ is a vector space, called the *n-dimensional coordinate space* over F.

A vector space $V(F)$ is *n-dimensional* over F provided V contains n elements $\nu_1, \nu_2, \ldots, \nu_n$ such that each element $\nu \in V$ is uniquely expressible in the form

$$\nu = a_1 \circ \nu_1 \oplus a_2 \circ \nu_2 \oplus \cdots \oplus a_n \circ \nu_n$$

for some $a_1,a_2,\ldots,a_n \in F$.

Two vector spaces $V(F)$ and $W(F)$ over the field of scalars F are *isomorphic* provided there is a one-to-one correspondence between the elements of V and the elements of W which is preserved under the arithmetic of the two spaces.

Basic Theorem.   An n-dimensional vector space $V(F)$ is isomorphic with the coordinate space $C_n(F)$ (of Example 2, above).

MATRICES AND DETERMINANTS

Dr. R. E. Bargmann

1. GENERAL DEFINITIONS

1.1. A matrix is an array of numbers, consisting of m rows and n columns. It is usually denoted by a bold-face capital letter, e.g.,

$$\mathbf{A} \qquad \Sigma \qquad \mathbf{M}$$

1.2. The (i, j) element of a matrix is the element occurring in row i and column j. It is usually denoted by a lower-case letter with subscripts, e.g.,

$$a_{ij} \qquad \sigma_{ij} \qquad m_{ij}$$

Exceptions to this convention will be stated where required.

1.3. A matrix is called rectangular if m (number of rows) $\neq n$ (number of columns).

1.4. A matrix is called square if $m = n$.

1.5a. In the transpose of a matrix $\mathbf{A}$, denoted by $\mathbf{A}'$, the element in the j'th row and i'th column of $\mathbf{A}$ is equal to the element in the i'th row and j'th column of $\mathbf{A}'$. Formally $(\mathbf{A}')_{ij} = (\mathbf{A})_{ji}$ where the symbol $(\mathbf{A}')_{ij}$ denotes the (i, j) element of $\mathbf{A}'$.

1.5b. The Hermitian conjugate of a matrix $\mathbf{A}$, denoted by $\mathbf{A}^H$ or $\mathbf{A}^\dagger$ is obtained by transposing $\mathbf{A}$ and replacing each element by its conjugate complex. Hence if

$$a_{kl} = u_{kl} + iv_{kl}$$

then

$$(\mathbf{A}^H)_{kl} = u_{lk} - iv_{lk}$$

where typical elements have been denoted by (k, l) to avoid confusion with $i = \sqrt{-1}$.

1.6a. A square matrix is called symmetric if $\mathbf{A} = \mathbf{A}'$.

1.6b. A square matrix is called Hermitian if $\mathbf{A} = \mathbf{A}^H$.

1.7. A matrix with m rows and 1 column is called a column vector and is usually denoted by bold faced, lower-case letters, e.g.,

$$\beta \qquad \mathbf{x} \qquad \mathbf{a}$$

1.8. A matrix with one row and n columns is called a row vector and is usually denoted by a primed, bold faced, lower-case letter, e.g.,

$$\mathbf{a}' \qquad \mathbf{c}' \qquad \mu'$$

1.9. A matrix with one row and one column is called a scalar, and is usually denoted by a lower-case letter, occasionally italicized.

1.10. The diagonal extending from upper left (NW) to lower right (SE) is called the principal diagonal of a square matrix.

1.11a. A matrix with all elements above the principal diagonal equal to zero is called a lower triangular matrix.

Example

$$\mathbf{T} = \begin{bmatrix} t_{11} & 0 & 0 \\ t_{21} & t_{22} & 0 \\ t_{31} & t_{32} & t_{33} \end{bmatrix} \text{ is lower triangular}$$

1.11b. The transpose of a lower triangular matrix is called an upper triangular matrix.

1.12. A square matrix with all off-diagonal elements equal to zero is called a diagonal matrix, denoted by the letter **D** with subscript indicating the typical element in the principal diagonal.

Example

$$\mathbf{D}_a = \begin{bmatrix} a_1 & 0 & 0 \\ 0 & a_2 & 0 \\ 0 & 0 & a_3 \end{bmatrix} \text{ is diagonal}$$

2. ADDITION, SUBTRACTION, AND MULTIPLICATION

2.1. Two matrices **A** and **B** can be added (subtracted) if the number of rows (columns) in **A** equals the number of rows (columns) in **B**.

$$\mathbf{A} \pm \mathbf{B} = \mathbf{C}$$

implies

$$a_{ij} \pm b_{ij} = c_{ij} \qquad i = 1, 2, \dots m$$
$$j = 1, 2, \dots n$$

2.2. Multiplication of a matrix or vector by a scalar implies multiplication of each element by the scalar. If

$$\mathbf{B} = \gamma \mathbf{A}$$

then

$$b_{ij} = \gamma a_{ij}$$

for all elements.

2.3a. Two matrices, **A** and **B**, can be multiplied if the number of columns in **A** equals the number of rows in **B**.

2.3b. Let **A** be of order $(m \times n)$ (have m rows and n columns) and **B** of order $(n \times p)$. Then the product of two matrices **C** = **AB**, is a matrix of order $(m \times p)$ with elements

$$c_{ij} = \sum_{k=1}^{n} a_{ik} b_{kj}$$

This states that c_{ij} is the scalar product of the i'th row vector of **A** and the j'th column vector of **B**.

Example

$$\begin{bmatrix} 3 & 4 & 2 \\ 2 & 3 & -1 \end{bmatrix} \begin{bmatrix} 1 & -2 & -4 \\ 0 & -1 & 2 \\ 6 & -3 & 9 \end{bmatrix} = \begin{bmatrix} 15 & -16 & 14 \\ -4 & -4 & -11 \end{bmatrix}$$

e.g.,

$$c_{23} = \begin{bmatrix} 2 & 3 & -1 \end{bmatrix} \begin{bmatrix} -4 \\ 2 \\ 9 \end{bmatrix}$$

$$= 2 \times (-4) + 3 \times 2 + (-1) \times 9 = -11$$

2.3c. In general, matrix multiplication is not commutative

$$\mathbf{AB} \neq \mathbf{BA}$$

2.3d. Matrix multiplication is associative

$$\mathbf{A(BC)} = \mathbf{(AB)C}$$

2.3e. The distributive law for multiplication and addition holds as in the case of scalars,

$$\mathbf{(A + B)C} = \mathbf{AC} + \mathbf{BC}$$
$$\mathbf{C(A + B)} = \mathbf{CA} + \mathbf{CB}$$

2.4. In some applications, the term-by-term product of two matrices **A** and **B** of identical order is defined as

$$\mathbf{C} = \mathbf{A} * \mathbf{B}$$

where

$$c_{ij} = a_{ij}b_{ij}$$

2.5. $(\mathbf{ABC})' = \mathbf{C'B'A'}$
2.6. $(\mathbf{ABC})^H = \mathbf{C}^H\mathbf{B}^H\mathbf{A}^H$
2.7. If both **A** and **B** are symmetric, then $(\mathbf{AB})' = \mathbf{BA}$. Note that the product of two symmetric matrices is generally not symmetric.

3.   RECOGNITION RULES AND SPECIAL FORMS

3.1. A column (row) vector with all elements equal to zero is called a null vector, and usually denoted by the symbol **0**.

3.2. A null matrix has all elements equal to zero.

3.3a. A diagonal matrix with all elements equal to one in the principal diagonal is called the identity matrix **I**.

3.3b. $\gamma\mathbf{I}$, i.e., a diagonal matrix with all diagonal elements equal to a constant γ, is called a scalar matrix.

3.4. A matrix which has only one element equal to one and all others equal to zero is called an elementary matrix $(\mathbf{EL})_{ij}$.

Example

$$(\mathbf{EL})_{23} = \begin{bmatrix} 0 & 0 & 0 & 0 & 0 \\ 0 & 0 & 1 & 0 & 0 \\ 0 & 0 & 0 & 0 & 0 \\ 0 & 0 & 0 & 0 & 0 \end{bmatrix}$$

The order of the matrix is usually implicit.

3.5a. The symbol **j** is reserved for a column vector with all elements equal to 1.

3.5b. The symbol **j'** is reserved for a row vector with all elements equal to 1.

3.6. An expression ending with a column vector is a column vector.

Example

$$\mathbf{ABx} = \mathbf{y}$$

(It is assumed that rule 2.3a is satisfied, else matrix multiplication would not be defined.)

3.7. An expression beginning with a row vector is a row vector.

Example

$$\mathbf{y'(A + BC)} = \mathbf{d'}$$

3.8. An expression beginning with a row vector and ending with a column vector, is a scalar.

Example

$$\mathbf{a'Bc} = \gamma$$

3.9a. If $\mathbf{Q}$ is a square matrix, the scalar $\mathbf{x'Qx}$ is called a quadratic form. If $\mathbf{Q}$ is non-symmetric, one can always find a symmetric matrix $\mathbf{Q^*}$ such that

$$\mathbf{x'Qx} = \mathbf{x'Q^*x}$$

where

$$(\mathbf{Q^*})_{ij} = \tfrac{1}{2}(q_{ij} + q_{ji})$$

3.9b. If $\mathbf{Q}$ is a square matrix the scalar $\mathbf{x^H Qx}$ is called a Hermitian form.

3.10. A scalar $\mathbf{x'Qy}$ is called a bilinear form.

3.11. The scalar $\mathbf{x'x} = \Sigma x_i^2$, i.e., the sum of squares of all elements of $\mathbf{x}$.

3.12. The scalar $\mathbf{x'y} = \Sigma x_i y_i$, i.e., the sum of products of elements in $\mathbf{x}$ by those in $\mathbf{y}$. $\mathbf{x}$ and $\mathbf{y}$ have the same number of elements.

3.13. The scalar $\mathbf{x'D_w x} = \Sigma w_i x_i^2$ is called a weighted sum of squares.

3.14. The scalar $\mathbf{x'D_w y} = \Sigma w_i x_i y_i$ is called a weighted sum of products.

3.15a. The vector $\mathbf{Aj}$ is a column vector whose elements are the row sums of $\mathbf{A}$.

3.15b. The vector $\mathbf{j'A}$ is a row vector whose elements are the column sums of $\mathbf{A}$.

3.15c. The scalar $\mathbf{j'Aj}$ is the sum of all elements in $\mathbf{A}$. Schematically

$\mathbf{A}$	$\mathbf{Aj}$
$\mathbf{j'A}$	$\mathbf{j'Aj}$

3.16a. If $\mathbf{B} = \mathbf{D_w A}$; then $b_{ij} = w_i a_{ij}$.

3.16b. If $\mathbf{B} = \mathbf{AD_w}$; then $b_{ij} = a_{ij} w_j$.

3.17. Interchanging summation and matrix notation:

If

$$\mathbf{ABCD} = \mathbf{E}$$

then

$$e_{ij} = \sum_k \sum_l \sum_m a_{ik} b_{kl} c_{lm} d_{mj}$$

The second subscript of an element must coincide with the first of the next one. Reordering and transposing may be required.

Example

If

$$e_{ij} = \sum_k \sum_l \sum_m a_{kl} b_{ki} c_{jm} d_{ml}$$

$$= \sum_k \sum_l \sum_m b_{ki} a_{kl} d_{ml} c_{jm}$$

Then

$$\mathbf{E} = \mathbf{B'AD'C'}$$

3.18a. $\mathbf{A'A}$ is a symmetric matrix whose (i,j) element is the scalar product of the i'th column vector and the j'th column vector of $\mathbf{A'}$.

3.18b. $\mathbf{AA'}$ is a symmetric matrix whose (i,j) element is the scalar product of the i'th row vector and the j'th row vector of $\mathbf{A}$.

4. DETERMINANTS

4.1a. A determinant $|\mathbf{A}|$ or $\det(\mathbf{A})$ is a scalar function of a square matrix defined in such a way that

$$|\mathbf{A}|\ |\mathbf{B}| = |\mathbf{AB}|$$

and

$$\begin{vmatrix} a_{11} & a_{12} \\ a_{21} & a_{22} \end{vmatrix} = a_{11}a_{22} - a_{12}a_{21}$$

4.1b. $|\mathbf{A}| = |\mathbf{A}'|$

4.2.

$$\begin{vmatrix} a_{11} & a_{12} & a_{13} \\ a_{21} & a_{22} & a_{23} \\ a_{31} & a_{32} & a_{33} \end{vmatrix} = \begin{aligned} & a_{11}a_{22}a_{33} + a_{12}a_{23}a_{31} + a_{13}a_{21}a_{32} \\ & - a_{13}a_{22}a_{31} - a_{11}a_{23}a_{32} - a_{12}a_{21}a_{33} \end{aligned}$$

4.3.

$$\begin{vmatrix} a_{11} & a_{12} & \cdots & a_{1n} \\ a_{21} & a_{22} & \cdots & a_{2n} \\ & & \cdots & \\ a_{n1} & a_{n2} & \cdots & a_{nm} \end{vmatrix} = \sum (-1)^{\delta} a_{1i_1} a_{2i_2} \cdots a_{ni_n}$$

where the sum is over all permutations

$$i_1 \neq i_2 \neq \cdots i_n$$

and δ denotes the number of exchanges necessary to bring the sequence $(i_1, i_2, \ldots i_n)$ back into the natural order $(1, 2, \ldots n)$.

4.4. If two rows (columns) in a matrix are exchanged, the determinant will change its sign.

4.5. A determinant does not change its value if a linear combination of other rows (columns) is added to any given row (column).

Example

$$\begin{vmatrix} a_{11} & a_{12} & a_{13} & a_{14} \\ b_{21} & b_{22} & b_{23} & b_{24} \\ a_{31} & a_{32} & a_{33} & a_{34} \\ a_{41} & a_{42} & a_{43} & a_{44} \end{vmatrix} = \begin{vmatrix} a_{11} & a_{12} & a_{13} & a_{14} \\ a_{21} & a_{22} & a_{23} & a_{24} \\ a_{31} & a_{32} & a_{33} & a_{34} \\ a_{41} & a_{42} & a_{43} & a_{44} \end{vmatrix}$$

where

$$b_{2i} = a_{2i} + \gamma_1 a_{1i} + \gamma_3 a_{3i} + \gamma_4 a_{4i}$$
$$i = 1, 2, 3, 4$$

$\gamma_1, \gamma_3, \gamma_4$ arbitrary.

4.6. If the i'th row (column) equals (a constant times) the j'th row (column) of a matrix, its determinant is equal to zero, $(i \neq j)$.

4.7. If, in a matrix $\mathbf{A}$, each element of a row (column) is multiplied by a constant γ, the determinant is multiplied by γ.

4.8. $|\gamma \mathbf{A}| = \gamma^n |\mathbf{A}|$ assuming that $\mathbf{A}$ is of order $(n \times n)$.

4.9. The cofactor of a square matrix $\mathbf{A}$, $\text{cof}_{ij}(\mathbf{A})$ is the determinant of a matrix obtained by striking the i'th row and j'th column of $\mathbf{A}$ and choosing positive (negative) sign if $i + j$ is even (odd).

Example

$$\text{cof}_{23} \begin{bmatrix} 2 & 4 & 3 \\ 6 & 1 & 5 \\ -2 & 1 & 3 \end{bmatrix} = - \begin{vmatrix} 2 & 4 \\ -2 & 1 \end{vmatrix}$$

$$= -(2 + 8) = -10$$

4.10. (Laplace Development)

$$|\mathbf{A}| = a_{i1}\text{cof}_{i1}(\mathbf{A}) + a_{i2}\text{cof}_{i2}(\mathbf{A}) + \cdots + a_{in}\text{cof}_{in}(\mathbf{A})$$
$$= a_{1j}\text{cof}_{1j}(\mathbf{A}) + a_{2j}\text{cof}_{2j}(\mathbf{A}) + \cdots + a_{nj}\text{cof}_{nj}(\mathbf{A})$$

for any row i or any column j.

4.11. Numerical Evaluation of the determinant of a symmetric matrix.

Note: If $\mathbf{A}$ is non-symmetric, form $\mathbf{A'A}$ or $\mathbf{AA'}$ by rule 3.18, obtain its determinant, and take the square root.

("Forward Doolittle Scheme", "left side")
Let

$$p_{11} = a_{11}, \quad p_{12} = a_{12} = a_{21}, \ldots p_{1n} = a_{1n}$$

$$
\begin{array}{ccccc}
p_{11} & p_{12} & p_{13} & \cdots & p_{1n} \\
1 & u_{12} & u_{13} & \cdots & u_{1n} \\
\hline
 & a_{22} & a_{23} & \cdots & a_{2n} \\
 & p_{22} & p_{23} & \cdots & p_{2n} \\
 & 1 & u_{23} & \cdots & u_{2n} \\
\hline
 & & a_{33} & \cdots & a_{3n} \\
 & & p_{33} & \cdots & p_{3n} \\
 & & 1 & \cdots & u_{3n} \\
\hline
 & & \cdot & \cdots & \cdot \\
 & & & & a_{nn} \\
 & & & & p_{nn} \\
 & & & & 1
\end{array}
$$

$$
\begin{aligned}
u_{1i} &= p_{1i}/p_{11} & i &= 1,2,\ldots n \\
p_{2i} &= a_{2i} - u_{12}p_{1i} & i &= 2,3,\ldots n \\
u_{2i} &= p_{2i}/p_{22} & \\
p_{3i} &= a_{3i} - u_{13}p_{1i} - u_{23}p_{2i} & i &= 3,4,\ldots n \\
u_{3i} &= p_{3i}/p_{33} & \\
p_{ki} &= a_{ki} - u_{1k}p_{1i} - u_{2k}p_{2i} - \cdots - u_{k-1,k}p_{k-1,i} & i &= k, k+1,\ldots n \\
 & & k &= 2,3,\ldots n \\
u_{ki} &= p_{ki}/p_{kk} &
\end{aligned}
$$

If, at some stage, $p_{kk} = 0$, reordering of rows and columns may be required. If the matrix is positive-definite (see 8.16) (always true for $\mathbf{AA'}$ or $\mathbf{A'A}$, see rule 10.24), none of the

p_{kk} will be zero. The p_{ii} are called pivots. Then

$$| A | = \prod_{i-1}^{n} p_{ii}$$

Further, if **A** is partitioned

$$A = \begin{bmatrix} A_{11} & A_{12} \\ A'_{12} & A_{22} \end{bmatrix}$$

where A_{11} is of order $(k \times k)$, then

$$| A_{11} | = \prod_{i-1}^{k} p_{ii}$$

(Numerical Examples: see 6.14.)

5. SINGULARITY AND RANK

5.1. A matrix **A** is called singular if there exists a vector $x \neq 0$ such that $Ax = 0$ or $A'x = 0$. Note $x \neq 0$ if a single element of x is unequal 0. If a matrix is not singular, it is called non-singular.

5.2. If a matrix A_1 can be formed by selection of r rows and columns of **A** such that $A_1 x \neq 0$ or $A'_1 x \neq 0$ for every $x \neq 0$, and if addition of an $(r + 1)st$ row and column would produce a singular matrix, r is called the rank of **A**.

Example

$$A = \begin{bmatrix} 2 & 4 & 6 \\ 1 & 3 & 7 \\ 3 & 7 & 13 \\ 1 & 1 & -1 \end{bmatrix}$$

Note that

$$[1, \quad 1, \quad -1] \begin{bmatrix} 2 & 4 & 6 \\ 1 & 3 & 7 \\ 3 & 7 & 13 \end{bmatrix} = [0 \quad 0 \quad 0]$$

and

$$[1, \quad -1, \quad -1] \begin{bmatrix} 2 & 4 & 6 \\ 1 & 3 & 7 \\ 1 & 1 & -1 \end{bmatrix} = [0 \quad 0 \quad 0]$$

but

$$\begin{bmatrix} 2 & 4 \\ 1 & 3 \end{bmatrix} \begin{bmatrix} x_1 \\ x_2 \end{bmatrix} \neq \begin{bmatrix} 0 \\ 0 \end{bmatrix}$$

or

$$[x_1 \quad x_2] \begin{bmatrix} 2 & 4 \\ 1 & 3 \end{bmatrix} \neq [0, \quad 0]$$

for any arbitrary

$$[x_1, \quad x_2] \neq [0, \quad 0].$$

Hence the matrix has rank 2.

5.3. If A has rank r and if A_1 is a non-singular submatrix consisting of r rows and columns of A, then A_1 is called a basis of A.

5.4a. The determinant of a square singular matrix is 0.

5.4b. The determinant of a non-singular matrix is $\neq 0$.

5.5. rank $(AB) \leq$ min [rank (A), rank (B)].

5.6. rank $(AA') =$ rank $(A'A) =$ rank (A).

5.7. $|A'A| = |AA'| = |A|^2$ if A is square.

5.8. $|A'A| = |AA'| \geq 0$ for every A with real elements.

6. INVERSION

(Regular Case, non-singular matrices)

6.1. If A is square and non-singular ($|A| \neq 0$) there exists a unique matrix A^{-1} such that $AA^{-1} = A^{-1}A = I$.

6.2. $(ABC)^{-1} = C^{-1}B^{-1}A^{-1}$ (provided that all inverses exist).

6.3. $(A^{-1})' = (A')^{-1}$

6.4. $Ax = b$ is a system of linear equations. If A is square and non-singular, there exists a unique solution

$$x = A^{-1}b$$

6.5. $(\gamma A)^{-1} = (1/\gamma)A^{-1}$

6.6. $|A^{-1}| = 1/|A|$

6.7. $D_w^{-1} = D_{1/w}$ where D is a diagonal matrix.

6.8. If

$$A = B + uv'$$

then

$$A^{-1} = B^{-1} - \lambda yz'$$

where

$$y = B^{-1}u, \quad z' = v'B^{-1},$$

and

$$\lambda = 1/(1 + z'u)$$

Example 6.8.1

$$A = \begin{bmatrix} 4 & 2 & 4 & 5 \\ 3 & 9 & 12 & 15 \\ 2 & 4 & 11 & 10 \\ 1 & 2 & 4 & 10 \end{bmatrix}$$

This matrix can be written as

$$\begin{bmatrix} 3 & 0 & 0 & 0 \\ 0 & 3 & 0 & 0 \\ 0 & 0 & 3 & 0 \\ 0 & 0 & 0 & 5 \end{bmatrix} + \begin{bmatrix} 1 \\ 3 \\ 2 \\ 1 \end{bmatrix} [1 \quad 2 \quad 4 \quad 5] = B + uv'$$

$$\mathbf{B}^{-1} = \begin{bmatrix} 1/3 & 0 & 0 & 0 \\ 0 & 1/3 & 0 & 0 \\ 0 & 0 & 1/3 & 0 \\ 0 & 0 & 0 & 1/5 \end{bmatrix}$$

$$\mathbf{y} = \mathbf{B}^{-1}\mathbf{u} = \begin{bmatrix} 1/3 \\ 1 \\ 2/3 \\ 1/5 \end{bmatrix}$$

$$\mathbf{z}' = \mathbf{v}'\mathbf{B}^{-1} = [1/3 \quad 2/3 \quad 4/3 \quad 1]$$

$$\mathbf{z}'\mathbf{u} = 1/3 \times 1 + 2/3 \times 3 + 4/3 \times 2 + 1 \times 1 = 6$$

$$\lambda = 1/7$$

$$\mathbf{A}^{-1} = \begin{bmatrix} 1/3 & 0 & 0 & 0 \\ 0 & 1/3 & 0 & 0 \\ 0 & 0 & 1/3 & 0 \\ 0 & 0 & 0 & 1/5 \end{bmatrix} - (1/7) \begin{bmatrix} 1/3 \\ 1 \\ 2/3 \\ 1/5 \end{bmatrix} [1/3 \quad 2/3 \quad 4/3 \quad 1]$$

$$= (1/315) \begin{bmatrix} 100 & -10 & -20 & -15 \\ -15 & 75 & -60 & -45 \\ -10 & -20 & 65 & -30 \\ -3 & -6 & -12 & 54 \end{bmatrix}$$

(This rule is especially useful if all off-diagonal elements are equal, then $\mathbf{u} = k\mathbf{j}$ and $\mathbf{v}' = \mathbf{j}'$ and $\mathbf{B}$ is diagonal.)

6.9. Let $\mathbf{B}$ (elements b_{ij}) have a known inverse, $\mathbf{B}^{-1}$ (elements b^{ij}). Let $\mathbf{A} = \mathbf{B}$ except for one element $a_{rs} = b_{rs} + k$. Then the elements of $\mathbf{A}^{-1}$ are

$$a^{ij} = b^{ij} - \frac{kb^{ir}b^{sj}}{1 + kb^{sr}}$$

6.10. (Partitioning)

Let

$$\mathbf{A} = \begin{matrix} (p) \\ (q) \end{matrix} \begin{matrix} (p) & (q) \\ \begin{bmatrix} \mathbf{B} & \mathbf{C} \\ \mathbf{D} & \mathbf{E} \end{bmatrix} \end{matrix}$$

(letters in parentheses denote order of the submatrices)

Let $\mathbf{B}^{-1}$ and $\mathbf{E}^{-1}$ exist. Then

$$\mathbf{A}^{-1} = \begin{bmatrix} \mathbf{X} & \mathbf{Y} \\ \mathbf{Z} & \mathbf{U} \end{bmatrix}$$

where

$$\mathbf{X} = (\mathbf{B} - \mathbf{C}\mathbf{E}^{-1}\mathbf{D})^{-1}$$
$$\mathbf{U} = (\mathbf{E} - \mathbf{D}\mathbf{B}^{-1}\mathbf{C})^{-1}$$
$$\mathbf{Y} = -\mathbf{B}^{-1}\mathbf{C}\mathbf{U}$$
$$\mathbf{Z} = -\mathbf{E}^{-1}\mathbf{D}\mathbf{X}$$

6.11. (Partitioning of Determinants)

Let

$$|\mathbf{A}| = \begin{vmatrix} \mathbf{B} & \mathbf{C} \\ \mathbf{D} & \mathbf{E} \end{vmatrix} \qquad \text{(same structure as in 6.10)}$$

Then

$$|\mathbf{A}| = |\mathbf{E}| \, |(\mathbf{B} - \mathbf{C}\mathbf{E}^{-1}\mathbf{D})| = |\mathbf{B}| \, |(\mathbf{E} - \mathbf{D}\mathbf{B}^{-1}\mathbf{C})|$$

6.12. Let

$$\mathbf{A} = \mathbf{B} + \mathbf{U}\mathbf{V}$$

where $\mathbf{B}(n \times n)$ has an inverse

$\mathbf{U}$ is of order $(n \times k)$, with k usually very small
$\mathbf{V}$ is of order $(k \times n)$

(the special case for $k = 1$ is treated in 6.8).

Then

$$\mathbf{A}^{-1} = \mathbf{B}^{-1} - \mathbf{Y}\boldsymbol{\Lambda}\mathbf{Z}$$

where

$$\mathbf{Y} = \mathbf{B}^{-1}\mathbf{U}(n \times k)$$
$$\mathbf{Z} = \mathbf{V}\mathbf{B}^{-1}(k \times n)$$

and

$$\boldsymbol{\Lambda}(k \times k) = [\mathbf{I} + \mathbf{Z}\mathbf{U}]^{-1}$$

6.13. Let a_{ij} denote the elements of $\mathbf{A}$ and a^{ij} those of $\mathbf{A}^{-1}$. Then

$$a^{ij} = \text{cof}_{ji}(\mathbf{A})/\,|\mathbf{A}|$$

where cof is the determinant defined in 4.9.

6.14. "Doolittle" Method of inverting symmetric matrices (see also 4.11). Let

$$p_{11} = a_{11}, \quad p_{12} = a_{12} = a_{21}, \ldots p_{1n} = a_{1n} = a_{n1}$$

Forward Solution

p_{11}	p_{12}	p_{13}	$\cdots$	p_{1n}	1				
1	u_{12}	u_{13}	$\cdots$	u_{1n}	u_{11}				
	a_{22}	a_{23}	$\cdots$	a_{2n}	0	1			
	p_{22}	p_{23}	$\cdots$	p_{2n}	p_{21}	$p_{2\text{II}}$			
	1	u_{23}	$\cdots$	u_{2n}	u_{21}	$u_{2\text{II}}$			
		a_{33}	$\cdots$	a_{3n}	0	0	1		
		p_{33}	$\cdots$	p_{3n}	p_{31}	$p_{3\text{II}}$	$p_{3\text{III}}$		
		1	$\cdots$	u_{3n}	u_{31}	$u_{3\text{II}}$	$u_{3\text{III}}$		
		$\cdot$	$\cdots$	$\cdot$	$\cdot$	$\cdots$	$\cdot$		
				a_{nn}	0	0	0	$\cdots$	1
				p_{nn}	p_{n1}	$p_{n\text{II}}$	$p_{n\text{III}}$	$\cdots$	p_{nN}
				1	u_{n1}	$u_{n\text{II}}$	$u_{n\text{III}}$	$\cdots$	u_{nN}

$$u_{1i} = p_{1i}/p_{11} \qquad\qquad i = 1, 2, \ldots n, \text{I}$$

$$p_{2i} = a_{2i} - u_{12}p_{1i} \qquad\quad i = 2, 3, \ldots n, \text{I}, \text{II}$$

$$u_{2i} = p_{2i}/p_{22}$$

$$p_{3i} = a_{3i} - u_{13}p_{1i} - u_{23}p_{2i} \qquad i = 3, 4, \ldots n, \text{I}, \text{II}, \text{III}$$

$$u_{3i} = p_{3i}/p_{33}$$

$$p_{ki} = a_{ki} - u_{1k}p_{1i} - u_{2k}p_{2i} - \cdots - u_{k-1,k}p_{k-1,i} \quad \begin{aligned} i &= k, k+1, \ldots n, \text{I}, \text{II}, \ldots K \\ k &= 2, 3, \ldots n \end{aligned}$$

$$u_{ki} = p_{ki}/p_{kk}$$

Backward Solution

(*j* refers to Arabic, *J* refers to Roman numerals)

The elements of A^{-1} are a^{ij}

$$a^{nj} = u_{nJ} \qquad\qquad \begin{aligned} j &= 1, 2, \ldots n; \\ J &= \text{I}, \text{II}, \ldots N \end{aligned}$$

$$a^{n-1,j} = u_{n-1,J} - u_{n-1,n}a^{nj} \qquad\qquad \begin{aligned} j &= 1, 2, \ldots (n-1); \\ J &= \text{I}, \text{II}, \ldots (N-1) \end{aligned}$$

$$a^{n-2,j} = u_{n-2,J} - u_{n-2,n}a^{nj} - u_{n-2,n-1}a^{n-1,j} \qquad \begin{aligned} j &= 1, 2, \ldots (n-2); \\ J &= \text{I}, \text{II}, \ldots (N-2) \end{aligned}$$

$$a^{n-k,j} = u_{n-k,J} - u_{n-k,n}a^{nj} - u_{n-k,n-1}a^{n-1,j} - \cdots - u_{n-k,n-k+1}a^{n-k+1,j} \quad \begin{aligned} j &= 1, 2, \ldots (n-k); \\ J &= \text{I}, \text{II}, \ldots (N-k); \\ k &= 1, 2, \ldots (n-1), \end{aligned}$$

and $a^{ji} = a^{ij}$.

Numerical Example 6.14.1.

Invert the Matrix

$$\begin{bmatrix} 25 & 30 & -10 \\ 30 & 40 & -6 \\ -10 & -6 & 17 \end{bmatrix}$$

a_1	25	30	-10	1		
u_1	1	1.2	-0.4	0.04		
	a_2	40	-6	0	1	
	p_2	4	6	-1.2	1	
	u_2	1	1.5	-0.3	0.25	
		a_3	17	0	0	1
		p_3	4	2.2	-1.5	1
		u_3	1	0.55	-0.375	0.25

1.61	-1.125	0.55
-1.125	0.8125	-0.375
0.55	-0.375	0.25

Enter row a_1.
Elements in u_1 = Elements in a_1 divided by $a_{11}(=25)$.
Enter row a_2.

$$p_{22} = 40 - 1.2 \times 30 = 4$$
$$p_{23} = -6 - 1.2 \times (-10) = 6$$
$$p_{21} = 0 - 1.2 \times 1 = -1.2$$
$$p_{211} = 1$$

Elements in u_2 = Elements in p_2 divided by $p_{22}(=4)$.
Enter row a_3.

$$p_{33} = 17 - (-0.4) \times (-10) - 1.5 \times 6 = 4$$
$$p_{31} = 0 - (-0.4) \times 1 - 1.5 \times (-1.2) = 2.2$$
$$p_{311} = 0 - 1.5 \times 1 = -1.5$$
$$p_{3111} = 1$$

Elements in u_3 = Elements in p_3 divided by $p_{33}(=4)$.
Copy the right-hand side of the last (third) u – row as the last column below the double line.

$$a^{21} = -0.3 - 1.5 \times 0.55 = -1.125$$
$$a^{22} = 0.25 - 1.5 \times (-0.375) = 0.8125$$
$$a^{23} = 0 - 1.5 \times 0.25 = -0.375 \quad \text{(check against } a^{32}\text{)}.$$

These are entered in the next to last (second) column below.

$$a^{11} = 0.04 - (-0.4) \times 0.55 - 1.2 \times (-1.125) = 1.61$$
$$a^{12} = 0 - (-0.4) \times (-0.375) - 1.2 \times 0.8125 = -1.125 \quad \text{(check against } a^{21}\text{)}$$
$$a^{13} = 0 - (-0.4) \times (0.25) - 1.2 \times (-0.375) = 0.55 \quad \text{(check against } a^{31}\text{)}.$$

6.15. A matrix is called orthogonal if $\mathbf{A}' = \mathbf{A}^{-1}$ (or $\mathbf{AA}' = \mathbf{I}$).

7.   TRACES

7.1. If $\mathbf{A}$ is a square matrix then the trace of $\mathbf{A}$ is $tr\ \mathbf{A} = \sum_i a_{ii}$, i.e., the sum of the diagonal elements.

7.2. If $\mathbf{A}$ is of order $(m \times k)$ and $\mathbf{B}$ of order $(k \times m)$ then $tr(\mathbf{AB}) = tr(\mathbf{BA})$.

7.3. If $\mathbf{A}$ is of order $(m \times k)$, $\mathbf{B}$ of order $(k \times r)$ and $\mathbf{C}$ of order $(r \times m)$, then

$$tr(\mathbf{ABC}) = tr(\mathbf{BCA}) = tr(\mathbf{CAB}).$$

7.3a. If $\mathbf{b}$ is a column vector and $\mathbf{c}'$ a row vector, then

$$tr(\mathbf{Abc}') = tr(\mathbf{bc}'\mathbf{A}) = \mathbf{c}'\mathbf{Ab}$$

since the trace of a scalar is the scalar.

7.4. $tr(\mathbf{A} + \gamma\mathbf{B}) = tr\mathbf{A} + \gamma tr\mathbf{B}$; where γ is a scalar.

7.5. $tr(\mathbf{EL})_{ij}\mathbf{A} = tr\mathbf{A}(\mathbf{EL})_{ij} = a_{ji}$; where $(\mathbf{EL})_{ij}$ is an elementary matrix as defined in 3.4.

7.6. $tr(\mathbf{EL})_{ij}\mathbf{A}(\mathbf{EL})_{rs}\mathbf{B} = a_{jr}b_{si}$

(These rules are useful in matrix differentiation)

7.7. The trace of the second order of a square matrix $\mathbf{A}$ is the sum of the determinants of all $\binom{n}{2}$ matrices of order (2×2) which can be formed by intersecting rows i and j with columns i and j.

$$tr_2 \mathbf{A} = \begin{vmatrix} a_{11} & a_{12} \\ a_{21} & a_{22} \end{vmatrix} + \begin{vmatrix} a_{11} & a_{13} \\ a_{31} & a_{33} \end{vmatrix}$$

$$+ \cdots + \begin{vmatrix} a_{11} & a_{1n} \\ a_{n1} & a_{nn} \end{vmatrix} + \begin{vmatrix} a_{22} & a_{23} \\ a_{32} & a_{33} \end{vmatrix}$$

$$+ \cdots + \begin{vmatrix} a_{22} & a_{2n} \\ a_{n2} & a_{nn} \end{vmatrix} + \cdots + \begin{vmatrix} a_{n-1,n-1} & a_{n-1,n} \\ a_{n,n-1} & a_{nn} \end{vmatrix}$$

7.8. The trace of the k'th order of a square matrix is the sum of the determinants of all $\binom{n}{k}$ matrices of order $(k \times k)$ which can be formed by intersecting any k rows of $\mathbf{A}$ with the same k columns.

$$tr_k \mathbf{A} = \sum \begin{vmatrix} a_{i_1 i_1} & a_{i_1 i_2} & \cdots & a_{i_1 i_k} \\ a_{i_2 i_1} & a_{i_2 i_2} & \cdots & a_{i_2 i_k} \\ \cdot & \cdot & \cdots & \cdot \\ a_{i_k i_1} & a_{i_k i_2} & \cdots & a_{i_k i_k} \end{vmatrix}$$

where the sum extends over all combinations of n elements taken k at a time in order

$$i_1 < i_2 < \cdots < i_k.$$

7.9. Rules 7.2 and 7.3 (cyclic exchange) are valid for trace of k'th order.
7.10. $tr_n \mathbf{A} = |\mathbf{A}|$ if $\mathbf{A}$ is of order $(n \times n)$.

8. CHARACTERISTIC ROOTS AND VECTORS

8.1. If $\mathbf{A}$ is a square matrix of order $(n \times n)$, then $|\mathbf{A} - \lambda\mathbf{I}| = 0$ is called the characteristic equation of the matrix $\mathbf{A}$. It is a polynomial of the n'th degree in λ.

8.2. The n roots of the characteristic equation (not necessarily distinct) are called the characteristic roots of $\mathbf{A}$

$$ch(\mathbf{A}) = \lambda_1, \lambda_2, \ldots \lambda_n$$

8.3. The characteristic equation of $\mathbf{A}$ can be obtained by the relation

$$\lambda^n - (tr\mathbf{A})\lambda^{n-1} + (tr_2\mathbf{A})\lambda^{n-2} - (tr_3\mathbf{A})\lambda^{n-3} \cdots - (-1)^n(tr_{n-1}\mathbf{A})\lambda + (-1)^n|\mathbf{A}| = 0$$

where tr_k is defined in 7.8.

Example 8.3.1

$$\mathbf{A} = \begin{bmatrix} 25 & 30 & -10 \\ 30 & 40 & -6 \\ -10 & -6 & 17 \end{bmatrix}$$

$tr\mathbf{A} = 25 + 40 + 17 = 82$
$tr_2\mathbf{A} = (25 \times 40 - 30 \times 30) + (25 \times 17 - 10 \times 10) + (40 \times 17 - 6 \times 6) = 1069$
$tr_3\mathbf{A} = |\mathbf{A}| = 25 \times 4 \times 4 = 400$

(cf. 6.14 and procedure stated in 4.11)

Hence

$$\lambda^3 - 82\lambda^2 + 1069\lambda - 400 = 0$$

The solutions (by Newton iteration) are

$$\lambda_1 = 65.86108$$
$$\lambda_2 = 15.75339$$
$$\lambda_3 = 0.38553$$

These are the characteristic roots of **A**.

8.4. $ch(\mathbf{A} + \gamma\mathbf{I}) = \gamma + ch(\mathbf{A})$

8.5. $ch(\mathbf{AB}) = ch(\mathbf{BA})$

(except that **AB** or **BA** may have additional roots equal to zero).

8.6. $ch(\mathbf{A}^{-1}) = 1/ch(\mathbf{A})$

8.7. If $\lambda_1, \lambda_2, \ldots \lambda_n$ are the roots of **A** then

$$\sum_i \lambda_i = tr\,\mathbf{A}$$

$$\sum_{i<j} \lambda_i\lambda_j = tr_2\mathbf{A}$$

$$\sum_{i<j<k} \lambda_i\lambda_j\lambda_k = tr_3\mathbf{A}$$

$$\prod_i \lambda_i = |\mathbf{A}|$$

8.8. If $\mathbf{x}'$ denotes the radius vector (running coordinates $[x, y, z]$) and if a matrix **Q** is positive-definite, then

$$(\mathbf{x}' - \mathbf{x}_0')\mathbf{Q}^{-1}(\mathbf{x} - \mathbf{x}_0) = 1$$

is the equation of an ellipsoid with center at $[x_0, y_0, z_0] = \mathbf{x}_0'$ and semi-axes equal to the square roots of the characteristic roots of **Q**.

8.9. The characteristic roots of a triangular (or diagonal) matrix are the diagonal elements of the matrix.

8.10. If **A** is a real matrix with positive roots, then

$$ch_{min}(\mathbf{AA}') \leq [ch_{min}(\mathbf{A})]^2 \leq [ch_{max}(\mathbf{A})]^2 \leq ch_{max}(\mathbf{AA}')$$

where ch_{min} denotes the smallest and ch_{max} the largest root.

8.11. The ratio of two quadratic forms (**B** non-singular)

$$u = \frac{\mathbf{x}'\mathbf{A}\mathbf{x}}{\mathbf{x}'\mathbf{B}\mathbf{x}}$$

attains stationary values at the roots of $\mathbf{B}^{-1}\mathbf{A}$. In particular

$$u_{max} = ch_{max}(\mathbf{B}^{-1}\mathbf{A}) \quad \text{and} \quad u_{min} = ch_{min}(\mathbf{B}^{-1}\mathbf{A})$$

8.12. The equation system

$$\mathbf{Ax} = \lambda\mathbf{x}$$

permits non-zero solutions only if λ is one of the characteristic roots of **A**. Such a solution **x** is called a characteristic vector.

8.13. If **x** is a solution to 8.12, so is $\gamma\mathbf{x}$ for an arbitrary scalar γ.

8.14. A solution **x** which has unit length ($\mathbf{x}'\mathbf{x} = 1$) is called the eigenvector associated with the characteristic root λ of **A**. The vector is frequently denoted by **e**.

8.15. A real symmetric matrix has real roots.

8.16. A matrix **A** is called positive-definite (abbreviated p.d.) if the quadratic form $\mathbf{x}'\mathbf{A}\mathbf{x} > 0$ for every $\mathbf{x} \neq \mathbf{0}$.

8.17. A matrix $\mathbf{A}$ is called positive-semidefinite (abbreviated p.s.d.) if the quadratic form $\mathbf{x'Ax} > 0$ and/or $\mathbf{x'Ax} = 0$ for some $\mathbf{x} \neq \mathbf{0}$.

8.18. A positive-definite real symmetric matrix has only positive characteristic roots.

8.19. If a real symmetric matrix is positive-semidefinite, it has no negative roots. The number of non-zero roots equals the rank of the matrix.

8.20. If all roots of a real symmetric matrix are distinct, the associated eigenvectors are distinct.

8.21. The matrix of eigenvectors

$$\mathbf{E} = [\mathbf{e}_1, \mathbf{e}_2, \ldots \mathbf{e}_n]$$

of a real symmetric matrix is (or can be chosen to be) orthogonal.

8.22. $\mathbf{AE} = \mathbf{ED}_\lambda$.

8.23. For a real symmetric matrix, $\mathbf{A} = \mathbf{ED}_\lambda\mathbf{E'}$ (decomposition into matrices of unit rank)

$$\mathbf{E'AE} = \mathbf{D}_\lambda$$

where $\mathbf{D}_\lambda$ denotes the diagonal matrix of characteristic roots ordered in the same way as the eigenvector columns in $\mathbf{E}$.

8.24. If $f(\lambda)$ is a polynomial in λ, then

$$f(\mathbf{A}) = \mathbf{ED}_{f(\lambda)}\mathbf{E}^{-1}$$

where λ are the characteristic roots of $\mathbf{A}$ and $\mathbf{E}$ is the matrix of associated eigenvectors. If $\mathbf{A}$ is symmetric, $\mathbf{E}^{-1} = \mathbf{E'}$.

Example 8.24.1

Consider the matrix in 8.3 (and 6.14).

$$\mathbf{A} = \begin{bmatrix} 25 & 30 & -10 \\ 30 & 40 & -6 \\ -10 & -6 & 17 \end{bmatrix}$$

The characteristic roots were found in Example 8.3.1,

$$\lambda_1 = 65.86108 \qquad \lambda_2 = 15.75339 \qquad \lambda_3 = 0.38553.$$

To find some $\mathbf{x}$ such that $\mathbf{Ax} = \lambda_1\mathbf{x}$, we arbitrarily set the first element of $\mathbf{x}$ equal to 1. Using only the first two rows of $\mathbf{A}$ we solve the equation system

$$25 + 30x_2 - 10x_3 = 65.86108$$
$$30 + 40x_2 - 6x_3 = 65.86108x_2$$

which yields $x_2 = 1.24294$ and $x_3 = -0.35729$. Substitution of these values into the third equation

$$-10 - 6x_2 + 17x_3 = 65.86108x_3$$

yields zero to five decimal places, indicating the accuracy of the first characteristic root. To reduce to unit length the characteristic vector

$$[1 \qquad 1.24294 \qquad -0.35729]$$

we divide each element by

$$\sqrt{1 + 1.24294^2 + 0.35729^2}$$

and thus obtain the first eigenvector

$$[0.61170 \qquad 0.76030 \qquad -0.21855]$$

This, written as a column vector, is e_1. Repeating the same process for the second and third eigenvectors we obtain

$$e_2 = \begin{bmatrix} -0.08659 \\ 0.33896 \\ 0.93681 \end{bmatrix} \qquad e_3 = \begin{bmatrix} 0.78634 \\ -0.55412 \\ 0.27318 \end{bmatrix}$$

The three vectors can be placed into the eigenvector matrix E, which is easily seen to be orthogonal.

9. CONDITIONAL INVERSES

9.1. Any matrix A (singular or non-singular, rectangular or square) has some conditional or generalized inverse $A^{(-1)}$ defined by the relation

$$AA^{(-1)}A = A.$$

9.2. If (and only if) A is square and non-singular, $A^{(-1)}$ is unique and equals A^{-1}. Otherwise there will be infinitely many matrices $A^{(-1)}$ which satisfy the defining relation 9.1.

9.3a. If A is rectangular $(n \times m)$ of rank m, with $m < n$, then $A^{(-1)}$ is of order $(m \times n)$ and $A^{(-1)}A = I(m \times m)$. Then $A^{(-1)}$ is called an inverse from the left. $AA^{(-1)} \neq I$ in this case.

9.3b. If A is rectangular $(n \times m)$ of rank n, with $m > n$, then $A^{(-1)}$ is of order $(m \times n)$ and $AA^{(-1)} = I(n \times n)$. Then $A^{(-1)}$ is called an inverse to the right. In this case,

$$A^{(-1)}A \neq I.$$

9.3c. For a square, singular matrix, $AA^{(-1)} \neq I$ and $A^{(-1)}A \neq I$.

Example 9.3.1

$$A = \begin{bmatrix} 3 \\ 2 \\ 1 \end{bmatrix}$$

The row vector $[1/3 \quad 0 \quad 0]$ is an inverse from the left. The row vector

$$[x \quad y \quad (1 - 3x - 2y)]$$

is a conditional inverse of the above matrix A for any values of x and y. It is called the generalized inverse of A.

Example 9.3.2

$$A = \begin{bmatrix} 1 & 2 & 3 \\ 2 & 5 & 6 \\ 3 & 7 & 9 \end{bmatrix}$$

A conditional inverse is

$$A^{(-1)} = \begin{bmatrix} 5 & -2 & 0 \\ -2 & 1 & 0 \\ 0 & 0 & 0 \end{bmatrix}$$

Here it was obtained by inversion of the basis (the 2×2 matrix in the upper left-hand corner) and replacement of the other elements by zeros.

9.4. A square matrix $\mathbf{A}$ is called idempotent if $\mathbf{AA} = \mathbf{A}^2 = \mathbf{A}$.

9.5. $\mathbf{AA}^{(-1)}$ and $\mathbf{A}^{(-1)}\mathbf{A}$ are idempotent.

9.6. All characteristic roots of idempotent matrices are either zero or one.

9.7. A system of linear equations (m equations in n unknowns)

$$\mathbf{Ax} = \mathbf{b}$$

is called consistent if there exists some solution $\mathbf{x}$ which satisfies the equation system.

Example 9.7.1
    The system

$$x + \quad y = 2$$
$$2x + 2y = 4 \qquad \text{is consistent.}$$

Example 9.7.2
    The system

$$x + \quad y = 2$$
$$2x + 2y = 5 \qquad \text{is inconsistent,}$$

for no pair of values (x, y) will satisfy this system.

9.8. If, in a system of equations (rectangular or square)

$$\mathbf{Ax} = \mathbf{b}$$

$\mathbf{AA}^{(-1)}\mathbf{b} = \mathbf{b}$ for some conditional inverse $\mathbf{A}^{(-1)}$, then $\mathbf{AA}^{(-1)}\mathbf{b} = \mathbf{b}$ for every conditional inverse of $\mathbf{A}$, and $\mathbf{Ax} = \mathbf{b}$ is consistent. Conversely, if $\mathbf{AA}^{(-1)}\mathbf{b} \neq \mathbf{b}$ for some conditional inverse $\mathbf{A}^{(-1)}$ then $\mathbf{AA}^{(-1)}\mathbf{b} \neq \mathbf{b}$ for every conditional inverse of $\mathbf{A}$, and $\mathbf{Ax} = \mathbf{b}$ is inconsistent.

9.9. If $\mathbf{Ax} = \mathbf{b}$ is consistent, then $\mathbf{x} = \mathbf{A}^{(-1)}\mathbf{b}$ is a solution (generally a different one for each $\mathbf{A}^{(-1)}$).

9.10. Let $\mathbf{y}$ ($p \times 1$) be a set of linear functions of the solutions $\mathbf{x}$ ($n \times 1$) of a consistent system of equations $\mathbf{Ax} = \mathbf{b}$, given by the relation $\mathbf{y} = \mathbf{Cx}$. Then $\mathbf{y} = \mathbf{Cx}$ is called unique if the same values of $\mathbf{y}$ will result regardless which solution $\mathbf{x}$ is used.

Example 9.10.1

$$3x + 4y + 5z = 22$$
$$x + \quad y + \quad z = 6$$

is a consistent system. One solution would be

$$x = 3 \quad y = 2 \quad z = 1$$

Another solution is

$$x = 2 \quad y = 4 \quad z = 0$$

The linear function

$$[7 \quad 9 \quad 11] \begin{bmatrix} x \\ y \\ z \end{bmatrix} = u$$

($7x + 9y + 11z = u$) will have the same value (50) regardless which of the two (or any other) solutions is substituted. Thus u is unique.

9.11. Let $\mathbf{Ax} = \mathbf{b}$ be a consistent system of equations. For $\mathbf{Cx} = \mathbf{y}$ to be a unique linear combination of the solution $\mathbf{x}$, it is necessary and sufficient that $\mathbf{CA}^{(-1)}\mathbf{A} = \mathbf{C}$. If this relation holds for some $\mathbf{A}^{(-1)}$ it will hold for every conditional inverse of $\mathbf{A}$. If it is violated for some $\mathbf{A}^{(-1)}$ it will be violated for every $\mathbf{A}^{(-1)}$, and y will be non-unique.

9.12. Let $\mathbf{A}$ be of rank r and select r rows and r columns which form a basis of $\mathbf{A}$. Then a conditional inverse of $\mathbf{A}$ can be obtained as follows: Invert the $(r \times r)$ matrix, place the inverse (without transposing) into the r rows corresponding to the column numbers and the r columns corresponding to the row numbers of the basis, and place zero into all remaining elements. Thus, if $\mathbf{A}$ is of order (5×4) and rank 3, and if rows $1, 2, 4$ and columns $2, 3, 4$ are selected as a basis, $\mathbf{A}^{(-1)}$, of order (4×5) will contain the inverse elements of the basis in rows $2, 3, 4$ and columns $1, 2, 4$, and zeros elsewhere. (See example 9.3.2)

9.13. If $\mathbf{A}$ is a square, singular matrix of order $(n \times n)$ and rank r, let $\mathbf{M}$ be a matrix of order $[n \times (n - r)]$ and $\mathbf{K}$ another matrix of order $[(n - r) \times n]$ chosen in such a way that $\mathbf{A} + \mathbf{MK}$ is non-singular. Then $(\mathbf{A} + \mathbf{MK})^{-1}$ is a conditional inverse of $\mathbf{A}$.

Example 9.13.1

$$\mathbf{A} = \begin{bmatrix} 3 & -1 & -1 & -1 \\ -1 & 3 & -1 & -1 \\ -1 & -1 & 3 & -1 \\ -1 & -1 & -1 & 3 \end{bmatrix}$$

is of order (4×4) and rank 3. Take $\mathbf{M} = \mathbf{j}$ (column vector of ones) and $\mathbf{K} = \mathbf{j}'$ (row vector of ones). Then $\mathbf{A} + \mathbf{MK} = \mathbf{A} + \mathbf{jj}' = 4\mathbf{I}$. Hence $(1/4)\,\mathbf{I}$ is a conditional inverse of $\mathbf{A}$.

9.14. The "Doolittle" method (see 6.14) can be employed to obtain a conditional inverse of a symmetric matrix. If, at any stage, the leading element of the p-row is zero, that cycle is disregarded.

Example 9.14.1

Invert, conditionally, the matrix

$$\mathbf{A} = \begin{bmatrix} 4 & 2 & -2 & 4 \\ 2 & 17 & 11 & 6 \\ -2 & 11 & 10 & 1 \\ 4 & 6 & 1 & 30 \end{bmatrix}$$

4	2	-2	4	1			
1	.5	-.5	1	.25			
	17	11	6	0	1		
	16	12	4	-.5	1		
	1	.75	.25	-.03125	.0625		
		10	1	0	0	1	
		0					
			30	0	0	0	1
			25	-.875	-.25	0	1
			1	-.035	-.01	0	.04

$$\begin{bmatrix} .29625 & -.0225 & 0 & -.035 \\ -.0225 & .065 & 0 & -.01 \\ 0 & 0 & 0 & 0 \\ -.035 & -.01 & 0 & .04 \end{bmatrix} = \mathbf{A}^{(-1)}$$

10. MATRIX DIFFERENTIATION

10.1a. If the elements of a matrix $\mathbf{Y}$ $(m \times n)$ are functions of a scalar, x, the expression

$$\partial \mathbf{Y}/\partial x$$

denotes a matrix of order $(m \times n)$ with elements $\partial y_{ij}/\partial x$.

10.1b. If the elements of a column (row) vector $\mathbf{y}$ $(\mathbf{y}')$ are functions of a scalar, x, the expression

$$\partial \mathbf{y}/\partial x \quad (\partial \mathbf{y}'/\partial x)$$

denotes a column (row) vector with elements $\partial y_i/\partial x$.

10.2a. If y is a scalar function of $m \times n$ variables, x_{ij}, arranged into a matrix $\mathbf{X}$, the expression

$$\partial y/\partial \mathbf{X}$$

denotes a matrix with elements $\partial y/\partial x_{ij}$.

(Note: Partial differentiation is performed with respect to the element in row i and column j of $\mathbf{X}$. If the same x-variable occurs in another place as, e.g., in a symmetric matrix, differentiation with respect to the distinct (repeated) variable is performed in two stages.)

Example 10.2.1

If $y = \mathbf{j}'\mathbf{X}\mathbf{j}$ (sum of all elements of a square matrix), $\partial y/\partial \mathbf{X}$ is a matrix of ones. If $\mathbf{X}$ is symmetric, one can introduce a new notation $x_{ij} = x_{ji} = z_{ij}$. Then

$$\begin{aligned} \partial y/\partial z_{ij} &= (\partial y/\partial x_{ij})(\partial x_{ij}/\partial z_{ij}) \\ &+ (\partial y/\partial x_{ji})(\partial x_{ji}/\partial z_{ij}) \\ &= 1 + 1 = 2 \quad (\text{if } i \neq j) \\ &= 1 \quad\quad\quad\ (\text{if } i = j) \end{aligned}$$

10.2b. If y is a scalar function of n variables, x_i, arranged into a column (row) vector $\mathbf{x}$ $(\mathbf{x}')$, the expression

$$\partial y/\partial \mathbf{x} \quad (\partial y/\partial \mathbf{x}')$$

denotes a column (row) vector with elements $\partial y/\partial x_i$.

10.3. If $\mathbf{y}$ is a column vector with m elements, each a function of n variables, x_i, arranged into a row vector $\mathbf{x}'$, the expression $\partial \mathbf{y}/\partial \mathbf{x}'$ denotes a matrix with m rows and n columns, with elements $\partial y_i/\partial x_j$.

10.4. $\partial \mathbf{Y}/\partial y_{ij} = (\mathbf{EL})_{ij}$ (see definition of $(\mathbf{EL})$ in 3.4).

10.5. $\partial \mathbf{UV}/\partial x = (\partial \mathbf{U}/\partial x)\mathbf{V} + \mathbf{U}(\partial \mathbf{V}/\partial x)$.

10.6. $\partial \mathbf{AY}/\partial x = \mathbf{A}(\partial \mathbf{Y}/\partial x)$ (if elements of $\mathbf{A}$ are not functions of x).

10.7. $\partial \mathbf{Y}'/\partial y_{ij} = (\mathbf{EL})_{ji}$

10.8. $\partial \mathbf{A}'\mathbf{YA}/\partial x = \mathbf{A}'(\partial \mathbf{Y}/\partial x)\mathbf{A}$

10.9. $\partial \mathbf{Y}'\mathbf{AY}/\partial x = (\partial \mathbf{Y}'/\partial x)\mathbf{AY} + \mathbf{Y}'\mathbf{A}(\partial \mathbf{Y}/\partial x)$

10.10. $\partial \mathbf{a}'\mathbf{x}/\partial \mathbf{x} = \mathbf{a}$

10.11. $\partial \mathbf{x}'\mathbf{x}/\partial \mathbf{x} = 2\mathbf{x}$

10.12. $\partial x'Ax/\partial x = Ax + A'x$

10.13. (Chain Rule No. 1) $\quad \partial y/\partial x' = (\partial y/\partial z')(\partial z/\partial x')$

10.14. $\partial Ax/\partial x' = A$

10.15. $\partial trX/\partial X = I$

10.16. $\partial trAX/\partial X = \partial trXA/\partial X = A'$

10.17. $\partial trAXB/\partial X = A'B'$

10.18. $\partial trX'AX/\partial X = AX + A'X$

10.19. $\partial \log |X|/\partial X = (X')^{-1} \quad$ (log to base e)

10.20. $\partial Y^{-1}/\partial x = -Y^{-1}(\partial Y/\partial x)Y^{-1}$

10.21. (Chain Rule No. 2)

$$\partial y/\partial x = tr(\partial y/\partial Z)(\partial Z'/\partial x)$$

where y and x are scalars. The scalar y is a function of $m \times n$ variables z_{ij}, and each of the z_{ij} is a function of x.

Example 10.21.1

Obtain $\log |R - FF'|/\partial F$, where R is symmetric.

By Chain Rule No. 2:

$\partial \log |R - FF'|/\partial f_{ij}$

$\quad = tr[\partial \log |R - FF'|/\partial(R - FF')][\partial(R - FF')/\partial f_{ij}] \quad$ (since R and FF' are symmetric)

$\quad = tr(R - FF')^{-1}[\partial(R - FF')/\partial f_{ij}] \quad$ (by 10.19)

$\quad = tr(R - FF')^{-1}[-(\partial F/\partial f_{ij})F' - F(\partial F'/\partial f_{ij})] \quad$ (by 10.5)

$\quad = tr(R - FF')^{-1}[-(EL)_{ij}F' - F(EL)_{ji}] \quad$ (by 10.4 and 10.7)

$\quad = -tr(R - FF')^{-1}(EL)_{ij}F' - tr(R - FF')^{-1}F(EL)_{ji}$

$\quad = -tr(EL)_{ij}F'(R - FF')^{-1} - tr(EL)_{ji}(R - FF')^{-1}F \quad$ (by 7.3)

$\quad = -[F'(R - FF')^{-1}]_{ji} - [(R - FF')^{-1}F]_{ij},$

where $[\ ]_{ij}$ denotes the (i, j) element of the matrix in brackets (by 7.5),

$\quad = -[(R - FF')^{-1}F]_{ij} - [(R - FF')^{-1}F]_{ij} \quad$ (since $R - FF'$ is symmetric)

$\quad = -2[(R - FF')^{-1}F]_{ij}.$

Hence, by definition 10.2a

$$\partial \log |R - FF'|/\partial F = -2(R - FF')^{-1}F.$$

10.22. $|\partial y/\partial x'| = J(y; x)$ is called the Jacobian or Functional Determinant used in variable transformation of multiple integrals. Formally, if y is a column vector with m elements, each a function of m variables x_i arranged into a row vector x',

$$dx_1 dx_2 \ldots dx_m = |\partial y/\partial x'|^{-1} dy_1 dy_2 \ldots dy_m.$$

10.23. For a scalar y (a function of m variables x_i) to attain a stationary value, it is necessary that

$$\partial y/\partial x = 0.$$

10.24. For a stationary value to be a minimum (maximum) it is necessary that

$$\partial(\partial y/\partial x)/\partial x' \quad (-\partial(\partial y/\partial x)/\partial x')$$

be a positive-definite matrix for the value of x satisfying 10.23.

Example 10.24.1

Find the values of β which minimize $u = x'x$ (the sum of squares of x_i) where $x = y - A\beta$ (with y and A known and fixed).

$$\partial u / \partial \beta' = (\partial u / \partial x')(\partial x / \partial \beta') \quad \text{(by Chain Rule No. 1)}$$
$$= -2x'A \quad \text{(by 10.11 and 10.14)}$$

Hence

$$\partial u / \partial \beta = -2A'x$$
$$= -2A'(y - A\beta).$$

Hence, for a stationary value, by 10.23, it is necessary that

$$A'A\hat{\beta} = A'y$$

where $\hat{\beta}$ denotes the values which make u stationary. Now,

$$\partial(\partial u / \partial \beta) / \partial \beta' = 2\partial(A'A\beta) / \partial \beta' = 2A'A.$$

If A has real elements, and if A'A is non-singular, then it is positive-definite (since, given an arbitrary real $x \neq 0$, $x'A'Ax = z'z$, with $z = Ax$; thus this is a sum of squares). Hence $\hat{\beta}$ minimizes u.

10.25. (Generalized Newton Iteration)

Let x_0' be an initial estimate (m elements) of the roots of the m equations

$$f(x') = 0$$

where the m elements of the column vector f are each functions of $x_1, x_2, \ldots x_m$. Then an improved root is

$$x_1 = x_0 - Q_0^{-1}f(x_0'),$$

where Q_0 is the matrix of derivatives $\partial f / \partial x'$ evaluated at $x = x_0$. The usual procedure consists of evaluating $f(x_0')$, then solving $Q_0 u = f(x_0')$ for u. Then $x_1 = x_0 - u$.

Example 10.25.1
   Solve

$$f_1(x, y) = x^3 - x^2 y + y^2 - 3.526 = 0$$
$$f_2(x, y) = x^3 + y^3 - 14.911 = 0$$

$$Q = \begin{bmatrix} 3x^2 - 2xy & 2y - x^2 \\ 3x^2 & 3y^2 \end{bmatrix}$$

Take $x_0 = 1$, $y_0 = 2$

$$f_1(x_0, y_0) = -0.526$$
$$f_2(x_0, y_0) = -5.911$$

$$Q_0 = \begin{bmatrix} -1 & 3 \\ 3 & 12 \end{bmatrix}$$

$$-u + 3v = -0.526$$
$$3u + 12v = -5.911$$

yields $u = -0.55$, $v = -0.36$.

Then,

$$x_1 = x_0 - u = 1.55$$
$$y_1 = y_0 - v = 2.36$$
$$f_1(x_1, y_1) = 0.0976$$
$$f_2(x_1, y_1) = 1.9572$$

$$Q_1 = \begin{bmatrix} -0.1085 & 2.3175 \\ 7.2075 & 16.7088 \end{bmatrix}$$

$$-0.1085u + 2.3175v = 0.0976$$
$$7.2075u + 16.7088v = 1.9572$$

yields $u = 0.157$, $v = 0.049$.

Then

$$x_2 = x_1 - u = 1.393$$
$$y_2 = y_1 - v = 2.311$$
$$f_1(x_2, y_2) = 0.03337$$
$$f_2(x_2, y_2) = 0.13443$$

$$Q_2 = \begin{bmatrix} -0.61710 & 2.68155 \\ 5.82135 & 16.02216 \end{bmatrix}$$

$$-0.61710u + 2.68155v = 0.03337$$
$$5.82135u + 16.02216v = 0.13443$$

yields $u = -0.0068$, $v = 0.0109$.

Then,

$$x_3 = x_2 - u = 1.3998$$
$$y_3 = y_2 - v = 2.3001$$

(The exact roots are $x = 1.4$ and $y = 2.3$).

11. STATISTICAL MATRIX FORMS

11.1. Let E denote the expectation operator, and let y be a set of p random variables. Then

$$E(\mathbf{y}) = \mu$$

states that $E(y_i) = \mu_i$ $(i = 1, 2, \ldots p)$.

11.2. Let var denote variance. Then

$$\text{var}(\mathbf{y}) = \Sigma$$

denotes a $p \times p$ symmetric matrix whose elements are $\text{cov}(y_i, y_j)$, and whose diagonal elements are $\text{var}(y_i)$, where cov denotes covariance.

11.3. $E(\mathbf{AY} + \mathbf{b}) = \mathbf{A}E(\mathbf{y}) + \mathbf{b} = \mathbf{A}\mu + \mathbf{b}$

11.4. $\text{var}(\mathbf{Ay} + \mathbf{b}) = \mathbf{A} \text{var}(\mathbf{y}) \mathbf{A}' = \mathbf{A}\Sigma\mathbf{A}'$

11.5. $\text{cov}(\mathbf{y}, \mathbf{z}')$ denotes a matrix with elements $\text{cov}(y_i, z_j)$.
$\text{cov}(\mathbf{z}, \mathbf{y}') = [\text{cov}(\mathbf{y}, \mathbf{z}')]'$.

11.6. $\text{cov}(\mathbf{Ay} + \mathbf{b}, \mathbf{z}'\mathbf{C} + \mathbf{d}') = \mathbf{A} \text{cov}(\mathbf{y}, \mathbf{z}') \mathbf{C}$

11.7. $\text{var}(\mathbf{y}) = E(\mathbf{yy}') - E(\mathbf{y})E(\mathbf{y}')$

11.8. $\text{cov}(\mathbf{y}, \mathbf{z}') = E(\mathbf{yz}') - E(\mathbf{y})E(\mathbf{z}')$

11.9. (Expected "sum of squares")

$$E(\mathbf{y}'\mathbf{Qy}) = tr[\mathbf{Q} \text{ var}(\mathbf{y})] + E(\mathbf{y}')\mathbf{Q}E(\mathbf{y}).$$

11.10. If a matrix $\mathbf{Q}$ is symmetric and positive-definite, one can find a lower triangular matrix $\mathbf{T}$ (with positive diagonal terms, for uniqueness) such that $\mathbf{TT}' = \mathbf{Q}$. The matrices $\mathbf{T}$ and $\mathbf{T}^{-1}$ can be obtained from the Doolittle pattern (6.14) (Gauss elimination or square-root method) as follows: In each cycle, divide the p-row (left and right hand side) by $\sqrt{p_{ii}}$ (instead of p_{ii} for the u-row). Thus obtain rows designated as t-rows. The left-hand side (Arabic subscripts) is **T'**, and the right-hand side (Roman subscripts) is **T**$^{-1}$

11.11. If a coordinate system **x** is oblique, and if the cosines between reference vectors (scalar products of basis vectors of unit length) are stated in a symmetric matrix **Q**, then **T**$^{-1}$**x** = **y** is an orthogonal system, where **T** is obtained from **Q** by 11.10.

11.12. The likelihood function of a sample of size n from a multivariate normal distribution (p responses), with common variance-covariance matrix $\Sigma(p \times p)$, and with means or main effects replaced by maximum-likelihood or least-squares estimates, can be written as

$$\log L = -\frac{np}{2} \log 2\pi - \frac{n}{2} \log |\Sigma| - \frac{n}{2} tr \Sigma^{-1} \mathbf{S}$$

where $\Sigma(p \times p)$ is the common variance-covariance matrix, and **S** is its maximum-likelihood estimate (matrix of sums of squares and products due to error, divided by sample size n).

11.13. If Σ has a structure under a model or null hypothesis, and if elements of Σ are to be estimated, by maximum-likelihood, two cases can be distinguished: (11.14) Σ^{-1} has the same structure (intraclass correlation, mixed model, compound symmetry, factor analysis). (11.15) Σ^{-1} has a different structure (autocorrelation, Simplex structure).

11.14. If the structure of Σ and Σ^{-1} is identical, and if u and v are elements (or functions of elements) of Σ^{-1} then estimates of Σ can be obtained from the relations (usually requiring Newton iteration, see 10.25):

$$\partial \log L/\partial u = \frac{n}{2} tr \mathbf{A}(\Sigma - \mathbf{S})$$

where $\mathbf{A} = \partial\Sigma^{-1}/\partial u$, is frequently an elementary matrix (see 3.4 and, especially, the rules 7.5 and 7.6).

$$\partial^2 \log L/\partial u \partial v = \frac{n}{2} tr(\partial \mathbf{A}/\partial v)(\Sigma - \mathbf{S}) + \frac{n}{2} tr \mathbf{A}\Sigma^{-1}\mathbf{B}\Sigma^{-1}$$

where $\mathbf{B} = \partial\Sigma^{-1}/\partial v$. These rules are useful to obtain Newton iterations and asymptotic variance-covariance matrices of the estimates.

11.15. If the structures of Σ and Σ^{-1} are different, then an estimate of Σ can be obtained from the relations

$$\partial \log L/\partial x = -\frac{n}{2} tr \mathbf{A}(\Sigma^{-1} - \mathbf{Q}),$$

where

$$\mathbf{Q} = \Sigma^{-1}\mathbf{S}\Sigma^{-1}$$

and

$$\mathbf{A} = \partial\Sigma/\partial x \quad \text{(see comments in 11.14).}$$

$$\partial^2 \log L/\partial x \partial y = -\frac{n}{2} tr(\partial \mathbf{A}/\partial y)(\Sigma^{-1} - \mathbf{Q}) + \frac{n}{2} tr \mathbf{A}\Sigma^{-1}\mathbf{B}(\Sigma^{-1} - \mathbf{Q}) - \frac{n}{2} tr \mathbf{A}\mathbf{Q}\mathbf{B}\Sigma^{-1},$$

where

$$\mathbf{B} = \partial\Sigma/\partial y$$

x and y are elements (or functions of elements) of Σ. The comments of 11.14 apply, but the iterative procedure is considerably more complex.

Suggestions for further reading:

A. S. Householder, *The Theory of Matrices in Numerical Analysis*, Blaisdell, 1964.

S. R. Searle, *Matrix Algebra for the Biological Sciences*, Wiley, 1966.

P. H. Schonemann, Matrix differentiation of traces and determinants, *Psychometrika*, 1966.

III. COMBINATORIAL ANALYSIS

POWERS OF NUMBERS

The larger numbers are expressed exponentially to at least seven significant figures.

The approximate value written as a whole number may be obtained by shifting the decimal point to the right by the number of places indicated in the exponent of 10 shown at the head of each group of values. For example: the approximate value of 33^8 is found in the table as 14.064086×10^{11}. Written as a whole number it is 1 406 408 600 000.

n	n^4	n^5	n^6	n^7	n^8	n^9
1	1	1	1	1	1	1
2	16	32	64	128	256	512
3	81	243	729	2187	6561	19683
4	256	1024	4096	16384	65536	262144
5	625	3125	15625	78125	390625	1953125
6	1296	7776	46656	279936	1679616	10077696
7	2401	16807	117649	823543	5764801	40353607
8	4096	32768	262144	2097152	16777216	134217728
9	6561	59049	531441	4782969	43046721	387420489
					$\times 10^8$	$\times 10^9$
10	10000	100000	1000000	10000000	1.000000	1.000000
11	14641	161051	1771561	19487171	2.143589	2.357948
12	20736	248832	2985984	35831808	4.299817	5.159780
13	28561	371293	4826809	62748517	8.157307	10.604499
14	38416	537824	7529536	105413504	14.757891	20.661047
15	50625	759375	11390625	170859375	25.628906	38.443359
16	65536	1048576	16777216	268435456	42.949673	68.719477
17	83521	1419857	24137569	410338673	69.757574	118.587876
18	104976	1889568	34012224	612220032	110.199606	198.359290
19	130321	2476099	47045881	893871739	169.835630	322.687698
				$\times 10^9$	$\times 10^{10}$	$\times 10^{11}$
20	160000	3200000	64000000	1.280000	2.560000	5.120000
21	194481	4084101	85766121	1.801089	3.782286	7.942800
22	234256	5153632	113379904	2.494358	5.487587	12.072692
23	279841	6436343	148035889	3.404825	7.831099	18.011527
24	331776	7962624	191102976	4.586471	11.007531	26.418075
25	390625	9765625	244140625	6.103516	15.258789	38.146973
26	456976	11881376	308915776	8.031810	20.882706	54.295037
27	531441	14348907	387420489	10.460353	28.242954	76.255975
28	614656	17210368	481890304	13.492929	37.780200	105.784560
29	707281	20511149	594823321	17.249876	50.024641	145.071460
			$\times 10^8$	$\times 10^{10}$	$\times 10^{11}$	$\times 10^{13}$
30	810000	24300000	7.290000	2.187000	6.561000	1.968300
31	923521	28629151	8.875037	2.751261	8.528910	2.643962
32	1048576	33554432	10.737418	3.435974	10.995116	3.518437
33	1185921	39135393	12.914680	4.261844	14.064086	4.641148
34	1336336	45435424	15.448044	5.252335	17.857939	6.071699
35	1500625	52521875	18.382656	6.433930	22.518754	7.881564
36	1679616	60466176	21.767823	7.836416	28.211099	10.155996
37	1874161	69343957	25.657264	9.493188	35.124795	12.996174
38	2085136	79235168	30.109364	11.441558	43.477921	16.521610
39	2313441	90224199	35.187438	13.723101	53.520093	20.872836
			$\times 10^9$	$\times 10^{10}$	$\times 10^{12}$	$\times 10^{14}$
40	2560000	102400000	4.096000	16.384000	6.553600	2.621440
41	2825761	115856201	4.750104	19.475427	7.984925	3.273819
42	3111696	130691232	5.489032	23.053933	9.682652	4.066714
43	3418801	147008443	6.321363	27.181861	11.688200	5.025926
44	3748096	164916224	7.256314	31.927781	14.048224	6.181218
45	4100625	184528125	8.303766	37.366945	16.815125	7.566806
46	4477456	205962976	9.474297	43.581766	20.047612	9.221902
47	4879681	229345007	10.779215	50.662312	23.811287	11.191305
48	5308416	254803968	12.230590	58.706834	28.179280	13.526055
49	5764801	282475249	13.841287	67.822307	33.232931	16.284136
50	6250000	312500000	15.625000	78.125000	39.062500	19.531250

POWERS OF NUMBERS (Continued)

n	n^4	n^5	n^6	n^7	n^8	n^9
			$\times 10^9$	$\times 10^{11}$	$\times 10^{13}$	$\times 10^{14}$
50	6250000	312500000	15.625000	7.812500	3.906250	19.531250
51	6765201	345025251	17.596288	8.974107	4.576794	23.341652
52	7311616	380204032	19.770610	10.280717	5.345973	27.799059
53	7890481	418195493	22.164361	11.747111	6.225969	32.997636
54	8503056	459165024	24.794911	13.389252	7.230196	39.043059
55	9150625	503284375	27.680641	15.224352	8.373394	46.053666
56	9834496	550731776	30.840979	17.270948	9.671731	54.161694
57	10556001	601692057	34.296447	19.548975	11.142916	63.514620
58	11316496	656356768	38.068693	22.079842	12.806308	74.276587
59	12117361	714924299	42.180534	24.886515	14.683044	86.629958
		$\times 10^8$	$\times 10^{10}$	$\times 10^{11}$	$\times 10^{13}$	$\times 10^{16}$
60	12960000	7.776000	4.665600	27.993600	16.796160	1.007770
61	13845841	8.445963	5.152037	31.427428	19.170731	1.169415
62	14776336	9.161328	5.680024	35.216146	21.834011	1.353709
63	15752961	9.924365	6.252350	39.389806	24.815578	1.563381
64	16777216	10.737418	6.871948	43.980465	28.147498	1.801440
65	17850625	11.602906	7.541889	49.022279	31.864481	2.071191
66	18974736	12.523326	8.265395	54.551607	36.004061	2.376268
67	20151121	13.501251	9.045838	60.607116	40.606768	2.720653
68	21381376	14.539336	9.886748	67.229888	45.716324	3.108710
69	22667121	15.640313	10.791816	74.463533	51.379837	3.545209
		$\times 10^8$	$\times 10^{10}$	$\times 10^{12}$	$\times 10^{14}$	$\times 10^{16}$
70	24010000	16.807000	11.764900	8.235430	5.764801	4.035361
71	25411681	18.042294	12.810028	9.095120	6.457535	4.584850
72	26873856	19.349176	13.931407	10.030613	7.222041	5.199870
73	28398241	20.730716	15.133423	11.047399	8.064601	5.887159
74	29986576	22.190066	16.420649	12.151280	8.991947	6.654041
75	31640625	23.730469	17.797852	13.348389	10.011292	7.508469
76	33362176	25.355254	19.269993	14.645195	11.130348	8.459064
77	35153041	27.067842	20.842238	16.048523	12.357363	9.515169
78	37015056	28.871744	22.519960	17.565569	13.701144	10.686892
79	38950081	30.770564	24.308746	19.203909	15.171088	11.985160
		$\times 10^8$	$\times 10^{10}$	$\times 10^{12}$	$\times 10^{14}$	$\times 10^{16}$
80	40960000	32.768000	26.214400	20.971520	16.777216	13.421773
81	43046721	34.867844	28.242954	22.876792	18.530202	15.009464
82	45212176	37.073984	30.400667	24.928547	20.441409	16.761955
83	47458321	39.390406	32.694037	27.136051	22.522922	18.694026
84	49787136	41.821194	35.129803	29.509035	24.787589	20.821575
85	52200625	44.370531	37.714952	32.057709	27.249053	23.161695
86	54700816	47.042702	40.456724	34.792782	29.921793	25.732742
87	57289761	49.842092	43.362620	37.725479	32.821167	28.554415
88	59969536	52.773192	46.440409	40.867560	35.963452	31.647838
89	62742241	55.840594	49.698129	44.231335	39.365888	35.035640
		$\times 10^9$	$\times 10^{11}$	$\times 10^{13}$	$\times 10^{15}$	$\times 10^{17}$
90	65610000	5.904900	5.314410	4.782969	4.304672	3.874205
91	68574961	6.240321	5.678693	5.167610	4.702525	4.279298
92	71639296	6.590815	6.063550	5.578466	5.132189	4.721614
93	74805201	6.956884	6.469902	6.017009	5.595818	5.204111
94	78074896	7.339040	6.898698	6.484776	6.095689	5.729948
95	81450625	7.737809	7.350919	6.983373	6.634204	6.302494
96	84934656	8.153727	7.827578	7.514475	7.213896	6.925340
97	88529281	8.587340	8.329720	8.079828	7.837434	7.602311
98	92236816	9.039208	8.858424	8.681255	8.507630	8.337478
99	96059601	9.509900	9.414801	9.320653	9.227447	9.135172
100	100000000	10.000000	10.000000	10.000000	10.000000	10.000000

POSITIVE POWERS OF TWO

n	2^n				
1	2				
2	4				
3	8				
4	16				
5	32				
6	64				
7	128				
8	256				
9	512				
10	1024				
11	2048				
12	4096				
13	8192				
14	16384				
15	32768				
16	65536				
17	13107	2			
18	26214	4			
19	52428	8			
20	10485	76			
21	20971	52			
22	41943	04			
23	83886	08			
24	16777	216			
25	33554	432			
26	67108	864			
27	13421	7728			
28	26843	5456			
29	53687	0912			
30	10737	41824			
31	21474	83648			
32	42949	67296			
33	85899	34592			
34	17179	86918	4		
35	34359	73836	8		
36	68719	47673	6		
37	13743	89534	72		
38	27487	79069	44		
39	54975	58138	88		
40	10995	11627	776		
41	21990	23255	552		
42	43980	46511	104		
43	87960	93022	208		
44	17592	18604	4416		
45	35184	37208	8832		
46	70368	74417	7664		
47	14073	74883	55328		
48	28147	49767	10656		
49	56294	99534	21312		
50	11258	99906	84262	4	

n	2^n						
51	22517	99813	68524	8			
52	45035	99627	37049	6			
53	90071	99254	74099	2			
54	18014	39850	94819	84			
55	36028	79701	89639	68			
56	72057	59403	79279	36			
57	14411	51880	75855	872			
58	28823	03761	51711	744			
59	57646	07523	03423	488			
60	11529	21504	60684	6976			
61	23058	43009	21369	3952			
62	46116	86018	42738	7904			
63	92233	72036	85477	5808			
64	18446	74407	37095	51616			
65	36893	48814	74191	03232			
66	73786	97629	48382	06464			
67	14757	39525	89676	41292	8		
68	29514	79051	79352	82585	6		
69	59029	58103	58705	65171	2		
70	11805	91620	71741	13034	24		
71	23611	83241	43482	26068	48		
72	47223	66482	86964	52136	96		
73	94447	32965	73929	04273	92		
74	18889	46593	14785	80854	784		
75	37778	93186	29571	61709	568		
76	75557	86372	59143	23419	136		
77	15111	57274	51828	64683	8272		
78	30223	14549	03657	29367	6544		
79	60446	29098	07314	58735	3088		
80	12089	25819	61462	91747	06176		
81	24178	51639	22925	83494	12352		
82	48357	03278	45851	66988	24704		
83	96714	06556	91703	33976	49408		
84	19342	81311	38340	66795	29881	6	
85	38685	62622	76681	33590	59763	2	
86	77371	25245	53362	67181	19526	4	
87	15474	25049	10672	53436	23905	28	
88	30948	50098	21345	06872	47810	56	
89	61897	00196	42690	13744	95621	12	
90	12379	40039	28538	02748	99124	224	
91	24758	80078	57076	05497	98248	448	
92	49517	60157	14152	10995	96496	896	
93	99035	20314	28304	21991	92993	792	
94	19807	04062	85660	84398	38598	7584	
95	39614	08125	71321	68796	77197	5168	
96	79228	16251	42643	37593	54395	0336	
97	15845	63250	28528	67518	70879	00672	
98	31691	26500	57057	35037	41758	01344	
99	63382	53001	14114	70074	83516	02688	
100	12676	50600	22822	94014	96703	20537	6
101	25353	01200	45645	88029	93406	41075	2

NEGATIVE POWERS OF TWO

n	2^{-n}							
0	1.0							
1	0.5							
2	0.25							
3	0.125							
4	0.0625							
5	0.03125							
6	0.01562	5						
7	0.00781	25						
8	0.00390	625						
9	0.00195	3125						
10	0.00097	65625						
11	0.00048	82812	5					
12	0.00024	41406	25					
13	0.00012	20703	125					
14	0.00006	10351	5625					
15	0.00003	05175	78125					
16	0.00001	52587	89062	5				
17	0.00000	76293	94531	25				
18	0.00000	38146	97265	625				
19	0.00000	19073	48632	8125				
20	0.00000	09536	74316	40625				
21	0.00000	04768	37158	20312	5			
22	0.00000	02384	18579	10156	25			
23	0.00000	01192	09289	55078	125			
24	0.00000	00596	04644	77539	0625			
25	0.00000	00298	02322	38769	53125			
26	0.00000	00149	01161	19384	76562	5		
27	0.00000	00074	50580	59692	38281	25		
28	0.00000	00037	25290	29846	19140	625		
29	0.00000	00018	62645	14923	09570	3125		
30	0.00000	00009	31322	57461	54785	15625		
31	0.00000	00004	65661	28730	77392	57812	5	
32	0.00000	00002	32830	64365	38696	28906	25	
33	0.00000	00001	16415	32182	69348	14453	125	
34	0.00000	00000	58207	66091	34674	07226	5625	
35	0.00000	00000	29103	83045	67337	03613	28125	
36	0.00000	00000	14551	91522	83668	51806	64062	5
37	0.00000	00000	07275	95761	41834	25903	32031	25
38	0.00000	00000	03637	97880	70917	12951	66015	625
39	0.00000	00000	01818	98940	35458	56475	83007	8125
40	0.00000	00000	00909	49470	17729	28237	91503	90625
41	0.00000	00000	00454	74735	08864	64118	95751	95312	5
42	0.00000	00000	00227	37367	54432	32059	47875	97656	25
43	0.00000	00000	00113	68683	77216	16029	73937	98828	125
44	0.00000	00000	00056	84341	88608	08014	86968	99414	0625
45	0.00000	00000	00028	42170	94304	04007	43484	49707	03125
46	0.00000	00000	00014	21085	47152	02003	71742	24853	51562	5
47	0.00000	00000	00007	10542	73576	01001	85871	12426	75781	25
48	0.00000	00000	00003	55271	36788	00500	92935	56213	37890	625
49	0.00000	00000	00001	77635	68394	00250	46467	78106	68945	3125
50	0.00000	00000	00000	88817	84197	00125	23233	89053	34472	65625

SUMS OF POWERS OF INTEGERS, $\sum_{k=1}^{n} k^m$

$(m = 1, 2, 3, 4); 1 \leq n \leq 40$

n	Σk	Σk^2	Σk^3	Σk^4
1	1	1	1	1
2	3	5	9	17
3	6	14	36	98
4	10	30	100	354
5	15	55	225	979
6	21	91	441	2275
7	28	140	784	4676
8	36	204	1296	8772
9	45	285	2025	15333
10	55	385	3025	25333
11	66	506	4356	39974
12	78	650	6084	60710
13	91	819	8281	89271
14	105	1015	11025	127687
15	120	1240	14400	178312
16	136	1496	18496	243848
17	153	1785	23409	327369
18	171	2109	29241	432345
19	190	2470	36100	562666
20	210	2870	44100	722666
21	231	3311	53361	917147
22	253	3795	64009	1151403
23	276	4324	76176	1431244
24	300	4900	90000	1763020
25	325	5525	105625	2153645
26	351	6201	123201	2610621
27	378	6930	142884	3142062
28	406	7714	164836	3756718
29	435	8555	189225	4463999
30	465	9455	216225	5273999
31	496	10416	246016	6197520
32	528	11440	278784	7246096
33	561	12529	314721	8432017
34	595	13685	354025	9768353
35	630	14910	396900	11268978
36	666	16206	443556	12948594
37	703	17575	494209	14822755
38	741	19019	549081	16907891
39	780	20540	608400	19221332
40	820	22140	672400	21781332

SUMS OF POWERS OF THE FIRST n INTEGERS

$$\sum_{k=1}^{n} k = 1 + 2 + 3 + \cdots + n = \frac{n(n+1)}{2}$$

$$\sum_{k=1}^{n} k^2 = 1^2 + 2^2 + 3^2 + \cdots + n^2 = \frac{n(n+1)(2n+1)}{6}$$

$$\sum_{k=1}^{n} k^3 = \frac{n^2(n+1)^2}{4}$$

$$\sum_{k=1}^{n} k^4 = \frac{n}{30}(n+1)(2n+1)(3n^2+3n-1).$$

$$\sum_{k=1}^{n} k^5 = \frac{n^2}{12}(n+1)^2(2n^2+2n-1).$$

$$\sum_{k=1}^{n} k^6 = \frac{n}{42}(n+1)(2n+1)(3n^4+6n^3-3n+1).$$

$$\sum_{k=1}^{n} k^7 = \frac{n^2}{24}(n+1)^2(3n^4+6n^3-n^2-4n+2).$$

$$\sum_{k=1}^{n} k^8 = \frac{n}{90}(n+1)(2n+1)(5n^6+15n^5+5n^4-15n^3-n^2+9n-3).$$

$$\sum_{k=1}^{n} k^9 = \frac{n^2}{20}(n+1)^2(2n^6+6n^5+n^4-8n^3+n^2+6n-3).$$

$$\sum_{k=1}^{n} k^{10} = \frac{n}{66}(n+1)(2n+1)(3n^8+12n^7+8n^6-18n^5$$
$$-10n^4+24n^3+2n^2-15n+5).$$

Note that

$$\sum_{k=1}^{n} k^p = 1^p + 2^p + 3^p + \cdots + n^p$$ is a function of n which can be conveniently generated

by use of the *following proposition*

If
$$\sum_{k=1}^{n} k^p = a_1 n^{p+1} + a_2 n^p + a_3 n^{p-1} + \cdots + a_{p+1} n$$

then

$$\sum_{k=1}^{n} k^{p+1} = \frac{p+1}{p+2} a_1 n^{p+2} + \frac{p+1}{p+1} a_2 n^{p+1} + \frac{p+1}{p} a_3 n^p$$
$$+ \cdots + \frac{p+1}{2} a_{p+1} n^2 + \left[1 - (p+1) \sum_{k=1}^{p+1} \frac{a_k}{(p+3-k)} \right] n$$

Example Since $\displaystyle\sum_{k=1}^{n} k = \tfrac{1}{2}n^2 + \tfrac{1}{2}n$, then

$$\sum_{k=1}^{n} k^2 = \tfrac{1}{3}n^3 + \tfrac{1}{2}n^2 + \tfrac{1}{6}n \text{ and from this result}$$

$$\sum_{k=1}^{n} k^3 = \tfrac{1}{4}n^4 + \tfrac{1}{2}n^3 + \tfrac{1}{4}n^2 \quad \text{etc.}$$

This proposition is extracted from a paper written by Michael A. Budin and Arnold J. Cantor entitled "Simplified Computation of Sums of Powers of Integers."

SUMS OF RECIPROCAL POWERS*

n	$\zeta(n) = \sum_{k=1}^{\infty} k^{-n}$				$\sum_{k=1}^{\infty} (-1)^{k-1} k^{-n}$			
1	∞				0.69314	71805	59945	30942
2	1.64493	40668	48226	43637	0.82246	70334	24113	21824
3	1.20205	69031	59594	28540	0.90154	26773	69695	71405
4	1.08232	32337	11138	19152	0.94703	28294	97245	91758
5	1.03692	77551	43369	92633	0.97211	97704	46909	30594
6	1.01734	30619	84449	13971	0.98555	10912	97435	10410
7	1.00834	92773	81922	82684	0.99259	38199	22830	28267
8	1.00407	73561	97944	33938	0.99623	30018	52647	89923
9	1.00200	83928	26082	21442	0.99809	42975	41605	33077
10	1.00099	45751	27818	08534	0.99903	95075	98271	56564
11	1.00049	41886	04119	46456	0.99951	71434	98060	75414
12	1.00024	60865	53308	04830	0.99975	76851	43858	19085
13	1.00012	27133	47578	48915	0.99987	85427	63265	11549
14	1.00006	12481	35058	70483	0.99993	91703	45979	71817
15	1.00003	05882	36307	02049	0.99996	95512	13099	23808
16	1.00001	52822	59408	65187	0.99998	47642	14906	10644
17	1.00000	76371	97637	89976	0.99999	23782	92041	01198
18	1.00000	38172	93264	99984	0.99999	61878	69610	11348
19	1.00000	19082	12716	55394	0.99999	80935	08171	67511
20	1.00000	09539	62033	87280	0.99999	90466	11581	52212
21	1.00000	04769	32986	78781	0.99999	95232	58215	54282
22	1.00000	02384	50502	72773	0.99999	97616	13230	82255
23	1.00000	01192	19925	96531	0.99999	98808	01318	43950
24	1.00000	00596	08189	05126	0.99999	99403	98892	39463
25	1.00000	00298	03503	51465	0.99999	99701	98856	96283
26	1.00000	00149	01554	82837	0.99999	99850	99231	99657
27	1.00000	00074	50711	78984	0.99999	99925	49550	48496
28	1.00000	00037	25334	02479	0.99999	99962	74753	40011
29	1.00000	00018	62659	72351	0.99999	99981	37369	41811
30	1.00000	00009	31327	43242	0.99999	99990	68682	28145
31	1.00000	00004	65662	90650	0.99999	99995	34340	33145
32	1.00000	00002	32831	18337	0.99999	99997	67169	89595
33	1.00000	00001	16415	50173	0.99999	99998	83584	85805
34	1.00000	00000	58207	72088	0.99999	99999	41792	39905
35	1.00000	00000	29103	85044	0.99999	99999	70896	18953
36	1.00000	00000	14551	92189	0.99999	99999	85448	09143
37	1.00000	00000	07275	95984	0.99999	99999	92724	04461
38	1.00000	00000	03637	97955	0.99999	99999	96362	02193
39	1.00000	00000	01818	98965	0.99999	99999	98181	01084
40	1.00000	00000	00909	49478	0.99999	99999	99090	50538
41	1.00000	00000	00454	74738	0.99999	99999	99545	25268
42	1.00000	00000	00227	37368	0.99999	99999	99772	62633

For $n > 42$, $\displaystyle\sum_{k=1}^{\infty} k^{-(n+1)} = \frac{1}{2}\left[1 + \sum_{k=1}^{\infty} k^{-n}\right]$, $\displaystyle\sum_{k=1}^{\infty} (-1)^{k-1} k^{-(n+1)} = \frac{1}{2}\left[1 + \sum_{k=1}^{\infty} (-1)^{k-1} k^{-n}\right]$

*Note: By definition Riemann's Zeta Function is $\zeta(p) = $ Zeta $(p) = 1 + \dfrac{1}{2^p} + \dfrac{1}{3^p} + \dfrac{1}{4^p} + \ldots$

SUMS OF RECIPROCAL POWERS

n	$\sum_{k=0}^{\infty} (2k+1)^{-n}$				$\sum_{k=0}^{\infty} (-1)^k (2k+1)^{-n}$			
1		∞			0.78539	81633	97448	310
2	1.23370	05501	36169	82735	0.91596	55941	77219	015
3	1.05179	97902	64644	99972	0.96894	61462	59369	380
4	1.01467	80316	04192	05455	0.98894	45517	41105	336
5	1.00452	37627	95139	61613	0.99615	78280	77088	064
6	1.00144	70766	40942	12191	0.99868	52222	18438	135
7	1.00047	15486	52376	55476	0.99955	45078	90539	909
8	1.00015	51790	25296	11930	0.99984	99902	46829	656
9	1.00005	13451	83843	77259	0.99994	96841	87220	090
10	1.00001	70413	63044	82549	0.99998	31640	26196	877
11	1.00000	56660	51090	10935	0.99999	43749	73823	699
12	1.00000	18858	48583	11958	0.99999	81223	50587	882
13	1.00000	06280	55421	80232	0.99999	93735	83771	841
14	1.00000	02092	40519	21150	0.99999	97910	87248	734
15	1.00000	00697	24703	12929	0.99999	99303	40842	624
16	1.00000	00232	37157	37916	0.99999	99767	75950	903
17	1.00000	00077	44839	45587	0.99999	99922	57782	104
18	1.00000	00025	81437	55666	0.99999	99974	19086	745
19	1.00000	00008	60444	11452	0.99999	99991	39660	745
20	1.00000	00002	86807	69746	0.99999	99997	13213	274
21	1.00000	00000	95601	16531	0.99999	99999	04403	029
22	1.00000	00000	31866	77514	0.99999	99999	68134	064
23	1.00000	00000	10622	20241	0.99999	99999	89377	965
24	1.00000	00000	03540	72294	0.99999	99999	96459	311
25	1.00000	00000	01180	23874	0.99999	99999	98819	768
26	1.00000	00000	00393	41247	0.99999	99999	99606	589
27	1.00000	00000	00131	13740	0.99999	99999	99868	863
28	1.00000	00000	00043	71245	0.99999	99999	99956	288
29	1.00000	00000	00014	57081	0.99999	99999	99985	429
30	1.00000	00000	00004	85694	0.99999	99999	99995	143
31	1.00000	00000	00001	61898	0.99999	99999	99998	381
32	1.00000	00000	00000	53966	0.99999	99999	99999	460
33	1.00000	00000	00000	17989	0.99999	99999	99999	820
34	1.00000	00000	00000	05996	0.99999	99999	99999	940
35	1.00000	00000	00000	01999	0.99999	99999	99999	980
36	1.00000	00000	00000	00666	0.99999	99999	99999	993
37	1.00000	00000	00000	00222	0.99999	99999	99999	998
38	1.00000	00000	00000	00074	0.99999	99999	99999	999
39	1.00000	00000	00000	00025				
40	1.00000	00000	00000	00008				
41	1.00000	00000	00000	00003				
42	1.00000	00000	00000	00001				

Factorials, Exact Values

n	$n!$
0	1 (by definition)
1	1
2	2
3	6
4	24
5	120
6	720
7	5040
8	40,320
9	362,880
10	3,628,800
11	39,916,800
12	479,001,600
13	6,227,020,800
14	87,178,291,200
15	1,307,674,368,000
16	20,922,789,888,000
17	355,687,428,096,000
18	6,402,373,705,728,000
19	121,645,100,408,832,000
20	2,432,902,008,176,640,000
21	51,090,942,171,709,440,000
22	1,124,000,727,777,607,680,000
23	25,852,016,738,884,976,640,000
24	620,448,401,733,239,439,360,000
25	15,511,210,043,330,985,984,000,000
26	403,291,461,126,605,635,584,000,000
27	10,888,869,450,418,352,160,768,000,000
28	304,888,344,611,713,860,501,504,000,000
29	8,841,761,993,739,701,954,543,616,000,000
30	265,252,859,812,191,058,636,308,480,000,000
31	8.22284×10^{33}
32	2.63131×10^{35}
33	8.68332×10^{36}
34	2.95233×10^{38}
35	1.03331×10^{40}
36	3.71993×10^{41}
37	1.37638×10^{43}
38	5.23023×10^{44}
39	2.03979×10^{46}

$\underline{n} = n! = e^{-n}n^n\sqrt{2\pi n}.$ approximately, known as Stirling's formula

$\log_e n! = n \log_e n - n$, approximately.

FACTORIALS AND THEIR COMMON LOGARITHMS

This table presents values of $n! = n(n-1)(n-2) \ldots 2 \cdot 1$ and its logarithm for numbers from 1 to 100. The values of $n!$ are expressed exponentially to 5 significant figures.

n	$n!$	$\log n!$	n	$n!$	$\log n!$
			50	3.0414×10^{64}	64.48307
1	1,0000	0.00000	51	1.5511×10^{66}	66.19065
2	2,0000	0.30103	52	8.0658×10^{67}	67.90665
3	6,0000	0.77815	53	4.2749×10^{69}	69.63092
4	2.4000×10	1.38021	54	2.3084×10^{71}	71.36332
5	1.2000×10^{2}	2.07918	55	1.2696×10^{73}	73.10368
6	7.2000×10^{2}	2.85733	56	7.1100×10^{74}	74.85187
7	5.0400×10^{3}	3.70243	57	4.0527×10^{76}	76.60774
8	4.0320×10^{4}	4.60552	58	2.3506×10^{78}	78.37117
9	3.6288×10^{5}	5.55976	59	1.3868×10^{80}	80.14202
10	3.6288×10^{6}	6.55976	60	8.3210×10^{81}	81.92017
11	3.9917×10^{7}	7.60116	61	5.0758×10^{83}	83.70550
12	4.7900×10^{8}	8.68034	62	3.1470×10^{85}	85.49790
13	6.2270×10^{9}	9.79428	63	1.9826×10^{87}	87.29724
14	8.7178×10^{10}	10.94041	64	1.2689×10^{89}	89.10342
15	1.3077×10^{12}	12.11650	65	8.2477×10^{90}	90.91633
16	2.0923×10^{13}	13.32062	66	5.4434×10^{92}	92.73587
17	3.5569×10^{14}	14.55107	67	3.6471×10^{94}	94.56195
18	6.4024×10^{15}	15.80634	68	2.4800×10^{96}	96.39446
19	1.2165×10^{17}	17.08509	69	1.7112×10^{98}	98.23331
20	2.4329×10^{68}	18.38612	70	1.1979×10^{100}	100.07841
21	5.1091×10^{19}	19.70834	71	8.5048×10^{101}	101.92966
22	1.1240×10^{21}	21.05077	72	6.1234×10^{103}	103.78700
23	2.5852×10^{22}	22.41249	73	4.4701×10^{105}	105.65032
24	6.2045×10^{23}	23.79271	74	3.3079×10^{107}	107.51955
25	1.5511×10^{25}	25.19065	75	2.4809×10^{109}	109.39461
26	4.0329×10^{26}	26.60562	76	1.8855×10^{111}	111.27543
27	1.0889×10^{28}	28.03698	77	1.4518×10^{113}	113.16192
28	3.0489×10^{29}	29.48414	78	1.1324×10^{115}	115.05401
29	8.8418×10^{30}	30.94654	79	8.9462×10^{116}	116.95164
30	2.6525×10^{32}	32.42366	80	7.1569×10^{118}	118.85473
31	8.2228×10^{33}	33.91502	81	5.7971×10^{120}	120.76321
32	2.6313×10^{35}	35.42017	82	4.7536×10^{122}	122.67703
33	8.6833×10^{36}	36.93869	83	3.9455×10^{124}	124.59610
34	2.9523×10^{38}	38.47016	84	3.3142×10^{126}	126.52038
35	1.0333×10^{40}	40.01423	85	2.8171×10^{128}	128.44980
36	3.7199×10^{41}	41.57054	86	2.4227×10^{130}	130.38430
37	1.3764×10^{43}	43.13874	87	2.1078×10^{132}	132.32382
38	5.2302×10^{44}	44.71852	88	1.8548×10^{134}	134.26830
39	2.0398×10^{46}	46.30959	89	1.6508×10^{136}	136.21769
40	8.1592×10^{47}	47.91165	90	1.4857×10^{138}	138.17194
41	3.3453×10^{49}	49.52443	91	1.3520×10^{140}	140.13098
42	1.4050×10^{51}	51.14768	92	1.2438×10^{142}	142.09476
43	6.0415×10^{52}	52.78115	93	1.1568×10^{144}	144.06325
44	2.6583×10^{54}	54.42460	94	1.0874×10^{146}	146.03638
45	1.1962×10^{56}	56.07781	95	1.0330×10^{148}	148.01410
46	5.5026×10^{57}	57.74057	96	9.9168×10^{149}	149.99637
47	2.5862×10^{59}	59.41267	97	9.6193×10^{151}	151.98314
48	1.2414×10^{61}	61.09391	98	9.4269×10^{153}	153.97437
49	6.0828×10^{62}	62.78410	99	9.3326×10^{155}	155.97000
50	3.0414×10^{64}	64.48307	100	9.3326×10^{157}	157.97000

$$n! = \left(\frac{n}{e}\right)^{n} \sqrt{2n\pi} + h; \, n = 1, 2, 3, \ldots \quad \left[0 < \frac{h}{n!} < \frac{1}{12n}\right], \quad \lim_{n \to \infty} \frac{n! e^{n}}{n^{n+\frac{1}{2}}} = \sqrt{2\pi}, \quad \lim_{n \to \infty} \frac{(n!)^{\frac{1}{n}}}{n} = \frac{1}{e}$$

RECIPROCALS OF FACTORIALS AND THEIR COMMON LOGARITHMS

This table presents the reciprocals of the factorials and their logarithms for numbers from 1 to 100.

n	$1/n!$	$\log(1/n!)$	n	$1/n!$	$\log(1/n!)$
1	1.	.00000	51	$.64470 \times 10^{-66}$	$\overline{67}.80935$
2	0.5	$\overline{1}.69897$	52	$.12398 \times 10^{-67}$	$\overline{68}.09335$
3	.16667	$\overline{1}.22185$	53	$.23392 \times 10^{-69}$	$\overline{70}.36908$
*4	$.41667 \times 10^{-1}$	$\overline{2}.61979$	54	$.43319 \times 10^{-71}$	$\overline{72}.63668$
5	$.83333 \times 10^{-2}$	$\overline{3}.92082$	55	$.78762 \times 10^{-73}$	$\overline{74}.89632$
6	$.13889 \times 10^{-2}$	$\overline{3}.14267$	56	$.14065 \times 10^{-74}$	$\overline{75}.14813$
7	$.19841 \times 10^{-3}$	$\overline{4}.29757$	57	$.24675 \times 10^{-76}$	$\overline{77}.39226$
8	$.24802 \times 10^{-4}$	$\overline{5}.39448$	58	$.42543 \times 10^{-78}$	$\overline{79}.62883$
9	$.27557 \times 10^{-5}$	$\overline{6}.44024$	59	$.72107 \times 10^{-80}$	$\overline{81}.85798$
10	$.27557 \times 10^{-6}$	$\overline{7}.44024$	60	$.12018 \times 10^{-81}$	$\overline{82}.07983$
11	$.25052 \times 10^{-7}$	$\overline{8}.39884$	61	$.19701 \times 10^{-83}$	$\overline{84}.29450$
12	$.20877 \times 10^{-8}$	$\overline{9}.31966$	62	$.31776 \times 10^{-85}$	$\overline{86}.50210$
13	$.16059 \times 10^{-9}$	$\overline{10}.20572$	63	$.50439 \times 10^{-87}$	$\overline{88}.70276$
14	$.11471 \times 10^{-10}$	$\overline{11}.05959$	64	$.78810 \times 10^{-89}$	$\overline{90}.89658$
15	$.76472 \times 10^{-12}$	$\overline{13}.88350$	65	$.12125 \times 10^{-90}$	$\overline{91}.08367$
16	$.47795 \times 10^{-13}$	$\overline{14}.67938$	66	$.18371 \times 10^{-92}$	$\overline{93}.26413$
17	$.28115 \times 10^{-14}$	$\overline{15}.44893$	67	$.27419 \times 10^{-94}$	$\overline{95}.43805$
18	$.15619 \times 10^{-15}$	$\overline{16}.19366$	68	$.40322 \times 10^{-96}$	$\overline{97}.60554$
19	$.82206 \times 10^{-17}$	$\overline{18}.91491$	69	$.58438 \times 10^{-98}$	$\overline{99}.76669$
20	$.41103 \times 10^{-18}$	$\overline{19}.61388$	70	$.83482 \times 10^{-100}$	$\overline{101}.92159$
21	$.19573 \times 10^{-19}$	$\overline{20}.29166$	71	$.11758 \times 10^{-101}$	$\overline{102}.07034$
22	$.88968 \times 10^{-21}$	$\overline{22}.94923$	72	$.16331 \times 10^{-103}$	$\overline{104}.21300$
23	$.38682 \times 10^{-23}$	$\overline{23}.58751$	73	$.22371 \times 10^{-105}$	$\overline{106}.34968$
24	$.16117 \times 10^{-23}$	$\overline{24}.20729$	74	$.30231 \times 10^{-107}$	$\overline{108}.48045$
25	$.64470 \times 10^{-25}$	$\overline{26}.80935$	75	$.40308 \times 10^{-109}$	$\overline{110}.60539$
26	$.24796 \times 10^{-26}$	$\overline{27}.39438$	76	$.53036 \times 10^{-111}$	$\overline{112}.72457$
27	$.91837 \times 10^{-28}$	$\overline{29}.96302$	77	$.68879 \times 10^{-113}$	$\overline{114}.83808$
28	$.32799 \times 10^{-29}$	$\overline{30}.51586$	78	$.88306 \times 10^{-115}$	$\overline{116}.94599$
29	$.11310 \times 10^{-30}$	$\overline{31}.05346$	79	$.11178 \times 10^{-116}$	$\overline{117}.04836$
30	$.37700 \times 10^{-32}$	$\overline{33}.57634$	80	$.13972 \times 10^{-118}$	$\overline{119}.14527$
31	$.12161 \times 10^{-33}$	$\overline{34}.08498$	81	$.17250 \times 10^{-120}$	$\overline{121}.23679$
32	$.38004 \times 10^{-35}$	$\overline{36}.57983$	82	$.21036 \times 10^{-122}$	$\overline{123}.32297$
33	$.11516 \times 10^{-36}$	$\overline{37}.06131$	83	$.25345 \times 10^{-124}$	$\overline{125}.40390$
34	$.33872 \times 10^{-38}$	$\overline{39}.52984$	84	$.30173 \times 10^{-126}$	$\overline{127}.47962$
35	$.96776 \times 10^{-40}$	$\overline{41}.98577$	85	$.35497 \times 10^{-128}$	$\overline{129}.55020$
36	$.26882 \times 10^{-41}$	$\overline{42}.42946$	86	$.41276 \times 10^{-130}$	$\overline{131}.61570$
37	$.72655 \times 10^{-43}$	$\overline{44}.86126$	87	$.47444 \times 10^{-132}$	$\overline{133}.67618$
38	$.19120 \times 10^{-44}$	$\overline{45}.28148$	88	$.53913 \times 10^{-134}$	$\overline{135}.73170$
39	$.49025 \times 10^{-46}$	$\overline{47}.69041$	89	$.60577 \times 10^{-136}$	$\overline{137}.78231$
40	$.12256 \times 10^{-47}$	$\overline{48}.08835$	90	$.67308 \times 10^{-138}$	$\overline{139}.82806$
41	$.29893 \times 10^{-49}$	$\overline{50}.47557$	91	$.73964 \times 10^{-140}$	$\overline{141}.86902$
42	$.71174 \times 10^{-51}$	$\overline{52}.85232$	92	$.80396 \times 10^{-142}$	$\overline{143}.90524$
43	$.16552 \times 10^{-52}$	$\overline{53}.21885$	93	$.86447 \times 10^{-144}$	$\overline{145}.93675$
44	$.37618 \times 10^{-54}$	$\overline{55}.57540$	94	$.91965 \times 10^{-146}$	$\overline{147}.96362$
45	$.83597 \times 10^{-56}$	$\overline{57}.92219$	95	$.96806 \times 10^{-148}$	$\overline{149}.98590$
46	$.18173 \times 10^{-57}$	$\overline{58}.25943$	96	$.10084 \times 10^{-149}$	$\overline{150}.00363$
47	$.38666 \times 10^{-59}$	$\overline{60}.58733$	97	$.10396 \times 10^{-151}$	$\overline{152}.01686$
48	$.80555 \times 10^{-61}$	$\overline{62}.90609$	98	$.10608 \times 10^{-153}$	$\overline{154}.02563$
49	$.16440 \times 10^{-62}$	$\overline{63}.21590$	99	$.10715 \times 10^{-155}$	$\overline{156}.03000$
50	$.32879 \times 10^{-64}$	$\overline{65}.51693$	100	$.10715 \times 10^{-157}$	$\overline{158}.03000$

* For example $\log \frac{1}{4!} = \overline{2}.61979 = .61979 - 2 = 8.61979 - 10$.

NUMBER OF PERMUTATIONS $P(n,m)$

This table contains the number of permutations of n distinct things taken m at a time, given by

$$P(n,m) = \frac{n!}{(n-m)!} = n(n-1) \cdots (n-m+1)$$

m \ n	0	1	2	3	4	5	6	7	8	9	10
0	1										
1	1	1									
2	1	2	2								
3	1	3	6	6							
4	1	4	12	24	24						
5	1	5	20	60	120	120					
6	1	6	30	120	360	720	720				
7	1	7	42	210	840	2520	5040	5040			
8	1	8	56	336	1680	6720	20160	40320	40320		
9	1	9	72	504	3024	15120	60480	1 81440	3 62880	3 62880	
10	1	10	90	720	5040	30240	1 51200	6 04800	18 14400	36 28800	36 28800
11	1	11	110	990	7920	55440	3 32640	16 63200	66 52800	199 58400	399 16800
12	1	12	132	1320	11880	95040	6 65280	39 91680	199 58400	798 33600	2395 00800
13	1	13	156	1716	17160	1 54440	12 35520	86 48640	518 91840	2594 59200	10378 36800
14	1	14	182	2184	24024	2 40240	21 62160	172 97280	1210 80960	7264 85760	36324 28800
15	1	15	210	2730	32760	3 60360	36 03600	324 32400	2594 59200	18162 14400	1 08972 86400

m \ n	11	12	13	14	15
8					
9					
10					
11	399 16800				
12	4790 01600	4790 01600			
13	31135 10400	62270 20800	62270 20800		
14	1 45297 15200	4 35891 45600	8 71782 91200	8 71782 91200	
15	5 44864 32000	21 79457 28000	65 38371 84000	130 76743 68000	130 76743 68000

NUMBER OF COMBINATIONS

This table contains the number of combinations of n distinct things taken m at a time, given by $\binom{n}{m} = C(n,m)$. For coefficients missing from the table, use the relation $\binom{n}{m} = \binom{n}{n-m}$.

m / n	0	1	2	3	4	5	6	7	8
1	1	1							
2	1	2	1						
3	1	3	3	1					
4	1	4	6	4	1				
5	1	5	10	10	5	1			
6	1	6	15	20	15	6	1		
7	1	7	21	35	35	21	7	1	
8	1	8	28	56	70	56	28	8	1
9	1	9	36	84	126	126	84	36	9
10	1	10	45	120	210	252	210	120	45
11	1	11	55	165	330	462	462	330	165
12	1	12	66	220	495	792	924	792	495
13	1	13	78	286	715	1287	1716	1716	1287
14	1	14	91	364	1001	2002	3003	3432	3003
15	1	15	105	455	1365	3003	5005	6435	6435
16	1	16	120	560	1820	4368	8008	11440	12870
17	1	17	136	680	2380	6188	12376	19448	24310
18	1	18	153	816	3060	8568	18564	31824	43758
19	1	19	171	969	3876	11628	27132	50388	75582
20	1	20	190	1140	4845	15504	38760	77520	1 25970
21	1	21	210	1330	5985	20349	54264	1 16280	2 03490
22	1	22	231	1540	7315	26334	74613	1 70544	3 19770
23	1	23	253	1771	8855	33649	1 00947	2 45157	4 90314
24	1	24	276	2024	10626	42504	1 34596	3 46104	7 35471
25	1	25	300	2300	12650	53130	1 77100	4 80700	10 81575
26	1	26	325	2600	14950	65780	2 30230	6 57800	15 62275
27	1	27	351	2925	17550	80730	2 96010	8 88030	22 20075
28	1	28	378	3276	20475	98280	3 76740	11 84040	31 08105
29	1	29	406	3654	23751	1 18755	4 75020	15 60780	42 92145
30	1	30	435	4060	27405	1 42506	5 93775	20 35800	58 52925
31	1	31	465	4495	31465	1 69911	7 36281	26 29575	78 88725
32	1	32	496	4960	35960	2 01376	9 06192	33 65856	105 18300
33	1	33	528	5456	40920	2 37336	11 07568	42 72048	138 84156
34	1	34	561	5984	46376	2 78256	13 44904	53 79616	181 56204
35	1	35	595	6545	52360	3 24632	16 23160	67 24520	235 35820
36	1	36	630	7140	58905	3 76992	19 47792	83 47680	302 60340
37	1	37	666	7770	66045	4 35897	23 24784	102 95472	386 08020
38	1	38	703	8436	73815	5 01942	27 60681	126 20256	489 03492
39	1	39	741	9139	82251	5 75757	32 62623	153 80937	615 23748
40	1	40	780	9880	91390	6 58008	38 38380	186 43560	769 04685
41	1	41	820	10660	101270	7 49398	44 96388	224 81940	955 48245
42	1	42	861	11480	111930	8 50668	52 45786	269 78328	1180 30185
43	1	43	903	12341	123410	9 62598	60 96454	322 24114	1450 08513
44	1	44	946	13244	135751	10 86008	70 59052	383 20568	1772 32627
45	1	45	990	14190	148995	12 21759	81 45060	453 79620	2155 53195
46	1	46	1035	15180	163185	13 70754	93 66819	535 24680	2609 32815
47	1	47	1081	16215	178365	15 33939	107 37573	628 91499	3144 57495
48	1	48	1128	17296	194580	17 12304	122 71512	736 29072	3773 48994
49	1	49	1176	18424	211876	19 06884	139 83816	859 00584	4509 78066
50	1	50	1225	19600	230300	21 18760	158 90700	998 84400	5368 78650

NUMBER OF COMBINATIONS

$$\binom{n}{m} = C(n,m)$$

m n	9	10	11	12	13
9	1				
10	10	1			
11	55	11	1		
12	220	66	12	1	
13	715	286	78	13	1
14	2002	1001	364	91	14
15	5005	3003	1365	455	105
16	11440	8008	4368	1820	560
17	24310	19448	12376	6188	2380
18	48620	43758	31824	18564	8568
19	92378	92378	75582	50388	27132
20	1 67960	1 84756	1 67960	1 25970	77520
21	2 93930	3 52716	3 52716	2 93930	2 03490
22	4 97420	6 46646	7 05432	6 46646	4 97420
23	8 17190	11 44066	13 52078	13 52078	11 44066
24	13 07504	19 61256	24 96144	27 04156	24 96144
25	20 42975	32 68760	44 57400	52 00300	52 00300
26	31 24550	53 11735	77 26160	96 57700	104 00600
27	46 86825	84 36285	130 37895	173 83860	200 58300
28	69 06900	131 23110	214 74180	304 21755	374 42160
29	100 15005	200 30010	345 97290	518 95935	678 63915
30	143 07150	300 45015	546 27300	864 93225	1197 59850
31	201 60075	443 52165	846 72315	1411 20525	2062 53075
32	280 48800	645 12240	1290 24480	2257 92840	3473 73600
33	385 67100	925 61040	1935 36720	3548 17320	5731 66440
34	524 51256	1311 28140	2860 97760	5483 54040	9279 83760
35	706 07460	1835 79396	4172 25900	8344 51800	14763 37800
36	941 43280	2541 86856	6008 05296	12516 77700	23107 89600
37	1244 03620	3483 30136	8549 92152	18524 82996	35624 67300
38	1630 11640	4727 33756	12033 22288	27074 75148	54149 50296
39	2119 15132	6357 45396	16760 56044	39107 97436	81224 25444
40	2734 38880	8476 60528	23118 01440	55868 53480	1 20332 22880
41	3503 43565	11210 99408	31594 61968	78986 54920	1 76200 76360
42	4458 91810	14714 42973	42805 61376	1 10581 16888	2 55187 31280
43	5639 21995	19173 34783	57520 04349	1 53386 78264	3 65768 48168
44	7098 30508	24812 56778	76693 39132	2 10906 82613	5 19155 26432
45	8861 63135	31901 87286	1 01505 95910	2 87600 21745	7 30062 09045
46	11017 16330	40763 50421	1 33407 83196	3 89106 17655	10 17662 30790
47	13626 49145	51780 66751	1 74171 33617	5 22514 00851	14 06768 48445
48	16771 06640	65407 15896	2 25952 00368	6 96685 34468	19 29282 49296
49	20544 55634	82178 22536	2 91359 16264	9 22637 34836	26 25967 83764
50	25054 33700	1 02722 78170	3 73537 38800	12 13996 51100	35 48605 18600

NUMBER OF COMBINATIONS

$$\binom{n}{m} = C(n,m)$$

n\m	14	15	16	17	18	19
14	1					
15	15	1				
16	120	16	1			
17	680	136	17	1		
18	3060	816	153	18	1	
19	11628	3876	969	171	19	1
20	38760	15504	4845	1140	190	20
21	1 16280	54264	20349	5985	1330	210
22	3 19770	1 70544	74613	26334	7315	1540
23	8 17190	4 90314	2 45157	1 00947	33649	8855
24	19 61256	13 07504	7 35471	3 46104	1 34596	42504
25	44 57400	32 68760	20 42975	10 81575	4 80700	1 77100
26	96 57700	77 26160	53 11735	31 24550	15 62275	6 57800
27	200 58300	173 83860	130 37895	84 36285	46 86825	22 20075
28	401 16600	374 42160	304 21755	214 74180	131 23110	69 06900
29	775 58760	775 58760	678 63915	518 95935	345 97290	200 30010
30	1454 22675	1551 17520	1454 22675	1197 59850	864 93225	546 27300
31	2651 82525	3005 40195	3005 40195	2651 82525	2062 53075	1411 20625
32	4714 35600	5657 22720	6010 60390	5657 22720	4714 35600	3473 73600
33	8188 09200	10371 58320	11668 03110	11668 03110	10371 58320	8188 09200
34	13919 75640	18559 67520	22039 61430	23336 06220	22039 61430	18559 67520
35	23199 59400	32479 43160	40599 28950	45375 67650	45375 67650	40599 28950
36	37962 97200	55679 02560	73078 72110	85974 96600	90751 35300	85974 96600
37	61070 86800	93641 99760	1 28757 74670	1 59053 68710	1 76726 31900	1 76726 31900
38	96695 54100	1 54712 86560	2 22399 74430	2 87811 43380	3 35780 00610	3 53452 63800
39	1 50845 04396	2 51408 40660	3 77112 60990	5 10211 17810	6 23591 43990	6 89232 64410
40	2 32069 29840	4 02253 45056	6 28521 01650	8 87323 78800	11 33802 61800	13 12824 08400
41	3 52401 52720	6 34322 74896	10 30774 46706	15 15844 80450	20 21126 40600	24 46626 70200
42	5 28602 29080	9 86724 27616	16 65097 21602	25 46619 27156	35 36971 21050	44 67753 10800
43	7 83789 60360	15 15326 56696	26 51821 49218	42 11716 48758	60 83590 48206	80 04724 31850
44	11 49558 08528	22 99116 17056	41 67148 05914	68 63537 97976	102 95306 96964	140 88314 80056
45	16 68713 34960	34 48674 25584	64 66264 22970	110 30686 03890	171 58844 94940	243 83621 77020
46	23 98775 44005	51 17387 60544	99 14938 48554	174 96950 26860	281 89530 98830	415 42466 71960
47	34 16437 74795	75 16163 04549	150 32326 09098	274 11888 75414	456 86481 25690	697 31997 70790
48	48 23206 23240	109 32600 79344	225 48489 13647	424 44214 84512	730 93370 01104	1154 78478 96480
49	67 52488 72536	157 55807 02584	334 81089 92991	649 92703 98159	1155 42584 85616	1885 16848 97584
50	93 78456 56300	225 08295 75120	492 36896 95575	984 73793 91150	1805 35288 83775	3040 59433 83200

NUMBER OF COMBINATIONS

$$\binom{n}{m} = C(n,m)$$

$n \backslash m$	25	24	23	22	21	20
20						1
21					1	21
22				1	22	231
23			1	23	253	1771
24		1	24	276	2024	10626
25	1	25	300	2300	12650	53130
26	26	325	2600	14950	65780	2 30230
27	351	2925	17550	80730	2 96010	8 88030
28	3276	20475	98280	3 76740	11 84040	31 08105
29	23751	1 18755	4 75020	15 60780	42 92145	100 15005
30	1 42506	5 93775	20 35800	58 52925	143 07150	300 45015
31	7 36281	26 29575	78 88725	201 60075	443 52165	846 72315
32	33 65856	105 18300	280 48800	645 12240	1290 24480	2257 92840
33	138 84156	385 67100	925 61040	1935 36720	3548 17320	5731 66440
34	524 51256	1311 28140	2860 97760	5483 54040	9279 83760	13919 75640
35	1835 79396	4172 25900	8344 51800	14763 37800	23199 59400	32479 43160
36	6008 05296	12516 77700	23107 89600	37962 97200	55679 02560	73078 72110
37	18524 82996	35624 67300	61070 86800	93641 99760	1 28757 74670	1 59053 68710
38	54149 50296	96695 54100	1 54712 86560	2 22399 74430	2 87811 43380	3 35780 00610
39	1 50845 04396	2 51408 40660	3 77112 60990	5 10211 17810	6 23591 43990	6 89232 64410
40	4 02253 45056	6 28521 01650	8 87323 78800	11 33802 61800	13 12824 08400	13 78465 28820
41	10 30774 46706	15 15844 80450	20 21126 40600	24 46626 70200	26 91289 37220	26 91289 37220
42	25 46619 27156	35 36971 21050	44 67753 10800	51 37916 07420	53 82578 74440	51 37916 07420
43	60 83590 48206	80 04724 31850	96 05669 18220	105 20494 81860	105 20494 81860	96 05669 18220
44	140 88314 80056	176 10393 50070	201 26164 00080	210 40989 63720	201 26164 00080	176 10393 50070
45	316 98708 30126	377 36557 50150	411 67153 63800	411 67153 63800	377 36557 50150	316 98708 30126
46	694 35265 80276	789 03711 13950	823 34307 27600	789 03711 13950	694 35265 80276	560 82330 07146
47	1483 38976 94226	1612 38018 41550	1612 38018 41550	1483 38976 94226	1255 17595 87422	976 24796 79106
48	3095 76995 35776	3224 76036 83100	3095 76995 35776	2738 56572 81648	2231 42392 66528	1673 56794 49896
49	6320 53032 18876	6320 53032 18876	5834 33568 17424	4969 98965 48176	3904 99187 16424	2827 75273 46376
50	12641 06064 37752	12154 86600 36300	10804 32533 65600	8874 98152 64600	6732 74460 62800	4712 92122 43960

Properties of Binomial Coefficients

$$(1 + x)^n = \binom{n}{0}x^0 + \binom{n}{1}x^n + \binom{n}{2}x^2 + \ldots + \binom{n}{n}x^n$$

$$\binom{n}{m} + \binom{n}{m+1} = \binom{n+1}{m+1}, \binom{n}{m} = \binom{n}{n-m}$$

This leads to Pascal's triangle

$$\binom{n}{0} + \binom{n}{1} + \binom{n}{2} + \ldots + \binom{n}{n} = 2^n$$

$$\binom{n}{0} - \binom{n}{1} + \binom{n}{2} - \ldots (-1)^n \binom{n}{n} = 0$$

$$\binom{n}{n} + \binom{n+1}{n} + \binom{n+2}{n} + \ldots + \binom{n+m}{n} = \binom{n+m+1}{n+1}$$

$$\binom{n}{0} + \binom{n}{2} + \binom{n}{4} + \ldots = 2^{n-1}$$

$$\binom{n}{1} + \binom{n}{3} + \binom{n}{5} + \ldots = 2^{n-1}$$

$$\binom{n}{0}^2 + \binom{n}{1}^2 + \binom{n}{2}^2 + \ldots + \binom{n}{n}^2 = \binom{2n}{n}$$

$$\binom{m}{0}\binom{n}{p} + \binom{m}{1}\binom{n}{p-1} + \ldots + \binom{m}{p}\binom{n}{0} = \binom{m+n}{p}$$

$$(1)\binom{n}{1} + (2)\binom{n}{2} + (3)\binom{n}{3} + \ldots + (n)\binom{n}{n} = n2^{n-1}$$

$$(1)\binom{n}{1} - (2)\binom{n}{2} + (3)\binom{n}{3} - \ldots (-1)^{n+1}(n)\binom{n}{n} = 0$$

POSITIONAL NOTATION

In our ordinary system of writing numbers, the value of any digit depends on its position in the number. The value of a digit in any position is ten times the value of the same digit one position to the right, or one-tenth the value of the same digit one position to the left. Thus, for example,

$$173.246 = 1 \times 10^2 + 7 \times 10^1 + 3 + 2 \times \frac{1}{10} + 4 \times \frac{1}{10^2} + 6 \times \frac{1}{10^3}.$$

There is no reason that a number other than 10 cannot be used as the *base*, or *radix*, of the number system. In fact, bases of 2, 8, and 16 are commonly used in working with digital computers. When the base used is not clear from the context, it is usually indicated as a parenthesized subscript or merely as a subscript. Thus

$$743_{(8)} = 7 \times 8^2 + 4 \times 8 + 3 = 7 \times 64 + 4 \times 8 + 3 = 448 + 32 + 3 = 483_{(10)}$$
$$1011.101_{(2)} = 1 \times 2^3 + 0 \times 2^2 + 1 \times 2 + 1 + 1 \times \tfrac{1}{2} + 0 \times \tfrac{1}{4} + 1 \times \tfrac{1}{8} = 11.625_{(10)}$$

CHANGE OF BASE

In this section, it is assumed that all calculations will be performed in base 10, since this is the only base in which most people can easily compute. However, there is no logical reason that some other base could not be used for the computations.

To convert a number from another base into base 10:

Simply write down the digits of the number, with each one multiplied by its appropriate positional value. Then perform the indicated computations in base 10, and write down the answer.

For examples, see the two examples in the previous section.

To convert a number from base 10 into another base:

The part of the number to the left of the point and the part to the right must be operated on separately. For the integer part (the part to the left of the point):

a. Divide the number by the new base, getting an integer quotient and remainder.
b. Write down the remainder as the last digit of the number in the new base.
c. Using the quotient from the last division in place of the original number, repeat the above two steps until the quotient becomes zero.

For the fractional part (the part to the right of the point):

a. Multiply the number by the new base.
b. Write down the integral part of the product as the first digit of the fractional part in the new base.
c. Using the fractional part of the last product in place of the original number, repeat the above two steps until the product becomes an integer, or until the desired number of places have been computed.

Examples:

These examples show a convenient method of arranging the computations.

1. Convert $103.118_{(10)}$ to base 8.

$$
\begin{array}{ll}
8 \ \underline{|103|} \ 7 & \qquad\qquad\qquad .118 \\
8 \ \underline{|12|} \ \ 4 & \qquad\qquad\qquad \underline{\ \ \ 8} \\
\ \ \ \ \ 1 & \quad 147.074324\ldots \qquad .944 \\
& \qquad\qquad\qquad \underline{\ \ \ 8}
\end{array}
$$

The calculation of the fractional part could be carried out as far as desired. It is a non-terminating fraction which will eventually repeat itself.

$$
\begin{array}{l}
7.552 \\
\underline{\ \ \ 8} \\
4.416 \\
\underline{\ \ \ 8} \\
3.328 \\
\underline{\ \ \ 8} \\
2.624 \\
\underline{\ \ \ 8} \\
4.992
\end{array}
$$

$$103.118_{(10)} = 147.074324\ldots_{(8)}$$

The calculations may be further shortened by not writing down the multiplier and divisor at each step of the algorithm, as shown in the next example.

2. Convert $275.824_{(10)}$ to base 5.

$$
\begin{array}{ll}
5 \ \underline{|275|} \ 0 & \qquad\qquad .824 \\
\ \ \ \underline{|55|} \ \ 0 & \qquad\quad 4.120 \\
\ \ \ \underline{|11|} \ \ 1 & \qquad\quad 0.600 \\
\ \ \ \ \ \ 2 & \qquad\quad 3.000
\end{array}
$$

$$275.824_{(10)} = 2100.403_{(5)}$$

To convert from one base to another (neither of which is 10):

The easiest procedure is usually to convert first to base 10, and then to the desired base. However, there are two exceptions to this:

1. If computational facility is possessed in either of the bases, it may be used instead of base 10, and the appropriate one of the above methods applied.
2. If the two bases are different powers of the same number, the conversion may be done digit-by-digit to the base which is the common root of both bases, and then digit-by-digit back to the other base.

Example: Convert $127.653_{(8)}$ to base 16. (For base 16, the letters A–F are used for the digits $10_{(10)} - 15_{(10)}$.)

The first step is to convert the number to base 2, simply by converting each digit to its binary equivalent:

$$127.653_{(8)} = 001 \ 010 \ 111 \cdot 110 \ 101 \ 011_{(2)}$$

Now by simply regrouping the binary number into groups of four binary digits, starting at the point, we convert to base 16:

$$127.653_{(8)} = 101 \ 0111 \cdot 1101 \ 0101 \ 1_{(2)} = 57.D58_{(16)}$$

$10^{\pm n}$ IN OCTAL SCALE

10^n	n	10^{-n}	10^n	n	10^{-n}
1	0	1.000 000 000 000 000	112 402 762 000	10	0.000 000 000 006 676
12	1	0.063 146 314 631 463	1 351 035 564 000	11	0.000 000 000 000 500
144	2	0.005 075 341 217 270	16 432 451 210 000	12	0.000 000 000 000 043
1 750	3	0.000 406 111 564 571	221 441 634 520 000	13	0.000 000 000 000 003
23 420	4	0.000 032 155 613 531	2 657 142 036 440 000	14	0.000 000 000 000 000
303 240	5	0.000 002 476 132 611	34 327 724 461 500 000	15	0.000 000 000 000 000
3 641 100	6	0.000 000 206 157 364	434 157 115 760 200 000	16	0.000 000 000 000 000
46 113 200	7	0.000 000 015 327 745	5 432 127 413 542 400 000	17	0.000 000 000 000 000
575 360 400	8	0.000 000 001 257 144	67 405 553 164 731 000 000	18	0.000 000 000 000 000
7 346 545 000	9	0.000 000 000 104 560			

2^n IN DECIMAL SCALE

n	2^n	n	2^n	n	2^n
0.001	1.00069 33874 62581	0.01	1.00695 55500 56719	0.1	1.07177 34625 36293
0.002	1.00138 72557 11335	0.02	1.01395 94797 90029	0.2	1.14869 83549 97035
0.003	1.00208 16050 79633	0.03	1.02101 21257 07193	0.3	1.23114 44133 44916
0.004	1.00277 63359 01078	0.04	1.02811 38266 56067	0.4	1.31950 79107 72894
0.005	1.00347 17845 09503	0.05	1.03526 49238 41377	0.5	1.4121 35623 73095
0.006	1.00416 75432 38973	0.06	1.04246 57608 41121	0.6	1.51571 65665 10398
0.007	1.00486 38204 23785	0.07	1.04971 66836 23067	0.7	1.62450 47927 12471
0.008	1.00556 05803 98468	0.08	1.05701 80405 61380	0.8	1.74110 11265 92248
0.009	1.00625 78234 97782	0.09	1.06437 01824 53360	0.9	1.86606 59830 73615

$n \log_{10} 2$, $n \log_2 10$ IN DECIMAL SCALE

n	$n\log_{10}2$	$n\log_2 10$	n	$n\log_{10}2$	$n\log_2 10$
1	0.30102 99957	3.32192 80949	6	1.80617 99740	19.93156 85693
2	0.60205 99913	6.64385 61898	7	2.10720 99696	23.25349 66642
3	0.90308 99870	9.96578 42847	8	2.40823 99653	26.57542 47591
4	1.20411 99827	13.28771 23795	9	2.70926 99610	29.89735 28540
5	1.50514 99783	16.60964 04744	10	3.01029 99566	33.21928 09480

ADDITION AND MULTIPLICATION TABLES

Binary Scale

Addition

$$0 + 0 = 0$$
$$0 + 1 = 1 + 0 = 1$$
$$1 + 1 = 10$$

Multiplication

$$0 \times 0 = 0$$
$$0 \times 1 = 1 \times 0 = 0$$
$$1 \times 1 = 1$$

Octal Scale

Addition

0	01	02	03	04	05	06	07
1	02	03	04	05	06	07	10
2	03	04	05	06	07	10	11
3	04	05	06	07	10	11	12
4	05	06	07	10	11	12	13
5	06	07	10	11	12	13	14
6	07	10	11	12	13	14	15
7	10	11	12	13	14	15	16

Multiplication

1	02	03	04	05	06	07
2	04	06	10	12	14	16
3	06	11	14	17	22	25
4	10	14	20	24	30	34
5	12	17	24	31	36	43
6	14	22	30	36	44	52
7	16	25	34	43	52	61

MATHEMATICAL CONSTANTS IN OCTAL SCALE

$\pi = (3.11037\ 552421)_{(8)}$

$\pi^{-1} = (0.24276\ 301556)_{(8)}$

$\sqrt{\pi} = (1.61337\ 611067)_{(8)}$

$\log_6 \pi = 1.11206\ 404435)_{(8)}$

$\log_2 \pi = (1.51544\ 163223)_{(8)}$

$\sqrt{10} = (3.12305\ 407267)_{(8)}$

$e = (2.55760\ 521305)_{(8)}$

$e^{-1} = (0.27426\ 530661)_{(8)}$

$\sqrt{e} = (1.51411\ 230704)_{(8)}$

$\log_{10} e = (0.33626\ 754251)_{(8)}$

$\log_2 e = (1.34252\ 166245)_{(8)}$

$\log_2 10 = (3.24464\ 741136)_{(8)}$

$\gamma = (0.44742\ 147707)_{(8)}$

$\log_6 \gamma = -(0.43127\ 233602)_{(8)}$

$\log_2 \gamma = -(0.62573\ 030645)_{(8)}$

$\sqrt{2} = (1.32404\ 746320)_{(8)}$

$\log_6 2 = (0.54271\ 027760)_{(8)}$

$\log_6 10 = (2.23273\ 067355)_{(8)}$

OCTAL-DECIMAL INTEGER CONVERSION TABLE

	0	1	2	3	4	5	6	7
0000	0000	0001	0002	0003	0004	0005	0006	0007
0010	0008	0009	0010	0011	0012	0013	0014	0015
0020	0016	0017	0018	0019	0020	0021	0022	0023
0030	0024	0025	0026	0027	0028	0029	0030	0031
0040	0032	0033	0034	0035	0036	0037	0038	0039
0050	0040	0041	0042	0043	0044	0045	0046	0047
0060	0048	0049	0050	0051	0052	0053	0054	0055
0070	0056	0057	0058	0059	0060	0061	0062	0063
0100	0064	0065	0066	0067	0068	0069	0070	0071
0110	0072	0073	0074	0075	0076	0077	0078	0079
0120	0080	0081	0082	0083	0084	0085	0086	0087
0130	0088	0089	0090	0091	0092	0093	0094	0095
0140	0096	0097	0098	0099	0100	0101	0102	0103
0150	0104	0105	0106	0107	0108	0109	0110	0111
0160	0112	0113	0114	0115	0116	0117	0118	0119
0170	0120	0121	0122	0123	0124	0125	0126	0127
0200	0128	0129	0130	0131	0132	0133	0134	0135
0210	0136	0137	0138	0139	0140	0141	0142	0143
0220	0144	0145	0146	0147	0148	0149	0150	0151
0230	0152	0153	0154	0155	0156	0157	0158	0159
0240	0160	0161	0162	0163	0164	0165	1066	0167
0250	0168	0169	0170	0171	0172	0173	0174	0175
0260	0176	0177	0178	0179	0180	0181	0182	0183
0270	0184	0185	0186	0187	0188	0189	0190	0191
0300	0192	0193	0194	0195	0196	0197	0198	0199
0310	0200	0201	0202	0203	0204	0205	0206	0207
0320	0208	0209	0210	0211	0212	0213	0214	0215
0330	0216	0217	0218	0219	0220	0221	0222	0223
0340	0224	0225	CC226	0227	0228	0229	0230	0231
0350	0232	0233	0234	0235	0236	0237	0238	0239
0360	0240	0241	0242	0243	0244	0245	0246	0247
0370	0248	0249	0250	0251	0252	0253	0254	0255

	0	1	2	3	4	5	6	7
0400	0256	0257	0258	0259	0260	0261	0262	0263
0410	0264	0265	0266	0267	0268	0269	0270	0271
0420	0272	0273	0274	0275	0276	0277	0278	0279
0430	0280	0281	0282	0283	0284	0285	0286	0287
0440	0288	0289	0290	0291	0292	0293	0294	0295
0450	0296	0297	0298	0299	0300	0301	0302	0303
0460	0304	0305	0306	0307	0308	0309	0310	0311
0470	0312	0313	0314	0315	0316	0317	0318	0319
0500	0320	0321	0322	0323	0324	0325	0326	0327
0510	0328	0329	0330	0331	0332	0333	0334	0335
0520	0336	0337	0338	0339	0340	0341	0342	0343
0530	0344	0345	0346	0347	0348	0349	0350	0351
0540	0352	0353	0354	0355	0356	0357	0358	0359
0550	0360	0361	0362	0363	0364	0365	0366	0367
0560	0368	0369	0370	0371	0372	0373	0374	0375
0570	0376	0377	0378	0379	0380	0381	0382	0383
0600	0384	0385	0386	0387	0388	0389	0390	0391
0610	0392	0393	0394	0395	0396	0397	0398	0399
0620	0400	0401	0402	0403	0404	0405	0406	0407
0630	0408	0409	0410	0411	0412	0413	0414	0415
0640	0416	0417	0418	0419	0420	0421	0422	0423
0650	0424	0425	0426	0427	0428	0429	0430	0431
0660	0432	0433	0434	0435	0436	0437	0438	0439
0670	0440	0441	0442	0443	0444	0445	0446	0447
0700	0448	0449	0450	0451	0452	0453	0454	0455
0710	0456	0457	0458	0459	0460	0461	0462	0463
0720	0464	0465	0466	0467	0468	0469	0470	0471
0730	0472	0473	0474	0475	0476	0477	0478	0479
0740	0480	0481	0482	0483	0484	0485	0486	0487
0750	0488	0489	0490	0491	0492	0493	0494	0495
0760	0496	0497	0498	0499	0500	0501	0502	0503
0770	0504	0505	0506	0507	0508	0509	0510	0511

0000	0000
to	to
0777	0511
(Octal)	(Decimal)

Octal	Decimal
10000	4096
20000	8192
30000	12288
40000	16384
50000	20480
60000	24576
70000	28672

	0	1	2	3	4	5	6	7
1000	0512	0513	0514	0515	0516	0517	0518	0519
1010	0520	0521	0522	0523	0524	0525	0526	0527
1020	0528	0529	0530	0531	0532	0533	0534	0535
1030	0536	0537	0538	0539	0540	0541	0542	0543
1040	0544	0545	0546	0547	0548	0549	0550	0551
1050	0552	0553	0554	0555	0556	0557	0558	0559
1060	0560	0561	0562	0563	0564	0565	0566	0567
1070	0568	0569	0570	0571	0572	0573	0574	0575
1100	0576	0577	0578	0579	0580	0581	0582	0583
1110	0584	0585	0586	0587	0588	0589	0590	0591
1120	0592	0593	0594	0595	0596	0597	0598	0599
1130	0600	0601	0602	0603	0604	0605	0606	0607
1140	0608	0609	0610	0611	0612	0613	0614	0615
1150	0616	0617	0618	0619	0620	0621	0622	0623
1160	0624	0625	0626	0627	0628	0629	0630	0631
1170	0632	0633	0634	0635	0636	0637	0638	0639
1200	0640	0641	0642	0643	0644	0645	0646	0647
1210	0648	0649	0650	0651	0652	0653	0654	0655
1220	0656	0657	0658	0659	0660	0661	0662	0663
1230	0664	0665	0666	0667	0668	0669	0670	0671
1240	0672	0673	0674	0675	0676	0677	0678	0679
1250	0680	0681	0682	0683	0684	0685	0686	0687
1260	0688	0689	0690	0691	0692	0693	0694	0695
1270	0696	0697	0698	0699	0700	0701	0702	0703
1300	0704	0705	0706	0707	0708	0709	0710	0711
1310	0712	0713	0714	0715	0716	0717	0718	0719
1320	0720	0721	0722	0723	0724	0725	0726	0727
1330	0728	0729	0730	0731	0732	0733	0734	0735
1340	0736	0737	0738	0739	0740	0741	0742	0743
1350	0744	0745	0746	0747	0748	0749	0750	0751
1360	0752	0753	0754	0755	0756	0757	0758	0759
1370	0760	0761	0762	0763	0764	0765	0766	0767

	0	1	2	3	4	5	6	7
1400	0768	0769	0770	0771	0772	0773	0774	0775
1410	0776	0777	0778	0779	0780	0781	0782	0783
1420	0784	0785	0786	0787	0788	0789	0790	0791
1430	0792	0793	0794	0795	0796	0797	0798	0799
1440	0800	0801	0802	0803	0804	0805	0806	0807
1450	0808	0809	0810	0811	0812	0813	0814	0815
1460	0816	0817	0818	0819	0820	0821	0822	0823
1470	0824	0825	0826	0827	0828	0829	0830	0831
1500	0832	0833	0834	0835	0836	0837	0838	0839
1510	0840	0841	0842	0843	0844	0845	0846	0847
1520	0848	0849	0850	0851	0852	0853	0854	0855
1530	0856	0857	0858	0859	0860	0861	0862	0863
1540	0864	0865	0866	0867	0868	0869	0870	0871
1550	0872	0873	0874	0875	0876	0877	0878	0879
1560	0880	0881	0882	0883	0884	0885	0886	0887
1570	0888	0889	0890	0891	0892	0893	0894	0895
1600	0896	0897	0898	0899	0900	0901	0902	0903
1610	0904	0905	0906	0907	0908	0909	0910	0911
1620	0612	0913	0914	0915	0916	0917	0918	0919
1630	0920	0921	0922	0923	0924	0925	0926	0927
1640	0928	0929	0930	0931	0932	0933	0934	0935
1650	0936	0937	0938	0939	0940	0941	0942	0943
1660	0944	0945	0946	0947	0948	0949	0950	0951
1670	0952	0953	0954	0955	0956	0957	0958	0959
1700	0960	0961	0962	0963	0964	0965	0966	0967
1710	0968	0969	0970	0971	0972	0973	0974	0975
1720	0976	0977	0978	0979	0980	0981	0982	0983
1730	0984	0985	0986	0987	0988	0989	0990	0991
1740	0992	0993	0994	0995	0996	0997	0998	0999
1750	1000	1001	1002	1003	1004	1005	1006	1007
1760	1008	1009	1010	1011	1012	1013	1014	1015
1770	1016	1017	1018	1019	1020	1021	1022	1023

1000	0512
to	to
1777	1023
(Octal)	(Decimal)

OCTAL-DECIMAL INTEGER CONVERSION TABLE
(Continued)

	0	1	2	3	4	5	6	7		0	1	2	3	4	5	6	7
2000	1024	1025	1026	1027	1028	1029	1030	1031	2400	1280	1281	1282	1283	1284	1285	1286	1287
2010	1032	1033	1034	1035	1036	1037	1038	1039	2410	1288	1289	1290	1291	1292	1293	1294	1295
2020	1040	1041	1042	1043	1044	1045	1046	1047	2420	1296	1297	1298	1299	1300	1301	1302	1303
2030	1048	1049	1050	1051	1052	1053	1054	1045	2430	1304	1305	1306	1307	1308	1309	1310	1311
2040	1056	1057	1058	1059	1060	1061	1062	1063	2440	1312	1313	1314	1315	1316	1317	1318	1319
2050	1064	1065	1066	1067	1068	1069	1070	1071	2450	1320	1321	1322	1323	1324	1325	1326	1327
2060	1072	1073	1074	1075	1076	1077	1078	1079	2460	1328	1329	1330	1331	1332	1333	1334	1335
2070	1080	1081	1082	1083	1084	1085	1086	1087	2470	1336	1337	1338	1339	1340	1341	1342	1343
2100	1088	1089	1090	1091	1092	1093	1094	1095	2500	1344	1345	1346	1347	1348	1349	1350	1351
2110	1096	1097	1098	1099	1100	1101	1102	1103	2510	1352	1353	1354	1355	1356	1357	1358	1359
2120	1104	1105	1106	1107	1108	1109	1110	1111	2520	1360	1361	1362	1363	1364	1365	1366	1367
2130	1112	1113	1114	1115	1116	1117	1118	1119	2530	1368	1369	1370	1371	1372	1373	1374	1375
2140	1120	1121	1122	1123	1124	1125	1126	1127	2540	1376	1377	1378	1379	1380	1381	1382	1383
2150	1128	1129	1130	1131	1132	1133	1134	1135	2550	1384	1385	1386	1387	1388	1389	1390	1391
2160	1136	1137	1138	1139	1140	1141	1142	1143	2560	1392	1393	1394	1395	1396	1397	1398	1399
2170	1144	1145	1146	1147	1148	1149	1150	1151	2570	1400	1401	1402	1403	1404	1405	1406	1407
2200	1152	1153	1154	1155	1156	1157	1158	1159	2600	1408	1409	1410	1411	1412	1413	1414	1415
2210	1160	1161	1162	1163	1164	1165	1166	1167	2610	1416	1417	1418	1419	1420	1421	1422	1423
2220	1168	1169	1170	1171	1172	1173	1174	1175	2620	1424	1425	1426	1427	1428	1429	1430	1431
2230	1176	1177	1178	1179	1180	1181	1182	1183	2630	1432	1433	1434	1435	1436	1437	1438	1439
2240	1184	1185	1186	1187	1188	1189	1190	1191	2640	1440	1441	1442	1443	1444	1445	1446	1447
2250	1192	1193	1194	1195	1196	1197	1198	1199	2650	1448	1449	1450	1451	1452	1453	1454	1455
2260	1200	1201	1202	1203	1204	1205	1206	1207	2660	1456	1457	1458	1459	1460	1461	1462	1463
2270	1208	1209	1210	1211	1212	1213	1214	1215	2670	1464	1465	1466	1467	1468	1469	1470	1471
2300	1216	1217	1218	1219	1220	1221	1222	1223	2700	1472	1473	1474	1475	1476	1477	1478	1479
2310	1224	1225	1226	1227	1228	1229	1230	1231	2710	1480	1481	1482	1483	1484	1485	1486	1487
2320	1232	1233	1234	1235	1236	1237	1238	1239	2720	1488	1489	1490	1491	1492	1493	1494	1495
2330	1240	1241	1242	1243	1244	1245	1246	1247	2730	1496	1497	1498	1499	1500	1501	1502	1503
2340	1248	1249	1250	1251	1252	1253	1254	1255	2740	1504	1505	1506	1507	1508	1509	1510	1511
2350	1256	1257	1258	1259	1260	1261	1262	1263	2750	1512	1513	1514	1515	1516	1517	1518	1519
2360	1264	1265	1266	1267	1268	1269	1270	1271	2760	1520	1521	1522	1523	1524	1525	1526	1527
2370	1272	1273	1274	1275	1276	1277	1278	1279	2770	1528	1529	1530	1531	1532	1533	1534	1535

2000	1024
to	to
2772	1535
(Octal)	(Decimal)

Octal	Decimal
10000	— 4096
20000	— 8192
30000	— 12288
40000	— 16384
50000	— 20480
60000	— 24576
70000	— 28672

	0	1	2	3	4	5	6	7		0	1	2	3	4	5	6	7
3000	1536	1537	1538	1539	1540	1541	1542	1543	3400	1792	1793	1794	1795	1796	1797	1798	1799
3010	1544	1545	1546	1547	1548	1549	1550	1551	3410	1800	1801	1802	1803	1804	1805	1806	1807
3020	1552	1553	1554	1555	1556	1557	1558	1559	3420	1808	1809	1810	1811	1812	1813	1814	1815
3030	1560	1561	1562	1563	1564	1565	1566	1567	3430	1816	1817	1818	1819	1820	1821	1822	1823
3040	1568	1569	1570	1571	1572	1573	1574	1575	3440	1824	1825	1826	1827	1828	1829	1830	1831
3050	1576	1577	1578	1579	1580	1581	1582	1583	3450	1832	1833	1834	1835	1836	1837	1838	1839
3060	1584	1585	1586	1587	1588	1589	1590	1591	3460	1840	1841	1842	1843	1844	1845	1846	1847
3070	1592	1593	1594	1595	1596	1597	1598	1599	3470	1848	1849	1850	1851	1852	1853	1954	1855
3100	1600	1601	1602	1603	1604	1605	1606	1607	3500	1856	1857	1858	1859	1860	1861	1862	1863
3110	1608	1609	1610	1611	1612	1613	1614	1615	3510	1864	1865	1866	1867	1868	1869	1870	1871
3120	1616	1617	1618	1619	1620	1621	1622	1623	3520	1872	1873	1874	1875	1876	1877	1878	1879
3130	1624	1625	1626	1627	1628	1629	1630	1631	3530	1880	1881	1882	1883	1884	1885	1886	1887
3140	1632	1633	1634	1635	1636	1637	1638	1639	3540	1888	1889	1890	1891	1892	1893	1894	1895
3150	1640	1641	1642	1643	1644	1645	1646	1647	3550	1896	1897	1898	1899	1900	1901	1902	1903
3160	1648	1649	1650	1651	1652	1653	1654	1655	3560	1904	1905	1906	1907	1908	1909	1910	1911
3170	1656	1657	1658	1659	1660	1661	1662	1663	3570	1912	1913	1914	1915	1916	1917	1918	1919
3200	1664	1665	1666	1667	1668	1669	1670	1671	3600	1920	1921	1922	1923	1924	1925	1926	1927
3210	1672	1673	1674	1675	1676	1677	1678	1679	3610	1928	1929	1930	1931	1932	1933	1934	1935
3220	1680	1681	1682	1683	1684	1685	1686	1687	3620	1936	1937	1938	1939	1940	1941	1942	1943
3230	1688	1689	1690	1691	1692	1693	1694	1695	3630	1944	1945	1946	1947	1948	1949	1950	1951
3240	1696	1697	1698	1699	1700	1701	1702	1703	3640	1952	1953	1954	1955	1956	1957	1958	1959
3250	1704	1705	1706	1707	1708	1709	1710	1711	3650	1960	1961	1962	1963	1964	1965	1966	1967
3260	1712	1713	1714	1715	1716	1717	1718	1719	3660	1968	1969	1970	1971	1972	1973	1974	1975
3270	1720	1721	1722	1723	1724	1725	1726	1727	3670	1976	1977	1978	1979	1980	1981	1982	1983
3300	1728	1729	1730	1731	1732	1733	1734	1735	3700	1984	1985	1986	1987	1988	1989	1990	1991
3310	1736	1737	1738	1739	1740	1741	1742	1743	3710	1992	1993	1994	1995	1996	1997	1998	1999
3320	1744	1745	1746	1747	1748	1749	1750	1751	3720	2000	2001	2002	2003	2004	2005	2006	2007
3330	1752	1753	1754	1755	1756	1757	1758	1759	3730	2008	2009	2010	2011	2012	2013	2014	2015
3340	1760	1761	1762	1763	1764	1765	1766	1767	3740	2016	2017	2018	2019	2020	2021	2022	2023
3350	1768	1769	1770	1771	1772	1773	1774	1775	3750	2024	2025	2026	2027	2028	2029	2030	2031
3360	1776	1777	1778	1779	1780	1781	1782	1783	3760	2032	2033	2034	2035	2036	2037	2038	2039
3370	1784	1785	1786	1787	1788	1789	1790	1791	3770	2040	2041	2042	2043	2044	2045	2046	2047

3000	1536
to	to
3777	2047
(Octal)	(Decimal)

OCTAL-DECIMAL INTEGER CONVERSION TABLE
(Continued)

	0	1	2	3	4	5	6	7		0	1	2	3	4	5	6	7
4000	2048	2049	2050	2051	2052	2053	2054	2055	4400	2304	2305	2306	2307	2308	2309	2310	2311
4010	2056	2057	2058	2059	2060	2061	2062	2063	4410	2312	2313	2314	2315	2316	2317	2318	2319
4020	2064	2065	2066	2067	2068	2069	2070	2071	4420	2320	2321	2322	2323	2324	2325	2326	2327
4030	2072	2073	2074	2075	2076	2077	2078	2079	4430	2328	2329	2330	2331	2332	2333	2334	2335
4040	2080	2081	2082	2083	2084	2085	2086	2087	4440	2336	2337	2338	2339	2340	2341	2342	2343
4050	2088	2089	2090	2091	2092	2093	2094	2095	4450	2344	2445	2346	2347	2348	2349	2350	2351
4060	2096	2097	2098	2099	2100	2101	2102	2103	4460	2352	2353	2354	2355	2356	2357	2358	2359
4070	2104	2105	2106	2107	2108	2109	2110	2111	4470	2360	2361	2362	2363	2364	2365	2366	2367
4100	2112	2113	2114	2115	2116	2117	2118	2119	4500	2368	2369	2370	2371	2372	2373	2374	2375
4110	2120	2121	2122	2123	2124	2125	2126	2127	4510	2376	2377	2378	2379	2380	2381	2382	2383
4120	2128	2129	2130	2131	2132	2133	2134	2135	4520	2384	2385	2386	2387	2388	2389	2390	2391
4130	2136	2137	2138	2139	2140	2141	2142	2143	4530	2392	2393	2394	2395	2396	2397	2398	2399
4140	2144	2145	2146	2147	2148	2149	2150	2151	4540	2400	2401	2402	2403	2404	2405	2406	2407
4150	2152	2153	2154	2155	2156	2157	2158	2159	4550	2408	2409	2410	2411	2412	2413	2114	2415
4160	2160	2161	2162	2163	2164	2165	2166	2167	4560	2416	2417	2418	2419	2420	2421	2422	2423
4170	2168	2169	2170	2171	2172	2173	2174	2175	4570	2424	2425	2426	2427	2428	2429	2430	2431
4200	2176	2177	2178	2179	2180	2181	2182	2183	4600	2432	2433	2434	2435	2436	2437	2438	2439
4210	2184	2185	2186	2187	2188	2189	2190	2191	4610	2440	2441	2442	2443	2444	2445	2446	2447
4220	2192	2193	2194	2195	2196	2197	2198	2199	4620	2448	2449	2450	2451	2452	2453	2454	2455
4230	2200	2201	2202	2203	2204	2205	2206	2207	4630	2456	2457	2458	2459	2460	2461	2462	2463
4240	2208	2209	2210	2211	2212	2213	2214	2215	4640	2464	2465	2466	2467	2468	2469	2470	2471
4250	2216	2217	2218	2219	2220	2221	2222	2223	4650	2472	2473	2474	2475	2476	2477	2478	2479
4260	2224	2225	2226	2227	2228	2229	2230	2231	4660	2480	2481	2482	2483	2484	2485	2486	2487
4270	2232	2233	2234	2235	2236	2237	2238	2239	4670	2488	2489	2490	2491	2492	2493	2494	2495
4300	2240	2241	2242	2243	2244	2245	2246	2247	4700	2496	2497	2498	2499	2500	2501	2502	2503
4310	2248	2249	2250	2251	2252	2253	2254	2255	4710	2504	2505	2506	2507	2508	2509	2510	2511
4320	2256	2257	2258	2259	2260	2261	2262	2263	4720	2512	2513	2514	2515	2416	2517	2518	2519
4330	2264	2265	2266	2267	2268	2269	2270	2271	4730	2520	2521	2522	2523	2524	2525	2526	2527
4340	2272	2273	2274	2275	2276	2277	2278	2279	4740	2528	2529	2530	2531	2532	2533	2534	2535
4350	2280	2281	2282	2283	2284	2285	2286	2287	4750	2536	2537	2538	2539	2540	2541	2542	2543
4360	2288	2289	2290	2291	2292	2293	2294	2295	4760	2544	2545	2546	2547	2548	2549	2550	2551
4370	2296	2297	2298	2299	2300	2301	2302	2303	4770	2552	2553	2554	2555	2556	2557	2558	2559

4000	2048
to	to
4777	2559
(Octal)	(Decimal)

Octal	Decimal
10000	4096
20000	8192
30000	12288
40000	16384
50000	20480
60000	24576
70000	28672

	0	1	2	3	4	5	6	7		0	1	2	3	4	5	6	7
5000	2560	2561	2562	2563	2564	2565	2566	2567	5400	2816	2817	2818	2819	2820	2821	2822	2823
5010	2568	2569	2570	2571	2572	2573	2574	2575	5410	2824	2825	2826	2827	2828	2829	2830	2831
5020	2576	2577	2578	2579	2580	2581	2582	2583	5420	2832	2833	2834	2835	2836	2837	2838	2839
5030	2584	2585	2586	2587	2588	2589	2590	2591	5430	2840	2841	2842	2843	2844	2845	2846	2847
5040	2592	2593	2594	2595	2596	2597	2598	2599	5440	2848	2849	2850	2851	2852	2853	2854	2855
5050	2600	2601	2602	2603	2604	2605	2606	2607	5450	2856	2857	2858	2859	2860	2861	2862	2863
5060	2608	2609	2610	2611	2612	2613	2614	2615	5460	2864	2865	2866	2867	2868	2869	2870	2871
5070	2616	2617	2618	2619	2620	2621	2622	2623	5470	2872	2873	2874	2875	2876	2877	2878	2879
5100	2624	2625	2626	2627	2628	2629	2630	2631	5500	2880	2881	2882	2883	2884	2885	2886	2887
5110	2632	2633	2634	2635	2636	2637	2638	2639	5510	2888	2889	2890	2891	2892	2893	2894	2895
5120	2640	2641	2642	2643	2644	2645	2646	2647	5520	2896	2897	2898	2899	2900	2901	2902	2903
5130	2648	2649	2650	2651	2652	2653	2654	2655	5530	2904	2905	2906	2907	2908	2909	2910	2911
5140	2656	2657	2658	2659	2660	2661	2662	2663	5540	2912	2913	2914	2915	2916	2917	2818	2919
5150	2664	2665	2666	2667	2668	2669	2670	2671	5550	2920	2921	2922	2923	2924	2925	2926	2927
5160	2672	2673	2674	2675	2676	2677	2678	2679	5560	2928	2929	2930	2931	2932	2933	2934	2935
5170	2680	2681	2682	2683	2684	2685	2686	2687	5570	2936	2937	2938	2939	2940	2941	2942	2943
5200	2688	2689	2690	2691	2692	2693	2694	2695	5600	2944	2945	2946	2947	2948	2949	2950	2951
5210	2696	2697	2698	2699	2700	2701	2702	2703	5610	2952	2953	2954	2955	2956	2957	2958	2959
5220	2704	2705	2706	2707	2708	2709	2710	2711	5620	2960	2961	2962	2963	2964	2965	2966	2967
5230	2712	2713	2714	2715	2716	2717	2718	2719	5630	2968	2969	2970	2971	2972	2973	2974	2975
5240	2720	2721	2722	2723	2724	2725	2726	2727	5640	2976	2977	2978	2979	2980	2981	2982	2983
5250	2728	2729	2730	2731	2732	2733	2734	2735	5650	2984	2985	2986	2987	2988	2989	2990	2991
5260	2736	2737	2738	2739	2740	2741	2742	2743	5660	2992	2993	2994	2995	2996	2997	2998	2999
5270	2744	2745	2746	2747	2748	2749	2750	2751	5670	3000	3001	3002	3003	3004	3005	3006	3007
5300	2752	2753	2754	2755	2756	2757	2758	2759	5700	3008	3009	3010	3011	3012	3013	3014	3015
5310	2760	2761	2762	2763	2764	2765	2766	2767	5710	3016	3017	3018	3019	3020	3021	3022	3023
5320	2768	2769	2770	2771	2772	2773	2774	2775	5720	3024	3025	3026	3027	3028	3029	3030	3031
5330	2776	2777	2778	2779	2780	2781	2782	2783	5730	3032	3033	3034	3035	2036	3037	3038	3039
5340	2784	2785	2786	2787	2788	2789	2790	2791	5740	3040	3041	3042	3043	3044	3045	3046	3047
5350	2792	2793	2794	2795	2796	2797	2798	2799	5750	3048	3049	3050	3051	3052	3053	3054	3055
5360	2800	2801	2802	2803	2804	2805	2806	2807	5760	3056	3057	3058	3059	3060	3061	3062	3063
5370	2808	2809	2810	2811	2812	2813	2814	2815	5770	3064	3065	3066	3067	3068	3069	3070	3071

5000	2560
to	to
5777	3071
(Octal)	(Decimal)

OCTAL-DECIMAL INTEGER CONVERSION TABLE
(Continued)

	0	1	2	3	4	5	6	7			0	1	2	3	4	5	6	7
6000	3072	3073	3074	3075	3076	3077	3078	3079		6400	3328	3329	3330	3331	3332	3333	3334	3335
6010	3080	3081	3082	3083	3084	3085	3086	3087		6410	3336	3337	3338	3339	3340	3341	3342	3343
6020	3088	3089	3090	3091	3092	3093	3094	3095		6420	3344	3345	3346	3347	3348	3349	3350	3351
6030	3096	3097	3098	3099	3100	3101	3102	3103		6430	3352	3353	3354	3355	3356	3357	3358	3359
6040	3104	3105	3106	3107	3108	3109	3110	3111		6440	3360	3361	3362	3363	3364	3365	3366	3367
6050	3112	3113	3114	3115	3116	3117	3118	3119		6450	3368	3369	3370	3371	3372	3373	3374	3375
6060	3120	3121	3122	3123	3124	3125	3126	3127		6460	3376	3377	3378	3379	3380	3381	3382	3383
6070	3128	3129	3130	3131	2132	3133	3134	3135		6470	3384	3385	3386	3387	3388	3389	3390	3391
6100	3136	3137	3138	3139	3140	3141	3142	3143		6500	3392	3393	3394	3395	3396	3397	3398	3399
6110	3144	3145	3146	3147	3148	3149	3150	3151		6510	3400	3401	3402	3403	3404	3405	3406	3407
6120	3152	3153	3154	3155	3156	3157	3158	3159		6520	3408	3409	3410	3411	3412	3413	3414	3415
6130	3160	3161	3162	3163	3164	3165	3166	3167		6530	3416	3417	3418	3419	3420	3421	3422	3423
6140	3168	3169	3170	3171	3172	3173	3174	3175		6540	3424	3425	3426	3427	3428	3429	3430	3431
6150	3176	3177	3178	3179	3180	3181	3182	4183		6550	3432	3433	3434	3435	3436	3437	3438	3439
6160	3184	3185	3186	3187	3188	3189	3190	3191		6560	3440	3441	3442	3443	3444	3445	3446	3447
6170	3192	3193	3194	3195	3196	3197	3198	3199		6570	3448	3449	3450	3451	3452	3453	3454	3455
6200	3200	3201	3202	3203	3204	3205	3206	3207		6600	3456	3457	3458	3459	3460	3461	3462	3463
6210	3208	3209	3210	3211	3212	3213	3214	3215		6610	3464	3465	3466	3467	3468	3469	3470	3471
6220	3216	3217	3218	3219	3220	3221	3222	3223		6620	3472	3473	3474	3475	3476	3477	3478	3479
6230	3224	3225	3226	3227	3228	3229	3230	3231		6630	3480	3481	3482	3483	3484	3485	3486	3487
6240	3232	3233	3234	3235	3236	3237	3238	3239		6640	3488	3489	3490	3491	3492	3493	3494	3495
6250	3240	3241	3442	3243	3244	3245	3246	3247		6650	3496	3497	3498	3499	3500	3501	3502	3503
6260	3248	3249	3250	3251	3252	3253	3254	3255		6660	3504	3505	3506	3507	3508	3509	3510	3511
6270	3256	3257	3258	3259	3260	3261	3262	3263		6670	3512	3513	3514	3515	3516	3517	3518	3519
6300	3264	3267	3266	3267	3268	3269	3270	3871		6700	3520	3521	3522	3523	3524	3525	3526	3527
6310	3272	3273	3274	3275	3276	3277	3278	3279		6710	3528	3529	3530	3531	3532	3533	3534	3535
6320	3280	3281	3282	3283	3284	3285	3286	3287		6720	3536	3537	3538	3539	3540	3541	3542	3543
6330	3288	3289	3290	3291	3292	3293	3294	3295		6730	3544	3545	3546	3547	3548	3549	3550	3551
6340	3296	3297	3298	3299	3300	3301	3302	3003		6740	3552	3553	3554	3555	3556	3557	3558	3559
6350	3304	3305	3306	3307	3308	3309	3310	3311		6750	3560	3561	3562	3563	3564	3565	3566	3567
6360	3312	3313	3314	3315	3316	3317	3318	3319		6760	3568	3569	3570	3571	3572	3573	3574	3575
6370	3320	3321	3322	3323	3324	3325	3326	3327		6770	3576	3577	3578	3579	3580	3581	3582	3583

Side notes (left margin):

6000	3072
to	to
6777	3583
(Octal)	(Decimal)

Octal	Decimal
10000	4096
20000	8192
30000	12288
40000	16384
50000	20480
60000	24576
70000	28672

7000	3584
to	to
7777	4095
(Octal)	(Decimal)

	0	1	2	3	4	5	6	7			0	1	2	3	4	5	6	7
7000	3584	3585	3586	3587	3588	3589	3590	3591		7400	3840	3841	3482	3843	3844	3845	3846	3847
7010	3592	3593	3594	3595	3596	3597	3598	3599		7410	3848	3849	3450	3851	3852	3853	3854	3855
7020	3600	3601	3602	3603	3604	3605	3606	3607		7420	3856	3857	3858	3859	3860	3861	3862	3863
7030	4608	3609	3610	3611	3612	3613	3614	3615		7430	3864	3865	3866	3867	3868	3869	3870	3871
7040	3616	3617	3618	3619	3620	3621	3622	3623		7440	3872	3873	3874	3875	3876	3877	3878	3879
7050	3624	3625	3626	3627	3628	3629	3630	3631		7450	3880	3881	3882	3883	3884	3885	3886	3887
7060	2632	3633	3634	3635	3636	3637	3638	3639		7460	3888	3889	3890	3891	3892	3893	3894	3895
7070	3640	3641	3642	3643	3644	3645	3646	3647		7470	3896	3897	3898	3899	3900	3901	3902	3903
7100	3648	3649	3650	3651	3652	3653	3654	3655		7500	3904	3905	3906	3907	3908	3909	3910	3911
7110	3656	3657	3658	3659	3660	3661	3662	3663		7510	3912	3913	3914	3915	3916	3917	3918	3919
7120	3664	3665	3666	3667	3668	3669	3670	3671		7520	3920	3921	3922	3923	3924	3925	3926	3927
7130	3672	3673	3674	3675	3676	3677	3678	3679		7530	3928	3929	3930	3931	3932	3933	3934	3935
7140	3680	3681	3682	3683	3684	3685	3686	3687		7540	3836	3937	3938	3939	3940	3941	3942	3943
7150	3688	3689	3690	3691	3692	3693	3694	3695		7550	3944	3945	3946	3947	3948	3949	3950	3951
7160	3696	3697	3698	3699	3700	3701	3702	3903		7560	3952	3953	3954	3955	3956	3957	3958	3959
7170	3704	3705	3706	3707	3708	3709	3710	3711		7570	3960	3961	3962	3963	3964	3965	3966	3967
7200	3712	3713	3714	3715	3716	3717	3718	3719		7600	3968	3969	4970	3971	3972	3973	3974	3975
7210	3720	3721	3722	3723	3724	3725	3726	3727		7610	3976	3977	3978	3979	3980	3981	3982	3983
7220	3728	3729	3730	3731	3732	3733	3734	3735		7620	3984	3985	3986	3987	3988	3989	3990	3991
7230	3736	3737	3738	3739	3740	3741	3742	3743		7630	3992	3993	3994	3995	3996	3997	3998	3999
7240	3744	3745	3746	3747	3748	3749	3750	3751		7640	4000	4001	4002	4003	4004	4005	4006	4007
7250	3752	3753	3754	3755	3756	3757	3758	3759		7650	4008	4009	4010	4011	4012	4013	4014	4015
7260	3760	3761	3762	3763	3764	3765	3766	3767		7660	4016	4017	4018	4019	4020	4021	4022	4023
7270	3768	3769	3770	3771	3772	3774	3774	3775		7670	4024	4025	4026	4027	4028	4029	4030	4031
7300	3776	3777	3778	3779	3780	3781	3782	3783		7700	4032	4033	4034	4035	4036	4037	4038	4039
7310	3784	3785	3786	3787	3788	3789	3790	3791		7710	4040	4041	4042	4043	4044	4045	4046	4047
7320	3792	3893	3794	3795	3796	3797	3798	3799		7720	4048	4049	4050	4051	4052	4053	4054	4055
7330	3800	3801	3802	3803	3804	3805	3806	3807		7730	4056	4057	4058	4059	4060	4061	4062	4063
7340	3808	3809	3810	3811	3812	3813	3814	3815		7740	4064	4065	4066	4067	4068	4069	4070	4071
7350	3816	3817	3818	3819	3820	3821	3822	3823		7750	4072	4073	4074	4075	4076	4077	4078	4079
7360	3824	3825	3826	3827	3828	3829	3830	3831		7760	4080	4081	4082	4083	4084	4085	4086	4087
7370	3832	3833	3834	3835	3836	3837	3838	3839		7770	4088	4089	4090	4091	4092	4093	4094	4095

OCTAL-DECIMAL FRACTION CONVERSION TABLE

This table covers the entries from $(.000)_8$ to $(.377)_8$. For entries from $(.400)_8$ to $(.777)_8$, cognizance should be made of the fact that $(.400)_8$ is $(.500)_{10}$. Hence if $(.637)_8$ is desired, find $(.237)_8$ in table, namely, $(.310456)_{10}$ and add $(.50000)_{10}$ for $(.400)_8$. Thus

$(.637)_8 = (.237)_8 + (.400)_8$
$= (.310456)_{10} + (.50000)_{10}$
$= (.810456)_{10}$.

OCTAL	DEC.	OCTAL	DEC.	OCTAL	DEC.	OCTAL	DEC.
.000	.000000	.100	.125000	.200	.250000	.300	.375000
.001	.001953	.101	.126953	.201	.251953	.301	.376953
.002	.003906	.102	.128906	.202	.253906	.302	.378906
.003	.005859	.103	.130859	.203	.255859	.303	.380859
.004	.007812	.104	.132812	.204	.257812	.304	.382812
.005	.009765	.105	.134765	.205	.259765	.305	.384765
.006	.011718	.106	.136718	.206	.261718	.306	.386718
.007	.013671	.107	.138671	.207	.263671	.307	.388671
.010	.015625	.110	.140625	.210	.265625	.310	.390625
.011	.017578	.111	.142578	.211	.267578	.311	.392578
.012	.019531	.112	.144531	.212	.269531	.312	.394531
.013	.021484	.113	.146484	.213	.271484	.313	.396484
.014	.023437	.114	.148437	.214	.273437	.314	.398437
.015	.025390	.115	.150390	.215	.275390	.315	.400490
.016	.027343	.116	.152343	.216	.277343	.316	.402343
.017	.029296	.117	.154296	.217	.279296	.317	.404296
.020	.031250	.120	.156250	.220	.281250	.320	.406250
.021	.033203	.121	.158203	.221	.283203	.321	.408203
.022	.035156	.122	.160156	.222	.285156	.322	.410156
.023	.037109	.123	.162109	.223	.287109	.323	.412109
.024	.039062	.124	.164062	.224	.289062	.324	.414062
.025	.041015	.125	.166015	.225	.291015	.325	.416015
.026	.042968	.126	.167968	.226	.292968	.326	.417968
.027	.044921	.127	.169921	.227	.294921	.327	.419921
.030	.046875	.130	.171875	.230	.294875	.330	.421875
.031	.048828	.131	.173828	.231	.298828	.331	.423828
.032	.050781	.132	.175781	.232	.300781	.332	.425781
.033	.052734	.133	.177734	.233	.302734	.333	.427734
.034	.054687	.134	.179687	.234	.304687	.334	.429687
.035	.056640	.135	.181640	.235	.306640	.335	.431640
.036	.058593	.136	.183593	.236	.308593	.336	.433593
.037	.060546	.137	.185546	.237	.310546	.337	.435546
.040	.062500	.140	.187500	.240	.312500	.340	.437500
.041	.064453	.141	.189453	.241	.314453	.341	.439453
.042	.066406	.142	.191406	.242	.316406	.342	.441406
.043	.068359	.143	.193359	.243	.318359	.343	.443359
.044	.070312	.144	.195312	.244	.320312	.344	.445312
.045	.072265	.145	.197265	.245	.322265	.345	.447265
.046	.074218	.146	.199218	.246	.324218	.346	.449218
.047	.076171	.147	.201171	.247	.326171	.347	.451171
.050	.078125	.150	.203125	.250	.328125	.350	.453125
.051	.080078	.151	.205078	.251	.330078	.351	.455078
.052	.082031	.152	.207031	.252	.332031	.352	.457031
.053	.083984	.153	.208984	.253	.333984	.353	.458984
.054	.085937	.154	.210937	.254	.335937	.354	.460937
.055	.087890	.155	.212890	.255	.337890	.355	.462890
.056	.089843	.156	.214843	.256	.339843	.356	.464843
.057	.091796	.157	.216796	.257	.341796	.357	.466796
.060	.093750	.160	.218750	.260	.343750	.360	.468750
.061	.095703	.161	.220703	.261	.345703	.361	.470703
.062	.097656	.162	.222656	.262	.347656	.362	.472656
.063	.099609	.163	.224609	.263	.349609	.363	.474609
.064	.101562	.164	.226562	.264	.351562	.364	.476562
.065	.103515	.165	.228515	.265	.353515	.365	.478515
.066	.105468	.166	.230468	.266	.355468	.366	.480468
.067	.107421	.167	.232421	.267	.357421	.367	.482421
.070	.109375	.170	.234375	.270	.359375	.370	.484375
.071	.111328	.171	.236328	.271	.361328	.371	.486328
.072	.113281	.172	.238281	.272	.363281	.372	.488281
.073	.115234	.173	.240234	.273	.365234	.373	.490234
.074	.117187	.174	.242187	.274	.367187	.374	.492187
.075	.119140	.175	.244140	.275	.369140	.375	.494140
.076	.121093	.176	.246093	.276	.371093	.376	.496093
.077	.123046	.177	.248046	.277	.373046	.377	.498046

OCTAL-DECIMAL FRACTION CONVERSION TABLE (Continued)

OCTAL	DEC.	OCTAL	DEC.	OCTAL	DEC.	OCTAL	DEC.
.000000	.000000	.000100	.000244	.000200	.000488	.000300	.000732
.000001	.000004	.000101	.000247	.000201	.000492	.000301	.000736
.000002	.000007	.000102	.000251	.000202	.000495	.000302	.000740
.000003	.000011	.000103	.000255	.000203	.000499	.000303	.000743
.000004	.000015	.000104	.000259	.000204	.000503	.000304	.000747
.000005	.000019	.000105	.000263	.000205	.000507	.000305	.000751
.000006	.000022	.000106	.000267	.000206	.000511	.000306	.000755
.000007	.000026	.000107	.000270	.000207	.000514	.000307	.000759
.000010	.000030	.000110	.000274	.000210	.000518	.000310	.000762
.000011	.000034	.000111	.000278	.000211	.000522	.000311	.000766
.000012	.000038	.000112	.000282	.000212	.000526	.000312	.000770
.000013	.000041	.000113	.000286	.000213	.000530	.000313	.000774
.000014	.000045	.000114	.000289	.000214	.000534	.000314	.000778
.000015	.000049	.000115	.000293	.000215	.000537	.000315	.000782
.000016	.000053	.000116	.000297	.000216	.000541	.000316	.000785
.000017	.000057	.000117	.000301	.000217	.000545	.000317	.000789
.000020	.000061	.000120	.000305	.000220	.000549	.000320	.000793
.000021	.000064	.000121	.000308	.000221	.000553	.000321	.000797
.000022	.000068	.000122	.000312	.000222	.000556	.000322	.000801
.000023	.000072	.000123	.000316	.000223	.000560	.000323	.000805
.000024	.000076	.000124	.000320	.000224	.000564	.000324	.000808
.000025	.000080	.000125	.000324	.000225	.000568	.000325	.000812
.000026	.000083	.000126	.000328	.000226	.000572	.000326	.000816
.000027	.000087	.000127	.000331	.000227	.000576	.000327	.000820
.000030	.000091	.000130	.000335	.000230	.000579	.000330	.000823
.000031	.000095	.000131	.000339	.000231	.000583	.000331	.000827
.000032	.000099	.000132	.000343	.000232	.000587	.000332	.000831
.000033	.000102	.000133	.000347	.000233	.000591	.000333	.000835
.000034	.000106	.000134	.000350	.000234	.000595	.000334	.000839
.000035	.000110	.000135	.000354	.000235	.000598	.000335	.000843
.000036	.000114	.000136	.000358	.000236	.000602	.000336	.000846
.000037	.000118	.000137	.000362	.000237	.000606	.000337	.000850
.000040	.000122	.000140	.000366	.000240	.000610	.000340	.000854
.000041	.000125	.000141	.000370	.000241	.000614	.000341	.000858
.000042	.000129	.000142	.000373	.000242	.000617	.000342	.000862
.000043	.000133	.000143	.000377	.000243	.000621	.000343	.000865
.000044	.000137	.000144	.000381	.000244	.000625	.000344	.000869
.000045	.000141	.000145	.000385	.000245	.000629	.000345	.000873
.000046	.000144	.000146	.000389	.000246	.000633	.000346	.000877
.000047	.000148	.000147	.000392	.000247	.000637	.000347	.000881
.000050	.000152	.000150	.000396	.000250	.000640	.000350	.000885
.000051	.000156	.000151	.000400	.000251	.000644	.000351	.000888
.000052	.000160	.000152	.000404	.000252	.000648	.000352	.000892
.000053	.000164	.000153	.000408	.000253	.000652	.000353	.000896
.000054	.000167	.000154	.000411	.000254	.000656	.000354	.000900
.000055	.000171	.000155	.000415	.000255	.000659	.000355	.000904
.000056	.000175	.000156	.000419	.000256	.000663	.000356	.000907
.000057	.000179	.000157	.000423	.000257	.000667	.000357	.000911
.000060	.000183	.000160	.000427	.000260	.000671	.000360	.000915
.000061	.000186	.000161	.000431	.000261	.000675	.000361	.000919
.000062	.000190	.000162	.000434	.000262	.000679	.000362	.000923
.000063	.000194	.000163	.000438	.000263	.000682	.000363	.000926
.000064	.000198	.000164	.000442	.000264	.000686	.000364	.000930
.000065	.000202	.000165	.000446	.000265	.000690	.000365	.000934
.000066	.000205	.000166	.000450	.000266	.000694	.000366	.000938
.000067	.000209	.000167	.000453	.000267	.000698	.000367	.000942
.000070	.000213	.000170	.000457	.000270	.000701	.000370	.000946
.000071	.000217	.000171	.000461	.000271	.000705	.000371	.000949
.000072	.000221	.000172	.000465	.000272	.000709	.000372	.000953
.000073	.000225	.000173	.000469	.000273	.000713	.000373	.000957
.000074	.000228	.000174	.000473	.000274	.000717	.000374	.000961
.000075	.000232	.000175	.000476	.000275	.000720	.000375	.000965
.000076	.000326	.000176	.000480	.000276	.000724	.000376	.000968
.000077	.000240	.000177	.000484	.000277	.000728	.000377	.000972

OCTAL-DECIMAL FRACTION CONVERSION TABLE (Continued)

OCTAL	DEC.	OCTAL	DEC.	OCTAL	DEC.	OCTAL	DEC.
000400	.000976	000500	.001220	000600	.001464	000700	.001708
000401	.000980	000501	.001224	000601	.001468	000701	.001712
000402	.000984	000502	.001228	000602	.001472	000702	.001716
000403	.000988	000503	.001232	000603	.001476	000703	.001720
000404	.000991	000504	.001235	000604	.001480	000704	.001724
000405	.000995	000505	.001239	000605	.001483	000705	.001728
000406	.000999	000506	.001243	000606	.001487	000706	.001731
000407	.001003	000507	.001247	000607	.001491	000707	.001735
000410	.001007	000510	.001251	000610	.001495	000710	.001739
000411	.001010	000511	.001255	000611	.001499	000711	.001743
000412	.001014	000512	.001258	000612	.001502	000712	.001747
000413	.001018	000513	.001262	000613	.001506	000713	.001750
000414	.001022	000514	.001266	000614	.001510	000714	.001754
000415	.001026	000515	.001270	000615	.001514	000715	.001758
000416	.001029	000516	.001274	000616	.001518	000716	.001762
000417	.001033	000517	.001277	000617	.001522	000717	.001766
000420	.001037	000520	.001281	000620	.001525	000720	.001770
000421	.001041	000521	.001285	000621	.001529	000721	.001733
000422	.001045	000522	.001289	000622	.001533	000722	.001777
000423	.001049	000523	.001293	000623	.001537	000723	.001781
000424	.001052	000524	.001296	000624	.001541	000724	.001785
000425	.001056	000525	.001300	000625	.001544	000725	.001789
000426	.001060	000526	.001304	000626	.001548	000726	.001792
000427	.001064	000527	.001308	000627	.001552	000727	.001796
000430	.001068	000530	.001312	000630	.001556	000730	.001800
000431	.001071	000531	.001316	000631	.001560	000731	.001804
000432	.001075	000532	.001319	000632	.001564	000732	.001808
000433	.001079	000533	.001323	000633	.001567	000733	.001811
000434	.001083	000534	.001327	000634	.001571	000734	.001815
000435	.001087	000535	.001331	000635	.001575	000735	.001819
000436	.001091	000536	.001335	000636	.001579	000736	.001823
000437	.001094	000537	.001338	000637	.001583	000737	.001827
000440	.001098	000540	.001342	000640	.001586	000740	.001831
000441	.001102	000541	.001346	000641	.001590	000741	.001834
000442	.001106	000542	.001350	000642	.001594	000742	.001838
000443	.001110	000543	.001354	000643	.001598	000743	.001842
000444	.001113	000544	.001358	000644	.001602	000744	.001846
000445	.001117	000545	.001361	000645	.001605	000745	.001850
000446	.001121	000546	.001365	000646	.001609	000746	.001853
000447	.001125	000547	.001369	000647	.001613	000747	.001857
000450	.001129	000550	.001373	000650	.001617	000750	.001861
000451	.001132	000551	.001377	000651	.001621	000751	.001865
000452	.001136	000552	.001380	000652	.001625	000752	.001869
000453	.001140	000553	.001384	000653	.001628	000753	.001873
000454	.001144	000554	.001388	000654	.001632	000754	.001876
000455	.001148	000555	.001392	000655	.001636	000755	.001880
000456	.001152	000556	.001396	000656	.001640	000756	.001884
000457	.001155	000557	.001399	000657	.001644	000757	.001888
000460	.001159	000560	.001403	000660	.001647	000760	.001892
000461	.001163	000561	.001407	000661	.001651	000761	.001895
000462	.001167	000562	.001411	000662	.001655	000762	.001899
000463	.001171	000563	.001415	000663	.001659	000763	.001903
000464	.001174	000564	.001419	000664	.001663	000764	.001907
000465	.001178	000565	.001422	000665	.001667	000765	.001911
000466	.001182	000566	.001426	000666	.001670	000766	.001914
000467	.001186	000567	.001430	000667	.001674	000767	.001918
000470	.001190	000570	.001434	000670	.001678	000770	.001922
000471	.001194	000571	.001438	000671	.001682	000771	.001926
000472	.001197	000572	.001441	000672	.001686	000772	.001930
000473	.001201	000573	.001445	000673	.001689	000773	.001934
000474	.001205	000574	.001449	000674	.001693	000774	.001937
000475	.001209	000575	.001453	000675	.001697	000775	.001941
000476	.001213	000576	.001457	000676	.001701	000776	.001945
000477	.001216	000577	.001461	000677	.001705	000777	.001949

I. HEXADECIMAL AND DECIMAL DIRECT CONVERSION TABLE

The following tables aid in converting hexadecimal (base 16) numbers to decimal, and the reverse. Note that the base 16 digits for the decimal values 10—15 are represented by the letters A—F, respectively.

This table provides direct conversion of decimal and hexadecimal numbers in the ranges:

HEXADECIMAL	DECIMAL
000 to FFF	0000 to 4095

For numbers outside the range of the table, add the following values to the table figures:

HEXADECIMAL	DECIMAL
1000	4096
2000	8192
3000	12288
4000	16384
5000	20480
6000	24576
7000	28672
8000	32768
9000	36864
A000	40960
B000	45056
C000	49152
D000	53248
E000	57344
F000	61440

	0	1	2	3	4	5	6	7	8	9	A	B	C	D	E	F
00—	0000	0001	0002	0003	0004	0005	0006	0007	0008	0009	0010	0011	0012	013	0014	0015
01—	0016	0017	0018	0019	0020	0021	0022	0023	0024	0025	0026	0027	0028	0029	0030	0031
02—	0032	0033	0034	0035	0036	0037	0038	0039	0040	0041	0042	0043	0044	0045	0046	0047
03—	0048	0049	0050	0051	0052	0053	0054	0055	0056	0057	0058	0059	0060	0061	0062	0063
04—	0064	0065	0066	0067	0068	0069	0070	0071	0072	0073	0074	0075	0076	0077	0078	0079
05—	0080	0081	0082	0083	0084	0085	0086	0087	0088	0089	0090	0091	0092	0093	0094	0095
06—	0096	0097	0098	0099	0100	0101	0102	0103	0104	0105	0106	0107	0108	0109	0110	0111
07—	0112	0113	0114	0115	0116	0117	0118	0119	0120	0121	0122	0123	0124	0125	0126	0127
08—	0128	0129	0130	0131	0132	0133	0134	0135	0136	0137	0138	0139	0140	0141	0142	0143
09—	0144	0145	0146	0147	0148	0149	0150	0151	0152	0153	0154	0155	0156	0157	0158	0159
0A—	0160	0161	0162	0163	0164	0165	0166	0167	0168	0169	0170	0171	0172	0173	0174	0175
0B—	0176	0177	0178	0179	0180	0181	0182	0183	0184	0185	0186	0187	0188	0189	0190	0191
0C—	0192	0193	0194	0195	0196	0197	0198	0199	0200	0201	0202	0203	0204	0205	0206	0207
0D—	0208	0209	0210	0211	0212	0213	0214	0215	0216	0217	0218	0219	0220	0221	0222	0223
0E—	0224	0225	0226	0227	0228	0229	0230	0231	0232	0233	0234	0235	0236	0237	0238	0239
0F—	0240	0241	0242	0243	0244	0245	0246	0247	0248	0249	0250	0251	0252	0253	0254	0255
10—	0256	0257	0258	0259	0260	0261	0262	0263	0264	0265	0266	0267	0268	0269	0270	0271
11—	0272	0273	0274	0275	0276	0277	0278	0279	0280	0281	0282	0283	0284	0285	0286	0287
12—	0288	0289	0290	0291	0292	0293	0294	0295	0296	0297	0298	0299	0300	0301	0302	0303
13—	0304	0305	0306	0307	0308	0309	0310	0311	0312	0313	0314	0315	0316	0317	0318	0319
14—	0320	0321	0322	0323	0324	0325	0326	0327	0328	0329	0330	0331	0332	0333	0334	0335
15—	0336	0337	0338	0339	0340	0341	0342	0343	0344	0345	0346	0347	0348	0349	350	0351
16—	0352	0353	0354	0355	0356	0357	0358	0359	0360	0361	0362	0363	0364	0365	0366	0367
17—	0368	0369	0370	0371	0372	0373	0374	0375	0376	0377	0378	0379	0380	0381	0382	0383
18—	0384	0385	0386	0387	0388	0389	0390	0391	0392	0393	0394	0395	0396	0397	0398	0399
19—	0400	0401	0402	0403	0404	0405	0406	0407	0408	0409	0410	0411	0412	0413	0414	0415
1A—	0416	0417	0418	0419	0420	0421	0422	0423	0424	0425	0426	0427	0428	0429	0430	0431
1B—	0432	0433	0434	0435	0436	0437	0438	0439	0440	0441	0442	0443	0444	0445	0446	0447
1C—	0448	0449	0450	0451	0452	0453	0454	0455	0456	0457	0458	0459	0460	0461	0462	0463
1D—	0464	0465	0466	0467	0468	0469	0470	0471	0472	0473	0474	0475	0476	0477	0478	0479
1E—	0480	0481	0482	0483	0484	0485	0486	0487	0488	0489	0490	0491	0492	0493	0494	0495
1F_	0496	0497	0498	0499	0500	0501	0502	0503	0504	0505	0506	0507	0508	0509	0510	0511
20—	0512	0513	0514	0515	0516	0517	0518	0519	0520	0521	0522	0523	0524	0525	0526	0527
21—	0528	0529	0530	0531	0532	0533	0534	0535	0536	0537	0538	0539	0540	0541	0542	0543
22—	0544	0545	0546	0547	0548	0549	0550	0551	0552	0553	0554	0555	0556	0557	0558	0559
23—	0560	0561	0562	0563	0564	0565	0566	0567	0568	0569	0570	0571	0572	0573	0574	0575
24—	0576	0577	0578	0579	0580	0581	0582	0583	0584	0585	0586	0587	0588	0589	0590	0591
25—	0592	0593	0594	0595	0596	0597	0598	0599	0600	0601	0602	0603	0604	0605	0606	0607
26—	0608	0609	0610	0611	0612	0613	0614	0615	0616	0617	0618	0619	0620	0621	0622	0623
27—	0624	0625	0626	0627	0628	0629	0630	0631	0632	0633	0634	0635	0636	0637	0638	0639
28—	0640	0641	0642	0643	0644	0645	0646	0647	0648	0649	0650	0651	0652	0653	0654	0655
29—	0656	0657	0658	0659	0660	0661	0662	0663	0664	0665	0666	0667	0668	0669	0670	0671
2A—	0672	0673	0674	0675	0676	0677	0678	0679	0680	0681	0682	0683	0684	0685	0686	0687

DIRECT CONVERSION TABLE (continued)

	0	1	2	3	4	5	6	7	8	9	A	B	C	D	E	F
2B—	0688	0689	0690	0691	0692	0693	0694	0695	0696	0697	0698	0699	0700	0701	0702	0703
2C—	0704	0705	0706	0707	0708	0709	0710	0711	0712	0713	0714	0715	0716	0717	0718	0719
2D—	0720	0721	0722	0723	0724	0725	0726	0727	0728	0729	0730	0731	0732	0733	0734	0735
2E—	0736	0737	0738	0739	0740	0741	0742	0743	0744	0745	0746	0747	0748	0749	0750	0751
2F—	0752	0753	0754	0755	0756	0757	0758	0759	0760	0761	0762	0763	0764	0765	0766	0767
30—	0768	0769	0770	0771	0772	0773	0774	0775	0776	0777	0778	0779	0780	0781	0782	0783
31—	0784	0785	0786	0787	0788	0789	0790	0791	0792	0793	0794	0795	0796	0797	0798	0799
32—	0800	0801	0802	0803	0804	0805	0806	0807	0808	0809	0810	0811	0812	0813	0814	0815
33—	0816	0817	0818	0819	0820	0821	0822	0823	0824	0825	0826	0827	0828	0829	0830	0831
34—	0832	0833	0834	0835	0836	0837	0838	0839	0840	0841	0842	0843	0844	0845	0846	0847
35—	0848	0849	0850	0851	0852	0853	0854	0855	0856	0857	0858	0859	0860	0861	0862	0863
36—	0864	0865	0866	0867	0868	0869	0870	0871	0872	0873	0874	0875	0876	0877	0878	0879
37—	0880	0881	0882	0883	0884	0885	0886	0887	0888	0889	0890	0891	0892	0893	0894	0895
38—	0896	0897	0898	0898	0900	0901	0902	0903	0904	0905	0906	0907	0908	0909	0910	0911
39—	0912	0913	0914	0915	0916	0917	0918	0919	0920	0921	0922	0923	0924	0925	0926	0927
3A—	0928	0929	0930	0931	0932	0933	0934	0935	0936	0937	0938	0939	0940	0941	0942	0943
3B—	0944	0945	0946	0947	0948	0949	0950	0951	0952	0953	0954	0955	0956	0957	0958	0959
3C—	0960	0961	0962	0963	0964	0965	0966	0967	0968	0969	0970	0971	0972	0973	0974	0975
3D—	0976	0977	0978	0979	0980	0981	0982	0983	0984	0985	0986	0987	0988	0989	0990	0991
3E—	0992	0993	0994	0995	0996	0997	0998	0999	1000	1001	1002	1003	1004	1005	1006	1007
3F—	1008	1009	1010	1011	1012	1013	1014	1015	1016	1017	1018	1019	1020	1021	1022	1023
40—	1024	1025	1026	1027	1028	1029	1030	1031	1032	1033	1034	1035	1036	1037	1038	1039
41—	1040	1041	1042	1043	1044	1045	1046	1047	1048	1049	1050	1051	1052	1053	1054	1055
42—	1056	1057	1058	1059	1060	1061	1062	1063	1064	1065	1066	1067	1068	1069	1070	1071
43—	1072	1073	1074	1075	1076	1077	1078	1079	1080	1081	1082	1083	1084	1085	1086	1087
44—	1088	1089	1090	1091	1092	1093	1094	1095	1096	1097	1098	1099	1100	1101	1102	1103
45—	1104	1105	1106	1107	1108	1109	1110	1111	1112	1113	1114	1115	1116	1117	1118	1119
46—	1120	1121	1122	1123	1124	1125	1126	1127	1128	1129	1130	1131	1132	1133	1134	1135
47—	1136	1137	1138	1139	1140	1141	1142	1143	1144	1145	1146	1147	1148	1149	1150	1151
48—	1152	1153	1154	1155	1156	1157	1158	1159	1160	1161	1162	1163	1164	1165	1166	1167
49—	1168	1169	1170	1171	1172	1173	1174	1175	1176	1177	1178	1179	1180	1181	1182	1183
4A—	1184	1185	1186	1187	1188	1189	1190	1191	1192	1193	1194	1195	1196	1197	1198	1199
4B—	1200	1201	1202	1203	1204	1205	1206	1207	1208	1209	1210	1211	1212	1213	1214	1215
4C—	1216	1217	1218	1219	1220	1221	1222	1223	1224	1225	1226	1227	1228	1229	1230	1231
4D—	1232	1233	1234	1235	1236	1237	1238	1239	1240	1241	1242	1243	1244	1245	1246	1247
4E—	1248	1249	1250	1251	1252	1253	1254	1255	1256	1257	1258	1259	1260	1261	1262	1263
4F—	1264	1265	1266	1267	1268	1269	1270	1271	1272	1273	1274	1275	1276	1277	1278	1279
50—	1280	1281	1282	1283	1284	1285	1286	1287	1288	1289	1290	1291	1292	1293	1294	1295
51—	1296	1297	1298	1299	1300	1301	1302	1303	1304	1305	1306	1307	1308	1309	1310	1311
52—	1312	1313	1314	1315	1316	1317	1318	1319	1320	1321	1322	1323	1324	1325	1326	1327
53—	1328	1329	1330	1331	1332	1333	1334	1335	1336	1337	1338	1339	1340	1341	1342	1343
54—	1344	1345	1346	1347	1348	1349	1350	1351	1352	1353	1354	1355	1356	1357	1358	1359
55—	1360	1361	1362	1363	1364	1365	1366	1367	1368	1369	1370	1371	1372	1373	1374	1375
56—	1376	1377	1378	1379	1380	1381	1382	1383	1384	1385	1386	1387	1388	1389	1390	1391
57—	1392	1393	1394	1395	1396	1397	1398	1399	1400	1401	1402	1403	1404	1405	1406	1407
58—	1408	1409	1410	1411	1412	1413	1414	1415	1416	1417	1418	1419	1420	1421	1422	1423
59—	1424	1425	1426	1427	1428	1429	1430	1431	1432	1433	1434	1435	1436	1437	1438	1439
5A—	1440	1441	1442	1443	1444	1445	1446	1447	1448	1449	1450	1451	1452	1453	1454	1455
5B—	1456	1457	1458	1459	1460	1461	1462	1463	1464	1465	1466	1467	1468	1469	1470	1471
5C—	1472	1473	1474	1475	1476	1477	1478	1479	1480	1481	1482	1483	1484	1485	1486	1487
5D—	1488	1489	1490	1491	1492	1493	1494	1495	1496	1497	1498	1499	1500	1501	1502	1503
5E—	1504	1505	1506	1507	1508	1509	1510	1511	1512	1513	1514	1515	1516	1517	1518	1519
5F—	1520	1521	1522	1523	1524	1525	1526	1527	1528	1529	1530	1531	1532	1533	1534	1535
60—	1536	1537	1538	1539	1540	1541	1542	1543	1544	1545	1546	1547	1548	1549	1550	1551
61—	1552	1553	1554	1555	1556	1557	1558	1559	1560	1561	1562	1563	1564	1565	1566	1567
62—	1568	1569	1570	1571	1572	1573	1574	1575	1576	1577	1578	1579	1580	1581	1582	1583
63—	1584	1585	1586	1587	1588	1589	1590	1591	1592	1593	1594	1595	1596	1597	1598	1599
64—	1600	1601	1602	1603	1604	1605	1606	1607	1608	1609	1610	1611	1612	1613	1614	1615
65—	1616	1617	1618	1619	1620	1621	1622	1623	1624	1625	1626	1627	1628	1629	1630	1631
66—	1632	1633	1634	1635	1636	1637	1638	1639	1640	1641	1642	1643	1644	1645	1646	1647
67—	1648	1649	1650	1651	1652	1653	1654	1655	1656	1657	1658	1659	1660	1661	1662	1663
68—	1664	1665	1666	1667	1668	1669	1670	1671	1672	1673	1674	1675	1676	1677	1678	1679
69—	1680	1681	1682	1683	1684	1685	1686	1687	1688	1689	1690	1691	1692	1693	1694	1695

DIRECT CONVERSION TABLE (Continued)

	0	1	2	3	4	5	6	7	8	9	A	B	C	D	E	F
6A—	1696	1697	1698	1699	1700	1701	1702	1703	1704	1705	1706	1707	1708	1709	1710	1711
6B—	1712	1713	1714	1715	1716	1717	1718	1719	1720	1721	1722	1723	1724	1725	1726	1727
6C—	1728	1729	1730	1731	1732	1733	1734	1735	1736	1737	1738	1739	1740	1741	1742	1743
6D—	1744	1745	1746	1747	1748	1749	1750	1751	1752	1753	1754	1755	1756	1757	1758	1759
6E—	1760	1761	1762	1763	1764	1765	1766	1767	1768	1769	1770	1771	1772	1773	1774	1775
6F—	1776	1777	1778	1779	1780	1781	1782	1783	1784	1785	1786	1787	1788	1789	1790	1791
70—	1792	1793	1794	1795	1796	1797	1798	1799	1800	1801	1802	1803	1804	1805	1806	1807
71—	1808	1809	1810	1811	1812	1813	1814	1815	1816	1817	1818	1819	1820	1821	1822	1823
72—	1824	1825	1826	1827	1828	1829	1830	1831	1832	1833	1834	1835	1836	1837	1838	1839
73—	1840	1841	1842	1843	1844	1845	1846	1847	1848	1849	1850	1851	1852	1853	1854	1855
74—	1856	1857	1858	1859	1960	1861	1862	1863	1864	1865	1866	1867	1868	1869	1870	1871
75—	1872	1873	1874	1875	1876	1877	1878	1879	1880	1881	1882	1883	1884	1885	1886	1887
76—	1888	1889	1890	1891	1892	1893	1894	1895	1896	1897	1898	1899	1900	1901	1902	1903
77—	1904	1905	1906	1907	1908	1909	1910	1911	1912	1913	1914	1915	1916	1917	1918	1919
78—	1920	1921	1922	1923	1924	1925	1926	1927	1928	1929	1930	1931	1932	1933	1934	1935
79—	1936	1937	1938	1939	1940	1941	1942	1943	1944	1945	1946	1947	1948	1949	1950	1951
7A—	1952	1953	1954	1955	1956	1957	1958	1959	1960	1961	1962	1963	1964	1965	1966	1967
7B—	1968	1969	1970	1971	1972	1973	1974	1975	1976	1977	1978	1979	1980	1981	1982	1983
7C—	1984	1985	1986	1987	1988	1989	1990	1991	1992	1993	1994	1995	1996	1997	1998	1999
7D—	2000	2001	2002	2003	2004	2005	2006	2007	2008	2009	2010	2011	2012	2013	2014	2015
7E—	2016	2017	2018	2019	2020	2021	2022	2023	2024	2025	2026	2027	2028	2029	2030	2031
7F—	2032	2033	2034	2035	2036	2037	2038	2039	2040	2041	2042	2043	2044	2045	2046	2047
80—	2048	2049	2050	2051	2052	2053	2054	2055	2056	2057	2058	2059	2060	2061	2062	2063
81—	2064	2065	2066	2067	2068	2069	2070	2071	2072	2073	2074	2075	2076	2077	2078	2079
82—	2080	2081	2082	2083	2084	2085	2086	2087	2088	2089	2090	2091	2092	2093	2094	2095
83—	2096	2097	2098	2099	2100	2101	2102	2103	2104	2105	2106	2107	2108	2109	2110	2111
84—	2112	2113	2114	2115	2116	2117	2118	2119	2120	2121	2122	2123	2124	2125	2126	2127
85—	2128	2129	2130	2131	2132	2133	2134	2135	2136	2137	2138	2139	2140	2141	2142	2143
86—	2144	2145	2146	2147	2148	2149	2150	2151	2152	2153	2154	2155	2156	2157	2158	2159
87—	2160	2161	2162	2163	2164	2165	2166	2167	2168	2169	2170	2171	2172	2173	2174	2175
88—	2176	2177	2178	2179	2180	2181	2182	2183	2184	2185	2186	2187	2188	2189	2190	2191
89—	2192	2193	2194	2195	2196	2197	2198	2199	2200	2201	2202	2203	2204	2205	2206	2207
8A—	2208	2209	2210	2211	2212	2213	2214	2215	2216	2217	2218	2219	2220	2221	2222	2223
8B—	2224	2225	2226	2227	2228	2229	2230	2231	2232	2233	2234	2235	2236	2237	2238	2239
8C—	2240	2241	2242	2243	2244	2245	2246	2247	2248	2249	2250	2251	2252	2253	2254	2255
8D—	2256	2257	2258	2259	2260	2261	2262	2263	2264	2265	2266	2267	2268	2269	2270	2271
8E—	2272	2273	2274	2275	2276	2277	2278	2279	2280	2281	2282	2283	2284	2285	2286	2287
8F—	2288	2289	2290	2291	2292	2293	2294	2295	2296	2297	2298	2299	2300	2301	2302	2303
90—	2304	2305	2306	2307	2308	2309	2310	2311	2312	2313	2314	2315	2316	2317	2318	2319
91—	2320	2321	2322	2323	2324	2325	2326	2327	2328	2329	2330	2331	2332	2333	2334	2335
92—	2336	2337	2338	2339	2340	2341	2342	2343	2344	2345	2346	2347	2348	2349	2350	2351
93—	2352	2353	2354	2355	2356	2357	2358	2359	2360	2361	2362	2363	2364	2365	2366	2367
94—	2368	2369	2370	2371	2372	2373	2374	2375	2376	2377	2378	2379	2380	2381	2382	2383
95—	2384	2385	2386	2387	2388	2389	2390	2391	2392	2393	2394	2395	2396	2397	2398	2399
96—	2400	2401	2402	2403	2404	2405	2406	2407	2408	2409	2410	2411	2412	2413	2414	2415
97—	2416	2417	2418	2419	2420	2421	2422	2423	2424	2425	2426	2427	2428	2429	2430	2431
98—	2432	2433	2434	2435	2436	2437	2438	2439	2440	2441	2442	2443	2444	2445	2446	2447
99	2448	2449	2450	2451	2452	2453	2454	2455	2456	2457	2458	2459	2560	2461	2462	2463
9A—	2464	2465	2466	2467	2468	2469	2470	2471	2472	2473	2474	2475	2476	2477	2478	2479
9B—	2480	2481	2482	2483	2484	2485	2486	2487	2488	2489	2490	2491	2492	2493	2494	2495
9C—	2496	2497	2498	2499	2500	2501	2502	2503	2504	2505	2506	2507	2508	2509	2510	2511
9D—	2512	2513	2514	2515	2516	2517	2518	2519	2520	2521	2522	2523	2524	2525	2526	2527
9E—	2528	2529	2530	2531	2532	2533	2534	2535	2536	2537	2538	2539	2540	2541	2542	2543
9F—	2544	2545	2546	2547	2548	2549	2550	2551	2552	2553	2554	2555	2556	2557	2558	2559
A0—	2560	2561	2562	2563	2564	2565	2566	2567	2568	2569	2570	2571	2572	2573	2574	2575
A1—	2576	2577	2578	2579	2580	2581	2582	2583	2584	2585	2586	2587	2588	2589	2590	2591
A2—	2592	2593	2594	2595	2596	2597	2598	2599	2600	2601	2602	2603	2604	2605	2606	2607
A3—	2608	2609	2610	2611	2612	2613	2614	2615	2616	2617	2618	2619	2620	2621	2622	2623
A4—	2624	2625	2626	2627	2628	2629	2630	2631	2632	2633	2634	2635	2636	2637	2638	2639
A5—	2640	2641	2642	2643	2644	2645	2646	2647	2648	2649	2650	2651	2652	2653	2654	2655
A6—	2656	2657	2658	2659	2660	2661	2662	2663	2664	2665	2666	2667	2668	2669	2670	2671
A7—	2672	2673	2674	2675	2676	2677	2678	2679	2680	2681	2682	2683	2684	2685	2686	2687
A8—	2688	2689	2690	2691	2692	2693	2694	2695	2696	2697	2698	2699	2700	2701	2702	2703

DIRECT CONVERSION TABLE (Continued)

	0	1	2	3	4	5	6	7	8	9	A	B	C	D	E	F
A9—	2704	2705	2706	2707	2708	2709	2710	2711	2712	2713	2714	2715	2716	2717	2718	2719
AA—	2720	2721	2722	2723	2724	2725	2726	2727	2728	2729	2730	2731	2732	2733	2734	2735
AB—	2736	2737	2738	2739	2740	2741	2742	2743	2744	2745	2746	2747	2748	2749	2750	2751
AC—	2752	2753	2754	2755	2756	2757	2758	2759	2760	2761	2762	2763	2764	2765	2766	2767
AD—	2768	2769	2770	2771	2772	2773	2774	2775	2776	2777	2778	2779	2780	2781	2782	2783
AE—	2784	2785	2786	2787	2788	2789	2790	2791	2792	2793	2794	2795	2796	2797	2798	2799
AF—	2800	2801	2802	2803	2804	2805	2806	2807	2808	2809	2810	2811	2812	2813	2814	2815
B0—	2816	2817	2818	2819	2820	2821	2822	2823	2824	2825	2826	2827	2828	2829	2830	2831
B1—	2832	2833	2834	2835	2836	2837	2838	2839	2840	2841	2842	2843	2844	2845	2846	2847
B2—	2848	2849	2850	2851	2852	2853	2854	2855	2856	2857	2858	2859	2860	2861	2862	2863
B3—	2864	2865	2866	2867	2868	2869	2870	2871	2872	2873	2874	2875	2876	2877	2878	2879
B4—	2800	2881	2882	2883	2884	2885	2886	2887	2888	2889	2890	2891	2892	2893	2894	2895
B5—	2896	2897	2898	2899	2900	2901	2902	2903	2904	2905	2906	2907	2908	2909	2910	2911
B6—	2912	2913	2914	2915	2916	2917	2918	2919	2920	2921	2922	2923	2924	2925	2926	2927
B7—	2928	2929	2930	2931	2932	2933	2934	2935	2936	2937	2938	2939	2940	2941	2942	2943
B8—	2944	2945	2946	2947	2948	2949	2950	2951	2952	2953	2954	2955	2956	2957	2958	2959
B9—	2960	2961	2962	2963	2964	2965	2966	2967	2968	2969	2970	2971	2972	2973	2974	2975
BA—	2976	2977	2978	2979	2980	2981	2982	2983	2984	2985	2986	2987	2988	2989	2990	2991
BB—	2992	2993	2994	2995	2996	2997	2998	2999	3000	3001	3002	3003	3004	3005	3006	3007
BC—	3008	3009	3010	3011	3012	3013	3014	3015	3016	3017	3018	3019	3020	3021	3022	3023
BD—	3024	3025	3026	3027	3028	3029	3030	3031	3032	3033	3034	3035	3036	3037	3038	3039
BE—	3040	3041	3042	3043	3044	3045	3046	3047	3048	3049	3050	3051	3052	3053	3054	3055
BF—	3056	3057	3058	3059	3060	3061	3062	3063	3064	3065	3066	3067	3068	3069	3070	3071
C0—	3072	3073	3074	3075	3076	3077	3078	3079	3080	3081	3082	3083	3084	3085	3086	3087
C1—	3088	3089	3090	3091	3092	3093	3094	3095	3096	3097	3098	3099	3100	3101	3102	3103
C2—	3104	3105	3106	3107	3108	3109	3110	3111	3112	3113	3114	3115	3116	3117	3118	3119
C3—	3120	3121	3122	3123	3124	3125	3126	3127	3128	3129	3130	3131	3132	3133	3134	3135
C4—	3136	3137	3138	3139	3140	3141	3142	3143	3144	3145	3146	3147	3148	3149	3150	3151
C5—	3152	3153	3154	3155	3156	3157	3158	3159	3160	3161	3162	3163	3164	3165	3166	3167
C6—	3168	3169	3170	3171	3172	3173	3174	3175	3176	3177	3178	3179	3180	3181	3182	3183
C7—	3184	3185	3186	3187	3188	3189	3190	3191	3192	3193	3194	3195	3196	3197	3198	3199
C8—	3200	3201	3202	3203	3204	3205	3206	3207	3208	3209	3210	3211	3212	3213	3214	3215
C9—	3216	3217	3218	3219	3220	3221	3222	3223	3224	3225	3226	3227	3228	3229	3230	3231
CA—	3232	3233	3234	3235	3236	3237	3238	3239	3240	3241	3242	3243	3244	3245	3246	3247
CB—	3248	3249	3250	3251	3252	3253	3254	3255	3256	3257	3258	3259	3260	3261	3262	3263
CC—	3264	3265	3266	3267	3268	3269	3270	3271	3272	3273	3274	3275	3276	3277	3278	3279
CD—	3280	3281	3282	3283	3284	3285	3286	3287	3288	3289	3290	3291	3292	3293	3294	3295
CE—	3296	3297	3298	3299	3300	3301	3302	3303	3304	3305	3306	3307	3308	3309	3310	3111
CF—	3312	3313	3314	3315	3316	3317	3318	3319	3320	3321	3322	3323	3324	3325	3326	3327
D0—	3328	3329	3330	3331	3332	3333	3334	3335	3336	3337	3338	3339	3340	3341	3342	3343
D1—	3344	3345	3346	3347	3348	3349	3350	3351	3352	3353	3354	3355	3356	3357	3358	3359
D2—	3360	3361	3362	3363	3364	3365	3366	3367	3368	3369	3370	3371	3372	3373	3374	3375
D3—	3376	3377	3378	3379	3380	3381	3382	3383	3384	3385	3386	3387	3388	3389	3390	3391
D4—	3392	3393	3394	3395	3396	3397	3398	3399	3400	3401	3402	3403	3404	3405	3406	3407
D5—	3408	3409	3410	3411	3412	3413	3414	3415	3416	3417	3418	3419	3420	3421	3422	3423
D6—	3424	3425	3426	3427	3428	3429	3430	3431	3432	3433	3434	3435	3436	3437	3438	3439
D7—	3440	3441	3442	3443	3444	3445	3446	3447	3448	3449	3450	3451	3452	3453	3454	3455
D8—	3456	3457	3458	3459	3460	3461	3462	3463	3464	3465	3466	3467	3468	3469	3470	3471
D9—	3472	3473	3474	3475	3476	3477	3478	3479	3480	3481	3482	3483	3484	3485	3486	3487
DA—	3488	3489	3490	3491	3492	3493	3494	3495	3496	3497	3498	3499	3500	3501	3502	3503
DB—	3504	3505	3506	3507	3508	3509	3510	3511	3512	3513	3514	3515	3516	3517	3518	3519
DC—	3520	3521	3522	3523	3524	3525	3526	3527	3528	3529	3530	3531	3532	3533	3534	3535
DD—	3536	3537	3538	3539	3540	3541	3542	3543	3544	3545	3546	3547	3548	3549	3550	3551
DE—	3552	3553	3554	3555	3556	3557	3558	3559	3560	3561	3562	3563	3564	3565	3566	3567
DF—	3568	3569	3570	3571	3572	3573	3574	3575	3576	3577	3578	3579	3580	3581	3582	3583
E0—	3584	3585	3586	3587	3588	3589	3590	3591	3592	3593	3594	3595	3596	3597	3598	3599
E1—	3600	3601	3602	3603	3604	3605	3606	3607	3608	3609	3610	3611	3612	3613	3614	3615
E2—	3616	3617	3618	3619	3620	3621	3622	3623	3624	3625	3626	3627	3628	3629	3630	32631
E3—	3632	3633	3634	3635	3636	3637	3638	3639	3640	3641	3642	3643	3644	3645	3646	3647
E4—	3648	3649	3650	3651	3652	3653	3654	3655	3656	3657	3658	3659	3660	3661	3662	3663
E5—	3664	3665	3666	3667	3668	3669	3670	3671	3672	3673	3674	3675	3676	3677	3678	3679
E6—	3680	3681	3682	3683	3684	3685	3686	3687	3688	3689	3690	3691	3692	3693	3694	3695
E7—	3696	3697	3698	3699	3700	3701	3702	3703	3704	3705	3706	3707	3708	3709	3710	3711
E8—	3712	3713	3714	3715	3716	3717	3718	3719	3720	3721	3722	3723	3724	3725	3726	3727
E9—	3728	3729	3730	3731	3732	3733	3734	3735	3736	3737	3738	3739	3740	3741	3742	3743

DIRECT CONVERSION TABLE (Continued)

	0	1	2	3	4	5	6	7	8	9	A	B	C	D	E	F
EA—	3744	3745	3746	3747	3748	3749	3750	3751	3752	3753	3754	3755	3756	3757	3758	3759
EB—	3760	3761	3762	3763	3764	3765	3766	3767	3768	3769	3770	3771	3772	3773	3774	3775
EC—	3776	3777	3778	3779	3780	3781	3782	3783	3784	3785	3786	3787	3788	3789	3790	3791
ED—	3792	3793	3794	3795	3796	3797	3798	3799	3800	3801	3802	3803	3804	3805	3806	3807
EE—	3808	3809	3810	3811	3812	3813	3814	3815	3816	3817	3818	3819	3820	3821	3822	3823
EF—	3824	3825	3826	3827	3828	3829	3830	3831	3832	3833	3834	3835	3836	3837	3838	3839
F0—	3840	3841	3842	3843	3844	3845	3846	3847	3848	3849	3850	3851	3852	3853	3854	3855
F1—	3856	3857	3858	3859	3860	3861	3862	3863	3864	3865	3866	3867	3868	3869	3870	3871
F2—	3872	3873	3874	3875	3876	3877	3878	3879	3880	3881	3882	3883	3884	3885	3886	3887
F3—	3888	3889	3890	3891	3892	3893	3894	3895	3896	3897	3898	3899	3900	3901	3902	3903
F4—	3904	3905	3906	3907	3908	3909	3910	3911	3912	3913	3914	3915	3916	3917	3918	3919
F5—	3920	3921	3922	3923	3924	3925	3926	3927	3928	3929	3930	3931	3932	3933	3934	3935
F6—	3936	3937	3938	3939	3940	3941	3942	3943	3944	3945	3946	3947	3948	3949	3950	3951
F7—	3952	3953	3954	3955	3956	3957	3958	3959	3960	3961	3962	3963	3964	3965	3966	3967
F8—	3968	3969	3970	3971	3972	3973	3974	3975	3976	3977	3978	3979	3980	3981	3982	3983
F9—	3984	3985	3986	3987	3988	3989	3990	3991	3992	3993	3994	3995	3996	3997	3998	3999
FA—	4000	4001	4002	4003	4004	4005	4006	4007	4008	4009	4010	4011	4012	4013	4014	4015
FB—	4016	4017	4018	4019	4020	4021	4022	4023	4024	4025	4026	4027	4028	4029	4030	4031
FC—	4032	4033	4034	4035	4036	4037	4038	4039	4040	4041	4042	4043	4044	4045	4046	4047
FD—	4048	4049	4050	4051	4052	4053	4054	4055	4056	4057	4058	4059	4060	4061	4062	4063
FE—	4064	4065	4066	4067	4068	4069	4070	4071	4072	4073	4074	4075	4076	4077	4078	4079
FF—	4080	4081	4082	4083	4084	4085	4086	4087	4088	4089	4090	4091	4092	4093	4094	4095

HEXADECIMAL AND DECIMAL INTEGER CONVERSION TABLE

	8		7		6		5		4		3		2		1
Hex	Decimal	Hex	Decimal	Hex	Decimal	Hex	Decimal	Hex	Decimal	Hex	Decimal	Hex	Decimal	Hex	Decimal
0	0	0	0	0	0	0	0	0	0	0	0	0	0	0	0
1	268,435,456	1	16,777,216	1	1,048,576	1	65,536	1	4,096	1	256	1	16	1	1
2	536,870,912	2	33,554,432	2	2,097,152	2	131,072	2	8,192	2	512	2	32	2	2
3	805,306,368	3	50,331,648	3	3,145,728	3	196,608	3	12,288	3	768	3	48	3	3
4	1,073,741,824	3	67,108,864	4	4,194,304	4	262,144	4	16,384	4	1,024	4	64	4	4
5	1,342,177,280	5	83,886,080	5	5,242,880	5	327,680	5	20,480	5	1,280	5	80	5	5
6	1,610,612,736	6	100,663,296	6	6,291,456	6	393,216	6	24,576	6	1,536	6	96	6	6
7	1,879,048,192	7	117,440,512	7	7,340,032	7	458,752	7	28,672	7	1,792	7	112	7	7
8	2,147,483,648	8	134,217,728	8	8,388,608	8	524,288	8	32,768	8	2,048	8	128	8	8
9	2,415,919,104	9	150,994,944	9	9,437,184	9	589,824	9	36,864	9	2,304	9	144	9	9
A	2,684,354,560	A	167,772,160	A	10,485,760	A	655,360	A	40,960	A	2,560	A	160	A	10
B	2,952,790,016	B	184,549,376	B	11,534,336	B	720,896	B	45,056	B	2,816	B	176	B	11
C	3,221,225,472	C	201,326,592	C	12,582,912	C	786,432	C	49,152	C	3,072	C	192	C	12
D	3,489,660,928	D	218,103,808	D	13,631,488	D	851,968	D	53,248	D	3,328	D	208	D	13
E	3,758,096,384	E	234,881,024	E	14,680,064	E	917,504	E	57,344	E	3,584	E	224	E	14
F	4,026,531,840	F	251,658,240	F	15,728,640	F	983,040	F	61,440	F	3,840	F	240	F	15

INTEGER CONVERSION TABLE (Continued)

TO CONVERT HEXADECIMAL TO DECIMAL

1. Locate the column of decimal numbers corresponding to the left-most digit or letter of the hexadecimal; select from this column and record the number that corresponds to the position of the hexadecimal digit or letter.
2. Repeat step 1 for the next (second from the left) position.
3. Repeat step 1 for the units (third from the left) position.
4. Add the numbers selected from the table to form the decimal number.

To convert integer numbers greater than the capacity of table, use the techniques below:

HEXADECIMAL TO DECIMAL

Successive cumulative multiplication from left to right, adding units position.

Example: $D34_{16} = 3380_{10}$

$$
\begin{array}{rr}
D = & 13 \\
& \times 16 \\ \hline
& 208 \\
3 = & +3 \\ \hline
& 211 \\
& \times 16 \\ \hline
& 3376 \\
4 = & +4 \\ \hline
& 3380
\end{array}
$$

TO CONVERT DECIMAL TO HEXADECIMAL

1. (a) Select from the table the highest decimal number that is equal to or less than the number to be converted.
   (b) Record the hexadecimal of the column containing the selected number.
   (c) Subtract the selected decimal from the number to be converted.
2. Using the remainder from step 1(c) repeat all of step 1 to develop the second position of the hexadecimal (and a remainder).
3. Using the remainder from step 2 repeat all of step 1 to develop the units position of the hexadecimal.
4. Combine terms to form the hexadecimal number.

DECIMAL TO HEXADECIMAL

Divide and collect the remainder in reverse order.

Example: $3380_{10} = X_{16}$

$$
\begin{array}{lll}
16 & \underline{|3380} & \text{remainder} \\
16 & \underline{|211} & 4 \\
16 & \underline{|13} & 3 \\
& D & \\
\end{array}
$$

$3380_{10} = D34_{16}$

EXAMPLE

Conversion of
Hexadecimal
Value   D34

1.	D	3328
2.	3	48
3.	4	4
4.	Decimal	3380

EXAMPLE

Conversion of
Decimal
Value   3380

1.	D	−3328
		52
2.	3	−48
		4
3.	4	−4
4.	Hexa-decimal	D34

INTEGER CONVERSION TABLE (Continued)

<u>POWERS OF 16 TABLE</u>

Example: $268{,}435{,}456_{10} = (2.68435456 \times 10^8)_{10} = 1000\ 0000_{16} = (10^7)_{16}$

16^n	n
1	0
16	1
256	2
4 096	3
65 536	4
1 048 576	5
16 777 216	6
268 435 456	7
4 294 967 296	8
68 719 476 736	9
1 099 511 627 776	10 = A
17 592 186 044 416	11 = B
281 474 976 710 656	12 = C
4 503 599 627 370 496	13 = D
72 057 594 037 927 936	14 = E
1 152 921 504 606 846 976	15 = F

Decimal Values

III. HEXADECIMAL AND DECIMAL FRACTION CONVERSION TABLE

	1		2			3				4				
Hex	Decimal	Hex	Decimal		Hex	Decimal			Hex	Decimal Equivalent				
.0	.0000	.00	.0000	0000	.000	.0000	0000	0000	.0000	.0000	0000	0000	0000
.1	.0625	.01	.0039	0625	.001	.0002	4414	0625	.0001	.0000	1525	8789	0625
.2	.1250	.02	.0078	1250	.002	.0004	8828	1250	.0002	.0000	3051	7578	1250
.3	.1875	.03	.0117	1875	.003	.0007	3242	1875	.0003	.0000	4577	6367	1875
.4	.2500	.04	.0156	2500	.004	.0009	7656	2500	.0004	.0000	6103	5156	2500
.5	.3125	.05	.0195	3125	.005	.0012	2070	3125	.0005	.0000	7629	3945	3125
.6	.3750	.06	.0234	3750	.006	.0014	6484	3750	.0006	.0000	9155	2734	3750
.7	.4375	.07	.0273	4375	.007	.0017	0898	4375	.0007	.0001	0681	1523	4375
.8	.5000	.08	.0312	5000	.008	.0019	5312	5000	.0008	.0001	2207	0312	5000
.9	.5625	.09	.0351	5625	.009	.0021	9726	5625	.0009	.0001	3732	9101	5625
.A	.6250	.0A	.0390	6250	.00A	.0024	4140	6250	.000A	.0001	5258	7890	6250
.B	.6875	.0B	.0429	6875	.00B	.0026	8554	6875	.000B	.0001	6784	6679	6875
.C	.7500	.0C	.0468	7500	.00C	.0029	2968	7500	.000C	.0001	8310	5468	7500
.D	.8125	.0D	.0507	8125	.00D	.0031	7382	8125	.000D	.0001	9836	4257	8125
.E	.8750	.0E	.0546	8750	.00E	.0034	1796	8750	.000E	.0002	1362	3046	8750
.F	.9375	.0F	.0585	9375	.00F	.0036	6210	9375	.000F	.0002	2888	1835	9375
	1		2			3				4				

<u>TO CONVERT .ABC HEXADECIMAL TO DECIMAL</u>

Find .A   in position 1   .6250
Find .0B   in position 2   .0429 6875
Find .00C in position 3   .0029 2968 7500
  .ABC Hex is equal to   .6708 9843 7500

FRACTION CONVERSION TABLE (Continued)

TO CONVERT .13 DECIMAL TO HEXADECIMAL

1. Find .1250 next lowest to	.1300	
subtract	− .1250	= .2 Hex
2. Find .0039 0625 next lowest to	.0050 0000	
	− .0039 0625	= .01
3. Find .0009 7656 2500	.0010 9375 0000	
	− .0009 7656 2500	= .004
4. Find .0001 0681 1523 4375	.0001 1718 7500 0000	
	− .0001 0681 1523 4375 = .0007	
	.0000 1037 5976 5625 = .2147 Hex	

5. .13 Decimal is approximately equal to ⎯⎯⎯⎯⎯⎯⎯⎯⎯⎯⎯⎯⎯↑

To convert fractions beyond the capacity of table, use techniques below:

HEXADECIMAL FRACTION TO DECIMAL

Convert the hexadecimal fraction to its decimal equivalent using the same technique as for integer numbers. Divide the results by 16^n (n is the number of fraction positions).

Example: $.8A7_{16} = .540771_{10}$

$$8A7_{16} = 2215_{10}$$
$$16^3 = 4096$$

$$\begin{array}{r} .540771 \\ 4096\overline{\smash{\big)}\,2215.000000} \end{array}$$

DECIMAL FRACTION TO HEXADECIMAL

Collect integer parts of product in the order of calculation.

Example: $.5408_{10} = .8A7_{16}$

$$
\begin{array}{l}
\quad\quad .5408 \\
\quad\quad \underline{\times 16} \\
8 \leftarrow \boxed{8}\ .6528 \\
\quad\quad \underline{\times 16} \\
A \leftarrow \boxed{10}\ .4448 \\
\quad\quad \underline{\times 16} \\
7 \leftarrow \boxed{7}\ .1168
\end{array}
$$

HEXADECIMAL ADDITION AND SUBTRACTION TABLE

Example: 6 + 2 = 8, 8 − 2 = 6, and 8 − 6 = 2

	1	2	3	4	5	6	7	8	9	A	B	C	D	E	F
1	02	03	04	05	06	07	08	09	0A	0B	0C	0D	0E	0F	10
2	03	04	05	06	07	08	09	0A	0B	0C	0D	0E	0F	10	11
3	04	05	06	07	08	09	0A	0B	0C	0D	0E	0F	10	11	12
4	05	06	07	08	09	0A	0B	0C	0D	0E	0F	10	11	12	13
5	06	07	08	09	0A	0B	0C	0D	0E	0F	10	11	12	13	14
6	07	08	09	0A	0B	0C	0D	0E	0F	10	11	12	13	14	15
7	08	09	0A	0B	0C	0D	0E	0F	10	11	12	13	14	15	16
8	09	0A	0B	0C	0D	0E	0F	10	11	12	13	14	15	16	17
9	0A	0B	0C	0D	0E	0F	10	11	12	13	14	15	16	17	18
A	0B	0C	0D	0E	0F	10	11	12	13	14	15	16	17	18	19
B	0C	0D	0E	0F	10	11	12	13	14	15	16	17	18	19	1A
C	0D	0E	0F	10	11	12	13	14	15	16	17	18	19	1A	1B
D	0E	0F	10	11	12	13	14	15	16	17	18	19	1A	1B	1C
E	0F	10	11	12	13	14	15	16	17	18	19	1A	1B	1C	1D
F	10	11	12	13	14	15	16	17	18	19	1A	1B	1C	1D	1E

HEXADECIMAL MULTIPLICATION TABLE

Example: 2 × 4 = 08, F × 2 = 1E

	1	2	3	4	5	6	7	8	9	A	B	C	D	E	F
1	01	02	03	04	05	06	07	08	09	0A	0B	0C	0D	0E	0F
2	02	04	06	08	0A	0C	0E	10	12	14	16	18	1A	1C	1E
3	03	06	09	0C	0F	12	15	18	1B	1E	21	24	27	2A	2D
4	04	08	0C	10	14	18	1C	20	24	28	2C	30	34	38	3C
5	05	0A	0F	14	19	1E	23	28	2D	32	37	3C	41	46	4B
6	06	0C	12	18	1E	24	2A	30	36	3C	42	48	4E	54	5A
7	07	0E	15	1C	23	2A	31	38	3F	46	4D	54	5B	62	69
08	08	10	18	20	28	30	38	40	48	50	58	60	68	70	78
9	09	12	1B	24	2D	36	3F	48	51	5A	63	6C	75	7E	87
A	0A	14	1E	28	32	3C	46	50	5A	64	6E	78	82	8C	96
B	0B	16	21	2C	37	42	4D	58	63	6E	79	84	8F	9A	A5
C	0C	18	24	30	3C	48	54	60	6C	78	84	90	9C	A8	B4
D	0D	1A	27	34	41	4E	5B	68	75	82	8F	9C	A9	B6	C3
E	0E	1C	2A	38	46	54	62	70	7E	8C	9A	A8	B6	C4	D2
F	0F	1E	2D	3C	4B	5A	69	78	87	96	A5	B4	C3	D2	E1

PRIMES

The following table contains all primes from 1 to 100,000. Taken from the Handbook of Mathematical Functions, Applied Mathematics Series 55, Permission received from National Bureau of Standards, Washington, D. C.

PRIMES

	0	1	2	3	4	5	6	7	8	9	10	11	12	13	14	15	16	17	18	19	20	21	22	23	24
1	2	547	1229	1993	2749	3581	4421	5281	6143	7001	7927	8837	9739	10663	11677	12569	13513	14533	15413	16411	17393	18329	19427	20359	21391
2	3	557	1231	1997	2753	3583	4423	5297	6151	7013	7933	8839	9743	10667	11681	12577	13523	14537	15427	16417	17401	18341	19429	20369	21397
3	5	563	1237	1999	2767	3593	4441	5303	6163	7019	7937	8849	9749	10687	11689	12583	13537	14543	15439	16421	17417	18353	19433	20389	21401
4	7	569	1249	2003	2777	3607	4447	5309	6173	7027	7949	8861	9767	10691	11699	12589	13553	14549	15443	16427	17419	18367	19441	20399	21407
5	11	571	1259	2011	2789	3613	4451	5323	6197	7039	7951	8863	9769	10709	11701	12601	13567	14551	15451	16433	17431	18371	19447	20407	21419
6	13	577	1277	2017	2791	3617	4457	5333	6199	7043	7963	8867	9781	10711	11717	12611	13577	14557	15461	16447	17443	18379	19457	20411	21433
7	17	587	1279	2027	2797	3623	4463	5347	6203	7057	7993	8887	9787	10723	11719	12613	13591	14561	15467	16451	17449	18397	19463	20431	21467
8	19	593	1283	2029	2801	3631	4481	5351	6211	7069	8009	8893	9791	10729	11731	12619	13597	14563	15473	16453	17467	18401	19469	20441	21481
9	23	599	1289	2039	2803	3637	4483	5381	6217	7079	8011	8923	9803	10733	11743	12637	13613	14591	15493	16477	17471	18413	19471	20443	21487
10	29	601	1291	2053	2819	3643	4493	5387	6221	7103	8017	8929	9811	10739	11777	12641	13619	14593	15497	16481	17477	18427	19477	20477	21491
11	31	607	1297	2063	2833	3659	4507	5393	6229	7109	8039	8933	9817	10753	11779	12647	13627	14621	15511	16487	17483	18433	19483	20479	21493
12	37	613	1301	2069	2837	3671	4513	5399	6247	7121	8053	8941	9829	10771	11783	12653	13633	14627	15527	16493	17489	18439	19489	20483	21499
13	41	617	1303	2081	2843	3673	4517	5407	6257	7127	8059	8951	9833	10781	11789	12659	13649	14629	15541	16519	17491	18443	19501	20507	21503
14	43	619	1307	2083	2851	3677	4519	5413	6263	7129	8069	8963	9839	10789	11801	12671	13669	14633	15551	16529	17497	18451	19507	20509	21517
15	47	631	1319	2087	2857	3691	4523	5417	6269	7151	8081	8969	9851	10799	11807	12689	13679	14639	15559	16547	17509	18457	19531	20521	21521
16	53	641	1321	2089	2861	3697	4547	5419	6271	7159	8087	8971	9857	10831	11813	12697	13681	14653	15569	16553	17519	18461	19541	20533	21523
17	59	643	1327	2099	2879	3701	4549	5431	6277	7177	8089	8999	9859	10837	11821	12703	13687	14657	15581	16561	17539	18481	19543	20543	21529
18	61	647	1361	2111	2887	3709	4561	5437	6287	7187	8093	9001	9871	10847	11827	12713	13691	14669	15583	16567	17551	18493	19553	20549	21557
19	67	653	1367	2113	2897	3719	4567	5441	6299	7193	8101	9007	9883	10853	11831	12721	13693	14683	15601	16573	17569	18503	19559	20551	21559
20	71	659	1373	2129	2903	3727	4583	5443	6301	7207	8111	9011	9887	10859	11833	12739	13697	14699	15607	16603	17573	18517	19571	20563	21563
21	73	661	1381	2131	2909	3733	4591	5449	6311	7211	8117	9013	9901	10861	11839	12743	13709	14713	15619	16607	17579	18521	19577	20593	21569
22	79	673	1399	2137	2917	3739	4597	5471	6317	7213	8123	9029	9907	10867	11863	12757	13711	14717	15629	16619	17581	18523	19583	20599	21577
23	83	677	1409	2141	2927	3761	4603	5477	6323	7219	8147	9041	9923	10883	11867	12763	13721	14723	15641	16631	17597	18539	19597	20611	21587
24	89	683	1423	2143	2939	3767	4621	5479	6329	7229	8161	9043	9929	10889	11887	12781	13723	14731	15643	16633	17599	18541	19603	20627	21589
25	97	691	1427	2153	2953	3769	4637	5483	6337	7237	8167	9049	9931	10891	11897	12791	13729	14737	15647	16649	17609	18553	19609	20639	21599
26	101	701	1429	2161	2957	3779	4639	5501	6343	7243	8171	9059	9941	10903	11903	12799	13751	14741	15649	16651	17623	18583	19661	20641	21601
27	103	709	1433	2179	2963	3793	4643	5503	6353	7247	8179	9067	9949	10909	11909	12809	13757	14747	15661	16657	17627	18587	19681	20663	21611
28	107	719	1439	2203	2969	3797	4649	5507	6359	7253	8191	9091	9967	10937	11923	12821	13759	14753	15667	16661	17657	18593	19687	20681	21613
29	109	727	1447	2207	2971	3803	4651	5519	6361	7283	8209	9103	9973	10939	11927	12823	13763	14759	15671	16673	17659	18617	19697	20693	21617
30	113	733	1451	2213	2999	3821	4657	5521	6367	7297	8219	9109	10007	10949	11933	12829	13781	14767	15679	16691	17669	18637	19699	20707	21647
31	127	739	1453	2221	3001	3823	4663	5527	6373	7307	8221	9127	10009	10957	11939	12841	13789	14771	15683	16693	17681	18661	19709	20717	21649
32	131	743	1459	2237	3011	3833	4673	5531	6379	7309	8231	9133	10037	10973	11941	12853	13799	14779	15727	16699	17683	18671	19717	20719	21661
33	137	751	1471	2239	3019	3847	4679	5557	6389	7321	8233	9137	10039	10979	11953	12889	13807	14783	15731	16703	17707	18679	19727	20731	21673
34	139	757	1481	2243	3023	3851	4691	5563	6397	7331	8237	9151	10061	10987	11959	12893	13829	14797	15733	16729	17713	18691	19739	20743	21683
35	149	761	1483	2251	3037	3853	4703	5569	6421	7333	8243	9157	10067	10993	11969	12899	13831	14813	15737	16741	17729	18701	19751	20747	21701
36	151	769	1487	2267	3041	3863	4721	5573	6427	7349	8263	9161	10069	11003	11971	12907	13841	14821	15739	16747	17737	18713	19753	20749	21713
37	157	773	1489	2269	3049	3877	4723	5581	6449	7351	8269	9173	10079	11027	11981	12911	13859	14827	15749	16759	17747	18719	19759	20753	21727
38	163	787	1493	2273	3061	3881	4729	5591	6451	7369	8273	9181	10091	11047	11987	12917	13873	14831	15761	16763	17749	18731	19763	20759	21737
39	167	797	1499	2281	3067	3889	4733	5623	6469	7393	8287	9187	10093	11057	12007	12919	13877	14843	15767	16787	17761	18743	19777	20771	21739
40	173	809	1511	2287	3079	3907	4751	5639	6473	7411	8291	9199	10099	11059	12011	12923	13879	14851	15773	16811	17783	18749	19793	20773	21751
41	179	811	1523	2293	3083	3911	4759	5641	6481	7417	8293	9203	10103	11069	12037	12941	13883	14867	15787	16823	17789	18757	19801	20807	21757
42	181	821	1531	2297	3089	3917	4783	5647	6491	7433	8297	9209	10111	11071	12041	12953	13901	14869	15791	16829	17791	18773	19813	20809	21767
43	191	823	1543	2309	3109	3919	4787	5651	6521	7451	8311	9221	10133	11083	12043	12959	13903	14879	15797	16831	17807	18787	19819	20849	21773
44	193	827	1549	2311	3119	3923	4789	5653	6529	7457	8317	9227	10139	11087	12049	12967	13907	14887	15803	16843	17827	18793	19841	20857	21787
45	197	829	1553	2333	3121	3929	4793	5657	6547	7459	8329	9239	10141	11093	12071	12973	13913	14891	15809	16871	17837	18797	19843	20873	21799
46	199	839	1559	2339	3137	3931	4799	5659	6551	7477	8353	9241	10151	11113	12073	12979	13921	14897	15817	16879	17839	18803	19853	20879	21803
47	211	853	1567	2341	3163	3943	4801	5669	6553	7481	8363	9257	10159	11117	12097	12983	13931	14923	15823	16883	17851	18839	19861	20887	21817
48	223	857	1571	2347	3167	3947	4813	5683	6563	7487	8369	9277	10163	11119	12101	13001	13933	14929	15859	16889	17863	18859	19867	20897	21821
49	227	859	1579	2351	3169	3967	4817	5689	6569	7489	8377	9281	10169	11131	12107	13003	13963	14939	15877	16901	17881	18869	19889	20899	21839
50	229	863	1583	2357	3181	3989	4831	5693	6571	7499	8387	9283	10177	11149	12109	13007	13967	14947	15881	16903	17891	18899	19891	20903	21841

PRIMES (continued)

	0	1	2	3	4	5	6	7	8	9	10	11	12	13	14	15	16	17	18	19	20	21	22	23	24
51	233	877	1597	2371	3187	4001	4861	5701	6577	7507	8389	9293	10181	11159	12113	13009	13997	14951	15887	16921	17903	18911	19913	20899	21851
52	239	881	1601	2377	3191	4003	4871	5711	6581	7517	8419	9311	10193	11161	12119	13033	13999	14957	15889	16927	17909	18913	19919	20903	21859
53	241	883	1607	2381	3203	4007	4877	5717	6599	7523	8423	9319	10211	11171	12143	13037	14009	14969	15901	16931	17911	18917	19927	20921	21863
54	251	887	1609	2383	3209	4013	4889	5737	6607	7529	8429	9323	10223	11173	12149	13043	14011	14983	15907	16937	17921	18919	19937	20929	21871
55	257	907	1613	2389	3217	4019	4903	5741	6619	7537	8431	9337	10243	11177	12157	13049	14029	15013	15913	16943	17923	18947	19949	20939	21881
56	263	911	1619	2393	3221	4021	4909	5743	6637	7541	8443	9341	10247	11197	12161	13063	14033	15017	15919	16963	17929	18959	19961	20947	21893
57	269	919	1621	2399	3229	4027	4919	5749	6653	7547	8447	9343	10253	11213	12163	13093	14051	15031	15923	16979	17939	18973	19963	20959	21911
58	271	929	1627	2411	3251	4049	4931	5779	6659	7549	8461	9349	10259	11239	12197	13099	14057	15053	15937	16981	17957	18979	19973	20963	21929
59	277	937	1637	2417	3253	4051	4933	5783	6661	7559	8467	9371	10267	11243	12203	13103	14071	15061	15959	16987	17959	19001	19979	20981	21937
60	281	941	1657	2423	3257	4057	4937	5791	6673	7561	8501	9377	10271	11251	12211	13109	14081	15073	15971	16993	17971	19009	19991	20983	21943
61	283	947	1663	2437	3259	4073	4943	5801	6679	7573	8513	9391	10273	11257	12227	13121	14083	15077	15973	17011	17977	19013	19993	21001	21961
62	293	953	1667	2441	3271	4079	4951	5807	6689	7577	8521	9397	10289	11261	12239	13127	14087	15083	15991	17021	17981	19031	19997	21011	21977
63	307	967	1669	2447	3299	4091	4957	5813	6691	7583	8527	9403	10301	11273	12241	13147	14107	15091	16001	17027	17987	19037	20011	21013	21991
64	311	971	1693	2459	3301	4093	4967	5821	6701	7589	8537	9413	10303	11279	12251	13151	14143	15101	16007	17029	17989	19051	20021	21017	21997
65	313	977	1697	2467	3307	4099	4969	5827	6703	7591	8539	9419	10313	11287	12253	13159	14149	15107	16033	17033	18013	19069	20023	21019	22003
66	317	983	1699	2473	3313	4111	4973	5839	6709	7603	8543	9421	10321	11299	12263	13163	14153	15121	16057	17041	18041	19073	20029	21023	22013
67	331	991	1709	2477	3319	4127	4987	5843	6719	7607	8563	9431	10331	11311	12269	13171	14159	15131	16061	17047	18043	19079	20047	21031	22027
68	337	997	1721	2503	3323	4129	4993	5849	6733	7621	8573	9433	10333	11317	12277	13177	14173	15137	16063	17053	18047	19081	20051	21059	22031
69	347	1009	1723	2521	3329	4133	4999	5851	6737	7639	8581	9437	10337	11321	12281	13183	14177	15139	16067	17077	18049	19087	20063	21061	22037
70	349	1013	1733	2531	3331	4139	5003	5857	6761	7643	8597	9439	10343	11329	12289	13187	14197	15149	16069	17093	18059	19121	20071	21067	22039
71	353	1019	1741	2539	3343	4153	5009	5861	6763	7649	8599	9461	10357	11351	12301	13217	14207	15161	16073	17099	18061	19139	20089	21089	22051
72	359	1021	1747	2543	3347	4157	5011	5867	6779	7669	8609	9463	10369	11353	12323	13219	14221	15173	16087	17107	18077	19141	20101	21101	22063
73	367	1031	1753	2549	3359	4159	5021	5869	6781	7673	8623	9467	10391	11369	12329	13229	14243	15187	16091	17117	18089	19157	20107	21107	22067
74	373	1033	1759	2551	3361	4177	5023	5879	6791	7681	8627	9473	10399	11383	12343	13241	14249	15193	16097	17123	18097	19163	20113	21121	22073
75	379	1039	1777	2557	3371	4201	5039	5881	6793	7687	8629	9479	10427	11393	12347	13249	14251	15199	16103	17137	18119	19181	20117	21139	22079
76	383	1049	1783	2579	3373	4211	5051	5897	6803	7691	8641	9491	10429	11399	12373	13259	14281	15217	16111	17159	18121	19183	20123	21143	22091
77	389	1051	1787	2591	3389	4217	5059	5903	6823	7699	8647	9497	10433	11411	12377	13267	14293	15227	16127	17167	18127	19207	20129	21149	22093
78	397	1061	1789	2593	3391	4219	5077	5923	6827	7703	8663	9511	10453	11423	12379	13291	14303	15233	16139	17183	18131	19211	20143	21157	22109
79	401	1063	1801	2609	3407	4229	5081	5927	6829	7717	8669	9521	10457	11437	12391	13297	14321	15241	16141	17189	18133	19213	20147	21163	22111
80	409	1069	1811	2617	3413	4231	5087	5939	6833	7723	8677	9533	10459	11443	12401	13309	14323	15259	16183	17191	18143	19219	20149	21169	22123
81	419	1087	1823	2621	3433	4241	5099	5953	6841	7727	8681	9539	10463	11447	12409	13313	14327	15263	16187	17203	18149	19231	20161	21179	22129
82	421	1091	1831	2633	3449	4243	5101	5981	6857	7741	8689	9547	10477	11467	12413	13327	14341	15269	16189	17207	18169	19237	20173	21187	22133
83	431	1093	1847	2647	3457	4253	5107	5987	6863	7753	8693	9551	10487	11471	12421	13331	14347	15271	16193	17209	18181	19249	20177	21191	22147
84	433	1097	1861	2657	3461	4259	5113	6007	6869	7757	8699	9587	10499	11483	12433	13337	14369	15277	16217	17231	18191	19259	20183	21193	22153
85	439	1103	1867	2659	3463	4261	5119	6011	6871	7759	8707	9601	10501	11489	12437	13339	14387	15287	16223	17239	18199	19267	20201	21211	22157
86	443	1109	1871	2663	3467	4271	5147	6029	6883	7789	8713	9613	10513	11491	12451	13367	14389	15289	16229	17257	18211	19273	20219	21221	22159
87	449	1117	1873	2671	3469	4273	5153	6037	6899	7793	8719	9619	10529	11497	12457	13381	14401	15299	16231	17291	18217	19289	20231	21227	22171
88	457	1123	1877	2677	3491	4283	5167	6043	6907	7817	8731	9623	10531	11503	12473	13397	14407	15307	16249	17293	18223	19301	20233	21247	22189
89	461	1129	1879	2683	3499	4289	5171	6047	6911	7823	8737	9629	10559	11519	12479	13399	14411	15313	16253	17299	18229	19309	20249	21269	22193
90	463	1151	1889	2687	3511	4297	5179	6053	6917	7829	8741	9631	10567	11527	12487	13411	14419	15319	16267	17317	18233	19319	20261	21277	22229
91	467	1153	1901	2689	3517	4327	5189	6067	6947	7841	8747	9643	10589	11549	12491	13417	14423	15329	16273	17321	18251	19333	20269	21283	22247
92	479	1163	1907	2693	3527	4337	5197	6073	6949	7853	8753	9649	10597	11551	12497	13421	14431	15331	16301	17327	18253	19373	20287	21313	22259
93	487	1171	1913	2699	3529	4339	5209	6079	6959	7867	8761	9661	10601	11579	12503	13441	14437	15349	16319	17333	18257	19379	20297	21317	22271
94	491	1181	1931	2707	3533	4349	5227	6089	6961	7873	8779	9677	10607	11587	12511	13451	14447	15359	16333	17341	18269	19381	20323	21319	22273
95	499	1187	1933	2711	3539	4357	5231	6091	6967	7877	8783	9679	10613	11593	12517	13457	14449	15361	16339	17351	18287	19387	20327	21323	22277
96	503	1193	1949	2713	3541	4363	5233	6101	6971	7879	8803	9689	10627	11597	12527	13463	14461	15373	16349	17359	18289	19391	20333	21341	22279
97	509	1201	1951	2719	3547	4373	5237	6113	6977	7883	8807	9697	10631	11617	12539	13469	14479	15377	16361	17377	18301	19403	20341	21347	22283
98	521	1213	1973	2729	3557	4391	5261	6121	6983	7901	8819	9719	10639	11621	12541	13477	14489	15383	16363	17383	18307	19417	20347	21377	22291
99	523	1217	1979	2731	3559	4397	5273	6131	6991	7907	8821	9721	10651	11633	12547	13487	14503	15391	16369	17387	18311	19421	20353	21379	22303
100	541	1223	1987	2741	3571	4409	5279	6133	6997	7919	8831	9733	10657	11657	12553	13499	14519	15401	16381	17389	18313	19423	20357	21383	22307

PRIMES (continued)

PRIMES (continued)

PRIMES (continued)

	25	26	27	28	29	30	31	32	33	34	35	36	37	38	39	40	41	42	43	44	45	46	47	48	49
1	22343	23327	24317	25409	26407	27457	28513	29453	30649	31607	32611	33617	34651	35771	36787	37831	38923	39979	41113	42083	43063	44203	45317	46451	47533
2	22349	23333	24329	25411	26417	27479	28517	29473	30661	31627	32621	33619	34667	35797	36791	37847	38933	39983	41117	42089	43067	44207	45319	46457	47543
3	22367	23339	24337	25423	26423	27481	28537	29483	30671	31643	32633	33623	34673	35801	36793	37853	38953	39989	41131	42101	43093	44221	45329	46471	47563
4	22369	23357	24359	25439	26431	27487	28541	29501	30677	31649	32647	33629	34679	35803	36809	37861	38959	40009	41141	42131	43103	44249	45337	46477	47569
5	22381	23369	24371	25447	26437	27509	28547	29527	30689	31657	32653	33637	34687	35809	36821	37871	38971	40013	41143	42139	43117	44257	45341	46489	47581
6	22391	23371	24373	25453	26449	27527	28549	29537	30697	31663	32687	33641	34693	35831	36833	37879	38977	40031	41149	42157	43151	44263	45343	46499	47591
7	22399	23399	24379	25457	26459	27529	28559	29567	30703	31667	32693	33647	34703	35837	36847	37889	38993	40037	41161	42169	43159	44267	45361	46507	47599
8	22409	23417	24391	25463	26479	27539	28571	29569	30707	31687	32707	33679	34721	35839	36857	37897	39019	40039	41177	42179	43177	44269	45377	46511	47609
9	22433	23431	24407	25469	26489	27541	28573	29573	30713	31699	32713	33703	34729	35851	36871	37907	39023	40063	41179	42187	43177	44273	45389	46523	47623
10	22441	23447	24413	25471	26497	27551	28579	29581	30727	31721	32717	33713	34739	35863	36877	37951	39041	40087	41183	42193	43189	44279	45403	46549	47629
11	22447	23459	24419	25523	26501	27581	28591	29587	30757	31723	32719	33721	34747	35869	36887	37957	39043	40093	41189	42197	43201	44281	45413	46559	47639
12	22453	23473	24421	25537	26513	27583	28597	29599	30763	31727	32749	33739	34757	35879	36899	37963	39047	40099	41201	42209	43207	44293	45427	46567	47653
13	22469	23497	24439	25541	26539	27611	28603	29611	30773	31729	32771	33749	34759	35897	36901	37967	39079	40111	41203	42221	43223	44351	45433	46573	47657
14	22481	23509	24443	25561	26557	27617	28607	29629	30781	31741	32779	33751	34763	35899	36913	37987	39089	40123	41213	42223	43237	44357	45439	46589	47659
15	22483	23531	24469	25577	26561	27631	28619	29633	30803	31751	32783	33757	34781	35911	36919	37991	39097	40127	41221	42227	43261	44371	45481	46591	47681
16	22501	23537	24473	25579	26573	27647	28621	29641	30809	31769	32789	33767	34807	35923	36923	37993	39103	40129	41227	42239	43271	44381	45491	46601	47699
17	22511	23539	24481	25583	26591	27653	28627	29663	30817	31771	32797	33769	34819	35933	36929	37997	39107	40151	41231	42257	43283	44389	45497	46619	47701
18	22531	23549	24499	25589	26597	27673	28631	29669	30829	31793	32801	33773	34841	35951	36931	38011	39113	40153	41233	42281	43291	44417	45503	46633	47711
19	22541	23557	24509	25601	26627	27689	28643	29671	30839	31799	32803	33791	34843	35963	36943	38039	39119	40163	41243	42283	43313	44449	45523	46639	47713
20	22543	23561	24517	25603	26633	27691	28649	29683	30841	31817	32831	33797	34847	35969	36947	38047	39133	40169	41257	42293	43319	44453	45533	46643	47717
21	22549	23563	24527	25609	26641	27697	28657	29717	30851	31847	32833	33809	34849	35977	36973	38053	39139	40177	41263	42299	43331	44483	45541	46649	47737
22	22567	23567	24533	25621	26647	27701	28661	29723	30853	31849	32839	33811	34871	35983	36979	38069	39157	40189	41269	42307	43391	44491	45553	46663	47741
23	22571	23581	24547	25633	26669	27733	28663	29741	30859	31859	32843	33827	34877	35993	36997	38083	39161	40193	41281	42323	43397	44497	45557	46679	47743
24	22573	23593	24551	25639	26681	27737	28669	29753	30869	31873	32869	33829	34883	35999	37003	38113	39163	40213	41299	42331	43399	44501	45569	46681	47777
25	22613	23599	24571	25643	26683	27739	28687	29759	30871	31883	32887	33851	34897	36007	37013	38119	39181	40231	41333	42337	43403	44507	45587	46687	47779
26	22619	23603	24593	25657	26687	27743	28697	29761	30881	31891	32909	33857	34913	36011	37019	38149	39191	40237	41341	42349	43411	44519	45589	46691	47791
27	22621	23609	24611	25667	26693	27749	28703	29789	30893	31957	32911	33863	34919	36013	37021	38153	39199	40241	41351	42359	43427	44531	45599	46703	47797
28	22637	23623	24623	25673	26699	27751	28711	29803	30911	31963	32917	33871	34939	36017	37039	38167	39209	40253	41357	42373	43441	44533	45613	46723	47807
29	22639	23627	24631	25679	26701	27763	28723	29819	30931	31973	32933	33889	34949	36037	37049	38177	39217	40277	41381	42379	43451	44537	45631	46727	47809
30	22643	23629	24659	25693	26711	27767	28729	29833	30937	31981	32939	33893	34961	36061	37057	38183	39227	40283	41387	42391	43457	44543	45641	46747	47819
31	22651	23633	24671	25703	26713	27773	28751	29837	30941	31991	32941	33911	34963	36067	37061	38189	39229	40289	41389	42397	43481	44549	45659	46751	47837
32	22669	23663	24677	25717	26717	27779	28753	29851	30949	32003	32957	33923	34981	36073	37087	38197	39233	40343	41399	42403	43487	44563	45667	46757	47843
33	22679	23669	24683	25733	26723	27791	28759	29863	30971	32009	32969	33931	35023	36083	37097	38201	39239	40351	41411	42407	43499	44579	45673	46769	47857
34	22691	23671	24691	25741	26729	27793	28771	29867	30977	32027	32971	33937	35027	36097	37117	38219	39241	40357	41413	42409	43517	44587	45677	46771	47869
35	22697	23677	24697	25747	26731	27799	28789	29873	30983	32029	32983	33941	35051	36107	37123	38231	39251	40361	41443	42433	43541	44617	45691	46807	47881
36	22699	23687	24709	25759	26737	27803	28793	29879	31013	32051	32987	33961	35053	36109	37139	38237	39293	40387	41453	42437	43543	44621	45697	46811	47903
37	22709	23689	24733	25763	26759	27809	28807	29881	31019	32057	32993	33967	35059	36131	37159	38239	39301	40423	41467	42443	43573	44623	45707	46817	47911
38	22717	23719	24749	25771	26777	27817	28813	29917	31033	32059	32999	33997	35069	36137	37171	38261	39313	40427	41479	42451	43577	44633	45737	46819	47917
39	22721	23741	24763	25793	26783	27823	28817	29921	31039	32063	33013	34019	35081	36151	37181	38273	39317	40429	41491	42457	43579	44641	45751	46829	47933
40	22727	23743	24767	25799	26801	27827	28837	29927	31051	32069	33023	34031	35083	36161	37189	38281	39341	40433	41507	42461	43591	44647	45757	46831	47939
41	22739	23747	24781	25801	26813	27847	28843	29947	31063	32077	33029	34033	35089	36187	37199	38287	39343	40459	41513	42463	43597	44651	45763	46853	47947
42	22741	23753	24793	25819	26821	27851	28859	29959	31069	32083	33037	34039	35099	36191	37201	38299	39359	40471	41519	42467	43607	44657	45767	46861	47951
43	22751	23761	24799	25841	26833	27883	28867	29983	31079	32089	33049	34057	35107	36209	37217	38303	39367	40483	41521	42473	43609	44683	45779	46867	47963
44	22769	23767	24809	25847	26839	27893	28871	29989	31081	32099	33053	34061	35111	36217	37223	38317	39371	40487	41539	42487	43613	44687	45817	46877	47969
45	22777	23773	24821	25849	26849	27901	28879	29999	31091	32117	33071	34123	35117	36229	37243	38321	39373	40493	41543	42491	43627	44699	45821	46889	47977
46	22783	23789	24841	25867	26861	27917	28901	30011	31121	32119	33073	34127	35129	36241	37253	38327	39383	40499	41549	42499	43633	44701	45823	46901	47981
47	22787	23801	24847	25873	26863	27919	28909	30013	31123	32141	33083	34129	35141	36251	37273	38329	39397	40507	41579	42509	43649	44711	45827	46919	48017
48	22807	23813	24851	25889	26879	27941	28921	30029	31139	32143	33091	34141	35149	36263	37277	38333	39409	40519	41593	42533	43651	44729	45833	46933	48023
49	22811	23819	24859	25903	26881	27943	28927	30047	31147	32159	33107	34147	35153	36269	37307	38351	39419	40529	41597	42557	43661	44741	45841	46957	48029
50	22817	23827	24877	25913	26891	27947	28933	30059	31151	32173	33113	34157	35159	36277	37309	38371	39419	40531	41603	42569	43669	44753	45853	46993	48049

PRIMES (continued)

	25	26	27	28	29	30	31	32	33	34	35	36	37	38	39	40	41	42	43	44	45	46	47	48	49
51	22853	23831	24889	25919	26893	27953	28949	30071	31121	32173	33119	34159	35171	36293	37337	38377	39439	40543	41609	42569	43669	44753	45863	46997	48073
52	22859	23833	24907	25931	26903	27961	28961	30089	31123	32183	33149	34171	35201	36299	37339	38393	39443	40559	41611	42571	43691	44771	45869	47017	48079
53	22861	23857	24911	25933	26921	27967	28979	30091	31139	32189	33151	34183	35221	36307	37357	38431	39451	40577	41617	42577	43711	44773	45887	47041	48091
54	22871	23869	24917	25939	26927	27983	29009	30097	31147	32191	33161	34211	35227	36313	37361	38447	39461	40583	41621	42589	43717	44777	45893	47051	48109
55	22877	23873	24923	25943	26947	27997	29017	30103	31151	32203	33179	34213	35251	36319	37363	38449	39499	40591	41627	42611	43721	44789	45943	47057	48119
56	22901	23879	24943	25951	26951	28001	29021	30109	31153	32213	33181	34217	35257	36341	37369	38453	39503	40597	41641	42641	43759	44797	45949	47059	48121
57	22907	23887	24953	25969	26959	28019	29023	30113	31159	32233	33191	34231	35267	36343	37379	38459	39509	40609	41647	42643	43777	44809	45953	47087	48131
58	22921	23893	24967	25981	26981	28027	29027	30119	31177	32237	33199	34253	35279	36353	37397	38461	39511	40627	41651	42649	43781	44819	45959	47093	48157
59	22937	23899	24971	25997	26987	28031	29033	30133	31181	32251	33203	34259	35281	36373	37409	38501	39521	40637	41659	42667	43783	44839	45971	47111	48163
60	22943	23909	24977	25999	26993	28051	29059	30137	31183	32257	33211	34261	35291	36383	37423	38543	39541	40639	41669	42677	43787	44843	45979	47119	48179
61	22961	23911	24979	26003	27011	28057	29063	30139	31189	32261	33223	34267	35311	36389	37441	38557	39551	40693	41681	42683	43789	44851	45989	47123	48187
62	22963	23917	24989	26017	27017	28069	29077	30161	31193	32297	33247	34273	35317	36433	37447	38561	39563	40697	41687	42689	43793	44867	46021	47129	48193
63	22973	23929	25013	26021	27031	28081	29101	30169	31219	32299	33287	34283	35323	36451	37463	38567	39569	40699	41719	42697	43801	44879	46027	47137	48197
64	22993	23957	25031	26029	27043	28087	29123	30181	31223	32303	33289	34297	35327	36457	37483	38569	39581	40709	41729	42701	43853	44887	46049	47143	48221
65	23003	23971	25033	26041	27059	28097	29129	30187	31231	32309	33301	34301	35339	36467	37489	38593	39607	40739	41737	42703	43867	44893	46051	47147	48239
66	23011	23977	25037	26053	27067	28099	29131	30197	31237	32321	33311	34303	35353	36469	37493	38603	39619	40751	41759	42709	43889	44909	46061	47149	48247
67	23017	23981	25057	26083	27073	28109	29137	30203	31247	32323	33317	34313	35363	36473	37501	38609	39623	40759	41761	42719	43891	44917	46073	47161	48259
68	23021	23993	25073	26099	27077	28111	29147	30211	31253	32327	33329	34319	35381	36479	37507	38611	39631	40763	41771	42727	43913	44927	46091	47189	48271
69	23027	24001	25087	26107	27091	28123	29153	30223	31259	32341	33337	34327	35393	36493	37511	38629	39659	40771	41777	42737	43933	44939	46093	47207	48281
70	23029	24007	25097	26111	27103	28151	29167	30241	31267	32353	33343	34337	35401	36497	37517	38639	39667	40787	41801	42743	43943	44953	46099	47221	48299
71	23039	24019	25111	26113	27107	28163	29173	30253	31271	32359	33347	34351	35407	36523	37529	38651	39671	40801	41809	42751	43951	44959	46103	47237	48311
72	23041	24023	25117	26119	27109	28181	29179	30259	31277	32363	33349	34361	35419	36527	37537	38653	39679	40813	41813	42767	43961	44963	46133	47251	48313
73	23053	24029	25121	26141	27127	28183	29191	30269	31307	32369	33353	34367	35423	36529	37547	38669	39703	40819	41843	42773	43963	44971	46141	47269	48337
74	23057	24043	25127	26153	27143	28201	29201	30271	31319	32371	33359	34369	35437	36541	37549	38671	39709	40823	41849	42787	43969	44983	46147	47279	48341
75	23059	24049	25147	26161	27179	28211	29207	30293	31321	32377	33377	34381	35447	36551	37561	38677	39719	40829	41851	42793	43973	44987	46153	47287	48353
76	23063	24061	25153	26171	27191	28219	29209	30307	31327	32381	33391	34403	35449	36559	37567	38693	39727	40841	41863	42797	43987	45007	46171	47293	48371
77	23071	24071	25163	26177	27197	28229	29221	30313	31333	32401	33403	34421	35461	36563	37571	38699	39733	40847	41879	42821	43991	45013	46181	47297	48383
78	23081	24077	25169	26183	27211	28277	29231	30319	31337	32411	33409	34429	35491	36571	37573	38707	39749	40849	41887	42829	43997	45053	46183	47303	48397
79	23087	24083	25171	26189	27239	28279	29243	30323	31357	32413	33413	34439	35507	36583	37579	38711	39761	40853	41893	42839	44017	45061	46187	47309	48407
80	23099	24091	25183	26203	27241	28283	29251	30341	31379	32423	33427	34457	35509	36587	37589	38713	39769	40867	41897	42841	44021	45077	46199	47317	48409
81	23117	24097	25189	26209	27253	28289	29269	30347	31387	32429	33457	34469	35521	36599	37591	38723	39779	40879	41903	42853	44027	45083	46219	47339	48413
82	23131	24103	25219	26227	27259	28297	29287	30367	31391	32441	33461	34471	35527	36607	37607	38729	39791	40883	41911	42859	44029	45119	46229	47351	48437
83	23143	24107	25229	26237	27271	28307	29297	30389	31393	32443	33469	34483	35531	36629	37619	38737	39799	40897	41927	42863	44041	45121	46237	47353	48449
84	23159	24109	25237	26249	27277	28309	29303	30391	31397	32467	33479	34487	35533	36637	37633	38747	39821	40903	41941	42899	44053	45127	46261	47363	48463
85	23167	24113	25243	26251	27281	28319	29311	30403	31469	32479	33487	34499	35537	36643	37643	38749	39827	40927	41947	42901	44059	45131	46271	47381	48473
86	23173	24121	25247	26261	27283	28349	29327	30427	31477	32491	33493	34501	35543	36677	37649	38767	39829	40933	41953	42923	44071	45137	46273	47387	48479
87	23189	24133	25253	26263	27299	28351	29333	30431	31481	32497	33503	34511	35569	36709	37657	38783	39839	40939	41957	42929	44087	45139	46279	47389	48481
88	23197	24137	25261	26267	27329	28387	29339	30449	31489	32503	33521	34513	35573	36713	37663	38791	39841	40949	41959	42937	44089	45161	46301	47407	48487
89	23201	24151	25301	26293	27337	28393	29347	30467	31511	32507	33529	34519	35591	36721	37691	38803	39847	40961	41969	42943	44101	45179	46307	47417	48491
90	23203	24169	25303	26297	27361	28403	29363	30469	31513	32531	33533	34537	35593	36739	37693	38821	39857	40973	41981	42953	44111	45181	46309	47419	48497
91	23209	24179	25307	26309	27367	28409	29383	30491	31517	32533	33547	34543	35597	36749	37699	38833	39877	40993	41983	42961	44119	45191	46327	47431	48523
92	23227	24181	25309	26317	27397	28411	29387	30493	31531	32537	33563	34549	35603	36761	37717	38839	39883	41011	41999	42967	44123	45197	46337	47441	48527
93	23251	24197	25321	26321	27407	28429	29389	30497	31541	32561	33569	34583	35617	36767	37747	38851	39887	41023	42013	42979	44129	45233	46349	47459	48533
94	23269	24203	25339	26339	27409	28433	29399	30509	31543	32563	33577	34589	35671	36779	37781	38861	39901	41039	42017	42989	44131	45247	46351	47491	48539
95	23279	24223	25343	26347	27427	28439	29401	30517	31547	32569	33581	34591	35677	36781	37783	38867	39929	41047	42019	43003	44159	45259	46381	47497	48541
96	23291	24229	25349	26357	27431	28447	29411	30529	31567	32573	33587	34603	35729	36787	37799	38873	39937	41051	42023	43013	44171	45263	46399	47501	48563
97	23293	24239	25357	26371	27437	28477	29423	30539	31573	32579	33589	34607	35731	36791	37811	38891	39953	41057	42043	43019	44179	45281	46411	47507	48571
98	23297	24247	25367	26387	27449	28493	29429	30553	31583	32587	33599	34613	35747	36793	37813	38903	39971	41077	42061	43037	44189	45289	46439	47513	48589
99	23311	24251	25373	26393	27457	28499	29437	30557	31601	32603	33601	34631	35753	36809	37831	38917	39979	41081	42071	43049	44201	45293	46441	47521	48593
100	23321	24281	25391	26399	27479	28513	29443	30559	31607	32609	33613	34649	35759	36821	37847	38921	39983	41113	42073	43051	44203	45307	46447	47527	48611

PRIMES (continued)

	50	51	52	53	54	55	56	57	58	59	60	61	62	63	64	65	66	67	68	69	70	71	72	73	74
1	48619	49667	50767	51817	52937	54001	55109	56197	57193	58243	59369	60509	61637	62791	63823	65071	66101	67247	68389	69497	70663	71719	72859	73999	75083
2	48623	49669	50773	51827	52951	54011	55117	56207	57203	58271	59377	60521	61643	62801	63839	65089	66109	67261	68399	69499	70667	71741	72869	74017	75109
3	48647	49681	50777	51829	52957	54013	55127	56237	57221	58309	59387	60539	61651	62819	63841	65101	66161	67271	68437	69539	70687	71761	72871	74021	75133
4	48649	49697	50789	51839	52963	54037	55147	56249	57223	58313	59393	60589	61657	62827	63853	65111	66169	67289	68443	69557	70709	71777	72883	74027	75149
5	48661	49711	50821	51853	52967	54049	55163	56263	57241	58321	59399	60601	61667	62851	63857	65119	66173	67307	68449	69623	70717	71789	72889	74047	75161
6	48673	49727	50833	51859	52973	54059	55171	56267	57251	58337	59407	60607	61673	62861	63863	65123	66179	67339	68473	69653	70729	71807	72893	74051	75167
7	48677	49739	50839	51869	52981	54083	55201	56269	57259	58363	59417	60611	61681	62869	63901	65141	66191	67343	68477	69661	70753	71809	72901	74071	75169
8	48679	49741	50849	51871	52999	54091	55207	56299	57269	58367	59419	60617	61687	62873	63907	65147	66221	67349	68483	69677	70769	71821	72907	74077	75181
9	48731	49747	50857	51893	53003	54101	55213	56311	57271	58369	59441	60623	61703	62897	63913	65167	66239	67369	68489	69691	70783	71837	72911	74093	75193
10	48733	49757	50867	51899	53017	54121	55217	56333	57283	58379	59443	60631	61717	62903	63929	65171	66271	67391	68491	69697	70793	71843	72923	74099	75209
11	48751	49783	50873	51907	53047	54133	55219	56359	57287	58391	59447	60637	61723	62921	63949	65173	66293	67399	68501	69709	70823	71849	72931	74101	75211
12	48757	49787	50891	51913	53051	54139	55229	56369	57301	58393	59453	60647	61729	62927	63977	65179	66301	67409	68507	69737	70841	71861	72937	74131	75217
13	48761	49789	50893	51929	53069	54151	55243	56377	57329	58403	59467	60649	61751	62929	63997	65183	66337	67411	68521	69739	70843	71867	72949	74143	75223
14	48767	49801	50909	51941	53077	54163	55249	56383	57331	58411	59471	60659	61757	62939	64007	65203	66343	67421	68531	69761	70849	71879	72953	74149	75227
15	48779	49807	50923	51949	53087	54167	55259	56393	57347	58417	59473	60661	61781	62969	64013	65213	66347	67427	68539	69763	70853	71881	72959	74159	75239
16	48781	49811	50929	51971	53089	54181	55291	56401	57349	58427	59497	60679	61813	62971	64019	65239	66359	67429	68543	69767	70867	71887	72977	74161	75253
17	48787	49823	50951	51977	53093	54193	55313	56417	57367	58439	59509	60689	61819	62981	64033	65257	66361	67433	68567	69779	70877	71899	72997	74167	75269
18	48799	49831	50957	51991	53101	54217	55331	56431	57373	58451	59513	60703	61837	62983	64037	65267	66373	67447	68581	69809	70879	71909	73009	74177	75277
19	48809	49843	50969	52009	53113	54251	55333	56437	57383	58453	59539	60719	61843	62987	64063	65269	66377	67453	68597	69821	70891	71917	73013	74189	75289
20	48817	49853	50971	52021	53117	54269	55337	56443	57389	58477	59557	60727	61861	62989	64067	65287	66383	67477	68611	69827	70901	71933	73019	74197	75307
21	48821	49871	50989	52027	53129	54277	55339	56453	57397	58481	59561	60733	61871	63029	64081	65293	66403	67481	68633	69829	70913	71941	73037	74201	75323
22	48823	49877	51001	52051	53147	54287	55343	56467	57413	58511	59567	60737	61879	63031	64091	65309	66413	67489	68639	69833	70919	71947	73039	74203	75329
23	48847	49891	51031	52057	53149	54293	55351	56473	57427	58537	59581	60757	61909	63059	64109	65323	66431	67493	68659	69847	70921	71963	73043	74209	75337
24	48857	49919	51043	52067	53161	54311	55373	56477	57457	58543	59611	60761	61927	63067	64123	65327	66449	67499	68669	69857	70937	71971	73061	74219	75347
25	48859	49921	51047	52069	53171	54319	55381	56479	57467	58549	59617	60763	61933	63073	64151	65353	66457	67511	68683	69859	70949	71983	73063	74231	75353
26	48869	49927	51059	52081	53173	54323	55399	56489	57487	58567	59621	60779	61949	63079	64153	65357	66463	67523	68687	69877	70951	71987	73079	74257	75367
27	48871	49937	51061	52103	53189	54331	55411	56501	57493	58573	59627	60793	61961	63097	64157	65371	66467	67531	68699	69899	70957	71993	73091	74279	75377
28	48883	49939	51071	52121	53197	54347	55439	56503	57503	58579	59629	60811	61967	63103	64171	65381	66491	67537	68711	69911	70969	71999	73121	74287	75389
29	48889	49943	51109	52127	53201	54361	55441	56509	57527	58601	59651	60821	61979	63113	64187	65393	66499	67547	68713	69929	70979	72019	73127	74293	75391
30	48907	49957	51131	52147	53231	54367	55457	56519	57529	58603	59659	60859	61981	63127	64189	65407	66509	67559	68729	69931	70981	72031	73133	74297	75401
31	48947	49991	51137	52153	53233	54371	55469	56527	57557	58613	59663	60869	61987	63131	64217	65413	66523	67567	68737	69941	70991	72043	73141	74311	75403
32	48953	49993	51151	52163	53257	54377	55487	56531	57559	58631	59669	60887	61991	63149	64223	65419	66529	67577	68743	69959	70997	72047	73181	74317	75407
33	48973	49999	51157	52177	53267	54401	55501	56533	57571	58657	59671	60889	62003	63179	64231	65423	66533	67579	68749	69991	70999	72053	73189	74323	75431
34	48989	50021	51169	52181	53269	54403	55511	56543	57587	58661	59693	60899	62011	63197	64237	65437	66541	67589	68767	69997	71011	72073	73237	74353	75437
35	48991	50023	51193	52183	53279	54409	55529	56569	57593	58679	59699	60901	62017	63199	64271	65447	66553	67601	68771	70001	71023	72077	73243	74357	75479
36	49003	50033	51197	52189	53281	54413	55541	56591	57601	58687	59707	60913	62039	63211	64279	65449	66569	67607	68777	70003	71039	72089	73259	74363	75503
37	49009	50047	51199	52201	53299	54419	55549	56597	57637	58693	59723	60917	62047	63241	64283	65479	66571	67619	68791	70009	71059	72091	73277	74377	75511
38	49019	50051	51203	52223	53309	54421	55579	56599	57641	58699	59729	60919	62053	63247	64301	65497	66587	67631	68813	70019	71069	72101	73291	74381	75521
39	49031	50053	51217	52237	53323	54437	55589	56611	57649	58711	59743	60923	62057	63277	64303	65519	66593	67651	68819	70039	71081	72103	73303	74383	75527
40	49033	50069	51229	52249	53327	54443	55603	56629	57653	58727	59747	60937	62081	63281	64319	65521	66601	67679	68821	70051	71089	72109	73309	74411	75533
41	49037	50077	51239	52253	53353	54449	55609	56633	57667	58733	59753	60943	62099	63299	64327	65537	66617	67699	68863	70061	71119	72139	73327	74413	75539
42	49043	50087	51241	52259	53359	54469	55619	56659	57679	58741	59771	60953	62119	63311	64333	65543	66629	67709	68879	70067	71129	72161	73331	74419	75541
43	49057	50093	51257	52267	53377	54493	55621	56663	57689	58757	59779	60961	62129	63313	64373	65551	66643	67723	68891	70079	71143	72167	73351	74441	75553
44	49069	50101	51263	52289	53381	54497	55631	56671	57697	58763	59791	61001	62131	63317	64381	65557	66653	67733	68897	70099	71147	72169	73361	74449	75557
45	49081	50111	51283	52291	53401	54499	55633	56681	57709	58771	59797	61007	62137	63331	64399	65563	66683	67741	68899	70111	71153	72173	73363	74453	75571
46	49103	50119	51287	52301	53407	54503	55639	56687	57713	58787	59809	61027	62141	63337	64403	65579	66697	67751	68903	70117	71161	72211	73369	74471	75577
47	49109	50123	51307	52313	53411	54517	55661	56701	57719	58789	59833	61031	62171	63347	64433	65581	66701	67757	68909	70121	71167	72221	73379	74489	75583
48	49117	50129	51329	52321	53419	54521	55663	56711	57727	58831	59863	61043	62189	63353	64439	65587	66713	67759	68917	70123	71171	72223	73387	74507	75611
49	49121	50131	51341	52361	53437	54539	55667	56713	57731	58889	59879	61051	62207	63361	64451	65599	66721	67763	68927	70139	71191	72227	73417	74509	75617
50	49123	50147	51343	52363	53441	54541	55673	56731	57737	58897	59887	61057	62213	63367	64453	65609	66733	67777	68947	70141	71209	72229	73421	74521	75619

PRIMES (continued)

	50	51	52	53	54	55	56	57	58	59	60	61	62	63	64	65	66	67	68	69	70	71	72	73	74
51	49139	50153	51341	52363	53453	54547	55681	56711	57751	58897	59921	61051	62191	63377	64483	65587	66733	67777	68927	70141	71233	72251	73421	74527	75629
52	49157	50159	51343	52369	53479	54559	55691	56713	57773	58901	59929	61057	62201	63389	64489	65599	66739	67783	68947	70157	71237	72253	73433	74531	75641
53	49169	50177	51347	52379	53503	54563	55697	56731	57781	58907	59951	61091	62207	63391	64499	65609	66749	67789	68963	70163	71249	72269	73453	74551	75653
54	49171	50207	51361	52387	53507	54577	55711	56737	57787	58909	59957	61099	62213	63397	64513	65617	66751	67801	68993	70177	71257	72271	73459	74561	75659
55	49177	50221	51383	52391	53527	54581	55717	56747	57791	58913	59971	61121	62219	63409	64553	65629	66763	67807	69001	70181	71261	72277	73471	74567	75679
56	49193	50231	51407	52433	53549	54583	55727	56767	57793	58921	59981	61129	62233	63419	64567	65647	66767	67819	69011	70183	71263	72287	73477	74573	75683
57	49199	50261	51413	52453	53551	54601	55731	56773	57803	58937	59999	61141	62273	63421	64577	65651	66797	67829	69019	70199	71287	72307	73483	74587	75689
58	49201	50263	51419	52457	53569	54617	55733	56779	57809	58943	60013	61151	62297	63439	64579	65657	66809	67843	69029	70201	71293	72313	73517	74597	75703
59	49207	50273	51421	52489	53591	54623	55739	56783	57829	58963	60017	61153	62299	63443	64591	65677	66821	67853	69031	70207	71317	72337	73523	74609	75707
60	49211	50287	51427	52501	53593	54629	55763	56807	57839	58967	60029	61169	62303	63463	64601	65687	66841	67867	69061	70223	71327	72341	73529	74611	75709
61	49223	50291	51431	52511	53597	54631	55787	56813	57847	58979	60037	61211	62311	63467	64609	65699	66851	67883	69067	70229	71329	72353	73547	74623	75721
62	49253	50311	51437	52517	53609	54647	55793	56821	57853	58991	60041	61223	62323	63473	64613	65707	66853	67891	69073	70237	71333	72367	73553	74653	75731
63	49261	50321	51439	52529	53611	54667	55799	56827	57859	58997	60077	61231	62327	63487	64621	65713	66863	67901	69109	70241	71339	72379	73561	74687	75743
64	49277	50329	51449	52541	53617	54673	55807	56843	57881	59009	60083	61253	62347	63493	64627	65717	66877	67927	69119	70249	71341	72383	73571	74699	75767
65	49279	50333	51461	52543	53623	54679	55813	56857	57899	59011	60089	61261	62351	63499	64633	65719	66883	67931	69127	70271	71347	72421	73583	74707	75773
66	49297	50341	51473	52553	53629	54709	55817	56873	57901	59021	60091	61283	62383	63521	64661	65729	66889	67933	69143	70289	71353	72431	73589	74713	75781
67	49307	50359	51479	52561	53633	54713	55819	56891	57917	59023	60101	61291	62401	63527	64663	65731	66919	67939	69149	70297	71359	72461	73597	74717	75787
68	49331	50377	51481	52567	53639	54721	55823	56897	57923	59029	60103	61297	62417	63533	64667	65761	66923	67943	69151	70309	71363	72467	73607	74719	75793
69	49333	50383	51487	52571	53651	54727	55829	56909	57943	59051	60107	61331	62423	63541	64679	65777	66931	67957	69163	70313	71387	72469	73609	74729	75797
70	49339	50387	51503	52579	53657	54751	55837	56911	57947	59053	60127	61333	62459	63559	64693	65789	66943	67961	69191	70321	71389	72481	73613	74731	75821
71	49363	50411	51511	52583	53681	54767	55843	56923	57973	59063	60133	61339	62467	63577	64709	65809	66947	67967	69193	70327	71399	72493	73637	74747	75833
72	49367	50417	51517	52609	53693	54773	55849	56929	57977	59069	60139	61343	62477	63587	64717	65827	66949	67979	69197	70351	71411	72497	73643	74759	75853
73	49369	50423	51521	52627	53699	54779	55871	56941	57991	59077	60149	61357	62483	63589	64747	65831	66959	67987	69203	70373	71413	72503	73651	74761	75869
74	49391	50441	51539	52639	53717	54787	55889	56957	58013	59083	60161	61363	62497	63599	64763	65837	66973	67993	69221	70379	71419	72533	73673	74771	75883
75	49393	50459	51551	52667	53719	54799	55897	56963	58027	59093	60167	61379	62501	63601	64781	65839	66977	68023	69233	70381	71429	72547	73679	74779	75913
76	49409	50461	51563	52673	53731	54829	55901	56983	58031	59107	60169	61381	62507	63607	64783	65843	67003	68041	69239	70393	71437	72551	73681	74797	75931
77	49411	50497	51577	52691	53759	54833	55903	56989	58043	59113	60209	61403	62533	63611	64793	65851	67021	68053	69247	70423	71443	72559	73693	74821	75937
78	49417	50503	51581	52697	53773	54851	55921	56993	58049	59119	60217	61409	62539	63617	64811	65867	67033	68059	69257	70429	71453	72577	73699	74827	75941
79	49429	50513	51593	52709	53777	54869	55927	57037	58057	59123	60223	61417	62549	63629	64817	65881	67043	68071	69259	70439	71471	72613	73709	74831	75967
80	49433	50527	51599	52711	53783	54877	55931	57041	58061	59141	60251	61441	62563	63647	64849	65899	67049	68087	69263	70451	71473	72617	73721	74843	75979
81	49451	50539	51607	52721	53791	54881	55933	57047	58067	59149	60259	61463	62581	63649	64853	65921	67057	68099	69313	70457	71479	72623	73727	74857	75983
82	49459	50549	51613	52727	53813	54907	55949	57059	58073	59159	60271	61469	62591	63659	64871	65927	67061	68111	69317	70459	71483	72643	73751	74861	75989
83	49463	50551	51631	52733	53819	54917	55967	57073	58099	59167	60289	61471	62597	63667	64877	65929	67073	68113	69337	70481	71503	72647	73757	74869	75991
84	49477	50581	51637	52747	53831	54919	55987	57089	58109	59183	60293	61483	62603	63671	64879	65951	67079	68141	69341	70487	71527	72649	73771	74873	75997
85	49481	50587	51647	52757	53849	54941	55997	57097	58111	59197	60317	61487	62617	63689	64891	65957	67103	68147	69371	70489	71537	72661	73783	74887	76001
86	49499	50591	51659	52769	53857	54949	56003	57107	58129	59207	60331	61493	62627	63691	64901	65963	67121	68161	69379	70501	71549	72671	73819	74891	76003
87	49523	50599	51673	52783	53861	54959	56009	57119	58147	59219	60337	61507	62633	63697	64919	65981	67129	68171	69383	70507	71551	72673	73823	74897	76031
88	49529	50627	51679	52807	53881	54973	56039	57131	58151	59221	60343	61511	62639	63703	64921	65983	67139	68207	69389	70529	71563	72679	73847	74903	76039
89	49531	50647	51683	52813	53887	54979	56041	57139	58153	59233	60353	61519	62653	63709	64927	65993	67141	68209	69401	70537	71569	72689	73849	74923	76079
90	49537	50651	51691	52817	53891	54983	56053	57143	58169	59239	60373	61543	62659	63719	64937	65983	67153	68213	69403	70549	71593	72701	73859	74929	76081
91	49547	50671	51713	52837	53897	55001	56081	57149	58171	59243	60383	61547	62683	63727	64951	65993	67157	68219	69427	70571	71597	72707	73867	74933	76091
92	49549	50683	51719	52859	53899	55009	56087	57163	58189	59263	60397	61553	62687	63737	64969	66029	67169	68227	69431	70573	71633	72719	73877	74941	76099
93	49559	50707	51721	52861	53917	55021	56093	57173	58193	59273	60413	61559	62701	63743	64997	66037	67181	68239	69439	70583	71647	72727	73883	74959	76103
94	49597	50723	51749	52879	53923	55049	56099	57179	58199	59281	60427	61561	62723	63761	65003	66041	67187	68261	69457	70589	71663	72733	73897	75011	76123
95	49603	50741	51767	52889	53927	55051	56101	57191	58207	59333	60443	61583	62731	63773	65011	66067	67189	68279	69463	70607	71671	72739	73907	75013	76129
96	49613	50753	51769	52901	53939	55057	56113	57149	58211	59341	60449	61603	62743	63781	65027	66071	67211	68281	69467	70619	71693	72763	73939	75017	76147
97	49627	50707	51787	52903	53951	55061	56123	57163	58217	59351	60457	61609	62753	63793	65029	66083	67213	68311	69473	70621	71699	72767	73943	75029	76157
98	49633	50723	51797	52919	53959	55073	56131	57173	58229	59357	60493	61613	62761	63803	65033	66089	67217	68329	69481	70627	71707	72797	73951	75037	76159
99	49639	50741	51803	52903	53987	55079	56149	57179	58231	59359	60497	61627	62773	63809	65053	66103	67219	68351	69491	70639	71711	72817	73961	75041	76163
100	49663	50753	51803	52919	53993	55103	56179	57191	58237	59359	60497	61631	62773	63809	65063	66103	67231	68371	69493	70657	71713	72823	73973	75079	76207

PRIMES (continued)

PRIMES (continued)

	75	76	77	78	79	80	81	82	83	84	85	86	87	88	89	90	91	92	93	94	95
1	76213	77359	78487	79627	80737	81817	82903	84131	85243	86381	87557	88807	89867	90989	92177	93187	94351	95443	96587	97829	98953
2	76231	77369	78497	79631	80747	81839	82913	84137	85247	86389	87559	88811	89891	90997	92179	93199	94379	95461	96589	97841	98963
3	76243	77377	78509	79633	80749	81847	82939	84143	85259	86399	87583	88813	89897	91009	92189	93229	94397	95467	96601	97843	98981
4	76249	77383	78511	79657	80761	81853	82963	84163	85297	86413	87587	88817	89899	91019	92203	93239	94399	95471	96643	97847	98993
5	76253	77417	78517	79669	80777	81869	82981	84179	85303	86423	87589	88819	89909	91033	92219	93241	94421	95479	96661	97849	98999
6	76259	77419	78539	79687	80779	81883	82997	84181	85313	86441	87613	88843	89917	91079	92221	93251	94427	95483	96667	97859	99013
7	76261	77431	78541	79691	80783	81899	83003	84191	85331	86453	87623	88853	89923	91081	92227	93253	94433	95507	96671	97861	99017
8	76283	77447	78553	79693	80789	81901	83009	84199	85333	86461	87629	88861	89939	91097	92233	93257	94439	95527	96697	97871	99023
9	76289	77471	78569	79697	80803	81919	83023	84211	85361	86467	87631	88867	89959	91099	92237	93263	94441	95531	96703	97879	99041
10	76303	77477	78571	79699	80809	81929	83047	84221	85363	86477	87641	88873	89963	91121	92243	93281	94447	95539	96731	97883	99053
11	76333	77479	78577	79757	80819	81931	83059	84223	85369	86491	87643	88883	89977	91127	92251	93283	94463	95549	96737	97919	99079
12	76343	77489	78583	79769	80831	81937	83063	84229	85381	86501	87649	88897	89983	91139	92269	93287	94477	95561	96739	97927	99083
13	76367	77491	78593	79777	80833	81943	83071	84239	85411	86509	87671	88903	89989	91141	92297	93307	94483	95569	96749	97931	99089
14	76369	77509	78607	79801	80849	81953	83077	84247	85427	86531	87679	88919	90001	91151	92311	93319	94513	95581	96757	97943	99103
15	76379	77513	78623	79811	80863	81967	83089	84263	85429	86533	87683	88937	90007	91153	92317	93323	94529	95597	96763	97961	99109
16	76387	77521	78643	79813	80897	81971	83093	84299	85439	86539	87691	88951	90011	91159	92333	93329	94531	95603	96769	97967	99119
17	76403	77527	78649	79817	80909	81973	83101	84307	85447	86561	87697	88969	90017	91163	92347	93337	94541	95617	96779	97973	99131
18	76421	77543	78653	79823	80911	82003	83117	84313	85451	86573	87701	88993	90019	91183	92353	93371	94543	95621	96787	97987	99133
19	76423	77549	78691	79829	80917	82007	83137	84317	85453	86579	87719	88997	90023	91193	92357	93377	94547	95629	96797	98009	99137
20	76441	77551	78697	79841	80923	82009	83177	84319	85469	86587	87721	89003	90031	91199	92363	93383	94559	95633	96799	98011	99139
21	76463	77557	78707	79843	80929	82013	83203	84347	85487	86599	87739	89009	90053	91229	92369	93407	94561	95651	96821	98017	99149
22	76471	77563	78713	79847	80933	82021	83207	84349	85513	86627	87743	89017	90059	91237	92377	93419	94573	95701	96823	98041	99173
23	76481	77569	78721	79861	80953	82031	83219	84377	85517	86629	87751	89021	90067	91243	92381	93427	94583	95707	96827	98047	99181
24	76487	77573	78737	79867	80963	82037	83221	84389	85523	86677	87767	89041	90071	91249	92383	93463	94597	95713	96847	98057	99191
25	76493	77587	78779	79873	80989	82039	83227	84391	85531	86689	87793	89051	90073	91253	92387	93479	94603	95717	96851	98081	99223
26	76507	77591	78781	79889	81001	82051	83231	84401	85549	86693	87797	89057	90089	91283	92399	93481	94613	95723	96857	98101	99233
27	76511	77611	78787	79901	81013	82067	83233	84407	85571	86711	87803	89069	90107	91291	92401	93487	94621	95731	96893	98123	99241
28	76519	77617	78791	79903	81017	82073	83243	84421	85577	86719	87811	89071	90121	91297	92413	93491	94649	95737	96907	98129	99251
29	76537	77621	78797	79907	81019	82129	83257	84431	85597	86729	87833	89083	90127	91303	92419	93493	94651	95747	96911	98143	99257
30	76541	77641	78803	79939	81023	82139	83267	84437	85601	86743	87853	89087	90149	91309	92431	93497	94687	95773	96931	98179	99259
31	76543	77647	78809	79943	81031	82141	83269	84443	85607	86753	87869	89101	90163	91331	92459	93503	94693	95783	96953	98207	99277
32	76561	77659	78823	79967	81041	82153	83273	84449	85619	86767	87877	89107	90173	91367	92461	93523	94709	95789	96959	98213	99289
33	76579	77681	78839	79973	81043	82163	83299	84457	85621	86771	87881	89113	90187	91369	92467	93529	94723	95791	96973	98221	99317
34	76597	77687	78853	79979	81047	82171	83311	84463	85627	86783	87887	89119	90191	91373	92479	93553	94727	95801	96979	98227	99347
35	76603	77689	78857	79987	81049	82183	83339	84467	85639	86813	87911	89123	90197	91381	92489	93557	94747	95803	96989	98251	99349
36	76607	77699	78877	79997	81071	82189	83341	84481	85643	86837	87917	89137	90199	91387	92503	93559	94771	95813	96997	98257	99367
37	76631	77711	78887	79999	81077	82193	83357	84499	85661	86843	87931	89153	90203	91397	92507	93563	94777	95819	97001	98269	99371
38	76649	77713	78893	80021	81083	82207	83383	84503	85667	86851	87943	89189	90217	91411	92551	93581	94781	95857	97003	98297	99377
39	76651	77719	78901	80039	81097	82217	83389	84509	85669	86857	87959	89203	90227	91423	92557	93601	94789	95869	97007	98299	99391
40	76667	77723	78919	80051	81101	82219	83399	84521	85691	86861	87961	89209	90239	91433	92567	93607	94793	95873	97021	98317	99397
41	76673	77731	78929	80071	81119	82223	83401	84523	85703	86869	87973	89213	90247	91453	92569	93629	94811	95881	97039	98321	99401
42	76679	77743	78941	80077	81131	82231	83407	84533	85711	86923	87977	89227	90263	91457	92581	93637	94819	95891	97073	98323	99409
43	76697	77747	78977	80107	81157	82237	83417	84551	85717	86927	87991	89231	90271	91463	92593	93683	94823	95911	97081	98327	99431
44	76717	77761	78979	80111	81163	82241	83423	84559	85733	86929	88001	89237	90281	91493	92623	93701	94837	95917	97103	98347	99439
45	76733	77773	78989	80141	81173	82261	83431	84589	85751	86939	88003	89261	90289	91499	92627	93703	94841	95923	97117	98369	99469
46	76753	77783	79031	80147	81181	82267	83437	84629	85781	86951	88007	89269	90313	91513	92639	93719	94847	95929	97127	98377	99487
47	76757	77797	79039	80149	81197	82279	83443	84631	85793	86959	88019	89273	90353	91529	92641	93739	94849	95947	97151	98387	99497
48	76771	77801	79043	80153	81199	82301	83449	84649	85817	86969	88037	89293	90359	91541	92647	93761	94873	95957	97157	98389	99523
49	76777	77813	79063	80167	81203	82307	83459	84653	85819	86981	88069	89303	90371	91571	92657	93763	94889	95959	97159	98407	99527
50	76781	77839	79087	80173	81223	82339	83471	84659	85829	86993	88079	89317	90373	91573	92669	93787	94903	95971	97169	98411	99529

PRIMES (continued)

	75	76	77	78	79	80	81	82	83	84	85	86	87	88	89	90	91	92	93	94	95
51	76801	77849	79087	80177	81233	82349	83477	84673	85831	87011	88093	89329	90377	91541	92671	93809	94907	95987	97171	98419	99551
52	76819	77863	79111	80191	81239	82351	83497	84691	85837	87013	88117	89363	90397	91571	92681	93811	94933	95989	97177	98429	99559
53	76829	77867	79133	80207	81281	82361	83537	84697	85843	87037	88129	89381	90401	91573	92683	93827	94949	96001	97187	98443	99563
54	76831	77893	79139	80209	81283	82373	83557	84701	85847	87041	88169	89387	90403	91577	92693	93851	94951	96013	97213	98453	99571
55	76837	77899	79147	80221	81293	82387	83561	84713	85853	87049	88177	89399	90407	91583	92699	93871	94961	96017	97231	98459	99577
56	76847	77929	79151	80231	81299	82393	83563	84719	85889	87071	88211	89413	90437	91591	92707	93887	94993	96043	97241	98467	99581
57	76871	77933	79153	80233	81307	82421	83579	84731	85903	87083	88223	89417	90439	91621	92717	93889	94999	96053	97259	98473	99607
58	76873	77951	79159	80239	81331	82457	83591	84737	85909	87103	88237	89431	90469	91631	92723	93893	95003	96059	97283	98479	99611
59	76883	77969	79181	80251	81343	82463	83597	84751	85931	87107	88241	89443	90473	91639	92737	93901	95009	96079	97301	98491	99623
60	76907	77977	79187	80263	81349	82469	83609	84761	85933	87119	88259	89449	90481	91673	92753	93911	95021	96097	97303	98507	99643
61	76913	77983	79193	80273	81353	82471	83617	84787	85991	87121	88261	89459	90499	91691	92761	93913	95027	96137	97327	98519	99661
62	76919	77999	79201	80279	81359	82483	83621	84793	85999	87133	88301	89477	90511	91703	92767	93923	95063	96149	97367	98533	99667
63	76943	78007	79229	80287	81371	82487	83639	84809	86011	87149	88321	89491	90523	91711	92779	93937	95071	96157	97369	98543	99679
64	76949	78017	79231	80309	81373	82493	83641	84811	86017	87151	88327	89501	90527	91733	92789	93941	95083	96167	97373	98561	99689
65	76961	78031	79241	80317	81401	82499	83653	84827	86027	87179	88337	89513	90529	91753	92791	93949	95087	96179	97379	98563	99707
66	76963	78041	79259	80329	81409	82507	83663	84857	86029	87181	88339	89519	90533	91757	92801	93967	95089	96181	97381	98573	99709
67	76991	78049	79273	80341	81421	82529	83689	84859	86069	87187	88379	89521	90547	91771	92809	93971	95093	96199	97387	98597	99713
68	77003	78059	79279	80347	81439	82531	83701	84869	86077	87211	88397	89527	90583	91801	92821	93979	95101	96211	97397	98621	99719
69	77017	78079	79283	80363	81457	82549	83717	84871	86083	87221	88411	89533	90599	91807	92831	93983	95107	96221	97423	98627	99721
70	77023	78101	79301	80369	81463	82559	83719	84913	86111	87223	88423	89561	90619	91811	92849	93997	95111	96223	97429	98639	99733
71	77029	78121	79309	80387	81509	82561	83737	84919	86113	87251	88427	89563	90631	91813	92857	94007	95131	96233	97441	98641	99761
72	77041	78137	79319	80407	81517	82567	83761	84947	86117	87253	88463	89567	90647	91823	92861	94021	95143	96259	97453	98663	99767
73	77047	78157	79333	80429	81527	82571	83773	84961	86131	87257	88469	89591	90659	91837	92863	94039	95153	96263	97459	98669	99787
74	77069	78163	79337	80447	81533	82591	83777	84967	86137	87277	88471	89597	90677	91841	92867	94043	95177	96269	97463	98689	99793
75	77081	78167	79349	80449	81547	82601	83791	84977	86143	87281	88493	89599	90679	91867	92893	94057	95189	96281	97499	98711	99809
76	77093	78173	79357	80471	81551	82609	83813	84979	86161	87293	88499	89603	90697	91873	92899	94063	95191	96289	97501	98713	99817
77	77101	78179	79367	80473	81553	82613	83833	84991	86171	87299	88513	89611	90703	91909	92921	94079	95203	96293	97511	98717	99823
78	77137	78191	79379	80489	81559	82619	83843	85009	86179	87313	88523	89627	90709	91921	92927	94099	95213	96323	97523	98729	99829
79	77141	78193	79393	80491	81563	82633	83857	85021	86183	87317	88547	89633	90731	91939	92941	94109	95219	96329	97547	98731	99833
80	77153	78203	79397	80513	81569	82651	83869	85027	86197	87323	88589	89653	90749	91943	92951	94111	95231	96331	97549	98737	99839
81	77167	78229	79411	80527	81611	82657	83873	85037	86201	87337	88591	89657	90787	91951	92957	94117	95233	96337	97553	98773	99859
82	77171	78233	79423	80537	81619	82699	83891	85049	86209	87359	88607	89659	90793	91957	92959	94121	95239	96353	97561	98779	99871
83	77191	78241	79427	80557	81629	82721	83903	85061	86239	87383	88609	89669	90803	91961	92987	94151	95257	96377	97571	98801	99877
84	77201	78259	79433	80567	81637	82723	83911	85081	86243	87403	88643	89671	90821	91967	92993	94153	95261	96401	97577	98809	99881
85	77213	78277	79451	80599	81647	82727	83921	85087	86249	87407	88651	89681	90823	91969	93001	94169	95267	96419	97579	98837	99901
86	77237	78283	79481	80603	81649	82729	83933	85091	86257	87421	88657	89689	90833	91997	93047	94201	95273	96431	97583	98849	99907
87	77239	78301	79493	80611	81667	82757	83939	85093	86263	87427	88661	89753	90841	92003	93053	94207	95279	96443	97607	98867	99923
88	77243	78307	79531	80621	81671	82759	83969	85103	86269	87433	88663	89759	90847	92009	93059	94219	95287	96451	97609	98869	99929
89	77249	78311	79537	80627	81677	82763	83983	85109	86287	87443	88667	89767	90863	92033	93077	94229	95311	96457	97613	98873	99961
90	77261	78317	79549	80629	81689	82781	83987	85121	86291	87473	88681	89779	90887	92041	93083	94253	95317	96461	97649	98887	99971
91	77263	78341	79559	80651	81701	82787	84011	85133	86293	87481	88721	89783	90901	92051	93089	94261	95327	96469	97651	98893	99989
92	77269	78347	79561	80657	81703	82799	84017	85147	86297	87491	88729	89797	90907	92077	93097	94273	95339	96479	97673	98897	99991
93	77279	78367	79579	80669	81707	82811	84047	85159	86311	87509	88741	89809	90911	92083	93103	94291	95369	96487	97687	98899	
94	77291	78401	79589	80671	81727	82813	84053	85193	86323	87511	88747	89819	90917	92107	93113	94307	95383	96493	97711	98909	
95	77317	78427	79601	80677	81737	82837	84059	85199	86341	87517	88771	89821	90931	92119	93131	94309	95393	96497	97729	98911	
96	77323	78437	79609	80681	81749	82847	84061	85201	86351	87523	88789	89833	90947	92143	93133	94321	95401	96517	97771	98927	
97	77339	78439	79613	80683	81761	82883	84067	85213	86353	87539	88793	89839	90971	92153	93139	94327	95413	96527	97777	98929	
98	77347	78467	79621	80687	81769	82889	84089	85223	86357	87541	88799	89849	90977	92173	93151	94331	95419	96553	97787	98939	
99	77351	78479		80701	81773	82891	84121	85229	86369	87547	88801				93169	94343	95429	96557	97789	98947	
100				80713	81799		84127	85237	86371	87553					93179	94349	95441	96581	97813		

FACTORS AND PRIMES

This table presents the prime factors of all factorable numbers and the mantissas of the common logarithms of all prime numbers from 1 to 2,000. The table runs across two facing pages. Thus, the factors of 258 are found on a line with 25 and under vertical column 8 to be $2 \cdot 3 \cdot 43$. If n is prime, the mantissa of its common logarithm is given. If n is not prime its prime factors are given.

n	0	1	2	3	4
0	....	0000000	3010300	4771213	2^3
1	$2 \cdot 5$	0413927	$2^3 \cdot 3$	1139434	$2 \cdot 7$
2	$2^3 \cdot 5$	$3 \cdot 7$	$2 \cdot 11$	3617278	$2^3 \cdot 3$
3	$2 \cdot 3 \cdot 5$	4913617	2^6	$3 \cdot 11$	$2 \cdot 17$
4	$2^3 \cdot 5$	6127839	$2 \cdot 3 \cdot 7$	6334685	$2^3 \cdot 11$
5	$2 \cdot 5^2$	$3 \cdot 17$	$2^3 \cdot 13$	7242759	$2 \cdot 3^3$
6	$2^3 \cdot 3 \cdot 5$	7853298	$2 \cdot 31$	$3^3 \cdot 7$	2^6
7	$2 \cdot 5 \cdot 7$	8512583	$2^3 \cdot 3^3$	8633229	$2 \cdot 37$
8	$2^4 \cdot 5$	3^4	$2 \cdot 41$	9190781	$2^3 \cdot 3 \cdot 7$
9	$2 \cdot 3^3 \cdot 5$	$7 \cdot 13$	$2^3 \cdot 23$	$3 \cdot 31$	$2 \cdot 47$
10	$2^3 \cdot 5^2$	0043214	$2 \cdot 3 \cdot 17$	0128372	$2^3 \cdot 13$
11	$2 \cdot 5 \cdot 11$	$3 \cdot 37$	$2^4 \cdot 7$	0530784	$2 \cdot 3 \cdot 19$
12	$2^3 \cdot 3 \cdot 5$	11^2	$2 \cdot 61$	$3 \cdot 41$	$2^3 \cdot 31$
13	$2 \cdot 5 \cdot 13$	1172713	$2^3 \cdot 3 \cdot 11$	$7 \cdot 19$	$2 \cdot 67$
14	$2^3 \cdot 5 \cdot 7$	$3 \cdot 47$	$2 \cdot 71$	$11 \cdot 13$	$2^4 \cdot 3^3$
15	$2 \cdot 3 \cdot 5^2$	1789769	$2^3 \cdot 19$	$3^3 \cdot 17$	$2 \cdot 7 \cdot 11$
16	$2^6 \cdot 5$	$7 \cdot 23$	$2 \cdot 3^4$	2121876	$2^3 \cdot 41$
17	$2 \cdot 5 \cdot 17$	$3^3 \cdot 19$	$2^3 \cdot 43$	2380461	$2 \cdot 3 \cdot 29$
18	$2^3 \cdot 3^3 \cdot 5$	2576786	$2 \cdot 7 \cdot 13$	$3 \cdot 61$	$2^3 \cdot 23$
19	$2 \cdot 5 \cdot 19$	2810334	$2^6 \cdot 3$	2855573	$2 \cdot 97$
20	$2^3 \cdot 5^2$	$3 \cdot 67$	$2 \cdot 101$	$7 \cdot 29$	$2^3 \cdot 3 \cdot 17$
21	$2 \cdot 3 \cdot 5 \cdot 7$	3242825	$2^3 \cdot 53$	$3 \cdot 71$	$2 \cdot 107$
22	$2^3 \cdot 5 \cdot 11$	$13 \cdot 17$	$2 \cdot 3 \cdot 37$	3483049	$2^6 \cdot 7$
23	$2 \cdot 5 \cdot 23$	$3 \cdot 7 \cdot 11$	$2^3 \cdot 29$	3673559	$2 \cdot 3^3 \cdot 13$
24	$2^4 \cdot 3 \cdot 5$	3820170	$2 \cdot 11^2$	3^5	$2^3 \cdot 61$
25	$2 \cdot 5^3$	3996737	$2^3 \cdot 3^3 \cdot 7$	$11 \cdot 23$	$2 \cdot 127$
26	$2^3 \cdot 5 \cdot 13$	$3^3 \cdot 29$	$2 \cdot 131$	4199557	$2^3 \cdot 3 \cdot 11$
27	$2 \cdot 3^3 \cdot 5$	4329693	$2^4 \cdot 17$	$3 \cdot 7 \cdot 13$	$2 \cdot 137$
28	$2^3 \cdot 5 \cdot 7$	4487063	$2 \cdot 3 \cdot 47$	4517864	$2^3 \cdot 71$
29	$2 \cdot 5 \cdot 29$	$3 \cdot 97$	$2^3 \cdot 73$	4668676	$2 \cdot 3 \cdot 7^3$
30	$2^3 \cdot 3 \cdot 5^2$	$7 \cdot 43$	$2 \cdot 151$	$3 \cdot 101$	$2^4 \cdot 19$
31	$2 \cdot 5 \cdot 31$	4927604	$2^3 \cdot 3 \cdot 13$	4955443	$2 \cdot 157$
32	$2^6 \cdot 5$	$3 \cdot 107$	$2 \cdot 7 \cdot 23$	$17 \cdot 19$	$2^3 \cdot 3^4$
33	$2 \cdot 3 \cdot 5 \cdot 11$	5198280	$2^3 \cdot 83$	$3^3 \cdot 37$	$2 \cdot 167$
34	$2^3 \cdot 5 \cdot 17$	$11 \cdot 31$	$2 \cdot 3^3 \cdot 19$	7^3	$2^3 \cdot 43$
35	$2 \cdot 5^2 \cdot 7$	$3^3 \cdot 13$	$2^4 \cdot 11$	5477747	$2 \cdot 3 \cdot 59$
36	$2^3 \cdot 3^3 \cdot 5$	19^2	$2 \cdot 181$	$3 \cdot 11^2$	$2^3 \cdot 7 \cdot 13$
37	$2 \cdot 5 \cdot 37$	$7 \cdot 53$	$2^3 \cdot 3 \cdot 31$	5717088	$2 \cdot 11 \cdot 17$
38	$2^3 \cdot 5 \cdot 19$	$3 \cdot 127$	$2 \cdot 191$	5831988	$2^7 \cdot 3$
39	$2 \cdot 3 \cdot 5 \cdot 13$	$17 \cdot 23$	$2^3 \cdot 7^3$	$3 \cdot 131$	$2 \cdot 197$
40	$2^4 \cdot 5^2$	6031444	$2 \cdot 3 \cdot 67$	$13 \cdot 31$	$2^3 \cdot 101$
41	$2 \cdot 5 \cdot 41$	$3 \cdot 137$	$2^3 \cdot 103$	$7 \cdot 59$	$2 \cdot 3^3 \cdot 23$
42	$2^3 \cdot 3 \cdot 5 \cdot 7$	6242821	$2 \cdot 211$	$3^3 \cdot 47$	$2^3 \cdot 53$
43	$2 \cdot 5 \cdot 43$	6344773	$2^4 \cdot 3^3$	6364879	$2 \cdot 7 \cdot 31$
44	$2^3 \cdot 5 \cdot 11$	$3^3 \cdot 7^3$	$2 \cdot 13 \cdot 17$	6464037	$2^3 \cdot 3 \cdot 37$
45	$2 \cdot 3^3 \cdot 5^2$	$11 \cdot 41$	$2^3 \cdot 113$	$3 \cdot 151$	$2 \cdot 227$
46	$2^3 \cdot 5 \cdot 23$	6637009	$2 \cdot 3 \cdot 7 \cdot 11$	6655810	$2^4 \cdot 29$
47	$2 \cdot 5 \cdot 47$	$3 \cdot 157$	$2^3 \cdot 59$	$11 \cdot 43$	$2 \cdot 3 \cdot 79$
48	$2^4 \cdot 3 \cdot 5$	$13 \cdot 37$	$2 \cdot 241$	$3 \cdot 7 \cdot 23$	$2^3 \cdot 11^2$
49	$2 \cdot 5 \cdot 7^2$	6910815	$2^3 \cdot 3 \cdot 41$	$17 \cdot 29$	$2 \cdot 13 \cdot 19$

FACTORS AND PRIMES (Continued)

n	5	6	7	8	9
0	6989700	$2 \cdot 3$	8450980	2^3	3^2
1	$3 \cdot 5$	2^4	2304489	$2 \cdot 3^2$	2787536
2	5^2	$2 \cdot 13$	3^3	$2^2 \cdot 7$	4623980
3	$5 \cdot 7$	$2^2 \cdot 3^2$	5682017	$2 \cdot 19$	$3 \cdot 13$
4	$3^2 \cdot 5$	$2 \cdot 23$	6720979	$2^4 \cdot 3$	7^2
5	$5 \cdot 11$	$2^3 \cdot 7$	$3 \cdot 19$	$2 \cdot 29$	7708520
6	$5 \cdot 13$	$2 \cdot 3 \cdot 11$	8260748	$2^2 \cdot 17$	$3 \cdot 23$
7	$3 \cdot 5^2$	$2^2 \cdot 19$	$7 \cdot 11$	$2 \cdot 3 \cdot 13$	8976271
8	$5 \cdot 17$	$2 \cdot 43$	$3 \cdot 29$	$2^3 \cdot 11$	9493900
9	$5 \cdot 19$	$2^5 \cdot 3$	9867717	$2 \cdot 7^2$	$3^2 \cdot 11$
10	$3 \cdot 5 \cdot 7$	$2 \cdot 53$	0293838	$2^2 \cdot 3^3$	0374265
11	$5 \cdot 23$	$2^2 \cdot 29$	$3^2 \cdot 13$	$2 \cdot 59$	$7 \cdot 17$
12	5^3	$2 \cdot 3^2 \cdot 7$	1038037	2^7	$3 \cdot 43$
13	$3^3 \cdot 5$	$2^2 \cdot 17$	1367206	$2 \cdot 3 \cdot 23$	1430148
14	$5 \cdot 29$	$2 \cdot 73$	$3 \cdot 7^2$	$2^2 \cdot 37$	1731863
15	$5 \cdot 31$	$2^2 \cdot 3 \cdot 13$	1958997	$2 \cdot 79$	$3 \cdot 53$
16	$3 \cdot 5 \cdot 11$	$2 \cdot 83$	2227165	$2^3 \cdot 3 \cdot 7$	13^2
17	$5^2 \cdot 7$	$2^4 \cdot 11$	$3 \cdot 59$	$2 \cdot 89$	2528530
18	$5 \cdot 37$	$2 \cdot 3 \cdot 31$	$11 \cdot 17$	$2^2 \cdot 47$	$3^3 \cdot 7$
19	$3 \cdot 5 \cdot 13$	$2^2 \cdot 7^2$	2944662	$2 \cdot 3^2 \cdot 11$	2988531
20	$5 \cdot 41$	$2 \cdot 103$	$3^2 \cdot 23$	$2^4 \cdot 13$	$11 \cdot 19$
21	$5 \cdot 43$	$2^3 \cdot 3^2$	$7 \cdot 31$	$2 \cdot 109$	$3 \cdot 73$
22	$3^2 \cdot 5^2$	$2 \cdot 113$	3560259	$2^3 \cdot 3 \cdot 19$	3598355
23	$5 \cdot 47$	$2^2 \cdot 59$	$3 \cdot 79$	$2 \cdot 7 \cdot 17$	3783979
24	$5 \cdot 7^2$	$2 \cdot 3 \cdot 41$	$13 \cdot 19$	$2^3 \cdot 31$	$3 \cdot 83$
25	$3 \cdot 5 \cdot 17$	2^8	4099331	$2 \cdot 3 \cdot 43$	$7 \cdot 37$
26	$5 \cdot 53$	$2 \cdot 7 \cdot 19$	$3 \cdot 89$	$2^3 \cdot 67$	4297523
27	$5^3 \cdot 11$	$2^2 \cdot 3 \cdot 23$	4424798	$2 \cdot 139$	$3^2 \cdot 31$
28	$3 \cdot 5 \cdot 19$	$2 \cdot 11 \cdot 13$	$7 \cdot 41$	$2^5 \cdot 3^2$	17^2
29	$5 \cdot 59$	$2^3 \cdot 37$	$3^3 \cdot 11$	$2 \cdot 149$	$13 \cdot 23$
30	$5 \cdot 61$	$2 \cdot 3^2 \cdot 17$	4871384	$2^2 \cdot 7 \cdot 11$	$3 \cdot 103$
31	$3^2 \cdot 5 \cdot 7$	$2^2 \cdot 79$	5010593	$2 \cdot 3 \cdot 53$	$11 \cdot 29$
32	$5^3 \cdot 13$	$2 \cdot 163$	$3 \cdot 109$	$2^3 \cdot 41$	$7 \cdot 47$
33	$5 \cdot 67$	$2^4 \cdot 3 \cdot 7$	5276299	$2 \cdot 13^2$	$3 \cdot 113$
34	$3 \cdot 5 \cdot 23$	$2 \cdot 173$	5403295	$2^3 \cdot 3 \cdot 29$	5428254
35	$5 \cdot 71$	$2^3 \cdot 89$	$3 \cdot 7 \cdot 17$	$2 \cdot 179$	5550944
36	$5 \cdot 73$	$2 \cdot 3 \cdot 61$	5646661	$2^4 \cdot 23$	$3^2 \cdot 41$
37	$3 \cdot 5^2$	$2^3 \cdot 47$	$13 \cdot 29$	$2 \cdot 3^3 \cdot 7$	5786392
38	$5 \cdot 7 \cdot 11$	$2 \cdot 193$	$3^2 \cdot 43$	$2^2 \cdot 97$	5899496
39	$5 \cdot 79$	$2^2 \cdot 3^2 \cdot 11$	5987905	$2 \cdot 199$	$3 \cdot 7 \cdot 19$
40	$3^4 \cdot 5$	$2 \cdot 7 \cdot 29$	$11 \cdot 37$	$2^3 \cdot 3 \cdot 17$	6117233
41	$5 \cdot 83$	$2^5 \cdot 13$	$3 \cdot 139$	$2 \cdot 11 \cdot 19$	6222140
42	$5^2 \cdot 17$	$2 \cdot 3 \cdot 71$	$7 \cdot 61$	$2^3 \cdot 107$	$3 \cdot 11 \cdot 13$
43	$3 \cdot 5 \cdot 29$	$2^2 \cdot 109$	$19 \cdot 23$	$2 \cdot 3 \cdot 73$	6424645
44	$5 \cdot 89$	$2 \cdot 223$	$3 \cdot 149$	$2^6 \cdot 7$	6522463
45	$5 \cdot 7 \cdot 13$	$2^2 \cdot 3 \cdot 19$	6599162	$2 \cdot 229$	$3^2 \cdot 17$
46	$3 \cdot 5 \cdot 31$	$2 \cdot 233$	6693169	$2^2 \cdot 3^2 \cdot 13$	$7 \cdot 67$
47	$5^2 \cdot 19$	$2^2 \cdot 7 \cdot 17$	$3^2 \cdot 53$	$2 \cdot 239$	6803355
48	$5 \cdot 97$	$2 \cdot 3^5$	6875290	$2^3 \cdot 61$	$3 \cdot 163$
49	$3^2 \cdot 5 \cdot 11$	$2^4 \cdot 31$	$7 \cdot 71$	$2 \cdot 3 \cdot 83$	6981005

FACTORS AND PRIMES (Continued)

n	0	1	2	3	4
50	$2^2 \cdot 5^3$	$3 \cdot 167$	$2 \cdot 251$	7015680	$2^3 \cdot 3^2 \cdot 7$
51	$2 \cdot 3 \cdot 5 \cdot 17$	$7 \cdot 73$	2^9	$3^3 \cdot 19$	$2 \cdot 257$
52	$2^3 \cdot 5 \cdot 13$	7168377	$2 \cdot 3^2 \cdot 29$	7185017	$2^2 \cdot 131$
53	$2 \cdot 5 \cdot 53$	$3^2 \cdot 59$	$2^2 \cdot 7 \cdot 19$	$13 \cdot 41$	$2 \cdot 3 \cdot 89$
54	$2^2 \cdot 3^3 \cdot 5$	7331973	$2 \cdot 271$	$3 \cdot 181$	$2^5 \cdot 17$
55	$2 \cdot 5^2 \cdot 11$	$19 \cdot 29$	$2^3 \cdot 3 \cdot 23$	$7 \cdot 79$	$2 \cdot 277$
56	$2^4 \cdot 5 \cdot 7$	$3 \cdot 11 \cdot 17$	$2 \cdot 281$	7505084	$2^2 \cdot 3 \cdot 47$
57	$2 \cdot 3 \cdot 5 \cdot 19$	7566361	$2^2 \cdot 11 \cdot 13$	$3 \cdot 191$	$2 \cdot 7 \cdot 41$
58	$2^2 \cdot 5 \cdot 29$	$7 \cdot 83$	$2 \cdot 3 \cdot 97$	$11 \cdot 53$	$2^3 \cdot 73$
59	$2 \cdot 5 \cdot 59$	$3 \cdot 197$	$2^4 \cdot 37$	7730547	$2 \cdot 3^3 \cdot 11$
60	$2^3 \cdot 3 \cdot 5^2$	7788745	$2 \cdot 7 \cdot 43$	$3^2 \cdot 67$	$2^2 \cdot 151$
61	$2 \cdot 5 \cdot 61$	$13 \cdot 47$	$2^2 \cdot 3^2 \cdot 17$	7874605	$2 \cdot 307$
62	$2^2 \cdot 5 \cdot 31$	$3^3 \cdot 23$	$2 \cdot 311$	$7 \cdot 89$	$2^4 \cdot 3 \cdot 13$
63	$2 \cdot 3^2 \cdot 5 \cdot 7$	8000294	$2^3 \cdot 79$	$3 \cdot 211$	$2 \cdot 317$
64	$2^7 \cdot 5$	8068580	$2 \cdot 3 \cdot 107$	8082110	$2^2 \cdot 7 \cdot 23$
65	$2 \cdot 5^2 \cdot 13$	$3 \cdot 7 \cdot 31$	$2^2 \cdot 163$	8149132	$2 \cdot 3 \cdot 109$
66	$2^2 \cdot 3 \cdot 5 \cdot 11$	8202015	$2 \cdot 331$	$3 \cdot 13 \cdot 17$	$2^3 \cdot 83$
67	$2 \cdot 5 \cdot 67$	$11 \cdot 61$	$2^5 \cdot 3 \cdot 7$	8280151	$2 \cdot 337$
68	$2^2 \cdot 5 \cdot 17$	$3 \cdot 227$	$2 \cdot 11 \cdot 31$	8344207	$2^2 \cdot 3^2 \cdot 19$
69	$2 \cdot 3 \cdot 5 \cdot 23$	8394780	$2^2 \cdot 173$	$3^2 \cdot 7 \cdot 11$	$2 \cdot 347$
70	$2^2 \cdot 5^2 \cdot 7$	8457180	$2 \cdot 3^3 \cdot 13$	$19 \cdot 37$	$2^6 \cdot 11$
71	$2 \cdot 5 \cdot 71$	$3^2 \cdot 79$	$2^3 \cdot 89$	$23 \cdot 3$	$2 \cdot 3 \cdot 7 \cdot 17$
72	$2^4 \cdot 3^2 \cdot 5$	$7 \cdot 103$	$2 \cdot 19^2$	$3 \cdot 241$	$2^2 \cdot 181$
73	$2 \cdot 5 \cdot 73$	$17 \cdot 43$	$2^2 \cdot 3 \cdot 61$	8651040	$2 \cdot 367$
74	$2^2 \cdot 5 \cdot 37$	$3 \cdot 13 \cdot 19$	$2 \cdot 7 \cdot 53$	8709888	$2^3 \cdot 3 \cdot 31$
75	$2 \cdot 3 \cdot 5^3$	8756399	$2^4 \cdot 47$	$3 \cdot 251$	$2 \cdot 13 \cdot 29$
76	$2^3 \cdot 5 \cdot 19$	8813847	$2 \cdot 3 \cdot 127$	$7 \cdot 109$	$2^2 \cdot 191$
77	$2 \cdot 5 \cdot 7 \cdot 11$	$3 \cdot 257$	$2^2 \cdot 193$	8881795	$2 \cdot 3^2 \cdot 43$
78	$2^2 \cdot 3 \cdot 5 \cdot 13$	$11 \cdot 71$	$2 \cdot 17 \cdot 23$	$3^3 \cdot 29$	$2^4 \cdot 7^2$
79	$2 \cdot 5 \cdot 79$	$7 \cdot 113$	$2^3 \cdot 3^2 \cdot 11$	$13 \cdot 61$	$2 \cdot 397$
80	$2^5 \cdot 5^2$	$3^2 \cdot 89$	$2 \cdot 401$	$11 \cdot 73$	$2^2 \cdot 3 \cdot 67$
81	$2 \cdot 3^4 \cdot 5$	9090209	$2^2 \cdot 7 \cdot 29$	$3 \cdot 271$	$2 \cdot 11 \cdot 37$
82	$2^2 \cdot 5 \cdot 41$	9143432	$2 \cdot 3 \cdot 137$	9153998	$2^3 \cdot 103$
83	$2 \cdot 5 \cdot 83$	$3 \cdot 277$	$2^6 \cdot 13$	$7^2 \cdot 17$	$2 \cdot 3 \cdot 139$
84	$2^3 \cdot 3 \cdot 5 \cdot 7$	29^2	$2 \cdot 421$	$3 \cdot 281$	$2^2 \cdot 211$
85	$2 \cdot 5^2 \cdot 17$	$23 \cdot 37$	$2^2 \cdot 3 \cdot 71$	9309490	$2 \cdot 7 \cdot 61$
86	$2^2 \cdot 5 \cdot 43$	$3 \cdot 7 \cdot 41$	$2 \cdot 431$	9360108	$2^5 \cdot 3^3$
87	$2 \cdot 3 \cdot 5 \cdot 29$	$13 \cdot 67$	$2^3 \cdot 109$	$3^2 \cdot 97$	$2 \cdot 19 \cdot 23$
88	$2^4 \cdot 5 \cdot 11$	9449759	$2 \cdot 3^2 \cdot 7^2$	9459607	$2^2 \cdot 13 \cdot 17$
89	$2 \cdot 5 \cdot 89$	$3^4 \cdot 11$	$2^2 \cdot 223$	$19 \cdot 47$	$2 \cdot 3 \cdot 149$
90	$2^2 \cdot 3^2 \cdot 5^2$	$17 \cdot 53$	$2 \cdot 11 \cdot 41$	$3 \cdot 7 \cdot 43$	$2^3 \cdot 113$
91	$2 \cdot 5 \cdot 7 \cdot 13$	9595184	$2^4 \cdot 3 \cdot 19$	$11 \cdot 83$	$2 \cdot 457$
92	$2^3 \cdot 5 \cdot 23$	$3 \cdot 307$	$2 \cdot 461$	$13 \cdot 71$	$2^2 \cdot 3 \cdot 7 \cdot 11$
93	$2 \cdot 3 \cdot 5 \cdot 31$	$7^2 \cdot 19$	$2^2 \cdot 233$	$3 \cdot 311$	$2 \cdot 467$
94	$2^2 \cdot 5 \cdot 47$	9735896	$2 \cdot 3 \cdot 157$	$23 \cdot 41$	$2^4 \cdot 59$
95	$2 \cdot 5^2 \cdot 19$	$3 \cdot 317$	$2^3 \cdot 7 \cdot 17$	9790929	$2 \cdot 3^2 \cdot 53$
96	$2^6 \cdot 3 \cdot 5$	31^2	$2 \cdot 13 \cdot 37$	$3^2 \cdot 107$	$2^2 \cdot 241$
97	$2 \cdot 5 \cdot 97$	9872192	$2^2 \cdot 3^5$	$7 \cdot 139$	$2 \cdot 487$
98	$2^2 \cdot 5 \cdot 7^2$	$3^2 \cdot 100$	$2 \cdot 491$	9925535	$2^3 \cdot 3 \cdot 41$
99	$2 \cdot 3^2 \cdot 5 \cdot 11$	9960737	$2^5 \cdot 31$	$3 \cdot 331$	$2 \cdot 7 \cdot 71$

FACTORS AND PRIMES (Continued)

n	5	6	7	8	9
50	$5 \cdot 101$	$2 \cdot 11 \cdot 23$	$3 \cdot 13^2$	$2^2 \cdot 127$	7067178
51	$5 \cdot 103$	$2^2 \cdot 3 \cdot 43$	$11 \cdot 47$	$2 \cdot 7 \cdot 37$	$3 \cdot 173$
52	$3 \cdot 5^2 \cdot 7$	$2 \cdot 263$	$17 \cdot 31$	$2^4 \cdot 3 \cdot 11$	23^2
53	$5 \cdot 107$	$2^3 \cdot 67$	$3 \cdot 179$	$2 \cdot 269$	$7^2 \cdot 11$
54	$5 \cdot 109$	$2 \cdot 3 \cdot 7 \cdot 13$	7379873	$2^2 \cdot 137$	$3^2 \cdot 61$
55	$3 \cdot 5 \cdot 37$	$2^2 \cdot 139$	7458552	$2 \cdot 3^2 \cdot 31$	$13 \cdot 43$
56	$5 \cdot 113$	$2 \cdot 283$	$3^4 \cdot 7$	$2^3 \cdot 71$	7551123
57	$5^2 \cdot 23$	$2^6 \cdot 3^2$	7611758	$2 \cdot 17^2$	$3 \cdot 193$
58	$3^2 \cdot 5 \cdot 13$	$2 \cdot 293$	7686381	$2^2 \cdot 3 \cdot 7^2$	$19 \cdot 31$
59	$5 \cdot 7 \cdot 17$	$2^2 \cdot 149$	$3 \cdot 199$	$2 \cdot 13 \cdot 23$	7774268
60	$5 \cdot 11^2$	$2 \cdot 3 \cdot 101$	7831887	$2^5 \cdot 19$	$3 \cdot 7 \cdot 29$
61	$3 \cdot 5 \cdot 41$	$2^3 \cdot 7 \cdot 11$	7902852	$2 \cdot 3 \cdot 103$	7916906
62	5^4	$2 \cdot 313$	$3 \cdot 11 \cdot 19$	$2^2 \cdot 157$	$17 \cdot 37$
63	$5 \cdot 127$	$2^2 \cdot 3 \cdot 53$	$7^2 \cdot 13$	$2 \cdot 11 \cdot 29$	$3^2 \cdot 71$
64	$3 \cdot 5 \cdot 43$	$2 \cdot 17 \cdot 19$	8109043	$2^3 \cdot 3^4$	$11 \cdot 59$
65	$5 \cdot 131$	$2^4 \cdot 41$	$3^2 \cdot 73$	$2 \cdot 7 \cdot 47$	8188854
66	$5 \cdot 7 \cdot 19$	$2 \cdot 3^2 \cdot 37$	$23 \cdot 29$	$2^2 \cdot 167$	$3 \cdot 223$
67	$3^3 \cdot 5^2$	$2^2 \cdot 13^2$	8305887	$2 \cdot 3 \cdot 113$	$7 \cdot 97$
68	$5 \cdot 137$	$2 \cdot 7^3$	$3 \cdot 229$	$2^4 \cdot 43$	$13 \cdot 53$
69	$5 \cdot 139$	$2^3 \cdot 3 \cdot 29$	$17 \cdot 41$	$2 \cdot 349$	$3 \cdot 233$
70	$3 \cdot 5 \cdot 47$	$2 \cdot 353$	$7 \cdot 101$	$2^3 \cdot 3 \cdot 59$	8506462
71	$5 \cdot 11 \cdot 13$	$2^2 \cdot 179$	$3 \cdot 239$	$2 \cdot 359$	8567289
72	$5^2 \cdot 29$	$2 \cdot 3 \cdot 11^2$	8615344	$2^3 \cdot 7 \cdot 13$	3^6
73	$3 \cdot 5 \cdot 7^2$	$2^5 \cdot 23$	$11 \cdot 67$	$2 \cdot 3^2 \cdot 41$	8686444
74	$5 \cdot 149$	$2 \cdot 373$	$3^2 \cdot 83$	$2^2 \cdot 11 \cdot 17$	$7 \cdot 107$
75	$5 \cdot 151$	$2^2 \cdot 3^3 \cdot 7$	8790959	$2 \cdot 379$	$3 \cdot 11 \cdot 23$
76	$3^2 \cdot 5 \cdot 17$	$2 \cdot 383$	$13 \cdot 59$	$2^8 \cdot 3$	8859263
77	$5^2 \cdot 31$	$2^3 \cdot 97$	$3 \cdot 7 \cdot 37$	$2 \cdot 389$	$19 \cdot 41$
78	$5 \cdot 157$	$2 \cdot 3 \cdot 131$	8959747	$2^2 \cdot 197$	$3 \cdot 263$
79	$3 \cdot 5 \cdot 53$	$2^2 \cdot 199$	9014583	$2 \cdot 3 \cdot 7 \cdot 19$	$17 \cdot 47$
80	$5 \cdot 7 \cdot 23$	$2 \cdot 13 \cdot 31$	$3 \cdot 269$	$2^3 \cdot 101$	9079485
81	$5 \cdot 163$	$2^4 \cdot 3 \cdot 17$	$19 \cdot 43$	$2 \cdot 409$	$3^2 \cdot 7 \cdot 13$
82	$3 \cdot 5^2 \cdot 11$	$2 \cdot 7 \cdot 59$	9175055	$2^2 \cdot 3^2 \cdot 23$	9185545
83	$5 \cdot 167$	$2^2 \cdot 11 \cdot 19$	$3^3 \cdot 31$	$2 \cdot 419$	9237620
84	$5 \cdot 13^2$	$2 \cdot 3^2 \cdot 47$	$7 \cdot 11^2$	$2^4 \cdot 53$	$3 \cdot 283$
85	$3^2 \cdot 5 \cdot 19$	$2^3 \cdot 107$	9329808	$2 \cdot 3 \cdot 11 \cdot 13$	9339932
86	$5 \cdot 173$	$2 \cdot 433$	$3 \cdot 17^2$	$2^2 \cdot 7 \cdot 31$	$11 \cdot 79$
87	$5^3 \cdot 7$	$2^2 \cdot 3 \cdot 73$	9429996	$2 \cdot 439$	$3 \cdot 293$
88	$3 \cdot 5 \cdot 59$	$2 \cdot 443$	9479236	$2^3 \cdot 3 \cdot 37$	$7 \cdot 127$
89	$5 \cdot 179$	$2^7 \cdot 7$	$3 \cdot 13 \cdot 23$	$2 \cdot 449$	$29 \cdot 31$
90	$5 \cdot 181$	$2 \cdot 3 \cdot 151$	9576073	$2^2 \cdot 227$	$3^2 \cdot 101$
91	$3 \cdot 5 \cdot 61$	$2^2 \cdot 229$	$7 \cdot 131$	$2 \cdot 3^3 \cdot 17$	9633155
92	$5^2 \cdot 37$	$2 \cdot 463$	$3^2 \cdot 103$	$2^5 \cdot 29$	9680157
93	$5 \cdot 11 \cdot 17$	$2^3 \cdot 3^2 \cdot 13$	9717396	$2 \cdot 7 \cdot 67$	$3 \cdot 313$
94	$3^3 \cdot 5 \cdot 7$	$2 \cdot 11 \cdot 43$	9763500	$2^2 \cdot 3 \cdot 79$	$13 \cdot 73$
95	$5 \cdot 191$	$2^2 \cdot 239$	$3 \cdot 11 \cdot 29$	$2 \cdot 479$	$7 \cdot 137$
96	$5 \cdot 193$	$2 \cdot 3 \cdot 7 \cdot 23$	9854265	$2^3 \cdot 11^2$	$3 \cdot 17 \cdot 19$
97	$3 \cdot 5^2 \cdot 13$	$2^4 \cdot 61$	9898946	$2 \cdot 3 \cdot 163$	$11 \cdot 89$
98	$5 \cdot 197$	$2 \cdot 17 \cdot 29$	$3 \cdot 7 \cdot 47$	$2^2 \cdot 13 \cdot 19$	$23 \cdot 43$
99	$5 \cdot 199$	$2^2 \cdot 3 \cdot 83$	9986952	$2 \cdot 499$	$3^3 \cdot 37$

FACTORS AND PRIMES (Continued)

n	0	1	2	3	4
100	$2^3 \cdot 5^2$	$7 \cdot 11 \cdot 13$	$2 \cdot 3 \cdot 167$	$17 \cdot 59$	$2^2 \cdot 251$
101	$2 \cdot 5 \cdot 101$	$3 \cdot 337$	$2^2 \cdot 11 \cdot 23$	0056094	$2 \cdot 3 \cdot 13^2$
102	$2^2 \cdot 3 \cdot 5 \cdot 17$	0090257	$2 \cdot 7 \cdot 73$	$3 \cdot 11 \cdot 31$	2^{10}
103	$2 \cdot 5 \cdot 103$	0132587	$2^3 \cdot 3 \cdot 43$	0141003	$2 \cdot 11 \cdot 47$
104	$2^4 \cdot 5 \cdot 13$	$3 \cdot 347$	$2 \cdot 521$	$7 \cdot 149$	$2^2 \cdot 3^2 \cdot 29$
105	$2 \cdot 3 \cdot 5^2 \cdot 7$	0216027	$2^2 \cdot 263$	$3^4 \cdot 13$	$2 \cdot 17 \cdot 31$
106	$2^2 \cdot 5 \cdot 53$	0257154	$2 \cdot 3^2 \cdot 59$	0265333	$2^3 \cdot 7 \cdot 19$
107	$2 \cdot 5 \cdot 107$	$3^2 \cdot 7 \cdot 17$	$2^4 \cdot 67$	$29 \cdot 37$	$2 \cdot 3 \cdot 179$
108	$2^3 \cdot 3^3 \cdot 5$	$23 \cdot 47$	$2 \cdot 541$	$3 \cdot 19^2$	$2^2 \cdot 271$
109	$2 \cdot 5 \cdot 109$	0378248	$2^2 \cdot 3 \cdot 7 \cdot 13$	0386202	$2 \cdot 547$
110	$2^2 \cdot 5^2 \cdot 11$	$3 \cdot 367$	$2 \cdot 19 \cdot 29$	0425755	$2^4 \cdot 3 \cdot 23$
111	$2 \cdot 3 \cdot 5 \cdot 37$	$11 \cdot 101$	$2^3 \cdot 139$	$3 \cdot 7 \cdot 53$	$2 \cdot 557$
112	$2^5 \cdot 5 \cdot 7$	$19 \cdot 59$	$2 \cdot 3 \cdot 11 \cdot 17$	0503798	$2^2 \cdot 281$
113	$2 \cdot 5 \cdot 113$	$3 \cdot 13 \cdot 29$	$2^2 \cdot 283$	$11 \cdot 103$	$2 \cdot 3^4 \cdot 7$
114	$2^2 \cdot 3 \cdot 5 \cdot 19$	$7 \cdot 163$	$2 \cdot 571$	$3^2 \cdot 127$	$2^3 \cdot 11 \cdot 13$
115	$2 \cdot 5^2 \cdot 23$	0610753	$2^7 \cdot 3^2$	0618293	$2 \cdot 577$
116	$2^3 \cdot 5 \cdot 29$	$3^3 \cdot 43$	$2 \cdot 7 \cdot 83$	0655797	$2^2 \cdot 3 \cdot 97$
117	$2 \cdot 3^2 \cdot 5 \cdot 13$	0685569	$2^2 \cdot 293$	$3 \cdot 17 \cdot 23$	$2 \cdot 587$
118	$2^2 \cdot 5 \cdot 59$	0722499	$2 \cdot 3 \cdot 197$	$7 \cdot 13^2$	$2^5 \cdot 37$
119	$2 \cdot 5 \cdot 7 \cdot 17$	$3 \cdot 397$	$2^3 \cdot 149$	0766404	$2 \cdot 3 \cdot 199$
120	$2^4 \cdot 3 \cdot 5^2$	0795430	$2 \cdot 601$	$3 \cdot 401$	$2^2 \cdot 7 \cdot 43$
121	$2 \cdot 5 \cdot 11^2$	$7 \cdot 173$	$2^2 \cdot 3 \cdot 101$	0838608	$2 \cdot 607$
122	$2^2 \cdot 5 \cdot 61$	$3 \cdot 11 \cdot 37$	$2 \cdot 13 \cdot 47$	0874265	$2^3 \cdot 3^2 \cdot 17$
123	$2 \cdot 3 \cdot 5 \cdot 41$	0902581	$2^4 \cdot 7 \cdot 11$	$3^2 \cdot 137$	$2 \cdot 617$
124	$2^3 \cdot 5 \cdot 31$	$17 \cdot 73$	$2 \cdot 3^3 \cdot 23$	$11 \cdot 113$	$2^2 \cdot 311$
125	$2 \cdot 5^4$	$3^2 \cdot 139$	$2^2 \cdot 313$	$7 \cdot 179$	$2 \cdot 3 \cdot 11 \cdot 19$
126	$2^2 \cdot 3^2 \cdot 5 \cdot 7$	$13 \cdot 97$	$2 \cdot 631$	$3 \cdot 421$	$2^4 \cdot 79$
127	$2 \cdot 5 \cdot 127$	$31 \cdot 41$	$2^3 \cdot 3 \cdot 53$	$19 \cdot 67$	$2 \cdot 7^2 \cdot 13$
128	$2^8 \cdot 5$	$3 \cdot 7 \cdot 61$	$2 \cdot 641$	1082267	$2^2 \cdot 3 \cdot 107$
129	$2 \cdot 3 \cdot 5 \cdot 43$	1109262	$2^2 \cdot 17 \cdot 19$	$3 \cdot 431$	$2 \cdot 647$
130	$2^2 \cdot 5^2 \cdot 13$	1142773	$2 \cdot 3 \cdot 7 \cdot 31$	1149444	$2^3 \cdot 163$
131	$2 \cdot 5 \cdot 131$	$3 \cdot 19 \cdot 23$	$2^5 \cdot 41$	$13 \cdot 101$	$2 \cdot 3^2 \cdot 73$
132	$2^3 \cdot 3 \cdot 5 \cdot 11$	1209028	$2 \cdot 661$	$3^3 \cdot 7^2$	$2^2 \cdot 331$
133	$2 \cdot 5 \cdot 7 \cdot 19$	11^3	$2^2 \cdot 3^2 \cdot 37$	$31 \cdot 43$	$2 \cdot 23 \cdot 29$
134	$2^2 \cdot 5 \cdot 67$	$3^2 \cdot 149$	$2 \cdot 11 \cdot 61$	$17 \cdot 79$	$2^6 \cdot 3 \cdot 7$
135	$2 \cdot 3^3 \cdot 5^2$	$7 \cdot 193$	$2^3 \cdot 13^2$	$3 \cdot 11 \cdot 41$	$2 \cdot 677$
136	$2^4 \cdot 5 \cdot 17$	1338581	$2 \cdot 3 \cdot 227$	$29 \cdot 47$	$2^2 \cdot 11 \cdot 31$
137	$2 \cdot 5 \cdot 137$	$3 \cdot 457$	$2^2 \cdot 7^3$	1376705	$2 \cdot 3 \cdot 229$
138	$2^2 \cdot 3 \cdot 5 \cdot 23$	1401937	$2 \cdot 691$	$3 \cdot 461$	$2^3 \cdot 173$
139	$2 \cdot 5 \cdot 139$	$13 \cdot 107$	$2^4 \cdot 3 \cdot 29$	$7 \cdot 199$	$2 \cdot 17 \cdot 41$
140	$2^3 \cdot 5^2 \cdot 7$	$3 \cdot 467$	$2 \cdot 701$	$23 \cdot 61$	$2^2 \cdot 3^3 \cdot 13$
141	$2 \cdot 3 \cdot 5 \cdot 47$	$17 \cdot 83$	$2^2 \cdot 353$	$3^2 \cdot 157$	$2 \cdot 7 \cdot 101$
142	$2^2 \cdot 5 \cdot 71$	$7^2 \cdot 29$	$2 \cdot 3^2 \cdot 79$	1532049	$2^4 \cdot 89$
143	$2 \cdot 5 \cdot 11 \cdot 13$	$3^3 \cdot 53$	$2^3 \cdot 179$	1562462	$2 \cdot 3 \cdot 239$
144	$2^5 \cdot 3^2 \cdot 5$	$11 \cdot 131$	$2 \cdot 7 \cdot 103$	$3 \cdot 13 \cdot 37$	$2^2 \cdot 19^2$
145	$2 \cdot 5^2 \cdot 29$	1616674	$2^2 \cdot 3 \cdot 11^2$	1622656	$2 \cdot 727$
146	$2^2 \cdot 5 \cdot 73$	$3 \cdot 487$	$2 \cdot 17 \cdot 43$	$7 \cdot 11 \cdot 19$	$2^3 \cdot 3 \cdot 61$
147	$2 \cdot 3 \cdot 5 \cdot 7^2$	1676127	$2^6 \cdot 23$	$3 \cdot 491$	$2 \cdot 11 \cdot 67$
148	$2^3 \cdot 5 \cdot 37$	1705551	$2 \cdot 3 \cdot 13 \cdot 19$	1711412	$2^2 \cdot 7 \cdot 53$
149	$2 \cdot 5 \cdot 149$	$3 \cdot 7 \cdot 71$	$2^2 \cdot 373$	1740598	$2 \cdot 3^2 \cdot 83$

FACTORS AND PRIMES (Continued)

n	5	6	7	8	9
100	$3 \cdot 5 \cdot 67$	$2 \cdot 503$	$19 \cdot 53$	$2^4 \cdot 3^2 \cdot 7$	0038912
101	$5 \cdot 7 \cdot 29$	$2^3 \cdot 127$	$3^2 \cdot 113$	$2 \cdot 509$	0081742
102	$5^2 \cdot 41$	$2 \cdot 3^3 \cdot 19$	$13 \cdot 79$	$2^2 \cdot 257$	$3 \cdot 7^3$
103	$3^2 \cdot 5 \cdot 23$	$2^2 \cdot 7 \cdot 37$	$17 \cdot 61$	$2 \cdot 3 \cdot 173$	0166155
104	$5 \cdot 11 \cdot 19$	$2 \cdot 523$	$3 \cdot 349$	$2^3 \cdot 131$	0207755
105	$5 \cdot 211$	$2^5 \cdot 3 \cdot 11$	$7 \cdot 151$	$2 \cdot 23^2$	$3 \cdot 353$
106	$3 \cdot 5 \cdot 71$	$2 \cdot 13 \cdot 41$	$11 \cdot 97$	$2^2 \cdot 3 \cdot 89$	0289777
107	$5^2 \cdot 43$	$2^2 \cdot 269$	$3 \cdot 359$	$2 \cdot 7^2 \cdot 11$	$13 \cdot 83$
108	$5 \cdot 7 \cdot 31$	$2 \cdot 3 \cdot 181$	0362295	$2^6 \cdot 17$	$3^2 \cdot 11^2$
109	$3 \cdot 5 \cdot 73$	$2^3 \cdot 137$	0402066	$2 \cdot 3^2 \cdot 61$	$7 \cdot 157$
110	$5 \cdot 13 \cdot 17$	$2 \cdot 7 \cdot 79$	$3^3 \cdot 41$	$2^2 \cdot 277$	0449315
111	$5 \cdot 223$	$2^2 \cdot 3^2 \cdot 31$	0480532	$2 \cdot 13 \cdot 43$	$3 \cdot 373$
112	$3^2 \cdot 5^3$	$2 \cdot 563$	$7^2 \cdot 23$	$2^3 \cdot 3 \cdot 47$	0526939
113	$5 \cdot 227$	$2^4 \cdot 71$	$3 \cdot 379$	$2 \cdot 569$	$17 \cdot 67$
114	$5 \cdot 229$	$2 \cdot 3 \cdot 191$	$31 \cdot 37$	$2^2 \cdot 7 \cdot 41$	$3 \cdot 383$
115	$3 \cdot 5 \cdot 7 \cdot 11$	$2^2 \cdot 17^2$	$13 \cdot 89$	$2 \cdot 3 \cdot 193$	$19 \cdot 61$
116	$5 \cdot 233$	$2 \cdot 11 \cdot 53$	$3 \cdot 389$	$2^4 \cdot 73$	$7 \cdot 167$
117	$5^2 \cdot 47$	$2^3 \cdot 3 \cdot 7^2$	$11 \cdot 107$	$2 \cdot 19 \cdot 31$	$3^2 \cdot 131$
118	$3 \cdot 5 \cdot 79$	$2 \cdot 593$	0744507	$2^2 \cdot 3^3 \cdot 11$	$29 \cdot 41$
119	$5 \cdot 239$	$2^3 \cdot 13 \cdot 23$	$3^2 \cdot 7 \cdot 19$	$2 \cdot 599$	$11 \cdot 109$
120	$5 \cdot 241$	$2 \cdot 3^2 \cdot 67$	$17 \cdot 71$	$2^3 \cdot 151$	$3 \cdot 13 \cdot 31$
121	$3^5 \cdot 5$	$2^6 \cdot 19$	0852906	$2 \cdot 3 \cdot 7 \cdot 29$	$23 \cdot 53$
122	$5^2 \cdot 7^2$	$2 \cdot 613$	$3 \cdot 409$	$2^2 \cdot 307$	0895519
123	$5 \cdot 13 \cdot 19$	$2^2 \cdot 3 \cdot 103$	0923697	$2 \cdot 619$	$3 \cdot 7 \cdot 59$
124	$3 \cdot 5 \cdot 83$	$2 \cdot 7 \cdot 89$	$29 \cdot 43$	$2^5 \cdot 3 \cdot 13$	0965624
125	$5 \cdot 251$	$2^3 \cdot 157$	$3 \cdot 419$	$2 \cdot 17 \cdot 37$	1000257
126	$5 \cdot 11 \cdot 23$	$2 \cdot 3 \cdot 211$	$7 \cdot 181$	$2^2 \cdot 317$	$3^3 \cdot 47$
127	$3 \cdot 5^2 \cdot 17$	$2^2 \cdot 11 \cdot 29$	1061909	$2 \cdot 3^2 \cdot 71$	1068705
128	$5 \cdot 257$	$2 \cdot 643$	$3^2 \cdot 11 \cdot 13$	$2^3 \cdot 7 \cdot 23$	1102529
129	$5 \cdot 7 \cdot 37$	$2^4 \cdot 3^4$	1129400	$2 \cdot 11 \cdot 59$	$3 \cdot 433$
130	$3^2 \cdot 5 \cdot 29$	$2 \cdot 653$	1162756	$2^2 \cdot 3 \cdot 109$	$7 \cdot 11 \cdot 17$
131	$5 \cdot 263$	$2^2 \cdot 7 \cdot 47$	$3 \cdot 439$	$2 \cdot 659$	1202448
132	$5^2 \cdot 53$	$2 \cdot 3 \cdot 13 \cdot 17$	1228709	$2^4 \cdot 83$	$3 \cdot 443$
133	$3 \cdot 5 \cdot 89$	$2^3 \cdot 167$	$7 \cdot 191$	$2 \cdot 3 \cdot 223$	$13 \cdot 103$
134	$5 \cdot 269$	$2 \cdot 673$	$3 \cdot 449$	$2^2 \cdot 337$	$19 \cdot 71$
135	$5 \cdot 271$	$2^2 \cdot 3 \cdot 113$	$23 \cdot 59$	$2 \cdot 7 \cdot 97$	$3^2 \cdot 151$
136	$3 \cdot 5 \cdot 7 \cdot 13$	$2 \cdot 683$	1357685	$2^3 \cdot 3^2 \cdot 19$	37^2
137	$5^3 \cdot 11$	$2^5 \cdot 43$	$3^4 \cdot 17$	$2 \cdot 13 \cdot 53$	$7 \cdot 197$
138	$5 \cdot 277$	$2 \cdot 3^2 \cdot 7 \cdot 11$	$19 \cdot 73$	$2^2 \cdot 347$	$3 \cdot 463$
139	$3^2 \cdot 5 \cdot 31$	$2^2 \cdot 349$	$11 \cdot 127$	$2 \cdot 3 \cdot 233$	1458177
140	$5 \cdot 281$	$2 \cdot 19 \cdot 37$	$3 \cdot 7 \cdot 67$	$2^7 \cdot 11$	1489110
141	$5 \cdot 283$	$2^3 \cdot 3 \cdot 59$	$13 \cdot 109$	$2 \cdot 709$	$3 \cdot 11 \cdot 43$
142	$3 \cdot 5^2 \cdot 19$	$2 \cdot 23 \cdot 31$	1544240	$2^2 \cdot 3 \cdot 7 \cdot 17$	1550322
143	$5 \cdot 7 \cdot 41$	$2^2 \cdot 359$	$3 \cdot 479$	$2 \cdot 719$	1580608
144	$5 \cdot 17^2$	$2 \cdot 3 \cdot 241$	1604685	$2^3 \cdot 181$	$3^2 \cdot 7 \cdot 23$
145	$3 \cdot 5 \cdot 97$	$2^4 \cdot 7 \cdot 13$	$31 \cdot 47$	$2 \cdot 3^6$	1640553
146	$5 \cdot 293$	$2 \cdot 733$	$3^2 \cdot 163$	$2^2 \cdot 367$	$13 \cdot 113$
147	$5^2 \cdot 59$	$2^2 \cdot 3^2 \cdot 41$	$7 \cdot 211$	$2 \cdot 739$	$3 \cdot 17 \cdot 29$
148	$3^3 \cdot 5 \cdot 11$	$2 \cdot 743$	1723110	$2^4 \cdot 3 \cdot 31$	1728947
149	$5 \cdot 13 \cdot 23$	$2^3 \cdot 11 \cdot 17$	$3 \cdot 499$	$2 \cdot 7 \cdot 107$	1758016

FACTORS AND PRIMES (Continued)

n	0	1	2	3	4
150	$2^3 \cdot 3 \cdot 5^2$	$19 \cdot 79$	$2 \cdot 751$	$3^2 \cdot 167$	$2^5 \cdot 47$
151	$2 \cdot 5 \cdot 151$	1792645	$2^3 \cdot 3^3 \cdot 7$	$17 \cdot 89$	$2 \cdot 757$
152	$2^4 \cdot 5 \cdot 19$	$3^2 \cdot 13^2$	$2 \cdot 761$	1826999	$2^2 \cdot 3 \cdot 127$
153	$2 \cdot 3^2 \cdot 5 \cdot 17$	1849752	$2^2 \cdot 383$	$3 \cdot 7 \cdot 73$	$2 \cdot 13 \cdot 59$
154	$2^2 \cdot 5 \cdot 7 \cdot 11$	$23 \cdot 67$	$2 \cdot 3 \cdot 257$	1883659	$2^3 \cdot 193$
155	$2 \cdot 5^2 \cdot 31$	$3 \cdot 11 \cdot 47$	$2^4 \cdot 97$	1911715	$2 \cdot 3 \cdot 7 \cdot 37$
156	$2^3 \cdot 3 \cdot 5 \cdot 13$	$7 \cdot 223$	$2 \cdot 11 \cdot 71$	$3 \cdot 521$	$2^2 \cdot 17 \cdot 23$
157	$2 \cdot 5 \cdot 157$	1961762	$2^2 \cdot 3 \cdot 131$	$11^2 \cdot 13$	$2 \cdot 787$
158	$2^2 \cdot 5 \cdot 79$	$3 \cdot 17 \cdot 31$	$2 \cdot 7 \cdot 113$	1994809	$2^4 \cdot 3^2 \cdot 11$
159	$2 \cdot 3 \cdot 5 \cdot 53$	$37 \cdot 43$	$2^3 \cdot 199$	$3^3 \cdot 59$	$2 \cdot 797$
160	$2^6 \cdot 5^2$	2043913	$2 \cdot 3 \cdot 89$	$7 \cdot 229$	$2^2 \cdot 401$
161	$2 \cdot 5 \cdot 7 \cdot 23$	$3^2 \cdot 179$	$2^2 \cdot 13 \cdot 31$	2076344	$2 \cdot 3 \cdot 269$
162	$2^2 \cdot 3^4 \cdot 5$	2097830	$2 \cdot 811$	$3 \cdot 541$	$2^3 \cdot 7 \cdot 29$
163	$2 \cdot 5 \cdot 163$	$7 \cdot 233$	$2^5 \cdot 3 \cdot 17$	$23 \cdot 71$	$2 \cdot 19 \cdot 43$
164	$2^2 \cdot 5 \cdot 41$	$3 \cdot 547$	$2 \cdot 821$	$31 \cdot 53$	$2^2 \cdot 3 \cdot 137$
165	$2 \cdot 3 \cdot 5^2 \cdot 11$	$13 \cdot 127$	$2^2 \cdot 7 \cdot 59$	$3 \cdot 19 \cdot 29$	$2 \cdot 827$
166	$2^2 \cdot 5 \cdot 83$	$11 \cdot 151$	$2 \cdot 3 \cdot 277$	2208922	$2^7 \cdot 13$
167	$2 \cdot 5 \cdot 167$	$3 \cdot 557$	$2^3 \cdot 11 \cdot 19$	$7 \cdot 239$	$2 \cdot 3^3 \cdot 31$
168	$2^4 \cdot 3 \cdot 5 \cdot 7$	41^2	$2 \cdot 29^2$	$3^2 \cdot 11 \cdot 17$	$2^2 \cdot 421$
169	$2 \cdot 5 \cdot 13^2$	$19 \cdot 89$	$2^2 \cdot 3^3 \cdot 47$	2286570	$2 \cdot 7 \cdot 11^2$
170	$2^2 \cdot 5^2 \cdot 17$	$3^5 \cdot 7$	$2 \cdot 23 \cdot 37$	$13 \cdot 131$	$2^3 \cdot 3 \cdot 71$
171	$2 \cdot 3^2 \cdot 5 \cdot 19$	$29 \cdot 59$	$2^4 \cdot 107$	$3 \cdot 571$	$2 \cdot 857$
172	$2^3 \cdot 5 \cdot 43$	2357809	$2 \cdot 3 \cdot 7 \cdot 41$	2362853	$2^2 \cdot 431$
173	$2 \cdot 5 \cdot 173$	$3 \cdot 577$	$2^2 \cdot 433$	2387986	$2 \cdot 3 \cdot 17^2$
174	$2^2 \cdot 3 \cdot 5 \cdot 29$	2407988	$2 \cdot 13 \cdot 67$	$3 \cdot 7 \cdot 83$	$2^4 \cdot 109$
175	$2 \cdot 5^3 \cdot 7$	$17 \cdot 103$	$2^3 \cdot 3 \cdot 73$	2437819	$2 \cdot 877$
176	$2^5 \cdot 5 \cdot 11$	$3 \cdot 587$	$2 \cdot 881$	$41 \cdot 43$	$2^2 \cdot 3^2 \cdot 7^2$
177	$2 \cdot 3 \cdot 5 \cdot 59$	$7 \cdot 11 \cdot 23$	$2^2 \cdot 443$	$3^2 \cdot 197$	$2 \cdot 887$
178	$2^2 \cdot 5 \cdot 89$	$13 \cdot 137$	$2 \cdot 3^4 \cdot 11$	2511513	$2^3 \cdot 223$
179	$2 \cdot 5 \cdot 179$	$3^2 \cdot 199$	$2^8 \cdot 7$	$11 \cdot 163$	$2 \cdot 3 \cdot 13 \cdot 23$
180	$2^3 \cdot 3^2 \cdot 5^2$	2555137	$2 \cdot 17 \cdot 53$	$3 \cdot 601$	$2^2 \cdot 11 \cdot 41$
181	$2 \cdot 5 \cdot 181$	2579185	$2^2 \cdot 3 \cdot 151$	$7^2 \cdot 37$	$2 \cdot 907$
182	$2^2 \cdot 5 \cdot 7 \cdot 13$	$3 \cdot 607$	$2 \cdot 911$	2607867	$2^5 \cdot 3 \cdot 19$
183	$2 \cdot 3 \cdot 5 \cdot 61$	2626883	$2^3 \cdot 229$	$3 \cdot 13 \cdot 47$	$2 \cdot 7 \cdot 131$
184	$2^4 \cdot 5 \cdot 23$	$7 \cdot 263$	$2 \cdot 3 \cdot 307$	$19 \cdot 97$	$2^2 \cdot 461$
185	$2 \cdot 5^2 \cdot 37$	$3 \cdot 617$	$2^2 \cdot 463$	$17 \cdot 109$	$2 \cdot 3^2 \cdot 103$
186	$2^2 \cdot 3 \cdot 5 \cdot 31$	2697464	$2 \cdot 7^2 \cdot 19$	$3^4 \cdot 23$	$2^3 \cdot 233$
187	$2 \cdot 5 \cdot 11 \cdot 17$	2720738	$2^4 \cdot 3^2 \cdot 13$	2725378	$2 \cdot 937$
188	$2^3 \cdot 5 \cdot 47$	$3^2 \cdot 11 \cdot 19$	$2 \cdot 941$	$7 \cdot 269$	$2^2 \cdot 3 \cdot 157$
189	$2 \cdot 3^3 \cdot 5 \cdot 7$	$31 \cdot 61$	$2^2 \cdot 11 \cdot 43$	$3 \cdot 631$	$2 \cdot 947$
190	$2^2 \cdot 5 \cdot 2 \cdot 19$	2789821	$2 \cdot 3 \cdot 317$	$11 \cdot 173$	$2^4 \cdot 7 \cdot 17$
191	$2 \cdot 5 \cdot 191$	$3 \cdot 7^2 \cdot 13$	$2^3 \cdot 239$	2817150	$2 \cdot 3 \cdot 11 \cdot 29$
192	$2^7 \cdot 3 \cdot 5$	$17 \cdot 113$	$2 \cdot 31^2$	$3 \cdot 641$	$2^2 \cdot 13 \cdot 37$
193	$2 \cdot 5 \cdot 193$	2857823	$2^2 \cdot 3 \cdot 7 \cdot 23$	2862319	$2 \cdot 967$
194	$2^2 \cdot 5 \cdot 97$	$3 \cdot 647$	$2 \cdot 971$	$29 \cdot 67$	$2^3 \cdot 3^5$
195	$2 \cdot 3 \cdot 5^2 \cdot 13$	2902573	$2^5 \cdot 61$	$3^2 \cdot 7 \cdot 31$	$2 \cdot 977$
196	$2^3 \cdot 5 \cdot 7^2$	$37 \cdot 53$	$2 \cdot 3^2 \cdot 109$	$13 \cdot 151$	$2^2 \cdot 491$
197	$2 \cdot 5 \cdot 197$	$3^3 \cdot 73$	$2^2 \cdot 17 \cdot 29$	2951271	$2 \cdot 3 \cdot 7 \cdot 47$
198	$2^2 \cdot 3^2 \cdot 5 \cdot 11$	$7 \cdot 283$	$2 \cdot 991$	$3 \cdot 661$	$2^6 \cdot 31$
199	$2 \cdot 5 \cdot 199$	$11 \cdot 181$	$2^3 \cdot 3 \cdot 83$	2995073	$2 \cdot 997$

FACTORS AND PRIMES (Continued)

n	5	6	7	8	9
150	$5 \cdot 7 \cdot 43$	$2 \cdot 3 \cdot 251$	$11 \cdot 137$	$2^2 \cdot 13 \cdot 29$	$3 \cdot 503$
151	$3 \cdot 5 \cdot 101$	$2^2 \cdot 379$	$37 \cdot 41$	$2 \cdot 3 \cdot 11 \cdot 23$	$7^2 \cdot 31$
152	$5^2 \cdot 61$	$2 \cdot 7 \cdot 109$	$3 \cdot 509$	$2^3 \cdot 191$	$11 \cdot 139$
153	$5 \cdot 307$	$2^9 \cdot 3$	$29 \cdot 53$	$2 \cdot 769$	$3^4 \cdot 19$
154	$3 \cdot 5 \cdot 103$	$2 \cdot 773$	$7 \cdot 13 \cdot 17$	$2^2 \cdot 3^2 \cdot 43$	1900514
155	$5 \cdot 311$	$2^2 \cdot 389$	$3^2 \cdot 173$	$2 \cdot 19 \cdot 41$	1928461
156	$5 \cdot 313$	$2 \cdot 3^3 \cdot 29$	1950690	$2^5 \cdot 7^2$	$3 \cdot 523$
157	$3^2 \cdot 5^2 \cdot 7$	$2^3 \cdot 197$	$19 \cdot 83$	$2 \cdot 3 \cdot 263$	1983821
158	$5 \cdot 317$	$2 \cdot 13 \cdot 61$	$3 \cdot 23^2$	$2^2 \cdot 397$	$7 \cdot 227$
159	$5 \cdot 11 \cdot 29$	$2^2 \cdot 3 \cdot 7 \cdot 19$	2033049	$2 \cdot 17 \cdot 47$	$3 \cdot 13 \cdot 41$
160	$3 \cdot 5 \cdot 107$	$2 \cdot 11 \cdot 73$	2060159	$2^3 \cdot 3 \cdot 67$	2065560
161	$5 \cdot 17 \cdot 19$	$2^4 \cdot 101$	$3 \cdot 7^2 \cdot 11$	$2 \cdot 809$	2092468
162	$5^3 \cdot 13$	$2 \cdot 3 \cdot 271$	2113876	$2^2 \cdot 11 \cdot 37$	$3^2 \cdot 181$
163	$3 \cdot 5 \cdot 109$	$2^2 \cdot 409$	2140487	$2 \cdot 3^2 \cdot 7 \cdot 13$	$11 \cdot 149$
164	$5 \cdot 7 \cdot 47$	$2 \cdot 823$	$3^3 \cdot 61$	$2^4 \cdot 103$	$17 \cdot 97$
165	$5 \cdot 331$	$2^3 \cdot 3^2 \cdot 23$	2193225	$2 \cdot 829$	$3 \cdot 7 \cdot 79$
166	$3^2 \cdot 5 \cdot 37$	$2 \cdot 7^2 \cdot 17$	2219356	$2^2 \cdot 3 \cdot 139$	2224563
167	$5^2 \cdot 67$	$2^2 \cdot 419$	$3 \cdot 13 \cdot 43$	$2 \cdot 839$	$23 \cdot 73$
168	$5 \cdot 337$	$2 \cdot 3 \cdot 281$	$7 \cdot 241$	$2^3 \cdot 211$	$3 \cdot 563$
169	$3 \cdot 5 \cdot 113$	$2^5 \cdot 53$	2296818	$2 \cdot 3 \cdot 283$	2301934
170	$5 \cdot 11 \cdot 31$	$2 \cdot 853$	$3 \cdot 569$	$2^2 \cdot 7 \cdot 61$	2327421
171	$5 \cdot 7^3$	$2^2 \cdot 3 \cdot 11 \cdot 13$	$17 \cdot 101$	$2 \cdot 859$	$3^2 \cdot 191$
172	$3 \cdot 5^2 \cdot 23$	$2 \cdot 863$	$11 \cdot 157$	$2^6 \cdot 3^3$	$7 \cdot 13 \cdot 19$
173	$5 \cdot 347$	$2^3 \cdot 7 \cdot 31$	$3^2 \cdot 193$	$2 \cdot 11 \cdot 79$	$37 \cdot 47$
174	$5 \cdot 349$	$2 \cdot 3^2 \cdot 97$	2422929	$2^2 \cdot 19 \cdot 23$	$3 \cdot 11 \cdot 53$
175	$3^3 \cdot 5 \cdot 13$	$2^2 \cdot 439$	$7 \cdot 251$	$2 \cdot 3 \cdot 293$	2452658
176	$5 \cdot 353$	$2 \cdot 883$	$3 \cdot 19 \cdot 31$	$2^3 \cdot 13 \cdot 17$	$29 \cdot 61$
177	$5^2 \cdot 71$	$2^4 \cdot 3 \cdot 37$	2496874	$2 \cdot 7 \cdot 127$	$3 \cdot 593$
178	$3 \cdot 5 \cdot 7 \cdot 17$	$2 \cdot 19 \cdot 47$	2521246	$2^2 \cdot 3 \cdot 149$	2526103
179	$5 \cdot 359$	$2^2 \cdot 449$	$3 \cdot 599$	$2 \cdot 29 \cdot 31$	$7 \cdot 257$
180	$5 \cdot 19^2$	$2 \cdot 3 \cdot 7 \cdot 43$	$13 \cdot 139$	$2^4 \cdot 113$	$3^3 \cdot 67$
181	$3 \cdot 5 \cdot 11^2$	$2^3 \cdot 227$	$23 \cdot 79$	$2 \cdot 3^2 \cdot 101$	$17 \cdot 107$
182	$5^2 \cdot 73$	$2 \cdot 11 \cdot 83$	$3^2 \cdot 7 \cdot 29$	$2^2 \cdot 457$	$31 \cdot 59$
183	$5 \cdot 367$	$2^2 \cdot 3^3 \cdot 17$	$11 \cdot 167$	$2 \cdot 919$	$3 \cdot 613$
184	$3^2 \cdot 5 \cdot 41$	$2 \cdot 13 \cdot 71$	2664669	$2^3 \cdot 3 \cdot 7 \cdot 11$	43^2
185	$5 \cdot 7 \cdot 53$	$2^6 \cdot 29$	$3 \cdot 619$	$2 \cdot 929$	$11 \cdot 13^2$
186	$5 \cdot 373$	$2 \cdot 3 \cdot 311$	2711443	$2^2 \cdot 467$	$3 \cdot 7 \cdot 89$
187	$3 \cdot 5^4$	$2^2 \cdot 7 \cdot 67$	2734643	$2 \cdot 3 \cdot 313$	2739268
188	$5 \cdot 13 \cdot 29$	$2 \cdot 23 \cdot 41$	$3 \cdot 17 \cdot 37$	$2^5 \cdot 59$	2762320
189	$5 \cdot 379$	$2^3 \cdot 3 \cdot 79$	$7 \cdot 271$	$2 \cdot 13 \cdot 73$	$3^2 \cdot 211$
190	$3 \cdot 5 \cdot 127$	$2 \cdot 953$	2803507	$2^2 \cdot 3^2 \cdot 53$	$23 \cdot 83$
191	$5 \cdot 383$	$2^2 \cdot 479$	$3^3 \cdot 71$	$2 \cdot 7 \cdot 137$	$19 \cdot 101$
192	$5^2 \cdot 7 \cdot 11$	$2 \cdot 3^2 \cdot 107$	$41 \cdot 47$	$2^3 \cdot 241$	$3 \cdot 643$
193	$3^2 \cdot 5 \cdot 43$	$2^4 \cdot 11^2$	$13 \cdot 149$	$2 \cdot 3 \cdot 17 \cdot 19$	$7 \cdot 277$
194	$5 \cdot 389$	$2 \cdot 7 \cdot 139$	$3 \cdot 11 \cdot 59$	$2^2 \cdot 487$	2898118
195	$5 \cdot 17 \cdot 23$	$2^2 \cdot 3 \cdot 163$	$19 \cdot 103$	$2 \cdot 11 \cdot 89$	$3 \cdot 653$
196	$3 \cdot 5 \cdot 131$	$2 \cdot 983$	$7 \cdot 281$	$2^4 \cdot 3 \cdot 41$	$11 \cdot 179$
197	$5^2 \cdot 79$	$2^3 \cdot 13 \cdot 19$	$3 \cdot 659$	$2 \cdot 23 \cdot 43$	2964458
198	$5 \cdot 397$	$2 \cdot 3 \cdot 331$	2981979	$2^2 \cdot 7 \cdot 71$	$3^2 \cdot 13 \cdot 17$
199	$3 \cdot 5 \cdot 7 \cdot 19$	$2^2 \cdot 499$	3003781	$2 \cdot 3^3 \cdot 37$	3008128

EXTENDED TABLES OF FACTORS AND PRIMES

The following procedure makes possible the determination of a number between 2009 and 19,949 as being either prime, or if not, what its factors will be. It is herewith included with the kind permission of its author, Professor Leonard Caners.

The following symbols will be used:

N is the number whose factors, if any, are to be determined.

A is N with the last digit dropped. Thus if $N = 17,873$, $A = 1787$.

R is the range and is the integral part of the square root of N with its last two digits dropped. Thus R of $17,873 = 13$.

K is the key number and is found in the table below.

P_1 is a possible factor corresponding to K.

The twin series are given in the table for the sake of completeness but are not written down in actual practice.

There are two steps as outlined below.

Step I

N	K	P_1	Series	Procedure
Any number ending in 1, 3, 7, or 9, within limits stated above	$A - R$	$10R + $ last digit	$K + n$; $P_1 - 10n$ $n = 0, 1, \ldots, 2R + 1$	Beginning with K read table of Factors and Primes from left to right and look for corresponding possible factors

Step II

N ending in	K	P_1	Series	Procedure
1	$(A - 2) - 3R$	$10R + 7$	$K + 3n$; $P_1 - 10n$ $n = 0, 1, \ldots, 2R + 1$	Same as in Step I except that only every *third* entry in table of Factors and Primes is examined for corresponding possible factors
3	$A - 3k$	$10R + 1$	$n = 0, 1, \ldots, 2R + 1$	
7	$(A - 2) - 3R$	$10R + 9$	$n = 0, 1, \ldots, 2R + 1$	
9	$A - 3R$	$10R + 3$	$n = 0, 1, \ldots, 2R + 1$	

As an example consider 7519. Using tables on preceding pages proceed as follows:

Step I

From Table $N = 7519$; $A = 751$; $R = 8$, $K = 743$; $P_1 = 89$ and the series obtained:

743	89
744	79
745	69
746	59
—	—
751	9
752	1
753	11
—	—
760	81

EXTENDED TABLES OF FACTORS AND PRIMES (Continued)

Examining the Table of Factors and Primes beginning with 743 note whether 743 has 89 as a factor; whether 744 has 79 as a factor, etc. Then continue to read from left to right keeping in mind the possible factors 69, 59, . . . 81.

Since none are found one concludes that 7519 has no factors within the given range ending in 9 or 1.

Step II

From Table $K = 727$ and $P_1 = 83$; the series obtained is:

727	83
730	73
733	63
—	—
751	3
754	7
—	—
778	87

Proceed exactly as in Step I. Begin with 727 and note whether it has 83 as a factor. Thereafter examine every *third* entry for the remaining corresponding possible factors 73, 63 . . . 3, 7, . . . 87. Since 730 yields the factor 73 one concludes that 73 is the factor of 7519. By division $7519 = 73 \times 103$. Had no factor been found in either Step I or Step II the conclusion would be that the number under consideration was prime.

Proof for Step I

Let N end in 1. Then, if N has a factor ending in 1, write

$$(10a + 1)(10b + 1) = N = 10A + 1$$
$$10ab + a + b = A$$

or

$$b(10a + 1) = (A - a)$$

This proves that any factor $10a + 1$ of N is also a factor of $A - a$. Let $a = (R - n)$, then $(10a + 1)$ becomes $(10R + 1) - 10n$ and $(A - a)$ becomes $(A - R) + n$, i.e., $P_1 - 10n$ and $K + n$ respectively as given in the table. Since $P_1 - 10n$ becomes a number ending in 9 when $P_1 < 10n$, all possible factors ending in 9 are also provided for.

The proof for Step II is similar. For possible factors ending in 3 or 7 write

$$(10a + 7)(10b + 3) = N = 10A + 1.$$

By identical reasoning this results in $P_1 - 10n$ and $K + 3n$ respectively given in the table. This completes the proof for numbers ending in 1.

Identical reasoning establishes the key numbers and series for ending in 3, 7, or 9.

A separate table giving primes from 1 to 100,000 is included on pages 86—93.

TOTIENT FUNCTION $\phi(n)$

Introductory facts

$\phi(n)$ is the number of integers not exceeding and relatively prime to n.

σ_k is the sum of the k'th powers of divisors of n.

σ_0 is usually denoted by $d(n)$ and specifies the number of divisors of n.

For example if $n = 10$, then the divisors are 1, 2, 5, 10 and the sum of the first powers is 18, i.e. $\sigma_0 = d(10) = 4$; $\sigma_1 = 18$; $\phi(10) = 4$.

n	$\phi(n)$	σ_0	σ_1	n	$\phi(n)$	σ_0	σ_1	n	$\phi(n)$	σ_0	σ_1	n	$\phi(n)$	σ_0	σ_1
1	1	1	1	41	40	2	42	81	54	5	121	121	110	3	133
2	1	2	3	42	12	8	96	82	40	4	126	122	60	4	186
3	2	2	4	43	42	2	44	83	82	2	84	123	80	4	168
4	2	3	7	44	20	6	84	84	24	12	224	124	60	6	224
5	4	2	6	45	24	6	78	85	64	4	108	125	100	4	156
6	2	4	12	46	22	4	72	86	42	4	132	126	36	12	312
7	6	2	8	47	46	2	48	87	56	4	120	127	126	2	128
8	4	4	15	48	16	10	124	88	40	8	180	128	64	8	255
9	6	3	13	49	42	3	57	89	88	2	90	129	84	4	176
10	4	4	18	50	20	6	93	90	24	12	234	130	48	8	252
11	10	2	12	51	32	4	72	91	72	4	112	131	130	2	132
12	4	6	28	52	24	6	98	92	44	6	168	132	40	12	336
13	12	2	14	53	52	2	54	93	60	4	128	133	108	4	160
14	6	4	24	54	18	8	120	94	46	4	144	134	66	4	204
15	8	4	24	55	40	4	72	95	72	4	120	135	72	8	240
16	8	5	31	56	24	8	120	96	32	12	252	136	64	8	270
17	16	2	18	57	36	4	80	97	96	2	98	137	136	2	138
18	6	6	39	58	28	4	90	98	42	6	171	138	44	8	288
19	18	2	20	59	58	2	60	99	60	6	156	139	138	2	140
20	8	6	42	60	16	12	168	100	40	9	217	140	48	12	336
21	12	4	32	61	60	2	62	101	100	2	102	141	92	4	192
22	10	4	36	62	30	4	96	102	32	8	216	142	70	4	216
23	22	2	24	63	36	6	104	103	102	2	104	143	120	4	168
24	8	8	60	64	32	7	127	104	48	8	210	144	48	15	403
25	20	3	31	65	48	4	84	105	48	8	192	145	112	4	180
26	12	4	42	66	20	8	144	106	52	4	162	146	72	4	222
27	18	4	40	67	66	2	68	107	106	2	108	147	84	6	228
28	12	6	56	68	32	6	126	108	36	12	280	148	72	6	266
29	28	2	30	69	44	4	96	109	108	2	110	149	148	2	150
30	8	8	72	70	24	8	144	110	40	8	216	150	40	12	372
31	30	2	32	71	70	2	72	111	72	4	152	151	150	2	152
32	16	6	63	72	24	12	195	112	48	10	248	152	72	8	300
33	20	4	48	73	72	2	74	113	112	2	114	153	96	6	234
34	16	4	54	74	36	4	114	114	36	8	240	154	60	8	288
35	24	4	48	75	40	6	124	115	88	4	144	155	120	4	192
36	12	9	91	76	36	6	140	116	56	6	210	156	48	12	392
37	36	2	38	77	60	4	96	117	72	6	182	157	156	2	158
38	18	4	60	78	24	8	168	118	58	4	180	158	78	4	240
39	24	4	56	79	78	2	80	119	96	4	144	159	104	4	216
40	16	8	90	80	32	10	186	120	32	16	360	160	64	12	378

TOTIENT FUNCTION $\phi(n)$ (Continued)

n	$\phi(n)$	σ_0	σ_1	n	$\phi(n)$	σ_0	σ_1	n	$\phi(n)$	σ_0	σ_1	n	$\phi(n)$	σ_0	σ_1
161	132	4	192	211	210	2	212	261	168	6	390	311	310	2	312
162	54	10	363	212	104	6	378	262	130	4	396	312	96	16	840
163	162	2	164	213	140	4	288	263	262	2	264	313	312	2	314
164	80	6	294	214	106	4	324	264	80	16	720	314	156	4	474
165	80	8	288	215	168	4	264	265	208	4	324	315	144	12	624
166	82	4	252	216	72	16	600	266	108	8	480	316	156	6	560
167	166	2	168	217	180	4	256	267	176	4	360	317	316	2	318
168	48	16	480	218	108	4	330	268	132	6	476	318	104	8	648
169	156	3	183	219	144	4	296	269	268	2	270	319	280	4	360
170	64	8	324	220	80	12	504	270	72	16	720	320	128	14	762
171	108	6	260	221	192	4	252	271	270	2	272	321	212	4	432
172	84	6	308	222	72	8	456	272	128	10	558	322	132	8	576
173	172	2	174	223	222	2	224	273	144	8	448	323	288	4	360
174	56	8	360	224	96	12	504	274	136	4	414	324	108	15	847
175	120	6	248	225	120	9	403	275	200	6	372	325	240	6	434
176	80	10	372	226	112	4	342	276	88	12	672	326	162	4	492
177	116	4	240	227	226	2	228	277	276	2	278	327	216	4	440
178	88	4	270	228	72	12	560	278	138	4	420	328	160	8	630
179	178	2	180	229	228	2	230	279	180	6	416	329	276	4	384
180	48	18	546	230	88	8	432	280	96	16	720	330	80	16	864
181	180	2	182	231	120	8	384	281	280	2	282	331	330	2	332
182	72	8	336	232	112	8	450	282	92	8	576	332	164	6	588
183	120	4	248	233	232	2	234	283	282	2	284	333	216	6	494
184	88	8	360	234	72	12	546	284	140	6	504	334	166	4	504
185	144	4	228	235	184	4	288	285	144	8	480	335	264	4	408
186	60	8	384	236	116	6	420	286	120	8	504	336	96	20	992
187	160	4	216	237	156	4	320	287	240	4	336	337	336	2	338
188	92	6	336	238	96	8	432	288	96	18	819	338	156	6	549
189	108	8	320	239	238	2	240	289	272	3	307	339	224	4	456
190	72	8	360	240	64	20	744	290	112	8	540	340	128	12	756
191	190	2	192	241	240	2	242	291	192	4	392	341	300	4	384
192	64	14	508	242	110	6	399	292	144	6	518	342	108	12	780
193	192	2	194	243	162	6	364	293	292	2	294	343	294	4	400
194	96	4	294	244	120	6	434	294	84	12	684	344	168	8	660
195	96	8	336	245	168	6	342	295	232	4	360	345	176	8	576
196	84	9	399	246	80	8	504	296	144	8	570	346	172	4	522
197	196	2	198	247	216	4	280	297	180	8	480	347	346	2	348
198	60	12	468	248	120	8	480	298	148	4	450	348	112	12	840
199	198	2	200	249	164	4	336	299	264	4	336	349	348	2	350
200	80	12	465	250	100	8	468	300	80	18	868	350	120	12	744
201	132	4	272	251	250	2	252	301	252	4	352	351	216	8	560
202	100	4	306	252	72	18	728	302	150	4	456	352	160	12	756
203	168	4	240	253	220	4	288	303	200	4	408	353	352	2	354
204	64	12	504	254	126	4	384	304	144	10	620	354	116	8	720
205	160	4	252	255	128	8	432	305	240	4	372	355	280	4	432
206	102	4	312	256	128	9	511	306	96	12	702	356	176	6	630
207	132	6	312	257	256	2	258	307	306	2	308	357	192	8	576
208	96	10	434	258	84	8	528	308	120	12	672	358	178	4	540
209	180	4	240	259	216	4	304	309	204	4	416	359	358	2	360
210	48	16	576	260	96	12	588	310	120	8	576	360	96	24	1170

TOTIENT FUNCTION $\phi(n)$ (Continued)

n	$\phi(n)$	σ_0	σ_1	n	$\phi(n)$	σ_0	σ_1	n	$\phi(n)$	σ_0	σ_1	n	$\phi(n)$	σ_0	σ_1
361	342	3	381	411	272	4	552	461	460	2	462	511	432	4	592
362	180	4	546	412	204	6	728	462	120	16	1152	512	256	10	1023
363	220	6	532	413	348	4	480	463	462	2	464	513	324	8	800
364	144	12	784	414	132	12	936	464	224	10	930	514	256	4	774
365	288	4	444	415	328	4	504	465	240	8	768	515	408	4	624
366	120	8	744	416	192	12	882	466	232	4	702	516	168	12	1232
367	366	2	368	417	276	4	560	467	466	2	468	517	460	4	576
368	176	10	744	418	180	8	720	468	144	18	1274	518	216	8	912
369	240	6	546	419	418	2	420	469	396	4	544	519	344	4	696
370	144	8	684	420	96	24	1344	470	184	8	864	520	192	16	1260
371	312	4	432	421	420	2	422	471	312	4	632	521	520	2	522
372	120	12	896	422	210	4	636	472	232	8	900	522	168	12	1170
373	372	2	374	423	276	6	624	473	420	4	528	523	522	2	524
374	160	8	648	424	208	8	810	474	156	8	960	524	260	6	924
375	200	8	624	425	320	6	558	475	360	6	620	525	240	12	992
376	184	8	720	426	140	8	864	476	192	12	1008	526	262	4	792
377	336	4	420	427	360	4	496	477	312	6	702	527	480	4	576
378	108	16	960	428	212	6	756	478	238	4	720	528	160	20	1488
379	378	2	380	429	240	8	672	479	478	2	480	529	506	3	553
380	144	12	840	430	168	8	792	480	128	24	1512	530	208	8	972
381	252	4	512	431	430	2	432	481	432	4	532	531	348	6	780
382	190	4	576	432	144	20	1240	482	240	4	726	532	216	12	1120
383	382	2	384	433	432	2	434	483	264	8	768	533	480	4	588
384	128	16	1020	434	180	8	768	484	220	9	931	534	176	8	1080
385	240	8	576	435	224	8	720	485	384	4	588	535	424	4	648
386	192	4	582	436	216	6	770	486	162	12	1092	536	264	8	1020
387	252	6	572	437	396	4	480	487	486	2	488	537	356	4	720
388	192	6	686	438	144	8	888	488	240	8	930	538	268	4	810
389	388	2	390	439	438	2	440	489	324	4	656	539	420	6	684
390	96	16	1008	440	160	16	1080	490	168	12	1026	540	144	24	1680
391	352	4	432	441	252	9	741	491	490	2	492	541	540	2	542
392	168	12	855	442	192	8	756	492	160	12	1176	542	270	4	816
393	260	4	528	443	442	2	444	493	448	4	540	543	360	4	728
394	196	4	594	444	144	12	1064	494	216	8	840	544	256	12	1134
395	312	4	480	445	352	4	540	495	240	12	936	545	432	4	660
396	120	18	1092	446	222	4	672	496	240	10	992	546	144	16	1344
397	396	2	398	447	296	4	600	497	420	4	576	547	546	2	548
398	198	4	600	448	192	14	1016	498	164	8	1008	548	272	6	966
399	216	8	640	449	448	2	450	499	498	2	500	549	360	6	806
400	160	15	961	450	120	18	1209	500	200	12	1092	550	200	12	1116
401	400	2	402	451	400	4	504	501	332	4	672	551	504	4	600
402	132	8	816	452	224	6	798	502	250	4	756	552	176	16	1440
403	360	4	448	453	300	4	608	503	502	2	504	553	468	4	640
404	200	6	714	454	226	4	684	504	144	24	1560	554	276	4	834
405	216	10	726	455	288	8	672	505	400	4	612	555	288	8	912
406	168	8	720	456	144	16	1200	506	220	8	864	556	276	6	980
407	360	4	456	457	456	2	458	507	312	6	732	557	556	2	558
408	128	16	1080	458	228	4	690	508	252	6	896	558	180	12	1248
409	408	2	410	459	288	8	720	509	508	2	510	559	504	4	616
410	160	8	756	460	176	12	1008	510	128	16	1296	560	192	20	1488

TOTIENT FUNCTION $\phi(n)$ (Continued)

n	$\phi(n)$	σ_0	σ_1	n	$\phi(n)$	σ_0	σ_1	n	$\phi(n)$	σ_0	σ_1	n	$\phi(n)$	σ_0	σ_1
561	320	8	864	611	552	4	672	661	660	2	662	711	468	6	1040
562	280	4	846	612	192	18	1638	662	330	4	996	712	352	8	1350
563	562	2	564	613	612	2	614	663	384	8	1008	713	660	4	768
564	184	12	1344	614	306	4	924	664	328	8	1260	714	192	16	1728
565	448	4	684	615	320	8	1008	665	432	8	960	715	480	8	1008
566	282	4	852	616	240	16	1440	666	216	12	1482	716	356	6	1260
567	324	10	968	617	616	2	618	667	616	4	720	717	476	4	960
568	280	8	1080	618	204	8	1248	668	332	6	1176	718	358	4	1080
569	568	2	570	619	618	2	620	669	444	4	896	719	718	2	720
570	144	16	1440	620	240	12	1344	670	264	8	1224	720	192	30	2418
571	570	2	572	621	396	8	960	671	600	4	744	721	612	4	832
572	240	12	1176	622	310	4	936	672	192	24	2016	722	342	6	1143
573	380	4	768	623	528	4	720	673	672	2	674	723	480	4	968
574	240	8	1008	624	192	20	1736	674	336	4	1014	724	360	6	1274
575	440	6	744	625	500	5	781	675	360	12	1240	725	560	6	930
576	192	21	1651	626	312	4	942	676	312	9	1281	726	220	12	1596
577	576	2	578	627	360	8	960	677	676	2	678	727	726	2	728
578	272	6	921	628	312	6	1106	678	224	8	1368	728	288	16	1680
579	384	4	776	629	576	4	684	679	576	4	784	729	486	7	1093
580	224	12	1260	630	144	24	1872	680	256	16	1620	730	288	8	1332
581	492	4	672	631	630	2	632	681	452	4	912	731	672	4	792
582	192	8	1176	632	312	8	1200	682	300	8	1152	732	240	12	1736
583	520	4	648	633	420	4	848	683	682	2	684	733	732	2	734
584	288	8	1110	634	316	4	954	684	216	18	1820	734	366	4	1104
585	288	12	1092	635	504	4	768	685	544	4	828	735	336	12	1368
586	292	4	882	636	208	12	1512	686	294	8	1200	736	352	12	1512
587	586	2	588	637	504	6	798	687	456	4	920	737	660	4	816
588	168	18	1596	638	280	8	1080	688	336	10	1364	738	240	12	1638
589	540	4	640	639	420	6	936	689	624	4	756	739	738	2	740
590	232	8	1080	640	256	16	1530	690	176	16	1728	740	288	12	1596
591	392	4	792	641	640	2	642	691	690	2	692	741	432	8	1120
592	288	10	1178	642	212	8	1296	692	344	6	1218	742	312	8	1296
593	592	2	594	643	642	2	644	693	360	12	1248	743	742	2	744
594	180	16	1440	644	264	12	1344	694	346	4	1044	744	240	16	1920
595	384	8	864	645	336	8	1056	695	552	4	840	745	592	4	900
596	296	6	1050	646	288	8	1080	696	224	16	1800	746	372	4	1122
597	396	4	800	647	646	2	648	697	640	4	756	747	492	6	1092
598	264	8	1008	648	216	20	1815	698	348	4	1050	748	320	12	1512
599	598	2	600	649	580	4	720	699	464	4	936	749	636	4	864
600	160	24	1860	650	240	12	1302	700	240	18	1736	750	200	16	1872
601	600	2	602	651	360	8	1024	701	700	2	702	751	750	2	752
602	252	8	1056	652	324	6	1148	702	216	16	1680	752	368	10	1488
603	396	6	884	653	652	2	654	703	648	4	760	753	500	4	1008
604	300	6	1064	654	216	8	1320	704	320	14	1524	754	336	8	1260
605	440	6	798	655	520	4	792	705	368	8	1152	755	600	4	912
606	200	8	1224	656	320	10	1302	706	352	4	1062	756	216	24	2240
607	606	2	608	657	432	6	962	707	600	4	816	757	756	2	758
608	288	12	1260	658	276	8	1152	708	232	12	1680	758	378	4	1140
609	336	8	960	659	658	2	660	709	708	2	710	759	440	8	1152
610	240	8	1116	660	160	24	2016	710	280	8	1296	760	288	16	1800

TOTIENT FUNCTION $\phi(n)$ (Continued)

n	$\phi(n)$	σ_0	σ_1	n	$\phi(n)$	σ_0	σ_1	n	$\phi(n)$	σ_0	σ_1	n	$\phi(n)$	σ_0	σ_1
761	760	2	762	811	810	2	812	861	480	8	1344	911	910	2	912
762	252	8	1536	812	336	12	1680	862	430	4	1296	912	288	20	2480
763	648	4	880	813	540	4	1088	863	862	2	864	913	820	4	1008
764	380	6	1344	814	360	8	1368	864	288	24	2520	914	456	4	1374
765	384	12	1404	815	648	4	984	865	688	4	1044	915	480	8	1488
766	382	4	1152	816	256	20	2232	866	432	4	1302	916	456	6	1610
767	696	4	840	817	756	4	880	867	544	6	1228	917	780	4	1056
768	256	18	2044	818	408	4	1230	868	360	12	1792	918	288	16	2160
769	768	2	770	819	432	12	1456	869	780	4	960	919	918	2	920
770	240	16	1728	820	320	12	1764	870	224	16	2160	920	352	16	2160
771	512	4	1032	821	820	2	822	871	792	4	952	921	612	4	1232
772	384	6	1358	822	272	8	1656	872	432	8	1650	922	460	4	1386
773	772	2	774	823	822	2	824	873	576	6	1274	923	840	4	1008
774	252	12	1716	824	408	8	1560	874	396	8	1440	924	240	24	2688
775	600	6	992	825	400	12	1488	875	600	8	1248	925	720	6	1178
776	384	8	1470	826	348	8	1440	876	288	12	2072	926	462	4	1392
777	432	8	1216	827	826	2	828	877	876	2	878	927	612	6	1352
778	388	4	1170	828	264	18	2184	878	438	4	1320	928	448	12	1890
779	720	4	840	829	828	2	830	879	584	4	1176	929	928	2	930
780	192	24	2352	830	328	8	1512	880	320	20	2232	930	240	16	2304
781	700	4	864	831	552	4	1112	881	880	2	882	931	756	6	1140
782	352	8	1296	832	384	14	1778	882	252	18	2223	932	464	6	1638
783	504	8	1200	833	672	6	1026	883	882	2	884	933	620	4	1248
784	336	15	1767	834	276	8	1680	884	384	12	1764	924	466	4	1404
785	624	4	948	835	664	4	1008	885	464	8	1440	935	640	8	1296
786	260	8	1584	836	360	12	1680	886	442	4	1332	936	288	24	2730
787	786	2	788	837	540	8	1280	887	886	2	888	937	936	2	938
788	392	6	1386	838	418	4	1260	888	288	16	2280	938	396	8	1632
789	524	4	1056	839	838	2	840	889	756	4	1024	939	624	4	1256
790	312	8	1440	840	192	32	2880	890	352	8	1620	940	368	12	2016
791	672	4	912	841	812	3	871	891	540	10	1452	941	940	2	942
792	240	24	2340	842	420	4	1266	892	444	6	1568	942	312	8	1896
793	720	4	868	843	560	4	1128	893	828	4	960	943	880	4	1008
794	396	4	1194	844	420	6	1484	894	296	8	1800	944	464	10	1860
795	416	8	1296	845	624	6	1098	895	712	4	1080	945	432	16	1920
796	396	6	1400	846	276	12	1872	896	384	16	2040	946	420	8	1584
797	796	2	798	847	660	6	1064	897	528	8	1344	947	946	2	948
798	216	16	1920	848	416	10	1674	898	448	4	1350	948	312	12	2240
799	736	4	864	849	564	4	1136	899	840	4	960	949	864	4	1036
800	320	18	1953	850	320	12	1674	900	240	27	2821	950	360	12	1860
801	528	6	1170	851	792	4	912	901	832	4	972	951	632	4	1272
802	400	4	1206	852	280	12	2016	902	400	8	1512	952	384	16	2160
803	720	4	888	853	852	2	854	903	504	8	1408	953	952	2	954
804	264	12	1904	854	360	8	1488	904	448	8	1710	954	312	12	2106
805	528	8	1152	855	432	12	1560	905	720	4	1092	955	760	4	1152
806	360	8	1344	856	424	8	1620	906	300	8	1824	956	476	6	1680
807	536	4	1080	857	856	2	858	907	906	2	908	957	560	8	1440
808	400	8	1530	858	240	16	2016	908	452	6	1596	958	478	4	1440
809	808	2	810	859	858	2	860	909	600	6	1326	959	816	4	1104
810	216	20	2178	860	336	12	1848	910	288	16	2016	960	256	28	3048

TOTIENT FUNCTION $\phi(n)$ (Continued)

n	$\phi(n)$	σ_0	σ_1	n	$\phi(n)$	σ_0	σ_1	n	$\phi(n)$	σ_0	σ_1	n	$\phi(n)$	σ_0	σ_1
961	930	3	993	971	970	2	972	981	648	6	1430	991	990	2	992
962	432	8	1596	972	324	18	2548	982	490	4	1476	992	480	12	2016
963	636	6	1404	973	828	4	1120	983	982	2	984	993	660	4	1328
964	480	6	1694	974	486	4	1464	984	320	16	2520	994	420	8	1728
965	768	4	1164	975	480	12	1736	985	784	4	1188	995	792	4	1200
966	264	16	2304	976	480	10	1922	986	448	8	1620	996	328	12	2352
967	966	2	968	977	976	2	978	987	552	8	1536	997	996	2	998
968	440	12	1995	978	324	8	1968	988	432	12	1960	998	498	4	1500
969	576	8	1440	979	880	4	1080	989	924	4	1056	999	648	8	1520
970	384	8	1764	980	336	18	2394	990	240	24	2808	1000	400	16	2340

From British Association for the Advancement of Science, Mathematical Tables, vol. VIII, Number-divisor tables, by permission of Cambridge University Press.

TABLES OF INDICES AND POWER RESIDUES

H. C. Williams, Ph.D.

1. Introduction

Let a and b be any two positive integers. If the largest integer that divides both a and b is unity, a and b are said to be *relatively prime*. If m is any positive integer, the *totient of m*, denoted by $\phi(m)$, is defined to be the number of positive integers less than m and relatively prime to m. If one writes

$$m = p_1^{\alpha_1} p_2^{\alpha_2} \dots p_n^{\alpha_n},$$

where $p_1, p_2, \dots, p_n$ are distinct primes, it can be shown that

$$\phi(m) = p_1^{\alpha_1 - 1} p_2^{\alpha_2 - 1} \dots p_n^{\alpha_n - 1}(p_1 - 1)(p_2 - 1) \dots (p_n - 1).$$

Two integers a and b are said to be *congruent modulo* an integer m if m is an integer divisor of $a - b$. This relation between a and b is denoted by

$$a \equiv b \pmod{m}.$$

If a is congruent to b modulo m and $0 \leq b < m$, b is called the residue of a modulo m. a and b are said to be distinct modulo m if m is not an integer divisor of $a - b$. A well-known result is the

Theorem. If a and m ($\geqslant 0$) are relatively prime integers, then

$$a^{\phi(m)} \equiv 1 \pmod{m}.$$

Corollary. If p is a prime which is not a divisor of an integer a, then

$$a^{p-1} \equiv 1 \pmod{p}.$$

If a and m (> 0) are relatively prime integers, and μ is the least positive integer for which

$$a^\mu \equiv 1 \pmod{m},$$

μ is called the *exponent* to which a belongs modulo m. If the exponent to which a belongs modulo m is $\phi(m)$, a is defined to be a *primitive root* modulo m (or a primitive root of m).
Theorem. The only integers which possess primitive roots are 2, 4, p^n, $2p^n$, where p is an odd prime.

If m does have a primitive root, it has $\phi(\phi(m))$ distinct primitive roots modulo m.

Let p be any prime, and let g be any primitive root of p. To each integer a relatively prime to p there corresponds a unique integer i such that

$$a \equiv g^i \pmod{p} \qquad (0 < i < p-1).$$

i is called the *index* to base g of a modulo p. This is written

$$i = \text{ind}_g a.$$

For example, consider the prime 11 which has a primitive root $g = 2$. Construct the table below, where

$$r_i \equiv g^i \pmod{p} \qquad (0 < r_i < p).$$

i	0	1	2	3	4	5	6	7	8	9	10
r_i	1	2	4	8	5	10	9	7	3	6	1

Note that the bottom row runs through all possible residues modulo 11, except zero. The index, then, of any number in this row is the corresponding entry in the top row. That is, $\text{ind}_2 1 = 0$, $\text{ind}_2 2 = 1$, $\text{ind}_2 3 = 8$, $\text{ind}_2 4 = 2$, $\text{ind}_2 5 = 4$, $\text{ind}_2 6 = 9$, etc. Indices possess the following important properties (analogous to those of logarithms).

TABLES OF INDICES AND POWER RESIDUES (Continued)

(1) $\text{ind}_g 1 = 0$

(2) $\text{ind}_g(-1) = (p-1)/2$

(3) $\text{ind}_g(ab) \equiv \text{ind}_g a + \text{ind}_g b \pmod{p-1}$

(4) $\text{ind}_g a^n \equiv n \, \text{ind}_g a \pmod{p-1}$

(5) $\text{ind}_g a \equiv \text{ind}_g g' \cdot \text{ind}_{g'} a \pmod{p-1}$,

where g' is any other primitive root of p.

The *power residue* of an integer b to base g is simply the integer r such that

$$r \equiv g^b \pmod{p} \qquad (0 < r < p).$$

Since the power residue of $\text{ind}_g a$ is congruent to a modulo p, it is clear that the concept of indices and power residues is analogous to that of logarithms and antilogarithms.

2. Use of the tables

In the tables that follow, the indices and power residues are given for all primes less than 100. (A table of indices and power residues for all primes and prime powers less than 2000 is given in [1].) In the tables which follow, the base g for the indices and power residues is chosen as the smallest primitive root of p.

To determine the index or power residue of an integer a modulo p, look at the appropriate table for prime p and select the entry in the column under j and in the row under i, where

$$a \equiv 10i + j \pmod{p} \qquad (0 \le i, j \le 9).$$

For example, the index modulo 97 of 134 ($\equiv 37 \pmod{97}$) is the entry under the number 7 and across from the number 3. This is found to be 91.

Indices and power residues can be used to simplify number-theoretic calculations. The following two examples illustrate the use of indices and power residues.

Example. Find an integer congruent to

$$(134)^{92} (54)^{67} \quad \text{modulo } (97).$$

Let

$$a \equiv (134)^{92} (54)^{67} \pmod{97};$$

then

$$\text{ind}_g a \equiv 92 \, \text{ind}_g 37 + 67 \, \text{ind}_g 54 \pmod{96}$$

$$\equiv 92 \,(91) + 67 \,(52) \pmod{96}$$

$$\equiv 48 \pmod{96}.$$

Hence

$$a \equiv g^{48} \equiv 96 \pmod{97}.$$

This is obtained by looking in the body of the table of indices under $p = 97$ and locating the index 48, and then reading the appropriate quadratic residue from the first column and top row.

Example. Find an integer x such that

$$44x^{21} \equiv 53 \pmod{73}.$$

If we take indices of both sides, we get

$$\text{ind}_g 44 + 21 \, \text{ind}_g x \equiv \text{ind}_g 53 \pmod{72}$$

$$71 + 21 \, \text{ind}_g x \equiv 53 \pmod{72}$$

$$21 \, \text{ind}_g x \equiv 54 \pmod{72}$$

$$7 \, \text{ind}_g x \equiv 18 \pmod{24}$$

TABLES OF INDICES AND POWER RESIDUES (Continued)

Multiplying by 7, we get

$$\text{ind}_g x \equiv 7(18) \equiv 6 \quad (\text{mod } 24).$$

Hence

$$x \equiv g^6, g^{30}, g^{54} \quad (\text{mod } 73)$$

and

$$x \equiv 3, 24, 46 \quad (\text{mod } 73).$$

REFERENCE

1. *A Table of Indices and Power Residues,* University of Oklahoma Mathematical Tables Project, W. W. Norton and Co., New York, N.Y., 1962.

INDICES FOR PRIMES 3 to 97

Prime 3
$g = 2$

Indices	0	1	2	3	4	5	6	7	8	9
0		0	1							

Prime 5
$g = 2$

Indices	0	1	2	3	4	5	6	7	8	9
0		0	1	3	2					

Prime 7
$g = 3$

Indices	0	1	2	3	4	5	6	7	8	9
0		0	2	1	4	5	3			

Prime 11
$g = 2$

Indices	0	1	2	3	4	5	6	7	8	9
0		0	1	8	2	4	9	7	3	6
1	5									

Prime 13
$g = 2$

Indices	0	1	2	3	4	5	6	7	8	9
0		0	1	4	2	9	5	11	3	8
1	10	7	6							

Prime 17
$g = 3$

Indices	0	1	2	3	4	5	6	7	8	9
0		0	14	1	12	5	15	11	10	2
1	3	7	13	4	9	6	8			

Prime 19
$g = 2$

Indices	0	1	2	3	4	5	6	7	8	9
0		0	1	13	2	16	14	6	3	8
1	17	12	15	5	7	11	4	10	9	

Prime 23
$g = 5$

Indices	0	1	2	3	4	5	6	7	8	9
0		0	2	16	4	1	18	19	6	10
1	3	9	20	14	21	17	8	7	12	15
2	5	13	11							

Prime 29
$g = 2$

Indices	0	1	2	3	4	5	6	7	8	9
0		0	1	5	2	22	6	12	3	10
1	23	25	7	18	13	27	4	21	11	9
2	24	17	26	20	8	16	19	15	14	

Prime 31
$g = 3$

Indices	0	1	2	3	4	5	6	7	8	9
0		0	24	1	18	20	25	28	12	2
1	14	23	19	11	22	21	6	7	26	4
2	8	29	17	27	13	10	5	3	16	9
3	14									

Prime 37
$g = 2$

Indices	0	1	2	3	4	5	6	7	8	9
0		0	1	26	2	23	27	32	3	16
1	24	30	28	11	33	13	4	7	17	35
2	25	22	31	15	29	10	12	6	34	21
3	14	9	5	20	8	19	18			

Prime 41
$g = 6$

Indices	0	1	2	3	4	5	6	7	8	9
0		0	26	15	12	22	1	39	38	30
1	8	3	27	31	25	37	24	33	16	9
2	34	14	29	36	13	4	17	5	11	7
3	23	28	10	18	19	21	2	32	35	6
4	20									

Prime 43
$g = 3$

Indices	0	1	2	3	4	5	6	7	8	9
0		0	27	1	12	25	28	35	39	2
1	10	30	13	32	20	26	24	38	29	19
2	37	36	15	16	40	8	17	3	5	41
3	11	34	9	31	23	18	14	7	4	33
4	22	6	21							

Prime 47
$g = 5$

Indices	0	1	2	3	4	5	6	7	8	9
0		0	18	20	36	1	38	32	8	40
1	19	7	10	11	4	21	26	16	12	45
2	37	6	25	5	28	2	29	14	22	35
3	39	3	44	27	34	33	30	42	17	31
4	9	15	24	13	43	41	23			

Prime 53
$g = 2$

Indices	0	1	2	3	4	5	6	7	8	9
0		0	1	17	2	47	18	14	3	34
1	48	6	19	24	15	12	4	10	35	37
2	49	31	7	39	20	42	25	51	16	46
3	13	33	5	23	11	9	36	30	38	41
4	50	45	32	22	8	29	40	44	21	28
5	43	27	26							

Prime 59
$g = 2$

Indices	0	1	2	3	4	5	6	7	8	9
0		0	1	50	2	6	51	18	3	42
1	7	25	52	45	19	56	4	40	43	38
2	8	10	26	15	53	12	46	34	20	28
3	57	49	5	17	41	24	44	55	39	37
4	9	14	11	33	27	48	16	23	54	36
5	13	32	47	22	35	31	21	30	29	

Prime 61
$g = 2$

Indices	0	1	2	3	4	5	6	7	8	9
0		0	1	6	2	22	7	49	3	12
1	23	15	8	40	50	28	4	47	13	26
2	24	55	16	57	9	44	41	18	51	35
3	29	59	5	21	48	11	14	39	27	46
4	25	54	56	43	17	34	58	20	10	38
5	45	53	42	33	19	37	52	32	36	31
6	30									

INDICES FOR PRIMES 3 to 97 (Continued)

Prime 67
$g = 2$

Indices

	0	1	2	3	4	5	6	7	8	9
0		0	1	39	2	15	40	23	3	12
1	16	59	41	19	24	54	4	64	13	10
2	17	62	60	28	42	30	20	51	25	44
3	55	47	5	32	65	38	14	22	11	58
4	18	53	63	9	61	27	29	50	43	46
5	31	37	21	57	52	8	26	49	45	36
6	56	7	48	35	6	34	33			

Prime 71
$g = 7$

Indices

	0	1	2	3	4	5	6	7	8	9
0		0	6	26	12	28	32	1	18	52
1	34	31	38	39	7	54	24	49	58	16
2	40	27	37	15	44	56	45	8	13	68
3	60	11	30	57	55	29	64	20	22	65
4	46	25	33	48	43	10	21	9	50	2
5	62	5	51	23	14	59	19	42	4	3
6	66	69	17	53	36	67	63	47	61	41
7	35									

Prime 73
$g = 5$

Indices

	0	1	2	3	4	5	6	7	8	9
0		0	8	6	16	1	14	33	24	12
1	9	55	22	59	41	7	32	21	20	62
2	17	39	63	46	30	2	67	18	49	35
3	15	11	40	61	29	34	28	64	70	65
4	25	4	47	51	71	13	54	31	38	66
5	10	27	3	53	26	56	57	68	43	5
6	23	58	19	45	48	60	69	50	37	52
7	42	44	36							

Prime 79
$g = 3$

Indices

	0	1	2	3	4	5	6	7	8	9
0		0	4	1	8	62	5	43	12	2
1	66	68	9	34	57	63	16	21	6	32
2	70	54	72	26	13	46	38	3	61	11
3	67	56	20	69	25	37	10	19	36	35
4	74	75	58	49	76	64	30	59	17	28
5	50	22	42	77	7	52	65	33	15	31
6	71	45	60	55	24	18	73	48	29	27
7	41	51	14	44	23	47	40	43	39	

Prime 83
$g = 2$

Indices

	0	1	2	3	4	5	6	7	8	9
0		0	1	72	2	27	73	8	3	62
1	28	24	74	77	9	17	4	56	63	47
2	29	80	25	60	75	54	78	52	10	12
3	18	38	5	14	57	35	64	20	48	67
4	30	40	81	71	26	7	61	23	76	16
5	55	46	79	59	53	51	11	37	3	34
6	19	66	39	70	6	22	15	45	58	50
7	36	33	65	69	21	44	49	32	68	43
8	31	42	41							

Prime 89
$g = 3$

Indices

	0	1	2	3	4	5	6	7	8	9
0		0	16	1	32	70	17	81	48	2
1	86	84	33	23	9	71	64	6	18	35
2	14	82	12	57	49	52	39	3	25	59
3	87	31	80	85	22	63	34	11	51	24
4	30	21	10	29	28	72	73	54	65	74
5	68	7	55	78	19	66	41	36	75	43
6	15	69	47	83	8	5	13	56	38	58
7	79	62	50	20	27	53	67	77	40	42
8	46	4	37	61	26	76	45	60	44	

Prime 97
$g = 5$

Indices

	0	1	2	3	4	5	6	7	8	9
0		0	34	70	68	1	8	31	6	44
1	35	86	42	25	65	71	40	89	78	81
2	69	5	24	77	76	2	59	18	3	13
3	9	46	74	60	27	32	16	91	19	95
4	7	85	39	4	58	45	15	84	14	62
5	36	63	93	10	52	87	37	55	47	67
6	43	64	80	75	12	26	94	57	61	51
7	66	11	50	28	29	72	53	21	33	30
8	41	88	23	17	73	90	38	83	92	54
9	76	56	49	20	22	82	48			

PRIMITIVE ROOTS FOR PRIMES 3 to 5003

In this table

   g denotes the least primitive root of p

   G denotes the least negative primitive root of p

   ϵ denotes whether 10, -10 both or neither are primitive roots of p

Introductory Facts

As noted in the preceding Totient and Indices Tables, the number of integers not exceeding and relatively prime to a fixed integer n is represented by $\phi(n)$. These integers form a group; the group is cyclic if and only if $n = 2, 4$, or n is of the form p^k or $2p^k$ where p is an odd prime. We refer to g as a primitive root of n if it generates that group i.e. if $g, g^2, \ldots, g^{\phi(n)}$ are distinct modulo n. There are $\phi(\phi(n))$ primitive roots of n. If g is a primitive root of p and $g^{p-1} \not\equiv 1 \pmod{p^2}$, then g is a primitive root of p^k for all k. If $g^{p-1} \equiv 1 \pmod{p^2}$ then $g + p$ is a primitive root of p^k for all k.

If g is a primitive root of p^k then either g or $g + p^k$, whichever is odd, is a primitive root of $2p^k$.

If g is a primitive root of n, then g^k is a primitive root of n if and only if k and $\phi(n)$ are relatively prime, and each primitive root of n is of this form, i.e. $(k, \phi(n)) = 1$.

p	$p-1$	g	$-G$	ϵ	p	$p-1$	g	$-G$	ϵ
3	2	2	1	-10	167	2·83	5	2	10
5	2²	2	2	—	173	2²·43	2	2	—
7	2·3	3	2	10	179	2·89	2	3	10
11	2·5	2	3	—	181	2²·3²·5	2	2	±10
13	2²·3	2	2	—	191	2·5·19	19	2	-10
17	2⁴	3	3	±10	193	2⁶·3	5	5	±10
19	2·3²	2	4	10	197	2²·7²	2	2	—
23	2·11	5	2	10	199	2·3²·11	3	2	-10
29	2²·7	2	2	±10	211	2·3·5·7	2	4	—
31	2·3·5	3	7	-10	223	2·3·37	3	9	10
37	2²·3²	2	2	—	227	2·113	2	3	-10
41	2³·5	6	6	—	229	2²·3·19	6	6	±10
43	2·3·7	3	9	-10	233	2³·29	3	3	±10
47	2·23	5	2	10	239	2·7·17	7	2	—
53	2²·13	2	2	—	241	2⁴·3·5	7	7	—
59	2·29	2	3	10	251	2·5³	6	3	—
61	2²·3·5	2	2	±10	257	2⁸	3	3	±10
67	2·3·11	2	4	-10	263	2·131	5	2	10
71	2·5·7	7	2	-10	269	2²·67	2	2	±10
73	2³·3²	5	5	—	271	2·3³·5	6	2	—
79	2·3·13	3	2	—	277	2²·3·23	5	5	—
83	2·41	2	3	-10	281	2³·5·7	3	3	—
89	2³·11	3	3	—	283	2·3·47	3	6	-10
97	2⁵·3	5	5	±10	293	2²·73	2	2	—
101	2²·5²	2	2	—	307	2·3²·17	5	7	-10
103	2·3·17	5	2	—	311	2·5·31	17	2	-10
107	2·53	2	3	-10	313	2³·3·13	10	10	±10
109	2²·3³	6	6	±10	317	2²·79	2	2	—
113	2⁴·7	3	3	±10	331	2·3·5·11	3	5	—
127	2·3²·7	3	9	—	337	2⁴·3·7	10	10	±10
131	2·5·13	2	3	10	347	2·173	2	3	-10
137	2³·17	3	3	—	349	2²·3·29	2	2	—
139	2·3·23	2	4	—	353	2⁵·11	3	3	—
149	2²·37	2	2	±10	359	2·179	7	2	-10
151	2·3·5²	6	5	-10	367	2·3·61	6	2	10
157	2²·3·13	5	5	—	373	2²·3·31	2	2	—
163	2·3⁴	2	4	-10	379	2·3³·7	2	4	10

PRIMITIVE ROOTS FOR PRIMES 3 to 5003 (Continued)

p	p−1	g	−G	ε	p	p−1	g	−G	ε
383	$2 \cdot 191$	5	2	10	769	$2^8 \cdot 3$	11	11	—
389	$2^2 \cdot 97$	2	2	±10	773	$2^2 \cdot 193$	2	2	—
397	$2^2 \cdot 3^2 \cdot 11$	5	5	—	787	$2 \cdot 3 \cdot 131$	2	4	−10
401	$2^4 \cdot 5^2$	3	3	—	797	$2^2 \cdot 199$	2	2	—
409	$2^3 \cdot 3 \cdot 17$	21	21	—	809	$2^3 \cdot 101$	3	3	—
419	$2 \cdot 11 \cdot 19$	2	3	10	811	$2 \cdot 3^4 \cdot 5$	3	5	10
421	$2^2 \cdot 3 \cdot 5 \cdot 7$	2	2	—	821	$2^2 \cdot 5 \cdot 41$	2	2	±10
431	$2 \cdot 5 \cdot 43$	7	5	−10	823	$2 \cdot 3 \cdot 137$	3	2	10
433	$2^4 \cdot 3^3$	5	5	±10	827	$2 \cdot 7 \cdot 59$	2	3	−10
439	$2 \cdot 3 \cdot 73$	15	5	−10	829	$2^2 \cdot 3^2 \cdot 23$	2	2	—
443	$2 \cdot 13 \cdot 17$	2	3	−10	839	$2 \cdot 419$	11	2	−10
449	$2^6 \cdot 7$	3	3	—	853	$2^2 \cdot 3 \cdot 71$	2	2	—
457	$2^3 \cdot 3 \cdot 19$	13	13	—	857	$2^3 \cdot 107$	3	3	±10
461	$2^2 \cdot 5 \cdot 23$	2	2	±10	859	$2 \cdot 3 \cdot 11 \cdot 13$	2	4	—
463	$2 \cdot 3 \cdot 7 \cdot 11$	3	2	—	863	$2 \cdot 431$	5	2	10
467	$2 \cdot 233$	2	3	−10	877	$2^2 \cdot 3 \cdot 73$	2	2	—
479	$2 \cdot 239$	13	2	−10	881	$2^4 \cdot 5 \cdot 11$	3	3	—
487	$2 \cdot 3^5$	3	2	10	883	$2 \cdot 3^2 \cdot 7^2$	2	4	−10
491	$2 \cdot 5 \cdot 7^2$	2	4	10	887	$2 \cdot 443$	5	2	10
499	$2 \cdot 3 \cdot 83$	7	5	10	907	$2 \cdot 3 \cdot 151$	2	4	—
503	$2 \cdot 251$	5	2	10	911	$2 \cdot 5 \cdot 7 \cdot 13$	17	3	−10
509	$2^2 \cdot 127$	2	2	±10	919	$2 \cdot 3^3 \cdot 17$	7	5	−10
521	$2^3 \cdot 5 \cdot 13$	3	3	—	929	$2^5 \cdot 29$	3	3	—
523	$2 \cdot 3^2 \cdot 29$	2	4	−10	937	$2^3 \cdot 3^2 \cdot 13$	5	5	±10
541	$2^2 \cdot 3^3 \cdot 5$	2	2	±10	941	$2^2 \cdot 5 \cdot 47$	2	2	±10
547	$2 \cdot 3 \cdot 7 \cdot 13$	2	4	—	947	$2 \cdot 11 \cdot 43$	2	3	−10
557	$2^2 \cdot 139$	2	2	—	953	$2^3 \cdot 7 \cdot 17$	3	3	±10
563	$2 \cdot 281$	2	3	−10	967	$2 \cdot 3 \cdot 7 \cdot 23$	5	2	—
569	$2^3 \cdot 71$	3	3	—.	971	$2 \cdot 5 \cdot 97$	6	3	10
571	$2 \cdot 3 \cdot 5 \cdot 19$	3	5	10	977	$2^4 \cdot 61$	3	3	±10
577	$2^6 \cdot 3^2$	5	5	±10	983	$2 \cdot 491$	5	2	10
587	$2 \cdot 293$	2	3	−10	991	$2 \cdot 3^2 \cdot 5 \cdot 11$	6	2	−10
593	$2^4 \cdot 37$	3	3	±10	997	$2^2 \cdot 3 \cdot 83$	7	7	—
599	$2 \cdot 13 \cdot 23$	7	2	−10	1009	$2^4 \cdot 3^2 \cdot 7$	11	11	—
601	$2^3 \cdot 3 \cdot 5^2$	7	7	—	1013	$2^2 \cdot 11 \cdot 23$	3	3	—
607	$2 \cdot 3 \cdot 101$	3	2	—	1019	$2 \cdot 509$	2	3	10
613	$2^2 \cdot 3^2 \cdot 17$	2	2	—	1021	$2^2 \cdot 3 \cdot 5 \cdot 17$	10	10	±10
617	$2^3 \cdot 7 \cdot 11$	3	3	—	1031	$2 \cdot 5 \cdot 103$	14	2	—
619	$2 \cdot 3 \cdot 103$	2	4	10	1033	$2^3 \cdot 3 \cdot 43$	5	5	±10
631	$2 \cdot 3^2 \cdot 5 \cdot 7$	3	9	−10	1039	$2 \cdot 3 \cdot 173$	3	2	−10
641	$2^7 \cdot 5$	3	3	—	1049	$2^3 \cdot 131$	3	3	—
643	$2 \cdot 3 \cdot 107$	11	7	—	1051	$2 \cdot 3 \cdot 5^2 \cdot 7$	7	5	10
647	$2 \cdot 17 \cdot 19$	5	2	10	1061	$2^2 \cdot 5 \cdot 53$	2	2	—
653	$2^2 \cdot 163$	2	2	—	1063	$2 \cdot 3^2 \cdot 59$	3	2	10
659	$2 \cdot 7 \cdot 47$	2	3	10	1069	$2^2 \cdot 3 \cdot 89$	6	6	±10
661	$2^2 \cdot 3 \cdot 5 \cdot 11$	2	2	—	1087	$2 \cdot 3 \cdot 181$	3	2	10
673	$2^5 \cdot 3 \cdot 7$	5	5	—	1091	$2 \cdot 5 \cdot 109$	2	4	10
677	$2^2 \cdot 13^2$	2	2	—	1093	$2^2 \cdot 3 \cdot 7 \cdot 13$	5	5	—
683	$2 \cdot 11 \cdot 31$	5	10	−10	1097	$2^3 \cdot 137$	3	3	±10
691	$2 \cdot 3 \cdot 5 \cdot 23$	3	6	—	1103	$2 \cdot 19 \cdot 29$	5	3	10
701	$2^2 \cdot 5^2 \cdot 7$	2	2	±10	1109	$2^2 \cdot 277$	2	2	±10
709	$2^2 \cdot 3 \cdot 59$	2	2	±10	1117	$2^2 \cdot 3^2 \cdot 31$	2	2	—
719	$2 \cdot 359$	11	2	−10	1123	$2 \cdot 3 \cdot 11 \cdot 17$	2	4	−10
727	$2 \cdot 3 \cdot 11^2$	5	7	10	1129	$2^3 \cdot 3 \cdot 47$	11	11	—
733	$2^2 \cdot 3 \cdot 61$	6	6	—	1151	$2 \cdot 5^2 \cdot 23$	17	2	−10
739	$2 \cdot 3^2 \cdot 41$	3	6	—	1153	$2^7 \cdot 3^2$	5	5	±10
743	$2 \cdot 7 \cdot 53$	5	2	10	1163	$2 \cdot 7 \cdot 83$	5	3	−10
751	$2 \cdot 3 \cdot 5^3$	3	2	—	1171	$2 \cdot 3^2 \cdot 5 \cdot 13$	2	4	10
757	$2^2 \cdot 3^3 \cdot 7$	2	2	—	1181	$2^2 \cdot 5 \cdot 59$	7	7	±10
761	$2^3 \cdot 5 \cdot 19$	6	6	—	1187	$2 \cdot 593$	2	3	−10

PRIMITIVE ROOTS FOR PRIMES 3 to 5003 (Continued)

p	$p-1$	g	$-G$	ϵ	p	$p-1$	g	$-G$	ϵ
1193	$2^3 \cdot 149$	3	3	± 10	1619	$2 \cdot 809$	2	3	10
1201	$2^4 \cdot 3 \cdot 5^2$	11	11	—	1621	$2^2 \cdot 3^4 \cdot 5$	2	2	± 10
1213	$2^2 \cdot 3 \cdot 101$	2	2	—	1627	$2 \cdot 3 \cdot 271$	3	6	—
1217	$2^6 \cdot 19$	3	3	± 10	1637	$2^2 \cdot 409$	2	2	—
1223	$2 \cdot 13 \cdot 47$	5	2	10	1657	$2^3 \cdot 3^2 \cdot 23$	11	11	—
1229	$2^2 \cdot 307$	2	2	± 10	1663	$2 \cdot 3 \cdot 277$	3	2	10
1231	$2 \cdot 3 \cdot 5 \cdot 41$	3	2	—	1667	$2 \cdot 7^2 \cdot 17$	2	3	-10
1237	$2^2 \cdot 3 \cdot 103$	2	2	—	1669	$2^2 \cdot 3 \cdot 139$	2	2	—
1249	$2^5 \cdot 3 \cdot 13$	7	7	—	1693	$2^2 \cdot 3^2 \cdot 47$	2	2	—
1259	$2 \cdot 17 \cdot 37$	2	3	10	1697	$2^5 \cdot 53$	3	3	± 10
1277	$2^2 \cdot 11 \cdot 29$	2	2	—	1699	$2 \cdot 3 \cdot 283$	3	6	—
1279	$2 \cdot 3^2 \cdot 71$	3	2	-10	1709	$2^2 \cdot 7 \cdot 61$	3	3	± 10
1283	$2 \cdot 641$	2	3	-10	1721	$2^3 \cdot 5 \cdot 43$	3	3	—
1289	$2^3 \cdot 7 \cdot 23$	6	6	—	1723	$2 \cdot 3 \cdot 7 \cdot 41$	3	6	—
1291	$2 \cdot 3 \cdot 5 \cdot 43$	2	4	10	1733	$2^2 \cdot 433$	2	2	—
1297	$2^4 \cdot 3^4$	10	10	± 10	1741	$2^2 \cdot 3 \cdot 5 \cdot 29$	2	2	± 10
1301	$2^2 \cdot 5^2 \cdot 13$	2	2	± 10	1747	$2 \cdot 3^2 \cdot 97$	2	4	—
1303	$2 \cdot 3 \cdot 7 \cdot 31$	6	2	10	1753	$2^3 \cdot 3 \cdot 73$	7	7	—
1307	$2 \cdot 653$	2	3	-10	1759	$2 \cdot 3 \cdot 293$	6	2	-10
1319	$2 \cdot 659$	13	2	-10	1777	$2^4 \cdot 3 \cdot 37$	5	5	± 10
1321	$2^3 \cdot 3 \cdot 5 \cdot 11$	13	13	—	1783	$2 \cdot 3^4 \cdot 11$	10	2	10
1327	$2 \cdot 3 \cdot 13 \cdot 17$	3	9	10	1787	$2 \cdot 19 \cdot 47$	2	3	-10
1361	$2^4 \cdot 5 \cdot 17$	3	3	—	1789	$2^2 \cdot 3 \cdot 149$	6	6	± 10
1367	$2 \cdot 683$	5	2	10	1801	$2^3 \cdot 3^2 \cdot 5^2$	11	11	—
1373	$2^2 \cdot 7^3$	2	2	—	1811	$2 \cdot 5 \cdot 181$	6	3	10
1381	$2^2 \cdot 3 \cdot 5 \cdot 23$	2	2	± 10	1823	$2 \cdot 911$	5	2	10
1399	$2 \cdot 3 \cdot 233$	13	5	-10	1831	$2 \cdot 3 \cdot 5 \cdot 61$	3	9	—
1409	$2^7 \cdot 11$	3	3	—	1847	$2 \cdot 13 \cdot 71$	5	2	10
1423	$2 \cdot 3^2 \cdot 79$	3	9	—	1861	$2^2 \cdot 3 \cdot 5 \cdot 31$	2	2	± 10
1427	$2 \cdot 23 \cdot 31$	2	3	-10	1867	$2 \cdot 3 \cdot 311$	2	4	-10
1429	$2^2 \cdot 3 \cdot 7 \cdot 17$	6	6	± 10	1871	$2 \cdot 5 \cdot 11 \cdot 17$	14	2	-10
1433	$2^3 \cdot 179$	3	3	± 10	1873	$2^4 \cdot 3^2 \cdot 13$	10	10	± 10
1439	$2 \cdot 719$	7	2	-10	1877	$2^2 \cdot 7 \cdot 67$	2	2	—
1447	$2 \cdot 3 \cdot 241$	3	2	10	1879	$2 \cdot 3 \cdot 313$	6	2	—
1451	$2 \cdot 5^2 \cdot 29$	2	3	—	1889	$2^5 \cdot 59$	3	3	—
1453	$2^2 \cdot 3 \cdot 11^2$	2	2	—	1901	$2^2 \cdot 5^2 \cdot 19$	2	2	—
1459	$2 \cdot 3^6$	3	6	—	1907	$2 \cdot 953$	2	3	-10
1471	$2 \cdot 3 \cdot 5 \cdot 7^2$	6	5	-10	1913	$2^3 \cdot 239$	3	3	± 10
1481	$2^3 \cdot 5 \cdot 37$	3	3	—	1931	$2 \cdot 5 \cdot 193$	2	3	—
1483	$2 \cdot 3 \cdot 13 \cdot 19$	2	4	—	1933	$2^2 \cdot 3 \cdot 7 \cdot 23$	5	5	—
1487	$2 \cdot 743$	5	2	10	1949	$2^2 \cdot 487$	2	2	± 10
1489	$2^4 \cdot 3 \cdot 31$	14	14	—	1951	$2 \cdot 3 \cdot 5^2 \cdot 13$	3	2	—
1493	$2^2 \cdot 373$	2	2	—	1973	$2^2 \cdot 17 \cdot 29$	2	2	—
1499	$2 \cdot 7 \cdot 107$	2	3	—	1979	$2 \cdot 23 \cdot 43$	2	3	10
1511	$2 \cdot 5 \cdot 151$	11	2	-10	1987	$2 \cdot 3 \cdot 331$	2	4	—
1523	$2 \cdot 761$	2	3	-10	1993	$2^3 \cdot 3 \cdot 83$	5	5	—
1531	$2 \cdot 3^2 \cdot 5 \cdot 17$	2	4	10	1997	$2^2 \cdot 499$	2	2	—
1543	$2 \cdot 3 \cdot 257$	5	2	10	1999	$2 \cdot 3^3 \cdot 37$	3	5	-10
1549	$2^2 \cdot 3^2 \cdot 43$	2	2	± 10	2003	$2 \cdot 7 \cdot 11 \cdot 13$	5	3	-10
1553	$2^4 \cdot 97$	3	3	± 10	2011	$2 \cdot 3 \cdot 5 \cdot 67$	3	5	—
1559	$2 \cdot 19 \cdot 41$	19	2	-10	2017	$2^5 \cdot 3^2 \cdot 7$	5	5	± 10
1567	$2 \cdot 3^3 \cdot 29$	3	2	10	2027	$2 \cdot 1013$	2	3	-10
1571	$2 \cdot 5 \cdot 157$	2	3	10	2029	$2^2 \cdot 3 \cdot 13^2$	2	2	± 10
1579	$2 \cdot 3 \cdot 263$	3	5	10	2039	$2 \cdot 1019$	7	2	-10
1583	$2 \cdot 7 \cdot 113$	5	2	10	2053	$2^2 \cdot 3^3 \cdot 19$	2	2	—
1597	$2^2 \cdot 3 \cdot 7 \cdot 19$	11	11	—	2063	$2 \cdot 1031$	5	2	10
1601	$2^6 \cdot 5^2$	3	3	—	2069	$2^3 \cdot 11 \cdot 47$	2	2	± 10
1607	$2 \cdot 11 \cdot 73$	5	2	10	2081	$2^5 \cdot 5 \cdot 13$	3	3	—
1609	$2^3 \cdot 3 \cdot 67$	7	7	—	2083	$2 \cdot 3 \cdot 347$	2	4	-10
1613	$2^2 \cdot 13 \cdot 31$	3	3	—	2087	$2 \cdot 7 \cdot 149$	5	2	—

PRIMITIVE ROOTS FOR PRIMES 3 to 5003 (Continued)

p	$p-1$	g	$-G$	ϵ	p	$p-1$	g	$-G$	ϵ
2089	$2^3 \cdot 3^2 \cdot 29$	7	7	—	2579	$2 \cdot 1289$	2	3	10
2099	$2 \cdot 1049$	2	3	10	2591	$2 \cdot 5 \cdot 7 \cdot 37$	7	2	—
2111	$2 \cdot 5 \cdot 211$	7	2	-10	2593	$2^5 \cdot 3^4$	7	7	± 10
2113	$2^6 \cdot 3 \cdot 11$	5	5	± 10	2609	$2^4 \cdot 163$	3	3	—
2129	$2^4 \cdot 7 \cdot 19$	3	3	—	2617	$2^3 \cdot 3 \cdot 109$	5	5	± 10
2131	$2 \cdot 3 \cdot 5 \cdot 71$	2	4	—	2621	$2^2 \cdot 5 \cdot 131$	2	2	± 10
2137	$2^3 \cdot 3 \cdot 89$	10	10	± 10	2633	$2^3 \cdot 7 \cdot 47$	3	3	± 10
2141	$2^2 \cdot 5 \cdot 107$	2	2	± 10	2647	$2 \cdot 3^3 \cdot 7^2$	3	2	—
2143	$2 \cdot 3^2 \cdot 7 \cdot 17$	3	9	10	2657	$2^5 \cdot 83$	3	3	± 10
2153	$2^3 \cdot 269$	3	3	± 10	2659	$2 \cdot 3 \cdot 443$	2	4	—
2161	$2^4 \cdot 3^3 \cdot 5$	23	23	—	2663	$2 \cdot 11^3$	5	2	10
2179	$2 \cdot 3^2 \cdot 11^2$	7	5	10	2671	$2 \cdot 3 \cdot 5 \cdot 89$	7	5	-10
2203	$2 \cdot 3 \cdot 367$	5	7	-10	2677	$2^2 \cdot 3 \cdot 223$	2	2	—
2207	$2 \cdot 1103$	5	2	10	2683	$2 \cdot 3^2 \cdot 149$	2	4	—
2213	$2^2 \cdot 7 \cdot 79$	2	2	—	2687	$2 \cdot 17 \cdot 79$	5	3	10
2221	$2^2 \cdot 3 \cdot 5 \cdot 37$	2	2	± 10	2689	$2^7 \cdot 3 \cdot 7$	19	19	—
2237	$2^2 \cdot 13 \cdot 43$	2	2	—	2693	$2^2 \cdot 673$	2	2	—
2239	$2 \cdot 3 \cdot 373$	3	2	-10	2699	$2 \cdot 19 \cdot 71$	2	3	10
2243	$2 \cdot 19 \cdot 59$	2	3	-10	2707	$2 \cdot 3 \cdot 11 \cdot 41$	2	4	-10
2251	$2 \cdot 3^2 \cdot 5^3$	7	5	10	2711	$2 \cdot 5 \cdot 271$	7	2	-10
2267	$2 \cdot 11 \cdot 103$	2	3	-10	2713	$2^3 \cdot 3 \cdot 113$	5	5	± 10
2269	$2^2 \cdot 3^4 \cdot 7$	2	2	± 10	2719	$2 \cdot 3^2 \cdot 151$	3	2	-10
2273	$2^5 \cdot 71$	3	3	± 10	2729	$2^3 \cdot 11 \cdot 31$	3	3	—
2281	$2^3 \cdot 3 \cdot 5 \cdot 19$	7	7	—	2731	$2 \cdot 3 \cdot 5 \cdot 7 \cdot 13$	3	5	10
2287	$2 \cdot 3^2 \cdot 127$	19	7	—	2741	$2^2 \cdot 5 \cdot 137$	2	2	± 10
2293	$2^2 \cdot 3 \cdot 191$	2	2	—	2749	$2^2 \cdot 3 \cdot 229$	6	6	—
2297	$2^3 \cdot 7 \cdot 41$	5	5	± 10	2753	$2^6 \cdot 43$	3	3	± 10
2309	$2^2 \cdot 577$	2	2	± 10	2767	$2 \cdot 3 \cdot 461$	3	9	10
2311	$2 \cdot 3 \cdot 5 \cdot 7 \cdot 11$	3	2	—	2777	$2^3 \cdot 347$	3	3	± 10
2333	$2^2 \cdot 11 \cdot 53$	2	2	—	2789	$2^2 \cdot 17 \cdot 41$	2	2	± 10
2339	$2 \cdot 7 \cdot 167$	2	3	10	2791	$2 \cdot 3^2 \cdot 5 \cdot 31$	6	7	—
2341	$2^2 \cdot 3^2 \cdot 5 \cdot 13$	7	7	± 10	2797	$2^2 \cdot 3 \cdot 233$	2	2	—
2347	$2 \cdot 3 \cdot 17 \cdot 23$	3	6	-10	2801	$2^4 \cdot 5^2 \cdot 7$	3	3	—
2351	$2 \cdot 5^2 \cdot 47$	13	3	-10	2803	$2 \cdot 3 \cdot 467$	2	4	-10
2357	$2^2 \cdot 19 \cdot 31$	2	2	—	2819	$2 \cdot 1409$	2	3	10
2371	$2 \cdot 3 \cdot 5 \cdot 79$	2	4	10	2833	$2^4 \cdot 3 \cdot 59$	5	5	± 10
2377	$2^3 \cdot 3^3 \cdot 11$	5	5	—	2837	$2^2 \cdot 709$	2	2	—
2381	$2^2 \cdot 5 \cdot 7 \cdot 17$	3	3	—	2843	$2 \cdot 7^2 \cdot 29$	2	4	-10
2383	$2 \cdot 3 \cdot 397$	5	13	10	2851	$2 \cdot 3 \cdot 5^2 \cdot 19$	2	4	10
2389	$2^2 \cdot 3 \cdot 199$	2	2	± 10	2857	$2^3 \cdot 3 \cdot 7 \cdot 17$	11	11	—
2393	$2^3 \cdot 13 \cdot 23$	3	3	—	2861	$2^2 \cdot 5 \cdot 11 \cdot 13$	2	2	± 10
2399	$2 \cdot 11 \cdot 109$	11	2	-10	2879	$2 \cdot 1439$	7	2	-10
2411	$2 \cdot 5 \cdot 241$	6	3	10	2887	$2 \cdot 3 \cdot 13 \cdot 37$	5	2	10
2417	$2^4 \cdot 151$	3	3	± 10	2897	$2^4 \cdot 181$	3	3	± 10
2423	$2 \cdot 7 \cdot 173$	5	2	10	2903	$2 \cdot 1451$	5	2	10
2437	$2^2 \cdot 3 \cdot 7 \cdot 29$	2	2	—	2909	$2^2 \cdot 727$	2	2	± 10
2441	$2^3 \cdot 5 \cdot 61$	6	6	—	2917	$2^2 \cdot 3^6$	5	5	—
2447	$2 \cdot 1223$	5	2	10	2927	$2 \cdot 7 \cdot 11 \cdot 19$	5	2	10
2459	$2 \cdot 1229$	2	3	10	2939	$2 \cdot 13 \cdot 113$	2	3	10
2467	$2 \cdot 3^2 \cdot 137$	2	4	—	2953	$2^3 \cdot 3^2 \cdot 41$	13	13	—
2473	$2^3 \cdot 3 \cdot 103$	5	5	± 10	2957	$2^2 \cdot 739$	2	2	—
2477	$2^2 \cdot 619$	2	2	—	2963	$2 \cdot 1481$	2	3	-10
2503	$2 \cdot 3^2 \cdot 139$	3	2	—	2969	$2^3 \cdot 7 \cdot 53$	3	3	—
2521	$2^3 \cdot 3^2 \cdot 5 \cdot 7$	17	17	—	2971	$2 \cdot 3^3 \cdot 5 \cdot 11$	10	5	10
2531	$2 \cdot 5 \cdot 11 \cdot 23$	2	3	—	2999	$2 \cdot 1499$	17	2	-10
2539	$2 \cdot 3^3 \cdot 47$	2	4	10	3001	$2^3 \cdot 3 \cdot 5^3$	14	14	—
2543	$2 \cdot 31 \cdot 41$	5	2	10	3011	$2 \cdot 5 \cdot 7 \cdot 43$	2	3	10
2549	$2^2 \cdot 7^2 \cdot 13$	2	2	± 10	3019	$2 \cdot 3 \cdot 503$	2	4	10
2551	$2 \cdot 3 \cdot 5^2 \cdot 17$	6	2	—	3023	$2 \cdot 1511$	5	2	10
2557	$2^2 \cdot 3^2 \cdot 71$	2	2	—	3037	$2^2 \cdot 3 \, 11 \cdot 23$	2	2	—

PRIMITIVE ROOTS FOR PRIMES 3 to 5003 (Continued)

p	p−1	g	−G	ε	p	p−1	g	−G	ε
3041	$2^5 \cdot 5 \cdot 19$	3	3	—	3541	$2^2 \cdot 3 \cdot 5 \cdot 59$	7	7	—
3049	$2^3 \cdot 3 \cdot 127$	11	11	—	3547	$2 \cdot 3^2 \cdot 197$	2	4	−10
3061	$2^2 \cdot 3^2 \cdot 5 \cdot 17$	6	6	—	3557	$2^2 \cdot 7 \cdot 127$	2	2	—
3067	$2 \cdot 3 \cdot 7 \cdot 73$	2	4	−10	3559	$2 \cdot 3 \cdot 593$	3	2	−10
3079	$2 \cdot 3^4 \cdot 19$	6	2	−10	3571	$2 \cdot 3 \cdot 5 \cdot 7 \cdot 17$	2	4	10
3083	$2 \cdot 23 \cdot 67$	2	3	−10	3581	$2^2 \cdot 5 \cdot 179$	2	2	±10
3089	$2^4 \cdot 193$	3	3	—	3583	$2 \cdot 3^2 \cdot 199$	3	2	—
3109	$2^2 \cdot 3 \cdot 7 \cdot 37$	6	6	—	3593	$2^3 \cdot 449$	3	3	±10
3119	$2 \cdot 1559$	7	2	−10	3607	$2 \cdot 3 \cdot 601$	5	11	10
3121	$2^4 \cdot 3 \cdot 5 \cdot 13$	7	7	—	3613	$2^2 \cdot 3 \cdot 7 \cdot 43$	2	2	—
3137	$2^6 \cdot 7^2$	3	3	±10	3617	$2^5 \cdot 113$	3	3	±10
3163	$2 \cdot 3 \cdot 17 \cdot 31$	3	6	−10	3623	$2 \cdot 1811$	5	2	10
3167	$2 \cdot 1583$	5	2	10	3631	$2 \cdot 3 \cdot 5 \cdot 11^2$	15	10	−10
3169	$2^5 \cdot 3^2 \cdot 11$	7	7	—	3637	$2^2 \cdot 3^2 \cdot 101$	2	2	—
3181	$2^2 \cdot 3 \cdot 5 \cdot 53$	7	7	—	3643	$2 \cdot 3 \cdot 607$	2	4	−10
3187	$2 \cdot 3^3 \cdot 59$	2	4	—	3659	$2 \cdot 31 \cdot 59$	2	3	10
3191	$2 \cdot 5 \cdot 11 \cdot 29$	11	5	—	3671	$2 \cdot 5 \cdot 367$	13	2	—
3203	$2 \cdot 1601$	2	3	−10	3673	$2^3 \cdot 3^3 \cdot 17$	5	5	±10
3209	$2^3 \cdot 401$	3	3	—	3677	$2^2 \cdot 919$	2	2	—
3217	$2^4 \cdot 3 \cdot 67$	5	5	—	3691	$2 \cdot 3^2 \cdot 5 \cdot 41$	2	4	—
3221	$2^2 \cdot 5 \cdot 7 \cdot 23$	10	10	±10	3697	$2 \cdot 43^2$	5	5	—
3229	$2^2 \cdot 3 \cdot 269$	6	6	—	3701	$2^2 \cdot 5^2 \cdot 37$	2	2	±10
3251	$2 \cdot 5^3 \cdot 13$	6	3	10	3709	$2^2 \cdot 3^2 \cdot 103$	2	2	±10
3253	$2^2 \cdot 3 \cdot 271$	2	2	—	3719	$2 \cdot 11 \cdot 13^2$	7	2	−10
3257	$2^3 \cdot 11 \cdot 37$	3	3	±10	3727	$2 \cdot 3^4 \cdot 23$	3	2	10
3259	$2 \cdot 3^2 \cdot 181$	3	5	10	3733	$2^2 \cdot 3 \cdot 311$	2	2	—
3271	$2 \cdot 3 \cdot 5 \cdot 109$	3	5	−10	3739	$2 \cdot 3 \cdot 7 \cdot 89$	7	5	—
3299	$2 \cdot 17 \cdot 97$	2	3	10	3761	$2^4 \cdot 5 \cdot 47$	3	3	—
3301	$2^2 \cdot 3 \cdot 5^2 \cdot 11$	6	6	±10	3767	$2 \cdot 7 \cdot 269$	5	2	10
3307	$2 \cdot 3 \cdot 19 \cdot 29$	2	4	−10	3769	$2^3 \cdot 3 \cdot 157$	7	7	—
3313	$2^4 \cdot 3^2 \cdot 23$	10	10	±10	3779	$2 \cdot 1889$	2	3	10
3319	$2 \cdot 3 \cdot 7 \cdot 79$	6	2	—	3793	$2^4 \cdot 3 \cdot 79$	5	5	—
3323	$2 \cdot 11 \cdot 151$	2	3	−10	3797	$2^2 \cdot 13 \cdot 73$	2	2	—
3329	$2^8 \cdot 13$	3	3	—	3803	$2 \cdot 1901$	2	3	−10
3331	$2 \cdot 3^2 \cdot 5 \cdot 37$	3	5	10	3821	$2^2 \cdot 5 \cdot 191$	3	3	±10
3343	$2 \cdot 3 \cdot 557$	5	11	10	3823	$2 \cdot 3 \cdot 7^2 \cdot 13$	3	9	—
3347	$2 \cdot 7 \cdot 239$	2	3	−10	3833	$2^3 \cdot 479$	3	3	±10
3359	$2 \cdot 23 \cdot 73$	11	2	−10	3847	$2 \cdot 3 \cdot 641$	5	2	10
3361	$2^5 \cdot 3 \cdot 5 \cdot 7$	22	22	—	3851	$2 \cdot 5^2 \cdot 7 \cdot 11$	2	4	—
3371	$2 \cdot 5 \cdot 337$	2	3	10	3853	$2^2 \cdot 3^2 \cdot 107$	2	2	—
3373	$2^2 \cdot 3 \cdot 281$	5	5	—	3863	$2 \cdot 1931$	5	2	10
3389	$2^2 \cdot 7 \cdot 11^2$	3	3	±10	3877	$2^2 \cdot 3 \cdot 17 \cdot 19$	2	2	—
3391	$2 \cdot 3 \cdot 5 \cdot 113$	3	5	−10	3881	$2^3 \cdot 5 \cdot 97$	13	13	—
3407	$2 \cdot 13 \cdot 131$	5	2	10	3889	$2^4 \cdot 3^5$	11	11	—
3413	$2^2 \cdot 853$	2	2	—	3907	$2 \cdot 3^2 \cdot 7 \cdot 31$	2	4	−10
3433	$2^3 \cdot 3 \cdot 11 \cdot 13$	5	5	±10	3911	$2 \cdot 5 \cdot 17 \cdot 23$	13	2	−10
3449	$2^3 \cdot 431$	3	3	—	3917	$2^2 \cdot 11 \cdot 89$	2	2	—
3457	$2^7 \cdot 3^3$	7	7	—	3919	$2 \cdot 3 \cdot 653$	3	2	—
3461	$2^2 \cdot 5 \cdot 173$	2	2	±10	3923	$2 \cdot 37 \cdot 53$	2	3	−10
3463	$2 \cdot 3 \cdot 577$	3	9	10	3929	$2^3 \cdot 491$	3	3	—
3467	$2 \cdot 1733$	2	3	−10	3931	$2 \cdot 3 \cdot 5 \cdot 131$	2	4	—
3469	$2^2 \cdot 3 \cdot 17^2$	2	2	±10	3943	$2 \cdot 3^3 \cdot 73$	3	9	10
3491	$2 \cdot 5 \cdot 349$	2	3	—	3947	$2 \cdot 1973$	2	3	−10
3499	$2 \cdot 3 \cdot 11 \cdot 53$	2	4	—	3967	$2 \cdot 3 \cdot 661$	6	2	10
3511	$2 \cdot 3^3 \cdot 5 \cdot 13$	7	2	−10	3989	$2^2 \cdot 997$	2	2	±10
3517	$2^2 \cdot 3 \cdot 293$	2	2	—	4001	$2^5 \cdot 5^3$	3	3	—
3527	$2 \cdot 41 \cdot 43$	5	2	10	4003	$2 \cdot 3 \cdot 23 \cdot 29$	2	4	—
3529	$2^3 \cdot 3^2 \cdot 7^2$	17	17	—	4007	$2 \cdot 2003$	5	2	10
3533	$2^2 \cdot 883$	2	2	—	4013	$2^2 \cdot 17 \cdot 59$	2	2	—
3539	$2 \cdot 29 \cdot 61$	2	3	10	4019	$2 \cdot 7^2 \cdot 41$	2	4	10

PRIMITIVE ROOTS FOR PRIMES 3 to 5003 (Continued)

p	$p-1$	g	$-G$	ϵ	p	$p-1$	g	$-G$	ϵ
4021	$2^2 \cdot 3 \cdot 5 \cdot 67$	2	2	—	4519	$2 \cdot 3^2 \cdot 251$	3	9	—
4027	$2 \cdot 3 \cdot 11 \cdot 61$	3	6	-10	4523	$2 \cdot 7 \cdot 17 \cdot 19$	5	3	-10
4049	$2^4 \cdot 11 \cdot 23$	3	3	—	4547	$2 \cdot 2273$	2	3	-10
4051	$2 \cdot 3^4 \cdot 5^2$	10	5	10	4549	$2^2 \cdot 3 \cdot 379$	6	6	—
4057	$2^3 \cdot 3 \cdot 13^2$	5	5	± 10	4561	$2^4 \cdot 3 \cdot 5 \cdot 19$	11	11	—
4073	$2^3 \cdot 509$	3	3	± 10	4567	$2 \cdot 3 \cdot 761$	3	7	10
4079	$2 \cdot 2039$	11	2	-10	4583	$2 \cdot 29 \cdot 79$	5	2	10
4091	$2 \cdot 5 \cdot 409$	2	3	10	4591	$2 \cdot 3^3 \cdot 5 \cdot 17$	11	2	-10
4093	$2^2 \cdot 3 \cdot 11 \cdot 31$	2	2	—	4597	$2^2 \cdot 3 \cdot 383$	5	5	—
4099	$2 \cdot 3 \cdot 683$	2	4	10	4603	$2 \cdot 3 \cdot 13 \cdot 59$	2	4	-10
4111	$2 \cdot 3 \cdot 5 \cdot 137$	12	2	-10	4621	$2^2 \cdot 3 \cdot 5 \cdot 7 \cdot 11$	2	2	—
4127	$2 \cdot 2063$	5	2	10	4637	$2^2 \cdot 19 \cdot 61$	2	2	—
4129	$2^5 \cdot 3 \cdot 43$	13	13	—	4639	$2 \cdot 3 \cdot 773$	3	2	-10
4133	$2^2 \cdot 1033$	2	2	—	4643	$2 \cdot 11 \cdot 211$	5	3	-10
4139	$2 \cdot 2069$	2	3	10	4649	$2^3 \cdot 7 \cdot 83$	3	3	—
4153	$2^3 \cdot 3 \cdot 173$	5	5	± 10	4651	$2 \cdot 3 \cdot 5^2 \cdot 31$	3	5	10
4157	$2^2 \cdot 1039$	2	2	—	4657	$2^4 \cdot 3 \cdot 97$	15	15	—
4159	$2 \cdot 3^3 \cdot 7 \cdot 11$	3	2	—	4663	$2 \cdot 3^2 \cdot 7 \cdot 37$	3	9	—
4177	$2^4 \cdot 3^2 \cdot 29$	5	5	± 10	4673	$2^6 \cdot 73$	3	3	± 10
4201	$2^3 \cdot 3 \cdot 5^2 \cdot 7$	11	11	—	4679	$2 \cdot 2339$	11	2	-10
4211	$2 \cdot 5 \cdot 421$	6	3	10	4691	$2 \cdot 5 \cdot 7 \cdot 67$	2	3	10
4217	$2^3 \cdot 17 \cdot 31$	3	3	± 10	4703	$2 \cdot 2351$	5	2	10
4219	$2 \cdot 3 \cdot 19 \cdot 37$	2	4	10	4721	$2^4 \cdot 5 \cdot 59$	6	6	—
4229	$2^2 \cdot 7 \cdot 151$	2	2	± 10	4723	$2 \cdot 3 \cdot 787$	2	4	-10
4231	$2 \cdot 3^2 \cdot 5 \cdot 47$	3	2	-10	4729	$2^3 \cdot 3 \cdot 197$	17	17	—
4241	$2^4 \cdot 5 \cdot 53$	3	3	—	4733	$2^2 \cdot 7 \cdot 13^2$	5	5	—
4243	$2 \cdot 3 \cdot 7 \cdot 101$	2	4	-10	4751	$2 \cdot 5^3 \cdot 19$	19	3	-10
4253	$2^2 \cdot 1063$	2	2	—	4759	$2 \cdot 3 \cdot 13 \cdot 61$	3	5	-10
4259	$2 \cdot 2129$	2	3	10	4783	$2 \cdot 3 \cdot 797$	6	2	10
4261	$2^2 \cdot 3 \cdot 5 \cdot 71$	2	2	± 10	4787	$2 \cdot 2393$	2	3	-10
4271	$2 \cdot 5 \cdot 7 \cdot 61$	7	3	-10	4789	$2^2 \cdot 3^2 \cdot 7 \cdot$	2	2	—
4273	$2^4 \cdot 3 \cdot 89$	5	5	—	4793	$2^3 \cdot 599$	3	3	± 10
4283	$2 \cdot 2141$	2	3	-10	4799	$2 \cdot 2399$	7	2	-10
4289	$2^6 \cdot 67$	3	3	—	4801	$2^6 \cdot 3 \cdot 5^2$	7	7	—
4297	$2^3 \cdot 3 \cdot 179$	5	5	—	4813	$2^2 \cdot 3 \cdot 401$	2	2	—
4327	$2 \cdot 3 \cdot 7 \cdot 103$	3	2	10	4817	$2^4 \cdot 7 \cdot 43$	3	3	± 10
4337	$2^4 \cdot 271$	3	3	± 10	4831	$2 \cdot 3 \cdot 5 \cdot 7 \cdot 23$	3	2	—
4339	$2 \cdot 3^2 \cdot 241$	10	5	10	4861	$2^2 \cdot 3^5 \cdot 5$	11	11	—
4349	$2^2 \cdot 1087$	2	2	± 10	4871	$2 \cdot 5 \cdot 487$	11	3	-10
4357	$2^2 \cdot 3^2 \cdot 11^2$	2	2	—	4877	$2^2 \cdot 23 \cdot 53$	2	2	—
4363	$2 \cdot 3 \cdot 727$	2	4	-10	4889	$2^3 \cdot 13 \cdot 47$	3	3	—
4373	$2^2 \cdot 1093$	2	2	—	4903	$2 \cdot 3 \cdot 19 \cdot 43$	3	2	—
4391	$2 \cdot 5 \cdot 439$	14	2	-10	4909	$2^2 \cdot 3 \cdot 409$	6	6	—
4397	$2^2 \cdot 7 \cdot 157$	2	2	—	4919	$2 \cdot 2459$	13	2	-10
4409	$2^3 \cdot 19 \cdot 29$	3	3	—	4931	$2 \cdot 5 \cdot 17 \cdot 29$	6	3	10
4421	$2^2 \cdot 5 \cdot 13 \cdot 17$	3	3	± 10	4933	$2^2 \cdot 3^2 \cdot 137$	2	2	—
4423	$2 \cdot 3 \cdot 11 \cdot 67$	3	7	10	4937	$2^3 \cdot 617$	3	3	± 10
4441	$2^3 \cdot 3 \cdot 5 \cdot 37$	21	21	—	4943	$2 \cdot 7 \cdot 353$	7	2	10
4447	$2 \cdot 3^2 \cdot 13 \cdot 19$	3	2	10	4951	$2 \cdot 3^2 \cdot 5^2 \cdot 11$	6	2	-10
4451	$2 \cdot 5^2 \cdot 89$	2	3	10	4957	$2^2 \cdot 3 \cdot 7 \cdot 59$	2	2	—
4457	$2^3 \cdot 557$	3	3	± 10	4967	$2 \cdot 13 \cdot 191$	5	3	10
4463	$2 \cdot 23 \cdot 97$	5	2	10	4969	$2^3 \cdot 3^3 \cdot 23$	11	11	—
4481	$2^7 \cdot 5 \cdot 7$	3	3	—	4973	$2^2 \cdot 11 \cdot 113$	2	2	—
4483	$2 \cdot 3^3 \cdot 83$	2	4	—	4987	$2 \cdot 3^2 \cdot 277$	2	4	-10
4493	$2^2 \cdot 1123$	2	2	—	4993	$2^7 \cdot 3 \cdot 13$	5	5	—
4507	$2 \cdot 3 \cdot 751$	2	4	—	4999	$2 \cdot 3 \cdot 7^2 \cdot 17$	3	9	—
4513	$2^5 \cdot 3 \cdot 47$	7	7	—	5003	$2 \cdot 41 \cdot 61$	2	3	-10
4517	$2^2 \cdot 1129$	2	2	—					

From Applied Mathematics Series—55, Primitive Roots, Factorization of $p-1$, pages 864, 866, 867. By permission of United States Department of Commerce, National Bureau of Standards, Washington, D.C.

IV. GEOMETRY
MENSURATION FORMULAS

Dr. Howard Eves

TRIANGLES

In the following: K = area, r = radius of the inscribed circle, R = radius of the circumscribed circle.

Right Triangle

$A + B = C = 90°$
$c^2 = a^2 + b^2$ (*Pythagorean relation*)
$a = \sqrt{(c + b)(c - b)}$
$K = \frac{1}{2}ab$

$r = \dfrac{ab}{a + b + c}$, $\quad R = \frac{1}{2}c$

$h = \dfrac{ab}{c}$, $\quad m = \dfrac{b^2}{c}$, $\quad n = \dfrac{a^2}{c}$

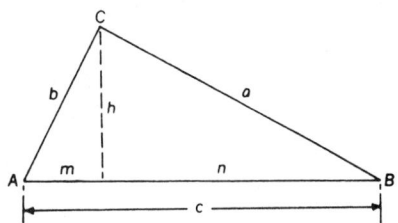

Equilateral Triangle

$A = B = C = 60°$
$K = \frac{1}{4}a^2\sqrt{3}$
$r = \frac{1}{6}a\sqrt{3}$, $\quad R = \frac{1}{3}a\sqrt{3}$
$h = \frac{1}{2}a\sqrt{3}$

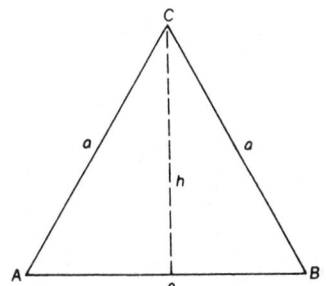

General Triangle

Let $s = \frac{1}{2}(a + b + c)$, h_c = length of altitude on side c, t_c = length of bisector of angle C, m_c = length of median to side c.

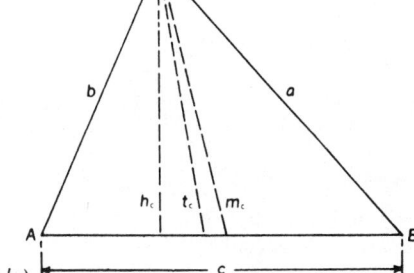

$A + B + C = 180°$
$c^2 = a^2 + b^2 - 2ab \cos C$
$\qquad$ (*law of cosines*)
$K = \frac{1}{2}h_c c = \frac{1}{2}ab \sin C$
$\quad = \dfrac{c^2 \sin A \sin B}{2 \sin C}$

$\quad = rs = \dfrac{abc}{4R}$

$\quad = \sqrt{s(s - a)(s - b)(s - c)}$ (*Heron's formula*)

Mensuration Formulas

$$r = c \sin \frac{A}{2} \sin \frac{B}{2} \sec \frac{C}{2} = \frac{ab \sin C}{2s} = (s - c) \tan \frac{C}{2}$$

$$= \sqrt{\frac{(s - a)(s - b)(s - c)}{s}} = \frac{K}{s} = 4R \sin \frac{A}{2} \sin \frac{B}{2} \sin \frac{C}{2}$$

$$R = \frac{c}{2 \sin C} = \frac{abc}{4\sqrt{s(s - a)(s - b)(s - c)}} = \frac{abc}{4K}$$

$$h_c = a \sin B = b \sin A = \frac{2K}{c}$$

$$t_c = \frac{2ab}{a + b} \cos \frac{C}{2} = \sqrt{ab\left\{1 - \frac{c^2}{(a + b)^2}\right\}}$$

$$m_c = \sqrt{\frac{a^2}{2} + \frac{b^2}{2} - \frac{c^2}{4}}$$

    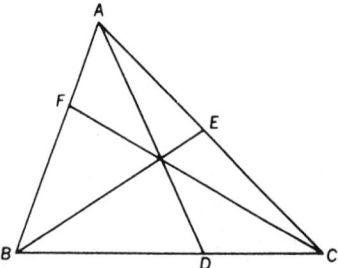

Menelaus' Theorem.   A necessary and sufficient condition for points D, E, F on the respective side lines BC, CA, AB of a triangle ABC to be collinear is that

$$BD \cdot CE \cdot AF = - DC \cdot EA \cdot FB,$$

where all segments in the formula are directed segments.

Ceva's Theorem.   A necessary and sufficient condition for AD, BE, CF, where D, E, F are points on the respective side lines BC, CA, AB of a triangle ABC, to be concurrent is that

$$BD \cdot CE \cdot AF = + DC \cdot EA \cdot FB,$$

where all segments in the formula are directed segments.

QUADRILATERALS

In the following: K = area, p and q are diagonals.

Rectangle

$$A = B = C = D = 90°$$
$$K = ab, \quad p = \sqrt{a^2 + b^2}$$

Mensuration Formulas

Parallelogram

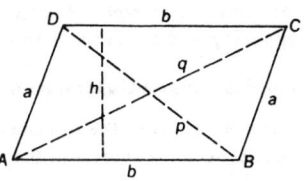

$$A = C, \quad B = D, \quad A + B = 180°$$
$$K = bh = ab \sin A = ab \sin B$$
$$h = a \sin A = a \sin B$$
$$p = \sqrt{a^2 + b^2 - 2ab \cos A}$$
$$q = \sqrt{a^2 + b^2 - 2ab \cos B} = \sqrt{a^2 + b^2 + 2ab \cos A}$$

Rhombus

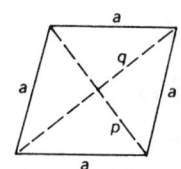

$$p^2 + q^2 = 4a^2$$
$$K = \tfrac{1}{2}pq$$

Trapezoid

$$m = \tfrac{1}{2}(a + b)$$
$$K = \tfrac{1}{2}(a + b)h = mh$$

General quadrilateral

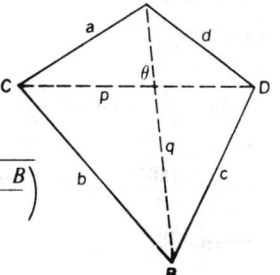

Let $s = \tfrac{1}{2}(a + b + c + d)$.
$$K = \tfrac{1}{2}pq \sin \theta$$
$$= \tfrac{1}{4}(b^2 + d^2 - a^2 - c^2) \tan \theta$$
$$= \tfrac{1}{4}\sqrt{4p^2q^2 - (b^2 + d^2 - a^2 - c^2)^2}$$

(Bretschneider's formula)

$$= \sqrt{(s - a)(s - b)(s - c)(s - d) - abcd \cos^2\left(\frac{A + B}{2}\right)}$$

Theorem. The diagonals of a quadrilateral with consecutive sides a, b, c, d are perpendicular if and only if $a^2 + c^2 = b^2 + d^2$.

Cyclic Quadrilateral

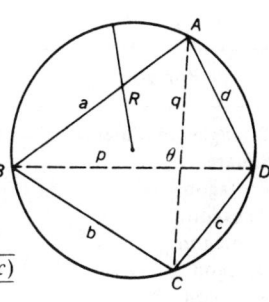

Let R = radius of the circumscribed circle.
$$A + C = B + D = 180°$$
$$K = \sqrt{(s - a)(s - b)(s - c)(s - d)}$$

(Brahmagupta's formula)

$$= \frac{\sqrt{(ac + bd)(ad + bc)(ab + cd)}}{4R}$$

$$p = \sqrt{\frac{(ac + bd)(ab + cd)}{ad + bc}}, \quad q = \sqrt{\frac{(ac + bd)(ad + bc)}{ab + cd}}$$

$$R = \tfrac{1}{4}\sqrt{\frac{(ac + bd)(ad + bc)(ab + cd)}{(s - a)(s - b)(s - c)(s - d)}}, \quad \sin \theta = \frac{2K}{ac + bd}$$

Mensuration Formulas

Ptolemy's Theorem. A convex quadrilateral with consecutive sides a, b, c, d and diagonals p and q is cyclic if and only if $ac + bd = pq$.

Cyclic-inscriptable Quadrilateral

Let r = radius of the inscribed circle, R = radius of the circumscribed circle, m = distance between the centers of the inscribed and the circumscribed circles.

$A + C = B + D = 180°$

$a + c = b + d$

$K = \sqrt{abcd}$

$$\frac{1}{(R - m)^2} + \frac{1}{(R + m)^2} = \frac{1}{r^2}$$

$$r = \frac{\sqrt{abcd}}{s}$$

$$R = \frac{1}{4} \sqrt{\frac{(ac + bd)(ad + bc)(ab + cd)}{abcd}}$$

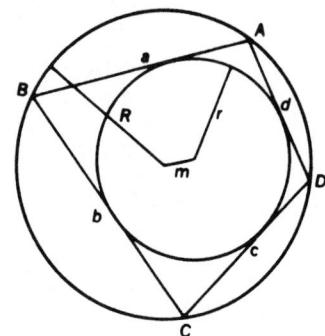

REGULAR POLYGONS

In the following: n = number of sides, s = length of each side, p = perimeter, θ = one of the vertex angles, r = radius of the inscribed circle, R = radius of the circumscribed circle, K = area.

$$\theta = \left(\frac{n - 2}{n}\right) 180°$$

$$s = 2r \tan \frac{180°}{n} = 2R \sin \frac{180°}{n}$$

$$p = ns$$

$$K = \tfrac{1}{4} ns^2 \cot \frac{180°}{n}$$

$$\quad = nr^2 \tan \frac{180°}{n}$$

$$\quad = \tfrac{1}{2} nR^2 \sin \frac{360°}{n}$$

$$r = \tfrac{1}{2} s \cot \frac{180°}{n}, \quad R = \tfrac{1}{2} s \csc \frac{180°}{n}$$

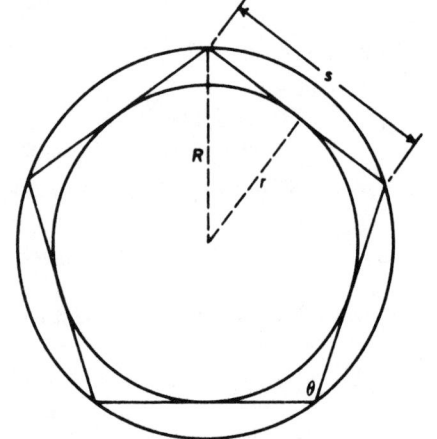

Polygon	n	K	r	R
Triangle (equilateral)	3	$0.43301s^2$	$0.28868s$	$0.57735s$
Square	4	$1.00000s^2$	$0.50000s$	$0.70711s$
Pentagon	5	$1.72048s^2$	$0.68819s$	$0.85065s$
Hexagon	6	$2.59808s^2$	$0.86603s$	$1.00000s$
Heptagon	7	$3.63391s^2$	$1.0383s$	$1.1524s$
Octagon	8	$4.82843s^2$	$1.2071s$	$1.3066s$
Nonagon	9	$6.18182s^2$	$1.3737s$	$1.4619s$
Decagon	10	$7.69421s^2$	$1.5388s$	$1.6180s$
Undecagon	11	$9.36564s^2$	$1.7028s$	$1.7747s$
Dodecagon	12	$11.19615s^2$	$1.8660s$	$1.9319s$

Mensuration Formulas

If s_k denotes the side of a regular polygon of k sides inscribed in a circle of radius R, then

$$s_{2n} = \sqrt{2R^2 - R\sqrt{4R^2 - s_n^2}}$$

If S_k denotes the side of a regular polygon of k sides circumscribed about a circle of radius r, then

$$S_{2n} = \frac{2rS_n}{2r + \sqrt{4r^2 + S_n^2}}$$

If p_k and P_k denote, respectively, the perimeters of regular polygons of k sides inscribed in and circumscribed about the same circle, then

$$P_{2n} = \frac{2p_n P_n}{p_n + P_n} \quad \text{and} \quad p_{2n} = \sqrt{p_n P_{2n}}.$$

If a_k and A_k denote, respectively, the areas of regular polygons of k sides inscribed in and circumscribed about the same circle, then

$$a_{2n} = \sqrt{a_n A_n} \quad \text{and} \quad A_{2n} = \frac{2a_{2n} A_n}{a_{2n} + A_n}.$$

CIRCLES

In the following: R = radius, D = diameter, C = circumference, K = area.

Circumference and Area of a Circle

$C = 2\pi R = \pi D \qquad (\pi = 3.14159\cdots)$
$K = \pi R^2 = \frac{1}{4}\pi D^2 = 0.7854 D^2$
$C = 2\sqrt{\pi K} = \dfrac{2K}{R}$

$K = \dfrac{C^2}{4\pi} = \frac{1}{2}CR$

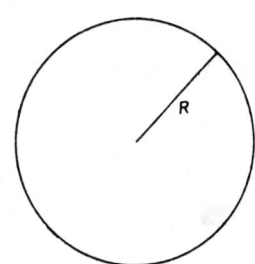

Sector and Segment of a Circle

Let the central angle θ be measured in radians ($\theta < \pi$).

$h = R - d, \quad d = R - h$
$s = R\theta$

$d = R\cos\dfrac{\theta}{2} = \frac{1}{2}c\cot\dfrac{\theta}{2}$

$\quad = \frac{1}{2}\sqrt{4R^2 - c^2}$

$c = 2R\sin\dfrac{\theta}{2} = 2d\tan\dfrac{\theta}{2}$

$\quad = 2\sqrt{R^2 - d^2} = \sqrt{4h(2R - h)}$

$\theta = \dfrac{s}{R} = 2\,\mathrm{Cos}^{-1}\dfrac{d}{R} = 2\,\mathrm{Tan}^{-1}\dfrac{c}{2d} = 2\,\mathrm{Sin}^{-1}\dfrac{c}{2R}$

$K\text{ (sector)} = \frac{1}{2}Rs = \frac{1}{2}R^2\theta$

$K\text{ (segment)} = \frac{1}{2}R^2(\theta - \sin\theta) = \frac{1}{2}(Rs - cd) = R^2\,\mathrm{Cos}^{-1}\dfrac{d}{R} - d\sqrt{R^2 - d^2}$

$\quad = R^2\,\mathrm{Cos}^{-1}\dfrac{R - h}{R} - (R - h)\sqrt{2Rh - h^2}$

Mensuration Formulas

Sector of an Annulus

$h = R_1 - R_2$

$K = \frac{1}{2}\theta(R_1 + R_2)(R_1 - R_2)$

$\quad = \frac{1}{2}\theta h(R_1 + R_2)$

$\quad = \frac{1}{2}h(s_1 + s_2)$

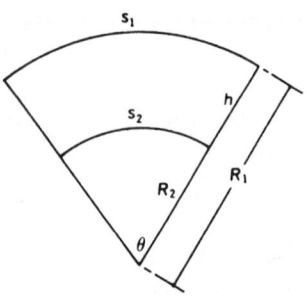

CONIC SECTIONS

Ellipse

Let p = circumference, K = area

$p = 2\pi \sqrt{\dfrac{a^2 + b^2}{2}}$ (approximately)

$\quad = 4aE$ (exactly)   See table of elliptic integral for E, using $k = \sqrt{a^2 - b^2}/a$.

$K = \pi ab$

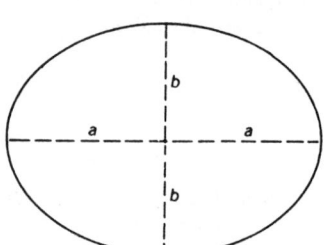

Parabolic Segment

$s = \sqrt{4x^2 + y^2} + \dfrac{y^2}{2x} \log_e \left[\dfrac{2x + \sqrt{4x^2 + y^2}}{y} \right]$

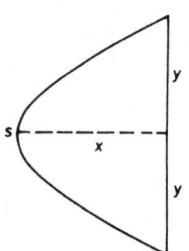

K (right segment) = $\frac{2}{3}xy$

K (oblique segment) = $\frac{4}{3}T$, where T is the area of the triangle with base along the chord of the segment and with opposite vertex at the point on the parabola at which the tangent to the parabola is parallel to the chord of the segment.

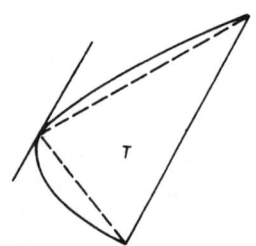

CAVALIERI'S THEOREM FOR THE PLANE

If two planar areas are included between a pair of parallel lines, and if the two segments cut off by the areas on any line parallel to the including lines are equal in length, then the two planar areas are equal.

Mensuration Formulas

PLANAR AREAS BY APPROXIMATION

Divide the planar area K into n strips by equidistant parallel chords of lengths $y_0, y_1, y_2, \ldots, y_n$ (where y_0 and/or y_n may be zero), and let h denote the common distance between the chords. Then, approximately:

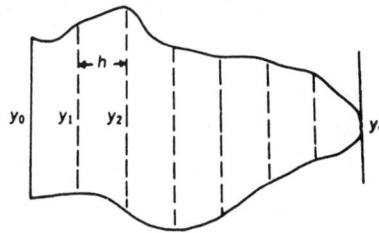

Trapezoidal Rule

$$K = h(\tfrac{1}{2}y_0 + y_1 + y_2 + \cdots + y_{n-1} + \tfrac{1}{2}y_n)$$

Durand's Rule

$$K = h(\tfrac{4}{10}y_0 + \tfrac{11}{10}y_1 + y_2 + y_3 + \cdots + y_{n-2} + \tfrac{11}{10}y_{n-1} + \tfrac{4}{10}y_n)$$

Simpson's rule (n even)

$$K = \tfrac{1}{3}h(y_0 + 4y_1 + 2y_2 + 4y_3 + 2y_4 + \cdots + 2y_{n-2} + 4y_{n-1} + y_n)$$

Weddle's Rule ($n = 6$)

$$K = \tfrac{3}{10}h(y_0 + 5y_1 + y_2 + 6y_3 + y_4 + 5y_5 + y_6)$$

SOLIDS BOUNDED BY PLANES

In the following: S = lateral surface, T = total surface, V = volume.

Cube

Let a = length of each edge.

$$T = 6a^2, \quad \text{diagonal of face} = a\sqrt{2}$$
$$V = a^3, \quad \text{diagonal of cube} = a\sqrt{3}$$

Rectangular Parallelepiped (or box)

Let a, b, c be the lengths of its edges.

$$T = 2(ab + bc + ca), \quad V = abc$$
$$\text{diagonal} = \sqrt{a^2 + b^2 + c^2}$$

Prism

S = (perimeter of right section) × (lateral edge)
V = (area of right section) × (lateral edge)
  = (area of base) × (altitude)

Truncated Triangular Prism

V = (area of right section) × $\tfrac{1}{3}$(sum of the three lateral edges)

Mensuration Formulas

Pyramid

S of regular pyramid $= \frac{1}{2}$ (perimeter of base) $\times$ (slant height)

$V = \frac{1}{3}$ (area of base) $\times$ (altitude)

Frustum of Pyramid

Let B_1 = area of lower base, B_2 = area of upper base, h = altitude.

S of regular figure $= \frac{1}{2}$ (sum of perimeters of bases) $\times$ (slant height)

$V = \frac{1}{3}h(B_1 + B_2 + \sqrt{B_1 B_2})$

Prismatoid

A *prismatoid* is a polyhedron having for bases two polygons in parallel planes, and for lateral faces triangles or trapezoids with one side lying in one base, and the opposite vertex or side lying in the other base, of the polyhedron. Let B_1 = area of lower base, M = area of midsection, B_2 = area of upper base, h = altitude.

$$V = \frac{1}{6}h(B_1 + 4M + B_2) \quad \text{(the } prismoidal\ formula\text{)}$$

Note: Since cubes, rectangular parallelepipeds, prisms, pyramids, and frustums of pyramids are all examples of prismatoids, the formula for the volume of a prismatoid subsumes most of the above volume formulae.

Regular Polyhedra

Let v = number of vertices, e = number of edges, f = number of faces, α = each dihedral angle, a = length of each edge, r = radius of the inscribed sphere, R = radius of the circumscribed sphere, A = area of each face, T = total area, V = volume.

$v - e + f = 2$ (the *Euler-Descartes formula*—actually holds for *any* convex polyhedron)

$$T = fA$$
$$V = \frac{1}{3}rfA = \frac{1}{3}rT$$

Name	Nature of Surface	T	V
Tetrahedron	4 equilateral triangles	$1.73205a^2$	$0.11785a^3$
Hexahedron (cube)	6 squares	$6.00000a^2$	$1.00000a^3$
Octahedron	8 equilateral triangles	$3.46410a^2$	$0.47140a^3$
Dodecahedron	12 regular pentagons	$20.64573a^2$	$7.66312a^3$
Icosahedron	20 equilateral triangles	$8.66025a^2$	$2.18169a^3$

Name	v	e	f	α	a	r
Tetrahedron	4	6	4	70° 32'	$1.633R$	$0.333R$
Hexahedron	8	12	6	90°	$1.155R$	$0.577R$
Octahedron	6	12	8	109° 28'	$1.414R$	$0.577R$
Dodecahedron	20	30	12	116° 34'	$0.714R$	$0.795R$
Icosahedron	12	30	20	138° 11'	$1.051R$	$0.795R$

Mensuration Formulas

Name	A	r	R	V
Tetrahedron	$\frac{1}{4}a^2\sqrt{3}$	$\frac{1}{12}a\sqrt{6}$	$\frac{1}{4}a\sqrt{6}$	$\frac{1}{12}a^3\sqrt{2}$
Hexahedron	a^2	$\frac{1}{2}a$	$\frac{1}{2}a\sqrt{3}$	a^3
Octahedron	$\frac{1}{4}a^2\sqrt{3}$	$\frac{1}{6}a\sqrt{6}$	$\frac{1}{2}a\sqrt{2}$	$\frac{1}{3}a^3\sqrt{2}$
Dodecahedron	$\frac{1}{4}a^2\sqrt{25+10\sqrt{5}}$	$\frac{1}{20}a\sqrt{250+110\sqrt{5}}$	$\frac{1}{4}a(\sqrt{15}+\sqrt{3})$	$\frac{1}{4}a^3(15+7\sqrt{5})$
Icosahedron	$\frac{1}{4}a^2\sqrt{3}$	$\frac{1}{12}a\sqrt{42+18\sqrt{5}}$	$\frac{1}{4}a\sqrt{10+2\sqrt{5}}$	$\frac{5}{12}a^3(3+\sqrt{5})$

CYLINDERS AND CONES

In the following: B_1 = area of lower base, B_2 = area of upper base, h = altitude, S = lateral surface, T = total surface, V = volume.

Cylinder

S = (perimeter of right section) × (lateral edge)
V = (area of right section) × (lateral edge)

Right Circular Cylinder

Let R = radius of base.

$$S = 2\pi Rh, \quad T = 2\pi R(R+h), \quad V = \pi R^2 h$$

Cone

$$V = \frac{1}{3}B_1 h$$

Right Circular Cone

Let R = radius of base, s = slant height.

$$s = \sqrt{R^2+h^2}$$
$$S = \pi Rs = \pi R\sqrt{R^2+h^2}$$
$$T = \pi R(R+s) = \pi R(R+\sqrt{R^2+h^2})$$
$$V = \frac{1}{3}\pi R^2 h$$

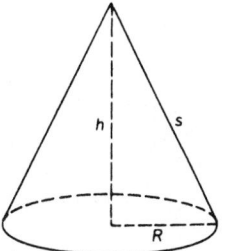

Frustum of Cone

$V = \frac{1}{3}h(B_1 + B_2 + \sqrt{B_1 B_2})$, where B_1 and B_2 are the areas of the bases.

Frustum of Right Circular Cone

Let R_1 = radius of lower base, R_2 = radius of upper base, s = slant height.

Mensuration Formulas

$$s = \sqrt{(R_1 - R_2)^2 + h^2}$$
$$S = \pi(R_1 + R_2)s$$
$$\quad = \pi(R_1 + R_2)\sqrt{(R_1 - R_2)^2 + h^2}$$
$$T = \pi[R_1^2 + R_2^2 + (R_1 + R_2)s]$$
$$\quad = \pi[R_1^2 + R_2^2 + (R_1 + R_2)\sqrt{(R_1 - R_2)^2 + h^2}]$$
$$V = \tfrac{1}{3}\pi h(R_1^2 + R_2^2 + R_1 R_2)$$

SPHERICAL FIGURES

In the following: R = radius of sphere, D = diameter of sphere, S = surface area, V = volume.

Sphere

$$D = 2R$$
$$S = 4\pi R^2 = \pi D^2 = 12.57R^2$$
$$V = \tfrac{4}{3}\pi R^3 = \tfrac{1}{6}\pi D^3 = 4.189R^3$$

Zone and Segment of One Base

$$S = 2\pi Rh = \pi Dh = \pi p^2$$
$$V = \tfrac{1}{3}\pi h^2(3R - h) = \tfrac{1}{6}\pi h(3a^2 + h^2)$$

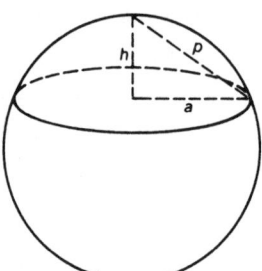

Zone and Segment of Two Bases

$$S = 2\pi Rh = \pi Dh$$
$$V = \tfrac{1}{6}\pi h(3a^2 + 3b^2 + h^2)$$

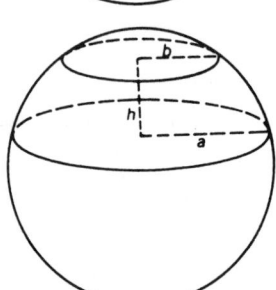

Lune

$$S = 2R^2\theta, \quad \theta \text{ in radians}$$

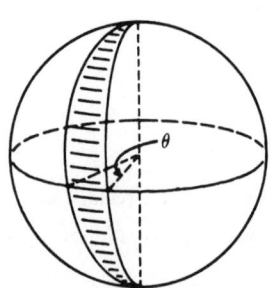

Mensuration Formulas

Spherical Sector

$$V = \tfrac{2}{3}\pi R^2 h = \tfrac{1}{6}\pi D^2 h$$

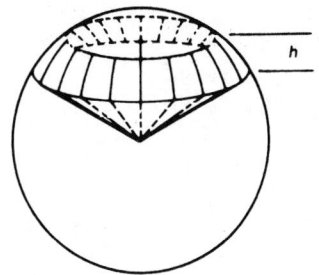

Spherical Triangle and Polygon

Let A, B, C be the angles, in radians, of the triangle; let θ = sum of angles, in radians, of a spherical polygon of n sides.

$$S = (A + B + C - \pi)R^2$$
$$S = [\theta - (n - 2)\pi]R^2$$

SPHEROIDS

Ellipsoid

Let a, b, c be the lengths of the semiaxes.

$$V = \tfrac{4}{3}\pi abc$$

Oblate Spheroid

An *oblate spheroid* is formed by the rotation of an ellipse about its minor axis. Let a and b be the major and minor semiaxes, respectively, and ϵ the eccentricity, of the revolving ellipse.

$$S = 2\pi a^2 + \pi\,\frac{b^2}{\epsilon}\,\log_e\frac{1 + \epsilon}{1 - \epsilon}$$

$$V = \tfrac{4}{3}\pi a^2 b$$

Prolate Spheroid

A *prolate spheroid* is formed by the rotation of an ellipse about its major axis. Let a and b be the major and minor semiaxes, respectively, and ϵ the eccentricity, of the revolving ellipse.

$$S = 2\pi b^2 + 2\pi\,\frac{ab}{\epsilon}\,\sin^{-1}\epsilon$$

$$V = \tfrac{4}{3}\pi ab^2$$

CIRCULAR TORUS

A *circular torus* is formed by the rotation of a circle about an axis in the plane of the circle and not cutting the circle. Let r be the radius of the revolving circle and let R be the distance of its center from the axis of rotation.

Mensuration Formulas

$$S = 4\pi^2 R r$$
$$V = 2\pi^2 R r^2$$

PAPPUS-GULDINUS THEOREMS

1. If a planar arc be revolved about an axis in its plane, but not cutting the arc, the area of the surface of revolution so formed is equal to the product of the length of the arc and the length of the path traced by the centroid of the arc.

2. If a planar area be revolved about an axis in its plane, but not intersecting the area, the volume of the solid of revolution so formed is equal to the product of the area and the length of the path traced by the centroid of the area.

CAVALIERI'S THEOREM FOR SPACE

If two solids are included between a pair of parallel planes, and if the two sections cut by them on any plane parallel to the including planes are equal in area, then the volumes of the solids are equal.

GENERAL PRISMATOID

A *general prismatoid* is a solid such that the area A_y of any section parallel to and distant y from a fixed plane can be expressed as a polynomial in y of degreee not higher than the third. That is,

$$A_y = ay^3 + by^2 + cy + d,$$

where a, b, c, d are constants which may be positive, zero, or negative. Let B_1 = area of lower base; M = area of midsection, B_2 = area of upper base, h = altitude.

$$V = \tfrac{1}{6}h(B_1 + 4M + B_2)$$

Note. All prismatoids, cylinders, cones, spheres, spheroids, and many other solids are general prismatoids.

CENTROIDS

If a geometrical figure possesses a center of symmetry, that point is the centroid of the figure.

If a geometrical figure possesses an axis of symmetry, the centroid of the figure lies on that axis.

Mensuration Formulas

Geometrical Figure	Location of Centroid
Perimeter of triangle	Center of the inscribed circle of the triangle whose vertices are the midpoints of the sides of the given triangle.
Arc of semicircle of radius R	Distance from diameter $= \dfrac{2R}{\pi}$
Arc of 2α radians of a circle of radius R	Distance from center of circle $= \dfrac{R \sin \alpha}{\alpha}$
Area of triangle	Intersection of the medians
Area of quadrilateral	Intersection of the diagonals of the parallelogram whose sides pass through adjacent trisection points of pairs of consecutive sides of the quadrilateral
Area of semicircle of radius R	Distance from diameter $= \dfrac{4R}{3\pi}$
Area of circular sector of radius R and central angle 2α radians	Distance from center of circle $= \dfrac{2R \sin \alpha}{3\alpha}$
Area of semiellipse of altitude h	Distance from base $= \dfrac{4h}{3\pi}$
Area of a quadrant of an ellipse of major and minor semiaxes a and b	Distance from minor axis $= \dfrac{4a}{3\pi}$, distance from major axis $= \dfrac{4b}{3\pi}$
Area of right parabolic segment of altitude h	Distance from base $= \frac{2}{5}h$
Lateral area of regular pyramid or right circular cone	Distance from base $= \frac{1}{3}h$
Area of hemisphere of radius R	Distance from base $= \frac{1}{2}R$
Volume of pyramid or cone	One fourth the way from the centroid of the base to the vertex of the pyramid or cone
Volume of frustum of pyramid or cone with d as the distance between the centroids of its bases and k as the ratio of similarity of the upper base to the lower base	On the line joining the centroids of the two bases at a distance from the centroid of the lower base $= \frac{1}{4}d\left(\dfrac{1 + 2k + 3k^2}{1 + k + k^2}\right)$
Volume of hemisphere of radius R	Distance from base $= \frac{3}{8}R$
Volume of revolution of altitude h obtained by revolving a semiellipse about its axis of symmetry	Distance from base $= \frac{3}{8}h$
Volume of paraboloid of revolution of altitude h	Distance from base $= \frac{1}{3}h$

V. TRIGONOMETRY
TRIGONOMETRY
DR. HOWARD EVES

PLANE TRIGONOMETRY

Angle

That part of a straight line lying entirely to one side of a point O on the line is called a *ray* (or a *half-line*); the point O is called the *origin* of the ray. A ray of origin O is identified by the notation OA, where A is any point of the ray.

If a ray OA is rotated, in a plane, about its origin O onto ray OB, an *angle AOB* is said to be generated. Ray OA is called the *initial side*, ray OB the *terminal side*, and point O the *vertex* of the angle. The angle is said to be *positive* or *negative* according as the generating rotation is counterclockwise or clockwise.

An angle is said to be in *standard position* if its vertex is at the origin O and its initial side is on the positive x-axis of a rectangular Cartesian coordinate system (see p. 542). If the terminal side of the angle falls on a coordinate axis, the angle is called a *quadrantal angle*; otherwise the angle is called a *first, second, third,* or *fourth quadrant angle* according as the terminal side falls in the first, second, third, or fourth quadrant of the coordinate system.

An angle of one *degree* is an angle in which the rotation is $1/360$ of one complete rotation.

A *straight angle* is an angle of 180° (180 degrees).

A *right angle* is an angle of 90°.

An *acute angle* is an angle between 0° and 90°.

An *obtuse angle* is an angle between 90° and 180°.

A *radian* is an angle subtended at the center of a circle by an arc whose length is equal to that of the radius.

$$180° = \pi \text{ radians}; \quad 1° = \frac{\pi}{180} \text{ radians}; \quad 1 \text{ radian} = \frac{180}{\pi} \text{ degrees}.$$

The Trigonometric Functions of an Acute Angle

In the right triangle ABC,

sine A = sin A = a/c

cosine A = cos A = b/c

tangent A = tan A = a/b

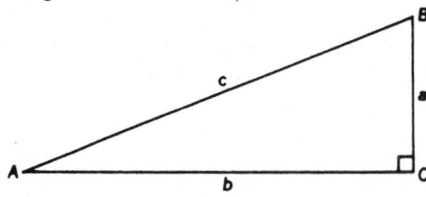

cosecant A = csc A = c/a

secant A = sec A = c/b

cotangent A = cot A = ctn A = b/a

exsecant A = exsec A = sec A − 1

versine A = vers A = 1 − cos A

coversine A = covers A = 1 − sin A

haversine A = hav A = $\frac{1}{2}$ vers A

Formulas for Use in Trigonometry

The Trigonometric Functions of an Arbitrary Angle

Let α be any angle in standard position and let $P(x,y)$ be any point on the terminal side of the angle. Denote the positive distance OP by r. Then

$$\sin \alpha = y/r \qquad \csc \alpha = r/y$$
$$\cos \alpha = x/r \qquad \sec \alpha = r/x$$
$$\tan \alpha = y/x \qquad \cot \alpha = \text{ctn } \alpha = x/y$$
$$\text{exsec } \alpha = \sec \alpha - 1 \qquad \text{covers } \alpha = 1 - \sin \alpha$$
$$\text{vers } \alpha = 1 - \cos \alpha \qquad \text{hav } \alpha = \tfrac{1}{2}\text{vers } \alpha$$
$$\text{cis } \alpha = \cos \alpha + i \sin \alpha = e^{i\alpha}, \alpha \text{ in radians}, i = \sqrt{-1}$$

RELATIONS BETWEEN CIRCULAR (OR INVERSE CIRCULAR) FUNCTIONS

$$\left(0 \leq x \leq \frac{\pi}{2}\right)$$

	$\sin x = a$	$\cos x = a$	$\tan x = a$
$\sin x$	a	$(1 - a^2)^{1/2}$	$a(1 + a^2)^{-1/2}$
$\cos x$	$(1 - a^2)^{1/2}$	a	$(1 + a^2)^{-1/2}$
$\tan x$	$a(1 - a^2)^{-1/2}$	$a^{-1}(1 - a^2)^{1/2}$	a
$\csc x$	a^{-1}	$(1 - a^2)^{-1/2}$	$a^{-1}(1 + a^2)^{1/2}$
$\sec x$	$(1 - a^2)^{-1/2}$	a^{-1}	$(1 + a^2)^{1/2}$
$\cot x$	$a^{-1}(1 - a^2)^{1/2}$	$a(1 - a^2)^{-1/2}$	a^{-1}

	$\csc x = a$	$\sec x = a$	$\cot x = a$
$\sin x$	a^{-1}	$a^{-1}(a^2 - 1)^{1/2}$	$(1 + a^2)^{-1/2}$
$\cos x$	$a^{-1}(a^2 - 1)^{1/2}$	a^{-1}	$a(1 + a^2)^{-1/2}$
$\tan x$	$(a^2 - 1)^{-1/2}$	$(a^2 - 1)^{1/2}$	a^{-1}
$\csc x$	a	$a(a^2 - 1)^{-1/2}$	$(1 + a^2)^{1/2}$
$\sec x$	$a(a^2 - 1)^{-1/2}$	a	$a^{-1}(1 + a^2)^{1/2}$
$\cot x$	$(a^2 - 1)^{1/2}$	$(a^2 - 1)^{-1/2}$	a

Examples:

If $\sec x = a$, then $\tan x = (a^2 - 1)^{1/2}$

$\text{arc tan } a = \text{arc cos }(1 + a^2)^{-1/2}$

Formulas for Use in Trigonometry

SIGNS OF THE TRIGONOMETRIC FUNCTIONS

Quadrant	sin	cos	tan	cot	sec	csc
I	+	+	+	+	+	+
II	+	−	−	−	−	+
III	−	−	+	+	−	−
IV	−	+	−	−	+	−

VARIATIONS OF THE TRIGONOMETRIC FUNCTIONS

Quadrant	sin	cos	tan	cot	sec	csc
I	$0 \to +1$	$+1 \to 0$	$0 \to +\infty$	$+\infty \to 0$	$+1 \to +\infty$	$+\infty \to +1$
II	$+1 \to 0$	$0 \to -1$	$-\infty \to 0$	$0 \to -\infty$	$-\infty \to -1$	$+1 \to +\infty$
III	$0 \to -1$	$-1 \to 0$	$0 \to +\infty$	$+\infty \to 0$	$-1 \to -\infty$	$-\infty \to -1$
IV	$-1 \to 0$	$0 \to +1$	$-\infty \to 0$	$0 \to -\infty$	$+\infty \to +1$	$-1 \to -\infty$

TRIGONOMETRIC FUNCTIONS OF SOME SPECIAL ANGLES

Angle	sin	cos	tan	cot	sec	csc
$0° = 0$	0	1	0	$\cdots$	1	$\cdots$
$15° = \dfrac{\pi}{12}$	$\dfrac{\sqrt{2}}{4}(\sqrt{3}-1)$	$\dfrac{\sqrt{2}}{4}(\sqrt{3}+1)$	$2-\sqrt{3}$	$2+\sqrt{3}$	$\sqrt{2}(\sqrt{3}-1)$	$\sqrt{2}(\sqrt{3}+1)$
$30° = \dfrac{\pi}{6}$	$1/2$	$\sqrt{3}/2$	$\sqrt{3}/3$	$\sqrt{3}$	$2\sqrt{3}/3$	2
$45° = \dfrac{\pi}{4}$	$\sqrt{2}/2$	$\sqrt{2}/2$	1	1	$\sqrt{2}$	$\sqrt{2}$
$60° = \dfrac{\pi}{3}$	$\sqrt{3}/2$	$1/2$	$\sqrt{3}$	$\sqrt{3}/3$	2	$2\sqrt{3}/3$
$75° = \dfrac{5\pi}{12}$	$\dfrac{\sqrt{2}}{4}(\sqrt{3}+1)$	$\dfrac{\sqrt{2}}{4}(\sqrt{3}-1)$	$2+\sqrt{3}$	$2-\sqrt{3}$	$\sqrt{2}(\sqrt{3}+1)$	$\sqrt{2}(\sqrt{3}-1)$
$90° = \dfrac{\pi}{2}$	1	0	$\cdots$	0	$\cdots$	1
$105° = \dfrac{7\pi}{12}$	$\dfrac{\sqrt{2}}{4}(\sqrt{3}+1)$	$-\dfrac{\sqrt{2}}{4}(\sqrt{3}-1)$	$-(2+\sqrt{3})$	$-(2-\sqrt{3})$	$-\sqrt{2}(\sqrt{3}+1)$	$\sqrt{2}(\sqrt{3}-1)$
$120° = \dfrac{2\pi}{3}$	$\sqrt{3}/2$	$-1/2$	$-\sqrt{3}$	$-\sqrt{3}/3$	-2	$2\sqrt{3}/3$
$135° = \dfrac{3\pi}{4}$	$\sqrt{2}/2$	$-\sqrt{2}/2$	-1	-1	$-\sqrt{2}$	$\sqrt{2}$
$150° = \dfrac{5\pi}{6}$	$1/2$	$-\sqrt{3}/2$	$-\sqrt{3}/3$	$-\sqrt{3}$	$-2\sqrt{3}/3$	2
$165° = \dfrac{11\pi}{12}$	$\dfrac{\sqrt{2}}{4}(\sqrt{3}-1)$	$-\dfrac{\sqrt{2}}{4}(\sqrt{3}+1)$	$-(2-\sqrt{3})$	$-(2+\sqrt{3})$	$-\sqrt{2}(\sqrt{3}-1)$	$\sqrt{2}(\sqrt{3}+1)$
$180° = \pi$	0	-1	0	$\cdots$	-1	$\cdots$
$270° = \dfrac{3\pi}{2}$	-1	0	$\cdots$	0	$\cdots$	-1

Formulas for Use in Trigonometry

Relations among the Functions

$$\sin x = \frac{1}{\csc x}$$

$$\csc x = \frac{1}{\sin x}$$

$$\cos x = \frac{1}{\sec x}$$

$$\sec x = \frac{1}{\cos x}$$

$$\tan x = \frac{1}{\cot x} = \frac{\sin x}{\cos x}$$

$$\sin^2 x + \cos^2 x = 1$$
$$1 + \tan^2 x = \sec^2 x$$

$$\cot x = \frac{1}{\tan x} = \frac{\cos x}{\sin x}$$

$$1 + \cot^2 x = \csc^2 x$$

$$* \; \sin x = \pm \sqrt{1 - \cos^2 x}$$
$$* \; \tan x = \pm \sqrt{\sec^2 x - 1}$$
$$* \; \cot x = \pm \sqrt{\csc^2 x - 1}$$

$$* \; \cos x = \pm \sqrt{1 - \sin^2 x}$$
$$* \; \sec x = \pm \sqrt{\tan^2 x + 1}$$
$$* \; \csc x = \pm \sqrt{\cot^2 x + 1}$$

$$\sin x = \cos(90° - x) = \sin(180° - x)$$
$$\cos x = \sin(90° - x) = -\cos(180° - x)$$
$$\tan x = \cot(90° - x) = -\tan(180° - x)$$
$$\cot x = \tan(90° - x) = -\cot(180° - x)$$

$$\csc x = \cot \frac{x}{2} - \cot x$$

*The sign in front of radical depends on quadrant in which x falls.

Reduction Formulas

$$\sin \alpha = + \cos(\alpha - 90°) = - \sin(\alpha - 180°) = - \cos(\alpha - 270°)$$
$$\cos \alpha = - \sin(\alpha - 90°) = - \cos(\alpha - 180°) = + \sin(\alpha - 270°)$$
$$\tan \alpha = - \cot(\alpha - 90°) = + \tan(\alpha - 180°) = - \cot(\alpha - 270°)$$
$$\cot \alpha = - \tan(\alpha - 90°) = + \cot(\alpha - 180°) = - \tan(\alpha - 270°)$$
$$\sec \alpha = - \csc(\alpha - 90°) = - \sec(\alpha - 180°) = + \csc(\alpha - 270°)$$
$$\csc \alpha = + \sec(\alpha - 90°) = - \csc(\alpha - 180°) = - \sec(\alpha - 270°)$$

FURTHER REDUCTION FORMULAS

	sin	cos	tan	cot	sec	csc
$- \alpha$	$- \sin \alpha$	$+ \cos \alpha$	$- \tan \alpha$	$- \cot \alpha$	$+ \sec \alpha$	$- \csc \alpha$
$90° + \alpha$	$+ \cos \alpha$	$- \sin \alpha$	$- \cot \alpha$	$- \tan \alpha$	$- \csc \alpha$	$+ \sec \alpha$
$90° - \alpha$	$+ \cos \alpha$	$+ \sin \alpha$	$+ \cot \alpha$	$+ \tan \alpha$	$+ \csc \alpha$	$+ \sec \alpha$
$180° + \alpha$	$- \sin \alpha$	$- \cos \alpha$	$+ \tan \alpha$	$+ \cot \alpha$	$- \sec \alpha$	$- \csc \alpha$
$180° - \alpha$	$+ \sin \alpha$	$- \cos \alpha$	$- \tan \alpha$	$- \cot \alpha$	$- \sec \alpha$	$+ \csc \alpha$
$270° + \alpha$	$- \cos \alpha$	$+ \sin \alpha$	$- \cot \alpha$	$- \tan \alpha$	$+ \csc \alpha$	$- \sec \alpha$
$270° - \alpha$	$- \cos \alpha$	$- \sin \alpha$	$+ \cot \alpha$	$+ \tan \alpha$	$- \csc \alpha$	$- \sec \alpha$
$360° + \alpha$	$+ \sin \alpha$	$+ \cos \alpha$	$+ \tan \alpha$	$+ \cot \alpha$	$+ \sec \alpha$	$+ \csc \alpha$
$360° - \alpha$	$- \sin \alpha$	$+ \cos \alpha$	$- \tan \alpha$	$- \cot \alpha$	$+ \sec \alpha$	$- \csc \alpha$

Formulas for Use in Trigonometry

The previous table may be summarized and extended by the following easily remembered rule:

$$f(\pm\alpha + n90°) = \pm g(\alpha)$$

where n may be any integer, positive, negative, or zero

f is any one of the six trigonometric functions: sin, cos, tan, cot, sec, or csc

α may be any real angle measure

If n is even, then g is the same function as f. If n is odd, then g is the *cofunction* of f.

(Sine and cosine, tangent and cotangent, secant and cosecant, are cofunctions of each other.)

The second $\pm$ sign is not necessarily the same as the first one, but is determined as follows: For a given function f, a given value of n, and a given choice of the first $\pm$ sign, the second $\pm$ sign will be the same for all values of α. Thus it is only necessary to check the sign for any one value of α, and the formula will be complete.

EXAMPLES:

$\tan(\alpha + 270°) = \pm \cot \alpha$. Since $n(=3)$ is odd, we use the cofunction. To determine the sign, assume a value of α in the first quadrant. Then $\alpha + 270°$ is in the fourth quadrant, where the tangent is negative, so a minus sign is required. Thus the formula becomes

$$\tan(\alpha + 270°) = -\cot \alpha, \quad \text{valid for all values of } \alpha.$$

$\cos(\alpha - 450°) = \pm \sin \alpha$. Again assuming a value of α in the first quadrant, we find that $\alpha - 450°$ is in the fourth quadrant. Thus $\cos(\alpha - 450°)$ would be positive, and no minus sign is needed. Hence the formula becomes

$$\cos(\alpha - 450°) = \sin \alpha.$$

$\sec(180° - \alpha) = \pm \sec \alpha$. Here $n(=2)$ is even, so we use the same function. To determine the sign, again assume a value of α in the first quadrant. Then $180° - \alpha$ is in the second quadrant, where the secant is negative. Thus the formula. valid for all values of α, is

$$\sec(180° - \alpha) = -\sec \alpha.$$

Fundamental Identities

Where a double sign appears in the following, the choice of sign depends upon the quadrant in which the angle terminates.

Reciprocal relations

$$\sin \alpha = \frac{1}{\csc \alpha}, \quad \cos \alpha = \frac{1}{\sec \alpha}, \quad \tan \alpha = \frac{1}{\cot \alpha}$$

$$\csc \alpha = \frac{1}{\sin \alpha}, \quad \sec \alpha = \frac{1}{\cos \alpha}, \quad \cot \alpha = \frac{1}{\tan \alpha}$$

Product relations

$$\sin \alpha = \tan \alpha \cos \alpha, \quad \cos \alpha = \cot \alpha \sin \alpha$$
$$\tan \alpha = \sin \alpha \sec \alpha, \quad \cot \alpha = \cos \alpha \csc \alpha$$
$$\sec \alpha = \csc \alpha \tan \alpha, \quad \csc \alpha = \sec \alpha \cot \alpha$$

Quotient relations

$$\sin \alpha = \frac{\tan \alpha}{\sec \alpha}, \quad \cos \alpha = \frac{\cot \alpha}{\csc \alpha}, \quad \tan \alpha = \frac{\sin \alpha}{\cos \alpha}$$

$$\csc \alpha = \frac{\sec \alpha}{\tan \alpha}, \quad \sec \alpha = \frac{\csc \alpha}{\cot \alpha}, \quad \cot \alpha = \frac{\cos \alpha}{\sin \alpha}$$

Formulas for Use in Trigonometry

Pythagorean relations

$$\sin^2\alpha + \cos^2\alpha = 1, \quad 1 + \tan^2\alpha = \sec^2\alpha, \quad 1 + \cot^2\alpha = \csc^2\alpha$$

Angle-sum and angle-difference relations

$$\sin(\alpha + \beta) = \sin\alpha\cos\beta + \cos\alpha\sin\beta$$
$$\sin(\alpha - \beta) = \sin\alpha\cos\beta - \cos\alpha\sin\beta$$
$$\cos(\alpha + \beta) = \cos\alpha\cos\beta - \sin\alpha\sin\beta$$
$$\cos(\alpha - \beta) = \cos\alpha\cos\beta + \sin\alpha\sin\beta$$

$$\tan(\alpha + \beta) = \frac{\tan\alpha + \tan\beta}{1 - \tan\alpha\tan\beta}$$

$$\tan(\alpha - \beta) = \frac{\tan\alpha - \tan\beta}{1 + \tan\alpha\tan\beta}$$

$$\cot(\alpha + \beta) = \frac{\cot\beta\cot\alpha - 1}{\cot\beta + \cot\alpha}$$

$$\cot(\alpha - \beta) = \frac{\cot\beta\cot\alpha + 1}{\cot\beta - \cot\alpha}$$

$$\sin(\alpha + \beta)\sin(\alpha - \beta) = \sin^2\alpha - \sin^2\beta = \cos^2\beta - \cos^2\alpha$$
$$\cos(\alpha + \beta)\cos(\alpha - \beta) = \cos^2\alpha - \sin^2\beta = \cos^2\beta - \sin^2\alpha$$

Double-angle relations

$$\sin 2\alpha = 2\sin\alpha\cos\alpha = \frac{2\tan\alpha}{1 + \tan^2\alpha}$$

$$\cos 2\alpha = \cos^2\alpha - \sin^2\alpha = 2\cos^2\alpha - 1 = 1 - 2\sin^2\alpha = \frac{1 - \tan^2\alpha}{1 + \tan^2\alpha}$$

$$\tan 2\alpha = \frac{2\tan\alpha}{1 - \tan^2\alpha}, \quad \cot 2\alpha = \frac{\cot^2\alpha - 1}{2\cot\alpha}$$

Multiple-angle relations

$$\sin 3\alpha = 3\sin\alpha - 4\sin^3\alpha$$
$$\cos 3\alpha = 4\cos^3\alpha - 3\cos\alpha$$
$$\sin 4\alpha = 4\sin\alpha\cos\alpha - 8\sin^3\alpha\cos\alpha$$
$$\cos 4\alpha = 8\cos^4\alpha - 8\cos^2\alpha + 1$$
$$\sin 5\alpha = 5\sin\alpha - 20\sin^3\alpha + 16\sin^5\alpha$$
$$\cos 5\alpha = 16\cos^5\alpha - 20\cos^3\alpha + 5\cos\alpha$$
$$\sin 6\alpha = 32\cos^5\alpha\sin\alpha - 32\cos^3\alpha\sin\alpha + 6\cos\alpha\sin\alpha$$
$$\cos 6\alpha = 32\cos^6\alpha - 48\cos^4\alpha + 18\cos^2\alpha - 1$$
$$\sin n\alpha = 2\sin(n - 1)\alpha\cos\alpha - \sin(n - 2)\alpha$$
$$\cos n\alpha = 2\cos(n - 1)\alpha\cos\alpha - \cos(n - 2)\alpha$$

$$\tan 3\alpha = \frac{3\tan\alpha - \tan^3\alpha}{1 - 3\tan^2\alpha}$$

$$\tan 4\alpha = \frac{4\tan\alpha - 4\tan^3\alpha}{1 - 6\tan^2\alpha + \tan^4\alpha}$$

$$\tan n\alpha = \frac{\tan(n - 1)\alpha + \tan\alpha}{1 - \tan(n - 1)\alpha\tan\alpha}$$

Formulas for Use in Trigonometry

Function-product relations

$$\sin\alpha\sin\beta = \tfrac{1}{2}\cos(\alpha - \beta) - \tfrac{1}{2}\cos(\alpha + \beta)$$
$$\cos\alpha\cos\beta = \tfrac{1}{2}\cos(\alpha - \beta) + \tfrac{1}{2}\cos(\alpha + \beta)$$
$$\sin\alpha\cos\beta = \tfrac{1}{2}\sin(\alpha + \beta) + \tfrac{1}{2}\sin(\alpha - \beta)$$
$$\cos\alpha\sin\beta = \tfrac{1}{2}\sin(\alpha + \beta) - \tfrac{1}{2}\sin(\alpha - \beta)$$

Function-sum and function-difference relations

$$\sin\alpha + \sin\beta = 2\sin\tfrac{1}{2}(\alpha + \beta)\cos\tfrac{1}{2}(\alpha - \beta)$$
$$\sin\alpha - \sin\beta = 2\cos\tfrac{1}{2}(\alpha + \beta)\sin\tfrac{1}{2}(\alpha - \beta)$$
$$\cos\alpha + \cos\beta = 2\cos\tfrac{1}{2}(\alpha + \beta)\cos\tfrac{1}{2}(\alpha - \beta)$$
$$\cos\alpha - \cos\beta = -2\sin\tfrac{1}{2}(\alpha + \beta)\sin\tfrac{1}{2}(\alpha - \beta)$$

$$\tan\alpha + \tan\beta = \frac{\sin(\alpha + \beta)}{\cos\alpha\cos\beta}, \qquad \tan\alpha - \tan\beta = \frac{\sin(\alpha - \beta)}{\cos\alpha\cos\beta}$$

$$\cot\alpha + \cot\beta = \frac{\sin(\alpha + \beta)}{\sin\alpha\sin\beta}, \qquad \cot\alpha - \cot\beta = \frac{\sin(\beta - \alpha)}{\sin\alpha\sin\beta}$$

$$\frac{\sin\alpha + \sin\beta}{\sin\alpha - \sin\beta} = \frac{\tan\tfrac{1}{2}(\alpha + \beta)}{\tan\tfrac{1}{2}(\alpha - \beta)}, \qquad \frac{\sin\alpha + \sin\beta}{\cos\alpha - \cos\beta} = \cot\tfrac{1}{2}(\beta - \alpha)$$

$$\frac{\sin\alpha + \sin\beta}{\cos\alpha + \cos\beta} = \tan\tfrac{1}{2}(\alpha + \beta), \qquad \frac{\sin\alpha - \sin\beta}{\cos\alpha + \cos\beta} = \tan\tfrac{1}{2}(\alpha - \beta)$$

Half-angle relations

$$\sin\frac{\alpha}{2} = \pm\sqrt{\frac{1 - \cos\alpha}{2}}, \qquad \cos\frac{\alpha}{2} = \pm\sqrt{\frac{1 + \cos\alpha}{2}}$$

$$\tan\frac{\alpha}{2} = \pm\sqrt{\frac{1 - \cos\alpha}{1 + \cos\alpha}} = \frac{1 - \cos\alpha}{\sin\alpha} = \frac{\sin\alpha}{1 + \cos\alpha}$$

$$\cot\frac{\alpha}{2} = \pm\sqrt{\frac{1 + \cos\alpha}{1 - \cos\alpha}} = \frac{1 + \cos\alpha}{\sin\alpha} = \frac{\sin\alpha}{1 - \cos\alpha}$$

Power relations

$$\sin^2\alpha = \tfrac{1}{2}(1 - \cos 2\alpha), \qquad \sin^3\alpha = \tfrac{1}{4}(3\sin\alpha - \sin 3\alpha)$$
$$\sin^4\alpha = \tfrac{1}{8}(3 - 4\cos 2\alpha + \cos 4\alpha)$$
$$\cos^2\alpha = \tfrac{1}{2}(1 + \cos 2\alpha), \qquad \cos^3\alpha = \tfrac{1}{4}(3\cos\alpha + \cos 3\alpha)$$
$$\cos^4\alpha = \tfrac{1}{8}(3 + 4\cos 2\alpha + \cos 4\alpha)$$
$$\tan^2\alpha = \frac{1 - \cos 2\alpha}{1 + \cos 2\alpha}, \qquad \cot^2\alpha = \frac{1 + \cos 2\alpha}{1 - \cos 2\alpha}$$

Exponential relations (α in radians), Euler's equation

$$e^{i\alpha} = \cos\alpha + i\sin\alpha, \qquad i = \sqrt{-1}$$

$$\sin\alpha = \frac{e^{i\alpha} - e^{-i\alpha}}{2i}, \qquad \cos\alpha = \frac{e^{i\alpha} + e^{-i\alpha}}{2}$$

$$\tan\alpha = -i\left(\frac{e^{i\alpha} - e^{-i\alpha}}{e^{i\alpha} + e^{-i\alpha}}\right) = -i\left(\frac{e^{2i\alpha} - 1}{e^{2i\alpha} + 1}\right)$$

Formulas for Use in Trigonometry

THE TRIGONOMETRIC FUNCTIONS IN TERMS OF ONE ANOTHER

Function	$\sin\alpha$	$\cos\alpha$	$\tan\alpha$	$\cot\alpha$	$\sec\alpha$	$\csc\alpha$
$\sin\alpha$	$\sin\alpha$	$\pm\sqrt{1-\cos^2\alpha}$	$\dfrac{\tan\alpha}{\pm\sqrt{1+\tan^2\alpha}}$	$\dfrac{1}{\pm\sqrt{1+\cot^2\alpha}}$	$\dfrac{\pm\sqrt{\sec^2\alpha-1}}{\sec\alpha}$	$\dfrac{1}{\csc\alpha}$
$\cos\alpha$	$\pm\sqrt{1-\sin^2\alpha}$	$\cos\alpha$	$\dfrac{1}{\pm\sqrt{1+\tan^2\alpha}}$	$\dfrac{\cot\alpha}{\pm\sqrt{1+\cot^2\alpha}}$	$\dfrac{1}{\sec\alpha}$	$\dfrac{\pm\sqrt{\csc^2\alpha-1}}{\csc\alpha}$
$\tan\alpha$	$\dfrac{\sin\alpha}{\pm\sqrt{1-\sin^2\alpha}}$	$\dfrac{\pm\sqrt{1-\cos^2\alpha}}{\cos\alpha}$	$\tan\alpha$	$\dfrac{1}{\cot\alpha}$	$\pm\sqrt{\sec^2\alpha-1}$	$\dfrac{1}{\pm\sqrt{\csc^2\alpha-1}}$
$\cot\alpha$	$\dfrac{\pm\sqrt{1-\sin^2\alpha}}{\sin\alpha}$	$\dfrac{\cos\alpha}{\pm\sqrt{1-\cos^2\alpha}}$	$\dfrac{1}{\tan\alpha}$	$\cot\alpha$	$\dfrac{1}{\pm\sqrt{\sec^2\alpha-1}}$	$\pm\sqrt{\csc^2\alpha-1}$
$\sec\alpha$	$\dfrac{1}{\pm\sqrt{1-\sin^2\alpha}}$	$\dfrac{1}{\cos\alpha}$	$\pm\sqrt{1+\tan^2\alpha}$	$\dfrac{\pm\sqrt{1+\cot^2\alpha}}{\cot\alpha}$	$\sec\alpha$	$\dfrac{\csc\alpha}{\pm\sqrt{\csc^2\alpha-1}}$
$\csc\alpha$	$\dfrac{1}{\sin\alpha}$	$\dfrac{1}{\pm\sqrt{1-\cos^2\alpha}}$	$\dfrac{\pm\sqrt{1+\tan^2\alpha}}{\tan\alpha}$	$\pm\sqrt{1+\cot^2\alpha}$	$\dfrac{\sec\alpha}{\pm\sqrt{\sec^2\alpha-1}}$	$\csc\alpha$

Note. The choice of sign depends upon the quadrant in which the angle terminates.

Principal Values of the Inverse Trigonometric Functions

The notation arcsin x (or $\sin^{-1}x$) is used to denote any angle whose sine is x; Arcsin x (or $\text{Sin}^{-1}x$) is usually used to denote the *principal value*. Similar notation is used for the other inverse trigonometric functions. The principal values of the inverse trigonometric functions are defined as follows:

$$-\pi/2 \leq \text{Arcsin } x \leq \pi/2, \qquad -1 \leq x \leq 1$$

$$0 \leq \text{Arccos } x \leq \pi, \qquad -1 \leq x \leq 1$$

$$-\pi/2 < \text{Arctan } x < \pi/2, \qquad -\infty < x < \infty$$

$$0 < \text{Arccsc } x \leq \pi/2, \qquad x \geq 1$$
$$-\pi < \text{Arccsc } x \leq -\pi/2, \qquad x \leq -1$$

$$0 \leq \text{Arcsec } x < \pi/2, \qquad x \geq 1$$
$$-\pi \leq \text{Arcsec } x < -\pi/2, \qquad x \leq -1$$

$$0 < \text{Arccot } x < \pi, \qquad -\infty < x < \infty$$

Note. There is no uniform agreement on the definitions of Arccsc x, Arcsec x, Arccot x for negative values of x.

Fundamental Identities Involving Principal Values

$$\text{Arcsin } x + \text{Arccos } x = \pi/2$$
$$\text{Arctan } x + \text{Arccot } x = \pi/2$$

If $\alpha = \text{Arcsin } x$, then

$$\sin\alpha = x, \qquad \cos\alpha = \sqrt{1-x^2}, \qquad \tan\alpha = \frac{x}{\sqrt{1-x^2}}$$

$$\csc\alpha = \frac{1}{x}, \qquad \sec\alpha = \frac{1}{\sqrt{1-x^2}}, \qquad \cot\alpha = \frac{\sqrt{1-x^2}}{x}$$

Formulas for Use in Trigonometry

If $\alpha = \text{Arccos } x$, then

$$\sin \alpha = \sqrt{1 - x^2}, \qquad \cos \alpha = x, \qquad \tan \alpha = \frac{\sqrt{1 - x^2}}{x}$$

$$\csc \alpha = \frac{1}{\sqrt{1 - x^2}}, \qquad \sec \alpha = \frac{1}{x}, \qquad \cot \alpha = \frac{x}{\sqrt{1 - x^2}}$$

If $\alpha = \text{Arctan } x$, then

$$\sin \alpha = \frac{x}{\sqrt{1 + x^2}}, \qquad \cos \alpha = \frac{1}{\sqrt{1 + x^2}}, \qquad \tan \alpha = x$$

$$\csc \alpha = \frac{\sqrt{1 + x^2}}{x}, \qquad \sec \alpha = \sqrt{1 + x^2}, \qquad \cot \alpha = \frac{1}{x}$$

Relations Between Principal Values of Inverse Trigonometric Functions

The following additional relations between principal values of the inverse trigonometric functions are useful:

$$\text{Arcsin } x = \text{Arccos}(-x) - \frac{\pi}{2} = \frac{\pi}{2} - \text{Arccos } x$$

$$= -\text{Arcsin}(-x) = \text{Arctan } \frac{x}{\sqrt{1 - x^2}}$$

$$= \frac{\pi}{2} - \text{Arccot } \frac{x}{\sqrt{1 - x^2}}$$

$$\text{Arctan } x = \text{Arccot}(-x) - \frac{\pi}{2} = \frac{\pi}{2} - \text{Arccot } x$$

$$= -\text{Arctan}(-x) = \text{Arcsin } \frac{x}{\sqrt{x^2 + 1}}$$

$$= \frac{\pi}{2} - \text{Arccos } \frac{x}{\sqrt{x^2 + 1}}$$

$$\text{Arccos } x = \frac{\pi}{2} + \text{Arcsin}(-x) = \frac{\pi}{2} - \text{Arcsin } x$$

$$= \pi - \text{Arccos}(-x) = \text{Arccot } \frac{x}{\sqrt{1 - x^2}}$$

$$= \frac{\pi}{2} - \text{Arctan } \frac{x}{\sqrt{1 - x^2}}$$

$$\text{Arccot } x = \frac{\pi}{2} + \text{Arctan}(-x) = \frac{\pi}{2} - \text{Arctan } x$$

$$= \pi - \text{Arccot}(-x) = \text{Arccos } \frac{x}{\sqrt{x^2 + 1}}$$

$$= \frac{\pi}{2} - \text{Arcsin } \frac{x}{\sqrt{x^2 + 1}}$$

Formulas for Use in Trigonometry

$$\text{Arccsc } x = \text{Arcsec } \frac{x}{\sqrt{x^2 - 1}}$$

$$\text{Arcsec } x = \text{Arccsc } \frac{x}{\sqrt{x^2 - 1}}$$

$$\cos(\text{Arcsin } x) = \sin(\text{Arccos } x) = \sqrt{1 - x^2}$$

$$\sec(\text{Arctan } x) = \csc(\text{Arccot } x) = \sqrt{x^2 + 1}$$

$$\tan(\text{Arcsec } x) = \cot(\text{Arccsc } x) = \sqrt{x^2 - 1}$$

The above are valid for x positive or negative. The following are valid only for $x \geq 0$.

$$\text{Arcsin } x = \text{Arccos } \sqrt{1 - x^2} = \text{Arccot } \frac{\sqrt{1 - x^2}}{x}$$

$$= \text{Arcsec } \frac{1}{\sqrt{1 - x^2}} = \text{Arccsc } \frac{1}{x}$$

$$= \frac{\pi}{2} - \text{Arcsin } \sqrt{1 - x^2}$$

$$\text{Arccos } x = \text{Arcsin } \sqrt{1 - x^2} = \text{Arctan } \frac{\sqrt{1 - x^2}}{x}$$

$$= \text{Arcsec } \frac{1}{x} = \text{Arccsc } \frac{1}{\sqrt{1 - x^2}}$$

$$= \frac{\pi}{2} - \text{Arccos } \sqrt{1 - x^2}$$

$$\text{Arctan } x = \text{Arccot } \frac{1}{x} = \text{Arccos } \frac{1}{\sqrt{x^2 + 1}}$$

$$= \text{Arcsec } \sqrt{x^2 + 1} = \text{Arccsc } \frac{\sqrt{x^2 + 1}}{x}$$

$$= \frac{\pi}{2} - \text{Arctan } \frac{1}{x}$$

$$\text{Arccot } x = \text{Arctan } \frac{1}{x} = \text{Arcsin } \frac{1}{\sqrt{x^2 + 1}}$$

$$= \text{Arcsec } \frac{\sqrt{x^2 + 1}}{x} = \text{Arccsc } \sqrt{x^2 + 1}$$

$$= \frac{\pi}{2} - \text{Arccot } \frac{1}{x}$$

$$\text{Arcsec } x = \text{Arctan } \sqrt{x^2 - 1} = \text{Arccot } \frac{1}{\sqrt{x^2 - 1}}$$

$$= \text{Arcsin } \frac{\sqrt{x^2 - 1}}{x} = \text{Arccos } \frac{1}{x} = \pi + \text{Arcsec}(-x)$$

$$= \frac{\pi}{2} - \text{Arccsc } x = -\frac{\pi}{2} - \text{Arccsc}(-x)$$

Formulas for Use in Trigonometry

$$\text{Arccsc } x = \text{Arctan } \frac{1}{\sqrt{x^2 - 1}} = \text{Arccot } \sqrt{x^2 - 1}$$

$$= \text{Arcsin } \frac{1}{x} = \text{Arccos } \frac{\sqrt{x^2 - 1}}{x} = \pi + \text{Arccsc}(-x)$$

$$= \frac{\pi}{2} - \text{Arcsec } x = -\frac{\pi}{2} - \text{Arcsec}(-x)$$

The following are valid if $x < 0$.

$$\text{Arcsin } x = -\text{Arccos } \sqrt{1 - x^2} = \text{Arccot } \frac{\sqrt{1 - x^2}}{x} - \pi$$

$$= -\pi - \text{Arccsc } \frac{1}{x} = -\text{Arcsec } \frac{1}{\sqrt{1 - x^2}}$$

$$= \text{Arcsin } \sqrt{1 - x^2} - \frac{\pi}{2}$$

$$\text{Arccos } x = \pi - \text{Arcsin } \sqrt{1 - x^2} = \pi + \text{Arctan } \frac{\sqrt{1 - x^2}}{x}$$

$$= \pi - \text{Arccsc } \frac{1}{\sqrt{1 - x^2}} = -\text{Arcsec } \frac{1}{x}$$

$$= \text{Arccos } \sqrt{1 - x^2} + \frac{\pi}{2}$$

$$\text{Arctan } x = \text{Arccot } \frac{1}{x} - \pi = -\text{Arccos } \frac{1}{\sqrt{x^2 + 1}}$$

$$= -\text{Arcsec } \sqrt{x^2 + 1} = -\pi - \text{Arccsc } \frac{\sqrt{x^2 + 1}}{x}$$

$$-\frac{\pi}{2} - \text{Arctan } \frac{1}{x}$$

$$\text{Arccot } x = \pi + \text{Arctan } \frac{1}{x} = \pi - \text{Arcsin } \frac{1}{\sqrt{x^2 + 1}}$$

$$= -\text{Arcsec } \frac{\sqrt{x^2 + 1}}{x} = \pi - \text{Arccsc } \sqrt{x^2 + 1}$$

$$= \frac{3\pi}{2} - \text{Arccot } \frac{1}{x}$$

$$\text{Arcsec } x = \text{Arctan } \sqrt{x^2 - 1} - \pi = \text{Arccot } \frac{1}{\sqrt{x^2 - 1}} - \pi$$

$$= -\pi - \text{Arcsin } \frac{\sqrt{x^2 - 1}}{x} = -\text{Arccos } \frac{1}{x} = \text{Arcsec}(-x) - \pi$$

$$= -\frac{3\pi}{2} - \text{Arccsc } x = -\frac{\pi}{2} - \text{Arccsc}(-x)$$

Formulas for Use in Trigonometry

$$\text{Arccsc } x = \text{Arctan } \frac{1}{\sqrt{x^2 - 1}} - \pi = \text{Arccot } \sqrt{x^2 - 1} - \pi$$

$$= -\pi - \text{Arcsin } \frac{1}{x} = -\text{Arccos } \frac{\sqrt{x^2 - 1}}{x} = \text{Arccsc}(-x) - \pi$$

$$= -\frac{3\pi}{2} - \text{Arcsec } x = -\frac{\pi}{2} - \text{Arcsec}(-x)$$

Plane Triangle Formulas

In the following, A, B, C denote the angles of any plane triangle, a, b, c the corresponding opposite sides, and $s = \frac{1}{2}(a + b + c)$.

Radius of inscribed circle:

$$r = \sqrt{\frac{(s - a)(s - b)(s - c)}{s}}$$

Radius of circumscribed circle:

$$R = \frac{a}{2 \sin A} = \frac{b}{2 \sin B} = \frac{c}{2 \sin C}$$

Law of sines:

$$\frac{a}{\sin A} = \frac{b}{\sin B} = \frac{c}{\sin C}$$

Law of cosines:

$$a^2 = b^2 + c^2 - 2bc \cos A, \qquad \cos A = \frac{b^2 + c^2 - a^2}{2bc}$$

$$b^2 = c^2 + a^2 - 2ca \cos B, \qquad \cos B = \frac{c^2 + a^2 - b^2}{2ca}$$

$$c^2 = a^2 + b^2 - 2ab \cos C, \qquad \cos C = \frac{a^2 + b^2 - c^2}{2ab}$$

Law of tangents:

$$\frac{b - c}{b + c} = \frac{\tan \frac{1}{2}(B - C)}{\tan \frac{1}{2}(B + C)}, \qquad \frac{c - a}{c + a} = \frac{\tan \frac{1}{2}(C - A)}{\tan \frac{1}{2}(C + A)}$$

$$\frac{a - b}{a + b} = \frac{\tan \frac{1}{2}(A - B)}{\tan \frac{1}{2}(A + B)}$$

Half-angle formulas:

$$\tan \tfrac{1}{2}A = \frac{r}{s - a}, \qquad \tan \tfrac{1}{2}B = \frac{r}{s - b}, \qquad \tan \tfrac{1}{2}C = \frac{r}{s - c}$$

$$\sin \tfrac{1}{2}A = \sqrt{\frac{(s - b)(s - c)}{bc}}, \qquad \cos \tfrac{1}{2}A = \sqrt{\frac{s(s - a)}{bc}}$$

$$\sin \tfrac{1}{2}B = \sqrt{\frac{(s - c)(s - a)}{ca}}, \qquad \cos \tfrac{1}{2}B = \sqrt{\frac{s(s - b)}{ca}}$$

$$\sin \tfrac{1}{2}C = \sqrt{\frac{(s - a)(s - b)}{ab}}, \qquad \cos \tfrac{1}{2}C = \sqrt{\frac{s(s - c)}{ab}}$$

Formulas for Use in Trigonometry

Area:

$$K = \tfrac{1}{2}bc \sin A = \tfrac{1}{2}ca \sin B = \tfrac{1}{2}ab \sin C$$

$$K = \frac{a^2 \sin B \sin C}{2 \sin A} = \frac{b^2 \sin C \sin A}{2 \sin B} = \frac{c^2 \sin A \sin B}{2 \sin C}$$

$$K = \sqrt{s(s-a)(s-b)(s-c)} = rs = \frac{abc}{4R}$$

Mollweide's formulas:

$$\frac{b-c}{a} = \frac{\sin \tfrac{1}{2}(B-C)}{\cos \tfrac{1}{2}A}, \qquad \frac{c-a}{b} = \frac{\sin \tfrac{1}{2}(C-A)}{\cos \tfrac{1}{2}B}$$

$$\frac{a-b}{c} = \frac{\sin \tfrac{1}{2}(A-B)}{\cos \tfrac{1}{2}C}$$

Newton's formulas:

$$\frac{b+c}{a} = \frac{\cos \tfrac{1}{2}(B-C)}{\sin \tfrac{1}{2}A}, \qquad \frac{c+a}{b} = \frac{\cos \tfrac{1}{2}(C-A)}{\sin \tfrac{1}{2}B}$$

$$\frac{a+b}{c} = \frac{\cos \tfrac{1}{2}(A-B)}{\sin \tfrac{1}{2}C}$$

Solution of Right Triangles

(a) Given acute angle A and opposite leg a.

$$B = 90° - A, \quad b = a/\tan A = a \cot A, \quad c = a/\sin A = a \csc A$$

(b) Given acute angle A and adjacent leg b.

$$B = 90° - A, \quad a = b \tan A, \quad c = b/\cos A = b \sec A$$

(c) Given acute angle A and hypotenuse c.

$$B = 90° - A, \quad a = c \sin A, \quad b = c \cos A$$

(d) Given legs a and b.

$$c = \sqrt{a^2 + b^2}, \quad \tan A = a/b, \quad B = 90° - A$$

(e) Given hypotenuse c and leg a.

$$b = \sqrt{(c+a)(c-a)}, \quad \sin A = a/c, \quad B = 90° - A$$

Solution of Oblique Triangles

(a) Given sides b and c and included angle A.

Nonlogarithmic solution

$$a^2 = b^2 + c^2 - 2bc \cos A, \quad \cos B = (c^2 + a^2 - b^2)/2ca,$$
$$\cos C = (a^2 + b^2 - c^2)/2ab$$

Logarithmic solution

$$\tfrac{1}{2}(B + C) = 90° - \tfrac{1}{2}A, \quad \tan \tfrac{1}{2}(B - C) = \frac{b-c}{b+c}\tan \tfrac{1}{2}(B + C),$$
$$B = \tfrac{1}{2}(B + C) + \tfrac{1}{2}(B - C), \quad C = \tfrac{1}{2}(B + C) - \tfrac{1}{2}(B - C),$$
$$a = (b \sin A)/\sin B, \quad K = \tfrac{1}{2}bc \sin A$$

Formulas for Use in Spherical Trigonometry

Check. $A + B + C = 180°$, or use Newton's formula or law of sines.

(b) Given angles B and C and included side a.

$$A = 180° - (B + C), \quad b = (a \sin B)/\sin A,$$
$$c = (a \sin C)/\sin A, \quad K = \frac{a^2 \sin B \sin C}{2 \sin A}$$

Check. $a = b \cos C + c \cos B$, or use Newton's formula or law of tangents.

(c) Given sides a and c and opposite angle A.

$$\sin C = (c \sin A)/a, \quad B = 180° - (A + C),$$
$$b = (a \sin B)/\sin A, \quad K = \tfrac{1}{2}ac \sin B$$

Check. $a = b \cos C + c \cos B$, or use Newton's formula or law of tangents.

Note. In this case there may be two solutions, for C may have two values:

$C_1 < 90°$ and $C_2 = 180° - C_1 > 90°$. If $A + C_2 > 180°$, use only C_1.

(d) Given the three sides a, b, c.

Nonlogarithmic solution

$$\cos A = (b^2 + c^2 - a^2)/2bc, \quad \cos B = (c^2 + a^2 - b^2)/2ca,$$
$$\cos C = (a^2 + b^2 - c^2)/2ab$$

Logarithmic solution

$$s = \tfrac{1}{2}(a + b + c), \quad r = \sqrt{\frac{(s - a)(s - b)(s - c)}{s}},$$
$$\tan \tfrac{1}{2}A = \frac{r}{s - a}, \quad \tan \tfrac{1}{2}B = \frac{r}{s - b}, \quad \tan \tfrac{1}{2}C = \frac{r}{s - c},$$
$$K = \sqrt{s(s - a)(s - b)(s - c)}$$

Check. $A + B + C = 180°$.

Relations Between Accuracy of Computed Lengths and Angles

When solving a triangle for any of its parts, the following should be observed:

Significant figures for sides	Angles to the nearest
2	degree
3	ten minutes
4	minute
5	tenth of a minute

SPHERICAL TRIGONOMETRY

Right Spherical Triangles

Let a, b, c be the sides of a right spherical triangle with opposite angles $A, B, C = 90°$, respectively, where each side is measured by the angle subtended at the center of the sphere.

$\sin a = \tan b \cot B,$	$\sin a = \sin A \sin c$
$\sin b = \tan a \cot A,$	$\sin b = \sin B \sin c$
$\cos A = \tan b \cot c,$	$\cos A = \cos a \sin B$
$\cos B = \tan a \cot c,$	$\cos B = \cos b \sin A$
$\cos c = \cot A \cot B,$	$\cos c = \cos a \cos b$

Formulas for Use in Spherical Trigonometry

Napier's Rules of Circular Parts

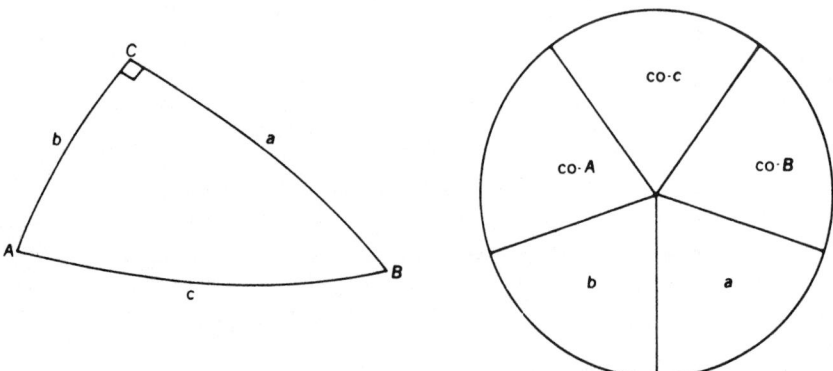

Arrange the five quantities a, b, co-A (complement of A), co-c, co-B of a right spherical triangle right-angled at C in cyclic order as pictured. If any one of these quantities is designated a *middle* part, then two of the other parts are *adjacent* to it, and the remaining two parts are *opposite* to it. The above formulas for a right spherical triangle may be recalled by the following two rules:

(a) The sine of any middle part is equal to the product of the *tangents* of the two *adjacent* parts.

(b) The sine of any middle part is equal to the product of the *cosines* of the two *opposite* parts.

Rules for Determining the Quadrant of a Calculated Part of a Right Spherical Triangle

(a) A leg and the angle opposite it are always of the same quadrant.

(b) If the hypotenuse if less than 90° the legs are of the same quadrant.

(c) If the hypotenuse is greater than 90°, the legs are of unlike quadrants.

Oblique Spherical Triangles

In the following, a, b, c represent the sides of any spherical triangle, A, B, C the corresponding opposite angles, $s = \frac{1}{2}(a + b + c)$, $S = \frac{1}{2}(A + B + C)$, Δ = area of triangle, E = spherical excess of triangle, R = radius of the sphere upon which the triangle lies, and a', b', c', A', B', C' are the corresponding parts of the polar triangle.

$$0° < a + b + c < 360°, \qquad 180° < A + B + C < 540°$$
$$E = A + B + C - 180°, \qquad \Delta = \pi R^2 E / 180$$
$$\tan \tfrac{1}{4}E = \sqrt{\tan \tfrac{s}{2} \tan \tfrac{1}{2}(s - a) \tan \tfrac{1}{2}(s - b) \tan \tfrac{1}{2}(s - c)}$$
$$A = 180° - a', \qquad B = 180° - b', \qquad C = 180° - c'$$
$$a = 180° - A', \qquad b = 180° - B', \qquad c = 180° - C'$$

Law of sines:

$$\frac{\sin a}{\sin A} = \frac{\sin b}{\sin B} = \frac{\sin c}{\sin C}$$

Law of cosines for sides:

$$\cos a = \cos b \cos c + \sin b \sin c \cos A$$
$$\cos b = \cos c \cos a + \sin c \sin a \cos B$$
$$\cos c = \cos a \cos b + \sin a \sin b \cos C$$

Formulas for Use in Spherical Trigonometry

Law of cosines for angles:

$$\cos A = -\cos B \cos C + \sin B \sin C \cos a$$
$$\cos B = -\cos C \cos A + \sin C \sin A \cos b$$
$$\cos C = -\cos A \cos B + \sin A \sin B \cos c$$

Law of tangents:

$$\frac{\tan \frac{1}{2}(B - C)}{\tan \frac{1}{2}(B + C)} = \frac{\tan \frac{1}{2}(b - c)}{\tan \frac{1}{2}(b + c)}, \quad \frac{\tan \frac{1}{2}(C - A)}{\tan \frac{1}{2}(C + A)} = \frac{\tan \frac{1}{2}(c - a)}{\tan \frac{1}{2}(c + a)}$$

$$\frac{\tan \frac{1}{2}(A - B)}{\tan \frac{1}{2}(A + B)} = \frac{\tan \frac{1}{2}(a - b)}{\tan \frac{1}{2}(a + b)}$$

Half-angle formulas:

$$\tan \tfrac{1}{2} A = \frac{k}{\sin(s - a)}, \quad \tan \tfrac{1}{2} B = \frac{k}{\sin(s - b)}, \quad \tan \tfrac{1}{2} C = \frac{k}{\sin(s - c)},$$

where

$$k^2 = \frac{\sin(s - a) \sin(s - b) \sin(s - c)}{\sin s} = (\tan r)^2$$

Half-side formulas:

$$\tan \tfrac{1}{2} a = K \cos(S - A), \quad \tan \tfrac{1}{2} b = K \cos(S - B),$$
$$\tan \tfrac{1}{2} c = K \cos(S - C),$$

where

$$K^2 = \frac{-\cos S}{\cos(S - A) \cos(S - B) \cos(S - C)} = (\tan R)^2$$

Gauss's formulas:

$$\frac{\sin \frac{1}{2}(a - b)}{\sin \frac{1}{2} c} = \frac{\sin \frac{1}{2}(A - B)}{\cos \frac{1}{2} C}, \quad \frac{\cos \frac{1}{2}(a - b)}{\cos \frac{1}{2} c} = \frac{\sin \frac{1}{2}(A + B)}{\cos \frac{1}{2} C}$$

$$\frac{\sin \frac{1}{2}(a + b)}{\sin \frac{1}{2} c} = \frac{\cos \frac{1}{2}(A - B)}{\sin \frac{1}{2} C}, \quad \frac{\cos \frac{1}{2}(a + b)}{\cos \frac{1}{2} c} = \frac{\cos \frac{1}{2}(A + B)}{\sin \frac{1}{2} C}$$

Napier's analogies:

$$\frac{\sin \frac{1}{2}(A - B)}{\sin \frac{1}{2}(A + B)} = \frac{\tan \frac{1}{2}(a - b)}{\tan \frac{1}{2} c}, \quad \frac{\sin \frac{1}{2}(a - b)}{\sin \frac{1}{2}(a + b)} = \frac{\tan \frac{1}{2}(A - B)}{\cot \frac{1}{2} C}$$

$$\frac{\cos \frac{1}{2}(A - B)}{\cos \frac{1}{2}(A + B)} = \frac{\tan \frac{1}{2}(a + b)}{\tan \frac{1}{2} c}, \quad \frac{\cos \frac{1}{2}(a - b)}{\cos \frac{1}{2}(a + b)} = \frac{\tan \frac{1}{2}(A + B)}{\cot \frac{1}{2} C}$$

Haversine formulas:

$$\text{hav } a = \text{hav}(b - c) + \sin b \sin c \text{ hav } A$$

$$\text{hav } A = \frac{\sin(s - b) \sin(s - c)}{\sin b \sin c}$$

$$= \frac{\text{hav } a - \text{hav}(b - c)}{\sin b \sin c}$$

$$= \text{hav}[180° - (B + C)] + \sin B \sin C \text{ hav } a$$

Formulas for Use in Spherical Trigonometry

Rules for Determining the Quadrant of a Calculated Part of an Oblique Spherical Triangle

(a) If $A > B > C$, then $a > b > c$.

(b) A side (angle) which differs more from 90° than does another side (angle) is in the same quadrant as its opposite angle (side).

(c) Half the sum of any two sides and half the sum of the opposite angles are in the same quadrant.

SUMMARY OF SOLUTION OF OBLIQUE SPHERICAL TRIANGLES

Given	Solution	Check
Three sides	Half-angle formulas.	Law of sines
Three angles	Half-side formulas.	Law of sines
Two sides and included angle	Napier's analogies (to find sum and difference of unknown angles), then law of sines (to find remaining side).	Gauss's formula
Two angles and included side	Napier's analogies (to find sum and difference of unknown sides), then law of sines (to find remaining angle).	Gauss's formula
Two sides and an opposite angle	Law of sines (to find an angle), then Napier's analogies (to find remaining angle and side). Note number of solutions.	Gauss's formula
Two angles and an opposite side	Law of sines (to find a side), then Napier's analogies (to find remaining side and angle). Note number of solutions.	Gauss's formula

DEGREES, MINUTES, AND SECONDS TO RADIANS

Units in degrees, minutes *or* seconds	Degrees to Radians	Minutes to Radians	Seconds to Radians
10	0.174 5329	0.002 9089	0.000 0485
20	0.349 0659	0.005 8178	0.000 0970
30	0.523 5988	0.008 7266	0.000 1454
40	0.698 1317	0.011 6355	0.000 1939
50	0.872 6646	0.014 5444	0.000 2424
60	1.047 1976	0.017 4533	0.000 2909
70	1.221 7305	(0.020 3622)	(0.000 3394)
80	1.396 2634	(0.023 2711)	(0.000 3879)
90	1.570 7963	(0.026 1799)	(0.000 4363)
100	1.745 3293	....	....
200	3.490 6585	....	....
300	5.235 9878	....	....

where n = 1, 2, 3, 4, etc. n (100°) = n (1.745 3293)

RADIANS TO DEGREES, MINUTES, AND SECONDS

Radians	1.0	0.1	0.01	0.001	0.0001
1	57° 17′ 44.8″	5° 43′ 46.5″	0° 34′ 22.6″	0° 03′ 26.3″	0° 00′ 20.6″
2	114° 35′ 29.6″	11° 27′ 33.0″	1° 08′ 45.3″	0° 06′ 52.5″	0° 00′ 41.3″
3	171° 53′ 14.4″	17° 11′ 19.4″	1° 43′ 07.9′	0° 10′ 18.8″	0° 01′ 01.9″
4	229° 10′ 59.2″	22° 55′ 05.9″	2° 17′ 30.6″	0° 13′ 45.1′	0° 01′ 22.5″
5	286° 28′ 44.0″	28° 38′ 52.4″	2° 51′ 53.2″	0° 17′ 11.3″	0° 01′ 43.1″
6	343° 46′ 28.8″	34° 22′ 38.9″	3° 26′ 15.9″	0° 20′ 37.6″	0° 02′ 03.8″
7	401° 04′ 13.6″	40° 06′ 25.4″	4° 00′ 38.5″	0° 24′ 03.9″	0° 02′ 24.4″
8	458° 21′ 58.4″	45° 50′ 11.8″	4° 35′ 01.2″	0° 27′ 30.1″	0° 02′ 45.0″
9	515° 39′ 43.3″	51° 33′ 58.3″	5° 09′ 23.8″	0° 30′ 56.4″	0° 03′ 05.6″

Example: If 3.214 is desired in degrees, minutes and seconds it is obtained as follows:

$$3 = 171° \ 53′ \ 14.4″$$
$$.2 = \ 11° \ 27′ \ 33.0″$$
$$.01 = \ \ 0° \ 34′ \ 22.6″$$
$$.004 = \ \ 0° \ 13′ \ 45.1″$$
$$\overline{3.214 = 184° \ \ 8′ \ 55.1″}$$

MILS—RADIANS—DEGREES

1 mil = 0.00098175 radians = 0.05625° = 3.375′ = 202.5″
1000 mils = 0.98175 radians = 56.25°
6400 mils = 360° = 2π radians
1 radian = 1018.6 mils
1° = 17.777778 mils
1′ = 0.296296 mils
1″ = 0.0049383 mils

DEGREES—RADIANS

1 radian = 57° 17′ 44″ .80625

		log
1 radian	= 57.29577 95131 degrees	1.75812 26324
1 radian	= 3437.74677 07849 minutes	3.53627 38828
1 radian	= 206264.80625 seconds	5.31442 51332
1 degree	= 0.01745 32925 19943 radians	8.24187 73676−10
1 minute	= 0.00029 08882 08666 radians	6.46372 61172−10
1 second	= 0.00000 48481 36811 radians	4.68557 48668−10

DEGREES AND DECIMAL FRACTIONS TO RADIANS

The table below facilitates conversion of an angle expressed in degrees and decimal fractions into radians. To convert 25.78 into radians, find the equivalents, successively, of 20°, 5°, 0°.7, 0°.08 and add.

Deg.	Radians	Deg.	Radians	Deg.	Radians	Deg.	Radians	Deg.	Radians
10	0.174533	1	0.017453	0.1	0.001745	0.01	0.000175	0.001	0.000017
20	0.349066	2	.034907	.2	.003491	.02	.000349	.002	.000035
30	0.523599	3	.052360	.3	.005236	.03	.000524	.003	.000052
40	0.698132	4	.069813	.4	.006981	.04	.000698	.004	.000070
50	0.872665	5	.087266	.5	.008727	.05	.000873	.005	.000087
60	1.047198	6	.104720	.6	.010472	.06	.001047	.006	.000105
70	1.221730	7	.122173	.7	.012217	.07	.001222	.007	.000122
80	1.396263	8	.139626	.8	.013963	.08	.001396	.008	.000140
90	1.570796	9	.157080	.9	.015708	.09	.001571	.009	.000157

RADIANS TO DEGREES AND DECIMALS

Radians	Degrees	Radians	Degrees	Radians	Degrees	Radians	Degrees
1	57.2958	0.1	5.7296	0.01	0.5730	0.001	0.0573
2	114.5916	.2	11.4592	.02	1.1459	.002	.1146
3	171.8873	.3	17.1887	.03	1.7189	.003	.1719
4	229.1831	.4	22.9183	.04	2.2918	.004	.2292
5	286.4789	.5	28.6479	.05	2.8648	.005	.2865
6	343.7747	.6	34.3775	.06	3.4377	.006	.3438
7	401.0705	.7	40.1070	.07	4.0107	.007	.4011
8	458.3662	.8	45.8366	.08	4.5837	.008	.4584
9	515.6620	.9	51.5662	.09	5.1566	.009	.5157
10	572.9578	1.0	57.2958	.10	5.7296	.010	.5730

RADIANS—DEGREES
Multiples and Fractions of π Radians in Degrees

Radians	Radians	Deg.	Radians	Radians	Deg.	Radians	Radians	Deg.
π	3.1416	180	π/2	1.5708	90	2π/3	2.0944	120
2π	6.2832	360	π/3	1.0472	60	3π/4	2.3562	135
3π	9.4248	540	π/4	0.7854	45	5π/6	2.6180	150
4π	12.5664	720	π/5	0.6283	36	7π/6	3.6652	210
5π	15.7080	900	π/6	0.5236	30	5π/4	3.9270	225
6π	18.8496	1080	π/7	0.4488	25.714	4π/3	4.1888	240
7π	21.9911	1260	π/8	0.3927	22.5	3π/2	4.7124	270
8π	25.1327	1440	π/9	0.3491	20	5π/3	5.2360	300
9π	28.2743	1620	π/10	0.3142	18	7π/4	5.4978	315
10π	31.4159	1800	π/12	0.2618	15	11π/6	5.7596	330

CONVERSION OF ANGLES FROM ARC TO TIME

Arc	Time	Arc	Time	Arc	Time	Arc	Time
°	h m	°	h m	″	s	″	s
′	m s	′	m s				
0	0 00	20	1 20	0	0.00	8	0.53
1	0 04	30	2 00	1	0.07	9	0.60
2	0 08	40	2 40	2	0.13	10	0.67
3	0 12	50	3 20	3	0.20	20	1.33
4	0 16	60	4 00	4	0.27	30	2.00
5	0 20	70	4 40	5	0.33	40	2.67
6	0 24	80	5 20	6	0.40	50	3.33
7	0 28	90	6 00	7	0.47	60	4.00
8	0 32	100	6 40				
9	0 36	200	13 20				
10	0 40	300	20 00				

NATURAL TRIGONOMETRIC FUNCTIONS TO FOUR PLACES

X radians	X degrees	sin x	cos x	tan x	cot x	sec x	csc x		
.0000	0° 00′	.0000	1.0000	.0000	—	1.000	—	90° 00′	1.5708
.0029	10	.0029	1.0000	.0029	343.8	1.000	343.8	50	1.5679
.0058	20	.0058	1.0000	.0058	171.9	1.000	171.9	40	1.5650
.0087	30	.0087	1.0000	.0087	114.6	1.000	114.6	30	1.5621
.0116	40	.0116	.9999	.0116	85.94	1.000	85.95	20	1.5592
.0145	50	.0145	.9999	.0145	68.75	1.000	68.76	10	1.5563
.0175	1° 00′	.0175	.9998	.0175	57.29	1.000	57.30	89° 00′	1.5533
.0204	10	.0204	.9998	.0204	49.10	1.000	49.11	50	1.5504
.0233	20	.0233	.9997	.0233	42.96	1.000	42.98	40	1.5475
.0262	30	.0262	.9997	.0262	38.19	1.000	38.20	30	1.5446
.0291	40	.0291	.9996	.0291	34.37	1.000	34.38	20	1.5417
.0320	50	.0320	.9995	.0320	31.24	1.001	31.26	10	1.5388
.0349	2° 00′	.0349	.9994	.0349	28.64	1.001	28.65	88° 00′	1.5359
.0378	10	.0378	.9993	.0378	26.43	1.001	26.45	50	1.5330
.0407	20	.0407	.9992	.0407	24.54	1.001	24.56	40	1.5301
.0436	30	.0436	.9990	.0437	22.90	1.001	22.93	30	1.5272
.0465	40	.0465	.9989	.0466	21.47	1.001	21.49	20	1.5243
.0495	50	.0494	.9988	.0495	20.21	1.001	20.23	10	1.5213
.0524	3° 00′	.0523	.9986	.0524	19.08	1.001	19.11	87° 00′	1.5184
.0553	10	.0552	.9985	.0553	18.07	1.002	18.10	50	1.5155
.0582	20	.0581	.9983	.0582	17.17	1.002	17.20	40	1.5126
.0611	30	.0610	.9981	.0612	16.35	1.002	16.38	30	1.5097
.0640	40	.0640	.9980	.0641	15.60	1.002	15.64	20	1.5068
.0669	50	.0669	.9978	.0670	14.92	1.002	14.96	10	1.5039
.0698	4° 00′	.0698	.9976	.0699	14.30	1.002	14.34	86° 00′	1.5010
.0727	10	.0727	.9974	.0729	13.73	1.003	13.76	50	1.4981
.0756	20	.0756	.9971	.0758	13.20	1.003	13.23	40	1.4952
.0785	30	.0785	.9969	.0787	12.71	1.003	12.75	30	1.4923
.0814	40	.0814	.9967	.0816	12.25	1.003	12.29	20	1.4893
.0844	50	.0843	.9964	.0846	11.83	1.004	11.87	10	1.4864
.0873	5° 00′	.0872	.9962	.0875	11.43	1.004	11.47	85° 00′	1.4835
.0902	10	.0901	.9959	.0904	11.06	1.004	11.10	50	1.4806
.0931	20	.0929	.9957	.0934	10.71	1.004	10.76	40	1.4777
.0960	30	.0958	.9954	.0963	10.39	1.005	10.43	30	1.4748
.0989	40	.0987	.9951	.0992	10.08	1.005	10.13	20	1.4719
.1018	50	.1016	.9948	.1022	9.788	1.005	9.839	10	1.4690
.1047	6° 00′	.1045	.9945	.1051	9.514	1.006	9.567	84° 00′	1.4661
.1076	10	.1074	.9942	.1080	9.255	1.006	9.309	50	1.4632
.1105	20	.1103	.9939	.1110	9.010	1.006	9.065	40	1.4603
.1134	30	.1132	.9936	.1139	8.777	1.006	8.834	30	1.4573
.1164	40	.1161	.9932	.1169	8.556	1.007	8.614	20	1.4544
.1193	50	.1190	.9929	.1198	8.345	1.007	8.405	10	1.4515
.1222	7° 00′	.1219	.9925	.1228	8.144	1.008	8.206	83° 00′	1.4486
.1251	10	.1248	.9922	.1257	7.953	1.008	8.016	50	1.4457
.1280	20	.1276	.9918	.1287	7.770	1.008	7.834	40	1.4428
.1309	30	.1305	.9914	.1317	7.596	1.009	7.661	30	1.4399
.1338	40	.1334	.9911	.1346	7.429	1.009	7.496	20	1.4370
.1367	50	.1363	.9907	.1376	7.269	1.009	7.337	10	1.4341
.1396	8° 00′	.1392	.9903	.1405	7.115	1.010	7.185	82° 00′	1.4312
.1425	10	.1421	.9899	.1435	6.968	1.010	7.040	50	1.4283
.1454	20	.1449	.9894	.1465	6.827	1.011	6.900	40	1.4254
.1484	30	.1478	.9890	.1495	6.691	1.011	6.765	30	1.4224
.1513	40	.1507	.9886	.1524	6.561	1.012	6.636	20	1.4195
.1542	50	.1536	.9881	.1554	6.435	1.012	6.512	10	1.4166
.1571	9° 00′	.1564	.9877	.1584	6.314	1.012	6.392	81° 00′	1.4137
.1600	10	.1593	.9872	.1614	6.197	1.013	6.277	50	1.4108
.1629	20	.1622	.9868	.1644	6.084	1.013	6.166	40	1.4079
.1658	30	.1650	.9863	.1673	5.976	1.014	6.059	30	1.4050
.1687	40	.1679	.9858	.1703	5.871	1.014	5.955	20	1.4021
.1716	50	.1708	.9853	.1733	5.769	1.015	5.855	10	1.3992
.1745	10° 00′	.1736	.9848	.1763	5.671	1.015	5.759	80° 00′	1.3963
		cos x	sin x	cot x	tan x	csc x	sec x	x degrees	x radians

NATURAL TRIGONOMETRIC FUNCTIONS TO FOUR PLACES (continued)

x radians	x degrees	sin x	cos x	tan x	cot x	sec x	csc x		
.1774	10	.1765	.9843	.1793	5.576	1.016	5.665	50	1.3934
.1804	20	.1794	.9838	.1823	5.485	1.016	5.575	40	1.3904
.1833	30	.1822	.9833	.1853	5.396	1.017	5.487	30	1.3875
.1862	40	.1851	.9827	.1883	5.309	1.018	5.403	20	1.3846
.1891	50	.1880	.9822	.1914	5.226	1.018	5.320	10	1.3817
.1920	11° 00′	.1908	.9816	.1944	5.145	1.019	5.241	79° 00′	1.3788
.1949	10	.1937	.9811	.1974	5.066	1.019	5.164	50	1.3759
.1978	20	.1965	.9805	.2004	4.989	1.020	5.089	40	1.3730
.2007	30	.1994	.9799	.2035	4.915	1.020	5.016	30	1.3701
.2036	40	.2022	.9793	.2065	3.843	1.021	4.945	20	1.3672
.2065	50	.2051	.9787	.2095	4.773	1.022	4.876	10	1.3643
.2094	12° 00′	.2079	.9781	.2126	4.705	1.022	4.810	78° 00′	1.3614
.2123	10	.2108	.9775	.2156	4.638	1.023	4.745	50	1.3584
.2153	20	.2136	.9769	.2186	4.574	1.024	4.682	40	1.3555
.2182	30	.2164	.9763	.2217	4.511	1.025	4.620	30	1.3526
.2211	40	.2193	.9757	.2247	4.449	1.025	4.560	20	1.3497
.2240	50	.2221	.9750	.2278	4.390	1.026	4.502	10	1.3468
.2269	13° 00′	.2250	.9744	.2309	4.331	1.026	4.445	77° 00′	1.3439
.2298	10	.2278	.9737	.2339	4.275	1.027	4.390	50	1.3410
.2327	20	.2306	.9730	.2370	4.219	1.028	4.336	40	1.3381
.2356	30	.2334	.9724	.2401	4.165	1.028	4.284	30	1.3352
.2385	40	.2363	.9717	.2432	4.113	1.029	4.232	20	1.3323
.2414	50	.2391	.9710	.2462	4.061	1.030	4.182	10	1.3294
.2443	14° 00′	.2419	.9703	.2493	4.011	1.031	4.134	76° 00′	1.3265
.2473	10	.2447	.9696	.2524	3.962	1.031	4.086	50	1.3235
.2502	20	.2476	.9689	.2555	3.914	1.032	4.039	40	1.3206
.2531	30	.2504	.9681	.2586	3.867	1.033	3.994	30	1.3177
.2560	40	.2532	.9674	.2617	3.821	1.034	3.950	20	1.3148
.2589	50	.2560	.9667	.2648	3.776	1.034	3.906	10	1.3119
.2618	15° 00′	.2588	.9659	.2679	3.732	1.035	3.864	75° 00′	1.3090
.2647	10	.2616	.9652	.2711	3.689	1.036	3.822	50	1.3061
.2676	20	.2644	.9644	.2732	3.647	1.037	3.782	40	1.3032
.2705	30	.2672	.9636	.2773	3.606	1.038	3.742	30	1.3003
.2734	40	.2700	.9628	.2805	3.566	1.039	3.703	20	1.2974
.2763	50	.2728	.9621	.2836	3.526	1.039	3.665	10	1.2945
.2793	16° 00′	.2756	.9613	.2867	3.487	1.040	3.628	74° 00′	1.2915
.2822	10	.2784	.9605	.2899	3.450	1.041	3.592	50	1.2886
.2851	20	.2812	.9596	.2931	3.412	1.042	3.556	40	1.2857
.2880	30	.2840	.9588	.2962	3.376	1.043	3.521	30	1.2828
.2909	40	.2868	.9580	.2994	3.340	1.044	3.487	20	1.2799
.2938	50	.2896	.9572	.3026	3.305	1.045	3.453	10	1.2770
.2967	17° 00′	.2924	.9563	.3057	3.271	1.046	3.420	73° 00′	1.2741
.2996	10	.2952	.9555	.3089	3.237	1.047	3.388	50	1.2712
.3025	20	.2979	.9546	.3121	4.204	1.048	3.356	40	1.2683
.3054	30	.3007	.9537	.3153	3.172	1.049	3.326	30	1.2654
.3083	40	.3035	.9528	.3185	3.140	1.049	3.295	20	1.2625
.3113	50	.3062	.9520	.3217	3.108	1.050	3.265	10	1.2595
.3142	18° 00′	.3090	.9511	.3249	3.078	1.051	3.236	72° 00′	1.2566
.3171	10	.3118	.9502	.3281	3.047	1.052	3.207	50	1.2537
.3200	20	.3145	.9492	.3314	3.018	1.053	3.179	40	1.2508
.3229	30	.3173	.9483	.3346	2.989	1.054	3.152	30	1.2479
.3258	40	.3201	.9474	.3378	2.960	1.056	3.124	20	1.2450
.3287	50	.3228	.9465	.3411	2.932	1.057	3.098	10	1.2421
.3316	19° 00′	.3256	.9455	.3443	2.904	1.058	3.072	71° 00′	1.2392
.3345	10	.3283	.9446	.3476	2.877	1.059	3.046	50	1.2363
.3374	20	.3311	.9436	.3508	2.850	1.060	3.021	40	1.2334
.3403	30	.3338	.9426	.3541	2.824	1.061	2.996	30	1.2305
.3432	40	.3365	.9417	.3574	2.798	1.062	2.971	20	1.2275
.3462	50	.3393	.9407	.3607	2.773	1.063	2.947	10	1.2246
.3491	20° 00′	.3420	.9397	.3640	2.747	1.064	2.924	70° 00′	1.2217
.3520	10	.3448	.9387	.3673	2.723	1.065	2.901	50	1.2188
		cos x	sin x	cot x	tan x	csc x	sec x	x degrees	x radians

NATURAL TRIGONOMETRIC FUNCTIONS TO FOUR PLACES (continued)

x radians	x degrees	sin x	cos x	tan x	cot x	sec x	csc x		
.3599	20	.3475	.9377	.3706	2.699	1.066	2.878	40	1.2159
.3578	30	.3502	.9367	.3739	2.675	1.068	2.855	30	1.2130
.3607	40	.3529	.9356	.3772	2.651	1.069	2.833	20	1.2101
.3636	50	.3557	.9346	.3805	2.628	1.070	2.812	10	1.2072
.3665	21° 00′	.3584	.9336	.3839	2.605	1.071	2.790	69° 00′	1.2043
.3694	10	.3611	.9325	.3872	2.583	1.072	2.769	50	1.2014
.3723	20	.3638	.9315	.3906	2.560	1.074	2.749	40	1.1985
.3752	30	.3665	.9304	.3939	2.539	1.075	2.729	30	1.1956
.3782	40	.3692	.9293	.3973	2.517	1.076	2.709	20	1.1926
.3811	50	.3719	.9283	.4006	2.496	1.077	2.689	10	1.1897
.3840	22° 00′	.3746	.9272	.4040	2.475	1.079	2.669	68° 00′	1.1868
.3869	10	.3773	.9261	.4074	2.455	1.080	2.650	50	1.1839
.3898	20	.3800	.9250	.4108	2.434	1.081	2.632	40	1.1810
.3927	30	.3827	.9239	.4142	2.414	1.082	2.613	30	1.1781
.3956	40	.3854	.9228	.4176	2.394	1.084	2.595	20	1.1752
.3985	50	.3881	.9216	.4210	2.375	1.085	2.577	10	1.1723
.4014	23° 00′	.3907	.9205	.4245	2.356	1.086	2.559	67° 00′	1.1694
.4043	10	.3934	.9194	.4279	2.337	1.088	2.542	50	1.1665
.4072	20	.3961	.9182	.4314	2.318	1.089	2.525	40	1.1636
.4102	30	.3987	.9171	.4348	2.300	1.090	2.508	30	1.1606
.4131	40	.4014	.9159	.4383	2.282	1.092	2.491	20	1.1577
.4160	50	.4041	.9147	.4417	2.264	1.093	2.475	10	1.1548
.4189	24° 00′	.4067	.9135	.4452	2.246	1.095	2.459	66° 00′	1.1519
.4218	10	.4094	.9124	.4487	2.229	1.096	2.443	50	1.1490
.4247	20	.4120	.9112	.4522	2.211	1.097	2.427	40	1.1461
.4276	30	.4147	.9100	.4557	2.194	1.099	2.411	30	1.1432
.4305	40	.4173	.9088	.4592	2.177	1.100	2.396	20	1.1403
.4334	50	.4200	.9075	.4628	2.161	1.102	2.381	10	1.1374
.4363	25° 00′	.4226	.9063	.4663	2.145	1.103	2.366	65° 00′	1.1345
.4392	10	.4253	.9051	.4699	2.128	1.105	2.352	50	1.1316
.4422	20	.4279	.9038	.4734	2.112	1.106	2.337	40	1.1286
.4451	30	.4305	.9026	.4770	2.097	1.108	2.323	30	1.1257
.4480	40	.4331	.9013	.4806	2.081	1.109	2.309	20	1.1228
.4509	50	.4358	.9001	.4841	2.066	1.111	2.295	10	1.1199
.4538	26° 00′	.4384	.8988	.4877	2.050	1.113	2.281	64° 00′	1.1170
.4567	10	.4410	.8975	.4913	2.035	1.114	2.268	50	1.1141
.4596	20	.4436	.8962	.4950	2.020	1.116	2.254	40	1.1112
.4625	30	.4462	.8949	.4986	2.006	1.117	2.241	30	1.1083
.4654	40	.4488	.8936	.5022	1.991	1.119	2.228	20	1.1054
.4683	50	.4514	.8923	.5059	1.977	1.121	2.215	10	1.1025
.4712	27° 00′	.4540	.8910	.5095	1.963	1.122	2.203	63° 00′	1.0996
.4741	10	.4566	.8897	.5132	1.949	1.124	2.190	50	1.0966
.4771	20	.4592	.8884	.5169	1.935	1.126	2.178	40	1.0937
.4800	30	.4617	.8870	.5206	1.921	1.127	2.166	30	1.0908
.4829	40	.4643	.8857	.5243	1.907	1.129	2.154	20	1.0879
.4858	50	.4669	.8843	.5280	1.894	1.131	2.142	10	1.0850
.4887	28° 00′	.4695	.8829	.5317	1.881	1.133	2.130	62° 00′	1.0821
.4916	10	.4720	.8816	.5354	1.868	1.134	2.118	50	1.0792
.4945	20	.4746	.8802	.5392	1.855	1.136	2.107	40	1.0763
.4974	30	.4772	.8788	.5430	1.842	1.138	2.096	30	1.0734
.5003	40	.4797	.8774	.5467	1.829	1.140	2.085	20	1.0705
.5032	50	.4823	.8760	.5505	1.816	1.142	2.074	10	1.0676
.5061	29° 00′	.4848	.8746	.5543	1.804	1.143	2.063	61° 00′	1.0647
.5091	10	.4874	.8732	.5581	1.792	1.145	2.052	50	1.0617
.5120	20	.4899	.8718	.5619	1.780	1.147	2.041	40	1.0588
.5149	30	.4924	.8704	.5658	1.767	1.149	2.031	30	1.0559
.5178	40	.4950	.8689	.5696	1.756	1.151	2.020	20	1.0530
.5207	50	.4975	.8675	.5735	1.744	1.153	2.010	10	1.0501
.5236	30° 00′	.5000	.8660	.5774	1.732	1.155	2.000	60° 00′	1.0472
.5265	10	.5025	.8646	.5812	1.720	1.157	1.990	50	1.0443
.5294	20	.5050	.8631	.5851	1.709	1.159	1.980	40	1.0414

| | | cos x | sin x | cot x | tan x | csc x | sec x | x degrees | x radians |

NATURAL TRIGONOMETRIC FUNCTIONS TO FOUR PLACES (continued)

x radians	x degrees	sin x	cos x	tan x	cot x	sec x	csc x		
.5323	30	.5075	.8616	.5890	1.698	1.161	1.970	30	1.0385
.5352	40	.5100	.8601	.5930	1.686	1.163	1.961	20	1.0356
.5381	50	.5125	.8587	.5969	1.675	1.165	1.951	10	1.0327
.5411	31° 00′	.5150	.8572	.6009	1.664	1.167	1.942	59° 00′	1.0297
.5440	10	.5175	.8557	.6048	1.653	1.169	1.932	50	1.0268
.5469	20	.5200	.8542	.6088	1.643	1.171	1.923	40	1.0239
.5498	30	.5225	.8526	.6128	1.632	1.173	1.914	30	1.0210
.5527	40	.5250	.8511	.6168	1.621	1.175	1.905	20	1.0181
.5556	50	.5275	.8496	.6208	1.611	1.177	1.896	10	1.0152
.5585	32° 00′	.5299	.8480	.6249	1.600	1.179	1.887	58° 00′	1.0123
.5614	10	.5324	.8465	.6289	1.590	1.181	1.878	50	1.0094
.5643	20	.5348	.8450	.6330	1.580	1.184	1.870	40	1.0065
.5672	30	.5373	.8434	.6371	1.570	1.186	1.861	30	1.0036
.5701	40	.5398	.8418	.6412	1.560	1.188	1.853	20	1.0007
.5730	50	.5422	.8403	.6453	1.550	1.190	1.844	10	.9977
.5760	33° 00′	.5446	.8397	.6494	1.540	1.192	1.836	57° 00′	.9948
.5789	10	.5471	.8371	.6536	1.530	1.195	1.828	50	.9919
.5818	20	.5495	.8355	.6577	1.520	1.197	1.820	40	.9890
.5847	30	.5519	.8339	.6619	1.511	1.199	1.812	30	.9861
.5876	40	.5544	.8323	.6661	1.501	1.202	1.804	20	.9832
.5905	50	.5568	.8307	.6703	1.492	1.204	1.796	10	.9803
.5934	34° 00′	.5592	.8290	.6745	1.483	1.206	1.788	56° 00′	.9774
.5963	10	.5616	.8274	.6787	1.473	1.209	1.781	50	.9745
.5992	20	.5640	.8258	.6830	1.464	1.211	1.773	40	.9716
.6021	30	.5664	.8241	.6873	1.455	1.213	1.766	30	.9687
.6050	40	.5688	.8225	.6916	1.446	1.216	1.758	20	.9657
.6080	50	.5712	.8208	.6959	1.437	1.218	1.751	10	.9628
.6109	35° 00′	.5736	.8192	.7002	1.428	1.221	1.743	55° 00′	.9599
.6138	10	.5760	.8175	.7046	1.419	1.223	1.736	50	.9570
.6167	20	.5783	.8158	.7089	1.411	1.226	1.729	40	.9541
.6196	30	.5807	.8141	.7133	1.402	1.228	1.722	30	.9512
.6225	40	.5831	.8124	.7177	1.393	1.231	1.715	20	.9483
.6254	50	.5854	.8107	.7221	1.385	1.233	1.708	10	.9454
.6283	36° 00′	.5878	.8090	.7265	1.376	1.236	1.701	54° 00′	.9425
.6312	10	.5901	.8073	.7310	1.368	1.239	1.695	50	.9396
.6341	20	.5925	.8056	.7355	1.360	1.241	1.688	40	.9367
.6370	30	.5948	.8039	.7400	1.351	1.244	1.681	30	.9338
.6400	40	.5972	.8021	.7445	1.343	1.247	1.675	20	.9308
.6429	50	.5995	.8004	.7490	1.335	1.249	1.668	10	.9279
.6458	37° 00′	.6018	.7986	.7536	1.327	1.252	1.662	53° 00′	.9250
.6487	10	.6041	.7969	.7581	1.319	1.255	1.655	50	.9221
.6516	20	.6065	.7951	.7627	1.311	1.258	1.649	40	.9192
.6545	30	.6088	.7934	.7673	1.303	1.260	1.643	30	.9163
.6574	40	.6111	.7916	.7720	1.295	1.263	1.636	20	.9134
.6603	50	.6134	.7898	.7766	1.288	1.266	1.630	10	.9105
.6632	38° 00′	.6157	.7880	.7813	1.280	1.269	1.624	52° 00′	.9076
.6661	10	.6180	.7862	.7860	1.272	1.272	1.618	50	.9047
.6690	20	.6202	.7844	.7907	1.265	1.275	1.612	40	.9018
.6720	30	.6225	.7826	.7954	1.257	1.278	1.606	30	.8988
.6749	40	.6248	.7808	.8002	1.250	1.281	1.601	20	.8959
.6778	50	.6271	.7790	.8050	1.242	1.284	1.595	10	.8930
.6807	39° 00′	.6293	.7771	.8098	1.235	1.287	1.589	51° 00′	.8901
.6836	10	.6316	.7753	.8146	1.228	1.290	1.583	50	.8872
.6865	20	.6338	.7735	.8195	1.220	1.293	1.578	40	.8843
.6894	30	.6361	.7716	.8243	1.213	1.296	1.572	30	.8814
.6923	40	.6383	.7698	.8292	1.206	1.299	1.567	20	.8785
.6952	50	.6406	.7679	.8342	1.199	1.302	1.561	10	.8756
.6981	40° 00′	.6428	.7660	.8391	1.192	1.305	1.556	50° 00′	.8727
.7010	10	.6450	.7642	.8441	1.185	1.309	1.550	50	.8698
.7039	20	.6472	.7623	.8491	1.178	1.312	1.545	40	.8668
.7069	30	.6494	.7604	.8541	1.171	1.315	1.540	30	.8639

		cos x	sin x	cot x	tan x	csc x	sec x	x degrees	x radians

NATURAL TRIGONOMETRIC FUNCTIONS TO FOUR PLACES (continued)

x radians	x degrees	sin x	cos x	tan x	cot x	sec x	csc x		
.7098	40	.6517	.7585	.8591	1.164	1.318	1.535	20	.8610
.7127	50	.6539	.7566	.8642	1.157	1.322	1.529	10	.8581
.7156	41° 00′	.6561	.7547	.8693	1.150	1.325	1.524	49° 00′	.8552
.7185	10	.6583	.7528	.8744	1.144	1.328	1.519	50	.8523
.7214	20	.6604	.7509	.8796	1.137	1.332	1.514	40	.8494
.7243	30	.6626	.7490	.8847	1.130	1.335	1.509	30	.8465
.7272	40	.6648	.7470	.8899	1.124	1.339	1.504	20	.8436
.7301	50	.6670	.7451	.8952	1.117	1.342	1.499	10	.8407
.7330	42° 00′	.6691	.7431	.9004	1.111	1.346	1.494	48° 00′	.8378
.7359	10	.6713	.7412	.9057	1.104	1.349	1.490	50	.8348
7389	20	.6734	.7392	.9110	1.098	1.353	1.485	40	.8319
.7418	30	.6756	.7373	.9163	1.091	1.356	1.480	30	.8290
.7447	40	.6777	.7353	.9217	1.085	1.360	1.476	20	.8261
.7476	50	.6799	.7333	.9271	1.079	1.364	1.471	10	.8232
.7505	43° 00′	.6820	.7314	.9325	1.072	1.367	1.466	47° 00′	.8203
.7534	10	.6841	.7294	.9380	1.066	1.371	1.462	50	.8174
.7563	20	.6862	.7274	.9435	1.060	1.375	1.457	40	.8145
.7592	30	.6884	.7254	.9490	1.054	1.379	1.453	30	.8116
.7621	40	.6905	.7234	.9545	1.048	1.382	1.448	20	.8087
.7650	50	.6926	.7214	.9601	1.042	1.386	1.444	10	.8058
.7679	44° 00′	.6947	.7193	.9657	1.036	1.390	1.440	46° 00′	.8029
.7709	10	.6967	.7173	.9713	1.030	1.394	1.435	50	.7999
.7738	20	.6988	.7153	.9770	1.024	1.398	1.431	40	.7970
.7767	30	.7009	.7133	.9827	1.018	1.402	1.427	30	.7941
.7796	40	.7030	.7112	.9884	1.012	1.406	1.423	20	.7912
.7825	50	.7050	.7092	.9942	1.006	1.410	1.418	10	.7883
.7854	45° 00′	.7071	.7071	1.0000	1.0000	1.414	1.414	45° 00′	.7854
		cos x	sin x	cot x	tan x	csc x	sec x	x degrees	x radians

VI. LOGARITHMIC, EXPONENTIAL, AND HYPERBOLIC FUNCTIONS

LAWS OF EXPONENTS

For a any real number and m a positive integer, the exponential a^m is defined as

$$\underbrace{a \cdot a \cdot a \cdots \cdot a}_{m \text{ terms}}$$

Using this definition, it is easy to show that the following three *laws of exponents* hold:

I. $a^m \cdot a^n = a^{m+n}$

II. $\dfrac{a^m}{a^n} = \begin{cases} a^{m-n} & \text{if } m > n \\ 1 & \text{if } m = n \\ \dfrac{1}{a^{n-m}} & \text{if } m < n \end{cases}$

III. $(a^m)^n = a^{mn}$

The n-th root function is defined as the inverse of the n-th power function; that is, if

$$b^n = a, \quad \text{then} \quad b = \sqrt[n]{a}.$$

If n is odd, there will be a unique real number satisfying the above definition for $\sqrt[n]{a}$, for any real value of a. If n is even, for positive values of a there will be two real values for $\sqrt[n]{a}$, one positive and one negative. By convention, the symbol $\sqrt[n]{a}$ is understood to mean the positive value. If n is even and a is negative, there are no real values for $\sqrt[n]{a}$.

If we now attempt to extend the definition of the exponential a^t to all rational values of the exponent t, in such a way that the three laws of exponents continue to hold, it is easily shown that the required definitions are:

$$a^0 = 1$$
$$a^{p/q} = \sqrt[q]{a^p}$$
$$a^{-t} = \frac{1}{a^t}$$

In order to avoid difficulties with imaginary numbers and division by zero, a must now be restricted to be positive, if p is odd, and q is even.

With this extended definition, it is possible to restate the second law of exponents in a simpler form:

II′. $\dfrac{a^m}{a^n} = a^{m-n}$

It is shown in advanced calculus that this definition may be further extended so that the exponent may be any real number, and the laws of exponents continue to hold. When the quantity a^x thus defined is viewed as a function of the exponent x, with the base a held constant, it is a continuous function. Also, if $a > 1$, the exponential function is monotone increasing, and if $0 < a < 1$, it is monotone decreasing.

IV. $a^{uv} = a^u$, where $u = x^v$ and $v = y^z$

LOGARITHMS

Any monotone function has a single-valued inverse function, which is also monotone. Furthermore, if the original function is continuous, so is the inverse. Therefore, the inverse function to the exponential function a^x exists for all positive values of a, except $a = 1$. This function is given the name *logarithm to the base a*, abbreviated $\log_a$. That is, if

$$x = a^y, \quad \text{then} \quad y = \log_a x.$$

This function is defined and continuous for all positive values of x. It is monotone increasing if $a > 1$, and monotone decreasing if $0 < a < 1$.

If the laws of exponents are rewritten in terms of logarithms, they become the *laws of logarithms*:

I. $\log_a(xy) = \log_a x + \log_a y$

II. $\log_a\left(\dfrac{x}{y}\right) = \log_a x - \log_a y$

III. $\log_a(x^n) = n \log_a x$

Logarithms derive their main usefulness in computation from the above laws, since they allow multiplication, division, and exponentiation to be replaced by the simpler operations of addition, subtraction, and multiplication, respectively. See the examples which follow.

Further recourse to the definition of logarithm leads to the following formula for change of base

$$\log_a x = \log_b x / \log_b a = (\log_b x) \cdot (\log_a b)$$

Two numbers are commonly used as bases for logarithms. Logarithms to the base 10 are most convenient for use in computation. These logarithms are called common or Briggsian logarithms.

The other usual base for logarithms is an irrational number denoted by e, whose value is approximately 2.71828.... These logarithms are called natural, Naperian, or hyperbolic logarithms, and occur in many formulas of higher mathematics. The abbreviation ln is frequently used for the natural logarithm function.

Other bases for logarithms, such as 2 and 3, occur in certain applications. These applications are rather specialized and separate tables for these bases are not given. Instead, the formulas for change of base are applied to common or natural logarithms.

If the formulas for change of base are applied to the two usual bases, the following formulas result:

$$\log_{10} x = \log_e x / \log_e 10 = (\log_{10} e)(\log_e x) = M \log_e x$$
$$= 0.43429\ 44819 \log_e x$$
$$\log_e x = \log_{10} x / \log_{10} e = (\log_e 10)(\log_{10} x) = \frac{1}{M} \log_{10} x$$
$$= 2.30258\ 50930 \log_{10} x$$

The following remarks apply to common logarithms.

Since most numbers are irrational powers of ten, a common logarithm, in general, consists of an integer, which is called the characteristic, and an endless decimal, the mantissa.

It is to be observed that the common logarithms of all numbers expressed by the same figures in the same order with the decimal point in different positions have different characteristics but the same mantissa. To illustrate:—if the decimal point stand after the first figure of a number, counting from the left, the characteristic is 0; if after two figures, it is 1; if after three figures, it is 2; and so forth. If the decimal point stands before the first significant figure the characteristic is −1, usually written $\bar{1}$; if there is one zero between the decimal point and the first significant figure it is $\bar{2}$, and so on. For example: log 256 = 2.40824, log 2.56 = 0.40824, log 0.256 = $\bar{1}$.40824, log 0.00256 = $\bar{3}$.40824. The two latter are often written log 0.256 = 9.40824 − 10, log 0.00256 = 7.40824 − 10.

Notice that, although the common logarithm of a number less than one is a negative number, it is customarily written as a negative characteristic and a *positive* mantissa, since the mantissa are usually given in tables as positive numbers. This is the reason that the negative sign is written above the characteristic, since it does not apply to the mantissa. Thus log 0.00256 = $\bar{3}$.40824 = 7.40824 − 10 = −2.59176.

A method of determining characteristics of logarithms is to write the number with one figure to the left of the decimal point multiplied by the appropriate power of 10. The characteristic is then the exponent used. For example:

$$256\ 000\ 000 = 2.56 \times 10^8 \qquad \log = 8.40824$$
$$0.000\ 000\ 256 = 2.56 \times 10^{-7} \qquad \log = \bar{7}.40824 \text{ or } 3.40824 - 10$$

Inasmuch as the characteristic may be determined by inspection, the mantissas only are given in tables of common logarithms.

*FOUR-PLACE MANTISSAS FOR COMMON LOGARITHMS OF DECIMAL FRACTIONS

N	0	1	2	3	4	5	6	7	8	9
.10	−1.000	−.9957	−.9914	−.9872	−.9830	−.9788	−.9747	−.9706	−.9666	−.9626
.11	−.9586	−.9547	−.9508	−.9469	−.9431	−.9393	−.9355	−.9318	−.9281	−.9245
.12	−.9208	−.9172	−.9136	−.9101	−.9066	−.9031	−.8996	−.8962	−.8928	−.8894
.13	−.8861	−.8827	−.8794	−.8761	−.8729	−.8697	−.8665	−.8633	−.8601	−.8570
.14	−.8539	−.8508	−.8477	−.8447	−.8416	−.8386	−.8356	−.8327	−.8297	−.8268
.15	−.8239	−.8210	−.8182	−.8153	−.8125	−.8097	−.8069	−.8041	−.8013	−.7986
.16	−.7959	−.7932	−.7905	−.7878	−.7852	−.7825	−.7799	−.7773	−.7747	−.7721
.17	−.7696	−.7670	−.7645	−.7620	−.7595	−.7570	−.7545	−.7520	−.7496	−.7471
.18	−.7447	−.7423	−.7399	−.7375	−.7352	−.7328	−.7305	−.7282	−.7258	−.7235
.19	−.7212	−.7190	−.7167	−.7144	−.7122	−.7100	−.7077	−.7055	−.7033	−.7011
.20	−.6990	−.6968	−.6946	−.6925	−.6904	−.6882	−.6861	−.6840	−.6819	−.6799
.21	−.6778	−.6757	−.6737	−.6716	−.6696	−.6676	−.6655	−.6635	−.6615	−.6596
.22	−.6576	−.6556	−.6536	−.6517	−.6498	−.6478	−.6459	−.6440	−.6421	−.6402
.23	−.6383	−.6364	−.6345	−.6326	−.6308	−.6289	−.6271	−.6253	−.6234	−.6216
.24	−.6198	−.6180	−.6162	−.6144	−.6126	−.6108	−.6091	−.6073	−.6055	−.6038
.25	−.6021	−.6003	−.5986	−.5969	−.5952	−.5935	−.5918	−.5901	−.5884	−.5867
.26	−.5850	−.5834	−.5817	−.5800	−.5784	−.5768	−.5751	−.5735	−.5719	−.5702
.27	−.5686	−.5670	−.5654	−.5638	−.5622	−.5607	−.5591	−.5575	−.5560	−.5544
.28	−.5528	−.5513	−.5498	−.5482	−.5467	−.5452	−.5436	−.5421	−.5406	−.5391
.29	−.5376	−.5361	−.5346	−.5331	−.5317	−.5302	−.5287	−.5272	−.5258	−.5243
.30	−.5229	−.5214	−.5200	−.5186	−.5171	−.5157	−.5143	−.5129	−.5114	−.5100
.31	−.5086	−.5072	−.5058	−.5045	−.5031	−.5017	−.5003	−.4989	−.4976	−.4962
.32	−.4949	−.4935	−.4921	−.4908	−.4895	−.4881	−.4868	−.4855	−.4841	−.4828
.33	−.4815	−.4802	−.4789	−.4776	−.4763	−.4750	−.4737	−.4724	−.4711	−.4698
.34	−.4685	−.4672	−.4660	−.4647	−.4634	−.4622	−.4609	−.4597	−.4584	−.4572
.35	−.4559	−.4547	−.4535	−.4522	−.4510	−.4498	−.4486	−.4473	−.4461	−.4449
.36	−.4437	−.4425	−.4413	−.4401	−.4389	−.4377	−.4365	−.4353	−.4342	−.4330
.37	−.4318	−.4306	−.4295	−.4283	−.4271	−.4260	−.4248	−.4237	−.4225	−.4214
.38	−.4202	−.4191	−.4179	−.4168	−.4157	−.4145	−.4134	−.4123	−.4112	−.4101
.39	−.4089	−.4078	−.4067	−.4056	−.4045	−.4034	−.4023	−.4012	−.4001	−.3990
.40	−.3979	−.3969	−.3958	−.3947	−.3936	−.3925	−.3915	−.3904	−.3893	−.3883
.41	−.3872	−.3862	−.3851	−.3840	−.3830	−.3820	−.3809	−.3799	−.3788	−.3778
.42	−.3768	−.3757	−.3747	−.3737	−.3726	−.3716	−.3706	−.3696	−.3686	−.3675
.43	−.3665	−.3655	−.3645	−.3635	−.3625	−.3615	−.3605	−.3595	−.3585	−.3575
.44	−.3565	−.3556	−.3546	−.3536	−.3526	−.3516	−.3507	−.3497	−.3487	−.3478
.45	−.3468	−.3458	−.3449	−.3439	−.3429	−.3420	−.3410	−.3401	−.3391	−.3382
.46	−.3372	−.3363	−.3354	−.3344	−.3335	−.3325	−.3316	−.3307	−.3298	−.3288
.47	−.3279	−.3270	−.3261	−.3251	−.3242	−.3233	−.3224	−.3215	−.3206	−.3197
.48	−.3188	−.3179	−.3170	−.3161	−.3152	−.3143	−.3134	−.3125	−.3116	−.3107
.49	−.3098	−.3089	−.3080	−.3072	−.3063	−.3054	−.3045	−.3036	−.3028	−.3019
.50	−.3010	−.3002	−.2993	−.2984	−.2976	−.2967	−.2958	−.2950	−.2941	−.2933
.51	−.2924	−.2916	−.2907	−.2899	−.2890	−.2882	−.2874	−.2865	−.2857	−.2848
.52	−.2840	−.2832	−.2823	−.2815	−.2807	−.2798	−.2790	−.2782	−.2774	−.2765
.53	−.2757	−.2749	−.2741	−.2733	−.2725	−.2716	−.2708	−.2700	−.2692	−.2684
.54	−.2676	−.2668	−.2660	−.2652	−.2644	−.2636	−.2628	−.2620	−.2612	−.2604

* This table gives the logarithms of the decimal fractions which are negative numbers.

For example log 0.61 = −0.2147 = 9.7853 − 10. It should be noted that the entries as given can be used conveniently to find cologarithms of positive numbers. Every positive number $N = P \cdot (10)^k$, where $0 < P \le 1$. Since colog $N = -$ log N, it follows that colog $N = -$ log $P - k$.

For example colog 0.61 = − log 0.61 = 0.2147; colog 61 = 0.2147 − 2; and colog 0.00061 = 3.2147.

*FOUR-PLACE MANTISSAS FOR COMMON LOGARITHMS OF DECIMAL FRACTIONS (Continued)

N	0	1	2	3	4	5	6	7	8	9
.55	−.2596	−.2588	−.2581	−.2573	−.2565	−.2557	−.2549	−.2541	−.2534	−.2526
.56	−.2518	−.2510	−.2503	−.2495	−.2487	−.2480	−.2472	−.2464	−.2457	−.2449
.57	−.2441	−.2434	−.2426	−.2418	−.2411	−.2403	−.2396	−.2388	−.2381	−.2373
.58	−.2366	−.2358	−.2351	−.2343	−.2336	−.2328	−.2321	−.2314	−.2306	−.2299
.59	−.2291	−.2284	−.2277	−.2269	−.2262	−.2255	−.2248	−.2240	−.2233	−.2226
.60	−.2218	−.2211	−.2204	−.2197	−.2190	−.2182	−.2175	−.2168	−.2161	−.2154
.61	−.2147	−.2140	−.2132	−.2125	−.2118	−.2111	−.2104	−.2097	−.2090	−.2083
.62	−.2076	−.2069	−.2062	−.2055	−.2048	−.2041	−.2034	−.2027	−.2020	−.2013
.63	−.2007	−.2000	−.1993	−.1986	−.1979	−.1972	−.1965	−.1959	−.1952	−.1945
.64	−.1938	−.1931	−.1925	−.1918	−.1911	−.1904	−.1898	−.1891	−.1884	−.1878
.65	−.1871	−.1864	−.1858	−.1851	−.1844	−.1838	−.1831	−.1824	−.1818	−.1811
.66	−.1805	−.1798	−.1791	−.1785	−.1778	−.1772	−.1765	−.1759	−.1752	−.1746
.67	−.1739	−.1733	−.1726	−.1720	−.1713	−.1707	−.1701	−.1694	−.1688	−.1681
.68	−.1675	−.1669	−.1662	−.1656	−.1649	−.1643	−.1637	−.1630	−.1624	−.1618
.69	−.1612	−.1605	−.1599	−.1593	−.1586	−.1580	−.1574	−.1568	−.1561	−.1555
.70	−.1549	−.1543	−.1537	−.1530	−.1524	−.1518	−.1512	−.1506	−.1500	−.1494
.71	−.1487	−.1481	−.1475	−.1469	−.1463	−.1457	−.1451	−.1445	−.1439	−.1433
.72	−.1427	−.1421	−.1415	−.1409	−.1403	−.1397	−.1391	−.1385	−.1379	−.1373
.73	−.1367	−.1361	−.1355	−.1349	−.1343	−.1337	−.1331	−.1325	−.1319	−.1314
.74	−.1308	−.1302	−.1296	−.1290	−.1284	−.1278	−.1273	−.1267	−.1261	−.1255
.75	−.1249	−.1244	−.1238	−.1232	−.1226	−.1221	−.1215	−.1209	−.1203	−.1198
.76	−.1192	−.1186	−.1180	−.1175	−.1169	−.1163	−.1158	−.1152	−.1146	−.1141
.77	−.1135	−.1129	−.1124	−.1118	−.1113	−.1107	−.1101	−.1096	−.1090	−.1085
.78	−.1079	−.1073	−.1068	−.1062	−.1057	−.1051	−.1046	−.1040	−.1035	−.1029
.79	−.1024	−.1018	−.1013	−.1007	−.1002	−.0996	−.0991	−.0985	−.0980	−.0975
.80	−.0969	−.0964	−.0958	−.0953	−.0947	−.0942	−.0937	−.0931	−.0926	−.0921
.81	−.0915	−.0910	−.0904	−.0899	−.0894	−.0888	−.0883	−.0878	−.0872	−.0867
.82	−.0862	−.0857	−.0851	−.0846	−.0841	−.0835	−.0830	−.0825	−.0820	−.0814
.83	−.0809	−.0804	−.0799	−.0794	−.0788	−.0783	−.0778	−.0773	−.0768	−.0762
.84	−.0757	−.0752	−.0747	−.0742	−.0737	−.0731	−.0726	−.0721	−.0716	−.0711
.85	−.0706	−.0701	−.0696	−.0691	−.0685	−.0680	−.0675	−.0670	−.0665	−.0660
.86	−.0655	−.0650	−.0645	−.0640	−.0635	−.0630	−.0625	−.0620	−.0615	−.0610
.87	−.0605	−.0600	−.0595	−.0590	−.0585	−.0580	−.0575	−.0570	−.0565	−.0560
.88	−.0555	−.0550	−.0545	−.0540	−.0535	−.0531	−.0526	−.0521	−.0516	−.0511
.89	−.0506	−.0501	−.0496	−.0491	−.0487	−.0482	−.0477	−.0472	−.0467	−.0462
.90	−.0458	−.0453	−.0448	−.0443	−.0438	−.0434	−.0429	−.0424	−.0419	−.0414
.91	−.0410	−.0405	−.0400	−.0395	−.0391	−.0386	−.0381	−.0376	−.0372	−.0367
.92	−.0362	−.0357	−.0353	−.0348	−.0343	−.0339	−.0334	−.0329	−.0325	−.0320
.93	−.0315	−.0311	−.0306	−.0301	−.0297	−.0292	−.0287	−.0283	−.0278	−.0273
.94	−.0269	−.0264	−.0259	−.0255	−.0250	−.0246	−.0241	−.0237	−.0232	−.0227
.95	−.0223	−.0218	−.0214	−.0209	−.0205	−.0200	−.0195	−.0191	−.0186	−.0182
.96	−.0177	−.0173	−.0168	−.0164	−.0159	−.0155	−.0150	−.0146	−.0141	−.0137
.97	−.0132	−.0128	−.0123	−.0119	−.0114	−.0110	−.0106	−.0101	−.0097	−.0092
.98	−.0088	−.0083	−.0079	−.0074	−.0070	−.0066	−.0061	−.0057	−.0052	−.0048
.99	−.0044	−.0039	−.0035	−.0031	−.0026	−.0022	−.0017	−.0013	−.0009	−.0004

FOUR-PLACE MANTISSAS FOR COMMON LOGARITHMS

N	0	1	2	3	4	5	6	7	8	9	1	2	3	4	5	6	7	8	9
											Proportional Parts								

N	0	1	2	3	4	5	6	7	8	9	1	2	3	4	5	6	7	8	9
10	0000	0043	0086	0128	0170	0212	0253	0294	0334	0374	*4	8	12	17	21	25	29	33	37
11	0414	0453	0492	0531	0569	0607	0645	0682	0719	0755	4	8	11	15	19	23	26	30	34
12	0792	0828	0864	0899	0934	0969	1004	1038	1072	1106	3	7	10	14	17	21	24	28	31
13	1139	1173	1206	1239	1271	1303	1335	1367	1399	1430	3	6	10	13	16	19	23	26	29
14	1461	1492	1523	1553	1584	1614	1644	1673	1703	1732	3	6	9	12	15	18	21	24	27
15	1761	1790	1818	1847	1875	1903	1931	1959	1987	2014	*3	6	8	11	14	17	20	22	25
16	2041	2068	2095	2122	2148	2175	2201	2227	2253	2279	3	5	8	11	13	16	18	21	24
17	2304	2330	2355	2380	2405	2430	2455	2480	2504	2529	2	5	7	10	12	15	17	20	22
18	2553	2577	2601	2625	2648	2672	2695	2718	2742	2765	2	5	7	9	12	14	16	19	21
19	2788	2810	2833	2856	2878	2900	2923	2945	2967	2989	2	4	7	9	11	13	16	18	20
20	3010	3032	3054	3075	3096	3118	3139	3160	3181	3201	2	4	6	8	11	13	15	17	19
21	3222	3243	3263	3284	3304	3324	3345	3365	3385	3404	2	4	6	8	10	12	14	16	18
22	3424	3444	3464	3483	3502	3522	3541	3560	3579	3598	2	4	6	8	10	12	14	15	17
23	3617	3636	3655	3674	3692	3711	3729	3747	3766	3784	2	4	6	7	9	11	13	15	17
24	3802	3820	3838	3856	3874	3892	3909	3927	3945	3962	2	4	5	7	9	11	12	14	16
25	3979	3997	4014	4031	4048	4065	4082	4099	4116	4133	2	3	5	7	9	10	12	14	15
26	4150	4166	4183	4200	4216	4232	4249	4265	4281	4298	2	3	5	7	8	10	11	13	15
27	4314	4330	4346	4362	4378	4393	4409	4425	4440	4456	2	3	5	6	8	9	11	13	14
28	4472	4487	4502	4518	4533	4548	4564	4579	4594	4609	2	3	5	6	8	9	11	12	14
29	4624	4639	4654	4669	4683	4698	4713	4728	4742	4757	1	3	4	6	7	9	10	12	13
30	4771	4786	4800	4814	4829	4843	4857	4871	4886	4900	1	3	4	6	7	9	10	11	13
31	4914	4928	4942	4955	4969	4983	4997	5011	5024	5038	1	3	4	6	7	8	10	11	12
32	5051	5065	5079	5092	5105	5119	5132	5145	5159	5172	1	3	4	5	7	8	9	11	12
33	5185	5198	5211	5224	5237	5250	5263	5276	5289	5302	1	3	4	5	6	8	9	10	12
34	5315	5328	5340	5353	5366	5378	5391	5403	5416	5428	1	3	4	5	6	8	9	10	11
35	5441	5453	5465	5478	5490	5502	5514	5527	5539	5551	1	2	4	5	6	7	9	10	11
36	5563	5575	5587	5599	5611	5623	5635	5647	5658	5670	1	2	4	5	6	7	8	10	11
37	5682	5694	5705	5717	5729	5740	5752	5763	5775	5786	1	2	3	5	6	7	8	9	10
38	5798	5809	5821	5832	5843	5855	5866	5877	5888	5899	1	2	3	5	6	7	8	9	10
39	5911	5922	5933	5944	5955	5966	5977	5988	5999	6010	1	2	3	4	5	7	8	9	10
40	6021	6031	6042	6053	6064	6075	6085	6096	6107	6117	1	2	3	4	5	6	8	9	10
41	6128	6138	6149	6160	6170	6180	6191	6201	6212	6222	1	2	3	4	5	6	7	8	9
42	6232	6243	6253	6263	6274	6284	6294	6304	6314	6325	1	2	3	4	5	6	7	8	9
43	6335	6345	6355	6365	6375	6385	6395	6405	6415	6425	1	2	3	4	5	6	7	8	9
44	6435	6444	6454	6464	6474	6484	6493	6503	6513	6522	1	2	3	4	5	6	7	8	9
45	6532	6542	6551	6561	6571	6580	6590	6599	6609	6618	1	2	3	4	5	6	7	8	9
46	6628	6637	6646	6656	6665	6675	6684	6693	6702	6712	1	2	3	4	5	6	7	7	8
47	6721	6730	6739	6749	6758	6767	6776	6785	6794	6803	1	2	3	4	5	5	6	7	8
48	6812	6821	6830	6839	6848	6857	6866	6875	6884	6893	1	2	3	4	4	5	6	7	8
49	6902	6911	6920	6928	6937	6946	6955	6964	6972	6981	1	2	3	4	4	5	6	7	8
50	6990	6998	7007	7016	7024	7033	7042	7050	7059	7067	1	2	3	3	4	5	6	7	8
51	7076	7084	7093	7101	7110	7118	7126	7135	7143	7152	1	2	3	3	4	5	6	7	8
52	7160	7168	7177	7185	7193	7202	7210	7218	7226	7235	1	2	2	3	4	5	6	7	7
53	7243	7251	7259	7267	7275	7284	7292	7300	7308	7316	1	2	2	3	4	5	6	6	7
54	7324	7332	7340	7348	7356	7364	7372	7380	7388	7396	1	2	2	3	4	5	6	6	7
N	0	1	2	3	4	5	6	7	8	9	1	2	3	4	5	6	7	8	9

*The use of proportional parts for log 1.01 to log 1.59 is less accurate than usual.

FOUR-PLACE MANTISSAS FOR COMMON LOGARITHMS (Continued)

N	0	1	2	3	4	5	6	7	8	9	1	2	3	4	5	6	7	8	9
											Proportional Parts								
55	7404	7412	7419	7427	7435	7443	7451	7459	7466	7474	1	2	2	3	4	5	5	6	7
56	7482	7490	7497	7505	7513	7520	7528	7536	7543	7551	1	2	2	3	4	5	5	6	7
57	7559	7566	7574	7582	7589	7597	7604	7612	7619	7627	1	2	2	3	4	5	5	6	7
58	7634	7642	7649	7657	7664	7672	7679	7686	7694	7701	1	1	2	3	4	4	5	6	7
59	7709	7716	7723	7731	7738	7745	7752	7760	7767	7774	1	1	2	3	4	4	5	6	7
60	7782	7789	7796	7803	7810	7818	7825	7832	7839	7846	1	1	2	3	4	4	5	6	6
61	7853	7860	7868	7875	7882	7889	7896	7903	7910	7917	1	1	2	3	4	4	5	6	6
62	7924	7931	7938	7945	7952	7959	7966	7973	7980	7987	1	1	2	3	3	4	5	6	6
63	7993	8000	8007	8014	8021	8028	8035	8041	8048	8055	1	1	2	3	3	4	5	5	6
64	8062	8069	8075	8082	8089	8096	8102	8109	8116	8122	1	1	2	3	3	4	5	5	6
65	8129	8136	8142	8149	8156	8162	8169	8176	8182	8189	1	1	2	3	3	4	5	5	6
66	8195	8202	8209	8215	8222	8228	8235	8241	8248	8254	1	1	2	3	3	4	5	5	6
67	8261	8267	8274	8280	8287	8293	8299	8306	8312	8319	1	1	2	3	3	4	5	5	6
68	8325	8331	8338	8344	8351	8357	8363	8370	8376	8382	1	1	2	3	3	4	4	5	6
69	8388	8395	8401	8407	8414	8420	8426	8432	8439	8445	1	1	2	2	3	4	4	5	6
70	8451	8457	8463	8470	8476	8482	8488	8494	8500	8506	1	1	2	2	3	4	4	5	6
71	8513	8519	8525	8531	8537	8543	8549	8555	8561	8567	1	1	2	2	3	4	4	5	5
72	8573	8579	8585	8591	8597	8603	8609	8615	8621	8627	1	1	2	2	3	4	4	5	5
73	8633	8639	8645	8651	8657	8663	8669	8675	8681	8686	1	1	2	2	3	4	4	5	5
74	8692	8698	8704	8710	8716	8722	8727	8733	8739	8745	1	1	2	2	3	4	4	5	5
75	8751	8756	8762	8768	8774	8779	8785	8791	8797	8802	1	1	2	2	3	3	4	5	5
76	8808	8814	8820	8825	8831	8837	8842	8848	8854	8859	1	1	2	2	3	3	4	5	5
77	8865	8871	8876	8882	8887	8893	8899	8904	8910	8915	1	1	2	2	3	3	4	4	5
78	8921	8927	8932	8938	8943	8949	8954	8960	8965	8971	1	1	2	2	3	3	4	4	5
79	8976	8982	8987	8993	8998	9004	9009	9015	9020	9025	1	1	2	2	3	3	4	4	5
80	9031	9036	9042	9047	9053	9058	9063	9069	9074	9079	1	1	2	2	3	3	4	4	5
81	9085	9090	9096	9101	9106	9112	9117	9122	9128	9133	1	1	2	2	3	3	4	4	5
82	9138	9143	9149	9154	9159	9165	9170	9175	9180	9186	1	1	2	2	3	3	4	4	5
83	9191	9196	9201	9206	9212	9217	9222	9227	9232	9238	1	1	2	2	3	3	4	4	5
84	9243	9248	9253	9258	9263	9269	9274	9279	9284	9289	1	1	2	2	3	3	4	4	5
85	9294	9299	9304	9309	9315	9320	9325	9330	9335	9340	1	1	2	2	3	3	4	4	5
86	9345	9350	9355	9360	9365	9370	9375	9380	9385	9390	1	1	2	2	3	3	4	4	5
87	9395	9400	9405	9410	9415	9420	9425	9430	9435	9440	0	1	1	2	2	3	3	4	4
88	9445	9450	9455	9460	9465	9469	9474	9479	9484	9489	0	1	1	2	2	3	3	4	4
89	9494	9499	9504	9509	9513	9518	9523	9528	9533	9538	0	1	1	2	2	3	3	4	4
90	9542	9547	9552	9557	9562	9566	9571	9576	9581	9586	0	1	1	2	2	3	3	4	4
91	9590	9595	9600	9605	9609	9614	9619	9624	9628	9633	0	1	1	2	2	3	3	4	4
92	9638	9643	9647	9652	9657	9661	9666	9671	9675	9680	0	1	1	2	2	3	3	4	4
93	9685	9689	9694	9699	9703	9708	9713	9717	9722	9727	0	1	1	2	2	3	3	4	4
94	9731	9736	9741	9745	9750	9754	9759	9763	9768	9773	0	1	1	2	2	3	3	4	4
95	9777	9782	9786	9791	9795	9800	9805	9809	9814	9818	0	1	1	2	2	3	3	4	4
96	9823	9827	9832	9836	9841	9845	9850	9854	9859	9863	0	1	1	2	2	3	3	4	4
97	9868	9872	9877	9881	9886	9890	9894	9899	9903	9908	0	1	1	2	2	3	3	4	4
98	9912	9917	9921	9926	9930	9934	9939	9943	9948	9952	0	1	1	2	2	3	3	4	4
99	9956	9961	9965	9969	9974	9978	9983	9987	9991	9996	0	1	1	2	2	3	3	3	4
N	0	1	2	3	4	5	6	7	8	9	1	2	3	4	5	6	7	8	9

ANTILOGARITHMS

	0	1	2	3	4	5	6	7	8	9	Proportional Parts 1	2	3	4	5	6	7	8	9
.00	1000	1002	1005	1007	1009	1012	1014	1016	1019	1021	0	0	1	1	1	1	2	2	2
.01	1023	1026	1028	1030	1033	1035	1038	1040	1042	1045	0	0	1	1	1	1	2	2	2
.02	1047	1050	1052	1054	1057	1059	1062	1064	1067	1069	0	0	1	1	1	1	2	2	2
.03	1072	1074	1076	1079	1081	1084	1086	1089	1091	1094	0	0	1	1	1	1	2	2	2
.04	1096	1099	1102	1104	1107	1109	1112	1114	1117	1119	0	1	1	1	1	2	2	2	2
.05	1122	1125	1127	1130	1132	1135	1138	1140	1143	1146	0	1	1	1	1	2	2	2	2
.06	1148	1151	1153	1156	1159	1161	1164	1167	1169	1172	0	1	1	1	1	2	2	2	2
.07	1175	1178	1180	1183	1186	1189	1191	1194	1197	1199	0	1	1	1	1	2	2	2	2
.08	1202	1205	1208	1211	1213	1216	1219	1222	1225	1227	0	1	1	1	1	2	2	2	3
.09	1230	1233	1236	1239	1242	1245	1247	1250	1253	1256	0	1	1	1	1	2	2	2	3
.10	1259	1262	1265	1268	1271	1274	1276	1279	1282	1285	0	1	1	1	1	2	2	2	3
.11	1288	1291	1294	1297	1300	1303	1306	1309	1312	1315	0	1	1	1	2	2	2	3	3
.12	1318	1321	1324	1327	1330	1334	1337	1340	1343	1346	0	1	1	1	2	2	2	3	3
.13	1349	1352	1355	1358	1361	1365	1368	1371	1374	1377	0	1	1	1	2	2	2	3	3
.14	1380	1384	1387	1390	1393	1396	1400	1403	1406	1409	0	1	1	1	2	2	2	3	3
.15	1413	1416	1419	1422	1426	1429	1432	1435	1439	1442	0	1	1	1	2	2	2	3	3
.16	1445	1449	1452	1455	1459	1462	1466	1469	1472	1476	0	1	1	1	2	2	2	3	3
.17	1479	1483	1486	1489	1493	1496	1500	1503	1507	1510	0	1	1	1	2	2	2	3	3
.18	1514	1517	1521	1524	1528	1531	1535	1538	1542	1545	0	1	1	1	2	2	2	3	3
.19	1549	1552	1556	1560	1563	1567	1570	1574	1578	1581	0	1	1	1	2	2	3	3	3
.20	1585	1589	1592	1596	1600	1603	1607	1611	1614	1618	0	1	1	1	2	2	3	3	3
.21	1622	1626	1629	1633	1637	1641	1644	1648	1652	1656	0	1	1	2	2	2	3	3	3
.22	1660	1663	1667	1671	1675	1679	1683	1687	1690	1694	0	1	1	2	2	2	3	3	3
.23	1698	1702	1706	1710	1714	1718	1722	1726	1730	1734	0	1	1	2	2	2	3	3	4
.24	1738	1742	1746	1750	1754	1758	1762	1766	1770	1774	0	1	1	2	2	2	3	3	4
.25	1778	1782	1786	1791	1795	1799	1803	1807	1811	1816	0	1	1	2	2	2	3	3	4
.26	1820	1824	1828	1832	1837	1841	1845	1849	1854	1858	0	1	1	2	2	3	3	3	4
.27	1862	1866	1871	1875	1879	1884	1888	1892	1897	1901	0	1	1	2	2	3	3	3	4
.28	1905	1910	1914	1919	1923	1928	1932	1936	1941	1945	0	1	1	2	2	3	3	4	4
.29	1950	1954	1959	1963	1968	1972	1977	1982	1986	1991	0	1	1	2	2	3	3	4	4
.30	1995	2000	2004	2009	2014	2018	2023	2028	2032	2037	0	1	1	2	2	3	3	4	4
.31	2042	2046	2051	2056	2061	2065	2070	2075	2080	2084	0	1	1	2	2	3	3	4	4
.32	2089	2094	2099	2104	2109	2113	2118	2123	2128	2133	0	1	1	2	2	3	3	4	4
.33	2138	2143	2148	2153	2158	2163	2168	2173	2178	2183	0	1	1	2	2	3	3	4	4
.34	2188	2193	2198	2203	2208	2213	2218	2223	2228	2234	1	1	2	2	3	3	4	4	5
.35	2239	2244	2249	2254	2259	2265	2270	2275	2280	2286	1	1	2	2	3	3	4	4	5
.36	2291	2296	2301	2307	2312	2317	2323	2328	2333	2339	1	1	2	2	3	3	4	4	5
.37	2344	2350	2355	2360	2366	2371	2377	2382	2388	2393	1	1	2	2	3	3	4	4	5
.38	2399	2404	2410	2415	2421	2427	2432	2438	2443	2449	1	1	2	2	3	3	4	4	5
.39	2455	2460	2466	2472	2477	2483	2489	2495	2500	2506	1	1	2	2	3	3	4	5	5
.40	2512	2518	2523	2529	2535	2541	2547	2553	2559	2564	1	1	2	2	3	4	4	5	5
.41	2570	2576	2582	2588	2594	2600	2606	2612	2618	2624	1	1	2	2	3	4	4	5	5
.42	2630	2636	2642	2649	2655	2661	2667	2673	2679	2685	1	1	2	2	3	4	4	5	6
.43	2692	2698	2704	2710	2716	2723	2729	2735	2742	2748	1	1	2	3	3	4	4	5	6
.44	2754	2761	2767	2773	2780	2786	2793	2799	2805	2812	1	1	2	3	3	4	4	5	6
.45	2818	2825	2831	2838	2844	2851	2858	2864	2871	2877	1	1	2	3	3	4	5	5	6
.46	2884	2891	2897	2904	2911	2917	2924	2931	2938	2944	1	1	2	3	3	4	5	5	6
.47	2951	2958	2965	2972	2979	2985	2992	2999	3006	3013	1	1	2	3	3	4	5	5	6
.48	3020	3027	3034	3041	3048	3055	3062	3069	3076	3083	1	1	2	3	4	4	5	6	6
.49	3090	3097	3105	3112	3119	3126	3133	3141	3148	3155	1	1	2	3	4	4	5	6	6
	0	1	2	3	4	5	6	7	8	9	1	2	3	4	5	6	7	8	9

NATURAL OR NAPERIAN LOGARITHMS

To find the natural logarithm of a number which is $\frac{1}{10}, \frac{1}{100}, \frac{1}{1000}$, etc. of a number whose logarithm is given, subtract from the given logarithm $\log_e 10$, $2 \log_e 10$, $3 \log_e 10$, etc.

To find the natural logarithm of a number which is 10, 100, 1000, etc. times a number whose logarithm is given, add to the given logarithm $\log_e 10$, $2 \log_e 10$, $3 \log_e 10$, etc.

$\log_e 10 = 2.30258\ 50930$	$6 \log_e 10 = 13.81551\ 05580$
$2 \log_e 10 = 4.60517\ 01860$	$7 \log_e 10 = 16.11809\ 56510$
$3 \log_e 10 = 6.90775\ 52790$	$8 \log_e 10 = 18.42068\ 07440$
$4 \log_e 10 = 9.21034\ 03720$	$9 \log_e 10 = 20.72326\ 58369$
$5 \log_e 10 = 11.51292\ 54650$	$10 \log_e 10 = 23.02585\ 09299$

1.00–4.99

N	0	1	2	3	4	5	6	7	8	9
1.0	0.00000	.00995	.01980	.02956	.03922	.04879	.05827	.06766	.07696	.08618
.1	.09531	.10436	.11333	.12222	.13103	.13976	.14842	.15700	.16551	.17395
.2	.18232	.19062	.19885	.20701	.21511	.22314	.23111	.23902	.24686	.25464
.3	.26236	.27003	.27763	.28518	.29267	.30010	.30748	.31481	.32208	.32930
.4	.33647	.34359	.35066	.35767	.36464	.37156	.37844	.38526	.39204	.39878
.5	.40547	.41211	.41871	.42527	.43178	.43825	.44469	.45108	.45742	.46373
.6	.47000	.47623	.48243	.48858	.49470	.50078	.50682	.51282	.51879	.52473
.7	.53063	.53649	.54232	.54812	.55389	.55962	.56531	.57098	.57661	.58222
.8	.58779	.59333	.59884	.60432	.60977	.61519	.62058	.62594	.63127	.63658
.9	.64185	.64710	.65233	.65752	.66269	.66783	.67294	.67803	.68310	.68813
2.0	0.69315	.69813	.70310	.70804	.71295	.71784	.72271	.72755	.73237	.73716
.1	.74194	.74669	.75142	.75612	.76081	.76547	.77011	.77473	.77932	.78390
.2	.78846	.79299	.79751	.80200	.80648	.81093	.81536	.81978	.82418	.82855
.3	.83291	.83725	.84157	.84587	.85015	.85442	.85866	.86289	.86710	.87129
.4	.87547	.87963	.88377	.88789	.89200	.89609	.90016	.90422	.90826	.91228
.5	.91629	.92028	.92426	.92822	.93216	.93609	.94001	.94391	.94779	.95166
.6	.95551	.95935	.96317	.96698	.97078	.97456	.97833	.98208	.98582	.98954
.7	.99325	.99695	* .00063	* .00430	* .00796	* .01160	* .01523	* .01885	* .02245	* .02604
.8	1.02962	.03318	.03674	.04028	.04380	.04732	.05082	.05431	.05779	.06126
.9	.06471	.06815	.07158	.07500	.07841	.08181	.08519	.08856	.09192	.09527
3.0	1.09861	.10194	.10526	.10856	.11186	.11514	.11841	.12168	.12493	.12817
.1	.13140	.13462	.13783	.14103	.14422	.14740	.15057	.15373	.15688	.16002
.2	.16315	.16627	.16938	.17248	.17557	.17865	.18173	.18479	.18784	.19089
.3	.19392	.19695	.19996	.20297	.20597	.20896	.21194	.21491	.21788	.22083
.4	.22378	.22671	.22964	.23256	.23547	.23837	.24127	.24415	.24703	.24990
.5	.25276	.25562	.25846	.26130	.26413	.26695	.26976	.27257	.27536	.27815
.6	.28093	.28371	.28647	.28923	.29198	.29473	.29746	.30019	.30291	.30563
.7	.30833	.31103	.31372	.31641	.31909	.32176	.32442	.32708	.32972	.33237
.8	.33500	.33763	.34025	.34286	.34547	.34807	.35067	.35325	.35584	.35841
.9	.36098	.36354	.36609	.36864	.37118	.37372	.37624	.37877	.38128	.38379
4.0	1.38629	.38879	.39128	.39377	.39624	.39872	.40118	.40364	.40610	.40854
.1	.41099	.41342	.41585	.41828	.42070	.42311	.42552	.42792	.43031	.43270
.2	.43508	.43746	.43984	.44220	.44456	.44692	.44927	.45161	.45395	.45629
.3	.45862	.46094	.46326	.46557	.46787	.47018	.47247	.47476	.47705	.47933
.4	.48160	.48387	.48614	.48840	.49065	.49290	.49515	.49739	.49962	.50185
.5	.50408	.50630	.50851	.51072	.51293	.51513	.51732	.51951	.52170	.52388
.6	.52606	.52823	.53039	.53256	.53471	.53687	.53902	.54116	.54330	.54543
.7	.54756	.54969	.55181	.55393	.55604	.55814	.56025	.56235	.56444	.56653
.8	.56862	.57070	.57277	.57485	.57691	.57898	.58104	.58309	.58515	.58719
.9	.58924	.59127	.59331	.59534	.59737	.59939	.60141	.60342	.60543	.60744

NATURAL OR NAPERIAN LOGARITHMS (Continued)

5.00–9.99

N	0	1	2	3	4	5	6	7	8	9
5.0	1 60944	61144	61343	61542	61741	61939	62137	62334	62531	62728
.1	62924	63120	63315	63511	63705	63900	64094	64287	64481	64673
.2	64866	65058	65250	65441	65632	65823	66013	66203	66393	66582
.3	66771	66959	67147	67335	67523	67710	67896	68083	68269	68455
.4	68640	68825	69010	69194	69378	69562	69745	69928	70111	70293
.5	70475	70656	70838	71019	71199	71380	71560	71740	71919	72098
.6	72277	72455	72633	72811	72988	73166	73342	73519	73695	73871
.7	74047	74222	74397	74572	74746	74920	75094	75267	75440	75613
.8	75786	75958	76130	76302	76473	76644	76815	76985	77156	77326
.9	77495	77665	77834	78002	78171	78339	78507	78675	78842	79009
6.0	1 79176	79342	79509	79675	79840	80006	80171	80336	80500	80665
.1	80829	80993	81156	81319	81482	81645	81808	81970	82132	82294
.2	82455	82616	82777	82938	83098	83258	83418	83578	83737	83896
.3	84055	84214	84372	84530	84688	84845	85003	85160	85317	85473
.4	85630	85786	85942	86097	86253	86408	86563	86718	86872	87026
.5	87180	87334	87487	87641	87794	87947	88099	88251	88403	88555
.6	88707	88858	89010	89160	89311	89462	89612	89762	89912	90061
.7	90211	90360	90509	90658	90806	90954	91102	91250	91398	91545
.8	91692	91839	91986	92132	92279	92425	92571	92716	92862	93007
.9	93152	93297	93442	93586	93730	93874	94018	94162	94305	94448
7.0	1 94591	94734	94876	95019	95161	95303	95445	95586	95727	95869
.1	96009	96150	96291	96431	96571	96711	96851	96991	97130	97269
.2	97408	97547	97685	97824	97962	98100	98238	98376	98513	98650
.3	98787	98924	99061	99198	99334	99470	99606	99742	99877	* 00013
.4	2 00148	00283	00418	00553	00687	00821	00956	01089	01223	01357
.5	01490	01624	01757	01890	02022	02155	02287	02419	02551	02683
.6	02815	02946	03078	03209	03340	03471	03601	03732	03862	03992
.7	04122	04252	04381	04511	04640	04769	04898	05027	05156	05284
.8	05412	05540	05668	05796	05924	06051	06179	06306	06433	06560
.9	06686	06813	06939	07065	07191	07317	07443	07568	07694	07819
8.0	2 07944	08069	08194	08318	08443	08567	08691	08815	08939	09063
.1	09186	09310	09433	09556	09679	09802	09924	10047	10169	10291
.2	10413	10535	10657	10779	10900	11021	11142	11263	11384	11505
.3	11626	11746	11866	11986	12106	12226	12346	12465	12585	12704
.4	12823	12942	13061	13180	13298	13417	13535	13653	13771	13889
.5	14007	14124	14242	14359	14476	14593	14710	14827	14943	15060
.6	15176	15292	15409	15524	15640	15756	15871	15987	16102	16217
.7	16332	16447	16562	16677	16791	16905	17020	17134	17248	17361
.8	17475	17589	17702	17816	17929	18042	18155	18267	18380	18493
.9	18605	18717	18830	18942	19054	19165	19277	19389	19500	19611
9.0	2 19722	19834	19944	20055	20166	20276	20387	20497	20607	20717
.1	20827	20937	21047	21157	21266	21375	21485	21594	21703	21812
.2	21920	22029	22138	22246	22354	22462	22570	22678	22786	22894
.3	23001	23109	23216	23324	23431	23538	23645	23751	23858	23965
.4	24071	24177	24284	24390	24496	24601	24707	24813	24918	25024
.5	25129	25234	25339	25444	25549	25654	25759	25863	25968	26072
.6	26176	26280	26384	26488	26592	26696	26799	26903	27006	27109
.7	27213	27316	27419	27521	27624	27727	27829	27932	28034	28136
.8	28238	28340	28442	28544	28646	28747	28849	28950	29051	29152
.9	29253	29354	29455	29556	29657	29757	29858	29958	30058	30158

HYPERBOLIC AND RELATED FUNCTIONS

Dr. Madhu S. Gupta

HYPERBOLIC FUNCTIONS

Geometrical Definition

Let O be the center, A the vertex, and P any point with coordinates (x,y) on the branch B'AB of the rectangular hyperbola $X^2 - Y^2 = a^2$. Set OM = x, MP = y and OA = a. The shaded area shown in the figure is given by

$$\text{Area OPAP}' = a^2 \log_e \frac{(x+y)}{a}$$

If the angle POP' in hyperbolic radians is denoted by u,

$$u = \frac{\text{area OPAP}'}{a^2} \text{ hyperbolic radians.}$$

The hyperbolic functions are defined by

hyperbolic sine of u = sinh u = y/a
hyperbolic cosine of u = cosh u = x/a

The approximate length of the hyperbolic curve is given by

$$\text{arc AP} = \frac{3}{2} y - \frac{1}{2} \tan^{-1} y$$

while the straight line distance is

$$\text{line AP} = \sqrt{\sinh^2 u + (\cosh u - 1)^2}$$

Exponential Definition

hyperbolic sine of u = sinh u = $\frac{1}{2} (e^u - e^{-u})$ $\operatorname{csch} u = \dfrac{1}{\sinh u}$,

hyperbolic cosine of u = cosh u = $\frac{1}{2} (e^u + e^{-u})$ $\operatorname{sech} u = \dfrac{1}{\cosh u}$,

hyperbolic tangent of u = tanh u = $\dfrac{\sinh u}{\cosh u} = \dfrac{e^u - e^{-u}}{e^u + e^{-u}}$ $\operatorname{coth} u = \dfrac{1}{\tanh u}$,

Domain and Range for Real Argument

Function	Domain (interval of u)	Range (interval of function)	Remarks
sinh u	$(-\infty, +\infty)$	$(-\infty, +\infty)$	
cosh u	$(-\infty, +\infty)$	$[1, +\infty)$	
tanh u	$(-\infty, +\infty)$	$(-1, +1)$	
cosech u	$(-\infty, 0)$	$(0, -\infty)$	Two branches, pole
	$(0, +\infty)$	$(+\infty, 0)$	at $u = 0$.
sech u	$(-\infty, +\infty)$	$(0, 1]$	
coth u	$(-\infty, 0)$	$(-1, -\infty)$	Two branches, pole
	$(0, +\infty)$	$(+\infty, 1)$	at $u = 0$

Hyperbolic Functions In Terms of One Another

Function	sinh z	cosh z	tanh z
sinh z =	sinh z	$\pm \sqrt{\cosh^2 z - 1}$	$\dfrac{\tanh z}{\sqrt{1 - \tanh^2 z}}$
cosh z =	$\sqrt{1 + \sinh^2 z}$	cosh z	$\dfrac{1}{\sqrt{1 - \tanh^2 z}}$
tanh z =	$\dfrac{\sinh z}{\sqrt{1 + \sinh^2 z}}$	$\pm \dfrac{\sqrt{\cosh^2 z - 1}}{\cosh z}$	tanh z
cosech z =	$\dfrac{1}{\sinh z}$	$\pm \dfrac{1}{\sqrt{\cosh^2 z - 1}}$	$\dfrac{\sqrt{1 - \tanh^2 z}}{\tanh z}$
sech z =	$\dfrac{1}{\sqrt{1 + \sinh^2 z}}$	$\dfrac{1}{\cosh z}$	$\sqrt{1 - \tanh^2 z}$
coth z =	$\dfrac{\sqrt{1 + \sinh^2 z}}{\sinh z}$	$\pm \dfrac{\cosh z}{\sqrt{\cosh^2 z - 1}}$	$\dfrac{1}{\tanh z}$

Function	cosech z	sech z	coth z
sinh z =	$\dfrac{1}{\cosh z}$	$\pm \dfrac{\sqrt{1 - \mathrm{sech}^2 z}}{\mathrm{sech}\, z}$	$\dfrac{\pm 1}{\sqrt{\coth^2 z - 1}}$
cosh z =	$\pm \dfrac{\sqrt{\mathrm{cosech}^2 z + 1}}{\mathrm{cosech}\, z}$	$\dfrac{1}{\mathrm{sech}\, z}$	$\pm \dfrac{\coth z}{\sqrt{\coth^2 z - 1}}$
tanh z =	$\dfrac{1}{\sqrt{\mathrm{cosech}^2 z + 1}}$	$\pm \sqrt{1 - \mathrm{sech}^2 z}$	$\dfrac{1}{\coth z}$
cosech z =	cosech z	$\pm \dfrac{\mathrm{sech}\, z}{\sqrt{1 - \mathrm{sech}^2 z}}$	$\pm \dfrac{\sqrt{\coth^2 z - 1}}{1}$
sech z =	$\pm \dfrac{\mathrm{cosec}\, z}{\sqrt{\mathrm{cosech}^2 z + 1}}$	sech z	$\pm \dfrac{\sqrt{\coth^2 z - 1}}{\coth z}$
coth z =	$\sqrt{\mathrm{cosech}^2 z + 1}$	$\pm \dfrac{1}{\sqrt{1 - \mathrm{sech}^2 z}}$	coth z

Whenever two signs are shown, choose $+$ sign if z is positive, $-$ sign if z is negative.

Special Values of Hyperbolic Functions

x	0	$\dfrac{\pi}{2} i$	πi	$\dfrac{3\pi}{2} i$	∞
sinh z	0	i	0	$-i$	∞
cosh z	1	0	-1	0	∞
tanh z	0	∞i	0	$-\infty i$	1
csch z	∞	$-i$	∞	i	0
sech z	1	∞	-1	∞	0
coth z	∞	0	∞	0	1

Symmetry and Periodicity

$$\sinh(-u) = -\sinh u, \qquad \operatorname{csch}(-u) = -\operatorname{csch} u$$
$$\cosh(-u) = \cosh u, \qquad \operatorname{sech}(-u) = \operatorname{sech} u$$
$$\tanh(-u) = -\tanh u, \qquad \coth(-u) = -\coth u$$

sinh u, cosh u, cosech u and sech u are periodic with a period $2\pi i$; tanh u and coth u are periodic with a period πi.

Fundamental Identities

Reciprocal Relations

$$\operatorname{csch} u = \frac{1}{\sinh u}, \qquad \operatorname{sech} u = \frac{1}{\cosh u}, \qquad \coth u = \frac{1}{\tanh u}$$

Product Relations

$$\sinh u = \tanh u \cosh u \qquad\qquad \cosh u = \coth u \sinh u$$
$$\tanh u = \sinh u \operatorname{sech} u \qquad\qquad \coth u = \cosh u \operatorname{cosech} u$$
$$\operatorname{sech} u = \operatorname{cosech} u \tanh u \qquad \operatorname{cosech} u = \operatorname{sech} u \coth u$$

Quotient Relations

$$\sinh u = \frac{\tanh u}{\operatorname{sech} u} \qquad \cosh u = \frac{\coth u}{\operatorname{cosech} u} \qquad \tanh u = \frac{\sinh u}{\cosh u}$$

$$\operatorname{cosech} u = \frac{\operatorname{sech} u}{\tanh u} \qquad \operatorname{sech} u = \frac{\operatorname{cosech} u}{\coth u} \qquad \coth u = \frac{\cosh u}{\sinh u}$$

Relations Between Squares of Functions

$$\cosh^2 u - \sinh^2 u = 1, \qquad \tanh^2 u + \operatorname{sech}^2 u = 1$$
$$\coth^2 u - \operatorname{csch}^2 u = 1, \qquad \operatorname{csch}^2 u - \operatorname{sech}^2 u = \operatorname{csch}^2 u \operatorname{sech}^2 u$$

Angle-Sum and Angle-Difference Relations

$$\sinh (u + v) = \sinh u \cosh v + \cosh u \sinh v$$
$$\sinh (u - v) = \sinh u \cosh v - \cosh u \sinh v$$
$$\cosh (u + v) = \cosh u \cosh v + \sinh u \sinh v$$
$$\cosh (u - v) = \cosh u \cosh v - \sinh u \sinh v$$

$$\tanh (u + v) = \frac{\tanh u + \tanh v}{1 + \tanh u \tanh v} = \frac{\sinh 2u + \sinh 2v}{\cosh 2u + \cosh 2v}$$

$$\tanh (u - v) = \frac{\tanh u - \tanh v}{1 - \tanh u \tanh v} = \frac{\sinh 2u - \sinh 2v}{\cosh 2u - \cosh 2v}$$

$$\coth (u + v) = \frac{1 + \coth u \coth v}{\coth u + \coth v} = \frac{\sinh 2u - \sinh 2v}{\cosh 2u - \cosh 2v}$$

$$\coth (u - v) = \frac{1 - \coth u \coth v}{\coth u - \coth v} = \frac{\sinh 2u + \sinh 2v}{\cosh 2u - \cosh 2v}$$

Multiple Angle Relations

$$\sinh 2u = 2 \sinh u \cosh u = \frac{2 \tanh u}{1 - \tanh^2 u}$$

$$\cosh 2u = \cosh^2 u + \sinh^2 u = 2 \cosh^2 u - 1 = 1 + 2 \sinh^2 u = \frac{1 + \tanh^2 u}{1 - \tanh^2 u}$$

$$\tanh 2u = \frac{2 \tanh u}{1 + \tanh^2 u}$$

$$\coth 2u = \frac{\coth^2 u + 1}{2 \coth u}$$

$$\sinh 3u = 3 \sinh u + 4 \sinh^3 u = \sinh u \,(4 \cosh^2 u - 1)$$
$$\cosh 3u = 4 \cosh^3 u - 3 \cosh u = \cosh u \,(1 + 4 \sinh^2 u)$$

$$\tanh 3u = \frac{3 \tanh u + \tanh^3 u}{1 + 3 \tanh^2 u}$$

$$\coth 3u = \frac{3 \coth u + \coth^3 u}{1 + 3 \coth^2 u}$$

$$\sinh 4u = 4 \sinh u \cosh u (2 \cosh^2 u - 1)$$
$$= 4 \sinh u \cosh u (1 + 2 \sinh^2 u)$$
$$= 4 \sinh u \cosh u (\cosh^2 u + \sinh^2 u)$$

$$\cosh 4u = 1 + 8 \cosh^2 u (\cosh^2 u - 1)$$
$$= 1 + 8 \sinh^2 u (\sinh^2 u + 1)$$
$$= \cosh^4 u + 6 \sinh^2 u \cosh^2 u + \sinh^4 u$$

$$\tanh 4u = \frac{4 \tanh u (1 + \tanh^2 u)}{1 + 6 \tanh^2 u + \tanh^4 u}$$

$$\coth 4u = \frac{\coth^4 u + 6 \coth^2 u + 1}{4 \coth u (\coth^2 u + 1)}$$

$$\sinh 5u = \sinh u (16 \sinh^4 u + 20 \sinh^2 u + 5)$$
$$= \sinh u (16 \cosh^4 u - 12 \cosh^2 u + 1)$$

$$\cosh 5u = \cosh u (16 \cosh^4 u - 20 \cosh^2 u + 5)$$
$$= \cosh u (16 \sinh^4 u + 12 \sinh^2 u + 1)$$

$$\sinh 6u = 2 \sinh u \cosh u (16 \cosh^4 u - 16 \cosh^2 u + 3)$$
$$= 2 \sinh u \cosh u (16 \sinh^4 u + 16 \sinh^2 u + 3)$$

$$\cosh 6u = 32 \cosh^6 u - 48 \cosh^4 u + 18 \cosh^2 u - 1$$
$$= 32 \sinh^6 u + 48 \sinh^4 u + 18 \sinh^2 u + 1$$

$$\sinh nu = \sinh u \left[(2 \cosh u)^{n-1} - \frac{(n-2)}{1!} \cdot (2 \cosh u)^{n-3} + \frac{(n-3)(n-4)}{2!} \right.$$
$$\left. (2 \cosh u)^{n-5} - \frac{(n-4)(n-5)(n-6)}{3!} (2 \cosh u)^{n-7} + \cdots \right].$$

$$\cosh nu = \frac{1}{2} \left[(2 \cosh u)^n - \frac{n}{1!} (2 \cosh u)^{n-2} + \frac{n(n-3)}{2!} (2 \cosh u)^{n-4} \right.$$
$$\left. - \frac{n(n-4)(n-5)}{3!} (2 \cosh u)^{n-6} + \cdots \right].$$

Half Angle Relations

$$\sinh \tfrac{1}{2} u = \pm \sqrt{\tfrac{1}{2}(\cosh u - 1)}$$
$$\cosh \tfrac{1}{2} u = \sqrt{\tfrac{1}{2}(\cosh u + 1)}$$

$$\tanh \frac{u}{2} = \frac{\sinh u}{1 + \cosh u} = \frac{\cosh u - 1}{\sinh u} = \pm \sqrt{\frac{\cosh u - 1}{\cosh u + 1}}$$

$$\coth \frac{u}{2} = \frac{1 + \cosh u}{\sinh u} = \frac{\sinh u}{\cosh u - 1} = \pm \sqrt{\frac{\cosh u + 1}{\cosh u - 1}}$$

Choose $+$ sign if u is positive, otherwise choose the $-$ sign.

Function Sum and Function Difference Relations

$$\sinh u + \sinh v = 2 \sinh \tfrac{1}{2}(u + v) \cosh \tfrac{1}{2}(u - v)$$
$$\sinh u - \sinh v = 2 \cosh \tfrac{1}{2}(u + v) \sinh \tfrac{1}{2}(u - v)$$
$$\cosh u + \cosh v = 2 \cosh \tfrac{1}{2}(u + v) \cosh \tfrac{1}{2}(u - v)$$
$$\cosh u - \cosh v = 2 \sinh \tfrac{1}{2}(u + v) \sinh \tfrac{1}{2}(u - v)$$

$$\tanh u + \tanh v = (1 + \tanh u \tanh v) \tanh (u + v) = \frac{\sinh (u + v)}{\cosh u \cosh v}$$

$$\tanh u - \tanh v = (1 - \tanh u \tanh v) \tanh (u - v) = \frac{\sinh (u - v)}{\cosh u \cosh v}$$

$$\coth u + \coth v = \frac{1 + \coth u \coth v}{\coth (u + v)} = \frac{\sinh (u + v)}{\sinh u \sinh v}$$

$$\coth u - \coth v = \frac{1 - \coth u \coth v}{\coth (u - v)} = \frac{\sinh (u - v)}{\sinh u \sinh v}$$

$$\sinh u + \cosh u = \frac{1 + \tanh \frac{1}{2}u}{1 - \tanh \frac{1}{2}u} = e^u \qquad \cosh u - \sinh u = \frac{1 - \tanh \frac{1}{2}u}{1 + \tanh \frac{1}{2}u} = e^{-u}$$

Function Product Relations

$$\sinh u \cosh v = \tfrac{1}{2} \sinh (u + v) + \tfrac{1}{2} \sinh (u - v)$$
$$\cosh u \sinh v = \tfrac{1}{2} \sinh (u + v) - \tfrac{1}{2} \sinh (u - v)$$
$$\cosh u \cosh v = \tfrac{1}{2} \cosh (u + v) + \tfrac{1}{2} \cosh (u - v)$$
$$\sinh u \sinh v = \tfrac{1}{2} \cosh (u + v) - \tfrac{1}{2} \cosh (u - v)$$
$$\sinh (u + v) \sinh (u - v) = \sinh^2 u - \sinh^2 v = \cosh^2 u - \cosh^2 v$$
$$\cosh (u + v) \cosh (u - v) = \sinh^2 u + \cosh^2 v = \cosh^2 u + \sinh^2 v$$

Power Relations

$$\sinh^2 u = \tfrac{1}{2}(\cosh 2u - 1)$$
$$\cosh^2 u = \tfrac{1}{2}(\cosh 2u + 1)$$
$$\sinh^3 u = \tfrac{1}{4}(-3 \sinh u + \sinh 3u)$$
$$\cosh^3 u = \tfrac{1}{4}(3 \cosh u + \cosh 3u)$$
$$\sinh^4 u = \tfrac{1}{8}(3 - 4 \cosh 2u + \cosh 4u)$$
$$\cosh^4 u = \tfrac{1}{8}(3 + 4 \cosh 2u + \cosh 4u)$$
$$\sinh^5 u = \tfrac{1}{16}(10 \sinh u - 5 \sinh 3u + \sinh 5u)$$
$$\cosh^5 u = \tfrac{1}{16}(10 \cosh u + 5 \cosh 3u + \cosh 5u)$$
$$\sinh^6 u = \tfrac{1}{32}(-10 + 15 \cosh 2u - 6 \cosh 4u + \cosh 6u)$$
$$\cosh^6 u = \tfrac{1}{32}(10 + 15 \cosh 2u + 6 \cosh 4u + \cosh 6u)$$
$$(\cosh u \pm \sinh u)^n = \cosh nu \pm \sinh nu$$

Relations with Circular Functions

$$\sinh iu = i \sin u, \qquad \sinh u = -i \sin iu$$
$$\cosh iu = \cos u, \qquad \cosh u = \cos iu$$
$$\tanh iu = i \tan u, \qquad \tanh u = -i \tan iu$$
$$\operatorname{cosech} iu = -i \operatorname{cosec} u \qquad \operatorname{cosech} u = i \operatorname{cosec} iu$$
$$\operatorname{sech} iu = \sec u \qquad \operatorname{sech} u = \sec iu$$
$$\coth iu = -i \cot u \qquad \coth u = i \coth iu$$

Hyperbolic Functions of Complex Argument

$$\sinh (u + iv) = \sinh u \cos v + i \cosh u \sin v$$
$$\sinh (u - iv) = \sinh u \cos v - i \cosh u \sin v$$
$$\cosh (u + iv) = \cosh u \cos v + i \sinh u \sin v$$
$$\cosh (u - iv) = \cosh u \cos v - i \sinh u \sin v$$

$$\tanh (u + iv) = \frac{\sinh 2u + i \sin 2v}{\cosh 2u + \cos 2v}$$

$$\tanh (u - iv) = \frac{\sinh 2u - i \sin 2v}{\cosh 2u + \cos 2v}$$

$$\coth (u + iv) = \frac{\sinh 2u - i \sin 2v}{\cosh 2u - \cos 2v}$$

$$\coth (u - iv) = \frac{\sinh 2u + i \sin 2v}{\cosh 2u - \cos 2v}$$

$$\sinh (u + \tfrac{1}{2}\pi i) = i \cosh u, \qquad \cosh (u + \tfrac{1}{2}\pi i) = i \sinh u$$
$$\sinh (u + \pi i) = -\sinh u, \qquad \cosh (u + \pi i) = -\cosh u$$
$$\sinh (u + 2\pi i) = \sinh u, \qquad \cosh (u + 2\pi i) = \cosh u$$

Series for Hyperbolic Functions

(see series expansions for sinh nu and cosh nu under multiple angle relations).

$$\sinh x = x + \frac{x^3}{3!} + \frac{x^5}{5!} + \frac{x^7}{7!} + \cdots + \frac{x^{2n+1}}{(2n+1)!} + \cdots \qquad |x| < \infty$$

$$\sinh ax = \frac{2}{\pi} \sinh \pi a \left[\frac{\sin x}{a^2 + 1^2} - \frac{2 \sin 2x}{a^2 + 2^2} + \frac{3 \sin 3x}{a^2 + 3^2} - + \cdots \right]$$

$$= \frac{2}{\pi} \sinh \pi a \sum_{n=1}^{\infty} (-1)^{n+1} \frac{n \sin nx}{n^2 + a^2}, \qquad |x| < \pi$$

$$\cosh x = 1 + \frac{x^2}{2!} + \frac{x^4}{4!} + \frac{x^6}{6!} + \cdots + \frac{x^{2n}}{(2n)!} + \cdots \qquad |x| < \infty$$

$$\cosh ax = \frac{2a}{\pi} \sinh \pi a \left[\frac{1}{2a^2} - \frac{\cos x}{a^2 + 1^2} + \frac{\cos 2x}{a^2 + 2^2} - \frac{\cos 3x}{a^2 + 3^2} + - \cdots \right]$$

$$= \frac{\sinh \pi a}{a\pi} + \frac{2a}{\pi} \sinh \pi a \sum_{n=1}^{\infty} (-1)^n \frac{\cos nx}{n^2 + a^2}, \qquad |x| < \pi$$

$$\tanh x = x - \frac{1}{3} x^3 + \frac{2}{15} x^5 - \frac{17}{315} x^7 + \frac{62}{2835} x^9 - \cdots$$
$$+ \frac{2^{2n}(2^{2n} - 1) B_{2n} x^{2n-1}}{(2n)!} \pm \cdots \quad (1) \qquad |x| < \frac{\pi}{2}$$

$$\tanh x = 1 - 2e^{-2x} + 2e^{-4x} - 2e^{-6x} + - \cdots$$

$$= 1 + 2 \sum_{n=1}^{\infty} (-1)^n e^{-2nx}, \qquad \mathrm{Re}\,(x) > 0$$

$$\tanh x = 2x \left[\frac{1}{\left(\frac{\pi}{2}\right)^2 + x^2} + \frac{1}{\left(\frac{3\pi}{2}\right)^2 + x^2} + \frac{1}{\left(\frac{5\pi}{2}\right)^2 + x^2} + \cdots \right]$$

$$= 2x \sum_{n=0}^{\infty} \frac{1}{\left(n + \frac{1}{2}\right)^2 \pi^2 + x^2}$$

$$\coth x = \frac{1}{x} + \frac{x}{3} - \frac{x^3}{45} + \frac{2x^5}{945} - \frac{x^7}{4725} + \cdots + \frac{2^{2n}}{(2n)!} B_{2n} x^{2n-1} \pm \cdots \quad (1)$$
$$0 < |x| < \pi$$

$$\coth x = 1 + 2e^{-2x} + 2e^{-4x} + 2e^{-6x} + \cdots$$

$$= 1 + 2 \sum_{n=1}^{\infty} e^{-2nx} \qquad \mathrm{Re}\,(x) > 0$$

$$\coth x = \frac{1}{x} + 2x \left[\frac{1}{\pi^2 + x^2} + \frac{1}{(2\pi)^2 + x^2} + \frac{1}{(3\pi)^2 + x^2} + \cdots \right]$$

$$= \frac{1}{x} + 2x \sum_{n=1}^{\infty} \frac{1}{(n\pi)^2 + x^2}$$

(1) B_{2n} denotes Bernoulli numbers.

$$\text{sech } x = 1 - \frac{1}{2!} x^2 + \frac{5}{4!} x^4 - \frac{61}{6!} x^6 + \frac{1385}{8!} x^8 - \cdots + \frac{E_{2n} x^{2n}}{(2n)!} \pm \cdots \text{ (2)}$$

$$|x| < \frac{\pi}{2}$$

$$\text{sech } x = 2e^{-x} - 2e^{-3x} + 2e^{-5x} - 2e^{-7x} + - \cdots$$

$$= 2 \sum_{n=0}^{\infty} (-1)^n e^{-(2n+1)x}, \text{Re } (x) > 0$$

$$\text{sech } x = 4\pi \left[\frac{1}{\pi^2 + 4x^2} - \frac{3}{(3\pi)^2 + 4x^2} + \frac{5}{(5\pi)^2 + 4x^2} - + \cdots \right]$$

$$= 4\pi \sum_{n=0}^{\infty} \frac{(-1)^n (2n+1)}{(2n+1)^2 \pi^2 + 4x^2}$$

$$\text{cosech } x = \frac{1}{x} - \frac{x}{6} + \frac{7x^3}{360} - \frac{31x^5}{15,120} + \cdots - \frac{2(2^{2n-1} - 1)}{(2n)!} B_{2n} x^{2n-1} + \cdots \text{ (1)}$$

$$0 < |x| < \pi$$

$$\text{cosech } x = 2e^{-x} + 2e^{-3x} + 2e^{-5x} + \cdots$$

$$= 2 \sum_{n=0}^{\infty} e^{-(2n+1)x}, \text{Re } (x) > 0$$

$$\text{cosech } x = \frac{1}{x} - \frac{2x}{\pi^2 + x^2} + \frac{2x}{(2\pi)^2 + x^2} - \frac{2x}{(3\pi)^2 + x^2} + - \cdots$$

$$= \frac{1}{x} + 2x \sum_{n=1}^{\infty} \frac{(-1)^n}{(n\pi)^2 + x^2}$$

[2] E_{2n} denotes Euler numbers.

EXPONENTIAL AND HYPERBOLIC FUNCTIONS AND THEIR COMMON LOGARITHMS

x	e^x Value	e^x $\log^{10}$	e^{-x} (value)	sinh x Value	sinh x $\log^{10}$	cosh x Value	cosh x $\log^{10}$	tanh x (value)
0.00	1.0000	0.00000	1.00000	0.0000	— ∞	1.0000	0.00000	0.00000
0.01	1.0101	.00434	0.99005	.0100	$\overline{2}$.00001	1.0001	.00002	.01000
0.02	1.0202	.00869	.98020	.0200	$\overline{2}$.30106	1.0002	.00009	.02000
0.03	1.0305	.01303	.97045	.0300	$\overline{2}$.47719	1.0005	.00020	.02999
0.04	1.0408	.01737	.96079	.0400	$\overline{2}$.60218	1.0008	.00035	.03998
0.05	1.0513	.02171	.95123	.0500	$\overline{2}$.69915	1.0013	.00054	.04996
0.06	1.0618	.02606	.94176	.0600	$\overline{2}$.77841	1.0018	.00078	.05993
0.07	1.0725	.03040	.93239	.0701	$\overline{2}$.84545	1.0025	.00106	.06989
0.08	1.0833	.03474	.92312	.0801	$\overline{2}$.90355	1.0032	.00139	.07983
0.09	1.0942	.03909	.91393	.0901	$\overline{2}$.95483	1.0041	.00176	.08976
0.10	1.1052	.04343	.90484	.1002	$\overline{1}$.00072	1.0050	.00217	.09967
0.11	1.1163	.04777	.89583	1102	$\overline{1}$.04227	1.0061	.00262	.10956
0.12	1.1275	.05212	.88692	.1203	$\overline{1}$.08022	1.0072	.00312	.11943
0.13	1.1388	.05646	.87809	.1304	$\overline{1}$.11517	1.0085	.00366	.12927
0.14	1.1503	.06080	.86936	.1405	$\overline{1}$.14755	1.0098	.00424	.13909
0.15	1.1618	.06514	.86071	.1506	$\overline{1}$.17772	1.0113	.00487	.14889
0.16	1.1735	.06949	.85214	.1607	$\overline{1}$.20597	1.0128	.00554	.15865
0.17	1.1853	.07383	.84366	.1708	$\overline{1}$.23254	1.0145	.00625	.16838
0.18	1.1972	.07817	.83527	.1810	$\overline{1}$.25762	1.0162	.00700	.17808
0.19	1.2092	.08252	.82696	.1911	$\overline{1}$.28136	1.0181	.00779	.18775
0.20	1.2214	.08686	.81873	.2013	$\overline{1}$.30392	1.0201	.00863	.19738
0.21	1.2337	.09120	.81058	.2115	$\overline{1}$.32541	1.0221	.00951	.20697
0.22	1.2461	.09554	.80252	.2218	$\overline{1}$.34592	1.0243	.01043	.21652
0.23	1.2586	.09989	.79453	.2320	$\overline{1}$.36555	1.0266	.01139	.22603
0.24	1.2712	.10423	.78663	.2423	$\overline{1}$.38437	1.0289	.01239	.23550
0.25	1.2840	.10857	.77880	.2526	$\overline{1}$.40245	1.0314	.01343	.24492
0.26	1.2969	.11292	.77105	.2629	$\overline{1}$.41986	1.0340	.01452	.25430
0.27	1.3100	.11726	.76338	.2733	$\overline{1}$.43663	1.0367	.01564	.26362
0.28	1.3231	12160	.75578	.2837	$\overline{1}$.45282	1.0395	.01681	.27291
0.29	1.3364	.12595	.74826	.2941	$\overline{1}$.46847	1.0423	.01801	.28213
0.30	1.3499	.13029	.74082	.3045	$\overline{1}$.48362	1.0453	.01926	.29131
0.31	1.3634	.13463	.73345	.3150	$\overline{1}$.49830	1.0484	.02054	.30044
0.32	1.3771	.13897	.72615	.3255	$\overline{1}$.51254	1.0516	.02187	.30951
0.33	1.3910	.14332	.71892	.3360	$\overline{1}$.52637	1.0549	.02323	.31852
0.34	1.4049	.14766	.71177	.3466	$\overline{1}$.53981	1.0584	.02463	.32748
0.35	1.4191	.15200	.70469	.3572	$\overline{1}$.55290	1.0619	.02607	.33638
0.36	1.4333	.15635	.69768	.3678	$\overline{1}$.56564	1.0655	.02755	.34521
0.37	1.4477	.16069	.69073	.3785	$\overline{1}$.57807	1.0692	.02907	.35399
0.38	1.4623	.16503	.68386	.3892	$\overline{1}$.59019	1.0731	.03063	.36271
0.39	1.4770	.16937	.67706	.4000	$\overline{1}$.60202	1.0770	.03222	.37136
0.40	1.4918	.17372	.67032	.4108	$\overline{1}$.61358	1.0811	.03385	.37995
0.41	1.5063	.17806	.66365	.4216	$\overline{1}$.62488	1.0852	.03552	.33847
0.42	1.5220	.18240	.65705	.4325	$\overline{1}$.63594	1.0895	.03723	.39693
0.43	1.5373	.18675	.65051	.4434	$\overline{1}$.64677	1.0939	.03897	.40532
0.44	1.5527	.19109	.64404	.4543	$\overline{1}$.65738	1.0984	.04075	.41364
0.45	1.5683	.19543	.63763	.4653	$\overline{1}$.66777	1.1030	.04256	.42190
0.46	1.5841	.19978	.63128	.4764	$\overline{1}$.67797	1.1077	.04441	.43008
0.47	1.6000	.20412	.62500	.4875	$\overline{1}$.68797	1.1125	.04630	.43820
0.48	1.6161	.20846	.61878	.4986	$\overline{1}$.69779	1.1174	.04822	.44624
0.49	1.6323	.21280	.61263	.5098	$\overline{1}$.70744	1.1225	.05018	.45422
0.50	1.6487	.21715	.60653	.5211	$\overline{1}$.71692	1.1276	.05217	.46212
0.51	1.6653	.22149	.60050	.5324	$\overline{1}$.72624	1.1329	.05419	.46995
0.52	1.6820	.22583	.59452	.5438	$\overline{1}$.73540	1.1383	.05625	.47770
0.53	1.6989	.23018	.58860	.5552	$\overline{1}$.74442	1.1438	.05834	.48538
0.54	1.7160	.23452	.58275	.5666	$\overline{1}$.75330	1.1494	.06046	.49299
0.55	1.7333	.23886	.57695	.5782	$\overline{1}$.76204	1.1551	.06262	.50052
0.56	1.7507	.24320	.57121	.5897	$\overline{1}$.77065	1.1609	.06481	.50798
0.57	1.7683	.24755	.56553	.6014	$\overline{1}$.77914	1.1669	.06703	.51536
0.58	1.7860	.25189	.55990	.6131	$\overline{1}$.78751	1.1730	.06929	.52267
0.59	1.8040	.25623	.55433	.6248	$\overline{1}$.79576	1.1792	.07157	.52990
0.60	1.8221	.26058	.54881	.6367	$\overline{1}$.80390	1.1855	.07389	.53705
0.61	1.8404	.26492	.54335	.6485	$\overline{1}$.81194	1.1919	.07624	.54413
0.62	1.8589	.26926	.53794	.6605	$\overline{1}$.81987	1.1984	.07861	.55113
0.63	1.8776	.27361	.53259	.6725	1.82770	1.2051	.08102	.55805

EXPONENTIAL AND HYPERBOLIC FUNCTIONS AND THEIR COMMON LOGARITHMS
(continued)

x	e^x Value	$\log^{10}$	e^{-x} (value)	sinh x Value	$\log^{10}$	cosh x Value	$\log^{10}$	tanh x (value)
0.64	1.8965	.27795	.52729	.6846	$\bar{1}$.83543	1.2119	.08346	.56490
0.65	1.9155	.28229	.52205	.6967	$\bar{1}$.84308	1.2188	.08593	.57167
0.66	1.9348	.28664	.51685	.7090	$\bar{1}$.85063	1.2258	.08843	.57836
0.67	1.9542	.29098	.51171	.7213	$\bar{1}$.85809	1.2330	.09095	.58498
0.68	1.9739	.29532	.50662	.7336	$\bar{1}$.86548	1.2402	.09351	.59152
0.69	1.9937	.29966	.50158	.7461	$\bar{1}$.87278	1.2476	.09609	.59798
0.70	2.0138	.30401	.49659	.7586	$\bar{1}$.88000	1.2552	.09870	.60437
0.71	2.0340	.30835	.49164	.7712	$\bar{1}$.88715	1.2628	.10134	.61068
0.72	2.0544	.31269	.48675	.7838	$\bar{1}$.89423	1.2706	.10401	.61691
0.73	2.0751	.31703	.48191	.7966	$\bar{1}$.90123	1.2785	.10670	.62307
0.74	2.0959	.32138	.47711	.8094	$\bar{1}$.90817	1.2865	.10942	.62915
0.75	2.1170	.32572	.47237	.8223	$\bar{1}$.91504	1.2947	.11216	.63515
0.76	2.1383	.33006	.46767	.8353	$\bar{1}$.92185	1.3030	.11493	.64108
0.77	2.1598	.33441	.46301	.8484	$\bar{1}$.92859	1.3114	.11773	.64693
0.78	2.1815	.33875	.45841	.8615	$\bar{1}$.93527	1.3199	.12055	.65271
0.79	2.2034	.34309	.45384	.8748	$\bar{1}$.94190	1.3286	.12340	.65841
0.80	2.2255	.34744	.44933	.8881	$\bar{1}$.94846	1.3374	.12627	.66404
0.81	2.2479	.35178	.44486	.9015	$\bar{1}$.95498	1.3464	.12917	.66959
0.82	2.2705	.35612	.44043	.9150	$\bar{1}$.96144	1.3555	.13209	.67507
0.83	2.2933	.36046	.43605	.9286	$\bar{1}$.96784	1.3647	.13503	.68048
0.84	2.3164	.36481	.43171	.9423	$\bar{1}$.97420	1.3740	.13800	.68581
0.85	2.3396	.36915	.42741	.9561	$\bar{1}$.98051	1.3835	.14099	.69107
0.86	2.3632	.37349	.42316	.9700	$\bar{1}$.98677	1.3932	.14400	.69626
0.87	2.3869	.37784	.41895	.9840	$\bar{1}$.99299	1.4029	.14704	.70137
0.88	2.4100	.38218	.41478	.9981	$\bar{1}$.99916	1.4128	.15009	.70642
0.89	2.4351	.38652	.41066	1.0122	0.00528	1.4229	.15317	.71139
0.90	2.4596	.39087	.40657	1.0265	.01137	1.4331	.15627	.71630
0.91	2.4843	.39521	.40242	1.0409	.01741	1.4434	.15939	.72113
0.92	2.5093	.39955	.39852	1.0554	.02341	1.4539	.16254	.72590
0.93	2.5345	.40389	.39455	1.0700	.02937	1.4645	.16570	.73059
0.94	2.5600	.40824	.39063	1.0847	.03530	1.4753	.16888	.73522
0.95	2.5857	.41258	.38674	1.0995	.04119	1.4862	.17208	.73978
0.96	2.6117	.41692	.38289	1.1144	.04704	1.4973	.17531	.74428
0.97	2.6379	.42127	.37908	1.1294	.05286	1.5085	.17855	.74870
0.98	2.6645	.42561	.37531	1.1446	.05864	1.5199	.18181	.75307
0.99	2.6912	.42995	.37158	1.1598	.06439	1.5314	.18509	.75736
1.00	2.7183	.43429	.36788	1.1752	.07011	1.5431	.18839	.76159
1.01	2.7456	.43864	.36422	1.1907	.07580	1.5549	.19171	.76576
1.02	2.7732	.44298	.36060	1.2063	.06146	1.5669	.19504	.76987
1.03	2.8011	.44732	.35701	1.2220	.08708	1.5790	.19839	.77391
1.04	2.8292	.45167	.35345	1.2379	.09268	1.5913	.20176	.77789
1.05	2.8577	.45601	.34994	1.2539	.09825	1.6038	.20515	.78181
1.06	2.8864	.46035	.34646	1.2700	.10379	1.6164	.20855	.78566
1.07	2.9154	.46470	.34301	1.2862	.10930	1.6292	.21197	.78946
1.08	2.9447	.46904	.33960	1.3025	.11479	1.6421	.21541	.79320
1.09	2.9743	.47338	.33622	1.3190	.12025	1.6552	.21886	.79688
1.10	3.0042	.47772	.33287	1.3356	.12569	1.6685	.22233	.80050
1.11	3.0344	.48207	.32956	1.3524	.13111	1.6820	.22582	.80406
1.12	3.0659	.48641	.32628	1.3693	.13649	1.6956	.22931	.80757
1.13	3.0957	.49075	.32303	1.3863	.14186	1.7083	.23283	.81102
1.14	3.1268	.49510	.31982	1.4035	.14720	1.7233	.23636	.81441
1.15	3.1582	.49944	.31644	1.4208	.15253	1.7374	.23990	.81775
1.16	3.1899	.50378	.31349	1.4382	.15783	1.7517	.24346	.82104
1.17	3.2220	.50812	.31037	1.4558	.16311	1.7662	.24703	.82427
1.18	3.2544	.51247	.30728	1.4735	.16836	1.7808	.25062	.82745
1.19	3.2871	.51681	.30422	1.4914	.17360	1.7957	.25422	.83058
1.20	3.3201	.52115	.30119	1.5095	.17882	1.8107	.25784	.83365
1.21	3.3535	.52550	.29820	1.5276	.18402	1.8258	.26146	.83668
1.22	3.3872	.52984	.29523	1.5460	.18920	1.8412	.26510	.83965
1.23	3.4212	.53418	.29229	1.5645	.19437	1.8568	.26876	.84258
1.24	3.4556	.53853	.28938	1.5831	.19951	1.8725	.27242	.83546
1.25	3.4903	.54287	.28650	1.6019	.20464	1.8884	.27610	.84828
1.26	3.5254	.54721	.28365	1.6209	.20975	1.9045	.27979	.85106

EXPONENTIAL AND HYPERBOLIC FUNCTIONS AND THEIR COMMON LOGARITHMS
(continued)

x	e^x Value	$\log^{10}$	e^{-x} (value)	sinh x Value	$\log^{10}$	cosh x Value	$\log^{10}$	tanh x (value)
1.27	3.5609	.55155	.28083	1.6400	.21485	1.9208	.28349	.85380
1.28	3.5996	.55590	.27804	1.6593	.21993	1.9373	.28721	.85648
1.29	3.6328	.56024	.27527	1.6788	.22499	1.9540	.29093	.85913
1.30	3.6693	.56458	.27253	1.6984	.23004	1.9709	.29467	.86172
1.31	3.7062	.56893	.26982	1.7182	.23507	1.9880	.29842	.86428
1.32	3.7434	.57327	.26714	1.7381	.24009	2.0053	.30217	.86678
1.33	3.7810	.57761	.26448	1.7583	.24509	2.0228	.30594	.86925
1.34	3.8190	.58195	.26185	1.7786	.25008	2.0404	.30972	.87167
1.35	3.8574	.58630	.25924	1.7991	.25505	2.0583	.31352	.87405
1.36	3.8962	.59064	.25666	1.8198	.26002	2.0764	.31732	.87639
1.37	3.9354	.59498	.25411	1.8406	.26496	2.0947	.32113	.87869
1.38	3.9749	.59933	.25158	1.8617	.26990	2.1132	.32495	.88095
1.39	4.0149	.60367	.24908	1.8829	.27482	2.1320	.32878	.88317
1.40	4.0552	.60801	.24660	1.9043	.27974	2.1509	.33262	.88535
1.41	4.0960	.61236	.24414	1.9259	.28464	2.1700	.33647	.88749
1.42	4.1371	.61670	.24171	1.9477	.28952	2.1894	.34033	.88960
1.43	4.1787	.62104	.23931	1.9697	.29440	2.2090	.34420	.89167
1.44	4.2207	.62538	.23693	1.9919	.29926	2.2288	.34807	.89370
1.45	4.2631	.62973	.23457	2.0143	30412	2.2488	.35196	.89569
1.46	4.3060	.63407	.23224	2.0369	.30896	2.2691	.35585	.89765
1.47	4.3492	.63841	.22993	2.0597	.31379	2.2896	.35976	.89958
1.48	4.3929	.64276	.22764	2.0827	.31862	2.3103	.36367	.90147
1.49	4.4371	.64710	.22537	2.1059	.32343	2.3312	.36759	.90332
1.50	4.4817	.65144	.22313	2.1293	.32823	2.3524	.37151	.90515
1.51	4.5267	.65578	.22091	2.1529	.33303	2.3738	.37545	.90694
1.52	4.5722	.66013	.21871	2.1768	.33781	2.3955	.37939	.90870
1.53	4.6182	.66447	.21654	2.2008	.34258	2.4174	.38334	.91042
1.54	4.6646	.66881	.21438	2.2251	.34735	2.4395	.38730	.91212
1.55	4.7115	.67316	.21225	2.2496	.35211	2.4619	.39126	.91379
1.56	4.7588	.67750	.21014	2.2743	.35686	2.4845	.39524	.91542
1.57	4.8066	.68184	.20805	2.2993	.36160	2.5073	.39921	.91703
1.58	4.8550	.68619	.20598	2.3245	.36633	2.5305	.40320	.91860
1.59	4.9037	.69053	.20393	2.3499	.37105	2.5538	.40719	.92015
1.60	4.9530	.69487	.20190	2.3756	.37577	2.5775	.41119	.92167
1.61	5.0028	.69921	.19989	2.4015	.38048	2.6013	.41520	.92316
1.62	5.0531	.70356	.19790	2.4276	.38518	2.6255	.41921	.92462
1.63	5.1039	.70790	.19593	2.4540	.38987	2.6499	.42323	.92606
1.64	5.1552	.71224	.19398	2.4806	.39456	2.6746	.42725	.92747
1.65	5.2070	.71659	.19205	2.5075	.39923	2.6995	.43129	.92886
1.66	5.2593	.72093	.19014	2.5346	.40391	2.7247	.43532	.93022
1.67	5.3122	.72527	.18825	2.5620	.40857	2.7502	.43937	.93155
1.68	5.3656	.72961	.18637	2.5896	.41323	2.7760	.44341	.93286
1.69	5.4195	.73396	.18452	2.6175	.41788	2.8020	.44747	.93415
1.70	5.4739	.73830	.18268	2.6456	.42253	2.8283	.45153	.93541
1.71	5.5290	.74264	.18087	2.6740	.42717	2.8549	.45559	.93665
1.72	5.5845	.74699	.17907	2.7027	.43180	2.8818	.45966	.93786
1.73	5.6407	.75133	.17728	2.7317	.43643	2.9090	.46374	.93906
1.74	5.6973	.75567	.17552	2.7609	.44105	2.9364	.46782	.94023
1.75	5.7546	.76002	.17377	2.7904	.44567	2.9642	.47191	.94138
1.76	5.8124	.76436	.17204	2.8202	.45028	2.9922	.47600	.94250
1.77	5.8709	.76870	.17033	2.8503	.45488	3.0206	.48009	.94361
1.78	5.9299	.77304	.16864	2.8806	.45948	3.0492	.48419	.94470
1.79	5.9895	.77739	.16696	2.9112	.46408	3.0782	.48830	.94576
1.80	6.0496	.78173	.16530	2.9422	.46867	3.1075	.49241	.94681
1.81	6.1104	.78607	.16365	2.9734	.47325	3.1371	.49652	.94783
1.82	6.1719	.79042	.16203	3.0049	.47783	3.1669	.50064	.94884
1.83	6.2339	.79476	.16041	3.0367	.48241	3.1972	.50476	.94983
1.84	6.2965	.79910	.15882	3.0689	.48698	3.2277	.50889	.95080
1.85	6.3598	.80344	.15724	3.1013	.49154	3.2585	.51302	.95175
1.86	6.4237	.80779	.15567	3.1340	.49610	3.2897	.51716	.95268
1.87	6.4383	.81213	.15412	3.1671	.50066	3.3212	.52130	.95359
1.88	6.5535	.81647	.15259	3.2005	.50521	3.3530	.52544	.95449
1.89	6.6194	.82082	.15107	3.2341	.50976	3.3852	.52959	.95537

EXPONENTIAL AND HYPERBOLIC FUNCTIONS AND THEIR COMMON LOGARITHMS
(continued)

x	e^x Value	e^x log^{10}	e^{-x} (value)	sinh x Value	sinh x log^{10}	cosh x Value	cosh x log^{10}	tanh x (value)
1.90	6.6859	.82516	.14957	3.2682	.51430	3.4177	.53374	.95624
1.91	6.7531	.82950	.14808	3.3025	.51884	3.4506	.53789	.95709
1.92	6.8210	.83385	.14661	3.3372	.52338	3.4838	.54205	.95792
1.93	6.8895	.83819	.14515	3.3722	.52791	3.5173	.54621	.95873
1.94	6.9588	.84253	.14370	3.4075	.53244	3.5512	.55038	.95953
1.95	7.0287	.84687	.14227	3.4432	.53696	3.5855	.55455	.96032
1.96	7.0993	.85122	.14086	3.4792	.54148	3.6201	.55872	.96109
1.97	7.1707	.85556	.13946	3.5156	.54600	3.6551	.56290	96185
1.98	7.2427	.85990	.13807	3.5923	.55051	3.6904	.56707	.96259
1.99	7.3155	.86425	.13670	3.5894	.55502	3.7261	.57126	.96331
2.00	7.3891	.86859	.13534	3.6269	.55953	3.7622	.57544	.96403
2.01	7.4633	.87293	.13399	3.6647	.56403	3.7987	.57963	.96473
2.02	7.5383	.87727	.13266	3.7028	.56853	3.8335	.58382	.96541
2.03	7.6141	.88162	.13134	3.7414	.57303	3.8727	.58802	.96609
2.04	7.6906	.88596	.13003	3.7803	.57753	3.9103	.59221	.96675
2.05	7.7679	.89030	.12873	3.8196	.58202	3.9483	.59641	.96740
2.06	7.8460	.89465	.12745	3.8593	.58650	3.9867	.60061	.96803
2.07	7.9248	.89899	.12619	3.8993	.59099	4.0255	.60482	.96865
2.08	8.0045	.90333	.12493	3.9398	.59547	4.0647	.60903	.96926
2.09	8.0849	.90768	.12369	3.9806	.59995	4.1043	.61324	.96986
2.10	8.1662	.91202	.12246	4.0219	.60443	4.1443	.61745	.97045
2.11	8.2482	.91636	.12124	4.0635	.60890	4.1847	.62167	.97103
2.12	8.3311	.92070	.12003	4.1056	.61337	4.2256	.62589	.97159
2.13	8.4149	.92505	.11884	4.1480	.61784	4.2669	.63011	.97215
2.14	8. 994	.92939	.11765	4.1909	.62231	4.3085	.63433	.97269
2.15	8.5849	.93373	.11648	4.2342	62677	4.3507	.63856	.97323
2.16	8.6711	.93808	.11533	4.2779	.63123	4.3932	.64278	.97375
2.17	8.7583	.94242	.11418	4.3221	.63569	4.4362	.64701	.97426
2.18	8.8463	.94676	.11304	4.3666	.64015	4.4797	.65125	.97477
2.19	8.9352	.95110	.11192	4.4116	.64460	4.5236	.65548	.97526
2.20	9.0250	.95545	.11080	4.4571	.64905	4.5679	.65972	.97574
2.21	9.1157	.95979	.10970	4.5030	.65350	4.6127	.66396	.97622
2.22	9.2073	.96413	.10861	4.5494	.65795	4.6580	.66820	.97668
2.23	9.2999	.96848	.10753	4.5962	.66240	4.7037	.67244	.97714
2.24	9.3933	.97282	.10646	4.6434	.66684	4.7499	.67668	.97759
2.25	9.4877	.97716	.10540	4.6912	.67128	4.7966	.68093	.97803
2.26	9.5831	.98151	.10435	4.7394	.67572	4.8437	.68518	.97846
2.27	9.6794	.98585	.10331	4.7880	.68016	4.8914	.68943	.97888
2.28	9.7767	.99019	.10228	4.8372	.68459	4.9395	.69368	.97929
7.29	9.8749	.99453	.10127	4.8868	.68903	4.9881	.69794	97970
2.30	9.9742	.99888	.10026	4.9370	.69346	5.0372	.70219	.98010
2.31	10.074	1.00322	.09926	4.9876	.69789	5.0868	.70645	.98049
2.32	10.176	1.00756	.09827	5.0387	.70232	5.1370	.71071	.98087
2.33	10.278	1.01191	.09730	5.0903	.70675	5.1876	.71497	.98124
2.34	10.381	1.01625	.09633	5.1425	.71117	5.2388	.71923	.98161
2.35	10.486	1.02059	.09537	5.1951	.71559	5.2905	.72349	.98197
2.36	10.591	1.02493	.09442	5.2483	.72002	5.3427	.72776	.98233
2.37	10.697	1.02928	.09348	5.3020	.72444	5.3954	.73203	.98267
2.38	10.805	1.03362	.09255	5.3562	.72885	5.4487	.73630	.98301
2.39	10.913	1.03796	.09163	5.4109	.73327	5.5026	.74056	.98335
2.40	11.023	1.04231	.09072	5.4662	.73769	5.5569	.74484	.98367
2.41	11.134	1.04665	.08982	5.5221	.74210	5.6119	.74911	.98400
2.42	11.246	1.05099	.08892	5.5785	.74652	5.6674	.75338	.98431
2.43	11.359	1.05534	08804	5.6354	.75093	5.7235	.75766	.98462
2.44	11.473	1.05968	.08716	5.6929	.75534	5.7801	.76194	.98492
2.45	11.588	1.06402	.08629	5.7510	.75975	5.8373	.76621	.98522
2.46	11.705	1.06836	.08543	5.8097	.76415	5.8951	.77049	.98551
2.47	11.822	1.07271	.08458	5.8689	.76856	5.9535	.77477	.98579
2.48	11.941	1.07705	.08374	5.9288	.77296	6.0125	.77906	.98607
2.49	12.061	1.08139	.08291	5.9892	.77737	6.0721	.78334	.98635
2.50	12.182	1.08574	.08208	6.0502	.78177	6.1323	.78762	.98661
2.51	12.305	1.09008	.08127	6.1118	.78617	6.1931	.79191	.98688
2.52	12.429	1.09442	.08046	6.1741	.79057	6.2545	.79619	.98714

EXPONENTIAL AND HYPERBOLIC FUNCTIONS AND THEIR COMMON LOGARITHMS
(continued)

x	e^x Value	$\log^{10}$	e^{-x} (value)	sinh x Value	$\log^{10}$	cosh x Value	$\log^{10}$	tanh x (value)
2.53	12.554	1.09877	.07966	6.2369	.79497	6.3166	.80048	.98739
2.54	12.680	1.10311	.07887	6.3004	.79937	6.3793	.80477	.98764
2.55	12.807	1.10745	.07808	6.3645	.80377	6.4426	.80906	.98788
2.56	12.936	1.11179	.07730	6.4293	.80816	6.5066	.81335	.98812
2.57	13.066	1.11614	.07654	6.4946	.81256	6.5712	.81764	.98835
2.58	13.197	1.12048	.07577	6.5607	.81695	6.6365	.82194	.98858
2.59	13.330	1.12482	.07502	6.6274	.82134	6.7024	.82623	.98881
2.60	13.464	1.12917	.07427	6.6947	.82573	6.7690	.83052	.98903
2.61	13.599	1.13351	.07353	6.7628	.83012	6.8363	.83482	.98924
2.62	13.736	1.13785	.07280	6.8315	.83451	6.9043	.83912	.98946
2.63	13.874	1.14219	.07208	6.9008	.83890	6.9729	.84341	.98966
2.64	14.013	1.14654	.07136	6.9709	.84329	7.0423	.84771	98987
2.65	14.154	1.15008	.07065	7.0417	.84768	7.1123	.85201	.99007
2.66	14.296	1.15522	.06995	7.1132	.85206	7.1831	.85631	.99026
2.67	14.440	1.15957	.06925	7.1854	.85645	7.2546	.86061	.99045
2.68	14.585	1.16391	.06856	7.2583	.86083	7.3268	.86492	.99064
2.69	14.732	1.16825	.06788	7.3319	.86522	7.3998	.86922	.99083
2.70	14.880	1.17260	.06721	7.4063	.86960	7.4735	.87352	.99101
2.71	15.029	1.17694	.06654	7.4814	.87398	7.5479	.87783	.99118
2.72	15.180	1.18128	.06587	7.5572	.87836	7.6231	.88213	.99136
2.73	15.333	1.18562	.06522	7.6338	.88274	7.6991	.89644	.99153
2.74	15.487	1.18997	.06457	7.7112	.88712	7.7758	.89074	.99170
2.75	15.643	1.19431	.06393	7.7894	.89150	7.8533	.89505	.99186
2.76	15.800	1.19865	.06329	7.8683	.89588	7.9316	.89936	.99202
2.77	15.959	1.20300	.06266	7.9480	.90026	8.0106	90367	.99218
2.78	16.119	1.20734	.06204	8.0285	.90463	8.0905	.90798	.99233
2.79	16.281	1.21168	.06142	8.1098	.90901	8.1712	.91229	.99248
2.80	16.445	1.21602	.06081	8.1919	.91339	8.2527	.91660	.99263
2.81	16.610	1.22037	.06020	8.2749	.91776	8.3351	92091	.99278
2.82	16.777	1.22471	.05961	8.3586	.92213	8.4182	.92522	.99292
2.83	16.945	1.22905	.05901	8.4432	.92651	8.5022	.92953	.99306
2.84	17.116	1.23340	.05843	8.5287	.93088	8.5871	.93385	.99320
2.85	17.288	1.23774	.05784	8.6150	.93525	8.6728	.93816	.99333
2.86	17.462	1.24208	.05727	8.7021	93963	8.7594	.94247	.99346
2.87	17.637	1.24643	.05670	8.7902	.94400	8.8469	.94679	.99359
2.88	17.814	1.25077	.05613	8.8791	.94837	8.9352	95110	.99372
2.89	17.993	1.25511	.05558	8.9689	.95274	9.0244	.95542	.99384
2.90	18.174	1.25945	.05502	9.0596	.95711	9.1146	.95974	.99396
2.91	18.357	1.26380	.05448	9.1512	.96148	9.2056	.96405	.99408
2.92	18.541	1.26814	.05393	9.2437	.96584	9.2976	.96837	.99420
2.93	18.728	1.27248	.05340	9.3371	.97021	9.3905	.97269	.99431
2.94	18.916	1.27683	.05287	9.4315	.97458	9.4844	.97701	.99443
2.95	19.106	1.28117	.05234	9.5268	.97895	9.5791	.98133	.99454
2.96	19.298	1.28551	.05182	9.6231	.98331	9.6749	.98565	.99464
2.97	19.492	1.28985	.05130	9.7203	.98768	9.7716	.98997	.99475
2.98	19.688	1.29420	.05079	9.8185	.99205	9.8693	.99429	.99485
2.99	19.886	1.29854	.05029	9.9177	.99641	9.9680	.99861	.99496
3.00	20.086	1.30288	.04979	10.018	1.00078	10.068	1.00293	0.99505
3.05	21.115	1.32460	.04736	10.534	1.02259	10.581	1.02454	0.99552
3.10	22.198	1.34631	.04505	11.076	1.04440	11.122	1.04616	0.99595
3.15	23.336	1.36803	.04285	11.647	1.06620	11.690	1.06779	0.99633
3.20	24.533	1.38974	.04076	12.246	1.08799	12.287	1.08943	0.99668
3.25	25.790	1.41146	.03877	12.876	1.10977	12.915	1.11108	0.99700
3.30	27.113	1.43317	.03688	13.538	1.13155	13.575	1.13273	0.99728
3.35	28.503	1.45489	.03508	14.234	1.15332	14.269	1.15439	0.99754
3.40	29.964	1.47660	.03337	14.965	1.17509	14.999	1.17605	0.99777
3.45	31.500	1.49832	.03175	15.734	1.19685	15.766	1.19772	0.99799
3.50	33.115	1.52003	.03020	16.543	1.21860	16.573	1.21940	0.99818
3.55	34.813	1.54175	.02872	17.392	1.24036	17.421	1.24107	0.99835
3.60	36.598	1.56346	.02732	18.286	1.26211	18.313	1.26275	0.99851
3.65	38.475	1.58517	.02599	19.224	1.28385	19.250	1.28444	9.99865
3.70	40.447	1.60689	.02472	20.211	1.30559	20.236	1.30612	0.99878
3.75	42.521	1.62860	.02352	21.249	1.32733	21.272	1.32781	0.99889

EXPONENTIAL AND HYPERBOLIC FUNCTIONS AND THEIR COMMON LOGARITHMS
(continued)

x	e^x Value	e^x $\log^{10}$	e^{-x} (value)	sinh x Value	sinh x $\log^{10}$	cosh x Value	cosh x $\log^{10}$	tanh x (value)
3.80	44.701	1.65032	.02237	22.339	1.34907	22.362	1.34951	0.99900
3.85	46.993	1.67203	.02128	23.486	1.37081	23.507	1.37120	0.99909
3.90	49.402	1.69375	.02024	24.691	1.39254	24.711	1.39290	0.99918
3.95	51.935	1.71546	.01925	25.958	1.41427	25.977	1.41459	0.09926
4.00	54.598	1.73718	.01832	27.290	1.43600	27.308	1.43629	0.99933
4.10	60.340	1.78061	.01657	30.162	1.47946	30.178	1.47970	0.99945
4.20	66.686	1.82404	.01500	33.336	1.52291	33.351	1.52310	0.99955
4.30	73.700	1.86747	.01357	36.843	1.56636	36.857	1.56652	0.99963
4.40	81.451	1.91090	.01227	40.719	1.60980	40.732	1.60993	0.99970
4.50	90.017	1.95433	.01111	45.003	1.65324	45.014	1.65335	0.99975
4.60	99.484	1.99775	.01005	49.737	1.69668	49.747	1.69677	0.99980
4.70	109.95	2.04118	.00910	54.969	1.74012	54.978	1.74019	0.99983
4.80	121.51	2.08461	.00823	60.751	1.78355	60.759	1.78361	0.99986
4.90	134.29	2.12804	.00745	67.141	1.82699	67.149	1.82704	0.99989
5.00	148.41	2.17147	.00674	74.203	1.87042	74.210	1.87046	0.99991
5.10	164.02	2.21490	.00610	82.008	1.91389	82.014	1.91389	0.99993
5.20	181.27	2.25833	.00552	90.633	1.95729	90.639	1.95731	0.99994
5.30	200.34	2.30176	.00499	100.17	2.00074	100.17	2.00074	0.99995
5.40	221.41	2.34519	.00452	110.70	2.04415	110.71	2.04417	0.99996
5.50	244.69	2.38862	.00409	122.34	2.08758	122.35	2.08760	0.99997
5.60	270.43	2.43205	.00370	135.21	2.13101	135.22	2.13103	0.99997
5.70	298.87	2.47548	.00335	149.43	2.17444	149.44	2.17445	0.99998
5.80	330.30	2.51891	.00303	165.15	2.21787	165.15	2.21788	0.99998
5.90	365.04	2.56234	.00274	182.52	2.26130	182.52	2.26131	0.99998
6.00	403.43	2.60577	.00248	201.71	2.30473	201.72	2.30474	0.99999
6.25	518.01	2.71434	.00193	259.01	2.41331	259.01	2.41331	0.99999
6.50	665.14	2.82291	.00150	332.57	2.52188	332.57	2.52189	1.00000
6.75	854.06	2.93149	.00117	427.03	2.63046	427.03	2.63046	1.00000
7.00	1096.6	3.04006	.00091	548.32	2.73904	548.32	2.73903	1.00000
7.50	1808.0	3.25721	.00055	904.02	2.95618	904.02	2.95618	1.00000
8.00	2981.0	3.47436	.00034	1490.5	3.17333	1490.5	3.17333	1.00000
8.50	4914.8	3.69150	.00020	2457.4	3.39047	2457.4	3.39047	1.00000
9.00	8103.1	3.90865	.00012	4051.5	3.60762	4051.5	3.60762	1.00000
9.50	13360.	4.12580	.00007	6679.9	3.82477	6679.9	3.82477	1.00000
10.00	22026.	4.34294	.00005	11013.	4.04191	11013.	4.04191	1.00000

INVERSE HYPERBOLIC FUNCTIONS

Definitions

If $x = \sinh y$, then $y = \sinh^{-1} x$.   Other inverse functions are denned similarly.

Domain and Range

Function	Domain	Range	Remarks
$\sinh^{-1} x$	$(-\infty, +\infty)$	$(-\infty, +\infty)$	odd function
$\cosh^{-1} x$	$[1, +\infty)$	$(-\infty, +\infty)$	even function double valued
$\tanh^{-1} x$	$(-1, 1)$	$(-\infty, +\infty)$	odd function
$\operatorname{cosech}^{-1} x$	$(-\infty, 0), (0, \infty)$	$(0, -\infty), (\infty, 0)$	odd function two branches, pole at $x = 0$
$\operatorname{sech}^{-1} x$	$(0, 1]$	$(-\infty, +\infty)$	double valued
$\coth^{-1} x$	$(-\infty, -1), (1, \infty)$	$(0, -\infty), (\infty, 0)$	odd function two branches

Graph of the Inverse Functions

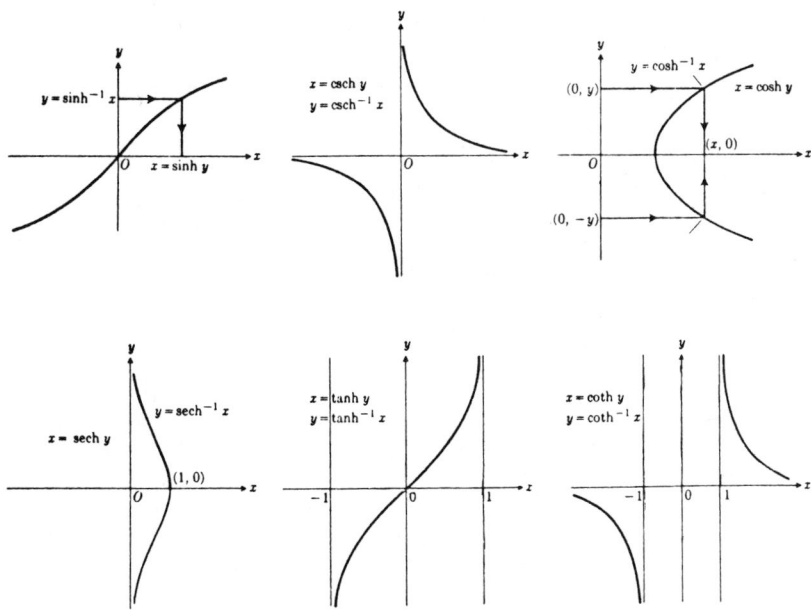

Inverse Hyperbolic Functions In Terms of One Another

Function	$\sinh^{-1} x$	$\cosh^{-1} x$ $+$ if $x > 0$ $-$ if $x < 0$	$\tanh^{-1} x$
$\sinh^{-1} x =$	$\sinh^{-1} x$	$\pm \cosh^{-1} \sqrt{x^2 + 1}$	$\tanh^{-1} \dfrac{x}{\sqrt{1 + x^2}}$
$\cosh^{-1} x =$	$\pm \sinh^{-1} \sqrt{x^2 - 1}$	$\cosh^{-1} x$	$\pm \tanh^{-1} \dfrac{\sqrt{x^2 - 1}}{x}$
$\tanh^{-1} x =$	$\sinh^{-1} \dfrac{x}{\sqrt{1 - x^2}}$	$\pm \cosh^{-1} \dfrac{1}{\sqrt{1 - x^2}}$	$\tanh^{-1} x$
$\operatorname{cosech}^{-1} x =$	$\sinh^{-1} \dfrac{1}{x}$	$\pm \cosh^{-1} \dfrac{\sqrt{x^2 + 1}}{x}$	$\tanh^{-1} \dfrac{1}{\sqrt{1 + x^2}}$
$\operatorname{sech}^{-1} x =$	$\pm \sinh^{-1} \dfrac{\sqrt{1 - x^2}}{x}$	$\cosh^{-1} \dfrac{1}{x}$	$\pm \tanh^{-1} \sqrt{1 - x^2}$
$\coth^{-1} x =$	$\sinh^{-1} \dfrac{1}{\sqrt{x^2 - 1}}$	$\pm \cosh^{-1} \dfrac{x}{\sqrt{x^2 - 1}}$	$\tanh^{-1} \dfrac{1}{x}$

Function	$\operatorname{cosech}^{-1} x$	$\operatorname{sech}^{-1} x$ $+$ if $x > 0$ $-$ if $x < 0$	$\coth^{-1} x$
$\sinh^{-1} x =$	$\operatorname{cosech}^{-1} \dfrac{1}{x}$	$\pm \operatorname{sech}^{-1} \dfrac{1}{\sqrt{1 + x^2}}$	$\coth^{-1} \dfrac{\sqrt{1 + x^2}}{x}$
$\cosh^{-1} x =$	$\pm \operatorname{cosech}^{-1} \dfrac{1}{\sqrt{x^2 - 1}}$	$\operatorname{sech}^{-1} \dfrac{1}{x}$	$\pm \coth^{-1} \dfrac{x}{\sqrt{x^2 - 1}}$
$\tanh^{-1} x =$	$\operatorname{cosech}^{-1} \dfrac{\sqrt{1 - x^2}}{x}$	$\pm \operatorname{sech}^{-1} \sqrt{1 - x^2}$	$\coth^{-1} \dfrac{1}{x}$
$\operatorname{cosech}^{-1} x =$	$\operatorname{cosech}^{-1} x$	$\pm \operatorname{sech}^{-1} \dfrac{x}{\sqrt{x^2 + 1}}$	$\coth^{-1} \sqrt{1 + x^2}$
$\operatorname{sech}^{-1} x =$	$\pm \operatorname{cosech}^{-1} \dfrac{x}{\sqrt{1 - x^2}}$	$\operatorname{sech}^{-1} x$	$\pm \coth^{-1} \dfrac{1}{\sqrt{1 - x^2}}$
$\coth^{-1} x =$	$\operatorname{cosech}^{-1} \sqrt{x^2 - 1}$	$\operatorname{sech}^{-1} \dfrac{\sqrt{x^2 - 1}}{x}$	$\coth^{-1} x$

Fundamental Identities

Relations with Logarithmic Functions

$$\sinh^{-1} x = \log_e (x + \sqrt{x^2 + 1})$$

$$\cosh^{-1} x = \log_e (x \pm \sqrt{x^2 - 1}), \quad x \geq 1. \quad \text{The plus sign is used for the principal value.}$$

$$\tanh^{-1} x = \tfrac{1}{2} \log_e \left(\frac{1 + x}{1 - x}\right), \quad x^2 < 1$$

$$\operatorname{csch}^{-1} x = \log_e \left(\frac{1 \pm \sqrt{1 + x^2}}{x}\right). \quad \text{The plus sign is used if } x > 0, \text{ the minus sign if } x < 0.$$

$$\operatorname{sech}^{-1} x = \log_e \left(\frac{1 \pm \sqrt{1 - x^2}}{x}\right), \quad 0 < x \leq 1. \quad \text{The plus sign is used for the principal values.}$$

$$\coth^{-1} x = \tfrac{1}{2} \log_e \left(\frac{x + 1}{x - 1}\right), \quad x^2 > 1$$

Relations with Circular Functions

$$\sinh^{-1} x = -i \sin^{-1} (ix) \qquad \sinh^{-1} (ix) = i \sin^{-1} x$$
$$\cosh^{-1} x = \pm i \cos^{-1} x \qquad \cosh^{-1} (ix) = \pm i \cos^{-1} (ix)$$
$$\tanh^{-1} x = -i \tan^{-1} (ix) \qquad \tanh^{-1} (ix) = i \tan^{-1} x$$
$$\operatorname{cosech}^{-1} x = i \operatorname{cosec}^{-1} (ix) \qquad \operatorname{cosech}^{-1} (ix) = -i \operatorname{cosec}^{-1} x$$
$$\operatorname{sech}^{-1} x = \pm i \sec^{-1} x \qquad \operatorname{sech}^{-1} (ix) = \pm i \sec^{-1} (ix)$$
$$\coth^{-1} x = i \coth^{-1} (ix) \qquad \coth^{-1} (ix) = -i \cot^{-1} (x)$$

Function Sum and Function Difference Relations

$$\sinh^{-1} x + \sinh^{-1} y = \sinh^{-1} (x \sqrt{1 + y^2} + y \sqrt{1 + x^2})$$
$$\sinh^{-1} x - \sinh^{-1} y = \sinh^{-1} (x \sqrt{1 + y^2} - y \sqrt{1 + x^2})$$
$$\cosh^{-1} x + \cosh^{-1} y = \cosh^{-1} (xy + \sqrt{(x^2 - 1)(y^2 - 1)})$$
$$\cosh^{-1} x - \cosh^{-1} y = \cosh^{-1} (xy - \sqrt{(x^2 - 1)(y^2 - 1)})$$
$$\tanh^{-1} x + \tanh^{-1} y = \tanh^{-1} \left(\frac{x + y}{1 + xy}\right)$$
$$\tanh^{-1} x - \tanh^{-1} y = \tanh^{-1} \left(\frac{x - y}{1 - xy}\right)$$
$$\sinh^{-1} x + \cosh^{-1} y = \sinh^{-1} (xy + \sqrt{(1 + x^2)(y^2 - 1)})$$
$$= \cosh^{-1} (y \sqrt{1 + x^2} + x \sqrt{y^2 - 1})$$
$$\sinh^{-1} x - \cosh^{-1} y = \sinh^{-1} (xy - \sqrt{(1 + x^2)(y^2 - 1)})$$
$$= \cosh^{-1} (y \sqrt{1 + x^2} - x \sqrt{y^2 - 1})$$
$$\tanh^{-1} x + \coth^{-1} y = \tanh^{-1} \left(\frac{xy + 1}{y + x}\right)$$
$$= \coth^{-1} \left(\frac{y + x}{xy + 1}\right)$$
$$\tanh^{-1} x - \coth^{-1} y = \tanh^{-1} \left(\frac{xy - 1}{y - x}\right)$$
$$= \coth^{-1} \left(\frac{y - x}{xy - 1}\right)$$

Series Expansions

$$\sinh^{-1} x = x - \frac{1}{2 \cdot 3} x^3 + \frac{1 \cdot 3}{2 \cdot 4 \cdot 5} x^5 - \frac{1 \cdot 3 \cdot 5}{2 \cdot 4 \cdot 6 \cdot 7} x^7 + \cdots$$

$$+ (-1)^n \cdot \frac{1 \cdot 3 \cdot 5 \ldots (2n-1)}{2 \cdot 4 \cdot 6 \ldots 2n(2n+1)} x^{2n+1} \pm \cdots \qquad |x| < 1$$

$$\sinh^{-1} x = \ln (2x) + \frac{1}{2} \cdot \frac{1}{2x^2} - \frac{1 \cdot 3}{2 \cdot 4} \cdot \frac{1}{4x^4} + \frac{1 \cdot 3 \cdot 5}{2 \cdot 4 \cdot 6} \cdot \frac{1}{6x^6} - \cdots$$

$$= \ln (2x) + \sum_{n=1}^{\infty} (-1)^{n+1} \frac{(2n)! x^{-2n}}{2^{2n}(n!)^2 2n}, \qquad |x| > 1$$

$$\cosh^{-1} x = \pm \left[\ln (2x) - \frac{1}{2 \cdot 2x^2} - \frac{1 \cdot 3}{2 \cdot 4 \cdot 4x^4} - \frac{1 \cdot 3 \cdot 5}{2 \cdot 4 \cdot 6 \cdot 6x^6} - \cdots \right] \qquad x > 1$$

$$\operatorname{cosech}^{-1} x = \frac{1}{x} - \frac{1}{2} \cdot \frac{1}{3x^3} + \frac{1 \cdot 3}{2 \cdot 4} \cdot \frac{1}{5x^5} - \frac{1 \cdot 3 \cdot 5}{2 \cdot 4 \cdot 6} \cdot \frac{1}{7x^7} + - \cdots$$

$$= \sum_{n=0}^{\infty} (-1)^n \frac{(2n)! x^{-2n-1}}{2^{2n}(n!)^2(2n+1)}, \qquad |x| > 1$$

$$\operatorname{cosech}^{-1} x = \ln \frac{2}{x} + \frac{1}{2} \cdot \frac{x^2}{2} - \frac{1 \cdot 3}{2 \cdot 4} \cdot \frac{x^4}{4} + \frac{1 \cdot 3 \cdot 5}{2 \cdot 4 \cdot 6} \cdot \frac{x^6}{6} - + \cdots$$

$$= \ln \frac{2}{x} + \sum_{n=1}^{\infty} \frac{(-1)^{n+1}(2n)! x^{2n}}{2^{2n}(n!)^2 2n}, \qquad 0 < x < 1$$

$$\operatorname{sech}^{-1} x = \ln \frac{2}{x} - \frac{1}{2} \frac{x^2}{2} - \frac{1 \cdot 3}{2 \cdot 4} \cdot \frac{x^4}{4} - \frac{1 \cdot 3 \cdot 5}{2 \cdot 4 \cdot 6} \cdot \frac{x^6}{6} - - \cdots$$

$$= \ln \frac{2}{x} - \sum_{n=1}^{\infty} \frac{(2n)! x^{2n}}{2^{2n}(n!)^2 2n}, \qquad 0 < x < 1$$

$$* \ \tanh^{-1} x = x + \frac{x^3}{3} + \frac{x^5}{5} + \frac{x^7}{7} + \cdots + \frac{x^{2n+1}}{2n+1} + \cdots \qquad |x| < 1$$

$$* \ \coth^{-1} x = \frac{1}{x} + \frac{1}{3x^3} + \frac{1}{5x^5} + \frac{1}{7x^7} + \cdots + \frac{1}{(2n+1)x^{2n+1}} + \cdots \qquad |x| > 1$$

GUDERMANNIAN FUNCTION

This function is useful because it relates circular and hyperbolic functions without the use of functions of imaginary argument.

Definition

$$\gamma = \text{the gudermannian of } x, \text{ written as gd } x$$

$$= 2 \tan^{-1} e^x - \frac{\pi}{2}$$

$$x = \text{gd}^{-1} \gamma$$

$$= \ln \tan \left(\frac{\pi}{4} + \frac{\gamma}{2} \right)$$

$$= \ln (\sec \gamma + \tan \gamma)$$

* Can also be written as arg tanh x and arg coth x respectively.

Special Values of Gudermannian Function

x	0	∞	$-\infty$
gd x	0	$\frac{1}{2}\pi$	$-\frac{1}{2}\pi$

Relations with Hyperbolic and Circular Functions

$$\sinh x = \tan (\text{gd } x) \qquad \text{cosech } x = \cot (\text{gd } x)$$
$$\cosh x = \sec (\text{gd } x) \qquad \text{sech } (x) = \cos (\text{gd } x)$$
$$\tanh x = \sin (\text{gd } x) \qquad \coth (x) = \text{cosec } (\text{gd } x)$$

Derivatives

$$\frac{d}{dx} (\text{gd } x) = \text{sech } x$$

$$\frac{d}{dx} (\text{gd}^{-1} \gamma) = \sec \gamma$$

Fundamental Identities

$$\tanh (\tfrac{1}{2}x) = \tan (\tfrac{1}{2}\text{gd } x)$$
$$e^x = \cosh x + \sinh x = \sec (\text{gd } x) + \tan (\text{gd } x)$$
$$= \tan \left(\frac{\pi}{4} + \frac{1}{2} \text{gd } x \right) = \frac{1 + \sin (\text{gd } x)}{\cos (\text{gd } x)} = \frac{1 + \tan (\tfrac{1}{2}\text{gd } x)}{1 - \tan (\tfrac{1}{2}\text{gd } x)}$$
$$\text{gd } x = 2 \tan^{-1} \left(\tanh \frac{1}{2} x \right) = \int_0^x \frac{dt}{\cosh t}$$
$$\text{gd}^{-1} \gamma = \int_0^\gamma \frac{dt}{\cos t}$$
$$i \, \text{gd}^{-1} \gamma = \text{gd } i\gamma, \text{ where } i = \sqrt{-1}.$$

If

$$\alpha + i\beta = \text{gd}(x + iy)$$

then

$$\tan \alpha = \frac{\sinh x}{\cos y} \qquad \tanh \beta = \frac{\sin y}{\cosh x}$$

$$\tanh x = \frac{\sin \alpha}{\cosh \beta} \qquad \tan y = \frac{\sinh \beta}{\cosh \alpha}$$

Series Expansions

$$\text{gd } x = x - \frac{1}{6} x^3 + \frac{1}{24} x^5 - \frac{61}{5040} x^7 + - \cdots$$

$$= \sum_{n=0}^{\infty} \frac{E_{2n}}{(2n + 1)!} x^{2n+1}, \quad |x| < 1 \; *$$

$$\text{gd } x = \frac{\pi}{2} - \text{sech } x - \frac{1}{2} \frac{\text{sech}^3 x}{3} - \frac{1 \cdot 3}{2 \cdot 4} \frac{\text{sech}^5 x}{5} + - \cdots$$

$$= \frac{\pi}{2} - \sum_{n=0}^{\infty} \frac{(2n)!}{2^{2n}(n!)^2} \frac{\text{sech}^{2n+1} x}{(2n + 1)} \quad x \text{ large}$$

*E_n denotes Euler numbers.

$$\text{gd } x = \frac{2}{1} \tanh \frac{x}{2} - \frac{2}{3} \tanh^3 \frac{x}{2} + \frac{2}{5} \tanh^5 \frac{x}{2} - \frac{2}{7} \tanh^7 \frac{x}{2} + - \cdots$$

$$= 2 \sum_{n=0}^{\infty} \frac{(-1)^n}{2n+1} \tanh^{2n+1} \frac{x}{2}$$

$$\text{gd}^{-1} \gamma = \gamma + \frac{1}{6} \gamma^3 + \frac{1}{24} \gamma^5 + \frac{61}{5040} \gamma^7 + \cdots$$

$$= \sum_{n=0}^{\infty} \frac{(-1)^n E_{2n} \gamma^{2n+1}}{(2n+1)!}, \qquad |\gamma| < \frac{\pi}{2} \quad *$$

$$\text{gd}^{-1} \gamma = \frac{2}{1} \tan \frac{\gamma}{2} + \frac{2}{3} \tan^3 \frac{\gamma}{2} + \frac{2}{5} \tan^5 \frac{\gamma}{2} + \cdots$$

$$= 2 \sum_{n=0}^{\infty} \frac{1}{2n+1} \tan^{2n+1} \frac{\gamma}{2}$$

*E_n are Euler's numbers.

References

1. For extensive tables of inverse hyperbolic functions: Tables of Inverse Hyperbolic Functions, Harvard University Computation Laboratory (Cambridge, Harvard University Press, 1949).
2. For tables of hyperbolic functions with complex argument: Tables of Complex Hyperbolic and Circular Functions, A. E. Kennelly (Cambridge, Harvard University Press, 1914).

INVERSE HYPERBOLIC FUNCTIONS

x	$\sinh^{-1} x$	$\tanh^{-1} x$	$\operatorname{cosech}^{-1} x$	$\operatorname{sech}^{-1} x$
0.0	0.00000	0.00000	∞	∞
0.01	0.01000	0.01000	5.29834	5.29829
0.02	0.02000	0.02000	4.60527	4.60507
0.03	0.03000	0.03001	4.19993	4.19948
0.04	0.03999	0.04002	3.91242	3.91162
0.05	0.04998	0.05004	3.68950	3.68825
0.06	0.05996	0.06007	3.50746	3.50566
0.07	0.06994	0.07011	3.35363	3.35118
0.08	0.07991	0.08017	3.22047	3.21727
0.09	0.08988	0.09024	3.10311	3.09906
0.10	0.09983	0.10034	2.99822	2.99322
0.11	0.10978	0.11045	2.90343	2.89738
0.12	0.11971	0.12058	2.81699	2.80979
0.13	0.12964	0.13074	2.73757	2.72912
0.14	0.13955	0.14093	2.66412	2.65432
0.15	0.14944	0.15114	2.59585	2.58459
0.16	0.15933	0.16139	2.53207	2.51927
0.17	0.16919	0.17167	2.47225	2.45780
0.18	0.17904	0.18198	2.41595	2.39975
0.19	0.18888	0.19234	2.36278	2.34473
0.20	0.19869	0.20273	2.31244	2.29243
0.21	0.20849	0.21317	2.26464	2.24258
0.22	0.21826	0.22366	2.21916	2.19495
0.23	0.22802	0.23419	2.17579	2.14933
0.24	0.23775	0.24477	2.13436	2.10554
0.25	0.24747	0.25541	2.09471	2.06344
0.26	0.25716	0.26611	2.05671	2.02288
0.27	0.26682	0.27686	2.02023	1.98374
0.28	0.27646	0.28768	1.98516	1.94591
0.29	0.28608	0.29857	1.95141	1.90930
0.30	0.29567	0.30952	1.91890	1.87382
0.31	0.30524	0.32055	1.88753	1.83939
0.32	0.31478	0.33165	1.85725	1.80594
0.33	0.32429	0.34283	1.82799	1.77340
0.34	0.33377	0.35409	1.79968	1.74172
0.35	0.34322	0.36544	1.77228	1.71083
0.36	0.35265	0.37689	1.74573	1.68070
0.37	0.36204	0.38842	1.71999	1.65127
0.38	0.37140	0.40006	1.69502	1.62250
0.39	0.38073	0.41180	1.67078	1.59436
0.40	0.39004	0.42365	1.64723	1.56680
0.41	0.39930	0.43561	1.62434	1.53979
0.42	0.40854	0.44769	1.60209	1.51331
0.43	0.41774	0.45990	1.58043	1.48731
0.44	0.42691	0.47223	1.55935	1.46178
0.45	0.43605	0.48470	1.53882	1.43669
0.46	0.44515	0.49731	1.51881	1.41200
0.47	0.45422	0.51007	1.49931	1.38771
0.48	0.46325	0.52298	1.48029	1.36379
0.49	0.47225	0.53606	1.46174	1.34021
0.50	0.48121	0.54931	1.44364	1.31696

INVERSE HYPERBOLIC FUNCTIONS (Continued)

x	$\sinh^{-1} x$	$\tanh^{-1} x$	$\operatorname{cosech}^{-1} x$	$\operatorname{sech}^{-1} x$
0.50	0.48121	0.54931	1.44364	1.31696
0.51	0.49014	0.56273	1.42596	1.29401
0.52	0.49903	0.57634	1.40870	1.27136
0.53	0.50788	0.59015	1.39183	1.24898
0.54	0.51670	0.60416	1.37535	1.22686
0.55	0.52548	0.61838	1.35924	1.20497
0.56	0.53422	0.63283	1.34348	1.18331
0.57	0.54293	0.64752	1.32807	1.16186
0.58	0.55160	0.66246	1.31299	1.14060
0.59	0.56023	0.67767	1.29824	1.11952
0.60	0.56882	0.69315	1.28380	1.09861
0.61	0.57738	0.70892	1.26965	1.07785
0.62	0.58590	0.72501	1.25580	1.05723
0.63	0.59438	0.74142	1.24223	1.03673
0.64	0.60282	0.75817	1.22894	1.01635
0.65	0.61122	0.77530	1.21591	0.99606
0.66	0.61959	0.79281	1.20314	0.97585
0.67	0.62792	0.81074	1.19062	0.95572
0.68	0.63620	0.82911	1.17834	0.93564
0.69	0.64446	0.84796	1.16629	0.91560
0.70	0.65267	0.86730	1.15448	0.89559
0.71	0.66084	0.88718	1.14288	0.87559
0.72	0.66897	0.90764	1.13151	0.85558
0.73	0.67707	0.92873	1.12034	0.83555
0.74	0.68513	0.95048	1.10938	0.81549
0.75	0.69315	0.97296	1.09861	0.79537
0.76	0.70113	0.99622	1.08804	0.77517
0.77	0.70907	1.02033	1.07766	0.75487
0.78	0.71697	1.04537	1.06746	0.73445
0.79	0.72484	1.07143	1.05744	0.71388
0.80	0.73267	1.09861	1.04759	0.69315
0.81	0.74046	1.12703	1.03792	0.67221
0.82	0.74821	1.15682	1.02840	0.65103
0.83	0.75592	1.18814	1.01905	0.62958
0.84	0.76360	1.22117	1.00986	0.60781
0.85	0.77124	1.25615	1.00082	0.58568
0.86	0.77884	1.29334	0.99193	0.56313
0.87	0.78640	1.33308	0.98319	0.54008
0.88	0.79393	1.37577	0.97459	0.51647
0.89	0.80142	1.42193	0.96613	0.49220
0.90	0.80887	1.47222	0.95780	0.46715
0.91	0.81628	1.52752	0.94961	0.44116
0.92	0.82366	1.58903	0.94154	0.41406
0.93	0.83100	1.65839	0.93361	0.38560
0.94	0.83830	1.73805	0.92580	0.35542
0.95	0.84557	1.83178	0.91810	0.32304
0.96	0.85280	1.94591	0.91053	0.28768
0.97	0.86000	2.09230	0.90307	0.24807
0.98	0.86716	2.29756	0.89573	0.20169
0.99	0.87428	2.64665	0.88850	0.14201
1.00	0.88137	∞	0.88137	0.00000

INVERSE HYPERBOLIC FUNCTIONS (Continued)

x	$\sinh^{-1} x$	$\cosh^{-1} x$	$\operatorname{cosech}^{-1} x$	$\coth^{-1} x$
1.00	0.88137	0.00000	0.88137	∞
1.01	0.88843	0.14130	0.87436	2.65165
1.02	0.89545	0.19967	0.86744	2.30756
1.03	0.90243	0.24434	0.86063	2.10730
1.04	0.90938	0.28191	0.85391	1.96591
1.05	0.91629	0.31492	0.84730	1.85679
1.06	0.92317	0.34470	0.84078	1.76806
1.07	0.93002	0.37202	0.83435	1.69340
1.08	0.93683	0.39738	0.82801	1.62905
1.09	0.94360	0.42114	0.82177	1.57255
1.10	0.95035	0.44357	0.81561	1.52226
1.11	0.95706	0.46485	0.80954	1.47698
1.12	0.96373	0.48513	0.80355	1.43584
1.13	0.97038	0.50453	0.79764	1.39817
1.14	0.97699	0.52316	0.79182	1.36346
1.15	0.98357	0.54110	0.78607	1.33129
1.16	0.99011	0.55840	0.78041	1.30134
1.17	0.99663	0.57514	0.77482	1.27334
1.18	1.00311	0.59135	0.76930	1.24706
1.19	1.00956	0.60708	0.76386	1.22232
1.20	1.01597	0.62236	0.75849	1.19895
1.21	1.02236	0.63724	0.75319	1.17682
1.22	1.02871	0.65173	0.74796	1.15582
1.23	1.03504	0.66586	0.74279	1.13584
1.24	1.04133	0.67966	0.73770	1.11680
1.25	1.04759	0.69315	0.73267	1.09861
1.26	1.05382	0.70634	0.72770	1.08122
1.27	1.06003	0.71924	0.72280	1.06456
1.28	1.06620	0.73189	0.71796	1.04857
1.29	1.07234	0.74428	0.71318	1.03321
1.30	1.07845	0.75643	0.70846	1.01844
1.31	1.08453	0.76836	0.70380	1.00422
1.32	1.09059	0.78007	0.69920	0.99050
1.33	1.09661	0.79157	0.69465	0.97727
1.34	1.10261	0.80288	0.69016	0.96448
1.35	1.10857	0.81400	0.68572	0.95212
1.36	1.11451	0.82494	0.68134	0.94016
1.37	1.12042	0.83570	0.67701	0.92857
1.38	1.12630	0.84630	0.67273	0.91734
1.39	1.13216	0.85673	0.66851	0.90645
1.40	1.13798	0.86701	0.66433	0.89588
1.41	1.14378	0.87715	0.66020	0.88561
1.42	1.14955	0.88714	0.65612	0.87563
1.43	1.15530	0.89699	0.65209	0.86593
1.44	1.16101	0.90670	0.64811	0.85649
1.45	1.16670	0.91629	0.64417	0.84730
1.46	1.17237	0.92575	0.64028	0.83835
1.47	1.17801	0.93509	0.63643	0.82962
1.48	1.18362	0.94432	0.63263	0.82111
1.49	1.18920	0.95343	0.62886	0.81282
1.50	1.19476	0.96242	0.62515	0.80472

INVERSE HYPERBOLIC FUNCTIONS (Continued)

x	$\sinh^{-1} x$	$\cosh^{-1} x$	$\operatorname{cosech}^{-1} x$	$\coth^{-1} x$
1.50	1.19476	0.96242	0.62515	0.80472
1.51	1.20030	0.97131	0.62147	0.79681
1.52	1.20581	0.98010	0.61783	0.78909
1.53	1.21129	0.98879	0.61424	0.78155
1.54	1.21675	0.99737	0.61068	0.77418
1.55	1.22218	1.00587	0.60716	0.76697
1.56	1.22759	1.01426	0.60368	0.75991
1.57	1.23298	1.02257	0.60024	0.75301
1.58	1.23834	1.03079	0.59684	0.74626
1.59	1.24367	1.03892	0.59347	0.73965
1.60	1.24898	1.04697	0.59014	0.73317
1.61	1.25427	1.05493	0.58685	0.72682
1.62	1.25954	1.06282	0.58359	0.72061
1.63	1.26478	1.07063	0.58036	0.71451
1.64	1.26999	1.07836	0.57717	0.70853
1.65	1.27519	1.08601	0.57401	0.70267
1.66	1.28036	1.09360	0.57089	0.69692
1.67	1.28551	1.10111	0.56780	0.69128
1.68	1.29064	1.10855	0.56474	0.68574
1.69	1.29574	1.11592	0.56171	0.68030
1.70	1.30082	1.12323	0.55871	0.67496
1.71	1.30588	1.13047	0.55574	0.66972
1.72	1.31092	1.13765	0.55281	0.66457
1.73	1.31593	1.14476	0.54990	0.65951
1.74	1.32093	1.15182	0.54702	0.65453
1.75	1.32590	1.15881	0.54417	0.64964
1.76	1.33085	1.16574	0.54135	0.64483
1.77	1.33578	1.17262	0.53856	0.64011
1.78	1.34069	1.17944	0.53579	0.63546
1.79	1.34557	1.18620	0.53305	0.63088
1.80	1.35044	1.19291	0.53034	0.62638
1.81	1.35529	1.19957	0.52766	0.62195
1.82	1.36011	1.20617	0.52500	0.61759
1.83	1.36492	1.21272	0.52237	0.61330
1.84	1.36970	1.21922	0.51976	0.60908
1.85	1.37447	1.22567	0.51718	0.60492
1.86	1.37921	1.23207	0.51462	0.60082
1.87	1.38394	1.23842	0.51208	0.59679
1.88	1.38864	1.24473	0.50957	0.59281
1.89	1.39333	1.25098	0.50709	0.58890
1.90	1.39800	1.25720	0.50462	0.58504
1.91	1.40265	1.26336	0.50218	0.58123
1.92	1.40728	1.26949	0.49977	0.57748
1.93	1.41188	1.27557	0.49737	0.57379
1.94	1.41648	1.28160	0.49500	0.57014
1.95	1.42105	1.28760	0.49265	0.56655
1.96	1.42560	1.29355	0.49032	0.56301
1.97	1.43014	1.29946	0.48801	0.55951
1.98	1.43466	1.30533	0.48572	0.55606
1.99	1.43915	1.31117	0.48346	0.55266
2.00	1.44364	1.31696	0.48121	0.54931

INVERSE HYPERBOLIC FUNCTIONS (Continued)

x	$\sinh^{-1} x$	$\cosh^{-1} x$	$\operatorname{cosech}^{-1} x$	$\coth^{-1} x$
2.00	1.44364	1.31696	0.48121	0.54931
2.10	1.48748	1.37286	0.45982	0.51805
2.20	1.52966	1.42542	0.44019	0.49041
2.30	1.57028	1.47504	0.42213	0.46578
2.40	1.60944	1.52208	0.40547	0.44365
2.50	1.64723	1.56680	0.39004	0.42365
2.60	1.68374	1.60944	0.37571	0.40547
2.70	1.71905	1.65019	0.36239	0.38885
2.80	1.75323	1.68924	0.34996	0.37361
2.90	1.78634	1.72671	0.33834	0.35956
3.00	1.81845	1.76275	0.32745	0.34657
3.10	1.84960	1.79746	0.31723	0.33452
3.20	1.87986	1.83094	0.30763	0.32331
3.30	1.90927	1.86328	0.29857	0.31285
3.40	1.93788	1.89456	0.29003	0.30307
3.50	1.96572	1.92485	0.28196	0.29389
3.60	1.99284	1.95421	0.27432	0.28527
3.70	2.01926	1.98270	0.26708	0.27716
3.80	2.04503	2.01037	0.26021	0.26950
3.90	2.07017	2.03727	0.25368	0.26226
4.00	2.09471	2.06344	0.24747	0.25541
4.10	2.11869	2.08892	0.24155	0.24892
4.20	2.14211	2.11375	0.23590	0.24275
4.30	2.16502	2.13796	0.23051	0.23689
4.40	2.18742	2.16158	0.22536	0.23131
4.50	2.20935	2.18464	0.22043	0.22599
4.60	2.23081	2.20717	0.21571	0.22092
4.70	2.25184	2.22920	0.21119	0.21607
4.80	2.27244	2.25073	0.20685	0.21143
4.90	2.29264	2.27180	0.20269	0.20699
5.00	2.31244	2.29243	0.19869	0.20273
5.10	2.33186	2.31263	0.19484	0.19865
5.20	2.35093	2.33243	0.19114	0.19473
5.30	2.36964	2.35183	0.18758	0.19097
5.40	2.38801	2.37086	0.18414	0.18735
5.50	2.40606	2.38953	0.18083	0.18386
5.60	2.42379	2.40784	0.17764	0.18051
5.70	2.44122	2.42583	0.17455	0.17727
5.80	2.45836	2.44349	0.17157	0.17415
5.90	2.47521	2.46084	0.16869	0.17114
6.00	2.49178	2.47789	0.16590	0.16824
6.10	2.50809	2.49465	0.16321	0.16543
6.20	2.52414	2.51113	0.16060	0.16271
6.30	2.53994	2.52734	0.15807	0.16008
6.40	2.55549	2.54329	0.15562	0.15754
6.50	2.57081	2.55898	0.15325	0.15508
6.60	2.58591	2.57443	0.15094	0.15269
6.70	2.60078	2.58964	0.14871	0.15038
6.80	2.61543	2.60462	0.14653	0.14813
6.90	2.62988	2.61938	0.14442	0.14596
7.00	2.64412	2.63392	0.14238	0.14384

GUDERMANNIAN FUNCTION

x	0	1	2	3	4	5	6	7	8	9
0.0	0.00000	0.01000	0.02000	0.03000	0.03999	0.04998	0.05996	0.06994	0.07991	0.08988
0.1	0.09983	0.10978	0.11971	0.12964	0.13954	0.14944	0.15932	0.16919	0.17904	0.18887
0.2	0.19868	0.20847	0.21825	0.22800	0.23773	0.24744	0.25712	0.26678	0.27641	0.28602
0.3	0.29560	0.30515	0.31467	0.32417	0.33363	0.34307	0.35247	0.36184	0.37117	0.38047
0.4	0.38974	0.39897	0.40817	0.41733	0.42645	0.43554	0.44459	0.45359	0.46256	0.47149
0.5	0.48038	0.48923	0.49803	0.50680	0.51552	0.52420	0.53284	0.54143	0.54997	0.55848
0.6	0.56694	0.57535	0.58372	0.59204	0.60031	0.60854	0.61672	0.62486	0.63294	0.64098
0.7	0.64897	0.65692	0.66481	0.67266	0.68045	0.68820	0.69590	0.70355	0.71115	0.71870
0.8	0.72620	0.73366	0.74106	0.74841	0.75571	0.76297	0.77017	0.77732	0.78443	0.79148
0.9	0.79848	0.80544	0.81234	0.81919	0.82599	0.83275	0.83945	0.84611	0.85271	0.85926
1.0	0.86577	0.87223	0.87863	0.88499	0.89130	0.89756	0.90377	0.90993	0.91604	0.92211
1.1	0.92813	0.93410	0.94002	0.94589	0.95172	0.95750	0.96323	0.96892	0.97455	0.98015
1.2	0.98569	0.99119	0.99665	1.00205	1.00742	1.01274	1.01801	1.02324	1.02842	1.03356
1.3	1.03866	1.04371	1.04872	1.05368	1.05860	1.06348	1.06832	1.07312	1.07787	1.08258
1.4	1.08725	1.09188	1.09647	1.10101	1.10552	1.10999	1.11441	1.11880	1.12315	1.12746
1.5	1.13173	1.13596	1.14015	1.14431	1.14843	1.15251	1.15655	1.16056	1.16453	1.16846
1.6	1.17236	1.17622	1.18005	1.18384	1.18760	1.19132	1.19500	1.19866	1.20228	1.20586
1.7	1.20941	1.21293	1.21642	1.21987	1.22330	1.22668	1.23004	1.23337	1.23666	1.23993
1.8	1.24316	1.24636	1.24954	1.25268	1.25579	1.25888	1.26193	1.26496	1.26795	1.27092
1.9	1.27386	1.27677	1.27966	1.28251	1.28534	1.28815	1.29092	1.29367	1.29639	1.29909
2.0	1.30176	1.30441	1.30703	1.30962	1.31219	1.31473	1.31726	1.31975	1.32222	1.32467
2.1	1.32710	1.32950	1.33188	1.33423	1.33656	1.33887	1.34116	1.34343	1.34567	1.34789
2.2	1.35009	1.35227	1.35443	1.35656	1.35868	1.36077	1.36285	1.36490	1.36694	1.36895
2.3	1.37095	1.37292	1.37488	1.37682	1.37873	1.38063	1.38251	1.38438	1.38622	1.38805
2.4	1.38986	1.39165	1.39342	1.39518	1.39691	1.39864	1.40034	1.40203	1.40370	1.40535
2.5	1.40699	1.40862	1.41022	1.41181	1.41339	1.41495	1.41649	1.41802	1.41954	1.42104
2.6	1.42252	1.42399	1.42545	1.42689	1.42832	1.42973	1.43113	1.43251	1.43388	1.43524
2.7	1.43659	1.43792	1.43924	1.44054	1.44183	1.44311	1.44438	1.44564	1.44688	1.44811
2.8	1.44933	1.45053	1.45173	1.45291	1.45408	1.45524	1.45638	1.45752	1.45864	1.45976
2.9	1.46086	1.46195	1.46303	1.46410	1.46516	1.46621	1.46725	1.46828	1.46930	1.47031
3.0	1.47130	1.47229	1.47327	1.47424	1.47520	1.47615	1.47709	1.47802	1.47894	1.47986
3.1	1.48076	1.48165	1.48254	1.48342	1.48428	1.48514	1.48600	1.48684	1.48767	1.48850
3.2	1.48932	1.49013	1.49093	1.49172	1.49251	1.49329	1.49406	1.49482	1.49558	1.49632
3.3	1.49706	1.49780	1.49852	1.49924	1.49995	1.50066	1.50135	1.50204	1.50273	1.50340
3.4	1.50407	1.50474	1.50539	1.50605	1.50669	1.50733	1.50796	1.50858	1.50920	1.50981
3.5	1.51042	1.51102	1.51161	1.51220	1.51279	1.51336	1.51393	1.51450	1.51506	1.51561
3.6	1.51616	1.51671	1.51724	1.51778	1.51830	1.51883	1.51934	1.51985	1.52036	1.52086
3.7	1.52136	1.52185	1.52234	1.52282	1.52330	1.52377	1.52424	1.52470	1.52516	1.52561
3.8	1.52606	1.52651	1.52695	1.52738	1.52782	1.52824	1.52867	1.52909	1.52950	1.52991
3.9	1.53032	1.53072	1.53112	1.53151	1.53190	1.53229	1.53267	1.53305	1.53343	1.53380
4.0	1.53417	1.53453	1.53489	1.53525	1.53561	1.53596	1.53630	1.53664	1.53698	1.53732
4.1	1.53765	1.53798	1.53831	1.53863	1.53895	1.53927	1.53958	1.53989	1.54020	1.54051
4.2	1.54081	1.54111	1.54140	1.54169	1.54198	1.54227	1.54255	1.54283	1.54311	1.54339
4.3	1.54366	1.54393	1.54420	1.54446	1.54472	1.54498	1.54524	1.54550	1.54575	1.54600
4.4	1.54624	1.54649	1.54673	1.54697	1.54721	1.54744	1.54767	1.54790	1.54813	1.54836
4.5	1.54858	1.54880	1.54902	1.54924	1.54945	1.54966	1.54987	1.55008	1.55029	1.55049
4.6	1.55069	1.55089	1.55109	1.55129	1.55148	1.55167	1.55186	1.55205	1.55224	1.55242
4.7	1.55261	1.55279	1.55297	1.55314	1.55332	1.55349	1.55367	1.55384	1.55400	1.55417
4.8	1.55434	1.55450	1.55466	1.55482	1.55498	1.55514	1.55530	1.55545	1.55560	1.55575
4.9	1.55590	1.55605	1.55620	1.55634	1.55649	1.55663	1.55677	1.55691	1.55705	1.55719

GUDERMANNIAN FUNCTION (Continued)

x	0	1	2	3	4	5	6	7	8	9
5.0	1.55732	1.55745	1.55759	1.55772	1.55785	1.55798	1.55811	1.55823	1.55836	1.55848
5.1	1.55860	1.55872	1.55884	1.55896	1.55908	1.55920	1.55931	1.55943	1.55954	1.55965
5.2	1.55976	1.55987	1.55998	1.56009	1.56020	1.56030	1.56041	1.56051	1.56061	1.56071
5.3	1.56081	1.56091	1.56101	1.56111	1.56120	1.56130	1.56139	1.56149	1.56158	1.56167
5.4	1.56176	1.56185	1.56194	1.56203	1.56212	1.56220	1.56229	1.56237	1.56246	1.56254
5.5	1.56262	1.56270	1.56278	1.56286	1.56294	1.56302	1.56310	1.56318	1.56325	1.56333
5.6	1.56340	1.56347	1.56355	1.56362	1.56369	1.56376	1.56383	1.56390	1.56397	1.56404
5.7	1.56410	1.56417	1.56424	1.56430	1.56437	1.56443	1.56449	1.56456	1.56462	1.56468
5.8	1.56474	1.56480	1.56486	1.56492	1.56498	1.56504	1.56509	1.56515	1.56521	1.56526
5.9	1.56532	1.56537	1.56543	1.56548	1.56553	1.56558	1.56564	1.56569	1.56574	1.56579
6.0	1.56584	1.56589	1.56594	1.56599	1.56603	1.56608	1.56613	1.56617	1.56622	1.56627
6.1	1.56631	1.56636	1.56640	1.56644	1.56649	1.56653	1.56657	1.56661	1.56666	1.56670
6.2	1.56674	1.56678	1.56682	1.56686	1.56690	1.56694	1.56697	1.56701	1.56705	1.56709
6.3	1.56712	1.56716	1.56720	1.56723	1.56727	1.56730	1.56734	1.56737	1.56741	1.56744
6.4	1.56747	1.56751	1.56754	1.56757	1.56760	1.56764	1.56767	1.56770	1.56773	1.56776
6.5	1.56779	1.56782	1.56785	1.56788	1.56791	1.56794	1.56796	1.56799	1.56802	1.56805
6.6	1.56808	1.56810	1.56813	1.56816	1.56818	1.56821	1.56823	1.56826	1.56828	1.56831
6.7	1.56833	1.56836	1.56838	1.56841	1.56843	1.56845	1.56848	1.56850	1.56852	1.56855
6.8	1.56857	1.56859	1.56861	1.56863	1.56866	1.56868	1.56870	1.56872	1.56874	1.56876
6.9	1.56878	1.56880	1.56882	1.56884	1.56886	1.56888	1.56890	1.56892	1.56894	1.56895
7.0	1.56897	1.56899	1.56901	1.56903	1.56904	1.56906	1.56908	1.56910	1.56911	1.56913
7.1	1.56915	1.56916	1.56918	1.56919	1.56921	1.56923	1.56924	1.56926	1.56927	1.56929
7.2	1.56930	1.56932	1.56933	1.56935	1.56936	1.56938	1.56939	1.56940	1.56942	1.56943
7.3	1.56945	1.56946	1.56947	1.56949	1.56950	1.56951	1.56952	1.56954	1.56955	1.56956
7.4	1.56957	1.56959	1.56960	1.56961	1.56962	1.56963	1.56965	1.56966	1.56967	1.56968
7.5	1.56969	1.56970	1.56971	1.56972	1.56973	1.56974	1.56975	1.56976	1.56978	1.56979
7.6	1.56980	1.56981	1.56982	1.56983	1.56983	1.56984	1.56985	1.56986	1.56987	1.56988
7.7	1.56989	1.56990	1.56991	1.56992	1.56993	1.56993	1.56994	1.56995	1.56996	1.56997
7.8	1.56998	1.56999	1.57000	1.57000	1.57001	1.57002	1.57002	1.57003	1.57004	1.57005
7.9	1.57005	1.57006	1.57007	1.57008	1.57008	1.57009	1.57010	1.57010	1.57011	1.57012
8.0	1.57013	1.57013	1.57014	1.57015	1.57015	1.57016	1.57016	1.57017	1.57018	1.57018
8.1	1.57019	1.57020	1.57020	1.57021	1.57021	1.57022	1.57022	1.57023	1.57024	1.57024
8.2	1.57025	1.57025	1.57026	1.57026	1.57027	1.57027	1.57028	1.57028	1.57029	1.57029
8.3	1.57030	1.57030	1.57031	1.57031	1.57032	1.57032	1.57033	1.57033	1.57034	1.57034
8.4	1.57035	1.57035	1.57036	1.57036	1.57036	1.57037	1.57037	1.57038	1.57038	1.57039
8.5	1.57039	1.57039	1.57040	1.57040	1.57041	1.57041	1.57041	1.57042	1.57042	1.57042
8.6	1.57043	1.57043	1.57044	1.57044	1.57044	1.57045	1.57045	1.57045	1.57046	1.57046
8.7	1.57046	1.57047	1.57047	1.57047	1.57048	1.57048	1.57048	1.57049	1.57049	1.57049
8.8	1.57049	1.57050	1.57050	1.57050	1.57051	1.57051	1.57051	1.57052	1.57052	1.57052
8.9	1.57052	1.57053	1.57053	1.57053	1.57053	1.57054	1.57054	1.57054	1.57054	1.57055
9.0	1.57055	1.57055	1.57055	1.57056	1.57056	1.57056	1.57056	1.57057	1.57057	1.57057
9.1	1.57057	1.57058	1.57058	1.57058	1.57058	1.57058	1.57059	1.57059	1.57059	1.57059
9.2	1.57059	1.57060	1.57060	1.57060	1.57060	1.57060	1.57061	1.57061	1.57061	1.57061
9.3	1.57061	1.57062	1.57062	1.57062	1.57062	1.57062	1.57062	1.57063	1.57063	1.57063
9.4	1.57063	1.57063	1.57063	1.57064	1.57064	1.57064	1.57064	1.57064	1.57064	1.57065
9.5	1.57065	1.57065	1.57065	1.57065	1.57065	1.57065	1.57066	1.57066	1.57066	1.57066
9.6	1.57066	1.57066	1.57066	1.57066	1.57067	1.57067	1.57067	1.57067	1.57067	1.57067
9.7	1.57067	1.57067	1.57068	1.57068	1.57068	1.57068	1.57068	1.57068	1.57068	1.57068
9.8	1.57069	1.57069	1.57069	1.57069	1.57069	1.57069	1.57069	1.57069	1.57069	1.57069
9.9	1.57070	1.57070	1.57070	1.57070	1.57070	1.57070	1.57070	1.57070	1.57070	1.57070

INVERSE GUDERMANNIAN FUNCTION

x	0	1	2	3	4	5	6	7	8	9
0.0	0.00000	0.01000	0.02000	0.03000	0.04001	0.05002	0.06004	0.07006	0.08009	0.09012
0.1	0.10017	0.11022	0.12029	0.13037	0.14046	0.15057	0.16069	0.17082	0.18098	0.19115
0.2	0.20135	0.21156	0.22180	0.23206	0.24234	0.25265	0.26298	0.27334	0.28373	0.29415
0.3	0.30460	0.31509	0.32561	0.33616	0.34675	0.35737	0.36804	0.37874	0.38949	0.40028
0.4	0.41111	0.42199	0.43292	0.44390	0.45493	0.46600	0.47714	0.48833	0.49957	0.51087
0.5	0.52224	0.53366	0.54515	0.55671	0.56834	0.58003	0.59180	0.60364	0.61555	0.62755
0.6	0.63962	0.65178	0.66402	0.67636	0.68878	0.70129	0.71390	0.72661	0.73942	0.75233
0.7	0.76535	0.77848	0.79172	0.80508	0.81856	0.83217	0.84590	0.85976	0.87376	0.88790
0.8	0.90218	0.91660	0.93118	0.94592	0.96082	0.97589	0.99113	1.00654	1.02215	1.03794
0.9	1.05392	1.07011	1.08651	1.10313	1.11997	1.13704	1.15435	1.17192	1.18974	1.20783
1.0	1.22619	1.24485	1.26380	1.28306	1.30265	1.32258	1.34285	1.36349	1.38451	1.40593
1.1	1.42776	1.45003	1.47275	1.49594	1.51963	1.54384	1.56860	1.59394	1.61987	1.64645
1.2	1.67370	1.70166	1.73037	1.75987	1.79022	1.82147	1.85367	1.88689	1.92120	1.95667
1.3	1.99340	2.03147	2.07100	2.11210	2.15491	2.19959	2.24630	2.29524	2.34666	2.40080
1.4	2.45800	2.51861	2.58307	2.65193	2.72583	2.80558	2.89219	2.98695	3.09160	3.20843
1.5	3.34068	3.49307	3.67286	3.89217	4.17343	4.56609	5.22169	7.82865		

VII. ANALYTIC GEOMETRY

ANALYTIC GEOMETRY

Dr. Howard Eves

RECTANGULAR COORDINATES IN A PLANE

Rectangular (Cartesian) Coordinates

Let $X'X$ (called the *x-axis*) and $Y'Y$ (called the *y-axis*) be two perpendicular lines (here taken horizontally and vertically, respectively) intersecting in point O (called the *origin*). Then any point P in the plane of the axes is located by the distance x (called the *abscissa*) and the distance y (called the *ordinate*) from $Y'Y$ and $X'X$, respectively, to P, where x is taken as positive to the right and negative to the left of $Y'Y$, and y is taken as positive above and negative below $X'X$. The ordered pair of numbers, (x,y), are called *rectangular coordinates* of the point P.

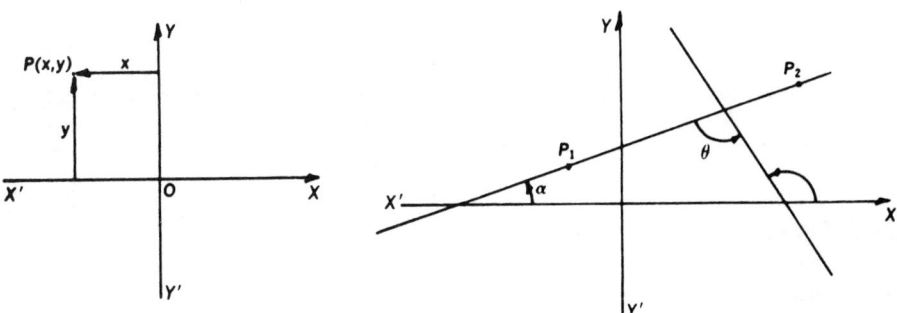

Points, Slopes, Angles

Let $P_1(x_1,y_1)$ and $P_2(x_2,y_2)$ be any two points and let α be the angle measured counter-clockwise from $X'X$ to P_1P_2.

Distance between P_1 and P_2:
$$\sqrt{(x_2 - x_1)^2 + (y_2 - y_1)^2}$$

Point dividing P_1P_2 in ratio $\dfrac{r}{s}$:
$$\left(\frac{rx_2 + sx_1}{r + s} , \frac{ry_2 + sy_1}{r + s} \right)$$

Midpoint of P_1P_2:
$$\left(\frac{x_1 + x_2}{2} , \frac{y_1 + y_2}{2} \right)$$

Slope m of P_1P_2:
$$m = \tan \alpha = \frac{y_2 - y_1}{x_2 - x_1}$$

Angle θ between two lines of slopes m_1 and m_2:
$$\tan \theta = \frac{m_2 - m_1}{1 + m_1 m_2}$$

For parallel lines: $m_1 = m_2$

For perpendicular lines: $m_1 m_2 = -1$

Points P_1, P_2, P_3 are collinear if and only if
$$\begin{vmatrix} x_1 & y_1 & 1 \\ x_2 & y_2 & 1 \\ x_3 & y_3 & 1 \end{vmatrix} = 0.$$

Formulas for Use in Analytic Geometry

Polygonal Areas

Area of triangle $P_1 P_2 P_3$:

$$\frac{1}{2}\begin{vmatrix} x_1 & y_1 & 1 \\ x_2 & y_2 & 1 \\ x_3 & y_3 & 1 \end{vmatrix} = \frac{1}{2}(x_1 y_2 + x_2 y_3 + x_3 y_1 - y_1 x_2 - y_2 x_3 - y_3 x_1)$$

Area of polygon $P_1 P_2 \cdots P_n$:

$$\frac{1}{2}(x_1 y_2 + x_2 y_3 + \cdots + x_{n-1} y_n + x_n y_1 - y_1 x_2 - y_2 x_3 - \cdots - y_{n-1} x_n - y_n x_1)$$

Note. The parenthesis in the last formula is remembered by the device

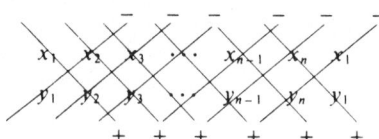

Here one adds the products of coordinates on the lines slanting downward to the right and subtracts the products of coordinates on the lines slanting upward to the right. The area is positive or negative according as $P_1 P_2 \cdots P_n$ is a counterclockwise or clockwise polygon.

Straight Lines

Line parallel to y-axis: $x = a$

Line parallel to x-axis: $y = b$

Slope y-intercept form: $y = mx + b$

Intercept form: $\dfrac{x}{a} + \dfrac{y}{b} = 1$

Point-slope form: $y - y_1 = m(x - x_1)$

Two-point form: $\dfrac{y - y_1}{x - x_1} = \dfrac{y_2 - y_1}{x_2 - x_1}$

or

$$\begin{vmatrix} x & y & 1 \\ x_1 & y_1 & 1 \\ x_2 & y_2 & 1 \end{vmatrix} = 0$$

Normal form: $x \cos \omega + y \sin \omega = p$

General form: $Ax + By + C = 0$

Slope: $m = -\dfrac{A}{B}$

Intercepts: $a = -\dfrac{C}{A}, \quad b = -\dfrac{C}{B}$

To reduce $Ax + By + C = 0$ to normal form, divide by $\pm \sqrt{A^2 + B^2}$, where the sign of the radical is chosen opposite to the sign of C when $C \neq 0$ and the same as the sign of B when $C = 0$.

Distance from $Ax + By + C = 0$ to P_1: $\dfrac{Ax_1 + By_1 + C}{\pm \sqrt{A^2 + B^2}}$

Formulas for Use in Analytic Geometry

Angle θ between lines $A_1x + B_1y + C_1 = 0$
and $A_2x + B_2y + C_2 = 0$

$$\tan \theta = \frac{A_1B_2 - A_2B_1}{A_1A_2 + B_1B_2}$$

Lines parallel: $A_1B_2 = A_2B_1$

Lines perpendicular: $A_1A_2 = -B_1B_2$

Lines $A_1x + B_1y + C_1 = 0$, $A_2x + B_2y + C_2 = 0$, $A_3x + B_3y + C_3 = 0$ are concurrent if and only if

$$\begin{vmatrix} A_1 & B_1 & C_1 \\ A_2 & B_2 & C_2 \\ A_3 & B_3 & C_3 \end{vmatrix} = 0.$$

Line of Best Fit

In seeking the straight line which best fits a given set of n points $P_1(x_1, y_1)$, $P_2(x_2, y_2)$, $\cdots$, $P_n(x_n, y_n)$, calculate

$$\bar{x} = \frac{x_1 + x_2 + \cdots + x_n}{n}, \quad \bar{y} = \frac{y_1 + y_2 + \cdots + y_n}{n},$$

$$m = \frac{(x_1y_1 + x_2y_2 + \cdots + x_ny_n) - n\bar{x}\bar{y}}{(x_1^2 + x_2^2 + \cdots + x_n^2) - n\bar{x}^2}.$$

Then the sought line is given by

$$y - \bar{y} = m(x - \bar{x}).$$

Circles

Center at origin, radius r: $x^2 + y^2 = r^2$

Center at (h,k), radius r: $(x - h)^2 + (y - k)^2 = r^2$

General form: $\begin{cases} Ax^2 + Ay^2 + Dx + Ey + F = 0, A \neq 0 \\ x^2 + y^2 + 2dx + 2ey + f = 0 \end{cases}$

Center: $(-d, -e)$

Radius: $r = \sqrt{d^2 + e^2 - f}$

Circle on P_1P_2 as diameter: $(x - x_1)(x - x_2) + (y - y_1)(y - y_2) = 0$

Three-point form:

$$\begin{vmatrix} x^2 + y^2 & x & y & 1 \\ x_1^2 + y_1^2 & x_1 & y_1 & 1 \\ x_2^2 + y_2^2 & x_2 & y_2 & 1 \\ x_3^2 + y_3^2 & x_3 & y_3 & 1 \end{vmatrix} = 0$$

Conic Sections

A *conic section* is the locus of a point P that moves in the plane of a fixed point F (called a *focus*) and a fixed line d (called a *directrix*), F not on d, such that the ratio of the distance of P from F to its distance from d is a constant e (called the *eccentricity*).

If $e = 1$, the conic is a *parabola*; if $e < 1$, an *ellipse*; if $e > 1$, a *hyperbola*.

Focus, $(0,0)$; directrix, $x = -a$: $x^2 + y^2 = e^2(x + a)^2$

Formulas for Use in Analytic Geometry

Parabolas (e = 1)

Let p = distance from the vertex to the focus, e = eccentricity.

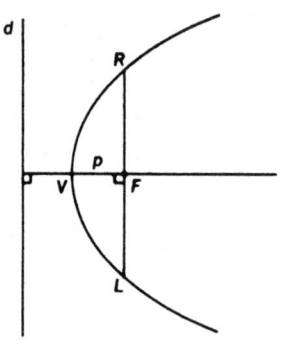

V: vertex
F: focus
d: directrix
LR: latus rectum
line VF: axis

Latus rectum:	$4p$
Distance from vertex to directrix:	p
Vertex at origin, focus at $(p,0)$:	$y^2 = 4px$
Vertex at origin, focus at $(-p,0)$:	$y^2 = -4px$
Vertex at origin, focus at $(0,p)$:	$x^2 = 4py$
Vertex at origin, focus at $(0,-p)$:	$x^2 = -4py$
Vertex, (h,k); focus, $(h + p,k)$:	$(y - k)^2 = 4p(x - h)$
Vertex, (h,k); focus, $(h - p,k)$:	$(y - k)^2 = -4p(x - h)$
Vertex, (h,k); focus, $(h,k + p)$:	$(x - h)^2 = 4p(y - k)$
Vertex, (h,k); focus, $(h,k - p)$:	$(x - h)^2 = -4p(y - k)$
General form, axis parallel to $X'X$:	$Cy^2 + Dx + Ey + F = 0$
General form, axis parallel to $Y'Y$:	$\begin{cases} Ax^2 + Dx + Ey + F = 0 \\ y = ax^2 + bx + c \end{cases}$
General form, axis oblique to coordinate axes:	$Ax^2 + Bxy + Cy^2 + Dx + Ey + F = 0$, $B^2 - 4AC = 0$

Ellipses (e < 1)

Let $2a$ = major axis, $2b$ = minor axis, e = eccentricity.

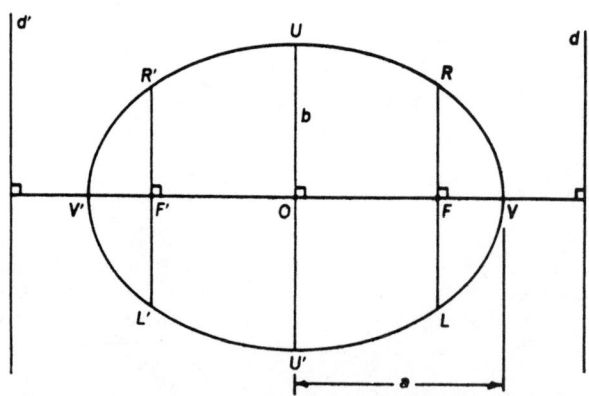

O: center
V, V': vertices
$V'V$: major axis = $2a$
$U'U$: minor axis = $2b$
F, F': foci
d, d': directrices
$LR, L'R'$: latera recta

Formulas for Use in Analytic Geometry

Eccentricity:	$e = \dfrac{\sqrt{a^2 - b^2}}{a}$
Latus rectum:	$\dfrac{2b^2}{a}$
Distance from center to either focus:	$\sqrt{a^2 - b^2}$
Distance from center to either directrix:	$\dfrac{a}{e}$
Sum of distances from any point on ellipse to the foci:	$2a$
Center at origin, foci on $X'X$:	$\dfrac{x^2}{a^2} + \dfrac{y^2}{b^2} = 1$
Center at origin, foci on $Y'Y$:	$\dfrac{x^2}{b^2} + \dfrac{y^2}{a^2} = 1$
Center at (h,k), major axis parallel to $X'X$:	$\dfrac{(x - h)^2}{a^2} + \dfrac{(y - k)^2}{b^2} = 1$
Center at (h,k), major axis parallel to $Y'Y$:	$\dfrac{(x - h)^2}{b^2} + \dfrac{(y - k)^2}{a^2} = 1$
General form, axes parallel to coordinate axes:	$Ax^2 + Cy^2 + Dx + Ey + F = 0,\, AC > 0$
General form, axes oblique to coordinate axes:	$Ax^2 + Bxy + Cy^2 + Dx + Ey + F = 0,$ $B^2 - 4AC < 0$

For a *circle*: $a = b$, $e = 0$, foci coincide at the center of the circle, directrices are at infinity.

Hyperbolas ($e > 1$)

Let $2a$ = transverse axis, $2b$ = conjugate axis, e = eccentricity.

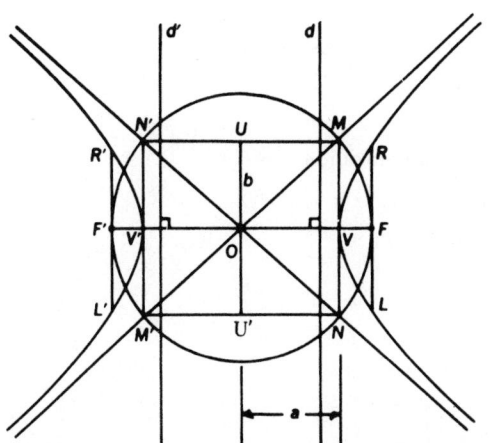

O: center
V, V': vertices
$V'V$: transverse axis = $2a$
$U'U$: conjugate axis = $2b$
F, F': foci
d, d': directrices
$LR, L'R'$: latera recta
lines $M'M$ and $N'N$: asymptotes

Formulas for Use in Analytic Geometry

Eccentricity:	$e = \dfrac{\sqrt{a^2 + b^2}}{a}$
Latus rectum:	$\dfrac{2b^2}{a}$
Distance from center to either focus:	$\sqrt{a^2 + b^2}$
Distance from center to either directrix:	$\dfrac{a}{e}$
Difference of distances of any point on hyperbola from foci:	$2a$
Center at origin, foci on $X'X$:	$\dfrac{x^2}{a^2} - \dfrac{y^2}{b^2} = 1$
Slopes of asymptotes:	$\pm \dfrac{b}{a}$
Center at origin, foci on $Y'Y$:	$\dfrac{y^2}{a^2} - \dfrac{x^2}{b^2} = 1$
Slopes of asymptotes:	$\pm \dfrac{a}{b}$
Center at (h,k), transverse axis parallel to $X'X$:	$\dfrac{(x - h)^2}{a^2} - \dfrac{(y - k)^2}{b^2} = 1$
Slopes of asymptotes:	$\pm \dfrac{b}{a}$
Center at (h, k), transverse axis parallel to $Y'Y$:	$\dfrac{(y - k)^2}{a^2} - \dfrac{(x - h)^2}{b^2} = 1$
Slopes of asymptotes:	$\pm \dfrac{a}{b}$
Center at origin, $X'X$ and $Y'Y$ for asymptotes:	$xy = c$
Center at (h,k), asymptotes parallel to $X'X$ and $Y'Y$:	$(x - h)(y - k) = c$
General form, axes parallel to coordinate axes:	$Ax^2 + Cy^2 + Dx + Ey + F = 0, AC < 0$
General form, axes oblique to coordinate axes:	$Ax^2 + Bxy + Cy^2 + Dx + Ey + F = 0,$ $B^2 - 4AC > 0$

For a *rectangular hyperbola*: $a = b$, $e = \sqrt{2}$, asymptotes are perpendicular.

General Equation of Second Degree

The nature of the graph of the general quadratic equation in x and y,

$$ax^2 + 2hxy + by^2 + 2gx + 2fy + c = 0,$$

is described in the following table in terms of the values of

$$\triangle = \begin{vmatrix} a & h & g \\ h & b & f \\ g & f & c \end{vmatrix}, \quad J = \begin{vmatrix} a & h \\ h & b \end{vmatrix},$$

$$I = a + b. \quad K = \begin{vmatrix} a & g \\ g & c \end{vmatrix} + \begin{vmatrix} b & f \\ f & c \end{vmatrix}.$$

Formulas for Use in Analytic Geometry

Case	$\triangle$	J	$\triangle/I$	K	Conic
1	$\neq 0$	> 0	< 0		real ellipse
2	$\neq 0$	> 0	> 0		imaginary ellipse
3	$\neq 0$	< 0			hyperbola
4	$\neq 0$	0			parabola
5	0	< 0			real intersecting lines
6	0	> 0			conjugate complex intersecting lines
7	0	0		< 0	real distinct parallel lines
8	0	0		> 0	conjugate complex parallel lines
9	0	0		0	coincident lines

In cases 1, 2, and 3, the center (x_0, y_0) of the conic is given by the simultaneous solution of the equations

$$ax + hy + g = 0, \quad hx + by + f = 0.$$

The equations of the axes of the conic are

$$y - y_0 = m(x - x_0), \quad y - y_0 = -\frac{1}{m}(x - x_0),$$

where m is the positive root of

$$hm^2 + (a - b)m - h = 0.$$

Transformation of Coordinates

To transform an equation of a curve from an old system of rectangular coordinates (x, y) to a new system of rectangular coordinates (x', y'), substitute for each old variable in the equation of the curve its expression in terms of the new variables.

Translation:
$$\begin{cases} x = x' + h \\ y = y' + k \end{cases}$$
The new axes are parallel to the old axes and the coordinates of the new origin in terms of the old system are (h, k).

Rotation:
$$\begin{cases} x = x' \cos \theta - y' \sin \theta \\ y = x' \sin \theta + y' \cos \theta \end{cases}$$
The new origin is coincident with the old origin and the new axes make an angle θ with the old axes.

To remove the xy-term from the equation

$$ax^2 + 2hxy + by^2 + 2gx + 2fy + c = 0,$$

rotate the coordinate axes about the origin through the acute angle $\theta = \arctan m$, where m is the positive root of

$$hm^2 + (a - b)m - h = 0.$$

OBLIQUE COORDINATES IN A PLANE

Oblique (Cartesian) Coordinates

Let $X'X$ (called the x-axis, here taken horizontally) and $Y'Y$ (called the y-axis) be two lines intersecting in point O (called the *origin*), and denote by ω the counterclockwise angle from $X'X$ to $Y'Y$. Then any point P in the plane of the axes is located by the distance x (called the *abscissa*) measured parallel to the x-axis and the distance y (called

Formulas for Use in Analytic Geometry

the *ordinate*) measured parallel to the y-axis from $Y'Y$ and $X'X$, respectively, to P, **where** x is taken as positive to the right and negative to the left of $Y'Y$, and y is taken as positive above and negative below $X'X$. The ordered pair of numbers, (x,y), are called *oblique co-ordinates* of the point P. If $\omega = 90°$, this coordinate system becomes a rectangular (Cartesian) coordinate system.

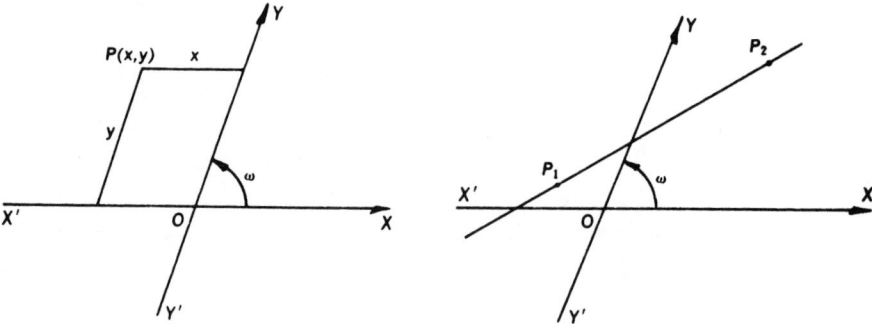

Points

Let $P_1(x_1,y_1)$ and $P_2(x_2,y_2)$ be any two points.

Distance between P_1 and P_2:

$$\sqrt{(x_2 - x_1)^2 + (y_2 - y_1)^2 + 2(x_2 - x_1)(y_2 - y_1)\cos \omega}$$

Point dividing $P_1 P_2$ in ratio $\dfrac{r}{s}$: $\left(\dfrac{rx_2 + sx_1}{r + s} , \dfrac{ry_2 + sy_1}{r + s} \right)$

Midpoint of $P_1 P_2$: $\left(\dfrac{x_1 + x_2}{2} , \dfrac{y_1 + y_2}{2} \right)$

Points P_1, P_2, P_3 are collinear if and only if $\begin{vmatrix} x_1 & y_1 & 1 \\ x_2 & y_2 & 1 \\ x_3 & y_3 & 1 \end{vmatrix} = 0.$

Polygonal Areas

Area of triangle $P_1 P_2 P_3$:

$$\sin \omega \begin{vmatrix} x_1 & y_1 & 1 \\ x_2 & y_3 & 1 \\ x_3 & y_3 & 1 \end{vmatrix} = \tfrac{1}{2}(\sin \omega)(x_1 y_2 + x_2 y_3 + x_3 y_1 - y_1 x_2 - y_2 x_3 - y_3 x_1)$$

Area of polygon $P_1 P_2 \cdots P_n$:

$$\tfrac{1}{2}(\sin \omega)(x_1 y_2 + x_2 y_3 + \cdots + x_{n-1} y_n + x_n y_1 - y_1 x_2 - y_2 x_3 - \cdots - y_{n-1} x_n - y_n x_1)$$

The area is positive or negative according as $P_1 P_2 \cdots P_n$ is a counterclockwise or clockwise polygon.

Straight Lines

Line parallel to y-axis: $x = a$

Line parallel to x-axis: $y = b$

Formulas for Use in Analytic Geometry

Intercept form: $\dfrac{x}{a} + \dfrac{y}{b} = 1$

Two-point form: $\dfrac{y - y_1}{x - x_1} = \dfrac{y_2 - y_1}{x_2 - x_1}$, or $\begin{vmatrix} x & y & 1 \\ x_1 & y_1 & 1 \\ x_2 & y_2 & 1 \end{vmatrix} = 0$

General form: $Ax + By + C = 0$

Intercepts: $a = -\dfrac{C}{A}$, $b = -\dfrac{C}{B}$

Distance from $Ax + By + C = 0$ to P_1: $\dfrac{(Ax_1 + By_1 + C)\sin \omega}{\pm \sqrt{A^2 + B^2 - 2AB \cos \omega}}$

Angle θ between lines $A_1 x + B_1 y + C_1 = 0$
and $A_2 x + B_2 y + C_2 = 0$:

$$\tan \theta = \frac{(A_1 B_2 - A_2 B_1)\sin \omega}{A_1 A_2 + B_1 B_2 - (A_1 B_2 + A_2 B_1)\cos \omega}$$

Lines parallel: $A_1 B_2 = A_2 B_1$

Lines perpendicular: $A_1 A_2 + B_1 B_2 = (A_1 B_2 + A_2 B_1)\cos \omega$

Lines $A_1 x + B_1 y + C_1 = 0$, $A_2 x + B_2 y + C_2 = 0$, $A_3 x + B_3 y + C_3 = 0$ are concurrent if and only if

$$\begin{vmatrix} A_1 & B_1 & C_1 \\ A_2 & B_2 & C_2 \\ A_3 & B_3 & C_3 \end{vmatrix} = 0.$$

Circles

Center at (h, k), radius r: $(x - h)^2 + (y - k)^2 + 2(x - h)(y - k)\cos \omega = r^2$

Transformation of Coordinates

Translation: $\begin{cases} x = x' + h \\ y = y' + k \end{cases}$ The new axes are parallel to the old axes and the coordinates of the new origin in terms of the old system are (h, k).

From one oblique system to another, origin fixed: $\begin{cases} x = \dfrac{x'\sin(\omega - \theta) + y'\sin(\omega - \omega' - \theta)}{\sin \omega} \\ y = \dfrac{x'\sin \theta + y'\sin(\omega' + \theta)}{\sin \omega} \end{cases}$

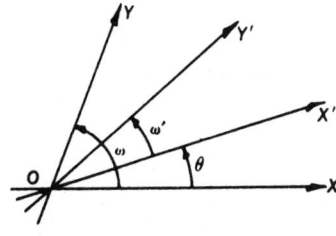

The old and new origins coincide; the old axes intersect at angle ω; the new axes intersect at angle ω'; the counterclockwise angle from x-axis to x'-axis is θ.

Formulas for Use in Analytic Geometry

POLAR COORDINATES IN A PLANE

Polar Coordinates

In a plane, let OX (called the *initial line*) be a fixed ray radiating from point O (called the *pole* or *origin*). Then any point P, other than O, in the plane is located by angle θ (called the *vectorial angle*) measured from OX to the line determined by O and P and the distance r (called the *radius vector*) from O to P, where θ is taken as positive if measured counterclockwise and negative if measured clockwise, and r is taken as positive if measured along the terminal side of angle θ and negative if measured along the terminal side of θ produced through the pole. Such an ordered pair of numbers, (r, θ), are called *polar coordinates* of the point P. The polar coordinates of the pole O are taken as $(0, \theta)$, where θ is arbitrary. It follows that, for a given initial line and pole, each point of the plane has infinitely many polar coordinates, but each pair of coordinates corresponds to only one point.

Example

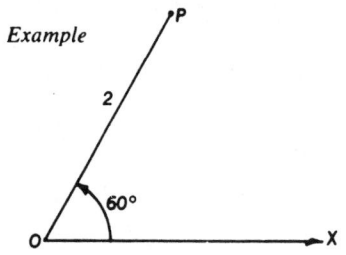

Some polar coordinates of P are: $(2, 60°)$, $(2, 420°)$, $(2, -300°)$, $(-2, 240°)$, $(-2, -120°)$.

Points

Distance between P_1 and P_2: $\sqrt{r_1^2 + r_2^2 - 2r_1 r_2 \cos(\theta_1 - \theta_2)}$
Points P_1, P_2, P_3 are collinear if and only if

$$r_2 r_3 \sin(\theta_3 - \theta_2) + r_3 r_1 \sin(\theta_1 - \theta_3) + r_1 r_2 \sin(\theta_2 - \theta_1) = 0.$$

Polygonal Areas

Area of triangle $P_1 P_2 P_3$:

$$\tfrac{1}{2}[r_1 r_2 \sin(\theta_2 - \theta_1) + r_2 r_3 \sin(\theta_3 - \theta_2) + r_3 r_1 \sin(\theta_1 - \theta_3)]$$

Area of polygon $P_1 P_2 \cdots P_n$:

$$\tfrac{1}{2}[r_1 r_2 \sin(\theta_2 - \theta_1) + r_2 r_3 \sin(\theta_3 - \theta_2) + \cdots + r_{n-1} r_n \sin(\theta_n - \theta_{n-1}) + r_n r_1 \sin(\theta_1 - \theta_n)]$$

The area is positive or negative according as $P_1 P_2 \cdots P_n$ is a counterclockwise or clockwise polygon.

Straight Lines

Let p = distance of line from O, ω = counterclockwise angle from OX to the perpendicular through O to the line.

Normal form: $r \cos(\theta - \omega) = p$

Two-point form: $r[r_1 \sin(\theta - \theta_1) - r_2 \sin(\theta - \theta_2)] = r_1 r_2 \sin(\theta_2 - \theta_1)$

Circles

Center at pole, radius a: $r = a$
Center at $(a, 0)$ and passing
through the pole: $r = 2a \cos \theta$

Formulas for Use in Analytic Geometry

Center at $\left(a, \dfrac{\pi}{2}\right)$ and passing

through the pole: $r = 2a \sin \theta$

Center (h, α), radius a: $r^2 - 2hr \cos(\theta - \alpha) + h^2 - a^2 = 0$

Conics

Let $2p$ = distance from directrix to focus, e = eccentricity.

Focus at pole, directrix to left of pole: $r = \dfrac{2ep}{1 - e \cos \theta}$

Focus at pole, directrix to right of pole: $r = \dfrac{2ep}{1 + e \cos \theta}$

Focus at pole, directrix below pole: $r = \dfrac{2ep}{1 - e \sin \theta}$

Focus at pole, directrix above pole: $r = \dfrac{2ep}{1 + e \sin \theta}$

Parabola with vertex at pole, directrix to left of pole: $r = \dfrac{4p \cos \theta}{\sin^2 \theta}$

Ellipse with center at pole, semiaxes a and b horizontal and vertical, respectively: $r^2 = \dfrac{a^2 b^2}{a^2 \sin^2 \theta + b^2 \cos^2 \theta}$

Hyperbola with center at pole, semiaxes a and b horizontal and vertical, respectively: $r^2 = \dfrac{a^2 b^2}{a^2 \sin^2 \theta - b^2 \cos^2 \theta}$

Relations Between Rectangular and Polar Coordinates

Let the positive x-axis coincide with the initial line and let r be nonnegative.

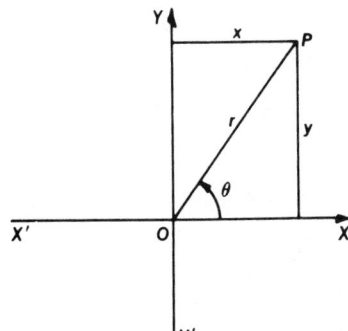

$x = r \cos \theta, \quad y = r \sin \theta,$

$r = \sqrt{x^2 + y^2}, \quad \theta = \arctan \dfrac{y}{x},$

$\sin \theta = \dfrac{y}{\sqrt{x^2 + y^2}}, \quad \cos \theta = \dfrac{x}{\sqrt{x^2 + y^2}}$

RECTANGULAR COORDINATES IN SPACE

Rectangular (Cartesian) Coordinates

Let $X'X$, $Y'Y$, $Z'Z$ (called the *x-axis*, the *y-axis*, and the *z-axis*, respectively) be three mutually perpendicular lines in space intersecting in a point O (called the *origin*), forming in this way three mutually perpendicular planes XOY, XOZ, YOZ (called the *xy-*

Formulas for Use in Analytic Geometry

plane, the *xz-plane*, and the *yz-plane*, respectively).   Then any point *P* of space is located by its signed distances *x*, *y*, *z* from the *yz*-plane, the *xz*-plane, and the *xy*-plane, respectively, where *x* and *y* are the rectangular coordinates with respect to the axes *X'X* and *Y'Y* of the orthogonal projection *P'* of *P* on the *xy*-plane (here taken horizontally) and *z* is taken as positive above and negative below the *xy*-plane.   The ordered triple of numbers, (x, y, z), are called *rectangular coordinates* of the point *P*.

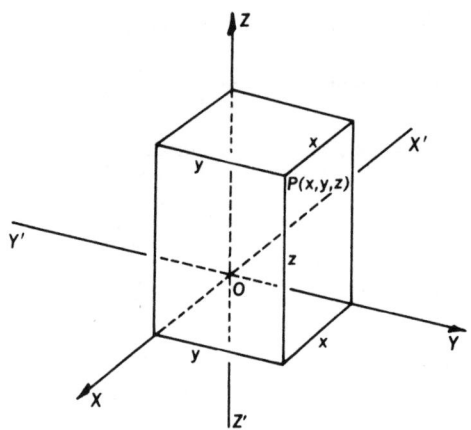

Points

Let $P_1(x_1, y_1, z_1)$ and $P_2(x_2, y_2, z_2)$ be any two points.

Distance between P_1 and P_2: $\sqrt{(x_2 - x_1)^2 + (y_2 - y_1)^2 + (z_2 - z_1)^2}$

Point dividing $P_1 P_2$ in ratio $\dfrac{r}{s}$: $\left(\dfrac{rx_2 + sx_1}{r + s}, \ \dfrac{ry_2 + sy_1}{r + s}, \ \dfrac{rz_2 + sz_1}{r + s} \right)$

Midpoint of $P_1 P_2$: $\left(\dfrac{x_1 + x_2}{2}, \ \dfrac{y_1 + y_2}{2}, \ \dfrac{z_1 + z_2}{2} \right)$

Points P_1, P_2, P_3 are collinear if and only if

$$x_2 - x_1 : y_2 - y_1 : z_2 - z_1 = x_3 - x_1 : y_3 - y_1 : z_3 - z_1.$$

Points P_1, P_2, P_3, P_4 are coplanar if and only if $\begin{vmatrix} x_1 & y_1 & z_1 & 1 \\ x_2 & y_2 & z_2 & 1 \\ x_3 & y_3 & z_3 & 1 \\ x_4 & y_4 & z_4 & 1 \end{vmatrix} = 0.$

Area of triangle $P_1 P_2 P_3$:

$$\frac{1}{2} \sqrt{ \begin{vmatrix} y_1 & z_1 & 1 \\ y_2 & z_2 & 1 \\ y_3 & z_3 & 1 \end{vmatrix}^2 + \begin{vmatrix} z_1 & x_1 & 1 \\ z_2 & x_2 & 1 \\ z_3 & x_3 & 1 \end{vmatrix}^2 + \begin{vmatrix} x_1 & y_1 & 1 \\ x_2 & y_2 & 1 \\ x_3 & y_3 & 1 \end{vmatrix}^2 }$$

Formulas for Use in Analytic Geometry

Volume of tetrahedron $P_1 P_2 P_3 P_4$: $\dfrac{1}{6} \begin{vmatrix} x_1 & y_1 & z_1 & 1 \\ x_2 & y_2 & z_2 & 1 \\ x_3 & y_3 & z_3 & 1 \\ x_4 & y_4 & z_4 & 1 \end{vmatrix}$

Direction Numbers and Direction Cosines

Let α, β, γ (called *direction angles*) be the angles that $P_1 P_2$, or any line parallel to $P_1 P_2$, makes with the x-, y-, and z-axis, respectively. Let d = distance between P_1 and P_2.

Direction cosines of $P_1 P_2$:

$$\cos \alpha = \frac{x_2 - x_1}{d}, \quad \cos \beta = \frac{y_2 - y_1}{d}, \quad \cos \gamma = \frac{z_2 - z_1}{d}$$

$$\cos^2 \alpha + \cos^2 \beta + \cos^2 \gamma = 1$$

If a, b, c are direction numbers of $P_1 P_2$, then:

$$a : b : c = x_2 - x_1 : y_2 - y_1 : z_2 - z_1$$
$$= \cos \alpha : \cos \beta : \cos \gamma$$

$$\cos \alpha = \frac{a}{\pm \sqrt{a^2 + b^2 + c^2}}, \quad \cos \beta = \frac{b}{\pm \sqrt{a^2 + b^2 + c^2}},$$

$$\cos \gamma = \frac{c}{\pm \sqrt{a^2 + b^2 + c^2}}$$

Angle between two lines with direction angles α_1, β_1, γ_1 and α_2, β_2, γ_2:

$$\cos \theta = \cos \alpha_1 \cos \alpha_2 + \cos \beta_1 \cos \beta_2 + \cos \gamma_1 \cos \gamma_2$$

For parallel lines: $\alpha_1 = \alpha_2$, $\beta_1 = \beta_2$, $\gamma_1 = \gamma_2$

For perpendicular lines:

$$\cos \alpha_1 \cos \alpha_2 + \cos \beta_1 \cos \beta_2 + \cos \gamma_1 \cos \gamma_2 = 0$$

Angle between two lines with directions (a_1, b_1, c_1) and (a_2, b_2, c_2):

$$\cos \theta = \frac{a_1 a_2 + b_1 b_2 + c_1 c_2}{\sqrt{a_1^2 + b_1^2 + c_1^2} \; \sqrt{a_2^2 + b_2^2 + c_2^2}}$$

$$\sin \theta = \frac{\sqrt{(b_1 c_2 - c_1 b_2)^2 + (c_1 a_2 - a_1 c_2)^2 + (a_1 b_2 - b_1 a_2)^2}}{\sqrt{a_1^2 + b_1^2 + c_1^2} \; \sqrt{a_2^2 + b_2^2 + c_2^2}}$$

For parallel lines: $a_1 : b_1 : c_1 = a_2 : b_2 : c_2$

For perpendicular lines: $a_1 a_2 + b_1 b_2 + c_1 c_2 = 0$

The direction

$$(b_1 c_2 - c_1 b_2, c_1 a_2 - a_1 c_2, a_1 b_2 - b_1 a_2)$$

is perpendicular to both directions (a_1, b_1, c_1) and (a_2, b_2, c_2).

The directions (a_1, b_1, c_1), (a_2, b_2, c_2), (a_3, b_3, c_3) are parallel to a common plane if and only if

$$\begin{vmatrix} a_1 & b_1 & c_1 \\ a_2 & b_2 & c_2 \\ a_3 & b_3 & c_3 \end{vmatrix} = 0.$$

Formulas for Use in Analytic Geometry

Straight Lines

Point-direction form:
$$\frac{x - x_1}{a} = \frac{y - y_1}{b} = \frac{z - z_1}{c}$$

Two-point form:
$$\frac{x - x_1}{x_2 - x_1} = \frac{y - y_1}{y_2 - y_1} = \frac{z - z_1}{z_2 - z_1}$$

Parametric form: $x = x_1 + ta, \ y = y_1 + tb, \ z = z_1 + tc$

General form:
$$\begin{cases} A_1 x + B_1 y + C_1 z + D_1 = 0 \\ A_2 x + B_2 y + C_2 z + D_2 = 0 \end{cases}$$

Direction of line: $(B_1 C_2 - C_1 B_2, C_1 A_2 - A_1 C_2, A_1 B_2 - B_1 A_2)$

Projection of segment $P_1 P_2$ on any line having the direction (a, b, c):

$$\frac{(x_2 - x_1)a + (y_2 - y_1)b + (z_2 - z_1)c}{\sqrt{a^2 + b^2 + c^2}}$$

Distance from point P_0 to line through P_1 in direction (a, b, c):

$$\sqrt{\frac{\begin{vmatrix} y_0 - y_1 & z_0 - z_1 \\ b & c \end{vmatrix}^2 + \begin{vmatrix} z_0 - z_1 & x_0 - x_1 \\ c & a \end{vmatrix}^2 + \begin{vmatrix} x_0 - x_1 & y_0 - y_1 \\ a & b \end{vmatrix}^2}{a^2 + b^2 + c^2}}$$

Distance between line through P_1 in direction (a_1, b_1, c_1) and line through P_2 in direction (a_2, b_2, c_2):

$$\pm \frac{\begin{vmatrix} x_2 - x_1 & y_2 - y_1 & z_2 - z_1 \\ a_1 & b_1 & c_1 \\ a_2 & b_2 & c_2 \end{vmatrix}}{\sqrt{\begin{vmatrix} b_1 & c_1 \\ b_2 & c_2 \end{vmatrix}^2 + \begin{vmatrix} c_1 & a_1 \\ c_2 & a_2 \end{vmatrix}^2 + \begin{vmatrix} a_1 & b_1 \\ a_2 & b_2 \end{vmatrix}^2}}$$

The line through P_1 in direction (a_1, b_1, c_1) and the line through P_2 in direction (a_2, b_2, c_2) intersect if and only if

$$\begin{vmatrix} x_2 - x_1 & y_2 - y_1 & z_2 - z_1 \\ a_1 & b_1 & c_1 \\ a_2 & b_2 & c_2 \end{vmatrix} = 0.$$

Planes

General form: $Ax + By + Cz + D = 0$

Direction of normal: (A, B, C)

Perpendicular to yz-plane: $By + Cz + D = 0$

Perpendicular to xz-plane: $Ax + Cz + D = 0$

Perpendicular to xy-plane: $Ax + By + D = 0$

Perpendicular to x-axis: $Ax + D = 0$

Perpendicular to y-axis: $By + D = 0$

Perpendicular to z-axis: $Cz + D = 0$

Intercept form:
$$\frac{x}{a} + \frac{y}{b} + \frac{z}{c} = 1$$

Plane through point P_1 and perpendicular to direction (a, b, c):

$$a(x - x_1) + b(y - y_1) + c(z - z_1) = 0$$

Formulas for Use in Analytic Geometry

Plane through point P_1 and parallel to directions (a_1, b_1, c_1) and (a_2, b_2, c_2):

$$\begin{vmatrix} x - x_1 & y - y_1 & z - z_1 \\ a_1 & b_1 & c_1 \\ a_2 & b_2 & c_2 \end{vmatrix} = 0$$

Plane through points P_1 and P_2 parallel to direction (a, b, c):

$$\begin{vmatrix} x - x_1 & y - y_1 & z - z_1 \\ x_2 - x_1 & y_2 - y_1 & z_2 - z_1 \\ a & b & c \end{vmatrix} = 0$$

Three-point form:

$$\begin{vmatrix} x & y & z & 1 \\ x_1 & y_1 & z_1 & 1 \\ x_2 & y_2 & z_2 & 1 \\ x_3 & y_3 & z_3 & 1 \end{vmatrix} = 0 \quad \text{or} \quad \begin{vmatrix} x - x_1 & y - y_1 & z - z_1 \\ x_2 - x_1 & y_2 - y_1 & z_2 - z_1 \\ x_3 - x_1 & y_3 - y_1 & z_3 - z_1 \end{vmatrix} = 0$$

Normal form (p = distance from origin to plane; α, β, γ are direction angles of perpendicular to plane from origin):

$$x \cos \alpha + y \cos \beta + z \cos \gamma = p$$

To reduce $Ax + By + Cz + D = 0$ to normal form, divide by $\pm \sqrt{A^2 + B^2 + C^2}$, where the sign of the radical is chosen opposite to the sign of D when $D \neq 0$, the same as the sign of C when $D = 0$ and $C \neq 0$, the same as the sign of B when $C = D = 0$.

Distance from point P_1 to plane $Ax + By + Cz + D = 0$:

$$\frac{Ax_1 + By_1 + Cz_1 + D}{\pm \sqrt{A^2 + B^2 + C^2}}$$

Angle θ between planes $A_1x + B_1y + C_1z + D_1 = 0$ and $A_2x + B_2y + C_2z + D_2 = 0$:

$$\cos \theta = \frac{A_1A_2 + B_1B_2 + C_1C_2}{\sqrt{A_1^2 + B_1^2 + C_1^2} \sqrt{A_2^2 + B_2^2 + C_2^2}}$$

Planes parallel: $A_1 : B_1 : C_1 = A_2 : B_2 : C_2$

Planes perpendicular: $A_1A_2 + B_1B_2 + C_1C_2 = 0$

Spheres

Center at origin, radius r: $x^2 + y^2 + z^2 = r^2$

Center at (g, h, k), radius r: $(x - g)^2 + (y - h)^2 + (z - k)^2 = r^2$

General form: $\begin{cases} Ax^2 + Ay^2 + Az^2 + Dx + Ey + Fz + M = 0, \quad A \neq 0 \\ x^2 + y^2 + z^2 + 2dx + 2ey + 2fz + m = 0 \end{cases}$

Center: $(-d, -e, -f)$

Radius: $r = \sqrt{d^2 + e^2 + f^2 - m}$

Formulas for Use in Analytic Geometry

Sphere on $P_1 P_2$ as diameter:

$$(x - x_1)(x - x_2) + (y - y_1)(y - y_2) + (z - z_1)(z - z_2) = 0$$

Four-point form:

$$\begin{vmatrix} x^2 + y^2 + z^2 & x & y & z & 1 \\ x_1^2 + y_1^2 + z_1^2 & x_1 & y_1 & z_1 & 1 \\ x_2^2 + y_2^2 + z_2^2 & x_2 & y_2 & z_2 & 1 \\ x_3^2 + y_3^2 + z_3^2 & x_3 & y_3 & z_3 & 1 \\ x_4^2 + y_4^2 + z_4^2 & x_4 & y_4 & z_4 & 1 \end{vmatrix} = 0$$

The Seventeen Quadric Surfaces in Standard Form

1. Real ellipsoid: $\qquad\qquad\quad x^2/a^2 + y^2/b^2 + z^2/c^2 = 1$
2. Imaginary ellipsoid: $\qquad\quad x^2/a^2 + y^2/b^2 + z^2/c^2 = -1$
3. Hyperboloid of one sheet: $\quad x^2/a^2 + y^2/b^2 - z^2/c^2 = 1$
4. Hyperboloid of two sheets: $\; x^2/a^2 + y^2/b^2 - z^2/c^2 = -1$
5. Real quadric cone: $\qquad\quad\; x^2/a^2 + y^2/b^2 - z^2/c^2 = 0$
6. Imaginary quadric cone: $\quad x^2/a^2 + y^2/b^2 + z^2/c^2 = 0$
7. Elliptic paraboloid: $\qquad\quad x^2/a^2 + y^2/b^2 + 2z = 0$
8. Hyperbolic paraboloid: $\quad\; x^2/a^2 - y^2/b^2 + 2z = 0$
9. Real elliptic cylinder: $\qquad x^2/a^2 + y^2/b^2 = 1$
10. Imaginary elliptic cylinder: $\; x^2/a^2 + y^2/b^2 = -1$
11. Hyperbolic cylinder: $\qquad\; x^2/a^2 - y^2/b^2 = -1$
12. Real intersecting planes: $\; x^2/a^2 - y^2/b^2 = 0$
13. Imaginary intersecting planes: $\; x^2/a^2 + y^2/b^2 = 0$
14. Parabolic cylinder: $\qquad\;\; x^2 + 2rz = 0$
15. Real parallel planes: $\qquad\; x^2 = a^2$
16. Imaginary parallel planes: $\;\; x^2 = -a^2$
17. Coincident planes: $\qquad\;\; x^2 = 0$

General Equation of Second Degree

The nature of the graph of the general quadratic equation in x, y, z,

$$ax^2 + by^2 + cz^2 + 2fyz + 2gzx + 2hxy + 2px + 2qy + 2rz + d = 0,$$

is described in the following table in terms of $\rho_3, \rho_4, \Delta, k_1, k_2, k_3$, where

$$e = \begin{bmatrix} a & h & g \\ h & b & f \\ g & f & c \end{bmatrix}, \quad E = \begin{bmatrix} a & h & g & p \\ h & b & f & q \\ g & f & c & r \\ p & q & r & d \end{bmatrix},$$

$$\rho_3 = \text{rank } e, \quad \rho_4 = \text{rank } E,$$
$$\Delta = \text{determinant of } E,$$

k_1, k_2, k_3 are the roots of $\begin{vmatrix} a - x & h & g \\ h & b - x & f \\ g & f & c - x \end{vmatrix} = 0.$

Formulas for Use in Analytic Geometry

Case	ρ_3	ρ_4	Sign of Δ	Nonzero k's same sign?	Quadric Surface
1	3	4	−	yes	Real ellipsoid
2	3	4	+	yes	Imaginary ellipsoid
3	3	4	+	no	Hyperboloid of one sheet
4	3	4	−	no	Hyperboloid of two sheets
5	3	3		no	Real quadric cone
6	3	3		yes	Imaginary quadric cone
7	2	4	−	yes	Elliptic paraboloid
8	2	4	+	no	Hyperbolic paraboloid
9	2	3		yes	Real elliptic cylinder
10	2	3		yes	Imaginary elliptic cylinder
11	2	3		no	Hyperbolic cylinder
12	2	2		no	Real intersecting planes
13	2	2		yes	Imaginary intersecting planes
14	1	3			Parabolic cylinder
15	1	2			Real parallel planes
16	1	2			Imaginary parallel planes
17	1	1			Coincident planes

Cylindrical and Conical Surfaces

Any equation in just two of the variables x, y, z represents a *cylindrical surface* whose elements are parallel to the axis of the missing variable.

Any equation homogeneous in the variables x, y, z represents a *conical surface* whose vertex is at the origin.

Transformation of Coordinates

To transform an equation of a surface from an old system of rectangular coordinates (x, y, z) to a new system of rectangular coordinates (x', y', z'), substitute for each old variable in the equation of the surface its expression in terms of the new variables.

Translation:

$x = x' + h$ The new axes are parallel to the old axes and the coordinates of
$y = y' + k$ the new origin in terms of the old system are (h, k, l).
$z = z' + l$

Rotation about the origin:

$x = \lambda_1 x' + \lambda_2 y' + \lambda_3 z'$ The new origin is coincident with the old origin and
$y = \mu_1 x' + \mu_2 y' + \mu_3 z'$ the x'-axis, y'-axis, z'-axis have direction cosines
$z = \nu_1 x' + \nu_2 y' + \nu_3 z'$ $(\lambda_1, \mu_1, \nu_1), (\lambda_2, \mu_2, \nu_2), (\lambda_3, \mu_3, \nu_3)$, respectively, with respect to the old system of axes.

$x' = \lambda_1 x + \mu_1 y + \nu_1 z$
$y' = \lambda_2 x + \mu_2 y + \nu_2 z$
$z' = \lambda_3 x + \mu_3 y + \nu_3 z$

Formulas for Use in Analytic Geometry

Cylindrical Coordinates

If (r, θ, z) are the cylindrical co-ordinates and (x, y, z) the rectangular coordinates of a point P, then

$$x = r \cos \theta, \quad r = \sqrt{x^2 + y^2},$$

$$y = r \sin \theta, \quad \theta = \arctan \frac{y}{x},$$

$$z = z, \qquad z = z.$$

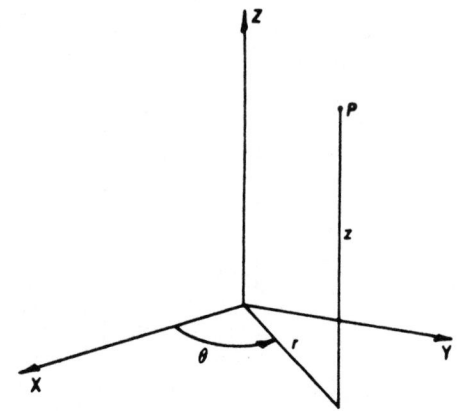

Spherical Coordinates

If (ρ, θ, ϕ) are the spherical co-ordinates and (x, y, z) the rectangular coordinates of a point P, then

$$x = \rho \cos \theta \sin \phi$$

$$y = \rho \sin \theta \sin \phi$$

$$z = \rho \cos \phi$$

$$\phi = \arccos \frac{z}{\sqrt{x^2 + y^2 + z^2}},$$

$$\theta = \arctan \frac{y}{x}$$

$$p^2 = x^2 + y^2 + z^2$$

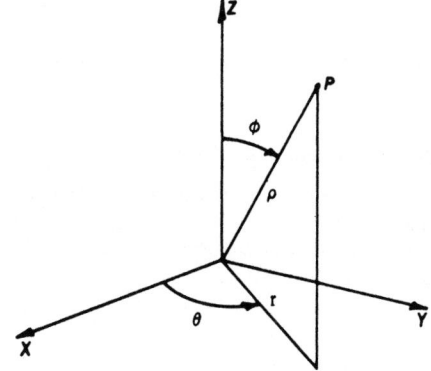

CURVES AND SURFACES

DR. HOWARD EVES

The curves and surfaces collected here for reference appear frequently in mathematical literature. The equations most generally associated with each figure are given. The equation of a plane curve when placed otherwise on the coordinate frame of reference may often be found from the given equation by the following rules.

RECTANGULAR COORDINATES

1. If a given curve is reflected in the x-axis, the new equation is obtained from the old by replacing y by $-y$.

2. If a given curve is reflected in the y-axis, the new equation is obtained from the old by replacing x by $-x$.

3. If a given curve is reflected in the origin, the new equation is obtained from the old by replacing x by $-x$ and y by $-y$.

4. If a given curve is reflected in the line $y = x$, the new equation is obtained from the old by interchanging x and y.

5. If a given curve is rotated about the origin through 90°, the new equation is obtained from the old by replacing x by y and y by $-x$.

6. If a given curve is rotated about the origin through $-90°$, the new equation is obtained from the old by replacing x by $-y$ and y by x.

7. If a given curve is translated a distance h in the x-direction, the new equation is obtained from the old by replacing x by $x - h$.

8. If a given curve is translated a distance k in the y-direction, the new equation is obtained from the old by replacing y by $y - k$.

9. If a given curve is altered by multiplying all the abscissas by a, the new equation is obtained from the old by replacing x by x/a.

10. If a given curve is altered by multiplying all the ordinates by b, the new equation is obtained from the old by replacing y by y/b.

POLAR COORDINATES

1. If a given curve is reflected in the polar axis, the new equation is obtained from the old by replacing θ by $-\theta$, or by replacing r by $-r$ and θ by $\pi - \theta$.

2. If a given curve is reflected in the 90° axis, the new equation is obtained from the old by replacing θ by $\pi - \theta$, or by replacing r by $-r$ and θ by $-\theta$.

3. If a given curve is reflected in the pole, the new equation is obtained from the old by replacing θ by $\pi + \theta$, or by replacing r by $-r$.

4. If a given curve is rotated about the pole through an angle α, the new equation is obtained from the old by replacing θ by $\theta - \alpha$.

PLANE CURVES

Archimedean spiral
See: Spiral of Archimedes

Astroid
See: Hypocycloid of four cusps

Curves and Surfaces

Bifolium

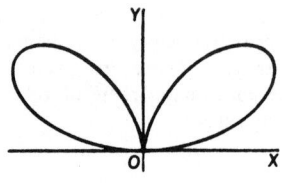

$$(x^2 + y^2)^2 = ax^2y$$
$$r = a \sin \theta \cos^2 \theta$$

Circle
(a)

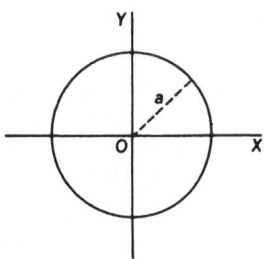

$$x^2 + y^2 = a^2$$
$$r = a$$

Cardioid

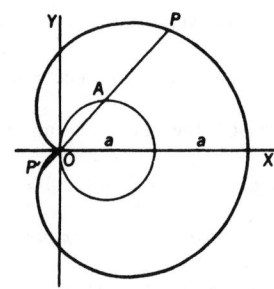

$$(x^2 + y^2 - ax)^2 = a^2(x^2 + y^2)$$
$$r = a(\cos \theta + 1)$$
or
$$r = a(\cos \theta - 1)$$
$$[P'A = AP = a]$$

(b)

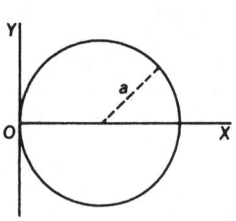

$$x^2 + y^2 = 2ax$$
$$r = 2a \cos \theta$$

(c)

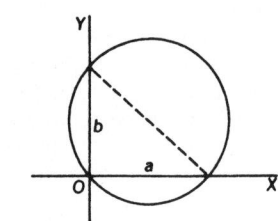

$$x^2 + y^2 = ax + by$$
$$r = a \cos \theta + b \sin \theta$$

Cassinian curves
  See: Ovals of Cassini

Catenary, Hyperbolic cosine

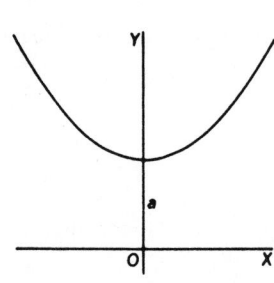

$$y = \frac{a}{2} (e^{x/a} + e^{-x/a}) = a \cosh \frac{x}{a}$$

Cissoid of Diocles

$$y^2(a - x) = x^3$$
$$r = a \sin \theta \tan \theta$$
$$[OP = AB]$$

Curves and Surfaces

Cochleoid, Oui-ja board curve

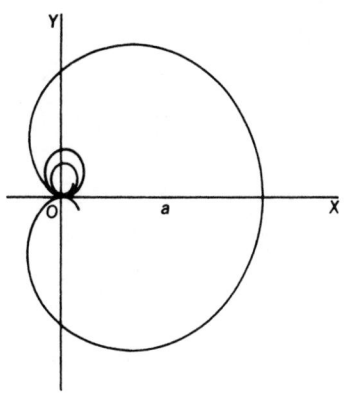

$$(x^2 + y^2) \tan^{-1}(y/x) = ay$$
$$r\theta = a \sin \theta$$

Companion to the cycloid

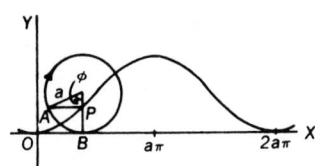

$$\begin{cases} x = a\phi \\ y = a(1 - \cos \phi) \end{cases}$$
$$[OB = \widehat{AB}]$$
(This is a sinusoid)

Conchoid of Nicomedes
(a) $a < b$

(b) $a > b$

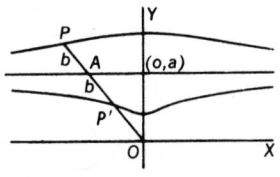

$$(y - a)^2(x^2 + y^2) = b^2 y^2$$
$$r = a \csc \theta \pm b$$
$$[P'A = AP = b]$$

Conic sections
 See: Circle; Ellipse; Hyperbola; Parabola

Cosecant curve

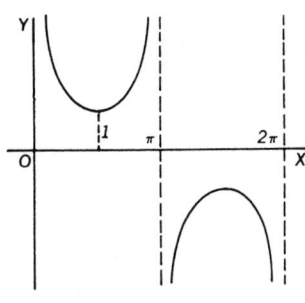

$$y = \csc x$$

Cosine curve

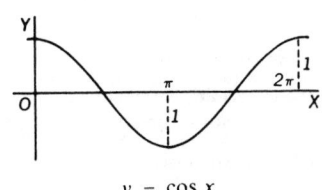

$$y = \cos x$$

Cotangent curve

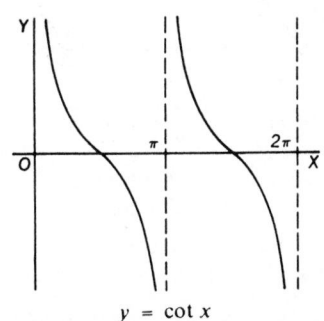

$$y = \cot x$$

Curves and Surfaces

Cubical parabola (special)

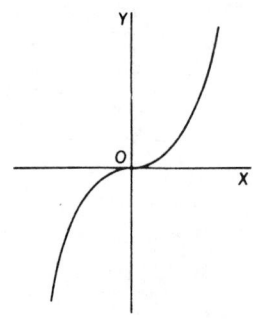

$$y = ax^3, \quad a > 0$$

$$r^2 = \frac{1}{a} \sec^2 \theta \tan \theta, \quad a > 0$$

Cubical parabola (general)

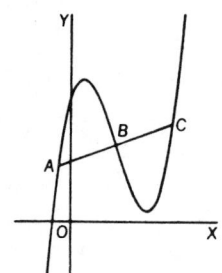

$$y = ax^3 + bx^2 + cx + d, \quad a > 0$$
$$[AB = BC]$$
$$(\text{abscissa of } B = -b/3a)$$

Curtate cycloid, Trochoids
See: Cycloid, curtate

Cycloid (cusp at origin)

$$x = a \arccos \frac{a - y}{a} \mp \sqrt{2ay - y^2}$$

$$\begin{cases} x = a(\phi - \sin \phi) \\ y = a(1 - \cos \phi) \end{cases}$$

(For one arch: arc length $= 8a$; area $= 3\pi a^2$)

Cycloid (vertex at origin)

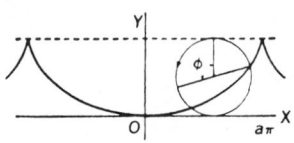

$$x = 2a \arcsin \sqrt{y/2a} + \sqrt{2ay - y^2}$$

$$\begin{cases} x = a(\phi + \sin \phi) \\ y = a(1 - \cos \phi) \end{cases}$$

Cycloid, curtate

$$\begin{cases} x = a\phi - b \sin \phi \\ y = a - b \cos \phi \end{cases}$$
$$a > b$$

Cycloid, prolate

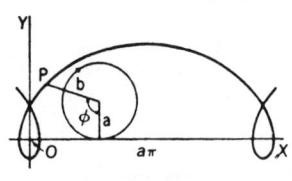

$$\begin{cases} x = a\phi - b \sin \phi \\ y = a - b \cos \phi \end{cases}$$
$$a < b$$

Deltoid
See: Hypocycloid of three cusps

Curves and Surfaces

Ellipse

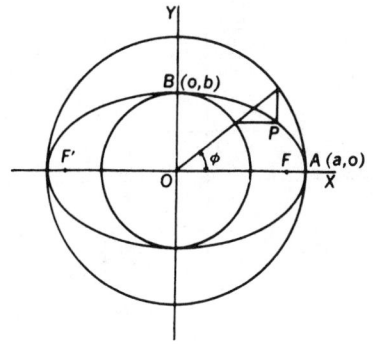

$$x^2/a^2 + y^2/b^2 = 1$$

$$\begin{cases} x = a \cos \phi \\ y = b \sin \phi \end{cases}$$

$$[BF' = BF = a, \quad PF' + PF = 2a]$$

Evolute of ellipse

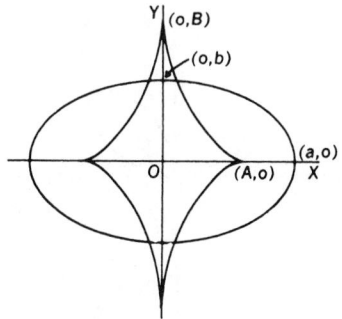

$$(ax)^{2/3} + (by)^{2/3} = (a^2 - b^2)^{2/3}$$

$$\begin{cases} x = A \cos^3 \phi \\ y = B \sin^3 \phi \end{cases}$$

$$[A = (a^2 - b^2)/a, \quad B = (a^2 - b^2)/b]$$

Exponential curve
(1) $a > 0$

Epicycloid

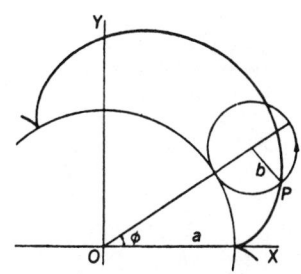

$$\begin{cases} x = (a + b) \cos \phi - b \cos\left(\dfrac{a + b}{b} \phi\right) \\ y = (a + b) \sin \phi - b \sin\left(\dfrac{a + b}{b} \phi\right) \end{cases}$$

(2) $a < 0$

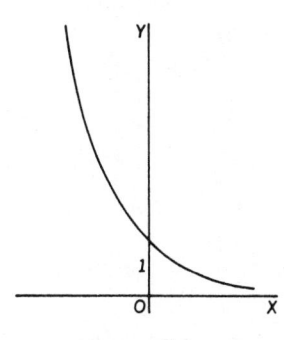

Equiangular spiral
See: Spiral, logarithmic or equiangular

Equilateral hyperbola
See: Hyperbola, equilateral or rectangular

$$y = e^{ax}$$

Curves and Surfaces

Folium of Descartes

Hyperbola

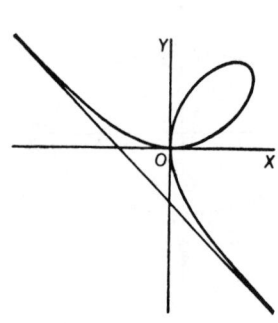

$$x^3 + y^3 - 3axy = 0$$

$$\begin{cases} x = 3a\phi/(1 + \phi^3) \\ y = 3a\phi^2/(1 + \phi^3) \end{cases}$$

$$r = \frac{3a \sin \theta \cos \theta}{\sin^3 \theta + \cos^3 \theta}$$

[asymptote: $x + y + a = 0$]

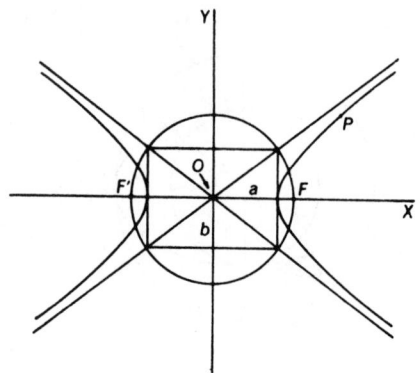

$$x^2/a^2 - y^2/b^2 = 1$$
$$[F'P - FP = 2a]$$

Hyperbola, equilateral or rectangular
(1)

Gamma function

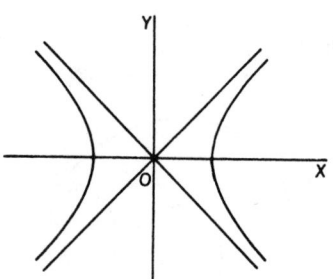

$$x^2 - y^2 = a^2$$

(2)

$$\Gamma(n) = \int_0^\infty x^{n-1} e^{-x} dx \quad (n > 0)$$

$$\Gamma(n) = \frac{\Gamma(n + 1)}{n} \quad (0 > n \neq -1, -2, -3, \ldots)$$

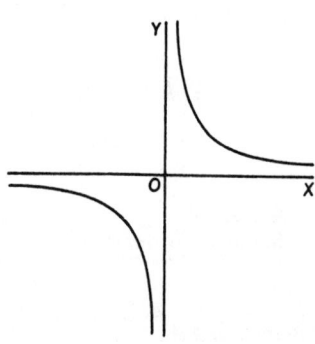

$$xy = k, \quad k > 0$$

Curves and Surfaces

(3)

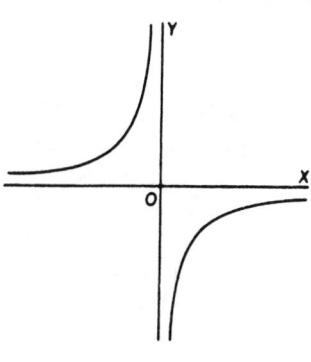

$$xy = k, \quad k < 0$$

Hyperbolic functions*

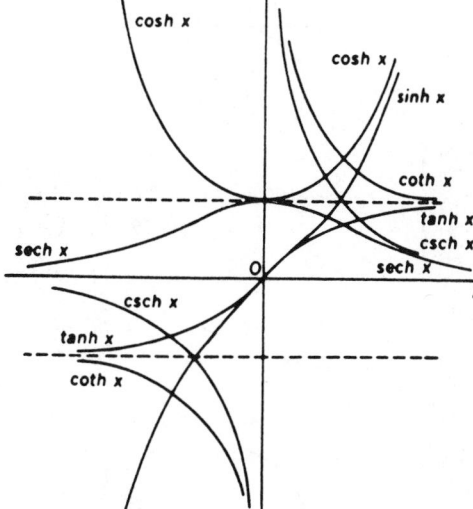

$$\sinh x = \frac{e^x - e^{-x}}{2} \qquad \operatorname{csch} x = \frac{2}{e^x - e^{-x}}$$

$$\cosh x = \frac{e^x + e^{-x}}{2} \qquad \operatorname{sech} x = \frac{2}{e^x + e^{-x}}$$

$$\tanh x = \frac{e^x - e^{-x}}{e^x + e^{-x}} \qquad \coth x = \frac{e^x + e^{-x}}{e^x - e^{-x}}$$

Hyperbolic spiral
See: Spiral, hyperbolic or reciprocal

*See page 181 for inverse hyperbolic functions.

Hypocycloid of three cusps, Deltoid

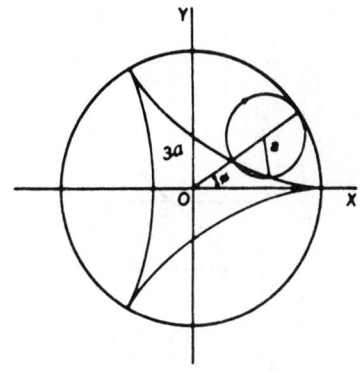

$$\begin{cases} x = 2a\cos\phi + a\cos 2\phi \\ y = 2a\sin\phi - a\sin 2\phi \end{cases}$$

Hypocycloid of four cusps, Astroid

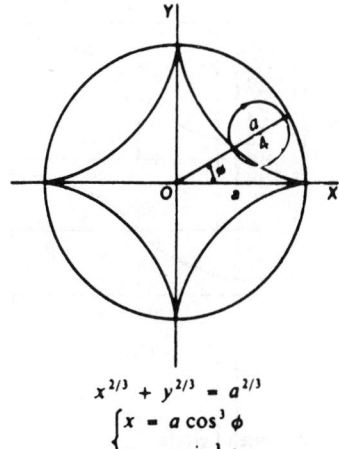

$$x^{2/3} + y^{2/3} = a^{2/3}$$
$$\begin{cases} x = a\cos^3\phi \\ y = a\sin^3\phi \end{cases}$$

Inverse cosine curve

$$y = \arccos x$$

Curves and Surfaces

Inverse sine curve

$$y = \arcsin x$$

Inverse tangent curve

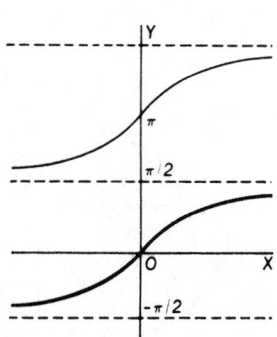

$$y = \arctan x$$

Involute of circle

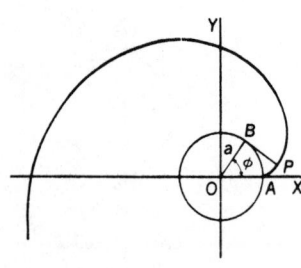

$$\begin{cases} x = a \cos \phi + a\phi \sin \phi \\ y = a \sin \phi - a\phi \cos \phi \end{cases}$$
$$[BP = \widehat{BA}]$$

Lemniscate of Bernoulli, Two-leaved rose

(a)

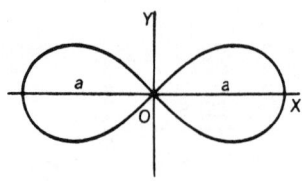

$$(x^2 + y^2)^2 = a^2(x^2 - y^2)$$
$$r^2 = a^2 \cos 2\theta$$

(b)

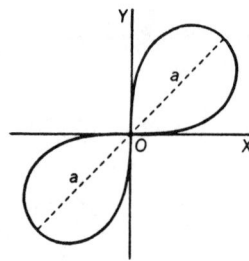

$$(x^2 + y^2)^2 = 2a^2xy$$
$$r^2 = a^2 \sin 2\theta$$

Limacon of Pascal

(1) $a > b$

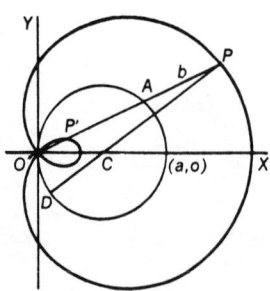

[If $a = 2b$, the curve is called the *trisectrix*, since then $\sphericalangle OPD = \frac{1}{3} \sphericalangle OCD$.]

(2) $a = b$

See: Cardioid

Curves and Surfaces

(3) $a < b$

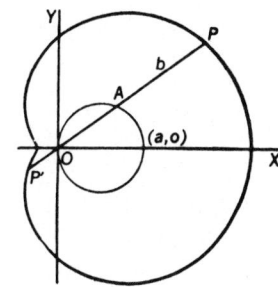

$$(x^2 + y^2 - ax)^2 = b^2(x^2 + y^2)$$
$$r = b + a \cos \theta$$
$$[P'A = AP = b]$$

Lituus

$$r^2\theta = a^2$$

Logarithmic curve

(1) $a > 1$

(2) $0 < a < 1$

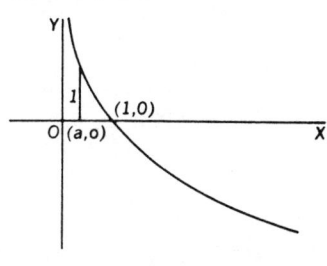

$$y = \log_a x$$

Logarithmic spiral
See: Spiral, logarithmic or equiangular

Nephroid

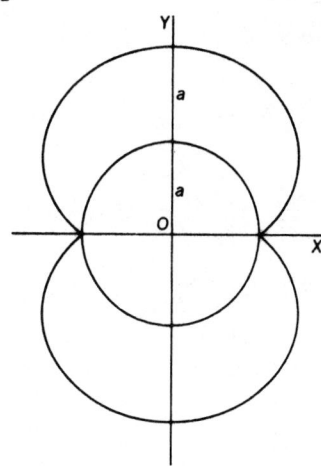

$$\begin{cases} x = \tfrac{1}{2}a(3 \cos \phi - \cos 3\phi) \\ y = \tfrac{1}{2}a(3 \sin \phi - \sin 3\phi) \end{cases}$$

[The nephroid is a 2-cusped epicycloid.]

Oui-ja board curve
See: Cochleoid

Ovals of Cassini
(1) $b > k$

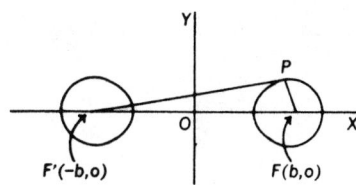

(2) $b = k$
See: Lemniscate of Bernoulli

(3) $b < k$

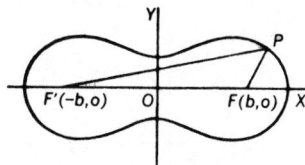

$$(x^2 + y^2 + b^2)^2 - 4b^2x^2 = k^4$$
$$r^4 + b^4 - 2r^2b^2 \cos 2\theta = k^4$$
$$[F'P \cdot FP = k^2]$$

[These curves are sections of a torus on planes parallel to the axis of the torus.]

Curves and Surfaces

Parabola

(1)

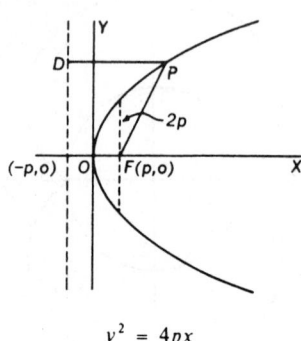

$$y^2 = 4px$$
$$[DP = FP]$$

(2)

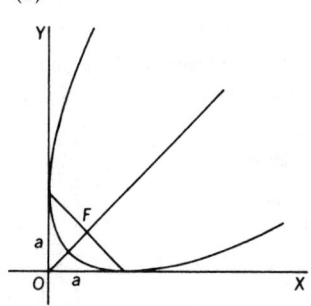

$$\pm x^{1/2} \pm y^{1/2} = a^{1/2}$$
$$(x - y)^2 - 2a(x + y) + a^2 = 0$$

(3)

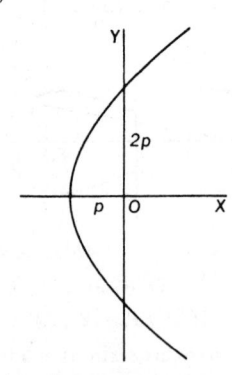

$$r = 2p/(1 - \cos \theta)$$

(4)

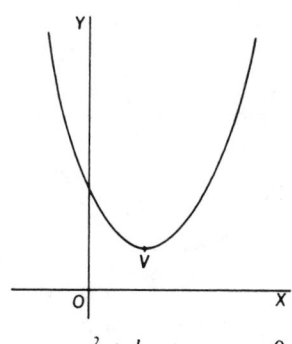

$$y = ax^2 + bx + c, \quad a > 0$$
$$[\text{abscissa of vertex} = -b/2a]$$

Parabolic spiral

See: Spiral, parabolic

Power functions

(1)

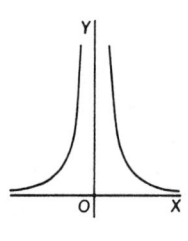

$$y = x^{-2}$$

(2) Equilateral hyperbola

$$y = x^{-1}$$

(3)

$$y = x^{-1/2}$$

Curves and Surfaces

(4) Cubical parabola

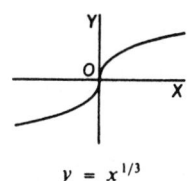

$$y = x^{1/3}$$

(5) Half of a parabola

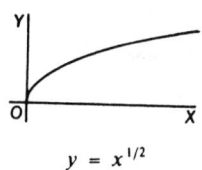

$$y = x^{1/2}$$

(6) Semicubical parabola

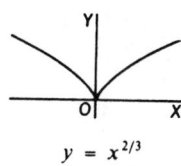

$$y = x^{2/3}$$

(7) Half of semicubical parabola

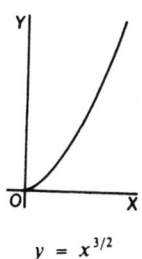

$$y = x^{3/2}$$

(8) Parabola

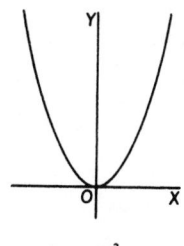

$$y = x^2$$

(9) Cubical parabola

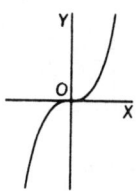

$$y = x^3$$

Probability curve

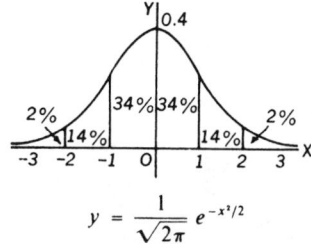

$$y = \frac{1}{\sqrt{2\pi}} e^{-x^2/2}$$

Prolate cycloid
  See: Cycloid, prolate

Pursuit curve
  See: Tractrix

Quadratrix of Hippias

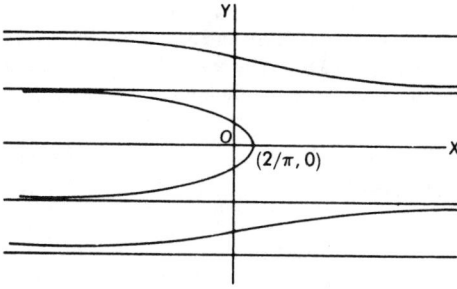

$$y = x \tan (\pi y/2)$$

Reciprocal spiral
  See: Spiral, hyperbolic or reciprocal

Rectangular hyperbola
  See: Hyperbola, equilateral or rectangular

Rose curves
  (1) Two-leaved
    See: Lemniscate of Bernoulli, Two-leaved rose

Curves and Surfaces

(2) Three-leaved

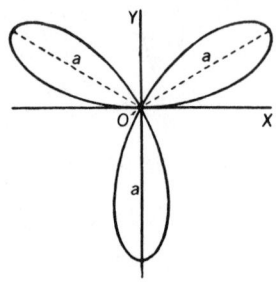

$r = a \sin 3\theta$

(3) Three-leaved

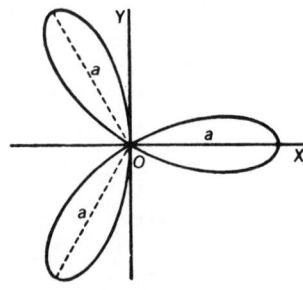

$r = a \cos 3\theta$

(4) Four-leaved

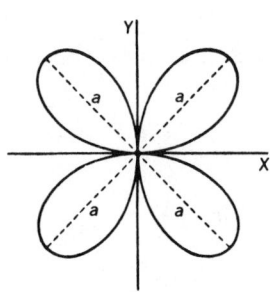

$r = a \sin 2\theta$

(5) Four-leaved

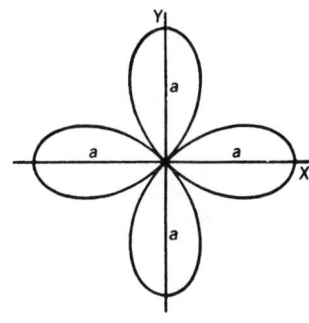

$r = a \cos 2\theta$

(6) *n*-leaved

The roses $r = a \sin n\theta$ and $r = a \cos n\theta$, have, for *n* an even integer, 2*n* leaves; for *n* an odd integer, *n* leaves. The roses $r^2 = a \sin n\theta$ and $r^2 = a \cos n\theta$, have, for *n* an even integer, *n* leaves; for *n* an odd integer, 2*n* leaves.

Secant curve

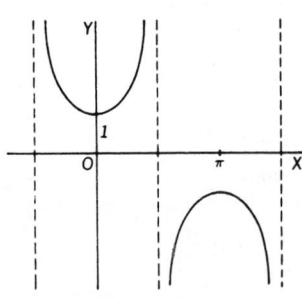

$y = \sec x$

Semicubical parabola

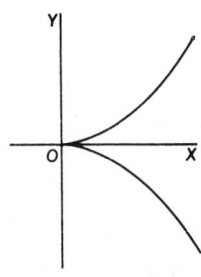

$$y^2 = ax^3$$

$$r = \frac{1}{a} \tan^2 \theta \sec \theta$$

Curves and Surfaces

Serpentine curve

$$(a^2 + x^2)y = abx$$

$$\begin{cases} x = a \cot \phi \\ y = b \sin \phi \cos \phi \end{cases}$$

Sine curve

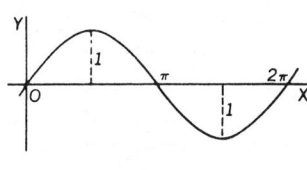

$$y = \sin x$$

Sinusoid

$$y = a \sin (bx + c)$$

Spiral of Archimedes

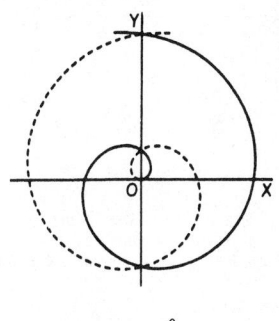

$$r = a\theta$$

Spiral, hyperbolic or reciprocal

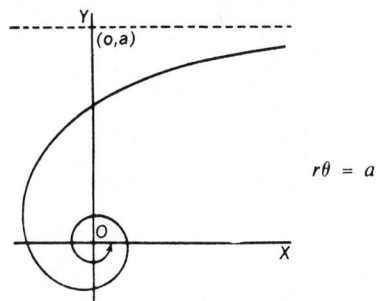

$$r\theta = a$$

Spiral, logarithmic or equiangular

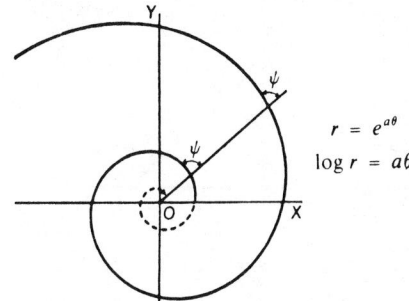

$$r = e^{a\theta}$$

$$\log r = a\theta$$

Spiral, parabolic

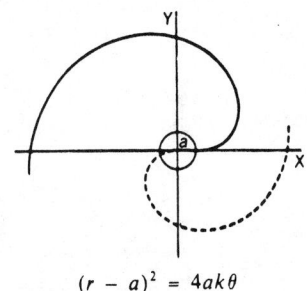

$$(r - a)^2 = 4ak\theta$$

Strophoid

$$y^2 = x^2 \frac{a - x}{a + x}$$

$$r = a \cos 2\theta \sec \theta$$

$$[P'A = AP = OA]$$

Curves and Surfaces

Tangent curve

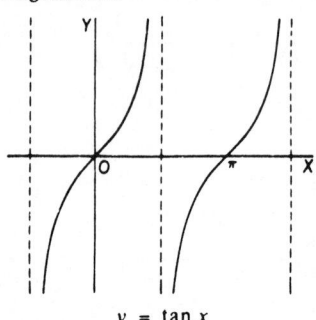

$y = \tan x$

Tractrix, Pursuit curve

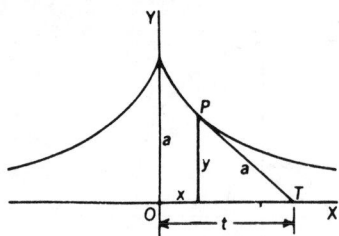

$$x = a \operatorname{sech}^{-1}(y/a) - \sqrt{a^2 - y^2}$$

$$\begin{cases} x = t - a \tanh(t/a) \\ y = a \operatorname{sech}(t/a) \end{cases}$$

$$[PT = a]$$

Trajectory (a parabola)

$$y = x \tan \alpha - gx^2/(2v_0^2 \cos^2 \alpha)$$
$$x = (v_0 \cos \alpha) t$$
$$y = (v_0 \sin \alpha) t - gt^2/2$$

Trigonometric functions
    See: Cosecant curve; Cosine curve; Cotangent curve; Secant curve Sine curve; Tangent curve

Trisectrix
    See: Limacon of Pascal (1)

Witch of Agnesi

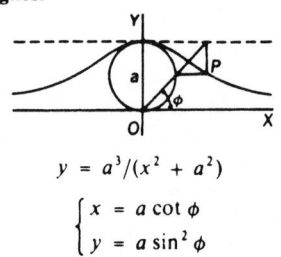

$$y = a^3/(x^2 + a^2)$$

$$\begin{cases} x = a \cot \phi \\ y = a \sin^2 \phi \end{cases}$$

QUADRIC SURFACES*

Ellipsoid

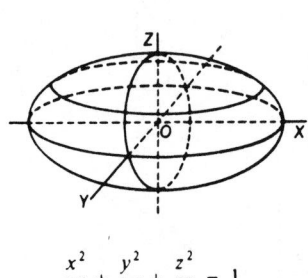

$$\frac{x^2}{a^2} + \frac{y^2}{b^2} + \frac{z^2}{c^2} = 1$$

Elliptic cone

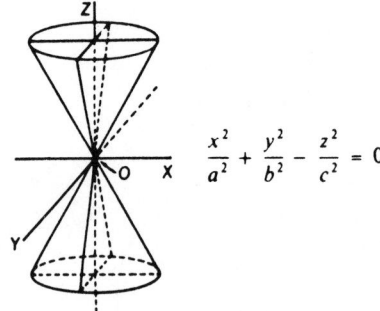

$$\frac{x^2}{a^2} + \frac{y^2}{b^2} - \frac{z^2}{c^2} = 0$$

*Each of the equations is given for the case where the origin is located at $(0, 0, 0)$, the center of the quadric surface. If, however, the center of the surface is at (h, k, l), replace x by $x - h$, y by $y - k$, and z by $z - l$, and the particular standardized form will be that of the surface with center at (h, k, l). For example, the elliptic paraboloid would be

$$\frac{(x - h)^2}{a^2} + \frac{(y - k)^2}{b^2} = c(z - l).$$

Curves and Surfaces

Elliptic cylinder

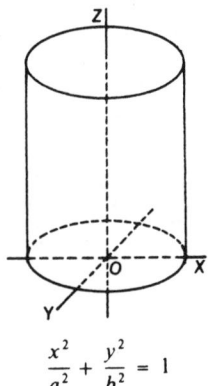

$$\frac{x^2}{a^2} + \frac{y^2}{b^2} = 1$$

Hyperboloid of one sheet

$$\frac{x^2}{a^2} + \frac{y^2}{b^2} - \frac{z^2}{c^2} = 1$$

Elliptic paraboloid

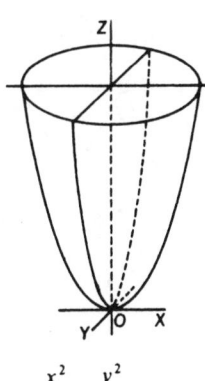

$$\frac{x^2}{a^2} + \frac{y^2}{b^2} = cz$$

Hyperboloid of two sheets

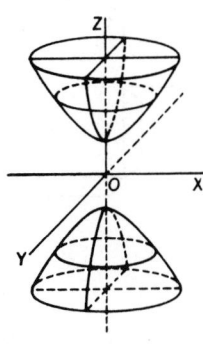

$$\frac{z^2}{c^2} - \frac{x^2}{a^2} - \frac{y^2}{b^2} = 1$$

Sphere

Hyperbolic paraboloid

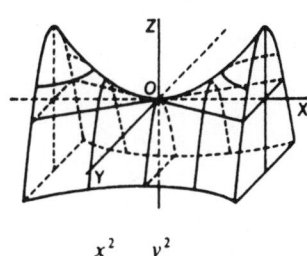

$$\frac{x^2}{a^2} - \frac{y^2}{b^2} = cz$$

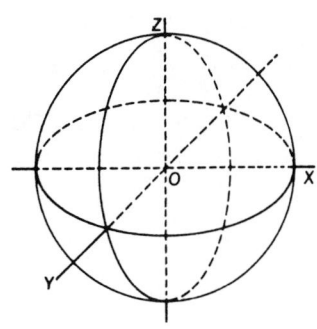

$$x^2 + y^2 + z^2 = a^2$$

Curves and Surfaces

PATTERNS OF REGULAR POLYHEDRA

Tetrahedron

Octahedron

Hexahedron, or **Cube**

Icosahedron

Dodecahedron

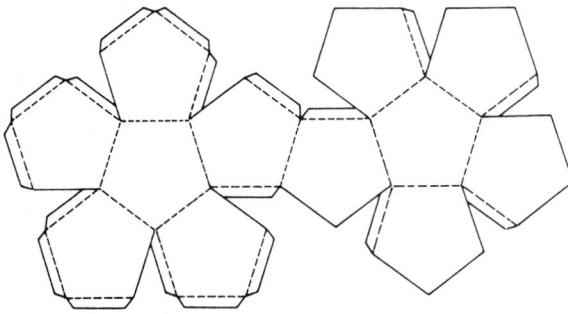

VIII. CALCULUS

Derivatives *

In the following formulas u, v, w represent functions of x, while a, c, n represent fixed real numbers. All arguments in the trigonometric functions are measured in radians, and all inverse trigonometric and hyperbolic functions represent principal values.

1. $\dfrac{d}{dx}(a) = 0$

2. $\dfrac{d}{dx}(x) = 1$

3. $\dfrac{d}{dx}(au) = a\dfrac{du}{dx}$

4. $\dfrac{d}{dx}(u + v - w) = \dfrac{du}{dx} + \dfrac{dv}{dx} - \dfrac{dw}{dx}$

5. $\dfrac{d}{dx}(uv) = u\dfrac{dv}{dx} + v\dfrac{du}{dx}$

6. $\dfrac{d}{dx}(uvw) = uv\dfrac{dw}{dx} + vw\dfrac{du}{dx} + uw\dfrac{dv}{dx}$ and so on to n factors

7. $\dfrac{d}{dx}\left(\dfrac{u}{v}\right) = \dfrac{v\dfrac{du}{dx} - u\dfrac{dv}{dx}}{v^2} = \dfrac{1}{v}\dfrac{du}{dx} - \dfrac{u}{v^2}\dfrac{dv}{dx}$

8. $\dfrac{d}{dx}(u^n) = nu^{n-1}\dfrac{du}{dx}$

9. $\dfrac{d}{dx}(\sqrt{u}) = \dfrac{1}{2\sqrt{u}}\dfrac{du}{dx}$

10. $\dfrac{d}{dx}\left(\dfrac{1}{u}\right) = -\dfrac{1}{u^2}\dfrac{du}{dx}$

11. $\dfrac{d}{dx}\left(\dfrac{1}{u^n}\right) = -\dfrac{n}{u^{n+1}}\dfrac{du}{dx}$

12. $\dfrac{d}{dx}\left(\dfrac{u^n}{v^m}\right) = \dfrac{u^{n-1}}{v^{m+1}}\left(nv\dfrac{du}{dx} - mu\dfrac{dv}{dx}\right)$

13. $\dfrac{d}{dx}(u^n v^m) = u^{n-1}v^{m-1}\left(nv\dfrac{du}{dx} + mu\dfrac{dv}{dx}\right)$

---

*Let $y = f(x)$ and $\dfrac{dy}{dx} = \dfrac{d[f(x)]}{dx} = f'(x)$ define respectively a function and its derivative for any value x in their common domain. The differential for the function at such a value x is accordingly defined as

$$dy = d[f(x)] = \dfrac{dy}{dx}\,dx = \dfrac{d[f(x)]}{dx}\,dx = f'(x)dx$$

Each derivative formula has an associated differential formula. For example, formula 6 above has the differential formula

$$d(uvw) = uv\,dw + vw\,du + uw\,dv$$

DERIVATIVES (Continued)

14. $\dfrac{d}{dx}[f(u)] = \dfrac{d}{du}[f(u)] \cdot \dfrac{du}{dx}$

15. $\dfrac{d^2}{dx^2}[f(u)] = \dfrac{df(u)}{du} \cdot \dfrac{d^2u}{dx^2} + \dfrac{d^2f(u)}{du^2} \cdot \left(\dfrac{du}{dx}\right)^2$

16. $\dfrac{d^n}{dx^n}[uv] = \dbinom{n}{0}v\dfrac{d^n u}{dx^n} + \dbinom{n}{1}\dfrac{dv}{dx}\dfrac{d^{n-1}u}{dx^{n-1}} + \dbinom{n}{2}\dfrac{d^2 v}{dx^2}\dfrac{d^{n-2}u}{dx^{n-2}}$

$$+ \cdots + \dbinom{n}{k}\dfrac{d^k v}{dx^k}\dfrac{d^{n-k}u}{dx^{n-k}} + \cdots + \dbinom{n}{n}u\dfrac{d^n v}{dx^n}$$

where $\dbinom{n}{r} = \dfrac{n!}{r!(n-r)!}$ the binomial coefficient, n non-negative integer and $\dbinom{n}{0} = 1$

17. $\dfrac{du}{dx} = \dfrac{1}{\dfrac{dx}{du}}$　　if $\dfrac{dx}{du} \neq 0$

18. $\dfrac{d}{dx}(\log_a u) = (\log_a e)\dfrac{1}{u}\dfrac{du}{dx}$

19. $\dfrac{d}{dx}(\log_e u) = \dfrac{1}{u}\dfrac{du}{dx}$

20. $\dfrac{d}{dx}(a^u) = a^u(\log_e a)\dfrac{du}{dx}$

21. $\dfrac{d}{dx}(e^u) = e^u\dfrac{du}{dx}$

22. $\dfrac{d}{dx}(u^v) = vu^{v-1}\dfrac{du}{dx} + (\log_e u)u^v\dfrac{dv}{dx}$

23. $\dfrac{d}{dx}(\sin u) = \dfrac{du}{dx}(\cos u)$

24. $\dfrac{d}{dx}(\cos u) = -\dfrac{du}{dx}(\sin u)$

25. $\dfrac{d}{dx}(\tan u) = \dfrac{du}{dx}(\sec^2 u)$

26. $\dfrac{d}{dx}(\cot u) = -\dfrac{du}{dx}(\csc^2 u)$

27. $\dfrac{d}{dx}(\sec u) = \dfrac{du}{dx}\sec u \cdot \tan u$

28. $\dfrac{d}{dx}(\csc u) = -\dfrac{du}{dx}\csc u \cdot \cot u$

29. $\dfrac{d}{dx}(\text{vers } u) = \dfrac{du}{dx}\sin u$

DERIVATIVES (Continued)

30. $\dfrac{d}{dx}(\text{arc sin } u) = \dfrac{1}{\sqrt{1 - u^2}} \dfrac{du}{dx}, \qquad \left(-\dfrac{\pi}{2} \le \text{arc sin } u \le \dfrac{\pi}{2} \right)$

31. $\dfrac{d}{dx}(\text{arc cos } u) = -\dfrac{1}{\sqrt{1 - u^2}} \dfrac{du}{dx}, \qquad (0 \le \text{arc cos } u \le \pi)$

32. $\dfrac{d}{dx}(\text{arc tan } u) = \dfrac{1}{1 + u^2} \dfrac{du}{dx}, \qquad \left(-\dfrac{\pi}{2} < \text{arc tan } u < \dfrac{\pi}{2} \right)$

33. $\dfrac{d}{dx}(\text{arc cot } u) = -\dfrac{1}{1 + u^2} \dfrac{du}{dx}, \qquad (0 \le \text{arc cot } u \le \pi)$

34. $\dfrac{d}{dx}(\text{arc sec } u) = \dfrac{1}{u\sqrt{u^2 - 1}} \dfrac{du}{dx}, \qquad \left(0 \le \text{arc sec } u < \dfrac{\pi}{2}, -\pi \le \text{arc sec } u < -\dfrac{\pi}{2} \right)$

35. $\dfrac{d}{dx}(\text{arc csc } u) = -\dfrac{1}{u\sqrt{u^2 - 1}} \dfrac{du}{dx}, \qquad \left(0 < \text{arc csc } u \le \dfrac{\pi}{2}, -\pi < \text{arc csc } u \le -\dfrac{\pi}{2} \right)$

36. $\dfrac{d}{dx}(\text{arc vers } u) = \dfrac{1}{\sqrt{2u - u^2}} \dfrac{du}{dx}, \qquad (0 \le \text{arc vers } u \le \pi)$

37. $\dfrac{d}{dx}(\sinh u) = \dfrac{du}{dx}(\cosh u)$

38. $\dfrac{d}{dx}(\cosh u) = \dfrac{du}{dx}(\sinh u)$

39. $\dfrac{d}{dx}(\tanh u) = \dfrac{du}{dx}(\text{sech}^2 u)$

40. $\dfrac{d}{dx}(\coth u) = -\dfrac{du}{dx}(\text{csch}^2 u)$

41. $\dfrac{d}{dx}(\text{sech } u) = -\dfrac{du}{dx}(\text{sech } u \cdot \tanh u)$

42. $\dfrac{d}{dx}(\text{csch } u) = -\dfrac{du}{dx}(\text{csch } u \cdot \coth u)$

43. $\dfrac{d}{dx}(\sinh^{-1} u) = \dfrac{d}{dx}[\log(u + \sqrt{u^2 + 1})] = \dfrac{1}{\sqrt{u^2 + 1}} \dfrac{du}{dx}$

44. $\dfrac{d}{dx}(\cosh^{-1} u) = \dfrac{d}{dx}[\log(u + \sqrt{u^2 - 1})] = \dfrac{1}{\sqrt{u^2 - 1}} \dfrac{du}{dx}, \qquad (u > 1, \cosh^{-1} u > 0)$

45. $\dfrac{d}{dx}(\tanh^{-1} u) = \dfrac{d}{dx}\left[\dfrac{1}{2}\log\dfrac{1 + u}{1 - u} \right] = \dfrac{1}{1 - u^2} \dfrac{du}{dx}, \qquad (u^2 < 1)$

46. $\dfrac{d}{dx}(\coth^{-1} u) = \dfrac{d}{dx}\left[\dfrac{1}{2}\log\dfrac{u + 1}{u - 1} \right] = \dfrac{1}{1 - u^2} \dfrac{du}{dx}, \qquad (u^2 > 1)$

47. $\dfrac{d}{dx}(\text{sech}^{-1} u) = \dfrac{d}{dx}\left[\log\dfrac{1 + \sqrt{1 - u^2}}{u} \right] = -\dfrac{1}{u\sqrt{1 - u^2}} \dfrac{du}{dx}, \qquad (0 < u < 1, \text{sech}^{-1} u > 0)$

DERIVATIVES (Continued)

48. $\dfrac{d}{dx}(\operatorname{csch}^{-1} u) = \dfrac{d}{dx}\left[\log \dfrac{1 + \sqrt{1 + u^2}}{u}\right] = -\dfrac{1}{|u|\sqrt{1 + u^2}}\dfrac{du}{dx}$

49. $\dfrac{d}{dq}\displaystyle\int_p^q f(x)\,dx = f(q),$ [p constant]

50. $\dfrac{d}{dp}\displaystyle\int_p^q f(x)\,dx = -f(p),$ [q constant]

51. $\dfrac{d}{da}\displaystyle\int_p^q f(x, a)\,dx = \int_p^q \dfrac{\partial}{\partial a}[f(x, a)]\,dx + f(q, a)\dfrac{dq}{da} - f(p, a)\dfrac{dp}{da}$

INTEGRATION

The following is a brief discussion of some integration techniques. A more complete discussion can be found in a number of good text books. However, the purpose of this introduction is simply to discuss a few of the important techniques which may be used, in conjunction with the integral table which follows, to integrate particular functions.

No matter how extensive the integral table, it is a fairly uncommon occurrence to find in the table the exact integral desired. Usually some form of transformation will have to be made. The simplest type of transformation, and yet the most general, is substitution. Simple forms of substitution, such as $y = ax$, are employed almost unconsciously by experienced users of integral tables. Other substitutions may require more thought. In some sections of the tables, appropriate substitutions are suggested for integrals which are similar to, but not exactly like, integrals in the table. Finding the right substitution is largely a matter of intuition and experience.

Several precautions must be observed when using substitutions:

1. Be sure to make the substitution in the dx term, as well as everywhere else in the integral.
2. Be sure that the function substituted is one-to-one and continuous. If this is not the case, the integral must be restricted in such a way as to make it true. See the example following.
3. With definite integrals, the limits should also be expressed in terms of the new dependent variable. With indefinite integrals, it is necessary to perform the reverse substitution to obtain the answer in terms of the original independent variable. This may also be done for definite integrals, but it is usually easier to change the limits.

Example:

$$\int \frac{x^4}{\sqrt{a^2 - x^2}} \, dx$$

Here we make the substitution $x = |a| \sin \theta$. Then $dx = |a| \cos \theta \, d\theta$, and

$$\sqrt{a^2 - x^2} = \sqrt{a^2 - a^2 \sin^2 \theta} = |a|\sqrt{1 - \sin^2 \theta} = |a \cos \theta|$$

Notice the absolute value signs. It is very important to keep in mind that a square root radical always denotes the positive square root, and to assure the sign is always kept positive. Thus $\sqrt{x^2} = |x|$. Failure to observe this is a common cause of errors in integration.

Notice also that the indicated substitution is not a one-to-one function, that is, it does not have a unique inverse. Thus we must restrict the range of θ in such a way as to make the function one-to-one. Fortunately, this is easily done by solving for θ

$$\theta = \sin^{-1} \frac{x}{|a|}$$

and restricting the inverse sine to the principal values, $-\frac{\pi}{2} \le \theta \le \frac{\pi}{2}$.

Thus the integral becomes

$$\int \frac{a^4 \sin^4 \theta |a| \cos \theta \, d\theta}{|a| |\cos \theta|}$$

Now, however, in the range of values chosen for θ, $\cos \theta$ is always positive. Thus we may remove the absolute value signs from $\cos \theta$ in the denominator. (This is one of the reasons that the principal values of the inverse trigonometric functions are defined as they are.)

Then the $\cos \theta$ terms cancel, and the integral becomes

$$a^4 \int \sin^4 \theta \, d\theta$$

By application of integral formulas 299 and 296, we integrate this to

$$-a^4 \frac{\sin^3 \theta \cos \theta}{4} - \frac{3a^4}{8} \cos \theta \sin \theta + \frac{3a^4}{8} \theta + C$$

We now must perform the inverse substitution to get the result in terms of x. We have

$$\theta = \sin^{-1} \frac{x}{|a|}$$

$$\sin \theta = \frac{x}{|a|}$$

Then

$$\cos \theta = \pm \sqrt{1 - \sin^2 \theta} = \pm \sqrt{1 - \frac{x^2}{a^2}} = \pm \frac{\sqrt{a^2 - x^2}}{|a|}.$$

Because of the previously mentioned fact that $\cos \theta$ is positive, we may omit the $\pm$ sign. The reverse substitution then produces the final answer

$$\int \frac{x^4}{\sqrt{a^2 - x^2}} \, dx = -\tfrac{1}{4}x^3 \sqrt{a^2 - x^2} - \tfrac{3}{8}a^2 x \sqrt{a^2 - x^2} + \frac{3a^4}{8} \sin^{-1} \frac{x}{|a|} + C.$$

Any rational function of x may be integrated, if the denominator is factored into linear and irreducible quadratic factors. The function may then be broken into partial fractions, and the individual partial fractions integrated by use of the appropriate formula from the integral table. See the section on partial fractions for further information.

Many integrals may be reduced to rational functions by proper substitutions. For example,

$$z = \tan \frac{x}{2}$$

will reduce any rational function of the six trigonometric functions of x to a rational function of z. (Frequently there are other substitutions which are simpler to use, but this one will always work. See integral formula number 484.)

Any rational function of x and $\sqrt{ax + b}$ may be reduced to a rational function of z by making the substitution

$$z = \sqrt{ax + b}.$$

Other likely substitutions will be suggested by looking at the form of the integrand.

The other main method of transforming integrals is integration by parts. This involves applying formula number 5 or 6 in the accompanying integral table. The critical factor in this method is the choice of the functions u and v. In order for the method to be successful, $v = \int dv$ and $\int v \, du$ must be easier to integrate than the original integral. Again, this choice is largely a matter of intuition and experience.

Example:

$$\int x \sin x \, dx$$

Two obvious choices are $u = x$, $dv = \sin x \, dx$, or $u = \sin x$, $dv = x \, dx$. Since a preliminary mental calculation indicates that $\int v \, du$ in the second choice would be more, rather than less, complicated than the original integral (it would contain x^2), we use the first choice.

$$u = x \qquad\qquad du = dx$$

$$dv = \sin x\, dx \qquad\qquad v = -\cos x$$

$$\int x \sin x\, dx = \int u\, dv = uv - \int v\, du = -x \cos x + \int \cos x\, dx$$

$$= \sin x - x \cos x$$

Of course, this result could have been obtained directly from the integral table, but it provides a simple example of the method. In more complicated examples the choice of u and v may not be so obvious, and several different choices may have to be tried Of course, there is no guarantee that any of them will work.

Integration by parts may be applied more than once, or combined with substitution. A fairly common case is illustrated by the following example.

Example:

$$\int e^x \sin x\, dx$$

Let

$$u = e^x \qquad \text{Then} \quad du = e^x\, dx$$

$$dv = \sin x\, dx \qquad\qquad v = -\cos x$$

$$\int e^x \sin x\, dx = \int u\, dv = uv - \int v\, du = -e^x \cos x + \int e^x \cos x\, dx$$

In this latter integral,

$$\text{let} \quad u = e^x \qquad\qquad \text{Then} \quad du = e^x\, dx$$

$$dv = \cos x\, dx \qquad\qquad v = \sin x$$

$$\int e^x \sin x\, dx = -e^x \cos x + \int e^x \cos x\, dx = -e^x \cos x + \int u\, dv$$

$$= -e^x \cos x + uv - \int v\, du$$

$$= -e^x \cos x + e^x \sin x - \int e^x \sin x\, dx$$

This looks as if a circular transformation has taken place, since we are back at the same integral we started from. However, the above equation can be solved algebraically for the required integral:

$$\int e^x \sin x\, dx = \tfrac{1}{2}(e^x \sin x - e^x \cos x)$$

In the second integration by parts, if the parts had been chosen as $u = \cos x$, $dv = e^x\, dx$, we would indeed have made a circular transformation, and returned to the starting place. In general, when doing repeated integration by parts, one should never choose the function u at any stage to be the same as the function v at the previous stage, or a constant times the previous v.

The following rule is called the extended rule for integration by parts. It is the result of $n + 1$ successive applications of integration by parts.

If

$$g_1(x) = \int g(x)\,dx, \qquad g_2(x) = \int g_1(x)\,dx,$$

$$g_3(x) = \int g_2(x)\,dx, \ldots, g_m(x) = \int g_{m-1}(x)\,dx, \ldots,$$

then

$$\int f(x) \cdot g(x)\,dx = f(x) \cdot g_1(x) - f'(x) \cdot g_2(x) + f''(x) \cdot g_3(x) - + \cdots$$

$$+ (-1)^n f^{(n)}(x) g_{n+1}(x) + (-1)^{n+1} \int f^{(n+1)}(x) g_{n+1}(x)\,dx.$$

A useful special case of the above rule is when $f(x)$ is a polynomial of degree n. Then $f^{(n+1)}(x) = 0$, and

$$\int f(x) \cdot g(x)\,dx = f(x) \cdot g_1(x) - f'(x) \cdot g_2(x) + f''(x) \cdot g_3(x) - + \cdots + (-1)^n f^{(n)}(x) g_{n+1}(x) + C$$

Example:

If $f(x) = x^2, g(x) = \sin x$

$$\int x^2 \sin x\,dx = -x^2 \cos x + 2x \sin x + 2 \cos x + C$$

Another application of this formula occurs if

$$f''(x) = af(x) \quad \text{and} \quad g''(x) = bg(x),$$

where a and b are unequal constants. In this case, by a process similar to that used in the above example for $\int e^x \sin x\,dx$, we get the formula

$$\int f(x) g(x)\,dx = \frac{f(x) \cdot g'(x) - f'(x) \cdot g(x)}{b - a} + C$$

This formula could have been used in the example mentioned. Here is another example.

Example:

If $f(x) = e^{2x}, g(x) = \sin 3x$, then $a = 4, b = -9$, and

$$\int e^{2x} \sin 3x\,dx = \frac{3 e^{2x} \cos 3x - 2 e^{2x} \sin 3x}{-9 - 4} + C = \frac{e^{2x}}{13}(2 \sin 3x - 3 \cos 3x) + C$$

The following additional points should be observed when using this table.

1. A constant of integration is to be supplied with the answers for indefinite integrals.
2. Logarithmic expressions are to base $e = 2.71828\ldots$, unless otherwise specified, and are to be evaluated for the absolute value of the arguments involved therein.
3. All angles are measured in radians, and inverse trigonometric and hyperbolic functions represent principal values, unless otherwise indicated.
4. If the application of a formula produces either a zero denominator or the square root of a negative number in the result, there is usually available another form of the answer which avoids this difficulty. In many of the results, the excluded values are specified, but when such are omitted it is presumed that one can tell what these should be, especially when difficulties of the type herein mentioned are obtained.
5. When inverse trigonometric functions occur in the integrals, be sure that any replacements made for them are strictly in accordance with the rules for such functions. This causes

little difficulty when the argument of the inverse trigonometric function is positive, since then all angles involved are in the first quadrant. However, if the argument is negative, special care must be used. Thus if $u > 0$,

$$\sin^{-1} u = \cos^{-1}\sqrt{1 - u^2} = \csc^{-1}\frac{1}{u}, \text{ etc.}$$

However, if $u < 0$,

$$\sin^{-1} u = -\cos^{-1}\sqrt{1 - u^2} = -\pi - \csc^{-1}\frac{1}{u}, \text{ etc.}$$

See the section on inverse trigonometric functions for a full treatment of the allowable substitutions.

6. In integrals 340–345 and some others, the right side includes expressions of the form

$$A \tan^{-1}[B + C \tan f(x)].$$

In these formulas, the $\tan^{-1}$ does not necessarily represent the principal value. Instead of always employing the principal branch of the inverse tangent function, one must instead use that branch of the inverse tangent function upon which $f(x)$ lies for any particular choice of x.

Example:

$$\int_0^{4\pi} \frac{dx}{2 + \sin x} = \frac{2}{\sqrt{3}}\tan^{-1}\frac{2\tan\frac{x}{2} + 1}{\sqrt{3}}\Bigg]_0^{4\pi}$$

$$= \frac{2}{\sqrt{3}}\left[\tan^{-1}\frac{2\tan 2\pi + 1}{\sqrt{3}} - \tan^{-1}\frac{2\tan 0 + 1}{\sqrt{3}}\right]$$

$$= \frac{2}{\sqrt{3}}\left[\frac{13\pi}{6} - \frac{\pi}{6}\right] = \frac{4\pi}{\sqrt{3}} = \frac{4\sqrt{3}\pi}{3}$$

Here

$$\tan^{-1}\frac{2\tan 2\pi + 1}{\sqrt{3}} = \tan^{-1}\frac{1}{\sqrt{3}} = \frac{13\pi}{6},$$

since $f(x) = 2\pi$; and

$$\tan^{-1}\frac{2\tan 0 + 1}{\sqrt{3}} = \tan^{-1}\frac{1}{\sqrt{3}} = \frac{\pi}{6},$$

since $f(x) = 0$.

7. B_n and E_n where used in Integrals represents the Bernoulli and Euler numbers as defined in the tables contained from pages 392—398.

INTEGRALS

ELEMENTARY FORMS

1. $\int a\,dx = ax$

2. $\int a \cdot f(x)\,dx = a \int f(x)\,dx$

3. $\int \phi(y)\,dx = \int \dfrac{\phi(y)}{y'}\,dy,$ where $y' = \dfrac{dy}{dx}$

4. $\int (u + v)\,dx = \int u\,dx + \int v\,dx,$ where u and v are any functions of x

5. $\int u\,dv = u \int dv - \int v\,du = uv - \int v\,du$

6. $\int u\dfrac{dv}{dx}dx = uv - \int v\dfrac{du}{dx}dx$

7. $\int x^n\,dx = \dfrac{x^{n+1}}{n+1},$ except $n = -1$

8. $\int \dfrac{f'(x)\,dx}{f(x)} = \log f(x),$ $(df(x) = f'(x)\,dx)$

9. $\int \dfrac{dx}{x} = \log x$

10. $\int \dfrac{f'(x)\,dx}{2\sqrt{f(x)}} = \sqrt{f(x)},$ $(df(x) = f'(x)\,dx)$

11. $\int e^x\,dx = e^x$

12. $\int e^{ax}\,dx = e^{ax}/a$

13. $\int b^{ax}\,dx = \dfrac{b^{ax}}{a\log b},$ $(b > 0)$

14. $\int \log x\,dx = x\log x - x$

15. $\int a^x \log a\,dx = a^x,$ $(a > 0)$

16. $\int \dfrac{dx}{a^2 + x^2} = \dfrac{1}{a}\tan^{-1}\dfrac{x}{a}$

INTEGRALS (Continued)

17. $\int \dfrac{dx}{a^2 - x^2} = \begin{cases} \dfrac{1}{a}\tanh^{-1}\dfrac{x}{a} \\ \text{or} \\ \dfrac{1}{2a}\log\dfrac{a + x}{a - x}, \quad (a^2 > x^2) \end{cases}$

18. $\int \dfrac{dx}{x^2 - a^2} = \begin{cases} -\dfrac{1}{a}\coth^{-1}\dfrac{x}{a} \\ \text{or} \\ \dfrac{1}{2a}\log\dfrac{x - a}{x + a}, \quad (x^2 > a^2) \end{cases}$

19. $\int \dfrac{dx}{\sqrt{a^2 - x^2}} = \begin{cases} \sin^{-1}\dfrac{x}{|a|} \\ \text{or} \\ -\cos^{-1}\dfrac{x}{|a|}, \quad (a^2 > x^2) \end{cases}$

20. $\int \dfrac{dx}{\sqrt{x^2 \pm a^2}} = \log\left(x + \sqrt{x^2 \pm a^2}\right)$

21. $\int \dfrac{dx}{x\sqrt{x^2 - a^2}} = \dfrac{1}{|a|}\sec^{-1}\dfrac{x}{a}$

22. $\int \dfrac{dx}{x\sqrt{a^2 \pm x^2}} = -\dfrac{1}{a}\log\left(\dfrac{a + \sqrt{a^2 \pm x^2}}{x}\right)$

FORMS CONTAINING $(a + bx)$

For forms containing $a + bx$, but not listed in the table, the substitution $u = \dfrac{a + bx}{x}$ may prove helpful.

23. $\int (a + bx)^n\, dx = \dfrac{(a + bx)^{n+1}}{(n + 1)b}, \quad (n \neq -1)$

24. $\int x(a + bx)^n\, dx$

$= \dfrac{1}{b^2(n + 2)}(a + bx)^{n+2} - \dfrac{a}{b^2(n + 1)}(a + bx)^{n+1}, \quad (n \neq -1, -2)$

25. $\int x^2(a + bx)^n\, dx = \dfrac{1}{b^3}\left[\dfrac{(a + bx)^{n+3}}{n + 3} - 2a\dfrac{(a + bx)^{n+2}}{n + 2} + a^2\dfrac{(a + bx)^{n+1}}{n + 1}\right]$

INTEGRALS (Continued)

26. $\int x^m(a + bx)^n \, dx =$
$$\begin{cases} \dfrac{x^{m+1}(a + bx)^n}{m + n + 1} + \dfrac{an}{m + n + 1} \int x^m(a + bx)^{n-1} \, dx \\[4pt] \text{or} \\[4pt] \dfrac{1}{a(n + 1)}\left[-x^{m+1}(a + bx)^{n+1} + (m + n + 2) \int x^m(a + bx)^{n+1} \, dx \right] \\[4pt] \text{or} \\[4pt] \dfrac{1}{b(m + n + 1)}\left[x^m(a + bx)^{n+1} - ma \int x^{m-1}(a + bx)^n \, dx \right] \end{cases}$$

27. $\displaystyle \int \frac{dx}{a + bx} = \frac{1}{b} \log (a + bx)$

28. $\displaystyle \int \frac{dx}{(a + bx)^2} = -\frac{1}{b(a + bx)}$

29. $\displaystyle \int \frac{dx}{(a + bx)^3} = -\frac{1}{2b(a + bx)^2}$

30. $\displaystyle \int \frac{x \, dx}{a + bx} = \begin{cases} \dfrac{1}{b^2}[a + bx - a \log (a + bx)] \\[4pt] \text{or} \\[4pt] \dfrac{x}{b} - \dfrac{a}{b^2} \log (a + bx) \end{cases}$

31. $\displaystyle \int \frac{x \, dx}{(a + bx)^2} = \frac{1}{b^2}\left[\log (a + bx) + \frac{a}{a + bx} \right]$

32. $\displaystyle \int \frac{x \, dx}{(a + bx)^n} = \frac{1}{b^2}\left[\frac{-1}{(n - 2)(a + bx)^{n-2}} + \frac{a}{(n - 1)(a + bx)^{n-1}} \right], \quad n \neq 1, 2$

33. $\displaystyle \int \frac{x^2 \, dx}{a + bx} = \frac{1}{b^3}\left[\frac{1}{2}(a + bx)^2 - 2a(a + bx) + a^2 \log (a + bx) \right]$

34. $\displaystyle \int \frac{x^2 \, dx}{(a + bx)^2} = \frac{1}{b^3}\left[a + bx - 2a \log (a + bx) - \frac{a^2}{a + bx} \right]$

35. $\displaystyle \int \frac{x^2 \, dx}{(a + bx)^3} = \frac{1}{b^3}\left[\log (a + bx) + \frac{2a}{a + bx} - \frac{a^2}{2(a + bx)^2} \right]$

36. $\displaystyle \int \frac{x^2 \, dx}{(a + bx)^n} = \frac{1}{b^3}\left[\frac{-1}{(n - 3)(a + bx)^{n-3}} + \frac{2a}{(n - 2)(a + bx)^{n-2}} - \frac{a^2}{(n - 1)(a + bx)^{n-1}} \right], \quad n \neq 1, 2, 3$

INTEGRALS (Continued)

37. $\displaystyle\int \frac{dx}{x(a + bx)} = -\frac{1}{a}\log\frac{a + bx}{x}$

38. $\displaystyle\int \frac{dx}{x(a + bx)^2} = \frac{1}{a(a + bx)} - \frac{1}{a^2}\log\frac{a + bx}{x}$

39. $\displaystyle\int \frac{dx}{x(a + bx)^3} = \frac{1}{a^3}\left[\frac{1}{2}\left(\frac{2a + bx}{a + bx}\right)^2 + \log\frac{x}{a + bx}\right]$

40. $\displaystyle\int \frac{dx}{x^2(a + bx)} = -\frac{1}{ax} + \frac{b}{a^2}\log\frac{a + bx}{x}$

41. $\displaystyle\int \frac{dx}{x^3(a + bx)} = \frac{2bx - a}{2a^2x^2} + \frac{b^2}{a^3}\log\frac{x}{a + bx}$

42. $\displaystyle\int \frac{dx}{x^2(a + bx)^2} = -\frac{a + 2bx}{a^2x(a + bx)} + \frac{2b}{a^3}\log\frac{a + bx}{x}$

FORMS CONTAINING $c^2 \pm x^2$, $x^2 - c^2$

43. $\displaystyle\int \frac{dx}{c^2 + x^2} = \frac{1}{c}\tan^{-1}\frac{x}{c}$

44. $\displaystyle\int \frac{dx}{c^2 - x^2} = \frac{1}{2c}\log\frac{c + x}{c - x}, \qquad (c^2 > x^2)$

45. $\displaystyle\int \frac{dx}{x^2 - c^2} = \frac{1}{2c}\log\frac{x - c}{x + c}, \qquad (x^2 > c^2)$

46. $\displaystyle\int \frac{x\,dx}{c^2 \pm x^2} = \pm\frac{1}{2}\log(c^2 \pm x^2)$

47. $\displaystyle\int \frac{x\,dx}{(c^2 \pm x^2)^{n+1}} = \mp\frac{1}{2n(c^2 \pm x^2)^n}$

48. $\displaystyle\int \frac{dx}{(c^2 \pm x^2)^n} = \frac{1}{2c^2(n - 1)}\left[\frac{x}{(c^2 \pm x^2)^{n-1}} + (2n - 3)\int\frac{dx}{(c^2 \pm x^2)^{n-1}}\right]$

49. $\displaystyle\int \frac{dx}{(x^2 - c^2)^n} = \frac{1}{2c^2(n - 1)}\left[-\frac{x}{(x^2 - c^2)^{n-1}} - (2n - 3)\int\frac{dx}{(x^2 - c^2)^{n-1}}\right]$

50. $\displaystyle\int \frac{x\,dx}{x^2 - c^2} = \frac{1}{2}\log(x^2 - c^2)$

51. $\displaystyle\int \frac{x\,dx}{(x^2 - c^2)^{n+1}} = -\frac{1}{2n(x^2 - c^2)^n}$

INTEGRALS (Continued)

FORMS CONTAINING $a + bx$ and $c + dx$

$$u = a + bx, \qquad v = c + dx, \qquad k = ad - bc$$

If $k = 0$, then $v = \dfrac{c}{a}u$

52. $\displaystyle \int \frac{dx}{u \cdot v} = \frac{1}{k} \cdot \log\left(\frac{v}{u}\right)$

53. $\displaystyle \int \frac{x\,dx}{u \cdot v} = \frac{1}{k}\left[\frac{a}{b}\log(u) - \frac{c}{d}\log(v)\right]$

54. $\displaystyle \int \frac{dx}{u^2 \cdot v} = \frac{1}{k}\left(\frac{1}{u} + \frac{d}{k}\log\frac{v}{u}\right)$

55. $\displaystyle \int \frac{x\,dx}{u^2 \cdot v} = \frac{-a}{bku} - \frac{c}{k^2}\log\frac{v}{u}$

56. $\displaystyle \int \frac{x^2\,dx}{u^2 \cdot v} = \frac{a^2}{b^2 ku} + \frac{1}{k^2}\left[\frac{c^2}{d}\log(v) + \frac{a(k - bc)}{b^2}\log(u)\right]$

57. $\displaystyle \int \frac{dx}{u^n \cdot v^m} = \frac{1}{k(m - 1)}\left[\frac{-1}{u^{n-1} \cdot v^{m-1}} - (m + n - 2)b \int \frac{dx}{u^n \cdot v^{m-1}}\right]$

58. $\displaystyle \int \frac{u}{v}\,dx = \frac{bx}{d} + \frac{k}{d^2}\log(v)$

59. $\displaystyle \int \frac{u^m\,dx}{v^n} = \begin{cases} \dfrac{-1}{k(n - 1)}\left[\dfrac{u^{m+1}}{v^{n-1}} + b(n - m - 2)\displaystyle\int \dfrac{u^m}{v^{n-1}}\,dx\right] \\ \qquad\qquad \text{or} \\ \dfrac{-1}{d(n - m - 1)}\left[\dfrac{u^m}{v^{n-1}} + mk\displaystyle\int \dfrac{u^{m-1}}{v^n}\,dx\right] \\ \qquad\qquad \text{or} \\ \dfrac{-1}{d(n - 1)}\left[\dfrac{u^m}{v^{n-1}} - mb\displaystyle\int \dfrac{u^{m-1}}{v^{n-1}}\,dx\right] \end{cases}$

FORMS CONTAINING $(a + bx^n)$

60. $\displaystyle \int \frac{dx}{a + bx^2} = \frac{1}{\sqrt{ab}}\tan^{-1}\frac{x\sqrt{ab}}{a}, \qquad (ab > 0)$

61. $\displaystyle \int \frac{dx}{a + bx^2} = \begin{cases} \dfrac{1}{2\sqrt{-ab}}\log\dfrac{a + x\sqrt{-ab}}{a - x\sqrt{-ab}}, \qquad (ab < 0) \\ \qquad\qquad \text{or} \\ \dfrac{1}{\sqrt{-ab}}\tanh^{-1}\dfrac{x\sqrt{-ab}}{a}, \qquad (ab < 0) \end{cases}$

INTEGRALS (Continued)

62. $\displaystyle\int \frac{dx}{a^2 + b^2x^2} = \frac{1}{ab}\tan^{-1}\frac{bx}{a}$

63. $\displaystyle\int \frac{x\,dx}{a + bx^2} = \frac{1}{2b}\log(a + bx^2)$

64. $\displaystyle\int \frac{x^2\,dx}{a + bx^2} = \frac{x}{b} - \frac{a}{b}\int \frac{dx}{a + bx^2}$

65. $\displaystyle\int \frac{dx}{(a + bx^2)^2} = \frac{x}{2a(a + bx^2)} + \frac{1}{2a}\int \frac{dx}{a + bx^2}$

66. $\displaystyle\int \frac{dx}{a^2 - b^2x^2} = \frac{1}{2ab}\log\frac{a + bx}{a - bx}$

67. $\displaystyle\int \frac{dx}{(a + bx^2)^{m+1}} = \begin{cases} \dfrac{1}{2ma}\dfrac{x}{(a + bx^2)^m} + \dfrac{2m - 1}{2ma}\displaystyle\int \dfrac{dx}{(a + bx^2)^m} \\[2ex] \quad\quad\quad\quad \text{or} \\[2ex] \dfrac{(2m)!}{(m!)^2}\left[\dfrac{x}{2a}\displaystyle\sum_{r=1}^{m}\dfrac{r!(r - 1)!}{(4a)^{m-r}(2r)!(a + bx^2)^r} + \dfrac{1}{(4a)^m}\displaystyle\int \dfrac{dx}{a + bx^2}\right] \end{cases}$

68. $\displaystyle\int \frac{x\,dx}{(a + bx^2)^{m+1}} = -\frac{1}{2bm(a + bx^2)^m}$

69. $\displaystyle\int \frac{x^2\,dx}{(a + bx^2)^{m+1}} = \frac{-x}{2mb(a + bx^2)^m} + \frac{1}{2mb}\int \frac{dx}{(a + bx^2)^m}$

70. $\displaystyle\int \frac{dx}{x(a + bx^2)} = \frac{1}{2a}\log\frac{x^2}{a + bx^2}$

71. $\displaystyle\int \frac{dx}{x^2(a + bx^2)} = -\frac{1}{ax} - \frac{b}{a}\int \frac{dx}{a + bx^2}$

72. $\displaystyle\int \frac{dx}{x(a + bx^2)^{m+1}} = \begin{cases} \dfrac{1}{2am(a + bx^2)^m} + \dfrac{1}{a}\displaystyle\int \dfrac{dx}{x(a + bx^2)^m} \\[2ex] \quad\quad\quad\quad \text{or} \\[2ex] \dfrac{1}{2a^{m+1}}\left[\displaystyle\sum_{r=1}^{m}\dfrac{a^r}{r(a + bx^2)^r} + \log\dfrac{x^2}{a + bx^2}\right] \end{cases}$

73. $\displaystyle\int \frac{dx}{x^2(a + bx^2)^{m+1}} = \frac{1}{a}\int \frac{dx}{x^2(a + bx^2)^m} - \frac{b}{a}\int \frac{dx}{(a + bx^2)^{m+1}}$

74. $\displaystyle\int \frac{dx}{a + bx^3} = \frac{k}{3a}\left[\frac{1}{2}\log\frac{(k + x)^3}{a + bx^3} + \sqrt{3}\tan^{-1}\frac{2x - k}{k\sqrt{3}}\right], \quad \left(k = \sqrt[3]{\frac{a}{b}}\right)$

75. $\displaystyle\int \frac{x\,dx}{a + bx^3} = \frac{1}{3bk}\left[\frac{1}{2}\log\frac{a + bx^3}{(k + x)^3} + \sqrt{3}\tan^{-1}\frac{2x - k}{k\sqrt{3}}\right], \quad \left(k = \sqrt[3]{\frac{a}{b}}\right)$

INTEGRALS (Continued)

76. $\displaystyle\int \frac{x^2\,dx}{a + bx^3} = \frac{1}{3b}\log\,(a + bx^3)$

77. $\displaystyle\int \frac{dx}{a + bx^4} = \frac{k}{2a}\left[\frac{1}{2}\log\frac{x^2 + 2kx + 2k^2}{x^2 - 2kx + 2k^2} + \tan^{-1}\frac{2kx}{2k^2 - x^2}\right],$

$$\left(ab > 0, k = \sqrt[4]{\frac{a}{4b}}\right)$$

78. $\displaystyle\int \frac{dx}{a + bx^4} = \frac{k}{2a}\left[\frac{1}{2}\log\frac{x + k}{x - k} + \tan^{-1}\frac{x}{k}\right], \qquad \left(ab < 0, k = \sqrt[4]{-\frac{a}{b}}\right)$

79. $\displaystyle\int \frac{x\,dx}{a + bx^4} = \frac{1}{2bk}\tan^{-1}\frac{x^2}{k}, \qquad \left(ab > 0, k = \sqrt{\frac{a}{b}}\right)$

80. $\displaystyle\int \frac{x\,dx}{a + bx^4} = \frac{1}{4bk}\log\frac{x^2 - k}{x^2 + k}, \qquad \left(ab < 0, k = \sqrt{-\frac{a}{b}}\right)$

81. $\displaystyle\int \frac{x^2\,dx}{a + bx^4} = \frac{1}{4bk}\left[\frac{1}{2}\log\frac{x^2 - 2kx + 2k^2}{x^2 + 2kx + 2k^2} + \tan^{-1}\frac{2kx}{2k^2 - x^2}\right],$

$$\left(ab > 0, k = \sqrt[4]{\frac{a}{4b}}\right)$$

82. $\displaystyle\int \frac{x^2\,dx}{a + bx^4} = \frac{1}{4bk}\left[\log\frac{x - k}{x + k} + 2\tan^{-1}\frac{x}{k}\right], \qquad \left(ab < 0, k = \sqrt[4]{-\frac{a}{b}}\right)$

83. $\displaystyle\int \frac{x^3\,dx}{a + bx^4} = \frac{1}{4b}\log\,(a + bx^4)$

84. $\displaystyle\int \frac{dx}{x(a + bx^n)} = \frac{1}{an}\log\frac{x^n}{a + bx^n}$

85. $\displaystyle\int \frac{dx}{(a + bx^n)^{m+1}} = \frac{1}{a}\int \frac{dx}{(a + bx^n)^m} - \frac{b}{a}\int \frac{x^n\,dx}{(a + bx^n)^{m+1}}$

86. $\displaystyle\int \frac{x^m\,dx}{(a + bx^n)^{p+1}} = \frac{1}{b}\int \frac{x^{m-n}\,dx}{(a + bx^n)^p} - \frac{a}{b}\int \frac{x^{m-n}\,dx}{(a + bx^n)^{p+1}}$

87. $\displaystyle\int \frac{dx}{x^m(a + bx^n)^{p+1}} = \frac{1}{a}\int \frac{dx}{x^m(a + bx^n)^p} - \frac{b}{a}\int \frac{dx}{x^{m-n}(a + bx^n)^{p+1}}$

INTEGRALS (Continued)

$$88. \int x^m(a + bx^n)^p \, dx = \begin{cases} \dfrac{1}{b(np + m + 1)}\left[x^{m-n+1}(a + bx^n)^{p+1} \right. \\ \qquad\qquad \left. - a(m - n + 1)\int x^{m-n}(a + bx^n)^p \, dx \right] \\ \qquad\qquad\qquad \text{or} \\ \dfrac{1}{np + m + 1}\left[x^{m+1}(a + bx^n)^p \right. \\ \qquad\qquad \left. + anp\int x^m(a + bx^n)^{p-1} \, dx \right] \\ \qquad\qquad\qquad \text{or} \\ \dfrac{1}{a(m + 1)}\left[x^{m+1}(a + bx^n)^{p+1} \right. \\ \qquad\qquad \left. - (m + 1 + np + n)b\int x^{m+n}(a + bx^n)^p \, dx \right] \\ \qquad\qquad\qquad \text{or} \\ \dfrac{1}{an(p + 1)}\left[-x^{m+1}(a + bx^n)^{p+1} \right. \\ \qquad\qquad \left. + (m + 1 + np + n)\int x^m(a + bx^n)^{p+1} \, dx \right] \end{cases}$$

FORMS CONTAINING $c^3 \pm x^3$

$$89. \int \frac{dx}{c^3 \pm x^3} = \pm\frac{1}{6c^2}\log\frac{(c \pm x)^3}{c^3 \pm x^3} + \frac{1}{c^2\sqrt{3}}\tan^{-1}\frac{2x \mp c}{c\sqrt{3}}$$

$$90. \int \frac{dx}{(c^3 \pm x^3)^2} = \frac{x}{3c^3(c^3 \pm x^3)} + \frac{2}{3c^3}\int \frac{dx}{c^3 \pm x^3}$$

$$91. \int \frac{dx}{(c^3 \pm x^3)^{n+1}} = \frac{1}{3nc^3}\left[\frac{x}{(c^3 \pm x^3)^n} + (3n - 1)\int \frac{dx}{(c^3 \pm x^3)^n} \right]$$

$$92. \int \frac{x \, dx}{c^3 \pm x^3} = \frac{1}{6c}\log\frac{c^3 \pm x^3}{(c \pm x)^3} \pm \frac{1}{c\sqrt{3}}\tan^{-1}\frac{2x \mp c}{c\sqrt{3}}$$

$$93. \int \frac{x \, dx}{(c^3 \pm x^3)^2} = \frac{x^2}{3c^3(c^3 \pm x^3)} + \frac{1}{3c^3}\int \frac{x \, dx}{c^3 \pm x^3}$$

$$94. \int \frac{x \, dx}{(c^3 \pm x^3)^{n+1}} = \frac{1}{3nc^3}\left[\frac{x^2}{(c^3 \pm x^3)^n} + (3n - 2)\int \frac{x \, dx}{(c^3 \pm x^3)^n} \right]$$

$$95. \int \frac{x^2 \, dx}{c^3 \pm x^3} = \pm\frac{1}{3}\log(c^3 \pm x^3)$$

INTEGRALS (Continued)

96. $\displaystyle\int \frac{x^2\,dx}{(c^3 \pm x^3)^{n+1}} = \mp\frac{1}{3n(c^3 \pm x^3)^n}$

97. $\displaystyle\int \frac{dx}{x(c^3 \pm x^3)} = \frac{1}{3c^3}\log\frac{x^3}{c^3 \pm x^3}$

98. $\displaystyle\int \frac{dx}{x(c^3 \pm x^3)^2} = \frac{1}{3c^3(c^3 \pm x^3)} + \frac{1}{3c^6}\log\frac{x^3}{c^3 \pm x^3}$

99. $\displaystyle\int \frac{dx}{x(c^3 \pm x^3)^{n+1}} = \frac{1}{3nc^3(c^3 \pm x^3)^n} + \frac{1}{c^3}\int \frac{dx}{x(c^3 \pm x^3)^n}$

100. $\displaystyle\int \frac{dx}{x^2(c^3 \pm x^3)} = -\frac{1}{c^3 x} \mp \frac{1}{c^3}\int \frac{x\,dx}{c^3 \pm x^3}$

101. $\displaystyle\int \frac{dx}{x^2(c^3 \pm x^3)^{n+1}} = \frac{1}{c^3}\int \frac{dx}{x^2(c^3 \pm x^3)^n} \mp \frac{1}{c^3}\int \frac{x\,dx}{(c^3 \pm x^3)^{n+1}}$

FORMS CONTAINING $c^4 \pm x^4$

102. $\displaystyle\int \frac{dx}{c^4 + x^4} = \frac{1}{2c^3\sqrt{2}}\left[\frac{1}{2}\log\frac{x^2 + cx\sqrt{2} + c^2}{x^2 - cx\sqrt{2} + c^2} + \tan^{-1}\frac{cx\sqrt{2}}{c^2 - x^2}\right]$

103. $\displaystyle\int \frac{dx}{c^4 - x^4} = \frac{1}{2c^3}\left[\frac{1}{2}\log\frac{c + x}{c - x} + \tan^{-1}\frac{x}{c}\right]$

104. $\displaystyle\int \frac{x\,dx}{c^4 + x^4} = \frac{1}{2c^2}\tan^{-1}\frac{x^2}{c^2}$

105. $\displaystyle\int \frac{x\,dx}{c^4 - x^4} = \frac{1}{4c^2}\log\frac{c^2 + x^2}{c^2 - x^2}$

106. $\displaystyle\int \frac{x^2\,dx}{c^4 + x^4} = \frac{1}{2c\sqrt{2}}\left[\frac{1}{2}\log\frac{x^2 - cx\sqrt{2} + c^2}{x^2 + cx\sqrt{2} + c^2} + \tan^{-1}\frac{cx\sqrt{2}}{c^2 - x^2}\right]$

107. $\displaystyle\int \frac{x^2\,dx}{c^4 - x^4} = \frac{1}{2c}\left[\frac{1}{2}\log\frac{c + x}{c - x} - \tan^{-1}\frac{x}{c}\right]$

108. $\displaystyle\int \frac{x^3\,dx}{c^4 \pm x^4} = \pm\frac{1}{4}\log(c^4 \pm x^4)$

FORMS CONTAINING $(a + bx + cx^2)$
$$X = a + bx + cx^2 \text{ and } q = 4ac - b^2$$

If $q = 0$, then $X = c\left(x + \dfrac{b}{2c}\right)^2$, and formulas starting with 23 should be used in place of these.

109. $\displaystyle\int \frac{dx}{X} = \frac{2}{\sqrt{q}}\tan^{-1}\frac{2cx + b}{\sqrt{q}}, \qquad (q > 0)$

INTEGRALS (Continued)

110. $$\int \frac{dx}{X} = \begin{cases} \dfrac{-2}{\sqrt{-q}} \tanh^{-1} \dfrac{2cx + b}{\sqrt{-q}} \\[2ex] \qquad\qquad \text{or} \\[2ex] \dfrac{1}{\sqrt{-q}} \log \dfrac{2cx + b - \sqrt{-q}}{2cx + b + \sqrt{-q}}, \quad (q < 0) \end{cases}$$

111. $$\int \frac{dx}{X^2} = \frac{2cx + b}{qX} + \frac{2c}{q} \int \frac{dx}{X}$$

112. $$\int \frac{dx}{X^3} = \frac{2cx + b}{q} \left(\frac{1}{2X^2} + \frac{3c}{qX} \right) + \frac{6c^2}{q^2} \int \frac{dx}{X}$$

113. $$\int \frac{dx}{X^{n+1}} = \begin{cases} \dfrac{2cx + b}{nqX^n} + \dfrac{2(2n - 1)c}{qn} \int \dfrac{dx}{X^n} \\[2ex] \qquad\qquad \text{or} \\[2ex] \dfrac{(2n)!}{(n!)^2} \left(\dfrac{c}{q} \right)^n \left[\dfrac{2cx + b}{q} \sum_{r=1}^{n} \left(\dfrac{q}{cX} \right)^r \left(\dfrac{(r - 1)!r!}{(2r)!} \right) + \int \dfrac{dx}{X} \right] \end{cases}$$

114. $$\int \frac{x\,dx}{X} = \frac{1}{2c} \log X - \frac{b}{2c} \int \frac{dx}{X}$$

115. $$\int \frac{x\,dx}{X^2} = -\frac{bx + 2a}{qX} - \frac{b}{q} \int \frac{dx}{X}$$

116. $$\int \frac{x\,dx}{X^{n+1}} = -\frac{2a + bx}{nqX^n} - \frac{b(2n - 1)}{nq} \int \frac{dx}{X^n}$$

117. $$\int \frac{x^2}{X}\,dx = \frac{x}{c} - \frac{b}{2c^2} \log X + \frac{b^2 - 2ac}{2c^2} \int \frac{dx}{X}$$

118. $$\int \frac{x^2}{X^2}\,dx = \frac{(b^2 - 2ac)x + ab}{cqX} + \frac{2a}{q} \int \frac{dx}{X}$$

119. $$\int \frac{x^m\,dx}{X^{n+1}} = -\frac{x^{m-1}}{(2n - m + 1)cX^n} - \frac{n - m + 1}{2n - m + 1} \cdot \frac{b}{c} \int \frac{x^{m-1}\,dx}{X^{n+1}}$$
$$+ \frac{m - 1}{2n - m + 1} \cdot \frac{a}{c} \int \frac{x^{m-2}\,dx}{X^{n+1}}$$

120. $$\int \frac{dx}{xX} = \frac{1}{2a} \log \frac{x^2}{X} - \frac{b}{2a} \int \frac{dx}{X}$$

121. $$\int \frac{dx}{x^2X} = \frac{b}{2a^2} \log \frac{X}{x^2} - \frac{1}{ax} + \left(\frac{b^2}{2a^2} - \frac{c}{a} \right) \int \frac{dx}{X}$$

122. $$\int \frac{dx}{xX^n} = \frac{1}{2a(n - 1)X^{n-1}} - \frac{b}{2a} \int \frac{dx}{X^n} + \frac{1}{a} \int \frac{dx}{xX^{n-1}}$$

INTEGRALS (Continued)

123. $\displaystyle\int \frac{dx}{x^m X^{n+1}} = -\frac{1}{(m-1)ax^{m-1}X^n} - \frac{n+m-1}{m-1}\cdot\frac{b}{a}\int \frac{dx}{x^{m-1}X^{n+1}}$

$$-\frac{2n+m-1}{m-1}\cdot\frac{c}{a}\int \frac{dx}{x^{m-2}X^{n+1}}$$

FORMS CONTAINING $\sqrt{a+bx}$

124. $\displaystyle\int \sqrt{a+bx}\, dx = \frac{2}{3b}\sqrt{(a+bx)^3}$

125. $\displaystyle\int x\sqrt{a+bx}\, dx = -\frac{2(2a-3bx)\sqrt{(a+bx)^3}}{15b^2}$

126. $\displaystyle\int x^2\sqrt{a+bx}\, dx = \frac{2(8a^2-12abx+15b^2x^2)\sqrt{(a+bx)^3}}{105b^3}$

127. $\displaystyle\int x^m\sqrt{a+bx}\, dx = \begin{cases} \dfrac{2}{b(2m+3)}\left[x^m\sqrt{(a+bx)^3} - ma\int x^{m-1}\sqrt{a+bx}\, dx\right] \\[2mm] \text{or} \\[2mm] \dfrac{2}{b^{m+1}}\sqrt{a+bx}\,\displaystyle\sum_{r=0}^{m}\frac{m!(-a)^{m-r}}{r!(m-r)!(2r+3)}(a+bx)^{r+1} \end{cases}$

128. $\displaystyle\int \frac{\sqrt{a+bx}}{x}\, dx = 2\sqrt{a+bx} + a\int \frac{dx}{x\sqrt{a+bx}}$

129. $\displaystyle\int \frac{\sqrt{a+bx}}{x^2}\, dx = -\frac{\sqrt{a+bx}}{x} + \frac{b}{2}\int \frac{dx}{x\sqrt{a+bx}}$

130. $\displaystyle\int \frac{\sqrt{a+bx}}{x^m}\, dx = -\frac{1}{(m-1)a}\left[\frac{\sqrt{(a+bx)^3}}{x^{m-1}} + \frac{(2m-5)b}{2}\int \frac{\sqrt{a+bx}}{x^{m-1}}\, dx\right]$

131. $\displaystyle\int \frac{dx}{\sqrt{a+bx}} = \frac{2\sqrt{a+bx}}{b}$

132. $\displaystyle\int \frac{x\, dx}{\sqrt{a+bx}} = -\frac{2(2a-bx)}{3b^2}\sqrt{a+bx}$

133. $\displaystyle\int \frac{x^2\, dx}{\sqrt{a+bx}} = \frac{2(8a^2-4abx+3b^2x^2)}{15b^3}\sqrt{a+bx}$

INTEGRALS (Continued)

134. $\displaystyle \int \frac{x^m \, dx}{\sqrt{a + bx}} = \begin{cases} \dfrac{2}{(2m + 1)b}\left[x^m\sqrt{a + bx} - ma \displaystyle\int \dfrac{x^{m-1}\, dx}{\sqrt{a + bx}} \right] \\[2mm] \text{or} \\[2mm] \dfrac{2(-a)^m\sqrt{a + bx}}{b^{m+1}} \displaystyle\sum_{r=0}^{m} \dfrac{(-1)^r m!(a + bx)^r}{(2r + 1)r!(m - r)!a^r} \end{cases}$

135. $\displaystyle \int \frac{dx}{x\sqrt{a + bx}} = \frac{1}{\sqrt{a}} \log\left(\frac{\sqrt{a + bx} - \sqrt{a}}{\sqrt{a + bx} + \sqrt{a}} \right), \qquad (a > 0)$

136. $\displaystyle \int \frac{dx}{x\sqrt{a + bx}} = \frac{2}{\sqrt{-a}} \tan^{-1} \sqrt{\frac{a + bx}{-a}}, \qquad (a < 0)$

137. $\displaystyle \int \frac{dx}{x^2\sqrt{a + bx}} = -\frac{\sqrt{a + bx}}{ax} - \frac{b}{2a}\int \frac{dx}{x\sqrt{a + bx}}$

138. $\displaystyle \int \frac{dx}{x^n\sqrt{a + bx}} = \begin{cases} -\dfrac{\sqrt{a + bx}}{(n - 1)ax^{n-1}} - \dfrac{(2n - 3)b}{(2n - 2)a}\displaystyle\int \dfrac{dx}{x^{n-1}\sqrt{a + bx}} \\[3mm] \text{or} \\[3mm] \dfrac{(2n - 2)!}{[(n - 1)!]^2}\left[-\dfrac{\sqrt{a + bx}}{a}\displaystyle\sum_{r=1}^{n-1} \dfrac{r!(r - 1)!}{x^r(2r)!}\left(-\dfrac{b}{4a} \right)^{n-r-1} \right. \\[3mm] \left. \qquad\qquad\qquad + \left(-\dfrac{b}{4a} \right)^{n-1}\displaystyle\int \dfrac{dx}{x\sqrt{a + bx}} \right] \end{cases}$

139. $\displaystyle \int (a + bx)^{\pm \frac{n}{2}} \, dx = \frac{2(a + bx)^{\frac{2 \pm n}{2}}}{b(2 \pm n)}$

140. $\displaystyle \int x(a + bx)^{\pm \frac{n}{2}} \, dx = \frac{2}{b^2}\left[\frac{(a + bx)^{\frac{4 \pm n}{2}}}{4 \pm n} - \frac{a(a + bx)^{\frac{2 \pm n}{2}}}{2 \pm n} \right]$

141. $\displaystyle \int \frac{dx}{x(a + bx)^{\frac{m}{2}}} = \frac{1}{a}\int \frac{dx}{x(a + bx)^{\frac{m-2}{2}}} - \frac{b}{a}\int \frac{dx}{(a + bx)^{\frac{m}{2}}}$

142. $\displaystyle \int \frac{(a + bx)^{\frac{n}{2}} \, dx}{x} = b\int (a + bx)^{\frac{n-2}{2}} \, dx + a\int \frac{(a + bx)^{\frac{n-2}{2}}}{x}\, dx$

143. $\displaystyle \int f(x, \sqrt{a + bx})\, dx = \frac{2}{b}\int f\left(\frac{z^2 - a}{b}, z \right) z \, dz, \qquad (z = \sqrt{a + bx})$

INTEGRALS (Continued)

FORMS CONTAINING $\sqrt{a + bx}$ and $\sqrt{c + dx}$

$$u = a + bx \qquad v = c + dx \qquad k = ad - bc$$

If $k = 0$, then $v = \dfrac{c}{a}u$, and formulas starting with 124 should be used in place of these.

144. $\displaystyle \int \frac{dx}{\sqrt{uv}} = \begin{cases} \dfrac{2}{\sqrt{bd}} \tanh^{-1} \dfrac{\sqrt{bduv}}{bv}, \ bd > o, \ k < o \\[4mm] \text{or} \\[2mm] \dfrac{2}{\sqrt{bd}} \tanh^{-1} \dfrac{\sqrt{bduv}}{du}, \ bd > o, \ k > o. \\[4mm] \text{or} \\[2mm] \dfrac{1}{\sqrt{bd}} \log \dfrac{(bv + \sqrt{bduv})^2}{v}, \qquad (bd > 0) \end{cases}$

145. $\displaystyle \int \frac{dx}{\sqrt{uv}} = \begin{cases} \dfrac{2}{\sqrt{-bd}} \tan^{-1} \dfrac{\sqrt{-bduv}}{bv} \\[4mm] \text{or} \\[2mm] -\dfrac{1}{\sqrt{-bd}} \sin^{-1} \left(\dfrac{2bdx + ad + bc}{|k|} \right), \qquad (bd < 0) \end{cases}$

146. $\displaystyle \int \sqrt{uv} \, dx = \frac{k + 2bv}{4bd} \sqrt{uv} - \frac{k^2}{8bd} \int \frac{dx}{\sqrt{uv}}$

147. $\displaystyle \int \frac{dx}{v\sqrt{u}} = \begin{cases} \dfrac{1}{\sqrt{kd}} \log \dfrac{d\sqrt{u} - \sqrt{kd}}{d\sqrt{u} + \sqrt{kd}} \\[4mm] \text{or} \\[2mm] \dfrac{1}{\sqrt{kd}} \log \dfrac{(d\sqrt{u} - \sqrt{kd})^2}{v}, \qquad (kd > 0) \end{cases}$

148. $\displaystyle \int \frac{dx}{v\sqrt{u}} = \frac{2}{\sqrt{-kd}} \tan^{-1} \frac{d\sqrt{u}}{\sqrt{-kd}}, \qquad (kd < 0)$

149. $\displaystyle \int \frac{x \, dx}{\sqrt{uv}} = \frac{\sqrt{uv}}{bd} - \frac{ad + bc}{2bd} \int \frac{dx}{\sqrt{uv}}$

150. $\displaystyle \int \frac{dx}{v\sqrt{uv}} = \frac{-2\sqrt{uv}}{kv}$

INTEGRALS (Continued)

151. $\int \dfrac{v \, dx}{\sqrt{uv}} = \dfrac{\sqrt{uv}}{b} - \dfrac{k}{2b} \int \dfrac{dx}{\sqrt{uv}}$

152. $\int \sqrt{\dfrac{v}{u}} \, dx = \dfrac{v}{|v|} \int \dfrac{v \, dx}{\sqrt{uv}}$

153. $\int v^m \sqrt{u} \, dx = \dfrac{1}{(2m + 3)d} \left(2v^{m+1} \sqrt{u} + k \int \dfrac{v^m \, dx}{\sqrt{u}} \right)$

154. $\int \dfrac{dx}{v^m \sqrt{u}} = -\dfrac{1}{(m-1)k} \left(\dfrac{\sqrt{u}}{v^{m-1}} + \left(m - \dfrac{3}{2} \right) b \int \dfrac{dx}{v^{m-1} \sqrt{u}} \right)$

155. $\int \dfrac{v^m \, dx}{\sqrt{u}} = \begin{cases} \dfrac{2}{b(2m+1)} \left[v^m \sqrt{u} - mk \int \dfrac{v^{m-1}}{\sqrt{u}} \, dx \right] \\ \quad \text{or} \\ \dfrac{2(m!)^2 \sqrt{u}}{b(2m+1)!} \displaystyle\sum_{r=0}^{m} \left(-\dfrac{4k}{b} \right)^{m-r} \dfrac{(2r)!}{(r!)^2} v^r \end{cases}$

FORMS CONTAINING $\sqrt{x^2 \pm a^2}$

156. $\int \sqrt{x^2 \pm a^2} \, dx = \frac{1}{2}[x\sqrt{x^2 \pm a^2} \pm a^2 \log(x + \sqrt{x^2 \pm a^2})]$

157. $\int \dfrac{dx}{\sqrt{x^2 \pm a^2}} = \log(x + \sqrt{x^2 \pm a^2})$

158. $\int \dfrac{dx}{x\sqrt{x^2 - a^2}} = \dfrac{1}{|a|} \sec^{-1} \dfrac{x}{a}$

159. $\int \dfrac{dx}{x\sqrt{x^2 + a^2}} = -\dfrac{1}{a} \log \left(\dfrac{a + \sqrt{x^2 + a^2}}{x} \right)$

160. $\int \dfrac{\sqrt{x^2 + a^2}}{x} \, dx = \sqrt{x^2 + a^2} - a \log \left(\dfrac{a + \sqrt{x^2 + a^2}}{x} \right)$

161. $\int \dfrac{\sqrt{x^2 - a^2}}{x} \, dx = \sqrt{x^2 - a^2} - |a| \sec^{-1} \dfrac{x}{a}$

162. $\int \dfrac{x \, dx}{\sqrt{x^2 \pm a^2}} = \sqrt{x^2 \pm a^2}$

163. $\int x\sqrt{x^2 \pm a^2} \, dx = \frac{1}{3}\sqrt{(x^2 \pm a^2)^3}$

INTEGRALS (Continued)

164. $\int \sqrt{(x^2 \pm a^2)^3}\, dx = \dfrac{1}{4}\left[x\sqrt{(x^2 \pm a^2)^3} \pm \dfrac{3a^2 x}{2}\sqrt{x^2 \pm a^2} \right.$

$$\left. + \dfrac{3a^4}{2}\log(x + \sqrt{x^2 \pm a^2}) \right]$$

165. $\int \dfrac{dx}{\sqrt{(x^2 \pm a^2)^3}} = \dfrac{\pm x}{a^2\sqrt{x^2 \pm a^2}}$

166. $\int \dfrac{x\, dx}{\sqrt{(x^2 \pm a^2)^3}} = \dfrac{-1}{\sqrt{x^2 \pm a^2}}$

167. $\int x\sqrt{(x^2 \pm a^2)^3}\, dx = \tfrac{1}{5}\sqrt{(x^2 \pm a^2)^5}$

168. $\int x^2\sqrt{x^2 \pm a^2}\, dx = \dfrac{x}{4}\sqrt{(x^2 \pm a^2)^3} \mp \dfrac{a^2}{8}x\sqrt{x^2 \pm a^2} - \dfrac{a^4}{8}\log(x + \sqrt{x^2 \pm a^2})$

169. $\int x^3\sqrt{x^2 + a^2}\, dx = (\tfrac{1}{5}x^2 - \tfrac{2}{15}a^2)\sqrt{(a^2 + x^2)^3}$

170. $\int x^3\sqrt{x^2 - a^2}\, dx = \dfrac{1}{5}\sqrt{(x^2 - a^2)^5} + \dfrac{a^2}{3}\sqrt{(x^2 - a^2)^3}$

171. $\int \dfrac{x^2\, dx}{\sqrt{x^2 \pm a^2}} = \dfrac{x}{2}\sqrt{x^2 \pm a^2} \mp \dfrac{a^2}{2}\log(x + \sqrt{x^2 \pm a^2})$

172. $\int \dfrac{x^3\, dx}{\sqrt{x^2 \pm a^2}} = \dfrac{1}{3}\sqrt{(x^2 \pm a^2)^3} \mp a^2\sqrt{x^2 \pm a^2}$

173. $\int \dfrac{dx}{x^2\sqrt{x^2 \pm a^2}} = \mp \dfrac{\sqrt{x^2 \pm a^2}}{a^2 x}$

174. $\int \dfrac{dx}{x^3\sqrt{x^2 + a^2}} = -\dfrac{\sqrt{x^2 + a^2}}{2a^2 x^2} + \dfrac{1}{2a^3}\log\dfrac{a + \sqrt{x^2 + a^2}}{x}$

175. $\int \dfrac{dx}{x^3\sqrt{x^2 - a^2}} = \dfrac{\sqrt{x^2 - a^2}}{2a^2 x^2} + \dfrac{1}{2|a^3|}\sec^{-1}\dfrac{x}{a}$

176. $\int x^2\sqrt{(x^2 \pm a^2)^3}\, dx = \dfrac{x}{6}\sqrt{(x^2 \pm a^2)^5} \mp \dfrac{a^2 x}{24}\sqrt{(x^2 \pm a^2)^3} - \dfrac{a^4 x}{16}\sqrt{x^2 \pm a^2}$

$$\mp \dfrac{a^6}{16}\log(x + \sqrt{x^2 \pm a^2})$$

177. $\int x^3\sqrt{(x^2 \pm a^2)^3}\, dx = \dfrac{1}{7}\sqrt{(x^2 \pm a^2)^7} \mp \dfrac{a^2}{5}\sqrt{(x^2 \pm a^2)^5}$

INTEGRALS (Continued)

178. $\displaystyle\int \frac{\sqrt{x^2 \pm a^2}\,dx}{x^2} = -\frac{\sqrt{x^2 \pm a^2}}{x} + \log\left(x + \sqrt{x^2 \pm a^2}\right)$

179. $\displaystyle\int \frac{\sqrt{x^2 + a^2}}{x^3}\,dx = -\frac{\sqrt{x^2 + a^2}}{2x^2} - \frac{1}{2a}\log\frac{a + \sqrt{x^2 + a^2}}{x}$

180. $\displaystyle\int \frac{\sqrt{x^2 - a^2}}{x^3}\,dx = -\frac{\sqrt{x^2 - a^2}}{2x^2} + \frac{1}{2|a|}\sec^{-1}\frac{x}{a}$

181. $\displaystyle\int \frac{\sqrt{x^2 \pm a^2}}{x^4}\,dx = \mp\frac{\sqrt{(x^2 \pm a^2)^3}}{3a^2 x^3}$

182. $\displaystyle\int \frac{x^2\,dx}{\sqrt{(x^2 \pm a^2)^3}} = \frac{-x}{\sqrt{x^2 \pm a^2}} + \log\left(x + \sqrt{x^2 \pm a^2}\right)$

183. $\displaystyle\int \frac{x^3\,dx}{\sqrt{(x^2 \pm a^2)^3}} = \sqrt{x^2 \pm a^2} \pm \frac{a^2}{\sqrt{x^2 \pm a^2}}$

184. $\displaystyle\int \frac{dx}{x\sqrt{(x^2 + a^2)^3}} = \frac{1}{a^2\sqrt{x^2 + a^2}} - \frac{1}{a^3}\log\frac{a + \sqrt{x^2 + a^2}}{x}$

185. $\displaystyle\int \frac{dx}{x\sqrt{(x^2 - a^2)^3}} = -\frac{1}{a^2\sqrt{x^2 - a^2}} - \frac{1}{|a^3|}\sec^{-1}\frac{x}{a}$

186. $\displaystyle\int \frac{dx}{x^2\sqrt{(x^2 \pm a^2)^3}} = -\frac{1}{a^4}\left[\frac{\sqrt{x^2 \pm a^2}}{x} + \frac{x}{\sqrt{x^2 \pm a^2}}\right]$

187. $\displaystyle\int \frac{dx}{x^3\sqrt{(x^2 + a^2)^3}} = -\frac{1}{2a^2 x^2\sqrt{x^2 + a^2}} - \frac{3}{2a^4\sqrt{x^2 + a^2}}$
$$+ \frac{3}{2a^5}\log\frac{a + \sqrt{x^2 + a^2}}{x}$$

188. $\displaystyle\int \frac{dx}{x^3\sqrt{(x^2 - a^2)^3}} = \frac{1}{2a^2 x^2\sqrt{x^2 - a^2}} - \frac{3}{2a^4\sqrt{x^2 - a^2}} - \frac{3}{2|a^5|}\sec^{-1}\frac{x}{a}$

189. $\displaystyle\int \frac{x^m}{\sqrt{x^2 \pm a^2}}\,dx = \frac{1}{m}x^{m-1}\sqrt{x^2 \pm a^2} \mp \frac{m-1}{m}a^2\int \frac{x^{m-2}}{\sqrt{x^2 \pm a^2}}\,dx$

190. $\displaystyle\int \frac{x^{2m}}{\sqrt{x^2 \pm a^2}}\,dx = \frac{(2m)!}{2^{2m}(m!)^2}\left[\sqrt{x^2 \pm a^2}\sum_{r=1}^{m}\frac{r!(r-1)!}{(2r)!}(\mp a^2)^{m-r}(2x)^{2r-1}\right.$
$$\left.+ (\mp a^2)^m \log\left(x + \sqrt{x^2 \pm a^2}\right)\right]$$

191. $\displaystyle\int \frac{x^{2m+1}}{\sqrt{x^2 \pm a^2}}\,dx = \sqrt{x^2 \pm a^2}\sum_{r=0}^{m}\frac{(2r)!(m!)^2}{(2m+1)!(r!)^2}(\mp 4a^2)^{m-r}x^{2r}$

INTEGRALS (Continued)

192. $\displaystyle\int \frac{dx}{x^m\sqrt{x^2 \pm a^2}} = \mp \frac{\sqrt{x^2 \pm a^2}}{(m-1)a^2 x^{m-1}} \mp \frac{(m-2)}{(m-1)a^2} \int \frac{dx}{x^{m-2}\sqrt{x^2 \pm a^2}}$

193. $\displaystyle\int \frac{dx}{x^{2m}\sqrt{x^2 \pm a^2}} = \sqrt{x^2 \pm a^2} \sum_{r=0}^{m-1} \frac{(m-1)!\,m!\,(2r)!\,2^{2m-2r-1}}{(r!)^2(2m)!\,(\mp a^2)^{m-r}x^{2r+1}}$

194. $\displaystyle\int \frac{dx}{x^{2m+1}\sqrt{x^2 + a^2}} = \frac{(2m)!}{(m!)^2}\left[\frac{\sqrt{x^2 + a^2}}{a^2} \sum_{r=1}^{m} (-1)^{m-r+1} \frac{r!\,(r-1)!}{2(2r)!\,(4a^2)^{m-r}x^{2r}}\right.$

$\displaystyle\left. + \frac{(-1)^{m+1}}{2^{2m}a^{2m+1}} \log \frac{\sqrt{x^2 + a^2} + a}{x}\right]$

195. $\displaystyle\int \frac{dx}{x^{2m+1}\sqrt{x^2 - a^2}} = \frac{(2m)!}{(m!)^2}\left[\frac{\sqrt{x^2 - a^2}}{a^2} \sum_{r=1}^{m} \frac{r!\,(r-1)!}{2(2r)!\,(4a^2)^{m-r}x^{2r}}\right.$

$\displaystyle\left. + \frac{1}{2^{2m}|a|^{2m+1}} \sec^{-1}\frac{x}{a}\right]$

196. $\displaystyle\int \frac{dx}{(x-a)\sqrt{x^2 - a^2}} = -\frac{\sqrt{x^2 - a^2}}{a(x-a)}$

197. $\displaystyle\int \frac{dx}{(x+a)\sqrt{x^2 - a^2}} = \frac{\sqrt{x^2 - a^2}}{a(x+a)}$

198. $\displaystyle\int f(x,\sqrt{x^2 + a^2})\,dx = a \int f(a\tan u, a\sec u)\sec^2 u\,du, \qquad \left(u = \tan^{-1}\frac{x}{a}, a > 0\right)$

199. $\displaystyle\int f(x,\sqrt{x^2 - a^2})\,dx = a \int f(a\sec u, a\tan u)\sec u\tan u\,du, \qquad \left(u = \sec^{-1}\frac{x}{a},\right.$

$\left. a > 0\right)$

FORMS CONTAINING $\sqrt{a^2 - x^2}$

200. $\displaystyle\int \sqrt{a^2 - x^2}\,dx = \frac{1}{2}\left[x\sqrt{a^2 - x^2} + a^2 \sin^{-1}\frac{x}{|a|}\right]$

201. $\displaystyle\int \frac{dx}{\sqrt{a^2 - x^2}} = \begin{cases} \sin^{-1}\dfrac{x}{|a|} \\[2mm] \text{or} \\[2mm] -\cos^{-1}\dfrac{x}{|a|} \end{cases}$

202. $\displaystyle\int \frac{dx}{x\sqrt{a^2 - x^2}} = -\frac{1}{a}\log\left(\frac{a + \sqrt{a^2 - x^2}}{x}\right)$

INTEGRALS (Continued)

203. $\displaystyle\int \frac{\sqrt{a^2 - x^2}}{x}\,dx = \sqrt{a^2 - x^2} - a\log\left(\frac{a + \sqrt{a^2 - x^2}}{x}\right)$

204. $\displaystyle\int \frac{x\,dx}{\sqrt{a^2 - x^2}} = -\sqrt{a^2 - x^2}$

205. $\displaystyle\int x\sqrt{a^2 - x^2}\,dx = -\tfrac{1}{3}\sqrt{(a^2 - x^2)^3}$

206. $\displaystyle\int \sqrt{(a^2 - x^2)^3}\,dx = \frac{1}{4}\left[x\sqrt{(a^2 - x^2)^3} + \frac{3a^2 x}{2}\sqrt{a^2 - x^2} + \frac{3a^4}{2}\sin^{-1}\frac{x}{|a|}\right]$

207. $\displaystyle\int \frac{dx}{\sqrt{(a^2 - x^2)^3}} = \frac{x}{a^2\sqrt{a^2 - x^2}}$

208. $\displaystyle\int \frac{x\,dx}{\sqrt{(a^2 - x^2)^3}} = \frac{1}{\sqrt{a^2 - x^2}}$

209. $\displaystyle\int x\sqrt{(a^2 - x^2)^3}\,dx = -\tfrac{1}{5}\sqrt{(a^2 - x^2)^5}$

210. $\displaystyle\int x^2\sqrt{a^2 - x^2}\,dx = -\frac{x}{4}\sqrt{(a^2 - x^2)^3} + \frac{a^2}{8}\left(x\sqrt{a^2 - x^2} + a^2\sin^{-1}\frac{x}{|a|}\right)$

211. $\displaystyle\int x^3\sqrt{a^2 - x^2}\,dx = (-\tfrac{1}{5}x^2 - \tfrac{2}{15}a^2)\sqrt{(a^2 - x^2)^3}$

212. $\displaystyle\int x^2\sqrt{(a^2 - x^2)^3}\,dx = -\frac{1}{6}x\sqrt{(a^2 - x^2)^5} + \frac{a^2 x}{24}\sqrt{(a^2 - x^2)^3}$

$$+ \frac{a^4 x}{16}\sqrt{a^2 - x^2} + \frac{a^6}{16}\sin^{-1}\frac{x}{|a|}$$

213. $\displaystyle\int x^3\sqrt{(a^2 - x^2)^3}\,dx = \frac{1}{7}\sqrt{(a^2 - x^2)^7} - \frac{a^2}{5}\sqrt{(a^2 - x^2)^5}$

214. $\displaystyle\int \frac{x^2\,dx}{\sqrt{a^2 - x^2}} = -\frac{x}{2}\sqrt{a^2 - x^2} + \frac{a^2}{2}\sin^{-1}\frac{x}{|a|}$

215. $\displaystyle\int \frac{dx}{x^2\sqrt{a^2 - x^2}} = -\frac{\sqrt{a^2 - x^2}}{a^2 x}$

216. $\displaystyle\int \frac{\sqrt{a^2 - x^2}}{x^2}\,dx = -\frac{\sqrt{a^2 - x^2}}{x} - \sin^{-1}\frac{x}{|a|}$

217. $\displaystyle\int \frac{\sqrt{a^2 - x^2}}{x^3}\,dx = -\frac{\sqrt{a^2 - x^2}}{2x^2} + \frac{1}{2a}\log\frac{a + \sqrt{a^2 - x^2}}{x}$

218. $\displaystyle\int \frac{\sqrt{a^2 - x^2}}{x^4}\,dx = -\frac{\sqrt{(a^2 - x^2)^3}}{3a^2 x^3}$

INTEGRALS (Continued)

219. $\displaystyle \int \frac{x^2\,dx}{\sqrt{(a^2-x^2)^3}} = \frac{x}{\sqrt{a^2-x^2}} - \sin^{-1}\frac{x}{|a|}$

220. $\displaystyle \int \frac{x^3\,dx}{\sqrt{a^2-x^2}} = -\frac{2}{3}(a^2-x^2)^{\frac{1}{2}} - x^2(a^2-x^2)^{\frac{1}{2}} = -\frac{1}{3}\sqrt{a^2-x^2}(x^2+2a^2)$

221. $\displaystyle \int \frac{x^3\,dx}{\sqrt{(a^2-x^2)^3}} = 2(a^2-x^2)^{\frac{1}{2}} + \frac{x^2}{(a^2-x^2)^{\frac{1}{2}}} = -\frac{a^2}{\sqrt{a^2-x^2}} + \sqrt{a^2-x^2}$

222. $\displaystyle \int \frac{dx}{x^3\sqrt{a^2-x^2}} = -\frac{\sqrt{a^2-x^2}}{2a^2x^2} - \frac{1}{2a^3}\log\frac{a+\sqrt{a^2-x^2}}{x}$

223. $\displaystyle \int \frac{dx}{x\sqrt{(a^2-x^2)^3}} = \frac{1}{a^2\sqrt{a^2-x^2}} - \frac{1}{a^3}\log\frac{a+\sqrt{a^2-x^2}}{x}$

224. $\displaystyle \int \frac{dx}{x^2\sqrt{(a^2-x^2)^3}} = \frac{1}{a^4}\left[-\frac{\sqrt{a^2-x^2}}{x} + \frac{x}{\sqrt{a^2-x^2}}\right]$

225. $\displaystyle \int \frac{dx}{x^3\sqrt{(a^2-x^2)^3}} = -\frac{1}{2a^2x^2\sqrt{a^2-x^2}} + \frac{3}{2a^4\sqrt{a^2-x^2}}$

$$-\frac{3}{2a^5}\log\frac{a+\sqrt{a^2-x^2}}{x}$$

226. $\displaystyle \int \frac{x^m}{\sqrt{a^2-x^2}}\,dx = -\frac{x^{m-1}\sqrt{a^2-x^2}}{m} + \frac{(m-1)a^2}{m}\int \frac{x^{m-2}}{\sqrt{a^2-x^2}}\,dx$

227. $\displaystyle \int \frac{x^{2m}}{\sqrt{a^2-x^2}}\,dx = \frac{(2m)!}{(m!)^2}\left[-\sqrt{a^2-x^2}\sum_{r=1}^{m}\frac{r!(r-1)!}{2^{2m-2r+1}(2r)!}a^{2m-2r}x^{2r-1}\right.$

$$\left. + \frac{a^{2m}}{2^{2m}}\sin^{-1}\frac{x}{|a|}\right]$$

228. $\displaystyle \int \frac{x^{2m+1}}{\sqrt{a^2-x^2}}\,dx = -\sqrt{a^2-x^2}\sum_{r=0}^{m}\frac{(2r)!(m!)^2}{(2m+1)!(r!)^2}(4a^2)^{m-r}x^{2r}$

229. $\displaystyle \int \frac{dx}{x^m\sqrt{a^2-x^2}} = -\frac{\sqrt{a^2-x^2}}{(m-1)a^2x^{m-1}} + \frac{m-2}{(m-1)a^2}\int \frac{dx}{x^{m-2}\sqrt{a^2-x^2}}$

230. $\displaystyle \int \frac{ax}{x^{2m}\sqrt{a^2-x^2}} = -\sqrt{a^2-x^2}\sum_{r=0}^{m-1}\frac{(m-1)!m!(2r)!2^{2m-2r-1}}{(r!)^2(2m)!a^{2m-2r}x^{2r+1}}$

231. $\displaystyle \int \frac{dx}{x^{2m+1}\sqrt{a^2-x^2}} = \frac{(2m)!}{(m!)^2}\left[-\frac{\sqrt{a^2-x^2}}{a^2}\sum_{r=1}^{m}\frac{r!(r-1)!}{2(2r)!(4a^2)^{m-r}x^{2r}}\right.$

$$\left. + \frac{1}{2^{2m}a^{2m+1}}\log\frac{a-\sqrt{a^2-x^2}}{x}\right]$$

INTEGRALS (Continued)

232. $\displaystyle\int \frac{dx}{(b^2 - x^2)\sqrt{a^2 - x^2}} = \frac{1}{2b\sqrt{a^2 - b^2}} \log \frac{(b\sqrt{a^2 - x^2} + x\sqrt{a^2 - b^2})^2}{b^2 - x^2},$

$$(a^2 > b^2)$$

233. $\displaystyle\int \frac{dx}{(b^2 - x^2)\sqrt{a^2 - x^2}} = \frac{1}{b\sqrt{b^2 - a^2}} \tan^{-1} \frac{x\sqrt{b^2 - a^2}}{b\sqrt{a^2 - x^2}},$ $\quad (b^2 > a^2)$

234. $\displaystyle\int \frac{dx}{(b^2 + x^2)\sqrt{a^2 - x^2}} = \frac{1}{b\sqrt{a^2 + b^2}} \tan^{-1} \frac{x\sqrt{a^2 + b^2}}{b\sqrt{a^2 - x^2}}$

235. $\displaystyle\int \frac{\sqrt{a^2 - x^2}}{b^2 + x^2} dx = \frac{\sqrt{a^2 + b^2}}{|b|} \sin^{-1} \frac{x\sqrt{a^2 + b^2}}{|a|\sqrt{x^2 + b^2}} - \sin^{-1} \frac{x}{|a|}$

236. $\displaystyle\int f(x, \sqrt{a^2 - x^2}) \, dx = a \int f(a \sin u, a \cos u) \cos u \, du, \quad \left(u = \sin^{-1} \frac{x}{a}, a > 0 \right)$

FORMS CONTAINING $\sqrt{a + bx + cx^2}$

$$X = a + bx + cx^2, q = 4ac - b^2, \text{and } k = \frac{4c}{q}$$

If $q = 0$, then $\sqrt{X} = \sqrt{c} \left| x + \dfrac{b}{2c} \right|$

237. $\displaystyle\int \frac{dx}{\sqrt{X}} = \begin{cases} \dfrac{1}{\sqrt{c}} \log \dfrac{2\sqrt{cX} + 2cx + b}{\sqrt{q}} \\[2mm] \text{or} \\[2mm] \dfrac{1}{\sqrt{c}} \sinh^{-1} \dfrac{2cx + b}{\sqrt{q}}, \quad (c > 0) \end{cases}$

238. $\displaystyle\int \frac{dx}{\sqrt{X}} = -\frac{1}{\sqrt{-c}} \sin^{-1} \frac{2cx + b}{\sqrt{-q}}, \quad (c < 0)$

239. $\displaystyle\int \frac{dx}{X\sqrt{X}} = \frac{2(2cx + b)}{q\sqrt{X}}$

240. $\displaystyle\int \frac{dx}{X^2\sqrt{X}} = \frac{2(2cx + b)}{3q\sqrt{X}} \left(\frac{1}{X} + 2k \right)$

241. $\displaystyle\int \frac{dx}{X^n\sqrt{X}} = \begin{cases} \dfrac{2(2cx + b)\sqrt{X}}{(2n - 1)qX^n} + \dfrac{2k(n - 1)}{2n - 1} \displaystyle\int \frac{dx}{X^{n-1}\sqrt{X}} \\[3mm] \text{or} \\[3mm] \dfrac{(2cx + b)(n!)(n - 1)!4^n k^{n-1}}{q[(2n)!]\sqrt{X}} \displaystyle\sum_{r=0}^{n-1} \dfrac{(2r)!}{(4kX)^r(r!)^2} \end{cases}$

INTEGRALS (Continued)

242. $\displaystyle \int \sqrt{X}\, dx = \frac{(2cx + b)\sqrt{X}}{4c} + \frac{1}{2k} \int \frac{dx}{\sqrt{X}}$

243. $\displaystyle \int X\sqrt{X}\, dx = \frac{(2cx + b)\sqrt{X}}{8c}\left(X + \frac{3}{2k}\right) + \frac{3}{8k^2}\int \frac{dx}{\sqrt{X}}$

244. $\displaystyle \int X^2\sqrt{X}\, dx = \frac{(2cx + b)\sqrt{X}}{12c}\left(X^2 + \frac{5X}{4k} + \frac{15}{8k^2}\right) + \frac{5}{16k^3}\int \frac{dx}{\sqrt{X}}$

245. $\displaystyle \int X^n\sqrt{X}\, dx = \begin{cases} \dfrac{(2cx + b)X^n\sqrt{X}}{4(n + 1)c} + \dfrac{2n + 1}{2(n + 1)k}\displaystyle\int X^{n-1}\sqrt{X}\, dx \\[2mm] \text{or} \\[2mm] \dfrac{(2n + 2)!}{[(n + 1)!]^2(4k)^{n+1}}\left[\dfrac{k(2cx + b)\sqrt{X}}{c}\displaystyle\sum_{r=0}^{n}\dfrac{r!(r + 1)!(4kX)^r}{(2r + 2)!} \right. \\[4mm] \hspace{6cm} \left. + \displaystyle\int\dfrac{dx}{\sqrt{X}}\right] \end{cases}$

246. $\displaystyle \int \frac{x\, dx}{\sqrt{X}} = \frac{\sqrt{X}}{c} - \frac{b}{2c}\int \frac{dx}{\sqrt{X}}$

247. $\displaystyle \int \frac{x\, dx}{X\sqrt{X}} = -\frac{2(bx + 2a)}{q\sqrt{X}}$

248. $\displaystyle \int \frac{x\, dx}{X^n\sqrt{X}} = -\frac{\sqrt{X}}{(2n - 1)cX^n} - \frac{b}{2c}\int \frac{dx}{X^n\sqrt{X}}$

249. $\displaystyle \int \frac{x^2\, dx}{\sqrt{X}} = \left(\frac{x}{2c} - \frac{3b}{4c^2}\right)\sqrt{X} + \frac{3b^2 - 4ac}{8c^2}\int \frac{dx}{\sqrt{X}}$

250. $\displaystyle \int \frac{x^2\, dx}{X\sqrt{X}} = \frac{(2b^2 - 4ac)x + 2ab}{cq\sqrt{X}} + \frac{1}{c}\int \frac{dx}{\sqrt{X}}$

251. $\displaystyle \int \frac{x^2\, dx}{X^n\sqrt{X}} = \frac{(2b^2 - 4ac)x + 2ab}{(2n - 1)cqX^{n-1}\sqrt{X}} + \frac{4ac + (2n - 3)b^2}{(2n - 1)cq}\int \frac{dx}{X^{n-1}\sqrt{X}}$

252. $\displaystyle \int \frac{x^3\, dx}{\sqrt{X}} = \left(\frac{x^2}{3c} - \frac{5bx}{12c^2} + \frac{5b^2}{8c^3} - \frac{2a}{3c^2}\right)\sqrt{X} + \left(\frac{3ab}{4c^2} - \frac{5b^3}{16c^3}\right)\int \frac{dx}{\sqrt{X}}$

253. $\displaystyle \int \frac{x^n\, dx}{\sqrt{X}} = \frac{1}{nc}x^{n-1}\sqrt{X} - \frac{(2n - 1)b}{2nc}\int \frac{x^{n-1}\, dx}{\sqrt{X}} - \frac{(n - 1)a}{nc}\int \frac{x^{n-2}\, dx}{\sqrt{X}}$

INTEGRALS (Continued)

254. $\displaystyle \int x\sqrt{X}\,dx = \frac{X\sqrt{X}}{3c} - \frac{b(2cx + b)}{8c^2}\sqrt{X} - \frac{b}{4ck}\int \frac{dx}{\sqrt{X}}$

255. $\displaystyle \int xX\sqrt{X}\,dx = \frac{X^2\sqrt{X}}{5c} - \frac{b}{2c}\int X\sqrt{X}\,dx$

256. $\displaystyle \int xX^n\sqrt{X}\,dx = \frac{X^{n+1}\sqrt{X}}{(2n + 3)c} - \frac{b}{2c}\int X^n\sqrt{X}\,dx$

257. $\displaystyle \int x^2\sqrt{X}\,dx = \left(x - \frac{5b}{6c}\right)\frac{X\sqrt{X}}{4c} + \frac{5b^2 - 4ac}{16c^2}\int \sqrt{X}\,dx$

258. $\displaystyle \int \frac{dx}{x\sqrt{X}} = -\frac{1}{\sqrt{a}}\log\frac{2\sqrt{aX} + bx + 2a}{x}, \qquad (a > 0)$

259. $\displaystyle \int \frac{dx}{x\sqrt{X}} = \frac{1}{\sqrt{-a}}\sin^{-1}\left(\frac{bx + 2a}{|x|\sqrt{-q}}\right), \qquad (a < 0)$

260. $\displaystyle \int \frac{dx}{x\sqrt{X}} = -\frac{2\sqrt{X}}{bx}, \qquad (a = 0)$

261. $\displaystyle \int \frac{dx}{x^2\sqrt{X}} = -\frac{\sqrt{X}}{ax} - \frac{b}{2a}\int \frac{dx}{x\sqrt{X}}$

262. $\displaystyle \int \frac{\sqrt{X}\,dx}{x} = \sqrt{X} + \frac{b}{2}\int \frac{dx}{\sqrt{X}} + a\int \frac{dx}{x\sqrt{X}}$

263. $\displaystyle \int \frac{\sqrt{X}\,dx}{x^2} = -\frac{\sqrt{X}}{x} + \frac{b}{2}\int \frac{dx}{x\sqrt{X}} + c\int \frac{dx}{\sqrt{X}}$

FORMS INVOLVING $\sqrt{2ax - x^2}$

264. $\displaystyle \int \sqrt{2ax - x^2}\,dx = \frac{1}{2}\left[(x - a)\sqrt{2ax - x^2} + a^2\sin^{-1}\frac{x - a}{|a|}\right]$

265. $\displaystyle \int \frac{dx}{\sqrt{2ax - x^2}} = \begin{cases} \cos^{-1}\dfrac{a - x}{|a|} \\[2mm] \text{or} \\[2mm] \sin^{-1}\dfrac{x - a}{|a|} \end{cases}$

INTEGRALS (Continued)

266. $\int x^n \sqrt{2ax - x^2}\, dx = \begin{cases} -\dfrac{x^{n-1}(2ax - x^2)^{\frac{3}{2}}}{n+2} + \dfrac{(2n+1)a}{n+2}\int x^{n-1}\sqrt{2ax - x^2}\, dx \\[2mm] \quad\text{or} \\[2mm] \sqrt{2ax - x^2}\left[\dfrac{x^{n+1}}{n+2} - \displaystyle\sum_{r=0}^{n} \dfrac{(2n+1)!(r!)^2 a^{n-r+1}}{2^{n-r}(2r+1)!(n+2)!n!}x^r\right] \\[4mm] \qquad + \dfrac{(2n+1)!a^{n+2}}{2^n n!(n+2)!}\sin^{-1}\dfrac{x-a}{|a|} \end{cases}$

267. $\int \dfrac{\sqrt{2ax - x^2}}{x^n}\, dx = \dfrac{(2ax - x^2)^{\frac{3}{2}}}{(3 - 2n)ax^n} + \dfrac{n-3}{(2n-3)a}\int \dfrac{\sqrt{2ax - x^2}}{x^{n-1}}\, dx$

268. $\int \dfrac{x^n\, dx}{\sqrt{2ax - x^2}} = \begin{cases} \dfrac{-x^{n-1}\sqrt{2ax - x^2}}{n} + \dfrac{a(2n-1)}{n}\int \dfrac{x^{n-1}}{\sqrt{2ax - x^2}}\, dx \\[2mm] \quad\text{or} \\[2mm] -\sqrt{2ax - x^2}\displaystyle\sum_{r=1}^{n} \dfrac{(2n)!r!(r-1)!a^{n-r}}{2^{n-r}(2r)!(n!)^2}x^{r-1} \\[4mm] \qquad + \dfrac{(2n)!a^n}{2^n(n!)^2}\sin^{-1}\dfrac{x-a}{|a|} \end{cases}$

269. $\int \dfrac{dx}{x^n\sqrt{2ax - x^2}} = \begin{cases} \dfrac{\sqrt{2ax - x^2}}{a(1 - 2n)x^n} + \dfrac{n-1}{(2n-1)a}\int \dfrac{dx}{x^{n-1}\sqrt{2ax - x^2}} \\[2mm] \quad\text{or} \\[2mm] -\sqrt{2ax - x^2}\displaystyle\sum_{r=0}^{n-1} \dfrac{2^{n-r}(n-1)!n!(2r)!}{(2n)!(r!)^2 a^{n-r}x^{r+1}} \end{cases}$

270. $\int \dfrac{dx}{(2ax - x^2)^{\frac{3}{2}}} = \dfrac{x - a}{a^2\sqrt{2ax - x^2}}$

271. $\int \dfrac{x\, dx}{(2ax - x^2)^{\frac{3}{2}}} = \dfrac{x}{a\sqrt{2ax - x^2}}$

MISCELLANEOUS ALGEBRAIC FORMS

272. $\int \dfrac{dx}{\sqrt{2ax + x^2}} = \log\left(x + a + \sqrt{2ax + x^2}\right)$

273. $\int \sqrt{ax^2 + c}\, dx = \dfrac{x}{2}\sqrt{ax^2 + c} + \dfrac{c}{2\sqrt{a}}\log\left(x\sqrt{a} + \sqrt{ax^2 + c}\right), \qquad (a > 0)$

274. $\int \sqrt{ax^2 + c}\, dx = \dfrac{x}{2}\sqrt{ax^2 + c} + \dfrac{c}{2\sqrt{-a}}\sin^{-1}\left(x\sqrt{-\dfrac{a}{c}}\right), \qquad (a < 0)$

INTEGRALS (Continued)

275. $\int \sqrt{\dfrac{1+x}{1-x}}\, dx = \sin^{-1} x - \sqrt{1-x^2}$

276. $\int \dfrac{dx}{x\sqrt{ax^n + c}} = \begin{cases} \dfrac{1}{n\sqrt{c}} \log \dfrac{\sqrt{ax^n + c} - \sqrt{c}}{\sqrt{ax^n + c} + \sqrt{c}} \\[2mm] \text{or} \\[2mm] \dfrac{2}{n\sqrt{c}} \log \dfrac{\sqrt{ax^n + c} - \sqrt{c}}{\sqrt{x^n}}, \qquad (c > 0) \end{cases}$

277. $\int \dfrac{dx}{x\sqrt{ax^n + c}} = \dfrac{2}{n\sqrt{-c}} \sec^{-1}\sqrt{-\dfrac{ax^n}{c}}, \qquad (c < 0)$

278. $\int \dfrac{dx}{\sqrt{ax^2 + c}} = \dfrac{1}{\sqrt{a}} \log (x\sqrt{a} + \sqrt{ax^2 + c}), \qquad (a > 0)$

279. $\int \dfrac{dx}{\sqrt{ax^2 + c}} = \dfrac{1}{\sqrt{-a}} \sin^{-1}\left(x\sqrt{-\dfrac{a}{c}}\right), \qquad (a < 0)$

280. $\int (ax^2 + c)^{m + \frac{1}{2}}\, dx = \begin{cases} \dfrac{x(ax^2 + c)^{m + \frac{1}{2}}}{2(m + 1)} + \dfrac{(2m + 1)c}{2(m + 1)} \int (ax^2 + c)^{m - \frac{1}{2}}\, dx \\[2mm] \text{or} \\[2mm] x\sqrt{ax^2 + c} \displaystyle\sum_{r=0}^{m} \dfrac{(2m + 1)!(r!)^2 c^{m-r}}{2^{2m - 2r + 1} m!(m + 1)!(2r + 1)!}(ax^2 + c)^r \\[2mm] + \dfrac{(2m + 1)!c^{m+1}}{2^{2m+1} m!(m + 1)!} \int \dfrac{dx}{\sqrt{ax^2 + c}} \end{cases}$

281. $\int x(ax^2 + c)^{m + \frac{1}{2}}\, dx = \dfrac{(ax^2 + c)^{m + \frac{3}{2}}}{(2m + 3)a}$

282. $\int \dfrac{(ax^2 + c)^{m + \frac{1}{2}}}{x}\, dx = \begin{cases} \dfrac{(ax^2 + c)^{m + \frac{1}{2}}}{2m + 1} + c \int \dfrac{(ax^2 + c)^{m - \frac{1}{2}}}{x}\, dx \\[2mm] \text{or} \\[2mm] \sqrt{ax^2 + c} \displaystyle\sum_{r=0}^{m} \dfrac{c^{m-r}(ax^2 + c)^r}{2r + 1} + c^{m+1} \int \dfrac{dx}{x\sqrt{ax^2 + c}} \end{cases}$

283. $\int \dfrac{dx}{(ax^2 + c)^{m + \frac{1}{2}}} = \begin{cases} \dfrac{x}{(2m - 1)c(ax^2 + c)^{m - \frac{1}{2}}} + \dfrac{2m - 2}{(2m - 1)c} \int \dfrac{dx}{(ax^2 + c)^{m - \frac{1}{2}}} \\[2mm] \text{or} \\[2mm] \dfrac{x}{\sqrt{ax^2 + c}} \displaystyle\sum_{r=0}^{m-1} \dfrac{2^{2m - 2r - 1}(m - 1)!m!(2r)!}{(2m)!(r!)^2 c^{m-r}(ax^2 + c)^r} \end{cases}$

INTEGRALS (Continued)

284. $\int \dfrac{dx}{x^m \sqrt{ax^2 + c}} = -\dfrac{\sqrt{ax^2 + c}}{(m-1)cx^{m-1}} - \dfrac{(m-2)a}{(m-1)c} \int \dfrac{dx}{x^{m-2}\sqrt{ax^2 + c}}$

285. $\int \dfrac{1 + x^2}{(1 - x^2)\sqrt{1 + x^4}} dx = \dfrac{1}{\sqrt{2}} \log \dfrac{x\sqrt{2} + \sqrt{1 + x^4}}{1 - x^2}$

286. $\int \dfrac{1 - x^2}{(1 + x^2)\sqrt{1 + x^4}} dx = \dfrac{1}{\sqrt{2}} \tan^{-1} \dfrac{x\sqrt{2}}{\sqrt{1 + x^4}}$

287. $\int \dfrac{dx}{x\sqrt{x^n + a^2}} = -\dfrac{2}{na} \log \dfrac{a + \sqrt{x^n + a^2}}{\sqrt{x^n}}$

288. $\int \dfrac{dx}{x\sqrt{x^n - a^2}} = -\dfrac{2}{na} \sin^{-1} \dfrac{a}{\sqrt{x^n}}$

289. $\int \sqrt{\dfrac{x}{a^3 - x^3}} dx = \dfrac{2}{3} \sin^{-1} \left(\dfrac{x}{a}\right)^{\frac{3}{2}}$

FORMS INVOLVING TRIGONOMETRIC FUNCTIONS

290. $\int (\sin ax)\, dx = -\dfrac{1}{a} \cos ax$

291. $\int (\cos ax)\, dx = \dfrac{1}{a} \sin ax$

292. $\int (\tan ax)\, dx = -\dfrac{1}{a} \log \cos ax = \dfrac{1}{a} \log \sec ax$

293. $\int (\cot ax)\, dx = \dfrac{1}{a} \log \sin ax = -\dfrac{1}{a} \log \csc ax$

294. $\int (\sec ax)\, dx = \dfrac{1}{a} \log (\sec ax + \tan ax) = \dfrac{1}{a} \log \tan \left(\dfrac{\pi}{4} + \dfrac{ax}{2}\right)$

295. $\int (\csc ax)\, dx = \dfrac{1}{a} \log (\csc ax - \cot ax) = \dfrac{1}{a} \log \tan \dfrac{ax}{2}$

296. $\int (\sin^2 ax)\, dx = -\dfrac{1}{2a} \cos ax \sin ax + \dfrac{1}{2} x = \dfrac{1}{2} x - \dfrac{1}{4a} \sin 2ax$

297. $\int (\sin^3 ax)\, dx = -\dfrac{1}{3a}(\cos ax)(\sin^2 ax + 2)$

298. $\int (\sin^4 ax)\, dx = \dfrac{3x}{8} - \dfrac{\sin 2ax}{4a} + \dfrac{\sin 4ax}{32a}$

299. $\int (\sin^n ax)\, dx = -\dfrac{\sin^{n-1} ax \cos ax}{na} + \dfrac{n-1}{n} \int (\sin^{n-2} ax)\, dx$

INTEGRALS (Continued)

300. $\displaystyle\int (\sin^{2m} ax)\,dx = -\frac{\cos ax}{a} \sum_{r=0}^{m-1} \frac{(2m)!(r!)^2}{2^{2m-2r}(2r+1)!(m!)^2} \sin^{2r+1} ax + \frac{(2m)!}{2^{2m}(m!)^2}x$

301. $\displaystyle\int (\sin^{2m+1} ax)\,dx = -\frac{\cos ax}{a} \sum_{r=0}^{m} \frac{2^{2m-2r}(m!)^2(2r)!}{(2m+1)!(r!)^2} \sin^{2r} ax$

302. $\displaystyle\int (\cos^2 ax)\,dx = \frac{1}{2a}\sin ax \cos ax + \frac{1}{2}x = \frac{1}{2}x + \frac{1}{4a}\sin 2ax$

303. $\displaystyle\int (\cos^3 ax)\,dx = \frac{1}{3a}(\sin ax)(\cos^2 ax + 2)$

304. $\displaystyle\int (\cos^4 ax)\,dx = \frac{3x}{8} + \frac{\sin 2ax}{4a} + \frac{\sin 4ax}{32a}$

305. $\displaystyle\int (\cos^n ax)\,dx = \frac{1}{na}\cos^{n-1} ax \sin ax + \frac{n-1}{n}\int (\cos^{n-2} ax)\,dx$

306. $\displaystyle\int (\cos^{2m} ax)\,dx = \frac{\sin ax}{a} \sum_{r=0}^{m-1} \frac{(2m)!(r!)^2}{2^{2m-2r}(2r+1)!(m!)^2} \cos^{2r+1} ax + \frac{(2m)!}{2^{2m}(m!)^2}x$

307. $\displaystyle\int (\cos^{2m+1} ax)\,dx = \frac{\sin ax}{a} \sum_{r=0}^{m} \frac{2^{2m-2r}(m!)^2(2r)!}{(2m+1)!(r!)^2} \cos^{2r} ax$

308. $\displaystyle\int \frac{dx}{\sin^2 ax} = \int (\csc^2 ax)\,dx = -\frac{1}{a}\cot ax$

309. $\displaystyle\int \frac{dx}{\sin^m ax} = \int (\csc^m ax)\,dx = -\frac{1}{(m-1)a}\cdot\frac{\cos ax}{\sin^{m-1} ax} + \frac{m-2}{m-1}\int \frac{dx}{\sin^{m-2} ax}$

310. $\displaystyle\int \frac{dx}{\sin^{2m} ax} = \int (\csc^{2m} ax)\,dx = -\frac{1}{a}\cos ax \sum_{r=0}^{m-1} \frac{2^{2m-2r-1}(m-1)!m!(2r)!}{(2m)!(r!)^2 \sin^{2r+1} ax}$

311. $\displaystyle\int \frac{dx}{\sin^{2m+1} ax} = \int (\csc^{2m+1} ax)\,dx =$

$\displaystyle\qquad -\frac{1}{a}\cos ax \sum_{r=0}^{m-1} \frac{(2m)!(r!)^2}{2^{2m-2r}(m!)^2(2r+1)!\sin^{2r+2} ax} + \frac{1}{a}\cdot\frac{(2m)!}{2^{2m}(m!)^2}\log\tan\frac{ax}{2}$

312. $\displaystyle\int \frac{dx}{\cos^2 ax} = \int (\sec^2 ax)\,dx = \frac{1}{a}\tan ax$

313. $\displaystyle\int \frac{dx}{\cos^n ax} = \int (\sec^n ax)\,dx = \frac{1}{(n-1)a}\cdot\frac{\sin ax}{\cos^{n-1} ax} + \frac{n-2}{n-1}\int \frac{dx}{\cos^{n-2} ax}$

314. $\displaystyle\int \frac{dx}{\cos^{2m} ax} = \int (\sec^{2m} ax)\,dx = \frac{1}{a}\sin ax \sum_{r=0}^{m-1} \frac{2^{2m-2r-1}(m-1)!m!(2r)!}{(2m)!(r!)^2 \cos^{2r+1} ax}$

INTEGRALS (Continued)

315. $\displaystyle\int \frac{dx}{\cos^{2m+1} ax} = \int (\sec^{2m+1} ax)\, dx =$

$$\frac{1}{a} \sin ax \sum_{r=0}^{m-1} \frac{(2m)!(r!)^2}{2^{2m-2r}(m!)^2(2r+1)!\cos^{2r+2} ax}$$

$$+ \frac{1}{a} \cdot \frac{(2m)!}{2^{2m}(m!)^2} \log(\sec ax + \tan ax)$$

316. $\displaystyle\int (\sin mx)(\sin nx)\, dx = \frac{\sin(m-n)x}{2(m-n)} - \frac{\sin(m+n)x}{2(m+n)}, \qquad (m^2 \neq n^2)$

317. $\displaystyle\int (\cos mx)(\cos nx)\, dx = \frac{\sin(m-n)x}{2(m-n)} + \frac{\sin(m+n)x}{2(m+n)}, \qquad (m^2 \neq n^2)$

318. $\displaystyle\int (\sin ax)(\cos ax)\, dx = \frac{1}{2a} \sin^2 ax$

319. $\displaystyle\int (\sin mx)(\cos nx)\, dx = -\frac{\cos(m-n)x}{2(m-n)} - \frac{\cos(m+n)x}{2(m+n)}, \qquad (m^2 \neq n^2)$

320. $\displaystyle\int (\sin^2 ax)(\cos^2 ax)\, dx = -\frac{1}{32a} \sin 4ax + \frac{x}{8}$

321. $\displaystyle\int (\sin ax)(\cos^m ax)\, dx = -\frac{\cos^{m+1} ax}{(m+1)a}$

322. $\displaystyle\int (\sin^m ax)(\cos ax)\, dx = \frac{\sin^{m+1} ax}{(m+1)a}$

323. $\displaystyle\int (\cos^m ax)(\sin^n ax)\, dx =$
$$\begin{cases}
\dfrac{\cos^{m-1} ax \, \sin^{n+1} ax}{(m+n)a} \\[2ex]
\qquad + \dfrac{m-1}{m+n} \displaystyle\int (\cos^{m-2} ax)(\sin^n ax)\, dx \\[2ex]
\text{or} \\[1ex]
-\dfrac{\sin^{n-1} ax \, \cos^{m+1} ax}{(m+n)a} \\[2ex]
\qquad + \dfrac{n-1}{m+n} \displaystyle\int (\cos^m ax)(\sin^{n-2} ax)\, dx
\end{cases}$$

324. $\displaystyle\int \frac{\cos^m ax}{\sin^n ax}\, dx =$
$$\begin{cases}
-\dfrac{\cos^{m+1} ax}{(n-1)a \sin^{n-1} ax} - \dfrac{m-n+2}{n-1} \displaystyle\int \dfrac{\cos^m ax}{\sin^{n-2} ax}\, dx \\[2ex]
\text{or} \\[1ex]
\dfrac{\cos^{m-1} ax}{a(m-n) \sin^{n-1} ax} + \dfrac{m-1}{m-n} \displaystyle\int \dfrac{\cos^{m-2} ax}{\sin^n ax}\, dx
\end{cases}$$

INTEGRALS (Continued)

325.
$$\int \frac{\sin^m ax}{\cos^n ax}\,dx = \begin{cases} \dfrac{\sin^{m+1} ax}{a(n-1)\cos^{n-1} ax} - \dfrac{m-n+2}{n-1}\int \dfrac{\sin^m ax}{\cos^{n-2} ax}\,dx \\[2mm] \text{or} \\[2mm] -\dfrac{\sin^{m-1} ax}{a(m-n)\cos^{n-1} ax} + \dfrac{m-1}{m-n}\int \dfrac{\sin^{m-2} ax}{\cos^n ax}\,dx \end{cases}$$

326. $\displaystyle \int \frac{\sin ax}{\cos^2 ax}\,dx = \frac{1}{a\cos ax} = \frac{\sec ax}{a}$

327. $\displaystyle \int \frac{\sin^2 ax}{\cos ax}\,dx = -\frac{1}{a}\sin ax + \frac{1}{a}\log\tan\left(\frac{\pi}{4} + \frac{ax}{2}\right)$

328. $\displaystyle \int \frac{\cos ax}{\sin^2 ax}\,dx = -\frac{1}{a\sin ax} = -\frac{\csc ax}{a}$

329. $\displaystyle \int \frac{dx}{(\sin ax)(\cos ax)} = \frac{1}{a}\log\tan ax$

330. $\displaystyle \int \frac{dx}{(\sin ax)(\cos^2 ax)} = \frac{1}{a}\left(\sec ax + \log\tan\frac{ax}{2}\right)$

331. $\displaystyle \int \frac{dx}{(\sin ax)(\cos^n ax)} = \frac{1}{a(n-1)\cos^{n-1} ax} + \int \frac{dx}{(\sin ax)(\cos^{n-2} ax)}$

332. $\displaystyle \int \frac{dx}{(\sin^2 ax)(\cos ax)} = -\frac{1}{a}\csc ax + \frac{1}{a}\log\tan\left(\frac{\pi}{4} + \frac{ax}{2}\right)$

333. $\displaystyle \int \frac{dx}{(\sin^2 ax)(\cos^2 ax)} = -\frac{2}{a}\cot 2ax$

334.
$$\int \frac{dx}{\sin^m ax \cos^n ax} = \begin{cases} -\dfrac{1}{a(m-1)(\sin^{m-1} ax)(\cos^{n-1} ax)} \\[2mm] \qquad + \dfrac{m+n-2}{m-1}\int \dfrac{dx}{(\sin^{m-2} ax)(\cos^n ax)} \\[2mm] \text{or} \\[2mm] \dfrac{1}{a(n-1)\sin^{m-1} ax \cos^{n-1} ax} \\[2mm] \qquad - \dfrac{m+n-2}{n-1}\int \dfrac{dx}{\sin^m ax \cos^{n-2} ax} \end{cases}$$

335. $\displaystyle \int \sin(a + bx)\,dx = -\frac{1}{b}\cos(a + bx)$

336. $\displaystyle \int \cos(a + bx)\,dx = \frac{1}{b}\sin(a + bx)$

337. $\displaystyle \int \frac{dx}{1 \pm \sin ax} = \mp\frac{1}{a}\tan\left(\frac{\pi}{4} \mp \frac{ax}{2}\right)$

INTEGRALS (Continued)

338. $\displaystyle\int \frac{dx}{1 + \cos ax} = \frac{1}{a}\tan\frac{ax}{2}$

339. $\displaystyle\int \frac{dx}{1 - \cos ax} = -\frac{1}{a}\cot\frac{ax}{2}$

*340. $\displaystyle\int \frac{dx}{a + b\sin x} = \begin{cases} \dfrac{2}{\sqrt{a^2 - b^2}}\tan^{-1}\dfrac{a\tan\dfrac{x}{2} + b}{\sqrt{a^2 - b^2}} \\[2em] \text{or} \\[1em] \dfrac{1}{\sqrt{b^2 - a^2}}\log\dfrac{a\tan\dfrac{x}{2} + b - \sqrt{b^2 - a^2}}{a\tan\dfrac{x}{2} + b + \sqrt{b^2 - a^2}} \end{cases}$

*341. $\displaystyle\int \frac{dx}{a + b\cos x} = \begin{cases} \dfrac{2}{\sqrt{a^2 - b^2}}\tan^{-1}\dfrac{\sqrt{a^2 - b^2}\tan\dfrac{x}{2}}{a + b} \\[2em] \text{or} \\[1em] \dfrac{1}{\sqrt{b^2 - a^2}}\log\left(-\dfrac{\sqrt{b^2 - a^2}\tan\dfrac{x}{2} + a + b}{\sqrt{b^2 - a^2}\tan\dfrac{x}{2} - a - b}\right) \end{cases}$

*342. $\displaystyle\int \frac{dx}{a + b\sin x + c\cos x}$

$$= \begin{cases} \dfrac{1}{\sqrt{b^2 + c^2 - a^2}}\log\dfrac{b - \sqrt{b^2 + c^2 - a^2} + (a - c)\tan\dfrac{x}{2}}{b + \sqrt{b^2 + c^2 - a^2} + (a - c)\tan\dfrac{x}{2}}, & \text{if } a^2 < b^2 + c^2, a \neq c \\[2em] \text{or} \\[1em] \dfrac{2}{\sqrt{a^2 - b^2 - c^2}}\tan^{-1}\dfrac{b + (a - c)\tan\dfrac{x}{2}}{\sqrt{a^2 - b^2 - c^2}}, & \text{if } a^2 > b^2 + c^2 \\[2em] \text{or} \\[1em] \dfrac{1}{a}\left[\dfrac{a - (b + c)\cos x - (b - c)\sin x}{a - (b - c)\cos x + (b + c)\sin x}\right], & \text{if } a^2 = b^2 + c^2, a \neq c. \end{cases}$$

*343. $\displaystyle\int \frac{\sin^2 x\, dx}{a + b\cos^2 x} = \frac{1}{b}\sqrt{\frac{a + b}{a}}\tan^{-1}\left(\sqrt{\frac{a}{a + b}}\tan x\right) - \frac{x}{b}, \qquad (ab > 0, \text{ or } |a| > |b|)$

*See note 6--page 237.

INTEGRALS (Continued)

*344. $\displaystyle\int \frac{dx}{a^2 \cos^2 x + b^2 \sin^2 x} = \frac{1}{ab} \tan^{-1}\left(\frac{b \tan x}{a}\right)$

*345. $\displaystyle\int \frac{\cos^2 cx}{a^2 + b^2 \sin^2 cx}\, dx = \frac{\sqrt{a^2 + b^2}}{ab^2 c} \tan^{-1} \frac{\sqrt{a^2 + b^2}\, \tan cx}{a} - \frac{x}{b^2}$

346. $\displaystyle\int \frac{\sin cx \cos cx}{a \cos^2 cx + b \sin^2 cx}\, dx = \frac{1}{2c(b - a)} \log (a \cos^2 cx + b \sin^2 cx)$

347. $\displaystyle\int \frac{\cos cx}{a \cos cx + b \sin cx}\, dx = \int \frac{dx}{a + b \tan cx} =$

$$\frac{1}{c(a^2 + b^2)}[acx + b \log (a \cos cx + b \sin cx)]$$

348. $\displaystyle\int \frac{\sin cx}{a \sin cx + b \cos cx}\, dx = \int \frac{dx}{a + b \cot cx} =$

$$\frac{1}{c(a^2 + b^2)}[acx - b \log (a \sin cx + b \cos cx)]$$

*349. $\displaystyle\int \frac{dx}{a \cos^2 x + 2b \cos x \sin x + c \sin^2 x} =$

$$\begin{cases} \dfrac{1}{2\sqrt{b^2 - ac}} \log \dfrac{c \tan x + b - \sqrt{b^2 - ac}}{c \tan x + b + \sqrt{b^2 - ac}}, \\ \qquad\qquad\qquad\qquad (b^2 > ac) \\ \text{or} \\ \dfrac{1}{\sqrt{ac - b^2}} \tan^{-1} \dfrac{c \tan x + b}{\sqrt{ac - b^2}}, \quad (b^2 < ac) \\ \text{or} \\ -\dfrac{1}{c \tan x + b}, \qquad (b^2 = ac) \end{cases}$$

350. $\displaystyle\int \frac{\sin ax}{1 \pm \sin ax}\, dx = \pm x + \frac{1}{a} \tan\left(\frac{\pi}{4} \mp \frac{ax}{2}\right)$

351. $\displaystyle\int \frac{dx}{(\sin ax)(1 \pm \sin ax)} = \frac{1}{a} \tan\left(\frac{\pi}{4} \mp \frac{ax}{2}\right) + \frac{1}{a} \log \tan \frac{ax}{2}$

352. $\displaystyle\int \frac{dx}{(1 + \sin ax)^2} = -\frac{1}{2a} \tan\left(\frac{\pi}{4} - \frac{ax}{2}\right) - \frac{1}{6a} \tan^3\left(\frac{\pi}{4} - \frac{ax}{2}\right)$

353. $\displaystyle\int \frac{dx}{(1 - \sin ax)^2} = \frac{1}{2a} \cot\left(\frac{\pi}{4} - \frac{ax}{2}\right) + \frac{1}{6a} \cot^3\left(\frac{\pi}{4} - \frac{ax}{2}\right)$

354. $\displaystyle\int \frac{\sin ax}{(1 + \sin ax)^2}\, dx = -\frac{1}{2a} \tan\left(\frac{\pi}{4} - \frac{ax}{2}\right) + \frac{1}{6a} \tan^3\left(\frac{\pi}{4} - \frac{ax}{2}\right)$

*See note 6--page 237.

INTEGRALS (Continued)

355. $\int \dfrac{\sin ax}{(1 - \sin ax)^2}\, dx = -\dfrac{1}{2a}\cot\left(\dfrac{\pi}{4} - \dfrac{ax}{2}\right) + \dfrac{1}{6a}\cot^3\left(\dfrac{\pi}{4} - \dfrac{ax}{2}\right)$

356. $\int \dfrac{\sin x\, dx}{a + b\sin x} = \dfrac{x}{b} - \dfrac{a}{b}\int \dfrac{dx}{a + b\sin x}$

357. $\int \dfrac{dx}{(\sin x)(a + b\sin x)} = \dfrac{1}{a}\log\tan\dfrac{x}{2} - \dfrac{b}{a}\int \dfrac{dx}{a + b\sin x}$

358. $\int \dfrac{dx}{(a + b\sin x)^2} = \dfrac{b\cos x}{(a^2 - b^2)(a + b\sin x)} + \dfrac{a}{a^2 - b^2}\int \dfrac{dx}{a + b\sin x}$

359. $\int \dfrac{\sin x\, dx}{(a + b\sin x)^2} = \dfrac{a\cos x}{(b^2 - a^2)(a + b\sin x)} + \dfrac{b}{b^2 - a^2}\int \dfrac{dx}{a + b\sin x}$

*360. $\int \dfrac{dx}{a^2 + b^2\sin^2 cx} = \dfrac{1}{ac\sqrt{a^2 + b^2}}\tan^{-1}\dfrac{\sqrt{a^2 + b^2}\,\tan cx}{a}$

*361. $\int \dfrac{dx}{a^2 - b^2\sin^2 cx} = \begin{cases} \dfrac{1}{ac\sqrt{a^2 - b^2}}\tan^{-1}\dfrac{\sqrt{a^2 - b^2}\,\tan cx}{a}, & (a^2 > b^2) \\[2mm] \text{or} \\[2mm] \dfrac{1}{2ac\sqrt{b^2 - a^2}}\log\dfrac{\sqrt{b^2 - a^2}\,\tan cx + a}{\sqrt{b^2 - a^2}\,\tan cx - a}, & (a^2 < b^2) \end{cases}$

362. $\int \dfrac{\cos ax}{1 + \cos ax}\, dx = x - \dfrac{1}{a}\tan\dfrac{ax}{2}$

363. $\int \dfrac{\cos ax}{1 - \cos ax}\, dx = -x - \dfrac{1}{a}\cot\dfrac{ax}{2}$

364. $\int \dfrac{dx}{(\cos ax)(1 + \cos ax)} = \dfrac{1}{a}\log\tan\left(\dfrac{\pi}{4} + \dfrac{ax}{2}\right) - \dfrac{1}{a}\tan\dfrac{ax}{2}$

365. $\int \dfrac{dx}{(\cos ax)(1 - \cos ax)} = \dfrac{1}{a}\log\tan\left(\dfrac{\pi}{4} + \dfrac{ax}{2}\right) - \dfrac{1}{a}\cot\dfrac{ax}{2}$

366. $\int \dfrac{dx}{(1 + \cos ax)^2} = \dfrac{1}{2a}\tan\dfrac{ax}{2} + \dfrac{1}{6a}\tan^3\dfrac{ax}{2}$

367. $\int \dfrac{dx}{(1 - \cos ax)^2} = -\dfrac{1}{2a}\cot\dfrac{ax}{2} - \dfrac{1}{6a}\cot^3\dfrac{ax}{2}$

368. $\int \dfrac{\cos ax}{(1 + \cos ax)^2}\, dx = \dfrac{1}{2a}\tan\dfrac{ax}{2} - \dfrac{1}{6a}\tan^3\dfrac{ax}{2}$

369. $\int \dfrac{\cos ax}{(1 - \cos ax)^2}\, dx = \dfrac{1}{2a}\cot\dfrac{ax}{2} - \dfrac{1}{6a}\cot^3\dfrac{ax}{2}$

*See note 6–page 237.

INTEGRALS (Continued)

370. $\displaystyle\int \frac{\cos x\, dx}{a + b\cos x} = \frac{x}{b} - \frac{a}{b}\int \frac{dx}{a + b\cos x}$

371. $\displaystyle\int \frac{dx}{(\cos x)(a + b\cos x)} = \frac{1}{a}\log\tan\left(\frac{x}{2} + \frac{\pi}{4}\right) - \frac{b}{a}\int \frac{dx}{a + b\cos x}$

372. $\displaystyle\int \frac{dx}{(a + b\cos x)^2} = \frac{b\sin x}{(b^2 - a^2)(a + b\cos x)} - \frac{a}{b^2 - a^2}\int \frac{dx}{a + b\cos x}$

373. $\displaystyle\int \frac{\cos x}{(a + b\cos x)^2}\, dx = \frac{a\sin x}{(a^2 - b^2)(a + b\cos x)} - \frac{b}{a^2 - b^2}\int \frac{dx}{a + b\cos x}$

*374. $\displaystyle\int \frac{dx}{a^2 + b^2 - 2ab\cos cx} = \frac{2}{c(a^2 - b^2)}\tan^{-1}\left(\frac{a + b}{a - b}\tan\frac{cx}{2}\right)$

*375. $\displaystyle\int \frac{dx}{a^2 + b^2\cos^2 cx} = \frac{1}{ac\sqrt{a^2 + b^2}}\tan^{-1}\frac{a\tan cx}{\sqrt{a^2 + b^2}}$

*376. $\displaystyle\int \frac{dx}{a^2 - b^2\cos^2 cx} = \begin{cases} \dfrac{1}{ac\sqrt{a^2 - b^2}}\tan^{-1}\dfrac{a\tan cx}{\sqrt{a^2 - b^2}}, & (a^2 > b^2) \\[2mm] \text{or} \\[2mm] \dfrac{1}{2ac\sqrt{b^2 - a^2}}\log\dfrac{a\tan cx - \sqrt{b^2 - a^2}}{a\tan cx + \sqrt{b^2 - a^2}}, & (b^2 > a^2) \end{cases}$

377. $\displaystyle\int \frac{\sin ax}{1 \pm \cos ax}\, dx = \mp \frac{1}{a}\log(1 \pm \cos ax)$

378. $\displaystyle\int \frac{\cos ax}{1 \pm \sin ax}\, dx = \pm \frac{1}{a}\log(1 \pm \sin ax)$

379. $\displaystyle\int \frac{dx}{(\sin ax)(1 \pm \cos ax)} = \pm \frac{1}{2a(1 \pm \cos ax)} + \frac{1}{2a}\log\tan\frac{ax}{2}$

380. $\displaystyle\int \frac{dx}{(\cos ax)(1 \pm \sin ax)} = \mp \frac{1}{2a(1 \pm \sin ax)} + \frac{1}{2a}\log\tan\left(\frac{\pi}{4} + \frac{ax}{2}\right)$

381. $\displaystyle\int \frac{\sin ax}{(\cos ax)(1 \pm \cos ax)}\, dx = \frac{1}{a}\log(\sec ax \pm 1)$

382. $\displaystyle\int \frac{\cos ax}{(\sin ax)(1 \pm \sin ax)}\, dx = - \frac{1}{a}\log(\csc ax \pm 1)$

383. $\displaystyle\int \frac{\sin ax}{(\cos ax)(1 \pm \sin ax)}\, dx = \frac{1}{2a(1 \pm \sin ax)} \pm \frac{1}{2a}\log\tan\left(\frac{\pi}{4} + \frac{ax}{2}\right)$

384. $\displaystyle\int \frac{\cos ax}{(\sin ax)(1 \pm \cos ax)}\, dx = - \frac{1}{2a(1 \pm \cos ax)} \pm \frac{1}{2a}\log\tan\frac{ax}{2}$

*See note 6–page 237.

INTEGRALS (Continued)

385. $\displaystyle\int \frac{dx}{\sin ax \pm \cos ax} = \frac{1}{a\sqrt{2}} \log \tan\left(\frac{ax}{2} \pm \frac{\pi}{8}\right)$

386. $\displaystyle\int \frac{dx}{(\sin ax \pm \cos ax)^2} = \frac{1}{2a} \tan\left(ax \mp \frac{\pi}{4}\right)$

387. $\displaystyle\int \frac{dx}{1 + \cos ax \pm \sin ax} = \pm\frac{1}{a} \log\left(1 \pm \tan\frac{ax}{2}\right)$

388. $\displaystyle\int \frac{dx}{a^2 \cos^2 cx - b^2 \sin^2 cx} = \frac{1}{2abc} \log\frac{b \tan cx + a}{b \tan cx - a}$

389. $\displaystyle\int x(\sin ax)\,dx = \frac{1}{a^2}\sin ax - \frac{x}{a}\cos ax$

390. $\displaystyle\int x^2(\sin ax)\,dx = \frac{2x}{a^2}\sin ax - \frac{a^2x^2 - 2}{a^3}\cos ax$

391. $\displaystyle\int x^3(\sin ax)\,dx = \frac{3a^2x^2 - 6}{a^4}\sin ax - \frac{a^2x^3 - 6x}{a^3}\cos ax$

392. $\displaystyle\int x^m \sin ax\,dx = \begin{cases} -\dfrac{1}{a}x^m \cos ax + \dfrac{m}{a}\displaystyle\int x^{m-1}\cos ax\,dx \\[2mm] \text{or} \\[2mm] \cos ax \displaystyle\sum_{r=0}^{\left[\frac{m}{2}\right]} (-1)^{r+1}\dfrac{m!}{(m-2r)!}\cdot\dfrac{x^{m-2r}}{a^{2r+1}} \\[4mm] +\sin ax \displaystyle\sum_{r=0}^{\left[\frac{m-1}{2}\right]} (-1)^r\dfrac{m!}{(m-2r-1)!}\cdot\dfrac{x^{m-2r-1}}{a^{2r+2}} \end{cases}$

Note: $[s]$ means greatest integer $\leq s$; $[3\frac{1}{2}] = 3$, $[\frac{1}{2}] = 0$, etc.

393. $\displaystyle\int x(\cos ax)\,dx = \frac{1}{a^2}\cos ax + \frac{x}{a}\sin ax$

394. $\displaystyle\int x^2(\cos ax)\,dx = \frac{2x \cos ax}{a^2} + \frac{a^2x^2 - 2}{a^3}\sin ax$

395. $\displaystyle\int x^3(\cos ax)\,dx = \frac{3a^2x^2 - 6}{a^4}\cos ax + \frac{a^2x^3 - 6x}{a^3}\sin ax$

396. $\displaystyle\int x^m(\cos ax)\,dx = \begin{cases} \dfrac{x^m \sin ax}{a} - \dfrac{m}{a}\displaystyle\int x^{m-1}\sin ax\,dx \\[2mm] \text{or} \\[2mm] \sin ax \displaystyle\sum_{r=0}^{\left[\frac{m}{2}\right]} (-1)^r\dfrac{m!}{(m-2r)!}\cdot\dfrac{x^{m-2r}}{a^{2r+1}} \\[4mm] +\cos ax \displaystyle\sum_{r=0}^{\left[\frac{m-1}{2}\right]} (-1)^r\dfrac{m!}{(m-2r-1)!}\cdot\dfrac{x^{m-2r-1}}{a^{2r+2}} \end{cases}$

See note integral 392.

INTEGRALS (Continued)

397. $\displaystyle\int \frac{\sin ax}{x}\,dx = \sum_{n=0}^{\infty} (-1)^n \frac{(ax)^{2n+1}}{(2n+1)(2n+1)!}$

398. $\displaystyle\int \frac{\cos ax}{x}\,dx = \log x + \sum_{n=1}^{x} (-1)^n \frac{(ax)^{2n}}{2n(2n)!}$

399. $\displaystyle\int x(\sin^2 ax)\,dx = \frac{x^2}{4} - \frac{x \sin 2ax}{4a} - \frac{\cos 2ax}{8a^2}$

400. $\displaystyle\int x^2(\sin^2 ax)\,dx = \frac{x^3}{6} - \left(\frac{x^2}{4a} - \frac{1}{8a^3}\right)\sin 2ax - \frac{x \cos 2ax}{4a^2}$

401. $\displaystyle\int x(\sin^3 ax)\,dx = \frac{x \cos 3ax}{12a} - \frac{\sin 3ax}{36a^2} - \frac{3x \cos ax}{4a} + \frac{3 \sin ax}{4a^2}$

402. $\displaystyle\int x(\cos^2 ax)\,dx = \frac{x^2}{4} + \frac{x \sin 2ax}{4a} + \frac{\cos 2ax}{8a^2}$

403. $\displaystyle\int x^2(\cos^2 ax)\,dx = \frac{x^3}{6} + \left(\frac{x^2}{4a} - \frac{1}{8a^3}\right)\sin 2ax + \frac{x \cos 2ax}{4a^2}$

404. $\displaystyle\int x(\cos^3 ax)\,dx = \frac{x \sin 3ax}{12a} + \frac{\cos 3ax}{36a^2} + \frac{3x \sin ax}{4a} + \frac{3 \cos ax}{4a^2}$

405. $\displaystyle\int \frac{\sin ax}{x^m}\,dx = -\frac{\sin ax}{(m-1)x^{m-1}} + \frac{a}{m-1}\int \frac{\cos ax}{x^{m-1}}\,dx$

406. $\displaystyle\int \frac{\cos ax}{x^m}\,dx = -\frac{\cos ax}{(m-1)x^{m-1}} - \frac{a}{m-1}\int \frac{\sin ax}{x^{m-1}}\,dx$

407. $\displaystyle\int \frac{x}{1 \pm \sin ax}\,dx = \mp \frac{x \cos ax}{a(1 \pm \sin ax)} + \frac{1}{a^2}\log (1 \pm \sin ax)$

408. $\displaystyle\int \frac{x}{1 + \cos ax}\,dx = \frac{x}{a}\tan \frac{ax}{2} + \frac{2}{a^2}\log \cos \frac{ax}{2}$

409. $\displaystyle\int \frac{x}{1 - \cos ax}\,dx = -\frac{x}{a}\cot \frac{ax}{2} + \frac{2}{a^2}\log \sin \frac{ax}{2}$

410. $\displaystyle\int \frac{x + \sin x}{1 + \cos x}\,dx = x \tan \frac{x}{2}$

411. $\displaystyle\int \frac{x - \sin x}{1 - \cos x}\,dx = -x \cot \frac{x}{2}$

412. $\displaystyle\int \sqrt{1 - \cos ax}\,dx = -\frac{2 \sin ax}{a\sqrt{1 - \cos ax}} = -\frac{2\sqrt{2}}{a}\cos\left(\frac{ax}{2}\right)$

413. $\displaystyle\int \sqrt{1 + \cos ax}\,dx = \frac{2 \sin ax}{a\sqrt{1 + \cos ax}} = \frac{2\sqrt{2}}{a}\sin\left(\frac{ax}{2}\right)$

INTEGRALS (Continued)

414. $\int \sqrt{1 + \sin x}\, dx = \pm 2\left(\sin\frac{x}{2} - \cos\frac{x}{2}\right),$

[use + if $(8k - 1)\dfrac{\pi}{2} < x \le (8k + 3)\dfrac{\pi}{2}$, otherwise $-$; k an integer]

415. $\int \sqrt{1 - \sin x}\, dx = \pm 2\left(\sin\frac{x}{2} + \cos\frac{x}{2}\right),$

[use + if $(8k - 3)\dfrac{\pi}{2} < x \le (8k + 1)\dfrac{\pi}{2}$, otherwise $-$; k an integer]

416. $\int \dfrac{dx}{\sqrt{1 - \cos x}} = \pm \sqrt{2} \log \tan \dfrac{x}{4},$

[use + if $4k\pi < x < (4k + 2)\pi$, otherwise $-$; k an integer]

417. $\int \dfrac{dx}{\sqrt{1 + \cos x}} = \pm \sqrt{2} \log \tan \left(\dfrac{x + \pi}{4}\right),$

[use + if $(4k - 1)\pi < x < (4k + 1)\pi$, otherwise $-$; k an integer]

418. $\int \dfrac{dx}{\sqrt{1 - \sin x}} = \pm \sqrt{2} \log \tan \left(\dfrac{x}{4} - \dfrac{\pi}{8}\right),$

[use + if $(8k + 1)\dfrac{\pi}{2} < x < (8k + 5)\dfrac{\pi}{2}$, otherwise $-$; k an integer]

419. $\int \dfrac{dx}{\sqrt{1 + \sin x}} = \pm \sqrt{2} \log \tan \left(\dfrac{x}{4} + \dfrac{\pi}{8}\right),$

[use + if $(8k - 1)\dfrac{\pi}{2} < x < (8k + 3)\dfrac{\pi}{2}$, otherwise $-$; k an integer]

420. $\int (\tan^2 ax)\, dx = \dfrac{1}{a} \tan ax - x$

421. $\int (\tan^3 ax)\, dx = \dfrac{1}{2a} \tan^2 ax + \dfrac{1}{a} \log \cos ax$

422. $\int (\tan^4 ax)\, dx = \dfrac{\tan^3 ax}{3a} - \dfrac{1}{a} \tan x + x$

423. $\int (\tan^n ax)\, dx = \dfrac{\tan^{n-1} ax}{a(n - 1)} - \int (\tan^{n-2} ax)\, dx$

424. $\int (\cot^2 ax)\, dx = -\dfrac{1}{a} \cot ax - x$

425. $\int (\cot^3 ax)\, dx = -\dfrac{1}{2a} \cot^2 ax - \dfrac{1}{a} \log \sin ax$

426. $\int (\cot^4 ax)\, dx = -\dfrac{1}{3a} \cot^3 ax + \dfrac{1}{a} \cot ax + x$

INTEGRALS (Continued)

427. $\int (\cot^n ax)\, dx = -\dfrac{\cot^{n-1} ax}{a(n-1)} - \int (\cot^{n-2} ax)\, dx$

428. $\int \dfrac{x}{\sin^2 ax}\, dx = \int x(\csc^2 ax)\, dx = -\dfrac{x \cot ax}{a} + \dfrac{1}{a^2} \log \sin ax$

429. $\int \dfrac{x}{\sin^n ax}\, dx = \int x(\csc^n ax)\, dx = -\dfrac{x \cos ax}{a(n-1)\sin^{n-1} ax}$

$$-\dfrac{1}{a^2(n-1)(n-2)\sin^{n-2} ax} + \dfrac{(n-2)}{(n-1)} \int \dfrac{x}{\sin^{n-2} ax}\, dx$$

430. $\int \dfrac{x}{\cos^2 ax}\, dx = \int x(\sec^2 ax)\, dx = \dfrac{1}{a} x \tan ax + \dfrac{1}{a^2} \log \cos ax$

431. $\int \dfrac{x}{\cos^n ax}\, dx = \int x(\sec^n ax)\, dx = \dfrac{x \sin ax}{a(n-1)\cos^{n-1} ax}$

$$-\dfrac{1}{a^2(n-1)(n-2)\cos^{n-2} ax} + \dfrac{n-2}{n-1} \int \dfrac{x}{\cos^{n-2} ax}\, dx$$

432. $\int \dfrac{\sin ax}{\sqrt{1 + b^2 \sin^2 ax}}\, dx = -\dfrac{1}{ab} \sin^{-1} \dfrac{b \cos ax}{\sqrt{1 + b^2}}$

433. $\int \dfrac{\sin ax}{\sqrt{1 - b^2 \sin^2 ax}}\, dx = -\dfrac{1}{ab} \log (b \cos ax + \sqrt{1 - b^2 \sin^2 ax})$

434. $\int (\sin ax)\sqrt{1 + b^2 \sin^2 ax}\, dx = -\dfrac{\cos ax}{2a} \sqrt{1 + b^2 \sin^2 ax}$

$$-\dfrac{1 + b^2}{2ab} \sin^{-1} \dfrac{b \cos ax}{\sqrt{1 + b^2}}$$

435. $\int (\sin ax)\sqrt{1 - b^2 \sin^2 ax}\, dx = -\dfrac{\cos ax}{2a} \sqrt{1 - b^2 \sin^2 ax}$

$$-\dfrac{1 - b^2}{2ab} \log (b \cos ax + \sqrt{1 - b^2 \sin^2 ax})$$

436. $\int \dfrac{\cos ax}{\sqrt{1 + b^2 \sin^2 ax}}\, dx = \dfrac{1}{ab} \log (b \sin ax + \sqrt{1 + b^2 \sin^2 ax})$

437. $\int \dfrac{\cos ax}{\sqrt{1 - b^2 \sin^2 ax}}\, dx = \dfrac{1}{ab} \sin^{-1} (b \sin ax)$

438. $\int (\cos ax)\sqrt{1 + b^2 \sin^2 ax}\, dx = \dfrac{\sin ax}{2a} \sqrt{1 + b^2 \sin^2 ax}$

$$+\dfrac{1}{2ab} \log (b \sin ax + \sqrt{1 + b^2 \sin^2 ax})$$

INTEGRALS (Continued)

439. $\int (\cos ax) \sqrt{1 - b^2 \sin^2 ax}\, dx = \dfrac{\sin ax}{2a} \sqrt{1 - b^2 \sin^2 ax} + \dfrac{1}{2ab} \sin^{-1} (b \sin ax)$

440. $\int \dfrac{dx}{\sqrt{a + b \tan^2 cx}} = \dfrac{\pm 1}{c\sqrt{a - b}} \sin^{-1} \left(\sqrt{\dfrac{a - b}{a}} \sin cx \right), \qquad (a > |b|)$

[use $+$ if $(2k - 1)\dfrac{\pi}{2} < x \le (2k + 1)\dfrac{\pi}{2}$, otherwise $-$; k an integer]

FORMS INVOLVING INVERSE TRIGONOMETRIC FUNCTIONS

441. $\int (\sin^{-1} ax)\, dx = x \sin^{-1} ax + \dfrac{\sqrt{1 - a^2 x^2}}{a}$

442. $\int (\cos^{-1} ax)\, dx = x \cos^{-1} ax - \dfrac{\sqrt{1 - a^2 x^2}}{a}$

443. $\int (\tan^{-1} ax)\, dx = x \tan^{-1} ax - \dfrac{1}{2a} \log (1 + a^2 x^2)$

444. $\int (\cot^{-1} ax)\, dx = x \cot^{-1} ax + \dfrac{1}{2a} \log (1 + a^2 x^2)$

445. $\int (\sec^{-1} ax)\, dx = x \sec^{-1} ax - \dfrac{1}{a} \log (ax + \sqrt{a^2 x^2 - 1})$

446. $\int (\csc^{-1} ax)\, dx = x \csc^{-1} ax + \dfrac{1}{a} \log (ax + \sqrt{a^2 x^2 - 1})$

447. $\int \left(\sin^{-1} \dfrac{x}{a} \right) dx = x \sin^{-1} \dfrac{x}{a} + \sqrt{a^2 - x^2}, \qquad (a > 0)$

448. $\int \left(\cos^{-1} \dfrac{x}{a} \right) dx = x \cos^{-1} \dfrac{x}{a} - \sqrt{a^2 - x^2}, \qquad (a > 0)$

449. $\int \left(\tan^{-1} \dfrac{x}{a} \right) dx = x \tan^{-1} \dfrac{x}{a} - \dfrac{a}{2} \log (a^2 + x^2)$

450. $\int \left(\cot^{-1} \dfrac{x}{a} \right) dx = x \cot^{-1} \dfrac{x}{a} + \dfrac{a}{2} \log (a^2 + x^2)$

451. $\int x[\sin^{-1} (ax)]\, dx = \dfrac{1}{4a^2}[(2a^2 x^2 - 1) \sin^{-1} (ax) + ax \sqrt{1 - a^2 x^2}]$

452. $\int x[\cos^{-1} (ax)]\, dx = \dfrac{1}{4a^2}[(2a^2 x^2 - 1) \cos^{-1} (ax) - ax \sqrt{1 - a^2 x^2}]$

INTEGRALS (Continued)

453. $\displaystyle\int x^n[\sin^{-1}(ax)]\,dx = \frac{x^{n+1}}{n+1}\sin^{-1}(ax) - \frac{a}{n+1}\int\frac{x^{n+1}\,dx}{\sqrt{1-a^2x^2}},$ $(n \neq -1)$

454. $\displaystyle\int x^n[\cos^{-1}(ax)]\,dx = \frac{x^{n+1}}{n+1}\cos^{-1}(ax) + \frac{a}{n+1}\int\frac{x^{n+1}\,dx}{\sqrt{1-a^2x^2}},$ $(n \neq -1)$

455. $\displaystyle\int x(\tan^{-1}ax)\,dx = \frac{1+a^2x^2}{2a^2}\tan^{-1}ax - \frac{x}{2a}$

456. $\displaystyle\int x^n(\tan^{-1}ax)\,dx = \frac{x^{n+1}}{n+1}\tan^{-1}ax - \frac{a}{n+1}\int\frac{x^{n+1}}{1+a^2x^2}\,dx$

457. $\displaystyle\int x(\cot^{-1}ax)\,dx = \frac{1+a^2x^2}{2a^2}\cot^{-1}ax + \frac{x}{2a}$

458. $\displaystyle\int x^n(\cot^{-1}ax)\,dx = \frac{x^{n+1}}{n+1}\cot^{-1}ax + \frac{a}{n+1}\int\frac{x^{n+1}}{1+a^2x^2}\,dx$

459. $\displaystyle\int\frac{\sin^{-1}(ax)}{x^2}\,dx = a\log\left(\frac{1-\sqrt{1-a^2x^2}}{x}\right) - \frac{\sin^{-1}(ax)}{x}$

460. $\displaystyle\int\frac{\cos^{-1}(ax)\,dx}{x^2} = -\frac{1}{x}\cos^{-1}(ax) + a\log\frac{1+\sqrt{1-a^2x^2}}{x}$

461. $\displaystyle\int\frac{\tan^{-1}(ax)\,dx}{x^2} = -\frac{1}{x}\tan^{-1}(ax) - \frac{a}{2}\log\frac{1+a^2x^2}{x^2}$

462. $\displaystyle\int\frac{\cot^{-1}ax}{x^2}\,dx = -\frac{1}{x}\cot^{-1}ax - \frac{a}{2}\log\frac{x^2}{a^2x^2+1}$

463. $\displaystyle\int(\sin^{-1}ax)^2\,dx = x(\sin^{-1}ax)^2 - 2x + \frac{2\sqrt{1-a^2x^2}}{a}\sin^{-1}ax$

464. $\displaystyle\int(\cos^{-1}ax)^2\,dx = x(\cos^{-1}ax)^2 - 2x - \frac{2\sqrt{1-a^2x^2}}{a}\cos^{-1}ax$

465. $\displaystyle\int(\sin^{-1}ax)^n\,dx = \begin{cases} x(\sin^{-1}ax)^n + \dfrac{n\sqrt{1-a^2x^2}}{a}(\sin^{-1}ax)^{n-1} \\ \qquad\qquad\qquad -n(n-1)\displaystyle\int(\sin^{-1}ax)^{n-2}\,dx \\[4pt] \qquad\qquad\text{or} \\ \displaystyle\sum_{r=0}^{\left[\frac{n}{2}\right]}(-1)^r\frac{n!}{(n-2r)!}x(\sin^{-1}ax)^{n-2r} \\ \qquad + \displaystyle\sum_{r=0}^{\left[\frac{n-1}{2}\right]}(-1)^r\frac{n!\sqrt{1-a^2x^2}}{(n-2r-1)!a}(\sin^{-1}ax)^{n-2r-1} \end{cases}$

Note : $[s]$ means greatest integer $\leq s$. Thus $[3.5]$ means 3; $[5] = 5$, $[\frac{1}{2}] = 0$.

INTEGRALS (Continued)

466. $\displaystyle\int (\cos^{-1} ax)^n \, dx = \begin{cases} x(\cos^{-1} ax)^n - \dfrac{n\sqrt{1 - a^2x^2}}{a}(\cos^{-1} ax)^{n-1} \\ \qquad\qquad\qquad -n(n-1)\displaystyle\int (\cos^{-1} ax)^{n-2} \, dx \\ \qquad\qquad \text{or} \\ \displaystyle\sum_{r=0}^{\left[\frac{n}{2}\right]} (-1)^r \dfrac{n!}{(n-2r)!} x(\cos^{-1} ax)^{n-2r} \\ \qquad - \displaystyle\sum_{r=0}^{\left[\frac{n-1}{2}\right]} (-1)^r \dfrac{n!\sqrt{1-a^2x^2}}{(n-2r-1)!a}(\cos^{-1} ax)^{n-2r-1} \end{cases}$

467. $\displaystyle\int \frac{1}{\sqrt{1 - a^2x^2}}(\sin^{-1} ax) \, dx = \frac{1}{2a}(\sin^{-1} ax)^2$

468. $\displaystyle\int \frac{x^n}{\sqrt{1 - a^2x^2}}(\sin^{-1} ax) \, dx = -\frac{x^{n-1}}{na^2}\sqrt{1 - a^2x^2} \sin^{-1} ax + \frac{x^n}{n^2 a}$

$$+ \frac{n-1}{na^2}\int \frac{x^{n-2}}{\sqrt{1 - a^2x^2}} \sin^{-1} ax \, dx$$

469. $\displaystyle\int \frac{1}{\sqrt{1 - a^2x^2}}(\cos^{-1} ax) \, dx = -\frac{1}{2a}(\cos^{-1} ax)^2$

470. $\displaystyle\int \frac{x^n}{\sqrt{1 - a^2x^2}}(\cos^{-1} ax) \, dx = -\frac{x^{n-1}}{na^2}\sqrt{1 - a^2x^2} \cos^{-1} ax - \frac{x^n}{n^2 a}$

$$+ \frac{n-1}{na^2}\int \frac{x^{n-2}}{\sqrt{1 - a^2x^2}} \cos^{-1} ax \, dx$$

471. $\displaystyle\int \frac{\tan^{-1} ax}{a^2x^2 + 1} \, dx = \frac{1}{2a}(\tan^{-1} ax)^2$

472. $\displaystyle\int \frac{\cot^{-1} ax}{a^2x^2 + 1} \, dx = -\frac{1}{2a}(\cot^{-1} ax)^2$

473. $\displaystyle\int x \sec^{-1} ax \, dx = \frac{x^2}{2} \sec^{-1} ax - \frac{1}{2a^2}\sqrt{a^2x^2 - 1}$

474. $\displaystyle\int x^n \sec^{-1} ax \, dx = \frac{x^{n+1}}{n+1} \sec^{-1} ax - \frac{1}{n+1}\int \frac{x^n \, dx}{\sqrt{a^2x^2 - 1}}$

475. $\displaystyle\int \frac{\sec^{-1} ax}{x^2} \, dx = -\frac{\sec^{-1} ax}{x} + \frac{\sqrt{a^2x^2 - 1}}{x}$

476. $\displaystyle\int x \csc^{-1} ax \, dx = \frac{x^2}{2} \csc^{-1} ax + \frac{1}{2a^2}\sqrt{a^2x^2 - 1}$

477. $\displaystyle\int x^n \csc^{-1} ax \, dx = \frac{x^{n+1}}{n+1} \csc^{-1} ax + \frac{1}{n+1}\int \frac{x^n \, dx}{\sqrt{a^2x^2 - 1}}$

INTEGRALS (Continued)

478. $\int \dfrac{\csc^{-1} ax}{x^2}\, dx = -\dfrac{\csc^{-1} ax}{x} - \dfrac{\sqrt{a^2 x^2 - 1}}{x}$

FORMS INVOLVING TRIGONOMETRIC SUBSTITUTIONS

479. $\int f(\sin x)\, dx = 2 \int f\!\left(\dfrac{2z}{1 + z^2}\right) \dfrac{dz}{1 + z^2}, \qquad \left(z = \tan \dfrac{x}{2}\right)$

480. $\int f(\cos x)\, dx = 2 \int f\!\left(\dfrac{1 - z^2}{1 + z^2}\right) \dfrac{dz}{1 + z^2}, \qquad \left(z = \tan \dfrac{x}{2}\right)$

*481. $\int f(\sin x)\, dx = \int f(u)\dfrac{du}{\sqrt{1 - u^2}}, \qquad (u = \sin x)$

*482. $\int f(\cos x)\, dx = -\int f(u)\dfrac{du}{\sqrt{1 - u^2}}, \qquad (u = \cos x)$

*483. $\int f(\sin x, \cos x)\, dx = \int f(u, \sqrt{1 - u^2})\dfrac{du}{\sqrt{1 - u^2}}, \qquad (u = \sin x)$

484. $\int f(\sin x, \cos x)\, dx = 2 \int f\!\left(\dfrac{2z}{1 + z^2}, \dfrac{1 - z^2}{1 + z^2}\right) \dfrac{dz}{1 + z^2}, \qquad \left(z = \tan \dfrac{x}{2}\right)$

LOGARITHMIC FORMS

485. $\int (\log x)\, dx = x \log x - x$

486. $\int x(\log x)\, dx = \dfrac{x^2}{2} \log x - \dfrac{x^2}{4}$

487. $\int x^2(\log x)\, dx = \dfrac{x^3}{3} \log x - \dfrac{x^3}{9}$

488. $\int x^n(\log ax)\, dx = \dfrac{x^{n+1}}{n + 1} \log ax - \dfrac{x^{n+1}}{(n + 1)^2}$

489. $\int (\log x)^2\, dx = x(\log x)^2 - 2x \log x + 2x$

490. $\displaystyle \int (\log x)^n\, dx = \begin{cases} x(\log x)^n - n \displaystyle\int (\log x)^{n-1}\, dx, \qquad (n \neq -1) \\[2ex] \text{or} \\[2ex] (-1)^n n!\, x \displaystyle\sum_{r=0}^{n} \dfrac{(-\log x)^r}{r!} \end{cases}$

*The square roots appearing in these formulas may be plus or minus, depending on the quadrant of x. Care must be used to give them the proper sign.

INTEGRALS (Continued)

491. $\int \dfrac{(\log x)^n}{x}\,dx = \dfrac{1}{n+1}(\log x)^{n+1}$

492. $\int \dfrac{dx}{\log x} = \log(\log x) + \log x + \dfrac{(\log x)^2}{2\cdot 2!} + \dfrac{(\log x)^3}{3\cdot 3!} + \cdots$

493. $\int \dfrac{dx}{x\log x} = \log(\log x)$

494. $\int \dfrac{dx}{x(\log x)^n} = -\dfrac{1}{(n-1)(\log x)^{n-1}}$

495. $\int \dfrac{x^m\,dx}{(\log x)^n} = -\dfrac{x^{m+1}}{(n-1)(\log x)^{n-1}} + \dfrac{m+1}{n-1}\int \dfrac{x^m\,dx}{(\log x)^{n-1}}$

496. $\int x^m(\log x)^n\,dx = \begin{cases} \dfrac{x^{m+1}(\log x)^n}{m+1} - \dfrac{n}{m+1}\displaystyle\int x^m(\log x)^{n-1}\,dx \\[2mm] \text{or} \\[2mm] (-1)^n\dfrac{n!}{m+1}x^{m+1}\displaystyle\sum_{r=0}^n \dfrac{(-\log x)^r}{r!(m+1)^{n-r}} \end{cases}$

497. $\int x^p\cos(b\,\ln x)\,dx = \dfrac{x^{p+1}}{(p+1)^2+b^2}\cdot[b\sin(b\,\ln x)+(p+1)\cos(b\,\ln x)]+c$

498. $\int x^p\sin(b\,\ln x)\,dx = \dfrac{x^{p+1}}{(p+1)^2+b^2}\cdot[(p+1)\sin(b\,\ln x)-b\cos(b\,\ln x)]+c$

499. $\int[\log(ax+b)]\,dx = \dfrac{ax+b}{a}\log(ax+b)-x$

500. $\int \dfrac{\log(ax+b)}{x^2}\,dx = \dfrac{a}{b}\log x - \dfrac{ax+b}{bx}\log(ax+b)$

501. $\int x^m[\log(ax+b)]\,dx = \dfrac{1}{m+1}\left[x^{m+1}-\left(-\dfrac{b}{a}\right)^{m+1}\right]\log(ax+b)$

$$-\dfrac{1}{m+1}\left(-\dfrac{b}{a}\right)^{m+1}\sum_{r=1}^{m+1}\dfrac{1}{r}\left(-\dfrac{ax}{b}\right)^r$$

502. $\int \dfrac{\log(ax+b)}{x^m}\,dx = -\dfrac{1}{m-1}\dfrac{\log(ax+b)}{x^{m-1}} + \dfrac{1}{m-1}\left(-\dfrac{a}{b}\right)^{m-1}\log\dfrac{ax+b}{x}$

$$+\dfrac{1}{m-1}\left(-\dfrac{a}{b}\right)^{m-1}\sum_{r=1}^{m-2}\dfrac{1}{r}\left(-\dfrac{b}{ax}\right)^r,\ (m>2)$$

503. $\int\left[\log\dfrac{x+a}{x-a}\right]dx = (x+a)\log(x+a)-(x-a)\log(x-a)$

504. $\int x^m\left[\log\dfrac{x+a}{x-a}\right]dx = \dfrac{x^{m+1}-(-a)^{m+1}}{m+1}\log(x+a)-\dfrac{x^{m+1}-a^{m+1}}{m+1}\log(x-a)$

$$+\dfrac{2a^{m+1}}{m+1}\sum_{r=1}^{\left[\frac{m+1}{2}\right]}\dfrac{1}{m-2r+2}\left(\dfrac{x}{a}\right)^{m-2r+2}$$

See note integral 392.

INTEGRALS (Continued)

505. $\displaystyle \int \frac{1}{x^2}\left[\log\frac{x+a}{x-a}\right]dx = \frac{1}{x}\log\frac{x-a}{x+a} - \frac{1}{a}\log\frac{x^2-a^2}{x^2}$

506. $\displaystyle \int (\log X)\,dx = \begin{cases} \left(x+\dfrac{b}{2c}\right)\log X - 2x + \dfrac{\sqrt{4ac-b^2}}{c}\tan^{-1}\dfrac{2cx+b}{\sqrt{4ac-b^2}}, \\ \hspace{6cm} (b^2-4ac<0) \\[0.3cm] \text{or} \\[0.3cm] \left(x+\dfrac{b}{2c}\right)\log X - 2x + \dfrac{\sqrt{b^2-4ac}}{c}\tanh^{-1}\dfrac{2cx+b}{\sqrt{b^2-4ac}}, \\ \hspace{6cm} (b^2-4ac>0) \\[0.3cm] \text{where} \\[0.2cm] X = a + bx + cx^2 \end{cases}$

507. $\displaystyle \int x^n(\log X)\,dx = \frac{x^{n+1}}{n+1}\log X - \frac{2c}{n+1}\int\frac{x^{n+2}}{X}dx - \frac{b}{n+1}\int\frac{x^{n+1}}{X}dx$

$$\text{where } X = a + bx + cx^2$$

508. $\displaystyle \int [\log(x^2+a^2)]\,dx = x\log(x^2+a^2) - 2x + 2a\tan^{-1}\frac{x}{a}$

509. $\displaystyle \int [\log(x^2-a^2)]\,dx = x\log(x^2-a^2) - 2x + a\log\frac{x+a}{x-a}$

510. $\displaystyle \int x[\log(x^2\pm a^2)]\,dx = \tfrac{1}{2}(x^2\pm a^2)\log(x^2\pm a^2) - \tfrac{1}{2}x^2$

511. $\displaystyle \int [\log(x+\sqrt{x^2\pm a^2})]\,dx = x\log(x+\sqrt{x^2\pm a^2}) - \sqrt{x^2\pm a^2}$

512. $\displaystyle \int x[\log(x+\sqrt{x^2\pm a^2})]\,dx = \left(\frac{x^2}{2}\pm\frac{a^2}{4}\right)\log(x+\sqrt{x^2\pm a^2}) - \frac{x\sqrt{x^2\pm a^2}}{4}$

513. $\displaystyle \int x^m[\log(x+\sqrt{x^2\pm a^2})]\,dx = \frac{x^{m+1}}{m+1}\log(x+\sqrt{x^2\pm a^2})$

$$- \frac{1}{m+1}\int\frac{x^{m+1}}{\sqrt{x^2\pm a^2}}dx$$

514. $\displaystyle \int\frac{\log(x+\sqrt{x^2+a^2})}{x^2}dx = -\frac{\log(x+\sqrt{x^2+a^2})}{x} - \frac{1}{a}\log\frac{a+\sqrt{x^2+a^2}}{x}$

515. $\displaystyle \int\frac{\log(x+\sqrt{x^2-a^2})}{x^2}dx = -\frac{\log(x+\sqrt{x^2-a^2})}{x} + \frac{1}{|a|}\sec^{-1}\frac{x}{a}$

INTEGRALS (Continued)

516. $\int x^n \log(x^2 - a^2)\,dx = \dfrac{1}{n+1}\Bigg[x^{n+1}\log(x^2 - a^2) - a^{n+1}\log(x-a)$

See note integral 392. $\qquad -(-a)^{n+1}\log(x+a) - 2\sum\limits_{r=0}^{\left[\frac{n}{2}\right]} \dfrac{a^{2r}x^{n-2r+1}}{n-2r+1}\Bigg]$

EXPONENTIAL FORMS

517. $\int e^x\,dx = e^x$

518. $\int e^{-x}\,dx = -e^{-x}$

519. $\int e^{ax}\,dx = \dfrac{e^{ax}}{a}$

520. $\int x\,e^{ax}\,dx = \dfrac{e^{ax}}{a^2}(ax - 1)$

521. $\int x^m e^{ax}\,dx = \begin{cases} \dfrac{x^m e^{ax}}{a} - \dfrac{m}{a}\int x^{m-1} e^{ax}\,dx \\[2mm] \qquad\quad \text{or} \\[2mm] e^{ax}\sum\limits_{r=0}^{m}(-1)^r \dfrac{m!\,x^{m-r}}{(m-r)!\,a^{r+1}} \end{cases}$

522. $\int \dfrac{e^{ax}\,dx}{x} = \log x + \dfrac{ax}{1!} + \dfrac{a^2 x^2}{2\cdot 2!} + \dfrac{a^3 x^3}{3\cdot 3!} + \cdots$

523. $\int \dfrac{e^{ax}}{x^m}\,dx = -\dfrac{1}{m-1}\dfrac{e^{ax}}{x^{m-1}} + \dfrac{a}{m-1}\int \dfrac{e^{ax}}{x^{m-1}}\,dx$

524. $\int e^{ax}\log x\,dx = \dfrac{e^{ax}\log x}{a} - \dfrac{1}{a}\int \dfrac{e^{ax}}{x}\,dx$

525. $\int \dfrac{dx}{1+e^x} = x - \log(1+e^x) = \log\dfrac{e^x}{1+e^x}$

526. $\int \dfrac{dx}{a+be^{px}} = \dfrac{x}{a} - \dfrac{1}{ap}\log(a+be^{px})$

527. $\int \dfrac{dx}{ae^{mx}+be^{-mx}} = \dfrac{1}{m\sqrt{ab}}\tan^{-1}\left(e^{mx}\sqrt{\dfrac{a}{b}}\right), \qquad (a>0, b>0)$

528. $\int \dfrac{dx}{ae^{mx}-be^{-mx}} = \begin{cases} \dfrac{1}{2m\sqrt{ab}}\log\dfrac{\sqrt{a}\,e^{mx}-\sqrt{b}}{\sqrt{a}\,e^{mx}+\sqrt{b}} \\[3mm] \qquad\quad \text{or} \\[3mm] \dfrac{-1}{m\sqrt{ab}}\tanh^{-1}\left(\sqrt{\dfrac{a}{b}}\,e^{mx}\right), \qquad (a>0, b>0) \end{cases}$

INTEGRALS (Continued)

529. $\int (a^x - a^{-x}) \, dx = \dfrac{a^x + a^{-x}}{\log a}$

530. $\int \dfrac{e^{ax}}{b + ce^{ax}} \, dx = \dfrac{1}{ac} \log (b + ce^{ax})$

531. $\int \dfrac{x \, e^{ax}}{(1 + ax)^2} \, dx = \dfrac{e^{ax}}{a^2(1 + ax)}$

532. $\int x \, e^{-x^2} \, dx = -\tfrac{1}{2} e^{-x^2}$

533. $\int e^{ax} [\sin (bx)] \, dx = \dfrac{e^{ax}[a \sin (bx) - b \cos (bx)]}{a^2 + b^2}$

534. $\int e^{ax} [\sin (bx)][\sin (cx)] \, dx = \dfrac{e^{ax}[(b - c) \sin (b - c)x + a \cos (b - c)x]}{2[a^2 + (b - c)^2]}$

$$- \dfrac{e^{ax}[(b + c) \sin (b + c)x + a \cos (b + c)x]}{2[a^2 + (b + c)^2]}$$

535. $\int e^{ax}[\sin (bx)][\cos (cx)] \, dx = \begin{cases} \dfrac{e^{ax}[a \sin (b - c)x - (b - c) \cos (b - c)x]}{2[a^2 + (b - c)^2]} \\[2mm] \quad + \dfrac{e^{ax}[a \sin (b + c)x - (b + c) \cos (b + c)x]}{2[a^2 + (b + c)^2]} \\[3mm] \qquad\qquad \text{or} \\[2mm] \dfrac{e^{ax}}{\rho}[(a \sin bx - b \cos bx)[\cos (cx - \alpha)] \\[2mm] \qquad\qquad - c(\sin bx) \sin (cx - \alpha)] \\[2mm] \text{where} \\[2mm] \rho = \sqrt{(a^2 + b^2 - c^2)^2 + 4a^2c^2}, \\[2mm] \rho \cos \alpha = a^2 + b^2 - c^2, \qquad \rho \sin \alpha = 2ac \end{cases}$

536. $\int e^{ax}[\sin (bx)][\sin (bx + c)] \, dx$

$$= \dfrac{e^{ax} \cos c}{2a} - \dfrac{e^{ax}[a \cos (2bx + c) + 2b \sin (2bx + c)]}{2(a^2 + 4b^2)}$$

537. $\int e^{ax}[\sin (bx)][\cos (bx + c)] \, dx$

$$= \dfrac{-e^{ax} \sin c}{2a} + \dfrac{e^{ax}[a \sin (2bx + c) - 2b \cos (2bx + c)]}{2(a^2 + 4b^2)}$$

538. $\int e^{ax}[\cos (bx)] \, dx = \dfrac{e^{ax}}{a^2 + b^2}[a \cos (bx) + b \sin (bx)]$

INTEGRALS (Continued)

539. $\int e^{ax}[\cos(bx)][\cos(cx)]\,dx = \dfrac{e^{ax}[(b-c)\sin(b-c)x + a\cos(b-c)x]}{2[a^2 + (b-c)^2]}$

$$+ \dfrac{e^{ax}[(b+c)\sin(b+c)x + a\cos(b+c)x]}{2[a^2 + (b+c)^2]}$$

540. $\int e^{ax}[\cos(bx)][\cos(bx+c)]\,dx$

$$= \dfrac{e^{ax}\cos c}{2a} + \dfrac{e^{ax}[a\cos(2bx+c) + 2b\sin(2bx+c)]}{2(a^2 + 4b^2)}$$

541. $\int e^{ax}[\cos(bx)][\sin(bx+c)]\,dx$

$$= \dfrac{e^{ax}\sin c}{2a} + \dfrac{e^{ax}[a\sin(2bx+c) - 2b\cos(2bx+c)]}{2(a^2 + 4b^2)}$$

542. $\int e^{ax}[\sin^n bx]\,dx = \dfrac{1}{a^2 + n^2 b^2}\Bigg[(a\sin bx - nb\cos bx)\,e^{ax}\sin^{n-1} bx$

$$+ n(n-1)b^2 \int e^{ax}[\sin^{n-2} bx]\,dx \Bigg]$$

543. $\int e^{ax}[\cos^n bx]\,dx = \dfrac{1}{a^2 + n^2 b^2}\Bigg[(a\cos bx + nb\sin bx)\,e^{ax}\cos^{n-1} bx$

$$+ n(n-1)b^2 \int e^{ax}[\cos^{n-2} bx]\,dx \Bigg]$$

544. $\int x^m e^x \sin x\,dx = \dfrac{1}{2}x^m e^x(\sin x - \cos x) - \dfrac{m}{2}\int x^{m-1} e^x \sin x\,dx$

$$+ \dfrac{m}{2}\int x^{m-1} e^x \cos x\,dx$$

545. $\int x^m e^{ax}[\sin bx]\,dx = \begin{cases} x^m e^{ax}\,\dfrac{a\sin bx - b\cos bx}{a^2 + b^2} \\[2mm] \qquad - \dfrac{m}{a^2 + b^2}\int x^{m-1} e^{ax}(a\sin bx - b\cos bx)\,dx \\[2mm] \qquad\qquad \text{or} \\[2mm] e^{ax}\sum\limits_{r=0}^{m}\dfrac{(-1)^r m!\,x^{m-r}}{\rho^{r+1}(m-r)!}\sin[bx - (r+1)\alpha] \\[2mm] \qquad\quad \text{where} \\[2mm] \rho = \sqrt{a^2 + b^2}, \qquad \rho\cos\alpha = a, \qquad \rho\sin\alpha = b \end{cases}$

546. $\int x^m e^x \cos x\,dx = \dfrac{1}{2}x^m e^x(\sin x + \cos x)$

$$- \dfrac{m}{2}\int x^{m-1} e^x \sin x\,dx - \dfrac{m}{2}\int x^{m-1} e^x \cos x\,dx$$

INTEGRALS (Continued)

547. $\displaystyle\int x^m e^{ax} \cos bx \, dx =$

$$\begin{cases} x^m e^{ax} \dfrac{a \cos bx + b \sin bx}{a^2 + b^2} \\[2mm] \qquad - \dfrac{m}{a^2 + b^2} \displaystyle\int x^{m-1} e^{ax}(a \cos bx + b \sin bx)\, dx \\[2mm] \text{or} \\[2mm] e^{ax} \displaystyle\sum_{r=0}^{m} \dfrac{(-1)^r m! x^{m-r}}{\rho^{r+1}(m-r)!} \cos[bx - (r+1)\alpha] \\[2mm] \text{where} \\[2mm] \rho = \sqrt{a^2 + b^2}, \qquad \rho \cos \alpha = a, \qquad \rho \sin \alpha = b \end{cases}$$

548. $\displaystyle\int e^{ax}(\cos^m x)(\sin^n x)\, dx =$

$$\begin{cases} \dfrac{e^{ax} \cos^{m-1} x \sin^n x[a \cos x + (m+n)\sin x]}{(m+n)^2 + a^2} \\[2mm] \quad - \dfrac{na}{(m+n)^2 + a^2} \displaystyle\int e^{ax}(\cos^{m-1} x)(\sin^{n-1} x)\, dx \\[2mm] \quad + \dfrac{(m-1)(m+n)}{(m+n)^2 + a^2} \displaystyle\int e^{ax}(\cos^{m-2} x)(\sin^n x)\, dx \\[2mm] \text{or} \\[2mm] \dfrac{e^{ax} \cos^m x \sin^{n-1} x[a \sin x - (m+n)\cos x]}{(m+n)^2 + a^2} \\[2mm] \quad + \dfrac{ma}{(m+n)^2 + a^2} \displaystyle\int e^{ax}(\cos^{m-1} x)(\sin^{n-1} x)\, dx \\[2mm] \quad + \dfrac{(n-1)(m+n)}{(m+n)^2 + a^2} \displaystyle\int e^{ax}(\cos^m x)(\sin^{n-2} x)\, dx \\[2mm] \text{or} \\[2mm] \dfrac{e^{ax}(\cos^{m-1} x)(\sin^{n-1} x)(a \sin x \cos x + m \sin^2 x - n \cos^2 x)}{(m+n)^2 + a^2} \\[2mm] \quad + \dfrac{m(m-1)}{(m+n)^2 + a^2} \displaystyle\int e^{ax}(\cos^{m-2} x)(\sin^n x)\, dx \\[2mm] \quad + \dfrac{n(n-1)}{(m+n)^2 + a^2} \displaystyle\int e^{ax}(\cos^m x)(\sin^{n-2} x)\, dx \\[2mm] \text{or} \\[2mm] \dfrac{e^{ax}(\cos^{m-1} x)(\sin^{n-1} x)(a \cos x \sin x + m \sin^2 x - n \cos^2 x)}{(m+n)^2 + a^2} \\[2mm] \quad + \dfrac{m(m-1)}{(m+n)^2 + a^2} \displaystyle\int e^{ax}(\cos^{m-2} x)(\sin^{n-2} x)\, dx \\[2mm] \quad + \dfrac{(n-m)(n+m-1)}{(m+n)^2 + a^2} \displaystyle\int e^{ax}(\cos^m x)(\sin^{n-2} x)\, dx \end{cases}$$

INTEGRALS (Continued)

549. $\int x \, e^{ax}(\sin bx) \, dx = \dfrac{x \, e^{ax}}{a^2 + b^2}(a \sin bx - b \cos bx)$

$$- \frac{e^{ax}}{(a^2 + b^2)^2}[(a^2 - b^2) \sin bx - 2ab \cos bx]$$

550. $\int x \, e^{ax}(\cos bx) \, dx = \dfrac{x \, e^{ax}}{a^2 + b^2}(a \cos bx + b \sin bx)$

$$- \frac{e^{ax}}{(a^2 + b^2)^2}[(a^2 - b^2) \cos bx + 2ab \sin bx]$$

551. $\displaystyle\int \frac{e^{ax}}{\sin^n x} \, dx = -\frac{e^{ax}[a \sin x + (n - 2)\cos x]}{(n - 1)(n - 2)\sin^{n-1} x} + \frac{a^2 + (n - 2)^2}{(n - 1)(n - 2)} \int \frac{e^{ax}}{\sin^{n-2} x} \, dx$

552. $\displaystyle\int \frac{e^{ax}}{\cos^n x} \, dx = -\frac{e^{ax}[a \cos x - (n - 2)\sin x]}{(n - 1)(n - 2)\cos^{n-1} x} + \frac{a^2 + (n - 2)^2}{(n - 1)(n - 2)} \int \frac{e^{ax}}{\cos^{n-2} x} \, dx$

553. $\displaystyle\int e^{ax} \tan^n x \, dx = e^{ax} \frac{\tan^{n-1} x}{n - 1} - \frac{a}{n - 1} \int e^{ax} \tan^{n-1} x \, dx - \int e^{ax} \tan^{n-2} x \, dx$

HYPERBOLIC FORMS

554. $\displaystyle\int (\sinh x) \, dx = \cosh x$

555. $\displaystyle\int (\cosh x) \, dx = \sinh x$

556. $\displaystyle\int (\tanh x) \, dx = \log \cosh x$

557. $\displaystyle\int (\coth x) \, dx = \log \sinh x$

558. $\displaystyle\int (\operatorname{sech} x) \, dx = \tan^{-1}(\sinh x)$

559. $\displaystyle\int \operatorname{csch} x \, dx = \log \tanh \left(\frac{x}{2}\right)$

560. $\displaystyle\int x(\sinh x) \, dx = x \cosh x - \sinh x$

561. $\displaystyle\int x^n(\sinh x) \, dx = x^n \cosh x - n \int x^{n-1}(\cosh x) \, dx$

562. $\displaystyle\int x(\cosh x) \, dx = x \sinh x - \cosh x$

563. $\displaystyle\int x^n(\cosh x) \, dx = x^n \sinh x - n \int x^{n-1}(\sinh x) \, dx$

INTEGRALS (Continued)

564. $\int (\operatorname{sech} x)(\tanh x)\, dx = -\operatorname{sech} x$

565. $\int (\operatorname{csch} x)(\coth x)\, dx = -\operatorname{csch} x$

566. $\int (\sinh^2 x)\, dx = \dfrac{\sinh 2x}{4} - \dfrac{x}{2}$

567. $\int (\sinh^m x)(\cosh^n x)\, dx = \begin{cases} \dfrac{1}{m+n}(\sinh^{m+1} x)(\cosh^{n-1} x) \\[2mm] \qquad + \dfrac{n-1}{m+n}\displaystyle\int (\sinh^m x)(\cosh^{n-2} x)\, dx \\[2mm] \text{or} \\[2mm] \dfrac{1}{m+n}\sinh^{m-1} x \cosh^{n+1} x \\[2mm] \qquad - \dfrac{m-1}{m+n}\displaystyle\int (\sinh^{m-2} x)(\cosh^n x)\, dx, \quad (m+n \neq 0) \end{cases}$

568. $\int \dfrac{dx}{(\sinh^m x)(\cosh^n x)} = \begin{cases} -\dfrac{1}{(m-1)(\sinh^{m-1} x)(\cosh^{n-1} x)} \\[2mm] \qquad - \dfrac{m+n-2}{m-1}\displaystyle\int \dfrac{dx}{(\sinh^{m-2} x)(\cosh^n x)}, \quad (m \neq 1) \\[2mm] \text{or} \\[2mm] \dfrac{1}{(n-1)\sinh^{m-1} x \cosh^{n-1} x} \\[2mm] \qquad + \dfrac{m+n-2}{n-1}\displaystyle\int \dfrac{dx}{(\sinh^m x)(\cosh^{n-2} x)}, \quad (n \neq 1) \end{cases}$

569. $\int (\tanh^2 x)\, dx = x - \tanh x$

570. $\int (\tanh^n x)\, dx = -\dfrac{\tanh^{n-1} x}{n-1} + \int (\tanh^{n-2} x)\, dx, \quad (n \neq 1)$

571. $\int (\operatorname{sech}^2 x)\, dx = \tanh x$

572. $\int (\cosh^2 x)\, dx = \dfrac{\sinh 2x}{4} + \dfrac{x}{2}$

573. $\int (\coth^2 x)\, dx = x - \coth x$

574. $\int (\coth^n x)\, dx = -\dfrac{\coth^{n-1} x}{n-1} + \int \coth^{n-2} x\, dx, \quad (n \neq 1)$

INTEGRALS (Continued)

575. $\int (\text{csch}^2 x)\, dx = -\text{ctnh } x$

576. $\int (\sinh mx)(\sinh nx)\, dx = \dfrac{\sinh(m+n)x}{2(m+n)} - \dfrac{\sinh(m-n)x}{2(m-n)},\qquad (m^2 \neq n^2)$

577. $\int (\cosh mx)(\cosh nx)\, dx = \dfrac{\sinh(m+n)x}{2(m+n)} + \dfrac{\sinh(m-n)x}{2(m-n)},\qquad (m^2 \neq n^2)$

578. $\int (\sinh mx)(\cosh nx)\, dx = \dfrac{\cosh(m+n)x}{2(m+n)} + \dfrac{\cosh(m-n)x}{2(m-n)},\qquad (m^2 \neq n^2)$

579. $\int \left(\sinh^{-1}\dfrac{x}{a}\right) dx = x \sinh^{-1}\dfrac{x}{a} - \sqrt{x^2 + a^2},\qquad (a > 0)$

580. $\int x\left(\sinh^{-1}\dfrac{x}{a}\right) dx = \left(\dfrac{x^2}{2} + \dfrac{a^2}{4}\right)\sinh^{-1}\dfrac{x}{a} - \dfrac{x}{4}\sqrt{x^2 + a^2},\qquad (a > 0)$

581. $\int x^n(\sinh^{-1} x)\, dx = \dfrac{x^{n+1}}{n+1}\sinh^{-1} x - \dfrac{1}{n+1}\int \dfrac{x^{n+1}}{(1+x^2)^{\frac{1}{2}}}\, dx,\qquad (n \neq -1)$

582. $\int \left(\cosh^{-1}\dfrac{x}{a}\right) dx = \begin{cases} x \cosh^{-1}\dfrac{x}{a} - \sqrt{x^2 - a^2}, & \left(\cosh^{-1}\dfrac{x}{a} > 0\right) \\[2mm] \qquad\qquad \text{or} \\[2mm] x \cosh^{-1}\dfrac{x}{a} + \sqrt{x^2 - a^2}, & \left(\cosh^{-1}\dfrac{x}{a} < 0\right), \qquad (a > 0) \end{cases}$

583. $\int x\left(\cosh^{-1}\dfrac{x}{a}\right) dx = \dfrac{2x^2 - a^2}{4}\cosh^{-1}\dfrac{x}{a} - \dfrac{x}{4}(x^2 - a^2)^{\frac{1}{2}}$

584. $\int x^n(\cosh^{-1} x)\, dx = \dfrac{x^{n+1}}{n+1}\cosh^{-1} x - \dfrac{1}{n+1}\int \dfrac{x^{n+1}}{(x^2 - 1)^{\frac{1}{2}}}\, dx,\qquad (n \neq -1)$

585. $\int \left(\tanh^{-1}\dfrac{x}{a}\right) dx = x \tanh^{-1}\dfrac{x}{a} + \dfrac{a}{2}\log(a^2 - x^2),\qquad \left(\left|\dfrac{x}{a}\right| < 1\right)$

586. $\int \left(\coth^{-1}\dfrac{x}{a}\right) dx = x \coth^{-1}\dfrac{x}{a} + \dfrac{a}{2}\log(x^2 - a^2),\qquad \left(\left|\dfrac{x}{a}\right| > 1\right)$

587. $\int x\left(\tanh^{-1}\dfrac{x}{a}\right) dx = \dfrac{x^2 - a^2}{2}\tanh^{-1}\dfrac{x}{a} + \dfrac{ax}{2},\qquad \left(\left|\dfrac{x}{a}\right| < 1\right)$

588. $\int x^n\left(\tanh^{-1} x\right) dx = \dfrac{x^{n+1}}{n+1}\tanh^{-1} x - \dfrac{1}{n+1}\int \dfrac{x^{n+1}}{1 - x^2}\, dx,\qquad (n \neq -1)$

589. $\int x\left(\coth^{-1}\dfrac{x}{a}\right) dx = \dfrac{x^2 - a^2}{2}\coth^{-1}\dfrac{x}{a} + \dfrac{ax}{2},\qquad \left(\left|\dfrac{x}{a}\right| > 1\right)$

590. $\int x^n(\coth^{-1} x)\, dx = \dfrac{x^{n+1}}{n+1}\coth^{-1} x + \dfrac{1}{n+1}\int \dfrac{x^{n+1}}{x^2 - 1}\, dx,\qquad (n \neq -1)$

INTEGRALS (Continued)

591. $\int (\text{sech}^{-1} x)\, dx = x\,\text{sech}^{-1} x + \sin^{-1} x$

592. $\int x\,\text{sech}^{-1} x\, dx = \dfrac{x^2}{2}\text{sech}^{-1} x - \dfrac{1}{2}\sqrt{1 - x^2}$

593. $\int x^n\,\text{sech}^{-1} x\, dx = \dfrac{x^{n+1}}{n+1}\text{sech}^{-1} x + \dfrac{1}{n+1}\int \dfrac{x^n}{(1 - x^2)^{\frac{1}{2}}}\, dx,\qquad (n \neq -1)$

594. $\int \text{csch}^{-1} x\, dx = x\,\text{csch}^{-1} x + \dfrac{x}{|x|}\sinh^{-1} x$

595. $\int x\,\text{csch}^{-1} x\, dx = \dfrac{x^2}{2}\text{csch}^{-1} x + \dfrac{1}{2}\dfrac{x}{|x|}\sqrt{1 + x^2}$

596. $\int x^n\,\text{csch}^{-1} x\, dx = \dfrac{x^{n+1}}{n+1}\text{csch}^{-1} x + \dfrac{1}{n+1}\dfrac{x}{|x|}\int \dfrac{x^n}{(x^2 + 1)^{\frac{1}{2}}}\, dx,\qquad (n \neq -1)$

DEFINITE INTEGRALS

597. $\displaystyle\int_0^\infty x^{n-1} e^{-x}\, dx = \int_0^1 \left(\log\frac{1}{x}\right)^{n-1} dx = \frac{1}{n}\prod_{m=1}^\infty \frac{\left(1 + \dfrac{1}{m}\right)^n}{1 + \dfrac{n}{m}}$

$$= \Gamma(n),\ n \neq 0, -1, -2, -3, \ldots \qquad \text{(Gamma Function)}$$

598. $\displaystyle\int_0^\infty t^n p^{-t}\, dt = \frac{n!}{(\log p)^{n+1}},\qquad (n = 0, 1, 2, 3, \ldots \text{ and } p > 0)$

599. $\displaystyle\int_0^\infty t^{n-1} e^{-(a+1)t}\, dt = \frac{\Gamma(n)}{(a+1)^n},\qquad (n > 0, a > -1)$

600. $\displaystyle\int_0^1 x^m\left(\log\frac{1}{x}\right)^n dx = \frac{\Gamma(n+1)}{(m+1)^{n+1}},\qquad (m > -1, n > -1)$

601. $\Gamma(n)$ is finite if $n > 0$, $\Gamma(n+1) = n\Gamma(n)$

602. $\Gamma(n)\cdot\Gamma(1 - n) = \dfrac{\pi}{\sin n\pi}$

603. $\Gamma(n) = (n - 1)!$ if $n = $ integer > 0

604. $\Gamma(\frac{1}{2}) = 2\displaystyle\int_0^\infty e^{-t^2}\, dt = \sqrt{\pi} = 1.7724538509\cdots = (-\frac{1}{2})!$

605. $\Gamma(n + \frac{1}{2}) = \dfrac{1\cdot 3\cdot 5 \ldots (2n - 1)}{2^n}\sqrt{\pi}\qquad n = 1, 2, 3, \ldots$

606. $\Gamma(-n + \frac{1}{2}) = \dfrac{(-1)^n 2^n \sqrt{\pi}}{1\cdot 3\cdot 5 \ldots (2n - 1)}\qquad n = 1, 2, 3, \ldots$

DEFINITE INTEGRALS (Continued)

607. $\displaystyle\int_0^1 x^{m-1}(1-x)^{n-1}\,dx = \int_0^\infty \frac{x^{m-1}}{(1+x)^{m+n}}\,dx = \frac{\Gamma(m)\Gamma(n)}{\Gamma(m+n)} = B(m,n)$

(Beta function)

608. $B(m,n) = B(n,m) = \dfrac{\Gamma(m)\Gamma(n)}{\Gamma(m+n)}$, where m and n are any positive real numbers.

609. $\displaystyle\int_a^b (x-a)^m(b-x)^n\,dx = (b-a)^{m+n+1}\frac{\Gamma(m+1)\cdot\Gamma(n+1)}{\Gamma(m+n+2)}$,

$$(m > -1, n > -1, b > a)$$

610. $\displaystyle\int_1^\infty \frac{dx}{x^m} = \frac{1}{m-1}, \qquad [m > 1]$

611. $\displaystyle\int_0^\infty \frac{dx}{(1+x)x^p} = \pi \csc p\pi, \qquad [p < 1]$

612. $\displaystyle\int_0^\infty \frac{dx}{(1-x)x^p} = -\pi \cot p\pi, \qquad [p < 1]$

613. $\displaystyle\int_0^\infty \frac{x^{p-1}\,dx}{1+x} = \frac{\pi}{\sin p\pi}$

$$= B(p, 1-p) = \Gamma(p)\Gamma(1-p), \qquad [0 < p < 1]$$

614. $\displaystyle\int_0^\infty \frac{x^{m-1}\,dx}{1+x^n} = \frac{\pi}{n\sin\dfrac{m\pi}{n}}, \qquad [0 < m < n]$

615. $\displaystyle\int_0^\infty \frac{x^a\,dx}{(m+x^b)^c} = \frac{m^{\frac{a+1-bc}{b}}}{b}\left[\frac{\Gamma\!\left(\dfrac{a+1}{b}\right)\Gamma\!\left(c-\dfrac{a+1}{b}\right)}{\Gamma(c)}\right]$

$$\left(a > -1, b > 0, m > 0, c > \frac{a+1}{b}\right)$$

616. $\displaystyle\int_0^\infty \frac{dx}{(1+x)\sqrt{x}} = \pi$

617. $\displaystyle\int_0^\infty \frac{a\,dx}{a^2+x^2} = \frac{\pi}{2}$, if $a > 0$; 0, if $a = 0$; $-\dfrac{\pi}{2}$, if $a < 0$

618. $\displaystyle\int_0^a (a^2-x^2)^{\frac{n}{2}}\,dx = \frac{1}{2}\int_{-a}^a (a^2-x^2)^{\frac{n}{2}}\,dx = \frac{1\cdot3\cdot5\ldots n}{2\cdot4\cdot6\ldots(n+1)}\cdot\frac{\pi}{2}\cdot a^{n+1}$ (n odd)

619. $\displaystyle\int_0^a x^m(a^2-x^2)^{\frac{n}{2}}\,dx = \begin{cases} \dfrac{1}{2}a^{m+n+1}B\!\left(\dfrac{m+1}{2}, \dfrac{n+2}{2}\right) \\[2mm] \text{or} \\[2mm] \dfrac{1}{2}a^{m+n+1}\dfrac{\Gamma\!\left(\dfrac{m+1}{2}\right)\Gamma\!\left(\dfrac{n+2}{2}\right)}{\Gamma\!\left(\dfrac{m+n+3}{2}\right)} \end{cases}$

DEFINITE INTEGRALS (Continued)

620. $\displaystyle\int_0^{\pi/2} (\sin^n x)\, dx = \begin{cases} \displaystyle\int_0^{\pi/2} (\cos^n x)\, dx \\[2mm] \text{or} \\[2mm] \dfrac{1\cdot 3\cdot 5\cdot 7\ldots(n-1)}{2\cdot 4\cdot 6\cdot 8\ldots(n)}\,\dfrac{\pi}{2}, \quad (n \text{ an even integer}, n \neq 0) \\[2mm] \text{or} \\[2mm] \dfrac{2\cdot 4\cdot 6\cdot 8\ldots(n-1)}{1\cdot 3\cdot 5\cdot 7\ldots(n)}, \quad (n \text{ an odd integer}, n \neq 1) \\[2mm] \text{or} \\[2mm] \dfrac{\sqrt{\pi}}{2}\,\dfrac{\Gamma\left(\dfrac{n+1}{2}\right)}{\Gamma\left(\dfrac{n}{2}+1\right)}, \quad (n > -1) \end{cases}$

621. $\displaystyle\int_0^{\infty} \frac{\sin mx\, dx}{x} = \frac{\pi}{2}, \text{ if } m > 0;\, 0, \text{ if } m = 0;\, -\frac{\pi}{2}, \text{ if } m < 0$

622. $\displaystyle\int_0^{\infty} \frac{\cos x\, dx}{x} = \infty$

623. $\displaystyle\int_0^{\infty} \frac{\tan x\, dx}{x} = \frac{\pi}{2}$

624. $\displaystyle\int_0^{\pi} \sin ax \cdot \sin bx\, dx = \int_0^{\pi} \cos ax \cdot \cos bx\, dx = 0, \quad (a \neq b;\, a, b \text{ integers})$

625. $\displaystyle\int_0^{\pi/a} [\sin(ax)][\cos(ax)]\, dx = \int_0^{\pi} [\sin(ax)][\cos(ax)]\, dx = 0$

626. $\displaystyle\int_0^{\pi} [\sin(ax)][\cos(bx)]\, dx = \frac{2a}{a^2 - b^2}, \text{ if } a - b \text{ is odd, or } 0 \text{ if } a - b \text{ is even}$

627. $\displaystyle\int_0^{\infty} \frac{\sin x \cos mx\, dx}{x}$

$$= 0, \text{ if } m < -1 \text{ or } m > 1;\, \frac{\pi}{4}, \text{ if } m = \pm 1;\, \frac{\pi}{2}, \text{ if } m^2 < 1$$

628. $\displaystyle\int_0^{\infty} \frac{\sin ax \sin bx}{x^2}\, dx = \frac{\pi a}{2}, \quad (a \leq b)$

629. $\displaystyle\int_0^{\pi} \sin^2 mx\, dx = \int_0^{\pi} \cos^2 mx\, dx = \frac{\pi}{2}$

630. $\displaystyle\int_0^{\infty} \frac{\sin^2(px)}{x^2}\, dx = \frac{\pi p}{2}$

DEFINITE INTEGRALS (Continued)

631. $\displaystyle\int_0^\infty \frac{\sin x}{x^p}\,dx = \frac{\pi}{2\Gamma(p)\sin(p\pi/2)},\qquad 0 < p < 1$

632. $\displaystyle\int_0^\infty \frac{\cos x}{x^p}\,dx = \frac{\pi}{2\Gamma(p)\cos(p\pi/2)},\qquad 0 < p < 1$

633. $\displaystyle\int_0^\infty \frac{1 - \cos px}{x^2}\,dx = \frac{\pi p}{2}$

634. $\displaystyle\int_0^\infty \frac{\sin px \cos qx}{x}\,dx = \left\{0,\quad q > p > 0;\quad \frac{\pi}{2},\quad p > q > 0;\quad \frac{\pi}{4},\quad p = q > 0\right\}$

635. $\displaystyle\int_0^\infty \frac{\cos(mx)}{x^2 + a^2}\,dx = \frac{\pi}{2|a|}\,e^{-|ma|}$

636. $\displaystyle\int_0^\infty \cos(x^2)\,dx = \int_0^\infty \sin(x^2)\,dx = \frac{1}{2}\sqrt{\frac{\pi}{2}}$

637. $\displaystyle\int_0^\infty \sin ax^n\,dx = \frac{1}{na^{1/n}}\Gamma(1/n)\sin\frac{\pi}{2n},\qquad n > 1$

638. $\displaystyle\int_0^\infty \cos ax^n\,dx = \frac{1}{na^{1/n}}\Gamma(1/n)\cos\frac{\pi}{2n},\qquad n > 1$

639. $\displaystyle\int_0^\infty \frac{\sin x}{\sqrt{x}}\,dx = \int_0^\infty \frac{\cos x}{\sqrt{x}}\,dx = \sqrt{\frac{\pi}{2}}$

640. (a) $\displaystyle\int_0^\infty \frac{\sin^3 x}{x}\,dx = \frac{\pi}{4}$ (b) $\displaystyle\int_0^\infty \frac{\sin^3 x}{x^2}\,dx = \frac{3}{4}\log 3$

641. $\displaystyle\int_0^\infty \frac{\sin^3 x}{x^3}\,dx = \frac{3\pi}{8}$

642. $\displaystyle\int_0^\infty \frac{\sin^4 x}{x^4}\,dx = \frac{\pi}{3}$

643. $\displaystyle\int_0^{\pi/2} \frac{dx}{1 + a\cos x} = \frac{\cos^{-1} a}{\sqrt{1 - a^2}},\qquad (a < 1)$

644. $\displaystyle\int_0^\pi \frac{dx}{a + b\cos x} = \frac{\pi}{\sqrt{a^2 - b^2}},\qquad (a > b \geq 0)$

645. $\displaystyle\int_0^{2\pi} \frac{dx}{1 + a\cos x} = \frac{2\pi}{\sqrt{1 - a^2}},\qquad (a^2 < 1)$

646. $\displaystyle\int_0^\infty \frac{\cos ax - \cos bx}{x}\,dx = \log\frac{b}{a}$

647. $\displaystyle\int_0^{\pi/2} \frac{dx}{a^2 \sin^2 x + b^2 \cos^2 x} = \frac{\pi}{2ab}$

DEFINITE INTEGRALS (Continued)

648. $\displaystyle\int_0^{\pi/2} \frac{dx}{(a^2 \sin^2 x + b^2 \cos^2 x)^2} = \frac{\pi(a^2 + b^2)}{4a^3b^3}$, $(a, b > 0)$

649. $\displaystyle\int_0^{\pi/2} \sin^{n-1} x \cos^{m-1} x \, dx = \frac{1}{2} B\left(\frac{n}{2}, \frac{m}{2}\right)$, *m* and *n* positive integers

650. $\displaystyle\int_0^{\pi/2} (\sin^{2n+1}\theta) \, d\theta = \frac{2 \cdot 4 \cdot 6 \dots (2n)}{1 \cdot 3 \cdot 5 \dots (2n+1)}$, $(n = 1, 2, 3 \dots)$

651. $\displaystyle\int_0^{\pi/2} (\sin^{2n}\theta) \, d\theta = \frac{1 \cdot 3 \cdot 5 \dots (2n-1)}{2 \cdot 4 \dots (2n)}\left(\frac{\pi}{2}\right)$, $(n = 1, 2, 3 \dots)$

652. $\displaystyle\int_0^{\pi/2} \frac{x}{\sin x} \, dx = 2\left\{\frac{1}{1^2} - \frac{1}{3^2} + \frac{1}{5^2} - \frac{1}{7^2} + \cdots\right\}$

653. $\displaystyle\int_0^{\pi/2} \frac{dx}{1 + \tan^m x} = \frac{\pi}{4}$

654. $\displaystyle\int_0^{\pi/2} \sqrt{\cos \theta} \, d\theta = \frac{(2\pi)^{\frac{1}{2}}}{[\Gamma(\frac{1}{4})]^2}$

655. $\displaystyle\int_0^{\pi/2} (\tan^h \theta) \, d\theta = \frac{\pi}{2 \cos\left(\dfrac{h\pi}{2}\right)}$, $(0 < h < 1)$

656. $\displaystyle\int_0^{\infty} \frac{\tan^{-1}(ax) - \tan^{-1}(bx)}{x} \, dx = \frac{\pi}{2} \log\frac{a}{b}$, $(a, b > 0)$

657. The area enclosed by a curve defined through the equation $x^{\frac{b}{c}} + y^{\frac{b}{c}} = a^{\frac{b}{c}}$ where $a > 0$, *c* a positive odd integer and *b* a positive even integer is given by

$$\frac{\left[\Gamma\left(\dfrac{c}{b}\right)\right]^2}{\Gamma\left(\dfrac{2c}{b}\right)}\left(\frac{2ca^2}{b}\right)$$

658. $I = \displaystyle\iiint_R x^{h-1} y^{m-1} z^{n-1} \, dv$, where *R* denotes the region of space bounded by

the co-ordinate planes and that portion of the surface $\left(\dfrac{x}{a}\right)^p + \left(\dfrac{y}{b}\right)^q + \left(\dfrac{z}{c}\right)^k = 1$,

which lies in the first octant and where *h, m, n, p, q, k, a, b, c,* denote positive real numbers is given by

$$\int_0^a x^{h-1} \, dx \int_0^{b\left[1-\left(\frac{x}{a}\right)^p\right]^{\frac{1}{q}}} y^m \, dy \int_0^{c\left[1-\left(\frac{x}{a}\right)^p-\left(\frac{y}{b}\right)^q\right]^{\frac{1}{k}}} z^{n-1} \, dz$$

$$= \frac{a^h b^m c^n}{pqk} \frac{\Gamma\left(\dfrac{h}{p}\right)\Gamma\left(\dfrac{m}{q}\right)\Gamma\left(\dfrac{n}{k}\right)}{\Gamma\left(\dfrac{h}{p} + \dfrac{m}{q} + \dfrac{n}{k} + 1\right)}$$

DEFINITE INTEGRALS (Continued)

659. $\displaystyle\int_0^\infty e^{-ax}\,dx = \frac{1}{a}$, $(a > 0)$

660. $\displaystyle\int_0^\infty \frac{e^{-ax} - e^{-bx}}{x}\,dx = \log\frac{b}{a}$, $(a, b > 0)$

661. $\displaystyle\int_0^\infty x^n e^{-ax}\,dx = \begin{cases} \dfrac{\Gamma(n+1)}{a^{n+1}}, & (n > -1, a > 0) \\[2ex] \qquad\text{or} \\[1ex] \dfrac{n!}{a^{n+1}}, & (a > 0, n\text{ positive integer}) \end{cases}$

662. $\displaystyle\int_0^\infty x^n \exp(-ax^p)\,dx = \frac{\Gamma(k)}{pa^k}$, $\left(n > -1, p > 0, a > 0, k = \dfrac{n+1}{p}\right)$

663. $\displaystyle\int_0^\infty e^{-a^2x^2}\,dx = \frac{1}{2a}\sqrt{\pi} = \frac{1}{2a}\Gamma\left(\frac{1}{2}\right)$, $(a > 0)$

663a. $\displaystyle\int_0^b e^{-ax^2}\,dx = \frac{1}{2}\sqrt{\frac{\pi}{a}}\ \text{erf}\,(b\sqrt{a})$ Error Function (see page 350)

663b. $\displaystyle\int_b^\infty e^{-ax^2}\,dx = \frac{1}{2}\sqrt{\frac{\pi}{a}}\ \text{erfc}\,(b\sqrt{a})$ Complimentary Error Function (see page 350)

664. $\displaystyle\int_0^\infty x e^{-x^2}\,dx = \tfrac{1}{2}$

665. $\displaystyle\int_0^\infty x^2 e^{-x^2}\,dx = \frac{\sqrt{\pi}}{4}$

666. $\displaystyle\int_0^\infty x^{2n} e^{-ax^2}\,dx = \frac{1\cdot 3\cdot 5\ldots(2n-1)}{2^{n+1}a^n}\sqrt{\frac{\pi}{a}}$

667. $\displaystyle\int_0^\infty x^{2n+1} e^{-ax^2}\,dx = \frac{n!}{2a^{n+1}}$, $(a > 0)$

668. $\displaystyle\int_0^1 x^m e^{-ax}\,dx = \frac{m!}{a^{m+1}}\left[1 - e^{-a}\sum_{r=0}^m \frac{a^r}{r!}\right]$

669. $\displaystyle\int_0^\infty e^{\left(-x^2 - \frac{a^2}{x^2}\right)}\,dx = \frac{e^{-2a}\sqrt{\pi}}{2}$, $(a \ge 0)$

670. $\displaystyle\int_0^\infty e^{-nx}\sqrt{x}\,dx = \frac{1}{2n}\sqrt{\frac{\pi}{n}}$

DEFINITE INTEGRALS (Continued)

671. $\displaystyle\int_0^\infty \frac{e^{-nx}}{\sqrt{x}}\,dx = \sqrt{\frac{\pi}{n}}$

672. $\displaystyle\int_0^\infty e^{-ax}(\cos mx)\,dx = \frac{a}{a^2 + m^2}, \qquad (a > 0)$

673. $\displaystyle\int_0^\infty e^{-ax}(\sin mx)\,dx = \frac{m}{a^2 + m^2}, \qquad (a > 0)$

674. $\displaystyle\int_0^\infty x\,e^{-ax}[\sin (bx)]\,dx = \frac{2ab}{(a^2 + b^2)^2}, \qquad (a > 0)$

675. $\displaystyle\int_0^\infty x\,e^{-ax}[\cos (bx)]\,dx = \frac{a^2 - b^2}{(a^2 + b^2)^2}, \qquad (a > 0)$

676. $\displaystyle\int_0^\infty x^n\,e^{-ax}[\sin (bx)]\,dx = \frac{n![(a + ib)^{n+1} - (a - ib)^{n+1}]}{2i(a^2 + b^2)^{n+1}}, \qquad (i^2 = -1, a > 0)$

677. $\displaystyle\int_0^\infty x^n\,e^{-ax}[\cos (bx)]\,dx = \frac{n![(a - ib)^{n+1} + (a + ib)^{n+1}]}{2(a^2 + b^2)^{n+1}}, \qquad (i^2 = -1, a > 0)$

678. $\displaystyle\int_0^\infty \frac{e^{-ax}\sin x}{x}\,dx = \cot^{-1} a, \qquad (a > 0)$

679. $\displaystyle\int_0^\infty e^{-a^2x^2} \cos bx\,dx = \frac{\sqrt{\pi}}{2a} \exp\left(-\frac{b^2}{4a^2}\right), \qquad (ab \neq 0)$

680. $\displaystyle\int_0^\infty e^{-t\cos\phi}\,t^{b-1} \sin (t \sin \phi)\,dt = [\Gamma(b)] \sin (b\phi), \qquad \left(b > 0,\ -\frac{\pi}{2} < \phi < \frac{\pi}{2}\right)$

681. $\displaystyle\int_0^\infty e^{-t\cos\phi}\,t^{b-1}[\cos (t \sin \phi)]\,dt = [\Gamma(b)] \cos (b\phi), \qquad \left(b > 0,\ -\frac{\pi}{2} < \phi < \frac{\pi}{2}\right)$

682. $\displaystyle\int_0^\infty t^{b-1} \cos t\,dt = [\Gamma(b)] \cos\left(\frac{b\pi}{2}\right), \qquad (0 < b < 1)$

683. $\displaystyle\int_0^\infty t^{b-1} (\sin t)\,dt = [\Gamma(b)] \sin\left(\frac{b\pi}{2}\right), \qquad (0 < b < 1)$

684. $\displaystyle\int_0^1 (\log x)^n\,dx = (-1)^n \cdot n!$

685. $\displaystyle\int_0^1 \left(\log\frac{1}{x}\right)^{\frac{1}{2}} dx = \frac{\sqrt{\pi}}{2}$

686. $\displaystyle\int_0^1 \left(\log\frac{1}{x}\right)^{-\frac{1}{2}} dx = \sqrt{\pi}$

687. $\displaystyle\int_0^1 \left(\log\frac{1}{x}\right)^n dx = n!$

688. $\displaystyle\int_0^1 x \log (1 - x)\,dx = -\tfrac{3}{4}$

689. $\displaystyle\int_0^1 x \log(1 + x)\, dx = \tfrac{1}{4}$

690. $\displaystyle\int_0^1 x^m(\log x)^n\, dx = \frac{(-1)^n n!}{(m + 1)^{n+1}}, \qquad m > -1, n = 0, 1, 2, \ldots$

If $n \neq 0, 1, 2, \ldots$ replace $n!$ by $\Gamma(n + 1)$.

691. $\displaystyle\int_0^1 \frac{\log x}{1 + x}\, dx = -\frac{\pi^2}{12}$

692. $\displaystyle\int_0^1 \frac{\log x}{1 - x}\, dx = -\frac{\pi^2}{6}$

693. $\displaystyle\int_0^1 \frac{\log(1 + x)}{x}\, dx = \frac{\pi^2}{12}$

694. $\displaystyle\int_0^1 \frac{\log(1 - x)}{x}\, dx = -\frac{\pi^2}{6}$

695. $\displaystyle\int_0^1 (\log x)[\log(1 + x)]\, dx = 2 - 2\log 2 - \frac{\pi^2}{12}$

696. $\displaystyle\int_0^1 (\log x)[\log(1 - x)]\, dx = 2 - \frac{\pi^2}{6}$

697. $\displaystyle\int_0^1 \frac{\log x}{1 - x^2}\, dx = -\frac{\pi^2}{8}$

698. $\displaystyle\int_0^1 \log\left(\frac{1 + x}{1 - x}\right) \frac{dx}{x} = \frac{\pi^2}{4}$

699. $\displaystyle\int_0^1 \frac{\log x\, dx}{\sqrt{1 - x^2}} = -\frac{\pi}{2}\log 2$

700. $\displaystyle\int_0^1 x^m\left[\log\left(\frac{1}{x}\right)\right]^n dx = \frac{\Gamma(n + 1)}{(m + 1)^{n+1}}, \qquad \text{if } m + 1 > 0, n + 1 > 0$

701. $\displaystyle\int_0^1 \frac{(x^p - x^q)\, dx}{\log x} = \log\left(\frac{p + 1}{q + 1}\right), \qquad (p + 1 > 0, q + 1 > 0)$

702. $\displaystyle\int_0^1 \frac{dx}{\sqrt{\log\left(\frac{1}{x}\right)}} = \sqrt{\pi}\ , (\text{same as integral 686})$

703. $\displaystyle\int_0^x \log\left(\frac{e^x + 1}{e^x - 1}\right) dx = \frac{\pi^2}{4}$

704. $\displaystyle\int_0^{\pi/2} (\log \sin x)\, dx = \int_0^{\pi/2} \log \cos x\, dx = -\frac{\pi}{2}\log 2$

705. $\displaystyle\int_0^{\pi/2} (\log \sec x)\, dx = \int_0^{\pi/2} \log \csc x\, dx = \frac{\pi}{2}\log 2$

DEFINITE INTEGRALS (Continued)

706. $\displaystyle\int_0^\pi x(\log \sin x)\,dx = -\frac{\pi^2}{2}\log 2$

707. $\displaystyle\int_0^{\pi/2} (\sin x)(\log \sin x)\,dx = \log 2 - 1$

708. $\displaystyle\int_0^{\pi/2} (\log \tan x)\,dx = 0$

709. $\displaystyle\int_0^\pi \log (a \pm b \cos x)\,dx = \pi \log \left(\frac{a + \sqrt{a^2 - b^2}}{2}\right),$ $(a \geq b)$

710. $\displaystyle\int_0^\pi \log (a^2 - 2ab \cos x + b^2)\,dx = \begin{cases} 2\pi \log a, & a \geq b > 0 \\ 2\pi \log b, & b \geq a > 0 \end{cases}$

711. $\displaystyle\int_0^\infty \frac{\sin ax}{\sinh bx}\,dx = \frac{\pi}{2b}\tanh\frac{a\pi}{2b}$

712. $\displaystyle\int_0^\infty \frac{\cos ax}{\cosh bx}\,dx = \frac{\pi}{2b}\operatorname{sech}\frac{a\pi}{2b}$

713. $\displaystyle\int_0^\infty \frac{dx}{\cosh ax} = \frac{\pi}{2a}$

714. $\displaystyle\int_0^\infty \frac{x\,dx}{\sinh ax} = \frac{\pi^2}{4a^2}$

715. $\displaystyle\int_0^\infty e^{-ax}(\cosh bx)\,dx = \frac{a}{a^2 - b^2},$ $(0 \leq |b| < a)$

716. $\displaystyle\int_0^\infty e^{-ax}(\sinh bx)\,dx = \frac{b}{a^2 - b^2},$ $(0 \leq |b| < a)$

717. $\displaystyle\int_0^\infty \frac{\sinh ax}{e^{bx} + 1}\,dx = \frac{\pi}{2b}\csc\frac{a\pi}{b} - \frac{1}{2a}$

718. $\displaystyle\int_0^\infty \frac{\sinh ax}{e^{bx} - 1}\,dx = \frac{1}{2a} - \frac{\pi}{2b}\cot\frac{a\pi}{b}$

719. $\displaystyle\int_0^{\pi/2} \frac{dx}{\sqrt{1 - k^2 \sin^2 x}} = \frac{\pi}{2}\left[1 + \left(\frac{1}{2}\right)^2 k^2 + \left(\frac{1\cdot3}{2\cdot4}\right)^2 k^4\right.$

$$\left. + \left(\frac{1\cdot3\cdot5}{2\cdot4\cdot6}\right)^2 k^6 + \cdots\right], \text{if } k^2 < 1$$

719a. $\displaystyle\int_0^{\frac{\pi}{2}} \frac{dx}{(1 - k^2 \operatorname{Sin}^2 x)^{3/2}} = \frac{\pi}{2}\left[1 + \left(\frac{1}{2}\right)^2 \cdot 3k^2 + \left(\frac{1\cdot3}{2\cdot4}\right)^2 \cdot 5k^4 + \right.$

$$\left. \left(\frac{1\cdot3\cdot5}{2\cdot4\cdot6}\right)^2 \cdot 7k^6 + \cdots\right], \text{ if } k^2 < 1$$

720. $\int_0^{\pi/2} \sqrt{1 - k^2 \sin^2 x}\, dx = \dfrac{\pi}{2}\left[1 - \left(\dfrac{1}{2}\right)^2 k^2 - \left(\dfrac{1 \cdot 3}{2 \cdot 4}\right)^2 \dfrac{k^4}{3}\right.$

$$\left. - \left(\dfrac{1 \cdot 3 \cdot 5}{2 \cdot 4 \cdot 6}\right)^2 \dfrac{k^6}{5} - \cdots \right], \text{ if } k^2 < 1$$

721. $\int_0^\infty e^{-x} \log x \, dx = -\gamma = -0.5772157\ldots$

722. $\int_0^\infty e^{-x^2} \log x \, dx = -\dfrac{\sqrt{\pi}}{4}(\gamma + 2 \log 2)$

723. $\int_0^\infty \left(\dfrac{1}{1 - e^{-x}} - \dfrac{1}{x}\right) e^{-x}\, dx = \gamma = 0.5772157\ldots$ 　　　[Euler's Constant]

724. $\int_0^\infty \dfrac{1}{x}\left(\dfrac{1}{1 + x} - e^{-x}\right) dx = \gamma = 0.5772157\ldots$

For n even:

725. $\int \cos^n x \, dx = \dfrac{1}{2^{n-1}} \sum_{k=0}^{\frac{n}{2}-1} \binom{n}{k} \dfrac{\sin (n - 2k)\, x}{(n - 2k)} + \dfrac{1}{2^n}\binom{n}{\frac{n}{2}} x$

726. $\int \sin^n x \, dx = \dfrac{1}{2^{n-1}} \sum_{k=0}^{\frac{n}{2}-1} \binom{n}{k} \dfrac{\sin \left[(n - 2k)\left(\frac{\pi}{2} - x\right)\right]}{2k - n} + \dfrac{1}{2^n}\binom{n}{\frac{n}{2}} x$

For n odd:

727. $\int \cos^n x \, dx = \dfrac{1}{2^{n-1}} \sum_{k=0}^{\frac{n-1}{2}} \binom{n}{k} \dfrac{\sin (n - 2k)\, x}{(n - 2k)}$

728. $\int \sin^n x \, dx = \dfrac{1}{2^{n-1}} \sum_{k=0}^{\frac{n-1}{2}} \binom{n}{k} \dfrac{\sin \left[(n - 2k)\left(\frac{\pi}{2} - x\right)\right]}{2k - n}$

SERIES EXPANSION

The expression in parentheses following certain of the series indicates the region of convergence. If not otherwise indicated it is to be understood that the series converges for all finite values of x.

BINOMIAL

$$(x + y)^n = x^n + nx^{n-1}y + \frac{n(n-1)}{2!}x^{n-2}y^2$$

$$+ \frac{n(n-1)(n-2)}{3!}x^{n-3}y^3 + \cdots \quad (y^2 < x^2)$$

$$(1 \pm x)^n = 1 \pm nx + \frac{n(n-1)x^2}{2!} \pm \frac{n(n-1)(n-2)x^3}{3!} + \cdots \text{ etc.} \quad (x^2 < 1)$$

$$(1 \pm x)^{-n} = 1 \mp nx + \frac{n(n+1)x^2}{2!} \mp \frac{n(n+1)(n+2)x^3}{3!} + \cdots \text{ etc.} \quad (x^2 < 1)$$

$$(1 \pm x)^{-1} = 1 \mp x + x^2 \mp x^3 + x^4 \mp x^5 + \cdots \qquad (x^2 < 1)$$
$$(1 \pm x)^{-2} = 1 \mp 2x + 3x^2 \mp 4x^3 + 5x^4 \mp 6x^5 + \cdots \qquad (x^2 < 1)$$

REVERSION OF SERIES

Let a series be represented by

$$y = a_1 x + a_2 x^2 + a_3 x^3 + a_4 x^4 + a_5 x^5 + a_6 x^6 + \cdots \quad (a_1 \neq 0)$$

to find the coefficients of the series

$$x = A_1 y + A_2 y^2 + A_3 y^3 + A_4 y^4 + \cdots$$

$$A_1 = \frac{1}{a_1} \qquad A_2 = -\frac{a_2}{a_1^3} \qquad A_3 = \frac{1}{a_1^5}(2a_2^2 - a_1 a_3)$$

$$A_4 = \frac{1}{a_1^7}(5a_1 a_2 a_3 - a_1^2 a_4 - 5a_2^3)$$

$$A_5 = \frac{1}{a_1^9}(6a_1^2 a_2 a_4 + 3a_1^2 a_3^2 + 14a_2^4 - a_1^3 a_5 - 21a_1 a_2^2 a_3)$$

$$A_6 = \frac{1}{a_1^{11}}(7a_1^3 a_2 a_5 + 7a_1^3 a_3 a_4 + 84a_1 a_2^3 a_3 - a_1^4 a_6 - 28a_1^2 a_2^2 a_4 - 28a_1^2 a_2 a_3^2 - 42a_2^5)$$

$$A_7 = \frac{1}{a_1^{13}}(8a_1^4 a_2 a_6 + 8a_1^4 a_3 a_5 + 4a_1^4 a_4^2 + 120a_1^2 a_2^3 a_4$$

$$+ 180a_1^2 a_2^2 a_3^2 + 132a_2^6 - a_1^5 a_7$$

$$- 36a_1^3 a_2^2 a_5 - 72a_1^3 a_2 a_3 a_4 - 12a_1^4 a_3^3 - 330a_1 a_2^4 a_3)$$

TAYLOR

1. $f(x) = f(a) + (x - a)f'(a) + \dfrac{(x - a)^2}{2!}f''(a) + \dfrac{(x - a)^3}{3!}f'''(a)$

$$+ \cdots + \frac{(x - a)^n}{n!}f^{(n)}(a) + \cdots \text{ (Taylor's Series)}$$

Series

(Increment form)

2. $f(x + h) = f(x) + hf'(x) + \dfrac{h^2}{2!} f''(x) + \dfrac{h^3}{3!} f'''(x) + \cdots$

$$= f(h) + xf'(h) + \dfrac{x^2}{2!} f''(h) + \dfrac{x^3}{3!} f'''(h) + \cdots$$

3. If $f(x)$ is a function possessing derivatives of all orders throughout the interval $a \leq x \leq b$, then there is a value X, with $a < X < b$, such that

$$f(b) = f(a) + (b - a)f'(a) + \frac{(b - a)^2}{2!} f''(a) + \cdots$$

$$+ \frac{(b - a)^{n-1}}{(n - 1)!} f^{(n-1)}(a) + \frac{(b - a)^n}{n!} f^{(n)}(X)$$

$$f(a + h) = f(a) + hf'(a) + \frac{h^2}{2!} f''(a) + \cdots + \frac{h^{n-1}}{(n - 1)!} f^{(n-1)}(a)$$

$$+ \frac{h^n}{n!} f^{(n)}(a + \theta h), \quad b = a + h, 0 < \theta < 1.$$

or

$$f(x) = f(a) + (x - a)f'(a) + \frac{(x - a)^2}{2!} f''(a) + \cdots + (x - a)^{n-1} \frac{f^{(n-1)}(a)}{(n - 1)!} + R_n,$$

where

$$R_n = \frac{f^{(n)}[a + \theta \cdot (x - a)]}{n!} (x - a)^n, \quad 0 < \theta < 1.$$

The above forms are known as Taylor's series with the remainder term.

4. *Taylor's series for a function of two variables*

If $\left(h \dfrac{\partial}{\partial x} + k \dfrac{\partial}{\partial y} \right) f(x, y) = h \dfrac{\partial f(x, y)}{\partial x} + k \dfrac{\partial f(x, y)}{\partial y}$;

$$\left(h \frac{\partial}{\partial x} + k \frac{\partial}{\partial y} \right)^2 f(x, y) = h^2 \frac{\partial^2 f(x, y)}{\partial x^2} + 2hk \frac{\partial^2 f(x, y)}{\partial x \, \partial y} + k^2 \frac{\partial^2 f(x, y)}{\partial y^2}$$

etc., and if $\left(h \dfrac{\partial}{\partial x} + k \dfrac{\partial}{\partial y} \right)^n f(x, y) \Big|_{\substack{x=a \\ y=b}}$ with the bar and subscripts means that after differentiation we are to replace x by a and y by b,

$$f(a + h, b + k) = f(a, b) + \left(h \frac{\partial}{\partial x} + k \frac{\partial}{\partial y} \right) f(x, y) \Big|_{\substack{x=a \\ y=b}} + \cdots$$

$$+ \frac{1}{n!} \left(h \frac{\partial}{\partial x} + k \frac{\partial}{\partial y} \right)^n f(x, y) \Big|_{\substack{x=a \\ y=b}} + \cdots$$

MACLAURIN

$$f(x) = f(0) + xf'(0) + \frac{x^2}{2!} f''(0) + \frac{x^3}{3!} f'''(0) + \cdots + x^{n-1} \frac{f^{(n-1)}(0)}{(n - 1)!} + R_n,$$

where

$$R_n = \frac{x^n f^{(n)}(\theta x)}{n!}, \quad 0 < \theta < 1.$$

Series

EXPONENTIAL

$$e = 1 + \frac{1}{1!} + \frac{1}{2!} + \frac{1}{3!} + \frac{1}{4!} + \cdots$$

$$e^x = 1 + x + \frac{x^2}{2!} + \frac{x^3}{3!} + \frac{x^4}{4!} + \cdots \qquad \text{(all real values of } x)$$

$$a^x = 1 + x \log_e a + \frac{(x \log_e a)^2}{2!} + \frac{(x \log_e a)^3}{3!} + \cdots$$

$$e^x = e^a \left[1 + (x - a) + \frac{(x - a)^2}{2!} + \frac{(x - a)^3}{3!} + \cdots \right]$$

LOGARITHMIC

$$\log_e x = \frac{x - 1}{x} + \frac{1}{2} \left(\frac{x - 1}{x}\right)^2 + \frac{1}{3} \left(\frac{x - 1}{x}\right)^3 + \cdots \qquad (x > \tfrac{1}{2})$$

$$\log_e x = (x - 1) - \tfrac{1}{2}(x - 1)^2 + \tfrac{1}{3}(x - 1)^3 - \cdots \qquad (2 \geq x > 0)$$

$$\log_e x = 2 \left[\frac{x - 1}{x + 1} + \frac{1}{3} \left(\frac{x - 1}{x + 1}\right)^3 + \frac{1}{5} \left(\frac{x - 1}{x + 1}\right)^5 + \cdots \right] \qquad (x > 0)$$

$$\log_e (1 + x) = x - \tfrac{1}{2}x^2 + \tfrac{1}{3}x^3 - \tfrac{1}{4}x^4 + \cdots \qquad (-1 < x \leq 1)$$

$$\log_e (n + 1) - \log_e (n - 1) = 2 \left[\frac{1}{n} + \frac{1}{3n^3} + \frac{1}{5n^5} + \cdots \right]$$

$$\log_e (a + x) = \log_e a + 2 \left[\frac{x}{2a + x} + \frac{1}{3} \left(\frac{x}{2a + x}\right)^3 + \frac{1}{5} \left(\frac{x}{2a + x}\right)^5 + \cdots \right]$$
$$(a > 0, -a < x < +\infty)$$

$$\log_e \frac{1 + x}{1 - x} = 2 \left[x + \frac{x^3}{3} + \frac{x^5}{5} + \cdots + \frac{x^{2n-1}}{2n - 1} + \cdots \right], \qquad -1 < x < 1$$

$$\log_e x = \log_e a + \frac{(x - a)}{a} - \frac{(x - a)^2}{2a^2} + \frac{(x - a)^3}{3a^3} - + \cdots, \qquad 0 < x \leq 2a$$

TRIGONOMETRIC

$$\sin x = x - \frac{x^3}{3!} + \frac{x^5}{5!} - \frac{x^7}{7!} + \cdots \qquad \text{(all real values of } x)$$

$$\cos x = 1 - \frac{x^2}{2!} + \frac{x^4}{4!} - \frac{x^6}{6!} + \cdots \qquad \text{(all real values of } x)$$

$$\tan x = x + \frac{x^3}{3} + \frac{2x^5}{15} + \frac{17x^7}{315} + \frac{62x^9}{2835} + \cdots + \frac{(-1)^{n-1} 2^{2n} (2^{2n} - 1) B_{2n}}{(2n)!} x^{2n-1} + \cdots,$$
$$\left[x^2 < \frac{\pi^2}{4}, \text{ and } B_n \text{ represents the } n\text{'th Bernoulli number.} \right]$$

$$\cot x = \frac{1}{x} - \frac{x}{3} - \frac{x^3}{45} - \frac{2x^5}{945} - \frac{x^7}{4725} - \cdots - \frac{(-1)^{n+1}2^{2n}}{(2n)!} B_{2n} x^{2n-1} - \cdots,$$
$$[x^2 < \pi^2, \text{ and } B_n \text{ represents the } n\text{'th Bernoulli number.}]$$

Series

$$\sec x = 1 + \frac{x^2}{2} + \frac{5}{24} x^4 + \frac{61}{720} x^6 + \frac{277}{8064} x^8 + \cdots + \frac{(-1)^n}{(2n)!} E_{2n} x^{2n} + \cdots ,$$

$$\left[x^2 < \frac{\pi^2}{4}, \text{ and } E_n \text{ represents the } n\text{'th Euler number.} \right]$$

$$\csc x = \frac{1}{x} + \frac{x}{6} + \frac{7}{360} x^3 + \frac{31}{15,120} x^5 + \frac{127}{604,800} x^7 + \cdots$$

$$+ \frac{(-1)^{n+1} 2 (2^{2n-1} - 1)}{(2n)!} B_{2n} x^{2n-1} + \cdots ,$$

$$[x^2 < \pi^2, \text{ and } B_n \text{ represents } n\text{'th Bernoulli number.}]$$

$$\sin x = x \left(1 - \frac{x^2}{\pi^2} \right) \left(1 - \frac{x^2}{2^2 \pi^2} \right) \left(1 - \frac{x^2}{3^2 \pi^2} \right) \cdots \qquad (x^2 < \infty)$$

$$\cos x = \left(1 - \frac{4x^2}{\pi^2} \right) \left(1 - \frac{4x^2}{3^2 \pi^2} \right) \left(1 - \frac{4x^2}{5^2 \pi^2} \right) \cdots \qquad (x^2 < \infty)$$

$$\sin^{-1} x = x + \frac{x^3}{2 \cdot 3} + \frac{1 \cdot 3}{2 \cdot 4 \cdot 5} x^5 + \frac{1 \cdot 3 \cdot 5}{2 \cdot 4 \cdot 6 \cdot 7} x^7 + \cdots \qquad \left(x^2 < 1, -\frac{\pi}{2} < \sin^{-1} x < \frac{\pi}{2} \right)$$

$$\cos^{-1} x = \frac{\pi}{2} - \left(x + \frac{x^3}{2 \cdot 3} + \frac{1 \cdot 3}{2 \cdot 4 \cdot 5} x^5 + \frac{1 \cdot 3 \cdot 5 x^7}{2 \cdot 4 \cdot 6 \cdot 7} + \cdots \right) \qquad (x^2 < 1, 0 < \cos^{-1} x < \pi)$$

$$\tan^{-1} x = x - \frac{x^3}{3} + \frac{x^5}{5} - \frac{x^7}{7} + \cdots \qquad (x^2 < 1)$$

$$\tan^{-1} x = \frac{\pi}{2} - \frac{1}{x} + \frac{1}{3x^3} - \frac{1}{5x^5} + \frac{1}{7x^7} - \cdots \qquad (x > 1)$$

$$\tan^{-1} x = -\frac{\pi}{2} - \frac{1}{x} + \frac{1}{3x^3} - \frac{1}{5x^5} + \frac{1}{7x^7} - \cdots \qquad (x < -1)$$

$$\cot^{-1} x = \frac{\pi}{2} - x + \frac{x^3}{3} - \frac{x^5}{5} + \frac{x^7}{7} - \cdots \qquad (x^2 < 1)$$

$$\log_e \sin x = \log_e x - \frac{x^2}{6} - \frac{x^4}{180} - \frac{x^6}{2835} - \cdots \qquad (x^2 < \pi^2)$$

$$\log_e \cos x = -\frac{x^2}{2} - \frac{x^4}{12} - \frac{x^6}{45} - \frac{17x^8}{2520} - \cdots \qquad \left(x^2 < \frac{\pi^2}{4} \right)$$

$$\log_e \tan x = \log_e x + \frac{x^2}{3} + \frac{7x^4}{90} + \frac{62x^6}{2835} + \cdots \qquad \left(x^2 < \frac{\pi^2}{4} \right)$$

$$e^{\sin x} = 1 + x + \frac{x^2}{2!} - \frac{3x^4}{4!} - \frac{8x^5}{5!} - \frac{3x^6}{6!} + \frac{56x^7}{7!} + \cdots$$

$$e^{\cos x} = e \left(1 - \frac{x^2}{2!} + \frac{4x^4}{4!} - \frac{31x^6}{6!} + \cdots \right)$$

$$e^{\tan x} = 1 + x + \frac{x^2}{2!} + \frac{3x^3}{3!} + \frac{9x^4}{4!} + \frac{37x^5}{5!} + \cdots \qquad \left(x^2 < \frac{\pi^2}{4} \right)$$

$$\sin x = \sin a + (x - a) \cos a - \frac{(x - a)^2}{2!} \sin a$$

$$- \frac{(x - a)^3}{3!} \cos a + \frac{(x - a)^4}{4!} \sin a + \cdots$$

VECTOR ANALYSIS

Definitions

Any quantity which is completely determined by its magnitude is called a *scalar*. Examples of such are mass, density, temperature, etc. Any quantity which is completely determined by its magnitude and direction is called a *vector*. Examples of such are velocity, acceleration, force, etc. A vector quantity is represented by a directed line segment, the length of which represents the magnitude of the vector. A vector quantity is usually represented by a boldfaced letter such as V. Two vectors V_1 and V_2 are equal to one another if they have equal magnitudes and are acting in the same directions. A negative vector, written as $-V$, is one which acts in the opposite direction to V, but is of equal magnitude to it. If we represent the magnitude of V by v, we write $|V| = v$. A vector parallel to V, but equal to the reciprocal of its magnitude is written as V^{-1} or as $\frac{1}{V}$.

The *unit vector* $\frac{V}{v}$ ($v \neq 0$) is that vector which has the same direction as V, but has a magnitude of unity (sometimes represented as V_0 or $\hat{v}$).

Vector Algebra

The vector sum of V_1 and V_2 is represented by $V_1 + V_2$. The vector sum of V_1 and $-V_2$, or the difference of the vector V_2 from V_1 is represented by $V_1 - V_2$.

If r is a scalar, then $rV = Vr$, and represents a vector r times the magnitude of V, in the same direction as V if r is positive, and in the opposite direction if r is negative. If r and s are scalars, V_1, V_2, V_3, vectors, then the following rules of scalars and vectors hold:

$$V_1 + V_2 = V_2 + V_1$$

$$(r + s)V_1 = rV_1 + sV_1; \qquad r(V_1 + V_2) = rV_1 + rV_2$$

$$V_1 + (V_2 + V_3) = (V_1 + V_2) + V_3 = V_1 + V_2 + V_3$$

Vectors in Space

A plane is described by two distinct vectors V_1 and V_2. Should these vectors not intersect each other, then one is displaced parallel to itself until they do (fig. 1.) Any other vector V lying in this plane is given by

$$V = rV_1 + sV_2$$

VECTOR ANALYSIS (Continued)

A *position vector* specifies the position in space of a point relative to a fixed origin. If therefore V_1 and V_2 are the position vectors of the points A and B, relative to the origin O, then any point P on the line AB has a position vector V given by

$$V = rV_1 + (1 - r)V_2$$

The scalar "r" can be taken as the parametric representation of P since $r = 0$ implies $P = B$ and $r = 1$ implies $P = A$. (fig. 2). If P divides the line AB in the ratio $r : s$ then

$$V = \left(\frac{r}{r + s}\right) V_1 + \left(\frac{s}{r + s}\right) V_2$$

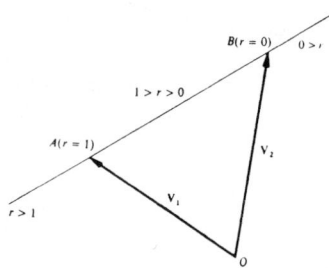

Fig. 1.   Fig. 2.

The vectors V_1, V_2, V_3, . . . , V_n are said to be *linearly dependent* if there exist scalars $r_1, r_2, r_3, \ldots, r_n$, not all zero, such that

$$r_1V_1 + r_2V_2 + \cdots + r_nV_n = 0$$

A vector V is linearly dependent upon the set of vectors V_1, V_2, V_3, . . . , V_n if

$$V = r_1V_1 + r_2V_2 + r_3V_3 + \cdots + r_nV_n$$

Three vectors are linearly dependent if and only if they are co-planar.

All points in space can be uniquely determined by linear dependence upon three *base vectors* i.e. three vectors any one of which is linearly independent of the other two. The simplest set of base vectors are the unit vectors along the coordinate Ox, Oy and Oz axes. These are usually designated by i, j and k respectively.

If V is a vector in space, and a, b and c are the respective magnitudes of the projections of the vector along the axes then

$$V = ai + bj + ck$$

and

$$v = \sqrt{a^2 + b^2 + c^2}$$

and the direction cosines of V are

$$\cos \alpha = a/v, \quad \cos \beta = b/v, \quad \cos \gamma = c/v.$$

The law of addition yields

$$V_1 + V_2 = (a_1 + a_2)i + (b_1 + b_2)j + (c_1 + c_2)k$$

The Scalar, Dot, or Inner Product of Two Vectors V_1 and V_2

This product is represented as $\mathbf{V}_1 \cdot \mathbf{V}_2$ and is defined to be equal to $v_1 v_2 \cos\theta$, where θ is the angle from $\mathbf{V}_1$ to $\mathbf{V}_2$, i.e.,

$$\mathbf{V}_1 \cdot \mathbf{V}_2 = v_1 v_2 \cos\theta$$

The following rules apply for this product:

$$\mathbf{V}_1 \cdot \mathbf{V}_2 = a_1 a_2 + b_1 b_2 + c_1 c_2 = \mathbf{V}_2 \cdot \mathbf{V}_1$$

It should be noted that this verifies that scalar multiplication is commutative.

$$(\mathbf{V}_1 + \mathbf{V}_2) \cdot \mathbf{V}_3 = \mathbf{V}_1 \cdot \mathbf{V}_3 + \mathbf{V}_2 \cdot \mathbf{V}_3$$
$$\mathbf{V}_1 \cdot (\mathbf{V}_2 + \mathbf{V}_3) = \mathbf{V}_1 \cdot \mathbf{V}_2 + \mathbf{V}_1 \cdot \mathbf{V}_3$$

If $\mathbf{V}_1$ is perpendicular to $\mathbf{V}_2$ then $\mathbf{V}_1 \cdot \mathbf{V}_2 = 0$, and if $\mathbf{V}_1$ is parallel to $\mathbf{V}_2$ then $\mathbf{V}_1 \cdot \mathbf{V}_2 = v_1 v_2 = r w_1^2$

In particular

and
$$i \cdot i = j \cdot j = k \cdot k = 1,$$
$$i \cdot j = j \cdot k = k \cdot i = 0$$

The Vector or Cross Product of Vectors V_1 and V_2

This product is represented as $\mathbf{V}_1 \times \mathbf{V}_2$ and is defined to be equal to $v_1 v_2 (\sin\theta)\mathbf{1}$, where θ is the angle from $\mathbf{V}_1$ to $\mathbf{V}_2$ and $\mathbf{1}$ is a unit vector perpendicular to the plane of $\mathbf{V}_1$ and $\mathbf{V}_2$ and so directed that a right-handed screw driven in the direction of $\mathbf{1}$ would carry $\mathbf{V}_1$ into $\mathbf{V}_2$, i.e.,

$$\mathbf{V}_1 \times \mathbf{V}_2 = v_1 v_2 (\sin\theta)\mathbf{1}$$

and
$$\tan\theta = \frac{|\mathbf{V}_1 \times \mathbf{V}_2|}{\mathbf{V}_1 \cdot \mathbf{V}_2}$$

The following rules apply for vector products:

$$\mathbf{V}_1 \times \mathbf{V}_2 = -\mathbf{V}_2 \times \mathbf{V}_1$$
$$\mathbf{V}_1 \times (\mathbf{V}_2 + \mathbf{V}_3) = \mathbf{V}_1 \times \mathbf{V}_2 + \mathbf{V}_1 \times \mathbf{V}_3$$
$$(\mathbf{V}_1 + \mathbf{V}_2) \times \mathbf{V}_3 = \mathbf{V}_1 \times \mathbf{V}_3 + \mathbf{V}_2 \times \mathbf{V}_3$$
$$\mathbf{V}_1 \times (\mathbf{V}_2 \times \mathbf{V}_3) = \mathbf{V}_2(\mathbf{V}_3 \cdot \mathbf{V}_1) - \mathbf{V}_3(\mathbf{V}_1 \cdot \mathbf{V}_2)$$
$$i \times i = j \times j = k \times k = 0.1 \text{ (zero vector)}$$
$$= 0$$

$$i \times j = k, \qquad j \times k = i, \qquad k \times i = j$$

If $\mathbf{V}_1 = a_1 i + b_1 j + c_1 k$, $\qquad \mathbf{V}_2 = a_2 i + b_2 j + c_2 k$, $\qquad \mathbf{V}_3 = a_3 i + b_3 j + c_3 k$,

then

$$\mathbf{V}_1 \times \mathbf{V}_2 = \begin{vmatrix} i & j & k \\ a_1 & b_1 & c_1 \\ a_2 & b_2 & c_2 \end{vmatrix} = (b_1 c_2 - b_2 c_1)i + (c_1 a_2 - c_2 a_1)j + (a_1 b_2 - a_2 b_1)k$$

It should be noted that, since $\mathbf{V}_1 \times \mathbf{V}_2 = -\mathbf{V}_2 \times \mathbf{V}_1$, the vector product is not commutative.

Scalar Triple Product

There is only one possible interpretation of the expression $\mathbf{V}_1 \cdot \mathbf{V}_2 \times \mathbf{V}_3$ and that is $\mathbf{V}_1 \cdot (\mathbf{V}_2 \times \mathbf{V}_3)$ which is obviously a scalar.

Further $\mathbf{V}_1 \cdot (\mathbf{V}_2 \times \mathbf{V}_3) = (\mathbf{V}_1 \times \mathbf{V}_2) \cdot \mathbf{V}_3 = \mathbf{V}_2 \cdot (\mathbf{V}_3 \times \mathbf{V}_1)$

$$= \begin{vmatrix} a_1 & b_1 & c_1 \\ a_2 & b_2 & c_2 \\ a_3 & b_3 & c_3 \end{vmatrix}$$

$$= v_1 v_2 v_3 \cos \phi \sin \theta,$$

Where θ is the angle between $\mathbf{V}_2$ and $\mathbf{V}_3$ and ϕ is the angle between $\mathbf{V}_1$ and the normal to the plane of $\mathbf{V}_2$ and $\mathbf{V}_3$.

This product is called the *scalar triple product* and is written as $[\mathbf{V}_1 \mathbf{V}_2 \mathbf{V}_3]$.

The determinant indicates that it can be considered as the volume of the parallelepiped whose three determining edges are $\mathbf{V}_1$, $\mathbf{V}_2$ and $\mathbf{V}_3$.

It also follows that cyclic permutation of the subscripts does not change the value of the scalar triple product so that

$$[\mathbf{V}_1 \mathbf{V}_2 \mathbf{V}_3] = [\mathbf{V}_2 \mathbf{V}_3 \mathbf{V}_1] = [\mathbf{V}_3 \mathbf{V}_1 \mathbf{V}_2]$$

but $[\mathbf{V}_1 \mathbf{V}_2 \mathbf{V}_3] = -[\mathbf{V}_2 \mathbf{V}_1 \mathbf{V}_3]$ etc.   and $[\mathbf{V}_1 \mathbf{V}_1 \mathbf{V}_2] \equiv 0$ etc.

Given three non-coplanar reference vectors $\mathbf{V}_1$, $\mathbf{V}_2$ and $\mathbf{V}_3$, the *reciprocal system is* given by $\mathbf{V}_1^*$, $\mathbf{V}_2^*$ and $\mathbf{V}_3^*$, where

$$1 = v_1 v_1^* = v_2 v_2^* = v_3 v_3^*$$

$$0 = v_1 v_2^* = v_1 v_3^* = v_2 v_1^* \quad \text{etc.}$$

$$\mathbf{V}_1^* = \frac{\mathbf{V}_2 \times \mathbf{V}_3}{[\mathbf{V}_1 \mathbf{V}_2 \mathbf{V}_3]}, \qquad \mathbf{V}_2^* = \frac{\mathbf{V}_3 \times \mathbf{V}_1}{[\mathbf{V}_1 \mathbf{V}_2 \mathbf{V}_3]}, \qquad \mathbf{V}_3^* = \frac{\mathbf{V}_1 \times \mathbf{V}_2}{[\mathbf{V}_1 \mathbf{V}_2 \mathbf{V}_3]}$$

The system $\mathbf{i}$, $\mathbf{j}$, $\mathbf{k}$ is its own reciprocal.

Vector Triple Product

The product $\mathbf{V}_1 \times (\mathbf{V}_2 \times \mathbf{V}_3)$ defines the *vector triple product*. Obviously, in this case, the brackets are vital to the definition.

$$\mathbf{V}_1 \times (\mathbf{V}_2 \times \mathbf{V}_3) = (\mathbf{V}_1 \cdot \mathbf{V}_3)\mathbf{V}_2 - (\mathbf{V}_1 \cdot \mathbf{V}_2)\mathbf{V}_3$$

$$= \begin{vmatrix} \mathbf{i} & \mathbf{j} & \mathbf{k} \\ a_1 & b_1 & c_1 \\ \begin{vmatrix} b_2 & c_2 \\ b_3 & c_3 \end{vmatrix} & \begin{vmatrix} c_2 & a_2 \\ c_3 & a_3 \end{vmatrix} & \begin{vmatrix} a_2 & b_2 \\ a_3 & b_3 \end{vmatrix} \end{vmatrix}$$

i.e. it is a vector, perpendicular to $\mathbf{V}_1$, lying in the plane of $\mathbf{V}_2$, $\mathbf{V}_3$.

Similarly $(\mathbf{V}_1 \times \mathbf{V}_2) \times \mathbf{V}_3 = \begin{vmatrix} \mathbf{i} & \mathbf{j} & \mathbf{k} \\ \begin{vmatrix} b_1 & c_1 \\ b_2 & c_2 \end{vmatrix} & \begin{vmatrix} c_1 & a_1 \\ c_2 & a_2 \end{vmatrix} & \begin{vmatrix} a_1 & b_1 \\ a_2 & b_2 \end{vmatrix} \\ a_3 & b_3 & c_3 \end{vmatrix}$

$$\mathbf{V}_1 \times (\mathbf{V}_2 \times \mathbf{V}_3) + \mathbf{V}_2 \times (\mathbf{V}_3 \times \mathbf{V}_1) + \mathbf{V}_3 \times (\mathbf{V}_1 + \mathbf{V}_2) \equiv 0$$

If $\mathbf{V}_1 \times (\mathbf{V}_2 \times \mathbf{V}_3) = (\mathbf{V}_1 \times \mathbf{V}_2) \times \mathbf{V}_3$ then $\mathbf{V}_1$, $\mathbf{V}_2$, $\mathbf{V}_3$ form an *orthogonal set*. Thus $\mathbf{i}$, $\mathbf{j}$, $\mathbf{k}$ form an orthogonal set.

Geometry of the Plane, Straight Line and Sphere

The position vectors of the fixed points A, B, C, D relative to O are $\mathbf{V}_1$, $\mathbf{V}_2$, $\mathbf{V}_3$, $\mathbf{V}_4$ and the position vector of the variable point P is $\mathbf{V}$.

The vector form of the equation of the straight line through A parallel to $\mathbf{V}_2$ is

$$\mathbf{V} = \mathbf{V}_1 + r\mathbf{V}_2$$

or
$$(\mathbf{V} - \mathbf{V}_1) = r\mathbf{V}_2$$

or
$$(\mathbf{V} - \mathbf{V}_1) \times \mathbf{V}_2 = 0$$

while that of the plane through A perpendicular to $\mathbf{V}_2$ is

$$(\mathbf{V} - \mathbf{V}_1) \cdot \mathbf{V}_2 = 0$$

The equation of the line AB is

$$\mathbf{V} = r\mathbf{V}_1 + (1 - r)\mathbf{V}_2$$

and those of the bisectors of the angles between $\mathbf{V}_1$ and $\mathbf{V}_2$ are

$$\mathbf{V} = r\left(\frac{\mathbf{V}_1}{v} \pm \frac{\mathbf{V}_2}{v_2}\right)$$

or
$$\mathbf{V} = r(\hat{\mathbf{v}}_1 \pm \hat{\mathbf{v}}_2)$$

The perpendicular from C to the line through A parallel to $\mathbf{V}_2$ has as its equation

$$\mathbf{V} = \mathbf{V}_1 - \mathbf{V}_3 - \hat{\mathbf{v}}_2 \cdot (\mathbf{V}_1 - \mathbf{V}_3)\hat{\mathbf{v}}_2.$$

The condition for the intersection of the two lines,

$$\mathbf{V} = \mathbf{V}_1 + r\mathbf{V}_3$$

and
$$\mathbf{V} = \mathbf{V}_2 + s\mathbf{V}_4$$

is
$$[(\mathbf{V}_1 - \mathbf{V}_2)\mathbf{V}_3\mathbf{V}_4] = 0.$$

The common perpendicular to the above two lines is the line of intersection of the two planes

$$[(\mathbf{V} - \mathbf{V}_1)\mathbf{V}_3(\mathbf{V}_3 \times \mathbf{V}_4)] = 0$$

and
$$[(\mathbf{V} - \mathbf{V}_2)\mathbf{V}_4(\mathbf{V}_3 \times \mathbf{V}_4)] = 0$$

and the length of this perpendicular is

$$\frac{[(\mathbf{V}_1 - \mathbf{V}_2)\mathbf{V}_3\mathbf{V}_4]}{|\mathbf{V}_3 \times \mathbf{V}_4|}.$$

The equation of the line perpendicular to the plane ABC is

$$\mathbf{V} = \mathbf{V}_1 \times \mathbf{V}_2 + \mathbf{V}_2 \times \mathbf{V}_3 + \mathbf{V}_3 \times \mathbf{V}_1$$

and the distance of the plane from the origin is

$$\frac{[\mathbf{V}_1\mathbf{V}_2\mathbf{V}_3]}{|(\mathbf{V}_2 - \mathbf{V}_1) \times (\mathbf{V}_3 - \mathbf{V}_1)|}.$$

In general the vector equation

$$\mathbf{V} \cdot \mathbf{V}_2 = r$$

defines the plane which is perpendicular to $\mathbf{V}_2$, and the perpendicular distance from A to this plane is

$$\frac{r - \mathbf{V}_1 \cdot \mathbf{V}_2}{v_2}.$$

The distance from A, measured along a line parallel to $\mathbf{V}_3$, is

$$\frac{r - \mathbf{V}_1 \cdot \mathbf{V}_2}{\mathbf{V}_2 \cdot \hat{\mathbf{v}}_3} \quad \text{or} \quad \frac{r - \mathbf{V}_1 \cdot \mathbf{V}_2}{v_2 \cos \theta}$$

where θ is the angle beween $\mathbf{V}_2$ and $\mathbf{V}_3$.
(If this plane contains the point C then $r = \mathbf{V}_3 \cdot \mathbf{V}_2$ and if it passes through the origin then $r = 0$.)

Given two planes

$$\mathbf{V} \cdot \mathbf{V}_1 = r$$
$$\mathbf{V} \cdot \mathbf{V}_2 = s$$

then any plane through the line of intersection of these two planes is given by

$$\mathbf{V} \cdot (\mathbf{V}_1 + \lambda \mathbf{V}_2) = r + \lambda s$$

where λ is a scalar parameter. In particular $\lambda = \pm v_1 / v_2$ yields the equation of the two planes bisecting the angle between the given planes.

The plane through A parallel to the plane of $\mathbf{V}_2$, $\mathbf{V}_3$ is

$$\mathbf{V} = \mathbf{V}_1 + r\mathbf{V}_2 + s\mathbf{V}_3$$
$$\text{or} \quad (\mathbf{V} - \mathbf{V}_1) \cdot \mathbf{V}_2 \times \mathbf{V}_3 = 0$$
$$\text{or} \quad [\mathbf{V}\mathbf{V}_2\mathbf{V}_3] - [\mathbf{V}_1\mathbf{V}_2\mathbf{V}_3] = 0$$

so that the expansion in rectangular Cartesian coordinates yields

$$\begin{vmatrix} (x - a_1) & (y - b_1) & (z - c_1) \\ a_2 & b_2 & c_2 \\ a_3 & b_3 & c_3 \end{vmatrix} = 0 \qquad (\mathbf{V} \equiv x\mathbf{i} + y\mathbf{j} + z\mathbf{k})$$

which is obviously the usual linear equation in x, y and z.
The plane through AB parallel to $\mathbf{V}_3$ is given by

$$[(\mathbf{V} - \mathbf{V}_1)(\mathbf{V}_1 - \mathbf{V}_2)\mathbf{V}_3] = 0$$
$$\text{or} \quad [\mathbf{V}\mathbf{V}_2\mathbf{V}_3] - [\mathbf{V}\mathbf{V}_1\mathbf{V}_3] - [\mathbf{V}_1\mathbf{V}_2\mathbf{V}_3] = 0$$

The plane through the three points A, B and C is

$$\mathbf{V} = \mathbf{V}_1 + s(\mathbf{V}_2 - \mathbf{V}_1) + t(\mathbf{V}_3 - \mathbf{V}_1)$$
$$\text{or} \quad \mathbf{V} = r\mathbf{V}_1 + s\mathbf{V}_2 + t\mathbf{V}_3 \qquad (r + s + t \equiv 1)$$
$$\text{or} \quad [(\mathbf{V} - \mathbf{V}_1)(\mathbf{V}_1 - \mathbf{V}_2)(\mathbf{V}_2 - \mathbf{V}_3)] = 0$$
$$\text{or} \quad [\mathbf{V}\mathbf{V}_1\mathbf{V}_2] + [\mathbf{V}\mathbf{V}_2\mathbf{V}_3] + [\mathbf{V}\mathbf{V}_3\mathbf{V}_1] - [\mathbf{V}_1\mathbf{V}_2\mathbf{V}_3] = 0$$

For four points A, B, C, D to be coplanar, then

$$r\mathbf{Y}_1 + s\mathbf{V}_2 + t\mathbf{V}_3 + u\mathbf{V}_4 \equiv 0 \equiv r + s + t + u$$

The following formulae relate to a sphere when the vectors are taken to lie in three dimensional space and to a circle when the space is two dimensional. For a circle in three dimensions take the intersection of the sphere with a plane.

The equation of a sphere with center O and radius OA is

$$\mathbf{V} \cdot \mathbf{V} = v_1^2 \qquad (\text{not } \mathbf{V} = \mathbf{V}_1)$$

or $\qquad (\mathbf{V} - \mathbf{V}_1) \cdot (\mathbf{V} + \mathbf{V}_1) = 0$

while that of a sphere with center B radius v_1 is

$$(\mathbf{V} - \mathbf{V}_2) \cdot (\mathbf{V} - \mathbf{V}_2) = v_1^2$$

or $\qquad \mathbf{V} \cdot (\mathbf{V} - 2\mathbf{V}_2) = v_1^2 - v_2^2$

If the above sphere passes through the origin then

$$\mathbf{V} \cdot (\mathbf{V} - 2\mathbf{V}_2) = 0$$

(note that in two dimensional polar coordinates this is simply)

$$r = 2a \cdot \cos\theta$$

while in three dimensional Cartesian coordinates it is

$$x^2 + y^2 + z^2 - 2(a_2x + b_2y + c_2x) = 0.$$

The equation of a sphere having the points A and B as the extremities of a diameter is

$$(\mathbf{V} - \mathbf{V}_1) \cdot (\mathbf{V} - \mathbf{V}_2) = 0.$$

The square of the length of the tangent from C to the sphere with center B and radius v_1 is given by

$$(\mathbf{V}_3 - \mathbf{V}_2) \cdot (\mathbf{V}_3 - \mathbf{V}_2) = v_1^2$$

The condition that the plane $\mathbf{V} \cdot \mathbf{V}_3 = s$ is tangential to the sphere $(\mathbf{V} - \mathbf{V}_2) \cdot (\mathbf{V} - \mathbf{V}_2) = v_1^2$ is

$$(s - \mathbf{V}_3 \cdot \mathbf{V}_2) \cdot (s - \mathbf{V}_3 \cdot \mathbf{V}_2) = v_1^2 v_3^2.$$

The equation of the tangent plane at D, on the surface of sphere $(\mathbf{V} - \mathbf{V}_2) \cdot (\mathbf{V} - \mathbf{V}_2) = v_1^2$, is

$$(\mathbf{V} - \mathbf{V}_4) \cdot (\mathbf{V}_4 - \mathbf{V}_2) = 0$$

or $\qquad \mathbf{V} \cdot \mathbf{V}_4 - \mathbf{V}_2 \cdot (\mathbf{V} + \mathbf{V}_4) = v_1^2 - v_2^2$

The condition that the two circles $(\mathbf{V} - \mathbf{V}_2) \cdot (\mathbf{V} - \mathbf{V}_2) = v_1^2$ and $(\mathbf{V} - \mathbf{V}_4) \cdot (\mathbf{V} - \mathbf{V}_4) = v_3^2$ intersect orthogonally is clearly

$$(\mathbf{V}_2 - \mathbf{V}_4) \cdot (\mathbf{V}_2 - \mathbf{V}_4) = v_1^2 + v_3^2$$

The polar plane of D with respect to the circle

$$(\mathbf{V} - \mathbf{V}_2) \cdot (\mathbf{V} - \mathbf{V}_2) = v_1^2 \quad \text{is}$$

$$\mathbf{V} \cdot \mathbf{V}_4 - \mathbf{V}_2 \cdot (\mathbf{V} + \mathbf{V}_4) = v_1^2 - v_2^2$$

Any sphere through the intersection of the two spheres $(\mathbf{V} - \mathbf{V}_2) \cdot (\mathbf{V} - \mathbf{V}_2) = v_1^2$ and $(\mathbf{V} - \mathbf{V}_4) \cdot (\mathbf{V} - \mathbf{V}_4) = v_3^2$ is given by

$$(\mathbf{V} - \mathbf{V}_2) \cdot (\mathbf{V} - \mathbf{V}_2) + \lambda(\mathbf{V} - \mathbf{V}_4) \cdot (\mathbf{V} - \mathbf{V}_4) = v_1^2 + \lambda v_3^2$$

while the radical plane of two such spheres is

$$\mathbf{V} \cdot (\mathbf{V}_2 - \mathbf{V}_4) = -\tfrac{1}{2}(v_1^2 - v_2^2 - v_3^2 + v_4^2)$$

Differentiation of Vectors

If $\mathbf{V}_1 = a_1\mathbf{i} + b_1\mathbf{j} + c_1\mathbf{k}$, and $\mathbf{V}_2 = a_2\mathbf{i} + b_2\mathbf{j} + c_2\mathbf{k}$, and if $\mathbf{V}_1$ and $\mathbf{V}_2$ are functions of the scalar t, then

$$\frac{d}{dt}(\mathbf{V}_1 + \mathbf{V}_2 + \cdots) = \frac{d\mathbf{V}_1}{dt} + \frac{d\mathbf{V}_2}{dt} + \cdots,$$

$$\text{where} \quad \frac{d\mathbf{V}_1}{dt} = \frac{da_1}{dt}\mathbf{i} + \frac{db_1}{dt}\mathbf{j} + \frac{dc_1}{dt}\mathbf{k}, \text{ etc.}$$

$$\frac{d}{dt}(\mathbf{V}_1 \cdot \mathbf{V}_2) = \frac{d\mathbf{V}_1}{dt} \cdot \mathbf{V}_2 + \mathbf{V}_1 \cdot \frac{d\mathbf{V}_2}{dt}$$

$$\frac{d}{dt}(\mathbf{V}_1 \times \mathbf{V}_2) = \frac{d\mathbf{V}_1}{dt} \times \mathbf{V}_2 + \mathbf{V}_1 \times \frac{d\mathbf{V}_2}{dt}$$

$$\mathbf{V} \cdot \frac{d\mathbf{V}}{dt} = v \cdot \frac{dv}{dt}$$

In particular, if $\mathbf{V}$ is a vector of constant length then the right hand side of the last equation is identically zero showing that $\mathbf{V}$ is perpendicular to its derivative.

The derivatives of the triple products are

$$\frac{d}{dt}[\mathbf{V}_1\mathbf{V}_2\mathbf{V}_3] = \left[\left(\frac{d\mathbf{V}_1}{dt}\right)\mathbf{V}_2\mathbf{V}_3\right] + \left[\mathbf{V}_1\left(\frac{d\mathbf{V}_2}{dt}\right)\mathbf{V}_3\right] + \left[\mathbf{V}_1\mathbf{V}_2\left(\frac{d\mathbf{V}_3}{dt}\right)\right]$$

and $\dfrac{d}{dt}\left\{\mathbf{V}_1 \times (\mathbf{V}_2 \times \mathbf{V}_3)\right\} = \left(\dfrac{d\mathbf{V}_1}{dt}\right) \times (\mathbf{V}_2 \times \mathbf{V}_3) + \mathbf{V}_1$

$$\times \left(\left(\frac{d\mathbf{V}_2}{dt}\right) \times \mathbf{V}_3\right) + \mathbf{V}_1 \times \left(\mathbf{V}_2 \times \left(\frac{d\mathbf{V}_3}{dt}\right)\right)$$

Geometry of Curves in Space

s = the *length of arc*, measured from some fixed point on the curve (fig. 3).
$\mathbf{V}_1$ = the position vector of the point A on the curve
$\mathbf{V}_1 + \delta\mathbf{V}_1$ = the position vector of the point P in the neighborhood of A
$\hat{\mathbf{t}}$ = the *unit tangent* to the curve at the point A, measured in the direction of s increasing.
The *normal plane* is that plane which is perpendicular to the unit tangent. The principal normal is defined as the intersection of the normal plane with the plane defined by $\mathbf{V}_1$ and $\mathbf{V}_1 + \delta\mathbf{V}_1$ in the limit as $\delta\mathbf{V}_1 - 0$.

$\hat{\mathbf{n}}$ = the *unit normal* (principal) at the point A. The plane defined by $\hat{\mathbf{t}}$ and $\hat{\mathbf{n}}$ is called the *osculating plane* (alternatively plane of curvature or local plane).

ρ = the radius of curvature at A
$\delta\theta$ = the angle subtended at the origin by $\delta\mathbf{V}_1$.

$$\kappa = \frac{d\theta}{ds} = \frac{1}{\rho}$$

$\hat{\mathbf{b}}$ = the *unit binormal* i.e. the unit vector which is parallel to $\hat{\mathbf{t}} \times \hat{\mathbf{n}}$ at the point A:
λ = the *torsion* of the curve at A

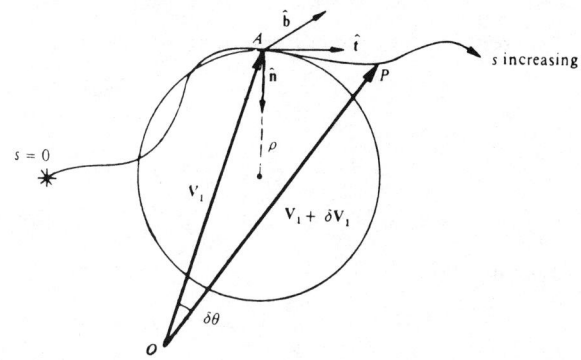

Figure 3.

Frenet's Formulae:

$$\frac{d\hat{\mathbf{t}}}{ds} = \kappa\hat{\mathbf{n}}$$

$$\frac{d\hat{\mathbf{n}}}{ds} = -\kappa\hat{\mathbf{t}} + \lambda\hat{\mathbf{b}}$$

$$\frac{d\hat{\mathbf{b}}}{ds} = -\lambda\hat{\mathbf{n}}$$

The following formulae are also applicable:

Unit tangent $\qquad\qquad\qquad \hat{\mathbf{t}} = \dfrac{d\mathbf{V}_1}{ds}$

Equation of the tangent $\qquad\qquad (\mathbf{V} - \mathbf{V}_1) \times \hat{\mathbf{t}} = 0$
$\qquad\qquad\qquad$ or $\qquad \mathbf{V} = \mathbf{V}_1 + q\hat{\mathbf{t}}$

Unit normal $\qquad\qquad\qquad \hat{\mathbf{n}} = \dfrac{1}{\kappa}\dfrac{d^2\mathbf{V}_1}{ds^2}$

Equation of the normal plane $\qquad (\mathbf{V} - \mathbf{V}_1) \cdot \hat{\mathbf{t}} = 0$

Equation of the normal $\qquad\qquad (\mathbf{V} - \mathbf{V}_1) \times \hat{\mathbf{n}} = 0$
$\qquad\qquad\qquad$ or $\qquad \mathbf{V} = \mathbf{V}_1 + r\hat{\mathbf{n}}$

Unit binormal $\qquad\qquad \hat{\mathbf{b}} = \hat{\mathbf{t}} \times \hat{\mathbf{n}}$

Equation of the binormal $\qquad\qquad (\mathbf{V} - \mathbf{V}_1) \times \hat{\mathbf{b}} = 0$
$\qquad\qquad$ or $\qquad\qquad \mathbf{V} = \mathbf{V}_1 + u\hat{\mathbf{b}}$
$\qquad\qquad$ or $\qquad\qquad \mathbf{V} = \mathbf{V}_1 + w\dfrac{d\mathbf{V}_1}{ds} \times \dfrac{d^2\mathbf{V}_1}{ds^2}$

Equation of the osculating plane:

$$[(\mathbf{V} - \mathbf{V}_1)\hat{\mathbf{t}}\hat{\mathbf{n}}] = 0$$
$$\text{or} \quad \left[(\mathbf{V} - \mathbf{V}_1)\left(\frac{d\mathbf{V}_1}{ds}\right)\left(\frac{d^2\mathbf{V}_1}{ds^2}\right) \right] = 0$$

A *geodetic line* on a surface is a curve, the osculating plane of which is everywhere normal to the surface.

The differential equation of the geodetic is

$$[\hat{\mathbf{n}} d\mathbf{V}_1 \, d^2\mathbf{V}_1] = 0$$

Differential Operators—Rectangular Coordinates

$$dS = \frac{\partial S}{\partial x} \cdot dx + \frac{\partial S}{\partial y} \cdot dy + \frac{\partial S}{\partial z} \cdot dz$$

By definition

$$\nabla \equiv \text{del} \equiv \mathbf{i} \frac{\partial}{\partial x} + \mathbf{j} \frac{\partial}{\partial y} + \mathbf{k} \frac{\partial}{\partial z}$$

$$\nabla^2 \equiv \text{Laplacian} \equiv \frac{\partial^2}{\partial x^2} + \frac{\partial^2}{\partial y^2} + \frac{\partial^2}{\partial z^2}$$

If S is a scalar function, then

$$\nabla S \equiv \text{grad } S \equiv \frac{\partial S}{dx} \mathbf{i} + \frac{\partial S}{dy} \mathbf{j} + \frac{\partial S}{dz} \mathbf{k}$$

Grad S defines both the direction and magnitude of the maximum rate of increase of S at any point. Hence the name *gradient* and also its vectorial nature. ∇S is independent of the choice of rectangular coordinates.

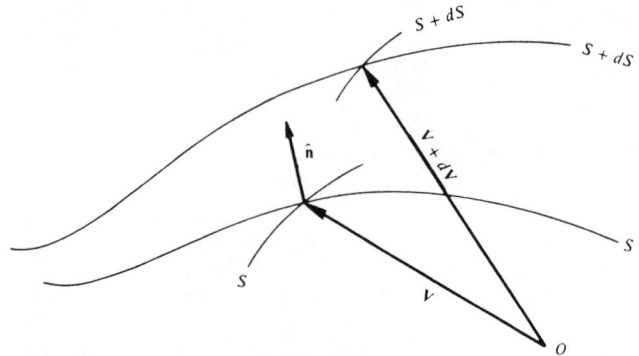

Figure 4

$$\nabla S = \frac{\partial S}{\partial n} \hat{\mathbf{n}}$$

where $\hat{\mathbf{n}}$ is the unit normal to the surface $S = $ constant, in the direction of S increasing. The total derivative of S at a point having the position vector $\mathbf{V}$ is given by (fig. 4)

$$dS = \frac{\partial S}{\partial n} \hat{\mathbf{n}} \cdot d\mathbf{V}$$

$$= d\mathbf{V} \cdot \nabla S$$

and the directional derivative of S in the direction of $\mathbf{U}$ is

$$\mathbf{U} \cdot \nabla S = \mathbf{U} \cdot (\nabla S) = (\mathbf{U} \cdot \nabla)S$$

Similarly the directional derivative of the vector $\mathbf{V}$ in the direction of $\mathbf{U}$ is

$$(\mathbf{U} \cdot \nabla)\mathbf{V}$$

The *distributive* law holds for finding a gradient. Thus if S and T are scalar functions

$$\nabla(S + T) = \nabla S + \nabla T$$

The *associative* law becomes the rule for differentiating a product:

$$\nabla(ST) = S\nabla T + T\nabla S$$

If V is a vector function with the magnitudes of the components parallel to the three co-ordinate axes V_x, V_y, V_z, then

$$\nabla \cdot V \equiv \text{div } V \equiv \frac{\partial V_x}{\partial x} + \frac{\partial V_y}{\partial y} + \frac{\partial V_z}{\partial z}$$

The divergence obeys the distributive law. Thus, if V and U are vectors functions, then

$$\nabla \cdot (V + U) = \nabla \cdot V + \nabla \cdot U$$
$$\nabla \cdot (SV) = (\nabla S) \cdot V + S(\nabla \cdot V)$$
$$\nabla \cdot (U \times V) = V \cdot (\nabla \times U) - U \cdot (\nabla \times V)$$

As with the gradient of a scalar, the divergence of a vector is invariant under a transformation from one set of rectangular coordinates to another.

$$\nabla \times V \equiv \text{curl } V \quad (\text{sometimes } \nabla \wedge V \text{ or rot } V)$$

$$\equiv \left(\frac{\partial V_z}{\partial y} - \frac{\partial V_y}{\partial z}\right)i + \left(\frac{\partial V_x}{\partial z} - \frac{\partial V_z}{\partial x}\right)j + \left(\frac{\partial V_y}{\partial x} - \frac{\partial V_x}{\partial y}\right)k$$

$$= \begin{vmatrix} i & j & k \\ \dfrac{\partial}{\partial x} & \dfrac{\partial}{\partial y} & \dfrac{\partial}{\partial z} \\ V_x & V_y & V_z \end{vmatrix}$$

The *curl* (or *rotation*) of a vector is a vector which is invariant under a transformation from one set of rectangular coordinates to another.

$$\nabla \times (U + V) = \nabla \times U + \nabla \times V$$
$$\nabla \times (SV) = (\nabla S) \times V + S(\nabla \times V)$$
$$\nabla \times (U \times V) = (V \cdot \nabla)U - (U \cdot \nabla)V + U(\nabla \cdot V) - V(\nabla \cdot U)$$

$$\text{grad } (U \cdot V) = \nabla(U \cdot V)$$
$$= (V \cdot \nabla)U + (U \cdot \nabla)V + V \times (\nabla \times U) + U \times (\nabla \times V)$$

If

$$V = V_x i + V_y j + V_z k$$
$$\nabla \cdot V = \nabla V_x \cdot i + \nabla V_y \cdot j + \nabla V_z \cdot k$$

and

$$\nabla \times V = \nabla V_x \times i + \nabla V_y \times j + \nabla V_z \times k$$

The operator ∇ can be used more than once. The number of possibilities where ∇ is used twice are

$$\nabla \cdot (\nabla\theta) \equiv \text{div grad } \theta$$
$$\nabla \times (\nabla\theta) \equiv \text{curl grad } \theta$$
$$\nabla(\nabla \cdot V) \equiv \text{grad div } V$$
$$\nabla \cdot (\nabla \times V) \equiv \text{div curl } V$$
$$\nabla \times (\nabla \times V) \equiv \text{curl curl } V$$

Thus: div grad $S \equiv \nabla \cdot (\nabla S) \equiv$ Laplacian $S \equiv \nabla^2 S$

$$\equiv \frac{\partial^2 S}{\partial x^2} + \frac{\partial^2 S}{\partial y^2} + \frac{\partial^2 S}{\partial z^2}$$

curl grad $S \equiv 0$;   curl curl $\mathbf{V} \equiv$ grad div $\mathbf{V} - \nabla^2 \mathbf{V}$;

div curl $\mathbf{V} \equiv \qquad 0$

Taylor's expansion in three dimensions can be written

$$f(\mathbf{V} + \mathbf{\varepsilon}) = e^{\mathbf{\varepsilon} \cdot \nabla} f(\mathbf{V})$$

where $\mathbf{V} = x\mathbf{i} + y\mathbf{j} + z\mathbf{k}$

and $\mathbf{\varepsilon} = h\mathbf{i} + l\mathbf{j} + m\mathbf{k}$

(note the analogy with $f_p = e^{phD} f_0$ in finite difference methods).

Orthogonal Curvilinear Coordinates

If at a point P there exist three uniform point functions u, v and w so that the surfaces $u = \text{const.}$, $v = \text{const.}$, and $w = \text{const.}$, intersect in three distinct curves through P then the surfaces are called the *coordinate surfaces* through P. The three lines of intersection are referred to as the *coordinate lines* and their tangents a, b, and c as the *coordinate axes*. When the coordinate axes form an orthogonal set the system is said to define *orthogonal curvilinear coordinates* at P.

Consider an infinitesimal volume enclosed by the surfaces u, v, w, $u + du$, $v + dv$, and $w + dw$ (fig. 5).

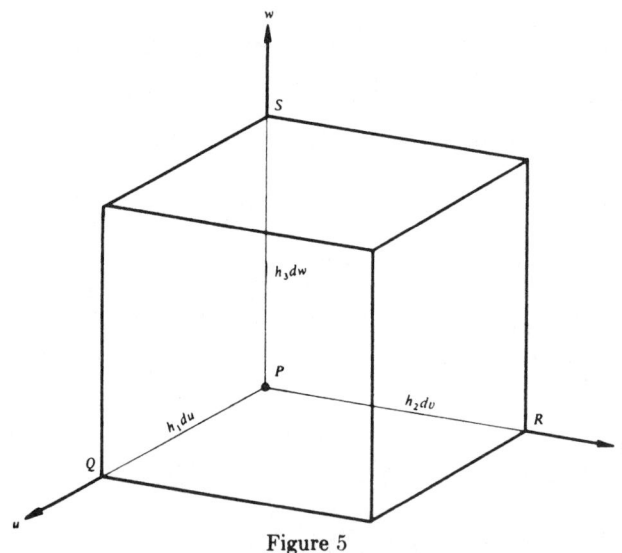

Figure 5

The surface $PRS \equiv u =$ const., and the face of the curvilinear figure immediately opposite this is $u + du =$ const. etc.

In terms of these surface constants

$$
\begin{aligned}
P &= P(u,v,w) \\
Q &= Q(u + du,v,w) \\
R &= R(u,v + dv,w) \\
S &= S(u,v,w + dw)
\end{aligned}
\qquad \text{and} \qquad
\begin{aligned}
PQ &= h_1 du \\
PR &= h_2 dv \\
PS &= h_3 dw
\end{aligned}
$$

where h_1, h_2, and h_3 are functions of u, v, and w.

In rectangular Cartesians $\mathbf{i}$, $\mathbf{j}$, $\mathbf{k}$

$$ h_1 = 1, \qquad h_2 = 1, \qquad h_3 = 1. $$

$$ \frac{\hat{\mathbf{a}}}{h_1}\frac{\partial}{\partial u} = \mathbf{i}\frac{\partial}{\partial x}, \qquad \frac{\hat{\mathbf{b}}}{h_2}\frac{\partial}{\partial v} = \mathbf{j}\frac{\partial}{\partial y}, \qquad \frac{\hat{\mathbf{c}}}{h_3}\frac{\partial}{\partial w} = \mathbf{k}\frac{\partial}{\partial z}. $$

In cylindrical coordinates $\hat{\mathbf{r}}$, $\hat{\boldsymbol{\phi}}$, $\hat{\mathbf{k}}$

$$ h_1 = 1, \qquad h_2 = r \qquad h_3 = 1. $$

$$ \frac{\hat{\mathbf{a}}}{h_1}\frac{\partial}{\partial u} = \hat{\mathbf{r}}\frac{\partial}{\partial r}, \qquad \frac{\hat{\mathbf{b}}}{h_2}\frac{\partial}{\partial v} = \frac{\hat{\boldsymbol{\phi}}}{r}\frac{\partial}{\partial \phi}, \qquad \frac{\hat{\mathbf{c}}}{h_3}\frac{\partial}{\partial w} = \hat{\mathbf{k}}\frac{\partial}{\partial z}. $$

In spherical coordinates $\hat{\mathbf{r}}$, $\hat{\boldsymbol{\theta}}$, $\hat{\boldsymbol{\phi}}$

$$ h_1 = 1, \qquad h_2 = r, \qquad h_3 = r\sin\theta. $$

$$ \frac{\hat{\mathbf{a}}}{h_1}\frac{\partial}{\partial u} = \hat{\mathbf{r}}\frac{\partial}{\partial r}, \qquad \frac{\hat{\mathbf{b}}}{h_2}\frac{\partial}{\partial v} = \frac{\hat{\boldsymbol{\phi}}}{r}\frac{\partial}{\partial \theta}, \qquad \frac{\hat{\mathbf{c}}}{h_3}\frac{\partial}{\partial w} = \frac{\hat{\boldsymbol{\phi}}}{r\sin\theta}\frac{\partial}{\partial \phi} $$

The general expressions for grad, div and curl together with those for ∇^2 and the directional derivative are, in orthogonal curvilinear coordinates, given by

$$ \nabla S = \frac{\hat{\mathbf{a}}}{h_1}\frac{\partial S}{\partial u} + \frac{\hat{\mathbf{b}}}{h_2}\frac{\partial S}{\partial v} + \frac{\hat{\mathbf{c}}}{h_3}\frac{\partial S}{\partial w} $$

$$ (\mathbf{V}\cdot\nabla)S = \frac{V_1}{h_1}\frac{\partial S}{\partial u} + \frac{V_2}{h_2}\frac{\partial S}{\partial v} + \frac{V_3}{h_3}\frac{\partial S}{\partial w} $$

$$ \nabla\cdot\mathbf{V} = \frac{1}{h_1 h_2 h_3}\left\{\frac{\partial}{\partial u}(h_2 h_3 V_1) + \frac{\partial}{\partial v}(h_3 h_1 V_2) + \frac{\partial}{\partial w}(h_1 h_2 V_3)\right. $$

$$ \nabla\times\mathbf{V} = \frac{\hat{\mathbf{a}}}{h_2 h_3}\left\{\frac{\partial}{\partial v}(h_3 V_3) - \frac{\partial}{\partial w}(h_2 V_2)\right\} + \frac{\hat{\mathbf{b}}}{h_3 h_1}\left\{\frac{\partial}{\partial w}(h_1 V_1) - \frac{\partial}{\partial u}(h_3 V_3)\right\} $$

$$ + \frac{\hat{\mathbf{c}}}{h_1 h_2}\left\{\frac{\partial}{\partial u}(h_2 V_2) - \frac{\partial}{\partial v}(h_1 V_1)\right\} $$

$$ \nabla^2 S = \frac{1}{h_1 h_2 h_3}\left\{\frac{\partial}{\partial u}\left(\frac{h_2 h_3}{h_1}\frac{\partial S}{\partial u}\right) + \frac{\partial}{\partial v}\left(\frac{h_3 h_1}{h_2}\frac{\partial S}{\partial v}\right) + \frac{\partial}{\partial w}\left(\frac{h_1 h_2}{h_3}\frac{\partial S}{\partial w}\right)\right\} $$

FORMULAS OF VECTOR ANALYSIS

	Rectangular coordinates	Cylindrical coordinates	Spherical coordinates
Conversion to rectangular coordinates		$x = r\cos\varphi \quad y = r\sin\varphi \quad z = z$	$x = r\cos\varphi\sin\theta \quad y = r\sin\varphi\sin\theta$ $z = r\cos\theta$
Gradient	$\nabla\phi = \dfrac{\partial\phi}{\partial x}\mathbf{i} + \dfrac{\partial\phi}{\partial y}\mathbf{j} + \dfrac{\partial\phi}{\partial z}\mathbf{k}$	$\nabla\phi = \dfrac{\partial\phi}{\partial r}\mathbf{r} + \dfrac{1}{r}\dfrac{\partial\phi}{\partial\varphi}\boldsymbol{\phi} + \dfrac{\partial\phi}{\partial z}\mathbf{k}$	$\nabla\phi = \dfrac{\partial\phi}{\partial r}\mathbf{r} + \dfrac{1}{r}\dfrac{\partial\phi}{\partial\theta}\boldsymbol{\theta} + \dfrac{1}{r\sin\theta}\dfrac{\partial\phi}{\partial\varphi}\boldsymbol{\phi}$
Divergence	$\nabla\cdot\mathbf{A} = \dfrac{\partial A_x}{\partial x} + \dfrac{\partial A_y}{\partial y} + \dfrac{\partial A_z}{\partial z}$	$\nabla\cdot\mathbf{A} = \dfrac{1}{r}\dfrac{\partial(rA_r)}{\partial r} + \dfrac{1}{r}\dfrac{\partial A_\varphi}{\partial\varphi} + \dfrac{\partial A_z}{\partial z}$	$\nabla\cdot\mathbf{A} = \dfrac{1}{r^2}\dfrac{\partial(r^2A_r)}{\partial r} + \dfrac{1}{r\sin\theta}\dfrac{\partial(A_\theta\sin\theta)}{\partial\theta} + \dfrac{1}{r\sin\theta}\dfrac{\partial A_\varphi}{\partial\varphi}$
Curl	$\nabla\times\mathbf{A} = \begin{vmatrix} \mathbf{i} & \mathbf{j} & \mathbf{k} \\[2pt] \dfrac{\partial}{\partial x} & \dfrac{\partial}{\partial y} & \dfrac{\partial}{\partial z} \\[4pt] A_x & A_y & A_z \end{vmatrix}$	$\nabla\times\mathbf{A} = \begin{vmatrix} \dfrac{1}{r}\mathbf{r} & \boldsymbol{\phi} & \dfrac{1}{r}\mathbf{k} \\[2pt] \dfrac{\partial}{\partial r} & \dfrac{\partial}{\partial\varphi} & \dfrac{\partial}{\partial z} \\[4pt] A_r & rA_\varphi & A_z \end{vmatrix}$	$\nabla\times\mathbf{A} = \begin{vmatrix} \dfrac{\mathbf{r}}{r^2\sin\theta} & \dfrac{\boldsymbol{\theta}}{r\sin\theta} & \dfrac{\boldsymbol{\phi}}{r} \\[2pt] \dfrac{\partial}{\partial r} & \dfrac{\partial}{\partial\theta} & \dfrac{\partial}{\partial\varphi} \\[4pt] A_r & rA_\theta & rA_\varphi\sin\theta \end{vmatrix}$
Laplacian	$\nabla^2\phi = \dfrac{\partial^2\phi}{\partial x^2} + \dfrac{\partial^2\phi}{\partial y^2} + \dfrac{\partial^2\phi}{\partial z^2}$	$\nabla^2\phi = \dfrac{1}{r}\dfrac{\partial}{\partial r}\left(r\dfrac{\partial\phi}{\partial r}\right) + \dfrac{1}{r^2}\dfrac{\partial^2\phi}{\partial\varphi^2} + \dfrac{\partial^2\phi}{\partial z^2}$	$\nabla^2\phi = \dfrac{1}{r^2}\dfrac{\partial}{\partial r}\left(r^2\dfrac{\partial\phi}{\partial r}\right) + \dfrac{1}{r^2\sin\theta}\dfrac{\partial}{\partial\theta}\left(\sin\theta\dfrac{\partial\phi}{\partial\theta}\right) + \dfrac{1}{r^2\sin^2\theta}\dfrac{\partial^2\phi}{\partial\varphi^2}$

Transformation of Integrals

s = the distance along some curve "C" in space and is measured from some fixed point.
S = a surface area
V = a volume contained by a specified surface
$\hat{t}$ = the unit tangent to C at the point P
$\hat{n}$ = the unit outward pointing normal
F = some vector function
ds = the vector element of curve ($= \hat{t}\, ds$)
dS = the vector element of surface ($= \hat{n}\, dS$)

Then

$$\int_{(c)} \mathbf{F} \cdot \hat{t}\, ds = \int_{(c)} \mathbf{F} \cdot d\mathbf{s}$$

and when

$$\mathbf{F} = \nabla\phi$$

$$\int_{(c)} (\nabla\phi) \cdot \hat{t}\, ds = \int_{(c)} d\phi$$

Gauss' Theorem (Green's Theorem)

When S defines a closed region having a volume V

$$\iiint_{(v)} (\nabla \cdot \mathbf{F})\, dV = \iint_{(s)} (\mathbf{F} \cdot \hat{n})\, dS = \iint_{(s)} \mathbf{F} \cdot d\mathbf{S}$$

also

$$\iiint_{(v)} (\nabla\phi)\, dV = \iint_{(s)} \phi\hat{n}\, dS$$

and

$$\iiint_{(v)} (\nabla \times \mathbf{F})\, dV = \iint_{(s)} (\hat{n} \times \mathbf{F})\, dS$$

Stokes' Theorem

When C is closed and bounds the open surface S.

$$\iint_{(s)} \hat{n} \cdot (\nabla \times \mathbf{F})\, dS = \int_{(c)} \mathbf{F} \cdot d\mathbf{s}$$

also

$$\iint_{(s)} (\hat{n} \times \nabla\phi)\, dS = \int_{(c)} \phi\, d\mathbf{s}$$

Green's Theorem

$$\iint_{(s)} (\nabla\phi \cdot \nabla\theta)\, dS = \iint_{(s)} \phi\hat{n} \cdot (\nabla\theta)\, dS = \iiint_{(v)} \phi(\nabla^2\theta)\, dV$$

$$= \iint_{(s)} \theta \cdot \hat{n}(\nabla\phi)\, dS = \iiint_{(v)} \theta(\nabla^2\phi)\, dV$$

MOMENT OF INERTIA FOR VARIOUS BODIES OF MASS

The mass of the body is indicated by m.

Body	Axis	Moment of inertia
Uniform thin rod	Normal to the length, at one end	$m\dfrac{l^2}{3}$
Uniform thin rod	Normal to the length, at the center	$m\dfrac{l^2}{12}$
Thin rectangular sheet, sides a and b	Through the center parallel to b	$m\dfrac{a^2}{12}$
Thin rectangular sheet, sides a and b	Through the center perpendicular to the sheet	$m\dfrac{a^2 + b^2}{12}$
Thin circular sheet of radius r	Normal to the plate through the center	$m\dfrac{r^2}{2}$
Thin circular sheet of radius r	Along any diameter	$m\dfrac{r^2}{4}$
Thin circular ring. Radii r_1 and r_2	Through center normal to plane of ring	$m\dfrac{r_1^2 + r_2^2}{2}$
Thin circular ring. Radii r_1 and r_2	Any diameter	$m\dfrac{r_1^2 + r_2^2}{4}$
Rectangular parallelopiped, edges a, b, and c	Through center perpendicular to face ab, (parallel to edge c)	$m\dfrac{a^2 + b^2}{12}$
Sphere, radius r	Any diameter	$m\dfrac{2}{5}r^2$
Spherical shell, external radius, r_1, internal radius r_2	Any diameter	$m\dfrac{2}{5}\dfrac{(r_1^5 - r_2^5)}{(r_1^3 - r_2^3)}$
Spherical shell, very thin, mean radius, r	Any diameter	$m\dfrac{2}{3}r^2$
Right circular cylinder of radius r, length l	The longitudinal axis of the solid	$m\dfrac{r^2}{2}$
Right circular cylinder of radius r, length l	Transverse diameter	$m\left(\dfrac{r^2}{4} + \dfrac{l^2}{12}\right)$
Hollow circular cylinder, length l, radii r_1 and r_2	The longitudinal axis of the figure	$m\dfrac{(r_1^2 + r_2^2)}{2}$
Thin cylindrical shell, length l, mean radius, r	The longitudinal axis of the figure	mr^2
Hollow circular cylinder, length l, radii r_1 and r_2	Transverse diameter	$m\left[\dfrac{r_1^2 + r_2^2}{4} + \dfrac{l^2}{12}\right]$
Hollow circular cylinder, length l, very thin, mean radius	Transverse diameter	$m\left(\dfrac{r^2}{2} + \dfrac{l^2}{12}\right)$
Elliptic cylinder, length l, transverse semiaxes a and b	Longitudinal axis	$m\left(\dfrac{a^2 + b^2}{4}\right)$
Right cone, altitude h, radius of base r	Axis of the figure	$m\dfrac{3}{10}r^2$
Spheroid of revolution, equatorial radius r	Polar axis	$m\dfrac{2r^2}{5}$
Ellipsoid, axes $2a$, $2b$, $2c$	Axis $2a$	$m\dfrac{(b^2 + c^2)}{5}$

IX. DIFFERENTIAL EQUATIONS

Differential equation	Method of solution
Separation of variables $f_1(x) g_1(y) dx + f_2(x) g_2(y) dy = 0$	$$\int \frac{f_1(x)}{f_2(x)} dx + \int \frac{g_2(y)}{g_1(y)} dy = c$$
Exact equation $M(x,y)dx + N(x,y)dy = 0$ where $\partial M/\partial y = \partial N/\partial x$	$$\int M \partial x + \int \left(N - \frac{\partial}{\partial y} \int M \partial x \right) dy = c$$ where ∂x indicates that the integration is to be performed with respect to x keeping y constant.
Linear first order equation $\frac{dy}{dx} + P(x)y = Q(x)$	$$ye^{\int Pdx} = \int Qe^{\int Pdx} dx + c$$
Bernoulli's equation $\frac{dy}{dx} + P(x)y = Q(x)y^n$	$$ve^{(1-n)\int Pdx} = (1-n)\int Qe^{(1-n)\int Pdx} dx + c$$ where $v = y^{1-n}$. If $n = 1$, the solution is $$\ln y = \int (Q - P) dx + c$$
Homogeneous equation $\frac{dy}{dx} = F\left(\frac{y}{x}\right)$	$$\ln x = \int \frac{dv}{F(v) - v} + c$$ where $v = y/x$. If $F(v) = v$, the solution is $y = cx$
Reducible to homogeneous $(a_1 x + b_1 y + c_1) dx + (a_2 x + b_2 y + c_2) dy = 0$ $\frac{a_1}{a_2} \neq \frac{b_1}{b_2}$	Set $u = a_1 x + b_1 y + c_1$, $v = a_2 x + b_2 y + c_2$ Eliminate x and y and the equation becomes homogenous
Reducible to separable $(a_1 x + b_1 y + c_1) dx + (a_2 x + b_2 y + c_2) dy = 0$ $\frac{a_1}{a_2} = \frac{b_1}{b_2}$	Set $u = a_1 x + b_1 y$ Eliminate x or y and equation becomes separable

$y\,F(xy)\,dx + x\,G(xy)dy = 0$	$\ln x = \displaystyle\int \frac{G(v)\,dv}{v\,\{G(v) - F(v)\,\}} + c$ where $v = xy$. If $G(v) = F(v)$, the solution is $xy = c$.
Linear, homogeneous second order equation $\dfrac{d^2 y}{dx^2} + b\,\dfrac{dy}{dx} + cy = 0$ b, c are real constants	Let m_1, m_2 be the roots of $m^2 + bm + c = 0$. Then there are 3 cases: Case 1. m_1, m_2 real and distinct: $$y = c_1 e^{m_1 x} + c_2 e^{m_2 x}$$ Case 2. m_1, m_2 real and equal: $$y = c_1 e^{m_1 x} + c_2 x e^{m_1 x}$$ Case 3. $m_1 = p + qi,\; m_2 = p - qi$: $$y = e^{px}(c_1 \cos qx + c_2 \sin qx)$$ where $p = -b/2,\; q = \sqrt{4c - b^2}/2$
Linear, nonhomogeneous second order equation $\dfrac{d^2 y}{dx^2} + b\,\dfrac{dy}{dx} + cy = R(x)$ b, c are real constants	There are 3 cases corresponding to those immediately above: Case 1. $$y = c_1 e^{m_1 x} + c_2 e^{m_2 x}$$ $$+ \frac{e^{m_1 x}}{m_1 - m_2} \int e^{-m_1 x} R(x)\,dx$$ $$+ \frac{e^{m_2 x}}{m_2 - m_1} \int e^{-m_2 x} R(x)\,dx$$ Case 2. $$y = c_1 e^{m_1 x} + c_2 x e^{m_1 x}$$ $$+ x e^{m_1 x} \int e^{-m_1 x} R(x)\,dx$$ $$- e^{m_1 x} \int x e^{-m_1 x} R(x)\,dx$$ Case 3. $$y = e^{px}(c_1 \cos qx + c_2 \sin qx)$$ $$+ \frac{e^{px} \sin qx}{q} \int e^{-px} R(x) \cos qx\,dx$$ $$- \frac{e^{px} \cos qx}{q} \int e^{-px} R(x) \sin qx\,dx$$

Euler or Cauchy equation $x^2 \dfrac{d^2 y}{dx^2} + bx \dfrac{dy}{dx} + cy = S(x)$	Putting $x = e^t$, the equation becomes $\dfrac{d^2 y}{dt^2} + (b - 1)\dfrac{dy}{dt} + cy = S(e^t)$ and can then be solved as a linear second order equation.
Bessel's equation $x^2 \dfrac{d^2 y}{dx^2} + x \dfrac{dy}{dx} + (\lambda^2 x^2 - n^2)y = 0$	$y = c_1 J_n(\lambda x) + c_2 Y_n(\lambda x)$ See pages 351, 355, 356, 385.
Transformed Bessel's equation $x^2 \dfrac{d^2 y}{dx^2} + (2p + 1)x \dfrac{dy}{dx} + (\alpha^2 x^{2r} + \beta^2)y = 0$	$y = x^{-p} \left\{ c_1 J_{q/r}\left(\dfrac{\alpha}{r} x^r\right) + c_2 Y_{q/r}\left(\dfrac{\alpha}{r} x^r\right) \right\}$ where $q = \sqrt{p^2 - \beta^2}$.
Legendre's equation $(1 - x^2)\dfrac{d^2 y}{dx^2} - 2x \dfrac{dy}{dx} + n(n + 1)y = 0$	$y = c_1 P_n(x) + c_2 Q_n(x)$ See page 374.

SPECIAL FORMULAS

Certain types of differential equations occur sufficiently often to justify the use of formulas for the corresponding particular solutions. The following set of tables I to XIV covers all first, second and nth order ordinary linear differential equations with constant coefficients for which the right members are of the form $P(x)e^{rx} \sin sx$ or $P(x)e^{rx} \cos sx$, where r and s are constants and $P(x)$ is a polynomial of degree n.

When the right member of a reducible linear partial differential equation with constant coefficients is not zero, particular solutions for certain types of right members are contained in tables XV to XXI. In these tables both F and P are used to denote polynomials, and it is assumed that no denominator is zero. In any formula the roles of x and y may be reversed throughout, changing a formula in which x dominates to one in which y dominates. Tables XIX, XX, XXI are applicable whether the equations are reducible or not.

The symbol $\binom{m}{n}$ stands for $\dfrac{m!}{(m-n)!n!}$ and is the $n + 1$ st coefficient in the expansion of $(a + b)^m$. Also $0! = 1$ by definition.

The tables as herewith given are those contained in the text *Differential Equations* by Ginn and Company (1955) and are published with their kind permission and that of the author, Professor Frederick H. Steen.

Solution of Linear Differential Equations with Constant Coefficients

Any linear differential equation with constant coefficients may be written in the form

$$p(D)y = R(x),$$

where D is the differential operator

$$Dy = \frac{dy}{dx},$$

$p(D)$ is a polynomial in D,
y is the dependent variable,
x is the independent variable,
$R(x)$ is an arbitrary function of x.

A power of D represents repeated differentiation, that is

$$D^n y = \frac{d^n y}{dx^n}.$$

For such an equation, the general solution may be written in the form

$$y = y_c + y_p,$$

where y_p is any particular solution, and y_c is called the *complementary function*. This complementary function is defined as the general solution of the *homogeneous equation*, which is the original differential equation with the right side replaced by zero, i.e.

$$p(D)y = 0$$

The complementary function y_c may be determined as follows:

1. Factor the polynomial $p(D)$ into real and complex linear factors, just as if D were a variable instead of an operator.

2. For each non-repeated linear factor of the form $(D - a)$, where a is real, write down a term of the form

$$ce^{ax},$$

where c is an arbitrary constant.

3. For each repeated real linear factor of the form $(D - a)^n$, write down n terms of the form

$$c_1 e^{ax} + c_2 x e^{ax} + c_3 x^2 e^{ax} + \cdots + c_n x^{n-1} e^{ax},$$

where the c_i's are arbitrary constants.

4. For each non-repeated conjugate complex pair of factors of the form $(D - a + ib)(D - a - ib)$, write down 2 terms of the form

$$c_1 e^{ax} \cos bx + c_2 e^{ax} \sin bx$$

5. For each repeated conjugate complex pair of factors of the form $(D - a + ib)^n (D - a - ib)^n$, write down $2n$ terms of the form

$$c_1 e^{ax} \cos bx + c_2 e^{ax} \sin bx + c_3 x e^{ax} \cos bx + c_4 x e^{ax} \sin bx + \cdots$$
$$+ c_{2n-1} x^{n-1} e^{ax} \cos bx + c_{2n} x^{n-1} e^{ax} \sin bx$$

6. The sum of all the terms thus written down is the complementary function y_c.

To find the particular solution y_p, use the following tables, as shown in the examples. For cases not shown in the tables, there are various methods of finding y_p. The most general method is called *variation of parameters*. The following example illustrates the method:

Find y_p for $(D^2 - 4)y = e^x$.

This example can be solved most easily by use of equation 63 in the tables following. However it is given here as an example of the method of variation of parameters.

The complementary function is

$$y_c = c_1 e^{2x} + c_2 e^{-2x}$$

To find y_p, replace the constants in the complementary function with unknown functions,

$$y_p = u e^{2x} + v e^{-2x}.$$

We now prepare to substitute this assumed solution into the original equation. We begin by taking all the necessary derivatives:

$$y_p = u e^{2x} + v e^{-2x}$$
$$y_p' = 2u e^{2x} - 2v e^{-2x} + u' e^{2x} + v' e^{-2x}$$

For each derivative of y_p except the highest, we set the sum of all the terms containing u' and v' to 0. Thus the above equation becomes

$$u' e^{2x} + v' e^{-2x} = 0 \quad \text{and} \quad y_p' = 2u e^{2x} - 2v e^{-2x}$$

Continuing to differentiate, we have

$$y_p'' = 4u e^{2x} + 4v e^{-2x} + 2u' e^{2x} - 2v' e^{-2x}$$

When we substitute into the original equation, all the terms not containing u' or v' cancel out. This is a consequence of the method by which y_p was set up.

Thus all that is necessary is to write down the terms containing u' or v' in the highest order derivative of y_p, multiply by the constant coefficient of the highest power of D in $p(D)$, and set it equal to $R(x)$. Together with the previous terms in u' and v' which were set equal to 0, this gives us as many linear equations in the first derivatives of the unknown functions as there are unknown functions. The first derivatives may then be solved for by algebra, and the unknown functions found by integration. In the present example, this becomes

$$u'e^{2x} + v'e^{-2x} = 0$$
$$2u'e^{2x} - 2v'e^{-2x} = e^x.$$

We eliminate v' and u' separately, getting

$$4u'e^{2x} = e^x$$
$$4v'e^{-2x} = -e^x.$$

Thus

$$u' = \tfrac{1}{4}e^{-x}$$
$$v' = -\tfrac{1}{4}e^{3x}.$$

Therefore, by integrating

$$u = -\tfrac{1}{4}e^{-x}$$
$$v = -\tfrac{1}{12}e^{3x}.$$

A constant of integration is not needed, since we need only one particular solution. Thus

$$y_p = ue^{2x} + ve^{-2x} = -\tfrac{1}{4}e^{-x}e^{2x} - \tfrac{1}{12}e^{3x}e^{-2x}$$
$$= -\tfrac{1}{4}e^x - \tfrac{1}{12}e^x = -\tfrac{1}{3}e^x,$$

and the general solution is

$$y = y_c + y_p = c_1 e^{2x} + c_2 e^{-2x} - \tfrac{1}{3}e^x.$$

The following examples illustrate the use of the tables.

Example 1.   Solve $(D^2 - 4)y = \sin 3x$.

Substitution of $q = -4, s = 3$ in formula 24 gives

$$y_p = \frac{\sin 3x}{-9 - 4},$$

wherefore the general solution is

$$y = c_1 e^{2x} + c_2 e^{-2x} - \frac{\sin 3x}{13}.$$

Example 2.   Obtain a particular solution of $(D^2 - 4D + 5)y = x^2 e^{3x} \sin x$.

Applying formula 40 with $a = 2, b = 1, r = 3, s = 1, P(x) = x^2, s + b = 2, s - b = 0, a - r = -1, (a - r)^2 + (s + b)^2 = 5, (a - r)^2 + (s - b)^2 = 1$, we have

$$y_p = \frac{e^{3x} \sin x}{2} \left[\left(\frac{2}{5} - \frac{0}{1} \right) x^2 + \left(\frac{2(-1)2}{25} - \frac{2(-1)0}{1} \right) 2x \right.$$
$$\left. + \left(\frac{3 \cdot 1 \cdot 2 - 2^3}{125} - \frac{3 \cdot 1 \cdot 0 - 0}{1} \right) 2 \right]$$
$$- \frac{e^{3x} \cos x}{2} \left[\left(\frac{-1}{5} - \frac{-1}{1} \right) x^2 + \left(\frac{1 - 4}{25} - \frac{1 - 0}{1} \right) 2x \right.$$
$$\left. + \left(\frac{-1 - 3(-1)4}{125} - \frac{-1 - 3(-1)0}{1} \right) 2 \right]$$

$$= (\tfrac{1}{5}x^2 - \tfrac{4}{25}x - \tfrac{2}{125}) e^{3x} \sin x + (-\tfrac{2}{5}x^2 + \tfrac{28}{25}x - \tfrac{136}{125}) e^{3x} \cos x.$$

The special formulas effect a very considerable saving of time in problems of this type.

Example 3.　Obtain a particular solution of $(D^2 - 4D + 5)y = x^2 e^{2x} \cos x$.　(Compare with Example 2.)

Formula 40 is not applicable here since for this equation $r = a$, $s = b$, wherefore the denominator $(a - r)^2 + (s - b)^2 = 0$.　We turn instead to formula 44.　Substituting $a = 2, b = 1$, $P(x) = x^2$ and replacing sin by cos, cos by $-\sin$, we obtain

$$y_p = \frac{e^{2x}\cos x}{4}\left(x^2 - \tfrac{2}{4}\right) + \frac{e^{2x}\sin x}{2}\int (x^2 - \tfrac{1}{2})\,dx$$

$$= \left(\frac{x^2}{4} - \frac{1}{8}\right) e^{2x}\cos x + \left(\frac{x^3}{6} - \frac{x}{4}\right) e^{2x}\sin x,$$

which is the required solution.

Example 4.　Find z_p for $(D_x - 3D_y)z = \ln (y + 3x)$.

Referring to Table XV we note that formula 69 (not 68) is applicable.　This gives

$$z_p = x \ln (y + 3x).$$

It is easily seen that $-\dfrac{y}{3}\ln (y + 3x)$ would serve equally well.

Example 5.　Solve $(D_x + 2D_y - 4)z = y \cos (y - 2x)$.

Since R in formula 76 contains a polynomial in x, not y, we rewrite the given equation in the form

$$(D_y + \tfrac{1}{2}D_x - 2)z = \tfrac{1}{2}y \cos (y - 2x).$$

Then

$$z_c = e^{2y}F(x - \tfrac{1}{2}y) = e^{2y}f(2x - y),$$

and by the formula

$$z_p = -\tfrac{1}{2}\cos (y - 2x)\cdot\left(\frac{y}{2} + \frac{\tfrac{1}{2}}{2}\right)$$

$$= -\tfrac{1}{8}(2y + 1)\cos (y - 2x).$$

Example 6.　Find z_p for $(D_x + 4D_y)^3 z = (2x - y)^2$.

Using formula 79, we obtain

$$z_p = \frac{\int\int\int u^2 du^3}{[2 + 4(-1)]^3} = \frac{u^5}{5\cdot 4\cdot 3\cdot(-8)} = -\frac{(2x - y)^5}{480}.$$

Example 7.　Find z_p for $(D_x^3 + 5D_x^2 D_y - 7D_x + 4)z = e^{2x+3y}$.

By formula 87

$$z_p = \frac{e^{2x+3y}}{2^3 + 5\cdot 2^2\cdot 3 - 7\cdot 2 + 4} = \frac{e^{2x+3y}}{58}.$$

Example 8.　Find z_p for

$$(D_x^4 + 6D_x^3 D_y + D_x D_y + D_y^2 + 9)z = \sin (3x + 4y).$$

Since every term in the left member is of *even* degree in the two operators D_x and D_y, formula 90 is applicable.

It gives

$$z_p = \frac{\sin (3x + 4y)}{(-9)^2 + 6(-9)(-12) + (-12) + (-16) + 9}$$

$$= \frac{\sin (3x + 4y)}{710}$$

DIFFERENTIAL EQUATIONS

TABLE I: $(D - a)y = R$

R	y_p
1. e^{rx}	$\dfrac{e^{rx}}{r-a}$
2. $\sin sx$*	$-\dfrac{a\sin sx + s\cos sx}{a^2+s^2} = -\dfrac{1}{\sqrt{a^2+s^2}}\sin\left(sx+\tan^{-1}\dfrac{s}{a}\right)$
3. $P(x)$	$-\dfrac{1}{a}\left[P(x) + \dfrac{P'(x)}{a} + \dfrac{P''(x)}{a^2} + \cdots + \dfrac{P^{(n)}(x)}{a^n}\right]$
4. $e^{rx}\sin sx$*	Replace a by $a - r$ in formula 2 and multiply by e^{rx}.
5. $P(x)e^{rx}$	Replace a by $a - r$ in formula 3 and multiply by e^{rx}.
6. $P(x)\sin sx$*	$-\sin sx\left[\dfrac{a}{a^2+s^2}P(x) + \dfrac{a^2-s^2}{(a^2+s^2)^2}P'(x) + \dfrac{a^3-3as^2}{(a^2+s^2)^3}P''(x) + \cdots \right.$ $\left. + \dfrac{a^k - \binom{k}{2}a^{k-2}s^2 + \binom{k}{4}a^{k-4}s^4 - \cdots - P^{(k-1)}(x)}{(a^2+s^2)^k} + \cdots\right]$ $-\cos sx\left[\dfrac{s}{a^2+s^2}P(x) + \dfrac{2as}{(a^2+s^2)^2}P'(x) + \dfrac{3a^2s-s^3}{(a^2+s^2)^3}P''(x) + \cdots\right.$ $\left.+ \dfrac{\binom{k}{1}a^{k-1}s - \binom{k}{3}a^{k-3}s^3 + \cdots - P^{(k-1)}(x)}{(a^2+s^2)^k} + \cdots\right]$
7. $P(x)e^{rx}\sin sx$*	Replace a by $a - r$ in formula 6 and multiply by e^{rx}.
8. e^{ax}	xe^{ax}
9. $e^{ax}\sin sx$*	$-\dfrac{e^{ax}\cos sx}{s}$
10. $P(x)e^{ax}$	$e^{ax}\displaystyle\int P(x)\,dx$
11. $P(x)e^{ax}\sin sx$*	$\dfrac{e^{ax}\sin sx}{s}\left[\dfrac{P'(x)}{s} - \dfrac{P'''(x)}{s^3} + \dfrac{P^v(x)}{s^5} - \cdots\right] - \dfrac{e^{ax}\cos sx}{s}\left[P(x) - \dfrac{P''(x)}{s^2} + \dfrac{P^{iv}(x)}{s^4} - \cdots\right]$

* For $\cos sx$ in R replace "sin" by "cos" and "cos" by "$-$ sin" in y_p.

$$D^n = \frac{d^n}{dx^n} \qquad \binom{m}{n} = \frac{m!}{(m-n)!n!} \qquad 0! = 1$$

DIFFERENTIAL EQUATIONS (Continued)

TABLE II: $(D - a)^2 y = R$

R	y_p
12. e^{rx}	$\dfrac{e^{rx}}{(r-a)^2}$
13. $\sin sx^*$	$\dfrac{1}{(a^2+s^2)^2}\left[(a^2-s^2)\sin sx + 2as\cos sx\right] = \dfrac{1}{a^2+s^2}\sin\left(sx + \tan^{-1}\dfrac{2as}{a^2-s^2}\right)$
14. $P(x)$	$\dfrac{1}{a^2}\left[P(x) + \dfrac{2P'(x)}{a} + \dfrac{3P''(x)}{a^2} + \cdots + \dfrac{(n+1)P^{(n)}(x)}{a^n}\right]$
15. $e^{rx}\sin sx^*$	Replace a by $a-r$ in formula 13 and multiply by e^{rx}.
16. $P(x)e^{rx}$	Replace a by $a-r$ in formula 14 and multiply by e^{rx}.
17. $P(x)\sin sx^*$	$\sin sx\left[\dfrac{a^2-s^2}{(a^2+s^2)^2}P(x) + 2\dfrac{a^3-3as^2}{(a^2+s^2)^3}P'(x) + 3\dfrac{a^4-6a^2s^2+s^4}{(a^2+s^2)^4}P''(x) + \cdots \right.$
	$\left. + (k-1)\dfrac{a^k - \binom{k}{2}a^{k-2}s^2 + \binom{k}{4}a^{k-4}s^4 - \cdots}{(a^2+s^2)^k}P^{(k-2)}(x) + \cdots\right]$
	$+ \cos sx\left[\dfrac{2as}{(a^2+s^2)^2}P(x) + 2\dfrac{3a^2s-s^3}{(a^2+s^2)^3}P'(x) + 3\dfrac{4a^3s-4as^3}{(a^2+s^2)^4}P''(x) + \cdots \right.$
	$\left. + (k-1)\dfrac{\binom{k}{1}a^{k-1}s - \binom{k}{3}a^{k-3}s^3 + \cdots}{(a^2+s^2)^k}P^{(k-2)}(x) + \cdots\right]$
18. $P(x)e^{rx}\sin sx^*$	Replace a by $a-r$ in formula 17 and multiply by e^{rx}.
19. e^{ax}	$\tfrac{1}{2}x^2 e^{ax}$
20. $e^{ax}\sin sx^*$	$-\dfrac{e^{ax}\sin sx}{s^2}$
21. $P(x)e^{ax}$	$e^{ax}\displaystyle\iint P(x)\,dx\,dx$
22. $P(x)e^{ax}\sin sx^*$	$-\dfrac{e^{ax}\sin sx}{s^2}\left[P(x) - \dfrac{3P''(x)}{s^2} + \dfrac{5P^{iv}(x)}{s^4} - \dfrac{7P^{vi}(x)}{s^6} + \cdots \right]$
	$-\dfrac{e^{ax}\cos sx}{s^2}\left[\dfrac{2P'(\,:\,)}{s} - \dfrac{4P'''(x)}{s^3} + \dfrac{6P^v(x)}{s^5} - \cdots\right]$

* For cos sx in R replace "sin" by "cos" and "cos" by "$-$ sin" in y_p.

DIFFERENTIAL EQUATIONS (Continued)

TABLE III: $(D^2 + q)y = R$

R	y_p
23. e^{rx}	$\dfrac{e^{rx}}{r^2 + q}$
24. $\sin sx$*	$\dfrac{\sin sx}{-s^2 + q}$
25. $P(x)$	$\dfrac{1}{q}\left[P(x) - \dfrac{P''(x)}{q} + \dfrac{P^{iv}(x)}{q^2} - \cdots + (-1)^k \dfrac{P^{(2k)}(x)}{q^k} \cdots \right]$
26. $e^{rx}\sin sx$*	$\dfrac{(r^2 - s^2 + q)e^{rx}\sin sx - 2\,rse^{rx}\cos sx}{(r^2 - s^2 + q)^2 + (2rs)^2} = \dfrac{e^{rx}}{\sqrt{(r^2 - s^2 + q)^2 + (2rs)^2}}\sin\left[sx - \tan^{-1}\dfrac{2rs}{r^2 - s^2 + q}\right]$
27. $P(x)e^{rx}$	$\dfrac{e^{rx}}{r^2 + q}\left[P(x) - \dfrac{2r}{r^2 + q}P'(x) + \dfrac{3r^2 - q}{(r^2 + q)^2}P''(x) - \dfrac{4r^3 - 4qr}{(r^2 + q)^3}P'''(x) \right.$ $\left. + \cdots + (-1)^{k-1}\dfrac{\binom{k}{1}r^{k-1} - \binom{k}{3}r^{k-3}q + \binom{k}{5}r^{k-5}q^2 - \cdots P^{(k-1)}(x)}{(r^2 + q)^{k-1}} + \cdots \right]$
28. $P(x)\sin sx$*	$\dfrac{\sin sx}{(-s^2 + q)}\left[P(x) - \dfrac{3s^2 + q}{(-s^2 + q)^2}P''(x) + \dfrac{5s^4 + 10s^2q + q^2}{(-s^2 + q)^4}P^{iv}(x) - \cdots \right.$ $\left. + (-1)^k\dfrac{4s^2 + 4q}{(-s^2 + q)^3}P'''(x) - \dfrac{\binom{2k+1}{1}s^{2k} + \binom{2k+1}{3}s^{2k-2}q + \binom{2k+1}{5}s^{2k-4}q^2 + \cdots}{(-s^2 + q)^{2k}}P^{(2k)}(x) + \cdots \right.$ $\left. - \dfrac{s\cos sx}{(-s^2 + q)}\left[\dfrac{2P'(x)}{(-s^2 + q)} - \dfrac{4s^2 + 4q}{(-s^2 + q)^3}P'''(x) - \cdots \right. \right.$ $\left. \left. + (-1)^{k+1}\dfrac{\binom{2k}{1}s^{2k-2} + \binom{2k}{3}s^{2k-4}q + \cdots}{(-s^2 + q)^{2k-1}}P^{(2k-1)}(x) + \cdots \right] \right]$

TABLE IV: $(D^2 + b^2)y = R$

29. $\sin bx$*	$-\dfrac{x\cos bx}{2b}$
30. $P(x)\sin bx$*	$\dfrac{\sin bx}{(2b)^2}\left[P(x) - \dfrac{P''(x)}{(2b)^2} + \dfrac{P^{iv}(x)}{(2b)^4} - \cdots \right] - \dfrac{\cos bx}{2b}\int\left[P(x) - \dfrac{P''(x)}{(2b)^2} + \cdots \right]dx$

*For $\cos sx$ in R replace "sin" by "cos" and "cos" by "− sin" in y_p.

DIFFERENTIAL EQUATIONS (Continued)

TABLE V: $(D^2 + pD + q)y = R$

R	y_p
31. e^{rx}	$\dfrac{e^{rx}}{r^2 + pr + q}$
32. $\sin sx$*	$\dfrac{(q - s^2)\sin sx - ps\cos sx}{(q - s^2)^2 + (ps)^2} = \dfrac{1}{\sqrt{(q - s^2)^2 + (ps)^2}}\sin\left(sx - \tan^{-1}\dfrac{ps}{q - s^2}\right)$
33. $P(x)$	$\dfrac{1}{q}\Bigg[P(x) - \dfrac{p}{q}P'(x) + \dfrac{p^2 - q}{q^2}P''(x) - \dfrac{p^3 - 2pq}{q^3}P'''(x) + \cdots$ $+ (-1)^n\dfrac{p^n - \binom{n}{1}p^{n-2}q + \binom{n}{2}p^{n-4}q^2 - \cdots}{q^n}P^{(n)}(x)\Bigg]$
34. $e^{rx}\sin sx$*	Replace p by $p + 2r$, q by $q + pr + r^2$ in formula 32 and multiply by e^{rx}.
35. $P(x)e^{rx}$	Replace p by $p + 2r$, q by $q + pr + r^2$ in formula 33 and multiply by e^{rx}.

TABLE VI: $(D - b)(D - a)y = R$

R	y_p
36. $P(x)\sin sx$*	$\dfrac{\sin sx}{b - a}\left[\left(\dfrac{a}{a^2 + s^2} - \dfrac{b}{b^2 + s^2}\right)P(x) + \left(\dfrac{a^2 - s^2}{(a^2 + s^2)^2} - \dfrac{b^2 - s^2}{(b^2 + s^2)^2}\right)P'(x)\right.$ $\left. + \left(\dfrac{a^3 - 3as^2}{(a^2 + s^2)^3} - \dfrac{b^3 - 3bs^2}{(b^2 + s^2)^3}\right)P''(x) + \cdots\right]$ $+ \dfrac{\cos sx}{b - a}\left[\left(\dfrac{s}{a^2 + s^2} - \dfrac{s}{b^2 + s^2}\right)P(x) + \left(\dfrac{2as}{(a^2 + s^2)^2} - \dfrac{2bs}{(b^2 + s^2)^2}\right)P'(x)\right.$ $\left. + \left(\dfrac{3a^2s - s^3}{(a^2 + s^2)^3} - \dfrac{3b^2s - s^3}{(b^2 + s^2)^3}\right)P''(x) + \cdots\right]$
37. $P(x)e^{rx}\sin sx$*	Replace a by $a - r$, b by $b - r$ in formula 36 and multiply by e^{rx}.
38. $P(x)e^{ax}$	$\dfrac{e^{ax}}{a - b}\left[\displaystyle\int P(x)\,dx + \dfrac{P(x)}{b - a} + \dfrac{P'(x)}{(b - a)^2} + \dfrac{P''(x)}{(b - a)^3} + \cdots + \dfrac{P^{(n)}(x)}{(b - a)^{n+1}}\right]$†

* For $\cos sx$ in R replace "sin" by "cos" and "cos" by "$-$ sin" in y_p.

† For additional terms, compare with formula 6.

DIFFERENTIAL EQUATIONS (Continued)

TABLE VII: $(D^2 - 2aD + a^2 + b^2)y = R$

R	y_p

39. $P(x)\sin sx$*

$$y_p = \frac{\sin sx}{2b}\left[\left(\frac{s+b}{a^2+(s+b)^2} - \frac{s-b}{a^2+(s-b)^2}\right)P(x) + \left(\frac{2a(s+b)}{[a^2+(s+b)^2]^2} - \frac{2a(s-b)}{[a^2+(s-b)^2]^2}\right)P'(x)\right.$$

$$+ \left(\frac{3a^2(s+b)-(s+b)^3}{[a^2+(s+b)^2]^3} - \frac{3a^2(s-b)-(s-b)^3}{[a^2+(s-b)^2]^3}\right)P''(x) + \cdots\right]$$

$$-\frac{\cos sx}{2b}\left[\left(\frac{a}{a^2+(s+b)^2} - \frac{a}{a^2+(s-b)^2}\right)P(x) + \left(\frac{a^2-(s+b)^2}{[a^2+(s+b)^2]^2} - \frac{a^2-(s-b)^2}{[a^2+(s-b)^2]^2}\right)P'(x)\right.$$

$$+ \left.\left(\frac{a^3-3a(s+b)^2}{[a^2+(s+b)^2]^3} - \frac{a^3-3a(s-b)^2}{[a^2+(s-b)^2]^3}\right)P''(x) + \cdots\right]^\dagger$$

40. $P(x)e^{rx}\sin sx$*

Replace a by $a - r$ in formula 39 and multiply by e^{rx}.

41. $P(x)e^{ax}$

$$\frac{e^{ax}}{b^2}\left[P(x) - \frac{P''(x)}{b^2} + \frac{P^{iv}(x)}{b^4} - \cdots\right]$$

42. $e^{ax}\sin sx$*

$$\frac{e^{ax}\sin sx}{-s^2+b^2}$$

43. $e^{ax}\sin bx$‡

$$-\frac{xe^{ax}\cos bx}{2b}$$

44. $P(x)e^{ax}\sin bx$*

$$\frac{e^{ax}\sin bx}{(2b)^2}\left[P(x) - \frac{P''(x)}{(2b)^2} + \frac{P^{iv}(x)}{(2b)^4} - \cdots\right] - \frac{e^{ax}\cos bx}{2b}\int\left[P(x) - \frac{P''(x)}{(2b)^2} + \frac{P^{iv}(x)}{(2b)^4} - \cdots\right]dx$$

* For cos sx in R replace "sin" by "cos" and "cos" by "$-$ sin" in y_p.

† For additional terms, compare with formula 6.

DIFFERENTIAL EQUATIONS (Continued)

TABLE VIII: $f(D)y = [D^n + a_{n-1}D^{n-1} + \cdots + a_1D + a_0]y = R$

R	y_p
45. e^{rx}	$\dfrac{e^{rx}}{f(r)}$
46. $\sin sx^*$	$\dfrac{[a_0 - a_2s^2 + a_4s^4 - \cdots]\sin sx - [a_1s - a_3s^3 + a_5s^5 + \cdots]\cos sx}{[a_0 - a_2s^2 + a_4s^4 - \cdots]^2 + [a_1s - a_3s^3 + a_5s^5 - \cdots]^2}$

TABLE IX: $f(D^2)y = R$

47. $\sin sx^*$	$\dfrac{\sin sx}{f(-s^2)} = \dfrac{\sin sx}{a_0 - a_2s^2 + \cdots \pm s^{2n}}$

TABLE X: $(D - a)^n y = R$

48. e^{rx}	$\dfrac{e^{rx}}{(r - a)^n}$
49. $\sin sx^*$	$\dfrac{(-1)^n}{(a^2+s^2)^n}\big\{[a^n - \binom{n}{2}a^{n-2}s^2 + \binom{n}{4}a^{n-4}s^4 - \cdots]\sin sx + [\binom{n}{1}a^{n-1}s - \binom{n}{3}a^{n-3}s^3 + \cdots]\cos sx\big\}$
50. $P(x)$	$\dfrac{(-1)^n}{a^n}\left[P(x) + \binom{n}{1}\dfrac{P'(x)}{a} + \binom{n+1}{2}\dfrac{P''(x)}{a^2} + \binom{n+2}{3}\dfrac{P'''(x)}{a^3} + \cdots\right]$
51. $e^{rx}\sin sx^*$	Replace a by $a - r$ in formula 49 and multiply by e^{rx}.
52. $e^{rx}P(x)$	Replace a by $a - r$ in formula 50 and multiply by e^{rx}.

* For $\cos sx$ in R replace "sin" by "cos" and "cos" by "$-\sin$" in y_p.

DIFFERENTIAL EQUATIONS (Continued)

53. $P(x)\sin sx$*

$(-1)^n \sin sx[A_n P(x) + \binom{n}{1}A_{n+1}P'(x) + \binom{n}{2}A_{n+2}P''(x) + \binom{n}{3}A_{n+3}P'''(x) + \cdots]$
$+ (-1)^n \cos sx[B_n P(x) + \binom{n}{1}B_{n+1}P'(x) + \binom{n}{2}B_{n+2}P''(x) + \binom{n}{3}B_{n+3}P'''(x) + \cdots]$

$A_1 = \dfrac{a}{a^2+s^2}$, $A_2 = \dfrac{a^2-s^2}{(a^2+s^2)^2}$, $\cdots$, $A_k = \dfrac{a^k - \binom{k}{2}a^{k-2}s^2 + \binom{k}{4}a^{k-4}s^4 - \cdots}{(a^2+s^2)^k}$

$B_1 = \dfrac{s}{a^2+s^2}$, $B_2 = \dfrac{2as}{(a^2+s^2)^2}$, $\cdots$, $B_k = \dfrac{\binom{k}{1}a^{k-1}s - \binom{k}{3}a^{k-3}s^3 + \cdots}{(a^2+s^2)^k}$

54. $P(x)e^{ax}\sin sx$* Replace a by $a - r$ in formula 53 and multiply by e^{rx}.

55. $e^{ax}P(x)$ $\qquad e^{ax}\underbrace{\int\int \cdots \int}_{n}P(x)\,dx^n$

56. $P(x)e^{ax}\sin sx$*

$\dfrac{(-1)^{\frac{n-1}{2}}e^{ax}\sin sx}{s^n}\left[\binom{n}{n-1}\dfrac{P'(x)}{s} - \binom{n+2}{n-1}\dfrac{P'''(x)}{s^3} + \binom{n+4}{n-1}\dfrac{P^v(x)}{s^5} - \cdots\right]$
$+ \dfrac{(-1)^{\frac{n+1}{2}}e^{ax}\cos sx}{s^n}\left[\binom{n-1}{n-1}P(x) - \binom{n+1}{n-1}\dfrac{P''(x)}{s^2} + \binom{n+3}{n-1}\dfrac{P^{iv}(x)}{s^4} - \cdots\right]$ (n odd)

$\dfrac{(-1)^{\frac{n}{2}}e^{ax}\sin sx}{s^n}\left[\binom{n-1}{n-1}P(x) - \binom{n+1}{n-1}\dfrac{P''(x)}{s^2} + \binom{n+3}{n-1}\dfrac{P^{iv}(x)}{s^4} - \cdots\right]$
$+ \dfrac{(-1)^{\frac{n}{2}}e^{ax}\cos sx}{s^n}\left[\binom{n}{n-1}\dfrac{P'(x)}{s} - \binom{n+2}{n-1}\dfrac{P'''(x)}{s^3} + \binom{n+4}{n-1}\dfrac{P^v(x)}{s^5} - \cdots\right]$ (n even)

TABLE XI: $(D - a)^r f(D)y = R$

57. e^{ax} $\qquad \dfrac{x^n}{n!}\cdot\dfrac{e^{ax}}{f(a)}$

* For cos sx in R replace "sin" by "cos" and "cos" by "− sin" in y_p.

DIFFERENTIAL EQUATIONS (Continued)

TABLE XII: $(D^2 + q)^n y = R$

R	y_p
58. e^{rx}	$e^{rx}/(r^2 + q)^n$
59. $\sin sx$*	$\sin sx/(q - s^2)^n$
60. $P(x)$	$\dfrac{1}{q^n}\left[P(x) - \binom{n}{1}\dfrac{P''(x)}{q} + \binom{n+1}{2}\dfrac{P^{iv}(x)}{q^2} - \binom{n+2}{3}\dfrac{P^{vi}(x)}{q^3} + \cdots\right]$
61. $e^{rx}\sin sx$*	$\dfrac{e^{rx}}{(A^2 + B^2)^n}\{[A^n - \binom{n}{2}A^{n-2}B^2 + \binom{n}{4}A^{n-4}B^4 - \cdots]\sin sx - [\binom{n}{1}A^{n-1}B - \binom{n}{3}A^{n-3}B^3 + \cdots]\cos sx\}$

$$A = r^2 - s^2 + q, \qquad B = 2rs$$

TABLE XIII: $(D^2 + b^2)^n y = R$

62. $\sin bx$*	$(-1)^{\frac{n+1}{2}}\dfrac{x^n \cos bx}{n!(2b)^n}$ (n odd), $\qquad (-1)^{\frac{n}{2}}\dfrac{x^n \sin bx}{n!(2b)^n}$ (n even)

TABLE XIV: $(D^n - q)y = R$

63. e^{rx}	$e^{rx}/(r^n - q)$
64. $P(x)$	$-\dfrac{1}{q}\left[P(x) + \dfrac{P^{(n)}(x)}{q} + \dfrac{P^{(2n)}(x)}{q^2} + \cdots\right]$
65. $\sin sx$*	$-\dfrac{q\sin sx + (-1)^{\frac{n-1}{2}}s^n\cos sx}{q^2 + s^{2n}}$ (n odd), $\qquad \dfrac{\sin sx}{(-s^2)^{n/2} - q}$ (n even)
66. $e^{rx}\sin sx$*	$\dfrac{Ae^{rx}\sin sx - Be^{rx}\cos sx}{A^2 + B^2} = \dfrac{e^{rx}}{\sqrt{A^2 + B^2}}\sin\left(sx - \tan^{-1}\dfrac{B}{A}\right)$

$$A = [r^n - \binom{n}{2}r^{n-2}s^2 + \binom{n}{4}r^{n-4}s^4 - \cdots] - q, \qquad B = [\binom{n}{1}r^{n-1}s - \binom{n}{3}r^{n-3}s^3 + \cdots]$$

* For cos sx in R replace "sin" by "cos" and "cos" by "− sin" in y_p.

DIFFERENTIAL EQUATIONS (Continued)

TABLE XV: $(D_x + mD_y)z = R$

R	z_p
67. e^{ax+by}	$\dfrac{e^{ax+by}}{a+mb}$
68. $f(ax+by)$	$\dfrac{\int f(u)du}{a+mb},\ u = ax + by$
69. $f(y-mx)$	$xf(y-mx)$
70. $\phi(x,y)f(y-mx)$	$f(y-mx)\int \phi(x, a+mx)dx \quad (a = y - mx$ after integration)

TABLE XVI: $(D_x + mD_y - k)z = R$

71. e^{ax+by}	$\dfrac{e^{ax+by}}{a+mb-k}$
72. $\sin(ax+by)$*	$-\dfrac{(a+bm)\cos(ax+by) + k\sin(ax+by)}{(a+bm)^2 + k^2}$
73. $e^{\alpha x+\beta y}\sin(ax+by)$*	Replace k in 72 by $k - \alpha - m\beta$ and multiply by $e^{\alpha x+\beta y}$
74. $e^{kx}f(ax+by)$	$\dfrac{e^{kx}\int f(u)du}{a+mb},\ u = ax + by$
75. $f(y-mx)$	$-\dfrac{f(y-mx)}{k}$
76. $P(x)f(y-mx)$	$-\dfrac{1}{k}f(y-mx)\left[P(x) + \dfrac{P'(x)}{k} + \dfrac{P''(x)}{k^2} + \cdots + \dfrac{P^{(n)}(x)}{k^n} \right]$
77. $e^{kx}f(y-mx)$	$xe^{kx}f(y-mx)$

* For $\cos(ax+by)$ replace "sin" by "cos," and "cos" by "$-\sin$" in z_p.

$$D_x = \frac{\partial}{\partial x}; \quad D_y = \frac{\partial}{\partial y}; \quad D_x^k D_y^r = \frac{\partial^{k+r}}{\partial_x^k \partial_y^r}.$$

DIFFERENTIAL EQUATIONS (Continued)

TABLE XVII: $(D_x + mD_y)^n z = R$

R	z_p
78. e^{ax+by}	$\dfrac{e^{ax+by}}{(a+mb)^n}$
79. $f(ax+by)$	$\dfrac{\int\int\cdots\int f(u)du^n}{(a+mb)^n}$, $\quad u = ax + by$
80. $f(y-mx)$	$\dfrac{x^n}{n!}f(y-mx)$
81. $\phi(x,y)f(y+mx)$	$f(y-mx)\int\int\cdots\int \phi(x, a+mx)dx^n \quad (a = y - mx \text{ after integration})$

TABLE XVIII: $(D_x + mD_y - k)^n z = R$

R	z_p
82. e^{ax+by}	$\dfrac{e^{ax+by}}{(a+mb-k)^n}$
83. $f(y-mx)$	$\dfrac{(-1)^n f(y-mx)}{k^n}$
84. $P(x)f(y-mx)$	$\dfrac{(-1)^n}{k^n}f(y-mx)\left[P(x) + \binom{n}{1}\dfrac{P'(x)}{k} + \binom{n+1}{2}\dfrac{P''(x)}{k^2} + \binom{n+2}{3}\dfrac{P'''(x)}{k^3} + \cdots\right]$
85. $e^{ax}f(ax+by)$	$\dfrac{e^{ax}\int\int\cdots\int f(u)du^n}{(a+mb)^n}$, $\quad u = ax + by$
86. $e^{ax}f(y-mx)$	$\dfrac{x^n}{n!}e^{ax}f(y-mx)$

DIFFERENTIAL EQUATIONS (Continued)

TABLE XIX: $[D_x^n + a_1 D_x^{n-1}D_y + a_2 D_x^{n-2}D_y^2 + \cdots + a^n D_y^n]z = R$

87. e^{ax+by}
$$\frac{e^{ax+by}}{a + a_1 a^{n-1}b + a_2 a^{n-2}b^2 + \cdots + a_n b^n}$$

88. $f(ax+by)$
$$\frac{\int\int \cdots \int f(u)du^n}{a^n + a_1 a^{n-1}b + a_2 a^{n-2}b^2 + \cdots + a^n b^n}, \quad (u = ax + by)$$

TABLE XX: $F(D_x, D_y)z = R$

89. e^{ax+by}
$$\frac{e^{ax+by}}{F(a, b)}$$

TABLE XXI: $F(D_x^2, D_x D_y, D_y^2)z = R$

90. $\sin(ax + by)$*
$$\frac{\sin(ax + by)}{F(-a^2, -ab, -b^2)}$$

* For $\cos(ax + by)$ replace "sin" by "cos", and "cos" by " $-\sin$" in z_r.

X. SPECIAL FUNCTIONS
COMPLEX VARIABLES

Complex Numbers
Cartesian Form

The cartesian form of a complex number is $z = x + iy$, where x and y are real numbers and i, called the imaginary unit, has the property that $i^2 = -1$. The real numbers x and y are called the real and imaginary parts of $x + iy$, respectively.

Polar Form

$z = re^{i\theta} = r(\cos\theta + i\sin\theta)$

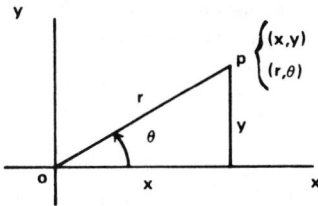

Modulus

$$r = |z| = (x^2 + y^2)^{1/2}$$

Argument

$$\theta = \arg z = \arctan\frac{y}{x}$$

Complex Conjugate

$$\bar{z} = x - iy, \quad |\bar{z}| = |z|, \quad \arg\bar{z} = -\arg z$$

Addition and Subtraction

$$z_1 \pm z_2 = (x_1 + iy_1) \pm (x_2 + iy_2) = (x_1 \pm x_2) + (y_1 \pm y_2)$$

Multiplication

$$z_1 z_2 = (x_1 + iy_1)(x_2 + iy_2) = (x_1 x_2 - y_1 y_2) + i(x_1 y_2 + x_2 y_1)$$

$$|z_1 z_2| = |z_1||z_2|, \quad \arg(z_1 z_2) = \arg z_1 + \arg z_2$$

Division

$$\frac{z_1}{z_2} = \frac{z_1 \bar{z}_2}{z_2 \bar{z}_2} = \frac{(x_1 x_2 + y_1 y_2) + i(x_2 y_1 - x_1 y_2)}{x_2^2 + y_2^2}$$

$$\left|\frac{z_1}{z_2}\right| = \frac{|z_1|}{|z_2|}, \quad \arg\left(\frac{z_1}{z_2}\right) = \arg z_1 - \arg z_2$$

Powers

$$z^n = r^n e^{in\theta} = r^n (\cos n\theta + i \sin n\theta) \quad \text{(DeMoivre's Theorem)}$$

Roots

$$z^{\frac{1}{n}} = r^{\frac{1}{n}} e^{i\theta/n} = r^{\frac{1}{n}} \left[\cos \frac{\theta + 2k\pi}{n} + i \sin \frac{\theta + 2k\pi}{n} , k = 1, 2, \ldots, n - 1 \right]$$

(Principal root if $-\pi < \theta < \pi$)

Functions of a Complex Variable
A complex function

$$w = f(z) = u(x, y) + iv(x, y) = |w| e^{i\phi}$$

$$(z = x + iy = |z| e^{i\theta})$$

associates one or more values of the complex dependent variable w with each value of the complex independent variable z in a given domain of definition.

Cauchy-Riemann Equations

$$\frac{\partial u}{\partial x} = \frac{\partial v}{\partial y} , \quad \frac{\partial u}{\partial y} = - \frac{\partial v}{\partial x}$$

A function $w = f(z)$ differentiable at each point of a certain neighborhood of a point z_o (i.e., at each point of a circle with center z_o and an arbitrary small radius) is said to be analytic at the point z_o. A function is called analytic in a connected domain if it is analytic at each point in the domain.

A necessary and sufficient condition that the function $f(z) = u(x,y) + iv(x,y)$ is analytic is that it satisfy the Cauchy-Riemann conditions.

Cauchy-Goursat Theorem
If a function $f(z)$ is analytic at all points within and on a simple closed curve C, then

$$\int_c f(z) \, dz = 0$$

Cauchy's Integral Formula
If $f(z)$ is analytic inside and on a simple closed curve C and if z_o is interior to C, then

$$F(z_0) = \frac{1}{2\pi i} \int_c \frac{f(z)}{z - z_0} \, dz$$

Also, the derivatives $f'(z), f''(z), \ldots$ of all orders exist, and

$$F^{(n)}(z_0) = \frac{n!}{2\pi i} \int_c \frac{f(z)}{(z - z_0)^{n+1}} \, dz$$

Taylor-Series Expansion

If f(z) is analytic inside and on a circle C of radius r about z = z_o, then there exists a unique and uniformly convergent series expansion in powers of z − z_o,

$$f(z) = \sum_{n=0}^{\infty} a_n (z - z_0)^n, \quad (|z - z_0| \leqslant r, z_0 \neq \infty)$$

where

$$a_n = \frac{1}{n!} f^n(z_0) = \frac{1}{2\pi i} \int_c \frac{f(s)}{(s - z_0)^{n+1}} ds$$

If M(r) is an upper bound on |f(z)| on C, then

$$|a_n| = \frac{1}{n!} |f^{(n)}(z_0)| < \frac{M(r)}{r^n} \quad \text{(Cauchy's Inequality)}$$

If Taylor's series is terminated with the term $a_{n-1} (z - z_o)^{n-1}$, the remainder $R_n(z)$ is given by

$$R_n(z) = \frac{(z - z_0)^n}{2\pi i} \int_c \frac{f(s)\, ds}{(s - z_0)^n (s - z)}$$

$$|R_n(z)| < \left(\frac{|z - z_0|}{r}\right)^n \frac{M(r)\, r}{r - |z - z_0|}$$

Laurent-Series Expansion

If f(z) is analytic throughout the annular region between and on the concentric circles C_1 and C_2 centered at z = z_o and radii r_1 and $r_2 < r_1$, respectively, there exists a unique series expansion in terms of positive and negative powers of z − z_o

$$f(z) = \sum_{n=0}^{\infty} a_n (z - z_0)^n + \sum_{n=1}^{\infty} b_n (z - z_0)^{-n}$$

where

$$a_n = \frac{1}{2\pi i} \int_c \frac{f(s)}{(s - z_0)^{n+1}} ds, \qquad b_n = \frac{1}{2\pi i} \int_c \frac{f(s)}{(s - z_0)^{-n+1}} ds$$

$$(n = 0, 1, 2, \ldots) \qquad\qquad (n = 1, 2, \ldots)$$

Zeros and Isolated Singularities

Zeros

The points z for which f(z) = 0 are called the zeros of f(z). A function f(z) analytic at z = z_o has a zero of order m, where m is a positive integer at z = z_o if and only if the first m coefficients a_o, a_1,..., a_{m-1} in the Taylor-series expansion about z = z_0 vanish.

Singularities

A singular point or singularity of the function f(z) is any point where f(z) is not analytic. An isolated singularity of f(z) at z = z_0 is

1. A removable singularity if and only if all coefficients b_n in the Laurent-series expansion of $f(z)$ about $z = z_0$ vanish.
2. A pole of order m (m = 1,2,...) if and only if $(z - z_0)^m f(z)$, but not $(z - z_0)^{m-1} f(z)$ is analytic at $z = z_0$, i.e., if and only if $b_m \neq 0$, $b_{m+1} = b_{m+2} = ... = 0$ in the Laurent-series expansion of $f(z)$ about $z = z_0$, or if $\frac{1}{f(z)}$ is analytic and has a zero of order m at $z = z_0$.
3. An isolated essential singularity if and only if the Laurent-series expansion of $f(z)$ about $z = z_0$ has an infinite number of terms involving negative powers of $z - z_0$.

Residues

Given a point $z = z_0$, where $f(z)$ is either analytic or has an isolated singularity, the residue of $f(z)$ at $z = z_0$ is the coefficient of $(z - z_0)^{-1}$ in the Laurent-series expansion of $f(z)$ about $z = z_0$, or

$$R_k = b_1 = \frac{1}{2\pi i} \int_C f(z)\, dz$$

If $f(z)$ is either analytic or has a removable singularity at $z = z_0$, then $b_1 = 0$. If $z = z_0$ is a pole of order m, then

$$b_1 = \frac{1}{(m-1)!} \frac{d^{m-1}}{dz^{m-1}} [(z - z_0)^m f(z)]_{z = z_0}$$

For every simple closed contour C enclosing at most a finite number of singularities $z_1, z_2, ..., z_n$ of a single-valued function $f(z)$ continuous on C,

$$\frac{1}{2\pi i} \int_C f(z)\, dz = \sum_{k=1}^{n} R_k$$

where the R_k are the residues of $f(z)$ at the singularities.

Mappings or Transformations

A function $w = f(z)$ maps points of the z-plane into corresponding points of the w-plane. At every point z such that $f(z)$ is analytic and $f'(z) \neq 0$, the mapping is conformal, i.e., the angle between two curves through such a point is reproduced in magnitude and sense by the angle between the corresponding curves in the w-plane.

A table giving real and imaginary parts, zeros, and singularities for frequently used functions of a complex variable and a table illustrating a number of special transformations of interest in various applications are provided.

Real and Imaginary Parts, Zeros, and Singularities for a Number of Frequently Used Functions

$$f(z) = u(x,y) + iv(x,y) \quad \text{of a Complex Variable } z = x + iy$$

Note: $|f(z)| = \sqrt{u^2 + v^2}$, $\quad \arg f(z) = \arctan \dfrac{v}{u}$

Function $f(z)$	$u(x,y)$	$v(x,y)$	Zeros (order m)	Isolated singularities
z	x	y	$z=0 \quad m=1$	Pole ($m=1$) at $z=\infty$
z^2	$x^2 - y^2$	$2xy$	$z=0 \quad m=2$	Pole ($m=2$) at $z=\infty$
$\dfrac{1}{z}$	$\dfrac{x}{x^2+y^2}$	$-\dfrac{y}{x^2+y^2}$	$z=\infty \quad m=1$	Pole ($m=1$) at $z=0$
$\dfrac{1}{z^2}$	$\dfrac{x^2-y^2}{(x^2+y^2)^2}$	$\dfrac{-2xy}{(x^2+y^2)^2}$	$z=\infty \quad m=2$	Pole ($m=2$) at $z=0$
$\dfrac{1}{z-(a+ib)}$ (a,b real)	$\dfrac{(x-a)}{(x-a)^2+(y-b)^2}$	$-\dfrac{(y-b)}{(x-a)^2+(y-b)^2}$	$z=\infty \quad m=1$	Pole ($m=1$) at $z=a+ib$
$\sqrt{z}$	$\pm\left(\dfrac{x+\sqrt{x^2+y^2}}{2}\right)^{1/2}$	$\pm\left(\dfrac{-x+\sqrt{x^2+y^2}}{2}\right)^{1/2}$	Zero of order 1 at $z=0$ (branch point)	Branch point ($m=1$) at $z=0$; Branch point ($m=1$) at $z=\infty$
e^z	$e^x \cos y$	$e^x \sin y$	. . . .	Essential singularity at $z=\infty$
$\sin z$	$\sin x \cosh y$	$\cos x \sinh y$	$z=k\pi \quad m=1$ ($k=0,\pm1,\pm2,\pm\ldots$)	Essential singularity at $z=\infty$
$\cos z$	$\cos x \cosh y$	$-\sin x \sinh y$	$z=(k+\tfrac12)\pi \quad m=1$ ($k=0,\pm1,\pm2,\pm\ldots$)	Essential singularity at $z=\infty$

Real and Imaginary Parts, Zeros, and Singularities for a Number of Frequently Used Functions

$$f(z) = u(x,y) + iv(x,y) \text{ of a Complex Variable } z = x + iy$$

Function $f(z)$	$u(x,y)$	$v(x,y)$	Zeros (order m)	Isolated singularities
$\sinh z$	$\sinh x \cos y$	$\cosh x \sin y$	$z = k\pi i$ $m = 1$ $(k = 0, \pm 1, \pm 2, \pm \ldots)$	Essential singularity at $z = \infty$
$\cosh z$	$\cosh x \cos y$	$\sinh x \sin y$	$z = (k + \tfrac{1}{2})\pi i$ $m = 1$ $(k = 0, \pm 1, \pm 2, \pm \ldots)$	Essential singularity at $z = \infty$
$\tan z$	$\dfrac{\sin 2x}{\cos 2x + \cosh 2y}$	$\dfrac{\sinh 2y}{\cos 2x + \cosh 2y}$	$z = k\pi$ $m = 1$ $(k = 0, \pm 1, \pm 2, \pm \ldots)$	Essential singularity at $z = \infty$ Poles $(m = 1)$ at $z = (k + \tfrac{1}{2})\pi$ $(k = 0, \pm 1, \pm 2, \pm \ldots)$
$\tanh z$	$\dfrac{\sinh 2x}{\cosh 2x + \cos 2y}$	$\dfrac{\sin 2y}{\cosh 2x + \cos 2y}$	$z = k\pi i$ $m = 1$ $(k = 0, \pm 1, \pm 2, \pm \ldots)$	Essential singularity at $z = \infty$ Poles $(m = 1)$ at $z = (k + \tfrac{1}{2})\pi i$ $(k = 0, \pm 1, \pm 2, \pm \ldots)$
$\log_e z$	$\tfrac{1}{2} \log_e (x^2 + y^2)$	$\arctan \dfrac{y}{x} + 2k\pi$ $(k = 0, \pm 1, \pm 2, + \ldots)$	$z = 1$ $m = 1$ (branch corresponding to $k = 0$ only)	Branch points of infinite order at $z = 0$, $z = \infty$; both are essential singularities

From Korn, G. A. and Korn, T. M., *Mathematical Handbook for Scientists & Engineers*, 2nd ed., McGraw-Hill, New York, 1968, 189. With permission.

Table of Transformations of Regions

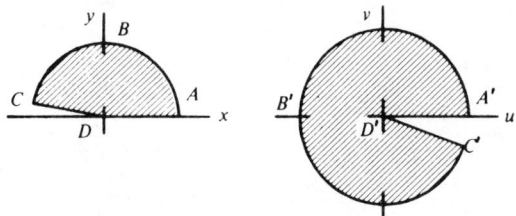

FIGURE 1. $\omega = z^2$.

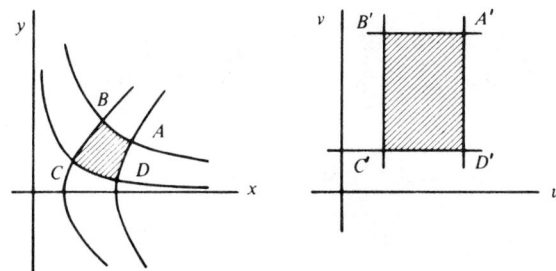

FIGURE 2. $\omega = z^2$.

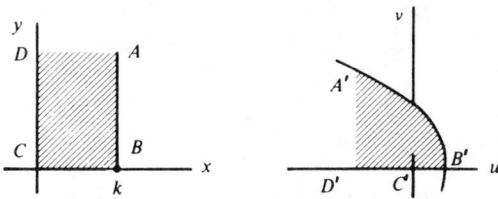

FIGURE 3. $\omega = z^2$; A′ B′ on parabola $\rho = \dfrac{2\,k^2}{1 + \cos \phi}$

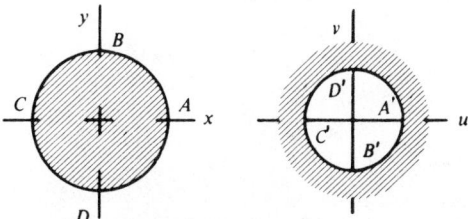

FIGURE 4. $\omega = 1/z$.

(From Churchill, R. V., Brown, J. W., and Verhey, R. F., *Complex Variables and Applications*, 34d ed., McGraw-Hill, New York, 1974, 314 – 324. With permission.)

Table of Transformations of Regions (continued)

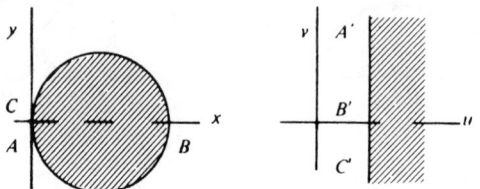

FIGURE 5. $\omega = 1/z$.

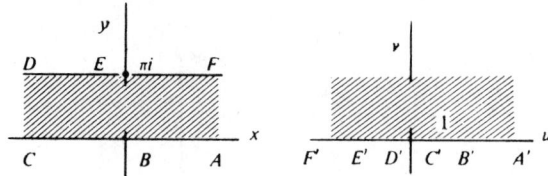

FIGURE 6. $\omega = e^z$.

FIGURE 7. $\omega = e^z$.

FIGURE 8. $\omega = e^z$.

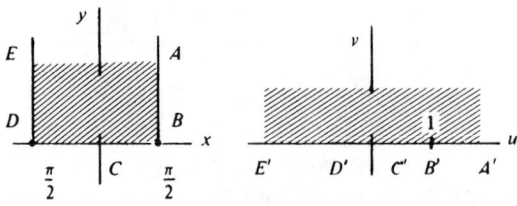

FIGURE 9. $\omega = \sin z$.

Table of Transformations of Regions (continued)

FIGURE 10. $\omega = \sin z$.

FIGURE 11. $\omega = \sin z$; BCD: $y = k$, $B'\, C'\, D'$ is on ellipse $\left(\dfrac{u}{\cosh k}\right)^2 + \left(\dfrac{v}{\sinh k}\right)^2 = 1$.

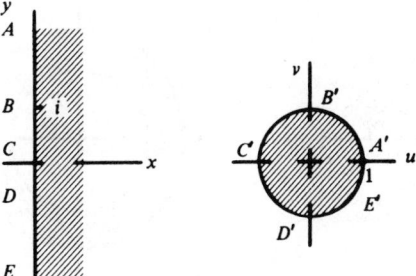

FIGURE 12. $\omega = \dfrac{z-1}{z+1}$.

FIGURE 13. $\omega = \dfrac{i-z}{i+z}$.

Table of Transformations of Regions (continued)

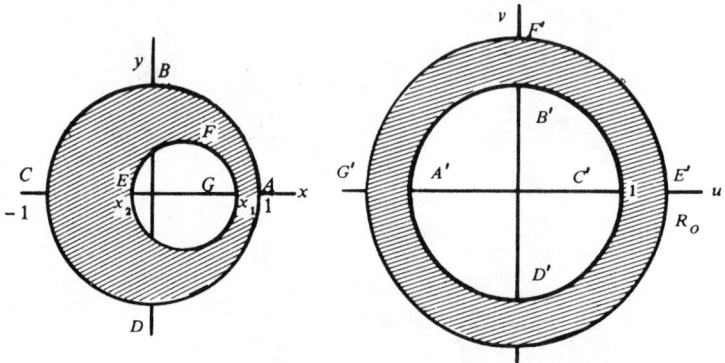

FIGURE 14. $\omega = \dfrac{z-a}{az-1}$; $a = \dfrac{1 + x_1 x_2 + \sqrt{(1 - x_1^2)(1 - x_2^2)}}{x_1 + x_2}$;

$R_0 = \dfrac{1 - x_1 x_2 + \sqrt{(1 - x_1^2)(1 - x_2^2)}}{x_1 - x_2}$ $\quad$ (a > 1 and R_0 > 1 when $-1 < x_2 < x_1 < 1$).

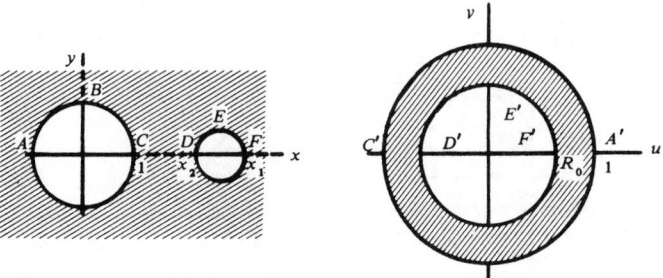

FIGURE 15. $\omega = \dfrac{z-a}{az-1}$; $a = \dfrac{1 + x_1 x_2 + \sqrt{(x_1^2 - 1)(x_2^2 - 1)}}{x_1 + x_2}$;

$R_0 = \dfrac{x_1 x_2 - 1 - \sqrt{(x_1^2 - 1)(x_2^2 - 1)}}{x_1 - x_2}$ $\quad$ ($x_2 < a < x_1$ and $0 < R_0 < 1$ when $1 < x_2 < x_1$).

FIGURE 16. $\omega = z + 1/z$.

Table of Transformations of Regions (continued)

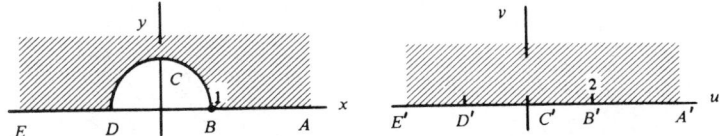

FIGURE 17. $\omega = z + 1/z$.

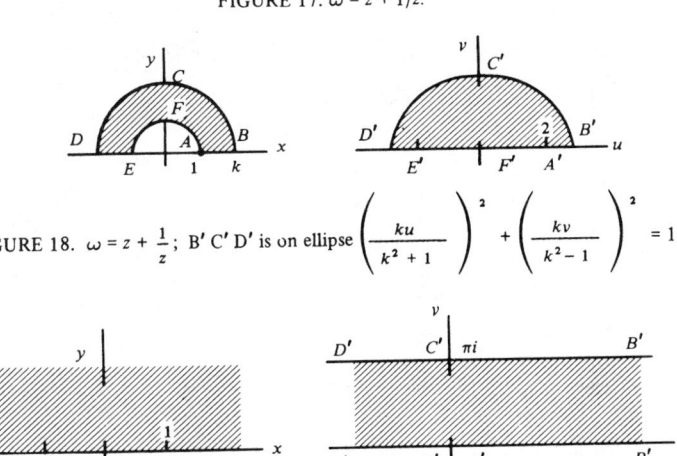

FIGURE 18. $\omega = z + \dfrac{1}{z}$; $B'\,C'\,D'$ is on ellipse $\left(\dfrac{ku}{k^2 + 1}\right)^2 + \left(\dfrac{kv}{k^2 - 1}\right)^2 = 1$.

FIGURE 19. $\omega = \log_e \dfrac{z - 1}{z + 1}$; $z = -\coth \dfrac{\omega}{2}$.

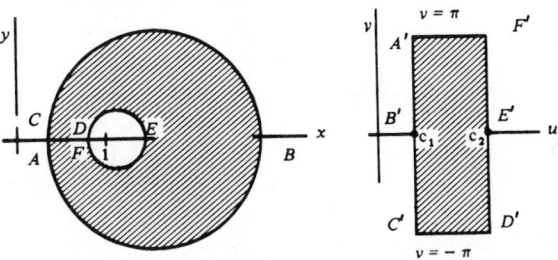

FIGURE 20. $\omega = \log_e \dfrac{z - 1}{z + 1}$; ABC is on circle $x^2 + y^2 - 2y \cot k = 1$.

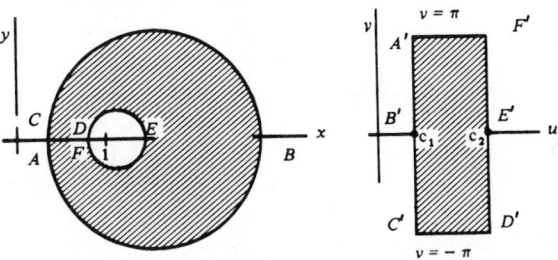

FIGURE 21. $\omega = \log_e \dfrac{z + 1}{z - 1}$; centers of circles at $z = \coth c_n$, radii: $\operatorname{csch} c_n$ $(n = 1, 2)$.

Table of Transformations of Regions (continued)

FIGURE 22. $\omega = k \log_e \dfrac{k}{1-k} + \log_e 2\,(1-k) + i\pi - k\log_e(z+1)$

$- (1-k)\log_e(z-1);\ x_1 = 2k-1.$

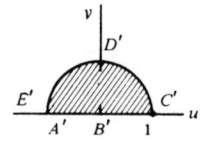

FIGURE 23. $\omega = \tan^2 \dfrac{z}{2} = \dfrac{1-\cos z}{1+\cos z}$

FIGURE 24. $\omega = \coth \dfrac{z}{2} = \dfrac{e^z+1}{e^z-1}$.

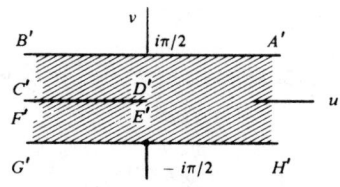

FIGURE 25. $\omega = \log_e \coth \dfrac{z}{2}.$

FIGURE 26. $\omega = \pi i + z - \log_e z.$

Table of Transformations of Regions (continued)

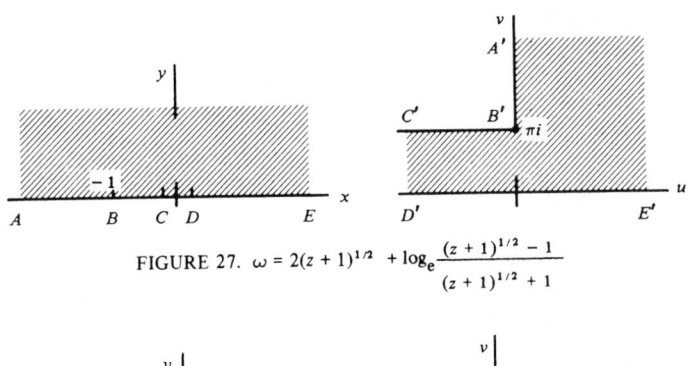

FIGURE 27. $\omega = 2(z + 1)^{1/2} + \log_e \dfrac{(z + 1)^{1/2} - 1}{(z + 1)^{1/2} + 1}$

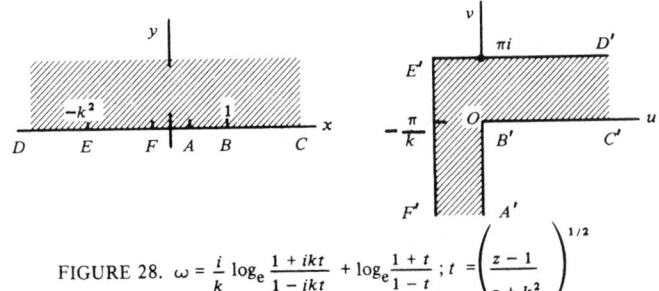

FIGURE 28. $\omega = \dfrac{i}{k} \log_e \dfrac{1 + ikt}{1 - ikt} + \log_e \dfrac{1 + t}{1 - t} \; ; t = \left(\dfrac{z - 1}{z + k^2} \right)^{1/2}$

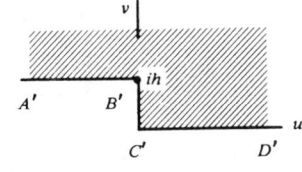

FIGURE 29. $\omega = \dfrac{h}{\pi}[(z^2 - 1)^{1/2} + \cosh^{-1} z]$.

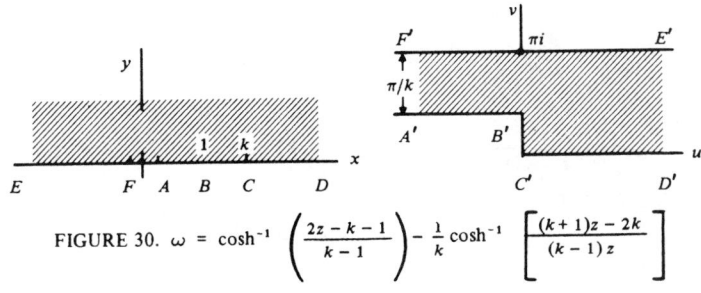

FIGURE 30. $\omega = \cosh^{-1} \left(\dfrac{2z - k - 1}{k - 1} \right) - \dfrac{1}{k} \cosh^{-1} \left[\dfrac{(k + 1)z - 2k}{(k - 1)z} \right]$

The Gamma Function

Definition: $\Gamma(n) = \int_0^\infty t^{n-1} e^{-t} dt \quad n > 0$

Recursion Formula: $\Gamma(n + 1) = n\Gamma(n)$

$\Gamma(n + 1) = n!$ if $n = 0,1,2,\ldots$ where $0! = 1$

For $n < 0$ the gamma function can be defined by using

$$\Gamma(n) = \frac{\Gamma(n + 1)}{n}$$

Graph:

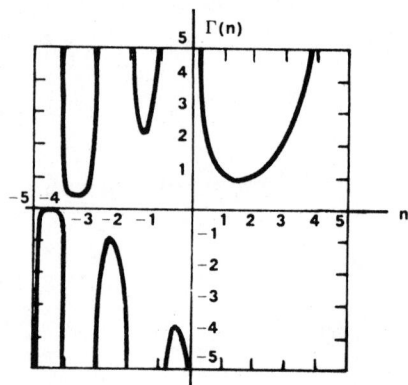

Special Values: $\Gamma(\tfrac{1}{2}) = \sqrt{\pi}$

$$\Gamma(m + \tfrac{1}{2}) = \frac{1 \cdot 3 \cdot 5 \cdots (2m - 1)}{2^m} \sqrt{\pi} \qquad m = 1,2,3,\ldots$$

$$\Gamma(-m + \tfrac{1}{2}) = \frac{(-1)^m 2^m \sqrt{\pi}}{1 \cdot 3 \cdot 5 \cdots (2m - 1)} \qquad m = 1,2,3,\ldots$$

Definition: $\Gamma(x + 1) = \lim\limits_{k \to \infty} \dfrac{1 \cdot 2 \cdot 3 \cdots k}{(x + 1)(x + 2) \cdots (x + k)} k^x$

$$\frac{1}{\Gamma(x)} = xe^{\gamma x} \prod_{m=1}^{\infty} \left\{ \left(1 + \frac{x}{m}\right) e^{-x/m} \right\}$$

This is an infinite product representation for the gamma function where γ is Euler's constant.

Properties:

$$\Gamma'(1) = \int_0^\infty e^{-x} \ln x \, dx = -\gamma$$

$$\frac{\Gamma'(x)}{\Gamma(x)} = -\gamma + \left(\frac{1}{1} - \frac{1}{x}\right) + \left(\frac{1}{2} - \frac{1}{x+1}\right) + \dots + \left(\frac{1}{n} - \frac{1}{x+n-1}\right) + \dots$$

$$\Gamma(x+1) = \sqrt{2\pi x} \; x^x e^{-x} \left\{1 + \frac{1}{12x} + \frac{1}{288x^2} - \frac{139}{51,840x^3} + \dots\right\}$$

This is called *Stirling's asymptotic series.*

If we let $x = n$ a positive integer, then a useful approximation for $n!$ where n is large [e.g. $n > 10$] is given by *Stirling's formula*

$$n! \approx \sqrt{2\pi n} \; n^n e^{-n}$$

GAMMA FUNCTION*

Values of $\Gamma(n) = \int_0^\infty e^{-x} x^{n-1} \, dx; \; \Gamma(n+1) = n\Gamma(n)$

n	$\Gamma(n)$	n	$\Gamma(n)$	n	$\Gamma(n)$	n	$\Gamma(n)$
1.00	1.00000	1.25	.90640	1.50	.88623	1.75	.91906
1.01	.99433	1.26	.90440	1.51	.88659	1.76	.92137
1.02	.98884	1.27	.90250	1.52	.88704	1.77	.92376
1.03	.98355	1.28	.90072	1.53	.88757	1.78	.92623
1.04	.97844	1.29	.89904	1.54	.88818	1.79	.92877
1.05	.97350	1.30	.89747	1.55	.88887	1.80	.93138
1.06	.96874	1.31	.89600	1.56	.88964	1.81	.93408
1.07	.96415	1.32	.89464	1.57	.89049	1.82	.93685
1.08	.95973	1.33	.89338	1.58	.89142	1.83	.93969
1.09	.95546	1.34	.89222	1.59	.89243	1.84	.94261
1.10	.95135	1.35	.89115	1.60	.89352	1.85	.94561
1.11	.94740	1.36	.89018	1.61	.89468	1.86	.94869
1.12	.94359	1.37	.88931	1.62	.89592	1.87	.95184
1.13	.93993	1.38	.88854	1.63	.89724	1.88	.95507
1.14	.93642	1.39	.88785	1.64	.89864	1.89	.95838
1.15	.93304	1.40	.88726	1.65	.90012	1.90	.96177
1.16	.92980	1.41	.88676	1.66	.90167	1.91	.96523
1.17	.92670	1.42	.88636	1.67	.90330	1.92	.96877
1.18	.92373	1.43	.88604	1.68	.90500	1.93	.97240
1.19	.92089	1.44	.88581	1.69	.90678	1.94	.97610
1.20	.91817	1.45	.88566	1.70	.90864	1.95	.97988
1.21	.91558	1.46	.88560	1.71	.91057	1.96	.98374
1.22	.91311	1.47	.88563	1.72	.91258	1.97	.98768
1.23	.91075	1.48	.88575	1.73	.91466	1.98	.99171
1.24	.90852	1.49	.88595	1.74	.91683	1.99	.99581
						2.00	1.00000

* For large positive values of x, $\Gamma(x)$ approximates Stirling's asymptotic series

$$x^x e^{-x} \sqrt{\frac{2\pi}{x}} \left[1 + \frac{1}{12x} + \frac{1}{288x^2} - \frac{139}{51840x^3} - \frac{571}{2488320x^4} + \dots\right]$$

The Beta Function

Definition: $B(m,n) = \int_0^1 t^{m-1}(1-t)^{n-1} dt \quad m > 0, n > 0$

Relationship with
Gamma Function $\qquad B(m,n) = \dfrac{\Gamma(m)\Gamma(n)}{\Gamma(m+n)}$

Properties:

$$B(m,n) = B(n,m)$$

$$B(m,n) = 2 \int_0^{\pi/2} \sin^{2m-1}\theta \, \cos^{2n-1}\theta \, d\theta$$

$$B(m,n) = \int_0^\infty \frac{t^{m-1}}{(1+t)^{m+n}} dt$$

$$B(m,n) = r^n(r+1)^m \int_0^1 \frac{t^{m-1}(1-t)^{n-1}}{(r+t)^{m+n}} dt$$

The Error Function

Definition: $\operatorname{erf} x = \dfrac{2}{\sqrt{\pi}} \int_0^x e^{-t^2} dt$

Series: $\operatorname{erf} x = \dfrac{2}{\sqrt{\pi}} \left(x - \dfrac{x^3}{3} + \dfrac{1}{2!} \dfrac{x^5}{5} - \dfrac{1}{3!} \dfrac{x^7}{7} + \ldots \right)$

Property: $\operatorname{erf} x = -\operatorname{erf}(-x)$

Relationship with Normal Probability Function f(t): $\displaystyle\int^x f(t)\, dt = \frac{1}{2}\operatorname{erf}\left(\frac{x}{\sqrt{2}}\right)$

To evaluate *erf* (2.3), one proceeds as follows: Since $\dfrac{x}{\sqrt{2}} = 2.3$, one finds $x = (2.3)(\sqrt{2}) = 3.25$. In the normal probability function table (page 551), one finds the entry 0.4994 opposite the value 3.25. Thus *erf* (2.3) = 2(0.4994) = 0.9988.

$$\operatorname{erfc} z = 1 - \operatorname{erf} z = \frac{2}{\sqrt{\pi}} \int_z^\infty e^{-t^2} dt$$

is known as the complementary error function.

BESSEL FUNCTIONS

1. **Bessel's** differential equation for a real variable x is

$$x^2 \frac{d^2 y}{dx^2} + x \frac{dy}{dx} + (x^2 - n^2)y = 0$$

2. When n is not an integer, two independent solutions of the equation are $J_n(x)$ and $J_{-n}(x)$, where

$$J_n(x) = \sum_{k=0}^{\infty} \frac{(-1)^k}{k!\,\Gamma(n + k + 1)} \left(\frac{x}{2}\right)^{n+2k}$$

3. If n is an integer $J_{-n}(x) = (-1)^n J_n(x)$, where

$$J_n(x) = \frac{x^n}{2^n n!} \left\{ 1 - \frac{x^2}{2^2 \cdot 1!(n + 1)} + \frac{x^4}{2^4 \cdot 2!(n + 1)(n + 2)} \right.$$
$$\left. - \frac{x^6}{2^6 \cdot 3!(n + 1)(n + 2)(n + 3)} + \cdots \right\}$$

4. For $n = 0$ and $n = 1$, this formula becomes

$$J_0(x) = 1 - \frac{x^2}{2^2(1!)^2} + \frac{x^4}{2^4(2!)^2} - \frac{x^6}{2^6(3!)^2} + \frac{x^8}{2^8(4!)^2} - \cdots$$

$$J_1(x) = \frac{x}{2} - \frac{x^3}{2^3 \cdot 1!2!} + \frac{x^5}{2^5 \cdot 2!3!} - \frac{x^7}{2^7 \cdot 3!4!} + \frac{x^9}{2^9 \cdot 4!5!} - \cdots$$

5. When x is large and positive, the following asymptotic series may be used

$$J_0(x) = \left(\frac{2}{\pi x}\right)^{\frac{1}{2}} \left\{ P_0(x) \cos\left(x - \frac{\pi}{4}\right) - Q_0(x) \sin\left(x - \frac{\pi}{4}\right) \right\}$$

$$J_1(x) = \left(\frac{2}{\pi x}\right)^{\frac{1}{2}} \left\{ P_1(x) \cos\left(x - \frac{3\pi}{4}\right) - Q_1(x) \sin\left(x - \frac{3\pi}{4}\right) \right\},$$

where

$$P_0(x) \sim 1 - \frac{1^2 \cdot 3^2}{2!(8x)^2} + \frac{1^2 \cdot 3^2 \cdot 5^2 \cdot 7^2}{4!(8x)^4} - \frac{1^2 \cdot 3^2 \cdot 5^2 \cdot 7^2 \cdot 9^2 \cdot 11^2}{6!(8x)^6} + \cdots$$

$$Q_0(x) \sim - \frac{1^2}{1!8x} + \frac{1^2 \cdot 3^2 \cdot 5^2}{3!(8x)^3} - \frac{1^2 \cdot 3^2 \cdot 5^2 \cdot 7^2 \cdot 9^2}{5!(8x)^5} + - \cdots$$

$$P_1(x) \sim 1 + \frac{1^2 \cdot 3 \cdot 5}{2!(8x)^2} - \frac{1^2 \cdot 3^2 \cdot 5^2 \cdot 7 \cdot 9}{4!(8x)^4} + \frac{1^2 \cdot 3^2 \cdot 5^2 \cdot 7^2 \cdot 9^2 \cdot 11 \cdot 13}{6!(8x)^6} - + \cdots$$

$$Q_1(x) \sim \frac{1 \cdot 3}{1!8x} - \frac{1^2 \cdot 3^2 \cdot 5 \cdot 7}{3!(8x)^3} + \frac{1^2 \cdot 3^2 \cdot 5^2 \cdot 7^2 \cdot 9 \cdot 11}{5!(8x)^5} - \cdots$$

[In $P_1(x)$ the signs alternate from + to − after the first term]

6. If $x > 25$, it is convenient to use the formulas

$$J_0(x) = A_0(x) \sin x + B_0(x) \cos x$$
$$J_1(x) = B_T(x) \sin x - A_1(x) \cos x,$$

where

$$A_0(x) = \frac{P_0(x) - Q_0(x)}{(\pi x)^{\frac{1}{2}}} \quad \text{and} \quad A_1(x) = \frac{P_1(x) - Q_1(x)}{(\pi x)^{\frac{1}{2}}}$$

$$B_0(x) = \frac{P_0(x) + Q_0(x)}{(\pi x)^{\frac{1}{2}}} \quad \text{and} \quad B_1(x) = \frac{P_1(x) + Q_1(x)}{(\pi x)^{\frac{1}{2}}}$$

7. The zeros of $J_0(x)$ and $J_1(x)$

If $j_{0,s}$ and $j_{1,s}$ are the s'th zeros of $J_0(x)$ and $J_1(x)$ respectively, and if $a = 4s - 1$, $b = 4s + 1$

$$j_{0,s} \sim \frac{1}{4} \pi a \left\{ 1 + \frac{2}{\pi^2 a^2} - \frac{62}{3\pi^4 a^4} + \frac{15,116}{15\pi^6 a^6} - \frac{12,554,474}{105\pi^8 a^8} + \frac{8,368,654,292}{315\pi^{10} a^{10}} - + \cdots \right\}$$

$$j_{1,s} \sim \frac{1}{4} \pi b \left\{ 1 - \frac{6}{\pi^2 b^2} + \frac{6}{\pi^4 b^4} - \frac{4716}{5\pi^6 b^6} + \frac{3,902,418}{35\pi^8 b^8} - \frac{895,167,324}{35\pi^{10} b^{10}} + \cdots \right\}$$

$$J_1(j_{0,s}) \sim \frac{(-1)^{s+1} 2^{\frac{1}{2}}}{\pi a^{\frac{1}{2}}} \left\{ 1 - \frac{56}{3\pi^4 a^4} + \frac{9664}{5\pi^6 a^6} - \frac{7,381,280}{21\pi^8 a^8} + \cdots \right\}$$

$$J_0(j_{1,s}) \sim \frac{(-1)^s 2^{\frac{1}{2}}}{\pi b^{\frac{1}{2}}} \left\{ 1 + \frac{24}{\pi^4 b^4} - \frac{19,584}{10\pi^6 b^6} + \frac{2,466,720}{7\pi^8 b^8} - \cdots \right\}$$

8. Table of zeros for $J_0(x)$ and $J_1(x)$

$$J_0(\alpha_n) = 0 \qquad J_1(\beta_n) = 0$$

Roots α_n	$J_1(\alpha_n)$	Roots β_n	$J_0(\beta_n)$
2.4048	0.5191	0.0000	1.0000
5.5201	-0.3403	3.8317	-0.4028
8.6537	0.2715	7.0156	0.3001
11.7915	-0.2325	10.1735	-0.2497
14.9309	0.2065	13.3237	0.2184
18.0711	-0.1877	16.4706	-0.1965
21.2116	0.1733	19.6159	0.1801

9. Recurrence formulas

$$J_{n-1}(x) + J_{n+1}(x) = \frac{2n}{x} J_n(x) \qquad nJ_n(x) + xJ_n'(x) = xJ_{n-1}(x)$$

$$J_{n-1}(x) - J_{n+1}(x) = 2J_n'(x) \qquad nJ_n(x) - xJ_n'(x) = xJ_{n+1}(x)$$

10. If J_n is written for $J_n(x)$ and $J_n^{(k)}$ is written for $\frac{d^k}{dx^k} \{J_n(x)\}$, then the following derivative relationships are important

$$J_0^{(r)} = -J_1^{(r-1)}$$

$$J_0^{(2)} = -J_0 + \frac{1}{x} J_1 = \frac{1}{2} (J_2 - J_0)$$

$$J_0^{(3)} = \frac{1}{x} J_0 + \left(1 - \frac{2}{x^2}\right) J_1 = \frac{1}{4} (-J_3 + 3J_1)$$

$$J_0^{(4)} = \left(1 - \frac{3}{x^2}\right) J_0 - \left(\frac{2}{x} - \frac{6}{x^3}\right) J_1 = \frac{1}{8} (J_4 - 4J_2 + 3J_0), \text{ etc.}$$

11. Half order Bessel functions

$$J_{\frac{1}{2}}(x) = \sqrt{\frac{2}{\pi x}} \sin x$$

$$J_{-\frac{1}{2}}(x) = \sqrt{\frac{2}{\pi x}} \cos x$$

$$J_{n+\frac{3}{2}}(x) = -x^{n+\frac{1}{2}} \frac{d}{dx} \{x^{-(n+\frac{1}{2})} J_{n+\frac{1}{2}}(x)\}$$

$$J_{n-\frac{1}{2}}(x) = x^{-(n+\frac{1}{2})} \frac{d}{dx} \{x^{n+\frac{1}{2}} J_{n+\frac{1}{2}}(x)\}$$

n	$\left(\dfrac{\pi x}{2}\right)^{\frac{1}{2}} J_{n+\frac{1}{2}}(x)$	$\left(\dfrac{\pi x}{2}\right)^{\frac{1}{2}} J_{-(n+\frac{1}{2})}(x)$
0	$\sin x$	$\cos x$
1	$\dfrac{\sin x}{x} - \cos x$	$-\dfrac{\cos x}{x} - \sin x$
2	$\left(\dfrac{3}{x^2} - 1\right)\sin x - \dfrac{3}{x}\cos x$	$\left(\dfrac{3}{x^2} - 1\right)\cos x + \dfrac{3}{x}\sin x$
3	$\left(\dfrac{15}{x^3} - \dfrac{6}{x}\right)\sin x - \left(\dfrac{15}{x^2} - 1\right)\cos x$	$-\left(\dfrac{15}{x^3} - \dfrac{6}{x}\right)\cos x - \left(\dfrac{15}{x^2} - 1\right)\sin x$
	etc.	

12. Additional solutions to Bessel's equation are

$Y_n(x)$ (also called Weber's function, and sometimes denoted by $N_n(x)$)

$H_n^{(1)}(x)$ and $H_n^{(2)}(x)$ (also called Hankel functions)

These solutions are defined as follows

$$Y_n(x) = \begin{cases} \dfrac{J_n(x) \cos(n\pi) - J_{-n}(x)}{\sin(n\pi)} & n \text{ not an integer} \\[2ex] \lim_{v \to n} \dfrac{J_v(x) \cos(v\pi) - J_{-v}(x)}{\sin(v\pi)} & n \text{ an integer} \end{cases}$$

$$H_n^{(1)}(x) = J_n(x) + iY_n(x)$$
$$H_n^{(2)}(x) = J_n(x) - iY_n(x)$$

The additional properties of these functions may all be derived from the above relations and the known properties of $J_n(x)$.

13. Complete solutions to Bessel's equation may be written as

$$c_1 J_n(x) + c_2 J_{-n}(x) \qquad \text{if } n \text{ is not an integer,}$$

or

or
$$\left.\begin{array}{l} c_1 J_n(x) + c_2 Y_n(x) \\[2mm] c_1 H_n^{(1)}(x) + c_2 H_n^{(2)}(x) \end{array}\right\} \text{for any value of } n$$

14. The modified (or hyperbolic) Bessel's differential equation is

$$x^2 \frac{d^2 y}{dx^2} + x \frac{dy}{dx} - (x^2 + n^2)y = 0$$

15. When n is not an integer, two independent solutions of the equation are $I_n(x)$ and $I_{-n}(x)$, where

$$I_n(x) = \sum_{k=0}^{\infty} \frac{1}{k! \Gamma(n + k + 1)} \left(\frac{x}{2}\right)^{n+2k}$$

16. If n is an integer,

$$I_n(x) = I_{-n}(x) = \frac{x^n}{2^n n!} \left\{1 + \frac{x^2}{2^2 \cdot 1!(n+1)} + \frac{x^4}{2^4 \cdot 2!(n+1)(n+2)} \right.$$
$$\left. + \frac{x^6}{2^6 \cdot 3!(n+1)(n+2)(n+3)} + \cdots\right\}$$

17. For $n = 0$ and $n = 1$, this formula becomes

$$I_0(x) = 1 + \frac{x^2}{2^2(1!)^2} + \frac{x^4}{2^4(2!)^2} + \frac{x^6}{2^6(3!)^2} + \frac{x^8}{2^8(4!)^2} + \cdots$$

$$I_1(x) = \frac{x}{2} + \frac{x^3}{2^3 \cdot 1!2!} + \frac{x^5}{2^5 \cdot 2!3!} + \frac{x^7}{2^7 \cdot 3!4!} + \frac{x^9}{2^9 \cdot 4!5!} + \cdots$$

18. Another solution to the modified Bessel's equation is

$$K_n(x) = \begin{cases} \dfrac{1}{2} \pi \dfrac{I_{-n}(x) - I_n(x)}{\sin(n\pi)} & n \text{ not an integer} \\[4mm] \lim_{v \to n} \dfrac{1}{2} \pi \dfrac{I_{-v}(x) - I_v(x)}{\sin(v\pi)} & n \text{ an integer} \end{cases}$$

This function is linearly independent of $I_n(x)$ for all values of n. Thus the complete solution to the modified Bessel's equation may be written as

$$c_1 I_n(x) + c_2 I_{-n}(x) \qquad n \text{ not an integer}$$

or

$$c_1 I_n(x) + c_2 K_n(x) \qquad \text{any } n$$

19. The following relations hold among the various Bessel functions:

$$I_n(z) = i^{-m} J_m(iz)$$

$$Y_n(iz) = (i)^{n+1} I_n(z) - \frac{2}{\pi} i^{-n} K_n(z)$$

Most of the properties of the modified Bessel function may be deduced from the known properties of $J_n(x)$ by use of these relations and those previously given.

20. Recurrence formulas

$$I_{n-1}(x) - I_{n+1}(x) = \frac{2n}{x} I_n(x) \qquad I_{n-1}(x) + I_{n+1}(x) = 2I_n'(x)$$

$$I_{n-1}(x) - \frac{n}{x} I_n(x) = I_n'(x) \qquad I_n'(x) = I_{n+1}(x) + \frac{n}{x} I_n(x)$$

BESSEL FUNCTIONS $J_0(x)$ AND $J_1(x)$

x	$J_0(x)$	$J_1(x)$	x	$J_0(x)$	$J_1(x)$	x	$J_0(x)$	$J_1(x)$
0.0	1.0000	.0000	5.0	−.1776	−.3276	10.0	−.2459	.0435
0.1	.9975	.0499	5.1	−.1443	−.3371	10.1	−.2490	.0184
0.2	.9900	.0995	5.2	−.1103	−.3432	10.2	−.2496	−.0066
0.3	.9776	.1483	5.3	−.0758	−.3460	10.3	−.2477	−.0313
0.4	.9604	.1960	5.4	−.0412	−.3453	10.4	−.2434	−.0555
0.5	.9385	.2423	5.5	−.0068	−.3414	10.5	−.2366	−.0789
0.6	.9120	.2867	5.6	.0270	−.3343	10.6	−.2276	−.1012
0.7	.8812	.3290	5.7	.0599	−.3241	10.7	−.2164	−.1224
0.8	.8463	.3688	5.8	.0917	−.3110	10.8	−.2032	−.1422
0.9	.8075	.4059	5.9	.1220	−.2951	10.9	−.1881	−.1603
1.0	.7652	.4401	6.0	.1506	−.2767	11.0	−.1712	−.1768
1.1	.7196	.4709	6.1	.1773	−.2559	11.1	−.1528	−.1913
1.2	.6711	.4983	6.2	.2017	−.2329	11.2	−.1330	−.2039
1.3	.6201	.5220	6.3	.2238	−.2081	11.3	−.1121	−.2143
1.4	.5669	.5419	6.4	.2433	−.1816	11.4	−.0902	−.2225
	.5118							
1.5	.4554	.5579	6.5	.2601	−.1538	11.5	−.0677	−.2284
1.6	.3980	.5699	6.6	.2740	−.1250	11.6	−.0446	−.2320
1.7	.3400	.5778	6.7	.2851	−.0953	11.7	−.0213	−.2333
1.8	.2818	.5815	6.8	.2931	−.0652	11.8	.0020	−.2323
1.9		.5812	6.9	.2981	−.0349	11.9	.0250	−.2290
	.2239							
2.0	.1666	.5767	7.0	.3001	−.0047	12.0	.0477	−.2234
2.1	.1104	.5683	7.1	.2991	.0252	12.1	.0697	−.2157
2.2	.0555	.5560	7.2	.2951	.0543	12.2	.0908	−.2060
2.3	.0025	.5399	7.3	.2882	.0826	12.3	.1108	−.1943
2.4		.5202	7.4	.2786	.1096	12.4	.1296	−.1807
2.5	−.0484	.4971	7.5	.2663	.1352	12.5	.1469	−.1655
2.6	−.0968	.4708	7.6	.2516	.1592	12.6	.1626	−.1487
2.7	−.1424	.4416	7.7	.2346	.1813	12.7	.1766	−.1307
2.8	−.1850	.4097	7.8	.2154	.2014	12.8	.1887	−.1114
2.9	−.2243	.3754	7.9	.1944	.2192	12.9	.1988	−.0912
3.0	−.2601	.3391	8.0	.1717	.2346	13.0	.2069	−.0703
3.1	−.2921	.3009	8.1	.1475	.2476	13.1	.2129	−.0489
3.2	−.3202	.2613	8.2	.1222	.2580	13.2	.2167	−.0271
3.3	−.3443	.2207	8.3	.0960	.2657	13.3	.2183	−.0052
3.4	−.3643	.1792	8.4	.0692	.2708	13.4	.2177	.0166
3.5	−.3801	.1374	8.5	.0419	.2731	13.5	.2150	.0380
3.6	−.3918	.0955	8.6	.0146	.2728	13.6	.2101	.0590
3.7	−.3992	.0538	8.7	−.0125	.2697	13.7	.2032	.0791
3.8	−.4026	.0128	8.8	−.0392	.2641	13.8	.1943	.0984
3.9	−.4018	−.0272	8.9	−.0653	.2559	13.9	.1836	.1165
4.0	−.3971	−.0660	9.0	−.0903	.2453	14.0	.1711	.1334
4.1	−.3887	−.1033	9.1	−.1142	.2324	14.1	.1570	.1488
4.2	−.3766	−.1386	9.2	−.1367	.2174	14.2	.1414	.1626
4.3	−.3610	−.1719	9.3	−.1577	.2004	14.3	.1245	.1747
4.4	−.3423	−.2028	9.4	−.1768	.1816	14.4	.1065	.1850
4.5	−.3205	−.2311	9.5	−.1939	.1613	14.5	.0875	.1934
4.6	−.2961	−.2566	9.6	−.2090	.1395	14.6	.0679	.1999
4.7	−.2693	−.2791	9.7	−.2218	.1166	14.7	.0476	.2043
4.8	−.2404	−.2985	9.8	−.2323	.0928	14.8	.0271	.2066
4.9	−.2097	−.3147	9.9	−.2403	.0684	14.9	.0064	.2069

BESSEL FUNCTIONS FOR SPHERICAL COORDINATES

$$j_n(x) = \sqrt{\frac{\pi}{2x}} J_{(n+\frac{1}{2})}(x), \quad y_n(x) = \sqrt{\frac{\pi}{2x}} Y_{(n+\frac{1}{2})}(x) = (-1)^{n+1} \sqrt{\frac{\pi}{2x}} J_{-(n+\frac{1}{2})}(x)$$

x	$j_0(x)$	$y_0(x)$	$j_1(x)$	$y_1(x)$	$j_2(x)$	$y_2(x)$
0.0	1.0000	$-\infty$	0.0000	$-\infty$	0.0000	$-\infty$
0.1	0.9983	-9.9500	0.0333	-100.50	0.0007	-3005.0
0.2	0.9933	-4.9003	0.0664	-25.495	0.0027	-377.52
0.4	0.9735	-2.3027	0.1312	-6.7302	0.0105	-48.174
0.6	0.9411	-1.3756	0.1929	-3.2337	0.0234	-14.793
0.8	0.8967	-0.8709	0.2500	-1.9853	0.0408	-6.5740
1.0	0.8415	-0.5403	0.3012	-1.3818	0.0620	-3.6050
1.2	0.7767	-0.3020	0.3453	-1.0283	0.0865	-2.2689
1.4	0.7039	-0.1214	0.3814	-0.7906	0.1133	-1.5728
1.6	0.6247	$+0.0182$	0.4087	-0.6133	0.1416	-1.1682
1.8	0.5410	0.1262	0.4268	-0.4709	0.1703	-0.9111
2.0	0.4546	0.2081	0.4354	-0.3506	0.1984	-0.7340
2.2	0.3675	0.2675	0.4345	-0.2459	0.2251	-0.6028
2.4	0.2814	0.3072	0.4245	-0.1534	0.2492	-0.4990
2.6	0.1983	0.3296	0.4058	-0.0715	0.2700	-0.4121
2.8	0.1196	0.3365	0.3792	$+0.0005$	0.2867	-0.3359
3.0	$+0.0470$	0.3300	0.3457	0.0630	0.2986	-0.2670
3.2	-0.0182	0.3120	0.3063	0.1157	0.3054	-0.2035
3.4	-0.0752	0.2844	0.2622	0.1588	0.3066	-0.1442
3.6	-0.1229	0.2491	0.2150	0.1921	0.3021	-0.0890
3.8	-0.1610	0.2081	0.1658	0.2158	0.2919	-0.0378
4.0	-0.1892	0.1634	0.1161	0.2301	0.2763	$+0.0091$
4.2	-0.2075	0.1167	0.0673	0.2353	0.2556	0.0514
4.4	-0.2163	0.0698	$+0.0207$	0.2321	0.2304	0.0884
4.6	-0.2160	$+0.0244$	-0.0226	0.2213	0.2013	0.1200
4.8	-0.2075	-0.0182	-0.0615	0.2037	0.1691	0.1456
5.0	-0.1918	-0.0567	-0.0951	0.1804	0.1347	0.1650
5.2	-0.1699	-0.0901	-0.1228	0.1526	0.0991	0.1781
5.4	-0.1431	-0.1175	-0.1440	0.1213	0.0631	0.1850
5.6	-0.1127	-0.1385	-0.1586	0.0880	$+0.0277$	0.1856
5.8	-0.0801	-0.1527	-0.1665	0.0538	-0.0060	0.1805
6.0	-0.0466	-0.1600	-0.1678	$+0.0199$	-0.0373	0.1700
6.2	-0.0134	-0.1607	-0.1629	-0.0125	-0.0654	0.1547
6.4	$+0.0182$	-0.1552	-0.1523	-0.0425	-0.0896	0.1353
6.6	0.0472	-0.1440	-0.1368	-0.0690	-0.1094	0.1126
6.8	0.0727	-0.1278	-0.1172	-0.0915	-0.1243	0.0875
7.0	0.0939	-0.1077	-0.0943	-0.1092	-0.1343	0.0609
7.2	0.1102	-0.0845	-0.0692	-0.1220	-0.1391	0.0337
7.4	0.1215	-0.0593	-0.0429	-0.1295	-0.1388	$+0.0068$
7.6	0.1274	-0.0331	-0.0163	-0.1317	-0.1338	-0.0189
7.8	0.1280	-0.0069	$+0.0095$	-0.1289	-0.1244	-0.0427
8.0	0.1237	$+0.0182$	0.0336	-0.1214	-0.1111	-0.0637

Taken from Vibration and Sound with the permission of Philip Morse, author, and McGraw-Hill Book Company, Inc., publisher.

HYPERBOLIC BESSEL FUNCTIONS

$$I_m(x) = i^{-m} J_m(ix)$$

x	$I_o(x)$	$I_1(x)$	$I_2(x)$
0.0	1.0000	0.0000	0.0000
0.1	1.0025	0.0501	0.0012
0.2	1.0100	0.1005	0.0050
0.4	1.0404	0.2040	0.0203
0.6	1.0920	0.3137	0.0464
0.8	1.1665	0.4329	0.0844
1.0	1.2661	0.5652	0.1357
1.2	1.3937	0.7147	0.2026
1.4	1.5534	0.8861	0.2875
1.6	1.7500	1.0848	0.3940
1.8	1.9896	1.3172	0.5260
2.0	2.2796	1.5906	0.6889
2.2	2.6291	1.9141	0.8891
2.4	3.0493	2.2981	1.1342
2.6	3.5533	2.7554	1.4337
2.8	4.1573	3.3011	1.7994
3.0	4.8808	3.9534	2.2452
3.2	5.7472	4.7343	2.7883
3.4	6.7848	5.6701	3.4495
3.6	8.0277	6.7927	4.2540
3.8	9.5169	8.1404	5.2325
4.0	11.302	9.7595	6.4222
4.2	13.442	11.706	7.8684
4.4	16.010	14.046	9.6258
4.6	19.093	16.863	11.761
4.8	22.794	20.253	14.355
5.0	27.240	24.336	17.506
5.2	32.584	29.254	21.332
5.4	39.009	35.182	25.978
5.6	46.738	42.328	31.620
5.8	56.038	50.946	38.470
6.0	67.234	61.342	46.787
6.2	80.718	73.886	56.884
6.4	96.962	89.026	69.141
6.6	116.54	107.30	84.021
6.8	140.14	129.38	102.08
7.0	168.59	156.04	124.01
7.2	202.92	188.25	150.63
7.4	244.34	227.17	182.94
7.6	294.33	274.22	222.17
7.8	354.68	331.10	269.79
8.0	427.56	399.87	327.60

Taken from Vibration and Sound with the permission of Philip Morse, author, and McGraw-Hill Book Company, Inc., publisher.

ELLIPTIC INTEGRALS OF THE FIRST, SECOND AND THIRD KIND

An elliptic integral has the form $\int R(x, \sqrt{f(x)})dx$, where R represents a rational function and $f(x) = a + bx + cx^2 + dx^3 + ex^4$, an algebraic function of the third or fourth degree.

1. Elliptic integrals of the *first kind* are represented by

$$F(k, \phi) = \int_0^\phi \frac{d\Phi}{\sqrt{1 - k^2 \sin^2 \Phi}}$$

$$= \int_0^x \frac{d\xi}{\sqrt{(1 - \xi^2)(1 - k^2\xi^2)}}, \quad x = \sin \phi, \; k^2 < 1.$$

2. Elliptic integrals of the second kind are represented by

$$E(k, \phi) = \int_0^\phi \sqrt{1 - k^2 \sin^2 \Phi} \, d\Phi$$

$$= \int_0^x \frac{\sqrt{1 - k^2\xi^2}}{\sqrt{1 - \xi^2}} \, d\xi, \quad x = \sin \phi, \; k^2 < 1.$$

3. Elliptic integrals of the third kind are represented as

$$\pi(k, n, \phi) = \int_0^\phi \frac{d\Phi}{(1 + n \sin^2 \Phi) \sqrt{1 - k^2 \sin^2 \Phi}},$$

$$k^2 < 1, \; n \text{ an integer.}$$

Elliptic integrals of the third kind are also presented as

$$\pi_1(k, n, x) = \int_0^x \frac{d\xi}{(1 + n\xi^2) \sqrt{(1 - \xi^2)(1 - k^2\xi^2)}},$$

$$x = \sin \phi, \; k^2 < 1, \; n \text{ an integer.}$$

4. The complete integrals are

$$K = F\left(k, \frac{\pi}{2}\right) = \frac{\pi}{2}\left[1 + \left(\frac{1}{2}\right)^2 k^2 + \left(\frac{3}{2 \cdot 4}\right)^2 k^4 \right.$$

$$\left. + \left(\frac{3 \cdot 5}{2 \cdot 4 \cdot 6}\right)^2 k^6 + \cdots \right]$$

$$E = E\left(k, \frac{\pi}{2}\right) = \frac{\pi}{2}\left[1 - \left(\frac{1}{2^2}\right)k^2 - \left(\frac{3^2}{2^2 \cdot 4^2}\right)\frac{k^4}{3}\right.$$

$$\left. - \left(\frac{3^2 \cdot 5^2}{2^2 \cdot 4^2 \cdot 6^2}\right)\frac{k^6}{5} - \left(\frac{3^2 \cdot 5^2 \cdot 7^2}{2^2 \cdot 4^2 \cdot 6^2 \cdot 8^2}\right)\frac{k^8}{7} - \cdots \right].$$

$$K' = F\left(\sqrt{1 - k^2}, \frac{\pi}{2}\right), \; E' = E\left(\sqrt{1 - k^2}, \frac{\pi}{2}\right)$$

5. The following relation holds between K, K', E, E', namely

$$KE' + EK' - KK' = \frac{\pi}{2} \quad \text{Legendre's relation}$$

E: see 2 above. $E' = \int_0^{\pi/2} (1 - k'^2 \sin^2 \phi)^{\frac{1}{2}}d\phi.$ $k' = \sqrt{(1 - k^2)}$

$K = \int_0^{\pi/2} (1 - k^2 \sin^2 \phi)^{-\frac{1}{2}}d\phi$ $K' = \int_0^{\pi/2} (1 - k'^2 \sin^2 \phi)^{-\frac{1}{2}}d\phi$

6. To evaluate elliptic integrals for values outside the range contained in the following tables, these relations are useful

$$F(k, \pi) = 2K; E(k, \pi) = 2E$$

$$F(k, \phi + m\pi) = mF(k, \pi) + F(k, \phi) = 2mK + F(k, \phi)$$
$$m = 0, 1, 2, 3, \ldots$$

$$E(k, \phi + m\pi) = mE(k, \pi) + E(k, \phi) = 2mE + E(k, \phi)$$
$$m = 0, 1, 2, 3, \ldots$$

7. If $u = F(k, \phi) = \displaystyle\int_0^\phi \frac{d\Phi}{\sqrt{1 - k^2 \sin^2 \Phi}}$ $(k^2 < 1)$,

= elliptic integral of the first kind.

$$u = \int_0^x \frac{dx}{\sqrt{(1 - \xi^2)(1 - k^2\xi^2)}}, \text{ where } x = \sin \phi.$$

ϕ is called the amplitude of u or am u.
k is called the modulus.

$$k' = \sqrt{1 - k^2} = \text{the complementary modulus.}$$

$\sin \phi = \text{sn } u = x$ $\tan \phi = \text{tn } u = \dfrac{x}{\sqrt{1 - x^2}}$.

$\cos \phi = \text{cn } u = \sqrt{1 - x^2}$. $\Delta\phi = \text{dn } u = \sqrt{1 - k^2x^2}$.
am $0 = 0$.   sn $0 = 0$.
cn $0 = 1$.   dn $0 = 1$.
am $(-u) = -$am u.   sn $(-u) = -$sn u.
cn $(-u) = $ cn u.   dn $(-u) = $ dn u.

tn $(-u) = -$tn u.
$\text{sn}^2 u + \text{cn}^2 u = 1$.
$\text{dn}^2 u + k^2 \text{ sn}^2 u = 1$.
$\text{dn}^2 u - k^2 \text{ cn}^2 u = 1 - k^2 = k'^2$.

$$\text{sn } u = u - (1 + k^2) \frac{u^3}{3!} + (1 + 14k^2 + k^4) \frac{u^5}{5!}$$
$$- (1 + 135k^2 + 135k^4 + k^6) \frac{u^7}{7!} + \cdots$$

Periods: $4k$ and $2ik'$

$$\text{cn } u = 1 - \frac{u^2}{2!} + (1 + 4k^2) \frac{u^4}{4!} - (1 + 44k^2 + 16k^4) \frac{u^6}{6!} + \cdots$$

Periods: $4k$ and $2k + 2ik'$

$$\text{dn } u = 1 - k^2 \frac{u^2}{2!} + k^2(4 + k^2) \frac{u^4}{4!} - k^2(16 + 44k^2 + k^4) \frac{u^6}{6!} + \cdots$$

Periods: $2k$ and $4ik'$

ELLIPTIC INTEGRALS OF THE FIRST KIND: $F(k, \phi)^*$

$$F(k, \phi) = \int_0^\phi \frac{d\Phi}{\sqrt{1 - k^2 \sin^2 \Phi}}, \qquad \theta = \sin^{-1} k$$

θ / ϕ	5°	10°	15°	20°	25°	30°	35°	40°	45°
1°	0.0175	0.0175	0.0175	0.0175	0.0175	0.0175	0.0175	0.0175	0.0175
2°	0.0349	0.0349	0.0349	0.0349	0.0349	0.0349	0.0349	0.0349	0.0349
3°	0.0524	0.0524	0.0524	0.0524	0.0524	0.0524	0.0524	0.0524	0.0524
4°	0.0698	0.0698	0.0698	0.0698	0.0698	0.0698	0.0698	0.0698	0.0698
5°	0.0873	0.0873	0.0873	0.0873	0.0873	0.0873	0.0873	0.0873	0.0873
6°	0.1047	0.1047	0.1047	0.1047	0.1048	0.1048	0.1048	0.1048	0.1048
7°	0.1222	0.1222	0.1222	0.1222	0.1222	0.1222	0.1223	0.1223	0.1223
8°	0.1396	0.1396	0.1397	0.1397	0.1397	0.1397	0.1398	0.1398	0.1399
9°	0.1571	0.1571	0.1571	0.1572	0.1572	0.1572	0.1573	0.1573	0.1574
10°	0.1745	0.1746	0.1746	0.1746	0.1747	0.1748	0.1748	0.1749	0.1750
11°	0.1920	0.1920	0.1921	0.1921	0.1922	0.1923	0.1924	0.1925	0.1926
12°	0.2095	0.2095	0.2095	0.2096	0.2097	0.2098	0.2099	0.2101	0.2102
13°	0.2269	0.2270	0.2270	0.2271	0.2272	0.2274	0.2275	0.2277	0.2279
14°	0.2444	0.2444	0.2445	0.2446	0.2448	0.2450	0.2451	0.2453	0.2456
15°	0.2618	0.2619	0.2620	0.2621	0.2623	0.2625	0.2628	0.2630	0.2633
16°	0.2793	0.2794	0.2795	0.2797	0.2799	0.2802	0.2804	0.2808	0.2811
17°	0.2967	0.2968	0.2970	0.2972	0.2975	0.2978	0.2981	0.2985	0.2989
18°	0.3142	0.3143	0.3145	0.3148	0.3151	0.3154	0.3159	0.3163	0.3167
19°	0.3317	0.3318	0.3320	0.3323	0.3327	0.3331	0.3336	0.3341	0.3347
20°	0.3491	0.3493	0.3495	0.3499	0.3503	0.3508	0.3514	0.3520	0.3526
21°	0.3666	0.3668	0.3671	0.3675	0.3680	0.3685	0.3692	0.3699	0.3706
22°	0.3840	0.3842	0.3846	0.3851	0.3856	0.3863	0.3871	0.3879	0.3887
23°	0.4015	0.4017	0.4021	0.4027	0.4033	0.4041	0.4049	0.4059	0.4068
24°	0.4190	0.4192	0.4197	0.4203	0.4210	0.4219	0.4229	0.4239	0.4250
25°	0.4364	0.4367	0.4372	0.4379	0.4387	0.4397	0.4408	0.4420	0.4433
26°	0.4539	0.4542	0.4548	0.4556	0.4565	0.4576	0.4588	0.4602	0.4616
27°	0.4714	0.4717	0.4724	0.4732	0.4743	0.4755	0.4769	0.4784	0.4800
28°	0.4888	0.4893	0.4899	0.4909	0.4921	0.4934	0.4950	0.4967	0.4985
29°	0.5063	0.5068	0.5075	0.5086	0.5099	0.5114	0.5132	0.5150	0.5170
30°	0.5238	0.5243	0.5251	0.5263	0.5277	0.5294	0.5313	0.5334	0.5356
31°	0.5412	0.5418	0.5427	0.5440	0.5456	0.5475	0.5496	0.5519	0.5543
32°	0.5587	0.5593	0.5603	0.5617	0.5635	0.5656	0.5679	0.5704	0.5731
33°	0.5762	0.5769	0.5780	0.5795	0.5814	0.5837	0.5862	0.5890	0.5920
34°	0.5937	0.5944	0.5956	0.5973	0.5994	0.6018	0.6046	0.6077	0.6109
35°	0.6111	0.6119	0.6133	0.6151	0.6173	0.6200	0.6231	0.6264	0.6300
36°	0.6286	0.6295	0.6309	0.6329	0.6353	0.6383	0.6416	0.6452	0.6491
37°	0.6461	0.6470	0.6486	0.6507	0.6534	0.6565	0.6602	0.6641	0.6684
38°	0.6636	0.6646	0.6662	0.6685	0.6714	0.6749	0.6788	0.6831	0.6877
39°	0.6810	0.6821	0.6839	0.6864	0.6895	0.6932	0.6975	0.7021	0.7071
40°	0.6985	0.6997	0.7016	0.7043	0.7076	0.7116	0.7162	0.7213	0.7267
41°	0.7160	0.7173	0.7193	0.7222	0.7258	0.7301	0.7350	0.7405	0.7463
42°	0.7335	0.7348	0.7370	0.7401	0.7440	0.7486	0.7539	0.7598	0.7661
43°	0.7510	0.7524	0.7548	0.7580	0.7622	0.7671	0.7728	0.7791	0.7859
44°	0.7685	0.7700	0.7725	0.7760	0.7804	0.7857	0.7918	0.7986	0.8059
45°	0.7859	0.7876	0.7903	0.7940	0.7987	0.8044	0.8109	0.8181	0.8260

* For useful information about these tables see preceding page.

ELLIPTIC INTEGRALS OF THE FIRST KIND: $F(k, \phi)$ (Continued)

$$F(k, \phi) = \int_0^\phi \frac{d\Phi}{\sqrt{1 - k^2 \sin^2 \Phi}}, \qquad \theta = \sin^{-1} k$$

ϕ \ θ	50°	55°	60°	65°	70°	75°	80°	85°	90°
1°	0.0175	0.0175	0.0175	0.0175	0.0175	0.0175	0.0175	0.0175	0.0175
2°	0.0349	0.0349	0.0349	0.0349	0.0349	0.0349	0.0349	0.0349	0.0349
3°	0.0524	0.0524	0.0524	0.0524	0.0524	0.0524	0.0524	0.0524	0.0524
4°	0.0698	0.0699	0.0699	0.0699	0.0699	0.0699	0.0699	0.0699	0.0699
5°	0.0873	0.0873	0.0873	0.0874	0.0874	0.0874	0.0874	0.0874	0.0874
6°	0.1048	0.1048	0.1049	0.1049	0.1049	0.1049	0.1049	0.1049	0.1049
7°	0.1224	0.1224	0.1224	0.1224	0.1224	0.1225	0.1225	0.1225	0.1225
8°	0.1399	0.1399	0.1400	0.1400	0.1400	0.1401	0.1401	0.1401	0.1401
9°	0.1575	0.1575	0.1576	0.1576	0.1577	0.1577	0.1577	0.1577	0.1577
10°	0.1751	0.1751	0.1752	0.1753	0.1753	0.1754	0.1754	0.1754	0.1754
11°	0.1927	0.1928	0.1929	0.1930	0.1930	0.1931	0.1931	0.1932	0.1932
12°	0.2103	0.2105	0.2106	0.2107	0.2108	0.2109	0.2109	0.2110	0.2110
13°	0.2280	0.2282	0.2284	0.2285	0.2286	0.2287	0.2288	0.2288	0.2289
14°	0.2458	0.2460	0.2462	0.2464	0.2465	0.2466	0.2467	0.2468	0.2468
15°	0.2636	0.2638	0.2641	0.2643	0.2645	0.2646	0.2647	0.2648	0.2648
16°	0.2814	0.2817	0.2820	0.2823	0.2825	0.2827	0.2828	0.2829	0.2830
17°	0.2993	0.2997	0.3000	0.3003	0.3006	0.3008	0.3010	0.3011	0.3012
18°	0.3172	0.3177	0.3181	0.3185	0.3188	0.3191	0.3193	0.3194	0.3195
19°	0.3352	0.3357	0.3362	0.3367	0.3371	0.3374	0.3377	0.3378	0.3379
20°	0.3533	0.3539	0.3545	0.3550	0.3555	0.3559	0.3561	0.3563	0.3564
21°	0.3714	0.3721	0.3728	0.3734	0.3740	0.3744	0.3747	0.3749	0.3750
22°	0.3896	0.3904	0.3912	0.3919	0.3926	0.3931	0.3935	0.3937	0.3938
23°	0.4078	0.4088	0.4097	0.4105	0.4113	0.4119	0.4123	0.4126	0.4127
24°	0.4261	0.4272	0.4283	0.4292	0.4301	0.4308	0.4313	0.4316	0.4317
25°	0.4446	0.4458	0.4470	0.4481	0.4490	0.4498	0.4504	0.4508	0.4509
26°	0.4630	0.4645	0.4658	0.4670	0.4681	0.4690	0.4697	0.4701	0.4702
27°	0.4816	0.4832	0.4847	0.4861	0.4873	0.4884	0.4891	0.4896	0.4897
28°	0.5003	0.5021	0.5038	0.5053	0.5067	0.5079	0.5087	0.5092	0.5094
29°	0.5190	0.5210	0.5229	0.5247	0.5262	0.5275	0.5285	0.5291	0.5293
30°	0.5379	0.5401	0.5422	0.5442	0.5459	0.5474	0.5484	0.5491	0.5493
31°	0.5568	0.5593	0.5617	0.5639	0.5658	0.5674	0.5686	0.5693	0.5696
32°	0.5759	0.5786	0.5812	0.5837	0.5858	0.5876	0.5889	0.5898	0.5900
33°	0.5950	0.5980	0.6010	0.6037	0.6060	0.6080	0.6095	0.6104	0.6107
34°	0.6143	0.6176	0.6208	0.6238	0.6265	0.6287	0.6303	0.6313	0.6317
35°	0.6336	0.6373	0.6408	0.6441	0.6471	0.6495	0.6513	0.6525	0.6528
36°	0.6531	0.6571	0.6610	0.6647	0.6679	0.6706	0.6726	0.6739	0.6743
37°	0.6727	0.6771	0.6814	0.6854	0.6890	0.6919	0.6941	0.6955	0.6960
38°	0.6925	0.6973	0.7019	0.7063	0.7102	0.7135	0.7159	0.7175	0.7180
39°	0.7123	0.7176	0.7227	0.7275	0.7318	0.7353	0.7380	0.7397	0.7403
40°	0.7323	0.7380	0.7436	0.7488	0.7535	0.7575	0.7604	0.7623	0.7629
41°	0.7524	0.7586	0.7647	0.7704	0.7756	0.7799	0.7831	0.7852	0.7859
42°	0.7727	0.7794	0.7860	0.7922	0.7979	0.8026	0.8062	0.8084	0.8092
43°	0.7931	0.8004	0.8075	0.8143	0.8204	0.8256	0.8295	0.8320	0.8328
44°	0.8136	0.8215	0.8293	0.8367	0.8433	0.8490	0.8533	0.8560	0.8569
45°	0.8343	0.8428	0.8512	0.8592	0.8665	0.8727	0.8774	0.8804	0.8814

ELLIPTIC INTEGRALS OF THE FIRST KIND: $F(k, \phi)$ (Continued)

$$F(k, \phi) = \int_0^\phi \frac{d\Phi}{\sqrt{1 - k^2 \sin^2 \Phi}}, \qquad \theta = \sin^{-1} k$$

θ / ϕ	5°	10°	15°	20°	25°	30°	35°	40°	45°
46°	0.8034	0.8052	0.8080	0.8120	0.8170	0.8230	0.8300	0.8378	0.8462
47°	0.8209	0.8227	0.8258	0.8300	0.8353	0.8418	0.8492	0.8575	0.8666
48°	0.8384	0.8403	0.8436	0.8480	0.8537	0.8606	0.8685	0.8773	0.8870
49°	0.8559	0.8579	0.8614	0.8661	0.8721	0.8794	0.8878	0.8972	0.9076
50°	0.8734	0.8756	0.8792	0.8842	0.8905	0.8982	0.9072	0.9173	0.9283
51°	0.8909	0.8932	0.8970	0.9023	0.9090	0.9172	0.9267	0.9374	0.9491
52°	0.9084	0.9108	0.9148	0.9204	0.9275	0.9361	0.9462	0.9575	0.9701
53°	0.9259	0.9284	0.9326	0.9385	0.9460	0.9551	0.9658	0.9778	0.9912
54°	0.9434	0.9460	0.9505	0.9567	0.9646	0.9742	0.9855	0.9982	1.0124
55°	0.9609	0.9637	0.9683	0.9748	0.9832	0.9933	1.0052	1.0187	1.0337
56°	0.9784	0.9813	0.9862	0.9930	1.0018	1.0125	1.0250	1.0393	1.0552
57°	0.9959	0.9989	1.0041	1.0112	1.0204	1.0317	1.0449	1.0600	1.0768
58°	1.0134	1.0166	1.0219	1.0295	1.0391	1.0509	1.0648	1.0807	1.0985
59°	1.0309	1.0342	1.0398	1.0477	1.0578	1.0702	1.0848	1.1016	1.1204
60°	1.0484	1.0519	1.0577	1.0660	1.0766	1.0896	1.1049	1.1226	1.1424
61°	1.0659	1.0695	1.0757	1.0843	1.0953	1.1089	1.1250	1.1436	1.1646
62°	1.0834	1.0872	1.0936	1.1026	1.1141	1.1284	1.1452	1.1648	1.1868
63°	1.1009	1.1049	1.1115	1.1209	1.1330	1.1478	1.1655	1.1860	1.2093
64°	1.1184	1.1225	1.1295	1.1392	1.1518	1.1674	1.1859	1.2073	1.2318
65°	1.1359	1.1402	1.1474	1.1575	1.1707	1.1869	1.2063	1.2288	1.2545
66°	1.1534	1.1579	1.1654	1.1759	1.1896	1.2065	1.2267	1.2503	1.2773
67°	1.1709	1.1756	1.1833	1.1943	1.2085	1.2262	1.2472	1.2719	1.3002
68°	1.1884	1.1932	1.2013	1.2127	1.2275	1.2458	1.2678	1.2936	1.3232
69°	1.2059	1.2109	1.2193	1.2311	1.2465	1.2655	1.2885	1.3154	1.3464
70°	1.2234	1.2286	1.2373	1.2495	1.2655	1.2853	1.3092	1.3372	1.3697
71°	1.2410	1.2463	1.2553	1.2680	1.2845	1.3051	1.3299	1.3592	1.3931
72°	1.2585	1.2640	1.2733	1.2864	1.3036	1.3249	1.3507	1.3812	1.4167
73°	1.2760	1.2817	1.2913	1.3049	1.3226	1.3448	1.3715	1.4033	1.4403
74°	1.2935	1.2994	1.3093	1.3234	1.3417	1.3647	1.3924	1.4254	1.4640
75°	1.3110	1.3171	1.3273	1.3418	1.3608	1.3846	1.4134	1.4477	1.4879
76°	1.3285	1.3348	1.3454	1.3603	1.3800	1.4045	1.4344	1.4700	1.5118
77°	1.3460	1.3525	1.3634	1.3788	1.3991	1.4245	1.4554	1.4923	1.5359
78°	1.3636	1.3702	1.3814	1.3974	1.4183	1.4445	1.4765	1.5147	1.5600
79°	1.3811	1.3879	1.3995	1.4159	1.4374	1.4645	1.4976	1.5372	1.5842
80°	1.3986	1.4056	1.4175	1.4344	1.4566	1.4846	1.5187	1.5597	1.6085
81°	1.4161	1.4234	1.4356	1.4530	1.4758	1.5046	1.5399	1.5823	1.6328
82°	1.4336	1.4411	1.4536	1.4715	1.4950	1.5247	1.5611	1.6049	1.6572
83°	1.4512	1.4588	1.4717	1.4901	1.5143	1.5448	1.5823	1.6276	1.6817
84°	1.4687	1.4765	1.4897	1.5086	1.5335	1.5649	1.6035	1.6502	1.7062
85°	1.4862	1.4942	1.5078	1.5272	1.5527	1.5850	1.6248	1.6730	1.7308
86°	1.5037	1.5120	1.5259	1.5457	1.5720	1.6052	1.6461	1.6957	1.7554
87°	1.5212	1.5297	1.5439	1.5643	1.5912	1.6253	1.6673	1.7184	1.7801
88°	1.5388	1.5474	1.5620	1.5829	1.6105	1.6454	1.6886	1.7412	1.8047
89°	1.5563	1.5651	1.5801	1.6015	1.6297	1.6656	1.7099	1.7640	1.8294
90°	1.5738	1.5828	1.5981	1.6200	1.6490	1.6858	1.7312	1.7868	1.8541

ELLIPTIC INTEGRALS OF THE FIRST KIND: $F(k, \phi)$ (Continued)

$$F(k, \phi) = \int_0^\phi \frac{d\Phi}{\sqrt{1 - k^2 \sin^2 \Phi}}, \qquad \theta = \sin^{-1} k$$

ϕ \ θ	50°	55°	60°	65°	70°	75°	80°	85°	90°
46°	0.8552	0.8643	0.8734	0.8821	0.8900	0.8968	0.9019	0.9052	0.9063
47°	0.8761	0.8860	0.8958	0.9053	0.9139	0.9212	0.9269	0.9304	0.9316
48°	0.8973	0.9079	0.9185	0.9287	0.9381	0.9461	0.9523	0.9561	0.9575
49°	0.9186	0.9300	0.9415	0.9525	0.9627	0.9714	0.9781	0.9824	0.9838
50°	0.9401	0.9523	0.9647	0.9766	0.9876	0.9971	1.0044	1.0091	1.0107
51°	0.9617	0.9748	0.9881	1.0010	1.0130	1.0233	1.0313	1.0364	1.0381
52°	0.9835	0.9976	1.0118	1.0258	1.0387	1.0499	1.0587	1.0642	1.0662
53°	1.0055	1.0205	1.0359	1.0509	1.0649	1.0771	1.0866	1.0927	1.0948
54°	1.0277	1.0437	1.0602	1.0764	1.0915	1.1048	1.1152	1.1219	1.1242
55°	1.0500	1.0672	1.0848	1.1022	1.1186	1.1331	1.1444	1.1517	1.1542
56°	1.0725	1.0908	1.1097	1.1285	1.1462	1.1619	1.1743	1.1823	1.1851
57°	1.0952	1.1147	1.1349	1.1551	1.1743	1.1914	1.2049	1.2136	1.2167
58°	1.1180	1.1389	1.1605	1.1822	1.2030	1.2215	1.2362	1.2458	1.2492
59°	1.1411	1.1632	1.1864	1.2097	1.2321	1.2522	1.2684	1.2789	1.2826
60°	1.1643	1.1879	1.2125	1.2376	1.2619	1.2837	1.3014	1.3129	1.3170
61°	1.1877	1.2128	1.2392	1.2660	1.2922	1.3159	1.3352	1.3480	1.3524
62°	1.2113	1.2379	1.2661	1.2949	1.3231	1.3490	1.3701	1.3841	1.3890
63°	1.2351	1.2633	1.2933	1.3242	1.3547	1.3828	1.4059	1.4214	1.4268
64°	1.2591	1.2890	1.3209	1.3541	1.3870	1.4175	1.4429	1.4599	1.4659
65°	1.2833	1.3149	1.3489	1.3844	1.4199	1.4532	1.4810	1.4998	1.5065
66°	1.3076	1.3411	1.3773	1.4153	1.4536	1.4898	1.5203	1.5411	1.5485
67°	1.3321	1.3675	1.4060	1.4467	1.4880	1.5274	1.5610	1.5840	1.5923
68°	1.3568	1.3942	1.4351	1.4786	1.5232	1.5661	1.6030	1.6287	1.6379
69°	1.3817	1.4212	1.4646	1.5111	1.5591	1.6059	1.6466	1.6752	1.6856
70°	1.4068	1.4484	1.4944	1.5441	1.5959	1.6468	1.6918	1.7237	1.7354
71°	1.4320	1.4759	1.5246	1.5777	1.6335	1.6891	1.7388	1.7745	1.7877
72°	1.4574	1.5036	1.5552	1.6118	1.6720	1.7326	1.7876	1.8277	1.8427
73°	1.4830	1.5315	1.5862	1.6465	1.7113	1.7774	1.8384	1.8837	1.9008
74°	1.5087	1.5597	1.6175	1.6818	1.7516	1.8237	1.8915	1.9427	1.9623
75°	1.5345	1.5882	1.6492	1.7176	1.7927	1.8715	1.9468	2.0050	2.0276
76°	1.5606	1.6168	1.6812	1.7540	1.8347	1.9207	2.0047	2.0711	2.0973
77°	1.5867	1.6457	1.7136	1.7909	1.8777	1.9716	2.0653	2.1414	2.1721
78°	1.6130	1.6748	1.7462	1.8284	1.9215	2.0240	2.1288	2.2164	2.2528
79°	1.6394	1.7040	1.7792	1.8664	1.9663	2.0781	2.1954	2.2969	2.3404
80°	1.6660	1.7335	1.8125	1.9048	2.0119	2.1339	2.2653	2.3836	2.4362
81°	1.6926	1.7631	1.8461	1.9438	2.0584	2.1913	2.3387	2.4775	2.5421
82°	1.7193	1.7929	1.8799	1.9831	2.1057	2.2504	2.4157	2.5795	2.6603
83°	1.7462	1.8228	1.9140	2.0229	2.1537	2.3110	2.4965	2.6911	2.7942
84°	1.7731	1.8528	1.9482	2.0630	2.2024	2.3731	2.5811	2.8136	2.9487
85°	1.8001	1.8830	1.9826	2.1035	2.2518	2.4366	2.6694	2.9487	3.1313
86°	1.8271	1.9132	2.0172	2.1442	2.3017	2.5013	2.7612	3.0978	3.3547
87°	1.8542	1.9435	2,0519	2.1852	2.3520	2.5670	2.8561	3.2620	3.6425
88°	1.8813	1.9739	2.0867	2.2263	2.4026	2.6336	2.9537	3.4412	4.0481
89°	1.9084	2.0043	2.1216	2.2675	2.4535	2.7007	3.0530	3.6328	4.7413
90°	1.9356	2.0347	2.1565	2.3088	2.5046	2.7681	3.1534	3.8317	———

ELLIPTIC INTEGRALS OF THE SECOND KIND: $E(k, \phi)$

$$E(k, \phi) = \int_0^\phi \sqrt{(1 - k^2 \sin^2 \Phi)}\,d\Phi, \quad \theta = \sin^{-1} k$$

θ / ϕ	5°	10°	15°	20°	25°	30°	35°	40°	45°
1°	0.0175	0.0175	0.0175	0.0175	0.0175	0.0175	0.0175	0.0175	0.0175
2°	0.0349	0.0349	0.0349	0.0349	0.0349	0.0349	0.0349	0.0349	0.0349
3°	0.0524	0.0524	0.0524	0.0524	0.0524	0.0524	0.0524	0.0523	0.0523
4°	0.0698	0.0698	0.0698	0.0698	0.0698	0.0698	0.0698	0.0698	0.0698
5°	0.0873	0.0873	0.0873	0.0873	0.0872	0.0872	0.0872	0.0872	0.0872
6°	0.1047	0.1047	0.1047	0.1047	0.1047	0.1047	0.1047	0.1046	0.1046
7°	0.1222	0.1222	0.1222	0.1221	0.1221	0.1221	0.1221	0.1220	0.1220
8°	0.1396	0.1396	0.1396	0.1396	0.1395	0.1395	0.1395	0.1394	0.1394
9°	0.1571	0.1571	0.1570	0.1570	0.1570	0.1569	0.1569	0.1568	0.1568
10°	0.1745	0.1745	0.1745	0.1744	0.1744	0.1743	0.1742	0.1742	0.1741
11°	0.1920	0.1920	0.1919	0.1918	0.1918	0.1917	0.1916	0.1915	0.1914
12°	0.2094	0.2094	0.2093	0.2093	0.2092	0.2091	0.2089	0.2088	0.2087
13°	0.2269	0.2268	0.2268	0.2267	0.2265	0.2264	0.2263	0.2261	0.2259
14°	0.2443	0.2443	0.2442	0.2441	0.2439	0.2437	0.2436	0.2433	0.2431
15°	0.2618	0.2617	0.2616	0.2615	0.2613	0.2611	0.2608	0.2606	0.2603
16°	0.2792	0.2791	0.2790	0.2788	0.2786	0.2784	0.2781	0.2778	0.2775
17°	0.2967	0.2966	0.2964	0.2962	0.2959	0.2956	0.2953	0.2949	0.2946
18°	0.3141	0.3140	0.3138	0.3136	0.3133	0.3129	0.3125	0.3121	0.3116
19°	0.3316	0.3314	0.3312	0.3309	0.3305	0.3301	0.3296	0.3291	0.3286
20°	0.3490	0.3489	0.3486	0.3483	0.3478	0.3473	0.3468	0.3462	0.3456
21°	0.3665	0.3663	0.3660	0.3656	0.3651	0.3645	0.3639	0.3632	0.3625
22°	0.3839	0.3837	0.3834	0.3829	0.3823	0.3817	0.3809	0.3802	0.3793
23°	0.4013	0.4011	0.4007	0.4002	0.3996	0.3988	0.3980	0.3971	0.3961
24°	0.4188	0.4185	0.4181	0.4175	0.4168	0.4159	0.4150	0.4139	0.4129
25°	0.4362	0.4359	0.4354	0.4348	0.4339	0.4330	0.4319	0.4308	0.4296
26°	0.4537	0.4533	0.4528	0.4520	0.4511	0.4500	0.4488	0.4475	0.4462
27°	0.4711	0.4707	0.4701	0.4693	0.4682	0.4670	0.4657	0.4643	0.4628
28°	0.4886	0.4881	0.4874	0.4865	0.4854	0.4840	0.4825	0.4809	0.4793
29°	0.5060	0.5055	0.5048	0.5037	0.5025	0.5010	0.4993	0.4975	0.4957
30°	0.5234	0.5229	0.5221	0.5209	0.5195	0.5179	0.5161	0.5141	0.5120
31°	0.5409	0.5403	0.5394	0.5381	0.5366	0.5348	0.5327	0.5306	0.5283
32°	0.5583	0.5577	0.5567	0.5553	0.5536	0.5516	0.5494	0.5470	0.5446
33°	0.5757	0.5751	0.5740	0.5725	0.5706	0.5684	0.5660	0.5634	0.5607
34°	0.5932	0.5924	0.5912	0.5896	0.5876	0.5852	0.5826	0.5797	0.5768
35°	0.6106	0.6098	0.6085	0.6067	0.6045	0.6019	0.5991	0.5960	0.5928
36°	0.6280	0.6272	0.6258	0.6238	0.6214	0.6186	0.6155	0.6122	0.6087
37°	0.6455	0.6445	0.6430	0.6409	0.6383	0.6353	0.6319	0.6283	0.6245
38°	0.6629	0.6619	0.6602	0.6580	0.6552	0.6519	0.6483	0.6444	0.6403
39°	0.6803	0.6792	0.6775	0.6750	0.6720	0.6685	0.6646	0.6604	0.6559
40°	0.6977	0.6966	0.6947	0.6921	0.6888	0.6851	0.6808	0.6763	0.6715
41°	0.7152	0.7139	0.7119	0.7091	0.7056	0.7016	0.6970	0.6921	0.6870
42°	0.7326	0.7313	0.7291	0.7261	0.7224	0.7180	0.7132	0.7079	0.7024
43°	0.7500	0.7486	0.7463	0.7431	0.7391	0.7345	0.7293	0.7237	0.7178
44°	0.7674	0.7659	0.7634	0.7600	0.7558	0.7508	0.7453	0.7393	0.7330
45°	0.7849	0.7832	0.7806	0.7770	0.7725	0.7672	0.7613	0.7549	0.7482

ELLIPTIC INTEGRALS OF THE SECOND KIND: $E(k, \phi)$ (Continued)

$$E(k, \phi) = \int_0^\phi \sqrt{(1 - k^2 \sin^2 \Phi)}d\Phi, \quad \theta = \sin^{-1} k$$

θ / ϕ	50°	55°	60°	65°	70°	75°	80°	85°	90°
1°	0.0175	0.0175	0.0175	0.0175	0.0175	0.0175	0.0175	0.0175	0.0175
2°	0.0349	0.0349	0.0349	0.0349	0.0349	0.0349	0.0349	0.0349	0.0349
3°	0.0523	0.0523	0.0523	0.0523	0.0523	0.0523	0.0523	0.0523	0.0523
4°	0.0698	0.0698	0.0698	0.0698	0.0698	0.0698	0.0698	0.0698	0.0698
5°	0.0872	0.0872	0.0872	0.0872	0.0872	0.0872	0.0872	0.0872	0.0872
6°	0.1046	0.1046	0.1046	0.1046	0.1046	0.1045	0.1045	0.1045	0.1045
7°	0.1220	0.1220	0.1219	0.1219	0.1219	0.1219	0.1219	0.1219	0.1219
8°	0.1394	0.1393	0.1393	0.1393	0.1392	0.1392	0.1392	0.1392	0.1392
9°	0.1567	0.1566	0.1566	0.1566	0.1565	0.1565	0.1565	0.1564	0.1564
10°	0.1740	0.1739	0.1739	0.1738	0.1738	0.1737	0.1737	0.1737	0.1736
11°	0.1913	0.1912	0.1911	0.1910	0.1909	0.1909	0.1908	0.1908	0.1908
12°	0.2085	0.2084	0.2083	0.2082	0.2081	0.2080	0.2080	0.2079	0.2079
13°	0.2258	0.2256	0.2254	0.2253	0.2252	0.2251	0.2250	0.2250	0.2250
14°	0.2429	0.2427	0.2425	0.2424	0.2422	0.2421	0.2420	0.2419	0.2419
15°	0.2601	0.2598	0.2596	0.2594	0.2592	0.2590	0.2589	0.2588	0.2588
16°	0.2771	0.2768	0.2765	0.2763	0.2761	0.2759	0.2757	0.2757	0.2756
17°	0.2942	0.2938	0.2935	0.2932	0.2929	0.2927	0.2925	0.2924	0.2924
18°	0.3112	0.3107	0.3103	0.3099	0.3096	0.3094	0.3092	0.3091	0.3090
19°	0.3281	0.3276	0.3271	0.3267	0.3263	0.3260	0.3258	0.3256	0.3256
20°	0.3450	0.3444	0.3438	0.3433	0.3429	0.3425	0.3422	0.3421	0.3420
21°	0.3618	0.3611	0.3604	0.3598	0.3593	0.3589	0.3586	0.3584	0.3584
22°	0.3785	0.3777	0.3770	0.3763	0.3757	0.3752	0.3749	0.3747	0.3746
23°	0.3952	0.3943	0.3935	0.3927	0.3920	0.3915	0.3911	0.3908	0.3907
24°	0.4118	0.4108	0.4098	0.4090	0.4082	0.4076	0.4071	0.4068	0.4067
25°	0.4284	0.4272	0.4261	0.4251	0.4243	0.4236	0.4230	0.4227	0.4226
26°	0.4449	0.4436	0.4423	0.4412	0.4402	0.4394	0.4389	0.4385	0.4384
27°	0.4613	0.4598	0.4584	0.4572	0.4561	0.4552	0.4545	0.4541	0.4540
28°	0.4776	0.4760	0.4744	0.4730	0.4718	0.4708	0.4701	0.4696	0.4695
29°	0.4938	0.4920	0.4903	0.4887	0.4874	0.4863	0.4855	0.4850	0.4848
30°	0.5100	0.5080	0.5061	0.5044	0.5029	0.5016	0.5007	0.5002	0.5000
31°	0.5261	0.5239	0.5218	0.5199	0.5182	0.5169	0.5159	0.5152	0.5150
32°	0.5421	0.5396	0.5373	0.5352	0.5334	0.5319	0.5308	0.5301	0.5299
33°	0.5580	0.5553	0.5528	0.5505	0.5485	0.5468	0.5456	0.5449	0.5446
34°	0.5738	0.5709	0.5681	0.5656	0.5634	0.5616	0.5603	0.5595	0.5592
35°	0.5895	0.5863	0.5833	0.5806	0.5782	0.5762	0.5748	0.5739	0.5736
36°	0.6051	0.6017	0.5984	0.5954	0.5928	0.5907	0.5891	0.5881	0.5878
37°	0.6207	0.6169	0.6134	0.6101	0.6073	0.6050	0.6032	0.6022	0.6018
38°	0.6361	0.6321	0.6282	0.6247	0.6216	0.6191	0.6172	0.6160	0.6157
39°	0.6515	0.6471	0.6429	0.6391	0.6357	0.6330	0.6310	0.6297	0.6293
40°	0.6667	0.6620	0.6575	0.6533	0.6497	0.6468	0.6446	0.6432	0.6428
41°	0.6818	0.6767	0.6719	0.6674	0.6636	0.6604	0.6580	0.6566	0.6561
42°	0.6969	0.6914	0.6862	0.6814	0.6772	0.6738	0.6712	0.6697	0.6691
43°	0.7118	0.7059	0.7003	0.6952	0.6907	0.6870	0.6843	0.6826	0.6820
44°	0.7266	0.7204	0.7144	0.7088	0.7040	0.7000	0.6971	0.6953	0.6947
45°	0.7414	0.7346	0.7282	0.7223	0.7171	0.7129	0.7097	0.7078	0.7071

ELLIPTIC INTEGRALS OF THE SECOND KIND: $E(k, \phi)$ (Continued)

$$E(k, \phi) = \int_0^\phi \sqrt{(1 - k^2 \sin^2 \Phi)}\,d\Phi, \quad \theta = \sin^{-1} k$$

θ \ ϕ	5°	10°	15°	20°	25°	30°	35°	40°	45°
46°	0.8023	0.8006	0.7977	0.7939	0.7891	0.7835	0.7772	0.7704	0.7633
47°	0.8197	0.8179	0.8149	0.8108	0.8057	0.7998	0.7931	0.7858	0.7782
48°	0.8371	0.8352	0.8320	0.8277	0.8223	0.8160	0.8089	0.8012	0.7931
49°	0.8545	0.8525	0.8491	0.8446	0.8389	0.8322	0.8247	0.8165	0.8079
50°	0.8719	0.8698	0.8663	0.8614	0.8554	0.8483	0.8404	0.8317	0.8227
51°	0.8894	0.8871	0.8834	0.8783	0.8719	0.8644	0.8560	0.8469	0.8373
52°	0.9068	0.9044	0.9004	0.8951	0.8884	0.8805	0.8716	0.8620	0.8518
53°	0.9242	0.9217	0.9175	0.9119	0.9048	0.8965	0.8872	0.8770	0.8663
54°	0.9416	0.9389	0.9345	0.9287	0.9212	0.9125	0.9026	0.8919	0.8806
55°	0.9590	0.9562	0.9517	0.9454	0.9376	0.9284	0.9181	0.9068	0.8949
56°	0.9764	0.9735	0.9687	0.9622	0.9540	0.9443	0.9335	0.9216	0.9091
57°	0.9938	0.9908	0.9858	0.9789	0.9703	0.9602	0.9488	0.9363	0.9232
58°	1.0112	1.0080	1.0028	0.9956	0.9866	0.9760	0.9641	0.9510	0.9372
59°	1.0286	1.0253	1.0198	1.0123	1.0029	1.9918	0.9793	0.9656	0.9511
60°	1.0460	1.0426	1.0368	1.0290	1.0191	1.0076	0.9945	0.9801	0.9650
61°	1.0634	1.0598	1.0538	1.0456	1.0354	1.0233	1.0096	0.9946	0.9787
62°	1.0808	1.0771	1.0708	1.0623	1.0516	1.0389	1.0246	1 0090	0.9924
63°	1.0982	1.0943	1.0878	1.0789	1.0678	1.0546	1.0397	1.0233	1.0060
64°	1.1156	1.1115	1.1048	1.0955	1.0839	1.0702	1.0547	1.0376	1.0195
65°	1.1330	1.1288	1.1218	1.1121	1.1001	1.0858	1.0696	1.0518	1.0329
66°	1.1504	1.1460	1.1387	1.1287	1.1162	1.1013	1.0845	1.0660	1.0463
67°	1.1678	1.1632	1.1557	1.1453	1.1323	1.1168	1.0993	1.0801	1.0596
68°	1.1852	1.1805	1.1726	1.1618	1.1483	1.1323	1.1141	1.0941	1.0728
69°	1.2026	1.1977	1.1896	1.1784	1.1644	1.1478	1.1289	1.1081	1.0859
70°	1.2200	1.2149	1.2065	1.1949	1.1804	1.1632	1.1436	1.1221	1.0990
71°	1.2374	1.2321	1.2234	1.2114	1.1964	1.1786	1.1583	1.1359	1.1120
72°	1.2548	1.2493	1.2403	1.2280	1.2124	1.1939	1.1729	1.1498	1.1250
73°	1.2722	1.2666	1.2573	1.2445	1.2284	1.2093	1.1875	1.1636	1.1379
74°	1.2896	1.2838	1.2742	1.2609	1.2443	1.2246	1.2021	1.1773	1.1507
75°	1.3070	1.3010	1.2911	1.2774	1.2603	1.2399	1.2167	1.1910	1.1635
76°	1.3244	1.3182	1.3080	1.2939	1.2762	1.2552	1.2312	1.2047	1.1762
77°	1.3418	1.3354	1.3249	1.3104	1.2921	1.2704	1.2457	1.2183	1.1889
78°	1.3592	1.3526	1.3417	1.3268	1.3080	1.2856	1.2601	1.2319	1.2015
79°	1.3765	1.3698	1.3586	1.3432	1.3239	1.3009	1.2746	1.2454	1.2141
80°	1.3939	1.3870	1.3755	1.3597	1.3398	1.3161	1.2890	1.2590	1.2266
81°	1.4113	1.4042	1.3924	1.3761	1.3556	1.3312	1.3034	1.2725	1.2391
82°	1.4287	1.4214	1.4093	1.3925	1.3715	1.3464	1.3177	1.2859	1.2516
83°	1.4461	1.4386	1.4261	1.4090	1.3873	1.3616	1.3321	1.2994	1.2640
84°	1.4635	1.4558	1.4430	1.4254	1.4032	1.3767	1.3464	1.3128	1.2765
85°	1.4809	1.4729	1.4598	1.4418	1.4190	1.3919	1.3608	1.3262	1.2889
86°	1.4983	1.4901	1.4767	1.4582	1.4348	1.4070	1.3751	1.3396	1.3012
87°	1.5156	1.5073	1.4936	1.4746	1.4507	1.4221	1.3894	1.3530	1.3136
88°	1.5330	1.5245	1.5104	1.4910	1.4665	1.4372	1.4037	1.3664	1.3260
89°	1.5504	1.5417	1.5273	1.5074	1.4823	1.4523	1.4180	1.3798	1.3383
90°	1.5678	1.5589	1.5442	1.5238	1.4981	1.4675	1.4323	1.3931	1.3506

ELLIPTIC INTEGRALS OF THE SECOND KIND: $E(k, \phi)$ (Continued)

$$E(k, \phi) = \int_0^\phi \sqrt{(1 - k^2 \sin^2 \Phi)}\,d\Phi, \quad \theta = \sin^{-1} k$$

θ / ϕ	50°	55°	60°	65°	70°	75°	80°	85°	90°
46°	0.7560	0.7488	0.7419	0.7356	0.7301	0.7255	0.7221	0.7200	0.7193
47°	0.7705	0.7628	0.7555	0.7488	0.7429	0.7380	0.7344	0.7321	0.7314
48°	0.7849	0.7768	0.7690	0.7618	0.7555	0.7502	0.7464	0.7440	0.7431
49°	0.7992	0.7905	0.7822	0.7746	0.7679	0.7623	0.7581	0.7556	0.7547
50°	0.8134	0.8042	0.7954	0.7872	0.7801	0.7741	0.7697	0.7670	0.7660
51°	0.8275	0.8177	0.8084	0.7997	0.7921	0.7858	0.7811	0.7781	0.7771
52°	0.8414	0.8311	0.8212	0.8120	0.8039	0.7972	0.7922	0.7891	0.7880
53°	0.8553	0.8444	0.8339	0.8241	0.8155	0.8084	0.8031	0.7998	0.7986
54°	0.8690	0.8575	0.8464	0.8361	0.8270	0.8194	0.8137	0.8102	0.8090
55°	0.8827	0.8705	0.8588	0.8479	0.8382	0.8302	0.8242	0.8204	0.8192
56°	0.8962	0.8834	0.8710	0.8595	0.8493	0.8408	0.8344	0.8304	0.8290
57°	0.9096	0.8961	0.8831	0.8709	0.8601	0.8511	0.8443	0.8401	0.8387
58°	0.9230	0.9088	0.8950	0.8822	0.8707	0.8612	0.8540	0.8496	0.8480
59°	0.9362	0.9213	0.9068	0.8932	0.8812	0.8711	0.8635	0.8588	0.8572
60°	0.9493	0.9336	0.9184	0.9042	0.8914	0.8808	0.8728	0.8677	0.8660
61°	0.9623	0.9459	0.9299	0.9149	0.9015	0.8903	0.8817	0.8764	0.8746
62°	0.9752	0.9580	0.9412	0.9254	0.9113	0.8995	0.8905	0.8849	0.8829
63°	0.9880	0.9700	0.9524	0.9358	0.9210	0.9085	0.8990	0.8930	0.8910
64°	1.0007	0.9818	0.9634	0.9460	0.9304	0.9173	0.9072	0.9009	0.8988
65°	1.0133	0.9936	0.9743	0.9561	0.9397	0.9258	0.9152	0.9086	0.9063
66°	1.0258	1.0052	0.9850	0.9659	0.9487	0.9341	0.9230	0.9159	0.9135
67°	1.0383	1.0167	0.9956	0.9756	0.9576	0.9422	0.9305	0.9230	0.9205
68°	1.0506	1.0281	1.0061	0.9852	0.9662	0.9501	0.9377	0.9299	0.9272
69°	1.0628	1.0394	1.0164	0.9946	0.9747	0.9578	0.9447	0.9364	0.9336
70°	1.0750	1.0506	1.0266	1.0038	0.9830	0.9652	0.9514	0.9427	0.9397
71°	1.0871	1.0617	1.0367	1.0129	0.9911	0.9724	0.9579	0.9487	0.9455
72°	1.0991	1.0727	1.0467	1.0218	0.9990	0.9794	0.9642	0.9544	0.9511
73°	1.1110	1.0836	1.0565	1.0306	1.0067	0.9862	0.9702	0.9599	0.9563
74°	1.1228	1.0944	1.0662	1.0392	1.0143	0.9928	0.9759	0.9650	0.9613
75°	1.1346	1.1051	1.0759	1.0477	1.0217	0.9992	0.9814	0.9699	0.9659
76°	1.1463	1.1158	1.0854	1.0561	1.0290	1.0053	0.9867	0.9745	0.9703
77°	1.1580	1.1263	1.0948	1.0643	1.0361	1.0113	0.9917	0.9789	0.9744
78°	1.1695	1.1368	1.1041	1.0724	1.0430	1.0171	0.9965	0.9829	0.9781
79°	1.1811	1.1472	1.1133	1.0805	1.0498	1.0228	1.0011	0.9867	0.9816
80°	1.1926	1.1576	1.1225	1.0884	1.0565	1.0282	1.0054	0.9902	0.9848
81°	1.2040	1.1678	1.1316	1.0962	1.0630	1.0335	1.0096	0.9935	0.9877
82°	1.2154	1.1781	1.1406	1.1040	1.0695	1.0387	1.0135	0.9965	0.9903
83°	1.2267	1.1883	1.1495	1.1116	1.0758	1.0437	1.0173	0.9992	0.9925
84°	1.2381	1.1984	1.1584	1.1192	1.0821	1.0486	1.0209	1.0017	0.9945
85°	1.2493	1.2085	1.1673	1.1267	1.0882	1.0534	1.0244	1.0039	0.9962
86°	1.2606	1.2186	1.1761	1.1342	1.0944	1.0581	1.0277	1.0060	0.9976
87°	1.2719	1.2286	1.1848	1.1417	1.1004	1.0628	1.0309	1.0078	0.9986
88°	1.2831	1.2386	1.1936	1.1491	1.1064	1.0673	1.0340	1.0095	0.9994
89°	1.2943	1.2487	1.2023	1.1565	1.1124	1.0719	1.0371	1.0111	0.9998
90°	1.3055	1.2587	1.2111	1.1638	1.1184	1.0764	1.0401	1.0127	1.0000

COMPLETE ELLIPTIC INTEGRALS

$$K = \int_0^{\pi/2} \frac{d\Phi}{\sqrt{1 - k^2 \sin^2 \Phi}} = F\left(k, \frac{\pi}{2}\right)$$

$\sin^{-1} k$	K	$\log K$	$\sin^{-1} k$	K	$\log K$
0°	1.5708	0.196120	**40°**	1.7868	0.252068
1	1.5709	0.196153	41	1.7992	0.255085
2	1.5713	0.196252	42	1.8122	0.258197
3	1.5719	0.196418	43	1.8256	0.261406
4	1.5727	0.196649	44	1.8396	0.264716
5	1.5738	0.196947	**45**	1.8541	0.268127
6	1.5751	0.197312	46	1.8691	0.271644
7	1.5767	0.197743	47	1.8848	0.275267
8	1.5785	0.198241	48	1.9011	0.279001
9	1.5805	0.198806	49	1.9180	0.282848
10	1.5828	0.199438	**50**	1.9356	0.286811
11	1.5854	0.200137	51	1.9539	0.290895
12	1.5882	0.200904	52	1.9729	0.295101
13	1.5913	0.201740	53	1.9927	0.299435
14	1.5946	0.202643	54	2.0133	0.303901
15	1.5981	0.203615	**55**	2.0347	0.308504
16	1.6020	0.204657	56	2.0571	0.313247
17	1.6061	0.205768	57	2.0804	0.318138
18	1.6105	0.206948	58	2.1047	0.323182
19	1.6151	0.208200	59	2.1300	0.328384
20	1.6200	0.209522	**60**	2.1565	0.333753
21	1.6252	0.210916	61	2.1842	0.339295
22	1.6307	0.212382	62	2.2132	0.345020
23	1.6365	0.213921	63	2.2435	0.350936
24	1.6426	0.215533	64	2.2754	0.357053
25	1.6490	0.217219	**65**	2.3088	0.363384
26	1.6557	0.218981	66	2.3439	0.369940
27	1.6627	0.220818	67	2.3809	0.376736
28	1.6701	0.222732	68	2.4198	0.383787
29	1.6777	0.224723	69	2.4610	0.391112
30	1.6858	0.226793	**70**	2.5046	0.398730
31	1.6941	0.228943	71	2.5507	0.406665
32	1.7028	0.231173	72	2.5998	0.414943
33	1.7119	0.233485	73	2.6521	0.423596
34	1.7214	0.235880	74	2.7081	0.432660
35	1.7312	0.238359	**75**	2.7681	0.442176
36	1.7415	0.240923	76	2.8327	0.452196
37	1.7522	0.243575	77	2.9026	0.462782
38	1.7633	0.246315	78	2.9786	0.474008
39	1.7748	0.249146	79	3.0617	0.485967
40	1.7868	0.252068	**80**	3.1534	0.498777

COMPLETE ELLIPTIC INTEGRALS (Continued)

$$K = \int_0^{\pi/2} \frac{d\Phi}{\sqrt{1 - k^2 \sin^2 \Phi}} = F\left(k, \frac{\pi}{2}\right)$$

$\sin^{-1} k$	K	$\log K$	$\sin^{-1} k$	K	$\log K$
80°	3.1534	0.498777	**85°**	3.8317	0.583396
81	3.2553	0.512591	86	4.0528	0.607751
82	3.3699	0.527613	87	4.3387	0.637355
83	3.5004	0.544120	88	4.7427	0.676027
84	3.6519	0.562514	89	5.4349	0.735192
85	3.8317	0.583396	**90**	∞	∞

Values of K for $\sin^{-1} k = 85°$ to $89°$ by $0.1°$ and $89°$ to $90°$ by minutes

$\sin^{-1} k$	K	$\log K$	$\sin^{-1} k$		K	$\log K$
85.0°	3.832	0.58343	**89°**	**0′**	5.435	0.73520
85.1	3.852	0.58569	89	2	5.469	0.73791
85.2	3.872	0.58794	89	4	5.504	0.74068
85.3	3.893	0.59028	89	6	5.540	0.74351
85.4	3.914	0.59262	89	8	5.578	0.74648
85.5	3.936	0.59506	**89**	**10**	5.617	0.74950
85.6	3.958	0.59748	89	12	5.658	0.75266
85.7	3.981	0.59999	89	14	5.700	0.75587
85.8	4.004	0.60249	89	16	5.745	0.75929
85.9	4.028	0.60509	89	18	5.791	0.76275
86.0	4.053	0.60778	**89**	**20**	5.840	0.76641
86.1	4.078	0.61045	89	22	5.891	0.77019
86.2	4.104	0.61321	89	24	5.946	0.77422
86.3	4.130	0.61595	89	26	6.003	0.77837
86.4	4.157	0.61878	89	28	6.063	0.78269
86.5	4.185	0.62170	**89**	**30**	6.128	0.78732
86.6	4.214	0.62469	89	32	6.197	0.79218
86.7	4.244	0.62778	89	34	6.271	0.79734
86.8	4.274	0.63083	89	36	6.351	0.80284
86.9	4.306	0.63407	89	38	6.438	0.80875
87.0	4.339	0.63739	**89**	**40**	6.533	0.81511
87.1	4.372	0.64068	89	41	6.584	0.81849
87.2	4.407	0.64414	89	42	6.639	0.82210
87.3	4.444	0.64777	89	43	6.696	0.82582
87.4	4.481	0.65137	89	44	6.756	0.82969
87.5	4.520	0.65514	**89**	**45**	6.821	0.83385
87.6	4.561	0.65916	89	46	6.890	0.83822
87.7	4.603	0.66304	89	47	6.964	0.84286
87.8	4.648	0.66727	89	48	7.044	0.84782
87.9	4.694	0.67154	89	49	7.131	0.85315
88.0	4.743	0.67605	**89**	**50**	7.226	0.85890
88.1	4.794	0.68070	89	51	7.332	0.86522
88.2	4.848	0.68556	89	52	7.449	0.87210
88.3	4.905	0.69064	89	53	7.583	0.87984
88.4	4.965	0.69592	89	54	7.737	0.88857
88.5	5.030	0.70157	**89**	**55**	7.919	0.89867
88.6	5.099	0.70749	89	56	8.143	0.91078
88.7	5.173	0.71374	89	57	8.430	0.92583
88.8	5.253	0.72041	89	58	8.836	0.94626
88.9	5.340	0.72754	89	59	9.529	0.97905
89.0	5.435	0.73520	**90**	**0**	∞	∞

COMPLETE ELLIPTIC INTEGRALS (Continued)

$$E = \int_0^{\pi/2} \sqrt{1 - k^2 \sin^2 \Phi} \cdot d\Phi = E\left(k, \frac{\pi}{2}\right)$$

$\sin^{-1} k$	E	$\log E$	$\sin^{-1} k$	E	$\log E$
0°	1.5708	0.196120	**45°**	1.3506	0.130541
1	1.5707	0.196087	46	1.3418	0.127690
2	1.5703	0.195988	47	1.3329	0.124788
3	1.5697	0.195822	48	1.3238	0.121836
4	1.5689	0.195591	49	1.3147	0.118836
5	1.5678	0.195293	**50**	1.3055	0.115790
6	1.5665	0.194930	51	1.2963	0.112698
7	1.5649	0.194500	52	1.2870	0.109563
8	1.5632	0.194004	53	1.2776	0.106386
9	1.5611	0.193442	54	1.2681	0.103169
10	1.5589	0.192815	**55**	1.2587	0.099915
11	1.5564	0.192121	56	1.2492	0.096626
12	1.5537	0.191362	57	1.2397	0.093303
13	1.5507	0.190537	58	1.2301	0.089950
14	1.5476	0.189646	59	1.2206	0.086569
15	1.5442	0.188690	**60**	1.2111	0.083164
16	1.5405	0.187668	61	1.2015	0.079738
17	1.5367	0.186581	62	1.1920	0.076293
18	1.5326	0.185428	63	1.1826	0.072834
19	1.5283	0.184210	64	1.1732	0.069364
20	1.5238	0.182928	**65**	1.1638	0.065889
21	1.5191	0.181580	66	1.1545	0.062412
22	1.5141	0.180168	67	1.1453	0.058937
23	1.5090	0.178691	68	1.1362	0.055472
24	1.5037	0.177150	69	1.1272	0.052020
25	1.4981	0.175545	**70**	1.1184	0.048589
26	1.4924	0.173876	71	1.1096	0.045183
27	1.4864	0.172144	72	1.1011	0.041812
28	1.4803	0.170348	73	1.0927	0.038481
29	1.4740	0.168489	74	1.0844	0.035200
30	1.4675	0.166567	**75**	1.0764	0.031976
31	1.4608	0.164583	76	1.0686	0.028819
32	1.4539	0.162537	77	1.0611	0.025740
33	1.4469	0.160429	78	1.0538	0.022749
34	1.4397	0.158261	79	1.0468	0.019858
35	1.4323	0.156031	**80**	1.0401	0.017081
36	1.4248	0.153742	81	1.0338	0.014432
37	1.4171	0.151393	82	1.0278	0.011927
38	1.4092	0.148985	83	1.0223	0.009584
39	1.4013	0.146519	84	1.0172	0.007422
40	1.3931	0.143995	**85**	1.0127	0.005465
41	1.3849	0.141414	86	1.0086	0.003740
42	1.3765	0.138778	87	1.0053	0.002278
43	1.3680	0.136086	88	1.0026	0.001121
44	1.3594	0.133340	89	1.0008	0.000326
45	1.3506	0.130541	**90**	1.0000	0.000000

SINE, COSINE, AND EXPONENTIAL INTEGRALS

$$Si(x) = \int_0^x \frac{\sin v}{v}\, dv; \qquad Ci(x) = \int_\infty^x \frac{\cos v}{v}\, dv;$$

$$Ei(x) = \int_{-\infty}^x \frac{e^v}{v}\, dv; \qquad -Ei(-x) = \int_x^\infty \frac{e^{-v}}{v}\, dv$$

x	$Si(x)$	$Ci(x)$	$Ei(x)$	$-Ei(-x)$
0.0	0.00000	$-\infty$	$-\infty$	$+\infty$
0.1	0.09994	-1.72787	-1.62281	1.82292
0.2	.19956	-1.04221	- .82176	1.22265
0.3	.29850	- .64917	- .30267	.90568
0.4	.39646	- .37881	.10477	.70238
0.5	.49311	- .17778	.45422	.55977
0.6	.58813	- .02227	.76988	.45438
0.7	.68122	.10051	1.06491	.37377
0.8	.77210	.19828	1.34740	.31060
0.9	.86047	.27607	1.62281	.26018
1.0	.94608	.33740	1.89512	.21938
1.1	1.02869	.38487	2.16738	.18599
1.2	1.10805	.42046	2.44209	.15841
1.3	1.18396	.44574	2.72140	.13545
1.4	1.25623	.46201	3.00721	.11622
1.5	1.32468	.47036	3.30129	.10002
1.6	1.38918	.47173	3.60532	.08631
1.7	1.44959	.46697	3.92096	.07465
1.8	1.50582	.45681	4.24987	.06471
1.9	1.55778	.44194	4.59371	.05620
2.0	1.60541	.42298	4.95423	.04890
2.1	1.64870	.40051	5.33324	.04261
2.2	1.68762	.37507	5.73261	.03719
2.3	1.72221	.34718	6.15438	.03250
2.4	1.75249	.31729	6.60067	.02844
2.5	1.77852	.28587	7.07377	.02491
2.6	1.80039	.25334	7.57611	.02185
2.7	1.81821	.22008	8.11035	.01918
2.8	1.83210	.18649	8.67930	.01686
2.9	1.84219	.15290	9.28602	.01482
3.0	1.84865	.11963	9.93383	.01305
3.1	1.85166	.08699	10.6263	.01149
3.2	1.85140	.05526	11.3673	.01013
3.3	1.84808	.02468	12.1610	.00894
3.4	1.84191	- .00452	13.0121	.00789
3.5	1.83313	- .03213	13.9254	.00697
3.6	1.82195	- .05797	14.9063	.00616
3.7	1.80862	- .08190	15.9606	.00545
3.8	1.79339	- .10378	17.0948	.00482
3.9	1.77650	- .12350	18.3157	.00427
4.0	1.75820	- .14098	19.6309	.00378
4.1	1.73874	- .15617	21.0485	.00335
4.2	1.71837	- .16901	22.5774	.00297
4.3	1.69732	- .17951	24.2274	.00263
4.4	1.67583	- .18766	26.0090	.00234

SINE, COSINE, AND EXPONENTIAL INTEGRALS (Continued)

x	$Si(x)$	$Ci(x)$	$Ei(x)$	$-Ei(-x)$
4.5	1.65414	− .19349	27.9337	.00207
4.6	1.63246	− .19705	30.0141	.00184
4.7	1.61100	− .19839	32.2639	.00164
4.8	1.58998	− .19760	34.6979	.00145
4.9	1.56956	− .19478	37.3325	.00129
5.0	1.54993	− .19003	40.1853	.00115
5.1	1.53125	− .18348	43.2757	.00102
5.2	1.51367	− .17525	46.6249	.00091
5.3	1.49732	− .16551	50.2557	.00081
5.4	1.48230	− .15439	54.1935	.00072
5.5	1.46872	− .14205	58.4655	.00064
5.6	1.45667	− .12867	63.1018	.00057
5.7	1.44620	− .11441	68.1350	.00051
5.8	1.43736	− .09944	73.6008	.00045
5.9	1.43018	− .08393	79.5382	.00040
6.0	1.42469	− .06806	85.9898	.00036
6.1	1.42087	− .05198	93.0020	.00032
6.2	1.41871	− .03587	100.626	.00029
6.3	1.41817	− .01989	108.916	.00026
6.4	1.41922	− .00418	117.935	.00023
6.5	1.42179	+ .01110	127.747	.00020
6.6	1.42582	+ .02582	138.426	.00018
6.7	1.43121	.03986	150.050	.00016
6.8	1.43787	.05308	162.707	.00014
6.9	1.44570	.06539	176.491	.00013
7.0	1.45460	.07670	191.505	.00012
7.1	1.46443	.08691	207.863	.00010
7.2	1.47509	.09596	225.688	.00009
7.3	1.48644	.10379	245.116	.00008
7.4	1.49834	.11036	266.296	.00007
7.5	1.51068	.11563	289.388	.00007
7.6	1.52331	.11960	314.572	.00006
7.7	1.53611	.12225	342.040	.00005
7.8	1.54894	.12359	372.006	.00005
7.9	1.56167	.12364	404.701	.00004
8.0	1.57419	.12243	440.380	.00004
8.1	1.58637	.12002	479.322	.00003
8.2	1.59810	.11644	521.831	.00003
8.3	1.60928	.11177	568.242	.00003
8.4	1.61981	.10607	681.919	.00002
8.5	1.62960	.09943	674.264	.00002
8.6	1.63857	.09194	734.714	.00002
8.7	1.64665	.08368	800.749	.00002
8.8	1.65379	.07476	872.895	.00002
8.9	1.65993	.06528	951.728	.00001
9.0	1.66504	.05535	1037.88	.00001
9.1	1.66908	.04507	1132.04	.00001
9.2	1.67205	.03455	1234.96	.00001
9.3	1.67393	.02391	1347.48	.00001
9.4	1.67473	.01325	1470.51	.00001

SINE, COSINE, AND EXPONENTIAL INTEGRALS (Continued)

x	Si(x)	Ci(x)	Ei(x)	-Ei(-x)
9.5	1.67446	.00268	1605.03	.00001
9.6	1.67316	- .00771	1752.14	.00001
9.7	1.67084	- .01780	1913.05	.00001
9.8	1.66757	- .02752	2089.05	.00001
9.9	1.66338	- .03676	2281.58	.00000
10.0	1.65835	- .04546	2492.23	.00000
10.5	1.62294	- .07828	3883.74	.00000
11.0	1.57831	- .08956	6071.41	.00000
11.5	1.53572	- .07857	9518.20	.00000
12.0	1.50497	- .04978	14959.5	.00000
12.5	1.49234	- .01141	23565.1	.00000
13.0	1.49936	+ .02676	37197.7	.00000
13.5	1.52291	+ .05576	58827.0	.00000
14.0	1.55621	.06940	93193.0	.00000
14.5	1.59072	.06554	147866.	.00000
15.0	1.61819	.04628	234955.	.00000

ORTHOGONAL POLYNOMIALS

I

Name: Legendre   *Symbol*: $P_n(x)$ *Interval*: $[-1, 1]$

Differential Equation: $(1 - x^2)y'' - 2xy' + n(n + 1)y = 0$

$$y = P_n(x)$$

Explicit Expression: $P_n(x) = \dfrac{1}{2^n} \displaystyle\sum_{m=0}^{[n/2]} (-1)^m \binom{n}{m}\binom{2n - 2m}{n} x^{n-2m}$

Recurrence Relation: $(n + 1)P_{n+1}(x) = (2n + 1)xP_n(x) - nP_{n-1}(x)$

Weight: 1 *Standardization*: $P_n(1) = 1$

Norm: $\displaystyle\int_{-1}^{+1} [P_n(x)]^2 \, dx = \dfrac{2}{2n + 1}$

Rodrigues' Formula: $P_n(x) = \dfrac{(-1)^n}{2^n n!} \dfrac{d^n}{dx^n} \{(1 - x^2)^n\}$

Generating Function: $R^{-1} = \displaystyle\sum_{n=0}^{\infty} P_n(x)z^n$; $-1 < x < 1$, $|z| < 1$,

$$R = \sqrt{1 - 2xz + z^2}.$$

Inequality: $|P_n(x)| \le 1$, $-1 \le x \le 1$.

II

Name: Tschebysheff, First Kind   *Symbol*: $T_n(x)$ *Interval*: $[-1, 1]$

Differential Equation: $(1 - x^2)y'' - xy' + n^2 y = 0$

$$y = T_n(x)$$

Explicit Expression: $\dfrac{n}{2} \displaystyle\sum_{m=0}^{[n/2]} (-1)^m \dfrac{(n - m - 1)!}{m!(n - 2m)!} (2x)^{n-2m} = \cos(n \arccos x) = T_n(x)$

Recurrence Relation: $T_{n+1}(x) = 2xT_n(x) - T_{n-1}(x)$

Weight: $(1 - x^2)^{-1/2}$ *Standardization*: $T_n(1) = 1$

Norm: $\displaystyle\int_{-1}^{+1} (1 - x^2)^{-1/2}[T_n(x)]^2 \, dx = \begin{cases} \pi/2, & n \ne 0 \\ \pi, & n = 0 \end{cases}$

Rodrigues' Formula: $\dfrac{(-1)^n(1 - x^2)^{1/2} \sqrt{\pi}}{2^n \Gamma(n + \frac{1}{2})} \dfrac{d^n}{dx^n} \{(1 - x^2)^{n-(1/2)}\} = T_n(x)$

Generating Function: $\dfrac{1 - xz}{1 - 2xz + z^2} = \displaystyle\sum_{n=0}^{\infty} T_n(x)z^n$, $-1 < x < 1$, $|z| < 1$.

Inequality: $|T_n(x)| \le 1$, $-1 \le x \le 1$.

Orthogonal Polynomials

III

Name: Tschebysheff, Second Kind   *Symbol*: $U_n(x)$ *Interval*: $[-1, 1]$

Differential Equation: $(1 - x^2)y'' - 3xy' + n(n + 2)y = 0$

$$y = U_n(x)$$

Explicit Expression: $U_n(x) = \sum_{m=0}^{[n/2]} (-1)^m \frac{(m - n)!}{m!(n - 2m)!} (2x)^{n-2m}$

$$U_n(\cos \theta) = \frac{\sin[(n + 1)\theta]}{\sin \theta}$$

Recurrence Relation: $U_{n+1}(x) = 2x U_n(x) - U_{n-1}(x)$

Weight: $(1 - x^2)^{1/2}$ *Standardization*: $U_n(1) = n + 1$

Norm: $\int_{-1}^{+1} (1 - x^2)^{1/2}[U_n(x)]^2 dx = \frac{\pi}{2}$

Rodrigues' Formula: $U_n(x) = \frac{(-1)^n(n + 1)\sqrt{\pi}}{(1 - x^2)^{1/2}2^{n+1}\Gamma(n + \frac{3}{2})} \frac{d^n}{dx^n}\{(1 - x^2)^{n+(1/2)}\}$

Generating Function: $\frac{1}{1 - 2xz + z^2} = \sum_{n=0}^{\infty} U_n(x)z^n, \; -1 < x < 1, \; |z| < 1.$

Inequality: $|U_n(x)| \le n + 1, \; -1 \le x \le 1.$

IV

Name: Jacobi   *Symbol*: $P_n^{(\alpha,\beta)}(x)$ *Interval*: $[-1, 1]$

Differential Equation:

$$(1 - x^2)y'' + [\beta - \alpha - (\alpha + \beta + 2)x]y' + n(n + \alpha + \beta + 1)y = 0$$
$$y = P_n^{(\alpha,\beta)}(x)$$

Explicit Expression: $P_n^{(\alpha,\beta)}(x) = \frac{1}{2^n} \sum_{m=0}^{n} \binom{n + \alpha}{m}\binom{n + \beta}{n - m}(x - 1)^{n-m}(x + 1)^m$

Recurrence Relation: $2(n + 1)(n + \alpha + \beta + 1)(2n + \alpha + \beta)P_{n+1}^{(\alpha,\beta)}(x)$

$$= (2n + \alpha + \beta + 1)[(\alpha^2 - \beta^2) + (2n + \alpha + \beta + 2)$$
$$\times (2n + \alpha + \beta)x]P_n^{(\alpha,\beta)}(x)$$
$$- 2(n + \alpha)(n + \beta)(2n + \alpha + \beta + 2)P_{n-1}^{(\alpha,\beta)}(x)$$

Weight: $(1 - x)^\alpha(1 + x)^\beta; \; \alpha, \beta > 1$ *Standardization*: $P_n^{(\alpha,\beta)}(x) = \binom{n + \alpha}{n}$

Norm: $\int_{-1}^{+1} (1 - x)^\alpha(1 + x)^\beta[P_n^{(\alpha,\beta)}(x)]^2 dx = \frac{2^{\alpha+\beta+1}\Gamma(n + \alpha + 1)\Gamma(n + \beta + 1)}{(2n + \alpha + \beta + 1)n!\Gamma(n + \alpha + \beta + 1)}$

Rodrigues' Formula: $P_n^{(\alpha,\beta)}(x) = \frac{(-1)^n}{2^n n!(1 - x)^\alpha(1 + x)^\beta} \frac{d^n}{dx^n}\{(1 - x)^{n+\alpha}(1 + x)^{n+\beta}\}$

Orthogonal Polynomials

IV (Continued)

Generating Function: $R^{-1}(1 - z + R)^{-\alpha}(1 + z + R)^{-\beta} = \sum_{n=0}^{\infty} 2^{-\alpha-\beta} P_n^{(\alpha,\beta)}(x) z^n,$

$$R = \sqrt{1 - 2xz + z^2}, |z| < 1$$

Inequality: $\max_{-1 \le x \le 1} |P_n^{(\alpha,\beta)}(x)| = \begin{cases} \binom{n+q}{n} \sim n^q \text{ if } q = \max(\alpha,\beta) \ge -\frac{1}{2} \\[2mm] |P_n^{(\alpha,\beta)}(x')| \sim n^{-1/2} \text{ if } q < -\frac{1}{2} \\[1mm] x' \text{ is one of the two maximum points nearest} \\[2mm] \dfrac{\beta - \alpha}{\alpha + \beta + 1} \end{cases}$

V

Name: Generalized Laguerre   *Symbol:* $L_n^{(\alpha)}(x)$ *Interval:* $[0, \infty]$

Differential Equation: $xy'' + (\alpha + 1 - x)y' + ny = 0$

$$y = L_n^{(\alpha)}(x)$$

Explicit Expression: $L_n^{(\alpha)}(x) = \sum_{m=0}^{n} (-1)^m \binom{n+\alpha}{n-m} \frac{1}{m!} x^m$

Recurrence Relation: $(n + 1) L_{n+1}^{(\alpha)}(x) = [(2n + \alpha + 1) - x] L_n^{(\alpha)}(x) - (n + \alpha) L_{n-1}^{(\alpha)}(x)$

Weight: $x^\alpha e^{-x}, \alpha > -1$ *Standardization:* $L_n^{(\alpha)}(x) = \frac{(-1)^n}{n!} x^n + \cdots$

Norm: $\int_0^\infty x^\alpha e^{-x} [L_n^{(\alpha)}(x)]^2 dx = \frac{\Gamma(n + \alpha + 1)}{n!}$

Rodrigues' Formula: $L_n^{(\alpha)}(x) = \frac{1}{n! x^\alpha e^{-x}} \frac{d^n}{dx^n} \{x^{n+\alpha} e^{-x}\}$

Generating Function: $(1 - z)^{-\alpha-1} \exp\left(\frac{xz}{z-1}\right) = \sum_{n=0}^{\infty} L_n^{(\alpha)}(x) z^n$

Inequality: $|L_n^{(\alpha)}(x)| \le \frac{\Gamma(n + \alpha + 1)}{n! \Gamma(\alpha + 1)} e^{x/2}; \quad \begin{array}{l} x \ge 0 \\ \alpha > 0 \end{array}$

$$|L_n^{(\alpha)}(x)| \le \left[2 - \frac{\Gamma(\alpha + n + 1)}{n! \Gamma(\alpha + 1)}\right] e^{x/2}; \quad \begin{array}{l} x \ge 0 \\ -1 < \alpha < 0 \end{array}$$

Orthogonal Polynomials

Name: Hermite *Symbol:* $H_n(x)$ *Interval:* $[-\infty, \infty]$

Differential Equation: $y'' - 2xy' + 2ny = 0$

Explicit Expression: $H_n(x) = \displaystyle\sum_{m=0}^{[n/2]} \frac{(-1)^m \, n! \, (2x)^{n-2m}}{m! \, (n-2m)!}$

Recurrence Relation: $H_{n+1}(x) = 2x \, H_n(x) - 2n H_{n-1}(x)$

Weight: e^{-x^2} *Standardization:* $H_n(1) = 2^n x^n + \ldots$

Norm: $\displaystyle\int_{-\infty}^{\infty} e^{-x^2} [H_n(x)]^2 \, dx = 2^n \, n! \, \sqrt{\pi}$

Rodriques' Formula: $H_n(x) = (-1)^n \, e^{x^2} \dfrac{d^n}{dx^n} (e^{-x^2})$

Generating Function: $e^{-z^2 + 2zx} = \displaystyle\sum_{n=0}^{\infty} H_n(x) \frac{z^n}{n!}$

Inequality: $|H_n(x)| < e^{\frac{x^2}{2}} \, k \, 2^{n/2} \, \sqrt{n!}$ $k \approx 1.086435$

Coefficients for Orthogonal Polynomials, and for x^n in Terms of Orthogonal Polynomials*

I. Legendre Polynomials: $P_n(x) = a_n^{-1} \sum_{m=0}^{n} c_m x^m$ $x^n = b_n^{-1} \sum_{m=0}^{n} d_m P_m(x)$

	a_n	x^0	x^1	x^2	x^3	x^4	x^5	x^6	x^7
b_n		1	1	3	5	35	63	231	429
P_0	1	1 1		1		7		33	
P_1	1		1 1		3		27		143
P_2	2	−1		3 2		20		110	
P_3	2		−3		5 2		28		182
P_4	8	3		−30		35 8		72	
P_5	8		15		−70		63 8		88
P_6	16	−5		105		−315		231 16	
P_7	16		−35		315		−693		429 16

$$P_6(x) = \frac{1}{16}[231x^6 - 315x^4 + 105x^2 - 5] \qquad x^6 = \frac{1}{231}[33P_0 + 110P_2 + 72P_4 + 16P_6]$$

II. Tschebysheff Polynomials: $T_n(x) = \sum_{m=0}^{n} c_m x^m$ $x^n = b_n^{-1} \sum_{m=0}^{n} d_m T_m(x)$

	x^0	x^1	x^2	x^3	x^4	x^5	x^6	x^7
b_n	1	1	2	4	8	16	32	64
T_0	1 1		1		3		10	
T_1		1 1		3		10		35
T_2	−1		2 1		4		15	
T_3		−3		4 1		5		21
T_4	1		−8		8 1		6	
T_5		5		−20		16 1		7
T_6	−1		18		−48		32 1	
T_7		−7		56		−112		64 1

$$T_6(x) = 32x^6 - 48x^4 + 18x^2 - 1 \qquad x^6 = \frac{1}{32}[10T_0 + 15T_2 + 6T_4 + T_6]$$

III. Tschebysheff Polynomials: $U_n(x) = \sum_{m=0}^{n} c_m x^m$ $x^n = b_n^{-1} \sum_{m=0}^{n} d_m U_m(x)$

	x^0	x^1	x^2	x^3	x^4	x^5	x^6	x^7
b_n	1	2	4	8	16	32	64	128
U_0	1 1		1		2		5	
U_1		2 1		2		5		14
U_2	−1		4 1		3		9	
U_3		−4		8 1		4		14
U_4	1		−12		16 1		5	
U_5		6		−32		32 1		6
U_6	−1		24		−80		64 1	
U_7		−8		80		−192		128 1

$$U_6(x) = 64x^6 - 80x^4 + 24x^2 - 1 \qquad x^6 = \frac{1}{64}[5U_0 + 9U_2 + 5U_4 + U_6]$$

Coefficients for Orthogonal Polynomials, and for x^n in Terms of Orthogonal Polynomials* (continued)

IV. Jacobi Polynomials $P_n^{(\alpha,\beta)}(x) = a_n^{-1} \sum_{m=0}^{n} c_m (x-1)^m$

	α_n	$(x-1)^0$	$(x-1)^1$	$(x-1)^2$	$(x-1)^3$	$(x-1)^4$	$(x-1)^5$	$(x-1)^6$
$P_0(\alpha,\beta)$	1	1						
$P_1(\alpha,\beta)$	2	$2(\alpha+1)$	$\alpha+\beta+2$					
$P_2(\alpha,\beta)$	8	$4(\alpha+1)_2$	$4(\alpha+\beta+3)(\alpha+2)$	$(\alpha+\beta+3)_2$				
$P_3(\alpha,\beta)$	48	$8(\alpha+1)_3$	$12(\alpha+\beta+4)(\alpha+2)_2$	$6(\alpha+\beta+4)_2(\alpha+3)$	$(\alpha+\beta+4)_3$			
$P_4(\alpha,\beta)$	384	$16(\alpha+1)_4$	$32(\alpha+\beta+5)(\alpha+2)_3$	$24(\alpha+\beta+5)_2(\alpha+3)_2$	$8(\alpha+\beta+5)_3(\alpha+4)$	$(\alpha+\beta+5)_4$		
$P_5(\alpha,\beta)$	3840	$32(\alpha+1)_5$	$80(\alpha+\beta+6)(\alpha+2)_4$	$80(\alpha+\beta+6)_2(\alpha+3)_3$	$40(\alpha+\beta+6)_3(\alpha+4)_2$	$10(\alpha+\beta+6)_4(\alpha+5)$	$(\alpha+\beta+6)_5$	
$P_6(\alpha,\beta)$	46080	$64(\alpha+1)_6$	$192(\alpha+\beta+7)(\alpha+2)_5$	$240(\alpha+\beta+7)_2(\alpha+3)_4$	$160(\alpha+\beta+7)_3(\alpha+4)_3$	$60(\alpha+\beta+7)_4(\alpha+5)_2$	$12(\alpha+\beta+7)_5(\alpha+6)$	$(\alpha+\beta+7)_6$

$$(m)_n = m(m+1)(m+2)\ldots(m+n-1)$$

$$P_5^{(1,1)}(x) = \frac{1}{3840}\left[(8)_5(x-1)^5 + 10(8)_4(6)(x-1)^4 + 40(8)_2(5)_2(x-1)^3 + 80(8)_2(4)_3(x-1)^2 + 80(8)(3)_4(x-1) + 32(2)_5\right]$$

$$P_5^{(1,1)}(x) = \frac{1}{3840}\left[95040(x-1)^5 + 475200(x-1)^4 + 864000(x-1)^3 + 691200(x-1)^2 + 230400(x-1) + 23040\right]$$

Coefficients for Orthogonal Polynomials, and for x^n in Terms of Orthogonal Polynomials* (continued)

V. Laguerre Polynomials: $L_n(x) = \sum_{m=0}^{n} c_m x^m \qquad x^n = b_n^{-1} \sum_{m=0}^{n} d_m L_m(x)$

	x^0	x^1	x^2	x^3	x^4	x^5	x^6	x^7
b_m	1	1	2	6	24	120	720	5040
L_0	1 1	1	2	6	24	120	720	5040
L_1	1	−1 −1	−4	−18	−96	−600	−4320	−35280
L_2	2	−4	1 2	18	144	1200	10800	105840
L_3	6	−18	9	−1 −6	−96	−1200	−14400	−176400
L_4	24	−96	72	−16	1 24	600	10800	17640
L_5	120	−600	600	−200	25	−1 −120	−4320	−105840
L_6	720	−4320	5400	−2400	450	−36	1 720	35280
L_7	5040	−35280	52920	−29400	7350	−882	49	−1 −5040

$$L_6(x) = x^6 - 36x^5 + 450x^4 - 2400x^3 + 5400x^2 - 4320x + 720$$
$$x^6 = \frac{1}{720}[720L_0 - 4320L_1 + 10800L_2 - 14400L_3 + 10800L_4 - 4320L_5 + 720L_6]$$

VI. Hermite polynomials: $H_n(x) = \sum_{m=0}^{n} c_m x^m \qquad x^n = b_n^{-1} \sum_{m=0}^{n} d_m H_m(x)$

	x^0	x^1	x^2	x^3	x^4	x^5	x^6	x^7
b_n	1	2	4	8	16	32	64	128
H_0	1 1		2		12		120	
H_1		2 1		6		60		840
H_2	−2		4 1		12		180	
H_3		−12		8 1		20		420
H_4	12		−48		16 1		30	
H_5		120		−160		32 1		42
H_6	−120		720		−480		64 1	
H_7		−1680		3360		−1344		128 1

$$H_6(x) = 64x^6 - 480x^4 + 720x^2 - 120 \qquad x^6 = \frac{1}{64}[120\,H_0 + 180\,H_2 + 30H_4 + H_6]$$

Abridged from Abramowitz, M. and Stegun, I. A., Eds., *Handbook of Mathematical Functions*, National Bureau of Standards, Washington, D. C., 1964.

LEGENDRE FUNCTIONS

In the following, m and n are positive integers.

1. The differential equation $(1 - z^2) \dfrac{d^2w}{dz^2} - 2z \dfrac{dw}{dz} + n(n + 1)z = 0$ is known as Legendre's differential equation. The Legendre polynomials $P_0(z)$, $P_1(z)$, $P_2(z)$, . . . are solutions of this equation, and are referred to as Surface Zonal Harmonics, for which tables are herewith given.

2. The solution of Legendre's equation can be stated as

$$w = AP_n(z) + BQ_n(z) \qquad |z| < 1$$

or

$$w = AP_n(z) + B\mathfrak{Q}_n(z) \qquad |z| > 1,$$

where A and B are arbitrary constants, $P_n(z)$ the Legendre polynomials, $Q_n(z)$ and $\mathfrak{Q}_n(z)$ Legendre functions of the second kind.

3. The differential equation $(1 - z^2) \dfrac{d^2u}{dz^2} - 2z \dfrac{du}{dz} + \left[n(n + 1) - \dfrac{m^2}{1 - z^2} \right] u = 0$ which is obtained from the Legendre equation in 1. after it has been differentiated m times and u replaced by $(1 - z^2)^{m/2} \left(\dfrac{d^m w}{dz^m} \right)$ is referred to as the "associated Legendre differential equation."

4. The solution for the "associated Legendre differential equation" is given by

$$u = AP_n^m(z) + BQ_n^m(z),$$

where A and B are arbitrary constants and $P_n^m(z)$, $Q_n^m(z)$ are called associated Legendre functions.

5. $P_n(z) = \displaystyle\sum_{1=0}^{m} (-1)^r \frac{(2n - 2r)!}{2^n(r!)(n - r_r)!(n - 2r)!} z^{n-2r} \quad m = \tfrac{1}{2}n,\ n$ even

$$m = \tfrac{1}{2}(n - 1),\ n \text{ odd}$$

$$Q_n(z) = \tfrac{1}{2}P_n(z) \log_e \frac{1 + z}{1 - z} - \sum_{r=1}^{n} \frac{1}{r} P_{r-1}(z)P_{n-r}(z)$$

$$= P_n(z)Q_0(z) - \sum_{r=1}^{n} \frac{1}{r} P_{r-1}(z)P_{n-r}(z)$$

$$Q_0(z) = \tfrac{1}{2} \log_e \frac{1 + z}{1 - z} = \tanh^{-1} z$$

$$\mathfrak{Q}_n(z) = \tfrac{1}{2}P_n(z) \log_e \frac{z + 1}{z - 1} - \sum_{r=1}^{n} \frac{1}{r} P_{r-1}(z) P_{n-r}(z)$$

$$= P_n(z)\mathfrak{Q}_0(z) - \sum_{r=1}^{n} \frac{1}{r} P_{r-1}(z)P_{n-r}(z)$$

$$\mathfrak{Q}_0(z) = \tfrac{1}{2} \log_e \frac{z + 1}{z - 1} = \operatorname{ctnh}^{-1} z$$

LEGENDRE FUNCTIONS (Continued)

6.

n	$P_n(z)$	$Q_n(z)$
0	1	$\dfrac{\log_e}{2}\dfrac{(1+z)}{(1-z)}$
1	z	$zQ_0(z) - 1$
2	$\dfrac{1}{2}(3z^2 - 1)$	$\dfrac{1}{2}(3z^2 - 1)Q_0(z) - \dfrac{3}{2}z$
3	$\dfrac{1}{2}(5z^3 - 3z)$	$\dfrac{1}{2}(5z^3 - 3z)Q_0(z) - \dfrac{5}{2}z^2 + \dfrac{2}{3}$
4	$\dfrac{1}{8}(35z^4 - 30z^2 + 3)$	$\dfrac{1}{8}(35z^4 - 30z^2 + 3)Q_0(z) - \dfrac{35}{8}z^3 + \dfrac{55}{24}z$
5	$\dfrac{1}{8}(63z^5 - 70z^3 + 15z)$	$\dfrac{1}{8}(63z^5 - 70z^3 + 15z)Q_0(z) - \dfrac{63}{8}z^4 + \dfrac{49}{8}z^2 - \dfrac{8}{15}$

7. $\dfrac{1}{(1 - 2xZ + Z^2)^{1/2}} = \sum P_n(x)Z^n$

If $x = \cos\theta = \frac{1}{2}(e^{i\theta} + e^{-i\theta})$, $i = \sqrt{-1}$, then

$$[1 - Z(e^{i\theta} + e^{-i\theta}) + Z^2]^{-1/2} = \sum_{n=0}^{\infty} P_n(\cos\theta)Z^n$$

$P_0(\cos\theta) = 1$

$P_1(\cos\theta) = \cos\theta$

$P_2(\cos\theta) = \dfrac{1}{4}(3\cos 2\theta + 1)$

$P_3(\cos\theta) = \dfrac{1}{8}(5\cos 3\theta + 3\cos\theta)$

$P_4(\cos\theta) = \dfrac{1}{64}(35\cos 4\theta + 20\cos 2\theta + 9)$

$$P_n(\cos\theta) = \frac{(2n)!}{2^{2n}(n!)^2}\left[\cos n\theta + 1/1\,\frac{n}{2n-1}\cos(n-2)\theta\right.$$
$$+ \frac{1\cdot 3}{1\cdot 2}\frac{n(n-1)}{(2n-1)(2n-3)}\cos(n-4)\theta$$
$$\left.+ \frac{1\cdot 3\cdot 5}{1\cdot 2\cdot 3}\frac{n(n-1)(n-2)}{(2n-1)(2n-3)(2n-5)}\cos(n-6)\theta + \cdots\right]$$

LEGENDRE FUNCTIONS (Continued)

8. $P_{2n+1}(0) = 0$

$$P_{2n}(0) = (-1)^n \frac{1 \cdot 3 \cdot 5 \cdot \cdot \cdot (2n-1)}{2 \cdot 4 \cdot 6 \cdot 8 \cdot \cdot \cdot (2n)}$$

$$P_n(1) = 1$$

$$P_n(-1) = (-1)^n$$

$$P_n(z) = \frac{1}{2^n n!} \frac{d^n}{dz^n} (z^2 - 1)^n \text{ (Rodrigues' formula)}$$

$$P_n^m(z) = (1 - z^2)^{m/2} \frac{d^m[P_n(z)]}{dz^m}$$

$$Q_n^m(z) = (1 - z^2)^{m/2} \frac{d^m[Q_n(z)]}{dz^m}$$

9. Important recurrence and orthogonality relations (note that w_n stands for either P_n or Q_n in the following)

$$(n+1)[w_{n+1}(z)] - (2n+1)z[w_n(z)] + n[w_{n-1}(z)] = 0$$

$$z\frac{d[w_n(z)]}{dz} - \frac{d[w_{n-1}(z)]}{dz} = n[w_n(z)]$$

$$\frac{d[w_{n+1}(z)]}{dz} - z\frac{d[w_n(z)]}{dz} = (n+1)[w_n(z)]$$

$$\frac{d[w_{n+1}(z)]}{dz} - \frac{d}{dz}[w_{n-1}(z)] = (2n+1)[w_n(z)]$$

$$(z^2 - 1)\frac{d}{dz}[w_n(z)] = nz[w_n(z)] - n[w_{n-1}(z)]$$

$$\int_{-1}^{1} [P_m(z)][P_n(z)]dz \begin{cases} = 0 & m \neq n \\ = \dfrac{2}{2n+1} & m = n \end{cases}$$

$$\int_{-1}^{1} [P_n^m(z)][P_r^m(z)]dz \begin{cases} = 0 & r \neq n \\ = \dfrac{2}{2n+1}\dfrac{(n+m)!}{(n-m)!} & r = n > m. \end{cases}$$

SURFACE ZONAL HARMONICS

$$P_n(x) = \frac{1}{2^n n!} \frac{d^n}{dx^n} (x^2 - 1)^n$$

x	$P_1(x)$	$P_2(x)$	$P_3(x)$	$P_4(x)$	$P_5(x)$
0	0	$-.5$	0	.375	0
.01	.01	$-.49985$	$-.0149975$	.37463	.018741
.02	.02	$-.4994$	$-.02998$	.37350	.037430
.03	.03	$-.49865$	$-.0449325$	.37163	.056014
.04	.04	$-.4976$	$-.05984$	.36901	.074441
.05	.05	$-.49625$	$-.0746875$	.36565	.092659
.06	.06	$-.4946$	$-.08946$	.36156	.11062
.07	.07	$-.49265$	$-.10414$	.35673	.12826
.08	.08	$-.4904$	$-.11872$	.35118	.14555
.09	.09	$-.48785$	$-.13318$	.34491	.16242
.10	.10	$-.485$	$-.1475$	.33794	.17883
.11	.11	$-.48185$	$-.16167$	.33027	.19473
.12	.12	$-.4784$	$-.17568$	.32191	.21008
.13	.13	$-.47465$	$-.18951$	.31287	.22482
.14	.14	$-.4706$	$-.20314$	.30318	.23891
.15	.15	$-.46625$	$-.21656$	.29284	.25232
.16	.16	$-.4616$	$-.22976$	.28187	.26499
.17	.17	$-.45665$	$-.24272$	.27028	.27688
.18	.18	$-.4514$	$-.25542$	.25809	.28796
.19	.19	$-.44585$	$-.26785$	.24533	.29818
.20	.20	$-.44$	$-.28$	.232	.30752
.21	.21	$-.43385$	$-.29185$	.21813	.31593
.22	.22	$-.4274$	$-.30338$	.20375	.32339
.23	.23	$-.42065$	$-.31458$	.18887	.32986
.24	.24	$-.4136$	$-.32544$	.17352	.33531
.25	.25	$-.40625$	$-.33594$	.15771	.33972
.26	.26	$-.3986$	$-.34606$	.14149	.34307
.27	.27	$-.39065$	$-.35579$	.12488	.34532
.28	.28	$-.3824$	$-.36512$	.10789	.34647
.29	.29	$-.37385$	$-.37403$	.09057	.34650
.30	.30	$-.365$	$-.3825$	.07294	.34539
.31	.31	$-.35585$	$-.39052$	.05503	.34312
.32	.32	$-.3464$	$-.39808$	.03688	.33970
.33	.33	$-.33665$	$-.40516$	.01851	.33512
.34	.34	$-.3266$	$-.41174$	$-.00004$	.32937
.35	.35	$-.31625$	$-.41781$	$-.01872$	.32245
.36	.36	$-.3056$	$-.42336$	$-.03752$	.31438
.37	.37	$-.29465$	$-.42837$	$-.05638$	.30514
.38	.38	$-.2834$	$-.43282$	$-.07528$	.29477
.39	.39	$-.27185$	$-.43670$	$-.09416$	.28326
.40	.40	$-.26$	$-.44$	$-.113$	.27064
.41	.41	$-.24785$	$-.44270$	$-.13175$	.25693
.42	.42	$-.2354$	$-.44478$	$-.15036$	.24215
.43	.43	$-.22265$	$-.44623$	$-.16880$	.22633
.44	.44	$-.2096$	$-.44704$	$-.18702$	.20951
.45	.45	$-.19625$	$-.44719$	$-.20497$	.19172
.46	.46	$-.1826$	$-.44666$	$-.22261$	.17301
.47	.47	$-.16865$	$-.44544$	$-.23989$	.15341
.48	.48	$-.1544$	$-.44352$	$-.25676$	.13298
.49	.49	$-.13985$	$-.44088$	$-.27316$	.11177

SURFACE ZONAL HARMONICS (Continued)

x	$P_6(x)$	$P_7(x)$	$P_8(x)$	$P_9(x)$	$P_{10}(x)$
0	− .3125	− 0	.2734	0	− .2461
.01	− .31184	− .021855	.2725	.0246	− .2447
.02	− .30988	− .043593	.2695	.0489	− .2407
.03	− .30661	− .065094	.2646	.0729	− .2340
.04	− .30205	− .086244	.2578	.0961	− .2247
.05	− .29622	− .10693	.2492	.1186	− .2130
.06	− .28913	− .12703	.2387	.1400	− .1989
.07	− .28081	− .14644	.2265	.1601	− .1826
.08	− .27130	− .16506	.2126	.1789	− .1642
.09	− .26063	− .18278	.1972	.1960	− .1440
.10	− .24883	− .19949	.1803	.2114	− .1221
.11	− .23595	− .21511	.1621	.2249	− .0989
.12	− .22204	− .22955	.1426	.2364	− .0745
.13	− .20715	− .24271	.1221	.2457	− .0492
.14	− .19133	− .25453	.1006	.2529	− .0233
.15	− .17465	− .26492	.0783	.2577	.0020
.16	− .15716	− .27383	.0554	.2601	.0293
.17	− .13894	− .28119	.0319	.2602	.0553
.18	− .12005	− .28695	.0082	.2579	.0808
.19	− .10057	− .29107	− .0157	.2531	.1055
.20	− .080576	− .29352	− .0396	.2460	.1291
.21	− .060144	− .29426	− .0632	.2365	.1513
.22	− .039357	− .29327	− .0865	.2247	.1718
.23	− .018300	− .29055	− .1093	.2108	.1905
.24	.002941	− .28610	− .1313	.1948	.2070
.25	.024277	− .27992	− .1525	.1768	.2212
.26	.045618	− .27203	− .1725	.1571	.2329
.27	.066872	− .26246	− .1914	.1357	.2419
.28	.087947	− .25124	− .2089	.1129	.2480
.29	.10875	− .23843	− .2248	.0888	.2513
.30	.12918	− .22407	− .2391	.0637	.2515
.31	.14915	− .20824	− .2515	.0378	.2487
.32	.16856	− .19100	− .2621	.0114	.2428
.33	.18732	− .17244	− .2706	− .0154	.2339
.34	.20534	− .15266	− .2770	− .0422	.2220
.35	.22251	− .13176	− .2812	− .0688	.2073
.36	.23875	− .10984	− .2831	− .0948	.1899
.37	.25397	− .087036	− .2826	− .1201	.1699
.38	.26808	− .063467	− .2798	− .1444	.1476
.39	.28100	− .039271	− .2746	− .1674	.1231
.40	.29264	− .014590	− .2670	− .1888	.0968
.41	.30291	.010424	− .2570	− .2083	.0690
.42	.31176	.035614	− .2447	− .2258	.0401
.43	.31909	.060820	− .2302	− .2410	.0103
.44	.32486	.085873	− .2134	− .2537	− .0200
.45	.32898	.11060	− .1945	− .2637	− .0503
.46	.33141	.13483	− .1737	− .2708	− .0803
.47	.33209	.15838	− .1510	− .2749	− .1095
.48	.33098	.18107	− .1267	− .2758	− .1375
.49	.32804	.20272	− .1008	− .2735	− .1639

SURFACE ZONAL HARMONICS (Continued)

x	$P_1(x)$	$P_2(x)$	$P_3(x)$	$P_4(x)$	$P_5(x)$
0.50	0.50	−0.125	−0.4375	−0.28906	0.08984
.51	.51	−.10985	−.43337	−.30440	.06726
.52	.52	−.0944	−.42848	−.31912	.04409
.53	53	−.07865	−.42281	−.33317	.02041
.54	.54	−.0626	−.41634	−.34649	−.00372
55	.55	−.04625	−.40906	−.35904	−.02819
.56	.56	−.0296	−.40096	−.37074	−.05294
.57	.57	−.01265	−.39202	−.38155	−.07786
.58	.58	.0046	−.38222	−.39140	−.10285
.59	.59	.02215	−.37155	−.40024	−.12781
.60	.60	.04	−.36	−.408	−.15264
.61	.61	.05815	−.34755	−.41462	−.17721
.62	.62	.0766	−.33418	−.42004	−.20142
.63	.63	.09535	−.31988	−.42418	−.22512
.64	.64	.1144	−.30464	−.42700	−.24819
.65	.65	.13375	−.28844	−.42841	−.27049
.66	.66	.1534	−.27126	−.42836	−.29188
.67	.67	.17335	−.25309	−.42676	−.31220
.68	.68	.1936	−.23392	−.42356	−.33131
.69	.69	.21415	−.21373	−.41869	−.34903
.70	.70	.235	−.1925	−.41206	−.36520
.71	.71	.25615	−.17022	−.40361	−.37964
.72	.72	.2776	−.14688	−.39327	−.39217
.73	.73	.29935	−.12246	−.38095	−.40260
.74	.74	.3214	−.09694	−.36659	−.41074
.75	.75	.34375	−.07031	−.35010	−.41638
.76	.76	.3664	−.04256	−.33140	−.41931
.77	.77	.38935	−.01367	−.31043	−.41932
.78	.78	.4126	.01638	−.28709	−.41618
.79	.79	.43615	.04760	−.26131	−.40966
.80	.80	.46	.08	−.233	−.39952
.81	.81	.48415	.11360	−.20208	−.38552
.82	.82	.5086	.14842	−.16847	−.36739
.83	.83	.53335	.18447	−.13207	−.34489
.84	.84	.5584	.22176	−.09281	−.31774
.85	.85	.58375	.26031	−.05060	−.28566
.86	.86	.6094	.30014	−.00534	−.24838
.87	.87	.63535	.34126	.04305	−.20559
.88	.88	.6616	.38368	.09467	−.15699
.89	.89	.68815	.42742	.14960	−.10228
.90	.90	.715	.4725	.20794	−.04114
.91	.91	.74215	.51893	.26978	0.02676
.92	.92	.7696	.56672	.33522	.10175
.93	.93	.79735	.61589	.40435	.18417
.94	.94	.8254	66646	.47728	.27438
.95	.95	.85373	.71844	.55409	.37274
.96	.96	.8824	.77184	.63489	.47962
.97	.97	.91135	.82668	.71978	.59539
.98	.98	.9406	.88298	.80886	.72045
.99	.99	.97015	.94075	.90223	.85518
100	1	1	1	1	1

SURFACE ZONAL HARMONICS (Continued)

x	$P_6(x)$	$P_7(x)$	$P_8(x)$	$P_9(x)$	$P_{10}(x)$
.50	0.32324	0.22314	−0.0736	−0.2679	−0.1882
.51	.31655	.24217	−.0454	−.2590	−.2101
.52	.30796	.25961	−.0163	−.2468	−.2291
.53	.29747	.27530	.0133	−.2314	−.2450
.54	.28506	.28906	.0432	−.2128	−.2573
.55	.27077	.30074	.0732	−.1913	−.2658
.56	.25460	.31016	.1029	−.1669	−.2701
.57	.23660	.31719	.1320	−.1399	−.2702
.58	.21681	.32169	.1601	−.1105	−.2659
.59	.19528	.32353	.1870	−.0791	−.2570
.60	.17210	.32260	.2133	−.0450	−.2433
.61	.14733	.31880	.2357	−.0118	−.2258
.63	.12109	.31207	.2568	.0234	−.2036
.63	.093475	.30232	.2753	.0589	−.1773
.64	.064623	.28954	.2909	.0943	−.1471
.65	.034675	.27371	.3032	.1290	−.1136
.66	.003790	.25483	.3120	.1625	−.0771
.67	−.027853	.23295	.3170	.1941	−.0382
.68	−.060059	.20813	.3179	.2233	.0024
.69	−.092615	.18049	.3145	.2495	.0440
.70	−.12529	.15016	.3067	.2721	.0858
.71	−.15782	.11731	.2943	.2904	.1269
.72	−.18994	.082166	.2771	.3039	.1663
.73	−.22136	.044990	.2553	.3120	.2030
.74	−.25175	.006087	.2287	.3143	.2360
.75	−.28078	−.034184	.1976	.3103	.2644
.76	−.30807	−.075411	.1621	.2997	.2869
.77	−.33325	−.11713	.1225	.2823	.3027
.78	−.35589	−.15881	.0791	.2578	.3108
.79	−.37557	−.19987	.0326	.2263	.3103
.80	−.39180	−.23965	−.0167	.1879	.3005
.81	−.40409	−.27743	−.0678	.1429	.2810
.82	−.41193	−.31240	−.1199	.0920	.2513
.83	−.41475	−.34368	−.1720	.0359	.1942
.84	−.41198	−.37033	−.2228	−.0243	.1617
.85	−.40300	−.39130	−.2710	−.0873	.1029
.86	−.38716	−.40545	−.3150	−.1513	.0362
.87	−.36379	−.41156	−.3530	−.2143	−.0366
.88	−.33217	−.40829	−.3830	−.2738	−.1130
.89	−.29156	−.39423	−.4028	−.3267	−.1899
.90	−.24116	−.36782	−.4097	−.3695	−.2631
.91	−.18018	−.32743	−.4010	−.3983	−.3277
.92	−.10774	−.27129	−.3737	−.4083	−.3773
.93	−.02295	−.19749	−.3243	−.3941	−.4046
.94	.07512	−.10404	−.2491	−.3498	−.4006
.95	.18745	.01123	−.1440	−.2684	−.3549
.96	.31506	.15060	−.0046	−.1422	−.2552
.97	.45899	.31650	.1740	.0375	−.0875
.98	.62035	.51151	.3971	.2804	.1647
.99	.80029	.73838	.6704	.5973	.5201
1.00	1	1	1	1	1

SURFACE ZONAL HARMONICS (Continued)

θ deg.	$P_1(\cos\theta)$	$P_2(\cos\theta)$	$P_3(\cos\theta)$	$P_4(\cos\theta)$	$P_5(\cos\theta)$
0	1	1	1	1	1
1	0.99985	0.99954	0.99909	0.99848	0.99772
2	.99939	.99817	.99635	.99392	.99088
3	.99863	.99589	.99179	.98634	.97954
4	.99756	.99270	.98543	.97577	.96377
5	.99619	.98861	.97728	.96227	.94368
6	.99452	.98361	.96736	.94589	.91939
7	.99255	.97772	.95569	.92670	.89108
8	.99027	.97095	.94232	.90480	.85893
9	.98769	.96329	.92726	.88026	.82315
10	.98481	.95477	.91057	.85321	.78399
11	.98163	.94539	.89228	.82376	.74170
12	.97815	.93516	.87244	.79204	.69656
13	.97437	.92410	.85111	.75819	.64888
14	.97030	.91221	.82833	.72235	.59895
15	.96593	.89952	.80416	.68470	.54713
16	.96126	.88604	.77868	.64537	.49373
17	.95630	.87178	.75194	.60456	.43911
18	.95106	.85676	.72401	.56244	.38363
19	.94552	.84101	.69497	.51918	.32763
20	.93969	.82453	.66488	.47498	.27149
21	.93358	.80736	.63384	.43002	.21556
22	.92718	.78950	.60190	.38450	.16019
23	.92050	.77099	.56917	.33862	.10573
24	.91355	.75185	.53572	.29256	.05252
25	.90631	.73209	.50163	.24653	.00088
26	.89879	.71175	.46699	.20072	− .04887
27	.89101	.69084	.43190	.15531	− .09642
28	.88295	.66939	.39644	.11051	− .14151
29	.87462	.64744	.36069	.06649	− .18388
30	.86603	.62500	.32476	.02344	− .22327
31	.85717	.60210	.28873	− .01847	− .25949
32	.84805	.57878	.25269	− .05907	− .29233
33	.83867	.55505	.21673	− .09820	− .32163
34	.82904	.53095	.18094	− .13570	− .34726
35	.81915	.50652	.14542	− .17142	− .36910
36	.80902	.48176	.11025	− .20524	− .38707
37	.79864	.45673	.07551	− .23701	− .40113
38	.78801	.43144	.04129	− .26664	− .41124
39	.77715	.40593	.00769	− .29400	− .41741
40	.76604	.38024	− .02523	− .31900	− .41968
41	.75471	.35438	− .05738	− .34157	− .41811
42	.74314	.32840	− .08869	− .36163	− .41279
43	.73135	.30232	− .11907	− .37913	− .40385
44	.71934	.27617	− .14845	− .39401	− .39141
45	.70711	.25000	− .17678	− .40625	− .37565
46	.69466	.22383	− .20397	− .41582	− .35677
47	.68200	.19768	− .22997	− .42273	− .33496
48	.66913	.17160	− .25471	− .42696	− .31048
49	.65606	.14562	− .27815	− .42856	− .28357

For $P_n(\cos\theta)$, use the definition of $P_n(x)$ given on the first page of this table, and put $x = \cos\theta$.

SURFACE ZONAL HARMONICS (Continued)

$\theta°$	$P_6(\cos\theta)$	$P_7(\cos\theta)$	$P_8(\cos\theta)$	$P_9(\cos\theta)$	$P_{10}(\cos\theta)$
0	1	1	1	1	1
1	0.99680	0.99574	0.9945	0.9932	0.9916
2	.98725	.98301	.9782	.9728	.9668
3	.97142	.96198	.9513	.9393	.9260
4	.94947	.93291	.9142	.8933	.8704
5	.92160	.89616	.8675	.8358	.8012
6	.88808	.85220	.8121	.7680	.7203
7	.84922	.80158	.7487	.6911	.6296
8	.80538	.74493	.6784	.6069	.5312
9	.75698	.68296	.6024	.5168	.4277
10	.70447	.61644	.5218	.4228	.3214
11	.64833	.54619	.4380	.3266	.2150
12	.58909	.47307	.3522	.2302	.1108
13	.52729	.39798	.2657	.1353	.0113
14	.46350	.32183	.1799	.0437	− .0813
15	.39831	.24554	.0962	− .0428	− .1651
16	.33229	.17001	.0157	− .1227	− .2381
17	.26606	.09614	− .0604	− .1946	− .2992
18	.20020	.02477	− .1310	− .2573	− .3471
19	.13529	− .04327	− .1951	− .3100	− .3813
20	.07190	− .10723	− .2518	− .3517	− .4013
21	.01059	− .16640	− .3005	− .3821	− .4073
22	− .04813	− .22017	− .3407	− .4009	− .3997
23	− .10376	− .26800	− .3718	− .4082	− .3793
24	− .15585	− .30942	− .3936	− .4042	− .3473
25	− .20398	− .34408	− .4062	− .3896	− .3052
26	− .24779	− .37172	− .4096	− .3650	− .2547
27	− .28694	− .39216	− .4041	− .3515	− .1975
28	− .32117	− .40534	− .3900	− .2902	− .1358
29	− .35025	− .41130	− .3680	− .2424	− .0716
30	− .37402	− .41018	− .3388	− .1896	− .0070
31	− .39238	− .40221	− .3031	− .1332	.0559
32	− .40527	− .38771	− .2619	− .0749	.1150
33	− .41269	− .36710	− .2162	− .0161	.1689
34	− .41471	− .34086	− .1670	.0415	.2157
35	− .41145	− .30956	− .1154	.0966	.2542
36	− .40307	− .27382	− .0627	.1476	.2833
37	− .38980	− .23432	− .0098	.1935	.3024
38	− .37191	− .19178	.0421	.2331	.3111
39	− .34972	− .14695	.0919	.2655	.3093
40	− .32357	− .10060	.1386	.2900	.2973
41	− .29387	− .05351	.1814	.3062	.2758
42	− .26104	− .00645	.2194	.3137	.2455
43	− .22554	.03982	.2519	.3127	.2077
44	− .18784	.08455	.2784	.3031	.1637
45	− .14844	.12706	.2983	.2855	.1151
46	− .10783	.16668	.3115	.2605	.0635
47	− .06654	.20283	.3176	.2288	.0107
48	− .02508	.23497	.3167	.1915	− .0416
49	.01606	.26263	.3090	.1495	− .0918

SURFACE ZONAL HARMONICS (Continued)

$\theta°$	$P_1(\cos \theta)$	$P_2(\cos \theta)$	$P_3(\cos \theta)$	$P_4(\cos \theta)$	$P_5(\cos \theta)$
50	0.64279	0.11976	−0.30022	−0.42753	−0.25449
51	.62932	.09407	− .32088	− .42394	− .22353
52	.61566	.06856	− .34009	− .41784	− .19097
53	.60182	.04327	− .35781	− .40929	− .15712
54	.58779	.01824	− .37399	− .39837	− .12229
55	.57358	− .00652	− .38861	− .38519	− .08679
56	.55919	− .03095	− .40164	− .36983	− .05093
57	.54464	− .05505	− .41307	− .35241	− .01503
58	.52992	− .07878	− .42286	− .33306	.02060
59	.51504	− .10210	− .43100	− .31189	.05566
60	.50000	− .12500	− .43750	− .28906	.08984
61	.48481	− .14744	− .44234	− .26471	.12287
62	.46947	− .16939	− .44552	− .23899	.15446
63	.45399	− .19084	− .44706	− .21205	.18436
64	.43837	− .21175	− .44695	− .18407	.21232
65	.42262	− .23209	− .44522	− .15521	.23811
66	.40674	− .25185	− .44188	− .12564	.26152
67	.39073	− .27099	− .43696	− .09554	.28238
68	.37461	− .28950	− .43049	− .06508	.30051
69	.35837	− .30736	− .42249	− .03444	.31577
70	.34202	− .32453	− .41301	− .00380	.32807
71	.32557	− .34101	− .40208	.02667	.33730
72	.30902	− .35676	− .38975	.05680	.34340
73	.29237	− .37178	− .37608	.08641	.34634
74	.27564	− .38604	− .36110	.11534	.34611
75	.25882	− .39952	− .34488	.14343	.34273
76	.24192	− .41221	− .32749	.17051	.33624
77	.22495	− .42410	− .30897	.19644	.32672
78	.20791	− .43516	− .28940	.22107	.31425
79	.19081	− .44539	− .26885	.24427	.29897
80	.17365	− .45477	− .24738	.26590	.28102
81	.15643	− .46329	− .22508	.28585	.26056
82	.13917	− .47095	− .20202	.30401	.23777
83	.12187	− .47772	− .17828	.32027	.21288
84	.10453	− .48361	− .15394	.33455	.18610
85	.08716	− .48861	− .12908	.34677	.15766
86	.06976	− .49270	− .10379	.35686	.12784
87	.05234	− .49589	− .07815	.36476	.09688
88	.03490	− .49817	− .05224	.37044	.06507
89	.01745	− .49954	− .02617	.37386	.03268
90	0	− .50000	0	.37500	0

SURFACE ZONAL HARMONICS (Continued)

$\theta°$	$P_6(\cos\theta)$	$P_7(\cos\theta)$	$P_8(\cos\theta)$	$P_9(\cos\theta)$	$P_{10}(\cos\theta)$
50	0.05638	0.28543	0.2947	0.1041	−0.1381
51	.09539	.30308	.2742	.0565	−.1792
52	.13265	.31535	.2480	.0080	−.2137
53	.16772	.32213	.2167	−.0400	−.2407
54	.20020	.32336	.1812	−.0863	−.2594
55	.22972	.31910	.1422	−.1296	−.2692
56	.25597	.30949	.1005	−.1689	−.2700
57	.27866	.29475	.0572	−.2032	−.2617
58	.29756	.27518	.0131	−.2315	−.2449
59	.31246	.25117	−.0309	−.2533	−.2201
60	.32324	.22314	−.0736	−.2679	−.1882
61	.32980	.19162	−.1144	−.2751	−.1504
62	.33210	.15715	−.1523	−.2747	−.1080
63	.33016	.12034	−.1865	−.2669	−.0624
64	.32403	.08181	−.2163	−.2518	−.0151
65	.31383	.04222	−.2411	−.2300	.0323
66	.29971	.00223	−.2605	−.2022	.0783
67	.28189	−.03748	−.2741	−.1690	.1213
68	.26062	−.07627	−.2816	−.1315	.1599
69	.23617	−.11348	−.2829	−.0906	.1929
70	.20888	−.14853	−.2780	−.0476	.2193
71	.17910	−.18082	−.2671	−.0035	.2382
72	.14721	−.20986	−.2504	.0404	.2491
73	.11363	−.23516	−.2283	.0829	.2516
74	.07878	−.25634	−.2014	.1230	.2457
75	.04310	−.27305	−.1702	.1595	.2316
76	.00704	−.28504	−.1355	.1915	.2099
77	−.02896	−.29214	−.0979	.2181	.1813
78	−.06444	−.29424	−.0583	.2387	.1468
79	−.09897	−.29133	−.0176	.2526	.1074
80	−.13212	−.28348	.0233	.2596	.0647
81	−.16348	−.27083	.0636	.2595	.0199
82	−.19267	−.25360	.1024	.2523	−.0254
83	−.21933	−.23211	.1389	.2383	−.0698
84	−.24313	.20671	.1722	.2177	−.1118
85	−.26378	−.17784	.2017	.1913	−.1499
86	−.28103	−.14598	.2268	.1597	−.1830
87	−.29467	−.11168	.2469	.1237	−.2099
88	−.30454	−.07551	.2615	.0844	−.2298
89	−.31050	−.03807	.2704	.0428	−.2420
90	−.31250	0	.2734	0	−.2461

For larger tables, see "Report of the British Association for the Advancement of Science," 1879, pp. 54–57, Philosophical Magazine, Dec., 1891, "Tafeln der Besselschen, Theta-, Kugel- und anderer Funktionen" by K. Hayashi and "Fünfstellige Funktionentafeln" by K. Hayashi.

BERNOULLI AND EULER NUMBERS—POLYNOMIALS

There are numerous sets of defined numbers and polynomials, among which the more important ones are those classified under the names of Bernoulli and Euler.

The *Bernoulli Polynomials* are generated by the defining condition

$$\frac{te^{tx}}{e^t - 1} = B_0(x) + B_1(x)t + B_2(x)\frac{t^2}{2!} + B_3(x)\frac{t^3}{3!} + \cdots$$

$$B_0(x) = 1, \quad B_1(x) = x - \tfrac{1}{2}, \quad B_2(x) = x^2 - x + \tfrac{1}{6}$$

$$B_3(x) = x^3 - \frac{3}{2}x^2 + \frac{x}{2}, \quad B_4(x) = x^4 - 2x^3 + x^2 - \tfrac{1}{30}, \ldots$$

The following useful relations should be noted

$$B'_n(x) = nB_{n-1}(x), \quad \int_a^x B_n(x)\,dx = \frac{1}{n+1}[B_{n+1}(x) - B_{n+1}(a)]$$

The Bernoulli numbers $B_0, B_1, B_2, \ldots$, can be obtained by putting $x = 0$ in the respective polynomials. A simpler method is to use the generating function

$$\frac{x}{e^x - 1} = \sum_{n=0}^{\infty} \frac{B_n x^n}{n!}$$

and read the coefficients from the expansion. Here,

$$B_0 = 1, \quad B_1 = -\tfrac{1}{2}, \quad B_2 = \tfrac{1}{6}, \quad B_4 = -\tfrac{1}{30},$$

$$B_6 = \tfrac{1}{42}, \quad B_8 = -\tfrac{1}{30}, \ldots B_{2n+1} = 0 \qquad (n \geq 1)$$

An important application for the Bernoulli coefficients is in its use involved for the Euler-Maclaurin Sum Formula:

$$\sum_{x=1}^{n-1} f(x) = \int_1^n f(x)\,dx + \left[\sum_{i=1}^{\infty} \frac{B_i}{i!} f^{(i-1)}(x)\right]_{x=1}^{x=n}$$

$$= \left[\int f(x)\,dx - \frac{1}{2}f(x) + \frac{1}{12}f'(x) - \frac{1}{720}f'''(x) \right.$$

$$\left. + \frac{1}{30,240}f^{(v)}(x) - \frac{1}{1,209,600}f^{(vii)}(x)\right]_{x=1}^{x=n}$$

Examples:

$$\sum_{x=1}^{n-1} \sqrt{x} = \sqrt{n}\left\{\frac{2}{3}n - \frac{1}{2} + \frac{1}{24n} - \frac{1}{1,920n^3}\right.$$

$$\left. + \frac{1}{9,216n^5} - \frac{11}{163,840n^7}\right\} - 0.207,886,224,977,355$$

correct to 12 places for $n \geq 10$.

$$\log_e(x!) = \log_e \Gamma(x + 1)$$

$$= \left(x + \frac{1}{2}\right)\log_e x - x + \frac{1}{12x} - \frac{1}{360x^3} + \frac{1}{1,260x^5} - \frac{1}{1,680x^7}$$

$$+ 0.918,938,533,205$$

accurate to 12 places for $x \geq 10$.

$f(x)$ (digamma function) $= \dfrac{d \log \Gamma(x)}{dx}$

$$= 1 + \frac{1}{2} + \frac{1}{3} + \cdots + \frac{1}{x-1} - \gamma$$

(Euler Constant) for x integer.

By Euler-Maclaurin

$$f(x) = \log_e x - \frac{1}{2x} - \frac{1}{12x^2} + \frac{1}{120x^4} - \frac{1}{252x^6} + \frac{1}{240x^8} - \frac{5}{660x^{10}} + \frac{691}{32,760x^{12}}$$

correct to 12 places for $x \geq 10$.

The Euler numbers together with their respective polynomials can be generated from

$$\frac{2e^{tx}}{e^t + 1} = \sum_{i=0}^{\infty} E_i(x) \frac{t^i}{i!}$$

and the relation

$$x^n = \frac{1}{2} [E_n(x + 1) + E_n(x)]$$

The Euler polynomials are

$$E_0(x) = 1, \quad E_1(x) = x - \frac{1}{2}, \quad E_2(x) = x^2 - x$$

$$E_3(x) = x^3 - \frac{3}{2}x^2 + \frac{1}{4}, \quad E_4(x) = x^4 - 2x^3 + x$$

$$E_5(x) = x^5 - \frac{5}{2}x^4 + \frac{5}{2}x^2 - \frac{1}{2}$$

Tables which follow record the first fifteen polynomials of $B_k(x)$ and $E_k(x)$. The first sixty Bernoulli and Euler numbers are given in a separate table. The value of $x^n/n!$ is also important and this is given in a succeeding table for values of x from 1 to 9 and n from 1 to 50.

COEFFICIENTS b_k OF THE BERNOULLI POLYNOMIALS $B_n(x) = \sum\limits_{k=0}^{n} b_k x^k$

n/k	0	1	2	3	4	5	6	7	8	9	10	11	12	13	14	15
0	1															
1	$-\frac{1}{2}$	1														
2	$\frac{1}{6}$	-1	1													
3	0	$\frac{1}{2}$	$-\frac{3}{2}$	1												
4	$-\frac{1}{30}$	0	1	-2	1											
5	0	$-\frac{1}{6}$	0	$\frac{5}{3}$	$-\frac{5}{2}$	1										
6	$\frac{1}{42}$	0	$-\frac{1}{2}$	0	$\frac{5}{2}$	-3	1									
7	0	$\frac{1}{6}$	0	$-\frac{7}{6}$	0	$\frac{7}{2}$	$-\frac{7}{2}$	1								
8	$-\frac{1}{30}$	0	$\frac{2}{3}$	0	$-\frac{7}{3}$	0	$\frac{14}{3}$	-4	1							
9	0	$-\frac{3}{10}$	0	2	0	$-\frac{21}{5}$	0	6	$-\frac{9}{2}$	1						
10	$\frac{5}{66}$	0	$-\frac{3}{2}$	0	5	0	-7	0	$\frac{15}{2}$	-5	1					
11	0	$\frac{5}{6}$	0	$-\frac{11}{2}$	0	11	0	-11	0	$\frac{55}{6}$	$-\frac{11}{2}$	1				
12	$-\frac{691}{2730}$	0	5	0	$-\frac{33}{2}$	0	22	0	$-\frac{33}{2}$	0	11	-6	1			
13	0	$-\frac{691}{210}$	0	$\frac{65}{3}$	0	$-\frac{429}{10}$	0	$-\frac{286}{7}$	0	$-\frac{143}{6}$	0	13	$-\frac{13}{2}$	1		
14	$\frac{7}{6}$	0	$-\frac{691}{30}$	0	$\frac{455}{6}$	0	$-\frac{1001}{10}$	0	$\frac{143}{2}$	0	$-\frac{1001}{30}$	0	$\frac{91}{6}$	-7	1	
15	0	$\frac{35}{2}$	0	$-\frac{691}{6}$	0	$\frac{455}{2}$	0	$-\frac{429}{2}$	0	$\frac{715}{6}$	0	$-\frac{91}{2}$	0	$\frac{35}{2}$	$-\frac{15}{2}$	1

COEFFICIENTS e_k OF THE EULER POLYNOMIALS $E_n(x) = \sum\limits_{k=0}^{n} e_k x^k$

n/k	0	1	2	3	4	5	6	7	8	9	10	11	12	13	14	15
0	1															
1	$-\frac{1}{2}$	1														
2	0	-1	1													
3	$\frac{1}{4}$	0	$-\frac{3}{2}$	1												
4	0	1	0	-2	1											
5	$-\frac{1}{2}$	0	$\frac{5}{2}$	0	$-\frac{5}{2}$	1										
6	0	-3	0	5	0	-3	1									
7	$\frac{17}{8}$	0	$-\frac{21}{2}$	0	$\frac{35}{4}$	0	$-\frac{7}{2}$	1								
8	0	17	0	-28	0	14	0	-4	1							
9	$-\frac{31}{2}$	0	$\frac{153}{2}$	0	-63	0	21	0	$-\frac{9}{2}$	1						
10	0	-155	0	255	0	-126	0	30	0	-5	1					
11	$\frac{691}{4}$	0	$-\frac{1705}{2}$	0	$\frac{2805}{2}$	0	-231	0	$\frac{165}{4}$	0	$-\frac{11}{2}$	1				
12	0	2073	0	-3410	0	1683	0	-396	0	55	0	-6	1			
13	$-\frac{5461}{2}$	0	$\frac{26949}{2}$	0	$-\frac{22165}{2}$	0	$\frac{7293}{2}$	0	$-\frac{1287}{2}$	0	$\frac{143}{2}$	0	$-\frac{13}{2}$	1		
14	0	-38227	0	62881	0	-31031	0	7293	0	-1001	0	91	0	-7	1	
15	$\frac{929569}{16}$	0	$-\frac{573405}{2}$	0	$\frac{943215}{4}$	0	$-\frac{155155}{2}$	0	$\frac{109395}{8}$	0	$-\frac{3003}{2}$	0	$\frac{455}{4}$	0	$-\frac{15}{2}$	1

BERNOULLI NUMBERS

$$B_n = N/D$$

n	N	D	B_n
0	1	1	(0) 1.0000 00000
1	-1	2	(-1) - 5.0000 00000*
2	1	6	(-1) 1.6666 66667
4	-1	30	(-2) - 3.3333 33333
6	1	42	(-2) 2.3809 52381
8	-1	30	(-2) - 3.3333 33333
10	5	66	(-2) 7.5757 57576
12	-691	2730	(-1) - 2.5311 35531
14	7	6	(0) 1.1666 66667
16	-3617	510	(0) - 7.0921 56863
18	43867	798	(1) 5.4971 17794
20	-1 74611	330	(2) - 5.2912 42424
22	8 54513	138	(3) 6.1921 23188
24	-2363 64091	2730	(4) - 8.6580 25311
26	85 53103	6	(6) 1.4255 17167
28	-2 37494 61029	870	(7) - 2.7298 23107
30	861 58412 76005	14322	(8) 6.0158 08739
32	-770 93210 41217	510	(10) - 1.5116 31577
34	257 76878 58367	6	(11) 4.2961 46431
36	-26315 27155 30534 77373	19 19190	(13) - 1.3711 65521
38	2 92999 39138 41559	6	(14) 4.8833 23190
40	-2 61082 71849 64491 22051	13530	(16) - 1.9296 57934
42	15 20097 64391 80708 02691	1806	(17) 8.4169 30476
44	-278 33269 57930 10242 35023	690	(19) - 4.0338 07185
46	5964 51111 59391 21632 77961	282	(21) 2.1150 74864
48	-560 94033 68997 81768 62491 27547	46410	(23) - 1.2086 62652
50	49 50572 05241 07964 82124 77525	66	(24) 7.5008 66746
52	-80116 57181 35489 95734 79249 91853	1590	(26) - 5.0387 78101
54	29 14996 36348 84862 42141 81238 12691	798	(28) 3.6528 77648
56	-2479 39292 93132 26753 68541 57396 63229	870	(30) - 2.8498 76930
58	84483 61334 88800 41862 04677 59940 36021	354	(32) 2.3865 42750
60	-121 52331 40483 75557 20403 04994 07982 02460 41491	567 86730	(34) - 2.1399 94926

*The floating decimal point notation is used here. For example for $n = 1$, $B_1 = -\frac{1}{2} = -.500000$
$= (-5.00000)(10^{-1}) = (-1) - 5.0000,0000$.

EULER NUMBERS

n	*En*
0	1
2	-1
4	5
6	-61
8	1385
10	-50521
12	27 02765
14	-1993 60981
16	1 93915 12145
18	-240 48796 75441
20	37037 11882 37525
22	-69 34887 43931 37901
24	15514 53416 35570 86905
26	-40 87072 50929 31238 92361
28	12522 59641 40362 98654 68285
30	-44 15438 93249 02310 45536 82821
32	17751 93915 79539 28943 66647 89665
34	-80 72329 92358 87898 06216 82474 53281
36	41222 06033 95177 02122 34707 96712 59045
38	-234 89580 52704 31082 52017 82857 61989 47741
40	1 48511 50718 11498 00178 77156 78140 58266 84425
42	-1036 46227 33519 61211 93979 57304 74518 59763 10201
44	7 94757 94225 97592 70360 80405 10088 07061 95192 73805
46	-6667 53751 66855 44977 43502 84747 73748 19752 41076 84661
48	60 96278 64556 85421 58691 68574 28768 43153 97653 90444 35185
50	-60532 85248 18862 18963 14383 78511 16490 88103 49822 51468 15121
52	650 61624 86684 60884 77158 70634 08082 29834 83644 23676 53855 76565
54	-7 54665 99390 08739 09806 14325 65889 73674 42122 40024 71169 98586 45581
56	9420 32189 64202 41204 20228 62376 90583 22720 93888 52599 64600 93949 05945
58	-126 22019 25180 62187 19903 40923 72874 89255 48234 10611 91825 59406 99649 20041
60	181089 11496 57923 04965 45807 74165 21586 88733 48734 92363 14106 00809 54542 31325

BERNOULLI AND EULER POLYNOMIALS

$$x^n/n!$$

n\x	2	3	4	5
1	(0) 2.0000 00000	(0) 3.0000 00000	(0) 4.0000 00000	0) 5.0000 00000
2	(0) 2.0000 00000	(0) 4.5000 00000	(0) 8.0000 00000	1) 1.2500 00000
3	(0) 1.3333 33333	(0) 4.5000 00000	1) 1.0666 66667	1) 2.0833 33333
4	(− 1) 6.6666 66667	(0) 3.3750 00000	1) 1.0666 66667	1) 2.6041 66667
5	(− 1) 2.6666 66667	(0) 2.0250 00000	0) 8.5333 33333	1) 2.6041 66667
6	(− 2) 8.8888 88889	(0) 1.0125 00000	0) 5.6888 88889	1) 2.1701 38889
7	(− 2) 2.5396 82540	(− 1) 4.3392 85714	0) 3.2507 93651	1) 1.5500 99206
8	(− 3) 6.3492 06349	(− 1) 1.6272 32143	0) 1.6253 96825	0) 9.6881 20040
9	(− 3) 1.4109 34744	(− 2) 5.4241 07143	(− 1) 7.2239 85891	0) 5.3822 88911
10	(− 4) 2.8218 69489	(− 2) 1.6272 32144	(− 1) 2.8895 94356	0) 2.6911 44455
11	(− 5) 5.1306 71797	(− 3) 4.4379 05844	(− 1) 1.0507 61584	0) 1.2232 47480
12	(− 6) 8.5511 19662	(− 3) 1.1094 76461	(− 2) 3.5025 38614	(− 1) 5.0968 64499
13	(− 6) 1.3155 56871	(− 4) 2.5603 30295	(− 2) 1.0777 04189	(− 1) 1.9603 32500
14	(− 7) 1.8793 66959	(− 5) 5.4864 22060	(− 3) 3.0791 54825	(− 2) 7.0011 87499
15	(− 8) 2.5058 22612	(− 5) 1.0972 84412	(− 4) 8.2110 79534	(− 2) 2.3337 29166
16	(− 9) 3.1322 78264	(− 6) 2.0574 08272	(− 4) 2.0527 69883	(− 3) 7.2929 03644
17	(−10) 3.6850 33252	(− 7) 3.6307 20481	(− 5) 4.8300 46785	(− 3) 2.1449 71660
18	(−11) 4.0944 81391	(− 8) 6.0512 00801	(− 5) 1.0733 43730	(− 4) 5.9582 54611
19	(−12) 4.3099 80412	(− 9) 9.5545 27582	(− 6) 2.2596 71011	(− 4) 1.5679 61740
20	(−13) 4.3099 80413	(− 9) 1.4331 79137	(− 7) 4.5193 42021	(− 5) 3.9199 04350
21	(−14) 4.1047 43250	(−10) 2.0473 98768	(− 8) 8.6082 70516	(− 6) 9.3331 05595
22	(−15) 3.7315 84772	(−11) 2.7919 07410	(− 8) 1.5651 40093	(− 6) 2.1211 60362
23	(−16) 3.2448 56324	(−12) 3.6416 18361	(− 9) 2.7219 82772	(− 7) 4.6112 18179
24	(−17) 2.7040 46937	(−13) 4.5520 22952	(−10) 4.5366 37953	(− 8) 9.6067 04540
25	(−18) 2.1632 37550	(−14) 5.4624 27543	(−11) 7.2586 20726	(− 8) 1.9213 40908
26	(−19) 1.6640 28884	(−15) 6.3028 01010	(−11) 1.1167 10881	(− 9) 3.6948 86362
27	(−20) 1.2326 13988	(−16) 7.0031 12233	(−12) 1.6543 86490	(−10) 6.8423 82151
28	(−22) 8.8043 85630	(−17) 7.5033 34535	(−13) 2.3634 09271	(−10) 1.2218 53956
29	(−23) 6.0719 90089	(−18) 7.7620 70209	(−14) 3.2598 74857	(−11) 2.1066 44751
30	(−24) 4.0479 93393	(−19) 7.7620 70209	(−15) 4.3464 99810	(−12) 3.5110 74585
31	(−25) 2.6116 08641	(−20) 7.5116 80847	(−16) 5.6083 86851	(−13) 5.6630 23524
32	(−26) 1.6322 55401	(−21) 7.0422 00795	(−17) 7.0104 83564	(−14) 8.8484 74257
33	(−28) 9.8924 56972	(−22) 6.4020 00722	(−18) 8.4975 55834	(−14) 1.3406 77918
34	(−29) 5.8190 92337	(−23) 5.6488 24167	(−19) 9.9971 24511	(−15) 1.9715 85173
35	(−30) 3.3251 95620	(−24) 4.8418 49286	(−19) 1.1425 28515	(−16) 2.8165 50246
36	(−31) 1.8473 30900	(−25) 4.0348 74405	(−20) 1.2694 76128	(−17) 3.9118 75343
37	(−33) 9.9855 72436	(−26) 3.2715 19788	(−21) 1.3724 06625	(−18) 5.2863 18032
38	(−34) 5.2555 64439	(−27) 2.5827 78779	(−22) 1.4446 38552	(−19) 6.9556 81619
39	(−35) 2.6951 61251	(−28) 1.9867 52908	(−23) 1.4816 80567	(−20) 8.9175 40539
40	(−36) 1.3475 80626	(−29) 1.4900 64681	(−24) 1.4816 80567	(−20) 1.1146 92567
41	(−38) 6.5735 64028	(−30) 1.0902 91230	(−25) 1.4455 42017	(−21) 1.3593 81180
42	(−39) 3.1302 68584	(−32) 7.7877 94498	(−26) 1.3767 06682	(−22) 1.6183 10928
43	(−40) 1.4559 38876	(−33) 5.4333 44999	(−27) 1.2806 57379	(−23) 1.8817 56893
44	(−42) 6.6179 03983	(−34) 3.7045 53408	(−28) 1.1642 33981	(−24) 2.1383 60106
45	(−43) 2.9412 90659	(−35) 2.4697 02271	(−29) 1.0348 74650	(−25) 2.3759 55673
46	(−44) 1.2788 22026	(−36) 1.6106 75395	(−31) 8.9989 09998	(−26) 2.5825 60514
47	(−46) 5.4417 95855	(−37) 1.0280 90677	(−32) 7.6586 46807	(−27) 2.7474 04803
48	(−47) 2.2674 14940	(−39) 6.4255 66736	(−33) 6.3822 05674	(−28) 2.8618 80003
49	(−49) 9.2547 54855	(−40) 3.9340 20450	(−34) 5.2099 63815	(−29) 2.9202 85717
50	(−50) 3.7019 10942	(−41) 2.3604 12270	(−35) 4.1679 71052	(−30) 2.9202 85717

BERNOULLI AND EULER POLYNOMIALS
$x^n/n!$

$n \backslash x$	6		7		8		9	
1	(0) 6.0000	00000	(0) 7.0000	00000	(0) 8.0000	00000	(0) 9.0000	00000
2*	(1) 1.8000	00000	(1) 2.4500	00000	(1) 3.2000	00000	(1) 4.0500	00000
3	(1) 3.6000	00000	(1) 5.7166	66667	(1) 8.5333	33333	(2) 1.2150	00000
4	(1) 5.4000	00000	(2) 1.0004	16667	(2) 1.7066	66667	(2) 2.7337	50000
5	(1) 6.4800	00000	(2) 1.4005	83333	(2) 2.7306	66667	(2) 4.9207	50000
6	(1) 6.4800	00000	(2) 1.6340	13889	(2) 3.6408	88889	(2) 7.3811	25000
7	(1) 5.5542	85714	(2) 1.6340	13889	(2) 4.1610	15873	(2) 9.4900	17857
8	(1) 4.1657	14286	(2) 1.4297	62153	(2) 4.1610	15873	(3) 1.0676	27009
9	(1) 2.7771	42857	(2) 1.1120	37230	(2) 3.6986	80776	(3) 1.0676	27009
10	(1) 1.6662	85714	(1) 7.7842	60610	(2) 2.9589	44621	(2) 9.6086	43080
11	(0) 9.0888	31169	(1) 4.9536	20388	(2) 2.1519	59724	(2) 7.8616	17066
12	(0) 4.5444	15584	(1) 2.8896	11893	(2) 1.4346	39816	(2) 5.8962	12799
13	(0) 2.0974	22577	(1) 1.5559	44865	(1) 8.8285	52715	(2) 4.0819	93476
14	(− 1) 8.9889	53903	(0) 7.7797	24327	(1) 5.0448	87266	(2) 2.6241	38663
15	(− 1) 3.5955	81561	(0) 3.6305	38019	(1) 2.6906	06542	(2) 1.5744	83198
16	(− 1) 1.3483	43085	(0) 1.5883	60383	(1) 1.3453	03271	(1) 8.8564	67988
17	(− 2) 4.7588	57949	(− 1) 6.5403	07461	(0) 6.3308	38921	(1) 4.6887	18347
18	(− 2) 1.5862	85983	(− 1) 2.5434	52902	(0) 2.8137	06187	(1) 2.3443	59173
19	(− 3) 5.0093	24157	(− 2) 9.3706	15954	(0) 1.1847	18395	(1) 1.1104	85924
20	(− 3) 1.5027	97247	(− 2) 3.2797	15584	(− 1) 4.7388	73579	(0) 4.9971	86660
21	(− 4) 4.2937	06421	(− 2) 1.0932	38528	(− 1) 1.8052	85173	(0) 2.1416	51426
22	(− 4) 1.1710	10841	(− 3) 3.4784	86224	(− 2) 6.5646	73356	(− 1) 8.7613	01286
23	(− 5) 3.0548	10892	(− 3) 1.0586	69721	(− 2) 2.2833	64645	(− 1) 3.4283	35286
24	(− 6) 7.6370	27230	(− 4) 3.0877	86685	(− 3) 7.6112	15485	(− 1) 1.2856	25732
25	(− 6) 1.8328	86535	(− 5) 8.6458	02719	(− 3) 2.4355	88956	(− 2) 4.6282	52637
26	(− 7) 4.2297	38158	(− 5) 2.3277	16117	(− 4) 7.4941	19863	(− 2) 1.6020	87451
27	(− 8) 9.3994	18129	(− 6) 6.0348	19562	(− 4) 2.2204	79959	(− 3) 5.3402	91503
28	(− 8) 2.0141	61028	(− 6) 1.5087	04890	(− 5) 6.3442	28454	(− 3) 1.7165	22269
29	(− 9) 4.1672	29712	(− 7) 3.6417	01460	(− 5) 1.7501	31987	(− 4) 5.3271	38075
30	(− 10) 8.3344	59424	(− 8) 8.4973	03406	(− 6) 4.6670	18634	(− 4) 1.5981	41423
31	(− 10) 1.6131	21179	(− 8) 1.9187	45930	(− 6) 1.2043	91905	(− 5) 4.6397	65421
32	(− 11) 3.0246	02211	(− 9) 4.1972	56723	(− 7) 3.0109	79764	(− 5) 1.3049	34025
33	(− 12) 5.4992	76746	(− 10) 8.9032	71836	(− 8) 7.2993	44881	(− 6) 3.5589	10976
34	(− 13) 9.7046	06022	(− 10) 1.8330	26555	(− 8) 1.7174	92913	(− 7) 9.4206	46701
35	(− 13) 1.6636	46746	(− 11) 3.6660	53108	(− 9) 3.9256	98086	(− 7) 2.4224	52008
36	(− 14) 2.7727	44578	(− 12) 7.1284	36600	(− 10) 8.7237	73527	(− 8) 6.0561	30022
37	(− 15) 4.4963	42559	(− 12) 1.3486	23141	(− 10) 1.8862	21303	(− 8) 1.4731	12708
38	(− 16) 7.0994	88250	(− 13) 2.4843	05785	(− 11) 3.9709	92217	(− 9) 3.4889	51151
39	(− 16) 1.0922	28962	(− 14) 4.4590	10384	(− 12) 8.1456	25061	(− 10) 8.0514	25733
40	(− 17) 1.6383	43443	(− 15) 7.8032	68172	(− 12) 1.6291	25012	(− 10) 1.8115	70790
41	(− 18) 2.3975	75770	(− 15) 1.3322	65298	(− 13) 3.1787	80512	(− 11) 3.9766	18807
42	(− 19) 3.4251	08241	(− 16) 2.2204	42162	(− 14) 6.0548	20021	(− 12) 8.5213	26014
43	(− 20) 4.7792	20803	(− 17) 3.6146	73288	(− 14) 1.1264	78144	(− 12) 1.7835	33352
44	(− 21) 6.5171	19276	(− 18) 5.7506	16594	(− 15) 2.0481	42079	(− 13) 3.6481	36401
45	(− 22) 8.6894	92369	(− 19) 8.9454	03592	(− 16) 3.6411	41473	(− 14) 7.2962	72804
46	(− 22) 1.1334	12048	(− 19) 1.3612	57068	(− 17) 6.3324	19955	(− 14) 1.4275	31635
47	(− 23) 1.4469	08998	(− 20) 2.0274	04144	(− 17) 1.0778	58716	(− 15) 2.7335	71217
48	(− 24) 1.8086	36247	(− 21) 2.9566	31045	(− 18) 1.7964	31193	(− 16) 5.1254	46033
49	(− 25) 2.2146	56629	(− 22) 4.2237	58634	(− 19) 2.9329	48887	(− 17) 9.4140	84548
50	(− 26) 2.6575	87955	(− 23) 5.9132	62088	(− 20) 4.6927	18219	(− 17) 1.6945	35219

*The floating decimal point notation is used here. For example (1) 1.8000,000 = (1.8000,000) 10.

STIRLING NUMBERS

Stirling numbers

The Stirling numbers are used for reducing factorials such as $x^{(n)}$ to polynomials in x and vice versa.

Stirling numbers of the first kind

The factorial polynomial $x^{(n)}$ is defined and represented by

$$x^{(n)} = x(x - 1)(x - 2)\cdots(x - n + 1)$$

where $x^{(0)}$ is 1 by definition.

If n is a non-negative integer, then

$$x^{(n)} = s_{n1}x + s_{n2}x^2 + \cdots + s_{nn}x^n.$$

Here the numbers $s_{n1}, s_{n2}, s_{n3}, \ldots$, are Stirling numbers of the first kind. A table listing these numbers with an example using same follows.

STIRLING NUMBERS OF THE FIRST KIND

n	s_{n1}	s_{n2}	s_{n3}	s_{n4}	s_{n5}	s_{n6}	s_{n7}	s_{n8}
1	1	0	0	0	0	0	0	0
2	-1	1	0	0	0	0	0	0
3	2	-3	1	0	0	0	0	0
4	-6	11	-6	1	0	0	0	0
5	24	-50	35	-10	1	0	0	0
6	-120	274	-225	85	-15	1	0	0
7	720	-1 764	1 624	-735	175	-21	1	0
8	-5 040	13 068	-13 132	6 769	-1 960	322	-28	1

The table may be continued by using the recurrence formula

$$s_{ni} = s_{n-1,i-1} - (n - 1)s_{n-1,i}, \quad i = 1, 2, \ldots, n$$

where $s_{n0} = 0$ for all n.

Example

Express $3x^{(3)} + 2x^{(1)}$ using Stirling's numbers of the first kind

$$3x^{(3)} = 3(2x - 3x^2 + x^3)$$
$$= 6x - 9x^2 + 3x^3$$
$$2x^{(1)} = 2x$$
$$\therefore 3x^{(3)} + 2x^{(1)} = 8x - 9x^2 + 3x^3$$

This may be verified by carrying out the indicated operations as follows

$$3x^{(3)} + 2x^{(1)} = 3(x)(x - 1)(x - 2) + 2x$$
$$= 3x^3 - 9x^2 + 6x + 2x$$
$$= 8x - 9x^2 + 3x^3$$

Stirling numbers of the second kind

For every non-negative integer n the function defined by x^n can be expressed as a linear combination of factorial powers of x not higher than the n'th. In other words

$$x^n = t_{n1}x^{(1)} + t_{n2}x^{(2)} + \cdots + t_{nn}x^{(n)}.$$

The numbers $t_{n1}, t_{n2}, \ldots, t_{nn}$ are called Stirling's numbers of the second kind.

A table listing these numbers with an example using same follows.

STIRLING NUMBERS OF THE SECOND KIND

n	t_{n1}	t_{n2}	t_{n3}	t_{n4}	t_{n5}	t_{n6}	t_{n7}	t_{n8}
1	1	0	0	0	0	0	0	0
2	1	1	0	0	0	0	0	0
3	1	3	1	0	0	0	0	0
4	1	7	6	1	0	0	0	0
5	1	15	25	10	1	0	0	0
6	1	31	90	65	15	1	0	0
7	1	63	301	350	140	21	1	0
8	1	127	966	1 701	1 050	266	28	1

This table may be continued by using the recurrence formula

$$t_{ni} = it_{n-1,i} + t_{n-1,i-1}, \quad i = 1, 2, \ldots, n$$

where $t_{n0} = 0$ for all n.

Example

Express $2x^3 - 3x^2 + x + 2$ by use of factorial powers

$$2x^3 = 2[x^{(1)} + 3x^{(2)} + x^{(3)}] = 2x^{(1)} + 6x^{(2)} + 2x^{(3)}$$
$$-3x^2 = -3[x^{(1)} + x^{(2)}] \qquad = -3x^{(1)} - 3x^{(2)}$$
$$x = x^{(1)} \qquad\qquad\quad = x^{(1)}$$
$$+2 = +2x^{(0)} \qquad\qquad = 2x^{(0)}$$
$$\therefore 2x^3 - 3x^2 + x + 2 = 2 + 3x^{(2)} + 2x^{(3)}$$

Fourier Series

(Also see Index for Cosine and Sine Transforms)
1. If $f(x)$ is a bounded periodic function of period 2L (i.e. $f(x + 2L) = f(x)$), and satisfies the Dirichlet conditions:

    a)In any period $f(x)$ is continuous, except possibly for a finite number of jump discontinuities

    b) In any period $f(x)$ has only a finite number of maxima and minima.
Then $f(x)$ may be represented by the Fourier series

$$\frac{a_0}{2} + \sum_{n=1}^{\infty} \left(a_n \cos \frac{n\pi x}{L} + b_n \sin \frac{n\pi x}{L} \right)$$

where a_n and b_n are as determined below. This series will converge to $f(x)$ at every point where $f(x)$ is continuous, and to

$$\frac{f(x^+) + f(x^-)}{2}$$

(i.e. the average of the left-hand and right-hand limits) at every point where $f(x)$ has a jump discontinuity.

$$a_n = \frac{1}{L} \int_{-L}^{L} f(x) \cos \frac{n\pi x}{L} \, dx, \, n = 0,1,2,3,\ldots;$$

$$b_n = \frac{1}{L} \int_{-L}^{L} f(x) \sin \frac{n\pi x}{L} \, dx, \, n = 1,2,3,\ldots$$

We may also write

$$a_n = \frac{1}{L} \int_{a}^{a+2L} f(x) \cos \frac{n\pi x}{L} \, dx \text{ and } b_n = \frac{1}{L} \int_{a}^{a+2L} f(x) \sin \frac{n\pi x}{L} \, dx,$$

where a is any real number. This if $a = 0$,

$$a_n = \frac{1}{L} \int_{0}^{2L} f(x) \cos \frac{n\pi x}{L} \, dx, \, n = 0,1,2,3,\ldots;$$

$$b_n = \frac{1}{L} \int_{0}^{2L} f(x) \sin \frac{n\pi x}{L} \, dx, \, n = 1,2,3,\ldots$$

2. If in addition to the above restrictions, $f(x)$ is even (i.e. $f(-x) = f(x)$), the Fourier series reduces to

$$\frac{a_0}{2} + \sum_{n=1}^{\infty} a_n \cos \frac{n\pi x}{L}$$

That is, $b_n = 0$. In this case, a simple formula for a_n, is

$$a_n = \frac{2}{L} \int_{0}^{L} f(x) \cos \frac{n\pi x}{L} \, dx, \, n = 0,1,2,3,\ldots$$

3. If in addition to the restrictions in (1), $f(x)$ is an odd function (i.e. $f(-x) = -f(x)$), then the Fourier series reduces to

$$\sum_{n=1}^{\infty} b_n \sin \frac{n\pi x}{L}$$

That is, $a_n = 0$. In this case, a simpler formula for the b_n is

$$b_n = \frac{2}{L} \int_0^L f(x) \sin \frac{n\pi x}{L} \, dx, \quad n = 1,2,3, \ldots$$

4. If in addition to the restrictions in (2) above, $f(x) = f(L - x)$, then a_n will be 0 for all even values of n, including n = 0. Thus in this case, the expansion reduces to

$$\sum_{n=1}^{\infty} a_{2m-1} \cos \frac{(2m - 1)\pi x}{L}$$

5. If in addition to the restrictions in (3) above, $f(x) = f(L - x)$, then b_n will be 0 for all even values of n. Thus in this case, the expansion reduces to

$$\sum_{n=1}^{\infty} b_{2m-1} \sin \frac{(2m - 1)\pi x}{L}$$

(The series in (4) and (5) are known as odd-harmonic series, since only the odd harmonics appear. Similar rules may be stated for even-harmonic series, but when a series appears in the even-harmonic form, it means that 2L has not been taken as the smallest period of $f(x)$. Since any integral multiple of a period is also a period, series obtained in this way will also work, but in general computation is simplified if 2L is taken to be the smallest period.)

6. If we write the Euler definitions for $\cos \theta$ and $\sin \theta$, we obtain the complex form of the Fourier Series known either as the "Complex Fourier Series" or the "Exponential Fourier Series" of $f(x)$. It is represented as

$$f(x) = \frac{1}{2} \sum_{n=-\infty}^{n=+\infty} c_n e^{i\omega_n x},$$

where

$$c_n = \frac{1}{L} \int_{-L}^{L} f(x) e^{-i\omega_n x} dx, \quad n = 0,\pm 1,\pm 2,\pm 3, \ldots$$

$$\text{with } \omega_n = \frac{n\pi}{L}, \quad n = 0,\pm 1,\pm 2, \ldots$$

The set of coefficients c_n is often referred to as the Fourier spectrum.

7. If both sine and cosine terms are present and if $f(x)$ is of period 2L and expandable by a Fourier series, it can be represented as

$$f(x) = \frac{a_0}{2} + \sum_{n=1}^{\infty} c_n \cos \left(\frac{n\pi x}{L} + \phi_n \right)$$

$$a_n = c_n \cos \phi_n, \quad b_n = -c_n \sin \phi_n, \quad c_n = \sqrt{a_n^2 + b_n^2}, \quad \phi_n = \text{arc} \tan \left(-\frac{b_n}{a_n} \right)$$

It can also be represented as

$$f(x) = \frac{a_0}{2} + \sum_{n=1}^{\infty} c_n \sin\left(\frac{n\pi x}{L} + \phi_n\right)$$

where $a_n = c_n \sin\phi_n$, $\quad b_n = c_n \cos\phi_n$, $\quad c_n = \sqrt{a_n^2 + b_n^2}$, $\quad \phi_n = \arctan\left(\frac{a_n}{b_n}\right)$

where the quadrant of ϕ_n is chosen so as to make the formulas for a_n, b_n, and c_n hold.

8. The following table of trigonometric identities should be helpful for developing Fourier Series.

	n**	n even	n odd	n/2 odd	n/2 even
$\sin n\pi$	0	0	0	0	0
$\cos n\pi$	$(-1)^n$	$+1$	-1	$+1$	$+1$
$\sin n\pi/2$*		0	$(-1)^{(n-1)/2}$	0	0
$\cos n\pi/2$*		$(-1)^{n/2}$	0	-1	$+1$
$\sin n\pi/4$		$\sqrt{2}/2\,(-1)^{(n^3+4n+11)/8}$		$(-1)^{(n-2)/4}$	0

*   A useful formula for $\sin n\pi/2$ and $\cos n\pi/2$ is given by

$$\sin\frac{n\pi}{2} = \frac{(i)^{n+1}}{2}\,[(-1)^n - 1] \text{ and } \cos\frac{n\pi}{2} = \frac{(i)^n}{2}\,[(-1)^n + 1], \text{ where } i^2 = -1.$$

**   n any integer.

AUXILIARY FORMULAS FOR FOURIER SERIES

$$1 = \frac{4}{\pi}\left[\sin\frac{\pi x}{k} + \frac{1}{3}\sin\frac{3\pi x}{k} + \frac{1}{5}\sin\frac{5\pi x}{k} + \cdots\right] \qquad [0 < x < k]$$

$$x = \frac{2k}{\pi}\left[\sin\frac{\pi x}{k} - \frac{1}{2}\sin\frac{2\pi x}{k} + \frac{1}{3}\sin\frac{3\pi x}{k} - \cdots\right] \qquad [-k < x < k]$$

$$x = \frac{k}{2} - \frac{4k}{\pi^2}\left[\cos\frac{\pi x}{k} + \frac{1}{3^2}\cos\frac{3\pi x}{k} + \frac{1}{5^2}\cos\frac{5\pi x}{k} + \cdots\right] \qquad [0 < x < k]$$

$$x^2 = \frac{2k^2}{\pi^3}\left[\left(\frac{\pi^2}{1} - \frac{4}{1}\right)\sin\frac{\pi x}{k} - \frac{\pi^2}{2}\sin\frac{2\pi x}{k} + \left(\frac{\pi^2}{3} - \frac{4}{3^3}\right)\sin\frac{3\pi x}{k}\right.$$
$$\left. - \frac{\pi^2}{4}\sin\frac{4\pi x}{k} + \left(\frac{\pi^2}{5} - \frac{4}{5^3}\right)\sin\frac{5\pi x}{k} + \cdots\right] [0 < x < k]$$

$$x^2 = \frac{k^2}{3} - \frac{4k^2}{\pi^2}\left[\cos\frac{\pi x}{k} - \frac{1}{2^2}\cos\frac{2\pi x}{k} + \frac{1}{3^2}\cos\frac{3\pi x}{k} - \frac{1}{4^2}\cos\frac{4\pi x}{k} + \cdots\right]$$
$$[-k < x < k]$$

$$1 - \frac{1}{3} + \frac{1}{5} - \frac{1}{7} + \cdots = \frac{\pi}{4}$$

$$1 + \frac{1}{2^2} + \frac{1}{3^2} + \frac{1}{4^2} + \cdots = \frac{\pi^2}{6}$$

$$1 - \frac{1}{2^2} + \frac{1}{3^2} - \frac{1}{4^2} + \cdots = \frac{\pi^2}{12}$$

$$1 + \frac{1}{3^2} + \frac{1}{5^2} + \frac{1}{7^2} + \cdots = \frac{\pi^2}{8}$$

$$\frac{1}{2^2} + \frac{1}{4^2} + \frac{1}{6^2} + \frac{1}{8^2} + \cdots = \frac{\pi^2}{24}$$

FOURIER EXPANSIONS FOR BASIC PERIODIC FUNCTIONS

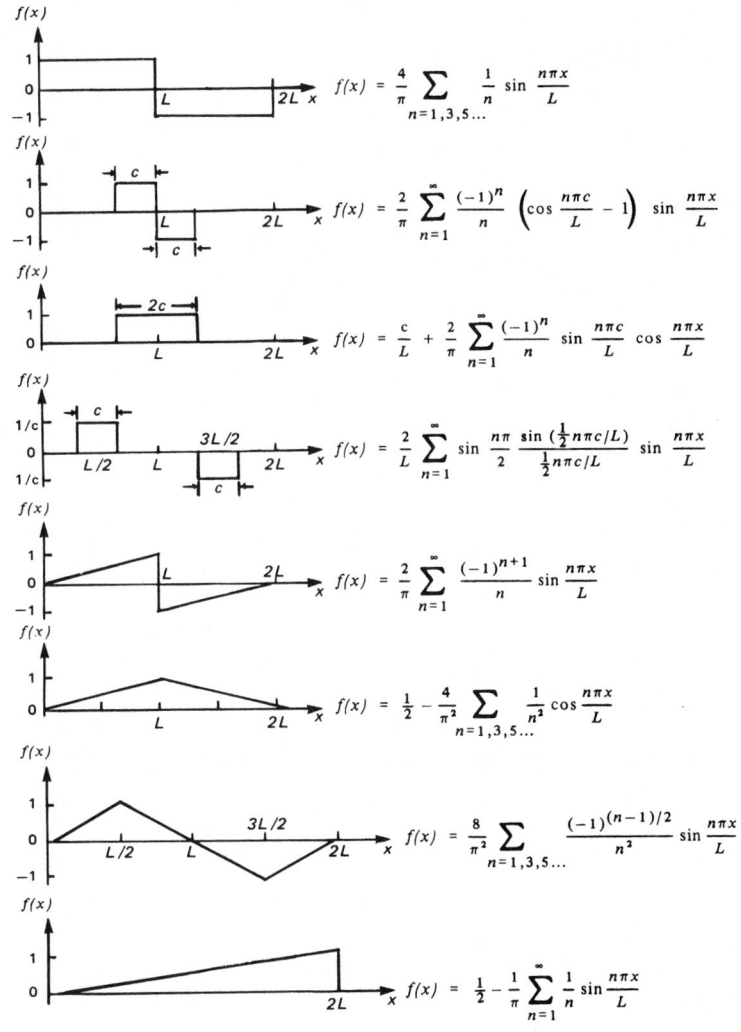

$$f(x) = \frac{4}{\pi} \sum_{n=1,3,5\ldots} \frac{1}{n} \sin \frac{n\pi x}{L}$$

$$f(x) = \frac{2}{\pi} \sum_{n=1}^{\infty} \frac{(-1)^n}{n} \left(\cos \frac{n\pi c}{L} - 1 \right) \sin \frac{n\pi x}{L}$$

$$f(x) = \frac{c}{L} + \frac{2}{\pi} \sum_{n=1}^{\infty} \frac{(-1)^n}{n} \sin \frac{n\pi c}{L} \cos \frac{n\pi x}{L}$$

$$f(x) = \frac{2}{L} \sum_{n=1}^{\infty} \sin \frac{n\pi}{2} \frac{\sin (\frac{1}{2}n\pi c/L)}{\frac{1}{2}n\pi c/L} \sin \frac{n\pi x}{L}$$

$$f(x) = \frac{2}{\pi} \sum_{n=1}^{\infty} \frac{(-1)^{n+1}}{n} \sin \frac{n\pi x}{L}$$

$$f(x) = \frac{1}{2} - \frac{4}{\pi^2} \sum_{n=1,3,5\ldots} \frac{1}{n^2} \cos \frac{n\pi x}{L}$$

$$f(x) = \frac{8}{\pi^2} \sum_{n=1,3,5\ldots} \frac{(-1)^{(n-1)/2}}{n^2} \sin \frac{n\pi x}{L}$$

$$f(x) = \frac{1}{2} - \frac{1}{\pi} \sum_{n=1}^{\infty} \frac{1}{n} \sin \frac{n\pi x}{L}$$

FOURIER EXPANSIONS FOR BASIC PERIODIC FUNCTIONS (Continued)

$$f(x) = \tfrac{1}{2}(1 + a) + \frac{2}{\pi^2(1-a)} \sum_{n=1}^{\infty} \frac{1}{n^2} \left[(-1)^n \cos n\pi a - 1\right] \cos \frac{n\pi x}{L} \; ; \left(a = \frac{c}{2L}\right)$$

$$f(x) = \frac{2}{\pi} \sum_{n=1}^{\infty} \frac{(-1)^{n-1}}{n} \left[1 + \frac{\sin n\pi a}{n\pi(1-a)}\right] \sin \frac{n\pi x}{L} \; ; \left(a = \frac{c}{2L}\right)$$

$$f(x) = \frac{1}{2} - \frac{4}{\pi^2(1-2a)} \sum_{n=1,3,5\ldots} \frac{1}{n^2} \cos n\pi a \cos \frac{n\pi x}{L} \; ; \left(a = \frac{c}{2L}\right)$$

$$f(x) = \frac{2}{\pi} \sum_{n=1}^{\infty} \frac{(-1)^n}{n} \left[1 + \frac{1+(-1)^n}{n\pi(1-2a)} \sin n\pi a\right] \sin \frac{n\pi x}{L} \; ; \left(a = \frac{c}{2L}\right)$$

$$f(x) = \frac{4}{\pi} \sum_{n=1}^{\infty} \frac{1}{n} \sin \frac{n\pi}{4} \sin n\pi a \sin \frac{n\pi x}{L} \; ; \left(a = \frac{c}{2L}\right)$$

$$f(x) = \frac{9}{\pi^2} \sum_{n=1}^{\infty} \frac{1}{n^2} \sin \frac{n\pi}{3} \sin \frac{n\pi x}{L} \; ; \left(a = \frac{c}{2L}\right)$$

$$f(x) = \frac{32}{3\pi^2} \sum_{n=1}^{\infty} \frac{1}{n^2} \sin \frac{n\pi}{4} \sin \frac{n\pi x}{L} \; ; \left(a = \frac{c}{2L}\right)$$

$$f(x) = \frac{1}{\pi} + \frac{1}{2} \sin \omega t - \frac{2}{\pi} \sum_{n=2,4,6\ldots} \frac{1}{n^2-1} \cos n\omega t$$

Extracted from graphs and formulas, pages 372, 373, *Differential Equations in Engineering Problems*, Salvadori and Schwarz, published by Prentice-Hall, Inc., 1954.

THE FOURIER TRANSFORMS

Dr. R. E. Gaskell

For a piecewise continuous function $F(x)$ over a finite interval $0 \leq x \leq \pi$, the *finite Fourier cosine transform* of $F(x)$ is

$$f_c(n) = \int_0^\pi F(x) \cos nx \, dx \quad (n = 0, 1, 2, \ldots). \tag{1}$$

If x ranges over the interval $0 \leq x \leq L$, the substitution $x' = \pi x / L$ allows the use of this definition, also. The inverse transform is written

$$\bar{F}(x) = \frac{1}{\pi} f_c(0) + \frac{2}{\pi} \sum_{n=1}^\infty f_c(n) \cos nx \quad (0 < x < \pi) \tag{2}$$

where $\bar{F}(x) = \dfrac{[F(x + 0) + F(x - 0)]}{2}$. We observe that $\bar{F}(x) = F(x)$ at points of continuity. The formula

$$f_c^{(2)}(n) = \int_0^\pi F''(x) \cos nx \, dx$$

$$= -n^2 f_c(n) - F'(0) + (-1)^n F'(\pi) \tag{3}$$

makes the finite Fourier cosine transform useful in certain boundary value problems.

Analogously, the *finite Fourier sine transform* of $F(x)$ is

$$f_s(n) = \int_0^\pi F(x) \sin nx \, dx \quad (n = 1, 2, 3, \ldots) \tag{4}$$

and

$$\bar{F}(x) = \frac{2}{\pi} \sum_{n=1}^\infty f_s(n) \sin nx \quad (0 < x < \pi) \tag{5}$$

Corresponding to (6) we have

$$f_s^{(2)}(n) = \int_0^\pi F''(x) \sin nx \, dx$$

$$= -n^2 f_s(n) - nF(0) - n(-1)^n F(\pi). \tag{6}$$

FOURIER TRANSFORMS

If $F(x)$ is defined for $x \geq 0$ and is piecewise continuous over any finite interval, and if

$$\int_0^\infty F(x) \, dx$$

is absolutely convergent, then

$$f_c(\alpha) = \sqrt{\frac{2}{\pi}} \int_0^\infty F(x) \cos (\alpha x) \, dx \tag{7}$$

is the *Fourier cosine transform* of $F(x)$. Furthermore,

$$\bar{F}(x) = \sqrt{\frac{2}{\pi}} \int_0^\infty f_c(\alpha) \cos (\alpha x) \, d\alpha. \tag{8}$$

The Fourier Transforms

If $\lim\limits_{x \to \infty} \dfrac{d^n F}{dx^n} = 0$, an important property of the Fourier cosine transform

$$f_c^{(2r)}(\alpha) = \sqrt{\frac{2}{\pi}} \int_0^\infty \left(\frac{d^{2r} F}{dx^{2r}}\right) \cos(\alpha x)\, dx$$

$$= -\sqrt{\frac{2}{\pi}} \sum_{n=0}^{r-1} (-1)^n a_{2r-2n-1} \alpha^{2n} + (-1)^r \alpha^{2r} f_c(\alpha) \tag{9}$$

where $\lim\limits_{x \to 0} \dfrac{d^r F}{dx^r} = a_r$, makes it useful in the solution of many problems.

Under the same conditions,

$$f_s(\alpha) = \sqrt{\frac{2}{\pi}} \int_0^\infty F(x) \sin(\alpha x)\, dx \tag{10}$$

defines the *Fourier sine transform* of $F(x)$, and

$$\bar{F}(x) = \sqrt{\frac{2}{\pi}} \int_0^\infty f_s(\alpha) \sin(\alpha x)\, d\alpha. \tag{11}$$

Corresponding to (12) we have

$$f_s^{(2r)}(\alpha) = \sqrt{\frac{2}{\pi}} \int_0^\infty \frac{d^{2r} F}{dx^{2r}} \sin(\alpha x)\, dx$$

$$= -\sqrt{\frac{2}{\pi}} \sum_{n=1}^{r} (-1)^n \alpha^{2n-1} a_{2r-2n} + (-1)^{r-1} \alpha^{2r} f_s(\alpha). \tag{12}$$

Similarly, if $F(x)$ is defined for $-\infty < x < \infty$, and if $\displaystyle\int_{-\infty}^{\infty} F(x)\, dx$ is absolutely convergent, then

$$f(\alpha) = \frac{1}{\sqrt{2\pi}} \int_{-\infty}^{\infty} F(x) e^{i\alpha x}\, dx \tag{13}$$

is the *Fourier transform* of $F(x)$, and

$$\bar{F}(x) = \frac{1}{\sqrt{2\pi}} \int_{-\infty}^{\infty} f(\alpha) e^{-i\alpha x}\, d\alpha. \tag{14}$$

Also, if

$$\lim_{|x| \to \infty} \left|\frac{d^n F}{dx^n}\right| = 0 \quad (n = 1, 2, \ldots, r-1),$$

then

$$f^{(r)}(\alpha) = \frac{1}{\sqrt{2\pi}} \int_{-\infty}^{\infty} F^{(r)}(x) e^{i\alpha x}\, dx = (-i\alpha)^r f(\alpha). \tag{15}$$

The Fourier Transforms

FINITE SINE TRANSFORMS

	$f_s(n)$	$F(x)$
1	$f_s(n) = \displaystyle\int_0^\pi F(x) \sin nx \, dx \; (n = 1, 2, \cdots)$	$F(x)$
2	$(-1)^{n+1} f_s(n)$	$F(\pi - x)$
3	$\dfrac{1}{n}$	$\dfrac{\pi - x}{\pi}$
4	$\dfrac{(-1)^{n+1}}{n}$	$\dfrac{x}{\pi}$
5	$\dfrac{1 - (-1)^n}{n}$	1
6	$\dfrac{2}{n^2} \sin \dfrac{n\pi}{2}$	$\begin{cases} x & \text{when } 0 < x < \pi/2 \\ \pi - x & \text{when } \pi/2 < x < \pi \end{cases}$
7	$\dfrac{(-1)^{n+1}}{n^3}$	$\dfrac{x(\pi^2 - x^2)}{6\pi}$
8	$\dfrac{1 - (-1)^n}{n^3}$	$\dfrac{x(\pi - x)}{2}$
9	$\dfrac{\pi^2 (-1)^{n-1}}{n} - \dfrac{2[1 - (-1)^n]}{n^3}$	x^2
10	$\pi(-1)^n \left(\dfrac{6}{n^3} - \dfrac{\pi^2}{n} \right)$	x^3
11	$\dfrac{n}{n^2 + c^2} [1 - (-1)^n e^{c\pi}]$	e^{cx}
12	$\dfrac{n}{n^2 + c^2}$	$\dfrac{\sinh c(\pi - x)}{\sinh c\pi}$
13	$\dfrac{n}{n^2 - k^2} \; (k \neq 0, 1, 2, \cdots)$	$\dfrac{\sin k(\pi - x)}{\sin k\pi}$
14	$\begin{cases} \dfrac{\pi}{2} & \text{when } n = m \\ 0 & \text{when } n \neq m \end{cases} \; (m = 1, 2, \cdots)$	$\sin mx$
15	$\dfrac{n}{n^2 - k^2} [1 - (-1)^n \cos k\pi]$ $(k \neq 1, 2, \cdots)$	$\cos kx$
16	$\begin{cases} \dfrac{n}{n^2 - m^2} [1 - (-1)^{n+m}] & \\ \qquad \text{when } n \neq m = 1, 2, \cdots \\ 0 & \text{when } n = m \end{cases}$	$\cos mx$
17	$\dfrac{n}{(n^2 - k^2)^2} \; (k \neq 0, 1, 2, \cdots)$	$\dfrac{\pi \sin kx}{2k \sin^2 k\pi} - \dfrac{x \cos k(\pi - x)}{2k \sin k\pi}$
18	$\dfrac{b^n}{n} \; (|b| \leq 1)$	$\dfrac{2}{\pi} \arctan \dfrac{b \sin x}{1 - b \cos x}$
19	$\dfrac{1 - (-1)^n}{n} b^n \; (|b| \leq 1)$	$\dfrac{2}{\pi} \arctan \dfrac{2b \sin x}{1 - b^2}$

The Fourier Transforms

FINITE COSINE TRANSFORMS

	$f_c(n)$	$F(x)$
1	$f_c(n) = \int_0^\pi F(x) \cos nx \, dx \quad (n = 0, 1, 2, \cdots)$	$F(x)$
2	$(-1)^n f_c(n)$	$F(\pi - x)$
3	0 when $n = 1, 2, \cdots; \; f_c(0) = \pi$	1
4	$\dfrac{2}{n} \sin \dfrac{n\pi}{2}; \; f_c(0) = 0$	$\begin{cases} 1 \text{ when } 0 < x < \pi/2 \\ -1 \text{ when } \pi/2 < x < \pi \end{cases}$
5	$-\dfrac{1 - (-1)^n}{n^2}; \; f_c(0) = \dfrac{\pi^2}{2}$	x
6	$\dfrac{(-1)^n}{n^2}; \; f_c(0) = \dfrac{\pi^2}{6}$	$\dfrac{x^2}{2\pi}$
7	$\dfrac{1}{n^2}; \; f_c(0) = 0$	$\dfrac{(\pi - x)^2}{2\pi} - \dfrac{\pi}{6}$
8	$3\pi^2 \dfrac{(-1)^n}{n^2} - 6 \dfrac{1 - (-1)^n}{n^4}; \; f_c(0) = \dfrac{\pi^4}{4}$	x^3
9	$\dfrac{(-1)^n e^c \pi - 1}{n^2 + c^2}$	$\dfrac{1}{c} e^{cx}$
10	$\dfrac{1}{n^2 + c^2}$	$\dfrac{\cosh c(\pi - x)}{c \sinh c\pi}$
11	$\dfrac{k}{n^2 - k^2}[(-1)^n \cos \pi k - 1]$ $(k \neq 0, 1, 2, \cdots)$	$\sin kx$
12	$\dfrac{(-1)^{n+m} - 1}{n^2 - m^2}; \; f_c(m) = 0 \quad (m = 1, 2, \cdots)$	$\dfrac{1}{m} \sin mx$
13	$\dfrac{1}{n^2 - k^2} \quad (k \neq 0, 1, 2, \cdots)$	$-\dfrac{\cos k(\pi - x)}{k \sin k\pi}$
14	0 when $n = 1, 2, \cdots;$ $f_c(m) = \dfrac{\pi}{2} \quad (m = 1, 2, \cdots)$	$\cos mx$

The Fourier Transforms

FOURIER SINE TRANSFORMS**

$F(x)$	$f_s(\alpha)$
1 $\begin{cases} 1 & (0 < x < a) \\ 0 & (x > a) \end{cases}$	$\sqrt{\dfrac{2}{\pi}}\left[\dfrac{1 - \cos \alpha}{\alpha}\right]$
2 $x^{p-1}\,(0 < p < 1)$	$\sqrt{\dfrac{2}{\pi}}\,\dfrac{\Gamma(p)}{\alpha^p}\sin\dfrac{p\pi}{2}$
3 $\begin{cases} \sin x & (0 < x < a) \\ 0 & (x > a) \end{cases}$	$\dfrac{1}{\sqrt{2\pi}}\left[\dfrac{\sin[a(1-\alpha)]}{1-\alpha} - \dfrac{\sin[a(1+\alpha)]}{1+\alpha}\right]$
4 e^{-x}	$\sqrt{\dfrac{2}{\pi}}\left[\dfrac{\alpha}{1+\alpha^2}\right]$
5 $xe^{-x^2/2}$	$\alpha e^{-\alpha^2/2}$
6 $\cos\dfrac{x^2}{2}$	$\sqrt{2}\left[\sin\dfrac{\alpha^2}{2}\,C\!\left(\dfrac{\alpha^2}{2}\right) - \cos\dfrac{\alpha^2}{2}\,S\!\left(\dfrac{\alpha^2}{2}\right)\right]^*$
7 $\sin\dfrac{x^2}{2}$	$\sqrt{2}\left[\cos\dfrac{\alpha^2}{2}\,C\!\left(\dfrac{\alpha^2}{2}\right) + \sin\dfrac{\alpha^2}{2}\,S\!\left(\dfrac{\alpha^2}{2}\right)\right]^*$

*$C(y)$ and $S(y)$ are the Fresnel integrals

$$C(y) = \frac{1}{\sqrt{2\pi}}\int_0^y \frac{1}{\sqrt{t}}\cos t\,dt,$$

$$S(y) = \frac{1}{\sqrt{2\pi}}\int_0^y \frac{1}{\sqrt{t}}\sin t\,dt.$$

**More extensive tables of the Fourier sine and cosine transforms can be found in Fritz Oberhettinger, "Tabellen zur-Fourier Transformation," Springer (1957).

FOURIER COSINE TRANSFORMS

$F(x)$	$f_c(\alpha)$
1 $\begin{cases} 1 & (0 < x < a) \\ 0 & (x > a) \end{cases}$	$\sqrt{\dfrac{2}{\pi}}\,\dfrac{\sin a\alpha}{\alpha}$
2 $x^{p-1}\ (0 < p < 1)$	$\sqrt{\dfrac{2}{\pi}}\,\dfrac{\Gamma(p)}{\alpha^p}\cos\dfrac{p\pi}{2}$
3 $\begin{cases} \cos x & (0 < x < a) \\ 0 & (x > a) \end{cases}$	$\dfrac{1}{\sqrt{2\pi}}\left[\dfrac{\sin[a(1-\alpha)]}{1-\alpha} + \dfrac{\sin[a(1+\alpha)]}{1+\alpha}\right]$
4 e^{-x}	$\sqrt{\dfrac{2}{\pi}}\left(\dfrac{1}{1+\alpha^2}\right)$
5 $e^{-x^2/2}$	$e^{-\alpha^2/2}$
6 $\cos\dfrac{x^2}{2}$	$\cos\left(\dfrac{\alpha^2}{2} - \dfrac{\pi}{4}\right)$
7 $\sin\dfrac{x^2}{2}$	$\cos\left(\dfrac{\alpha^2}{2} + \dfrac{\pi}{4}\right)$

The Fourier Transforms

FOURIER TRANSFORMS*

$F(x)$	$f(\alpha)$
1 $\dfrac{\sin ax}{x}$	$\begin{cases} \sqrt{\dfrac{\pi}{2}} & \mid \alpha \mid < a \\ 0 & \mid \alpha \mid > a \end{cases}$
2 $\begin{cases} e^{iwx} & (p < x < q) \\ 0 & (x < p, x > q) \end{cases}$	$\dfrac{i}{\sqrt{2\pi}} \, \dfrac{e^{ip(w+\alpha)} - e^{iq(w+\alpha)}}{(w + \alpha)}$
3 $\begin{cases} e^{-cx+iwx} & (x > 0) \\ 0 & (x < 0) \end{cases} \quad (c > 0)$	$\dfrac{i}{\sqrt{2\pi}(w + \alpha + ic)}$
4 $e^{-px^2} \quad R(p) > 0$	$\dfrac{1}{\sqrt{2p}} \, e^{-\alpha^2/4p}$
5 $\cos px^2$	$\dfrac{1}{\sqrt{2p}} \cos\left[\dfrac{\alpha^2}{4p} - \dfrac{\pi}{4}\right]$
6 $\sin px^2$	$\dfrac{1}{\sqrt{2p}} \cos\left[\dfrac{\alpha^2}{4p} + \dfrac{\pi}{4}\right]$
7 $\mid x \mid^{-p} \quad (0 < p < 1)$	$\sqrt{\dfrac{2}{\pi}} \, \dfrac{\Gamma(1 - p) \sin \dfrac{p\pi}{2}}{\mid \alpha \mid^{(1-p)}}$
8 $\dfrac{e^{-a\mid x \mid}}{\sqrt{\mid x \mid}}$	$\dfrac{\sqrt{\sqrt{(a^2 + \alpha^2)} + a}}{\sqrt{a^2 + \alpha^2}}$
9 $\dfrac{\cosh ax}{\cosh \pi x} \quad (-\pi < a < \pi)$	$\sqrt{\dfrac{2}{\pi}} \, \dfrac{\cos \dfrac{a}{2} \cosh \dfrac{\alpha}{2}}{\cosh \alpha + \cos a}$
10 $\dfrac{\sinh ax}{\sinh \pi x} \quad (-\pi < a < \pi)$	$\dfrac{1}{\sqrt{2\pi}} \, \dfrac{\sin a}{\cosh \alpha + \cos a}$
11 $\begin{cases} \dfrac{1}{\sqrt{a^2 - x^2}} & (\mid x \mid < a) \\ 0 & (\mid x \mid > a) \end{cases}$	$\sqrt{\dfrac{\pi}{2}} \, J_0(a\alpha)$
12 $\dfrac{\sin[b\sqrt{a^2 + x^2}]}{\sqrt{a^2 + x^2}}$	$\begin{cases} 0 & (\mid \alpha \mid > b) \\ \sqrt{\dfrac{\pi}{2}} \, J_0(a\sqrt{b^2 - \alpha^2}) & (\mid \alpha \mid < b) \end{cases}$
13 $\begin{cases} P_n(x) & (\mid x \mid < 1) \\ 0 & (\mid x \mid > 1) \end{cases}$	$\dfrac{i^n}{\sqrt{\alpha}} \, J_{n+\frac{1}{2}}(\alpha)$
14 $\begin{cases} \dfrac{\cos[b\sqrt{a^2 - x^2}]}{\sqrt{a^2 - x^2}} & (\mid x \mid < a) \\ 0 & (\mid x \mid > a) \end{cases}$	$\sqrt{\dfrac{\pi}{2}} \, J_0(a\sqrt{a^2 + b^2})$
15 $\begin{cases} \dfrac{\cosh[b\sqrt{a^2 - x^2}]}{\sqrt{a^2 - x^2}} & (\mid x \mid < a) \\ 0 & (\mid x \mid > a) \end{cases}$	$\sqrt{\dfrac{\pi}{2}} \, J_0(a\sqrt{\alpha^2 - b^2})$

*More extensive tables of Fourier transforms can be found in W. Magnus and F. Oberhettinger, "Formulas and Theorems of the Special Functions of Mathematical Physics," pp. 116–120. Chelsea (1949).

The Fourier Transforms

The following functions appear among the entries of the tables on transforms.

Function	Definition	Name
$Ei(x)$	$\displaystyle\int_{-\infty}^{x} \frac{e^{v}}{v}\, dv;$ or sometimes defined as $$-Ei(-x) = \int_{x}^{\infty} \frac{e^{-v}}{v}\, dv$$	Sine, Cosine, and Exponential Integral tables pages 371—373
$Si(x)$	$\displaystyle\int_{0}^{x} \frac{\sin v}{v}\, dv$	Sine, Cosine, and Exponential Integral tables pages 371—373
$Ci(x)$	$\displaystyle\int_{\infty}^{x} \frac{\cos v}{v}\, dv;$ or sometimes defined as negative of this integral	Sine, Cosine, and Exponential Integral tables pages 371—373
$erf(x)$	$\displaystyle\frac{2}{\sqrt{\pi}} \int_{0}^{x} e^{-v^{2}}\, dv$	Error function
$erfc(x)$	$1 - erf(x) = \dfrac{2}{\sqrt{\pi}} \displaystyle\int_{x}^{\infty} e^{-v^{2}}\, dv$	Complementary function to error function
$L_{n}(x)$	$\dfrac{e^{x}}{n!} \dfrac{d^{n}}{dx^{n}} (x^{n} e^{-x}),\ \ n = 0, 1, \cdots$	Laguerre polynomial of degree n

THE LAPLACE TRANSFORM

Dr. R. E. Gaskell

If $F(t)$ is a piecewise continuous real-valued function of the real variable $t (0 \leq t < \infty)$, and if $F(t)$ is of exponential order, that is if $|F(t)| < Me^{at} (t > T; M, a, T$ positive constants) then the *Laplace transform* of $F(t)$,

$$L\{F(t)\} = f(s) = \int_0^\infty e^{-st} F(t) \, dt, \tag{1}$$

exists in the half-plane of the complex variable s for which the real part of s is greater than some fixed value s_0, i.e., $R(s) \geq s_0$. Furthermore

$$F(t) = \frac{1}{2\pi i} \int_{a-i\infty}^{a+i\infty} e^{st} f(s) \, ds, \tag{2}$$

where $a > s_0$. The important property

$$L\{F^{(r)}(t)\} = \int_0^\infty e^{-st} \left(\frac{d^r F}{dt^r}\right) dt$$
$$= s^r f(s) - \sum_{n=0}^{r-1} s^{r-1-n} F^{(n)}(+0) \tag{3}$$

makes the Laplace transform very useful for solving linear differential equations with constant coefficients, and many boundary value problems.

The Laplace Transform
LAPLACE OPERATIONS*

	$F(t)$	$f(s)$
1	$F(t)$	$\int_0^\infty e^{-st} F(t)\,dt$
2	$AF(t) + BG(t)$	$Af(s) + Bg(s)$
3	$F'(t)$	$sf(s) - F(+0)$
4	$F^{(n)}(t)$	$s^n f(s) - s^{n-1}F(+0) - s^{n-2}F'(+0) - \cdots$ $- F^{(n-1)}(+0)$
5	$\int_0^t F(\tau)\,d\tau$	$\dfrac{1}{s} f(s)$
6	$\int_0^t \int_0^r F(\lambda)\,d\lambda\,d\tau$	$\dfrac{1}{s^2} f(s)$
7	$\int_0^t F_1(t - \tau) F_2(\tau)\,d\tau = F_1 * F_2$	$f_1(s) f_2(s)$
8	$tF(t)$	$-f'(s)$
9	$t^n F(t)$	$(-1)^n f^{(n)}(s)$
10	$\dfrac{1}{t} F(t)$	$\int_s^\infty f(x)\,dx$
11	$e^{at} F(t)$	$f(s - a)$
12	$F(t - b)$, where $F(t) = 0$ when $t < 0$	$e^{-bs} f(s)$
13	$\dfrac{1}{c} F\left(\dfrac{t}{c}\right)$	$f(cs)$
14	$\dfrac{1}{c} e^{(bt)/c} F\left(\dfrac{t}{c}\right)$	$f(cs - b)$
15	$F(t + a) = F(t)$	$\dfrac{\int_0^a e^{-st} F(t)\,dt}{1 - e^{-as}}$
16	$F(t + a) = -F(t)$	$\dfrac{\int_0^a e^{-st} F(t)\,dt}{1 + e^{-as}}$
17	$F_1(t)$, the half-wave rectification of $F(t)$ in No. 16	$\dfrac{f(s)}{1 - e^{-as}}$
18	$F_2(t)$, the full-wave rectification of $F(t)$ in No. 16	$f(s) \coth \dfrac{as}{2}$
19	$\displaystyle\sum_1^m \dfrac{p(a_n)}{q'(a_n)} e^{a_n t}$	$\dfrac{p(s)}{q(s)}, q(s) = (s - a_1)(s - a_2)\cdots(s - a_m)$
20	$e^{at} \displaystyle\sum_{n=1}^r \dfrac{\phi^{(r-n)}(a)}{(r - n)!} \dfrac{t^{n-1}}{(n - 1)!} + \cdots$	$\dfrac{p(s)}{q(s)} = \dfrac{\phi(s)}{(s - a)^r}$

*These tables of Laplace Operations, Laplace Transforms, and Finite Fourier sine and cosine transforms were taken from "Modern Operational Mathematics in Engineering", by permission of the author, R. V. Churchill, and the publisher, McGraw-Hill Book Company, Inc.

LAPLACE TRANSFORMS

	$f(s)$	$F(t)$
1	$\dfrac{1}{s}$	$\mu(t)$, unit step function
2	$\dfrac{1}{s^2}$	t
3	$\dfrac{1}{s^n}$ $(n = 1, 2, \ldots)$	$\dfrac{t^{n-1}}{(n-1)!}$
4	$\dfrac{1}{\sqrt{s}}$	$\dfrac{1}{\sqrt{\pi t}}$
5	$s^{-3/2}$	$2\sqrt{\dfrac{t}{\pi}}$
6	$s^{-[n+(1/2)]}$ $(n = 1, 2, \ldots)$	$\dfrac{2^n t^{n-(1/2)}}{1 \cdot 3 \cdot 5 \cdots (2n-1)\sqrt{\pi}}$
7	$\dfrac{\Gamma(k)}{s^k}$ $(k > 0)$	t^{k-1}
8	$\dfrac{1}{s-a}$	e^{at}
9	$\dfrac{1}{(s-a)^2}$	te^{at}
10	$\dfrac{1}{(s-a)^n}$ $(n = 1, 2, \ldots)$	$\dfrac{1}{(n-1)!} t^{n-1} e^{at}$
11	$\dfrac{\Gamma(k)}{(s-a)^k}$ $(k > 0)$	$t^{k-1} e^{at}$
12*	$\dfrac{1}{(s-a)(s-b)}$	$\dfrac{1}{a-b}(e^{at} - e^{bt})$
13*	$\dfrac{s}{(s-a)(s-b)}$	$\dfrac{1}{a-b}(ae^{at} - be^{bt})$
14*	$\dfrac{1}{(s-a)(s-b)(s-c)}$	$-\dfrac{(b-c)e^{at} + (c-a)e^{bt} + (a-b)e^{ct}}{(a-b)(b-c)(c-a)}$
15	$\dfrac{1}{s^2+a^2}$	$\dfrac{1}{a}\sin at$
16	$\dfrac{s}{s^2+a^2}$	$\cos at$
17	$\dfrac{1}{s^2-a^2}$	$\dfrac{1}{a}\sinh at$
18	$\dfrac{s}{s^2-a^2}$	$\cosh at$

*Here a, b, and (in 14) c represent distinct constants.

The Laplace Transforms

LAPLACE TRANSFORMS (Continued)

	$f(s)$	$F(t)$
19	$\dfrac{1}{s(s^2 + a^2)}$	$\dfrac{1}{a^2}(1 - \cos at)$
20	$\dfrac{1}{s^2(s^2 + a^2)}$	$\dfrac{1}{a^3}(at - \sin at)$
21	$\dfrac{1}{(s^2 + a^2)^2}$	$\dfrac{1}{2a^3}(\sin at - at \cos at)$
22	$\dfrac{s}{(s^2 + a^2)^2}$	$\dfrac{t}{2a} \sin at$
23	$\dfrac{s^2}{(s^2 + a^2)^2}$	$\dfrac{1}{2a}(\sin at + at \cos at)$
24	$\dfrac{s^2 - a^2}{(s^2 + a^2)^2}$	$t \cos at$
25	$\dfrac{s}{(s^2 + a^2)(s^2 + b^2)} \quad (a^2 \neq b^2)$	$\dfrac{\cos at - \cos bt}{b^2 - a^2}$
26	$\dfrac{1}{(s - a)^2 + b^2}$	$\dfrac{1}{b} e^{at} \sin bt$
27	$\dfrac{s - a}{(s - a)^2 + b^2}$	$e^{at} \cos bt$
27.1	$\dfrac{1}{[(s + a)^2 + b^2]^n}$	$\dfrac{-e^{-at}}{4^{n-1}b^{2n}} \sum_{r=1}^{n} \binom{2n - r - 1}{n - 1}(-2t)^{r-1} \dfrac{d^r}{dt^r}[\cos(bt)]$
27.2	$\dfrac{s}{[(s + a)^2 + b^2]^n}$	$\dfrac{e^{-at}}{4^{n-1}b^{2n}} \left\{ \sum_{r=1}^{n} \binom{2n - r - 1}{n - 1} \dfrac{1}{(r-1)!} \right.$ $(-2t)^{r-1} \dfrac{d^r}{dt^r}[a \cos(bt) + b \sin(bt)]$ $-2b \sum_{r=1}^{n-1} \dfrac{1}{(r-1)!} \binom{2n - r - 2}{n - 1}$ $\left. (-2t)^{r-1} \dfrac{d^r}{dt^r}[\sin bt] \right\}$
28	$\dfrac{3a^2}{s^3 + a^3}$	$e^{-at} - e^{(at)/2}\left(\cos \dfrac{at\sqrt{3}}{2} - \sqrt{3} \sin \dfrac{at\sqrt{3}}{2} \right)$
29	$\dfrac{4a^3}{s^4 + 4a^4}$	$\sin at \cosh at - \cos at \sinh at$
30	$\dfrac{s}{s^4 + 4a^4}$	$\dfrac{1}{2a^2} \sin at \sinh at$

The Laplace Transforms

LAPLACE TRANSFORMS (Continued)

	$f(s)$	$F(t)$
31	$\dfrac{1}{s^4 - a^4}$	$\dfrac{1}{2a^3}(\sinh at - \sin at)$
32	$\dfrac{s}{s^4 - a^4}$	$\dfrac{1}{2a^2}(\cosh at - \cos at)$
33	$\dfrac{8a^3 s^2}{(s^2 + a^2)^3}$	$(1 + a^2 t^2)\sin at - \cos at$
34*	$\dfrac{1}{s}\left(\dfrac{s-1}{s}\right)^n$	$L_n(t) = \dfrac{e^t}{n!}\dfrac{d^n}{dt^n}(t^n e^{-t})$
35	$\dfrac{s}{(s-a)^{3/2}}$	$\dfrac{1}{\sqrt{\pi t}}e^{at}(1 + 2at)$
36	$\sqrt{s-a} - \sqrt{s-b}$	$\dfrac{1}{2\sqrt{\pi t^3}}(e^{bt} - e^{at})$
37	$\dfrac{1}{\sqrt{s}+a}$	$\dfrac{1}{\sqrt{\pi t}} - ae^{a^2 t}\,\mathrm{erfc}\,(a\sqrt{t})$
38	$\dfrac{\sqrt{s}}{s - a^2}$	$\dfrac{1}{\sqrt{\pi t}} + ae^{a^2 t}\,\mathrm{erf}\,(a\sqrt{t})$
39	$\dfrac{\sqrt{s}}{s + a^2}$	$\dfrac{1}{\sqrt{\pi t}} - \dfrac{2a}{\sqrt{\pi}}e^{-a^2 t}\displaystyle\int_0^{a\sqrt{t}} e^{\lambda^2}\,d\lambda$
40	$\dfrac{1}{\sqrt{s}(s - a^2)}$	$\dfrac{1}{a}e^{a^2 t}\,\mathrm{erf}\,(a\sqrt{t})$
41	$\dfrac{1}{\sqrt{s}(s + a^2)}$	$\dfrac{2}{a\sqrt{\pi}}e^{-a^2 t}\displaystyle\int_0^{a\sqrt{t}} e^{\lambda^2}\,d\lambda$
42	$\dfrac{b^2 - a^2}{(s - a^2)(b + \sqrt{s})}$	$e^{a^2 t}[b - a\,\mathrm{erf}\,(a\sqrt{t})] - be^{b^2 t}\,\mathrm{erfc}\,(b\sqrt{t})$
43	$\dfrac{1}{\sqrt{s}(\sqrt{s}+a)}$	$e^{a^2 t}\,\mathrm{erfc}\,(a\sqrt{t})$
44	$\dfrac{1}{(s+a)\sqrt{s+b}}$	$\dfrac{1}{\sqrt{b-a}}e^{-at}\,\mathrm{erf}\,(\sqrt{b-a}\sqrt{t})$
45	$\dfrac{b^2 - a^2}{\sqrt{s}(s - a^2)(\sqrt{s}+b)}$	$e^{a^2 t}\left[\dfrac{b}{a}\,\mathrm{erf}\,(a\sqrt{t}) - 1\right] + e^{b^2 t}\,\mathrm{erfc}\,(b\sqrt{t})$
46†	$\dfrac{(1-s)^n}{s^{n+(1/2)}}$	$\dfrac{n!}{(2n)!\sqrt{\pi t}}H_{2n}(\sqrt{t})$
47	$\dfrac{(1-s)^n}{s^{n+(3/2)}}$	$-\dfrac{n!}{\sqrt{\pi}(2n+1)!}H_{2n+1}(\sqrt{t})$

*$L_n(t)$ is the Laguerre polynomial of degree n.

†$H_n(x)$ is the Hermite polynomial, $H_n(x) = e^{x^2}\dfrac{d^n}{dx^n}(e^{-x^2})$.

The Laplace Transforms

LAPLACE TRANSFORMS (Continued)

	$f(s)$	$F(t)$
48*	$\dfrac{\sqrt{s + 2a}}{\sqrt{s}} - 1$	$ae^{-at}[I_1(at) + I_0(at)]$
49	$\dfrac{1}{\sqrt{s + a}\,\sqrt{s + b}}$	$e^{-(1/2)(a + b)t} I_0\left(\dfrac{a - b}{2}\,t\right)$
50	$\dfrac{\Gamma(k)}{(s + a)^k(s + b)^k} \quad (k \geq 0)$	$\sqrt{\pi}\left(\dfrac{t}{a - b}\right)^{k - (1/2)} e^{-(1/2)(a + b)t} I_{k - (1/2)}\left(\dfrac{a - b}{2}\,t\right)$
51	$\dfrac{1}{(s + a)^{1/2}(s + b)^{3/2}}$	$te^{-(1/2)(a + b)t}\left[I_0\left(\dfrac{a - b}{2}\,t\right) + I_1\left(\dfrac{a - b}{2}\,t\right)\right]$
52	$\dfrac{\sqrt{s + 2a} - \sqrt{s}}{\sqrt{s + 2a} + \sqrt{s}}$	$\dfrac{1}{t}\,e^{-at}I_1(at)$
53	$\dfrac{(a - b)^k}{(\sqrt{s + a} + \sqrt{s + b})^{2k}} \quad (k > 0)$	$\dfrac{k}{t}\,e^{-(1/2)(a + b)t} I_k\left(\dfrac{a - b}{2}\,t\right)$
54	$\dfrac{(\sqrt{s + a} + \sqrt{s})^{-2\nu}}{\sqrt{s}\,\sqrt{s + a}} \quad (\nu > -1)$	$\dfrac{1}{a^\nu}\,e^{-(1/2)(at)} I_\nu\left(\dfrac{1}{2}\,at\right)$
55	$\dfrac{1}{\sqrt{s^2 + a^2}}$	$J_0(at)$
56	$\dfrac{(\sqrt{s^2 + a^2} - s)^\nu}{\sqrt{s^2 + a^2}} \quad (\nu > -1)$	$a^\nu J_\nu(at)$
57	$\dfrac{1}{(s^2 + a^2)^k} \quad (k > 0)$	$\dfrac{\sqrt{\pi}}{\Gamma(k)}\left(\dfrac{t}{2a}\right)^{k - (1/2)} J_{k - (1/2)}(at)$
58	$(\sqrt{s^2 + a^2} - s)^k (k > 0)$	$\dfrac{ka^k}{t}\,J_k(at)$
59	$\dfrac{(s - \sqrt{s^2 - a^2})^\nu}{\sqrt{s^2 - a^2}} \quad (\nu > -1)$	$a^\nu I_\nu(at)$
60	$\dfrac{1}{(s^2 - a^2)^k} \quad (k > 0)$	$\dfrac{\sqrt{\pi}}{\Gamma(k)}\left(\dfrac{t}{2a}\right)^{k - (1/2)} I_{k - (1/2)}(at)$
61	$\dfrac{e^{-ks}}{s}$	$S_k(t) = \begin{cases} 0 \text{ when } 0 < t < k \\ 1 \text{ when } t > k \end{cases}$
62	$\dfrac{e^{-ks}}{s^2}$	$\begin{cases} 0 \text{ when } 0 < t < k \\ t - k \text{ when } t > k \end{cases}$
63	$\dfrac{e^{-ks}}{s^\mu} \quad (\mu > 0)$	$\begin{cases} 0 \qquad\qquad \text{when } 0 < t < k \\ \dfrac{(t - k)^{\mu - 1}}{\Gamma(\mu)} \text{ when } t > k \end{cases}$
64	$\dfrac{1 - e^{-ks}}{s}$	$\begin{cases} 1 \text{ when } 0 < t < k \\ 0 \text{ when } t > k \end{cases}$

*$I_n(x) = i^{-n}J_n(ix)$, where J_n is Bessel's function of the first kind.

The Laplace Transforms

LAPLACE TRANSFORMS (Continued)

	$f(s)$	$F(t)$
65	$\dfrac{1}{s(1 - e^{-ks})} = \dfrac{1 + \coth \frac{1}{2}ks}{2s}$	$S(k, t) = n$ when $(n - 1)k < t < nk\,(n = 1, 2, \ldots)$
66	$\dfrac{1}{s(e^{ks} - a)}$	$\begin{cases} 0 \text{ when } 0 < t < k \\ 1 + a + a^2 + \cdots + a^{n-1} \\ \quad \text{when } nk < t < (n + 1)k\,(n = 1, 2, \ldots) \end{cases}$
67	$\dfrac{1}{s} \tanh ks$	$M(2k, t) = (-1)^{n-1}$ when $2k(n - 1) < t < 2kn$ $(n = 1, 2, \ldots)$
68	$\dfrac{1}{s(1 + e^{-ks})}$	$\dfrac{1}{2} M(k, t) + \dfrac{1}{2} = \dfrac{1 - (-1)^n}{2}$ when $(n - 1)k < t < nk$
69*	$\dfrac{1}{s^2} \tanh ks$	$H(2k, t)$
70	$\dfrac{1}{s \sinh ks}$	$2S(2k, t + k) - 2 = 2(n - 1)$ when $(2n - 3)k < t < (2n - 1)k$ $(t > 0)$
71	$\dfrac{1}{s \cosh ks}$	$M(2k, t + 3k) + 1 = 1 + (-1)^n$ when $(2n - 3)k < t < (2n - 1)k$ $(t > 0)$
72	$\dfrac{1}{s} \coth ks$	$2S(2k, t) - 1 = 2n - 1$ when $2k(n - 1) < t < 2kn$
73	$\dfrac{k}{s^2 + k^2} \coth \dfrac{\pi s}{2k}$	$\lvert \sin kt \rvert$
74	$\dfrac{1}{(s^2 + 1)(1 - e^{-\pi s})}$	$\begin{cases} \sin t \text{ when } (2n - 2)\pi < t < (2n - 1)\pi \\ 0 \quad \text{when } (2n - 1)\pi < t < 2n\pi \end{cases}$
75	$\dfrac{1}{s} e^{-k/s}$	$J_0(2\sqrt{kt})$
76	$\dfrac{1}{\sqrt{s}} e^{-k/s}$	$\dfrac{1}{\sqrt{\pi t}} \cos 2\sqrt{kt}$
77	$\dfrac{1}{\sqrt{s}} e^{k/s}$	$\dfrac{1}{\sqrt{\pi t}} \cosh 2\sqrt{kt}$
78	$\dfrac{1}{s^{3/2}} e^{-k/s}$	$\dfrac{1}{\sqrt{\pi k}} \sin 2\sqrt{kt}$
79	$\dfrac{1}{s^{3/2}} e^{k/s}$	$\dfrac{1}{\sqrt{\pi k}} \sinh 2\sqrt{kt}$
80	$\dfrac{1}{s^{\mu}} e^{-k/s}(\mu > 0)$	$\left(\dfrac{t}{k}\right)^{(\mu-1)/2} J_{\mu-1}(2\sqrt{kt})$

*$H(2k, t) = k + (r - k)(-1)^n$ where $t = 2kn + r; 0 \le r < 2k; n = 0, 1, 2, \ldots$.

The Laplace Transforms

LAPLACE TRANSFORMS (Continued)

	$f(s)$	$F(t)$
81	$\dfrac{1}{s^\mu} e^{k/s} (\mu > 0)$	$\left(\dfrac{t}{k}\right)^{(\mu-1)/2} I_{\mu-1}(2\sqrt{kt})$
82	$e^{-k\sqrt{s}} (k > 0)$	$\dfrac{k}{2\sqrt{\pi t^3}} \exp\left(-\dfrac{k^2}{4t}\right)$
83	$\dfrac{1}{s} e^{-k\sqrt{s}} (k \geq 0)$	$\operatorname{erfc}\left(\dfrac{k}{2\sqrt{t}}\right)$
84	$\dfrac{1}{\sqrt{s}} e^{-k\sqrt{s}} (k \geq 0)$	$\dfrac{1}{\sqrt{\pi t}} \exp\left(-\dfrac{k^2}{4t}\right)$
85	$s^{-3/2} e^{-k\sqrt{s}} (k \geq 0)$	$2\sqrt{\dfrac{t}{\pi}} \exp\left(-\dfrac{k^2}{4t}\right) - k \operatorname{erfc}\left(\dfrac{k}{2\sqrt{t}}\right)$
86	$\dfrac{a e^{-k\sqrt{s}}}{s(a+\sqrt{s})} (k \geq 0)$	$-e^{ak} e^{a^2 t} \operatorname{erfc}\left(a\sqrt{t} + \dfrac{k}{2\sqrt{t}}\right) + \operatorname{erfc}\left(\dfrac{k}{2\sqrt{t}}\right)$
87	$\dfrac{e^{-k\sqrt{s}}}{\sqrt{s}(a+\sqrt{s})} (k \geq 0)$	$e^{ak} e^{a^2 t} \operatorname{erfc}\left(a\sqrt{t} + \dfrac{k}{2\sqrt{t}}\right)$
88	$\dfrac{e^{-k\sqrt{s(s+a)}}}{\sqrt{s(s+a)}}$	$\begin{cases} 0 & \text{when } 0 < t < k \\ e^{-(1/2)(at)} I_0(\tfrac{1}{2} a\sqrt{t^2-k^2}) & \text{when } t > k \end{cases}$
89	$\dfrac{e^{-k\sqrt{s^2+a^2}}}{\sqrt{s^2+a^2}}$	$\begin{cases} 0 & \text{when } 0 < t < k \\ J_0(a\sqrt{t^2-k^2}) & \text{when } t > k \end{cases}$
90	$\dfrac{e^{-k\sqrt{s^2-a^2}}}{\sqrt{s^2-a^2}}$	$\begin{cases} 0 & \text{when } 0 < t < k \\ I_0(a\sqrt{t^2-k^2}) & \text{when } t > k \end{cases}$
91	$\dfrac{e^{-k(\sqrt{s^2+a^2}-s)}}{\sqrt{s^2+a^2}} (k \geq 0)$	$J_0(a\sqrt{t^2+2kt})$
92	$e^{-ks} - e^{-k\sqrt{s^2+a^2}}$	$\begin{cases} 0 & \text{when } 0 < t < k \\ \dfrac{ak}{\sqrt{t^2-k^2}} J_1(a\sqrt{t^2-k^2}) & \text{when } t > k \end{cases}$
93	$e^{-k\sqrt{s^2+a^2}} - e^{-ks}$	$\begin{cases} 0 & \text{when } 0 < t < k \\ \dfrac{ak}{\sqrt{t^2-k^2}} I_1(a\sqrt{t^2-k^2}) & \text{when } t > k \end{cases}$
94	$\dfrac{a^\nu e^{-k\sqrt{s^2-a^2}}}{\sqrt{s^2+a^2}(\sqrt{s^2+a^2}+s)^\nu}$ $(\nu > -1)$	$\begin{cases} 0 & \text{when } 0 < t < k \\ \left(\dfrac{t-k}{t+k}\right)^{(1/2)\nu} J_\nu(a\sqrt{t^2-k^2}) & \text{when } t > k \end{cases}$
95	$\dfrac{1}{s} \log s$	$\Gamma'(1) - \log t \; [\Gamma'(1) = -0.5772]$
96	$\dfrac{1}{s^k} \log s \; (k > 0)$	$t^{k-1}\left\{\dfrac{\Gamma'(k)}{[\Gamma(k)]^2} - \dfrac{\log t}{\Gamma(k)}\right\}$
97	$\dfrac{\log s}{s-a} \; (a > 0)$	$e^{at}[\log a - \operatorname{Ei}(-at)]$

The Laplace Transforms

LAPLACE TRANSFORMS (Continued)

	$f(s)$	$F(t)$
98	$\dfrac{\log s}{s^2 + 1}$	$\cos t\,\mathrm{Si}(t) - \sin t\,\mathrm{Ci}(t)$
99	$\dfrac{s \log s}{s^2 + 1}$	$-\sin t\,\mathrm{Si}(t) - \cos t\,\mathrm{Ci}(t)$
100	$\dfrac{1}{s} \log (1 + ks)\,(k > 0)$	$-\mathrm{Ei}\left(-\dfrac{t}{k}\right)$
101	$\log \dfrac{s - a}{s - b}$	$\dfrac{1}{t}\,(e^{bt} - e^{at})$
102	$\dfrac{1}{s} \log (1 + k^2 s^2)$	$-2\mathrm{Ci}\left(\dfrac{t}{k}\right)$
103	$\dfrac{1}{s} \log (s^2 + a^2)\ \ (a > 0)$	$2 \log a - 2\mathrm{Ci}(at)$
104	$\dfrac{1}{s^2} \log (s^2 + a^2)\ \ (a > 0)$	$\dfrac{2}{a}\,[at \log a + \sin at - at\,\mathrm{Ci}(at)]$
105	$\log \dfrac{s^2 + a^2}{s^2}$	$\dfrac{2}{t}\,(1 - \cos at)$
106	$\log \dfrac{s^2 - a^2}{s^2}$	$\dfrac{2}{t}\,(1 - \cosh at)$
107	$\arctan \dfrac{k}{s}$	$\dfrac{1}{t} \sin kt$
108	$\dfrac{1}{s} \arctan \dfrac{k}{s}$	$\mathrm{Si}(kt)$
109	$e^{k^2 s^2} \mathrm{erfc}\,(ks)\ \ (k > 0)$	$\dfrac{1}{k \sqrt{\pi}} \exp\left(-\dfrac{t^2}{4k^2}\right)$
110	$\dfrac{1}{s}\,e^{k^2 s^2} \mathrm{erfc}\,(ks)\ \ (k > 0)$	$\mathrm{erf}\left(\dfrac{t}{2k}\right)$
111	$e^{ks} \mathrm{erfc}\,(\sqrt{ks})\ \ (k > 0)$	$\dfrac{\sqrt{k}}{\pi \sqrt{t}(t + k)}$
112	$\dfrac{1}{\sqrt{s}} \mathrm{erfc}\,(\sqrt{ks})$	$\begin{cases} 0 & \text{when } 0 < t < k \\ (\pi t)^{-1/2} & \text{when } t > k \end{cases}$
113	$\dfrac{1}{\sqrt{s}}\,e^{ks} \mathrm{erfc}\,(\sqrt{ks})\,(k > 0)$	$\dfrac{1}{\sqrt{\pi(t + k)}}$
114	$\mathrm{erf}\left(\dfrac{k}{\sqrt{s}}\right)$	$\dfrac{1}{\pi t} \sin (2k \sqrt{t})$
115	$\dfrac{1}{\sqrt{s}}\,e^{k^2/s} \mathrm{erfc}\left(\dfrac{k}{\sqrt{s}}\right)$	$\dfrac{1}{\sqrt{\pi t}}\,e^{-2k \sqrt{t}}$

The Laplace Transforms

LAPLACE TRANSFORMS (Continued)

	$f(s)$	$F(t)$
115.1	$-e^{as} \text{Ei}(-as)$	$\dfrac{1}{t+a}$; $(a > 0)$
115.2	$\dfrac{1}{a} + se^{as} \text{Ei}(-as)$	$\dfrac{1}{(t+a)^2}$; $(a > 0)$
115.3	$\left[\dfrac{\pi}{2} - \text{Si}(s)\right]\cos s + \text{Ci}(s)\sin s$	$\dfrac{1}{t^2+1}$
116*	$K_0(ks)$	$\begin{cases} 0 & \text{when } 0 < t < k \\ (t^2 - k^2)^{-1/2} & \text{when } t > k \end{cases}$
117	$K_0(k\sqrt{s})$	$\dfrac{1}{2t}\exp\left(-\dfrac{k^2}{4t}\right)$
118	$\dfrac{1}{s}e^{ks}K_1(ks)$	$\dfrac{1}{k}\sqrt{t(t+2k)}$
119	$\dfrac{1}{\sqrt{s}}K_1(k\sqrt{s})$	$\dfrac{1}{k}\exp\left(-\dfrac{k^2}{4t}\right)$
120	$\dfrac{1}{\sqrt{s}}e^{k/s}K_0\left(\dfrac{k}{s}\right)$	$\dfrac{2}{\sqrt{\pi t}}K_0(2\sqrt{2kt})$
121	$\pi e^{-ks}I_0(ks)$	$\begin{cases} [t(2k - t)]^{-1/2} & \text{when } 0 < t < 2k \\ 0 & \text{when } t > 2k \end{cases}$
122**	$e^{-ks}I_1(ks)$	$\begin{cases} \dfrac{k-t}{\pi k\sqrt{t(2k-t)}} & \text{when } 0 < t < 2k \\ 0 & \text{when } t > 2k \end{cases}$

*$K_n(x)$ is Bessel's function of the second kind for the imaginary argument.
**Several additional transforms, especially those involving other Bessel functions, can be found in the tables by G. A. Campbell and R. M. Foster, "Fourier Integrals for Practical Applications", or "Vol. 1, Bateman Manuscript Project, Transform Tables, McGraw-Hill, 1955", or N. W. McLachlan and P. Humbert, "Formulaire pour le calcul symbolique". In the tables by Campbell and Foster, only those entries containing the condition $0 < g$ or $k < g$, where g is our t, are Laplace transforms.

THE Z TRANSFORM

B. Girling

When $F(t)$, a continuous function of time, is sampled at regular intervals of period T the usual Laplace transform techniques are modified. The diagramatic form of a simple sampler together with its associated input-output waveforms is shown below

$$\frac{1}{T} \equiv F_s \qquad \text{the sampling frequency}$$

Defining the set of impulse functions $\delta_T(t)$ by

$$\delta_T(t) \equiv \sum_{n=0}^{\infty} \delta(t - nT)$$

the input-output relationship of the sampler becomes

$$F^*(t) = F(t) \cdot \delta_T(t)$$

$$= \sum_{n=0}^{\infty} F(nT) \cdot \delta(t - nT).$$

While for a given $F(t)$ and T the $F^*(t)$ is unique, the converse is not true.

The Laplace transform can be used to define $F^*(s)$ as follows

$$L\{F^*(t)\} \equiv f^*(s)$$

$$= \sum_{n=0}^{\infty} F(nT) \cdot e^{-nTs}.$$

The variable 'z' is introduced by means of the transformation

$$z = e^{Ts}$$

and since any function of s can now be replaced by a corresponding function of z we have

$$f(z) = \sum_{n=0}^{\infty} F(nT) \cdot z^{-n}$$

where $\qquad f^*(s) \equiv f(z)$

and $\qquad s = \frac{1}{T} \ln z$

The Z operator can now be defined in terms of the Laplace operator by the relationship

$$Z\{F(t)\} \equiv L\{F^*(t)\}$$

The Z Transform

THE Z TRANSFORM (Continued)

An alternative definition (quoted without proof) is

$$Z\{F(t)\} = \sum \text{residues of} \left[\left(\frac{1}{1 - e^{Tz}z^{-1}} \right) \cdot f(z) \right]$$

The inverse z transform

$$Z^{-1}\{f(z)\} \equiv F^*(t)$$

$$= \frac{1}{2\pi j} \oint f(z) \cdot z^{n-1} \, dz$$

where the contour of integration encloses all the singularities of the integrand. In the following table Greek letters denote constants.

$F(t)$	$f(z) = Z\{F(t)\}$
$\alpha F(t)$	$\alpha f(z)$
$F(t) + G(t)$	$f(z) + g(z)$
$F(t + T)$	$zf(z) - zF(0)$
$F(t + 2T)$	$z^2 f(z) - z^2 F(0) - zF(T)$
$F(t + mT)$	$z^m f(z) - \displaystyle\sum_{r=0}^{m-1} z^{m-r} F(rT)$
	$= z^m f(z)$ when $F(rT) = 0, 0 \le r \le m - 1$
$F(t - mT)$	$z^{-m} f(z)$
$e^{\alpha t} F(t)$	$f(e^{-\alpha T} z)$
$e^{-\alpha t} F(t)$	$f(e^{\alpha T} z)$
$t \cdot F(t)$	$-Tz \dfrac{d}{dz} f(z)$
$t^{-1} F(t)$	$-\dfrac{1}{T} \displaystyle\int_0^z \dfrac{f(z)}{z} \, dz$
$\displaystyle\sum_{m=0}^{T/t} F(mT)$	$\left(\dfrac{z}{z - 1} \right) f(z)$

The following limits are also valid

$$\lim_{t \to 0} F(t) = \lim_{z \to \infty} f(z)$$

$$\lim_{t \to \infty} F^*(t) = \lim_{z \to 1} \left[\left(\frac{z - 1}{z} \right) f(z) \right]$$

In the table which follows, the Heaviside unit step function is defined by

$$H(t - nT) \equiv \begin{cases} 1; & t \ge nT \\ 0; & t < nT. \end{cases}$$

The Z Transform

THE Z TRANSFORM (Continued)

$F(t)$	$f(z)$
$\delta(t)$	1
$\delta(t - mT)$	$\dfrac{1}{z^m}$
$H(t)$	$\dfrac{z}{z - 1}$
$H(t - T)$	$\dfrac{1}{z - 1}$
$H(t - mT)$	$\dfrac{z}{z^m \cdot (z - 1)}$
$H(t) - H(t - T)$	1
$H(t) - H(t - 2T)$	$1 + \dfrac{1}{z}$
$H(t - mT) - H(t - \overline{m + 1}T)$	$\dfrac{1}{z}m$
$\dfrac{T}{t} H(t - T)$	$\ln\left(\dfrac{z}{z - 1}\right)$
t	$\dfrac{Tz}{(z - 1)^2}$
t^2	$\dfrac{T^2 z(z + 1)}{(z - 1)^3}$
t^3	$\dfrac{T^3 z(z^2 + 4z + 1)}{(z - 1)^4}$
t^n	$(-1)^n \lim\limits_{x \to 0} \dfrac{\partial^n}{\partial x^n}\left(\dfrac{z}{z - e^{-xT}}\right)$
$1 - a^{\omega t}$	$\dfrac{z(1 - a^{\omega T})}{(z - 1)(z - a^{\omega T})}$
$a^{\omega t}$	$\dfrac{z}{(z - a^{\omega T})}$
$ta^{\omega t}$	$\dfrac{Tza^{\omega T}}{(z - a^{\omega T})^2}$
$t^2 a^{\omega t}$	$\dfrac{T^2 a^{\omega T} z(z + a^{\omega T})}{(z - a^{\omega T})^3}$
$\sin \omega t$	$\dfrac{z \sin \omega T}{z^2 - 2z \cos \omega T + 1}$
$\cos \omega t$	$\dfrac{z(z - \cos \omega T)}{z^2 - 2z \cos \omega T + 1}$
$\sinh \omega t$	$\dfrac{z \sinh \omega T}{z^2 - 2z \cosh \omega T + 1}$
$\cosh \omega t$	$\dfrac{z(z - \cosh \omega T)}{z^2 - 2z \cosh \omega T + 1}$
$e^{-\alpha t} \sin \omega t$	$\dfrac{ze^{-\alpha T} \sin \omega T}{z^2 - 2ze^{-\alpha T} \cos \omega T + e^{-2\alpha T}}$
$e^{-\alpha t} \cos \omega t$	$\dfrac{z(z - e^{-\alpha T} \cos \omega T)}{z^2 - 2ze^{-\alpha T} \cos \omega T + e^{-2\alpha T}}$
$e^{-\alpha t} \sinh \omega t$	$\dfrac{ze^{-\alpha T} \sinh \omega T}{z^2 - 2ze^{-\alpha T} \cosh \omega T + e^{-2\alpha T}}$
$e^{-\alpha t} \cosh \omega t$	$\dfrac{z(z - e^{-\alpha T} \cosh \omega T)}{z^2 - 2ze^{-\alpha T} \cosh \omega T + e^{-2\alpha T}}$

The Z Transform

THE Z TRANSFORM (Continued)

$F(t)$	$f(z)$
$-\dfrac{1}{a}[\delta(t) - a^{t/T}]$	$\dfrac{1}{z - a}$
$\dfrac{1}{(a - b)}\left[a^{\left(\frac{t}{T}-1\right)} - b^{\left(\frac{t}{T}-1\right)}\right]$	$\dfrac{1}{(z - a)(z - b)}$
$\dfrac{1}{(a - b)}\left[a^{\frac{t}{T}} - b^{\frac{t}{T}}\right]$	$\dfrac{z}{(z - a)(z - b)}$
$\dfrac{1}{(a - b)}\left[(a - c)a^{\left(\frac{t}{T}-1\right)} - (b - c)b^{\left(\frac{t}{T}-1\right)}\right]$	$\dfrac{z - c}{(z - a)(z - b)}$
$\dfrac{1}{(a - b)}\left[a^{\left(\frac{t}{T}+1\right)} - b^{\left(\frac{t}{T}+1\right)}\right]$	$\dfrac{z^2}{(z - a)(z - b)}$
$\dfrac{1}{\left(\frac{t}{T}\right)!}$	$e^{1/z}$
$\dfrac{1}{\left(\frac{2t}{T}\right)!}$	$\cosh(z^{-\frac{1}{2}})$

Methods of evaluating inverse z transforms.

(1) Cauchy's residue theorem.

For $t = nT$,

$$G(nT) = \sum_{\text{all } z_k} [\text{residues of } g(z)z^{n-1} \text{ at } z_k]$$

where the z_k define all the poles of $g(z)z^{n-1}$.

(2) Partial fractions.

Expand $g(z)/z$ into partial fractions. The product of z with each of the partial fractions will then be recognizable from the standard forms in the table of z transforms. Note however that the continuous functions obtained are only valid at the sampling instants.

(3) Power series expansion by long division using detached coefficients.

$g(z)$ is expanded into a power series in z^{-1} and the coefficient of the term in z^{-n} is the value of $g(nT)$ i.e. the value of $G(t)$ at the nth sampling instant.

The z transform as a means of determining approximately the inverse Laplace transform.

Since
$$z \equiv e^{Ts}$$

$$s^{-1} = \frac{T}{2}\left[\frac{1}{v} - \frac{v}{3} - \frac{4v^3}{45} - \frac{44v^5}{945} - \cdots\right]$$

where

$$v \equiv \frac{1 - z^{-1}}{1 + z^{-1}},$$

the series being very rapid in its convergence. Given $g(s)$, to find its inverse Laplace transform the following operations are carried out:-

(i) Divide the numerator and denominator of $g(s)$ by the highest power of s yielding as an alternative form for $g(s)$ the quotient of two polynomials in s^{-1}.

(ii) Chose as a numerical value of T, that which makes $2\pi/T$ much larger than the imaginary part of the poles of $G(s)$.

(iii) Substitute into the alternative form for $g(s)$ obtained in (i) above the expansion for s^{-n} determined from the following short table of approximations.

THE Z TRANSFORM (Continued)

Do not at this stage insert the numerical value for T as tabulations with different intervals may be required.

(iv) Divide by T.

(v) Insert the chosen value for T and divide the numerator by the denominator.

(vi) The coefficient of z^{-n} is the required value of the function at $t = nT$.

s^{-n}	z transform (approximate)
s^{-1}	$\dfrac{T}{2}\left[\dfrac{1 + z^{-1}}{1 - z^{-1}}\right]$
s^{-2}	$\dfrac{T^2}{12}\left[\dfrac{1 + 10z^{-1} + z^{-2}}{(1 - z^{-1})^2}\right]$
s^{-3}	$\dfrac{T^3}{3}\left[\dfrac{z^{-1} + z^{-2}}{(1 - z^{-1})^3}\right]$
s^{-4}	$\dfrac{T^4}{144}\left[\dfrac{1 + 20z^{-1} + 102z^{-2} + 20z^{-3} + z^{-4}}{(1 - z^{-1})^4}\right]$
s^{-5}	$\dfrac{T^5}{24}\left[\dfrac{z^{-1} + 11z^{-2} + 11z^{-3} + z^{-4}}{(1 - z^{-1})^5}\right]$
s^{-6}	$\dfrac{T^6}{4}\left[\dfrac{z^{-2} + 2z^{-3} + z^{-4}}{(1 - z^{-1})^6}\right]$
s^{-7}	$\dfrac{T^7}{8}\left[\dfrac{z^{-2} + 3z^{-3} + 3z^{-4} + z^{-5}}{(1 - z^{-1})^7}\right]$

Additional material on Z-transforms can be found in the papers by Boxer, R. and Thaler, S., A simplified method of solving linear and nonlinear systems. *Proc. IEE,* 1956, 89–101, and Boxer, R., A note on numerical transform calculus, *Proc. IEE,* 1957, 1401–1406.

XI. NUMERICAL METHODS

FINITE DIFFERENCES

Uniform interval h.

If a function $f(x)$ is tabulated at a uniform interval h, that is, for arguments given by $x_n = x_0 + nh$, where n is an integer, then the function $f(x)$ may be denoted by f_n. This can be generalized so that for all values of p, and in particular for $0 \leq p \leq 1$,

$$f(x_0 + ph) = f(x_p) = f_p ,$$

where the argument designated x_0 can be chosen quite arbitrarily.

The notation $x = a(h)b(H)C$ means that the arguments run from a to b inclusive at the uniform interval h and thereafter continue to C at the uniform interval H.

The statement $f(x)$ $4D$ means that the function $f(x)$ is to be tabulated and the answer rounded off to four places of decimals.

The statement $f(x)$ $5S$ means that the function $f(x)$ is to be tabulated with the answer being rounded off to five significant figures.

The following table lists and defines the standard operators used in numerical analysis.

Symbol	Function	Definition
E	Displacement	$Ef_p = f_{p+1}$
Δ	Forward difference	$\Delta f_p = f_{p+1} - f_p$
∇	Backward difference	$\nabla f_p = f_p - f_{p-1}$
$\wedge$	Divided difference	
δ	Central difference	$\delta f_p = f_{p+\frac{1}{2}} - f_{p-\frac{1}{2}}$
μ	Average	$\mu f_p = \frac{1}{2}(f_{p+\frac{1}{2}} + f_{p-\frac{1}{2}})$
Δ^{-1}	Backward sum	$\Delta^{-1}f_p = \Delta^{-1}f_{p-1} + f_{p-1}$
∇^{-1}	Forward sum	$\nabla^{-1}f_p = \nabla^{-1}f_{p-1} + f_p$
δ^{-1}	Central sum	$\delta^{-1}f_p = \delta^{-1}f_{p-1} + f_{p-\frac{1}{2}}$
D	Differentiation	$Df_p = \frac{d}{dx}f(x) = \frac{1}{h}\frac{d}{dp}f_p$
$I(=D^{-1})$	Integration	$If_p = \int^x f(x)dx = h\int^p f_p dp$
$J(=\Delta D^{-1})$	Definite integration	$Jf_p = h\int_p^{p+1} f_p dp$

I, Δ^{-1}, ∇^{-1} and δ^{-1} all imply the existence of an arbitrary constant which is determined by the initial conditions of the problem.

Where no confusion can arise the f can be omitted as, for example in writing Δ_p for Δf_p. Higher differences are formed by successive operations, e.g.,

$$\begin{aligned}
\Delta^2 f_p &= \Delta_p^2 \\
&= \Delta \cdot \Delta_p \\
&= \Delta(f_{p+1} - f_p) \\
&= \Delta_{p+1} - \Delta_p \\
&= f_{p+2} - f_{p+1} - f_{p+1} + f_p .
\end{aligned}$$

Thus $\Delta_p^2 = f_{p+2} - 2f_{p+1} + f_p$.

Note that $f_p \equiv \Delta_p^0 \equiv \nabla_p^0 \equiv \delta_p^0$.

The disposition of the differences and sums relative to the function values is as shown (the arguments are omitted in these cases in the interests of clarity). In manuscript working double spacing is recommended.

Calculus of Finite Differences

Forward difference scheme

$$\Delta_{-1}^{-2} \quad\quad f_{-2} \quad\quad \Delta_{-3}^{2}$$
$$\quad\quad \Delta_{-1}^{-1} \quad\quad \Delta_{-2} \quad\quad \Delta_{-3}^{3}$$
$$\Delta_{0}^{-2} \quad\quad f_{-1} \quad\quad \Delta_{-2}^{2}$$
$$\quad\quad \Delta_{0}^{-1} \quad\quad \Delta_{-1} \quad\quad \Delta_{-2}^{3}$$
$$\Delta_{1}^{-2} \quad\quad f_{0} \quad\quad \Delta_{-1}^{2}$$
$$\quad\quad \Delta_{1}^{-1} \quad\quad \Delta_{0} \quad\quad \Delta_{-1}^{3}$$
$$\Delta_{2}^{-2} \quad\quad f_{1} \quad\quad \Delta_{0}^{2}$$
$$\quad\quad \Delta_{2}^{-1} \quad\quad \Delta_{1} \quad\quad \Delta_{0}^{3}$$
$$\Delta_{3}^{-2} \quad\quad f_{2} \quad\quad \Delta_{1}^{2}$$

Backward difference scheme

$$\nabla_{-3}^{-2} \quad\quad f_{-2} \quad\quad \nabla_{-1}^{2}$$
$$\quad\quad \nabla_{-2}^{-1} \quad\quad \nabla_{-1} \quad\quad \nabla_{0}^{3}$$
$$\nabla_{-2}^{-2} \quad\quad f_{-1} \quad\quad \nabla_{0}^{2}$$
$$\quad\quad \nabla_{-1}^{-1} \quad\quad \nabla_{0} \quad\quad \nabla_{1}^{3}$$
$$\nabla_{-1}^{-2} \quad\quad f_{0} \quad\quad \nabla_{1}^{2}$$
$$\quad\quad \nabla_{0}^{-1} \quad\quad \nabla_{1} \quad\quad \nabla_{2}^{3}$$
$$\nabla_{0}^{-2} \quad\quad f_{1} \quad\quad \nabla_{2}^{2}$$
$$\quad\quad \nabla_{1}^{-1} \quad\quad \nabla_{2} \quad\quad \nabla_{3}^{3}$$
$$\nabla_{1}^{-2} \quad\quad f_{2} \quad\quad \nabla_{3}^{2}$$

Central difference scheme

$$\delta_{-2}^{-2} \quad\quad f_{-2} \quad\quad \delta_{-2}^{2} \quad\quad \delta_{-2}^{4}$$
$$\quad\quad \delta_{-1\frac{1}{2}}^{-1} \quad\quad \delta_{-1\frac{1}{2}} \quad\quad \delta_{-1\frac{1}{2}}^{3}$$
$$\delta_{-1}^{-2} \quad\quad f_{-1} \quad\quad \delta_{-1}^{2} \quad\quad \delta_{-1}^{4}$$
$$\quad\quad \delta_{-\frac{1}{2}}^{-1} \quad\quad \delta_{-\frac{1}{2}} \quad\quad \delta_{-\frac{1}{2}}^{3}$$
$$\delta_{0}^{-2} \quad\quad f_{0} \quad\quad \delta_{0}^{2} \quad\quad \delta_{0}^{4}$$
$$\quad\quad \delta_{\frac{1}{2}}^{-1} \quad\quad \delta_{\frac{1}{2}} \quad\quad \delta_{\frac{1}{2}}^{3}$$
$$\delta_{1}^{-2} \quad\quad f_{1} \quad\quad \delta_{1}^{2} \quad\quad \delta_{1}^{4}$$
$$\quad\quad \delta_{1\frac{1}{2}}^{-1} \quad\quad \delta_{1\frac{1}{2}} \quad\quad \delta_{1\frac{1}{2}}^{3}$$
$$\delta_{2}^{-2} \quad\quad f_{2} \quad\quad \delta_{2}^{2} \quad\quad \delta_{2}^{4}$$

In the forward difference scheme the subscripts are seen to move forward into the difference table and no fractional subscripts occur. In the backward difference scheme the subscripts lie on diagonals slanting backwards into the table while in the central difference scheme the subscripts maintain their position and the odd order subscripts are fractional.

All three however are merely alternative ways of labeling the same numerical quantities as any difference is the result of subtracting the number diagonally above it in the preceding column from that diagonally below it in the preceding column or, alternatively, it is the sum of the number diagonally above it in the subsequent column with that immediately above it in its own column.

In general $\Delta_{p-\frac{1}{2}n}^{n} \equiv \delta_{p}^{n} \equiv \nabla_{p+\frac{1}{2}n}^{n}$.

If a polynomial of degree r is tabulated exactly i.e., without any round-off errors, then the rth differences are constant.

Tabulate $f(x)3D$ for $x = -.4\,(.2)\,.8$ where $f(x) = x^3 - .3x^2 + .07x - .123$.

x	f	δ	δ^2	δ^3	δ^4
$-.4$	$-.263$				
		106			
$-.2$	$-.157$		-72		
		34		48	
$+0$	$-.123$		-24		0
		10		48	
$.2$	$-.113$		$+24$		0
		34		48	
$.4$	$-.079$		72		0
		106		48	
$.6$	$+.027$		120		
		226			
$.8$	$.253$				

Calculus of Finite Differences

Had the function been rounded off to two places of decimals then the third differences would not have been constant. The differences are conventionally expressed in units of the least significant decimal as shown. This obviates the need to write down non-significant zeros. In any well tabulated function the differences decrease in magnitude.

The effect of an error term e in any function value is superimposed upon the difference table in a manner shown in the following table:

f	δ	δ^2	δ^3	δ^4	δ^5
0		0		0	
	0		0		$+1e$
0		0		$+1e$	
	0		$+1e$		$-5e$
0		$+1e$		$-4e$	
	$+1e$		$-3e$		$+10e$
$+e$		$-2e$		$+6e$	
	$-1e$		$+3e$		$-10e$
0		$+1e$		$-4e$	
	0		$-1e$		$+5e$
0		0		$+1e$	
	0		0		$-1e$
0		0		0	

In particular since round-off can contribute an error of half a unit (of the least significant decimal) in the function values, reference to the table of binomial coefficients will show that the maximum effect of this upon the twelfth differences (say) is $924(\frac{1}{2}) = 462$. This could give trouble if the problem does not require this to be multiplied by a small constant and is in fact one of the reasons why numerical differentiation is unreliable.

The following table enables the simpler operators to be expressed in terms of the others:

	E	Δ	δ, μ	∇
E	—	$1 + \Delta$	$1 + \mu\delta + \frac{1}{2}\delta^2$	$(1 - \nabla)^{-1}$
Δ	$E - 1$	—	$\mu\delta + \frac{1}{2}\delta^2$	$\nabla(1 - \nabla)^{-1}$
δ	$E^{\frac{1}{2}} - E^{-\frac{1}{2}}$	$\Delta(1 + \Delta)^{-\frac{1}{2}}$	$2(\mu^2 - 1)^{\frac{1}{2}}$	$\nabla(1 - \nabla)^{-\frac{1}{2}}$
∇	$-E^{-1}$	$\Delta(1 + \Delta)^{-1}$	$\mu\delta - \frac{1}{2}\delta^2$	—
μ	$\frac{1}{2}(E^{\frac{1}{2}} + E^{-\frac{1}{2}})$	$\frac{1}{2}(2 + \Delta)(1 + \Delta)^{-\frac{1}{2}}$	$(1 + \frac{1}{4}\delta^2)^{\frac{1}{2}}$	$\frac{1}{2}(2 - \nabla)(1 - \nabla)^{-\frac{1}{2}}$

In addition to the above there are other identities by means of which the above table can be extended, viz.,

$$E = e^{hD} = \Delta\nabla^{-1}$$

$$\mu = E^{-\frac{1}{2}} + \frac{1}{2}\delta = E^{\frac{1}{2}} - \frac{1}{2}\delta = \cosh(\tfrac{1}{2}hD)$$

$$\delta = E^{-\frac{1}{2}}\Delta = E^{\frac{1}{2}}\nabla = (\Delta\nabla)^{\frac{1}{2}} = 2\sinh(\tfrac{1}{2}hD).$$

Note the emergence of Taylor's series from

$$f_p = E^p f_0$$

$$= e^{phD} f_0$$

$$= f_0 + phDf_0 + \frac{1}{2!}p^2h^2D^2f_0 + \cdots.$$

Calculus of Finite Differences

FUNCTION BUILD-UP FROM DIFFERENCES

Backward differences will be used here since the notation is simpler in this case.

If a function is tabulated as far as f_0 say, then the difference table can be built up. Assuming the differences up to and including ∇_0'' have been formed, if ∇_1'' is known it follows from the definition of backward differences that f_1 can be found from

$$f_1 = f_0 + \nabla_0 + \nabla_0^2 + \nabla_0^3 + \nabla_0^4 + \cdots + \nabla_0^{n-1} + \nabla_1^n .$$

For example, in the cubic tabulated earlier if we take $x_0 = .8$ then $f_0 = .253$ and f_1 can be built-up using the above scheme as follows:

$$f_1 = .253 + (226 + 120 + 48)(10^{-3})$$
$$= .647$$

INTERPOLATION

Finite difference interpolation entails taking a given set of points and fitting a function to them. This function is usualy a polynomial, although it is rarely found explicitly as such. Central differences formulae are in general to be preferred to those involving either forward or backward differences, although the latter may be essential at the extremities of a table where the central differences may not extend far enough.

The most useful of the central differences formulae are those of *Bessel* and *Everett*, the latter particularly so since it only utilizes even order differences. Nevertheless all central difference formulae stopping at the same difference are equivalent.

Notation used:

$$\Delta^r_{-m_r} \equiv \delta^r_{(r/2)-m_r} \equiv \nabla^r_{r-m_r}$$

$$p = \frac{x - x_0}{h} = 1 - q \quad (\text{usually } 0 \leqq p \leqq 1) .$$

Any number of finite difference interpolation formulae can be obtained from the following schematic (shown for central differences only, but easily extensible by the above identities):

$$y_p = \sum_{r=0} \binom{p + m_{r-1}}{r} \cdot \delta^r_{(r/2)-m_r}$$

$$= f_{-m_r} + \binom{p + m_0}{1} \delta_{\frac{1}{2}-m_1} + \binom{p + m_1}{2} \delta^2_{1-m_2} + \binom{p + m_2}{3} \delta^3_{1\frac{1}{2}-m_3} \cdots ,$$

where the m_r are integers so chosen that the binomial coefficient term $\binom{p + m_{r-1}}{r}$ contains all the linear factors occurring in the preceding term $\binom{p + m_{r-2}}{r - 1}$. Obviously $m_{r+1} = m_r$ or $1 + m_r$.

Further formulae are obtained by taking linear combinations of the formulae obtained from the above schematic, or by using the standard identity transformations upon chosen terms of one of the formulae.

Another way of obtaining interpolation formulae is to apply the standard identity transformations to the operator E in the operational form of the interpolation formula, viz., $f_p = E^p f_0$.

Newton's forward formula

$$f_p = f_0 + p\Delta_0 + \frac{1}{2!} p(p - 1)\Delta_0^2 + \frac{1}{3!} p(p - 1)(p - 2)\Delta_0^3 \cdots \quad 0 \leqq p \leqq 1$$

Calculus of Finite Differences

Newton's backward formula

$$f_p = f_0 + p\nabla_0 + \frac{1}{2!}\,p(p+1)\nabla_0^2 + \frac{1}{3!}\,p(p+1)(p+2)\nabla_0^3 \cdots \qquad 0 \leqq p \leqq 1$$

Gauss' forward formula

$$f_p = f_0 + p\delta_{\frac{1}{2}} + G_2\delta_0^2 + G_3\delta_{\frac{1}{2}}^3 + G_4\delta_0^4 + G_5\delta_{\frac{1}{2}}^5 \cdots \qquad\qquad 0 \leqq p \leqq 1$$

Gauss' backward formula

$$f_p = f_0 + p\delta_{-\frac{1}{2}} + G_2^*\delta_0^2 + G_3\delta_{-\frac{1}{2}}^3 + G_4^*\delta_0^4 + G_5\delta_{-\frac{1}{2}}^5 \cdots \qquad\qquad 0 \leqq p \leqq 1$$

In the above $G_{2n} = \begin{pmatrix} p+n-1 \\ 2n \end{pmatrix}$

$$G_{2n}^* = \begin{pmatrix} p+n \\ 2n \end{pmatrix}$$

$$G_{2n+1} = \begin{pmatrix} p+n \\ 2n+1 \end{pmatrix}$$

Stirling's formula

$$f_p = f_0 + \tfrac{1}{2}p(\delta_{\frac{1}{2}} + \delta_{-\frac{1}{2}}) + \tfrac{1}{2}p^2\delta_0^2 + S_3(\delta_{\frac{1}{2}}^3 + \delta_{-\frac{1}{2}}^3) + S_4\delta_0^4 + \cdots \qquad -\tfrac{1}{2} \leqq p \leqq \tfrac{1}{2}$$

Steffenson's formula

$$f_p = f_0 + \tfrac{1}{2}p(p+1)\delta_{\frac{1}{2}} - \tfrac{1}{2}(p-1)p\delta_{-\frac{1}{2}} + (S_3 + S_4)\delta_{\frac{1}{2}}^3 + (S_3 - S_4)\delta_{-\frac{1}{2}}^3 \cdots -\tfrac{1}{2} \leqq p \leqq \tfrac{1}{2}.$$

In the above $S_{2n+1} = \dfrac{1}{2}\begin{pmatrix} p+n \\ 2n+1 \end{pmatrix}$

$$S_{2n+2} = \frac{p}{2n+2}\begin{pmatrix} p+n \\ 2n+1 \end{pmatrix}$$

$$S_{2n+1} + S_{2n+2} = \begin{pmatrix} p+n+1 \\ 2n+2 \end{pmatrix}$$

$$S_{2n+1} - S_{2n+2} = -\begin{pmatrix} p+n \\ 2n+2 \end{pmatrix}$$

Bessel's formula

$$f_p = f_0 + p\delta_{\frac{1}{2}} + B_2(\delta_0^2 + \delta_1^2) + B_3\delta_{\frac{1}{2}}^3 + B_4(\delta_0^4 + \delta_1^4) + B_5\delta_{\frac{1}{2}}^5 + \cdots \qquad 0 \leqq p \leqq 1$$

Everett's formula

$$f_p = (1-p)f_0 + pf_1 + E_2\delta_0^2 + F_2\delta_1^2 + E_4\delta_0^4 + F_4\delta_1^4 + E_6\delta_0^6 + F_6\delta_1^6 + \cdots \qquad 0 \leqq p \leqq 1$$

The coefficients in the above two formulae are related to each other and to the coefficients in the Gaussian formulae by the identities

$$\begin{aligned}
B_{2n} &\equiv \tfrac{1}{2}G_{2n} \equiv \tfrac{1}{2}(E_{2n} + F_{2n}) \\
B_{2n+1} &\equiv G_{2n+1} - \tfrac{1}{2}G_{2n} \equiv \tfrac{1}{2}(F_{2n} - E_{2n}) \\
E_{2n} &\equiv G_{2n} - G_{2n+1} \equiv B_{2n} - B_{2n+1} \\
F_{2n} &\equiv G_{2n+1} \equiv B_{2n} + B_{2n+1}
\end{aligned}$$

Also for $q \equiv 1 - p$ the following symmetrical relationships hold:

$$\begin{aligned}
B_{2n}(p) &\equiv B_{2n}(q) \\
B_{2n+1}(p) &\equiv -B_{2n+1}(q) \\
E_{2n}(p) &\equiv F_{2n}(q) \\
F_{2n}(p) &\equiv E_{2n}(q)
\end{aligned}$$

as can be seen from the tables of these coefficients.

p	B_2	B_3	B_4	B_5	B_6	B_7	$(1-p)$
0.00	-0.000000	0.0000000	0.000000	-0.000000	-0.00000	0.00000	1.00
0.01	2475	8085	415	81	8	1	0.99
0.02	4900	15680	825	158	17	2	0.98
0.03	7275	22795	1230	231	25	3	0.97
0.04	9600	29440	1631	300	33	4	0.96
0.05	-0.011875	0.0035625	0.002026	-0.000365	-0.00041	0.00005	0.95
0.06	14100	41360	2416	425	49	6	0.94
0.07	16275	46655	2801	482	57	7	0.93
0.08	18400	51520	3180	534	64	8	0.92
0.09	20475	55965	3552	583	72	8	0.91
0.10	-0.022500	0.0060000	0.003919	-0.000627	-0.00080	0.00009	0.90
0.11	24475	63635	4279	667	87	10	0.89
0.12	26400	66880	4632	704	94	10	0.88
0.13	28275	69745	4979	737	101	11	0.87
0.14	30100	72240	5319	766	109	11	0.86
0.15	-0.031875	0.0074375	0.005651	-0.000791	-0.00115	0.00012	0.85
0.16	33600	76160	5976	813	122	12	0.84
0.17	35275	77605	6294	831	129	12	0.83
0.18	36900	78720	6604	845	135	12	0.82
0.19	38475	79515	6906	856	142	13	0.81
0.20	-0.040000	0.0080000	0.007200	-0.000864	-0.00148	0.00013	0.80
0.21	41475	80185	7486	868	154	13	0.79
0.22	42900	80080	7763	870	160	13	0.78
0.23	44275	79695	8033	868	165	13	0.77
0.24	45600	79040	8293	862	171	13	0.76
0.25	-0.046875	0.0078125	0.008545	-0.000554	-0.00176	0.00013	0.75
0.26	48100	76960	8788	844	181	12	0.74
0.27	49275	75555	9022	830	186	12	0.73
0.28	50400	73920	9247	814	191	12	0.72
0.29	51475	72065	9462	795	196	12	0.71
0.30	-0.052500	0.0070000	0.009669	-0.000773	-0.00200	0.00011	0.70
0.31	53475	67735	9866	750	204	11	0.69
0.32	54400	65280	10053	724	208	11	0.68
0.33	55275	62645	10231	696	212	10	0.67
0.34	56100	59840	10399	666	216	10	0.66
0.35	-0.056875	0.0056875	0.010557	-0.000633	-0.00219	0.00009	0.65
0.36	57600	53760	10706	600	222	9	0.64
0.37	58275	50505	10844	564	225	8	0.63
0.38	58900	47120	10973	527	228	8	0.62
0.39	59475	43615	11092	488	231	7	0.61
0.40	-0.060000	0.0040000	0.011200	-0.000448	-0.00233	0.00007	0.60
0.41	60475	36285	11298	407	235	6	0.59
0.42	60900	32480	11386	364	237	5	0.58
0.43	61275	28595	11464	321	239	5	0.57
0.44	61600	24640	11532	277	240	4	0.56
0.45	-0.061875	0.0020625	0.011589	-0.000232	-0.00241	0.00003	0.55
0.46	62100	16560	11635	186	242	3	0.54
0.47	62275	12455	11672	140	243	2	0.53
0.48	62400	8320	11698	94	244	1	0.52
0.49	62475	4165	11714	47	244	1	0.51
0.50	-0.062500	0.0000000	0.011719	-0.000000	-0.00244	0.00000	0.50
$(1-p)$	B_2	$-B_3$	B_4	$-B_5$	B_6	$-B_7$	p

Bessel's formula (*unmodified*)

(a) $f_p = f_0 + p\delta_{\frac{1}{2}} + B_2(\delta_0^2 + \delta_1^2) + B_3\delta_{\frac{1}{2}}^3 + B_4(\delta_0^4 + \delta_1^4)$
$$+ B_5\delta_{\frac{1}{2}}^5 + B_6(\delta_0^6 + \delta_1^6) + B_7\delta_{\frac{1}{2}}^7 + \cdots .$$

The end terms can be neglected,i.e.,they contribute less than half a unit in the last place of decimals, if the differences are less than the values shown in the following list:

$$
\begin{array}{lll}
\text{Neglect} & B_7\delta_{\frac{1}{2}}^7 \text{ if } \delta^7 < 3500 \\
& B_6(\delta_0 + \delta_1) & \delta^6 < 100 \\
& B_5\delta_{\frac{1}{2}}^5 & \delta^5 < 500 \\
& B_4(\delta_0^4 + \delta_1^4) & \delta^4 < 20 \\
& B_3\delta_{\frac{1}{2}}^3 & \delta^3 < 60 \\
& B_2(\delta_0^2 + \delta_1^2) & \delta^2 < 4
\end{array}
$$

A powerful simplification is that of throwback. If the higher differences are less than a specified value they can be combined with the lower order ones as follows:

If $\quad \delta^6 < 10{,}000 \quad$ use $\quad \delta_m^4 \equiv \delta^4 - 0.20697\delta^6$

and if $\delta^6 < 1{,}000^*$ use $\quad \delta_m^4 \equiv \delta^4 - 0.2\delta^6$
in the modified form of Bessel's formula

(b) $f_p = f_0 + p\delta_{\frac{1}{2}} + B_2(\delta_0^2 + \delta_1^2) + B_3\delta_{\frac{1}{2}}^3 + B_4(\delta_{m0}^4 + \delta_{m1}^4) + B_5\delta_{\frac{1}{2}}^5$.

If $\delta^4 < 1{,}000$ and $\delta^6 < 1{,}000^*$ use $\delta_m^2 \equiv \delta^2 - 0.18393\delta^4 + 0.03808\delta^6$
and if $\delta^4 < 1{,}000^*$ use $\delta_m^2 \equiv \delta^2 - 0.18393\delta^4$
in the modified form of Bessel's formula

(c) $f_p = f_0 + p\delta_{\frac{1}{2}} + B_2(\delta_{m0}^2 + \delta_{m1}^2) + B_3\delta_{\frac{1}{2}}^3$.

---

* Higher even order differences are negligible. Throwback involving odd order differences is of little practical use.

p	E_2	F_2	E_4	F_4	E_6	F_6	$(1 - p)$
0.00	−0.000000	−0.0000000	0.000000	0.000000	−0.00000	−0.00000	1.00
0.01	32835	16665	496	33	9	7	0.99
0.02	64680	33320	983	67	19	14	0.98
0.03	95545	49955	1461	100	28	21	0.97
0.04	125440	66560	1931	133	37	29	0.96
0.05	−0.0154375	−0.0083125	0.002391	0.001661	−0.00046	−0.00036	0.95
0.06	182360	99640	2842	199	55	43	0.94
0.07	209405	116095	3283	232	64	50	0.93
0.08	235520	132480	3714	264	72	57	0.92
0.09	260715	148785	4135	297	80	64	0.91
0.10	−0.0285000	−0.0165000	0.004546	0.003292	−0.00089	−0.00070	0.90
0.11	308385	181115	4946	361	97	77	0.89
0.12	330880	197120	5336	393	105	84	0.88
0.13	352495	213005	5716	424	112	91	0.87
0.14	373240	228760	6085	455	120	97	0.86
0.15	−0.0393125	−0.0244375	0.006442	0.004860	−0.00127	−0.00104	0.85
0.16	412160	259840	6789	516	134	110	0.84
0.17	430355	275145	7125	546	141	117	0.83
0.18	447720	290280	7449	576	148	123	0.82
0.19	464265	305235	7762	605	154	129	0.81
0.20	−0.0480000	−0.0320000	0.008064	0.006336	−0.00161	−0.00135	0.80
0.21	494935	334565	8354	662	167	141	0.79
0.22	509080	348920	8633	689	172	147	0.78
0.23	522445	363055	8900	716	178	153	0.77
0.24	535040	376960	9156	743	184	158	0.76
0.25	−0.0546875	−0.0390625	0.009399	0.007690	−0.00189	−0.00164	0.75
0.26	557960	404040	9632	794	194	169	0.74
0.27	568305	417195	9852	819	199	174	0.73
0.28	577920	430080	10060	843	203	179	0.72
0.29	586815	442685	10257	867	207	184	0.71
0.30	−0.0595000	−0.0455000	0.010442	0.008895	−0.00212	−0.00189	0.70
0.31	602485	467015	10615	912	215	193	0.69
0.32	609280	478720	10777	933	219	198	0.68
0.33	615395	490105	10927	954	222	202	0.67
0.34	620840	501160	11065	973	226	206	0.66
0.35	−0.0625625	−0.0511875	0.011191	0.009924	−0.00229	−0.00210	0.65
0.36	629760	522240	11305	1011	231	213	0.64
0.37	633255	532245	11408	1028	234	217	0.63
0.38	636120	541880	11500	1045	236	220	0.62
0.39	638365	551135	11580	1060	238	223	0.61
0.40	−0.0640000	−0.0560000	0.011648	0.010752	−.00240	−0.00226	0.60
0.41	641035	568465	11705	1089	241	229	0.59
0.42	641480	576520	11751	1102	242	232	0.58
0.43	641345	584155	11785	1114	243	234	0.57
0.44	640640	591360	11808	1125	244	236	0.56
0.45	−0.0639375	−0.0598125	0.011820	0.011357	−0.00245	−0.00238	0.55
0.46	637560	604440	11822	1145	245	240	0.54
0.47	635205	610295	11812	1153	245	241	0.53
0.48	632320	615680	11792	1160	245	242	0.52
0.49	628915	620585	11760	1167	245	243	0.51
0.50	−0.0625000	−0.0625000	0.011719	0.011719	−0.00244	−0.00244	0.50
$(1 - p)$	F_2	E_2	F_4	E_4	F_6	E_6	p

Everett's formula (unmodified)

(a) $f_p = (1 - p)f_0 + pf_1 + E_2\delta_0^2 + F_2\delta_1^2 + E_4\delta_0^4 + F_4\delta_1^4 + E_6\delta_0^6 + F_6\delta_1^6 + \cdots$

As with Bessel's formula, end terms can be neglected as follows:

$$\text{Neglect } \quad E_6\delta_0^6 + F_6\delta_1^6 \quad \text{if} \quad \delta^6 < 100$$
$$E_4\delta_0^4 + F_4\delta_1^4 \qquad \delta^4 < 20$$
$$E_2\delta_0^2 + F_2\delta_1^2 \qquad \delta^2 < 4$$

The corresponding throwback formulae are

(b) $\quad f_p = (1 - p)f_0 + pf_1 + E_2\delta_0^2 + F_2\delta_1^2 + E_4\delta_{m0}^4 + F_4\delta_{m1}^4,$

where $\delta_m^4 \equiv \delta^4 - 0.20697\delta^6 \quad$ providing $\delta^6 < 10,000^*$

or $\quad \delta_m^4 \equiv \delta^4 - 0.2\delta^6 \qquad$ providing $\delta^6 < 1,000^*$;

(c) $\quad f_p = (1 - p)f_0 + pf_1 + E_2\delta_{m0}^4 + F_2\delta_{m1}^2$

where $\delta_m^2 \equiv \delta^2 - 0.18393\delta^4 + 0.03808\delta^6 \quad$ if $\quad \delta^4, \delta^6 < 1,000^*$.

Generalized Throwback

Using 0.184 instead of the more precise value of 0.18393 we obtain a very simple but nevertheless accurate interpolation formulae

$$f \equiv (1 - p)f_0 + pf_1 + E_2\delta_{m0}^2 + F_2\delta_{m1}^2 + P_4\theta_0^4 + Q_4\theta_1^4,$$

where $\quad \delta_m^2 \equiv \delta^2 - 0.184\delta^4 + 0.03882\delta^6 - 0.0083\delta^8 + 0.0019\delta^{10}$

and $\quad 100\theta^4 \equiv \delta^4 - 0.2783\delta^6 + 0.0685\delta^8 - 0.0168\delta^{10}$

and $\quad P_4 \equiv 100(E_4 + 0.184E_2); \quad Q_4 \equiv 100(F_4 + 0.184F_2).$

Symmetric formulae for interpolation to halves (sub-tabulation to halves)

When $p = \frac{1}{2}$ is substituted into Bessel's interpolation formula the odd coefficients B_{2n+1} all become zero and the resulting formula is

$$f_{\frac{1}{2}} = \left(1 - \frac{1}{8}\delta^2 + \frac{3}{128}\delta^4 - \frac{5}{1024}\delta^6 + \frac{35}{32768}\delta^8 - \cdots\right)\mu f_{\frac{1}{2}}.$$

If this is truncated after one, two, three terms etc. the following formulae and error terms are obtained:

Error

$f_{\frac{1}{2}} = \frac{1}{2}(f_0 + f_1)$ $\qquad\qquad -\dfrac{1}{8}\mu\delta_{\frac{1}{2}}^2$

$f_{\frac{1}{2}} = (-f_{-1} + 9f_0 + 9f_1 - f_2)/16$ $\qquad\qquad +\dfrac{3}{128}\mu\delta_{\frac{1}{2}}^4$

$f_{\frac{1}{2}} = (3f_{-2} - 25f_{-1} + 150f_0 + 150f_1 - 25f_2 + 3f_3)/256$ $\qquad -\dfrac{5}{1024}\mu\delta_{\frac{1}{2}}^6$

$f_{\frac{1}{2}} = (-5f_{-3} + 49f_{-2} - 245f_{-1} + 1225f_0 + 1225f_1 - 245f_2 + 49f_3 - 5f_4)/2048$ $\quad +\dfrac{35}{32768}\mu\delta_{\frac{1}{2}}^8$

---

* Higher order differences are negligible.

Similarly, unsymmetric formulae for subtabulation to halves can be obtained from Newton's formula by substituting $p = \frac{1}{2}$ and truncating, e.g.,

Error

$$f_{\frac{1}{2}} = \left(1 + \frac{1}{2}\Delta - \frac{1}{8}\Delta^2 + \frac{1}{16}\Delta^3 - \frac{5}{128}\Delta^4 + \frac{7}{256}\Delta^5 \cdots \right) f_0$$

$f_{\frac{1}{2}} = (3f_0 + 6f_1 - f_2)/8$ $\qquad\qquad\qquad\qquad\qquad \dfrac{+1}{16}\Delta_0^3$

$f_{\frac{1}{2}} = (5f_0 + 15f_1 - 5f_2 + f_3)/16$ $\qquad\qquad\qquad \dfrac{-5}{128}\Delta_0^4$

$f_{\frac{1}{2}} = (35f_0 + 140f_1 - 70f_2 + 28f_3 - 5f_4)/128$ $\qquad \dfrac{+7}{256}\Delta_0^5$

The formula obtained by considering the first two terms only of the series is identical with the first one derived from Bessel's formula.

Calculus of Finite Differences

Interpolation techniques which do not require the function to be tabulated for equal interval of the argument

a) Lagrangian Polynomials

The interpolated value is obtained from a set of points which bridge the required point. The nearer the argument of the required value is to the center of the range of arguments of the function values used the better.

For an odd number of points
$$f(x) = \sum_{r=-n}^{n} L_r f_r .$$

For an even number of points
$$f(x) = \sum_{r=-n}^{n+1} L_r f_r .$$

The interpolating polynomial is of degree $2n$ in the first case and $2n + 1$ in the second. Further, it must pass through the given points $f_{-n}, f_{1-n}, f_{2-n}, \cdots , f_n$ or f_{1+n} as the case may be.

The coefficient L_r associated with the function value f_r is given by

$$L_r = \frac{(x - x_{-n})(x - x_{1-n}) \cdots (x - x_{r-1})(x - x_{r+1}) \cdots (x - x_{n-1})(x - x_n)}{(x_r - x_{-n})(x_r - x_{1-n}) \cdots (x_r - x_{r-1})(x_r - x_{r+1}) \cdots (x_r - x_{n-1})(x_r - x_n)}$$

for the first case with an additional factor $(x - x_{1+n})/(x_r - x_{1+n})$ in the second.

The error involved is equal to the $(2n + 2)$th. derivative, at some point in the range, multiplied by

$$(x - x_{-n})(x - x_{1-n}) \cdots (x - x_{1-n})/(2n + 2)!$$

in the case of the even number of points, and the $(2n + 1)$th. derivative, again at some point in the range, multiplied by

$$(x - x_{-n})(x - x_{1-n}) \cdots (x - x_n)/(2n + 1)!$$

in the other case.

In both cases the multipliers are functions which oscillate with an amplitude which increases substantially as the argument of the required point departs from the center of the range. When the arguments are spaced at equal intervals h and the point x is nearer to x_0 than to the other points, then $L_r(p)$ can be tabulated for $p = (x - x_0)/h$.

If the degree of the approximating polynomial is known the method is very powerful, otherwise it is best avoided.

b) Divided differences

The layout of a divided difference table is similar to that of an ordinary finite difference table.

x_{-1} f_{-1}		Δ^2_{-1}	Δ^4_{-1}
	$\Delta_{-\frac{1}{2}}$		$\Delta^3_{-\frac{1}{2}}$
x_0 f_0		Δ^2_0	Δ^4_0
	$\Delta_{\frac{1}{2}}$		$\Delta^3_{\frac{1}{2}}$
x_1 f_1		Δ^2_1	Δ^4_1

Calculus of Finite Differences

where the $\triangle$'s are defined as follows:

$$\triangle_r^0 \equiv f_r, \qquad \triangle_{r+\frac{1}{2}} \equiv (f_{r+1} - f_r)/(x_{r+1} - x_r),$$

and in general
$$\triangle_r^{2n} \equiv (\triangle_{r+\frac{1}{2}}^{2n-1} - \triangle_{r-\frac{1}{2}}^{2n-1})/(x_{r+n} - x_{r-n})$$

and
$$\triangle_{r+\frac{1}{2}}^{2n+1} \equiv (\triangle_{r+1}^{2n} - \triangle_r^{2n})/(x_{r+1+n} - x_{r-n}).$$

Divided differences can with advantage be replaced by adjusted divided differences.

c) *Adjusted divided differences*
These differences are a modified form of the above and, when the interval of tabulation becomes constant, they reduce to ordinary central differences. Formulae analogous to all the existing formulae involving forward, central and backward differences can be obtained by means of Sheppard's rules which are stated below.

x_{-1}	p_{-1}	f_{-1}		δ_{-1}^2		δ_{-1}^4	
			$\delta_{-\frac{1}{2}}$		$\delta_{-\frac{1}{2}}^3$		
x_0	p_0	f_0		δ_0^2		δ_0^4	
			$\delta_{\frac{1}{2}}$		$\delta_{\frac{1}{2}}^3$		
x_1	p_1	f_1		δ_1^2		δ_1^4	
			$\delta_{1\frac{1}{2}}$		$\delta_{1\frac{1}{2}}^3$		
x_2	p_2	f_2		δ_2^2		δ_2^4	

where h is the total range of arguments divided by the number of intervals in that range, the result being rounded to a suitable figure and $x_k \cong p_k \cdot h$ or $(x/h)_k = p_k + w_k$ where the w's are used to shift the origin, if necessary, and to round-off the p's.

Define
$$\delta_r \equiv \frac{1}{(p_{r+\frac{1}{2}} - p_{r-\frac{1}{2}})} (f_{r+\frac{1}{2}} - f_{r-\frac{1}{2}})$$

and
$$\delta_r^2 \equiv \frac{2}{(p_{r+1} - p_{r-1})} (\delta_{r+\frac{1}{2}} - \delta_{r-\frac{1}{2}}).$$

In general
$$\delta_r^{2n+1} \equiv \frac{2n+1}{(p_{r+\frac{1}{2}+n} - p_{r-\frac{1}{2}-n})} (\delta_{r+\frac{1}{2}}^{2n} - \delta_{r-\frac{1}{2}}^{2n}),$$

$$\delta_r^{2n} \equiv \frac{2n}{(p_{r+n} - p_{r-n})} (\delta_{r+\frac{1}{2}}^{2n-1} - \delta_{r+\frac{1}{2}}^{2n-1}).$$

The formula will be in the form

$$f(x) = f_0 + \sum_{r=1}^{N} \left\{ \prod (p - p_j \cdot) \frac{\delta_r}{r!} \right\},$$

where the product part of each term of the formula consists of r factors and the p_j's and s are chosen as follows:

a) When $r = 1$, $j = 0$ and $s = +\frac{1}{2}$, or $-\frac{1}{2}$, thereafter:—

Calculus of Finite Differences

b) r is increased by unity and s is either increased or decreased by $\frac{1}{2}$. Thus the p's, involved in the new divided difference of the series, are all those which are necessary for the computation of the divided difference used in the *preceding term* plus one more added either to the beginning or to the end of the set.

c) The product part of the term consists of factors $(p - p_i)$ such that all the p's necessary for the evaluation of the *previous* divided difference are involved. For example, Gauss' forward difference interpolation formula in terms of adjusted divided differences is obtained by following the path shown below

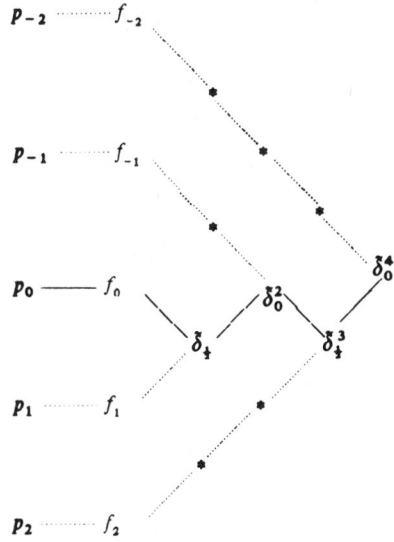

The solid line indicates the path chosen through the difference table.

$$f(x) = f_0 + (p - p_0)\delta_{\frac{1}{2}} + \frac{1}{2!} \cdot (p - p_0)(p - p_1)\delta_0^2 + \frac{1}{3!} \cdot (p - p_0)(p - p_1)(p - p_{-1})\delta_{\frac{1}{2}}^3$$

$$+ \frac{1}{4!} \cdot (p - p_0)(p - p_1)(p - p_{-1})(p - p_2)\delta_0^4 \cdots$$

Similarly Gauss' backward difference interpolation formula is

$$f(x) = f_0 + (p - p_0)\delta_{-\frac{1}{2}} + \frac{1}{2!} \cdot (p - p_0)(p - p_{-1})\delta_0^2 + \frac{1}{3!} \cdot (p - p_0)(p - p_{-1})(p - p_1)\delta_{-\frac{1}{2}}^3$$

$$+ \frac{1}{4!} \cdot (p - p_0)(p - p_{-1})(p - p_1)(p - p_{-2})\delta_0^4 \cdots,$$

and Stirling's formula is

$$f(x) = f_0 + \frac{(p - p_0)}{2}[\delta_{\frac{1}{2}} + \delta_{-\frac{1}{2}}] + \frac{1}{2!} \cdot \frac{(p - p_0)}{2}[(p - p_{-1}) + (p - p_1)]\delta_0^2$$

$$+ \frac{1}{3!} \cdot \frac{(p - p_1)(p - p_0)(p - p_{-1})}{2}[\delta_{\frac{1}{2}}^3 + \delta_{-\frac{1}{2}}^3]$$

$$+ \frac{1}{4!} \cdot \frac{(p - p_1)(p - p_0)(p - p_{-1})}{2}[(p - p_{-2}) + (p - p_2)]\delta_0^4 \cdots$$

Calculus of Finite Differences

Replacing the odd order differences, in Gauss' forward formula, by combinations of the previous even order differences the formula analogous to Everett's is obtained, i.e.,

$$f(x) = \left[1 - \frac{(p - p_0)}{(p_1 - p_0)}\right] f_0 + \frac{(p - p_0)}{(p_1 - p_0)} f_1 - \frac{1}{2!} \frac{(p - p_0)(p - p_1)(p - p_2)}{(p_2 - p_{-1})} \delta_0^2$$
$$+ \frac{1}{2!} \frac{(p - p_0)(p - p_1)(p - p_{-1})}{(p_2 - p_{-1})} \delta_1^2 - \cdots$$

d) Iterative linear interpolation

Neville's modification of Aiken's method of iterative linear interpolation is one of the most powerful methods of interpolation when the arguments are unevenly spaced as no prior knowledge of the order of the approximating polynomial is necessary nor is a difference table required.

The values obtained are successive approximations to the required result and the process terminates when there is no appreciable change. These values are of course useless if a new interpolation is required when the procedure must be started afresh.

Defining
$$f_{r,s} \equiv \frac{(x_s - x)f_r - (x_r - x)f_s}{(x_s - x_r)}$$

$$f_{r,s,t} \equiv \frac{(x_t - x)f_{r,s} - (x_r - x)f_{s,t}}{(x_t - x_r)}$$

$$f_{r,s,t,u} \equiv \frac{(x_u - x)f_{r,s,t} - (x_r - x)f_{s,t,u}}{(x_u - x_r)},$$

the computation is laid out as follows:

x_{-1}	$(x_{-1} - x)$	f_{-1}			
			$f_{-1,0}$		
x_0	$(x_0 - x)$	f_0		$f_{-1\,0,1}$	
			$f_{0,1}$		$f_{-1\,0\,1,2}$
x_1	$(x_1 - x)$	f_1		$f_{0,1,2}$	
			$f_{1,2}$		
x_2	$(x_2 - x)$	f_2			

As the iterates tend to their limit the common leading figures can be omitted.

e) Gauss' trigonometric interpolation formula

This is of greatest value when the function is periodic, i.e., a Fourier series expansion is possible.

$$f(x) = \sum_{r=0}^{n} C_r f_r,$$

where $C_r = N_r(x)/N_r(x_r)$ and

$$N_r(x) = \left[\sin \frac{(x - x_0)}{2}\right] \left[\sin \frac{(x - x_1)}{2}\right] \cdots \left[\sin \frac{(x - x_{r-1})}{2}\right]$$
$$\left[\sin \frac{(x - x_{r+1})}{2}\right] \cdots \left[\sin \frac{(x - x_n)}{2}\right].$$

Calculus of Finite Differences

This is similar to the Lagrangian formula.

f) Reciprocal differences

These are used when the quotient of two polynomials will give a better representation of the interpolating function than a simple polynomial expression.

A convenient layout is as shown below:

x_{-1}	f_{-1}				
		$\rho_{-\frac{1}{2}}$			
x_0	f_0		ρ_0^2		
		$\rho_{\frac{1}{2}}$		$\rho_{\frac{1}{2}}^3$	
x_1	f_1		ρ_1^2		ρ_1^4
		$\rho_{1\frac{1}{2}}$		$\rho_{1\frac{1}{2}}^3$	
x_2	f_2		ρ_2^2		
		$\rho_{2\frac{1}{2}}$			
x_3	f_3				

where

$$\rho_{r+\frac{1}{2}} \equiv \frac{x_{r+1} - x_r}{f_{r+1} - f_r}$$

and

$$\rho_r^2 \equiv \frac{x_{r+1} - x_{r-1}}{f_{r+\frac{1}{2}} - f_{r-\frac{1}{2}}} + f_r$$

In general

$$\rho_{r+\frac{1}{2}}^{2n+1} \equiv \frac{x_{r+n+1} - x_{r-n}}{\rho_{r+1}^{2n} - \rho_r^{2n}} + \rho_{r+\frac{1}{2}}^{2n-1}$$

$$\rho_r^{2n} \equiv \frac{x_{r+n} - x_{r-n}}{\rho_{r+\frac{1}{2}}^{2n-1} - \rho_{r-\frac{1}{2}}^{2n-1}} + \rho_r^{2n-2} .$$

The interpolation formula is expressed in the form of a continued fraction expansion.

The expansion corresponding to Newton's forward difference interpolation formula, in the sense of the differences involved, is

$$f(x) = f_0 + \cfrac{(x - x_0)}{\rho_{\frac{1}{2}} + \cfrac{(x_2 - x_1)}{\rho_1 - f_0 + \cfrac{(x - x_2)}{\rho_{1\frac{1}{2}}^3 - \rho_{\frac{1}{2}} + \cfrac{(x_4 - x_3)}{\rho_2^4 - \rho_1^2 + (x - x_4)}}}}$$
$$\text{etc.}$$

while that corresponding to Gauss' forward formula is

$$f(x) = f_0 + \cfrac{(x - x_0)}{\rho_{\frac{1}{2}} + \cfrac{(x_2 - x_1)}{\rho_0^2 - f_0 + \cfrac{(x_3 - x_{-1})}{\rho_{\frac{1}{2}}^3 - \rho_{\frac{1}{2}} + \cfrac{(x_4 - x_2)}{\rho_0^4 - \rho_0^2 + (x - x_{-2})}}}}$$
$$\text{etc.}$$

Calculus of Finite Differences

Inverse interpolation

Any method of interpolation which does not require the arguments to be evenly spaced will be satisfactory, by simply interchanging the roles of the arguments and the function values.

Alternative (i) Sub-tabulate the function until linear interpolation is adequate and simple ratio and proportion will yield the result.

Alternative (ii) Find an approximate value for p from

$$p \cong (f_p - f_0)/(f_1 - f_0)$$

and then iterate using *any* of the standard interpolation formulae; e.g., Bessel

$$p = [f_p - f_0 - B_2(\delta_0^2 + \delta_1^2) - B_3\delta_{\frac{1}{2}}^3 - \cdots \text{etc.}]/\delta_{\frac{1}{2}}$$

where the Bessel's coefficients on the right hand side are evaluated for the approximate p.
Everrett

$$p = [f_p - f_0 - E_2\delta_0^2 - F_2\delta_1^2 - E_4\delta^4 - F_4\delta_0^4 \cdots]/\delta_{\frac{1}{2}}$$

Newton forward

$$p = [f_p - f_0 - \frac{1}{2!} p(p - 1)\Delta_0^2 - \frac{1}{3!} p(p - 1)(p - 2)\Delta_0^3 \cdots]/\Delta_0$$

Newton backward

$$p = [f_p - f_0 - \frac{1}{2!} p(p + 1)\nabla_0^2 - \frac{1}{3!} p(p + 1)(p + 2)\nabla_0^3 \cdots]/\nabla_0.$$

Note that the divisors are in fact identical.

Lozenge Diagram — Interpolation

The following figure shows a scheme for writing down any of the standard interpolation formulas by associating it with a prescribed path through the diagram, called a lozenge diagram.

y_{-4}	$(u+4)_1$	$\Delta^2 y_{-5}$	$(u+5)_3$	$\Delta^4 y_{-6}$	$(u+6)_5$	$\Delta^6 y_{-7}$	$(u+7)_7$
1	Δy_{-4}	$(u+4)_2$	$\Delta^3 y_{-5}$	$(u+5)_4$	$\Delta^5 y_{-6}$	$(u+6)_6$	$\Delta^7 y_{-7}$
y_{-3}	$(u+3)_1$	$\Delta^2 y_{-4}$	$(u+4)_3$	$\Delta^4 y_{-5}$	$(u+5)_5$	$\Delta^6 y_{-6}$	$(u+6)_7$
1	Δy_{-3}	$(u+3)_2$	$\Delta^3 y_{-4}$	$(u+4)_4$	$\Delta^5 y_{-5}$	$(u+5)_6$	$\Delta^7 y_{-6}$
y_{-2}	$(u+2)_1$	$\Delta^2 y_{-3}$	$(u+3)_3$	$\Delta^4 y_{-4}$	$(u+4)_5$	$\Delta^6 y_{-5}$	$(u+5)_7$
1	Δy_{-2}	$(u+2)_2$	$\Delta^3 y_{-3}$	$(u+3)_4$	$\Delta^5 y_{-4}$	$(u+4)_6$	$\Delta^7 y_{-5}$
y_{-1}	$(u+1)_1$	$\Delta^2 y_{-2}$	$(u+2)_3$	$\Delta^4 y_{-3}$	$(u+3)_5$	$\Delta^6 y_{-4}$	$(u+4)_7$
1	Δy_{-1}	$(u+1)_2$	$\Delta^3 y_{-2}$	$(u+2)_4$	$\Delta^5 y_{-3}$	$(u+3)_6$	$\Delta^7 y_{-4}$
y_0	$(u)_1$	$\Delta^2 y_{-1}$	$(u+1)_3$	$\Delta^4 y_{-2}$	$(u+2)_5$	$\Delta^6 y_{-3}$	$(u+3)_7$
1	Δy_0	$(u)_2$	$\Delta^3 y_{-1}$	$(u+1)_4$	$\Delta^5 y_{-2}$	$(u+2)_6$	$\Delta^7 y_{-3}$
y_1	$(u-1)_1$	$\Delta^2 y_0$	$(u)_3$	$\Delta^4 y_{-1}$	$(u+1)_5$	$\Delta^6 y_{-2}$	$(u+2)_7$
1	Δy_1	$(u-1)_2$	$\Delta^3 y_0$	$(u)_4$	$\Delta^5 y_{-1}$	$(u+1)_6$	$\Delta^7 y_{-2}$
y_2	$(u-2)_1$	$\Delta^2 y_1$	$(u-1)_3$	$\Delta^4 y_0$	$(u)_5$	$\Delta^6 y_{-1}$	$(u+1)_7$
1	Δy_2	$(u-2)_2$	$\Delta^3 y_1$	$(u-1)_4$	$\Delta^5 y_0$	$(u)_6$	$\Delta^7 y_{-1}$
y_3	$(u-3)_1$	$\Delta^2 y_2$	$(u-2)_3$	$\Delta^4 y_1$	$(u-1)_5$	$\Delta^6 y_0$	$(u)_7$
1	Δy_3	$(u-3)_2$	$\Delta^3 y_2$	$(u-2)_4$	$\Delta^5 y_1$	$(u-1)_6$	$\Delta^7 y_0$
y_4	$(u-4)_1$	$\Delta^2 y_3$	$(u-3)_3$	$\Delta^4 y_2$	$(u-2)_5$	$\Delta^6 y_1$	$(u-1)_7$

→ Gregory-Newton (Forward)　　→→ Stirling

→→ Gregory-Newton (Backward)　　...→... Bessel

~~~ Gauss (I)　　　$(u+k)_s \equiv \dfrac{1}{s!}\,(u+k)^{[s]}$

Lozenge diagram showing paths for some of the standard interpolation formulas. (From Kunz, K. S., *Numerical Analysis*, McGraw-Hill, New York, 1957, 75–77, 80, 81. With permission.)

To convert a path through the lozenge to an interpolation formula the following rules are formulated:

1. Each time a difference column is crossed from left to right a term is added.
2. If a path enters a difference column (from the left) at a positive slope, the term added is the product of the difference, say $\Delta^k y_{-p}$, at which the column is crossed and the factorial $(u + p - 1)_k$ lying just below that difference.
3. If a path enters a difference column (from the left) at a positive slope, the term added is the product of the difference, say $\Delta^k y_{-p}$, at which the column is crossed and the factorial $(u + p)_k$ lying just above that difference.
4. If a path enters a difference column horizontally (from the left), the term added is the product of the difference, say $\Delta^k y_{-p}$, at which the column is crossed and the average of the two factorials $(u + p)_k$ and $(u + p-1)_k$ lying, respectively, just above and just below that difference.

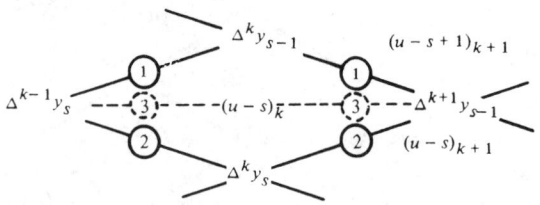

5. If a path crosses a difference column (from left to right) between two differences, say $\Delta^k y_{-(p+1)}$ and $\Delta^k y_{-p}$, then the added term is the product of the average of these two differences and the factorial $(u + p)_k$ at which the column is crossed.
6. Any portion of a path traversed from right to left gives rise to the same terms as would arise from going along this portion from left to right except that the sign of each term is changed.
7. The zero-difference column corresponding to the tabulated values may be treated by the same rules as any other difference columns provided one thinks of the lozenge as being entered just to the left of this column. Thus this column can be crossed by a path making a positive, negative, or zero slope, just as is true of the other columns.

Examples

Write down the interpolation formulas whose paths are shown on the lozenge diagram.

It is clear that, since the lozenge employs descending differences, all formulas will be in terms of descending differences. If one wishes the central-difference formulas to appear as they have been written in the earlier sections of the chapter, one should use central-difference notation for the differences.

Gregory-Newton (Forward) — Applying Rules 1, 3, and 7 to the diagonal path that slopes downward from y_0, one obtains the formula

$$y = y_0 + (u)_1\,\Delta y_0 + (u)_2\,\Delta^2 y_0 + (u)_3\,\Delta^3 y_0 + \ldots + (u)_m \Delta^m y_0$$

Note: $(u)_r = u^{[r]}/r!$

Gregory-Newton (Backward) — Employing Rules 1, 2, and 7 to the diagonal path that slopes upward from y_0, one obtains the formula

$$y = y_0 + (u)_1\,\Delta y_{-1} + (u + 1)_2\,\Delta^2 y_{-2} + (u + 2)_3\,\Delta^3 y_{-3} + \ldots$$

$$+ (u + m - 1)_m\,\Delta^m y_{-m}$$

Gauss (I) — Employing Rules 1, 2, 3, and 7 to the zigzag path shown, one has

$$y = y_0 + (u)_1 \, \Delta y_0 + (u)_2 \, \Delta^2 y_{-1} + (u+1)_3 \, \Delta^3 y_{-1} + (u+1)_4 \, \Delta^4 y_{-2} + \dots$$

$$+ (u+k-1)_{2k-1} \, \Delta^{2k-1} y_{-k+1} + (u+k-1)_{2k} \, \Delta^{2k} y_{-k} + \dots$$

where, as before, the series is terminated at any desired difference.

Stirling's — Employing Rules 1, 4, 5, and 7 to the horizontal path through y_0,

$$y = y_0 + (u)_1 \, \frac{\Delta y_{-1} + \Delta y_0}{2} + \frac{(u)_2 + (u+1)_2}{2} \, \Delta^2 y_{-1}$$

$$+ (u+1)_3 \, \frac{\Delta^2 y_{-2} + \Delta^3 y_{-1}}{2} + \dots$$

$$+ (u+k-1)_{2k-1} \, \frac{\Delta^{2k-1} y_{-k} + \Delta^{2k-1} y_{-k+1}}{2}$$

$$+ \frac{(u+k-1)_{2k} + (u+k)_{2k}}{2} \, \Delta^{2k} y_{-k} + \dots$$

Now

$$(u+k-1)_{2k-1} = \frac{1}{(2k-1)!} \, u(u^2-1)(u^2-4)\dots[u^2-(k-1)^2]$$

and

$$\frac{(u+k-1)_{2k} + (u+k)_{2k}}{2} = \frac{1}{2k!} \, u^2(u^2-1)(u^2-4)\dots[u^2-(k-1)^2]$$

Therefore, one may write

$$y = y_0 + u \, \frac{\Delta y_{-1} + \Delta y_0}{2} + \frac{1}{2!} \, u^2 \, \Delta^2 y_{-1} + \frac{1}{3!} \, u \, (u^2-1) \, \frac{\Delta^3 y_{-2} + \Delta^3 y_{-1}}{2}$$

$$+ \frac{1}{4!} \, u^2(u^2-1) \, \Delta^4 y_{-2} + \dots$$

$$+ \frac{1}{(2k-1)!} \, u(u^2-1)(u^2-4)\dots[u^2-(k-1)^2] \, \frac{\Delta^{2k-1} y_{-k} + \Delta^{2k-1} y_{-k+1}}{2}$$

$$+ \frac{1}{(2k)!} \, u^2(u^2-1)(u^2-4)\dots[u^2-(k-1)^2] \, \Delta^{2k} y_{-k} + \dots$$

This is the expression of Stirling's formula when descending differences are employed.

Bessel's — Employing the rules above to the horizontal path through Δy_0, one has

$$y = \frac{y_0 + y_1}{2} + \frac{(u)_1 + (u-1)_1}{2} \, \Delta y_0 + (u)_2 \, \frac{\Delta^2 y_{-1} + \Delta^2 y_0}{2}$$

$$+ \frac{(u+1)_3 + (u)_3}{2} \, \Delta^3 y_{-1} + \dots$$

$$+ \frac{(u+k-1)_{2k-1} + (u+k-2)_{2k-1}}{2} \, \Delta^{2k-1} y_{-k+1}$$

$$+ (u+k-1)_{2k} \, \frac{\Delta^{2k} y_{-k} + \Delta^{2k} y_{-k+1}}{2}$$

or

$$y = \frac{y_0 + y_1}{2} + (u - \tfrac{1}{2}) \Delta y_0 + \frac{1}{2!} u^{[2]} \frac{\Delta^2 y_{-1} + \Delta^2 y_0}{2}$$

$$+ \frac{1}{3!} (u - \tfrac{1}{2}) u^{[2]} \Delta^3 y_{-1} + \frac{1}{4!} (u + 1)^{[4]} \frac{\Delta^4 y_{-2} + \Delta^4 y_{-1}}{2} + \dots$$

$$+ \frac{1}{(2k)!} (u + k - 1)^{[2k]} \frac{\Delta^{2k} y_{-k} + \Delta^{2k} y_{-k+1}}{2}$$

$$+ \frac{1}{(2k+1)!} (u - \tfrac{1}{2}) (u + k - 1)^{[2k]} \Delta^{2k+1} y_{-k} + \dots$$

Remainder Term

The remainder term for a series terminated on a single difference, say the mth difference, is just the (m + 1)th term of the series if the series were extended, with, however, $h^{m+1} f^{m+1} (\xi)$ replacing the (m + 1)th difference (or mean difference). For a formula terminated on the mean of two differences, one must average the error terms for those formulas ending on each of the two differences.

DIFFERENTIATION FORMULAS

The notation used is defined as follows:

$$h^n \frac{d^n}{dx^n} f(x_0 + ph) \equiv h^n \frac{d^n}{dx^n} f_p \equiv \frac{d^n}{dp^n} f_p$$

Derivatives at tabular points.

$$
\begin{aligned}
h f_0^{(1)} &= \left(\Delta - \frac{\Delta^2}{2} + \frac{\Delta^3}{3} - \frac{\Delta^4}{4} + \frac{\Delta^5}{5} - \frac{\Delta^6}{6} \cdots \right) f_0 \\
&= \left(\mu\delta - \tfrac{1}{6}\mu\delta^3 + \tfrac{1}{30}\mu\delta^5 - \tfrac{1}{140}\mu\delta^7 \cdots \right) f_0 \\
&= \left(\nabla + \frac{\nabla^2}{2} + \frac{\nabla^3}{3} + \frac{\nabla^4}{4} + \frac{\nabla^5}{5} + \frac{\nabla^6}{6} \cdots \right) f_0
\end{aligned}
$$

$$
\begin{aligned}
h^2 f_0^{(2)} &= \left(\Delta^2 - \Delta^3 + \tfrac{11}{12}\Delta^4 - \tfrac{5}{6}\Delta^5 + \tfrac{137}{180}\Delta^6 - \tfrac{7}{10}\Delta^7 \cdots \right) f_0 \\
&= \left(\delta^2 - \tfrac{1}{12}\delta^4 + \tfrac{1}{90}\delta^6 - \tfrac{1}{560}\delta^8 \cdots \right) f_0 \\
&= \left(\nabla^2 + \nabla^3 + \tfrac{11}{12}\nabla^4 + \tfrac{5}{6}\nabla^5 + \tfrac{137}{180}\nabla^6 + \tfrac{7}{10}\nabla^7 \cdots \right) f_0
\end{aligned}
$$

$$
\begin{aligned}
h^3 f_0^{(3)} &= \left(\Delta^3 - \tfrac{3}{2}\Delta^4 + \tfrac{21}{12}\Delta^5 - \tfrac{45}{24}\Delta^6 + \tfrac{348}{180}\Delta^7 - \tfrac{79}{40}\Delta^8 \cdots \right) f_0 \\
&= \left(\mu\delta^3 - \tfrac{1}{4}\mu\delta^5 + \tfrac{7}{120}\mu\delta^7 - \tfrac{41}{3024}\mu\delta^9 \cdots \right) f_0 \\
&= \left(\nabla^3 + \tfrac{3}{2}\nabla^4 + \tfrac{21}{12}\nabla^5 + \tfrac{45}{24}\nabla^6 + \tfrac{348}{180}\nabla^7 + \tfrac{79}{40}\nabla^8 \cdots \right) f_0
\end{aligned}
$$

Higher derivatives can be found by direct multiplication of the above formulae e.g.

$$h^5 f_0^{(5)} = h^3 \frac{d^3}{dp^3} \left(h^2 \frac{d^2}{dp^2} f_0 \right)$$

$$\therefore h^5 f_0^{(5)} = \left(\mu\delta^3 - \tfrac{1}{4}\mu\delta^5 + \tfrac{7}{120}\mu\delta^7 \cdots \right) \left(\delta^2 - \tfrac{1}{12}\delta^4 + \tfrac{1}{90}\delta^6 - \tfrac{1}{560}\delta^8 \cdots \right) f_0$$

$$= \left(\mu\delta^5 - \tfrac{1}{3}\mu\delta^7 + \tfrac{13}{144}\mu\delta^9 \cdots \right) f_0$$

The identity $\mu^2 \equiv 1 + \tfrac{1}{4}\delta^2$ is used to ensure that no powers of 'μ,' other than the first, appear in any formula.

$$h^4 f_0^{(4)} = \left(\delta^4 - \tfrac{1}{6}\delta^6 + \tfrac{7}{240}\delta^8 - \tfrac{41}{7560}\delta^{10} \cdots \right) f_0$$

$$h^6 f_0^{(6)} = \left(\delta^6 - \tfrac{1}{4}\delta^8 + \tfrac{13}{240}\delta^{10} \cdots \right) f_0$$

$$h^7 f_0^{(7)} = \left(\mu\delta^7 - \tfrac{5}{12}\mu\delta^9 + \tfrac{31}{240}\mu\delta^{11} \cdots \right) f_0$$

The preceding formulae can be truncated, as in the examples, and the differences expressed in terms of the function values. The resulting formulae are of the type

$$h^n f_0^{(n)} = \sum_{r=1}^{k} a_r \cdot f_r + \epsilon$$

where

$$\sum_{r=1}^{k} a_r = 0$$

and the principal part of the error 'ϵ' is the first neglected difference. It is still necessary for the differences to be converging.

In the following formulae only the order of the differences constituting the error term are indicated.

$$hf_0^{(1)} \simeq (f_1 - f_0) - \tfrac{1}{2}\Delta^2$$
$$\simeq \tfrac{1}{2}(-f_2 + 4f_1 - 3f_0) + \tfrac{1}{3}\Delta^3$$
$$\simeq \tfrac{1}{6}(2f_3 - 9f_2 + 18f_1 - 11f_0) - \tfrac{1}{4}\Delta^4$$
$$\simeq \tfrac{1}{2}(f_1 - f_{-1}) - \tfrac{1}{6}\mu\delta^3$$
$$\simeq \tfrac{1}{12}(-f_2 + 8f_1 - 8f_{-1} + f_{-2}) + \tfrac{1}{30}\mu\delta^5$$
$$\simeq \tfrac{1}{60}(f_3 - 9f_2 + 45f_1 - 45f_{-1} + 9f_{-2} - f_{-3}) - \tfrac{1}{140}\mu\delta^7$$
$$\simeq (f_0 - f_{-1}) + \tfrac{1}{2}\nabla^2$$
$$\simeq \tfrac{1}{2}(3f_0 - 4f_{-1} + f_{-2}) + \tfrac{1}{3}\nabla^3$$
$$\simeq \tfrac{1}{6}(11f_0 - 18f_{-1} + 9f_{-2} - 2f_{-3}) + \tfrac{1}{4}\nabla^4$$

$$h^2 f_0^{(2)} \simeq (f_2 - 2f_1 + f_0) - \Delta^3$$
$$\simeq (-f_3 + 4f_2 - 5f_1 + 2f_0) + \tfrac{11}{12}\Delta^4$$
$$\simeq (11f_4 - 56f_3 + 114f_2 - 104f_1 + 35f_0) - \tfrac{5}{6}\Delta^5$$
$$\simeq (f_1 - 2f_0 + f_{-1}) - \tfrac{1}{12}\delta^4$$
$$\simeq \tfrac{1}{12}(-f_2 + 16f_1 - 30f_0 + 16f_{-1} - f_{-2}) + \tfrac{1}{90}\delta^6$$
$$\simeq \tfrac{1}{180}(2f_3 - 27f_2 + 270f_1 - 490f_0 + 270f_{-1} - 27f_{-2} + 2f_{-3}) - \tfrac{1}{560}\delta^8$$
$$\simeq (f_0 - 2f_{-1} + f_{-2}) + \nabla^3$$
$$\simeq (2f_0 - 5f_{-1} + 4f_{-2} - f_{-3}) + \tfrac{11}{12}\nabla^4$$
$$\simeq (35f_0 - 104f_{-1} + 114f_{-2} - 56f_{-3} + 11f_{-4}) + \tfrac{5}{6}\nabla^5$$

$$h^3 f_0^{(3)} \simeq (f_3 - 3f_2 + 3f_1 - f_0) - \tfrac{3}{2}\Delta^4$$
$$\simeq \tfrac{1}{2}(-3f_4 + 14f_3 - 24f_2 + 18f_1 - 5f_0) + \tfrac{21}{12}\Delta^5$$
$$\simeq \tfrac{1}{2}(f_2 - 2f_1 + 2f_{-1} - f_{-2}) - \tfrac{1}{4}\mu\delta^5$$
$$\simeq \tfrac{1}{8}(-f_3 + 8f_2 - 13f_1 + 13f_{-1} - 8f_{-2} + f_{-3}) + \tfrac{7}{120}\mu\delta^7$$
$$\simeq (f_0 - 3f_{-1} + 3f_{-2} - f_{-3}) + \tfrac{3}{2}\nabla^4$$
$$\simeq \tfrac{1}{2}(5f_0 - 18f_{-1} + 24f_{-2} - 14f_{-3} + 3f_{-4}) + \tfrac{21}{12}\nabla^5$$

For derivatives at half-way points there exist analogous formulae. The operators act upon f_0 and f_1, in the case of the forward and backward differences, and upon $f_{1/2}$ in the case of the central differences δ_0^{2n+1} being meaningless.

$$hf_{1/2}^{(1)} = (\Delta - \tfrac{1}{24}\Delta^3 + \tfrac{1}{24}\Delta^4 - \tfrac{71}{1920}\Delta^5 \cdots)f_0$$
$$= (\delta - \tfrac{1}{24}\delta^3 + \tfrac{3}{640}\delta^5 - \tfrac{5}{7168}\delta^7 \cdots)f_{1/2}$$
$$= (\nabla - \nabla^2 + \tfrac{23}{24}\nabla^3 + \tfrac{11}{12}\nabla^4 + \tfrac{563}{840}\nabla^5 \cdots)f_0$$
$$= (\nabla - \tfrac{1}{24}\nabla^3 - \tfrac{1}{24}\nabla^4 - \tfrac{71}{1920}\nabla^5 \cdots)f_1$$

$$h^2 f_{1/2}^{(2)} = (\Delta^2 - \tfrac{1}{12}\Delta^4 + \tfrac{1}{12}\Delta^5 - \tfrac{13}{180}\Delta^6 \cdots)f_0$$
$$= (\mu\delta^2 - \tfrac{5}{24}\mu\delta^4 + \tfrac{259}{5760}\mu\delta^6 - \tfrac{3229}{322560}\mu\delta^8 \cdots)f_{1/2}$$
$$= (\nabla^2 - \tfrac{1}{12}\nabla^4 - \tfrac{1}{12}\nabla^5 - \tfrac{13}{180}\nabla^6 \cdots)f_1$$

$$h^3 f_{1/2}^{(3)} = (\Delta^3 - \tfrac{1}{8}\Delta^5 + \tfrac{1}{8}\Delta^6 - \tfrac{203}{1920}\Delta^7 \cdots)f_0$$
$$= (\delta^3 - \tfrac{1}{8}\delta^5 + \tfrac{37}{1920}\delta^7 - \tfrac{2229}{967680}\delta^9 \cdots)f_{1/2}$$
$$= (\nabla^3 - \tfrac{1}{8}\nabla^5 - \tfrac{1}{8}\nabla^6 - \tfrac{203}{1920}\nabla^7 \cdots)f_1$$

As for tabular values, these formulae can be used to yield higher derivatives by multiplication of the operator series. Derivative formulae involving function values can also be obtained by truncation of the above series.

$$hf_{1/2}^{(1)} \simeq \tfrac{1}{24}(-f_3 + 3f_2 + 21f_1 - 23f_0) - \tfrac{1}{24}\Delta^4$$
$$\simeq \tfrac{1}{24}(f_4 - 5f_3 + 9f_2 + 13f_1 - 22f_0) - \tfrac{71}{1920}\Delta^5$$
$$\simeq (f_1 - f_0) - \tfrac{1}{24}\delta^3$$
$$\simeq \tfrac{1}{24}(-f_2 + 27f_1 - 27f_0 + f_{-1}) + \tfrac{3}{640}\delta^5$$
$$\simeq \tfrac{1}{1920}(3f_3 - 95f_2 + 2190f_1 - 2190f_0 + 95f_{-1} - 3f_{-2}) - \tfrac{5}{7168}\delta^7$$
$$\simeq (f_0 - f_{-1}) + \nabla^2$$
$$\simeq \tfrac{1}{24}(23f_1 - 21f_0 - 3f_{-1} + f_{-2}) - \tfrac{1}{24}\nabla^4$$
$$\simeq \tfrac{1}{24}(22f_1 - 17f_0 - 9f_{-1} + 5f_{-2} - f_{-3}) - \tfrac{71}{1920}\nabla^5$$

$$h^2 f_{1/2}^{(2)} \simeq (f_2 - 2f_1 + f_0) - \tfrac{1}{12}\Delta^4$$
$$\simeq \tfrac{1}{12}(-f_4 + 4f_3 + 6f_2 - 20f_1 + 11f_0) + \tfrac{1}{12}\Delta^5$$
$$\simeq \tfrac{1}{2}(f_2 - f_1 - f_0 + f_{-1}) - \tfrac{5}{24}\mu\delta^4$$
$$\simeq \tfrac{1}{48}(5f_3 + 33f_2 - 38f_1 - 38f_0 + 33f_{-1} + 5f_{-2}) + \tfrac{259}{5760}\mu\delta^6$$
$$\simeq (f_1 - 2f_0 + f_{-1}) - \tfrac{1}{12}\nabla^4$$
$$\simeq \tfrac{1}{12}(11f_1 - 20f_0 + 6f_{-1} + 4f_{-2} - f_{-3}) - \tfrac{1}{12}\nabla^5$$

$$h^3 f_{1/2}^{(3)} \simeq (f_3 - 3f_2 + 3f_1 - f_0) - \tfrac{1}{8}\Delta^5$$
$$\simeq (f_2 - 3f_1 + 3f_0 - f_{-1}) - \tfrac{1}{8}\delta^5$$
$$\simeq \tfrac{1}{8}(-f_3 + 13f_2 - 34f_1 + 34f_0 - 13f_{-1} + f_{-2}) + \tfrac{37}{1920}\delta^7$$
$$\simeq (f_1 - 3f_0 + 3f_{-1} - f_{-2}) - \tfrac{1}{8}\nabla^5$$

To calculate the derivative at an intermediate point 'p' the values of the derivative at tabular and half-way points can be evaluated and then interpolated, or the following formulae which involve the derivatives of Bessel's coefficients can be used. B'_r denotes the first derivative and B''_r the second etc. Note that the formula for the fourth derivative involves $B'_4 - \tfrac{1}{24}$ which is the same as B_6^{IV}

$$hf'_p = \delta_{1/2} + \tfrac{1}{2}(p - \tfrac{1}{2})(\delta_0^2 + \delta_1^2) + B'_3\delta_{1/2}^3 + B'_4(\delta_0^4 + \delta_1^4) + B'_5\delta_{1/2}^5$$
$$+ B'_6(\delta_0^6 + \delta_1^6) + B'_7\delta_{1/2}^7 + \cdots$$

$$h^2 f''_p = \delta_0^2 + p\delta_{1/2}^3 + B''_4(\delta_0^4 + \delta_1^4) + B''_5\delta_{1/2}^5 + B''_6(\delta_0^6 + \delta_1^6) + B''_7\delta_{1/2}^7 + \cdots$$

$$h^3 f'''_p = \delta_{1/2}^3 + \tfrac{1}{2}(p - \tfrac{1}{2})(\delta_0^4 + \delta_1^4) + B'''_5\delta_{1/2}^5 + B'''_6(\delta_0^6 + \delta_1^6) + B'''_7\delta_{1/2}^7 + \cdots$$

$$h^4 f_p = \delta_0^4 + p\delta_{1/2}^5 + (B'_4 - 0.417)(\delta_0^6 + \delta_1^6) + \cdots$$

To find the value of p at which a derivative has a given value a technique of successive approximation using these tables can be employed as an alternative to inverse interpolation in a table of the appropriate derivative.

Starting values for this procedure are given by

$$p \simeq \tfrac{1}{2} + 2(h^n f_p^{(n)} - \delta_{1/2}^n)/(\delta_0^{n+1} + \delta_1^{n+1}) \quad \text{when } n \text{ is odd}$$

and

$$p \simeq (h^n f_p^{(n)} - \delta_0^n)/\delta_{1/2}^{n+1} \quad \text{when } n \text{ is even}$$

DIFFERENTIATION TABLES FOR NON-TABULAR POINTS

p	B'_3	B'_4	B'_5	B'_6	B'_7	$(1 - p)$
.00	+ .083333	+ .041667	− .00833	− .0083	+ .0012	1.00
.01	78383	41238	792	83	11	.99
.02	73533	40784	750	82	11	.98
.03	68783	40306	709	81	10	.97
.04	64133	39805	667	81	10	.96
.05	+ .059583	+ .039281	− .00626	− .0080	+ .0009	.95
.06	55133	38735	585	79	9	.94
.07	50783	38166	544	78	8	.93
.08	46533	37576	504	77	7	.92
.09	42383	36965	464	76	7	.91
.10	+ .038333	+ .036333	− .00425	− .0075	+ .0006	.90
.11	34383	35682	385	74	6	.89
.12	30533	35011	347	72	5	.88
.13	26783	34321	309	71	5	.87
.14	23133	33612	271	70	4	.86
.15	+ .019583	+ .032885	− .00234	− .0068	+ .0004	.85
.16	16133	32141	198	67	3	.84
.17	12783	31380	162	66	3	.83
.18	9533	30603	128	64	2	.82
.19	6383	29809	93	63	1	.81
.20	+ .003333	+ .029000	− .00060	− .0061	+ .0001	.80
.21	+ 383	28176	− 27	59	+ 1	.79
.22	− 2467	27337	+ 4	58	− 0	.78
.23	5217	26485	35	56	0	.77
.24	7867	25619	65	54	1	.76
.25	− .010417	+ .024740	+ .00094	− .0052	− .0001	.75
.26	12867	23848	123	51	2	.74
.27	15217	22944	150	49	2	.73
.28	17467	22029	176	47	3	.72
.29	19617	21103	201	45	3	.71
.30	− .021667	+ .020167	+ .00225	− .0043	− .0003	.70
.31	23617	19220	249	41	4	.69
.32	25467	18264	271	39	4	.68
.33	27217	17299	292	37	4	.67
.34	28867	16325	311	35	5	.66
.35	− .030417	+ .015344	+ .00330	− .0033	− .0005	.65
.36	31867	14355	348	31	5	.64
.37	33217	13359	364	29	5	.63
.38	34467	12356	380	27	6	.62
.39	35617	11347	394	24	6	.61
.40	− .036667	+ .010333	+ .00407	− .0022	− .0006	.60
.41	37617	9314	418	20	6	.59
.42	38467	8291	429	18	6	.58
.43	39217	7263	438	16	7	.57
.44	39867	6232	446	13	7	.56
.45	− .040417	+ .005198	+ .00453	− .0011	− .0007	.55
.46	40867	4161	459	9	7	.54
.47	41217	3123	463	7	7	.53
.48	41467	2083	466	4	7	.52
.49	41617	1042	468	2	7	.51
.50	− .041667	+ .000000	+ .00469	− .0000	− .0007	.50
$(1 - p)$	B'_3	$-B'_4$	B'_5	$-B'_6$	B'_7	p

DIFFERENTIATION TABLES FOR NON-TABULAR POINTS

p	B_4''	B_5''	B_6''	B_7''	$(1 - p)$
.00	−.041667	+.04167	+.0056	−.0056	1.00
.01	44142	4164	62	56	.99
.02	46567	4157	68	56	.98
.03	48942	4145	74	56	.97
.04	51267	4128	80	57	.96
.05	−.053542	+.04106	+.0086	−.0057	.95
.06	55767	4080	91	57	.94
.07	57942	4050	97	56	.93
.08	60067	4015	103	56	.92
.09	62142	3976	108	56	.91
.10	−.064167	+.03933	+.0113	−.0056	.90
.11	66142	3886	119	55	.89
.12	68067	3835	124	55	.88
.13	69942	3781	129	54	.87
.14	71767	3722	134	54	.86
.15	−.073542	+.03660	+.0139	−.0053	.85
.16	75267	3595	143	52	.84
.17	76942	3526	148	51	.83
.18	78567	˙3454	152	51	.82
.19	80142	3378	157	50	.81
.20	−.081667	+.03300	+.0161	−.0049	.80
.21	83142	3219	165	48	.79
.22	84567	3134	169	46	.78
.23	85942	3047	173	45	.77
.24	87267	2957	176	44	.76
.25	−.088542	+.02865	+.0180	−.0043	.75
.26	89767	2770	184	42	.74
.27	90942	2672	187	40	.73
.28	92067	2573	190	39	.72
.29	93142	2471	193	37	.71
.30	−.094167	+.02367	+.0196	−.0036	.70
.31	95142	2261	199	34	.69
.32	96067	2153	201	33	.68
.33	96942	2043	204	31	.67
.34	97767	1932	206	29	.66
.35	−.098542	+.01819	+.0209	−.0028	.65
.36	99267	1704	211	26	.64
.37	99942	1588	213	24	.63
.38	100567	1471	214	23	.62
.39	101142	1353	216	21	.61
.40	−.101667	+.01233	+.0218	−.0019	.60
.41	102142	1113	219	17	.59
.42	102567	991	220	15	.58
.43	102942	869	221	13	.57
.44	103267	746	222	11	.56
.45	−.103542	+.00623	+.0223	−.0010	.55
.46	103767	499	224	8	.54
.47	103942	375	224	6	.53
.48	104067	250	225	4	.52
.49	104142	125	225	2	.51
.50	−.104167	+.00000	+.0225	−.0000	.50
$(1 - p)$	B_4''	$-B_5''$	B_6''	$-B_7''$	p

DIFFERENTIATION TABLES FOR NON-TABULAR POINTS

p	B_5'''	B_6'''	B_7'''	$(1 - p)$
.00	$-.00000$	$+.0625$	$-.0042$	1.00
.01	495	617	33	.99
.02	980	608	25	.98
.03	1455	599	17	.97
.04	1920	590	9	.96
.05	$-.02375$	$+.0580$	$-.0001$	.95
.06	2820	571	$+$ 7	.94
.07	3255	561	14	.93
.08	3680	551	22	.92
.09	4095	540	29	.91
.10	$-.04500$	$+.0530$	$+.0037$	.90
.11	4895	519	44	.89
.12	5280	508	51	.88
.13	5655	497	58	.87
.14	6020	486	65	.86
.15	$-.06375$	$+.0475$	$+.0071$	.85
.16	6720	463	78	.84
.17	7055	451	84	.83
.18	7380	439	90	.82
.19	7695	427	96	.81
.20	$-.08000$	$+.0415$	$+.0102$	.80
.21	8295	403	108	.79
.22	8580	390	114	.78
.23	8855	377	119	.77
.24	9120	365	124	.76
.25	$-.09375$	$+.0352$	$+.0129$	.75
.26	9620	338	134	.74
.27	9855	325	139	.73
.28	10080	312	143	.72
.29	10295	299	148	.71
.30	$-.10500$	$+.0285$	$+.0152$	.70
.31	10695	271	156	.69
.32	10880	258	159	.68
.33	11055	244	163	.67
.34	11220	230	166	.66
.35	$-.11375$	$+.0216$	.0169	.65
.36	11520	202	172	.64
.37	11655	188	175	.63
.38	11780	174	178	.62
.39	11895	159	180	.61
.40	$-.12000$	$+.0145$	$+.0182$	.60
.41	12095	131	184	.59
.42	12180	116	186	.58
.43	12255	102	188	.57
.44	12320	87	189	.56
.45	$-.12375$	$+.0073$	$+.0190$	.55
.46	12420	58	191	.54
.47	12455	44	192	.53
.48	12480	29	192	.52
.49	12495	15	193	.51
.50	$-.12500$	$+.0000$	$+.0193$	.50
$(1 - p)$	B_5'''	B_6'''	B_7'''	p

Numerical Differentiation/Numerical Integration

Caution

Numerical differentiation is error magnifying and many guarding figures are usually necessary. This is due to two factors namely:

    a) the interval h enters each formula in the form $1/h^n$

    b) each formula starts with the nth order difference.

Both of these combine to make numerical differentiation unreliable. e.g. Suppose the formula $f^{(2)} = (\Delta^2 - \Delta^3 + \frac{11}{12}\Delta^4)/h^2$ is used with $h = 0.1$ and an error of 5×10^{-4} can be tolerated in the derivative. For an error of e in each of the tabulated values

$$5 \times 10^{-4} = \frac{1}{0.01}(2e + 3e + \tfrac{11}{12}6e)$$

$$= 100(\tfrac{21}{2}e)$$

$$= 1050e$$

and therefore $e \simeq 5 \times 10^{-7}$ i.e. the function must be tabulated to *six* places of decimals before the second derivative can be correct to *three*.

If, on the other hand, h had been unity in magnitude then

$$5 \times 10^{-4} = 10.5e$$

i.e. $e \simeq 5 \times 10^{-5}$ and the function would need only one guarding figure to produce the required degree of accuracy in the second derivative.

Obviously this effect is magnified for higher derivatives. In any case, the largest value of h, which permits the function to be well represented by a converging table of differences, should be used.

INTEGRATION FORMULAS

Integration is a smoothing procedure and as such errors in tabulated values tend to be cancelled out.

Notation used:

$$\int_{x_0}^{x_n} f(x) \cdot dx = h \int_0^n f_p \cdot dp$$

where

$$f_p \equiv f(x_0 + ph) \equiv f(x)$$

$$\int_0^n f_p \cdot dp = \tfrac{1}{2}f_0 + f_1 + f_2 + \cdots + f_{n-1} + \tfrac{1}{2}f_n + \tfrac{1}{12}(\Delta_0 - \nabla_n) - \tfrac{1}{24}(\Delta_0^2 + \nabla_n^2)$$

$$+ \tfrac{19}{720}(\Delta_0^3 - \nabla_n^3) - \tfrac{3}{160}(\Delta_0^4 + \nabla_n^4) \cdots$$

$$= \tfrac{1}{2}f_0 + f_1 + f_2 + \cdots + f_{n-1} + \tfrac{1}{2}f_n + \tfrac{1}{12}(\mu\delta_0 - \mu\delta_n)$$

$$- \tfrac{11}{720}(\mu\delta_0^3 - \mu\delta_n^3) + \tfrac{191}{60480}(\mu\delta_0^5 - \mu\delta_n^5) - \cdots$$

In particular

$$\int_0^1 f_p \cdot dp = (1 + \tfrac{1}{2}\Delta - \tfrac{1}{12}\Delta^2 + \tfrac{1}{24}\Delta^3 - \tfrac{19}{720}\Delta^4 + \tfrac{3}{160}\Delta^5 - \tfrac{863}{60480}\Delta^6 + \cdots)f_0$$

$$= (1 + \tfrac{1}{2}\nabla + \tfrac{5}{12}\nabla^2 + \tfrac{3}{8}\nabla^3 + \tfrac{251}{720}\nabla^4 + \tfrac{95}{288}\nabla^5 + \tfrac{19087}{60480}\nabla^6 \cdots)f_0$$

$$= (1 - \tfrac{1}{2}\nabla - \tfrac{1}{12}\nabla^2 - \tfrac{1}{24}\nabla^3 - \tfrac{19}{720}\nabla^4 - \tfrac{3}{160}\nabla^5 - \tfrac{863}{60480}\nabla^6 \cdots)f_1$$

$$= (\mu - \tfrac{1}{12}\mu\delta^2 + \tfrac{11}{720}\mu\delta^4 - \tfrac{191}{60480}\mu\delta^6 + \cdots)f_{1/2}$$

$$\int_0^{n+(1/2)} f_p \cdot dp = \tfrac{1}{2}f_0 + f_1 + f_2 \cdots + f_n + (\tfrac{1}{12}\mu\delta - \tfrac{11}{720}\mu\delta^3 + \tfrac{191}{60480}\mu\delta^5 \cdots)f_0$$

$$+ (\tfrac{1}{24}\delta - \tfrac{17}{5760}\delta^3 + \tfrac{367}{967680}\delta^5 \cdots)f_{n+(1/2)}$$

Numerical Integration

In particular

$$\int_0^{1/2} f_p \cdot dp = \tfrac{1}{2} f_0 + (\tfrac{1}{8}\delta - \tfrac{1}{24}\mu\delta^2 + \tfrac{1}{384}\delta^3 + \tfrac{11}{1440}\mu\delta^4 - \tfrac{13}{46080}\delta^5 \cdots) f_{1/2}$$

Symmetric range integrals

$$\int_{-1/2}^{1/2} f_p \cdot dp = (1 + \tfrac{1}{24}\delta^2 - \tfrac{17}{5760}\delta^4 + \tfrac{367}{967680}\delta^6 - \tfrac{27859}{464486400}\delta^8 \cdots) f_0$$

$$\int_{-1}^{1} f_p \cdot dp = 2(1 + \tfrac{1}{6}\delta^2 - \tfrac{1}{180}\delta^4 + \tfrac{1}{1512}\delta^6 - \tfrac{23}{226800}\delta^8 + \cdots) f_0$$

$$\int_{-2}^{2} f_p \cdot dp = 4(1 + \tfrac{2}{3}\delta^2 + \tfrac{7}{90}\delta^4 - \tfrac{2}{945}\delta^6 + \tfrac{13}{56700}\delta^8 - \cdots) f_0$$

$$\int_{-3}^{3} f_p \cdot dp = 6(1 + \tfrac{3}{2}\delta^2 + \tfrac{11}{20}\delta^4 + \tfrac{41}{840}\delta^6 - \tfrac{3}{2800}\delta^8 + \cdots) f_0$$

$$\int_{-4}^{4} f_p \cdot dp = 8(1 + \tfrac{8}{3}\delta^2 + \tfrac{217}{90}\delta^4 + \tfrac{92}{189}\delta^6 + \tfrac{989}{28350}\delta^8 + \cdots) f_0$$

The differences in the above formulae can be replaced by their function values, after truncation of the series, if extensive differencing is to be avoided.

When this is done, the formulae take on the forms

$$\sum_m A_m \cdot f_m$$

Some typical formulae of this type, used in the iterative starting of the solution of ordinary differential equations, can be found on pages 634. These are essentially quadrature formulae as are the predictor corrector formulae of pages 641. *

When the limits involved in the integrals are not tabular or half-way points, formulae analogous to Bessel's interpolation formula can be used, the corresponding coefficients being designated by B^* etc. Single integration.

$$\int_0^p f_p \cdot dp = \tfrac{1}{2}p(f_0 + f_1)' + B_1^*\delta_{1/2} + B_2^*(\delta_0^2 + \delta_1^2) + B_3^*\delta_{1/2}^3$$

$$+ B_4^*(\delta_0^4 + \delta_1^4) + B_5^*\delta_{1/2}^5 + B_6^*(\delta_0^6 + \delta_1^6)$$

$$\iint_0^p f_p \cdot d^2p = B_0^{**}(f_0 + f_1) + B_1^{**}\delta_{1/2} + B_2^{**}(\delta_0 + \delta_1) + B_3^{**}\delta_{1/2}$$

$$+ B_4^{**}(\delta_0 + \delta_1) + B_5^{**}\delta_{1/2}$$

*The pages are from Beyer, William H., *CRC Handbook of Mathematical Sciences*, 6th Ed., CRC Press, Boca Raton, 1987.

INTEGRATION TABLES FOR NON-TABULAR POINTS

p	B_1^*	B_2^*	B_3^*	B_4^*	B_5^*	B_6^*
.00	− .000000	− .000000	+ .000000	+ .00000	− .00000	− .0000
.01	4950	12	4	0	0	0
.02	9800	49	16	1	0	0
.03	14550	110	35	2	0	0
.04	19200	195	61	3	1	0
.05	− .023750	− .000302	+ .000094	+ .00005	− .00001	− .0000
.06	28200	432	133	7	1	0
.07	32550	584	177	10	2	0
.08	36800	757	226	13	2	0
.09	40950	952	279	16	3	0
.10	− .045000	− .001167	+ .000338	+ .00020	− .00003	− .0000
.11	48950	1402	399	24	4	0
.12	52800	1656	465	29	5	1
.13	56550	1929	533	33	6	1
.14	60200	2221	604	39	6	1
.15	− .063750	− .002531	+ .000677	+ .00044	− .00007	− .0001
.16	67200	2859	753	50	8	1
.17	70550	3203	830	56	9	1
.18	73800	3564	908	62	10	1
.19	76950	3941	987	69	10	1
.20	− .080000	− .004333	+ .001067	+ .00076	− .00011	− .0002
.21	82950	4741	1147	84	12	2
.22	85800	5163	1227	91	13	2
.23	88550	5599	1307	99	14	2
.24	91200	6048	1386	107	15	2
.25	− .093750	− .006510	+ .001465	+ .00116	− .00016	− .0002
.26	96200	6985	1542	124	16	3
.27	98550	7472	1619	133	17	3
.28	100800	7971	1693	142	18	3
.29	102950	8480	1766	152	19	3
.30	− .105000	− .009000	+ .001838	+ .00161	− .00020	− .0003
.31	106950	9530	1906	171	20	4
.32	108800	10069	1973	181	21	4
.33	110550	10618	2037	191	22	4
.34	112200	11175	2098	202	23	4
.35	− .113750	− .011740	+ .002157	+ .00212	− .00023	− .0004
.36	115200	12312	2212	223	24	5
.37	116550	12891	2264	233	24	5
.38	117800	13477	2313	244	25	5
.39	118950	14069	2358	255	25	5
.40	− .120000	− .014667	+ .002400	+ .00266	− .00026	− .0005
.41	120950	15269	2438	278	26	6
.42	121800	15876	2473	289	27	6
.43	122550	16487	2503	301	27	6
.44	123200	17101	2530	312	27	6
.45	− .123750	− .017719	+ .002552	+ .00324	− .00028	− .0007
.46	124200	18339	2571	335	28	7
.47	124550	18961	2585	347	28	7
.48	124800	19584	2596	359	28	7
.49	124950	20208	2602	370	28	8
.50	− .125000	− .020833	+ .002604	+ .00382	− .00028	− .0008

INTEGRATION TABLES FOR NON-TABULAR POINTS (Continued)

p	B_1^*	B_2^*	B_3^*	B_4^*	B_5^*	B_6^*
.50	−.125000	−.020833	+.002604	+.00382	−.00028	−.0008
.51	124950	21458	2602	394	28	8
.52	124800	22083	2596	405	28	8
.53	124550	22706	2585	417	28	9
.54	124200	23328	2571.	429	28	9
.55	−.123750	−.023948	+.002552	+.00440	−.00028	−.0009
.56	123200	24565	2530	452	27	9
.57	122550	25180	2503	463	27	10
.58	121800	25791	2473	475	27	10
.59	120950	26398	2438	486	26	10
.60	−.120000	−.027000	+.002400	+.00497	−.00026	−.0010
.61	118950	27597	2358	509	25	11
.62	117800	28189	2313	520	25	11
.63	116550	28775	2264	530	24	11
.64	115200	29355	2212	541	24	11
.65	−.113750	−.029927	+.002157	+.00552	−.00023	−.0011
.66	112200	30492	2098	562	23	12
.67	110550	31049	2037	573	22	12
.68	108800	31597	1973	583	21	12
.69	106950	32137	1906	593	20	12
.70	−.105000	−.032667	+.001838	+.00603	−.00020	−.0012
.71	102950	33187	1766	612	19	13
.72	100800	33696	1693	621	18	13
.73	98550	34194	1619	631	17	13
.74	96200	34681	1542	640	16	13
.75	−.093750	−.035156	+.001465	+.00648	−.00016	−.0013
.76	91200	35619	1386	657	15	14
.77	88550	36068	1307	665	14	14
.78	85800	36504	1227	673	13	14
.79	82950	36926	1147	680	12	14
.80	−.080000	−.037333	+.001067	+.00688	−.00011	−.0014
.81	76950	37726	987	695	10	14
.82	73800	38103	908	701	10	15
.83	70550	38464	830	708	9	15
.84	67200	38808	753	714	8	15
.85	−.063750	−.039135	+.000677	+.00720	−.00007	−.0015
.86	60200	39445	604	725	6	15
.87	56550	39737	533	730	6	15
.88	52800	40011	465	735	5	15
.89	48950	40265	399	740	4	15
.90	−.045000	−.040500	+.000337	+.00744	−.00003	−.0015
.91	40950	40715	279	748	3	15
.92	36800	40909	226	751	2	16
.93	32550	41083	177	754	2	16
.94	28200	41235	133	757	1	16
.95	−.023750	−.041365	+.000094	+.00759	−.00001	−.0016
.96	19200	41472	61	761	1	16
.97	14550	41556	35	762	0	16
.98	9800	41617	16	763	0	16
.99	4950	41654	4	764	0	16
1.00	−.000000	−.041667	+.000000	+.00764	−.00000	−.0016

INTEGRATION TABLES FOR NON-TABULAR POINTS

p	B_0^{**}	B_1^{**}	B_2^{**}	B_3^{**}	B_4^{**}	B_5^{**}
.00	+ .000000	− .000000	− .000000	+ .00000	+ .00000	− .0000
.01	25	25	0	0	0	0
.02	100	99	0	0	0	0
.03	225	220	1	0	0	0
.04	400	389	3	0	0	0
.05	+ .000625	− .000604	− .000005	+ .00000	+ .00000	− .0000
.06	900	864	9	0	0	0
.07	1225	1168	14	0	0	0
.08	1600	1515	20	1	0	0
.09	2025	1904	29	1	0	0
.10	+ .002500	− .002333	− .000040	+ .00001	+ .00001	− .0000
.11	3025	2803	52	2	1	0
.12	3600	3312	68	2	1	0
.13	4225	3859	86	2	1	0
.14	4900	4443	106	3	2	0
.15	+ .005625	− .005063	− .000130	+ .00004	+ .00002	− .0000
.16	6400	5717	157	4	3	0
.17	7225	6406	187	5	3	0
.18	8100	7128	221	6	4	0
.19	9025	7882	259	7	4	0
.20	+ .010000	− .008667	− .000300	+ .00008	+ .00005	− .0000
.21	11025	9481	345	9	6	0
.22	12100	10325	395	10	7	0
.23	13225	11197	449	12	8	0
.24	14400	12096	507	13	9	0
.25	+ .015625	− .013021	− .000570	+ .00014	+ .00010	− .0000
.26	16900	13971	637	16	11	0
.27	18225	14945	709	17	12	0
.28	19600	15941	787	19	14	0
.29	21025	16960	869	21	15	0
.30	+ .022500	− .018000	− .000956	+ .00023	+ .00017	− .0000
.31	24025	19060	1049	25	19	0
.32	25600	20139	1147	26	20	0
.33	27225	21235	1250	28	22	0
.34	28900	22349	1359	31	24	0
.35	+ .030625	− .023479	− .001474	+ .00033	+ .00026	− .0000
.36	32400	24624	1594	35	28	0
.37	34225	25783	1720	37	31	0
.38	36100	26955	1852	39	33	0
.39	38025	28138	1990	42	36	0
.40	+ .040000	− .029333	− .002133	+ .00044	+ .00038	− .0000
.41	42025	30538	2283	47	41	0
.42	44100	31752	2439	49	44	1
.43	46225	32974	2601	51	47	1
.44	48400	34203	2768	54	50	1
.45	+ .050625	− .035438	− .002943	+ .00057	+ .00053	− .0001
.46	52900	36677	3123	59	56	1
.47	55225	37921	3309	62	60	1
.48	57600	39168	3502	64	63	1
.49	60025	40417	3701	67	67	1
.50	+ .062500	− .041667	− .003906	+ .00069	+ .00071	− .0001

INTEGRATION TABLES FOR NON-TABULAR POINTS (Continued)

p	B_0^{**}	B_1^{**}	B_2^{**}	B_3^{**}	B_4^{**}	B_5^{**}
.50	+.062500	−.041667	−.003906	+.00069	+.00071	−.0001
.51	65025	42916	4118	72	74	1
.52	67600	44165	4335	75	78	1
.53	70225	45412	4559	77	83	1
.54	72900	46656	4790	80	87	1
.55	+.075625	−.047896	−.005026	+.00082	+.00091	−.0001
.56	78400	49131	5268	85	96	1
.57	81225	50359	5517	87	100	1
.58	84100	51581	5772	90	105	1
.59	87025	52795	6033	92	110	1
.60	+.090000	−.054000	−.006300	+.00095	+.00115	−.0001
.61	93025	55195	6573	97	120	1
.62	96100	56379	6852	100	125	1
.63	99225	57550	7137	102	130	1
.64	102400	58709	7427	104	135	1
.65	+.105625	−.059854	−.007724	+.00106	+.00141	−.0001
.66	108900	60984	8026	108	146	1
.67	112225	62098	8334	110	152	1
.68	115600	63195	8647	112	158	1
.69	119025	64274	8966	114	164	1
.70	+.122500	−.065333	−.009290	+.00116	+.00170	−.0001
.71	126025	66373	9619	118	176	1
.72	129600	67392	9953	120	182	1
.73	133225	68389	10293	121	188	1
.74	136900	69363	10637	123	195	1
.75	+.140625	−.070313	−.010986	+.00125	+.00201	−.0001
.76	144400	71237	11340	126	207	1
.77	148225	72136	11699	127	214	1
.78	152100	73008	12062	129	221	1
.79	156025	73852	12429	130	228	1
.80	+.160000	−.074667	−.012800	+.00131	+.00234	−.0001
.81	164025	75451	13175	132	241	1
.82	168100	76205	13554	133	248	1
.83	172225	76927	13937	134	255	1
.84	176400	77616	14324	134	262	1
.85	+.180625	−.078271	−.014713	+.00135	+.00270	−.0001
.86	184900	78891	15106	136	277	1
.87	189225	79474	15502	136	284	1
.88	193600	80021	15901	137	291	1
.89	198025	80530	16302	137	299	1
.90	+.202500	−.081000	−.016706	+.00138	+.00306	−.0001
.91	207025	81430	17112	138	314	1
.92	211600	81819	17520	138	321	1
.93	216225	82165	17930	138	329	1
.94	220900	82469	18342	139	336	1
.95	+.225625	−.082729	−.018755	+.00139	+.00344	−.0001
.96	230400	82944	19169	139	351	1
.97	235225	83113	19584	139	359	1
.98	240100	83235	20000	139	367	1
.99	245025	83308	20417	139	374	1
1.00	+.250000	−.083333	−.020833	+.00139	+.00382	−.0001

GAUSS-TYPE WEIGHTS ABSCISSAE

Quadrature formulae using unevenly spaced ordinates. Some high accuracy formulae involve the use of abscissae which are unevenly spaced throughout the interval. The interval itself is usually subject to a transformation and various 'weighting functions' are involved.

To change the interval (a, b) in x to that of (θ, ϕ) in t the transformation

$$t = \frac{(a\theta - b\phi)}{(a - b)} + \frac{(\theta - \phi)x}{(a - b)}$$

is used.

Some of the more popular weighting functions and their associated intervals are given below. The general formulae are of two main types derived from

$$\int_a^b W(x) \cdot F(x) \cdot dx = \int_\theta^\phi \omega(t) \cdot f(t) \cdot dt$$

namely

$$\int_\theta^\phi \omega(t) \cdot f(t) \cdot dt = \sum_t \{H_t \cdot f(x_t)\}$$

and

$$\int_\theta^\phi \omega(t) \cdot f(t) \cdot dt = H \sum_t \{f(x_t) \pm f(-x_t)\}$$

$\omega(t)$	(θ, ϕ)	x_t are the zeros of:
1	$(-1, 1)$	$P_n(x)$
$t^{1/2}$	$(0, 1)$	$x^{-1/2} \cdot P_{2n+1}(\sqrt{x})$
$t^{-1/2}$	$(0, 1)$	$P_n(\sqrt{x})$
$(1 - t^2)^{1/2}$	$(-1, 1)$	$S_n(x)$
$(1 - t^2)^{-1/2}$	$(-1, 1)$	$T_n(x)$
e^{-t}	$(0, \infty)$	$L_n(x)$
e^{-t^2}	$(-\infty, \infty)$	$H_n(x)$

Some useful tables of abscissae x_t and their corresponding H_t are as follows.

Gaussian Quadrature.

$$\int_{-1}^{1} f(x) \cdot dx = \sum_{1}^{n} \{H_i \cdot f(x_i)\}$$

The x_i occur in pairs symmetrically placed with respect to the origin.

$\pm x_i$	H_i
	$n = 2$
0.5773503	1.0000000
	$n = 3$
0.7745967	0.5555556
0.0000000	0.8888889
	$n = 4$
0.8611363	0.3478548
0.3399810	0.6521452
	$n = 5$
0.9061798	0.2369269
0.5384693	0.4786287
0.0000000	0.5688889
	$n = 6$
0.9324695	0.1713245
0.6612094	0.3607616
0.2386192	0.4679139
	$n = 7$
0.9491079	0.1294850
0.7415312	0.2797054
0.4058452	0.3818301
0.0000000	0.4179592
	$n = 8$
0.9602899	0.1012285
0.7966665	0.2223810
0.5255324	0.3137066
0.1834346	0.3626838
	$n = 9$
0.9681602	0.0812744
0.8360311	0.1806482
0.6133714	0.2606107
0.3242534	0.3123471
0.0000000	0.3302394
	$n = 10$
0.9739065	0.0666713
0.8650634	0.1494513
0.6794096	0.2190864
0.4333954	0.2692602
0.1488743	0.2955242
	$n = 11$
0.9782287	0.0556686
0.8870626	0.1255804
0.7301520	0.1862902
0.5190961	0.2331938
0.2695432	0.2628045
0.0000000	0.2729251
	$n = 12$
0.9815606	0.0471753
0.9041173	0.1069393
0.7699027	0.1600783
0.5873180	0.2031674
0.3678315	0.2334925
0.1253334	0.2491470

$\pm x_i$	H_i
n = 13	
0.9841831	0.0404840
0.9175984	0.0921215
0.8015781	0.1388735
0.6423493	0.1781460
0.4484928	0.2078160
0.2304583	0.2262832
0.0000000	0.2325516
n = 14	
0.9862838	0.0351195
0.9284349	0.0801581
0.8272013	0.1215186
0.6872929	0.1572032
0.5152486	0.1855384
0.3191124	0.2051985
0.1080549	0.2152639
n = 15	
0.9879925	0.0307532
0.9372734	0.0703660
0.8482066	0.1071592
0.7244177	0.1395707
0.5709722	0.1662692
0.3941513	0.1861610
0.2011941	0.1984315
0.0000000	0.2025782
n = 16	
0.9894009	0.0271525
0.9445750	0.0622535
0.8656312	0.0951585
0.7554044	0.1246290
0.6178762	0.1495960
0.4580168	0.1691565
0.2816036	0.1826034
0.0950125	0.1894506

Laguerre Quadrature.

$$\int_0^\infty e^{-x} \cdot f(x) \cdot dx = \sum_1^n \{H_i \cdot f(x_i)\}$$

x_i	H_i
n = 2	
0.5857864	0.8535534
3.4142136	0.1464466
n = 3	
0.4157746	0.7110930
2.2942804	0.2785177
6.2899451	0.0103893
n = 4	
0.3225477	0.6031541
1.7457611	0.3574187
4.5366203	0.0388879
9.3950709	0.0005393
n = 5	
0.2635603	0.5217556
1.4134031	0.3986668
3.5964258	0.0759424
7.0858100	0.0036118
12.6408008	0.0000234
n = 6	
0.2228466	0.4589647
1.1889321	0.4170008
2.9927363	0.1133734
5.7751436	0.0103992
9.8374674	0.0002610
15.9828740	0.0000009

Hermitian Quadrature.

$$e^{-x^2} \cdot f(x) \cdot dx = H_i \cdot f(x_i)$$

The abscissae are symmetrically placed with respect to the origin.

$\pm x_i$	H_i
$n = 2$	
0.7071068	0.8862269
$n = 3$	
0.0000000	1.1816359
1.2247449	0.2954090
$n = 4$	
0.5246476	0.8049141
1.6506801	0.0813128
$n = 5$	
0.0000000	0.9453087
0.9585725	0.3936193
2.0201829	0.0199532
$n = 6$	
0.4360774	0.7246296
1.3358491	0.1570673
2.3506050	0.0045300
$n = 7$	
0.0000000	0.8102646
0.8162879	0.4256073
1.6735516	0.0545156
2.6519614	0.0009718
$n = 8$	
0.3811870	0.6611470
1.1571937	0.2078023
1.9816568	0.0170780
2.9306374	0.0001996
$n = 9$	
0.0000000	0.7202352
0.7235510	0.4326516
1.4685533	0.0884745
2.2665806	0.0049436
3.1909932	0.0000396
$n = 10$	
0.3429013	0.6108626
1.0366108	0.2401386
1.7566836	0.0338744
2.5327317	0.0013436
3.4361591	0.0000076
$n = 11$	
0.0000000	0.6547593
0.6568096	0.4293598
1.3265571	0.1172279
2.0259480	0.0119114
2.7832901	0.0003468
3.6684708	0.0000014
$n = 12$	
0.3142404	0.5701352
0.9477884	0.2604923
1.5976826	0.0516080
2.2795071	0.0039054
3.0206370	0.0000857
3.8897249	0.0000003

Radau Quadrature.

$$\int_{-1}^{1} f(x) \cdot dx = H_1 \cdot f(-1) + H_n \cdot f(1) + \sum_{2}^{n-1} \{H_i \cdot f(x_i)\}$$

$\pm x_i$	H_i
$n = 2$	
1.0000000	1.0000000
$n = 3$	
1.0000000	0.3333333
0.0000000	1.3333333
$n = 4$	
1.0000000	0.1666667
0.4472136	0.8333333
$n = 5$	
1.0000000	0.1000000
0.6546537	0.5444444
0.0000000	0.7111111
$n = 6$	
1.0000000	0.0666667
0.7650553	0.3784750
0.2852315	0.5548584
$n = 7$	
1.0000000	0.0476190
0.8302239	0.2768260
0.4688488	0.4317454
0.0000000	0.4876190
$n = 8$	
1.0000000	0.0357143
0.8717402	0.2107042
0.5917002	0.3411227
0.2092992	0.4124588
$n = 9$	
1.0000000	0.0277778
0.8997580	0.1654954
0.6771863	0.2745387
0.3631175	0.3464285
0.0000000	0.3715193
$n = 10$	
1.0000000	0.0222222
0.9195339	0.1333060
0.7387739	0.2248893
0.4779249	0.2920427
0.1652790	0.3275398
$n = 11$	
1.0000000	0.0181818
0.9340014	0.1096123
0.7844835	0.1871699
0.5652353	0.2480481
0.2957581	0.2868791
0.0000000	0.3002176

Chebyshev-Radau Quadrature.

$$\int_{-1}^{1} x \cdot f(x) \cdot dx = H \cdot \sum_{1}^{n} \{f(x_i) - f(-x_i)\}$$

x_i	H
$n = 1$	
0.7745967	0.4303315
$n = 2$	
0.5002990	0.2393715
0.8922365	
$n = 3$	
0.4429861	
0.7121545	0.1599145
0.9293066	
$n = 4$	
0.3549416	
0.6433097	
0.7783202	0.1223363
0.9481574	

Chebyshev Quadrature.

$$\int_{-1}^{1} f(x) \cdot dx = \frac{2}{n} \cdot \sum_{1}^{n} f(x_i)$$

The abscissae are skew symmetric with respect to the origin.

x_i	x_i
$n = 2$	$n = 6$
-0.5773503	-0.8662468
$+0.5773503$	-0.4225187
$n = 3$	-0.2666354
-0.7071068	$+0.2666354$
0.0000000	$+0.4225187$
$+0.7071068$	$+0.8662468$
$n = 4$	$n = 7$
-0.7946545	-0.8838617
-0.1875925	-0.5296568
$+0.1875925$	-0.3239118
$+0.7946545$	0.0000000
$n = 5$	$+0.3239118$
-0.8324975	$+0.5296568$
-0.3745414	$+0.8838617$
0.0000000	
$+0.3745414$	
$+0.8324975$	

THE NUMERICAL SOLUTION OF DIFFERENTIAL EQUATIONS

Introduction

The aim is to produce a numerical approximation to the solution of the differential equation, correct to a specified number of decimals.

The principal factors affecting accuracy are
- a) the form of the equation,
- b) the interval of tabulation,
- c) the formula chosen to effect the integration.

The main types of equation considered here are classified as follows

TABLE I

Differential equations

I.V.* = Initial value problems, sometimes referred to as Marching problems.
B.V.' = Boundary value problems, sometimes referred to as Jury problems.

Ordinary differential equations

With initial value problems, all the conditions required to determine uniquely the constants arising from the integration procedure are given at one point. With boundary value problems these conditions are given at two or more points.

For ordinary boundary value problems the solution can usually be based upon initial value techniques as follows. One of the boundary points is chosen as the principal point and the variables which are given at the other boundary point(s) are estimated at this point. This is repeated for a number of different estimates and a combination of the resulting solutions is chosen so that the numerical values satisfy both the differential equation and also all the original boundary conditions.

The principal methods of solving ordinary initial value differential equations to be considered are classified as follows. Purely analytical techniques will not be dealt with.

In the direct methods the value at any point is obtained from the value at the preceeding point without any iteration. In the case of the Taylor's series approach it is a simple matter to include a running check on previously computed values. With the Runge-Kutta and Chebyshev techniques checking is more difficult. For linear differential equations, or any for which repeated differentiation is practical, the Taylors series method can be used with a

TABLE II

Ordinary Initial value differential equations

large step length. The basic disadvantages of direct methods are that the amount of calculation can be heavy and previously computed values are ignored. In addition a prior knowledge of the order of the approximation is necessary for the most efficient use of the basic Runga-Kutta approach and the direct Chebyshev method requires normalization of the range of the argument to either $(-1, +1)$ or $(0, +1)$.

With the iterative methods to be described, initial approximations are made and these are then refined until successive approximations agree to the required number of decimals. This is carried out either a point at a time or simultaneously over the whole range. They have the advantage of being self correcting in the sense that small computational errors are eliminated in subsequent iterations.

In this group of methods the predictor-corrector methods are particularly suitable for desk machine operation, especially with the more complicated non-linear differential equation. Their accuracy is controlled by the corrector formula which has associated with it an indication of the maximum interval to ensure convergence. These formulae are expressed either in terms of ordinates or backward and or central differences.

The deferred corrector methods are particularly suitable for desk machine work and are highly recommended. Relaxation methods are seldom used for initial value problems but they are naturally applicable to boundary value problems and in fact an initial value problem has to be converted to a boundary value one if relaxation is to be used.

Some predictor-corrector methods can be modified to be non-iterative but all will require special starting techniques to get under way.

General observations applicable to all methods

There will always be an optimum interval "h" of the argument (independent variable) and the method chosen should be able to take into account the need for changing this as the solution proceeds.

Build-up error due to rounding-off of differences can cause trouble. Two or three guarding figures should be held and there should always be running and terminal checks incorporated in any solution.

The stability of the method i.e. the convergence to the wanted solution, depends upon the differential equation as well as the method chosen. Starting with the last computed value and integrating in the reverse direction back to the original origin will check this.

The truncation error due to using a finite approximation to an infinite series will reduce the number of significant decimals obtained. However, this can be corrected at a later stage.

Any order differential equation can be reduced to a number of simultaneous differential equations of the first order and so the solution of first order differential equations is considered in detail. In some cases there will however be a loss of convenience if such a reduction is employed.

e.g.   Given $y'' = xy - \sin x$ with $y(0) = 1, \quad y'(0) = 0.$

This reduces to $y' = w$ with $y(0) = 1$

$z' = v$ $z(0) = 0$

$v' = -z$ $v(0) = 1$

$w' = xy - z$ $w(0) = 0$

DIRECT METHODS

Taylor's series

Applicable to all linear equations and those non-linear equations whose higher derivatives can be easily found.

e.g. $y' = f(x,y)$ i.e. $y^{(1)} = f(x,y^{(0)})$

then $y^{(n+1)} = \dfrac{\partial y^{(n)}}{\partial x} + y^{(1)} \dfrac{\partial y^{(n)}}{\partial y}$

(since $y^{(n)}$ can be reduced to a function of x and y only.)

Finally $x_1 = x_0 + h$

and $y_1 = y_0 + \dfrac{hy_0^{(1)}}{1!} + \dfrac{h^2 y_0^{(2)}}{2!} + \dfrac{h^3 y_0^{(3)}}{3!} + \dfrac{h^4 y_0^{(4)}}{4!} + \cdots$

In practice the computational procedure is simplified by introducing the reduced derivatives defined by

$$\tau^{(n)} \equiv \frac{h^n y^{(n)}}{n!} \qquad\qquad (\tau^{(0)} \equiv y)$$

from which it follows that $\dfrac{d\tau^{(n)}}{dx} = \dfrac{(n+1)\tau^{(n+1)}}{h}$

For linear equations a recurrence relationship is obtained by means of Leibnitz's theorem to generate any particular $\tau^{(n)}$ from the preceeding τ's. Thus, given the differential equation and the initial conditions, the sequence $\tau^{(0)}, \tau^{(1)}, \tau^{(2)}, \tau^{(3)}, \ldots, \tau^{(n)}$ is computed until the terms cease to have any significance with regard to the number of places of decimals required.

If the Taylor's series is re-arranged then not only can the new function value be computed but a running check on the previously computed value be obtained with a minimum of effort. This can also be applied to as many of the derivatives as are desired.

$$y_1 = (\tau_0^{(0)} + \tau_0^{(2)} + \tau_0^{(4)} + \tau_0^{(6)} \cdots) + (\tau_0^{(1)} + \tau_0^{(3)} + \tau_0^{(5)} + \cdots)$$
$$\tau_1^{(1)} = (2\tau_0^{(2)} + 4\tau_0^{(4)} + 6\tau_0^{(6)} + \cdots) + (\tau_0^{(1)} + 3\tau_0^{(3)} + 5\tau_0^{(5)} + \cdots)$$

The checking formulae corresponding to the above pair are

$$y_{-1} = (\tau_0^{(0)} + \tau_0^{(2)} + \tau_0^{(4)} + \tau_0^{(6)} \cdots) - (\tau_0^{(1)} + \tau_0^{(3)} + \tau_0^{(5)} \cdots)$$
$$\tau_{-1}^{(1)} = (2\tau_0^{(2)} + 4\tau_0^{(4)} + 6\tau_0^{(6)} + \cdots) - (\tau_0^{(1)} + 3\tau_0^{(3)} + 5\tau_0^{(5)} + \cdots)$$

It will be seen that the sums inside the brackets which are used to evaluate the y_1 and the $\tau_1^{(1)}$ are also used to evaluate the y_{-1} and the $\tau_{-1}^{(1)}$. A shift of origin from (x_0, y_0) to (x_1, y_1) is then made, in accordance with the usual procedure for advancing the solution of a differential equation, and the process repeated. If too many terms are necessary, before the τ's assume negligible proportions, then the interval of tabulation "h" should be reduced. Conversely, if only a few terms have significance, then "h" should be increased.

Computational layout for one such stage

x_0			y_0	
	$\tau_0^{(0)}$	$\tau_0^{(1)}$		
	$\tau_0^{(2)}$	$\tau_0^{(3)}$		
	$\tau_0^{(4)}$	$\tau_0^{(5)}$		
	$\cdots$	$\cdots\cdots$		
	$\tau_0^{(2n)}$	$\tau_0^{(2n+1)}$		
x_1	$\displaystyle\sum_{r=0}^{n}\tau_0^{(2n)}$	$\displaystyle\sum_{r=0}^{n}\tau_0^{(2n+1)}$	y_1	y_{-1}
	$\displaystyle\sum_{r=0}^{n}2r\tau_0^{(2r)}$	$\displaystyle\sum_{r=0}^{n}(2r+1)\tau_0^{(2r+1)}$	$\tau_1^{(1)}$	$\tau_{-1}^{(1)}$

Method of Runge-Kutta

An nth order Runge-Kutta process has an error of $0(h^{n+1})$. If $y' = f(x,y)$ then $y_1 = y_0 + K$, where K is the weighted mean of "n" evaluations of $h \cdot y'$ taken at specified points. There are an infinity of such formulae and the weights, and the constants necessary to determine the specified points, are tabulated for some simple cases only.

At any stage of the numerical solution, only the function value at the beginning of the stage need be known. This means that no special starting technique is necessary, but against this must be set the fact that the function must be evaluated "n" times per step. Further, previously computed values are not used to check the computation. Error analysis is not easy and the usual check is simply one of repeating the calculations at a different interval (one simple formula involving an error check is given at the end). Alternatively a finite difference check can be used.

If the functions are not smooth or if a frequent change in step length, particularly when such a change is expected to be a decrease, is envisaged then this process is of particular importance.

Second order systems   Error $= 0(h^3)$

Given $y' = f(x,y)$ and y_0
Then $x_1 = x_0 + h$ and $y_1 = y_0 + K$
where $K = \omega_1 k_1 + \omega_2 k_2$ $(\omega_1 + \omega_2 = 1)$
and $k_r = h \cdot f(x_0 + a_r h, y_0 + b_r k_1)$

Six typical systems are listed

(i)

r	a_r	b_r	ω_r
1	0	0	-1
2	$\frac{1}{4}$	$\frac{1}{4}$	2

(ii)

r	a_r	b_r	ω_r
1	0	0	0
2	$\frac{1}{2}$	$\frac{1}{2}$	1

(iii)

r	a_r	b_r	ω_r
1	0	0	$\frac{2}{3}$
2	$\frac{3}{4}$	$\frac{3}{4}$	$\frac{1}{3}$

(iv)

r	a_r	b_r	ω_r
1	0	0	$\frac{1}{2}$
2	1	1	$\frac{1}{2}$

(v)

r	a_r	b_r	ω_r
1	0	0	$\frac{1}{4}$
2	$\frac{2}{3}$	$\frac{2}{3}$	$\frac{3}{4}$

(vi)

r	a_r	b_r	ω_r
1	0	0	$-\frac{1}{2}$
2	$\frac{1}{3}$	$\frac{1}{3}$	$1\frac{1}{2}$

Third order systems   Error $= 0(h^4)$

Given $y' = f(x,y)$ and y_0
Then $x_1 = x_0 + h$ and $y_1 = y_0 + K$
where $K = \omega_1 k_1 + \omega_2 k_2 + \omega_3 k_3$ $(\omega_1 + \omega_2 + \omega_3 = 1)$
and $k_r = h \cdot f(x_0 + a_r h, y_0 + b_r k_1 + c_r k_2)$
Four typical systems are listed

(i)

r	a_r	b_r	c_r	ω_r
1	0	0	0	$\frac{2}{3}$
2	$\frac{1}{4}$	$\frac{1}{4}$	0	$-\frac{4}{3}$
3	$\frac{1}{2}$	$\frac{1}{10}$	$\frac{2}{5}$	$\frac{5}{3}$

(ii)

r	a_r	b_r	c_r	ω_r
1	0	0	0	$\frac{1}{4}$
2	$\frac{1}{3}$	$\frac{1}{3}$	0	0
3	$\frac{2}{3}$	0	$\frac{2}{3}$	$\frac{3}{4}$

(iii)	r	a_r	b_r	c_r	ω_r
	1	0	0	0	$\frac{1}{6}$
	2	$\frac{1}{2}$	$\frac{1}{2}$	0	$\frac{2}{3}$
	3	1	-1	2	$\frac{1}{6}$

(iv)	r	a_r	b_r	c_r	ω_r
	1	0	0	0	$\frac{1}{4}$
	2	$\frac{2}{3}$	$\frac{2}{3}$	0	$\frac{1}{2}$
	3	$\frac{2}{3}$	$-\frac{1}{3}$	1	$\frac{1}{4}$

Fourth order systems   Error $= (h^5)$

Given $y' = f(x,y)$ and y_0
Then $x_1 = x_0 + h$ and $y_1 = y_0 + K$
where $K = \omega_1 k_1 + \omega_2 k_2 + \omega_3 k_3 + \omega_4 k_4$ $(\omega_1 + \omega_2 + \omega_3 + \omega_4 = 1)$
and $k_r = h \cdot f(x_0 + a_r, y_0 + b_r k_1 + c_r k_2 + d_r k_3)$

Four typical systems are listed. The third is of particular importance both from the point of view of simplicity of numerical constants and of and the sequential relationships between the various k's.

(i)	r	a_r	b_r	c_r	d_r	ω_r
	1	0	0	0	0	$\frac{1}{8}$
	2	$\frac{1}{3}$	$\frac{1}{3}$	0	0	$\frac{3}{8}$
	3	$\frac{2}{3}$	$-\frac{1}{3}$	1	0	$\frac{3}{8}$
	4	1	1	-1	1	$\frac{1}{8}$

(ii)	r	a_r	b_r	c_r	d_r	ω_r
	1	0	0	0	0	$\frac{1}{6}$
	2	1	1	0	0	0
	3	$\frac{1}{2}$	$\frac{3}{8}$	$\frac{1}{8}$	0	$\frac{2}{3}$
	4	1	$-\frac{1}{2}$	$-\frac{1}{2}$	2	$\frac{1}{6}$

(iii)	r	a_r	b_r	c_r	d_r	ω_r
	1	0	0	0	0	$\frac{1}{6}$
	2	$\frac{1}{2}$	$\frac{1}{2}$	0	0	$\frac{1}{3}$
	3	$\frac{1}{2}$	0	$\frac{1}{2}$	0	$\frac{1}{3}$
	4	1	0	0	1	$\frac{1}{6}$

(iv)	r	a_r	b_r	c_r	d_r	ω_r
	1	0	0	0	0	0
	2	$\frac{1}{2}$	$\frac{1}{2}$	0	0	$\frac{2}{3}$
	3	0	$-\frac{1}{2}$	$\frac{1}{2}$	0	$\frac{1}{6}$
	4	1	$-\frac{1}{2}$	$1\frac{1}{2}$	1	$\frac{1}{6}$

Fifth order systems   Error $= 0(h^6)$

The number of terms required to form the weighted mean "K" increases, for orders greater than the fourth and, in addition, the coefficients are much less easy to handle.
The following system requires one additional term.
Given $y' = f(x,y)$ and y_0
Then $x_1 = x_0 + h$, and $y_1 = y_0 + K$
where $K = \omega_1 k_1 + \omega_2 k_2 + \omega_3 k_3 + \omega_4 k_4 + \omega_5 k_5 + \omega_6 k_6$
$(\omega_1 + \omega_2 + \omega_3 + \omega_4 + \omega_5 + \omega_6 = 1)$
and $k_r = h \cdot f(x_0 + a_r h, y_0 + b_r k_1 + c_r k_2 + d_r k_3 + e_r k_4 + f_r k_5)$

r	a_r	b_r	c_r	d_r	e_r	f_r	ω_r
1	0	0	0	0	0	0	$23/192$
2	$\frac{1}{3}$	$\frac{1}{3}$	0	0	0	0	0
3	$\frac{2}{5}$	$\frac{4}{25}$	$\frac{6}{25}$	0	0	0	$125/192$
4	1	$\frac{1}{4}$	-3	$\frac{15}{4}$	0	0	0
5	$\frac{2}{3}$	$\frac{2}{27}$	$\frac{10}{9}$	$-\frac{50}{81}$	$\frac{8}{81}$	0	$-27/64$
6	$\frac{4}{5}$	$\frac{2}{25}$	$\frac{12}{25}$	$\frac{2}{15}$	$\frac{8}{75}$	0	$125/192$

An example of computational layout

Consider formula (iii) of the fourth order systems. On substituting the values from the table the resulting formulae are as follows

$$y' = f(x,y)$$
$$x_1 = x_0 + h$$
$$k_1 = h \cdot f(x_0, y_0)$$
$$k_2 = h \cdot f(x_0 + \tfrac{1}{2}h,\ y_0 + \tfrac{1}{2}k_1)$$
$$k_3 = h \cdot f(x_0 + \tfrac{1}{2}h,\ y_0 + \tfrac{1}{2}k_2)$$
$$k_4 = h \cdot f(x_0 + h,\ y_0 + k_3)$$
$$y_1 = y_0 + \tfrac{1}{6}(k_1 + 2k_2 + 2k_3 + k_4)$$

and the layout of one state of the calculation is

x	y	$k_r = hy'$	K
x_0	y_0	k_1	
$x_0 + \tfrac{1}{2}h$	$y_0 + \tfrac{1}{2}k_1$	k_2	
$x_0 + \tfrac{1}{2}h$	$y_0 + \tfrac{1}{2}k_2$	k_3	
$x_0 + h$	$y_0 + k_3$	k_4	
			$(k_1 + 2k_2 + 2k_3 + k_4)$
$x_1 = x_0 + h$	$y_1 = y_0 + K$		

The starting values for this stage are underlined.

Extension of the Runge-Kutta approach to simultaneous differential equations

Consider again table (iii) of the fourth order systems. It can be extended to cover any number of simultaneous D.E's. The extension to two is shown in detail and the general case can be easily deduced from it.

$$\text{Given}\quad y' = f(x,y,z)$$
$$\text{and}\quad z' = g(x,y,z)$$
$$x_1 = x_0 + h$$
$$\text{we obtain}\quad y_1 = y_0 + K$$
$$\text{and}\quad z_1 = z_0 + M$$

where $\quad K = \omega_1 k_1 + \omega_2 k_2 + \omega_3 k_3 + \omega_4 k_4$

$\qquad\qquad M = \omega_1 m_1 + \omega_2 m_2 + \omega_3 m_3 + \omega_4 m_4$

and $\quad k_1 = h \cdot f(x_0, y_0, z_0)$

$\qquad\qquad k_2 = h \cdot f(x_0 + \tfrac{1}{2}h, y_0 + \tfrac{1}{2}k_1, z_0 + \tfrac{1}{2}m_1)$

$\qquad\qquad k_3 = h \cdot f(x_0 + \tfrac{1}{2}h, y_0 + \tfrac{1}{2}k_2, z_0 + \tfrac{1}{2}m_2)$

$\qquad\qquad k_4 = h \cdot f(x_0 + h, y_0 + k_3, z_0 + m_3)$

and $\quad m_1 = h \cdot g(x_0, y_0, z_0)$

$\qquad\qquad m_2 = h \cdot g(x_0 + \tfrac{1}{2}h, y_0 + \tfrac{1}{2}k_1, z_0 + \tfrac{1}{2}m_1)$

$\qquad\qquad m_3 = h \cdot g(x_0 + \tfrac{1}{2}h, y_0 + \tfrac{1}{2}k_2, z_0 + \tfrac{1}{2}m_2)$

$\qquad\qquad m_4 = h \cdot g(x_0 + h, y_0 + k_3, z_0 + m_3)$

and the computational layout will be similar to the previous one

x	y	z	$k_r = hf$ $K = \Sigma \omega_r k_r$	$m_r = hg$ $M = \Sigma \omega_r m_r$
x_0	y_0	z_0	k_1	m_1
$x_0 + \tfrac{1}{2}h$	$y_0 + \tfrac{1}{2}k_1$	$z_0 + \tfrac{1}{2}m_1$	k_2	m_2
$x_0 + \tfrac{1}{2}h$	$y_0 + \tfrac{1}{2}k_2$	$z_0 + \tfrac{1}{2}m_2$	k_3	m_3
$x_0 + h$	$y_0 + k_3$	$z_0 + m_3$	k_4	m_4
			"K"	"M"
$x_1 = x_0 + h$	$y_1 = y_0 + K$	$z_1 = z_0 + M$		

The use of Runge-Kutta techniques for higher order differential equations

A schematic for the general second order differential equation is shown.

Given $y'' = f(x, y, y')$ and y_0, y_0' the reduced derivatives can be used i.e.

$$\tau^{(n)} \equiv \frac{h^n}{n!} \cdot y^{(n)}$$

Then $\quad y'' = f\left(x, y, \dfrac{\tau^{(1)}}{h}\right)$

and $\quad x_1 = x_0 + h$

$\qquad\quad y_1 = y_0 + \tau_0^{(1)} + K$

$\qquad\quad \tau_1^{(1)} = \tau_0^{(1)} + K'$

where $\quad K = \displaystyle\sum_{r=1}^{4} \omega_r k_r \qquad\qquad \left(1 = \displaystyle\sum_{r=1}^{4} \omega_r\right)$

and $\quad K' = \displaystyle\sum_{r=1}^{4} \omega_r' k_r \qquad\qquad \left(1 = \displaystyle\sum_{r=1}^{4} \omega_r'\right)$

$\quad k_r = \dfrac{h^2}{2} \cdot f(x_0 + a_r h, y_0 + b_r \tau_0^{(1)} + c_r k_1 + d_r k_2 + e_r k_3, \{\tau_0^{(1)} + g_r k_{r-1}\}/h)$

r	a_r	b_r	c_r	d_r	e_r	g_r	ω_r	ω_r'
1	0	0	0	0	0	0	0	$\frac{1}{3}$
2	$\frac{1}{2}$	$\frac{1}{2}$	$\frac{1}{4}$	0	0	1	$\frac{1}{3}$	$\frac{2}{3}$
3	$\frac{1}{2}$	$\frac{1}{2}$	$\frac{1}{4}$	0	0	1	$\frac{1}{3}$	$\frac{3}{2}$
4	1	1	0	0	1	2	$\frac{1}{3}$	$\frac{1}{3}$

The computational layout being as follows

x	y	τ	k, K, K'
x_0	y_0	$\tau_0^{(1)}$	k_1
$x_0 + \frac{1}{2}h$	$y_0 + \frac{1}{2}\tau_0^{(1)} + \frac{1}{4}k_1$	$\tau_0^{(1)} + k_1$	k_2
$x_0 + \frac{1}{2}h$	$y_0 + \frac{1}{2}\tau_0^{(1)} + \frac{1}{4}k_1$	$\tau_0^{(1)} + k_2$	k_3
$x_0 + h$	$y_0 + \tau_0^{(1)} + k_3$	$\tau_0^{(1)} + 2k_3$	k_4
			K
			K'

$$x_1 = x_0 + h \qquad y_1 = y_0 + \tau_0^{(1)} + K\tau_1^{(1)} = \tau_0^{(1)} + K'$$

where
$$K = \omega_1 k_1 + \omega_2 k_2 + \omega_3 k_3 + \omega_4 k_4$$
$$K' = \omega_1' k_1 + \omega_2' k_2 + \omega_3' k_3 + \omega_4' k_4$$

Chebyshev Polynomials (1)

The Chebyshev polynomial of degree r in x where $-1 \leqq x \leqq 1$ is denoted by $T_r \equiv T_r(x)$.

$$T_r(x) \equiv \cos{(r \cdot \cos^{-1} x)}$$
$$\text{and } 2x \cdot T_r = T_{r+1} + T_{r-1}$$

The shifted Chebyshev polynomials of degree r in x where $0 \leqq x \leqq 1$ are denoted by $T_r^* \equiv T_r^*(x)$.

$$T_r^*(x) \equiv \cos{(r \cdot \cos^{-1} (2x - 1))}$$
$$\text{and } 2(2x - 1) \cdot T_r^* = T_{r+1}^* + T_{r-1}^*$$

N.B. $T_r^*(x^2) = T_{2r}(x)$

Both types of polynomials can be used for linear differential equations over a finite interval. The equation is assumed to have polynomial coefficients—if not then suitable polynomial approximations should be inserted. The finite range must first be normalized to either $(-1,1)$ or $(0,1)$.

a) Chebyshev polynomials

$$T_0 = 1$$
$$T_r(1) = 1$$
$$T_r(-1) = (-1)^r$$
$$T_{2r}(0) = (-1)^r$$
$$T_{2r+1}(0) = 0$$

The solution of the equation $y^{(1)} = f(x,y)$ is assumed to have the form

$$y = \tfrac{1}{2}a_0 + a_1 T_1 + a_2 T_2 + a_3 T_3 + a_4 T_4 + \cdots$$

where $a_r = 0$ for all $r > N$

i.e.
$$y = \tfrac{1}{2}a_0 + a_1 T_1 + a_2 T_2 + \cdots + a_N T_N.$$

similarly
$$y^{(1)} = \tfrac{1}{2}a_0^{(1)} + \sum_{r=1}^{N} a_r^{(1)} T_r, \text{ etc.}$$

Writing $C_r(y^{(s)}) \equiv$ the coefficient of T_r in the expansion of $y^{(s)}$ (the s th derivative of y with respect to x)

$$C_r(y^{(s)}) = a_r^{(s)} \tag{1}$$

Further
$$C_r(xy) = \tfrac{1}{2}(a_{r+1} + a_{r-1})$$

and
$$C_r(x^2 y) = \tfrac{1}{4}(a_{r+2} + 2a_r + a_{r-2})$$

in general
$$C_r(x^p y^{(s)}) = 2^{-p} \sum_{i=0}^{p} \binom{p}{i} a_{|r-p+2i|}^{(s)} \qquad \left(\begin{matrix} r = 0,1,2 \cdots \\ s = 1,2, \cdots \end{matrix} \right) \tag{2}$$

In addition the Chebyshev recurrence relationship itself yields

$$a_{r-1}^{(s)} = 2r \cdot a_r^{(s-1)} + a_{r+1}^{(s)} \tag{3}$$

Method of solution

(i) Obtain a relationship between the a's and the $a^{(1)}$'s from $C_r\{y^{(1)} - f(x,y)\} = 0$, e.g. If $(x^2 + 1)y^{(1)} - 4xy = 0$.

Then
$$a_{r-2}^{(1)} + 6a_r^{(1)} + a_{r+2}^{(1)} - 8a_{r-1} - 8a_{r+1} = 0 \tag{4}$$
since
$$C_r\{x^2 y^{(1)}\} + C_r\{y^{(1)}\} - 4C_r\{xy\} = 0$$

(ii) From (3) with $s = 1$.

$$a_{r-1}^{(1)} = 2ra_r + a_{r+1}^{(1)} \tag{5}$$

(iii) Substitute (5) into (4) in such a manner that the suffix of one of the a's is *less* than all the other suffices. The above example yields

$$2(r - 5)a_{r-1} = 8a_{r+1} - 7a_r^{(1)} - a_{r+2}^{(1)} \tag{4a}$$

(iv) Equations (4a) and (5) are then used to generate the a's and $a^{(1)}$'s by recurrence *backwards* from some arbitrarily chosen values of a_N and $a_N^{(1)}$.

e.g.   Set $a_N = 1$, $\quad a_N^{(1)} = 1 \quad$ and $\quad a_r = a_r^{(1)} = 0$, $\quad$ all $r > N$

The values found will however be far too large, in general, so a scale factor has to be determined.

(v) The initial conditions will be given either at the origin or at the extremities of the range.

Noting that
$$y(0) \;\; = \tfrac{1}{2}a_0 - a_2 + a_4 - a_6 + a_8 \cdots$$
$$y(1) \;\; = \tfrac{1}{2}a_0 + a_1 + a_2 + a_3 + a_4 \cdots$$
$$y(-1) = \tfrac{1}{2}a_0 - a_1 + a_2 - a_3 + a_4 \cdots$$

If $y(0)$ is given then the scale factor is

$$K = y(0)/(\tfrac{1}{2}a_0 - a_1 + a_2 - a_3 + a_4 \cdots)$$

where the values inside the brackets are the values just computed.

(vi) The values for $a_r^{(1)}$ just computed, when multiplied by K, should satisfy the given equation at the origin i.e. $y^{(1)} = f(x,y)$ at $x = 0$, $y = y(0)$,

or $y^{(1)}(0) = K(\frac{1}{2}a_0^{(1)} - a_2^{(1)} + a_4^{(1)} - a_6^{(1)} + \cdots)$

This in general will not be the case and so the computation is repeated with different starting values for the a_N and the $a_N^{(1)}$. A linear combination of the two sets is then chosen so that both the a's *and* the $a^{(1)}$'s satisfy the given conditions.

The method can be extended to equations of higher degree if the necessary $a_r^{(s)}$ are tabulated. This will, of course, necessitate a linear combination of $s + 1$ sets of results.

(b) Shifted Chebyshev polynomials
   Fundamental values

$$T_0^* = 1$$

$$T_r^*(1) = 1$$

$$T_{2r}^*(\tfrac{1}{2}) = (-1)^r$$

$$T_{2r+1}^*(\tfrac{1}{2}) = 0$$

$$T_{2r}^*(0) = 1$$

$$T_{2r+1}^*(0) = -1$$

And correspondingly

$$y = \tfrac{1}{2}a_0 + a_1 T_1^* + a_2 T_2^* + \cdots + a_N T_N^*$$
$$C_r^*(y^{(s)}) = a_r^{(s)}$$

$$C_r^*(x^p y^{(s)}) = 2^{-2p} \sum_{i=0}^{2p} \binom{2p}{i} a_{|r-p+i|}^{(s)} \qquad \left(\begin{array}{l} r = 0,1,2 \cdots \\ s = 1,2, \cdots \end{array}\right)$$

also $a_{r-1}^{(s)} = 4r \ a_r^{(s-1)} + a_{r+1}^{(s)}$

In addition the initial values yield

$$y(0) = \tfrac{1}{2}a_0 - a_1 + a_2 - a_3 + \cdots$$

$$y(\tfrac{1}{2}) = \tfrac{1}{2}a_0 - a_2 + a_4 - a_6 + \cdots$$

$$y(1) = \tfrac{1}{2}a_0 + a_1 + a_2 + a_3 + \cdots$$

The computational procedure being identical with that of the preceding section.

ITERATIVE METHODS

With the iterative methods of solution of differential equations, two fundamental approaches exist
   a) Point iteration.
   b) Block iteration.
In the former, the solution at each point is refined as far as is necessary before the next point is considered. The latter, on the other hand, involves successive sweeps over the whole range of integration until no further improvement is detected.

With either group of methods the number of iterations should be small, i.e. if more than three or four applications of the iterative formula in question are necessary then the interval of tabulation should be reduced—in practice this is usually taken to mean halved.

The restriction on the number of iterations does not apply to the Chebyshev method since here the coefficients of an approximating polynomial are being determined and thus the iterations are continued until the required number of significant places is obtained. The solution of the differential equation is then obtained by direct substitution into the polynomial.

When only one starting value is given, as is usual at the beginning of the tabulation of a first order equation, then special starting techniques are necessary for the point iteration approach as a knowledge of the function at several consecutive points is necessary before it can be evaluated at the next point. Either one of the direct methods previously tabulated can be invoked or an iterative starting formula used.

With the iterative predictor-corrector methods, the starting formulae are of the same type.

Doubling the interval of tabulation does not give any trouble with the point iteration schemes whereas halving the interval requires the use of an interpolation routine.

The block iteration schemes require a fresh start to be made if the interval is to be changed.

Iterative Starting Formulae

Notation used:
$$x_r \equiv x_0 + rh$$
$$y_r \equiv y(x_r)$$
$$f_r \equiv f(x_r,y_r) \equiv hy'_r$$
$$E_r \equiv \text{The truncation error in the expression for } y_r.$$

The superscript (ν) denotes the νth iterate.

Since the iterative starting formulae require initial values to be inserted the first iterative values are obtained from

$$y_r^{(1)} = y_0 + rf_0 \qquad r = 1(1)n - 1$$

This enables "n" starting values to be determined, including the given value y_0, for use with the following groups of formulae.

It will be seen that the values of y_0 and f_0 are unaltered as they will be the given values; f_0 being simply a function of h, x_0 and y_0 determined by the differential equation in question. Further, as each of the other values are refined, they are used in the succeeding equations.

E.g., anticipating the table associated with $n = 3$ in group 1, we obtain, on writing out the formulae in full

$$y_1^{(\nu+1)} = \left(y_0 + \frac{5}{12}f_0\right) + \frac{(8f_1^{(\nu)} - f_2^{(\nu)})}{12} + \frac{\delta^3}{24}$$

$$y_2^{(\nu+1)} = \left(y_0 + \frac{1}{3}f_0\right) + \frac{4}{3}f_1^{(\nu+1)} + \frac{1}{3}f_2^{(\nu)} - \frac{\delta^4}{90}$$

The worst error term in the above is $\delta^3/24$ and thus for the contribution from this source to be less than $1/2$ unit in the last significant figure $\delta^3/24 < 1/2$ i.e. $\delta^3 < 12$. If this is not so then the interval h must be reduced.

The coefficients A_{rs} (and A_{rs}^*) can be expressed as rational fractions in the form $A_{rs} = $ Numerator of $A_{rs}/D_r \equiv$ Num. A_{rs}/D_r. The tabulation will therefore be of

Num. A_{rs}	D_r	E_r
$s = 0(1)n - 1$ $r = 1(1)n - 1$	$r = 1(1)n - 1$	$r = 1(1)n - 1$

where E_r indicates the principal error term associated with f_r.

Group 1

$$y_1^{(\nu+1)} = y_0 + A_{10}f_0 + \sum_{s=1}^{n-1} A_{1s}f_s^{(\nu)} + E_1$$

$$y_r^{(\nu+1)} = y_0 + A_{r0}f_0 + \sum_{s=1}^{r-1} A_{rs}f_s^{(\nu+1)} + \sum_{s=r}^{n-1} A_{rs}f_s^{(\nu)} + E_r, \quad r = 2(1)n - 1$$

$n = 2$

	Num. A_{rs}		D_r	E_r
r $\diagdown$ s	0	1		
1	1	1	2	$-\dfrac{1}{12}\delta^2$

Requires $\delta^2 < 6$

$n = 3$

	Num. A_{rs}			D_r	E_r
r $\diagdown$ s	0	1	2		
1	5	8	-1	12	$\dfrac{1}{24}\delta^3$
2	1	4	1	3	$-\dfrac{1}{90}\delta^4$

Requires $\delta^3 < 12$

$n = 4$

	Num. A_{rs}				D_r	E_r
r $\diagdown$ s	0	1	2	3		
1	9	19	-5	1	24	$-\dfrac{19}{720}\delta^4$
2	1	4	1	0	3	$-\dfrac{1}{90}\delta^4$
3	3	9	9	3	8	$-\dfrac{3}{80}\delta^4$

Requires $\delta^4 < 13$

$n = 5$

	Num. A_{rs}					D_r	E_r
r $\diagdown$ s	0	1	2	3	4		
1	251	646	-264	106	-19	720	$\dfrac{3}{160}\delta^5$
2	29	124	24	4	-1	90	$\dfrac{1}{90}\delta^5$
3	27	102	72	42	-3	80	$\dfrac{3}{160}\delta^5$
4	14	64	24	64	14	45	$-\dfrac{1}{105}\delta^6$

Requires $\delta^5 < 27$

$n = 6$

	Num. A_{rs}						D_r	E_r
r $\diagdown$ s	0	1	2	3	4	5		
1	493	1337	-618	302	-83	9	1440	$-\dfrac{14}{695}\delta^6$
2	28	129	14	14	-6	1	90	$-\dfrac{1}{105}\delta^6$
3	51	219	114	114	-21	3	160	$-\dfrac{3}{224}\delta^6$
4	28	128	48	128	28	0	90	$-\dfrac{1}{105}\delta^6$
5	95	375	250	250	375	95	288	$-\dfrac{1}{42}\delta^6$

Requires $\delta^6 < 21$

Group 2

The formulae of this group involve the function values as well as the derivatives and consequently tend to have smaller truncation errors.

$$y_r^{(\nu+1)} = \sum_{s=0}^{r-1} A_{rs}^* y_s^{(\nu+1)} + \sum_{s=0}^{r-1} A_{rs} f_s^{(\nu+1)} + \sum_{s=r}^{n-1} A_{rs} f_s^{(\nu)} + E_r, \qquad r = 1(1)n-1$$

$n = 4$

s	Num. A_{rs}			Num. A_{rs}				D_r	E_r
r	0	1	2	0	1	2	3		
1	24	0	0	9	19	-5	1	24	$-\dfrac{19}{720}\delta^4$
2	33	24	0	10	57	24	-1	57	$\dfrac{1}{342}\delta^5$
3	11	27	-27	3	27	27	3	11	$-\dfrac{1}{513}\delta^6$

Requires $\delta^4 < 18$

$n = 5$

s	Num. A_{rs}^*				Num. A_{rs}					D_r	E_r
r	0	1	2	3	0	1	2	3	4		
1	720	0	0	0	251	646	-264	106	-19	720	$\dfrac{3}{160}\delta^5$
2	990	1440	0	0	281	2056	1176	-104	11	2430	$-\dfrac{1}{729}\delta^6$
3	550	2160	-1350	0	141	1656	2376	456	-9	1360	$\dfrac{1}{2539}\delta^7$
4	25	160	0	-160	6	96	216	96	6	25	$-\dfrac{1}{2625}\delta^8$

Requires $\delta^5 < 27$

$n = 6$

s	Num. A_{rs}^*				
r	0	1	2	3	4
1	1440	0	0	0	0
2	24390	53280	0	0	0
3	9550	51570	-17550	0	0
4	3425	29560	14040	-35960	0
5	137	1625	2000	-2000	-1625

s	Num. A_{rs}						D_r	E_r
r	0	1	2	3	4	5		
1	475	1427	-798	482	-173	27	1440	$-\dfrac{1}{70}\delta^6$
2	6589	58528	41608	-5752	1223	-136	77670	$\dfrac{31}{290}\delta^7$
3	2337	33687	62352	16512	-693	45	43570	$-\dfrac{1}{9072}\delta^8$
4	786	15540	45720	29280	3210	-36	11065	$\dfrac{1}{16800}\delta^9$
5	30	750	3000	3000	750	30	137	$-\dfrac{1}{12659}\delta^{10}$

Requires $\delta^6 < 35$

Group 3

In this group neither y_r nor f_r appears on the right hand side i.e. $A_{ss}^* \equiv A_{ss} \equiv 0$.

$$y_r^{(\nu+1)} = \sum_{s=0}^{r-1} A_{rs}^* y_s^{(\nu+1)} + \sum_{s=r+1}^{n-1} A_{rs}^* y^{(\nu)} + \sum_{s=0}^{r-1} A_{rs} f^{(\nu+1)} + \sum_{s=r+1}^{n-1} A_{rs} f^{(\nu)} + E_r$$

$n = 3$

	Num. A_{rs}^*			Num. A_{rs}			D_r	E_r
r \ s	0	1	2	0	1	2		
1	2	0	2	1	0	-1	4	$\dfrac{1}{24}\delta^3$
2	5	-4	0	2	4	0	1	$\dfrac{1}{12}\delta^3$

Requires $\delta^3 < 6$

$n = 4$

	Num. A_{rs}^*				Num. A_{rs}				D_r	E_r
r \ s	0	1	2	3	0	1	2	3		
1	8	0	0	19	3	0	-27	-6	27	$\dfrac{1}{180}\delta^5$
2	19	0	0	8	6	27	0	-3	27	$\dfrac{1}{180}\delta^5$
3	10	9	-18	0	3	18	9	0	1	$\dfrac{1}{20}\delta^5$

Requires $\delta^5 < 10$

$n = 5$

	Num. A_{rs}^*					Num. A_{rs}					D_r	E_r
r \ s	0	1	2	3	4	0	1	2	3	4		
1	19	0	-216	224	69	6	0	-216	-192	-18	96	$\dfrac{1}{1120}\delta^7$
2	11	16	0	16	11	3	24	0	-24	-3	54	$\dfrac{1}{2520}\delta^7$
3	69	224	-216	0	19	18	192	216	0	-6	96	$\dfrac{1}{805}\delta^7$
4	47	192	-108	-128	0	12	144	216	48	0	3	$\dfrac{1}{70}\delta^7$

Requires $\delta^7 < 35$

Group 4

In this group the starting values are symmetrically placed with respect to the origin. These formulae usually have a better truncation error and their coefficients exhibit a certain degree of skew symmetry.

Assuming that y_r, and hence f_r, are found before y_{-r} and f_{-r} the formulae used are, for $N \equiv (n-1)/2$ where n denotes the odd number of points involved, as follows

$$y_r^{(\nu+1)} = y_0 + \sum_{s=-N}^{-r} A_{rs} f_s^{(\nu)} + \sum_{s=-r+1}^{r-1} A_{rs} f_s^{(\nu+1)} + \sum_{s=r}^{N} A_{rs} f_s^{(\nu)} + E_r$$

which is followed immediately by

$$y_{-r}^{(\nu+1)} = y_0 + \sum_{s=-N}^{-r} A_{rs} f_s^{(\nu)} + \sum_{s=-r+1}^{r} A_{rs} f_s^{(\nu+1)} + \sum_{s=r+1}^{N} A_{rs} f_s^{(r)} + E_r$$

The formulae are tabulated in the order in which they are to be used i.e. $r = 1, -1, 2, -2, 3, -3$.

$n = 3$

r \ s	-1	0	1	D_r	E_r
1	-1	8	5	12	$-\dfrac{1}{24}\delta^3$
-1	-5	-8	1	12	$-\dfrac{1}{24}\delta^3$

(Num. A_{rs})

Requires $\delta^3 < 12$

$n = 5$

r \ s	-2	-1	0	1	2	D_r	E_r
1	11	-74	456	346	-19	720	$\dfrac{1}{144}\delta^5$
-1	19	-346	-456	74	-11	720	$\dfrac{1}{144}\delta^5$
2	-1	4	24	124	29	90	$-\dfrac{1}{90}\delta^5$
-2	-29	-124	-24	-4	1	90	$-\dfrac{1}{90}\delta^5$

(Num. A_{rs})

Requires $\delta^5 < 45$

$n = 7$

r \ s	-3	-2	-1	0	1	2	3	D_r	E_r
1	-191	1608	-6771	37504	30819	-2760	271	60480	$\dfrac{1}{633}\delta^7$
-1	-271	2760	-30819	-37504	6771	-1608	191	60480	$\dfrac{1}{633}\delta^7$
2	5	-30	33	1328	4863	1398	-37	3780	$\dfrac{1}{8172}\delta^7$
-2	37	-1398	-4863	-1328	-33	30	-5	3780	$\dfrac{1}{8172}\delta^7$
3	-29	216	-729	2176	1161	3240	685	2240	$\dfrac{9}{896}\delta^7$
-3	-685	-3240	-1161	-2176	729	-216	29	2240	$\dfrac{9}{896}\delta^7$

(Num. A_{rs})

Requires $\delta^7 < 50$

Group 5

As group 4, with the addition of function values. The same observations apply. y_0 and f_0 do not alter from cycle to cycle. Defining N the same as for group 4, the formulae used are:

$$y_r^{(\nu+1)} = \sum_{s=-N}^{-r} A_{rs}^* y_s^{(\nu)} + \sum_{s=-r+1}^{r-1} A_{rs}^* y_s^{(\nu+1)} + \sum_{s=r}^{N} A_{rs}^* y_s^{(\nu)}$$

$$+ \sum_{s=-N}^{-r} A_{rs} f_s^{(\nu)} + \sum_{s=-r+1}^{r-1} A_{rs} f_s^{(\nu+1)} + \sum_{s=r}^{N} A_{rs} f_s^{(\nu)} + E_r$$

$n = 5$ Num. A_{rs}^{*}

r \ s	-2	-1	0	1	2
1	-85	0	540	0	-135
-1	-135	0	540	0	-85
2	0	1360	1350	-2160	0
-2	0	-2160	1350	1360	0

Num. A_{rs}

r \ s	-2	-1	0	1	2	D_r	E_r
1	-24	-144	216	336	36	320	$-\dfrac{1}{1643}\,\delta^7$
-1	-36	-336	-216	144	24	320	$-\dfrac{1}{1643}\,\delta^7$
2	-9	456	2376	1656	141	550	$-\dfrac{1}{1067}\,\delta^7$
-2	-141	-1656	-2376	-456	9	550	$-\dfrac{1}{1067}\,\delta^7$

Requires $\delta^7 < 533$

The coefficients become unwieldy for higher values of n.

Continuing the solution

Two formulae are used to continue the solution once sufficient starting values have been obtained. The first, the "predictor," is used to obtain an estimate of the next value. It is used once only and can be appreciably less accurate than the second, the "corrector," which determines the precision.

The corrector is used iteratively until sufficient significant figures are obtained.

Predictors and correctors can involve either backward differences, central differences or function values.

Predictor-corrector formulae involving backward differences

A typical predictor formula is

$$y_1 = y_0 + \left(1 + \frac{1}{2}\nabla + \frac{5}{12}\nabla^2 + \frac{3}{8}\nabla^3 + \frac{251}{720}\nabla^4 + \frac{95}{288}\nabla^5 + \frac{19087}{60480}\nabla^6 + \cdots\right)f_0$$

this is followed by

$$f_1 = h \cdot y_1',$$

where y' is defined as a function of x and y.

PREDICTOR-CORRECTOR METHODS

This predicted value of f_1 is used to generate all the backward differences ∇_1^r for $r = 1(1)6$.

These are then used with a corrector formula such as

$$y_1 = y_0 + \left(1 - \frac{1}{2}\nabla - \frac{1}{12}\nabla^2 - \frac{1}{24}\nabla^3 - \frac{19}{720}\nabla^4 - \frac{3}{160}\nabla^5 - \frac{863}{60480}\nabla^6 - \cdots\right)f_1$$

to recompute y_1 and thus f_1. Note that all the backward differences ∇_1^r must then be recomputed before the corrector is applied once more.

The numerical coefficients tend to be rather high and round-off errors can become troublesome if differences beyond ∇^6 are significant.

An alternative method of *prediction* when one particular column of differences is nearly constant (say for example $\nabla^6 \sim k$) is to use the recurrence formula

$$\nabla_1^{r-1} = \nabla_1^r + \nabla_0^{r-1}$$

to generate the required differences. The overall effect is as if

$$f_1 = (1 + \nabla + \nabla^2 + \nabla^3 + \nabla^4 + \nabla^5]f_0 + k$$

had been used as a predictor.

Even when ∇^6 is not constant it can usually be estimated with sufficient accuracy from the preceding entries in the column, i.e., it is extrapolated from a knowledge of the previous differences, and is then used in the predictor

$$f_1 = (1 + \nabla + \nabla^2 + \nabla^3 + \nabla^4 + \nabla^5)f_0 + \nabla^6 f.$$

The corrector quoted in the example is the first of a group of such formulae having the general form

$$y_1 = y_r + \sum_{s=0} A_{rs}\nabla_s f_1 \qquad r < 0.$$

Truncating the infinite series at $s = 6$, we have

r \ s	0	1	2	3	4	5	6
0	1	$-\dfrac{1}{2}$	$-\dfrac{1}{12}$	$-\dfrac{1}{24}$	$-\dfrac{19}{720}$	$-\dfrac{3}{160}$	$-\dfrac{863}{60480}$
-1	2	-2	$\dfrac{1}{3}$	0	$-\dfrac{1}{90}$	$-\dfrac{1}{90}$	$-\dfrac{37}{3780}$
-2	3	$-\dfrac{9}{2}$	$\dfrac{9}{4}$	$-\dfrac{3}{8}$	$-\dfrac{3}{80}$	$-\dfrac{3}{160}$	$-\dfrac{29}{2240}$
-3	4	-8	$\dfrac{20}{3}$	$-\dfrac{8}{3}$	$\dfrac{14}{45}$	0	$-\dfrac{8}{945}$
-4	5	$-\dfrac{25}{2}$	$\dfrac{175}{12}$	$-\dfrac{225}{24}$	$\dfrac{425}{144}$	$-\dfrac{95}{288}$	$-\dfrac{275}{12096}$
-5	6	-18	27	-24	$\dfrac{123}{10}$	$-\dfrac{33}{10}$	$\dfrac{41}{140}$

Caption above table: A_{rs}

Predictor-corrector formulae involving central differences

In these formulae, the predictors and the correctors have the same form. In fact the corrector has the same coefficients as the predictor on the previous line of the table with the addition of one more term, together with an estimate of the error.

The formulae involved are

Predictor
$$y_1 = y_{1-2r} + \sum_{s=0}^{r-1} A_{rs}\delta^{2s}f_{1-r}$$

Corrector
$$y_1 = y_{3-2r} + \sum_{s=0}^{r-1} B_{rs}\delta^{2s}f_{2-r} + \text{Error} \ (\equiv B_{rr}\delta^{2r})$$

A_{rs}

r \ s	0	1	2	3	4
2	4	$\frac{8}{3}$			
3	6	9	$\frac{33}{10}$		
4	8	$\frac{64}{3}$	$\frac{868}{45}$	$\frac{736}{189}$	
5	10	$\frac{125}{3}$	$\frac{875}{18}$	$\frac{17225}{756}$	$\frac{20225}{4536}$

B_{rs}

r \ s	0	1	2	3	4	5
2	2	$\frac{1}{3}$	$\frac{-1}{90}$			
3	4	$\frac{8}{3}$	$\frac{14}{45}$	$\frac{-8}{945}$		
4	6	9	$\frac{33}{10}$	$\frac{41}{140}$	$\frac{-9}{1400}$	
5	8	$\frac{64}{3}$	$\frac{868}{45}$	$\frac{736}{189}$	$\frac{3956}{14175}$	$\frac{-2368}{467775}$

e.g. Suppose that enough starting values have been obtained to indicate that the sixth differences are of the order of 50 (say).

The corrector corresponding to $r = 3$ has an error term of magnitude $8\delta^6/945$ which is less than $\frac{1}{2}$ when $\delta^6 = 50$.

Therefore label the last computed value y_0 and use the predictor

$$y_1 = y_{-5} + 6f_{-2} + 9\delta^2_{-2} + \frac{33}{10}\delta^4_{-2} \quad (r = 3 \text{ in the above table}).$$

From this value of y_1, generate f_1 ($= hy'_1$) and carry the differences back to the sixth differences column.

The corrector to use is then

$$y_1 = y_{-3} + 4f_{-1} + \frac{8}{3}\delta^2_{-1} + \frac{14}{45}\delta^4_{-1} \quad (r = 3 \text{ above}).$$

Note that the error term should strictly be expressed in terms of δ^6_{-1} and so an adequate check cannot be carried out until the next term has been computed.

Note also that, in common with all predictor-corrector methods, any form of predictor can be used, as the refinement depends only upon the corrector.

Predictor-corrector formulae involving function values

The general form of the simplest type of predictor is

$$y_1 = y_r + \sum_{s=r}^{0} A_{rs}f_s + E_r \qquad < 0$$

			A_{rs}				E_r
s	0	-1	-2	-3	-4	-5	
r							
0	1						$\dfrac{1}{2}\delta$
-1	2	0					$\dfrac{1}{3}\delta^2$
-2	$\dfrac{9}{4}$	0	$\dfrac{3}{4}$				$\dfrac{3}{8}\delta^3$
-3	$\dfrac{8}{3}$	$-\dfrac{4}{3}$	$\dfrac{8}{3}$	0			$\dfrac{14}{45}\delta^4$
-4	$\dfrac{55}{24}$	$\dfrac{5}{24}$	$\dfrac{5}{24}$	$\dfrac{55}{24}$	0		$\dfrac{95}{144}\delta^5$
-5	$\dfrac{33}{10}$	$-\dfrac{42}{10}$	$\dfrac{78}{10}$	$-\dfrac{42}{10}$	$\dfrac{33}{10}$	0	$\dfrac{41}{140}\delta^6$

An alternative group of predictor formulae have the form

$$y_1 = y_0 + \sum_{s=r}^{0} A_{rs}f_s + E_r \qquad (r < 0)$$

			A_{rs}			E_r
s	0	-1	-2	-3	-4	
r						
-1	$\dfrac{3}{2}$	$-\dfrac{1}{2}$				$\dfrac{5}{12}\delta^2$
-2	$\dfrac{23}{12}$	$-\dfrac{4}{3}$	$\dfrac{5}{12}$			$\dfrac{3}{8}\delta^3$
-3	$\dfrac{55}{24}$	$-\dfrac{59}{24}$	$\dfrac{37}{24}$	$-\dfrac{3}{8}$		$\dfrac{25}{72}\delta^4$
-4	$\dfrac{1901}{720}$	$-\dfrac{1387}{360}$	$\dfrac{327}{90}$	$-\dfrac{637}{360}$	$\dfrac{251}{720}$	$\dfrac{95}{288}\delta^5$

The correctors fall roughly into main groups. The first group is similar to the predictors tabulated above in that the emphasis is upon a weighted mean of the derivatives rather than the function values.

Group 1

$$y_1 = y_r + \sum_{s=r}^{0} A_{rs}f_s + E_r \qquad (r < 0)$$

				A_{rs}				E_r
s	1	0	-1	-2	-3	-4	-5	
r								
0	$\dfrac{1}{2}$	$\dfrac{1}{2}$						$\dfrac{-1}{12}\delta^2$
-1	$\dfrac{1}{3}$	$\dfrac{4}{3}$	$\dfrac{1}{3}$					$\dfrac{-1}{90}\delta^4$
-2	$\dfrac{3}{8}$	$\dfrac{9}{8}$	$\dfrac{9}{8}$	$\dfrac{3}{8}$				$\dfrac{-3}{80}\delta^4$
-3	$\dfrac{14}{45}$	$\dfrac{64}{45}$	$\dfrac{24}{45}$	$\dfrac{64}{45}$	$\dfrac{14}{45}$			$\dfrac{-1}{105}\delta^6$
-4	$\dfrac{95}{288}$	$\dfrac{375}{288}$	$\dfrac{125}{144}$	$\dfrac{125}{144}$	$\dfrac{375}{288}$	$\dfrac{95}{288}$		$\dfrac{-1}{44}\delta^6$
-5	$\dfrac{41}{140}$	$\dfrac{54}{35}$	$\dfrac{27}{140}$	$\dfrac{68}{35}$	$\dfrac{27}{140}$	$\dfrac{54}{35}$	$\dfrac{41}{140}$	$\dfrac{-1}{140}\delta^8$
-6	$\dfrac{3}{10}$	$\dfrac{3}{2}$	$\dfrac{3}{10}$	$\dfrac{9}{5}$	$\dfrac{3}{10}$	$\dfrac{3}{2}$	$\dfrac{3}{10}$	$\dfrac{-1}{140}\delta^6$

The second group involves the computation of a weighted mean of the function value as well as the derivatives.

Group 2

$$y_1 = \sum_{s=-4}^{0} A_{rs}^* y_s + \sum_{s=-4}^{1} A_{rs} f_s + E_r$$

A_{rs}^*

r \ s	−4	−3	−2	−1	0
1	0	0	0	−1	2
2	0	0	1	$\dfrac{27}{11}$	$\dfrac{-27}{11}$
3	0	1	$\dfrac{32}{5}$	0	$\dfrac{-32}{5}$
4	1	$\dfrac{1625}{137}$	$\dfrac{2000}{137}$	$\dfrac{-2000}{137}$	$\dfrac{-1625}{137}$
5	0	0	0	$\dfrac{1}{5}$	$\dfrac{4}{5}$
6	0	0	0	$\dfrac{-19}{13}$	$\dfrac{32}{13}$
7	0	0	$\dfrac{32}{5}$	$\dfrac{-27}{5}$	0
8	0	0	$\dfrac{136}{55}$	$\dfrac{27}{11}$	$\dfrac{-216}{55}$

A_{rs} | | | | | | E_r

r \ s	−4	−3	−2	−1	0	1	E_r
1	0	0	0	$\dfrac{1}{2}$	0	$\dfrac{-1}{2}$	$\dfrac{-1}{12}\delta^3$
2	0	0	$\dfrac{3}{11}$	$\dfrac{27}{11}$	$\dfrac{27}{11}$	$\dfrac{3}{11}$	$\dfrac{-1}{513}\delta^6$
3	0	$\dfrac{6}{25}$	$\dfrac{96}{25}$	$\dfrac{216}{25}$	$\dfrac{96}{25}$	$\dfrac{6}{25}$	$\dfrac{-1}{2625}\delta^8$
4	$\dfrac{30}{137}$	$\dfrac{750}{137}$	$\dfrac{3000}{137}$	$\dfrac{3000}{137}$	$\dfrac{750}{137}$	$\dfrac{30}{137}$	$\dfrac{-1}{12659}\delta^{10}$
5	0	0	0	0	$\dfrac{4}{5}$	$\dfrac{2}{5}$	$\dfrac{-1}{30}\delta^3$
6	0	0	$\dfrac{4}{39}$	−1	0	$\dfrac{17}{39}$	$\dfrac{-19}{390}\delta^4$
7	0	0	$\dfrac{12}{5}$	$\dfrac{27}{5}$	0	$\dfrac{3}{5}$	$\dfrac{-1}{30}\delta^4$
8	0	$\dfrac{-9}{550}$	$\dfrac{228}{275}$	$\dfrac{1188}{275}$	$\dfrac{828}{275}$	$\dfrac{141}{550}$	$\dfrac{-1}{1067}\delta^7$

Iterative methods

Should it become necessary to halve the interval, because the error term is becoming significant or the number of iterations required is becoming excessive, then interpolation becomes necessary.

This interpolation, actually subtabulation to halves, is based upon previously computed values and the formulae used can take several forms. One such form is as follows

$$y_k = \frac{1}{D_r} \sum_{s=-n}^{0} A_{rs}y_s + E_r, \qquad\qquad (r = 1(1)n)$$

where $k \equiv (1 - 2r)/2$, and E_r denotes the principal error term.

$n=2$ $\;$ s	0	A_{rs} -1	-2	D_r	E_r
r					
1	3	6	-1	8	$\dfrac{-1}{16}\nabla_0^3$
2	-1	6	3	8	$\dfrac{1}{16}\nabla_0^3$

$n=3$ $\;$ s	0	A_{rs} -1	-2	-3	D_r	E_r
r						
1	5	15	-5	1	16	$\dfrac{-5}{128}\nabla_0^4$
2	-1	9	9	-1	16	$\dfrac{3}{128}\nabla_0^4$
3	1	-5	15	5	16	$\dfrac{-5}{128}\nabla_0^4$

DEFERRED-CORRECTOR METHODS

$n=4$ $\;$ s	0	-1	A_{rs} -2	-3	-4	D_r	E_r
r							
1	35	140	-70	28	-5	128	$\dfrac{-7}{256}\nabla_0^5$
2	-5	60	90	-20	3	128	$\dfrac{3}{256}\nabla_0^5$
3	3	-20	90	60	-5	128	$\dfrac{-3}{256}\nabla_0^5$
4	-5	28	-70	140	35	128	$\dfrac{7}{256}\nabla_0^5$

For a given "n" there will be $2n + 1$ values available at the new interval to continue the solution.

Deferred-correction methods

One of the most powerful of the iterative methods is that of "deferred correction." This is a block iteration method, a complete set of function values being obtained from a recurrence relationship, their differences formed and corrections applied from these differences.

Central difference corrections are the most useful. Let the first order differential equation be

$$y' + g(x) \cdot y = k(x)$$

The first recurrence relation, assuming an initial y only given, is

$$y_1\left(1 + \frac{1}{2}hg_1\right) - y_0\left(1 - \frac{1}{2}hg_0\right) = \frac{1}{2}h(k_0 + k_1)$$

This is used to generate y_r for both positive and negative values of r if required. When the required range of values of y_r has been covered, with sufficient additional terms to generate all the differences required, a difference table is formed and the correction terms $C(y_1)$ tabulated from

$$C(y_{\frac{1}{2}}) \equiv \frac{1}{12}\,\delta^3_{\frac{1}{2}} - \frac{1}{120}\,\delta^5_{\frac{1}{2}} + \frac{1}{840}\,\delta^7_{\frac{1}{2}} - \frac{1}{5040}\,\delta^9_{\frac{1}{2}} \cdots$$

The correction terms $C(y_{\frac{1}{2}})$ are corrections to the recurrence relation. The corrections to the function values y_r are η_r i.e. True value = Approximate value + η

where
$$\eta_1\left(1 + \frac{1}{2}hg_1\right) - \eta_0\left(1 - \frac{1}{2}hg_0\right) + C(y_{\frac{1}{2}}) = 0$$

In this formula the initial η_0 is zero and the recurrence relation can be used in either direction.

New $C(y_{\frac{1}{2}})$ are then computed and the correction process repeated until there is no change in the values of $C(y_{\frac{1}{2}})$. At this point the computed values and the differences derived there-from should be checked for consistency with the differential equation. The method of deferred correction is particularly useful for linear differential equations as its convergence is extremely rapid, even for very large intervals. If more starting values are known formulae which have even faster convergence can be employed. Two such formulae are as follows: Two starting values given

Predictor
$$y_1\left(1 + \frac{1}{3}hg_1\right) + \frac{4}{3}hg_0 y_0 - y_{-1}\left(1 - \frac{1}{3}hg_{-1}\right) = \frac{1}{3}h(k_1 + 4k_0 + k_{-1})$$

$$C(y_0) \equiv \frac{1}{180}(\delta^5_{-\frac{1}{2}} + \delta^5_{\frac{1}{2}}) - \frac{1}{630}(\delta^7_{-\frac{1}{2}} + \delta^7_{\frac{1}{2}}) + \frac{1}{2510}(\delta^9_{-\frac{1}{2}} + \delta^9_{\frac{1}{2}}) \cdots$$

Corrector
$$\eta_1\left(1 + \frac{1}{3}hg_1\right) + \frac{4}{3}hg_0\eta_0 - \eta_{-1}\left(1 - \frac{1}{3}hg_{-1}\right) + C(y_0) = 0.$$

Three starting values given

Predictor
$$y_1 + y_0(9 + 6hg_0) - y_{-1}(9 - 6hg_{-1}) - y_{-2} = 6h(k_0 + k_{-1})$$

$$C(y_{-\frac{1}{2}}) \equiv -\frac{1}{10}\,\delta^5_{-\frac{1}{2}} + \frac{1}{70}\,\delta^7_{-\frac{1}{2}} - \frac{1}{420}\,\delta^9_{-\frac{1}{2}} + \cdots$$

Corrector
$$\eta_1 + \eta_0(9 + 6hg_0) - \eta_{-1}(9 - 6hg_{-1}) - \eta_{-2} + C(y_{-\frac{1}{2}}) = 0$$

The use of the deferred correction technique for higher order differential equations. Second order differential equations.

Two starting values given e.g. $y'' + m \cdot y' + g \cdot y = k$ where y_0 and y_{-1} are known and $y \equiv y(x)$; $m \equiv m(x)$; $g \equiv g(x)$; $k \equiv k(x)$.

Predictor
$$y_1\left(1 + \frac{1}{2}hm_0\right) - y_0(2 - h^2g_0) + y_{-1}\left(1 - \frac{1}{2}hm_0\right) = h^2k_0$$

$$C(y_0) \equiv \left[-\frac{1}{12}\,\delta^4_0 + \frac{1}{90}\,\delta^6_0 - \frac{1}{560}\,\delta^8_0 + \frac{1}{3150}\,\delta^{10}_0\right]$$

$$+ hg_0\left[-\frac{1}{12}(\delta^3_{\frac{1}{2}} + \delta^3_{-\frac{1}{2}}) + \frac{1}{60}(\delta^5_{\frac{1}{2}} + \delta^5_{-\frac{1}{2}}) - \frac{1}{280}(\delta^7_{\frac{1}{2}} + \delta^7_{-\frac{1}{2}}) + \frac{1}{1260}(\delta^9_{\frac{1}{2}} + \delta^9_{-\frac{1}{2}})\right].$$

Corrector
$$\eta_1\left(1 + \frac{1}{2}hm_0\right) - \eta_0(2 - h^2g_0) + \eta_{-1}\left(1 - \frac{1}{2}hm_0\right) + C(y_0) = 0.$$

Three starting values require the known functions $m(x)$, $g(x)$ $g(x)$ and $k(x)$ to be tabulated at half way points and the advantage in speed of convergence is relatively slight.

Predictor
$$y_1\left(1 - \frac{1}{12}hm_{-\frac{1}{2}} - \frac{1}{8}h^2g_{-\frac{1}{2}}\right) - y_0\left(1 - \frac{9}{4}hm_{-\frac{1}{2}} - \frac{9}{8}h^2g_{-\frac{1}{2}}\right)$$

$$- y_{-1}\left(1 + \frac{9}{4}hm_{-\frac{1}{2}} - \frac{9}{8}h^2g_{-\frac{1}{2}}\right) + y_{-2}\left(1 + \frac{1}{12}hm_{-\frac{1}{2}} - \frac{1}{8}h^2g_{-\frac{1}{2}}\right) = 2h^2k_{-\frac{1}{2}}$$

$$C(y_{-\frac{1}{2}}) \equiv \left[\frac{-5}{24} (\delta_0^4 + \delta_{-1}^4) + \frac{259}{5760} (\delta_0^6 + \delta_{-1}^6) - \frac{3229}{322560} (\delta_0^8 + \delta_{-1}^8) \right.$$

$$+ \frac{117469}{51609600} (\delta_0^{10} + \delta_{-1}^{10}) \Big] + hm_{-\frac{1}{2}} \left[\frac{3}{320} \delta_{-\frac{1}{2}}^5 - \frac{5}{3584} \delta_{-\frac{1}{2}}^7 + \frac{35}{147456} \delta_{-\frac{1}{2}}^9 \right]$$

$$+ h^2 g_{-\frac{1}{2}} \left[\frac{3}{128} (\delta_0^4 + \delta_{-1}^4) - \frac{5}{1024} (\delta_0^6 + \delta_{-1}^6) + \frac{35}{32768} (\delta_0^8 + \delta_{-1}^8) \right]$$

Corrector $\quad \eta_1 \left(1 - \frac{1}{12} hm_{-\frac{1}{2}} - \frac{1}{8} h^2 g_{-\frac{1}{2}} \right) - \eta_0 \left(1 - \frac{9}{4} hm_{-\frac{1}{2}} - \frac{9}{8} h^2 g_{-\frac{1}{2}} \right)$

$$- \eta_{-1} \left(1 + \frac{9}{4} hm_{-\frac{1}{2}} - \frac{9}{8} h^2 g_{-\frac{1}{2}} \right) + \eta_{-2} \left(1 + \frac{1}{12} hm_{-\frac{1}{2}} - \frac{1}{8} h^2 g_{-\frac{1}{2}} \right) + C(y_{-\frac{1}{2}}) = 0$$

CHEBYSHEV METHODS

In general, for second order differential equations, recurrence relations involving an even number of known values are simpler than those involving an odd number of such values. The formulae for four starting values are given below and they are seen to be much simpler than those for three values. Further the correction terms should have more rapid convergence properties.

Predictor $\quad y_1(1 + hm_{-1}) - y_0(16 + 8hm_{-1}) + y_{-1}(30 - 12h^2 g_{-1})$

$$+ y_{-2}(16 - 8hm_{-1}) + y_{-3}(1 - hm_{-1}) = -12h^2 k_{-1}$$

$$C(y_{-1}) \equiv \left[-\frac{4}{30} \delta_{-1}^6 + \frac{3}{140} \delta_{-1}^8 - \frac{2}{525} \delta_{-1}^{10} + \frac{1}{1386} \delta_{-1}^{12} \right]$$

$$+ hm_{-1} \left[-\frac{1}{5} (\delta_{-\frac{1}{2}}^5 + \delta_{-1\frac{1}{2}}^5) + \frac{3}{70} (\delta_{-\frac{1}{2}}^7 + \delta_{-1\frac{1}{2}}^7) \right.$$

$$\left. - \frac{1}{105} (\delta_{-\frac{1}{2}}^9 + \delta_{-1\frac{1}{2}}^9) + \frac{1}{462} (\delta_{-\frac{1}{2}}^{11} + \delta_{-1\frac{1}{2}}^{11}) \right].$$

Corrector $\quad \eta_1(1 + hm_{-1}) - \eta_0(16 + 8hm_{-1}) + \eta_{-1}(30 - 12h^2 g_{-1})$

$$+ \eta_{-2}(16 - 8hm_{-1}) + \eta_{-3}(1 - hm_{-1}) + C(y_{-1}) = 0$$

Iterative Chebyshev

The recurrence relationships used are identical with those set up in the direct Chebyshev method. The first value of $a_0^{(s)}$ is obtained from the first term of the series for the initial value of $y^{(s)}$, all the other terms being initially set at zero. e.g. Consider the case when $a_r^{(s)}$ are required for $s = 0, 1, 2$ and 3. (The initial values of y, y', y'' being known at $x = -1$.) The computational sequence is as follows

Set all $a_r^{(3)} = 0$
Obtain $a_0^{(2)}$ from $y''(-1) = \frac{1}{2} a_0^{(2)}$
Use the Chebyshev recurrence formula to obtain $a_1^{(1)}$ from this value of $a_0^{(2)}$
Obtain $a_0^{(1)}$ from $y'(-1) = \frac{1}{2} a_0^{(1)} - a_1^{(1)}$
Use the Chebyshev formula again to obtain both $a_1^{(0)}$ and $a_2^{(0)}$
Obtain $a_0^{(0)}$ from $y(-1) = \frac{1}{2} a_1^{(0)} - a_1^{(0)} + a_2^{(0)}$
Now utilise the recurrence relation given by the differential equation to generate $a_0^{(3)}$.

The cycle is now repeated each series being increased by one term if desired. The determining factor being the number of significant decimals required in the result. The method is in general slower than the direct Chebyshev process but it has the merit that no predetermined knowledge of the number of terms required is necessary—further computational errors die away as the method is truly iterative, whereas in the direct approach they can nullify all the working.

Direct Chebyshev method

This method is suitable for a differential equation of any order. The range of the arguments must however be normalized to $-1 \leq x \leq 1$ (or $0 \leq x \leq 1$ if the "shifted" Chebyshev polynomials are to be used).

A polynomial approximation to the analytical solution is sought, the degree of the polynomial N being decided beforehand.

Assume

$$y(x) = \tfrac{1}{2}a_0 + \sum_{r=1}^{N} a_r \cdot T_r(x)$$

$$y'(x) = \tfrac{1}{2}a_0' + \sum_{r=1}^{N} a_r' \cdot T_r(x)$$

$$y''(x) = \tfrac{1}{2}a_0'' + \sum_{r=1}^{N} a_r'' \cdot T_r(x) \qquad \text{etc.}$$

where the a's are constants.

Writing $y^{(0)}$, $y^{(1)}$, $y^{(2)}$ for $y(x)$, $y'(x)$, $y''(x)$ etc., $a_r^{(0)}$, $a_r^{(1)}$, $a_r^{(2)}$ for a_r, a_r', a_r'', etc., and T_r for $T_r(x)$.

The recurrence relationship for the Chebyshev polynomials can be written as

$$2xT_r = T_{|r-1|} + T_{r+1} \qquad (r = 0,1,2, \ldots)$$

further

$$2 \int T_r \cdot dx = \frac{T_{r+1}}{(r+1)} - \frac{T_{r-1}}{(r-1)} \qquad (r > 1)$$

$$= \tfrac{1}{2}T_2 \qquad (r = 1)$$

$$= 2T_1 \qquad (r = 0)$$

Thus $2r \cdot a_r^{(s)} = a_{r-1}^{(s+1)} - a_{r+1}^{(s+1)} \qquad (r > 1)$

If, in addition, the notation $C_r(x^p y^{(s)})$ is introduced to denote the coefficient of T_r in the expansion of $x^p y^{(s)}$ *and twice this coefficient when $r = 0$* then

$$C_r(y^{(0)}) = a_r$$

$$C_r(y^{(s)}) = a_r^{(s)}$$

$$C_r(x^p y^{(s)}) = \frac{1}{2^p} \sum_{k=0}^{p} \binom{p}{k} \cdot a_{|r-p+2k|}^{(s)}$$

Method of use of Chebyshev polynomials

Suppose the differential equation is

$$f(x) \cdot y'' + g(x) \cdot y' + h(x) \cdot y = 0$$

i.e.

$$fy^{(2)} + gy^{(1)} + hy^{(0)} = 0$$

where f, g and h are polynomials in x (or can be approximated to by such polynomials).

Then

$$C_r(fy^{(2)}) + C_r(gy^{(1)}) + C_r(hy^{(0)}) = 0$$

will yield a recurrence relationship based upon the differential equation. The Chebyshev polynomials themselves yield the second recurrence relationship, namely

$$2r \cdot a_r^{(s)} = a_{r-1}^{(s+1)} - a_{r+1}^{(s+1)}$$

To start the procedure, assume that

$$a_r^{(s)} = 0 \qquad r > N$$

and assign arbitrary integer values to $a_N^{(1)}$ and $a_N^{(2)}$. The recurrence relationships are used to generate $a_r^{(s)}$ for $r = N - 1, N - 2$, etc.

The formulae for the initial conditions are

$$y^{(s)}(-1) = \tfrac{1}{2}a_0^{(s)} - a_1^{(s)} + a_2^{(s)} - a_3^{(s)} + \cdots$$

$$y^{(s)}(0) = \tfrac{1}{2}a_0^{(s)} - a_2^{(s)} + a_4^{(s)} - a_6^{(s)} + \cdots$$

$$y^{(s)}(1) = \tfrac{1}{2}a_0^{(s)} + a_1^{(s)} + a_2^{(s)} + a_3^{(s)} + \cdots$$

It will be found that the series obtained do not satisfy the given initial conditions. Therefore a second set of coefficients must be obtained by repeating the process for different arbitrary starting values and a linear combination of the two sets will yield the required solution.

$$T_0 = 1 \qquad\qquad\qquad T_{r+1} - 2xT_r + T_{r-1} = 0$$

$$T_1 = x$$

$$T_2 = 2x^2 - 1$$

$$T_3 = 4x^3 - 3x$$

$$T_4 = 8x^4 - 8x^2 + 1$$

$$T_5 = 16x^5 - 20x^3 + 5x$$

$$T_6 = 32x^6 - 48x^4 + 18x^2 - 1$$

If the "shifted" Chebyshev polynomials T_r^* are to be used then

$$y(x) = \tfrac{1}{2}a_0 + \sum_{r=1}^{N} a_r T_r^*$$

$$4r \cdot a_r^{(s)} = a_{r-1}^{(s+1)} - a_{r+1}^{(s+1)}$$

$$C_r(x^p y^{(s)}) = \frac{1}{2^p} \sum_{k=0}^{2p} \binom{2p}{k} a_{|r-p+k|}^{(s)}$$

with

$$y^{(s)}(0) = \tfrac{1}{2}a_0^{(s)} - a_1^{(s)} + a_2^{(s)} - a_3^{(s)} \cdots$$

$$y^{(s)}(\tfrac{1}{2}) = \tfrac{1}{2}a_0^{(s)} - a_2^{(s)} + a_4^{(s)} - a_6^{(s)} \cdots$$

$$y^{(s)}(1) = \tfrac{1}{2}a_0^{(s)} + a_1^{(s)} + a_2^{(s)} + a_3^{(s)} \cdots$$

$$T_r^*(x) = T_r(2x - 1) = \cos\{r \cdot \arccos(2x - 1)\}$$

$$T_0^* = 1 \qquad\qquad\qquad (4x - 2)T_r^* = T_{r-1}^* + T_{r+1}^*$$

$$T_1^* = 2x - 1$$

$$T_2^* = 8x^2 - 8x + 1$$

$$T_3^* = 32x^3 - 48x^2 + 18x - 1$$

$$T_4^* = 128x^4 - 256x^3 + 160x^2 - 32x + 1$$

The approach is otherwise the same.

INDIRECT METHODS

MONTE CARLO

Applicable to first order equations i.e. quadrature type, for which an upper bound can be set for the function. e.g. $y' = f(x)$; $a \le x \le b$; $0 \le f(x) < e$.

The range $[a,b]$ is subdivided into n intervals, not necessarily equal, such that $x_0 = a$ and $x_n = b$. For the sub-interval $[x_i, x_{i+1}]$ the procedure is as follows:

Set N_i equal to zero and after each trial increase N_i by unity so that it will always indicate the number of completed trials.

Set T_i equal to zero and after each trial increase T_i by unity *only if the trial was successful* otherwise allow it to retain its previous value.

A trial consists of selecting two random numbers r_1 and r_2. The first of these is selected from a uniform (rectangular) distribution in the range $[x_i, x_{i+1}]$ and the second from a uniform distribution in the range $[0, e]$. If $r_2 \leq f(r_1)$ then the trial is deemed to be successful—otherwise it is a failure.

As $N_i \to \infty$,

$$\frac{T_i}{N_i} e(x_{i+1} - x_i) \to \int_{x_i}^{x_{i+1}} f(x) \cdot dx$$

and hence

$$y_{i+1} = y_i + \frac{T_i e(x_{i+1} - x_i)}{N_i} \qquad \text{as } N_i \to \infty.$$

If the function has a negative lower bound such that $-d \leq f(x) \leq e$ then a simple axis transformation is necessary i.e. replace $f(x)$ by $d + f(x)$ and e by $(e + d)$ in the above, giving

$$y_{i+1} = y_i + \frac{T_i(e + d)(x_{i+1} - x_i)}{N_i} \qquad \text{as } N_i \to \infty.$$

In general, the range of values for which a uniform distribution is required will not be standard and a transformation will be necessary. Such a transformation is obtained as follows:

if r^* is a random number from a uniform distribution in the range $[a,b]$ then r a random number from a uniform distribution in the range $[s,t]$ can be obtained from

$$r = \left(\frac{bs - at}{b - a}\right) - r^*\left(\frac{s - t}{b - a}\right)$$

In particular, if the given range is $[0, 1]$ then

$$r = s + r(t - s)$$

while if the given range is $[-1, -1]$ then

$$r = \tfrac{1}{2}(s + t) + \tfrac{1}{2}r(t - s).$$

In all *Monte Carlo* techniques the number of trials must be large—usually several thousand are required.

PARTIAL DIFFERENTIAL EQUATIONS

Introduction

In the section dealing with finite differences and their applications, some attention has been paid to the derivation of the formulae quoted and a few words of explanation of their use given. Formulae of interest to users of high speed digital computers have been given, as well as those for desk computation.

Physical phenomena frequently give rise to partial differential equations, rather than ordinary ones. The "field" equations of Laplace and Poisson being particular examples. The analytical solution of partial differential equations is frequently tedious, if not impossible, even in those cases where an analytical solution is feasible, a numerical treatment may well be quicker.

Partial differential equations in practice are often reduced to simultaneous equations in two dimensions, one of which is frequently time-like. It is this type of equation which will be considered here.

The classification of partial differential equations is, by analogy with the conic sections, into elliptic, parabolic and hyperbolic equations.

The physical criterion for this grouping is one of boundary conditions. It is also convenient to define the *characteristics* of the equation under consideration. If these are real and distinct then the classification is that of hyperbolic, if real and equal then it is parabolic, while if they are complex it is elliptic.

Consider partial differential equations in two dimensions.

a) Second order equation.
Notation used:

$$p = \frac{\partial u}{\partial x}; \quad q = \frac{\partial u}{\partial y}; \quad r = \frac{\partial^2 u}{\partial x^2}; \quad s = \frac{\partial^2 u}{\partial x \partial y}; \quad t = \frac{\partial^2 u}{\partial y^2}$$

A, B, C and D are functions of u, x, y, p and q.

The physical problem is determined by a second order partial differential equation, the general form of which is

$$A \cdot r + B \cdot s + C \cdot t = D$$

The geometry of the space in which the equation holds yields two more equations:

$$dp = d\left(\frac{\partial u}{\partial x}\right) = r \cdot dx + s \cdot dy; \qquad \text{and similarly, } dq = s \cdot dx + t \cdot dy$$

In matrix form these can be expressed as

$$\begin{bmatrix} A & B & C \\ dx & dy & 0 \\ 0 & dx & dy \end{bmatrix} \begin{bmatrix} r \\ s \\ t \end{bmatrix} = \begin{bmatrix} D \\ dp \\ dq \end{bmatrix}$$

At any point at which the determinant of the 3×3 matrix is zero

i.e.

$$\begin{vmatrix} A & B & C \\ dx & dy & 0 \\ 0 & dx & dy \end{vmatrix} = 0,$$

a necessary condition for the equations to have a solution is that the rank of the following matrix is two.

PARTIAL DIFFERENTIAL EQUATIONS (Continued)

$$\begin{bmatrix} A & B & C & D \\ dx & dy & 0 & dp \\ 0 & dx & dy & dq \end{bmatrix}$$

This condition can be stated in an alternative fashion as follows. The equations have a solution if any of the following three determinental equations are satisfied

$$\begin{vmatrix} A & B & D \\ dx & dy & dp \\ 0 & dx & dq \end{vmatrix} = 0$$

$$\begin{vmatrix} A & D & C \\ dx & dp & 0 \\ 0 & dq & dy \end{vmatrix} = 0$$

$$\begin{vmatrix} D & B & C \\ dp & dy & 0 \\ dq & dx & dy \end{vmatrix} = 0.$$

The equation

$$\begin{vmatrix} A & B & C \\ dx & dy & 0 \\ 0 & dx & dy \end{vmatrix} = 0$$

can be written in the form

$$A\left(\frac{dy}{dx}\right)^2 - B\left(\frac{dy}{dx}\right) + C = 0$$

and thus for the discriminant Δ defined by

$$\Delta \equiv B^2 - 4AC$$

there exist three possibilities

(i) $\Delta > 0$, in which case two real distinct values can be obtained for $\frac{dy}{dx}$, corresponding to real characteristics, and the equation is said to be hyperbolic.

(ii) $\Delta = 0$, when the equation is said to be parabolic.

(iii) $\Delta < 0$, when the equation is said to be elliptic.

Simple examples of these equations are

Hyperbolic
$$\frac{\partial^2 u}{\partial x^2} - \frac{\partial^2 u}{\partial y^2} = 0$$

Parabolic
$$\frac{\partial^2 u}{\partial x^2} - \frac{\partial u}{\partial y} = 0$$

Elliptic
$$\frac{\partial^2 u}{\partial x^2} + \frac{\partial^2 u}{\partial y^2} = 0$$

PARTIAL DIFFERENTIAL EQUATIONS (Continued)

In the above simple forms A, B, C and D are constants while in fact they can depend upon the solution, and its first derivatives, as well as position in the region. Thus the classification of the equation *can* depend upon the solution itself.

b) Two simultaneous first order equations.
The techniques are similar to those employed in section (*a*) above.

A, B, C, D and E are functions of u, v, x, y, $\dfrac{\partial u}{\partial x}$, $\dfrac{\partial u}{\partial y}$, $\dfrac{\partial v}{\partial x}$, $\dfrac{\partial v}{\partial y}$ and the general form of the

equations are

$$A_1 \frac{\partial u}{\partial x} + B_1 \frac{\partial u}{\partial y} + C_1 \frac{\partial v}{\partial x} + D_1 \frac{\partial v}{\partial y} = E_1$$

$$A_2 \frac{\partial u}{\partial x} + B_2 \frac{\partial u}{\partial y} + C_2 \frac{\partial v}{\partial x} + D_2 \frac{\partial v}{\partial y} = E_2.$$

The geometry of the space yields, as before

$$du = \frac{\partial u}{\partial x} \cdot dx + \frac{\partial u}{\partial y} \cdot dy$$

$$dv = \frac{\partial v}{\partial x} \cdot dx + \frac{\partial v}{\partial y} \cdot dy$$

The discriminant Δ now being given by

$$\Delta \equiv (A_1 D_2 - A_2 D_1 + B_1 C_2 - B_2 C_1) - 4(A_1 C_2 - A_2 C_1)(B_1 D_2 - B_2 D_1).$$

Δ decides the class into which the two equations fall in the same manner as in the previous case.

i.e. Hyperbolic   if $\Delta > 0$
     Parabolic   if $\Delta = 0$
     Elliptic   if $\Delta < 0$.

An elegant method for the solution of hyperbolic equations, based on the determination of the equations of the characteristics, exists but will not be discussed further here.

Elliptic equations are best treated numerically by iteration. This enables both the interval to be adjusted arbitrarily and also the powerful convergence techniques of numerical analysis to be invoked.

Parabolic and hyperbolic equations on the other hand can be covered by step-by-step methods. These latter fall into two main groups. On the one hand, there are those methods which yield a direct solution, and, on the other, those which yield the solution implicitly.

In general, however, elliptic equations arise when the boundary conditions are specified on a contour enclosing a region, which need not be simply connected, i.e. elliptic equations are of the boundary value type.

The hyperbolic equations are of the initial value type, and require the solution over a domain having an open boundary.

For parabolic equations the boundary is also open, but in the main only in one direction, the boundary conditions themselves being mixed.

Elliptic Partial Differential Equations

A square mesh of side "*h*" is superimposed upon the region to enable the points to be labelled with respect to an arbitrary origin.

ELLIPTIC DIFFERENTIAL EQUATIONS (Continued)

This presupposes that the boundary is formed from the sides of such a mesh. If such is not the case, the procedure must be modified at the boundary. This will be discussed at the end of this section.

The emphasis here will be on the equations of Poisson and Laplace, although the methods involved can easily be extended to any elliptic partial differential equation. In essence, the Taylor's series expansion for a number of mesh points is used to express the partial derivatives occurring in the equation at the origin, in terms of the function values at neighboring points, and higher partial derivatives at the origin. These function values are used to replace the differential equation by a finite difference equation, which is cast in the form of an iteration formula, the higher derivatives consituting the truncation error term.

Consider the equation

$$\nabla^2 u(x,y) = f(x,y)$$

where

$$\nabla^2 \equiv \frac{\partial^2}{\partial x^2} + \frac{\partial^2}{\partial y^2}$$

The differential equation is to be replaced by the iteration formula having the form

$$A_{00}u_{00} = \sum_{s=-n}^{n} \sum_{r=-n}^{n}{}^{*} A_{rs}u_{rs} - Bh^2f_{00} + \text{error term}$$

(the asterisk attached to the double summation indicating that the term involving u_{00} is to be omitted from the sum). In practice n will be restricted to 1 or 2.

Notation used:

$$x_r = x_0 + rh$$

$$y_r = y_0 + sh$$

$$(r,s) = (x_r,y_s)$$

$$f_{00} = f(x_0,y_0)$$

$$u_{rs} = u(x_r,y_s)$$

$$A_{rs} = \text{Integer weight associated with } u_{rs}$$

$$B = \text{Integer constant.}$$

The principal part of the error term will be of the form

$$h^4(\theta\nabla^4 + \phi\mathfrak{D}^4)u_{00}$$

where

$$\mathfrak{D}^4 \equiv \frac{\partial^4}{\partial x^2 \partial y^2} \text{ and } \theta, \phi \text{ are constants.}$$

ELLIPTIC DIFFERENTIAL EQUATIONS (Continued)

A_{rs}, B, θ and ϕ are tabulated below.

Restricting the values of the weights to the doubly symmetric case, i.e. $A_{rs} = A_{sr} = A|_r| |_s|$, and assuming the validity of the Taylor's expansion in the neighborhood of u_{00}, integer values can be obtained for A_{rs} and B, and rational fractions for θ and ϕ. However, the assumptions of the existence of the Taylor's expansion implies that $u(x,y)$ can be adequately represented by a polynomial in x and y over the region in question. Thus if a square region, centered on an arbitrary origin, is considered, the terms involving odd powers of either variable will contribute nothing to the sum providing the coordinates involved are specially selected.

The significant part of the expansion is therefore

$$u_{rs} = \left\{ 1 + \frac{h^2}{2!}\left(r^2 \frac{\partial^2}{\partial x^2} + s^2 \frac{\partial^2}{\partial y^2} \right) + \frac{h^4}{4!}\left(r^4 \frac{\partial^4}{\partial x^4} + 6r^2s^2 \frac{\partial^4}{\partial x^2 \partial y^2} + s^4 \frac{\partial^4}{\partial y^4} \right) \cdots \right\} u_{00}$$

The coordinate groupings that are used are as follows:

(i) $(0,1)$, $(1,0)$, $(0,-1)$ and $(-1,0)$
(ii) $(1,1)$, $(1,-1)$, $(-1,1)$ and $(-1,-1)$
(iii) $(0,2)$, $(2,0)$, $(0,-2)$ and $(-2,0)$
(iv) $(2,2)$, $(2,-2)$, $(-2,2)$ and $(-2,-2)$
(v) $(2,1)$, $(1,2)$, $(-1,2)$, $(-2,1)$, $(-2,-1)$, $(-1,-2)$, $(1,-2)$ and $(2,-1)$.

Group 1. The general form is

A_{rs}

r \ s	-1	0	1
1	1	α	1
0	α	$4(1+\alpha)$	α
-1	1	α	1

$B = (\alpha + 2)$
$\theta = -(\alpha + 2)/12$
$\phi = (\alpha - 4)/6$

in particular

A_{rs}

r \ s	-1	0	1
1	1	0	1
0	0	4	0
-1	1	0	1

$B = 2$
$\theta = -1/6$
$\phi = -2/3$

A_{rs}

r \ s	-1	0	1
1	1	2	1
0	2	12	2
-1	1	2	1

$B = 4$
$\theta = -1/3$
$\phi = -1/3$

A_{rs}

r \ s	-1	0	1
1	1	3	1
0	3	16	3
-1	1	3	1

$B = 5$
$\theta = -5/12$
$\phi = -1/6$

ELLIPTIC DIFFERENTIAL EQUATIONS (Continued)

A_{rs}

r \ s	−1	0	1	
1	1	4	1	$B = 6$
0	4	20	4	$\theta = -1/2$
−1	1	4	1	$\phi = 0$

A_{rs}

r \ s	−1	0	1	
1	1	6	1	$B = 8$
0	6	28	6	$\theta = -2/3$
−1	1	6	1	$\phi = 1/3$

Group 2.   The general form is

A_{rs}

r \ s	−1	0	1	
1	α	1	α	$B = (1 + 2\alpha)$
0	1	$4(1 + \alpha)$	1	$\theta = -(1 + 2\alpha)/12$
−1	α	1	α	$\phi = (1 - 4\alpha)/6$

In particular

A_{rs}

r \ s	−1	0	1	
1	0	1	0	$B = 1$
0	1	4	1	$\theta = -1/2$
−1	0	1	0	$\phi = 1/6$

A_{rs}

r \ s	−1	0	1	
1	1	1	1	$B = 3$
0	1	8	1	$\theta = -1/4$
−1	1	1	1	$\phi = -1/2$

A_{rs}

r \ s	−1	0	1	
1	2	1	2	$B = 5$
0	1	12	1	$\theta = -5/12$
−1	2	1	2	$\phi = -7/6$

A_{rs}

r \ s	−1	0	1	
1	4	1	4	$B = 9$
0	1	20	1	$\theta = -3/4$
−1	4	1	4	$\phi = -5/3$

ELLIPTIC DIFFERENTIAL EQUATIONS (Continued)

A_{rs}			
r \ s	-1	0	1
1	8	1	8
0	1	36	1
-1	8	1	8

$B = 17$

$\theta = -17/12$

$\phi = -31/6$

Group 3.　The general form is

A_{rs}			
r \ s	1	0	-1
1	β	α	β
0	α	$4(\alpha + \beta)$	α
-1	β	α	β

$B = \alpha + 2\beta$

$\theta = -(\alpha + 2\beta)/12$

$\phi = (\alpha - 4\beta)/6$

In particular

A_{rs}			
r \ s	-1	0	1
1	2	3	2
0	3	20	3
-1	2	3	2

$B = 7$

$\theta = -7/2$

$\phi = -5/6$

A_{rs}			
r \ s	-1	0	1
1	2	5	2
0	5	28	5
-1	2	5	2

$B = 9$

$\theta = -3/4$

$\phi = -1/2$

A_{rs}			
r \ s	-1	0	1
1	3	4	3
0	4	28	4
-1	3	4	3

$B = 10$

$\theta = -5/6$

$\phi = -4/3$

A_{rs}			
r \ s	-1	0	1
1	3	5	3
0	5	32	5
-1	3	5	3

$B = 11$

$\theta = -11/12$

$\phi = -7/3$

A_{rs}			
r \ s	-1	0	1
1	4	5	4
0	5	36	5
-1	4	5	4

$B = 13$

$\theta = -13/12$

$\phi = -11/6$

ELLIPTIC DIFFERENTIAL EQUATIONS (Continued)

While negative weights can be used in all groups care must be taken that the subtraction of comparable terms does not reduce the number of significant decimals left in the result.

The above formulae are of the nine-point type. To increase the accuracy, twenty-five-point formulae can be used. For these the error term is taken to be

$$\{h^4(\theta\nabla^4 + \phi\mathfrak{D}^4) + h^6(\eta\nabla^6 + \gamma\mathfrak{D}^4\nabla^2)\}u_{00}$$

The twenty-five-point formulae which form the basic set are

A_{rs}

r \ s	−2	−1	0	1	2	
2	0	0	0	0	0	$B = 1$
1	0	0	1	0	0	$\theta = -1/12$
0	0	1	4	1	0	$\phi = 1/6$
−1	0	0	1	0	0	$\eta = -1/360$
−2	0	0	0	0	0	$\gamma = 1/120$

A_{rs}

r \ s	−2	−1	0	1	2	
2	0	0	0	0	0	$B = 2$
1	0	1	0	1	0	$\theta = -1/6$
0	0	0	4	0	0	$\phi = -2/3$
−1	0	1	0	1	0	$\eta = -1/180$
−2	0	0	0	0	0	$\gamma = -1/15$

A_{rs}

r \ s	−2	−1	0	1	2	
2	0	1	0	1	0	$B = 10$
1	1	0	0	0	1	$\theta = -17/6$
0	0	0	8	0	0	$\phi = -7/3$
−1	1	0	0	0	1	$\eta = -13/36$
−2	0	1	0	1	0	$\gamma = -7/12$

ELLIPTIC DIFFERENTIAL EQUATIONS (Continued)

r \\ s	-2	-1	0	1	2	
2	0	0	1	0	0	$B = 4$
1	0	0	0	0	0	$\theta = -4/3$
0	1	0	4	0	1	$\phi = 8/3$
-1	0	0	0	0	0	$\eta = -8/45$
-2	0	0	1	0	0	$\gamma = 8/15$

A_{rs}

r \\ s	-2	-1	0	1	2	
2	1	0	0	0	1	$B = 8$
1	0	0	0	0	0	$\theta = -8/3$
0	0	0	4	0	0	$\phi = -32/3$
-1	0	0	0	0	0	$\eta = -16/45$
-2	1	0	0	0	1	$\gamma = -64/15$

A_{rs}

Any linear combination of the above five sets can be used.

Group 4   The general form is

r \\ s	-2	-1	0	1	2	
2	μ	κ	ρ	κ	μ	$B = \alpha + 2\beta + 4\rho + 8\mu + 10\kappa$
1	κ	β	α	β	κ	$\theta = -(\alpha + 2\beta + 16\rho + 32\mu + 34\kappa)/12$
0	ρ	α	$4(\alpha + \beta + \rho + \mu + 2\kappa)$	α	ρ	$\phi = (\alpha - 4\beta + 16\rho - 64\mu - 14\kappa)/6$
-1	κ	β	α	β	κ	$\eta = -(\alpha + 2\beta + 64\rho + 128\mu + 130\kappa)/360$
-2	μ	κ	ρ	κ	μ	$\gamma = (\alpha - 8\beta + 64\rho - 512\mu - 70\kappa)/120$

A_{rs}

In particular θ and ϕ can be reduced to zero simultaneously if either *a*) $\rho = -1$, $\alpha = 16$, $\mu = 0 = \beta = \kappa$.

r \\ s	-2	-1	0	1	2	
2	0	0	-1	0	0	$B = 12$
1	0	0	16	0	0	$\theta = 0$
0	-1	16	60	16	-1	$\phi = 0$
-1	0	0	16	0	0	$\eta = 2/15$
-2	0	0	-1	0	0	$\gamma = -2/5$

A_{rs}

ELLIPTIC DIFFERENTIAL EQUATIONS (Continued)

or   *b)* $\mu = -1$, $\beta = 16$, $\alpha = 0 = \rho = \kappa$.

A_{rs}

r \ s	-2	-1	0	1	2	
2	-1	0	0	0	-1	$B = 24$
1	0	16	0	16	0	$\theta = 0$
0	0	0	60	0	0	$\phi = 0$
-1	0	16	0	16	0	$\eta = 4/15$
-2	-1	0	0	0	-1	$\gamma = 16/5$

or   *c)* $\rho = -1 = \mu$, $\alpha = 16 = \beta$.

A_{rs}

r \ s	-2	-1	0	1	2	
2	-1	0	-1	0	-1	$B = 36$
1	0	16	16	16	0	$\theta = 0$
0	-1	16	120	16	-1	$\phi = 0$
-1	0	16	16	16	0	$\eta = 3/5$
-2	-1	0	-1	0	-1	$\gamma = 14/5$

When working with digital computers it is frequently advantageous to have, as weights, powers of two. The following sets of weights yield this, and in addition the overall divisor A_{00} is also a power of two.

A_{rs}

r \ s	-2	-1	0	1	2	
2	0	1	2	1	0	$B = 14$
1	1	0	0	0	1	$\theta = -11/2$
0	2	0	16	0	2	$\phi = 3$
-1	1	0	0	0	1	$\eta = -43/60$
-2	1	1	2	1	0	$\gamma = 29/60$

A_{rs}

r \ s	-2	-1	0	1	2	
2	0	1	2	1	0	$B = 22$
1	1	4	0	4	1	$\theta = -37/6$
0	2	0	32	0	2	$\phi = 1/3$
-1	1	4	0	4	1	$\eta = -133/180$
-2	0	1	2	1	0	$\gamma = 13/60$

ELLIPTIC DIFFERENTIAL EQUATIONS (Continued)

A_{rs}

r \ s	-2	-1	0	1	2	
2	0	1	2	1	0	$B = 18$
1	1	0	4	0	1	$\theta = -35/6$
0	2	4	32	4	2	$\phi = 11/3$
-1	1	0	4	0	1	$\eta = -131/180$
-2	0	1	2	1	0	$\gamma = 31/60$

A_{rs}

r \ s	-2	-1	0	1	2	
2	0	1	2	1	0	$B = 34$
1	1	4	8	4	1	$\theta = -41/3$
0	2	8	64	8	2	$\phi = 5/3$
-1	1	4	8	4	1	$\eta = -137/180$
-2	0	1	2	1	0	$\gamma = 17/60$

A_{rs}

r \ s	-2	-1	0	1	2	
2	0	0	1	0	0	$B = 8$
1	0	1	2	1	0	$\theta = -5/3$
0	1	2	16	2	1	$\phi = 7/3$
-1	0	1	2	1	0	$\eta = -17/90$
-2	1	0	1	0	0	$\gamma = 29/60$

A_{rs}

r \ s	-2	-1	0	1	2	
2	0	1	0	1	0	$B = 13$
1	1	1	1	1	1	$\theta = -37/12$
0	0	1	16	1	0	$\phi = -17/6$
-1	1	1	1	1	1	$\eta = -133/360$
-2	0	1	0	1	0	$\gamma = -77/120$

ELLIPTIC DIFFERENTIAL EQUATIONS (Continued)

For desk machine working the value of A_{00} should be chosen so as to simplify the process of division. Some typical sets of weights in which A_{00} is 100 are

A_{rs}

s \ r	-2	-1	0	1	2	
2	1	7	10	7	1	$B = 118$
1	7	0	0	0	7	$\theta = -215/6$
0	10	0	100	0	10	$\phi = -1/6$
-1	7	0	0	0	7	$\eta = -839/180$
-2	1	7	10	7	1	$\gamma = -181/60$

A_{rs}

s \ r	-2	-1	0	1	2	
2	0	1	5	1	0	$B = 56$
1	1	8	10	8	1	$\theta = -35/3$
0	5	10	100	10	5	$\phi = 22/3$
-1	1	8	10	8	1	$\eta = -119/90$
-2	0	1	5	1	0	$\gamma = 49/30$

A_{rs}

s \ r	-2	-1	0	1	2	
2	0	5	0	5	0	$B = 70$
1	5	5	10	5	5	$\theta = -95/6$
0	0	10	100	10	0	$\phi = -40/3$
-1	5	5	10	5	5	$\eta = -67/36$
-2	0	5	0	5	0	$\gamma = -19/6$

Starting the solution

Any rough estimate can be used to start the solution. In the absence of such an estimate all the interior points can be set at zero. In the case of Laplace's equation, straight lines can be drawn through any point to cut the boundary. The estimated value of the function at that point is then obtained by simple ratio and proportion.

Continuing the solution.

A systematic sweep through the region is essential, although the actual direction of travel chosen is immaterial for all practical purposes. It is important however that once the value at a specific point has been recomputed the new value should immediately replace the old.

Refining the mesh.

Once all the values at the mesh points have converted to the degree of accuracy permitted by the interval "h," the mesh can be subdivided in the following fashion and convergence to more accurate values obtained.

ELLIPTIC DIFFERENTIAL EQUATIONS (Continued)

Fig. 1 shows the mesh of side h, near a boundary where it is required to produce a mesh of side $\frac{1}{2}h$

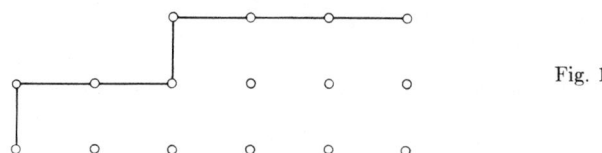

Fig. 1

The points marked with a $+$ in Fig. 2 can be inserted by means of the first formula of Group 1.

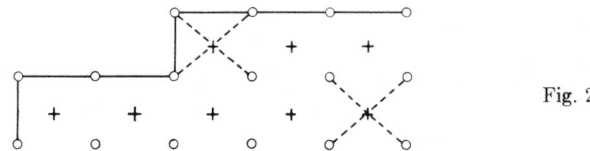

Fig. 2

The points marked with a $\bullet$ in Fig. 3 can then be inserted by means of the first formula of Group 2.

Fig. 3

Finally the boundary conditions enable the values at the new mesh points on the boundary to be inserted. These are indicated by $\bullet$ in Fig. 4.

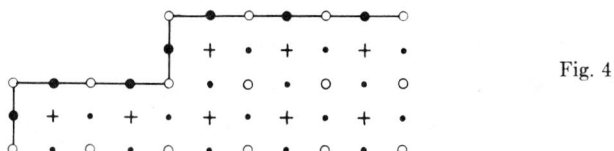

Fig. 4

Improving the numerical solution

(i) Aitken's δ^2 process.

If $u^{(1)}$, $u^{(2)}$ and $u^{(3)}$ are three successive approximations for a given h to u, then a better approximation is given by

$$u = u^{(3)} - \frac{[u^{(3} - u^{(2)}]^2}{u^{(3)} - 2u^{(2)} + u^{(1)}}$$

(ii) Richardson's deferred approach to the limit.

If $u_{(1)}$ is the value obtained for a mesh size h and $u_{(2)}$ is the value when the mesh size is $\frac{1}{2}h$ then a better value for u is given by

$$u = u_{(2)} + \frac{1}{3}[u_{(2)} - u_{(1)}]$$

ELLIPTIC DIFFERENTIAL EQUATIONS (Continued)

If, in addition, $u_{(3)}$ is the value obtained for a mesh size $\frac{1}{4}h$ then the improved value is given by

$$u = u_{(3)} + \frac{4}{9}\left[u_{(3)} - u_{(2)}\right] - \frac{1}{45}\left[u_{(3)} - u_{(1)}\right]$$

It is not necessary to refine the mesh over the entire region. In most cases only specially selected areas will need refining.

(iii) Difference correction.

The technique here is the same as is described in the section on ordinary differential equations. The derivatives in the error term are replaced by their finite difference equivalents, in both the x and y directions, and these constitute the difference correction.

Non-rectangular boundaries.

In some cases a transformation of coordinates will produce a boundary which will fit a rectangular mesh at the expense of increased complexity of the partial differential equation.

In others a mesh which is not rectangular can be employed, the usual alternatives being triangular and hexagonal.

Otherwise the rectangular mesh can be preserved for the mean body of the calculation and the iterative formula modified on the boundary. Thus two basic forms will be needed at a curved boundary.

Case 1.

$$A_0 u_0 = -Bf_0 + \sum_{r=1}^{4} A_r u_r + 0(h^3)$$

$$h \geq H_i \qquad (i = 1,2,3,4)$$
$$h_i = H_i/h$$

$$A_0 = (h_1 + h_3)(h_2 + h_4)(h_1 h_3 + h_2 h_4)$$
$$B = \tfrac{1}{2}h_1 h_2 h_3 h_4(h_1 + h_3)(h_2 + h_4)$$
$$A_1 = h_2 h_3 h_4(h_2 + h_4)$$
$$A_2 = h_3 h_4 h_1(h_3 + h_1)$$
$$A_3 = h_4 h_1 h_2(h_4 + h_2)$$
$$A_4 = h_1 h_2 h_3(h_1 + h_3)$$

Case 2

The formulae are the same as in Case 1; it is only the orientation of the mesh which is changed

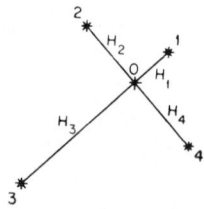

ELLIPTIC DIFFERENTIAL EQUATIONS (Continued)

Triangular mesh formulae for Poisson's equation

The points are numbered as shown

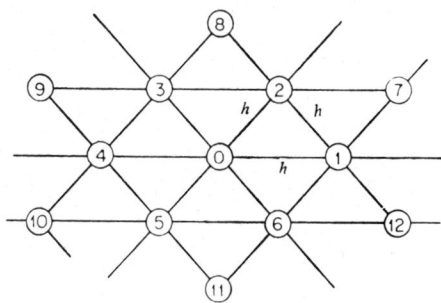

The iteration formula for the above mesh is

$$A_0 = \Sigma A_r u_r - B h^2 f_0 + \epsilon$$

a) Summation extends over $r = 1(1)6$

$$A_0 = 6, \qquad A_r = 1, \qquad B = 3/2$$

$$\epsilon = -\frac{32}{32} h^4 \nabla_0^4$$

b) Summation extends over $r = 7(1)12$

$$A_0 = 6, \qquad A_r = 1, \qquad B = 9/2$$

$$\epsilon = -\frac{27}{32} h^4 \nabla_0^4$$

c) Summation extends over $r = 1(1)12$

$$A_0 = 48, \qquad A_r = 9 \qquad (r = 1(1)6)$$

$$B = 8 \qquad A_r = -1 \qquad (r = 7(1)12)$$

$$\epsilon = -\frac{h^6}{3840} \left(11 \frac{\partial^6}{\partial x^6} + 15 \frac{\partial^6}{\partial x^4 \partial y^2} + 45 \frac{\partial^6}{\partial x^2 \partial y^4} + 9 \frac{\partial^6}{\partial y^6} \right) u_0$$

Hexagonal mesh formulae for Poisson's equation

The points are numbered as shown

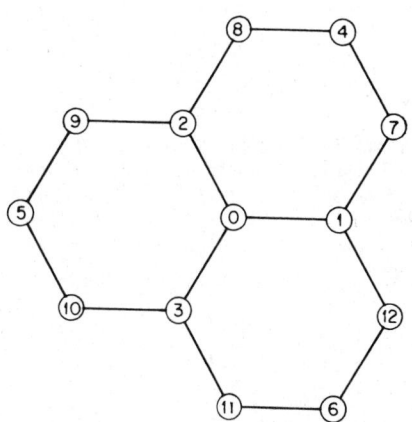

ELLIPTIC DIFFERENTIAL EQUATIONS (Continued)

The iteration formula for the above mesh being

$$A_0 = \Sigma A_r u_r - Bh^2 f_0 + \epsilon$$

a) Summation extends over $r = 1(1)3$

$$A_0 = 3, \qquad A_r = 1, \qquad B = 3/4$$

$$\epsilon = -\frac{h^3}{8}\left(\frac{\partial^3}{\partial x^3} - 3\frac{\partial^3}{\partial x \partial y^2}\right)u_0$$

b) Summation extends over $r = 4(1)6$

$$A_0 = 3, \qquad A_r = 1, \qquad B = 3$$

$$\epsilon = -h^3\left(\frac{\partial^3}{\partial x^3} - 3\frac{\partial^3}{\partial x \partial y^2}\right)u_0$$

c) Summation extends over $r = 1(1)6$

$$A_0 = 21, \qquad A_r = 8 \qquad (r = 1(1)3)$$

$$B = 3, \qquad A_r = -1 \qquad (r = 4(1)6)$$

$$\epsilon = \frac{h^4}{8}\left(3\frac{\partial^4}{\partial x^4} + \frac{\partial^4}{\partial x^2 \partial y^2} + 3\frac{\partial^4}{\partial y^4}\right)u_0$$

PARABOLIC DIFFERENTIAL EQUATIONS

Parabolic and Hyperbolic Partial Differential Equations

While this section will be restricted to partial differential equations with two independent variables, the techniques involved can easily be extended to those with three or more.

For simplicity, a rectangular mesh will be superimposed upon the region of integration. The pivotal points will have co-ordinates (x_s, t_r) where, for the intervals "h" and "k,"

$$x_s = x_0 + sh$$

$$t_r = t_0 + rk$$

$$f_{s,r} = f(x_s, t_r).$$

If the derivatives, with respect to either x or t, are replaced by their finite difference approximations, the result will be a set of simultaneous ordinary differential equations.

If, however, all the derivatives are replaced by their relevant approximations, a difference equation corresponding to the original differential equations is obtained. It should be noted, of course, that the approximation chosen will not be unique. Some typical examples are as follows,

$$\left(\frac{\partial f}{\partial t}\right)_{s,r} = (f_{s,r+1} - f_{s,r})/k$$

or

$$= (f_{s,r} - f_{s,r-1})/k$$

PARABOLIC DIFFERENTIAL EQUATIONS (Continued)

or $\qquad = (f_{s,r+1} - f_{s,r-1})/2k$

$$\left(\frac{\partial^2 f}{\partial x^2}\right)_{s,r} = (f_{s+1,r} - 2f_{s,r} + f_{s-1,r})/h^2$$

or $\qquad = (2f_{s,r} - 5f_{s-1,r} + 4f_{s-2,r} - f_{s-3,r})/h^2$

or $\qquad = (11f_{s+1,r} - 20f_{s,r} + 6f_{s-1,r} + 4f_{s-2,r} - f_{s-3,r})/12h^2$

and so forth.

Parabolic Partial Differential Equations

The examples in this section will be concerned in the main, with the simple but nevertheless typical one-dimensional heat equation given by:

$$\frac{\partial f}{\partial t} = \frac{\partial^2 f}{\partial x^2}$$

with the initial conditions $\qquad f = I(x) \qquad\qquad [x_0 \leqslant x \leqslant x_n,\ t = 0]$

and the boundary conditions $\qquad f = B(t) \qquad\qquad [t > 0, \quad x = x_0]$

$$f = B^*(t) \qquad\qquad [t > 0, \quad x = x_n]$$

Without loss of generality, x_0 can be replaced by 0 so that

$$x_s = sh, \quad t_r = rk,$$

and $\qquad\qquad I(x_s) = f_{s,0}, \quad B(t_r) = f_{0,r}, \quad B^*(t_r) = f_{n,r}.$

Two decisions have now to be made.

(*a*) Is the relationship between the values of "*f*" at the pivotal points to be an implicit one or an explicit one? That is to say, if the solution is being determined in the direction of *t* increasing, is the value at $f_{s,r}$ going to involve other values for which $t = rk$, or is it only going to involve those points for which $t < rk$?

(*b*) How many points are going to be involved at any one time?

A small number of points will mean less computational labor, but generally at the expense of the truncation error.

The explicit formulae are more direct than the implicit ones, but may require the mesh size to be unacceptably small in order to ensure the stability of the solution. In some cases the explicit form is unstable for all meshes. On the other hand, the implicit formulae are stable but they require the solution of large numbers of simultaneous equations.

Some typical explicit formulae

i. $\qquad\qquad f_{s,r+1} = f_{s,r} + (k/h^2)(f_{s-1,r} - 2f_{s,r} + f_{s+1,r})$

PARABOLIC DIFFERENTIAL EQUATIONS (Continued)

Stable if $0 < k/h^2 \leqq 1/2$

Truncation error $= 0(k) + 0(h^2)$

In particular when $k/h^2 = 1/2$ the point pattern is simplified by the omission of the pivot $f_{s,r}$.

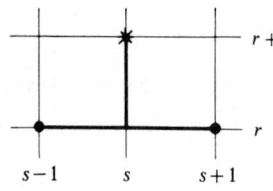

$$f_{s,r+1} = \tfrac{1}{2}(f_{s-1,r} + f_{s+1,r})$$

Milne has shown that an improved truncation error results when $k/h^2 = 1/6$

$$f_{s,r+1} = (1/6)(f_{s-1,r} + 4f_{s,r} + f_{s+1,r})$$

Truncation error $= 0(k^2) + 0(h^4)$

ii.
$$f_{s,r+1} = \frac{(h^2 - 2k)f_{s,r-1} + 2k(f_{s-1,r} + f_{s+1,r})}{(h^2 + 2k)}$$

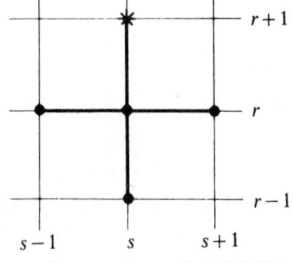

Always stable, but $f_{s,r-1}$ is required.

Truncation error $= 0(k) + 0(h^2) + 0(k/h)$

iii. $f_{s,r+1} = f_{s,r} - (1/12)(k/h^2)(f_{s-2,r} - 16f_{s-1,r} + 30f_{s,r} - 16f_{s+1,r} + f_{s+2,r})$

Stable if $0 < (k/h^2) \leq 3/8$

Truncation error $= 0(k) + 0(h^4)$

If the above mesh is used for the main body of the computation, then unsymmetric formulae are required at the ends of the range of s. The formula for the left hand side is shown below. (The formula for the right hand side is the mirror image.)

$$f_{s,r+1} = f_{s,r} + (1/12)(k/h^2)(11f_{s-1,r} - 20f_{s,r} + 6f_{s+1,r} + 4f_{s+2,r} - f_{s+3,r})$$

Stable if $0 < (k/h^2) \leq 2/7$

Truncation error $= 0(h^3) + 0(k)$

PARABOLIC DIFFERENTIAL EQUATIONS (Continued)

The truncation error of the unsymmetrical case will of course determine the overall truncation error if all three formulae are to be used in the one problem. The same observation will hold for the stability requirements.

One way of reducing the truncation error is to use additional, previously computed values; i.e., instead of using only those for which $t = rk$, increase the number of pivotal values involved by incorporating those for which $t = (r - 1)k$, $(r - 2)k$ etc. This method was used in example ii. However, it is generally unwise as such formulae tend toward high instability.

Some typical implicit formulae

These have the merit of stability but require the solution of a number of simultaneous equations. However, when matrix methods are used, often only one inversion is required. This simplifies the problem considerably.

i. $(k/h^2)(f_{s+1,r+1} + f_{s-1,r+1} + f_{s+1,r} + f_{s-1,r})$

$$- 2[1 + (k/h^2)]f_{s,r+1} + 2[1 - (k/h^2)]f_{s,r} = 0$$

Always stable

Truncation error $= 0(k^2) + 0(h^2)$

ii. $$f_{s,r+1} - f_{s,r} = (k/h^2)(f_{s-1,r+1} - 2f_{s,r+1} + f_{s+1,r+1})$$

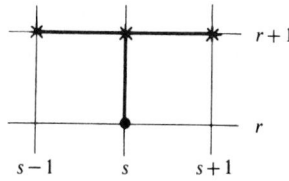

Always stable

Truncation error $= 0(k) + 0(h^2))$

iii. $12(f_{s,r+1} - f_{s,r}) + (k/h^2)(f_{s-2,r+1} - 16f_{s-1,r+1} + 30f_{s,r+1}$

$$- 16f_{s+1,r+1} + f_{s+2,r+1}) = 0$$

Always stable

Truncation error $= 0(k) + 0(h^4)$

As in the explicit case, unsymmetrical forms of the above formula are required at the extremities of the range. Only one will be quoted here (the other is merely a mirror image):

HYPERBOLIC DIFFERENTIAL EQUATIONS (Continued)

$$12(f_{s,r+1} - f_{s,r}) = (k/h^2)(11f_{s-1,r+1} - 20f_{s,r+1} + 6f_{s+1,r+1} + 4f_{s+2,r+1} - f_{s+3,r+1})$$

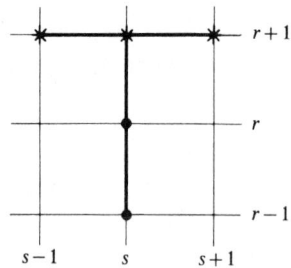

Always stable

Truncation error $= 0(k) + 0(h^3)$

iv. $[18(k/h^2) - 1](f_{s,r+1} - f_{s,r}) - [6(k/h^2) - 1](f_{s,r} - f_{s,r-1})$
$$= 12(k^2/h^4)(f_{s+1,r+1} - 2f_{s,r+1} + f_{s-1,r+1})$$

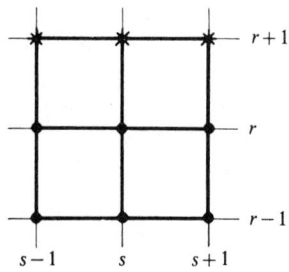

Always stable

Truncation error $= 0(k^2) + 0(h^4)$

v. An implicit method in its own right which can be used as a check on (iv) above is given by

$(3f_{s+1,r+1} - 4f_{s+1,r} + f_{s+1,r-1}) + (30f_{s,r+1} - 40f_{s,r} + 10f_{s,r-1})$
$$+ (3f_{s-1,r+1} - 4f_{s,r+1} + f_{s-1,r-1}) = 24(k/h^2)(f_{s+1,r+1} - 2f_{s,r+1} + f_{s-1,r+1})$$

Always stable

Truncation error $= 0(k^2) + 0(h^4)$

Hyperbolic Partial Differential Equations

The methods used in the parabolic case carry over into the hyperbolic case; therefore, only one example of each will be quoted.

Consider

$$(\partial^2 f/\partial x^2) = (\partial^2 f/\partial t^2)$$

with appropriate boundary conditions.

An explicit formula:

$$f_{s,r+1} = 2f_{s,r} - f_{s,r-1} + (k^2/h)(f_{s-1,r} - 2f_{s,r} + f_{s+1,r})$$

PARABOLIC AND HYPERBOLIC DIFFERENTIAL EQUATIONS (Continued)

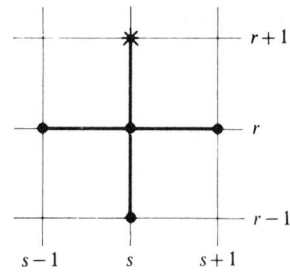

Stable if $0 < (k/h)^2 \leq 1$

Truncation error $= 0(h^4) + 0(k^4)$

An implicit formula:

$$(f_{s,r+1} - 2f_{s,r} + f_{s,r-1}) = (k/h)^2(f_{s-1,r+1} - 2f_{s,r+1} + f_{s+1,r+1})$$

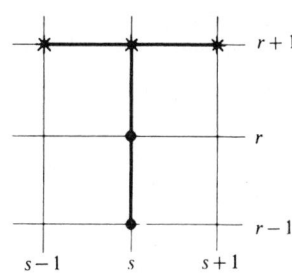

Always stable

Truncation error $= 0(h^4) + 0(k^4)$

Mixed Boundary Conditions for Parabolic and Hyperbolic Differential Equations

When the boundary conditions involve a derivative some slight modifications are necessary to take this condition into account.

Example 1 $\quad \dfrac{\partial f}{\partial t} = \dfrac{\partial^2 f}{\partial x^2};$

$\qquad\qquad f = I(x), \qquad\qquad\qquad [t = 0, \quad 0 \leq x \leq nh]$

$\qquad\qquad f = B(t), \qquad\qquad\qquad [t > 0, \quad x = 0]$

$\qquad f + A(\partial f/\partial x) = B^*(t), \qquad\qquad [t > 0, \quad x = nh]$

The derivative can be replaced by a finite difference approximation as follows

$$f_{n,r} + \frac{A(f_{n,r} - f_{n-1,r})}{k} = B^*(t_r)$$

which can be rewritten as $f_{n,r} = \dfrac{(k/A)B^*(t_r) + f_{n-1,r}}{(1 + k/A)}$

This enables the end points to be computed. A more accurate approximation to the derivative can be used of course, e.g.,

$$f_{n,r} + \frac{A(6f_{n,r} - 10f_{n-1,r} + 5f_{n-2,r} - f_{n-3,r})}{6k} = B^*(t_r)$$

Example 2. $\quad \dfrac{\partial f}{\partial t} = \dfrac{\partial^2 f}{\partial x^2};$ $\qquad f + A\dfrac{\partial f}{\partial t} = I(x), \qquad\qquad [t = 0, 0 \leq x \leq nh]$

$\qquad\qquad\qquad\qquad\qquad f = B(t), \qquad\qquad\qquad [t > 0, \quad x = 0]$

$\qquad\qquad\qquad\qquad\qquad f = B^*(t), \qquad\qquad\qquad [t > 0, \quad x = nh]$

PARABOLIC AND HYPERBOLIC DIFFERENTIAL EQUATIONS (Continued)

In this example the unconditionally stable form (ii) of the explicit set can be used. This is rewritten to give

$$f_{s,-1} = \frac{(h^2 + 2k)}{(h^2 - 2k)} \left(f_{s,1} - \frac{2k}{(h^2 + 2k)} (f_{s-1,0} + f_{s+1,0}) \right)$$

The initial conditions yield

$$f_{s,0} + (A/2k)(f_{s,1} - f_{s,-1}) = I(x_s)$$

or

$$f_{s,-1} = (2k/A)[f_{s,0} - I(x_s)] + f_{s,1}$$

Eliminating $f_{s,-1}$ from these two equations will yield an expression for $f_{s,1}[1 \leq s \leq (n-1)]$ and thereafter explicit formula (ii) can be used without modification.

MONTE CARLO TECHNIQUES FOR PARTIAL DIFFERENTIAL EQUATIONS

(i) Elliptic Equations.

The two dimensional case will be discussed here—the extension to more than two dimensions follows by increasing the number of the directions of the random walks by two for each added dimension.

The finite difference approximations

$$\frac{\partial^2 u}{\partial x^2} = \frac{u_{i+1,j} - 2u_{i,j} + u_{i-1,j}}{h_1^2}$$

and

$$\frac{\partial^2 u}{\partial y^2} = \frac{u_{i,j+1} - 2u_{i,j} + u_{i,j-1}}{h_2^2}$$

when substituted into $\nabla^2 u = 0$, yield

$$u_{i,j} = \frac{h_2^2 u_{i+1,j}}{2(h_1^2 + h_2^2)} + \frac{h_2^2 u_{i-1,j}}{2(h_1^2 + h_2^2)} + \frac{h_1^2 u_{i,j+1}}{2(h_1^2 + h_2^2)} + \frac{h_1^2 u_{i,j-1}}{2(h_1^2 + h_2^2)}$$

and, defining

$$p_1 = p_2 = \frac{h_2^2}{2(h_1^2 + h_2^2)}$$

$$p_3 = p_4 = \frac{h_1^2}{2(h_1^2 + h_2^2)}$$

It can be seen that $\sum_{i=1}^{4} p_i = 1$, which is the condition for carrying out a random walk along the four directions x increasing, x decreasing, y increasing and y decreasing. Thus to determine $u_{i,j}$ the value of u at the point with coordinates (x_i, y_j) the procedure is as follows; Set both T and N to zero initially.

For each walk completed add 1 to N.

A walk is completed when the boundary is reached and the value of u *at that point on the boundary* has been added to T. As the number of completed walks increases, $N \rightarrow \infty$ and $\frac{T}{N} \rightarrow u_{i,j}$.

For the equation $\nabla^2 u = f$ use the relationship

$$\frac{h_1^2 h_2^2}{2(h_1^2 + h_2^2)} f_{i,j} + u_{i,j} = p_1 u_{i+1,j} + p_2 u_{i-1,j} + p_3 u_{i,j+1} + p_4 u_{i,j-1}$$

As before the expression on the left hand side is the limiting value of the ratio $\frac{T}{N}$ as $N \rightarrow \infty$.

MONTE CARLO TECHNIQUES (Continued)

(ii) Parabolic equations.

Formula (ii) on page 511 yields, as a finite difference representation of

$$\frac{\partial f_{s,r}}{\partial t} = \frac{\partial^2 f_{s,r}}{\partial x^2}$$

$$f_{s,r+1} = \left(\frac{h^2 - 2k}{h^2 + 2k}\right) f_{s,r-1} + \left(\frac{2k}{h^2 + 2k}\right) f_{s-1,r} + \left(\frac{2k}{h^2 + 2k}\right) f_{s+1,r}$$

This can be written as

$$f_{s,r+1} = p_1 f_{s-1,r} + p_2 f_{s+1,r} + p_3 f_{s,r-1}$$

where as before $\displaystyle\sum_{r=1}^{3} p_r = 1$

for

$$p_1 = p_2 = \left(\frac{2k}{h^2 + 2k}\right); \qquad p_3 = \left(\frac{h^2 - 2k}{h^2 + 2k}\right).$$

The three directions are x increasing, x decreasing and t decreasing. In other words progress is restricted to be either towards the boundaries (along the x directions) or back towards the initial conditions along the direction of t decreasing. As before, N will be the total number of completed walks and T will be the sum of the boundary values or initial values reached.

XII. PROBABILITY AND STATISTICS

DESCRIPTIVE STATISTICS

a) Ungrouped Data

The formulas of this section designated as *a*) apply to a random sample of size n, denoted by x_i, $i = 1, 2, \ldots, n$.

b) Grouped Data

The formulas of this section designated as *b*) apply to data grouped into a frequency distribution having class marks x_i, $i = 1, 2, \ldots, k$, and corresponding class frequencies f_i, $i = 1, 2, \ldots, k$. The total number of observations given by

$$n = \sum_{i=1}^{k} f_i$$

In the formulas that follow, c denotes the width of the class interval, x_o denotes one of the class marks taken to be the computing origin, and $u_i = \dfrac{x_i - x_o}{c}$. Then coded class marks are obtained by replacing the original class marks with the integers $\ldots, -3, -2, -1, 0, 1, 2, 3, \ldots$ where 0 corresponds to class mark x_o in the original scale.

Mean (Arithmetic Mean)

a) $\bar{x} = \dfrac{1}{n} \sum_{i=1}^{n} x_i = \dfrac{x_1 + x_2 + \cdots + x_n}{n}$

b.1) $\bar{x} = \dfrac{1}{n} \sum_{i=1}^{k} f_i x_i = \dfrac{f_1 x_1 + f_2 x_2 + \cdots + f_k x_k}{n}$

If data is coded

b.2) $\bar{x} = x_o + c \dfrac{\displaystyle\sum_{i=1}^{k} f_i u_i}{n}$

Weighted Mean (Weighted Arithmetic Mean)

If with each value x_i is associated a weighting factor $w_i \geq 0$, then $\displaystyle\sum_{i=1}^{n} w_i$ is the total weight, and

a) $\bar{x} = \dfrac{\displaystyle\sum_{i=1}^{n} w_i x_i}{\displaystyle\sum_{i=1}^{n} w_i} = \dfrac{w_1 x_1 + w_2 x_2 + \cdots + w_n x_n}{w_1 + w_2 + \cdots + w_n}$

Geometric Mean

a) G.M. $= \sqrt[n]{x_1 \cdot x_2 \cdots x_n}$

In logarithmic form

$$\log \text{ (G.M.)} = \frac{1}{n} \sum_{i=1}^{n} \log x_i = \frac{\log x_1 + \log x_2 + \cdots + \log x_n}{n}$$

b) $\text{G.M.} = \sqrt[n]{x_1^{f_1} \cdot x_2^{f_2} \cdots x_k^{f_k}}$

In logarithmic form

$$\log \text{ (G.M.)} = \frac{1}{n} \sum_{i=1}^{k} f_i \log x_i = \frac{f_1 \log x_1 + f_2 \log x_2 + \cdots + f_k \log x_k}{n}$$

Harmonic Mean

a) $\text{H.M.} = \dfrac{n}{\displaystyle\sum_{i=1}^{n} \dfrac{1}{x_i}} = \dfrac{n}{\dfrac{1}{x_1} + \dfrac{1}{x_2} + \cdots + \dfrac{1}{x_n}}$

b) $\text{H.M.} = \dfrac{n}{\displaystyle\sum_{i=1}^{k} \dfrac{f_i}{x_i}} = \dfrac{n}{\dfrac{f_1}{x_1} + \dfrac{f_2}{x_2} + \cdots + \dfrac{f_k}{x_k}}$

Relation Between Arithmetic, Geometric, and Harmonic Mean

$\text{H.M.} \leq \text{G.M.} \leq \bar{x}$, (Equality sign holds only if all sample values are identical.)

Mode

a) A mode M_o of a sample of size n is a value which occurs with greatest frequency, i.e., it is the most common value. A mode may not exist, and even if it does exist it may not be unique.

b) $M_o = L + c \dfrac{\Delta_1}{\Delta_1 + \Delta_2}$,

where L is the lower class boundary of the modal class (class containing the mode),
Δ_1 is the excess of modal frequency over frequency of next lower class,
Δ_2 is the excess of modal frequency over frequency of next higher class.

Median

a) If the sample is arranged in ascending order of magnitude, then the median M_d is given by the $\dfrac{n+1}{2}$ nd value. When n is odd, the median is the middle value of the set of ordered data; when n is even, the median is usually taken as the mean of the two middle values of the set of ordered data.

b) $M_d = L + c \dfrac{\dfrac{n}{2} - F_c}{f_m}$,

where L is lower class boundary of median class (class containing the median),
F_c is the sum of the frequencies of all classes lower than the median class,
f_m is the frequency of the median class.

Empirical Relation Between Mean, Median, and Mode

$$\text{Mean} - \text{Mode} = 3 \, (\text{Mean} - \text{Median})$$

Quartiles

a) If the data is arranged in ascending order of magnitude, the jth quartile Q_j, $j = 1$, 2, or 3, is given by the $\dfrac{j(n+1)}{4}$ th value. It may be necessary to interpolate between successive values.

b) The jth quartile Q_j, $j = 1$, 2, or 3, is obtained from formula b) for the median by counting $\dfrac{jn}{4}$ cases starting at the bottom of the distribution.

Deciles

a) If the sample is arranged in ascending order of magnitude, the jth decile D_j, $j = 1, 2, \ldots$, or 9, is given by the $\dfrac{j(n+1)}{10}$ th value. It may be necessary to interpolate between successive values.

b) The jth decile D_j, $j = 1, 2, \ldots$, or 9, is obtained from formula b) for the median by counting $\dfrac{jn}{10}$ cases starting at the bottom of the distribution.

Percentiles

a) If the sample is arranged in ascending order of magnitude, the jth percentile P_j, $j = 1. 2, \ldots$, or 99 is given by the $\dfrac{j(n+1)}{100}$ th value. It may be necessary to interpolate between successive values.

b) The jth percentile P_j, $j = 1, 2, \ldots$, or 99, is obtained from formulas b) for the median by counting $\dfrac{jn}{100}$ cases starting at the bottom of the distribution.

Mean Deviation

a)
$$\text{M.D.} = \frac{1}{n} \sum_{i=1}^{n} |x_i - \bar{x}|$$

or

$$\text{M.D.} = \frac{1}{n} \sum_{i=1}^{n} |x_i - M_d|$$

where $\bar{x}$ is the mean and M_d is the median of the sample.

b)
$$\text{M.D.} = \frac{1}{n} \sum_{i=1}^{k} f_i |x_i - \bar{x}|$$

or

$$\text{M.D.} = \frac{1}{n} \sum_{i=1}^{k} f_i |x_i - M_d|$$

where $\bar{x}$ is the mean and M_d the median of the sample.

Standard Deviation

a) $s = \sqrt{\dfrac{\sum\limits_{i=1}^{n} (x_i - \bar{x})^2}{n - 1}}$, where $\bar{x}$ is the mean of the sample.

For computational purposes,

$$s = \sqrt{\dfrac{\sum\limits_{i=1}^{n} x_i^2 - n\bar{x}^2}{n - 1}}$$

$$s = \sqrt{\dfrac{n \sum\limits_{i=1}^{n} x_i^2 - \left(\sum\limits_{i=1}^{n} x_i\right)^2}{n(n - 1)}}$$

b) $s = \sqrt{\dfrac{\sum\limits_{i=1}^{k} f_i(x_i - \bar{x})^2}{n - 1}}$, where $\bar{x}$ is the mean of the sample.

For computational purposes

$$s = \sqrt{\dfrac{\sum\limits_{i=1}^{k} f_i x_i^2 - n\bar{x}^2}{n - 1}}$$

$$s = \sqrt{\dfrac{n \sum\limits_{i=1}^{k} f_i x_i^2 - \left(\sum\limits_{i=1}^{k} f_i x_i\right)^2}{n(n - 1)}}$$

If data is coded,

$$s = c \sqrt{\dfrac{n \sum\limits_{i=1}^{k} f_i u_i^2 - \left(\sum\limits_{i=1}^{k} f_i u_i\right)^2}{n(n - 1)}}$$

Variance

The variance is the square of the standard deviation.

Range

The range of a set of values is the difference between the largest and smallest values in the set.

Root Mean Square

a) R.M.S. $= \left[\dfrac{1}{n} \sum\limits_{i=1}^{n} x_i^2\right]^{\frac{1}{2}}$

b) R.M.S. $= \left[\dfrac{1}{n} \sum\limits_{i=1}^{k} f_i x_i^2\right]^{\frac{1}{2}}$

Interquartile Range

$$Q_3 - Q_1,$$

where Q_1 and Q_3 are the first and third quartiles.

Quartile Deviation (Semi-Interquartile Range)

$$\frac{Q_3 - Q_1}{2},$$

where Q_1 and Q_3 are the first and third quartiles.

Coefficient of Variation

$$V = \frac{100s}{\bar{x}},$$

where $\bar{x}$ is the mean and s the standard deviation of the sample.

Coefficient of Quartile Variation

$$V = 100 \frac{Q_3 - Q_1}{Q_3 + Q_1},$$

where Q_1 and Q_3 are the first and third quartiles.

Standardized Variable (Standard Scores)

$$z = \frac{x_i - \bar{x}}{s},$$

where $\bar{x}$ is the mean and s the standard deviation of the sample.

Moments

a) The rth moment about the origin is given by

$$m'_r = \frac{1}{n} \sum_{i=1}^{n} x_i^r$$

The rth moment about the mean $\bar{x}$ is given by

$$m_r = \frac{1}{n} \sum_{i=1}^{n} (x_i - \bar{x})^r$$

If $\sum_{i=1}^{n} (x_i - \bar{x})^r$ is expanded by use of the binomial theorem, moments about the mean may be expressed in terms of moments about the origin.

b) The rth moment about the origin is given by

$$m'_r = \frac{1}{n} \sum_{i=1}^{k} f_i x_i^r$$

The rth moment about the mean $\bar{x}$ is given by

$$m_r = \frac{1}{n} \sum_{i=1}^{k} f_i (x_i - \bar{x})^r$$

If $\displaystyle\sum_{i=1}^{k} f_i(x_i - \bar{x})^r$ is expanded by use of the binomial theorem, moments **about the** mean may be expressed in terms of moments about the origin.

If data is coded

$$m_r' = c^r \frac{\displaystyle\sum_{i=1}^{k} f_i u_i^r}{n}$$

Coefficient of Skewness

$$\alpha_3 = \frac{m_3}{(m_2)^{3/2}},$$

where m_2 and m_3 are the second and third moments about the mean of the sample.

Coefficient of Momental Skewness

$$\frac{\alpha_3}{2} = \frac{m_3}{2(m_2)^{3/2}},$$

where m_2 and m_3 are the second and third moments about the mean of the sample.

Pearson's First Coefficient of Skewness

$$S_{k_1} = \frac{3(\bar{x} - M_o)}{s},$$

where $\bar{x}$ is the mean, M_o the mode, and s the standard deviation of the sample.

Pearson's Second Coefficient of Skewness

$$S_{k_2} = \frac{3(\bar{x} - M_d)}{s},$$

where $\bar{x}$ is the mean, M_d the median, and s the standard deviation of the sample.

Quartile Coefficient of Skewness

$$S_{k_Q} = \frac{Q_3 - 2Q_2 + Q_1}{Q_3 - Q_1},$$

where Q_1, Q_2, and Q_3 are the first, second, and third quartiles.

Coefficient of Kurtosis

$$\alpha_4 = \frac{m_4}{(m_2)^2},$$

where m_2 and m_4 are the second and fourth moments about the mean of the sample.

Coefficient of Excess (Kurtosis)

$$\alpha_4 - 3 = \frac{m_4}{(m_2)^2} - 3,$$

where m_2 and m_4 are the second and fourth moments about the mean of the sample.

Sheppards Corrections for Grouping

Let all class intervals be of equal length c. If the distribution of x has a high order of contact with the x-axis at both tails, (i.e., if the distribution of x has tails which are very

nearly tangent to the x-axis), one may improve the grouped data approximation to the variance by adding Sheppard's correction $-\dfrac{c^2}{12}$. Thus

$$\text{corrected variance} = \text{grouped data variance} - \frac{c^2}{12}$$

Analogous corrections for grouped data sample moments

$$m'_r = \frac{1}{n} \sum_{i=1}^{k} f_i x_i^r \qquad \text{and} \qquad m_r = \frac{1}{n} \sum_{i=1}^{k} f_i(x_i - \bar{x})^r$$

yield improved estimates m'_{r_c} and m_{r_c} given by

$$m'_{1_c} = m'_1 \qquad\qquad m_{1_c} = m_1$$

$$m'_{2_c} = m'_2 - \frac{c^2}{12} \qquad\qquad m_{2_c} = m_2 - \frac{c^2}{12}$$

$$m'_{3_c} = m'_3 - \frac{c^2}{4} m'_1 \qquad\qquad m_{3_c} = m_3$$

$$m'_{4_c} = m'_4 - \frac{c^2}{2} m'_1 + \frac{7c^4}{240} \qquad m_{4_c} = m_4 - \frac{c^2}{2} m_2 + \frac{7c^4}{240}$$

Curve Fitting, Regression, and Correlation

The following formulas apply to a set of n ordered pairs $\{(x_i,y_i)\}$, $i = 1, 2, \ldots, n$. The assumptions of normal regression analysis are that the x's are fixed variables, and the y's are independent random variables having normal distributions with common variance σ^2. The assumptions of normal correlation analysis are that $\{(x_i,y_i)\}$ constitute a random sample from a bivariate normal population.

Curve Fitting

1. Polynomial Function

$$y = b_0 + b_1 x + b_2 x^2 + \cdots + b_m x^m$$

For a polynomial function fit by the method of least squares, the values of $b_0, b_1, \ldots, b_m$ are obtained by solving the system of $m + 1$ normal equations

$$nb_0 + b_1\Sigma x_i + b_2\Sigma x_i^2 + \cdots + b_m\Sigma x_i^m = \Sigma y_i$$
$$b_0\Sigma x_i + b_1\Sigma x_i^2 + b_2\Sigma x_i^3 + \cdots + b_m\Sigma x_i^{m+1} = \Sigma x_i y_i$$
$$\cdots\cdots\cdots\cdots\cdots\cdots\cdots\cdots\cdots\cdots\cdots$$
$$b_0\Sigma x_i^m + b_1\Sigma x_i^{m+1} + b_2\Sigma x_i^{m+2} + \cdots + b_m\Sigma x_i^{2m} = \Sigma x_i^m y_i$$

2. Straight Line

$$y = b_0 + b_1 x$$

For a straight line fit by the method of least squares, the values b_0 and b_1 are obtained by solving the normal equations

$$nb_0 + b_1\Sigma x_i = \Sigma y_i$$
$$b_0\Sigma x_i + b_1\Sigma x_i^2 = \Sigma x_i y_i$$

The solutions of these normal equations are

$$b_1 = \frac{n\Sigma x_i y_i - (\Sigma x_i)(\Sigma y_i)}{n\Sigma x_i^2 - (\Sigma x_i)^2}$$

$$b_0 = \frac{\Sigma y_i}{n} - b_1 \frac{\Sigma x_i}{n} = \bar{y} - b_1\bar{x}$$

3. Exponential Curve

$$y = ab^x$$

or

$$\log y = \log a + (\log b)x$$

For an exponential curve fit by the method of least squares, the values $\log a$ and $\log b$ are obtained by fitting a straight line to the set of ordered pairs $\{(x_i, \log y_i)\}$.

4. Power Function

$$y = ax^b$$

or

$$\log y = \log a + b \log x$$

For a power function fit by the method of least squares, the values $\log a$ and b are obtained by fitting a straight line to the set of ordered pairs $\{(\log x_i, \log y_i)\}$.

Regression and Correlation

1. Simple Linear Regression.

For a regression of y on x

$$E(y/x) = b_0 + b_1 x,$$

where $E(y/x)$ is the mean of the distribution of y for a given x.

Standard Error of Estimate

$$s_e = \sqrt{\frac{\Sigma[y_i - (b_0 + b_1 x_i)]^2}{n - 2}},$$

where b_0 and b_1 are given by

$$b_1 = \frac{n\Sigma x_i y_i - (\Sigma x_i)(\Sigma y_i)}{n\Sigma x_i^2 - (\Sigma x_i)^2}$$

$$b_0 = \frac{\Sigma y_i}{n} - b_1 \frac{\Sigma x_i}{n} = \bar{y} - b_1 \bar{x}$$

2. Correlation.

An estimate of the population correlation coefficient ρ is given by

$$r = \frac{\Sigma(x_i - \bar{x})(y_i - \bar{y})}{\sqrt{[\Sigma(x_i - \bar{x})^2][\Sigma(y_i - \bar{y})^2]}}$$

or by the computing formula

$$r = \frac{n\Sigma x_i y_i - (\Sigma x_i)(\Sigma y_i)}{\sqrt{[n\Sigma x_i^2 - (\Sigma x_i)^2][n\Sigma y_i^2 - (\Sigma y_i)^2]}}$$

For grouped data

$$r = \frac{n\Sigma f x_i y_i - (\Sigma f_x x_i)(\Sigma f_y y_i)}{\sqrt{[n\Sigma f_x x_i^2 - (\Sigma f_x x_i)^2][n\Sigma f_y y_i^2 - (\Sigma f_y y_i)^2]}}$$

where f_x and f_y denote the frequencies corresponding to the class marks x and y, and f denotes the frequency of the corresponding cell of the correlation table.

If the data is coded

$$r = \frac{n\Sigma f uv - (\Sigma f_u u)(\Sigma f_v v)}{\sqrt{[n\Sigma f_u u^2 - (\Sigma f_u u)^2][n\Sigma f_v v^2 - (\Sigma f_v v)^2]}}$$

where the u's and v's are coded class marks. The frequencies f_u and f_v are defined analogous to f_x and f_y.

PROBABILITY

Definitions

A sample space S associated with an experiment is a set S of elements such that any outcome of the experiment corresponds to one and only one element of the set. An event E is a subset of a sample space S. An element in a sample space is called a sample point or a simple event (Unit subset of S).

Definition of Probability

If an experiment can occur in n mutually exclusive and equally likely ways, and if exactly m of these ways correspond to an event E, then the probability of E is given by

$$P(E) = \frac{m}{n}.$$

If E is a subset of S, and if to each unit subset of S, a non-negative number, called its probability, is assigned, and if E is the union of two or more different simple events, then the probability of E, denoted by $P(E)$, is the sum of the probabilities of those simple events whose union is E.

Marginal and Conditional Probability

Suppose a sample space S is partioned into rs disjoint subsets where the general subset is denoted by $E_i \cap F_j$. Then the marginal probability of E_i is defined as

$$P(E_i) = \sum_{j=1}^{s} P(E_i \cap F_j)$$

and the marginal probability of F_j is defined as

$$P(F_j) = \sum_{i=1}^{r} P(E_i \cap F_j)$$

The conditional probability of E_i, given that F_j has occurred, is defined as

$$P(E_i/F_j) = \frac{P(E_i \cap F_j)}{P(F_j)} , \qquad P(F_j) \neq 0$$

and that of F_j, given that E_i has occurred, is defined as

$$P(F_j/E_i) = \frac{P(E_i \cap F_j)}{P(E_i)} , \qquad P(E_i) \neq 0 .$$

Probability Theorems

1. If ϕ is the null set, $P(\phi) = 0$.
2. If S is the sample space, $P(S) = 1$.
3. If E and F are two events

$$P(E \cup F) = P(E) + P(F) - P(E \cap F).$$

4 If E and F are mutually exclusive events,

$$P(E \cup F) = P(E) + P(F).$$

5. If E and E' are complementary events,

$$P(E) = 1 - P(E').$$

6. The conditional probability of an event E, given an event F, is denoted by $P(E/F)$ and is defined as

$$P(E/F) = \frac{P(E \cap F)}{P(F)},$$

where $P(F) \neq 0$.

7. Two events E and F are said to be independent if and only if

$$P(E \cap F) = P(E) \cdot P(F).$$

E is said to be statistically independent of F if $P(E/F) = P(E)$ and $P(F/E) = P(F)$.

8. The events $E_1, E_2, \ldots, E_n$ are called mutually independent for all combinations if and only if every combination of these events taken any number at a time is independent.

9. *Bayes Theorem.*

If $E_1, E_2, \ldots, E_n$ are n mutually exclusive events whose union is the sample space S, and E is any arbitrary event of S such that $P(E) \neq 0$, then

$$P(E_k/E) = \frac{P(E_k) \cdot P(E/E_k)}{\sum\limits_{j=1}^{n} [P(E_j) \cdot P(E/E_j)]}$$

Random Variable

A function whose domain is a sample space S and whose range is some set of real numbers is called a random variable, denoted by $\mathbf{X}$. The function $\mathbf{X}$ transforms sample points of S into points on the x-axis. $\mathbf{X}$ will be called a discrete random variable if it is a random variable that assumes only a finite or denumerable number of values on the x-axis. $\mathbf{X}$ will be called a continuous random variable if it assumes a continuum of values on the x-axis.

Probability Function (Discrete Case)

The random variable $\mathbf{X}$ will be called a discrete random variable if there exists a function f such that $f(x_i) \geq 0$ and $\sum\limits_{i} f(x_i) = 1$ for $i = 1, 2, 3, \ldots$ and such that for any event E,

$$P(E) = P[\mathbf{X} \text{ is in } E] = \sum\limits_{E} f(x)$$

where $\sum\limits_{E}$ means sum $f(x)$ over those values x_i that are in E and where $f(x) = P[\mathbf{X} = x]$. The probability that the value of $\mathbf{X}$ is some real number x, is given by $f(x) = P[\mathbf{X} = x]$, where f is called the probability function of the random variable $\mathbf{X}$.

Cumulative Distribution Function (Discrete Case)

The probability that the value of a random variable $\mathbf{X}$ is less than or equal to some real number x is defined as

$$F(x) = P(\mathbf{X} \leq x)$$
$$= \Sigma f(x_i), \qquad -\infty < x < \infty,$$

where the summation extends over those values of i such that $x_i \leq x$.

Probability Density (Continuous Case)

The random variable $\mathbf{X}$ will be called a continuous random variable if there exists a function f such that $f(x) \geq 0$ and $\int_{-\infty}^{\infty} f(x)\, dx = 1$ for all x in interval $-\infty < x < \infty$ and such that for any event E

$$P(E) = P(\mathbf{X} \text{ is in } E) = \int_E f(x)\, dx.$$

$f(x)$ is called the probability density of the random variable $\mathbf{X}$. The probability that $\mathbf{X}$ assumes any given value of x is equal to zero and the probability that it assumes a value on the interval from a to b, including or excluding either end point, is equal to

$$\int_a^b f(x)\, dx.$$

Cumulative Distribution Function (Continuous Case)

The probability that the value of a random variable $\mathbf{X}$ is less than or equal to some real number x is defined as

$$F(x) = P(\mathbf{X} \leq x), \qquad -\infty < x < \infty$$
$$= \int_{-\infty}^{x} f(x)\, dx.$$

From the cumulative distribution, the density, if it exists, can be found from

$$f(x) = \frac{dF(x)}{dx}.$$

From the cumulative distribution

$$P(a \leq \mathbf{X} \leq b) = P(\mathbf{X} \leq b) - P(\mathbf{X} \leq a)$$
$$= F(b) - F(a)$$

Mathematical Expectation

A. Expected Value

Let $\mathbf{X}$ be a random variable with density $f(x)$. Then the expected value of $\mathbf{X}$, $E(\mathbf{X})$, is defined to be

$$E(\mathbf{X}) = \sum_x x f(x)$$

if $\mathbf{X}$ is discrete and

$$E(\mathbf{X}) = \int_{-\infty}^{\infty} x f(x)\, dx$$

if $\mathbf{X}$ is continuous. The expected value of a function g of a random variable $\mathbf{X}$ is defined as

$$E[g(\mathbf{X})] = \sum_x g(x) \cdot f(x)$$

if $\mathbf{X}$ is discrete and

$$E[g(\mathbf{X})] = \int_{-\infty}^{\infty} g(x) \cdot f(x)\, dx$$

if $\mathbf{X}$ is continuous.

Theorems

1. $E[aX + bY] = aE(X) + bE(Y)$
2. $E[X \cdot Y] = E(X) \cdot E(Y)$ if X and Y are statistically independent.

B. MOMENTS

a. Moments About the Origin. The moments about the origin of a probability distribution are the expected values of the random variable which has the given distribution. The rth moment of X, usually denoted by μ'_r, is defined as

$$\mu'_r = E[X^r] = \sum_x x^r f(x)$$

if X is discrete and

$$\mu'_r = E[X^r] = \int_{-\infty}^{\infty} x^r f(x)\, dx$$

if X is continuous.

The first moment, μ'_1, is called the mean of the random variable X and is usually denoted by μ.

b. Moments About the Mean. The rth moment about the mean, usually denoted by μ_r, is defined as

$$\mu_r = E[(X - \mu)^r] = \sum_x (x - \mu)^r f(x)$$

if X is discrete and

$$\mu_r = E[(X - \mu)^r] = \int_{-\infty}^{\infty} (x - \mu)^r f(x)\, dx$$

if X is continuous.

The second moment about the mean, μ_2, is given by

$$\mu_2 = E[(X - \mu)^2] = \mu'_2 - \mu^2$$

and is called the variance of the random variable X, and is denoted by σ^2. The square root of the variance, σ, is called the standard deviation.

Theorems

1. $\sigma^2_{cX} = c^2 \sigma^2_X$
2. $\sigma^2_{c+X} = \sigma^2_X$
3. $\sigma^2_{aX+b} = a^2 \sigma^2_X$

c. Factorial Moments. The rth factorial moment of a probability distribution is defined as

$$\mu'_{(r)} = E[X^{[r]}] = \sum_x x^{[r]} f(x)$$

if X is discrete and

$$\mu'_{(r)} = E[X^{[r]}] = \int_{-\infty}^{\infty} x^{[r]} f(x)\, dx$$

if X is continuous, where the symbol $x^{[r]}$ denotes the factorial expression

$$x^{[r]} = x(x - 1)(x - 2) \cdots (x - r + 1), r = 1, 2, 3, \ldots$$

C. GENERATING FUNCTIONS

a. Moment Generating Functions. The moment generating function (m.g.f.) of the random variable X is defined as

$$m_x(t) = E(e^{tX}) = \sum_x e^{tx} f(x)$$

if X is discrete and

$$m_x(t) = E(e^{tX}) = \int_{-\infty}^{\infty} e^{tx} f(x)\, dx$$

if X is continuous.

$E(e^{tX})$ is the expected value of e^{tX}. If $m_x(t)$ and its derivatives exist, $|t| < h^2$, the rth moment about the origin is

$$\mu'_r = m_x^{(r)}(0), \qquad r = 0, 1, 2, \ldots$$

where $m_x^{(r)}(0)$ is the rth derivative of $m_x(t)$ with respect to t, evaluated at $t = 0$. For

$$
\begin{aligned}
m_x(t) &= E(e^{tX}) \\
&= E\left[1 + Xt + \frac{(Xt)^2}{2!} + \cdots\right] \\
&= 1 + \mu'_1 t + \mu'_2 \frac{t^2}{2} + \cdots
\end{aligned}
$$

Thus, the moments μ'_r appear as coefficients of $\dfrac{t^r}{r!}$, and $m_x(t)$ may be regarded as generating the moments ν_r. The moments μ_r may be generated by the generating function

$$M_x(t) = E[e^{t(X - \mu)}] = e^{-\mu t} E(e^{tX}) = e^{-\mu t} m_x(t) .$$

b. Factorial Moment Generating Function. The factorial moment generating function is defined as

$$E(t^X) = \sum_x t^x f(x) \qquad \text{(probability generation function)}$$

if X is discrete and

$$E(t^X) = \int_{-\infty}^{\infty} t^x f(x)\, dx$$

if X is continuous.

The rth factorial moment is obtained from the factorial moment generating function by differentiating it r times with respect to t and then evaluating the result when $t = 1$.

Theorems

1. If c is a constant, the m.g.f. of $c + X$ is $e^{ct} m_x(t)$.
2. If c is a constant, the m.g.f. of cX is $m_x(ct)$.
3. If $Y = \sum_{i=1}^{n} X_i$, and $m_x(t)$ is the m.g.f. of X_i, where $X_1, \ldots, X_n$ is a random sample from $f(x)$, then the m.g.f. of Y is $[m_x(t)]^n$.

D. CUMULANT GENERATING FUNCTION

Let $m_x(t)$ be a m.g.f. If $\ln m_x(t)$ can be expanded in the form

$$c(t) = \ln m_x(t) = \kappa_1 t + \kappa_2 \frac{t^2}{2!} + \kappa_3 \frac{t^3}{3!} + \cdots + \kappa_r \frac{t^r}{r!} + \cdots,$$

then $c(t)$ is called the cumulant generating function (semi-invariant generating function) and κ_r are called the cumulants (semi-invariants) of a distribution.

$$\kappa_r = c^{(r)}(0)$$

where $c^{(r)}(0)$ is the rth derivative of $c(t)$ with respect to t evaluated at $t = 0$.

E. Characteristic Functions

The characteristic function of a distribution is defined as

$$\phi(t) = E(e^{itX}) = \sum_x e^{its} \cdot f(x)$$

if **X** is discrete and

$$\phi(t) = E(e^{itX}) = \int_{-\infty}^{\infty} e^{its} \cdot f(x) \, dx$$

if **X** is continuous.

Here t is a real number, $i^2 = -1$, and $e^{itX} = \cos(t\mathbf{X}) + i\sin(t\mathbf{X})$. The characteristic function also generates moments, if they exist for

$$i^r \mu'_r = \phi^{(r)}(0)$$

where $\phi^{(r)}(0)$ is the rth derivative of $\phi(t)$ with respect to t evaluated at $t = 0$.

Multivariate Distributions

A. Discrete Case

The k-dimensional random variable $(\mathbf{X}_1, \mathbf{X}_2, \ldots, \mathbf{X}_k)$ is a k-dimensional discrete random variable if it assumes values only at a finite or denumerable number of points $(x_1, x_2, \ldots, x_k)$. Define

$$P[\mathbf{X}_1 = x_1, \mathbf{X}_2 = x_2, \ldots, \mathbf{X}_k = x_k] = f(x_1, x_2, \ldots, x_k)$$

for every value that the random variable can assume. $f(x_1, x_2, \ldots, x_k)$ is called the joint density of the k-dimensional random variable. If E is any subset of the set of values that the random variable can assume, then

$$P(E) = P[(\mathbf{X}_1, \mathbf{X}_2, \ldots, \mathbf{X}_k) \text{ is in } E] = \sum_E f(x_1, x_2, \ldots, x_k)$$

where the sum is over all those points in E. The cumulative distribution is defined as

$$F(x_1, x_2, \ldots, x_k) = \sum_{x_1} \sum_{x_2} \cdots \sum_{x_k} f(x_1, x_2, \ldots, x_k).$$

B. Continuous Case

The k random variables $\mathbf{X}_1, \mathbf{X}_2, \ldots, \mathbf{X}_k$ are said to be jointly distributed if there exists a function f such that $f(x_1, x_2, \ldots, x_k) \geq 0$ for all $-\infty < x_i < \infty$, $i = 1, 2, \ldots, k$ and such that for any event E

$$P(E) = P[(\mathbf{X}_1, \mathbf{X}_2, \ldots, \mathbf{X}_k) \text{ is in } E]$$
$$= \int_E f(x_1, x_2, \ldots, x_k) \, dx_1 \, dx_2 \cdots dx_k.$$

$f(x_1, x_2, \ldots, x_k)$ is called the joint density of the random variables $\mathbf{X}_1, \mathbf{X}_2, \ldots, \mathbf{X}_k$.

The cumulative distribution is defined as

$$F(x_1, x_2, \ldots, x_k) = \int_{-\infty}^{x_1} \int_{-\infty}^{x_2} \cdots \int_{-\infty}^{x_k} f(x_1, x_2, \ldots, x_k) \, dx_k \cdots dx_2 \, dx_1.$$

Given the cumulative distribution, the density may be found by

$$f(x_1, x_2, \ldots, x_k) = \frac{\partial}{\partial x_1} \cdot \frac{\partial}{\partial x_2} \cdots \frac{\partial}{\partial x_k} F(x_1, x_2, \ldots, x_k) .$$

Moments

The rth moment of X_i, say, is defined as

$$E(X_i^r) = \sum_{x_1} \sum_{x_2} \cdots \sum_{x_k} x_i^r f(x_1, x_2, \ldots, x_k)$$

if the X_i are discrete and

$$E(X_i^r) = \int_{-\infty}^{\infty} \int_{-\infty}^{\infty} \cdots \int_{-\infty}^{\infty} x_i^r f(x_1, x_2, \ldots, x_k) \, dx_k \cdots dx_2 \, dx_1$$

if the X_i are continuous.

Joint moments about the origin are defined as

$$E(X_1^{r_1} X_2^{r_2} \cdots X_k^{r_k})$$

where $r_1 + r_2 + \cdots + r_k$ is the order of the moment.

Joint moments about the mean are defined as

$$E[(X_1 - \mu_1)^{r_1} (X_2 - \mu_2)^{r_2} \cdots (X_k - \mu_k)^{r_k}].$$

Marginal and Conditional Distributions

If the random variables $X_1, X_2, \ldots, X_k$ have the joint density function $f(x_1, x_2, \ldots, x_k)$, then the marginal distribution of the subset of the random variables, say, $X_1, X_2, \ldots, X_p$, $(p < k)$, is given by

$$g(x_1, x_2, \ldots, x_p) = \sum_{x_{p+1}} \sum_{x_{p+1}} \cdots \sum_{x_k} f(x_1, x_2, \ldots, x_k)$$

if the X's are discrete, and

$$g(x_1, x_2, \ldots, x_p) = \int_{-\infty}^{\infty} \int_{-\infty}^{\infty} \cdots \int_{-\infty}^{\infty} f(x_1, x_2, \ldots, x_k) \, dx_{p+1} \cdots dx_{k-1} \, dx_k$$

if the X's are continuous.

The conditional distribution of a certain subset of the random variables is the joint distribution of this subset under the condition that the remaining variables are given certain values. The conditional distribution of $X_1, X_2, \ldots, X_p$ given $X_{p+1}, X_{p+2}, \ldots, X_k$ is

$$h(x_1, x_2, \ldots, x_p | x_{p+1}, x_{p+2}, \ldots, x_k) = \frac{f(x_1, x_2, \ldots, x_k)}{g(x_{p+1}, x_{p+2}, \ldots, x_k)}$$

if $g(x_{p+1}, x_{p+2}, \ldots, x_k) \neq 0$.

The variance σ_{ii} of X_i and the covariance σ_{ij} of X_i and X_j are given by

$$\sigma_{ii} = \sigma_i^2 = E[(X_i - \mu_i)^2]$$

and

$$\sigma_{ij} = \rho_{ij} \sigma_i \sigma_j = E[(X_i - \mu_i)(X_j - \mu_j)]$$

where ρ_{ij} is the correlation coefficient and σ_i and σ_j are the standard deviations of X_i and X_j.

A joint m.g.f. is defined as

$$m(t_1, t_2, \ldots, t_k) = E[e^{t_1 \mathbf{X}_1 + t_2 \mathbf{X}_2 + \cdots + t_k \mathbf{X}_k}]$$

if it exists for all values of t_i such that $|t_i| < h^2$.

The rth moment of $\mathbf{X}_i$ may be obtained by differentiating the m.g.f. r times with respect to t_i and then evaluating the result when all t's are set equal to zero. Similarly, a joint moment would be found by differentiating the m.g.f. r_1 times with respect to t_1, $\ldots$, r_k times with respect to t_k, and then evaluating the result when all t's are set equal to zero.

Probability Distributions

A. Discrete Case

1. *Discrete Uniform Distribution.* If the random variable $\mathbf{X}$ has a probability function given by

$$P(\mathbf{X} = x) = f(x) = \frac{1}{n}, \qquad x = x_1, x_2, \ldots, x_n,$$

then the variable $\mathbf{X}$ is said to possess a discrete uniform distribution.

Properties

When $x_i = i$ for $i = 1, 2, \ldots,$ and n

$$\text{Mean} = \mu = \frac{n+1}{2}$$

$$\text{Variance} = \sigma^2 = \frac{n^2 - 1}{12}$$

$$\text{Standard Deviation} = \sigma = \sqrt{\frac{n^2 - 1}{12}}$$

$$\text{Moment Generating Function} = m_x(t) = \frac{e^t(1 - e^{nt})}{n(1 - e^t)}$$

2. *Binomial Distribution.* If the random variable $\mathbf{X}$ has a probability function given by

$$P(\mathbf{X} = x) = f(x) = \binom{n}{x} \theta^x (1 - \theta)^{n-x}, \qquad x = 0, 1, 2, \ldots, n$$

where

$$\binom{n}{x} = \frac{n!}{x!(n-x)!},$$

then the variable $\mathbf{X}$ is said to possess a binomial distribution. $f(x)$ is the general term of the expansion of $[\theta + (1 - \theta)]^n$.

Properties

$$\text{Mean} = \mu = n\theta$$
$$\text{Variance} = \sigma^2 = n\theta(1 - \theta)$$
$$\text{Standard Deviation} = \sigma = \sqrt{n\theta(1 - \theta)}$$
$$\text{Moment Generating Function} = m_x(t) = [\theta e^t + (1 - \theta)]^n$$

3. *Geometric Distribution.* If the random variable $\mathbf{X}$ has a probability function given by

$$P(\mathbf{X} = x) = f(x) = \theta(1 - \theta)^{x-1}, \qquad x = 1, 2, 3, \ldots,$$

then the variable $\mathbf{X}$ is said to possess a geometric distribution.

Properties

$$\text{Mean} = \mu = \frac{1}{\theta}$$

$$\text{Variance} = \sigma^2 = \frac{1 - \theta}{\theta^2}$$

$$\text{Standard Deviation} = \sigma = \sqrt{\frac{1 - \theta}{\theta^2}}$$

$$\text{Moment Generating Function} = m_x(t) = \frac{\theta e^t}{1 - e^t(1 - \theta)}$$

4. *Multinomial Distribution.* If a set of random variables $\mathbf{X}_1, \mathbf{X}_2, \ldots, \mathbf{X}_n$ has a probability function given by

$$P(\mathbf{X}_1 = x_1, \mathbf{X}_2 = x_2, \ldots, \mathbf{X}_n = x_n) = f(x_1, x_2, \ldots, x_n) = \frac{N!}{\prod\limits_{i=1}^{n} x_i!} \prod_{i=1}^{n} \theta_i^{x_i}$$

where x_i are positive integers and each $\theta_i > 0$ for $i = 1, 2, \ldots, n$ and

$$\sum_{i=1}^{n} \theta_i = 1, \qquad \sum_{i=1}^{n} x_i = N,$$

then the joint distribution of $\mathbf{X}_1, \mathbf{X}_2, \ldots, \mathbf{X}_n$ is called the multinomial distribution. $f(x_1, x_2, \ldots, x_n)$ is the general term of the expansion of $(\theta_1 + \theta_2 + \cdots + \theta_n)^N$.

Properties

$$\text{Mean of } \mathbf{X}_i = \mu_i = N\theta_i$$
$$\text{Variance of } \mathbf{X}_i = \sigma_i^2 = N\theta_i(1 - \theta_i)$$
$$\text{Covariance of } \mathbf{X}_i \text{ and } \mathbf{X}_j = \sigma_{ij}^2 = -N\theta_i\theta_j$$
$$\text{Joint Moment Generating Function} = (\theta_1 e^{t_1} + \cdots + \theta_n e^{t_n})^N$$

5. *Poisson Distribution.* If the random variable $\mathbf{X}$ has a probability function given by

$$P(\mathbf{X} = x) = f(x) = \frac{e^{-\lambda}\lambda^x}{x!}, \qquad \lambda > 0, x = 0, 1, \ldots,$$

then the variable $\mathbf{X}$ is said to possess a Poisson distribution.

Properties

$$\text{Mean} = \mu = \lambda$$
$$\text{Variance} = \sigma^2 = \lambda$$
$$\text{Standard Deviation} = \sigma = \sqrt{\lambda}$$
$$\text{Moment Generating Function} = m_x(t) = e^{\lambda(e^t - 1)}$$

6. *Hypergeometric Distribution.* If the random variable $\mathbf{X}$ has a probability function given by

$$P(\mathbf{X} = x) = f(x) = \frac{\dbinom{k}{x}\dbinom{N - k}{n - x}}{\dbinom{N}{n}}, \qquad x = 0, 1, 2, \ldots, [n, k],$$

where $[n, k]$ means the smaller of the two numbers n, k, then the variable $\mathbf{X}$ is said to possess a hypergeometric distribution.

Properties

$$\text{Mean} = \mu = \frac{kn}{N}$$

$$\text{Variance} = \sigma^2 = \frac{k(N - k)n(N - n)}{N^2(N - 1)}$$

$$\text{Standard Deviation} = \sigma = \sqrt{\frac{k(N - k)n(N - n)}{N^2(N - 1)}}$$

7. *Negative Binomial Distribution.* If the random variable **X** has a probability function given by

$$P(\mathbf{X} = x) = f(x) = \binom{x + r - 1}{r - 1} \theta^r (1 - \theta)^x, \qquad x = 0, 1, 2, \ldots ;$$

then the variable **X** is said to possess a negative binomial distribution, known also as the Pascal or Pólya distribution.

Properties

$$\text{Mean} = \mu = \frac{r}{\theta}$$

$$\text{Variance} = \sigma^2 = \frac{r}{\theta}\left(\frac{1}{\theta} - 1\right) = \frac{r(1 - \theta)}{\theta^2}$$

$$\text{Standard Deviation} = \sigma = \sqrt{\frac{r}{\theta}\left(\frac{1}{\theta} - 1\right)} = \sqrt{\frac{r(1 - \theta)}{\theta^2}}$$

$$\text{Moment Generating Function} = m_x(t) = e^{tr}\theta^r[1 - (1 - \theta)e^t]^{-r}$$

B. CONTINUOUS CASE

1. *Uniform Distribution.* A random variable **X** is said to be distributed as the uniform distribution if the density function is given by

$$f(x) = \frac{1}{\beta - \alpha}, \qquad \alpha < x < \beta,$$

where α and β are parameters with $\alpha < \beta$.

Properties

$$\text{Mean} = \mu = \frac{\alpha + \beta}{2}$$

$$\text{Variance} = \sigma^2 = \frac{(\beta - \alpha)^2}{12}$$

$$\text{Standard Deviation} = \sigma = \sqrt{\frac{(\beta - \alpha)^2}{12}}$$

$$\text{Moment Generating Function} = m_x(t) = \frac{2}{(\beta - \alpha)t} \sinh\left[\frac{(\beta - \alpha)t}{2}\right] e^{\frac{\alpha + \beta}{2}t} = \frac{e^{\beta t} - e^{\alpha t}}{(\beta - \alpha)t}$$

2. *Normal Distribution.* A random variable **X** is said to be normally distributed if its density function is given by

$$f(x) = \frac{1}{\sqrt{2\pi}\,\sigma} e^{-(x - \mu)^2/2\sigma^2}, \qquad -\infty < x < \infty$$

where μ and σ are parameters, called the mean and the standard deviation or the random variable **X**, respectively.

Properties

$$\text{Mean} = \mu$$
$$\text{Variance} = \sigma^2$$
$$\text{Standard Deviation} = \sigma$$

$$\text{Moment Generating Function} = m_x(t) = e^{t\mu + \frac{\sigma^2 t^2}{2}}$$

Cumulative Distribution

$$F(x) = \int_{-\infty}^{x} \frac{1}{\sqrt{2\pi}\,\sigma} e^{-(x-\mu)^2/2\sigma^2} dx$$

Set $y = \dfrac{x - \mu}{\sigma}$ to obtain the cumulative standard normal.

3. *Gamma Distribution.* A random variable **X** is said to be distributed as the gamma distribution if the density function is given by

$$f(x) = \frac{1}{\Gamma(\alpha + 1)\beta^{\alpha+1}} x^\alpha e^{-x/\beta}, \qquad 0 < x < \infty$$

where α and β are parameters with $\alpha > -1$ and $\beta > 0$.

Properties

$$\text{Mean} = \mu = \beta(\alpha + 1)$$
$$\text{Variance} = \sigma^2 = \beta^2(\alpha + 1)$$
$$\text{Standard Deviation} = \sigma = \beta\sqrt{\alpha + 1}$$
$$\text{Moment Generating Function} = m_x(t) = (1 - \beta t)^{-(\alpha+1)}, \qquad t < \frac{1}{\beta}.$$

4. *Exponential Distribution.* A random variable **X** is said to be distributed as the exponential distribution if the density function is given by

$$f(x) = \frac{1}{\theta} e^{-x/\theta}, \qquad x > 0$$

where θ is a parameter and $\theta > 0$.

Properties

$$\text{Mean} = \mu = \theta$$
$$\text{Variance} = \sigma^2 = \theta^2$$
$$\text{Standard Deviation} = \sigma = \sqrt{\theta^2}$$
$$\text{Moment Generating Function} = m_x(t) = (1 - \theta t)^{-1}$$

5. *Beta Distribution.* A random variable **X** is said to be distributed as the beta distribution if the density function is given by

$$f(x) = \frac{\Gamma(\alpha + \beta + 2)}{\Gamma(\alpha + 1)\Gamma(\beta + 1)} x^\alpha (1 - x)^\beta, \qquad 0 < x < 1$$

where α and β are parameters with $\alpha > -1$ and $\beta > -1$.

Properties

$$\text{Mean} = \mu = \frac{\alpha + 1}{\alpha + \beta + 2}$$

$$\text{Variance} = \sigma^2 = \frac{(\alpha + 1)(\beta + 1)}{(\alpha + \beta + 2)^2(\alpha + \beta + 3)}$$

$$r\text{th moment about the origin} = \nu_r = \frac{\Gamma(\alpha + \beta + 2)\Gamma(\alpha + r + 1)}{\Gamma(\alpha + \beta + r + 2)\Gamma(\alpha + 1)}.$$

Sampling Distributions

Population—A finite or infinite set of elements of a random variable **X**.

Random Sample—If the random variables X_1, X_2, . . . , X_n have a joint density,

$$g(x_1, x_2, \ldots, x_n) = f(x_1)f(x_2) \cdots f(x_n)$$

where the density of each X_i is $f(x)$, then $X_1, X_2, \ldots, X_n$ is said to be a random sample of size n from the population with density $f(x)$.

Sampling Distributions

A random sample is selected from a population in which the form of the probability function is known, and from the joint density of the random variables a distribution, called the sampling distribution, of a function of the random variables is derived.

1. *Chi-Square Distribution.* If $Y_1, Y_2, \ldots, Y_n$ are normally and independently distributed with mean 0 and variance 1, then

$$\chi^2 = \sum_{i=1}^{n} Y_i^2$$

is distributed as Chi-Square (χ^2) with n degrees of freedom. The density function is given by

$$f(\chi^2) = \frac{(\chi^2)^{\frac{1}{2}(n-2)}}{2^{\frac{n}{2}}\Gamma\left(\frac{n}{2}\right)} e^{-x^2/2}, \qquad 0 < \chi^2 < \infty .$$

Properties

$$\text{Mean} = \mu = n$$
$$\text{Variance} = \sigma^2 = 2n$$

Reproductive Property of χ^2 - Distribution

If $\chi_1^2, \chi_2^2, \ldots, \chi_k^2$ are independently distributed according to χ^2 - distributions with $n_1, n_2, \ldots, n_k$ degrees of freedom, respectively, then $\sum_{j=1}^{k} \chi_j^2$ is distributed according to a χ^2 - distribution with $n = \sum_{j=1}^{k} n_j$ degrees of freedom.

2. *Snedecor's F-Distribution*. If a random variable X is distributed as χ^2 with m degrees of freedom (χ_m^2) and a random variable Y is distributed as χ^2 with n degrees of freedom (χ_n^2) and if X and Y are independent, then $F = \dfrac{X/m}{Y/n}$ is distributed as Snedecor's F with m and n degrees of freedom, denoted by $F(m, n)$. The density function of the F-distribution is given by

$$f(F) = \frac{\Gamma\left(\dfrac{m+n}{2}\right)\left(\dfrac{m}{n}\right)^{m/2} F^{(m-2)/2}}{\Gamma\left(\dfrac{m}{2}\right)\Gamma\left(\dfrac{n}{2}\right)\left(1 + \dfrac{m}{n}F\right)^{(m+n)/2}}, \qquad 0 < F < \infty.$$

Properties

$$\text{Mean} = \mu = \frac{n}{n-2}, \qquad n > 2$$

$$\text{Variance} = \sigma^2 = \frac{2n^2(m+n-2)}{m(n-2)^2(n-4)}, \qquad n > 4 .$$

The transformation $w = \dfrac{mF/n}{1 + \dfrac{mF}{n}}$ transforms the F-density into a Beta density.

3. *Student's t-Distribution*. If a random variable X is normally distributed with mean 0 and variance σ^2, and if Y^2/σ^2 is distributed as χ^2 with n degrees of freedom and if X and Y are independent, then

$$t = \frac{X\sqrt{n}}{Y}$$

is distributed as Student's t with n degrees of freedom. The density function is given by

$$f(t) = \frac{\Gamma\left(\dfrac{n+1}{2}\right)}{\sqrt{n\pi}\,\Gamma\left(\dfrac{n}{2}\right)\left(1 + \dfrac{t^2}{n}\right)^{\frac{1}{2}(n+1)}}, \qquad -\infty < t < \infty .$$

Properties

$$\text{Mean} = \mu = 0$$

$$\text{Variance} = \sigma^2 = \frac{n}{n-2}, \qquad n > 2 .$$

SUMMARY OF SIGNIFICANCE TESTS: TESTING FOR THE VALUE OF A SPECIFIED PARAMETER

Hypothesis	Conditions	Test Statistic	Distribution of Test Statistic	Critical Region
1. $\mu = \mu_0$	Known σ	$z = \dfrac{(\bar{x} - \mu_0)\sqrt{n}}{\sigma}$	Normal	$z > z_\alpha$ if we wish to reject when $\mu > \mu_0$ $z < -z_\alpha$ if we wish to reject when $\mu < \mu_0$ $|z| > z_{\alpha/2}$ if we wish to reject when $\mu \neq \mu_0$
2. $\mu = \mu_0$	Unknown σ	$t = \dfrac{(\bar{x} - \mu_0)\sqrt{n}}{s}$	Student's t with $(n-1)$ d.f.	$t > t_{\alpha,n-1}$ if we wish to reject when $\mu > \mu_0$ $t < -t_{\alpha,n-1}$ if we wish to reject when $\mu < \mu_0$ $|t| > t_{\alpha/2,n-1}$ if we wish to reject when $\mu \neq \mu_0$
3. $\sigma = \sigma_0$		$\chi^2 = \dfrac{(n-1)s^2}{\sigma_0^2}$	χ^2 with $n-1$ d.f.	$\chi^2 > \chi^2_{\alpha,n-1}$ if we wish to reject when $\sigma > \sigma_0$ $\chi^2 < \chi^2_{1-\alpha,n-1}$ if we wish to reject when $\sigma < \sigma_0$ $\chi^2 < \chi^2_{1-\alpha/2,n-1}$ or $\chi^2 > \chi^2_{\alpha/2,n-1}$ if we wish to reject when $\sigma \neq \sigma_0$
4. $\theta = \theta_0$	Large sample. (For small samples, exact tests are based on tables of binomial probabilities)	$z = \dfrac{\dfrac{x}{n} - \theta_0}{\sqrt{\dfrac{\theta_0(1-\theta_0)}{n}}}$ Continuity correction: Replace x in numerator of formula with $x - \frac{1}{2}$ or $x + \frac{1}{2}$, whichever makes z numerically smallest.	Normal	$z > z_\alpha$ if we wish to reject when $\theta > \theta_0$ $z < -z_\alpha$ if we wish to reject when $\theta < \theta_0$ $|z| > z_{\alpha/2}$ if we wish to reject when $\theta \neq \theta_0$

SUMMARY OF SIGNIFICANCE TESTS: COMPARISON OF TWO POPULATIONS

Hypothesis	Conditions	Test Statistic	Distribution of Test Statistic	Critical Region
1. $\mu_x = \mu_y$	Known σ_x and σ_y	$z = \dfrac{\bar{x} - \bar{y}}{\sqrt{\dfrac{\sigma_x^2}{n_x} + \dfrac{\sigma_y^2}{n_y}}}$	Normal	$z > z_\alpha$ if we wish to reject when $\mu_x > \mu_y$ $z < -z_\alpha$ if we wish to reject when $\mu_x < \mu_y$ $\lvert z \rvert > z_{\alpha/2}$ if we wish to reject when $\mu_x \neq \mu_y$
2. $\mu_x = \mu_y$	Unknown σ_x and σ_y $\sigma_x = \sigma_y$	$t = \dfrac{\bar{x} - \bar{y}}{\sqrt{\dfrac{(n_x-1)s_x^2 + (n_y-1)s_y^2}{n_x + n_y - 2}}\,\sqrt{\dfrac{1}{n_x} + \dfrac{1}{n_y}}}$	Student's t with $n - 1$ d.f.	$t > t_{\alpha, n_x+n_y-2}$ if wish to reject when $\mu_x > \mu_y$ $t < -t_{\alpha, n_x+n_y-2}$ if we wish to reject when $\mu_x < \mu_y$ $\lvert t \rvert > t_{\alpha/2, n_x+n_y-2}$ if we wish to reject when $\mu_x \neq \mu_y$
3. $\mu_x = \mu_y$	Unknown σ_x and σ_y $\sigma_x \neq \sigma_y$	$t = \dfrac{\bar{x} - \bar{y}}{\sqrt{\dfrac{s_x^2}{n_x} + \dfrac{s_y^2}{n_y}}}$	Student's t with ν d.f.	$t > t_{\alpha, \nu}$ if we wish to reject when $\mu_x > \mu_y$ $t < -t_{\alpha, \nu}$ if we wish to reject when $\mu_x < \mu_y$ $\lvert t \rvert > t_{\alpha/2, \nu}$ if we wish to reject when $\mu_x \neq \mu_y$ where d.f. ν is given by closest integer to $\nu = -2 + \dfrac{\left(\dfrac{s_x^2}{n_x} + \dfrac{s_y^2}{n_y}\right)^2}{\dfrac{\left(\dfrac{s_x^2}{n_x}\right)^2}{n_x + 1} + \dfrac{\left(\dfrac{s_y^2}{n_y}\right)^2}{n_y + 1}}$
4. $\mu_x = \mu_y$	Correlated pairs	$t = \dfrac{\bar{d}\sqrt{n}}{s_d}$ where $d_i = x_i - y_i$	Student's t with $n - 1$ d.f.	
5. $\sigma_x^2 = \sigma_y^2$		$F = \dfrac{s_x^2}{s_y^2}$ In a two-sided test, put larger mean square in the numerator	F with $n_x - 1$ and $n_y - 1$ d.f.	$F > F_{\alpha, n_x-1, n_y-1}$ if we wish to reject when $\sigma_x > \sigma_y$ $F > F_{\alpha/2, n_x-1, n_y-1}$ if $s_x^2 > s_y^2$ and we wish to reject when $\sigma_x \neq \sigma_y$ $F > F_{\alpha/2, n_y-1, n_x-1}$ if $s_x^2 < s_y^2$ and we wish to reject when $\sigma_x \neq \sigma_y$
6. $\theta_1 = \theta_2$	Large sample	$z = \dfrac{\dfrac{x_1}{n_1} - \dfrac{x_2}{n_2}}{\sqrt{\dfrac{\dfrac{x_1}{n_1}\left(1 - \dfrac{x_1}{n_1}\right)}{n_1} + \dfrac{\dfrac{x_2}{n_2}\left(1 - \dfrac{x_2}{n_2}\right)}{n_2}}}$ Continuity Correction: Replace x in numerator of formula with $x - \frac{1}{2}$ or $x + \frac{1}{2}$, whichever makes z numerically smallest.	Normal	$z > z_\alpha$ if we wish to reject when $\theta_1 > \theta_2$ $z < -z_\alpha$ if we wish to reject when $\theta_1 < \theta_2$ $\lvert z \rvert > z_{\alpha/2}$ if we wish to reject when $\theta_1 \neq \theta_2$

SUMMARY OF CONFIDENCE INTERVALS

Parameter	Conditions	Point Estimate	Confidence Interval
1. μ	Known σ	$\bar{x}$	$\bar{x} - z_{\alpha/2} \dfrac{\sigma}{\sqrt{n}} < \mu < \bar{x} + z_{\alpha/2} \dfrac{\sigma}{\sqrt{n}}$
2. μ	Unknown σ	$\bar{x}$	$\bar{x} - t_{\alpha/2} \dfrac{s}{\sqrt{n}} < \mu < \bar{x} + t_{\alpha/2} \dfrac{s}{\sqrt{n}}$
3. $\mu_x - \mu_y$	$\sigma_x = \sigma_y$ known	$\bar{x} - \bar{y}$	$\bar{x} - \bar{y} - z_{\alpha/2} \sqrt{\dfrac{\sigma_x^2}{n_x} + \dfrac{\sigma_y^2}{n_y}} < \mu_x - \mu_y$ $< \bar{x} - \bar{y} + z_{\alpha/2} \sqrt{\dfrac{\sigma_x^2}{n_x} + \dfrac{\sigma_y^2}{n_y}}$
4. $\mu_x - \mu_y$	$\sigma_x = \sigma_y$ unknown	$\bar{x} - \bar{y}$	$\bar{x} - \bar{y} - t_{\alpha/2} \dfrac{\sqrt{(n_x - 1)s_x^2 + (n_y - 1)s_y^2}}{\sqrt{\dfrac{n_x n_y (n_x + n_y - 2)}{n_x + n_y}}} < \mu_x - \mu_y < \bar{x} - \bar{y} + t_{\alpha/2} \dfrac{\sqrt{(n_x - 1)s_x^2 + (n_y - 1)s_y^2}}{\sqrt{\dfrac{n_x n_y (n_x + n_y - 2)}{n_x + n_y}}}$
5. $\mu_d = \mu_x - \mu_y$	Correlated pairs σ_x and σ_y unknown	$\bar{d} = \bar{x} - \bar{y}$	$\bar{d} - t_{\alpha/2} \dfrac{s_d}{\sqrt{n}} < \mu_d < \bar{d} + t_{\alpha/2} \dfrac{s_d}{\sqrt{n}}$
6. σ		s	$\sqrt{\dfrac{(n-1)s^2}{\chi^2_{\alpha/2;n-1}}} < \sigma < \sqrt{\dfrac{(n-1)s^2}{\chi^2_{1-\alpha/2;n-1}}}$
7. $\dfrac{\sigma_x^2}{\sigma_y^2}$		$\dfrac{s_x^2}{s_y^2}$	$\dfrac{s_x^2}{s_y^2} \dfrac{1}{F_{\alpha/2;n_x-1,n_y-1}} < \dfrac{\sigma_x^2}{\sigma_y^2} < \dfrac{s_x^2}{s_y^2} \dfrac{1}{F_{1-\alpha/2;n_x-1,n_y-1}}$
8. θ	Large sample	$\dfrac{x}{n}$	$\dfrac{x}{n} - z_{\alpha/2} \sqrt{\dfrac{\dfrac{x}{n}\left(1 - \dfrac{x}{n}\right)}{n}} < \theta < \dfrac{x}{n} + z_{\alpha/2} \sqrt{\dfrac{\dfrac{x}{n}\left(1 - \dfrac{x}{n}\right)}{n}}$
9. $\theta_1 - \theta_2$	Large sample	$\dfrac{x_1}{n_1} - \dfrac{x_2}{n_2}$	$\dfrac{x_1}{n_1} - \dfrac{x_2}{n_2} - z_{\alpha/2} \sqrt{\dfrac{\dfrac{x_1}{n_1}\left(1 - \dfrac{x_1}{n_1}\right)}{n_1} + \dfrac{\dfrac{x_2}{n_2}\left(1 - \dfrac{x_2}{n_2}\right)}{n_2}} < \theta_1 - \theta_2 < \dfrac{x_1}{n_1} - \dfrac{x_2}{n_2} + z_{\alpha/2} \sqrt{\dfrac{\dfrac{x_1}{n_1}\left(1 - \dfrac{x_1}{n_1}\right)}{n_1} + \dfrac{\dfrac{x_2}{n_2}\left(1 - \dfrac{x_2}{n_2}\right)}{n_2}}$

ANALYSIS OF VARIANCE (ANOVA) TABLES

The analysis of variance (ANOVA) table containing the sum of squares, degrees of freedom, mean square, expectations, etc., present the initial analysis in a compact form. This kind of tabular representation is customarily used to set out the results of analysis of variance calculations. Appropriate ANOVA tables for various experimental design models are presented here. In the tables, the use of "dot notation" indicates a summing over all observations in the population, i.e., when summing over a suffix, that suffix is replaced by a dot. Small letters refer to observations, whereas capital letters refer to observation totals.

ANALYSIS OF VARIANCE AND EXPECTED MEAN SQUARES FOR THE ONE-WAY CLASSIFICATION

Model: $y_{ij} = \mu + \alpha_i + \epsilon_{ij}$ $(i = 1, 2, \ldots, k; j = 1, 2, \ldots, n_i)$

Source of variation	Degrees of freedom	Sum of squares	Mean square	Test statistic
Between groups	$k - 1$	$S_1 = \sum_i n_i(\bar{y}_i - \bar{y}_{..})^2 = \sum_i \left(\frac{Y_i^2}{n_i}\right) - \frac{Y^2}{n}$	$s_1^2 = \dfrac{S_1}{k - 1}$	$F = \dfrac{s_1^2}{s_e^2}$
Within groups	$n - k$	$S_e = \sum_i \sum_j (\bar{y}_{ij} - \bar{y}_i)^2 = \sum_i \sum_j y_{ij}^2 - \sum_i \left(\frac{Y_i^2}{n_i}\right)$	$s_e^2 = \dfrac{S_e}{n - k}$	
Total	$n - 1$	$S = \sum_i \sum_j (y_{ij} - \bar{y})^2 = \sum_i \sum_j y_{ij}^2 - \frac{Y^2}{n}$		

Source of variation	Degrees of freedom	Mean square	Expected mean square for Fixed model	Expected mean square for Random model
Between groups	$k - 1$	s_1^2	$\sigma^2 + \dfrac{\sum_i n_i\alpha_i^2}{k - 1}$	$\sigma^2 + \dfrac{1}{k - 1}\left(n - \dfrac{\sum_i n_i^2}{n}\right)\sigma_\alpha^2$
Within groups	$n - k$	s_e^2	σ^2	σ^2
Total	$n - 1$			

Notation:

$$Y_i = \sum_j y_{ij} \; ; \quad Y = \sum_i \sum_j y_{ij} \; ; \quad \bar{y}_i = \frac{1}{n_i} \sum_j y_{ij} = \frac{1}{n_i} Y_i \; ;$$

$$n = \sum_i n_i \; ; \quad \bar{y} = \frac{1}{n} \sum_i \sum_j y_{ij} = \frac{Y}{n}$$

ANALYSIS OF VARIANCE AND EXPECTED MEAN SQUARES FOR THE TWO-WAY CLASSIFICATION WITH ONE OBSERVATION PER CELL

Model: $y_{ij} = \mu + \alpha_i + \beta_j + \epsilon_{ij}$ $\qquad (i = 1, 2, \ldots c; j = 1, 2, \ldots, r)$

Source of variation	Degrees of freedom	Sum of squares	Mean square	Test statistic
Column effects	$c - 1$	$SSC = \dfrac{\sum_i Y_i^2}{r} - \dfrac{Y^2}{cr}$	$s_1^2 = \dfrac{SSC}{c - 1}$	$\dfrac{s_1^2}{s_e^2}$
Row effects	$r - 1$	$SSR = \dfrac{\sum_j Y_j^2}{c} - \dfrac{Y^2}{cr}$	$s_2^2 = \dfrac{SSR}{r - 1}$	$\dfrac{s_2^2}{s_e^2}$
Error	$(c - 1)(r - 1)$	$SSE = SST - SSC - SSR$	$s_e^2 = \dfrac{SSE}{(c - 1)(r - 1)}$	
Total	$cr - 1$	$SST = \sum_i \sum_j y_{ij}^2 - \dfrac{Y^2}{cr}$		

Expected mean square for

Source of variation	Degrees of freedom	Mean square	Fixed model	Mixed model (α)	Random model
Column effects	$c - 1$	s_1^2	$\sigma^2 + r\left(\dfrac{\sum_i \alpha_i^2}{c - 1}\right)$	$\sigma^2 + r\left(\dfrac{\sum_i \alpha_i^2}{c - 1}\right)$	$\sigma^2 + r\sigma_\alpha^2$
Row effects	$r - 1$	s_2^2	$\sigma^2 + c\left(\dfrac{\sum_j \beta_j^2}{r - 1}\right)$	$\sigma^2 + c\sigma_\beta^2$	$\sigma^2 + c\sigma_\beta^2$
Error	$(c - 1)(r - 1)$	s_e^2	σ^2	σ^2	σ^2
Total	$cr - 1$				

ANALYSIS OF VARIANCE AND EXPECTED MEAN SQUARES FOR NESTED CLASSIFICATIONS WITH UNEQUAL SAMPLES

Model: $y_{iju} = \mu + \alpha_i + \delta_{ij} + \epsilon_{iju}$ $(i = 1, 2, \ldots, k; j = 1, 2, \ldots, n_i; u = 1, 2, \ldots, n_{ij})$

Source of variation	Degrees of freedom	Sum of squares	Mean square	Expected mean square for fixed model (α, δ)
Between main groups	$k - 1$	$S_1 = \sum_i \frac{Y_i^2}{n_i} - \frac{Y^2}{n}$	$s_1^2 = \frac{S_1}{k - 1}$	$\sigma^2 + \dfrac{\sum_i n_i \alpha_i^2}{k - 1}$
Subgroups within main groups (experimental error)	$\sum_i n_i - k$	$S_2 = \sum_i \sum_j \frac{Y_{ij}^2}{n_{ij}} - \sum_i \frac{Y_i^2}{n_i}$	$s_2^2 = \dfrac{S_2}{\sum_i n_i - k}$	$\sigma^2 + \dfrac{\sum_i \sum_j n_{ij}\delta_{ij}^2}{\sum_i n_i - k}$
Within subgroups (sampling error)	$n - \sum_i n_i$	$S_e = \sum_i \sum_j \sum_u y_{iju}^2 - \sum_i \sum_j \frac{Y_{ij}^2}{n_{ij}}$	$s_e^2 = \dfrac{S_3}{n - \sum_i n_i}$	σ^2
Total	$n - 1$	$S = \sum_i \sum_j \sum_u y_{iju}^2 - \frac{Y^2}{n}$		

Source of variation	Degrees of freedom	Mean square	Expected mean square for		
			Mixed model (α)	Mixed model (δ)	Random model
Between main groups	$k - 1$	s_1^2	$\sigma^2 + b\sigma_\delta^2 + \dfrac{\sum_i n_i \alpha_i^2}{k - 1}$	$\sigma^2 + c\delta_\alpha^2$	$\sigma^2 + b\sigma_\delta^2 + c\sigma_\alpha^2$
Experimental error	$\sum_i n_i - k$	s_2^2	$\sigma^2 + a\sigma_\delta^2$	$\sigma^2 + \dfrac{\sum_i \sum_j n_{ij}\delta_{ij}^2}{\sum_i n_i - k}$	$\sigma^2 + a\sigma_\delta^2$
Sampling error	$n - \sum_i n_i$	s_e^2	σ^2	σ^2	σ^2
Total	$n - 1$				

where

$$a = \frac{n - \sum_i \dfrac{\sum_j n_{ij}^2}{n_i}}{\sum_i n_i - k}$$

$$b = \frac{\sum_i \dfrac{\sum_j n_{ij}^2}{n_i} - \dfrac{\sum_i \sum_j n_{ij}^2}{n}}{k - 1}$$

$$c = \frac{n - \dfrac{\sum_i n_i^2}{n}}{k - 1}$$

ANALYSIS OF VARIANCE AND EXPECTED MEAN SQUARES FOR NESTED CLASSIFICATIONS WITH EQUAL SAMPLES

Model: $y_{iju} = \mu + \alpha_i + \delta_{ij} + \epsilon_{iju}$ $(i = 1, 2, \ldots, k; j = 1, 2, \ldots, n; u = 1, 2, \ldots, r)$

Source of variation	Degrees of freedom	Sum of squares	Mean square	Expected mean square for fixed model (α, δ)
Between main groups	$k - 1$	$S_1 = \sum_i \dfrac{Y_i^2}{nr} - \dfrac{Y^2}{knr}$	$s_1^2 = \dfrac{S_1}{k - 1}$	$\sigma^2 + nr\dfrac{\sum_i \alpha_i^2}{k - 1}$
Experimental error	$k(n - 1)$	$S_2 = \dfrac{\sum_i \sum_j Y_{ij}^2}{r} - \dfrac{\sum_i Y_i^2}{nr}$	$s_2^2 = \dfrac{S_2}{k(n - 1)}$	$\sigma^2 + r\dfrac{\sum_i \sum_j \delta_{ij}^2}{k(n - 1)}$
Sampling error	$kn(r - 1)$	$S_e = \sum_i \sum_j \sum_u y_{iju}^2 - \dfrac{\sum_i \sum_j Y_{ij}^2}{r}$	$s_e^2 = \dfrac{S_e}{kn(r - 1)}$	σ^2
Total	$kn(r - 1)$	$S = \sum_i \sum_j \sum_u y_{iju}^2 - \dfrac{Y^2}{knr}$		

Source of variation	Degrees of freedom	Mean square	Expected mean square for		
			Mixed model (α)	Mixed model (δ)	Random model
Between main groups	$k - 1$	s_1^2	$\sigma^2 + r\sigma_\delta^2 + nr\left(\dfrac{\sum_i \alpha_i^2}{k - 1}\right)$	$\sigma^2 + nr\sigma_\alpha^2$	$\sigma^2 + r\sigma_\delta^2 + nr\sigma_\alpha^2$
Experimental error	$k(n - 1)$	s_2^2	$\sigma^2 + r\sigma_\delta^2$	$\sigma^2 + \dfrac{r\sum_i \sum_j \delta_{ij}^2}{k(n - 1)}$	$\sigma^2 + r\sigma_\delta^2$
Sampling error	$kn(r - 1)$	s_e^2	σ^2	σ^2	σ^2
Total	$knr - 1$				

where

$$a = b = r$$
$$c = nr$$

ANALYSIS OF VARIANCE AND EXPECTED MEAN SQUARES FOR A FIXED MODEL TWO-FACTOR FACTORIAL EXPERIMENT IN A ONE-WAY CLASSIFICATION DESIGN

Model: $y_{iju} = \mu + \alpha_i + \beta_j + (\alpha\beta)_{ij} + \epsilon_{iju}$
$(i = 1, 2, \ldots, c; j = 1, 2, \ldots, r; u = 1, 2, \ldots, n)$

Source of variation	Degrees of freedom	Sum of squares	Mean square	Expected mean square for fixed model $[\alpha, \beta, (\alpha\beta)]$
Treatment combinations	$cr - 1$	$SSTr$	$s_0^2 = \dfrac{SSTr}{cr - 1}$	$\sigma^2 + n\dfrac{\sum\limits_i^c \sum\limits_j^r (\mu_{ij} - \mu)^2}{cr - 1}$
Factor A	$c - 1$	SSA	$s_1^2 = \dfrac{SSA}{c - 1}$	$\sigma^2 + rn\dfrac{\sum\limits_i^c \alpha_i^2}{c - 1}$
Factor B	$r - 1$	SSB	$s_2^2 = \dfrac{SSB}{r - 1}$	$\sigma^2 + cn\dfrac{\sum\limits_j^r \beta_j^2}{r - 1}$
Interaction	$(c - 1)(r - 1)$	$SSAB = SSTr - SSA - SSB$	$s_3^2 = \dfrac{SSAB}{(c - 1)(r - 1)}$	$\sigma^2 + n\dfrac{\sum\limits_i^c \sum\limits_j^r (\alpha\beta)_{ij}^2}{(c - 1)(r - 1)}$
Within (error)	$cr(n - 1)$	$SSW = SST - SSTr$	$s_e^2 = \dfrac{SSW}{cr(n - 1)}$	σ^2
Total	$crn - 1$	SST		

where

$$SSTr = \frac{\sum\limits_i^c \sum\limits_j^r Y_{ij}^2}{n} - \frac{Y^2}{crn} \qquad SSA = \frac{\sum\limits_i^c Y_{i.}^2}{rn} - \frac{Y^2}{crn}$$

$$SSB = \frac{\sum\limits_j^r Y_{.j}^2}{cn} - \frac{Y^2}{crn} \qquad SST = \sum\limits_i^c \sum\limits_j^r \sum\limits_u^n y_{iju}^2 - \frac{Y^2}{crn}$$

$$Y_{ij} = \sum\limits_u^n y_{iju} \qquad Y_{i.} = \sum\limits_j^r \sum\limits_u^n y_{iju} \qquad Y_{.j} = \sum\limits_i^c \sum\limits_u^n y_{iju}$$

ANALYSIS OF VARIANCE AND EXPECTED MEAN SQUARES FOR A FIXED MODEL TWO-FACTOR FACTORIAL EXPERIMENT IN A ONE-WAY CLASSIFICATION DESIGN (continued)

Source of variation	Mean square	Expected mean square for	
		Random model	Mixed model (α)
Factor A	$s_1^2 = \dfrac{SSA}{c-1}$	$\sigma^2 + n\sigma_{\alpha\beta}^2 + rn\sigma_\alpha^2$	$\sigma^2 + n\sigma_{\alpha\beta}^2 + rn\dfrac{\sum \alpha_i^2}{c-1}$
Factor B	$s_2^2 = \dfrac{SSB}{r-1}$	$\sigma^2 + n\sigma_{\alpha\beta}^2 + cn\sigma_\beta^2$	$\sigma^2 + cn\sigma_\beta^2$
Interaction	$s_3^2 = \dfrac{SSAB}{(c-1)(r-1)}$	$\sigma^2 + n\sigma_{\alpha\beta}^2$	$\sigma^2 + n\sigma_{\alpha\beta}^2$
Within (error)	$s_e^2 = \dfrac{SSW}{cr(n-1)}$	σ^2	σ^2
Total	$s_5^2 = \dfrac{SST}{crn-1}$		

ANALYSIS OF VARIANCE AND EXPECTED MEAN SQUARES FOR A THREE-FACTOR FACTORIAL EXPERIMENT IN A COMPLETELY RANDOMIZED DESIGN

Model: $y_{ijku} = \mu + \alpha_i + \beta_j + \gamma_k + (\alpha\beta)_{ij} + (\alpha\gamma)_{ik} + (\beta\gamma)_{jk} + (\alpha\beta\gamma)_{ijk} + \epsilon_{ijku}$
$(i = 1, 2, \ldots, c; j = 1, 2, \ldots, r; k = 1, 2, \ldots, l; u = 1, 2, \ldots, n)$

Source of variation	Degrees of freedom	Sum of squares	Mean square	Expected mean square for *Fixed Model*
Factor A	$c-1$	SSA	s_1^2	$\sigma^2 + rln\dfrac{\sum_i \alpha_i^2}{c-1}$
Factor B	$r-1$	SSB	s_2^2	$\sigma^2 + cln\dfrac{\sum_j \beta_j^2}{r-1}$
Factor C	$l-1$	SSC	s_3^2	$\sigma^2 + crn\dfrac{\sum_k \gamma_k^2}{l-1}$
Interaction $A \times B$	$(c-1)(r-1)$	SSAB	s_4^2	$\sigma^2 + ln\dfrac{\sum_i \sum_j (\alpha\beta)_{ij}^2}{(c-1)(r-1)}$

ANALYSIS OF VARIANCE AND EXPECTED MEAN SQUARES FOR A THREE-FACTOR FACTORIAL EXPERIMENT IN A COMPLETELY RANDOMIZED DESIGN (continued)

Source of variation	Degrees of freedom	Sum of squares	Mean square		Expected mean square for *Fixed Model*
Interaction $A \times C$	$(c - 1)(l - 1)$	SSAC	s_5^2	$\sigma^2 + rn$	$\dfrac{\sum_i \sum_k (\alpha\beta)_{ik}^2}{(c - 1)(l - 1)}$
Interaction $B \times C$	$(r - 1)(l - 1)$	SSBC	s_6^2	$\sigma^2 + cn$	$\dfrac{\sum_j \sum_k (\beta\gamma)_{jk}^2}{(r - 1)(l - 1)}$
Interaction $A \times B \times C$	$(c - 1)(r - 1)(l - 1)$	SSABC	s_7^2	$\sigma^2 + n$	$\dfrac{\sum_i \sum_j \sum_k (\alpha\beta\gamma)_{ijk}^2}{(c - 1)(r - 1)(l - 1)}$
Within (error)	$crl(n - 1)$	SSE	s_e^2	σ^2	
Total	$crln - 1$	SST			

where

$$SST = \sum_i \sum_j \sum_k \sum_n y_{ijkn}^2 - \frac{Y^2}{crln}$$

$$SSA = \frac{\sum_i Y_i^2}{rln} - \frac{Y^2}{crln}$$

$$SSB = \frac{\sum_j Y_j^2}{cln} - \frac{Y^2}{crln}$$

$$SSC = \frac{\sum_k Y_k^2}{crn} - \frac{Y^2}{crln}$$

$$SSTr(ABC) = \frac{\sum_i \sum_j \sum_k Y_{ijk}^2}{n} - \frac{Y^2}{crln}$$

$$SSTr(AB) = \frac{\sum_i \sum_j Y_{ij}^2}{ln} - \frac{Y^2}{crln}$$

ANALYSIS OF VARIANCE AND EXPECTED MEAN SQUARES FOR A THREE-FACTOR FACTORIAL EXPERIMENT IN A COMPLETELY RANDOMIZED DESIGN (continued)

$$SSTr(AC) = \frac{\sum_i \sum_k Y_{i.k.}^2}{rn} - \frac{Y^2}{crln}$$

$$SSTr(BC) = \frac{\sum_j \sum_k Y_{.jk.}^2}{cn} - \frac{Y^2}{crln}$$

$$SSAB = SSTr(AB) - SSA - SSB$$
$$SSAC = SSTr(AC) - SSA - SSC$$
$$SSBC = SSTr(BC) - SSB - SSC$$
$$SSABC = SSTr(ABC) - SSA - SSB - SSC - SSAB - SSAC - SSBC$$
$$SSE = SST - SSTr(ABC)$$

Source of variation	Mean square	Expected mean square for the		
		Random model	Mixed model (α)	Mixed model (α,β)
Factor A	$s_1^2 = \dfrac{SSA}{c-1}$	$\sigma^2 + n\sigma_{\alpha\beta\gamma}^2 + ln\sigma_{\alpha\beta}^2$ $+ rn\sigma_{\alpha\gamma}^2 + rln\sigma_{\alpha}^2$	$\sigma^2 + n\sigma_{\alpha\beta\gamma}^2 + ln\sigma_{\alpha\beta}^2$ $+ rn\sigma_{\alpha\gamma}^2 + rln\dfrac{\sum_i \alpha_i^2}{c-1}$	$\sigma^2 + rn\sigma_{\alpha\gamma}^2$ $+ rln\dfrac{\sum_i \alpha_i^2}{c-1}$
Factor B	$s_2^2 = \dfrac{SSB}{r-1}$	$\sigma^2 + n\sigma_{\alpha\beta\gamma}^2 + ln\sigma_{\alpha\beta}^2$ $+ cn\sigma_{\beta\gamma}^2 + cln\sigma_{\beta}^2$	$\sigma^2 + cn\sigma_{\beta\gamma}^2 + cln\sigma_{\beta}^2$	$\sigma^2 + cn\sigma_{\beta\gamma}^2$ $+ cln\dfrac{\sum_j \beta_j^2}{r-1}$
Factor C	$s_3^2 = \dfrac{SSC}{l-1}$	$\sigma^2 + n\sigma_{\alpha\beta\gamma}^2 + rn\sigma_{\alpha\gamma}^2$ $+ cn\sigma_{\beta\gamma}^2 + crn\sigma_{\gamma}^2$	$\sigma^2 + cn\sigma_{\beta\gamma}^2 + crn\sigma_{\gamma}^2$	$\sigma^2 + crn\sigma_{\gamma}^2$
$A \times B$	$s_4^2 = \dfrac{SSAB}{(c-1)(r-1)}$	$\sigma^2 + n\sigma_{\alpha\beta\gamma}^2 + ln_{\alpha\beta}^2$	$\sigma^2 + n\sigma_{\alpha\beta\gamma}^2 + ln_{\alpha\beta}^2$	$\sigma^2 + n\sigma_{\alpha\beta\gamma}^2$ $+ ln\dfrac{\sum_i \sum_j (\alpha\beta)_{ij}^2}{(c-1)(r-1)}$
$A \times C$	$s_5^2 = \dfrac{SSAC}{(c-1)(l-1)}$	$\sigma^2 + n\sigma_{\alpha\beta\gamma}^2 + rn\sigma_{\alpha\gamma}^2$	$\sigma^2 + n\sigma_{\alpha\beta\gamma}^2 + rn\sigma_{\alpha\gamma}^2$	$\sigma^2 + rn\sigma_{\alpha\gamma}^2$
$B \times C$	$s_6^2 = \dfrac{SSBC}{(r-1)(l-1)}$	$\sigma^2 + n\sigma_{\alpha\beta\gamma}^2 + cn\sigma_{\beta\gamma}^2$	$\sigma^2 + cn\sigma_{\beta\gamma}^2$	$\sigma^2 + cn\sigma_{\beta\gamma}^2$
$A \times B \times C$	$s_7^2 = \dfrac{SSABC}{(c-1)(r-1)(l-1)}$	$\sigma^2 + n\sigma_{\alpha\beta\gamma}^2$	$\sigma^2 + n\sigma_{\alpha\beta\gamma}^2$	$\sigma^2 + n\sigma_{\alpha\beta\gamma}^2$
Within (error)	$s_e^2 = \dfrac{SSE}{crl(n-1)}$	σ^2	σ^2	σ^2
Total	$s_0^2 = \dfrac{SST}{crln-1}$			

ANALYSIS OF VARIANCE AND EXPECTED MEAN SQUARES
FOR A $t \times t$ LATIN SQUARE

Model: $y_{ij(k)} = \mu + \alpha_i + \beta_j + \gamma_{(k)} + \epsilon_{ij(k)}$
$(i = 1, 2, \ldots, t; j = 1, 2, \ldots, t; k = 1, 2, \ldots, t)$

Source of variation	Degrees of freedom	Sum of squares	Mean square	Expected mean square for fixed model
Columns	$t - 1$	$SSC = \dfrac{\sum_i Y_i^2}{t} - \dfrac{Y^2}{t^2}$	$s_1^2 = \dfrac{SSC}{t - 1}$	$\sigma^2 + t\dfrac{\sum_i \alpha_i^2}{t - 1}$
Rows	$t - 1$	$SSR = \dfrac{\sum_j Y_j^2}{t} - \dfrac{Y^2}{t^2}$	$s_2^2 = \dfrac{SSR}{t - 1}$	$\sigma^2 + t\dfrac{\sum_j \beta_j^2}{t - 1}$
Treatments	$t - 1$	$SSTr = \dfrac{\sum_k Y_{(k)}^2}{t} - \dfrac{Y^2}{t^2}$	$s_3^2 = \dfrac{SSTr}{t - 1}$	$\sigma^2 + t\dfrac{\sum_k \gamma_k^2}{t - 1}$
Error	$(t - 1)(t - 2)$	$SSE = SST - SSC - SSR - SSTr$	$s_e^2 = \dfrac{SSE}{(t - 1)(t - 2)}$	σ^2
Total	$t^2 - 1$	$SST = \sum_i \sum_j y_{ij(k)}^2 - \dfrac{Y^2}{t^2}$		

Source of variation	Mean square	Expected mean square for Random model	Expected mean square for Mixed model (γ)	Expected mean square for Mixed model (α, γ)
Columns	$s_1^2 = \dfrac{SSC}{t - 1}$	$\sigma^2 + t\sigma_\alpha^2$	$\sigma^2 + t\sigma_\alpha^2$	$\sigma^2 + t\dfrac{\sum_i \alpha_i^2}{t - 1}$
Rows	$s_2^2 = \dfrac{SSR}{t - 1}$	$\sigma^2 + t\sigma_\beta^2$	$\sigma^2 + t\sigma_\beta^2$	$\sigma^2 + t\sigma_\beta^2$
Treatments	$s_3^2 = \dfrac{SSTr}{t - 1}$	$\sigma^2 + t\sigma_\gamma^2$	$\sigma^2 + t\dfrac{\sum_k \gamma_k^2}{t - 1}$	$\sigma^2 + t\dfrac{\sum_k \gamma_k^2}{t - 1}$
Error	$s_e^2 = \dfrac{SSE}{(t - 1)(t - 2)}$	σ^2	σ^2	σ^2

ANALYSIS OF VARIANCE FOR A GRAECO-LATIN SQUARE

Model: $y_{ijuk} = \mu + \alpha_i + \beta_j + \gamma_u + \delta_k + \epsilon_{ijuk}$ $(i, j, u, k = 1, 2, \ldots, n)$

Source of variation	Degrees of freedom	Sum of squares	Mean square
Factor I (rows)	$n - 1$	$S_1 = \dfrac{\sum_i Y^2_{i\ldots}}{n} - \dfrac{Y^2}{n^2}$	$s^2_1 = \dfrac{S_1}{n-1}$
Factor II (columns)	$n - 1$	$S_2 = \dfrac{\sum_j Y^2_{j}}{n} - \dfrac{Y^2}{n^2}$	$s^2_2 = \dfrac{S_2}{n-1}$
Factor III (Latin letters)	$n - 1$	$S_3 = \dfrac{\sum_u Y^2_{u}}{n-1} - \dfrac{Y^2}{n^2}$	$s^2_3 = \dfrac{S_3}{n-1}$
Factor IV (Greek letters)	$n - 1$	$S_4 = \dfrac{\sum_k Y^2_{k}}{n} - \dfrac{Y^2}{n^2}$	$s^2_4 = \dfrac{S_4}{n-1}$
Residual	$(n-1)(n-3)$	$S_r = $ difference	$s^2_e = \dfrac{S_r}{(n-1)(n-3)}$
Total	$n^2 - 1$	$S = \sum_i \sum_j y^2_{ijuk} - \dfrac{Y^2}{n^2}$	

ANALYSIS OF VARIANCE FOR A YOUDEN SQUARE

Model: $y_{iju} = \mu + \alpha_i + \beta_j + \gamma_u + \epsilon_{iju}$

$(i = 1, 2, \ldots, b; j = 1, 2, \ldots, t(= b); u = 1, 2, \ldots, k(<t))$

Source of variation	Degrees of freedom	Sum of squares	Mean square
Blocks (crude)		$S_1 = \sum_i \dfrac{Y^2_i}{k} - \dfrac{Y^2}{bk}$	
Treatments (adjusted)	$t - 1$	$S_2 = \dfrac{t-1}{bk^2(k-1)} \sum_j \left(kY^2_j - \sum_{i(j)} Y^2_i \right)$	$s^2_1 = \dfrac{S_2}{t-1}$
Treatments (crude)		$S_3 = \sum_j \dfrac{Y^2_j}{r} - \dfrac{Y^2}{tr}$	
Blocks (adjusted)	$b - 1$	$S_4 = \dfrac{b-1}{bk^2(k-1)} \sum_i \left(rY^2_i - \sum_{j(i)} Y^2_j \right)$	$s^2_2 = \dfrac{S_4}{b-1}$
Factor II (γ)	$k - 1$	$S_5 = \dfrac{\sum_u Y^2_{u}}{k} - \dfrac{Y^2}{bk}$	$s^2_3 = \dfrac{S_5}{k-1}$

ANALYSIS OF VARIANCE FOR A YOUDEN SQUARE (continued)

Source of variation	Degrees of freedom	Sum of squares	Mean square
Residual	$bk - t - b - k + 2$	$\begin{aligned} S_r &= S - (S_1 + S_2 + S_5) \\ &= S - (S_3 + S_4 + S_5) \end{aligned}$	$s_r^2 = \dfrac{S_r}{bk - t - b - k + 2}$
Total	$bk - 1$	$S = \sum_i \sum_j y_{iju}^2 - \dfrac{Y^2}{bk}$	

(Note that $S_1 + S_2 = S_3 + S_4$)

ANALYSIS OF VARIANCE FOR BALANCED INCOMPLETE BLOCK (BIB)

Model: $y_{iju} = \mu + \alpha_i + \beta_j + \epsilon_{iju}$ $(i = 1, 2, \ldots, b; j = 1, 2, \ldots, t; u = n_{ij})$

Source of variation	Degrees of freedom	Sum of squares	Mean square
Blocks	$b - 1$	$S_1 = \dfrac{\sum_i Y_i^2}{k} - \dfrac{Y^2}{bk}$	$s_1^2 = \dfrac{S_1}{b - 1}$
Treatments (adjusted)	$t - 1$	$S_2 = \dfrac{t - 1}{bk^2(k - 1)} \sum_j \left[kY_j - \sum_{u_{ji}} Y_i \right]^2$	$s_2^2 = \dfrac{S_2}{t - 1}$
Residual	$bk - t - b + 1$	$S_r = $ difference	$s_r^2 = \dfrac{S_r}{bk - t - b + 1}$
Total	$bk - 1$	$S = \sum_i \sum_j y_{iju}^2 - \dfrac{Y^2}{bk}$	

where

t = number of treatment levels
b = number of blocks
k = number of treatment levels per block
r = number of replications of each treatment level
λ = number of blocks in which any given pair of treatment levels appear together
$bk = tr$
$r(k - 1) = \lambda(t - 1)$

THE NORMAL PROBABILITY FUNCTION
AND RELATED FUNCTIONS

This table gives values of:

a) $f(x)$ = the probability density of a standardized random variable

$$= \frac{1}{\sqrt{2\pi}} e^{-\frac{1}{2}x^2}$$

For negative values of x, one uses the fact that $f(-x) = f(x)$.

b) $F(x)$ = the cumulative distribution function of a standardized normal random variable

$$= \int_{-\infty}^{x} \frac{1}{\sqrt{2\pi}} e^{-\frac{1}{2}t^2} dt$$

For negative values of x, one uses the relationship $F(-x) = 1 - F(x)$. Values of x corresponding to a few special values of $F(x)$ are given in a separate table following the main table. (See page 560.)

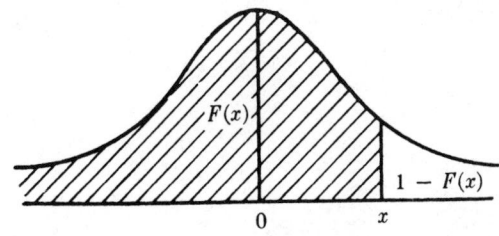

c) $f'(x)$ = the first derivative of $f(x)$ with respect to x

$$= -\frac{x}{\sqrt{2\pi}} e^{-\frac{1}{2}x^2} = -xf(x)$$

d) $f''(x)$ = the second derivative of $f(x)$ with respect to x

$$= \frac{(x^2 - 1)}{\sqrt{2\pi}} e^{-\frac{1}{2}x^2} = (x^2 - 1)f(x)$$

e) $f'''(x)$ = the third derivative of $f(x)$ with respect to x

$$= \frac{3x - x^3}{\sqrt{2\pi}} e^{-\frac{1}{2}x^2} = (3x - x^3)f(x)$$

f) $f^{iv}(x)$ = the fourth derivative of $f(x)$ with respect to x

$$= \frac{x^4 - 6x^2 + 3}{\sqrt{2\pi}} e^{-\frac{1}{2}x^2} = (x^4 - 6x^2 + 3)f(x)$$

It should be noted that other probability integrals can be evaluated by the use of these tables. For example,

$$\int_0^z f(t)dt = \tfrac{1}{2} \, \mathrm{erf}\left(\frac{x}{\sqrt{2}}\right),$$

where $\mathrm{erf}\left(\dfrac{x}{\sqrt{2}}\right)$ represents the error function associated with the normal curve.

To evaluate erf (2.3) one proceeds as follows: Since $\dfrac{x}{\sqrt{2}} = 2.3$, one finds $x = (2.3)(\sqrt{2}) = 3.25$. In the entry opposite $x = 3.25$, the value 0.9994 is given. Subtracting 0.5000 from the tabular value, one finds the value 0.4994. Thus erf (2.3) = 2(0.4994) = 0.9988.

NORMAL DISTRIBUTION AND RELATED FUNCTIONS

x	$F(x)$	$1 - F(x)$	$f(x)$	$f'(x)$	$f''(x)$	$f'''(x)$	$f^{IV}(x)$
.00	.5000	.5000	.3989	− .0000	− .3989	.0000	1.1968
.01	.5040	.4960	.3989	− .0040	− .3989	.0120	1.1965
.02	.5080	.4920	.3989	− .0080	− .3987	.0239	1.1956
.03	.5120	.4880	.3988	− .0120	− .3984	.0359	1.1941
.04	.5160	.4840	.3986	− .0159	− .3980	.0478	1.1920
.05	.5199	.4801	.3984	− .0199	− .3975	.0597	1.1894
.06	.5239	.4761	.3982	− .0239	− .3968	.0716	1.1861
.07	.5279	.4721	.3980	− .0279	− .3960	.0834	1.1822
.08	.5319	.4681	.3977	− .0318	− .3951	.0952	1.1778
.09	.5359	.4641	.3973	− .0358	− .3941	.1070	1.1727
.10	.5398	.4602	.3970	− .0397	− .3930	.1187	1.1671
.11	.5438	.4562	.3965	− .0436	− .3917	.1303	1.1609
.12	.5478	.4522	.3961	− .0475	− .3904	.1419	1.1541
.13	.5517	.4483	.3956	− .0514	− .3889	.1534	1.1468
.14	.5557	.4443	.3951	− .0553	− .3873	.1648	1.1389
.15	.5596	.4404	.3945	− .0592	− .3856	.1762	1.1304
.16	.5636	.4364	.3939	− .0630	− .3838	.1874	1.1214
.17	.5675	.4325	.3932	− .0668	− .3819	.1986	1.1118
.18	.5714	.4286	.3925	− .0707	− .3798	.2097	1.1017
.19	.5753	.4247	.3918	− .0744	− .3777	.2206	1.0911
.20	.5793	.4207	.3910	− .0782	− .3754	.2315	1.0799
.21	.5832	.4168	.3902	− .0820	− .3730	.2422	1.0682
.22	.5871	.4129	.3894	− .0857	− .3706	.2529	1.0560
.23	.5910	.4090	.3885	− .0894	− .3680	.2634	1.0434
.24	.5948	.4052	.3876	− .0930	− .3653	.2737	1.0302
.25	.5987	.4013	.3867	− .0967	− .3625	.2840	1.0165
.26	.6026	.3974	.3857	− .1003	− .3596	.2941	1.0024
.27	.6064	.3936	.3847	− .1039	− .3566	.3040	0.9878
.28	.6103	.3897	.3836	− .1074	− .3535	.3138	0.9727
.29	.6141	.3859	.3825	− .1109	− .3504	.3235	0.9572
.30	.6179	.3821	.3814	− .1144	− .3471	.3330	0.9413
.31	.6217	.3783	.3802	− .1179	− .3437	.3423	0.9250
.32	.6255	.3745	.3790	− .1213	− .3402	.3515	0.9082
.33	.6293	.3707	.3778	− .1247	− .3367	.3605	0.8910
.34	.6331	.3669	.3765	− .1280	− .3330	.3693	0.8735
.35	.6368	.3632	.3752	− .1313	− .3293	.3779	0.8556
.36	.6406	.3594	.3739	− .1346	− .3255	.3864	0.8373
.37	.6443	.3557	.3725	− .1378	− .3216	.3947	0.8186
.38	.6480	.3520	.3712	− .1410	− .3176	.4028	0.7996
.39	.6517	.3483	.3697	− .1442	− .3135	.4107	0.7803
.40	.6554	.3446	.3683	− .1473	− .3094	.4184	0.7607
.41	.6591	.3409	.3668	− .1504	− .3051	.4259	0.7408
.42	.6628	.3372	.3653	− .1534	− .3008	.4332	0.7206
.43	.6664	.3336	.3637	− .1564	− .2965	.4403	0.7001
.44	.6700	.3300	.3621	− .1593	− .2920	.4472	0.6793
.45	.6736	.3264	.3605	− .1622	− .2875	.4539	0.6583
.46	.6772	.3228	.3589	− .1651	− .2830	.4603	0.6371
.47	.6808	.3192	.3572	− .1679	− .2783	.4666	0.6156
.48	.6844	.3156	.3555	− .1707	− .2736	.4727	0.5940
.49	.6879	.3121	.3538	− .1734	− .2689	.4785	0.5721
.50	.6915	.3085	.3521	− .1760	− .2641	.4841	0.5501

NORMAL DISTRIBUTION AND RELATED FUNCTIONS

x	$F(x)$	$1 - F(x)$	$f(x)$	$f'(x)$	$f''(x)$	$f'''(x)$	$f^{IV}(x)$
.50	.6915	.3085	.3521	− .1760	− .2641	.4841	.5501
.51	.6950	.3050	.3503	− .1787	− .2592	.4895	.5279
.52	.6985	.3015	.3485	− .1812	− .2543	.4947	.5056
.53	.7019	.2981	.3467	− .1837	− .2493	.4996	.4831
.54	.7054	.2946	.3448	− .1862	− .2443	.5043	.4605
.55	.7088	.2912	.3429	− .1886	− .2392	.5088	.4378
.56	.7123	.2877	.3410	− .1920	− .2341	.5131	.4150
.57	.7157	.2843	.3391	− .1933	− .2289	.5171	.3921
.58	.7190	.2810	.3372	− .1956	− .2238	.5209	.3691
.59	.7224	.2776	.3352	− .1978	− .2185	.5245	.3461
.60	.7257	.2743	.3332	− .1999	− .2133	.5278	.3231
.61	.7291	.2709	.3312	− .2020	− .2080	.5309	.3000
.62	.7324	.2676	.3292	− .2041	− .2027	.5338	.2770
.63	.7357	.2643	.3271	− .2061	− .1973	.5365	.2539
.64	.7389	.2611	.3251	− .2080	− .1919	.5389	.2309
.65	.7422	.2578	.3230	− .2099	− .1865	.5411	.2078
.66	.7454	.2546	.3209	− .2118	− .1811	.5431	.1849
.67	.7486	.2514	.3187	− .2136	− .1757	.5448	.1620
.68	.7517	.2483	.3166	− .2153	− .1702	.5463	.1391
.69	.7549	.2451	.3144	− .2170	− .1647	.5476	.1164
.70	.7580	.2420	.3123	− .2186	− .1593	.5486	.0937
.71	.7611	.2389	.3101	− .2201	− .1538	.5495	.0712
.72	.7642	.2358	.3079	− .2217	− .1483	.5501	.0487
.73	.7673	.2327	.3056	− .2231	− .1428	.5504	.0265
.74	.7704	.2296	.3034	− .2245	− .1373	.5506	.0043
.75	.7734	.2266	.3011	− .2259	− .1318	.5505	− .0176
.76	.7764	.2236	.2989	− .2271	− .1262	.5502	− .0394
.77	.7794	.2206	.2966	− .2284	− .1207	.5497	− .0611
.78	.7823	.2177	.2943	− .2296	− .1153	.5490	− .0825
.79	.7852	.2148	.2920	− .2307	− .1098	.5481	− .1037
.80	.7881	.2119	.2897	− .2318	− .1043	.5469	− .1247
.81	.7910	.2090	.2874	− .2328	− .0988	.5456	− .1455
.82	.7939	.2061	.2850	− .2337	− .0934	.5440	− .1660
.83	.7967	.2033	.2827	− .2346	− .0880	.5423	− .1862
.84	.7995	.2005	.2803	− .2355	− .0825	.5403	− .2063
.85	.8023	.1977	.2780	− .2363	− .0771	.5381	− .2260
.86	.8051	.1949	.2756	− .2370	− .0718	.5358	− .2455
.87	.8078	.1922	.2732	− .2377	− .0664	.5332	− .2646
.88	.8106	.1894	.2709	− .2384	− .0611	.5305	− .2835
.89	.8133	.1867	.2685	− .2389	− .0558	.5276	− .3021
.90	.8159	.1841	.2661	− .2395	− .0506	.5245	− .3203
.91	.8186	.1814	.2637	− .2400	− .0453	.5212	− .3383
.92	.8212	.1788	.2613	− .2404	− .0401	.5177	− .3559
.93	.8238	.1762	.2589	− .2408	− .0350	.5140	− .3731
.94	.8264	.1736	.2565	− .2411	− .0299	.5102	− .3901
.95	.8289	.1711	.2541	− .2414	− .0248	.5062	− .4066
.96	.8315	.1685	.2516	− .2416	− .0197	.5021	− .4228
.97	.8340	.1660	.2492	− .2417	− .0147	.4978	− .4387
.98	.8365	.1635	.2468	− .2419	− .0098	.4933	− .4541
.99	.8389	.1611	.2444	− .2420	− .0049	.4887	− .4692
1.00	.8413	.1587	.2420	− .2420	.0000	.4839	− .4839

NORMAL DISTRIBUTION AND RELATED FUNCTIONS

x	$F(x)$	$1 - F(x)$	$f(x)$	$f'(x)$	$f''(x)$	$f'''(x)$	$f^{iv}(x)$
1.00	.8413	.1587	.2420	−.2420	.0000	.4839	−.4839
1.01	.8438	.1562	.2396	−.2420	.0048	.4790	−.4983
1.02	.8461	.1539	.2371	−.2419	.0096	.4740	−.5122
1.03	.8485	.1515	.2347	−.2418	.0143	.4688	−.5257
1.04	.8508	.1492	.2323	−.2416	.0190	.4635	−.5389
1.05	.8531	.1469	.2299	−.2414	.0236	.4580	−.5516
1.06	.8554	.1446	.2275	−.2411	.0281	.4524	−.5639
1.07	.8577	.1423	.2251	−.2408	.0326	.4467	−.5758
1.08	.8599	.1401	.2227	−.2405	.0371	.4409	−.5873
1.09	.8621	.1379	.2203	−.2401	.0414	.4350	−.5984
1.10	.8643	.1357	.2179	−.2396	.0458	.4290	−.6091
1.11	.8665	.1335	.2155	−.2392	.0500	.4228	−.6193
1.12	.8686	.1314	.2131	−.2386	.0542	.4166	−.6292
1.13	.8708	.1292	.2107	−.2381	.0583	.4102	−.6386
1.14	.8729	.1271	.2083	−.2375	.0624	.4038	−.6476
1.15	.8749	.1251	.2059	−.2368	.0664	.3973	−.6561
1.16	.8770	.1230	.2036	−.2361	.0704	.3907	−.6643
1.17	.8790	.1210	.2012	−.2354	.0742	.3840	−.6720
1.18	.8810	.1190	.1989	−.2347	.0780	.3772	−.6792
1.19	.8830	.1170	.1965	−.2339	.0818	.3704	−.6861
1.20	.8849	.1151	.1942	−.2330	.0854	.3635	−.6926
1.21	.8869	.1131	.1919	−.2322	.0890	.3566	−.6986
1.22	.8888	.1112	.1895	−.2312	.0926	.3496	−.7042
1.23	.8907	.1093	.1872	−.2303	.0960	.3425	−.7094
1.24	.8925	.1075	.1849	−.2293	.0994	.3354	−.7141
1.25	.8944	.1056	.1826	−.2283	.1027	.3282	−.7185
1.26	.8962	.1038	.1804	−.2273	.1060	.3210	−.7224
1.27	.8980	.1020	.1781	−.2262	.1092	.3138	−.7259
1.28	.8997	.1003	.1758	−.2251	.1123	.3065	−.7291
1.29	.9015	.0985	.1736	−.2240	.1153	.2992	−.7318
1.30	.9032	.0968	.1714	−.2228	.1182	.2918	−.7341
1.31	.9049	.0951	.1691	−.2216	.1211	.2845	−.7361
1.32	.9066	.0934	.1669	−.2204	.1239	.2771	−.7376
1.33	.9082	.0918	.1647	−.2191	.1267	.2697	−.7388
1.34	.9099	.0901	.1626	−.2178	.1293	.2624	−.7395
1.35	.9115	.0885	.1604	−.2165	.1319	.2550	−.7399
1.36	.9131	.0869	.1582	−.2152	.1344	.2476	−.7400
1.37	.9147	.0853	.1561	−.2138	.1369	.2402	−.7396
1.38	.9162	.0838	.1539	−.2125	.1392	.2328	−.7389
1.39	.9177	.0823	.1518	−.2110	.1415	.2254	−.7378
1.40	.9192	.0808	.1497	−.2096	.1437	.2180	−.7364
1.41	.9207	.0793	.1476	−.2082	.1459	.2107	−.7347
1.42	.9222	.0778	.1456	−.2067	.1480	.2033	−.7326
1.43	.9236	.0764	.1435	−.2052	.1500	.1960	−.7301
1.44	.9251	.0749	.1415	−.2037	.1519	.1887	−.7274
1.45	.9265	.0735	.1394	−.2022	.1537	.1815	−.7243
1.46	.9279	.0721	.1374	−.2006	.1555	.1742	−.7209
1.47	.9292	.0708	.1354	−.1991	.1572	.1670	−.7172
1.48	.9306	.0694	.1334	−.1975	.1588	.1599	−.7132
1.49	.9319	.0681	.1315	−.1959	.1604	.1528	−.7089
1.50	.9332	.0668	.1295	−.1943	.1619	.1457	−.7043

NORMAL DISTRIBUTION AND RELATED FUNCTIONS

x	$F(x)$	$1 - F(x)$	$f(x)$	$f'(x)$	$f''(x)$	$f'''(x)$	$f^{\text{iv}}(x)$
1.50	.9332	.0668	.1295	−.1943	.1619	.1457	−.7043
1.51	.9345	.0655	.1276	−.1927	.1633	.1387	−.6994
1.52	.9357	.0643	.1257	−.1910	.1647	.1317	−.6942
1.53	.9370	.0630	.1238	−.1894	.1660	.1248	−.6888
1.54	.9382	.0618	.1219	−.1877	.1672	.1180	−.6831
1.55	.9394	.0606	.1200	−.1860	.1683	.1111	−.6772
1.56	.9406	.0594	.1182	−.1843	.1694	.1044	−.6710
1.57	.9418	.0582	.1163	−.1826	.1704	.0977	−.6646
1.58	.9429	.0571	.1145	−.1809	.1714	.0911	−.6580
1.59	.9441	.0559	.1127	−.1792	.1722	.0846	−.6511
1.60	.9452	.0548	.1109	−.1775	.1730	.0781	−.6441
1.61	.9463	.0537	.1092	−.1757	.1738	.0717	−.6368
1.62	.9474	.0526	.1074	−.1740	.1745	.0654	−.6293
1.63	.9484	.0516	.1057	−.1723	.1751	.0591	−.6216
1.64	.9495	.0505	.1040	−.1705	.1757	.0529	−.6138
1.65	.9505	.0495	.1023	−.1687	.1762	.0468	−.6057
1.66	.9515	.0485	.1006	−.1670	.1766	.0408	−.5975
1.67	.9525	.0475	.0989	−.1652	.1770	.0349	−.5891
1.68	.9535	.0465	.0973	−.1634	.1773	.0290	−.5806
1.69	.9545	.0455	.0957	−.1617	.1776	.0233	−.5720
1.70	.9554	.0446	.0940	−.1599	.1778	.0176	−.5632
1.71	.9564	.0436	.0925	−.1581	.1779	.0120	−.5542
1.72	.9573	.0427	.0909	−.1563	.1780	.0065	−.5452
1.73	.9582	.0418	.0893	−.1546	.1780	.0011	−.5360
1.74	.9591	.0409	.0878	−.1528	.1780	−.0042	−.5267
1.75	.9599	.0401	.0863	−.1510	.1780	−.0094	−.5173
1.76	.9608	.0392	.0848	−.1492	.1778	−.0146	−.5079
1.77	.9616	.0384	.0833	−.1474	.1777	−.0196	−.4983
1.78	.9625	.0375	.0818	−.1457	.1774	−.0245	−.4887
1.79	.9633	.0367	.0804	−.1439	.1772	−.0294	−.4789
1.80	.9641	.0359	.0790	−.1421	.1769	−.0341	−.4692
1.81	.9649	.0351	.0775	−.1403	.1765	−.0388	−.4593
1.82	.9656	.0344	.0761	−.1386	.1761	−.0433	−.4494
1.83	.9664	.0336	.0748	−.1368	.1756	−.0477	−.4395
1.84	.9671	.0329	.0734	−.1351	.1751	−.0521	−.4295
1.85	.9678	.0322	.0721	−.1333	.1746	−.0563	−.4195
1.86	.9686	.0314	.0707	−.1316	.1740	−.0605	−.4095
1.87	.9693	.0307	.0694	−.1298	.1734	−.0645	−.3995
1.88	.9699	.0301	.0681	−.1281	.1727	−.0685	−.3894
1.89	.9706	.0294	.0669	−.1264	.1720	−.0723	−.3793
1.90	.9713	.0287	.0656	−.1247	.1713	−.0761	−.3693
1.91	.9719	.0281	.0644	−.1230	.1705	−.0797	−.3592
1.92	.9726	.0274	.0632	−.1213	.1697	−.0832	−.3492
1.93	.9732	.0268	.0620	−.1196	.1688	−.0867	−.3392
1.94	.9738	.0262	.0608	−.1179	.1679	−.0900	−.3292
1.95	.9744	.0256	.0596	−.1162	.1670	−.0933	−.3192
1.96	.9750	.0250	.0584	−.1145	.1661	−.0964	−.3093
1.97	.9756	.0244	.0573	−.1129	.1651	−.0994	−.2994
1.98	.9761	.0239	.0562	−.1112	.1641	−.1024	−.2895
1.99	.9767	.0233	.0551	−.1096	.1630	−.1052	−.2797
2.00	.9772	.0228	.0540	−.1080	.1620	−.1080	−.2700

NORMAL DISTRIBUTION AND RELATED FUNCTIONS

x	$F(x)$	$1 - F(x)$	$f(x)$	$f'(x)$	$f''(x)$	$f'''(x)$	$f^{IV}(x)$
2.00	.9773	.0227	.0540	−.1080	.1620	−.1080	−.2700
2.01	.9778	.0222	.0529	−.1064	.1609	−.1106	−.2603
2.02	.9783	.0217	.0519	−.1048	.1598	−.1132	−.2506
2.03	.9788	.0212	.0508	−.1032	.1586	−.1157	−.2411
2.04	.9793	.0207	.0498	−.1016	.1575	−.1180	−.2316
2.05	.9798	.0202	.0488	−.1000	.1563	−.1203	−.2222
2.06	.9803	.0197	.0478	−.0985	.1550	−.1225	−.2129
2.07	.9808	.0192	.0468	−.0969	.1538	−.1245	−.2036
2.08	.9812	.0188	.0459	−.0954	.1526	−.1265	−.1945
2.09	.9817	.0183	.0449	−.0939	.1513	−.1284	−.1854
2.10	.9821	.0179	.0440	−.0924	.1500	−.1302	−.1765
2.11	.9826	.0174	.0431	−.0909	.1487	−.1320	−.1676
2.12	.9830	.0170	.0422	−.0894	.1474	−.1336	−.1588
2.13	.9834	.0166	.0413	−.0879	.1460	−.1351	−.1502
2.14	.9838	.0162	.0404	−.0865	.1446	−.1366	−.1416
2.15	.9842	.0158	.0396	−.0850	.1433	−.1380	−.1332
2.16	.9846	.0154	.0387	−.0836	.1419	−.1393	−.1249
2.17	.9850	.0150	.0379	−.0822	.1405	−.1405	−.1167
2.18	.9854	.0146	.0371	−.0808	.1391	−.1416	−.1086
2.19	.9857	.0143	.0363	−.0794	.1377	−.1426	−.1006
2.20	.9861	.0139	.0355	−.0780	.1362	−.1436	−.0927
2.21	.9864	.0136	.0347	−.0767	.1348	−.1445	−.0850
2.22	.9868	.0132	.0339	−.0754	.1333	−.1453	−.0774
2.23	.9871	.0129	.0332	−.0740	.1319	−.1460	−.0700
2.24	.9875	.0125	.0325	−.0727	.1304	−.1467	−.0626
2.25	.9878	.0122	.0317	−.0714	.1289	−.1473	−.0554
2.26	.9881	.0119	.0310	−.0701	.1275	−.1478	−.0484
2.27	.9884	.0116	.0303	−.0689	.1260	−.1483	−.0414
2.28	.9887	.0113	.0297	−.0676	.1245	−.1486	−.0346
2.29	.9890	.0110	.0290	−.0664	.1230	−.1490	−.0279
2.30	.9893	.0107	.0283	−.0652	.1215	−.1492	−.0214
2.31	.9896	.0104	.0277	−.0639	.1200	−.1494	−.0150
2.32	.9898	.0102	.0270	−.0628	.1185	−.1495	−.0088
2.33	.9901	.0099	.0264	−.0616	.1170	−.1496	−.0027
2.34	.9904	.0096	.0258	−.0604	.1155	−.1496	.0033
2.35	.9906	.0094	.0252	−.0593	.1141	−.1495	.0092
2.36	.9909	.0091	.0246	−.0581	.1126	−.1494	.0149
2.37	.9911	.0089	.0241	−.0570	.1111	−.1492	.0204
2.38	.9913	.0087	.0235	−.0559	.1096	−.1490	.0258
2.39	.9916	.0084	.0229	−.0548	.1081	−.1487	.0311
2.40	.9918	.0082	.0224	−.0538	.1066	−.1483	.0362
2.41	.9920	.0080	.0219	−.0527	.1051	−.1480	.0412
2.42	.9922	.0078	.0213	−.0516	.1036	−.1475	.0461
2.43	.9925	.0075	.0208	−.0506	.1022	−.1470	.0508
2.44	.9927	.0073	.0203	−.0496	.1007	−.1465	.0554
2.45	.9929	.0071	.0198	−.0486	.0992	−.1459	.0598
2.46	.9931	.0069	.0194	−.0476	.0978	−.1453	.0641
2.47	.9932	.0068	.0189	−.0467	.0963	−.1446	.0683
2.48	.9934	.0066	.0184	−.0457	.0949	−.1439	.0723
2.49	.9936	.0064	.0180	−.0448	.0935	−.1432	.0762
2.50	.9938	.0062	.0175	−.0438	.0920	−.1424	.0800

NORMAL DISTRIBUTION AND RELATED FUNCTIONS

x	$F(x)$	$1 - F(x)$	$f(x)$	$f'(x)$	$f''(x)$	$f'''(x)$	$f^{iv}(x)$
2.50	.9938	.0062	.0175	− .0438	.0920	− .1424	.0800
2.51	.9940	.0060	.0171	− .0429	.0906	− .1416	.0836
2.52	.9941	.0059	.0167	− .0420	.0892	− .1408	.0871
2.53	.9943	.0057	.0163	− .0411	.0878	− .1399	.0905
2.54	.9945	.0055	.0158	− .0403	.0864	− .1389	.0937
2.55	.9946	.0054	.0155	− .0394	.0850	− .1380	.0968
2.56	.9948	.0052	.0151	− .0386	.0836	− .1370	.0998
2.57	.9949	.0051	.0147	− .0377	.0823	− .1360	.1027
2.58	.9951	.0049	.0143	− .0369	.0809	− .1350	.1054
2.59	.9952	.0048	.0139	− .0361	.0796	− .1339	.1080
2.60	.9953	.0047	.0136	− .0353	.0782	− .1328	.1105
2.61	.9955	.0045	.0132	− .0345	.0769	− .1317	.1129
2.62	.9956	.0044	.0129	− .0338	.0756	− .1305	.1152
2.63	.9957	.0043	.0126	− .0330	.0743	− .1294	.1173
2.64	.9959	.0041	.0122	− .0323	.0730	− .1282	.1194
2.65	.9960	.0040	.0119	− .0316	.0717	− .1270	.1213
2.66	.9961	.0039	.0116	− .0309	.0705	− .1258	.1231
2.67	.9962	.0038	.0113	− .0302	.0692	− .1245	.1248
2.68	.9963	.0037	.0110	− .0295	.0680	− .1233	.1264
2.69	.9964	.0036	.0107	− .0288	.0668	− .1220	.1279
2.70	.9965	.0035	.0104	− .0281	.0656	− .1207	.1293
2.71	.9966	.0034	.0101	− .0275	.0644	− .1194	.1306
2.72	.9967	.0033	.0099	− .0269	.0632	− .1181	.1317
2.73	.9968	.0032	.0096	− .0262	.0620	− .1168	.1328
2.74	.9969	.0031	.0093	− .0256	.0608	− .1154	.1338
2.75	.9970	.0030	.0091	− .0250	.0597	− .1141	.1347
2.76	.9971	.0029	.0088	− .0244	.0585	− .1127	.1356
2.77	.9972	.0028	.0086	− .0238	.0574	− .1114	.1363
2.78	.9973	.0027	.0084	− .0233	.0563	− .1100	.1369
2.79	.9974	.0026	.0081	− .0227	.0552	− .1087	.1375
2.80	.9974	.0026	.0079	− .0222	.0541	− .1073	.1379
2.81	.9975	.0025	.0077	− .0216	.0531	− .1059	.1383
2.82	.9976	.0024	.0075	− .0211	.0520	− .1045	.1386
2.83	.9977	.0023	.0073	− .0206	.0510	− .1031	.1389
2.84	.9977	.0023	.0071	− .0201	.0500	− .1017	.1390
2.85	.9978	.0022	.0069	− .0196	.0490	− .1003	.1391
2.86	.9979	.0021	.0067	− .0191	.0480	− .0990	.1391
2.87	.9979	.0021	.0065	− .0186	.0470	− .0976	.1391
2.88	.9980	.0020	.0063	− .0182	.0460	− .0962	.1389
2.89	.9981	.0019	.0061	− .0177	.0451	− .0948	.1388
2.90	.9981	.0019	.0060	− .0173	.0441	− .0934	.1385
2.91	.9982	.0018	.0058	− .0168	.0432	− .0920	.1382
2.92	.9982	.0018	.0056	− .0164	.0423	− .0906	.1378
2.93	.9983	.0017	.0055	− .0160	.0414	− .0893	.1374
2.94	.9984	.0016	.0053	− .0156	.0405	− .0879	.1369
2.95	.9984	.0016	.0051	− .0152	.0396	− .0865	.1364
2.96	.9985	.0015	.0050	− .0148	.0388	− .0852	.1358
2.97	.9985	.0015	.0048	− .0144	.0379	− .0838	.1352
2.98	.9986	.0014	.0047	− .0140	.0371	− .0825	.1345
2.99	.9986	.0014	.0046	− .0137	.0363	− .0811	.1337
3.00	.9987	.0013	.0044	− .0133	.0355	− .0798	.1330

NORMAL DISTRIBUTION AND RELATED FUNCTIONS

x	$F(x)$	$1 - F(x)$	$f(x)$	$f'(x)$	$f''(x)$	$f'''(x)$	$f^{IV}(x)$
3.00	.9987	.0013	.0044	− .0133	.0355	− .0798	.1330
3.01	.9987	.0013	.0043	− .0130	.0347	− .0785	.1321
3.02	.9987	.0013	.0042	− .0126	.0339	− .0771	.1313
3.03	.9988	.0012	.0040	− .0123	.0331	− .0758	.1304
3.04	.9988	.0012	.0039	− .0119	.0324	− .0745	.1294
3.05	.9989	.0011	.0038	− .0116	.0316	− .0732	.1285
3.06	.9989	.0011	.0037	− .0113	.0309	− .0720	.1275
3.07	.9989	.0011	.0036	− .0110	.0302	− .0707	.1264
3.08	.9990	.0010	.0035	− .0107	.0295	− .0694	.1254
3.09	.9990	.0010	.0034	− .0104	.0288	− .0682	.1243
3.10	.9990	.0010	.0033	− .0101	.0281	− .0669	.1231
3.11	.9991	.0009	.0032	− .0099	.0275	− .0657	.1220
3.12	.9991	.0009	.0031	− .0096	.0268	− .0645	.1208
3.13	.9991	.0009	.0030	− .0093	.0262	− .0633	.1196
3.14	.9992	.0008	.0029	− .0091	.0256	− .0621	.1184
3.15	.9992	.0008	.0028	− .0088	.0249	− .0609	.1171
3.16	.9992	.0008	.0027	− .0086	.0243	− .0598	.1159
3.17	.9992	.0008	.0026	− .0083	.0237	− .0586	.1146
3.18	.9993	.0007	.0025	− .0081	.0232	− .0575	.1133
3.19	.9993	.0007	.0025	− .0079	.0226	− .0564	.1120
3.20	.9993	.0007	.0024	− .0076	.0220	− .0552	.1107
3.21	.9993	.0007	.0023	− .0074	.0215	− .0541	.1093
3.22	.9994	.0006	.0022	− .0072	.0210	− .0531	.1080
3.23	.9994	.0006	.0022	− .0070	.0204	− .0520	.1066
3.24	.9994	.0006	.0021	− .0068	.0199	− .0509	.1053
3.25	.9994	.0006	.0020	− .0066	.0194	− .0499	.1039
3.26	.9994	.0006	.0020	− .0064	.0189	− .0488	.1025
3.27	.9995	.0005	.0019	− .0062	.0184	− .0478	.1011
3.28	.9995	.0005	.0018	− .0060	.0180	− .0468	.0997
3.29	.9995	.0005	.0018	− .0059	.0175	− .0458	.0983
3.30	.9995	.0005	.0017	− .0057	.0170	− .0449	.0969
3.31	.9995	.0005	.0017	− .0055	.0166	− .0439	.0955
3.32	.9995	.0005	.0016	− .0054	.0162	− .0429	.0941
3.33	.9996	.0004	.0016	− .0052	.0157	− .0420	.0927
3.34	.9996	.0004	.0015	− .0050	.0153	− .0411	.0913
3.35	.9996	.0004	.0015	− .0049	.0149	− .0402	.0899
3.36	.9996	.0004	.0014	− .0047	.0145	− .0393	.0885
3.37	.9996	.0004	.0014	− .0046	.0141	− .0384	.0871
3.38	.9996	.0004	.0013	− .0045	.0138	− .0376	.0857
3.39	.9997	.0003	.0013	− .0043	.0134	− .0367	.0843
3.40	.9997	.0003	.0012	− .0042	.0130	− .0359	.0829
3.41	.9997	.0003	.0012	− .0041	.0127	− .0350	.0815
3.42	.9997	.0003	.0012	− .0039	.0123	− .0342	.0801
3.43	.9997	.0003	.0011	− .0038	.0120	− .0334	.0788
3.44	.9997	.0003	.0011	− .0037	.0116	− .0327	.0774
3.45	.9997	.0003	.0010	− .0036	.0113	− .0319	.0761
3.46	.9997	.0003	.0010	− .0035	.0110	− .0311	.0747
3.47	.9997	.0003	.0010	− .0034	.0107	− .0304	.0734
3.48	.9997	.0003	.0009	− .0033	.0104	− .0297	.0721
3.49	.9998	.0002	.0009	− .0032	.0101	− .0290	.0707
3.50	.9998	.0002	.0009	− .0031	.0098	− .0283	.0694

NORMAL DISTRIBUTION AND RELATED FUNCTIONS

x	$F(x)$	$1 - F(x)$	$f(x)$	$f'(x)$	$f''(x)$	$f'''(x)$	$f^{iv}(x)$
3.50	.9998	.0002	.0009	− .0031	.0098	− .0283	.0694
3.51	.9998	.0002	.0008	− .0030	.0095	− .0276	.0681
3.52	.9998	.0002	.0008	− .0029	.0093	− .0269	.0669
3.53	.9998	.0002	.0008	− .0028	.0090	− .0262	.0656
3.54	.9998	.0002	.0008	− .0027	.0087	− .0256	.0643
3.55	.9998	.0002	.0007	− .0026	.0085	− .0249	.0631
3.56	.9998	.0002	.0007	− .0025	.0082	− .0243	.0618
3.57	.9998	.0002	.0007	− .0024	.0080	− .0237	.0606
3.58	.9998	.0002	.0007	− .0024	.0078	− .0231	.0594
3.59	.9998	.0002	.0006	− .0023	.0075	− .0225	.0582
3.60	.9998	.0002	.0006	− .0022	.0073	− .0219	.0570
3.61	.9998	.0002	.0006	− .0021	.0071	− .0214	.0559
3.62	.9999	.0001	.0006	− .0021	.0069	− .0208	.0547
3.63	.9999	.0001	.0005	− .0020	.0067	− .0203	.0536
3.64	.9999	.0001	.0005	− .0019	.0065	− .0198	.0524
3.65	.9999	.0001	.0005	− .0019	.0063	− .0192	.0513
3.66	.9999	.0001	.0005	− .0018	.0061	− .0187	.0502
3.67	.9999	.0001	.0005	− .0017	.0059	− .0182	.0492
3.68	.9999	.0001	.0005	− .0017	.0057	− .0177	.0481
3.69	.9999	.0001	.0004	− .0016	.0056	− .0173	.0470
3.70	.9999	.0001	.0004	− .0016	.0054	− .0168	.0460
3.71	.9999	.0001	.0004	− .0015	.0052	− .0164	.0450
3.72	.9999	.0001	.0004	− .0015	.0051	− .0159	.0440
3.73	.9999	.0001	.0004	− .0014	.0049	− .0155	.0430
3.74	.9999	.0001	.0004	− .0014	.0048	− .0150	.0420
3.75	.9999	.0001	.0004	− .0013	.0046	− .0146	.0410
3.76	.9999	.0001	.0003	− .0013	.0045	− .0142	.0401
3.77	.9999	.0001	.0003	− .0012	.0043	− .0138	.0392
3.78	.9999	.0001	.0003	− .0012	.0042	− .0134	.0382
3.79	.9999	.0001	.0003	− .0012	.0041	− .0131	.0373
3.80	.9999	.0001	.0003	− .0011	.0039	− .0127	.0365
3.81	.9999	.0001	.0003	− .0011	.0038	− .0123	.0356
3.82	.9999	.0001	.0003	− .0010	.0037	− .0120	.0347
3.83	.9999	.0001	.0003	− .0010	.0036	− .0116	.0339
3.84	.9999	.0001	.0003	− .0010	.0034	− .0113	.0331
3.85	.9999	.0001	.0002	− .0009	.0033	− .0110	.0323
3.86	.9999	.0001	.0002	− .0009	.0032	− .0107	.0315
3.87	.9999	.0001	.0002	− .0009	.0031	− .0104	.0307
3.88	.9999	.0001	.0002	− .0008	.0030	− .0100	.0299
3.89	1.0000	.0000	.0002	− .0008	.0029	− .0098	.0292
3.90	1.0000	.0000	.0002	− .0008	.0028	− .0095	.0284
3.91	1.0000	.0000	.0002	− .0008	.0027	− .0092	.0277
3.92	1.0000	.0000	.0002	− .0007	.0026	− .0089	.0270
3.93	1.0000	.0000	.0002	− .0007	.0026	− .0086	.0263
3.94	1.0000	.0000	.0002	− .0007	.0025	− .0084	.0256
3.95	1.0000	.0000	.0002	− .0006	.0024	− .0081	.0250
3.96	1.0000	.0000	.0002	− .0006	.0023	− .0079	.0243
3.97	1.0000	.0000	.0002	− .0006	.0022	− .0076	.0237
3.98	1.0000	.0000	.0001	− .0006	.0022	− .0074	.0230
3.99	1.0000	.0000	.0001	− .0006	.0021	− .0072	.0224
4.00	1.0000	.0000	.0001	− .0005	.0020	− .0070	.0218

x	1.282	1.645	1.960	2.326	2.576	3.090
$F(x)$	.90	.95	.975	.99	.995	.999
$2[1 - F(x)]$	.20	.10	.05	.02	.01	.002

CUMULATIVE TERMS, BINOMIAL DISTRIBUTION

This table contains the values of $\sum_{x=x'}^{n} \binom{n}{x} \theta^x (1 - \theta)^{n-x}$ for specified values of n, x', and θ. If $\theta >$
0.5, the values for $\sum_{x=x'}^{n} \binom{n}{x} \theta^x (1 - \theta)^{n-x}$ are obtained using the corresponding results obtained
from

$$1 - \sum_{x=n-x'+1}^{n} \binom{n}{x} (1 - \theta)^x \theta^{n-x}$$

Individual terms of the binomial distribution for specified x', n, and θ can be found from

$$\sum_{x=x}^{n} \binom{n}{x} \theta^x (1 - \theta)^{n-x} - \sum_{x=x'+1}^{n} \binom{n}{x} \theta^x (1 - \theta)^{n-x}$$

n	x'	.05	.10	.15	.20	.25	.30	.35	.40	.45	.50
2	1	.0975	.1900	.2775	.3600	.4375	.5100	.5775	.6400	.6975	.7500
	2	.0025	.0100	.0225	.0400	.0625	.0900	.1225	.1600	.2025	.2500
3	1	.1426	.2710	.3859	.4880	.5781	.6570	.7254	.7840	.8336	.8750
	2	.0072	.0280	.0608	.1040	.1562	.2160	.2818	.3520	.4252	.5000
	3	.0001	.0010	.0034	.0080	.0156	.0270	.0429	.0640	.0911	.1250
4	1	.1855	.3439	.4780	.5904	.6836	.7599	.8215	.8704	.9085	.9375
	2	.0140	.0523	.1095	.1808	.2617	.3483	.4370	.5248	.6090	.6875
	3	.0005	.0037	.0120	.0272	.0508	.0837	.1265	.1792	.2415	.3125
	4	.0000	.0001	.0005	.0016	.0039	.0081	.0150	.0256	.0410	.0625
5	1	.2262	.4095	.5563	.6723	.7627	.8319	.8840	.9222	.9497	.9688
	2	.0226	.0815	.1648	.2627	.3672	.4718	.5716	.6630	.7438	.8125
	3	.0012	.0086	.0266	.0579	.1035	.1631	.2352	.3174	.4069	.5000
	4	.0000	.0005	.0022	.0067	.0156	.0308	.0540	.0870	.1312	.1875
	5	.0000	.0000	.0001	.0003	.0010	.0024	.0053	.0102	.0185	.0312
6	1	.2649	.4686	.6229	.7379	.8220	.8824	.9246	.9533	.9723	.9844
	2	.0328	.1143	.2235	.3446	.4661	.5798	.6809	.7667	.8364	.8906
	3	.0022	.0158	.0473	.0989	.1694	.2557	.3529	.4557	.5585	.6562
	4	.0001	.0013	.0059	.0170	.0376	.0705	.1174	.1792	.2553	.3438
	5	.0000	.0001	.0004	.0016	.0046	.0109	.0223	.0410	.0692	.1094
	6	.0000	.0000	.0000	.0001	.0002	.0008	.0018	.0041	.0083	.0156
7	1	.3017	.5217	.6794	.7903	.8665	.9176	.9510	.9720	.9848	.9922
	2	.0444	.1497	.2834	.4233	.5551	.6706	.7662	.8414	.8976	.9375
	3	.0038	.0257	.0738	.1480	.2436	.3529	.4677	.5801	.6836	.7734
	4	.0002	.0027	.0121	.0333	.0706	.1260	.1998	.2898	.3917	.5000
	5	.0000	.0002	.0012	.0047	.0129	.0288	.0556	.0963	.1529	.2266
	6	.0000	.0000	.0001	.0004	.0013	.0038	.0090	.0188	.0357	.0625
	7	.0000	.0000	.0000	.0000	.0001	.0002	.0006	.0016	.0037	.0078
8	1	.3366	.5695	.7275	.8322	.8999	.9424	.9681	.9832	.9916	.9961
	2	.0572	.1869	.3428	.4967	.6329	.7447	.8309	.8936	.9368	.9648
	3	.0058	.0381	.1052	.2031	.3215	.4482	.5722	.6846	.7799	.8555
	4	.0004	.0050	.0214	.0563	.1138	.1941	.2936	.4059	.5230	.6367
	5	.0000	.0004	.0029	.0104	.0273	.0580	.1061	.1737	.2604	.3633
	6	.0000	.0000	.0002	.0012	.0042	.0113	.0253	.0498	.9885	.1445
	7	.0000	.0000	.0000	.0001	.0004	.0013	.0036	.0085	.0181	.0352
	8	.0000	.0000	.0000	.0000	.0000	.0001	.0002	.0007	.0017	.0039

Linear interpolation will be accurate at most to two decimal places.

CUMULATIVE TERMS, BINOMIAL DISTRIBUTION (Continued)

θ

n	x'	.05	.10	.15	.20	.25	.30	.35	.40	.45	.50
9	1	.3698	.6126	.7684	.8658	.9249	.9596	.9793	.9899	.9954	.9980
	2	.0712	.2252	.4005	.5638	.6997	.8040	.8789	.9295	.9615	.9805
	3	.0084	.0530	.1409	.2618	.3993	.5372	.6627	.7682	.8505	.9102
	4	.0006	.0083	.0339	.0856	.1657	.2703	.3911	.5174	.6386	.7461
	5	.0000	.0009	.0056	.0196	.0489	.0988	.1717	.2666	.3786	.5000
	6	.0000	.0001	.0006	.0031	.0100	.0253	.0536	.0994	.1658	.2539
	7	.0000	.0000	.0000	.0003	.0013	.0043	.0112	.0250	.0498	.0898
	8	.0000	.0000	.0000	.0000	.0001	.0004	.0014	.0038	.0091	.0195
	9	.0000	.0000	.0000	.0000	.0000	.0000	.0001	.0003	.0008	.0020
10	1	.4013	.6513	.8031	.8926	.9437	.9718	.9865	.9940	.9975	.9990
	2	.0861	.2639	.4557	.6242	.7560	.8507	.9140	.9536	.9767	.9893
	3	.0115	.0702	.1798	.3222	.4744	.6172	.7384	.8327	.9004	.9453
	4	.0010	.0128	.0500	.1209	.2241	.3504	.4862	.6177	.7340	.8281
	5	.0001	.0016	.0099	.0328	.0781	.1503	.2485	.3669	.4956	.6230
	6	.0000	.0001	.0014	.0064	.0197	.0473	.0949	.1662	.2616	.3770
	7	.0000	.0000	.0001	.0009	.0035	.0106	.0260	.0548	.1020	.1719
	8	.0000	.0000	.0000	.0001	.0004	.0016	.0048	.0123	.0274	.0547
	9	.0000	.0000	.0000	.0000	.0000	.0001	.0005	.0017	.0045	.0107
	10	.0000	.0000	.0000	.0000	.0000	.0000	.0000	.0001	.0003	.0010
11	1	.4312	.6862	.8327	.9141	.9578	.9802	.9912	.9964	.9986	.9995
	2	.1019	.3026	.5078	.6779	.8029	.8870	.9394	.9698	.9861	.9941
	3	.0152	.0896	.2212	.3826	.5448	.6873	.7999	.8811	.9348	.9673
	4	.0016	.0185	.0694	.1611	.2867	.4304	.5744	.7037	.8089	.8867
	5	.0001	.0028	.0159	.0504	.1146	.2103	.3317	.4672	.6029	.7256
	6	.0000	.0003	.0027	.0117	.0343	.0782	.1487	.2465	.3669	.5000
	7	.0000	.0000	.0003	.0020	.0076	.0216	.0501	.0994	.1738	.2744
	8	.0000	.0000	.0000	.0002	.0012	.0043	.0122	.0293	.0610	.1133
	9	.0000	.0000	.0000	.0000	.0001	.0006	.0020	.0059	.0148	.0327
	10	.0000	.0000	.0000	.0000	.0000	.0000	.0002	.0007	.0022	.0059
	11	.0000	.0000	.0000	.0000	.0000	.0000	.0000	.0000	.0002	.0005
12	1	.4596	.7176	.8578	.9313	.9683	.9862	.9943	.9978	.9992	.9998
	2	.1184	.3410	.5565	.7251	.8416	.9150	.9576	.9804	.9917	.9968
	3	.0196	.1109	.2642	.4417	.6093	.7472	.8487	.9166	.9579	.9807
	4	.0022	.0256	.0922	.2054	.3512	.5075	.6533	.7747	.8655	.9270
	5	.0002	.0043	.0239	.0726	.1576	.2763	.4167	.5618	.6956	.8062
	6	.0000	.0005	.0046	.0194	.0544	.1178	.2127	.3348	.4731	.6128
	7	.0000	.0001	.0007	.0039	.0143	.0386	.0846	.1582	.2607	.3872
	8	.0000	.0000	.0001	.0006	.0028	.0095	.0255	.0573	.1117	.1938
	9	.0000	.0000	.0000	.0001	.0004	.0017	.0056	.0153	.0356	.0730
	10	.0000	.0000	.0000	.0000	.0000	.0002	.0008	.0028	.0079	.0193
	11	.0000	.0000	.0000	.0000	.0000	.0000	.0001	.0003	.0011	.0032
	12	.0000	.0000	.0000	.0000	.0000	.0000	.0000	.0000	.0001	.0002

CUMULATIVE TERMS, BINOMIAL DISTRIBUTION (Continued)

θ

n	x′	.05	.10	.15	.20	.25	.30	.35	.40	.45	.50
13	1	.4867	.7458	.8791	.9450	.9762	.9903	.9963	.9987	.9996	.9999
	2	.1354	.3787	.6017	.7664	.8733	.9363	.9704	.9874	.9951	.9983
	3	.0245	.1339	.3080	.4983	.6674	.7975	.8868	.9421	.9731	.9888
	4	.0031	.0342	.1180	.2527	.4157	.5794	.7217	.8314	.9071	.9539
	5	.0003	.0065	.0342	.0991	.2060	.3457	.4995	.6470	.7721	.8666
	6	.0000	.0009	.0075	.0300	.0802	.1654	.2841	.4256	.5732	.7095
	7	.0000	.0001	.0013	.0070	.0243	.0624	.1295	.2288	.3563	.5000
	8	.0000	.0000	.0002	.0012	.0056	.0182	.0462	.0977	.1788	.2905
	9	.0000	.0000	.0000	.0002	.0010	.0040	.0126	.0321	.0698	.1334
	10	.0000	.0000	.0000	.0000	.0001	.0007	.0025	.0078	.0203	.0461
	11	.0000	.0000	.0000	.0000	.0000	.0001	.0003	.0013	.0041	.0112
	12	.0000	.0000	.0000	.0000	.0000	.0000	.0000	.0001	.0005	.0017
	13	.0000	.0000	.0000	.0000	.0000	.0000	.0000	.0000	.0000	.0001
14	1	.5123	.7712	.8972	.9560	.9822	.9932	.9976	.9992	.9998	.9999
	2	.1530	.4154	.6433	.8021	.8990	.9525	.9795	.9919	.9971	.9991
	3	.0301	.1584	.3521	.5519	.7189	.8392	.9161	.9602	.9830	.9935
	4	.0042	.0441	.1465	.3018	.4787	.6448	.7795	.8757	.9368	.9713
	5	.0004	.0092	.0467	.1298	.2585	.4158	.5773	.7207	.8328	.9102
	6	.0000	.0015	.0115	.0439	.1117	.2195	.3595	.5141	.6627	.7880
	7	.0000	.0002	.0022	.0116	.0383	.0933	.1836	.3075	.4539	.6047
	8	.0000	.0000	.0003	.0024	.0103	.0315	.0753	.1501	.2586	.3953
	9	.0000	.0000	.0000	.0004	.0022	.0083	.0243	.0583	.1189	.2120
	10	.0000	.0000	.0000	.0000	.0003	.0017	.0060	.0175	.0426	.0898
	11	.0000	.0000	.0000	.0000	.0000	.0002	.0011	.0039	.0114	.0287
	12	.0000	.0000	.0000	.0000	.0000	.0000	.0001	.0006	.0022	.0065
	13	.0000	.0000	.0000	.0000	.0000	.0000	.0000	.0001	.0003	.0009
	14	.0000	.0000	.0000	.0000	.0000	.0000	.0000	.0000	.0000	.0001
15	1	.5367	.7941	.9126	.9648	.9866	.9953	.9984	.9995	.9999	1.0000
	2	.1710	.4510	.6814	.8329	.9198	.9647	.9858	.9948	.9983	.9995
	3	.0362	.1841	.3958	.6020	.7639	.8732	.9383	.9729	.9893	.9963
	4	.0055	.0556	.1773	.3518	.5387	.7031	.8273	.9095	.9576	.9824
	5	.0006	.0127	.0617	.1642	.3135	.4845	.6481	.7827	.8796	.9408
	6	.0001	.0022	.0168	.0611	.1484	.2784	.4357	.5968	.7392	.8491
	7	.0000	.0003	.0036	.0181	.0566	.1311	.2452	.3902	.5478	.6964
	8	.0000	.0000	.0006	.0042	.0173	.0500	.1132	.2131	.3465	.5000
	9	.0000	.0000	.0001	.0008	.0042	.0152	.0422	.0950	.1818	.3036
	10	.0000	.0000	.0000	.0001	.0008	.0037	.0124	.0338	.0769	.1509
	11	.0000	.0000	.0000	.0000	.0001	.0007	.0028	.0093	.0255	.0592
	12	.0000	.0000	.0000	.0000	.0000	.0001	.0005	.0019	.0063	.0176
	13	.0000	.0000	.0000	.0000	.0000	.0000	.0001	.0003	.0011	.0037
	14	.0000	.0000	.0000	.0000	.0000	.0000	.0000	.0000	.0001	.0005
	15	.0000	.0000	.0000	.0000	.0000	.0000	.0000	.0000	.0000	.0000

CUMULATIVE TERMS, BINOMIAL DISTRIBUTION (Continued)

θ

n	x′	.05	.10	.15	.20	.25	.30	.35	.40	.45	.50
16	1	.5599	.8147	.9257	.9719	.9900	.9967	.9990	.9997	.9999	1.0000
	2	.1892	.4853	.7161	.8593	.9365	.9739	.9902	.9967	.9990	.9997
	3	.0429	.2108	.4386	.6482	.8029	.9006	.9549	.9817	.9934	.9979
	4	.0070	.0684	.2101	.4019	.5950	.7541	.8661	.9349	.9719	.9894
	5	.0009	.0170	.0791	.2018	.3698	.5501	.7108	.8334	.9147	.9616
	6	.0001	.0033	.0235	.0817	.1897	.3402	.5100	.6712	.8024	.8949
	7	.0000	.0005	.0056	.0267	.0796	.1753	.3119	.4728	.6340	.7228
	8	.0000	.0001	.0011	.0070	.0271	.0744	.1594	.2839	.4371	.5982
	9	.0000	.0000	.0002	.0015	.0075	.0257	.0671	.1423	.2559	.4018
	10	.0000	.0000	.0000	.0002	.0016	.0071	.0229	.0583	.1241	.2272
	11	.0000	.0000	.0000	.0000	.0003	.0016	.0062	.0191	.0486	.1051
	12	.0000	.0000	.0000	.0000	.0000	.0003	.0013	.0049	.0149	.0384
	13	.0000	.0000	.0000	.0000	.0000	.0000	.0002	.0009	.0035	.0106
	14	.0000	.0000	.0000	.0000	.0000	.0000	.0000	.0001	.0006	.0021
	15	.0000	.0000	.0000	.0000	.0000	.0000	.0000	.0000	.0001	.0003
	16	.0000	.0000	.0000	.0000	.0000	.0000	.0000	.0000	.0000	.0000
17	1	.5819	.8332	.9369	.9775	.9925	.9977	.9993	.9998	1.0000	1.0000
	2	.2078	.5182	.7475	.8818	.9499	.9807	.9933	.9979	.9994	.9999
	3	.0503	.2382	.4802	.6904	.8363	.9226	.9673	.9877	.9959	.9988
	4	.0088	.0826	.2444	.4511	.6470	.7981	.8972	.9536	.9816	.9936
	5	.0012	.0221	.0987	.2418	.4261	.6113	.7652	.8740	.9404	.9755
	6	.0001	.0047	.0319	.1057	.2347	.4032	.5803	.7361	.8529	.9283
	7	.0000	.0008	.0083	.0377	.1071	.2248	.3812	.5522	.7098	.8338
	8	.0000	.0001	.0017	.0109	.0402	.1046	.2128	.3595	.5257	.6855
	9	.0000	.0000	.0003	.0026	.0124	.0403	.0994	.1989	.3374	.5000
	10	.0000	.0000	.0000	.0005	.0031	.0127	.0383	.0919	.1834	.3145
	11	.0000	.0000	.0000	.0001	.0006	.0032	.0120	.0348	.0826	.1662
	12	.0000	.0000	.0000	.0000	.0001	.0007	.0030	.0106	.0301	.0717
	13	.0000	.0000	.0000	.0000	.0000	.0001	.0006	.0025	.0086	.0245
	14	.0000	.0000	.0000	.0000	.0000	.0000	.0001	.0005	.0019	.0064
	15	.0000	.0000	.0000	.0000	.0000	.0000	.0000	.0001	.0003	.0012
	16	.0000	.0000	.0000	.0000	.0000	.0000	.0000	.0000	.0000	.0001
	17	.0000	.0000	.0000	.0000	.0000	.0000	.0000	.0000	.0000	.0000
18	1	.6028	.8499	.9464	.9820	.9944	.9984	.9996	.9999	1.0000	1.0000
	2	.2265	.5497	.7759	.9009	.9605	.9858	.9954	.9987	.9997	.9999
	3	.0581	.2662	.5203	.7287	.8647	.9400	.9764	.9918	.9975	.9993
	4	.0109	.0982	.2798	.4990	.6943	.8354	.9217	.9672	.9880	.9962
	5	.0015	.0282	.1206	.2836	.4813	.6673	.8114	.9058	.9589	.9846
	6	.0002	.0064	.0419	.1329	.2825	.4656	.6450	.7912	.8923	.9519
	7	.0000	.0012	.0118	.0513	.1390	.2783	.4509	.6257	.7742	.8811
	8	.0000	.0002	.0027	.0163	.0569	.1407	.2717	.4366	.6085	.7597
	9	.0000	.0000	.0005	.0043	.0193	.0596	.1391	.2632	.4222	.5927
	10	.0000	.0000	.0001	.0009	.0054	.0210	.0597	.1347	.2527	.4073
	11	.0000	.0000	.0000	.0002	.0012	.0061	.0212	.0576	.1280	.2403
	12	.0000	.0000	.0000	.0000	.0002	.0014	0062	.0203	.0537	.1189
	13	.0000	.0000	.0000	.0000	.0000	.0003	.0014	.0058	.0183	.0481
	14	.0000	.0000	.0000	.0000	.0000	.0000	.0003	.0013	.0049	.0154
	15	.0000	.0000	.0000	.0000	.0000	.0000	.0000	.0002	.0010	.0038

CUMULATIVE TERMS, BINOMIAL DISTRIBUTION (Continued)

θ

n	x'	.05	.10	.15	.20	.25	.30	.35	.40	.45	.50
18	16	.0000	.0000	.0000	.0000	.0000	.0000	.0000	.0000	.0001	.0007
	17	.0000	.0000	.0000	.0000	.0000	.0000	.0000	.0000	.0000	.0001
	18	.0000	.0000	.0000	.0000	.0000	.0000	.0000	.0000	.0000	.0000
19	1	.6226	.8649	.9544	.9856	.9958	.9989	.9997	.9999	1.0000	1.0000
	2	.2453	.5797	.8015	.9171	.9690	.9896	.9969	.9992	.9998	1.0000
	3	0.665	.2946	.5587	.7631	.8887	.9538	.9830	.9945	.9985	.9996
	4	0.132	.1150	.3159	.5449	.7369	.8668	.9409	.9770	.9923	.9978
	5	.0020	.0352	.1444	.3267	.5346	.7178	.8500	.9304	.9720	.9904
	6	.0002	.0086	.0537	.1631	.3322	.5261	.7032	.8371	.9223	.9682
	7	.0000	.0017	.0163	.0676	.1749	.3345	.5188	.6919	.8273	.9165
	8	.0000	.0003	.0041	.0233	.0775	.1820	.3344	.5122	.6831	.8204
	9	.0000	.0000	.0008	.0067	.0287	.0839	.1855	.3325	.5060	.6762
	10	.0000	.0000	.0001	.0016	.0089	.0326	.0875	.1861	.3290	.5000
19	11	.0000	.0000	.0000	.0003	.0023	.0105	.0347	.0885	.1841	.3238
	12	.0000	.0000	.0000	.0000	.0005	.0028	.0114	.0352	.0871	.1796
	13	.0000	.0000	.0000	.0000	.0001	.0006	.0031	.0116	.0342	.0835
	14	.0000	.0000	.0000	.0000	.0000	.0001	.0007	.0031	.0109	.0318
	15	.0000	.0000	.0000	.0000	.0000	.0000	.0001	.0006	.0028	.0096
	16	.0000	.0000	.0000	.0000	.0000	.0000	.0000	.0001	.0005	.0022
	17	.0000	.0000	.0000	.0000	.0000	.0000	.0000	.0000	.0001	.0004
	18	.0000	.0000	.0000	.0000	.0000	.0000	.0000	.0000	.0000	.0000
	19	.0000	.0000	.0000	.0000	.0000	.0000	.0000	.0000	.0000	.0000
20	1	.6415	.8784	.9612	.9885	.9968	.9992	.9998	1.0000	1.0000	1.0000
	2	.2642	.6083	.8244	.9308	.9757	.9924	.9979	.9995	.9999	1.0000
	3	.0755	.3231	.5951	.7939	.9087	.9645	.9879	.9964	.9991	.9998
	4	.0159	.1330	.3523	.5886	.7748	.8929	.9556	.9840	.9951	.9987
	5	.0026	.0432	.1702	.3704	.5852	.7625	.8818	.9490	.9811	.9941
	6	.0003	.0113	.0673	.1958	.3828	.5836	.7546	.8744	.9447	.9793
	7	.0000	.0024	.0219	.0867	.2142	.3920	.5834	.7500	.8701	.9423
	8	.0000	.0004	.0059	.0321	.1018	.2277	.3990	.5841	.7480	.8684
	9	.0000	.0001	.0013	.0100	.0409	.1133	.2376	.4044	.5857	.7483
	10	.0000	.0000	.0002	.0026	.0139	.0480	.1218	.2447	.4086	.5881
	11	.0000	.0000	.0000	.0006	.0039	.0171	.0532	.1275	.2493	.4119
	12	.0000	.0000	.0000	.0001	.0009	.0051	.0196	.0565	.1308	.2517
	13	.0000	.0000	.0000	.0000	.0002	.0013	.0060	.0210	.0580	.1316
	14	.0000	.0000	.0000	.0000	.0000	.0003	.0015	.0065	.0214	.0577
	15	.0000	.0000	.0000	.0000	.0000	.0000	.0003	.0016	.0064	.0207
	16	.0000	.0000	.0000	.0000	.0000	.0000	.0000	.0003	.0015	.0059
	17	.0000	.0000	.0000	.0000	.0000	.0000	.0000	.0000	.0003	.0013
	18	.0000	.0000	.0000	.0000	.0000	.0000	.0000	.0000	.0000	.0002
	19	.0000	.0000	.0000	.0000	.0000	.0000	.0000	.0000	.0000	.0000
	20	.0000	.0000	.0000	.0000	.0000	.0000	.0000	.0000	.0000	.0000

CUMULATIVE TERMS, POISSON DISTRIBUTION

This table contains the values of $\sum\limits_{x=x'}^{\infty} \dfrac{e^{-\lambda}\lambda^x}{x!}$

for specified values of x' and λ. Individual terms of the Poisson distribution for specified x' and λ can be found from

$$\sum_{x=x'}^{\infty} \frac{e^{-\lambda}\lambda^x}{x!} - \sum_{x=x'+1}^{\infty} \frac{e^{-\lambda}\lambda^x}{x!}$$

λ

x'	0.1	0.2	0.3	0.4	0.5	0.6	0.7	0.8	0.9	1.0
0	1.0000	1.0000	1.0000	1.0000	1.0000	1.0000	1.0000	1.0000	1.0000	1.0000
1	.0952	.1813	.2592	.3297	.3935	.4512	.5034	.5507	.5934	.6321
2	.0047	.0175	.0369	.0616	.0902	.1219	.1558	.1912	.2275	.2642
3	.0002	.0011	.0036	.0079	.0144	.0231	.0341	.0474	.0629	.0803
4	.0000	.0001	.0003	.0008	.0018	.0034	.0058	.0091	.0135	.0190
5	.0000	.0000	.0000	.0001	.0002	.0004	.0008	.0014	.0023	.0037
6	.0000	.0000	.0000	.0000	.0000	.0000	.0001	.0002	.0003	.0006
7	.0000	.0000	.0000	.0000	.0000	.0000	.0000	.0000	.0000	.0001

λ

x'	1.1	1.2	1.3	1.4	1.5	1.6	1.7	1.8	1.9	2.0
0	1.0000	1.0000	1.0000	1.0000	1.0000	1.0000	1.0000	1.0000	1.0000	1.0000
1	.6671	.6988	.7275	.7534	.7769	.7981	.8173	.8347	.8504	.8647
2	.3010	.3374	.3732	.4082	.4422	.4751	.5068	.5372	.5663	.5940
3	.0996	.1205	.1429	.1665	.1912	.2166	.2428	.2694	.2963	.3233
4	.0257	.0338	.0431	.0537	.0656	.0788	.0932	.1087	.1253	.1429
5	.0054	.0077	.0107	.0143	.0186	.0237	.0296	.0364	.0441	.0527
6	.0010	.0015	.0022	.0032	.0045	.0060	.0080	.0104	.0132	.0166
7	.0001	.0003	.0004	.0006	.0009	.0013	.0019	.0026	.0034	.0045
8	.0000	.0000	.0001	.0001	.0002	.0003	.0004	.0006	.0008	.0011
9	.0000	.0000	.0000	.0000	.0000	.0000	.0001	.0001	.0002	.0002

λ

x'	2.1	2.2.	2.3	2.4	2.5	2.6	2.7	2.8	2.9	3.0
0	1.0000	1.0000	1.0000	1.0000	1.0000	1.0000	1.0000	1.0000	1.0000	1.0000
1	.8775	.8892	.8997	.9093	.9179	.9257	.9328	.9392	.9450	.9502
2	.6204	.6454	.6691	.6916	.7127	.7326	.7513	.7689	.7854	.8009
3	.3504	.3773	.4040	.4303	.4562	.4816	.5064	.5305	.5540	.5768
4	.1614	.1806	.2007	.2213	.2424	.2640	.2859	.3081	.3304	.3528
5	.0621	.0725	.0838	.0959	.1088	.1226	.1371	.1523	.1682	.1847
6	.0204	.0249	.0300	.0357	.0420	.0490	.0567	.0651	.0742	.0839
7	.0059	.0075	.0094	.0116	.0142	.0172	.0206	.0244	.0287	.0335
8	.0015	.0020	.0026	.0033	.0042	.0053	.0066	.0081	.0099	.0119
9	.0003	.0005	.0006	.0009	.0011	.0015	.0019	.0024	.0031	.0038
10	.0001	.0001	.0001	.0002	.0003	.0004	.0005	.0007	.0009	.0011
11	.0000	.0000	.0000	.0000	.0001	.0001	.0001	.0002	.0002	.0003
12	.0000	.0000	.0000	.0000	.0000	.0000	.0000	.0000	.0001	.0001

λ

x'	3.1	3.2	3.3	3.4	3.5	3.6	3.7	3.8	3.9	4.0
0	1.0000	1.0000	1.0000	1.0000	1.0000	1.0000	1.0000	1.0000	1.0000	1.0000
1	.9550	.9592	.9631	.9666	.9698	.9727	.9753	.9776	.9798	.9817
2	.8153	.8288	.8414	.8532	.8641	.8743	.8838	.8926	.9008	.9084
3	.5988	.6201	.6406	.6603	.6792	.6973	.7146	.7311	.7469	.7619
4	.3752	.3975	.4197	.4416	.4634	.4848	.5058	.5265	.5468	.5665

CUMULATIVE TERMS, POISSON DISTRIBUTION (Continued)

λ

x′	3.1	3.2	3.3	3.4	3.5	3.6	3.7	3.8	3.9	4.0
5	.2018	.2194	.2374	.2558	.2746	.2936	.3128	.3322	.3516	.3712
6	.0943	.1054	.1171	.1295	.1424	.1559	.1699	.1844	.1994	.2149
7	.0388	.0446	.0510	.0579	.0653	.0733	.0818	.0909	.1005	.1107
8	.0142	.0168	.0198	.0231	.0267	.0308	.0352	.0401	.0454	.0511
9	.0047	.0057	.0069	.0083	.0099	.0117	.0137	.0160	.0185	.0214
10	.0014	.0018	.0022	.0027	.0033	.0040	.0048	.0058	.0069	.0081
11	.0004	.0005	.0006	.0008	.0010	.0013	.0016	.0019	.0023	.0028
12	.0001	.0001	.0002	.0002	.0003	.0004	.0005	.0006	.0007	.0009
13	.0000	.0000	.0000	.0001	.0001	.0001	.0001	.0002	.0002	.0003
14	.0000	.0000	.0000	.0000	.0000	.0000	.0000	.0000	.0001	.0001

λ

x′	4.1	4.2	4.3	4.4	4.5	4.6	4.7	4.8	4.9	5.0
0	1.0000	1.0000	1.0000	1.0000	1.0000	1.0000	1.0000	1.0000	1.0000	1.0000
1	.9834	.9850	.9864	.9877	.9889	.9899	.9909	.9918	.9926	.9933
2	.9155	.9220	.9281	.9337	.9389	.9437	.9482	.9523	.9561	.9596
3	.7762	.7898	.8026	.8149	.8264	.8374	.8477	.8575	.8667	.8753
4	.5858	.6046	.6228	.6406	.6577	.6743	.6903	.7058	.7207	.7350
5	.3907	.4102	.4296	.4488	.4679	.4868	.5054	.5237	.5418	.5595
6	.2307	.2469	.2633	.2801	.2971	.3142	.3316	.3490	.3665	.3840
7	.1214	.1325	.1442	.1564	.1689	.1820	.1954	.2092	.2233	.2378
8	.0573	.0639	.0710	.0786	.0866	.0951	.1050	.1133	.1231	.1334
9	.0245	.0279	.0317	.0358	.0403	.0451	.0503	.0558	.0618	.0681
10	.0095	.0111	.0129	.0149	.0171	.0195	.0222	.0251	.0283	.0318
11	.0034	.0041	.0048	.0057	.0067	.0078	.0090	.0104	.0120	.0137
12	.0011	.0014	.0017	.0020	.0024	.0029	.0034	.0040	.0047	.0055
13	.0003	.0004	.0005	.0007	.0008	.0010	.0012	.0014	.0017	.0020
14	.0001	.0001	.0002	.0002	.0003	.0003	.0004	.0005	.0006	.0007
15	.0000	.0000	.0000	.0001	.0001	.0001	.0001	.0001	.0002	.0002
16	.0000	.0000	.0000	.0000	.0000	.0000	.0000	.0000	.0001	.0001

λ

x′	5.1	5.2	5.3	5.4	5.5	5.6	5.7	5.8	5.9	6.0
0	1.0000	1.0000	1.0000	1.0000	1.0000	1.0000	1.0000	1.0000	1.0000	1.0000
1	.9939	.9945	.9950	.9955	.9959	.9963	.9967	.9970	.9973	.9975
2	.9628	.9658	.9686	.9711	.9734	.9756	.9776	.9794	.9811	.9826
3	.8835	.8912	.8984	.9052	.9116	.9176	.9232	.9285	.9334	.9380
4	.7487	.7619	.7746	.7867	.7983	.8094	.8200	.8300	.8396	.8488
5	.5769	.5939	.6105	.6267	.6425	.6579	.6728	.6873	.7013	.7149
6	.4016	.4191	.4365	.4539	.4711	.4881	.5050	.5217	.5381	.5543
7	.2526	.2676	.2829	.2983	.3140	.3297	.3456	.3616	.3776	.3937
8	.1440	.1551	.1665	.1783	.1905	.2030	.2159	.2290	.2424	.2560
9	.0748	.0819	.0894	.0974	.1056	.1143	.1234	.1328	.1426	.1528

CUMULATIVE TERMS, POISSON DISTRIBUTION (Continued)

λ

x	5.1	5.2	5.3	5.4	5.5	5.6	5.7	5.8	5.9	6.0
10	.0356	.0397	.0441	.0488	.0538	.0591	.0648	.0708	.0772	.0839
11	.0156	.0177	.0200	.0225	.0253	.0282	.0314	.0349	.0386	.0426
12	.0063	.0073	.0084	.0096	.0110	.0125	.0141	.0160	.0179	.0201
13	.0024	.0028	.0033	.0038	.0045	.0051	.0059	.0068	.0078	.0088
14	.0008	.0010	.0012	.0014	.0017	.0020	.0023	.0027	.0031	.0036
15	.0003	.0003	.0004	.0005	.0006	.0007	.0009	.0010	.0012	.0014
16	.0001	.0001	.0001	.0002	.0002	.0002	.0003	.0004	.0004	.0005
17	.0000	.0000	.0000	.0001	.0001	.0001	.0001	.0001	.0001	.0002
18	.0000	.0000	.0000	.0000	.0000	.0000	.0000	.0000	.0000	.0001

λ

x'	6.1	6.2	6.3	6.4	6.5	6.6	6.7	6.8	6.9	7.0
0	1.0000	1.0000	1.0000	1.0000	1.0000	1.0000	1.0000	1.0000	1.0000	1.0000
1	.9978	.9980	.9982	.9983	.9985	.9986	.9988	.9989	.9990	.9991
2	.9841	.9854	.9866	.9877	.9887	.9897	.9905	.9913	.9920	.9927
3	.9423	.9464	.9502	.9537	.9570	.9600	.9629	.9656	.9680	.9704
4	.8575	.8658	.8736	.8811	.8882	.8948	.9012	.9072	.9129	.9182
5	.7281	.7408	.7531	.7649	.7763	.7873	.7978	.8080	.8177	.8270
6	.5702	.5859	.6012	.6163	.6310	.6453	.6594	.6730	.6863	.6993
7	.4098	.4258	.4418	.4577	.4735	.4892	.5047	.5201	.5353	.5503
8	.2699	.2840	.2983	.3127	.3272	.3419	.3567	.3715	.3864	.4013
9	.1633	.1741	.1852	.1967	.2084	.2204	.2327	.2452	.2580	.2709
10	.0910	.0984	.1061	.1142	.1226	.1314	.1404	.1498	.1505	.1695
11	.0469	.0514	.0563	.0614	.0668	.0726	.0786	.0849	.0916	.0985
12	.0224	.0250	.0277	.0307	.0339	.0373	.0409	.0448	.0490	.0534
13	.0100	.0113	.0127	.0143	.0160	.0179	.0199	.0221	.0245	.0270
14	.0042	.0048	.0055	.0063	.0071	.0080	.0091	.0102	.0115	.0128
15	.0016	.0019	.0022	.0026	.0030	.0034	.0039	.0044	.0050	.0057
16	.0006	.0007	.0008	.0010	.0012	.0014	.0016	.0018	.0021	.0024
17	.0002	.0003	.0003	.0004	.0004	.0005	.0006	.0007	.0008	.0010
18	.0001	.0001	.0001	.0001	.0002	.0002	.0002	.0003	.0003	.0004
19	.0000	.0000	.0000	.0000	.0001	.0001	.0001	.0001	.0001	.0001

λ

x'	7.1	7.2	7.3	7.4	7.5	7.6	7.7	7.8	7.9	8.0
0	1.0000	1.0000	1.0000	1.0000	1.0000	1.0000	1.0000	1.0000	1.0000	1.0000
1	.9992	.9993	.9993	.9994	.9994	.9995	.9995	.9996	.9996	.9997
2	.9933	.9939	.9944	.9949	.9953	.9957	.9961	.9964	.9967	.9970
3	.9725	.9745	.9764	.9781	.9797	.9812	.9826	.9839	.9851	.9862
4	.9233	.9281	.9326	.9368	.9409	.9446	.9482	.9515	.9547	.9576
5	.8359	.8445	.8527	.8605	.8679	.8751	.8819	.8883	.8945	.9004
6	.7119	.7241	.7360	.7474	.7586	.7693	.7797	.7897	.7994	.8088
7	.5651	.5796	.5940	.6080	.6218	.6354	.6486	.6616	.6743	.6866
8	.4162	.4311	.4459	.4607	.4754	.4900	.5044	.5188	.5330	.5470
9	.2840	.2973	.3108	.3243	.3380	.3518	.3657	.3796	.3935	.4075
10	.1798	.1904	.2012	.2123	.2236	.2351	.2469	.2589	.2710	.2834
11	.1058	.1133	.1212	.1293	.1378	.1465	.1555	.1648	.1743	.1841
12	.0580	.0629	.0681	.0735	.0792	.0852	.0915	.0980	.1048	.1119
13	.0297	.0327	.0358	.0391	.0427	.0464	.0504	.0546	.0591	.0638
14	.0143	.0159	.0176	.0195	.0216	.0238	.0261	.0286	.0313	.0342

CUMULATIVE TERMS, POISSON DISTRIBUTION (Continued)

λ

x'	7.1	7.2	7.3	7.4	7.5	7.6	7.7	7.8	7.9	8.0
15	.0065	.0073	.0082	.0092	.0103	.0114	.0127	.0141	.0156	.0173
16	.0028	.0031	.0036	.0041	.0046	.0052	.0059	.0066	.0074	.0082
17	.0011	.0013	.0015	.0017	.0020	.0022	.0026	.0029	.0033	.0037
18	.0004	.0005	.0006	.0007	.0008	.0009	.0011	.0012	.0014	.0016
19	.0002	.0002	.0002	.0003	.0003	.0004	.0004	.0005	.0006	.0006
20	.0001	.0001	.0001	.0001	.0001	.0001	.0002	.0002	.0002	.0003
21	.0000	.0000	.0000	.0000	.0000	.0000	.0001	.0001	.0001	.0001

λ

x'	8.1	8.2	8.3	8.4	8.5	8.6	8.7	8.8	8.9	9.0
0	1.0000	1.0000	1.0000	1.0000	1.0000	1.0000	1.0000	1.0000	1.0000	1.0000
1	.9997	.9997	.9998	.9998	.9998	.9998	.9998	.9998	.9999	.9999
2	.9972	.9975	.9977	.9979	.9981	.9982	.9984	.9985	.9987	.9988
3	.9873	.9882	.9891	.9900	.9907	.9914	.9921	.9927	.9932	.9938
4	.9604	.9630	.9654	.9677	.9699	.9719	.9738	.9756	.9772	.9788
5	.9060	.9113	.9163	.9211	.9256	.9299	.9340	.9340	.9416	.9450
6	.8178	.8264	.8347	.8427	.8504	.8578	.8648	.8716	.8781	.8843
7	.6987	.7104	.7219	.7330	.7438	.7543	.7645	.7744	.7840	.7932
8	.5609	.5746	.5881	.6013	.6144	.6272	.6398	.6522	.6643	.6761
9	.4214	.4353	.4493	.4631	.4769	.4906	.5042	.5177	.5311	.5443
10	.2959	.3085	.3212	.3341	.3470	.3600	.3731	.3863	.3994	.4126
11	.1942	.2045	.2150	.2257	.2366	.2478	.2591	.2706	.2822	.2940
12	.1193	.1269	.1348	.1429	.1513	.1600	.1689	.1780	.1874	.1970
13	.0687	.0739	.0793	.0850	.0909	.0971	.1035	.1102	.1171	.1242
14	.0372	.0405	.0439	.0476	.0514	.0555	.0597	.0642	.0689	.0739
15	.0190	.0209	.0229	.0251	.0274	.0299	.0325	.0353	.0383	.0415
16	.0092	.0102	.0113	.0125	.0138	.0152	.0168	.0184	.0202	.0220
17	.0042	.0047	.0053	.0059	.0066	.0074	.0082	.0091	.0101	.0111
18	.0018	.0021	.0023	.0027	.0030	.0034	.0038	.0043	.0048	.0053
19	.0008	.0009	.0010	.0011	.0013	.0015	.0017	.0019	.0022	.0024
20	.0003	.0003	.0004	.0005	.0005	.0006	.0007	.0008	.0009	.0011
21	.0001	.0001	.0002	.0002	.0002	.0002	.0003	.0003	.0004	.0004
22	.0000	.0000	.0001	.0001	.0001	.0001	.0001	.0001	.0002	.0002
23	.0000	.0000	.0000	.0000	.0000	.0000	.0000	.0000	.0001	.0001

λ

x'	9.1	9.2	9.3	9.4	9.5	9.6	9.7	9.8	9.9	10
0	1.0000	1.0000	1.0000	1.0000	1.0000	1.0000	1.0000	1.0000	1.0000	1.0000
1	.9999	.9999	.9999	.9999	.9999	.9999	.9999	.9999	1.0000	1.0000
2	.9989	.9990	.9991	.9991	.9992	.9993	.9993	.9994	.9995	.9995
3	.9942	.9947	.9951	.9955	.9958	.9962	.9965	.9967	.9970	.9972
4	.9802	.9816	.9828	.9840	.9851	.9862	.9871	.9880	.9889	.9897
5	.9483	.9514	.9544	.9571	.9597	.9622	.9645	.9667	.9688	.9707
6	.8902	.8959	.9014	.9065	.9115	.9162	.9207	.9250	.9290	.9329
7	.8022	.8108	.8192	.8273	.8351	.8426	.8498	.8567	.8634	.8699
8	.6877	.6990	.7101	.7208	.7313	.7416	.7515	.7612	.7706	.7798
9	.5574	.5704	.5832	.5958	.6082	.6204	.6324	.6442	.6558	.6672

CUMULATIVE TERMS, POISSON DISTRIBUTION (Continued)

λ

x′	9.1	9.2	9.3	9.4	9.5	9.6	9.7	9.8	9.9	10
10	.4258	.4389	.4521	.4651	.4782	.4911	.5040	.5168	.5295	.5421
11	.3059	.3180	.3301	.3424	.3547	.3671	.3795	.3920	.4045	.4170
12	.2068	.2168	.2270	.2374	.2480	.2588	.2697	.2807	.2919	.3032
13	.1316	.1393	.1471	.1552	.1636	.1721	.1809	.1899	.1991	.2084
14	.0790	.0844	.0900	.0958	.1019	.1081	.1147	.1214	.1284	.1355
15	.0448	.0483	.0520	.0559	.0600	.0643	.0688	.0735	.0784	.0835
16	.0240	.0262	.0285	.0309	.0335	.0362	.0391	.0421	.0454	.0487
17	.0122	.0135	.0148	.0162	.0177	.0194	.0211	.0230	.0249	.0270
18	.0059	.0066	.0073	.0081	.0089	.0098	.0108	.0119	.0130	.0143
19	.0027	.0031	.0034	.0038	.0043	.0048	.0053	.0059	.0065	.0072
20	.0012	.0014	.0015	.0017	.0020	.0022	.0025	.0028	.0031	.0035
21	.0005	.0006	.0007	.0008	.0009	.0010	.0011	.0013	.0014	.0016
22	.0002	.0002	.0003	.0003	.0004	.0004	.0005	.0005	.0006	.0007
23	.0001	.0001	.0001	.0001	.0001	.0002	.0002	.0002	.0003	.0003
24	.0000	.0000	.0000	.0000	.0001	.0001	.0001	.0001	.0001	.0001

λ

x′	11	12	13	14	15	16	17	18	19	20
0	1.0000	1.0000	1.0000	1.0000	1.0000	1.0000	1.0000	1.0000	1.0000	1.0000
1	1.0000	1.0000	1.0000	1.0000	1.0000	1.0000	1.0000	1.0000	1.0000	1.0000
2	.9998	.9999	1.0000	1.0000	1.0000	1.0000	1.0000	1.0000	1.0000	1.0000
3	.9988	.9995	.9998	.9999	1.0000	1.0000	1.0000	1.0000	1.0000	1.0000
4	.9951	.9977	.9990	.9995	.9998	.9999	1.0000	1.0000	1.0000	1.0000
5	.9849	.9924	.9963	.9982	.9991	.9996	.9998	.9999	1.0000	1.0000
6	.9625	.9797	.9893	.9945	.9972	.9986	.9993	.9997	.9998	.9999
7	.9214	.9542	.9741	.9858	.9924	.9960	.9979	.9990	.9995	.9997
8	.8568	.9105	.9460	.9684	.9820	.9900	.9946	.9971	.9985	.9992
9	.7680	.8450	.9002	.9379	.9626	.9780	.9874	.9929	.9961	.9979
10	.6595	.7576	.8342	.8906	.9301	.9567	.9739	.9846	.9911	.9950
11	.5401	.6528	.7483	.8243	.8815	.9226	.9509	.9696	.9817	.9892
12	.4207	.5384	.6468	.7400	.8152	.8730	.9153	.9451	.9653	.9786
13	.3113	.4240	.5369	.6415	.7324	.8069	.8650	.9083	.9394	.9610
14	.2187	.3185	.4270	.5356	.6368	.7255	.7991	.8574	.9016	.9339
15	.1460	.2280	.3249	.4296	.5343	.6325	.7192	.7919	.8503	.8951
16	.0926	.1556	.2364	.3306	.4319	.5333	.6285	.7133	.7852	.8435
17	.0559	.1013	.1645	.2441	.3359	.4340	.5323	.6250	.7080	.7789
18	.0322	.0630	.1095	.1728	.2511	.3407	.4360	.5314	.6216	.7030
19	.0177	.0374	.0698	.1174	.1805	.2577	.3450	.4378	.5305	.6186
20	.0093	.0213	.0427	.0765	.1248	.1878	.2637	.3491	.4394	.5297
21	.0047	.0116	.0250	.0479	.0830	.1318	.1945	.2693	.3528	.4409
22	.0023	.0061	.0141	.0288	.0531	.0892	.1385	.2009	.2745	.3563
23	.0010	.0030	.0076	.0167	.0327	.0582	.0953	.1449	.2069	.2794
24	.0005	.0015	.0040	.0093	.0195	.0367	.0633	.1011	.1510	.2125
25	.0002	.0007	.0020	.0050	.0112	.0223	.0406	.0683	.1067	.1568
26	.0001	.0003	.0010	.0026	.0062	.0131	.0252	.0446	.0731	.1122
27	.0000	.0001	.0005	.0013	.0033	.0075	.0152	.0282	.0486	.0779
28	.0000	.0001	.0002	.0006	.0017	.0041	.0088	.0173	.0313	.0525
29	.0000	.0000	.0001	.0003	.0009	.0022	.0050	.0103	.0195	.0343
30	.0000	.0000	.0000	.0001	.0004	.0011	.0027	.0059	.0118	.0218
31	.0000	.0000	.0000	.0001	.0002	.0006	.0014	.0033	.0070	.0135
32	.0000	.0000	.0000	.0000	.0001	.0003	.0007	.0018	.0040	.0081
33	.0000	.0000	.0000	.0000	.0000	.0001	.0004	.0010	.0022	.0047
34	.0000	.0000	.0000	.0000	.0000	.0001	.0002	.0005	.0012	.0027
35	.0000	.0000	.0000	.0000	.0000	.0000	.0001	.0002	.0006	.0015
36	.0000	.0000	.0000	.0000	.0000	.0000	.0000	.0001	.0003	.0008
37	.0000	.0000	.0000	.0000	.0000	.0000	.0000	.0001	.0002	.0004
38	.0000	.0000	.0000	.0000	.0000	.0000	.0000	.0000	.0001	.0002
39	.0000	.0000	.0000	.0000	.0000	.0000	.0000	.0000	.0000	.0001
40	.0000	.0000	.0000	.0000	.0000	.0000	.0000	.0000	.0000	.0001

PERCENTAGE POINTS, STUDENT'S *t*-DISTRIBUTION

This table gives values of t such that

$$F(t) = \int_{-\infty}^{t} \frac{\Gamma\left(\frac{n+1}{2}\right)}{\sqrt{n\pi}\ \Gamma\left(\frac{n}{2}\right)} \left(1 + \frac{x^2}{n}\right)^{-\frac{n+1}{2}} dx$$

for n, the number of degrees of freedom, equal to 1, 2, . . ., 30, 40, 60, 120, ∞; and for $F(t) = 0.60, 0.75, 0.90, 0.95, 0.975, 0.99, 0.995,$ and 0.9995. The *t*-distribution is symmetrical, so that $F(-t) = 1 - F(t)$

F \ n	.60	.75	.90	.95	.975	.99	.995	.9995
1	.325	1.000	3.078	6.314	12.706	31.821	63.657	636.619
2	.289	.816	1.886	2.920	4.303	6.965	9.925	31.598
3	.277	.765	1.638	2.353	3.182	4.541	5.841	12.924
4	.271	.741	1.533	2.132	2.776	3.747	4.604	8.610
5	.267	.727	1.476	2.015	2.571	3.365	4.032	6.869
6	.265	.718	1.440	1.943	2.447	3.143	3.707	5.959
7	.263	.711	1.415	1.895	2.365	2.998	3.499	5.408
8	.262	.706	1.397	1.860	2.306	2.896	3.355	5.041
9	.261	.703	1.383	1.833	2.262	2.821	3.250	4.781
10	.260	.700	1.372	1.812	2.228	2.764	3.169	4.587
11	.260	.697	1.363	1.796	2.201	2.718	3.106	4.437
12	.259	.695	1.356	1.782	2.179	2.681	3.055	4.318
13	.259	.694	1.350	1.771	2.160	2.650	3.012	4.221
14	.258	.692	1.345	1.761	2.145	2.624	2.977	4.140
15	.258	.691	1.341	1.753	2.131	2.602	2.947	4.073
16	.258	.690	1.337	1.746	2.120	2.583	2.921	4.015
17	.257	.689	1.333	1.740	2.110	2.567	2.898	3.965
18	.257	.688	1.330	1.734	2.101	2.552	2.878	3.922
19	.257	.688	1.328	1.729	2.093	2.539	2.861	3.883
20	.257	.687	1.325	1.725	2.086	2.528	2.845	3.850
21	.257	.686	1.323	1.721	2.080	2.518	2.831	3.819
22	.256	.686	1.321	1.717	2.074	2.508	2.819	3.792
23	.256	.685	1.319	1.714	2.069	2.500	2.807	3.767
24	.256	.685	1.318	1.711	2.064	2.492	2.797	3.745
25	.256	.684	1.316	1.708	2.060	2.485	2.787	3.725
26	.256	.684	1.315	1.706	2.056	2.479	2.779	3.707
27	.256	.684	1.314	1.703	2.052	2.473	2.771	3.690
28	.256	.683	1.313	1.701	2.048	2.467	2.763	3.674
29	.256	.683	1.311	1.699	2.045	2.462	2.756	3.659
30	.256	.683	1.310	1.697	2.042	2.457	2.750	3.646
40	.255	.681	1.303	1.684	2.021	2.423	2.704	3.551
60	.254	.679	1.296	1.671	2.000	2.390	2.660	3.460
120	.254	.677	1.289	1.658	1.980	2.358	2.617	3.373
∞	.253	.674	1.282	1.645	1.960	2.326	2.576	3.291

*   This table is abridged from the "Statistical Tables" of R. A. Fisher and Frank Yates published by Oliver & Boyd. Ltd., Edinburgh and London, 1938. It is here published with the kind permission of the authors and their publishers.

CHI SQUARE DISTRIBUTION

PERCENTAGE POINTS, CHI-SQUARE DISTRIBUTION

$$F(x^2) = \int_0^{x^2} \frac{1}{2^{\frac{n}{2}} \Gamma\left(\frac{n}{2}\right)} z^{\frac{n-2}{2}} e^{-\frac{z}{2}} dz$$

n	.995	.990	.975	.950	.900	.750	.500	.250	.100	.050	.025	.010	.005
1	7.88	6.63	5.02	3.84	2.71	1.32	.455	.102	.0158	.00393	.000982	.000157	.0000393
2	10.6	9.21	7.38	5.99	4.61	2.77	1.39	.575	.211	.103	.0506	.0201	.0100
3	12.8	11.3	9.35	7.81	6.25	4.11	2.37	1.21	.584	.352	.216	.115	.0717
4	14.9	13.3	11.1	9.49	7.78	5.39	3.36	1.92	1.06	.711	.484	.297	.207
5	16.7	15.1	12.8	11.1	9.24	6.63	4.35	2.67	1.61	1.15	.831	.554	.412
6	18.5	16.8	14.4	12.6	10.6	7.84	5.35	3.45	2.20	1.64	1.24	.872	.676
7	20.3	18.5	16.0	14.1	12.0	9.04	6.35	4.25	2.83	2.17	1.69	1.24	.989
8	22.0	20.1	17.5	15.5	13.4	10.2	7.34	5.07	3.49	2.73	2.18	1.65	1.34
9	23.6	21.7	19.0	16.9	14.7	11.4	8.34	5.90	4.17	3.33	2.70	2.09	1.73
10	25.2	23.2	20.5	18.3	16.0	12.5	9.34	6.74	4.87	3.94	3.25	2.56	2.16
11	26.8	24.7	21.9	19.7	17.3	13.7	10.3	7.58	5.58	4.57	3.82	3.05	2.60
12	28.3	26.2	23.3	21.0	18.5	14.8	11.3	8.44	6.30	5.23	4.40	3.57	3.07
13	29.8	27.7	24.7	22.4	19.8	16.0	12.3	9.30	7.04	5.89	5.01	4.11	3.57
14	31.3	29.1	26.1	23.7	21.1	17.1	13.3	10.2	7.79	6.57	5.63	4.66	4.07
15	32.8	30.6	27.5	25.0	22.3	18.2	14.3	11.0	8.55	7.26	6.26	5.23	4.60
16	34.3	32.0	28.8	26.3	23.5	19.4	15.3	11.9	9.31	7.96	6.91	5.81	5.14
17	35.7	33.4	30.2	27.6	24.8	20.5	16.3	12.8	10.1	8.67	7.56	6.41	5.70
18	37.2	34.8	31.5	28.9	26.0	21.6	17.3	13.7	10.9	9.39	8.23	7.01	6.26
19	38.6	36.2	32.9	30.1	27.2	22.7	18.3	14.6	11.7	10.1	8.91	7.63	6.84
20	40.0	37.6	34.2	31.4	28.4	23.8	19.3	15.5	12.4	10.9	9.59	8.26	7.43
21	41.4	38.9	35.5	32.7	29.6	24.9	20.3	16.3	13.2	11.6	10.3	8.90	8.03
22	42.8	40.3	36.8	33.9	30.8	26.0	21.3	17.2	14.0	12.3	11.0	9.54	8.64
23	44.2	41.6	38.1	35.2	32.0	27.1	22.3	18.1	14.8	13.1	11.7	10.2	9.26
24	45.6	43.0	39.4	36.4	33.2	28.2	23.3	19.0	15.7	13.8	12.4	10.9	9.89
25	46.9	44.3	40.6	37.7	34.4	29.3	24.3	19.9	16.5	14.6	13.1	11.5	10.5
26	48.3	45.6	41.9	38.9	35.6	30.4	25.3	20.8	17.3	15.4	13.8	12.2	11.2
27	49.6	47.0	43.2	40.1	36.7	31.5	26.3	21.7	18.1	16.2	14.6	12.9	11.8
28	51.0	48.3	44.5	41.3	37.9	32.6	27.3	22.7	18.9	16.9	15.3	13.6	12.5
29	52.3	49.6	45.7	42.6	39.1	33.7	28.3	23.6	19.8	17.7	16.0	14.3	13.1
30	53.7	50.9	47.0	43.8	40.3	34.8	29.3	24.5	20.6	18.5	16.8	15.0	13.8

F-DISTRIBUTION

PERCENTAGE POINTS, F-DISTRIBUTION

$$F(F) = \int_0^F \frac{\Gamma\left(\frac{m+n}{2}\right)}{\Gamma\left(\frac{m}{2}\right)\Gamma\left(\frac{n}{2}\right)} m^{\frac{m}{2}} n^{\frac{n}{2}} x^{\frac{m}{2}-1}(n+mx)^{-\frac{m+n}{2}}\, dx = .90$$

n \ m	1	2	3	4	5	6	7	8	9	10	12	15	20	24	30	40	60	120	∞
1	39.86	49.50	53.59	55.83	57.24	58.20	58.91	59.44	59.86	60.19	60.71	61.22	61.74	62.00	62.26	62.53	62.79	63.06	63.33
2	8.53	9.00	9.16	9.24	9.29	9.33	9.35	9.37	9.38	9.39	9.41	9.42	9.44	9.45	9.46	9.47	9.47	9.48	9.49
3	5.54	5.46	5.39	5.34	5.31	5.28	5.27	5.25	5.24	5.23	5.22	5.20	5.18	5.18	5.17	5.16	5.15	5.14	5.13
4	4.54	4.32	4.19	4.11	4.05	4.01	3.98	3.95	3.94	3.92	3.90	3.87	3.84	3.83	3.82	3.80	3.79	3.78	3.76
5	4.06	3.78	3.62	3.52	3.45	3.40	3.37	3.34	3.32	3.30	3.27	3.24	3.21	3.19	3.17	3.16	3.14	3.12	3.10
6	3.78	3.46	3.29	3.18	3.11	3.05	3.01	2.98	2.96	2.94	2.90	2.87	2.84	2.82	2.80	2.78	2.76	2.74	2.72
7	3.59	3.26	3.07	2.96	2.88	2.83	2.78	2.75	2.72	2.70	2.67	2.63	2.59	2.58	2.56	2.54	2.51	2.49	2.47
8	3.46	3.11	2.92	2.81	2.73	2.67	2.62	2.59	2.56	2.54	2.50	2.46	2.42	2.40	2.38	2.36	2.34	2.32	2.29
9	3.36	3.01	2.81	2.69	2.61	2.55	2.51	2.47	2.44	2.42	2.38	2.34	2.30	2.28	2.25	2.23	2.21	2.18	2.16
10	3.29	2.92	2.73	2.61	2.52	2.46	2.41	2.38	2.35	2.32	2.28	2.24	2.20	2.18	2.16	2.13	2.11	2.08	2.06
11	3.23	2.86	2.66	2.54	2.45	2.39	2.34	2.30	2.27	2.25	2.21	2.17	2.12	2.10	2.08	2.05	2.03	2.00	1.97
12	3.18	2.81	2.61	2.48	2.39	2.33	2.28	2.24	2.21	2.19	2.15	2.10	2.06	2.04	2.01	1.99	1.96	1.93	1.90
13	3.14	2.76	2.56	2.43	2.35	2.28	2.23	2.20	2.16	2.14	2.10	2.05	2.01	1.98	1.96	1.93	1.90	1.88	1.85
14	3.10	2.73	2.52	2.39	2.31	2.24	2.19	2.15	2.12	2.10	2.05	2.01	1.96	1.94	1.91	1.89	1.86	1.83	1.80
15	3.07	2.70	2.49	2.36	2.27	2.21	2.16	2.12	2.09	2.06	2.02	1.97	1.92	1.90	1.87	1.85	1.82	1.79	1.76
16	3.05	2.67	2.46	2.33	2.24	2.18	2.13	2.09	2.06	2.03	1.99	1.94	1.89	1.87	1.84	1.81	1.78	1.75	1.72
17	3.03	2.64	2.44	2.31	2.22	2.15	2.10	2.06	2.03	2.00	1.96	1.91	1.86	1.84	1.81	1.78	1.75	1.72	1.69
18	3.01	2.62	2.42	2.29	2.20	2.13	2.08	2.04	2.00	1.98	1.93	1.89	1.84	1.81	1.78	1.75	1.72	1.69	1.66
19	2.99	2.61	2.40	2.27	2.18	2.11	2.06	2.02	1.98	1.96	1.91	1.86	1.81	1.79	1.76	1.73	1.70	1.67	1.63
20	2.97	2.59	2.38	2.25	2.16	2.09	2.04	2.00	1.96	1.94	1.89	1.84	1.79	1.77	1.74	1.71	1.68	1.64	1.61
21	2.96	2.57	2.36	2.23	2.14	2.08	2.02	1.98	1.95	1.92	1.87	1.83	1.78	1.75	1.72	1.69	1.66	1.62	1.59
22	2.95	2.56	2.35	2.22	2.13	2.06	2.01	1.97	1.93	1.90	1.86	1.81	1.76	1.73	1.70	1.67	1.64	1.60	1.57
23	2.94	2.55	2.34	2.21	2.11	2.05	1.99	1.95	1.92	1.89	1.84	1.80	1.74	1.72	1.69	1.66	1.62	1.59	1.55
24	2.93	2.54	2.33	2.19	2.10	2.04	1.98	1.94	1.91	1.88	1.83	1.78	1.73	1.70	1.67	1.64	1.61	1.57	1.53
25	2.92	2.53	2.32	2.18	2.09	2.02	1.97	1.93	1.89	1.87	1.82	1.77	1.72	1.69	1.66	1.63	1.59	1.56	1.52
26	2.91	2.52	2.31	2.17	2.08	2.01	1.96	1.92	1.88	1.86	1.81	1.76	1.71	1.68	1.65	1.61	1.58	1.54	1.50
27	2.90	2.51	2.30	2.17	2.07	2.00	1.95	1.91	1.87	1.85	1.80	1.75	1.70	1.67	1.64	1.60	1.57	1.53	1.49
28	2.89	2.50	2.29	2.16	2.06	2.00	1.94	1.90	1.87	1.84	1.79	1.74	1.69	1.66	1.63	1.59	1.56	1.52	1.48
29	2.89	2.50	2.28	2.15	2.06	1.99	1.93	1.89	1.86	1.83	1.78	1.73	1.68	1.65	1.62	1.58	1.55	1.51	1.47
30	2.88	2.49	2.28	2.14	2.05	1.98	1.93	1.88	1.85	1.82	1.77	1.72	1.67	1.64	1.61	1.57	1.54	1.50	1.46
40	2.84	2.44	2.23	2.09	2.00	1.93	1.87	1.83	1.79	1.76	1.71	1.66	1.61	1.57	1.54	1.51	1.47	1.42	1.38
60	2.79	2.39	2.18	2.04	1.95	1.87	1.82	1.77	1.74	1.71	1.66	1.60	1.54	1.51	1.48	1.44	1.40	1.35	1.29
120	2.75	2.35	2.13	1.99	1.90	1.82	1.77	1.72	1.68	1.65	1.60	1.55	1.48	1.45	1.41	1.37	1.32	1.26	1.19
∞	2.71	2.30	2.08	1.94	1.85	1.77	1.72	1.67	1.63	1.60	1.55	1.49	1.42	1.38	1.34	1.30	1.24	1.17	1.00

$F = \dfrac{S_1^2}{S_2^2} = \dfrac{S1/m}{S2/n}$, where $S_1^2 = S1/m$ and $S_2^2 = S2/n$ are independent mean squares estimating a common variance σ^2 and based on m and n degrees of freedom, respectively. This table also provides values corresponding to $F(F) = .10, .05, .025, .01, .005, .001$ since $F_{1-\alpha}$ for m and n degrees of freedom is the reciprocal of F_α for n and m degrees of freedom. Thus $F_{.05}(4,7) = \dfrac{1}{F_{.95}(7,4)} = \dfrac{1}{6.09} = .164$

F-Distribution

PERCENTAGE POINTS, F-DISTRIBUTION (Continued)

$$F(F) = \int_0^F \frac{\Gamma\left(\frac{m+n}{2}\right)}{\Gamma\left(\frac{m}{2}\right)\Gamma\left(\frac{n}{2}\right)} m^{\frac{m}{2}} n^{\frac{n}{2}} x^{\frac{m}{2}-1} (n+mx)^{-\frac{m+n}{2}}\, dx = .95$$

n \ m	1	2	3	4	5	6	7	8	9	10	12	15	20	24	30	40	60	120	∞
1	161.4	199.5	215.7	224.6	230.2	234.0	236.8	238.9	240.5	241.9	243.9	245.9	248.0	249.1	250.1	251.1	252.2	253.3	254.3
2	18.51	19.00	19.16	19.25	19.30	19.33	19.35	19.37	19.38	19.40	19.41	19.43	19.45	19.45	19.46	19.47	19.48	19.49	19.50
3	10.13	9.55	9.28	9.12	9.01	8.94	8.89	8.85	8.81	8.79	8.74	8.70	8.66	8.64	8.62	8.59	8.57	8.55	8.53
4	7.71	6.94	6.59	6.39	6.26	6.16	6.09	6.04	6.00	5.96	5.91	5.86	5.80	5.77	5.75	5.72	5.69	5.66	5.63
5	6.61	5.79	5.41	5.19	5.05	4.95	4.88	4.82	4.77	4.74	4.68	4.62	4.56	4.53	4.50	4.46	4.43	4.40	4.36
6	5.99	5.14	4.76	4.53	4.39	4.28	4.21	4.15	4.10	4.06	4.00	3.94	3.87	3.84	3.81	3.77	3.74	3.70	3.67
7	5.59	4.74	4.35	4.12	3.97	3.87	3.79	3.73	3.68	3.64	3.57	3.51	3.44	3.41	3.38	3.34	3.30	3.27	3.23
8	5.32	4.46	4.07	3.84	3.69	3.58	3.50	3.44	3.39	3.35	3.28	3.22	3.15	3.12	3.08	3.04	3.01	2.97	2.93
9	5.12	4.26	3.86	3.63	3.48	3.37	3.29	3.23	3.18	3.14	3.07	3.01	2.94	2.90	2.86	2.83	2.79	2.75	2.71
10	4.96	4.10	3.71	3.48	3.33	3.22	3.14	3.07	3.02	2.98	2.91	2.85	2.77	2.74	2.70	2.66	2.62	2.58	2.54
11	4.84	3.98	3.59	3.36	3.20	3.09	3.01	2.95	2.90	2.85	2.79	2.72	2.65	2.61	2.57	2.53	2.49	2.45	2.40
12	4.75	3.89	3.49	3.26	3.11	3.00	2.91	2.85	2.80	2.75	2.69	2.62	2.54	2.51	2.47	2.43	2.38	2.34	2.30
13	4.67	3.81	3.41	3.18	3.03	2.92	2.83	2.77	2.71	2.67	2.60	2.53	2.46	2.42	2.38	2.34	2.30	2.25	2.21
14	4.60	3.74	3.34	3.11	2.96	2.85	2.76	2.70	2.65	2.60	2.53	2.46	2.39	2.35	2.31	2.27	2.22	2.18	2.13
15	4.54	3.68	3.29	3.06	2.90	2.79	2.71	2.64	2.59	2.54	2.48	2.40	2.33	2.29	2.25	2.20	2.16	2.11	2.07
16	4.49	3.63	3.24	3.01	2.85	2.74	2.66	2.59	2.54	2.49	2.42	2.35	2.28	2.24	2.19	2.15	2.11	2.06	2.01
17	4.45	3.59	3.20	2.96	2.81	2.70	2.61	2.55	2.49	2.45	2.38	2.31	2.23	2.19	2.15	2.10	2.06	2.01	1.96
18	4.41	3.55	3.16	2.93	2.77	2.66	2.58	2.51	2.46	2.41	2.34	2.27	2.19	2.15	2.11	2.06	2.02	1.97	1.92
19	4.38	3.52	3.13	2.90	2.74	2.63	2.54	2.48	2.42	2.38	2.31	2.23	2.16	2.11	2.07	2.03	1.98	1.93	1.88
20	4.35	3.49	3.10	2.87	2.71	2.60	2.51	2.45	2.39	2.35	2.28	2.20	2.12	2.08	2.04	1.99	1.95	1.90	1.84
21	4.32	3.47	3.07	2.84	2.68	2.57	2.49	2.42	2.37	2.32	2.25	2.18	2.10	2.05	2.01	1.96	1.92	1.87	1.81
22	4.30	3.44	3.05	2.82	2.66	2.55	2.46	2.40	2.34	2.30	2.23	2.15	2.07	2.03	1.98	1.94	1.89	1.84	1.78
23	4.28	3.42	3.03	2.80	2.64	2.53	2.44	2.37	2.32	2.27	2.20	2.13	2.05	2.01	1.96	1.91	1.86	1.81	1.76
24	4.26	3.40	3.01	2.78	2.62	2.51	2.42	2.36	2.30	2.25	2.18	2.11	2.03	1.98	1.94	1.89	1.84	1.79	1.73
25	4.24	3.39	2.99	2.76	2.60	2.49	2.40	2.34	2.28	2.24	2.16	2.09	2.01	1.96	1.92	1.87	1.82	1.77	1.71
26	4.23	3.37	2.98	2.74	2.59	2.47	2.39	2.32	2.27	2.22	2.15	2.07	1.99	1.95	1.90	1.85	1.80	1.75	1.69
27	4.21	3.35	2.96	2.73	2.57	2.46	2.37	2.31	2.25	2.20	2.13	2.06	1.97	1.93	1.88	1.84	1.79	1.73	1.67
28	4.20	3.34	2.95	2.71	2.56	2.45	2.36	2.29	2.24	2.19	2.12	2.04	1.96	1.91	1.87	1.82	1.77	1.71	1.65
29	4.18	3.33	2.93	2.70	2.55	2.43	2.35	2.28	2.22	2.18	2.10	2.03	1.94	1.90	1.85	1.81	1.75	1.70	1.64
30	4.17	3.32	2.92	2.69	2.53	2.42	2.33	2.27	2.21	2.16	2.09	2.01	1.93	1.89	1.84	1.79	1.74	1.68	1.62
40	4.08	3.23	2.84	2.61	2.45	2.34	2.25	2.18	2.12	2.08	2.00	1.92	1.84	1.79	1.74	1.69	1.64	1.58	1.51
60	4.00	3.15	2.76	2.53	2.37	2.25	2.17	2.10	2.04	1.99	1.92	1.84	1.75	1.70	1.65	1.59	1.53	1.47	1.39
120	3.92	3.07	2.68	2.45	2.29	2.17	2.09	2.02	1.96	1.91	1.83	1.75	1.66	1.61	1.55	1.50	1.43	1.35	1.25
∞	3.84	3.00	2.60	2.37	2.21	2.10	2.01	1.94	1.88	1.83	1.75	1.67	1.57	1.52	1.46	1.39	1.32	1.22	1.00

F-Distribution

PERCENTAGE POINTS, F-DISTRIBUTION (Continued)

$$F(F) = \int_0^F \frac{\Gamma\left(\frac{m+n}{2}\right)}{\Gamma\left(\frac{m}{2}\right)\Gamma\left(\frac{n}{2}\right)} m^{\frac{m}{2}} n^{\frac{n}{2}} x^{\frac{m}{2}-1} (n+mx)^{-\frac{m+n}{2}}\, dx = .975$$

m \ n	1	2	3	4	5	6	7	8	9	10	12	15	20	24	30	40	60	120	∞
1	647.8	799.5	864.2	899.6	921.8	937.1	948.2	956.7	963.3	968.6	976.7	984.9	993.1	997.2	1001	1006	1010	1014	1018
2	38.51	39.00	39.17	39.25	39.30	39.33	39.36	39.37	39.39	39.40	39.41	39.43	39.45	39.46	39.46	39.47	39.48	39.49	39.50
3	17.44	16.04	15.44	15.10	14.88	14.73	14.62	14.54	14.47	14.42	14.34	14.25	14.17	14.12	14.08	14.04	13.99	13.95	13.90
4	12.22	10.65	9.98	9.60	9.36	9.20	9.07	8.98	8.90	8.84	8.75	8.66	8.56	8.51	8.46	8.41	8.36	8.31	8.26
5	10.01	8.43	7.76	7.39	7.15	6.98	6.85	6.76	6.68	6.62	6.52	6.43	6.33	6.28	6.23	6.18	6.12	6.07	6.02
6	8.81	7.26	6.60	6.23	5.99	5.82	5.70	5.60	5.52	5.46	5.37	5.27	5.17	5.12	5.07	5.01	4.96	4.90	4.85
7	8.07	6.54	5.89	5.52	5.29	5.12	4.99	4.90	4.82	4.76	4.67	4.57	4.47	4.42	4.36	4.31	4.25	4.20	4.14
8	7.57	6.06	5.42	5.05	4.82	4.65	4.53	4.43	4.36	4.30	4.20	4.10	4.00	3.95	3.89	3.84	3.78	3.73	3.67
9	7.21	5.71	5.08	4.72	4.48	4.32	4.20	4.10	4.03	3.96	3.87	3.77	3.67	3.61	3.56	3.51	3.45	3.39	3.33
10	6.94	5.46	4.83	4.47	4.24	4.07	3.95	3.85	3.78	3.72	3.62	3.52	3.42	3.37	3.31	3.26	3.20	3.14	3.08
11	6.72	5.26	4.63	4.28	4.04	3.88	3.76	3.66	3.59	3.53	3.43	3.33	3.23	3.17	3.12	3.06	3.00	2.94	2.88
12	6.55	5.10	4.47	4.12	3.89	3.73	3.61	3.51	3.44	3.37	3.28	3.18	3.07	3.02	2.96	2.91	2.85	2.79	2.72
13	6.41	4.97	4.35	4.00	3.77	3.60	3.48	3.39	3.31	3.25	3.15	3.05	2.95	2.89	2.84	2.78	2.72	2.66	2.60
14	6.30	4.86	4.24	3.89	3.66	3.50	3.38	3.29	3.21	3.15	3.05	2.95	2.84	2.79	2.73	2.67	2.61	2.55	2.49
15	6.20	4.77	4.15	3.80	3.58	3.41	3.29	3.20	3.12	3.06	2.96	2.86	2.76	2.70	2.64	2.59	2.52	2.46	2.40
16	6.12	4.69	4.08	3.73	3.50	3.34	3.22	3.12	3.05	2.99	2.89	2.79	2.68	2.63	2.57	2.51	2.45	2.38	2.32
17	6.04	4.62	4.01	3.66	3.44	3.28	3.16	3.06	2.98	2.92	2.82	2.72	2.62	2.56	2.50	2.44	2.38	2.32	2.25
18	5.98	4.56	3.95	3.61	3.38	3.22	3.10	3.01	2.93	2.87	2.77	2.67	2.56	2.50	2.44	2.38	2.32	2.26	2.19
19	5.92	4.51	3.90	3.56	3.33	3.17	3.05	2.96	2.88	2.82	2.72	2.62	2.51	2.45	2.39	2.33	2.27	2.20	2.13
20	5.87	4.46	3.86	3.51	3.29	3.13	3.01	2.91	2.84	2.77	2.68	2.57	2.46	2.41	2.35	2.29	2.22	2.16	2.09
21	5.83	4.42	3.82	3.48	3.25	3.09	2.97	2.87	2.80	2.73	2.64	2.53	2.42	2.37	2.31	2.25	2.18	2.11	2.04
22	5.79	4.38	3.78	3.44	3.22	3.05	2.93	2.84	2.76	2.70	2.60	2.50	2.39	2.33	2.27	2.21	2.14	2.08	2.00
23	5.75	4.35	3.75	3.41	3.18	3.02	2.90	2.81	2.73	2.67	2.57	2.47	2.36	2.30	2.24	2.18	2.11	2.04	1.97
24	5.72	4.32	3.72	3.38	3.15	2.99	2.87	2.78	2.70	2.64	2.54	2.44	2.33	2.27	2.21	2.15	2.08	2.01	1.94
25	5.69	4.29	3.69	3.35	3.13	2.97	2.85	2.75	2.68	2.61	2.51	2.41	2.30	2.24	2.18	2.12	2.05	1.98	1.91
26	5.66	4.27	3.67	3.33	3.10	2.94	2.82	2.73	2.65	2.59	2.49	2.39	2.28	2.22	2.16	2.09	2.03	1.95	1.88
27	5.63	4.24	3.65	3.31	3.08	2.92	2.80	2.71	2.63	2.57	2.47	2.36	2.25	2.19	2.13	2.07	2.00	1.93	1.85
28	5.61	4.22	3.63	3.29	3.06	2.90	2.78	2.69	2.61	2.55	2.45	2.34	2.23	2.17	2.11	2.05	1.98	1.91	1.83
29	5.59	4.20	3.61	3.27	3.04	2.88	2.76	2.67	2.59	2.53	2.43	2.32	2.21	2.15	2.09	2.03	1.96	1.89	1.81
30	5.57	4.18	3.59	3.25	3.03	2.87	2.75	2.65	2.57	2.51	2.41	2.31	2.20	2.14	2.07	2.01	1.94	1.87	1.79
40	5.42	4.05	3.46	3.13	2.90	2.74	2.62	2.53	2.45	2.39	2.29	2.18	2.07	2.01	1.94	1.88	1.80	1.72	1.64
60	5.29	3.93	3.34	3.01	2.79	2.63	2.51	2.41	2.33	2.27	2.17	2.06	1.94	1.88	1.82	1.74	1.67	1.58	1.48
120	5.15	3.80	3.23	2.89	2.67	2.52	2.39	2.30	2.22	2.16	2.05	1.94	1.82	1.76	1.69	1.61	1.53	1.43	1.31
∞	5.02	3.69	3.12	2.79	2.57	2.41	2.29	2.19	2.11	2.05	1.94	1.83	1.71	1.64	1.57	1.48	1.39	1.27	1.00

F-Distribution

PERCENTAGE POINTS, F-DISTRIBUTION (Continued)

$$F(F) = \int_0^F \frac{\Gamma\left(\frac{m+n}{2}\right)}{\Gamma\left(\frac{m}{2}\right)\Gamma\left(\frac{n}{2}\right)}\, m^{\frac{m}{2}} n^{\frac{n}{2}} x^{\frac{m}{2}-1}(n+mx)^{-\frac{m+n}{2}}\, dx = .99$$

m\n	1	2	3	4	5	6	7	8	9	10	12	15	20	24	30	40	60	120	∞
1	4052	4999.5	5403	5625	5764	5859	5928	5982	6022	6056	6106	6157	6209	6235	6261	6287	6313	6339	6366
2	98.50	99.00	99.17	99.25	99.30	99.33	99.36	99.37	99.39	99.40	99.42	99.43	99.45	99.46	99.47	99.47	99.48	99.49	99.50
3	34.12	30.82	29.46	28.71	28.24	27.91	27.67	27.49	27.35	27.23	27.05	26.87	26.69	26.60	26.50	26.41	26.32	26.22	26.13
4	21.20	18.00	16.69	15.98	15.52	15.21	14.98	14.80	14.66	14.55	14.37	14.20	14.02	13.93	13.84	13.75	13.65	13.56	13.46
5	16.26	13.27	12.06	11.39	10.97	10.67	10.46	10.29	10.16	10.05	9.89	9.72	9.55	9.47	9.38	9.29	9.20	9.11	9.02
6	13.75	10.92	9.78	9.15	8.75	8.47	8.26	8.10	7.98	7.87	7.72	7.56	7.40	7.31	7.23	7.14	7.06	6.97	6.88
7	12.25	9.55	8.45	7.85	7.46	7.19	6.99	6.84	6.72	6.62	6.47	6.31	6.16	6.07	5.99	5.91	5.82	5.74	5.65
8	11.26	8.65	7.59	7.01	6.63	6.37	6.18	6.03	5.91	5.81	5.67	5.52	5.36	5.28	5.20	5.12	5.03	4.95	4.86
9	10.56	8.02	6.99	6.42	6.06	5.80	5.61	5.47	5.35	5.26	5.11	4.96	4.81	4.73	4.65	4.57	4.48	4.40	4.31
10	10.04	7.56	6.55	5.99	5.64	5.39	5.20	5.06	4.94	4.85	4.71	4.56	4.41	4.33	4.25	4.17	4.08	4.00	3.91
11	9.65	7.21	6.22	5.67	5.32	5.07	4.89	4.74	4.63	4.54	4.40	4.25	4.10	4.02	3.94	3.86	3.78	3.69	3.60
12	9.33	6.93	5.95	5.41	5.06	4.82	4.64	4.50	4.39	4.30	4.16	4.01	3.86	3.78	3.70	3.62	3.54	3.45	3.36
13	9.07	6.70	5.74	5.21	4.86	4.62	4.44	4.30	4.19	4.10	3.96	3.82	3.66	3.59	3.51	3.43	3.34	3.25	3.17
14	8.86	6.51	5.56	5.04	4.69	4.46	4.28	4.14	4.03	3.94	3.80	3.66	3.51	3.43	3.35	3.27	3.18	3.09	3.00
15	8.68	6.36	5.42	4.89	4.56	4.32	4.14	4.00	3.89	3.80	3.67	3.52	3.37	3.29	3.21	3.13	3.05	2.96	2.87
16	8.53	6.23	5.29	4.77	4.44	4.20	4.03	3.89	3.78	3.69	3.55	3.41	3.26	3.18	3.10	3.02	2.93	2.84	2.75
17	8.40	6.11	5.18	4.67	4.34	4.10	3.93	3.79	3.68	3.59	3.46	3.31	3.16	3.08	3.00	2.92	2.83	2.75	2.65
18	8.29	6.01	5.09	4.58	4.25	4.01	3.84	3.71	3.60	3.51	3.37	3.23	3.08	3.00	2.92	2.84	2.75	2.66	2.57
19	8.18	5.93	5.01	4.50	4.17	3.94	3.77	3.63	3.52	3.43	3.30	3.15	3.00	2.92	2.84	2.76	2.67	2.58	2.49
20	8.10	5.85	4.94	4.43	4.10	3.87	3.70	3.56	3.46	3.37	3.23	3.09	2.94	2.86	2.78	2.69	2.61	2.52	2.42
21	8.02	5.78	4.87	4.37	4.04	3.81	3.64	3.51	3.40	3.31	3.17	3.03	2.88	2.80	2.72	2.64	2.55	2.46	2.36
22	7.95	5.72	4.82	4.31	3.99	3.76	3.59	3.45	3.35	3.26	3.12	2.98	2.83	2.75	2.67	2.58	2.50	2.40	2.31
23	7.88	5.66	4.76	4.26	3.94	3.71	3.54	3.41	3.30	3.21	3.07	2.93	2.78	2.70	2.62	2.54	2.45	2.35	2.26
24	7.82	5.61	4.72	4.22	3.90	3.67	3.50	3.36	3.26	3.17	3.03	2.89	2.74	2.66	2.58	2.49	2.40	2.31	2.21
25	7.77	5.57	4.68	4.18	3.85	3.63	3.46	3.32	3.22	3.13	2.99	2.85	2.70	2.62	2.54	2.45	2.36	2.27	2.17
26	7.72	5.53	4.64	4.14	3.82	3.59	3.42	3.29	3.18	3.09	2.96	2.81	2.66	2.58	2.50	2.42	2.33	2.23	2.13
27	7.68	5.49	4.60	4.11	3.78	3.56	3.39	3.26	3.15	3.06	2.93	2.78	2.63	2.55	2.47	2.38	2.29	2.20	2.10
28	7.64	5.45	4.57	4.07	3.75	3.53	3.36	3.23	3.12	3.03	2.90	2.75	2.60	2.52	2.44	2.35	2.26	2.17	2.06
29	7.60	5.42	4.54	4.04	3.73	3.50	3.33	3.20	3.09	3.00	2.87	2.73	2.57	2.49	2.41	2.33	2.23	2.14	2.03
30	7.56	5.39	4.51	4.02	3.70	3.47	3.30	3.17	3.07	2.98	2.84	2.70	2.55	2.47	2.39	2.30	2.21	2.11	2.01
40	7.31	5.18	4.31	3.83	3.51	3.29	3.12	2.99	2.89	2.80	2.66	2.52	2.37	2.29	2.20	2.11	2.02	1.92	1.80
60	7.08	4.98	4.13	3.65	3.34	3.12	2.95	2.82	2.72	2.63	2.50	2.35	2.20	2.12	2.03	1.94	1.84	1.73	1.60
120	6.85	4.79	3.95	3.48	3.17	2.96	2.79	2.66	2.56	2.47	2.34	2.19	2.03	1.95	1.86	1.76	1.66	1.53	1.38
∞	6.63	4.61	3.78	3.32	3.02	2.80	2.64	2.51	2.41	2.32	2.18	2.04	1.88	1.79	1.70	1.59	1.47	1.32	1.00

F-Distribution

PERCENTAGE POINTS, F-DISTRIBUTION (Continued)

$$F(F) = \int_0^F \frac{\Gamma\left(\frac{m+n}{2}\right)}{\Gamma\left(\frac{m}{2}\right)\Gamma\left(\frac{n}{2}\right)} m^{\frac{m}{2}} n^{\frac{n}{2}} z^{\frac{m}{2}-1} (n+mz)^{-\frac{m+n}{2}}\, dz = .995$$

m \ n	1	2	3	4	5	6	7	8	9	10	12	15	20	24	30	40	60	120	∞
1	16211	20000	21615	22500	23056	23437	23715	23925	24091	24224	24426	24630	24836	24940	25044	25148	25253	25359	25465
2	198.5	199.0	199.2	199.2	199.3	199.3	199.4	199.4	199.4	199.4	199.4	199.4	199.4	199.5	199.5	199.5	199.5	199.5	199.5
3	55.55	49.80	47.47	46.19	45.39	44.84	44.43	44.13	43.88	43.69	43.39	43.08	42.78	42.62	42.47	42.31	42.15	41.99	41.83
4	31.33	26.28	24.26	23.15	22.46	21.97	21.62	21.35	21.14	20.97	20.70	20.44	20.17	20.03	19.89	19.75	19.61	19.47	19.32
5	22.78	18.31	16.53	15.56	14.94	14.51	14.20	13.96	13.77	13.62	13.38	13.15	12.90	12.78	12.66	12.53	12.40	12.27	12.14
6	18.63	14.54	12.92	12.03	11.46	11.07	10.79	10.57	10.39	10.25	10.03	9.81	9.59	9.47	9.36	9.24	9.12	9.00	8.88
7	16.24	12.40	10.88	10.05	9.52	9.16	8.89	8.68	8.51	8.38	8.18	7.97	7.75	7.65	7.53	7.42	7.31	7.19	7.08
8	14.69	11.04	9.60	8.81	8.30	7.95	7.69	7.50	7.34	7.21	7.01	6.81	6.61	6.50	6.40	6.29	6.18	6.06	5.95
9	13.61	10.11	8.72	7.96	7.47	7.13	6.88	6.69	6.54	6.42	6.23	6.03	5.83	5.73	5.62	5.52	5.41	5.30	5.19
10	12.83	9.43	8.08	7.34	6.87	6.54	6.30	6.12	5.97	5.85	5.66	5.47	5.27	5.17	5.07	4.97	4.86	4.75	4.64
11	12.23	8.91	7.60	6.88	6.42	6.10	5.86	5.68	5.54	5.42	5.24	5.05	4.86	4.76	4.65	4.55	4.44	4.34	4.23
12	11.75	8.51	7.23	6.52	6.07	5.76	5.52	5.35	5.20	5.09	4.91	4.72	4.53	4.43	4.33	4.23	4.12	4.01	3.90
13	11.37	8.19	6.93	6.23	5.79	5.48	5.25	5.08	4.94	4.82	4.64	4.46	4.27	4.17	4.07	3.97	3.87	3.76	3.65
14	11.06	7.92	6.68	6.00	5.56	5.26	5.03	4.86	4.72	4.60	4.43	4.25	4.06	3.96	3.86	3.76	3.66	3.55	3.44
15	10.80	7.70	6.48	5.80	5.37	5.07	4.85	4.67	4.54	4.42	4.25	4.07	3.88	3.79	3.69	3.58	3.48	3.37	3.26
16	10.58	7.51	6.30	5.64	5.21	4.91	4.69	4.52	4.38	4.27	4.10	3.92	3.73	3.64	3.54	3.44	3.33	3.22	3.11
17	10.38	7.35	6.16	5.50	5.07	4.78	4.56	4.39	4.25	4.14	3.97	3.79	3.61	3.51	3.41	3.31	3.21	3.10	2.98
18	10.22	7.21	6.03	5.37	4.96	4.66	4.44	4.28	4.14	4.03	3.86	3.68	3.50	3.40	3.30	3.20	3.10	2.99	2.87
19	10.07	7.09	5.92	5.27	4.85	4.56	4.34	4.18	4.04	3.93	3.76	3.59	3.40	3.31	3.21	3.11	3.00	2.89	2.78
20	9.94	6.99	5.82	5.17	4.76	4.47	4.26	4.09	3.96	3.85	3.68	3.50	3.32	3.22	3.12	3.02	2.92	2.81	2.69
21	9.83	6.89	5.73	5.09	4.68	4.39	4.18	4.01	3.88	3.77	3.60	3.43	3.24	3.15	3.05	2.95	2.84	2.73	2.61
22	9.73	6.81	5.65	5.02	4.61	4.32	4.11	3.94	3.81	3.70	3.54	3.36	3.18	3.08	2.98	2.88	2.77	2.66	2.55
23	9.63	6.73	5.58	4.95	4.54	4.26	4.05	3.88	3.75	3.64	3.47	3.30	3.12	3.02	2.92	2.82	2.71	2.60	2.48
24	9.55	6.66	5.52	4.89	4.49	4.20	3.99	3.83	3.69	3.59	3.42	3.25	3.06	2.97	2.87	2.77	2.66	2.55	2.43
25	9.48	6.60	5.46	4.84	4.43	4.15	3.94	3.78	3.64	3.54	3.37	3.20	3.01	2.92	2.82	2.72	2.61	2.50	2.38
26	9.41	6.54	5.41	4.79	4.38	4.10	3.89	3.73	3.60	3.49	3.33	3.15	2.97	2.87	2.77	2.67	2.56	2.45	2.33
27	9.34	6.49	5.36	4.74	4.34	4.06	3.85	3.69	3.56	3.45	3.28	3.11	2.93	2.83	2.73	2.63	2.52	2.41	2.29
28	9.28	6.44	5.32	4.70	4.30	4.02	3.81	3.65	3.52	3.41	3.25	3.07	2.89	2.79	2.69	2.59	2.48	2.37	2.25
29	9.23	6.40	5.28	4.66	4.26	3.98	3.77	3.61	3.48	3.38	3.21	3.04	2.86	2.76	2.66	2.56	2.45	2.33	2.21
30	9.18	6.35	5.24	4.62	4.23	3.95	3.74	3.58	3.45	3.34	3.18	3.01	2.82	2.73	2.63	2.52	2.42	2.30	2.18
40	8.83	6.07	4.98	4.37	3.99	3.71	3.51	3.35	3.22	3.12	2.95	2.78	2.60	2.50	2.40	2.30	2.18	2.06	1.93
60	8.49	5.79	4.73	4.14	3.76	3.49	3.29	3.13	3.01	2.90	2.74	2.57	2.39	2.29	2.19	2.08	1.96	1.83	1.69
120	8.18	5.54	4.50	3.92	3.55	3.28	3.09	2.93	2.81	2.71	2.54	2.37	2.19	2.09	1.98	1.87	1.75	1.61	1.43
∞	7.88	5.30	4.28	3.72	3.35	3.09	2.90	2.74	2.62	2.52	2.36	2.19	2.00	1.90	1.79	1.67	1.53	1.36	1.00

F-Distribution

PERCENTAGE POINTS, *F*-DISTRIBUTION (Continued)

$$F(F) = \int_0^F \frac{\Gamma\left(\frac{m+n}{2}\right)}{\Gamma\left(\frac{m}{2}\right)\Gamma\left(\frac{n}{2}\right)} m^{\frac{m}{2}} n^{\frac{n}{2}} x^{\frac{m}{2}-1} (n+mx)^{-\frac{m+n}{2}} \, dx = .999$$

n\m	1	2	3	4	5	6	7	8	9	10	12	15	20	24	30	40	60	120	∞
1	4053*	5000*	5404*	5625*	5764*	5859*	5929*	5981*	6023*	6056*	6107*	6158*	6209*	6235*	6261*	6287*	6313*	6340*	6366*
2	998.5	999.0	999.2	999.2	999.3	999.3	999.4	999.4	999.4	999.4	999.4	999.4	999.4	999.5	999.5	999.5	999.5	999.5	999.5
3	167.0	148.5	141.1	137.1	134.6	132.8	131.6	130.6	129.9	129.2	128.3	127.4	126.4	125.9	125.4	125.0	124.5	124.0	123.5
4	74.14	61.25	56.18	53.44	51.71	50.53	49.66	49.00	48.47	48.05	47.41	46.76	46.10	45.77	45.43	45.09	44.75	44.40	44.05
5	47.18	37.12	33.20	31.09	29.75	28.84	28.16	27.64	27.24	26.92	26.42	25.91	25.39	25.14	24.87	24.60	24.33	24.06	23.79
6	35.51	27.00	23.70	21.92	20.81	20.03	19.46	19.03	18.69	18.41	17.99	17.56	17.12	16.89	16.67	16.44	16.21	15.99	15.75
7	29.25	21.69	18.77	17.19	16.21	15.52	15.02	14.63	14.33	14.08	13.71	13.32	12.93	12.73	12.53	12.33	12.12	11.91	11.70
8	25.42	18.49	15.83	14.39	13.49	12.86	12.40	12.04	11.77	11.54	11.19	10.84	10.48	10.30	10.11	9.92	9.73	9.53	9.33
9	22.86	16.39	13.90	12.56	11.71	11.13	10.70	10.37	10.11	9.89	9.57	9.24	8.90	8.72	8.55	8.37	8.19	8.00	7.81
10	21.04	14.91	12.55	11.28	10.48	9.92	9.52	9.20	8.96	8.75	8.45	8.13	7.80	7.64	7.47	7.30	7.12	6.94	6.76
11	19.69	13.81	11.56	10.35	9.58	9.05	8.66	8.35	8.12	7.92	7.63	7.32	7.01	6.85	6.68	6.52	6.35	6.17	6.00
12	18.64	12.97	10.80	9.63	8.89	8.38	8.00	7.71	7.48	7.29	7.00	6.71	6.40	6.25	6.09	5.93	5.76	5.59	5.42
13	17.81	12.31	10.21	9.07	8.35	7.86	7.49	7.21	6.98	6.80	6.52	6.23	5.93	5.78	5.63	5.47	5.30	5.14	4.97
14	17.14	11.78	9.73	8.62	7.92	7.43	7.08	6.80	6.58	6.40	6.13	5.85	5.56	5.41	5.25	5.10	4.94	4.77	4.60
15	16.59	11.34	9.34	8.25	7.57	7.09	6.74	6.47	6.26	6.08	5.81	5.54	5.25	5.10	4.95	4.80	4.64	4.47	4.31
16	16.12	10.97	9.00	7.94	7.27	6.81	6.46	6.19	5.98	5.81	5.55	5.27	4.99	4.85	4.70	4.54	4.39	4.23	4.06
17	15.72	10.66	8.73	7.68	7.02	6.56	6.22	5.96	5.75	5.58	5.32	5.05	4.78	4.63	4.48	4.33	4.18	4.02	3.85
18	15.38	10.39	8.49	7.46	6.81	6.35	6.02	5.76	5.56	5.39	5.13	4.87	4.59	4.45	4.30	4.15	4.00	3.84	3.67
19	15.08	10.16	8.28	7.26	6.62	6.18	5.85	5.59	5.39	5.22	4.97	4.70	4.43	4.29	4.14	3.99	3.84	3.68	3.51
20	14.82	9.95	8.10	7.10	6.46	6.02	5.69	5.44	5.24	5.08	4.82	4.56	4.29	4.15	4.00	3.86	3.70	3.54	3.38
21	14.59	9.77	7.94	6.95	6.32	5.88	5.56	5.31	5.11	4.95	4.70	4.44	4.17	4.03	3.88	3.74	3.58	3.42	3.26
22	14.38	9.61	7.80	6.81	6.19	5.76	5.44	5.19	4.99	4.83	4.58	4.33	4.06	3.92	3.78	3.63	3.48	3.32	3.15
23	14.19	9.47	7.67	6.69	6.08	5.65	5.33	5.09	4.89	4.73	4.48	4.23	3.96	3.82	3.68	3.53	3.38	3.22	3.05
24	14.03	9.34	7.55	6.59	5.98	5.55	5.23	4.99	4.80	4.64	4.39	4.14	3.87	3.74	3.59	3.45	3.29	3.14	2.97
25	13.88	9.22	7.45	6.49	5.88	5.46	5.15	4.91	4.71	4.56	4.31	4.06	3.79	3.66	3.52	3.37	3.22	3.06	2.89
26	13.74	9.12	7.36	6.41	5.80	5.38	5.07	4.83	4.64	4.48	4.24	3.99	3.72	3.59	3.44	3.30	3.15	2.99	2.82
27	13.61	9.02	7.27	6.33	5.73	5.31	5.00	4.76	4.57	4.41	4.17	3.92	3.66	3.52	3.38	3.23	3.08	2.92	2.75
28	13.50	8.93	7.19	6.25	5.66	5.24	4.93	4.69	4.50	4.35	4.11	3.86	3.60	3.46	3.32	3.18	3.02	2.86	2.69
29	13.39	8.85	7.12	6.19	5.59	5.18	4.87	4.64	4.45	4.29	4.05	3.80	3.54	3.41	3.27	3.12	2.97	2.81	2.64
30	13.29	8.77	7.05	6.12	5.53	5.12	4.82	4.58	4.39	4.24	4.00	3.75	3.49	3.36	3.22	3.07	2.92	2.76	2.59
40	12.61	8.25	6.60	5.70	5.13	4.73	4.44	4.21	4.02	3.87	3.64	3.40	3.15	3.01	2.87	2.73	2.57	2.41	2.23
60	11.97	7.76	6.17	5.31	4.76	4.37	4.09	3.87	3.69	3.54	3.31	3.08	2.83	2.69	2.55	2.41	2.25	2.08	1.89
120	11.38	7.32	5.79	4.95	4.42	4.04	3.77	3.55	3.38	3.24	3.02	2.78	2.53	2.40	2.26	2.11	1.95	1.76	1.54
∞	10.83	6.91	5.42	4.62	4.10	3.74	3.47	3.27	3.10	2.96	2.74	2.51	2.27	2.13	1.99	1.84	1.66	1.45	1.00

* Multiply these entries by 100.

Table of Random Units

RANDOM UNITS

Use of Table. If one wishes to select a random sample of N items from a universe of M items, the following procedure may be applied. ($M > N$.)

1. Decide upon some arbitrary scheme of selecting entries from the table. For example, one may decide to use the entries in the first line, second column; second line, third column; third line, fourth column; etc.

2. Assign numbers to each of the items in the universe from 1 to M. Thus, if $M = 500$, the items would be numbered from 001 to 500, and therefore, each designated item is associated with a three digit number.

3. Decide upon some arbitrary scheme of selecting positional digits from each entry chosen according to Step 1. Thus, if $M = 500$, one may decide to use the first, third, and fourth digit of each entry selected, and as a consequence a three digit number is created for each entry choice.

4. If the number formed is $\leq M$, the correspondingly designated item in the universe is chosen for the random sample of N items. If a number formed is $> M$ or is a repeated number of one already chosen, it is passed over and the next desirable number is taken. This process is continued until the random sample of N items is selected.

Table of Random Units

A TABLE OF 14,000 RANDOM UNITS

Line/Col.	(1)	(2)	(3)	(4)	(5)	(6)	(7)	(8)	(9)	(10)	(11)	(12)	(13)	(14)
1	10480	15011	01536	02011	81647	91646	69179	14194	62590	36207	20969	99570	91291	90700
2	22368	46573	25595	85393	30995	89198	27982	53402	93965	34095	52666	19174	39615	99505
3	24130	48360	22527	97265	76393	64809	15179	24830	49340	32081	30680	19655	63348	58629
4	42167	93093	06243	61680	07856	16376	39440	53537	71341	57004	00849	74917	97758	16379
5	37570	39975	81837	16656	06121	91782	60468	81305	49684	60672	14110	06927	01263	54613
6	77921	06907	11008	42751	27756	53498	18602	70659	90655	15053	21916	81825	44394	42880
7	99562	72905	56420	69994	98872	31016	71194	18738	44013	48840	63213	21069	10634	12952
8	96301	91977	05463	07972	18876	20922	94595	56869	69014	60045	18425	84903	42508	32307
9	89579	14342	63661	10281	17453	18103	57740	84378	25331	12566	58678	44947	05585	56941
10	85475	36857	43342	53988	53060	59533	38867	62300	08158	17983	16439	11458	18593	64952
11	28918	69578	88231	33276	70997	79936	56865	05859	90106	31595	01547	85590	91610	78188
12	63553	40961	48235	03427	49626	69445	18663	72695	52180	20847	12234	90511	33703	90322
13	09429	93969	52636	92737	88974	33488	36320	17617	30015	08272	84115	27156	30613	74952
14	10365	61129	87529	85689	48237	52267	67689	93394	01511	26358	85104	20285	29975	89868
15	07119	97336	71048	08178	77233	13916	47564	81056	97735	85977	29372	74461	28551	90707
16	51085	12765	51821	51259	77452	16308	60756	92144	49442	53900	70960	63990	75601	40719
17	02368	21382	52404	60268	89368	19885	55322	44819	01188	65255	64835	44919	05944	55157
18	01011	54092	33362	94904	31273	04146	18594	29852	71585	85030	51132	01915	92747	64951
19	52162	53916	46369	58586	23216	14513	83149	98736	23495	64350	94738	17752	35156	35749
20	07056	97628	33787	09998	42698	06691	76988	13602	51851	46104	88916	19509	25625	58104
21	48663	91245	85828	14346	09172	30168	90229	04734	59193	22178	30421	61666	99904	32812
22	54164	58492	22421	74103	47070	25306	76468	26384	58151	06646	21524	15227	96909	44592
23	32639	32363	05597	24200	13363	38005	94342	28728	35806	06912	17012	64161	18296	22851
24	29334	27001	87637	87308	58731	00256	45834	15398	46557	41135	10367	07684	36188	18510
25	02488	33062	28834	07351	19731	92420	60952	61280	50001	67658	32586	86679	50720	94953
26	81525	72295	04839	96423	24878	82651	66566	14778	76797	14780	13300	87074	79666	95725
27	29676	20591	68086	26432	46901	20849	89768	81536	86645	12659	92259	57102	80428	25280
28	00742	57392	39064	66432	84673	40027	32832	61362	98947	96067	64760	64584	96096	98253
29	05366	04213	25669	26422	44407	44048	37937	63904	45766	66134	75470	66520	34693	90449
30	91921	26418	64117	94305	26766	25940	39972	22209	71500	64568	91402	42416	07844	69618
31	00582	04711	87917	77341	42206	35126	74087	99547	81817	42607	43808	76655	62028	76630
32	00725	69884	62797	56170	86324	88072	76222	36086	84637	93161	76038	65855	77919	88006
33	69011	65797	95876	55293	18988	27354	26575	08625	40801	59920	29841	80150	12777	48501
34	25976	57948	29888	88604	67917	48708	18912	82271	65424	69774	33611	54262	85963	03547
35	09763	83473	73577	12908	30883	18317	28290	35797	05998	41688	34952	37888	38917	88050
36	91567	42595	27958	30134	04024	86385	29880	99730	55536	84855	29080	09250	79656	73211
37	17955	56349	90999	49127	20044	59931	06115	20542	18059	02008	73708	83517	36103	42791
38	46503	18584	18845	49618	02304	51038	20655	58727	28168	15475	56942	53389	20562	87338
39	92157	89634	94824	78171	84610	82834	09922	25417	44137	48413	25555	21246	35509	20468
40	14577	62765	35605	81263	39667	47358	56873	56307	61607	49518	89656	20103	77490	18062
41	98427	07523	33362	64270	01638	92477	66969	98420	04880	45585	46565	04102	46880	45709
42	34914	63976	88720	82765	34476	17032	87589	40836	32427	70002	70663	88863	77775	69348
43	70060	28277	39475	46473	23219	53416	94970	25832	69975	94884	19661	72828	00102	66794
44	53976	54914	06990	67245	68350	82948	11398	42878	80287	88267	47363	46634	06541	97809
45	76072	29515	40980	07391	58745	25774	22987	80059	39911	96189	41151	14222	60697	59583
46	90725	52210	83974	29992	65831	38857	50490	83765	55657	14361	31720	57375	56228	41546
47	64364	67412	33339	31926	14883	24413	59744	92351	97473	89286	35931	04110	23726	51900
48	08962	00358	31662	25388	61642	34072	81249	35648	56891	69352	48373	45578	78547	81788
49	95012	68379	93526	70765	10593	04542	76463	54328	02349	17247	28865	14777	62730	92277
50	15664	10493	20492	38391	91132	21999	59516	81652	27195	48223	46751	22923	32261	85653

Table of Random Units

A TABLE OF 14,000 RANDOM UNITS (Continued)

Line/Col.	(1)	(2)	(3)	(4)	(5)	(6)	(7)	(8)	(9)	(10)	(11)	(12)	(13)	(14)
51	16408	81899	04153	53381	79401	21438	83035	92350	36693	31238	59649	91754	72772	02338
52	18629	81953	05520	91962	04739	13092	97662	24822	94730	06496	35090	04822	86772	98289
53	73115	35101	47498	87637	99016	71060	88824	71013	18735	20286	23153	72924	35165	43040
54	57491	16703	23167	49323	45021	33132	12544	41035	80780	45393	44812	12515	98931	91202
55	30405	83946	23792	14422	15059	45799	22716	19792	09983	74353	68668	30429	70735	25499
56	16631	35006	85900	98275	32388	52390	16815	69298	82732	38480	73817	32523	41961	44437
57	96773	20206	42559	78985	05300	22164	24369	54224	35083	19687	11052	91491	60383	19746
58	38935	64202	14349	82674	66523	44133	00697	35552	35970	19124	63318	29686	03387	59846
59	31624	76384	17403	53363	44167	64486	64758	75366	76554	31601	12614	33072	60332	92325
60	78919	19474	23632	27889	47914	02584	37680	20801	72152	39339	34806	08930	85001	87820
61	03931	33309	57047	74211	63445	17361	62825	39908	05607	91284	68833	25570	38818	46920
62	74426	33278	43972	10119	89917	15665	52872	73823	73144	88662	88970	74492	51805	99378
63	09066	00903	20795	95452	92648	45454	09552	88815	16553	51125	79375	97596	16296	66092
64	42238	12426	87025	14267	20979	04508	64535	31355	86064	29472	47689	05974	52468	16834
65	16153	08002	26504	41744	81959	65642	74240	56302	00033	67107	77510	70625	28725	34191
66	21457	40742	29820	96783	29400	21840	15035	34537	33310	06116	95240	15957	16572	06004
67	21581	57802	02050	89728	17937	37621	47075	42080	97403	48626	68995	43805	33386	21597
68	55612	78095	83197	33732	05810	24813	86902	60397	16489	03264	88525	42786	05269	92532
69	44657	66999	99324	51281	84463	60563	79312	93454	68876	25471	93911	25650	12682	73572
70	91340	84979	46949	81973	37949	61023	43997	15263	80644	43942	89203	71795	99533	50501
71	91227	21199	31935	27022	84067	05462	35216	14486	29891	68607	41867	14951	91696	85065
72	50001	38140	66321	19924	72163	09538	12151	06878	91903	18749	34405	56087	82790	70925
73	65390	05224	72958	28609	81406	39147	25549	48542	42627	45233	57202	94617	23772	07896
74	27504	96131	83944	41575	10573	08619	64482	73923	36152	05184	94142	25299	84387	34925
75	37169	94851	39117	89632	00959	16487	65536	49071	39782	17095	02330	74301	00275	48280
76	11508	70225	51111	38351	19444	66499	71945	05422	13442	78675	84081	66938	93654	59894
77	37449	30362	06694	54690	04052	53115	62757	95348	78662	11163	81651	50245	34971	52924
78	46515	70331	85922	38329	57015	15765	97161	17869	45349	61796	66345	81073	49106	79860
79	30986	81223	42416	58353	21532	30502	32305	86482	05174	07901	54339	58861	74818	46942
80	63798	64995	46583	09765	44160	78128	83991	42865	92520	83531	80377	35909	81250	54238
81	82486	84846	99254	67632	43218	50076	21361	64816	51202	88124	41870	52689	51275	83556
82	21885	32906	92431	09060	64297	51674	64126	62570	26123	05155	59194	52799	28225	85762
83	60336	98782	07408	53458	13564	59089	26445	29789	85205	41001	12535	12133	14645	23541
84	43937	46891	24010	25560	86355	33941	25786	54990	71899	15475	95434	98227	21824	19585
85	97656	63175	89303	16275	07100	92063	21942	18611	47348	20203	18534	03862	78095	50136
86	03299	01221	05418	38982	55758	92237	26759	86367	21216	98442	08303	56613	91511	75928
87	79626	06486	03574	17668	07785	76020	79924	25651	83325	88428	85076	72811	22717	50585
88	85636	68335	47539	03129	65651	11977	02510	26113	99447	68645	34327	15152	55230	93448
89	18039	14367	61337	06177	12143	46609	32989	74014	64708	00533	35398	58408	13261	47908
90	08362	15656	60627	36478	65648	16764	53412	09013	07832	41574	17639	82163	60859	75567
91	79556	29068	04142	16268	15387	12856	66227	38358	22478	73373	88732	09443	82558	05250
92	92608	82674	27072	32534	17075	27698	98204	63863	11951	34648	88022	56148	34925	57031
93	23982	25835	40055	67006	12293	02753	14827	22235	35071	99704	37543	11601	35503	85171
94	09915	96306	05908	97901	28395	14186	00821	80703	70426	75647	76310	88717	37890	40129
95	50937	33300	26695	62247	69927	76123	50842	43834	86654	70959	79725	93872	28117	19233
96	42488	78077	69882	61657	34136	79180	97526	43092	04098	73571	80799	76536	71255	64239
97	46764	86273	63003	93017	31204	36692	40202	35275	57306	55543	53203	18098	47625	88684
98	03237	45430	55417	63282	90816	17349	88298	90183	36600	78406	06216	95787	42579	90730
99	86591	81482	52667	61583	14972	90053	89534	76036	49199	43716	97548	04379	46370	28672
100	38534	01715	94964	87288	65680	43772	39560	12918	86537	62738	19636	51132	25739	56947

Table of Random Units

A TABLE OF 14,000 RANDOM UNITS (Continued)

Line/Col.	(1)	(2)	(3)	(4)	(5)	(6)	(7)	(8)	(9)	(10)	(11)	(12)	(13)	(14)
101	13284	16834	74151	92027	24670	36665	00770	22878	02179	51602	07270	76517	97275	45960
102	21224	00370	30420	03883	96648	89428	41583	17564	27395	63904	41548	49197	82277	24120
103	99052	47887	81085	64933	66279	80432	65793	83287	34142	13241	30590	97760	35848	91983
104	00199	50993	98603	38452	87890	94624	69721	57484	67501	77638	44331	11257	71131	11059
105	60578	06483	28733	37867	07936	98710	98539	27186	31237	80612	44488	97819	70401	95419
106	91240	18312	17441	01929	18163	69201	31211	54288	39296	37318	65724	90401	79017	62077
107	97458	14229	12063	59611	32249	90466	33216	19358	02591	54263	88449	01912	07436	50813
108	35249	38646	34475	72417	60514	69257	12489	51924	86871	92446	36607	11458	30440	52639
109	38980	46600	11759	11900	46743	27860	77940	39298	97838	95145	32378	68038	89351	37005
110	10750	52745	38749	87365	58959	53731	89295	59062	39404	13198	59960	70408	29812	83126
111	36247	27850	73958	20673	37800	63835	71051	84724	52492	22342	78071	17456	96104	18327
112	70994	66986	99744	72438	01174	42159	11392	20724	54322	36923	70009	23233	65438	59685
113	99638	94702	11463	18148	81386	80431	90628	52506	02016	85151	88598	47821	00265	82525
114	72055	15774	43857	99805	10419	76939	25993	03544	21560	83471	43989	90770	22965	44247
115	24038	65541	85788	55835	38835	59399	13790	35112	01324	39520	76210	22467	83275	32286
116	74976	14631	35908	28221	39470	91548	12854	30166	09073	75887	36782	00268	97121	57676
117	35553	71628	70189	26436	63407	91178	90348	55359	80392	41012	36270	77786	89578	21059
118	35676	12797	51434	82976	42010	26344	92920	92155	58807	54644	58581	95331	78629	73344
119	74815	67523	72985	23183	02446	63594	98924	20633	58842	85961	07648	70164	34994	67662
120	45246	88048	65173	50989	91060	89894	36063	32819	68559	99221	49475	50558	34698	71800
121	76509	47069	86378	41797	11910	49672	88575	97966	32466	10083	54728	81972	58975	30761
122	19689	90332	04315	21358	97248	11188	39062	63312	52496	07349	79178	33692	57352	72862
123	42751	35318	97513	61537	54955	08159	00337	80778	27507	95478	21252	12746	37554	97775
124	11946	22681	45045	13964	57517	59419	58045	44067	58716	58840	45557	96345	33271	53464
125	96518	48688	20996	11090	48396	57177	83867	86464	14342	21545	46717	72364	86954	55580
126	35726	58643	76869	84622	39098	36083	72505	92265	23107	60278	05822	46760	44294	07672
127	39737	42750	48968	70536	84864	64952	38404	94317	65402	13589	01055	79044	19308	83623
128	97025	66492	56177	04049	80312	48028	26408	43591	75528	65341	49044	95495	81256	53214
129	62814	08075	09788	56350	76787	51591	54509	49295	85830	59860	30883	89660	96142	18354
130	25578	22950	15227	83291	41737	79599	96191	71845	86899	70694	24290	01551	80092	82118
131	68763	69576	88991	49662	46704	63362	56625	00481	73323	91427	15264	06969	57048	54149
132	17900	00813	64361	60725	88974	61005	99709	30666	26451	11528	44323	34778	60342	60388
133	71944	60227	63551	71109	05624	43836	58254	26160	32116	63403	35404	57146	10909	07346
134	54684	93691	85132	64399	29182	44324	14491	55226	78793	34107	30374	48429	51376	09559
135	25946	27623	11258	65204	52832	50880	22273	05554	99521	73791	85744	29276	70326	60251
136	01353	39318	44961	44972	91766	90262	56073	06606	51826	18893	83448	31915	97764	75091
137	99083	88191	27662	99113	57174	35571	99884	13951	71057	53961	61448	74909	07322	80960
138	52021	45406	37945	75234	24327	86978	22644	87779	23753	99926	63898	54886	18051	96314
139	78755	47744	43776	83098	03225	14281	83637	55984	13300	52212	58781	14905	46502	04472
140	25282	69106	59180	16257	22810	43609	12224	25643	89884	31149	85423	32581	34374	70873
141	11959	94202	02743	86847	79725	51811	12998	76844	05320	54236	53891	70226	38632	84776
142	11644	13792	98190	01424	30078	28197	55583	05197	47714	68440	22016	79204	06862	94451
143	06307	97912	68110	59812	95448	43244	31262	88880	13040	16458	43813	89416	42482	33939
144	76285	75714	89585	99296	52640	46518	55486	90754	88932	19937	57119	23251	55619	23679
145	55322	07589	39600	60866	63007	20007	66819	84164	61131	81429	60676	42807	78286	29015
146	78017	90928	90220	92503	83375	26986	74399	30885	88567	29169	72816	53357	15428	86932
147	44768	43342	20696	26331	43140	69744	82928	24988	94237	46138	77426	39039	55596	12655
148	25100	19336	14605	86603	51680	97678	24261	02464	86563	74812	60069	71674	15478	47642
149	83612	46623	62876	85197	07824	91392	58317	37726	84628	42221	10268	20692	15699	29167
150	41347	81666	82961	60413	71020	83658	02415	33322	66036	98712	46795	16308	28413	05417

Table of Random Units

A TABLE OF 14,000 RANDOM UNITS (Continued)

Line/Col.	(1)	(2)	(3)	(4)	(5)	(6)	(7)	(8)	(9)	(10)	(11)	(12)	(13)	(14)
151	38128	51178	75096	13609	16110	73533	42564	59870	29399	67834	91055	89917	51096	89011
152	60950	00455	73254	96067	50717	13878	03216	78274	65863	37011	91283	33914	91303	49326
153	90524	17320	29832	96118	75792	25326	22940	24904	80523	38928	91374	55597	97567	38914
154	49897	18278	67160	39408	97056	43517	84426	59650	20247	19293	02019	14790	02852	05819
155	18494	99209	81060	19488	65596	59787	47939	91225	98768	43688	00438	05548	09443	82897
156	65373	72984	30171	37741	70203	94094	87261	30056	58124	70133	18936	02138	59372	09075
157	40653	12843	04213	70925	95360	55774	76439	61768	52817	81151	52188	31940	54273	49032
158	51638	22238	56344	44587	83231	50317	74541	07719	25472	41602	77318	15145	57515	07633
159	69742	99303	62578	83575	30337	07488	51941	84316	42067	49692	28616	29101	03013	73449
160	58012	74072	67488	74580	47992	69482	58624	17106	47538	13452	22620	24260	40155	74716
161	18348	19855	42887	08279	43206	47077	42637	45606	00011	20662	14642	49984	94509	56380
162	59614	09193	58064	29086	44385	45740	70752	05663	49081	26960	57454	99264	24142	74648
163	75688	28630	39210	52897	62748	72658	98059	67202	72789	01869	13496	14663	87645	89713
164	13941	77802	69101	70061	35460	34576	15412	81304	58757	35498	94830	75521	00603	97701
165	96656	86420	96475	86458	54463	96419	55417	41375	76886	19008	66877	35934	59801	00497
166	03363	82042	15942	14549	38324	87094	19069	67590	11087	68570	22591	65232	85915	91499
167	70366	08390	69155	25496	13240	57407	91407	49160	07379	34444	94567	66035	38918	65708
168	47870	36605	12927	16043	53257	93796	52721	73120	48025	76074	95605	67422	41646	14557
169	79504	77606	22761	30518	28373	73898	30550	76684	77366	32276	04690	61667	64798	66276
170	46967	74841	50923	15339	37755	98995	40162	89561	69199	42257	11647	47603	48779	97907
171	14558	50769	35444	59030	87516	48193	02945	00922	48189	04724	21263	20892	92955	90251
172	12440	25057	01132	38611	28135	68089	10954	10097	54243	06460	50856	65435	79377	53890
173	32293	29938	68653	10497	98919	46587	77701	99119	93165	67788	17638	23097	21468	36992
174	10640	21875	72462	77981	56550	55999	87310	69643	45124	00349	25748	00844	96831	30651
175	47615	23169	39571	56972	20628	21788	51736	33133	72696	32605	41569	76148	91544	21121
176	16948	11128	71624	72754	49084	96303	27830	45817	67867	18062	87453	17226	72904	71474
177	21258	61092	66634	70335	92448	17354	83432	49608	66520	06442	59664	20420	39201	69549
178	15072	48853	15178	30730	47481	48490	41436	25015	49932	20474	53821	51015	79841	32405
179	99154	57412	09858	65671	70655	71479	63520	31357	56968	06729	34465	70685	04184	25250
180	08759	61089	23706	32994	35426	36666	63988	98844	37533	08269	27021	45886	22835	78451
181	67323	57839	61114	62192	47547	58023	64630	34886	98777	75442	95592	06141	45096	73117
182	09255	13986	84834	20764	72206	89393	34548	93438	88730	61805	78955	18952	46436	58740
183	36304	74712	00374	10107	85061	69228	81969	92216	03568	39630	81869	52824	50937	27954
184	15884	67429	86612	47367	10242	44880	12060	44309	46629	55105	66793	93173	00480	13311
185	18745	32031	35303	08134	33925	03044	59929	95418	04917	57596	24878	61733	92834	64454
186	72934	40086	88292	65728	38300	42323	64068	98373	48971	09049	59943	36538	05976	82118
187	17626	02944	20910	57662	80181	38579	24580	90529	52303	50436	29401	57824	86039	81062
188	27117	61399	50967	41399	81636	16663	15634	79717	94696	59240	25543	97989	63306	90946
189	93995	18678	90012	63645	85701	85269	62263	68331	00389	72571	15210	20769	44686	96176
190	67392	89421	09623	80725	62620	84162	87368	29560	00519	84545	08004	24526	41252	14521
191	04910	12261	37566	80016	21245	69377	50420	85658	55263	68667	78770	04533	14513	18099
192	81453	20283	79929	59839	23875	13245	46808	74124	74703	35769	95588	21014	37078	39170
193	19480	75790	48539	23703	15537	48885	02861	86587	74539	65227	90799	58789	96257	02708
194	21456	13162	74608	81011	55512	07481	93551	72189	76261	91206	89941	15132	37738	59284
195	89406	20912	46189	76376	25538	87212	20748	12831	57166	35026	16817	79121	18929	40628
196	09866	07414	55977	16419	01101	69343	13305	94302	80703	57910	36933	57771	42546	03003
197	86541	24681	23421	13521	28000	94917	07423	57523	97234	63951	42876	46829	09781	58160
198	10414	96941	06205	72222	57167	83902	07460	69507	10600	08858	07685	44472	64220	27040
199	49942	06683	41479	58982	56288	42853	92196	20632	62045	78812	35895	51851	83534	10689
200	23995	68882	42291	23374	24299	27024	67460	94783	40937	16961	26053	78749	46704	21983

FACTORS FOR COMPUTING CONTROL LIMITS

A. Control Charts for Measurement

If the process mean and standard deviation, μ and σ, are known, and it is assumed that the underlying distribution is normal, it is possible to assert with probability $1 - \alpha$ that the mean of a random sample of size n will fall between $\bar{x} - z_{\alpha/2}\dfrac{\sigma}{\sqrt{n}}$ and $\bar{x} + z_{\alpha/2}\dfrac{\sigma}{\sqrt{n}}$. These two limits on $\bar{x}$ provide upper and lower control limits. In actual practice, μ and σ are usually unknown and it is necessary to estimate their values from a large sample taken while the process is "in control." The central line of an $\bar{x}$-chart is given by μ and the lower and upper three-sigma control limits are given by $\mu - A\sigma$ and $\mu + A\sigma$, respectively, where $A = \dfrac{3}{\sqrt{n}}$ and n is the sample size. Where the population parameters are unknown, it is necessary to estimate these parameters on the basis of preliminary samples. If k samples are used, each of size n, denote the mean of the ith sample by $\bar{x}_i$ and the grand mean of the k sample means by $\bar{\bar{x}}$, i.e.

$$\bar{\bar{x}} = \frac{1}{k} \sum_{i=1}^{k} \bar{x}_i$$

Denote the range of the ith sample by R_i and by $\bar{R}$ the mean of the k sample ranges, i.e.

$$\bar{R} = \frac{1}{k} \sum_{i=1}^{k} R_i$$

Since $\bar{\bar{x}}$ is an unbiased estimate of the population mean μ, the central line for the $\bar{x}$-chart is given by $\bar{\bar{x}}$. The statistic R does not provide an unbiased estimate of σ, but $A_2\bar{R}$ is an unbiased estimate of $\dfrac{3\sigma}{\sqrt{n}}$. The constant multiplier A_2 depends on the assumption of normality. Thus, the central line and the lower and upper three sigma limits, LCL and UCL, for an $\bar{x}$-chart (with μ and σ estimated from past date) are given by

$$\text{central line} = \bar{\bar{x}}$$
$$\text{LCL} = \bar{\bar{x}} - A_2\bar{R}$$
$$\text{UCL} = \bar{\bar{x}} + A_2\bar{R}$$

The central line and control limits of an R chart are based on the distribution of the range of samples of size n from a normal population. The mean and standard deviation of the sampling distribution of R are given by $d_2\sigma$ and $d_3\sigma$, respectively, when σ is known. Here d_2 and d_3 are constants which depend on the size of the sample. The set of control chart values for an R chart (with σ known) is given by

$$\text{central line} = d_2\sigma$$
$$\text{LCL} = D_1\sigma$$
$$\text{UCL} = D_2\sigma$$

where $D_1 = d_2 - 3d_3$ and $D_2 = d_2 + 3d_3$.

If σ is unknown, the control chart values for an R chart are given by

$$\text{central line} = \bar{R}$$
$$\text{LCL} = D_3\bar{R}$$
$$\text{UCL} = D_4\bar{R},$$

where $D_3 = \dfrac{D_1}{d_2}$ and $D_4 = \dfrac{D_2}{d_2}$.

The central line and control limits of an s-chart are based on estimates obtained from the samples. A pooled estimate of the population variance is obtained from the k samples, i.e.

$$s_p^2 = \frac{\sum_i (n_i - 1)s_i^2}{\sum_i (n_i - 1)}, \qquad i = 1, 2, \ldots, k$$

If the sample sizes are all equal, the pooled estimate is

$$s_p^2 = \frac{1}{k} \sum_i s_i^2$$

The control chart values for an s-chart are given by

$$\text{central line} = C_2' s_p$$
$$\text{LCL} = B_2' s_p$$
$$\text{UCL} = B_4' s_p$$

If one uses the biased estimator of the variance s_p', as is often done in quality control work, the control chart values are given by

$$\text{central line} = c_2 s_p'$$
$$\text{LCL} = B_2 s_p'$$
$$\text{UCL} = B_4 s_p'$$

B. Control Charts for Attributes

Control limits for a fraction-defective chart are based on the sampling theory for proportions, using the normal curve approximation to the binomial. If k samples are taken, the estimator of p is given by

$$\bar{p} = \frac{\sum_i x_i}{\sum_i n_i}, \qquad i = 1, 2, \ldots, k$$

where x_i is the number of defectives in the ith sample of size n_i. The central line and control limits of a fraction defective chart based on analysis of past data are given by

$$\text{central line} = \bar{p}$$
$$\text{LCL} = \bar{p} - 3\sqrt{\frac{\bar{p}(1 - \bar{p})}{n_i}}$$
$$\text{UCL} = \bar{p} + 3\sqrt{\frac{\bar{p}(1 - \bar{p})}{n_i}}$$

When the sample sizes are approximately equal, n_i is replaced by $\bar{n} = \frac{1}{k} \sum_i n_i$.

Equivalent to the p chart for the fraction defective is the control chart for the number of defective. Here, if p is estimated by $\bar{p}$, the control chart values for a number-of-defectives chart are given by

$$\text{central line} = \bar{n}\bar{p}$$
$$\text{LCL} = \bar{n}\bar{p} - 3\sqrt{\bar{n}\bar{p}(1 - \bar{p})}$$
$$\text{UCL} = \bar{n}\bar{p} + 3\sqrt{\bar{n}\bar{p}(1 - \bar{p})}$$

In many cases it is necessary to control the number of defects per unit C, where C is taken to be a value of a random variable having a Poisson distribution. If k is the number of units available for estimating λ, the parameter of the Poisson distribution, and if C_i is the number of defects in the ith unit, then λ is estimated by

$$\bar{C} = \frac{1}{k} \sum_{i=1}^{k} C_i$$

and the control-chart values for the C-chart are

$$\text{central line} = \bar{C}$$
$$\text{LCL} = \bar{C} - 3\sqrt{\bar{C}}$$
$$\text{UCL} = \bar{C} + 3\sqrt{\bar{C}}$$

This table presents values of the factors for computing control limits for various sample sizes n.

Number of observations in sample, n	$\bar{X}$ chart		R chart			s chart			$\hat{\sigma}$ chart (biased)		
	Factors for control limits		Factor for central line	Factors for control limits		Factor for central line	Factors for control limits		Factor for central line	Factors for control limits	
	A	A_2	d_2	D_3	D_4	c_2'	B_2'	B_4'	c_2	B_2	B_4
2	2.121	1.880	1.128	0	3.267	0.798	0	2.298	0.5642	0	3.267
3	1.732	1.023	1.693	0	2.575	0.886	0	2.111	0.7236	0	2.568
4	1.500	0.729	2.059	0	2.282	0.921	0	1.982	0.7979	0	2.266
5	1.342	0.577	2.326	0	2.115	0.940	0	1.889	0.8407	0	2.089
6	1.225	0.483	2.534	0	2.004	0.951	0.085	1.817	0.8686	0.030	1.970
7	1.134	0.419	2.704	0.076	1.924	0.960	0.158	1.762	0.8882	0.118	1.882
8	1.061	0.373	2.847	0.136	1.864	0.965	0.215	1.715	0.9027	0.185	1.815
9	1.000	0.337	2.970	0.184	1.816	0.969	0.262	1.676	0.9139	0.239	1.761
10	0.949	0.308	3.078	0.223	1.777	0.973	0.302	1.644	0.9227	0.284	1.716
11	0.905	0.285	3.173	0.256	1.744	0.976	0.336	1.616	0.9300	0.321	1.679
12	0.866	0.266	3.258	0.284	1.716	0.977	0.365	1.589	0.9359	0.354	1.646
13	0.832	0.249	3.336	0.308	1.692	0.980	0.392	1.568	0.9410	0.382	1.618
14	0.802	0.235	3.407	0.329	1.671	0.981	0.414	1.548	0.9453	0.406	1.594
15	0.775	0.223	3.472	0.348	1.652	0.982	0.434	1.530	0.9490	0.428	1.572
16	0.750	0.212	3.532	0.364	1.636	0.984	0.454	1.514	0.9523	0.448	1.552
17	0.728	0.203	3.588	0.379	1.621	0.984	0.469	1.499	0.9551	0.466	1.534
18	0.707	0.194	3.640	0.392	1.608	0.986	0.486	1.486	0.9576	0.482	1.518
19	0.688	0.187	3.689	0.404	1.596	0.986	0.500	1.472	0.9599	0.497	1.503
20	0.671	0.180	3.735	0.414	1.586	0.987	0.513	1.461	0.9619	0.510	1.490
21	0.655	0.173	3.778	0.425	1.575	0.988	0.525	1.451	0.9638	0.523	1.477
22	0.640	0.167	3.819	0.434	1.566	0.988	0.536	1.440	0.9655	0.534	1.466
23	0.626	0.162	3.858	0.443	1.557	0.989	0.546	1.432	0.9670	0.545	1.455
24	0.612	0.157	3.895	0.452	1.548	0.989	0.556	1.422	0.9684	0.555	1.445
25	0.600	0.153	3.931	0.459	1.541	0.990	0.566	1.414	0.9696	0.565	1.435

XIII. FINANCIAL TABLES

INTEREST TABLES FROM ¼% TO 20%

SIMPLE INTEREST

If P is the principal placed at interest at a rate i (expressed as a decimal), for a period of n years

The amount,

$$A = P (1 + ni)$$

Present value,

$$P = \frac{A}{1 + ni}$$

COMPOUND INTEREST

At interest compounded annually the **amount,—**

$$A = P (1 + i)^n$$

At interest compounded q times per year,—

$$A = P \left(1 + \frac{i}{q}\right)^{nq}$$

At interest compounded annually the **present value,—**

$$P = \frac{A}{(1 + i)^n} = A (1 + i)^{-n} = Av^n. \quad v = \frac{1}{1 + i}$$

At interest compounded q times per year,—

$$P = A \left(1 + \frac{i}{q}\right)^{-nq}$$

* The **amount of an annuity of 1 per annum,—**

$$s_{\overline{n}|i} = \frac{(1 + i)^n - 1}{i}$$

* The **present value of an annuity,—**

$$a_{\overline{n}|i} = \frac{1 - (1 + i)^{-n}}{i}$$

The **annuity whose present value is 1,—**

$$\frac{1}{a_{\overline{n}|i}} = \frac{1}{s_{\overline{n}|i}} + i = \frac{i}{(1 - v^n)}$$

Compound amount of 1 for fractional periods,—$(1+i)^{1/p}$

* This information can be constructed by use of tables $(1 + i)^n$ and $(1 + i)^{-n}$ as may be observed from the formula structures. For example $s_{\overline{50}|.07} = \dfrac{(1.07)^{50} - 1}{.07}$. Here $(1.07)^{50}$ is obtained from the entries under $(1 + i)^n$, where $i = .07$ and $n = 50$ and is equal to 29.45702506. Accordingly $s_{\overline{50}|.07} = \dfrac{28.45702506}{.07} = 406.528929$ Similarly $a_{\overline{n}|}$, may be evaluated by use of entries for $(1 + i)^{-n}$ and carrying out the appropriate arithmetic.

AMOUNT AT COMPOUND INTEREST $(1 + i)^{n}$*

The following table gives the amount after a term of n periods on unit original principal at rate of interest i.

Periods	Rate i				
n	0.0025(1/4%)	0.004167(5/12%)	0.005(1/2%)	0.005833(7/12%)	0.0075(3/4%)
1	1.00250000	1.00416667	1.00500000	1.00583333	1.00750000
2	1.00500625	1.00835069	1.01002500	1.01170069	1.01505625
3	1.00751877	1.01255216	1.01507513	1.01760228	1.02266917
4	1.01003756	1.01677112	1.02015050	1.02353830	1.03033919
5	1.01256266	1.02100767	1.02525125	1.02950894	1.03806673
6	1.01509406	1.02526187	1.03037751	1.03551440	1.04585224
7	1.01763180	1.02953379	1.03552940	1.04155490	1.05369613
8	1.02017588	1.03382352	1.04070704	1.04763064	1.06159885
9	1.02272632	1.03813111	1.04591058	1.05374182	1.06956084
10	1.02528313	1.04245666	1.05114013	1.05988865	1.07758255
11	1.02784634	1.04680023	1.05639583	1.06607133	1.08566441
12	1.03041596	1.05116190	1.06167781	1.07229008	1.09380690
13	1.03299200	1.05554174	1.06698620	1.07854511	1.10201045
14	1.03557448	1.05993983	1.07232113	1.08483662	1.11027553
15	1.03816341	1.06435625	1.07768274	1.09116483	1.11860259
16	1.04075882	1.06879106	1.08307115	1.09752996	1.12699211
17	1.04336072	1.07324436	1.08848651	1.10393222	1.13544455
18	1.04596912	1.07771621	1.09392894	1.11037182	1.14396039
19	1.04858404	1.08220670	1.09939858	1.11684899	1.15254009
20	1.05120550	1.08671589	1.10489558	1.12336395	1.16118414
21	1.05383352	1.09124387	1.11042006	1.12991690	1.16989302
22	1.05646810	1.09579072	1.11597216	1.13650808	1.17866722
23	1.05910927	1.10035652	1.12155202	1.14313771	1.18750723
24	1.06175704	1.10494134	1.12715978	1.14980602	1.19641353
25	1.06441144	1.10954526	1.13279558	1.15651322	1.20538663
26	1.06707247	1.11416836	1.13845955	1.16325955	1.21442703
27	1.06974015	1.11881073	1.14415185	1.17004523	1.22353523
28	1.07241450	1.12347244	1.14987261	1.17687049	1.23271175
29	1.07509553	1.12815358	1.15562197	1.18373557	1.24195709
30	1.07778327	1.13285422	1.16140008	1.19064069	1.25127176
31	1.08047773	1.13757444	1.16720708	1.19758610	1.26065630
32	1.08317892	1.14231434	1.17304312	1.20457202	1.27011122
33	1.08588687	1.14707398	1.17890833	1.21159869	1.27963706
34	1.08860159	1.15185346	1.18480288	1.21866634	1.28923434
35	1.09132309	1.15665284	1.19072689	1.22577523	1.29890359
36	1.09405140	1.16147223	1.19668052	1.23292559	1.30864537
37	1.09678653	1.16631170	1.20266393	1.24011765	1.31846021
38	1.09952850	1.17117133	1.20867725	1.24735167	1.32834866
39	1.10227732	1.17605121	1.21472063	1.25462789	1.33831128
40	1.10503301	1.18095142	1.22079424	1.26194655	1.34834861
41	1.10779559	1.18587206	1.22689821	1.26930791	1.35846123
42	1.11056508	1.19081319	1.23303270	1.27671220	1.36864969
43	1.11334149	1.19577491	1.23919786	1.28415969	1.37891456
44	1.11612485	1.20075731	1.24539385	1.29165062	1.38925642
45	1.11891516	1.20576046	1.25162082	1.29918525	1.39967584
46	1.12171245	1.21078446	1.25787892	1.30676383	1.41017341
47	1.12451673	1.21582940	1.26416832	1.31438662	1.42074971
48	1.12732802	1.22089536	1.27048916	1.32205388	1.43140533
49	1.13014634	1.22598242	1.27684161	1.32976586	1.44214087
50	1.13297171	1.23109068	1.28322581	1.33752283	1.45295693

*The $A_{n\,\neg i}$ table may be constructed from this table by use of the formula $\dfrac{(1 + i)^{n} - 1}{i}$

See page 587.

AMOUNT AT COMPOUND INTEREST $(1 + i)^n$ (Continued)

Periods n	0.0025(1/4%)	0.004167(5/12%)	0.005(1/2%)	0.005833(7/12%)	0.0075(3/4%)
51	1.13580414	1.23622022	1.28964194	1.34532504	1.46385411
52	1.23864365	1.24137114	1.29609014	1.35317277	1.47483301
53	1.14149026	1.24654352	1.30257060	1.36106628	1.48589426
54	1.14434398	1.25173745	1.30908346	1.36900583	1.49703847
55	1.14720484	1.25695302	1.31562887	1.37699170	1.50826626
56	1.15007285	1.26219033	1.32220702	1.38502415	1.51957825
57	1.15294804	1.26744946	1.32881805	1.39310346	1.53097509
58	1.15583041	1.27273050	1.33546214	1.40122990	1.54245740
59	1.15871998	1.27803354	1.34213946	1.40940374	1.55402583
60	1.16161678	1.28335868	1.34885015	1.41762526	1.56568103
61	1.16452082	1.28870601	1.35559440	1.42589474	1.57742363
62	1.16743213	1.29407561	1.36237238	1.43421246	1.58925431
63	1.17035071	1.29946760	1.36918424	1.44257870	1.60117372
64	1.17327658	1.30488204	1.37603016	1.45099374	1.61318252
65	1.17620977	1.31031905	1.38291031	1.45945787	1.62528139
66	1.17915030	1.31577872	1.38982486	1.46797138	1.63747100
67	1.18209817	1.32126113	1.39677399	1.47653454	1.64975203
68	1.18505342	1.32676638	1.40375785	1.48514766	1.66212517
69	1.18801605	1.33229458	1.41077664	1.49381102	1.67459111
70	1.19098609	1.33784580	1.41783053	1.50252492	1.68715055
71	1.19396356	1.34342016	1.42491968	1.51128965	1.69980418
72	1.19694847	1.34901774	1.43204428	1.52010550	1.71255271
73	1.19994084	1.35463865	1.43920450	1.52897279	1.72539685
74	1.20294069	1.36028298	1.44640052	1.53789179	1.73833733
75	1.20594804	1.36595082	1.45363252	1.54686283	1.75137486
76	1.20896291	1.37164229	1.46090069	1.55588620	1.76451017
77	1.21198532	1.37735746	1.46820519	1.56496220	1.77774400
78	1.21501528	1.38309645	1.47554622	1.57409115	1.79107708
79	1.21805282	1.38885935	1.48292395	1.58327334	1.80451915
80	1.22109795	1.39464627	1.49033857	1.59250910	1.81804398
81	1.22415070	1.40045729	1.49779026	1.60179874	1.83167931
82	1.22721108	1.40629253	1.50527921	1.61114257	1.84541691
83	1.23027910	1.41215209	1.51280561	1.62054090	1.85925753
84	1.23335480	1.41803605	1.52036964	1.62999405	1.87320196
85	1.23643819	1.42394454	1.52797148	1.63950235	1.88725098
86	1.23952928	1.42987764	1.53561134	1.64906612	1.90140536
87	1.24262811	1.43583546	1.54328940	1.65868567	1.91566590
88	1.24573468	1.44181811	1.55100585	1.66836134	1.93003339
89	1.24884901	1.44782568	1.55876087	1.67809344	1.94450865
90	1.25197114	1.45385829	1.56655468	1.68788232	1.95909246
91	1.25510106	1.45991603	1.57438745	1.69772830	1.97378565
92	1.25823882	1.46599902	1.58225939	1.70763172	1.98858905
93	1.26138441	1.47210735	1.59017069	1.71759290	2.00350346
94	1.26453787	1.47824113	1.59812154	1.72761219	2.01852974
95	1.26769922	1.48440047	1.60611215	1.73768993	2.03366871
96	1.27086847	1.49058547	1.61414271	1.74782646	2.04892123
97	1.27404564	1.49679624	1.62221342	1.75802211	2.06428814
98	1.27723075	1.50303289	1.63032449	1.76827724	2.07977030
99	1.28042383	1.50929553	1.63847611	1.77859219	2.09536858
100	1.28362489	1.51558426	1.64666849	1.78896731	2.11108384

AMOUNT AT COMPOUND INTEREST $(1 + i)^n$ (Continued)

Periods			Rate i		
n	0.01(1%)	0.001125(1 1/8%)	0.0125(1 1/4%)	0.015(1 1/2%)	0.0175(1 3/4%)
1	1.01000000	1.01125000	1.01250000	1.01500000	1.01750000
2	1.02010000	1.02262656	1.02515625	1.03022500	1.03530625
3	1.03030100	1.03413111	1.03797070	1.04567838	1.05342411
4	1.04060401	1.04576509	1.05094534	1.06136355	1.07185903
5	1.05101005	1.05752994	1.06408215	1.07728400	1.09061656
6	1.06152015	1.06942716	1.07738318	1.09344326	1.10970235
7	1.07213535	1.08145821	1.09085047	1.10984491	1.12912215
8	1.08285671	1.09362462	1.10448610	1.12649259	1.14888178
9	1.09368527	1.10592789	1.11829218	1.14338998	1.16898721
10	1.10462213	1.11836958	1.13227083	1.16054083	1.18944449
11	1.11566835	1.13095124	1.14642422	1.17794894	1.21025977
12	1.12682503	1.14367444	1.16075452	1.19561817	1.23143931
13	1.13809328	1.15654078	1.17526390	1.21355244	1.25298950
14	1.14947421	1.16955186	1.18995475	1.23175573	1.27491682
15	1.16096896	1.18270932	1.20482918	1.25023207	1.29722786
16	1.17257864	1.19601480	1.21988955	1.26898555	1.31992935
17	1.18430443	1.20946997	1.23513741	1.28802033	1.34302811
18	1.19614748	1.22307650	1.25057739	1.30734064	1.36653111
19	1.20810895	1.23683611	1.26620961	1.32695075	1.39044540
20	1.22019004	1.25075052	1.28203723	1.34685501	1.41477820
21	1.23239194	1.26482146	1.29806270	1.36705783	1.43953681
22	1.24471586	1.27905071	1.31428848	1.38756370	1.46472871
23	1.25716302	1.29344003	1.33071709	1.40837715	1.49036146
24	1.26973465	1.30799123	1.34735105	1.42950281	1.51644279
25	1.28243200	1.32270613	1.36419294	1.45094535	1.54298054
26	1.29525631	1.33758657	1.38124535	1.47270953	1.56998269
27	1.30820888	1.35263442	1.39851092	1.49480018	1.59745739
28	1.32129097	1.46785156	1.41599230	1.51722218	1.62541290
29	1.33450388	1.38323989	1.43369221	1.53998051	1.65385762
30	1.34784892	1.39880134	1.45161336	1.56308022	1.68280013
31	1.36132740	1.41453785	1.46975853	1.58652642	1.71224913
32	1.37494068	1.43045140	1.48813051	1.61032432	1.74221349
33	1.38869009	1.44654398	1.50673214	1.63447918	1.77270223
34	1.40257699	1.46281760	1.52556629	1.65899637	1.80372452
35	1.41660276	1.47927430	1.54463587	1.68388132	1.83528970
36	1.43076878	1.49591613	1.56394382	1.70913954	1.86740727
37	1.44507647	1.51274519	1.58349312	1.73477663	1.90008689
38	1.45952724	1.52976357	1.60328678	1.76079828	1.93333841
39	1.47412251	1.54697341	1.62332787	1.78721025	1.96717184
40	1.48886373	1.56437687	1.64361946	1.81401841	2.00159734
41	1.50375237	1.58197611	1.66416471	1.84122868	2.03662530
42	1.51878989	1.59977334	1.68496677	1.86884712	2.07226624
43	1.53397779	1.61777079	1.70602885	1.89687982	2.10853090
44	1.54931757	1.63597071	1.72735421	1.92533302	2.14543019
45	1.56481075	1.65437538	1.74894614	1.95421301	2.18297522
46	1.58045885	1.67298710	1.77080797	1.98352621	2.22117728
47	1.59626344	1.69180821	1.79294306	2.01327910	2.26004789
48	1.61222608	1.71084105	1.81535485	2.04347829	2.29959872
49	1.62834834	1.73008801	1.83804679	2.07413046	2.33984170
50	1.64463182	1.74955150	1.86102237	2.10524242	2.38078893

AMOUNT AT COMPOUND INTEREST $(1 + i)^n$ (Continued)

Periods n	0.01(1%)	0.001125(1 1/8%)	0.0125(1 1/4%)	0.015(1 1/2%)	0.0175(1 3/4%)
			Rate i		
51	1.66107814	1.76923395	1.88428515	2.13682106	2.42245274
52	1.67768892	1.78913784	1.90783872	2.16887337	2.46484566
53	1.69446581	1.80926564	1.93168670	2.20140647	2.50798046
54	1.71141047	1.82961988	1.95583279	2.23442757	2.55187012
55	1.72852457	1.85020310	1.98028070	2.26794398	2.59652785
56	1.74580982	1.87101788	2.00503420	2.30196314	2.64196708
57	1.76326792	1.89206684	2.03009713	2.33649259	2.68820151
58	1.78090060	1.91335259	2.05547335	2.37153998	2.73524503
59	1.79870960	1.93487780	2.08116676	2.40711308	2.78311182
60	1.81669670	1.95664518	2.10718135	2.44321978	2.83181628
61	1.83486367	1.97865744	2.13352111	2.47986807	2.88137306
62	1.85321230	2.00091733	2.16019013	2.51706609	2.93179709
63	1.87174443	2.02342765	2.18719250	2.55482208	2.98310354
64	1.89046187	2.04619121	2.21453241	2.59314442	3.03530785
65	1.90936649	2.06921087	2.24221407	2.63204158	3.08842574
66	1.92846015	2.09248949	2.27024174	2.67152221	3.14247319
67	1.94774475	2.11602999	2.29861976	2.71159504	3.19746647
68	1.96722220	2.13983533	2.32735251	2.75226896	3.25342213
69	1.98689442	2.16390848	2.35644442	2.79355300	3.31035702
70	2.00676337	2.18825245	2.38589997	2.83545629	3.36828827
71	2.02683100	2.21287029	2.41572372	2.87798814	3.42723331
72	2.04709931	2.23776508	2.44592027	2.92115696	3.48720990
73	2.06757031	2.26293994	2.47649427	2.96497533	3.54823607
74	2.08824601	2.28839801	2.50745045	3.00944996	3.61033020
75	2.10912847	2.31414249	2.53879358	3.05459171	3.67351098
76	2.13021975	2.34017659	2.57052850	3.10041059	3.73779742
77	2.15152195	2.36650358	2.60266011	3.14691674	3.80320888
78	2.17303717	2.39312675	2.63519336	3.19412050	3.86976503
79	2.19476754	2.42004942	2.66813327	3.24203230	3.93748592
80	2.21671522	2.44727498	2.70148494	3.29066279	4.00639192
81	2.23888237	2.47480682	2.73525350	3.34002273	4.07650378
82	2.26127119	2.50264840	2.76944417	3.39012307	4.14784260
83	2.28388390	2.53080319	2.80406222	3.44097492	4.22042984
84	2.30672274	2.55927473	2.83911300	3.49258954	4.29428737
85	2.32978997	2.58806657	2.87460191	3.54497838	4.36943740
86	2.35308787	2.61718232	2.91053444	3.59815306	4.44590255
87	2.37661875	2.64662562	2.94691612	3.65212535	4.52370584
88	2.40038494	2.67640016	2.98375257	3.70690723	4.60287070
89	2.42438879	2.70650966	3.02104948	3.76251084	4.68342093
90	2.44863267	2.73695789	3.05881260	3.81894851	4.76538080
91	2.47311900	2.76774867	3.09704775	3.87623273	4.84877496
92	2.49785019	2.79888584	3.13576085	3.93437622	4.93362853
93	2.52282869	2.83037331	3.17495786	3.99339187	5.01996703
94	2.54805698	2.86221501	3.21464483	4.05329275	5.10781645
95	2.57353755	2.89441492	3.25482789	4.11409214	5.19720324
96	2.59927293	2.92697709	3.29551324	4.17580352	5.28815429
97	2.62526565	2.95990559	3.33670716	4.23844057	5.38069699
98	2.65151831	2.99320452	3.37841600	4.30201718	5.47485919
99	2.67803349	3.02687807	3.42064620	4.36654744	5.57066923
100	2.70481383	3.06093045	3.46340427	4.43204565	5.66815594

AMOUNT AT COMPOUND INTEREST $(1 + i)^n$ (Continued)

Periods n	Rate i			
	0.02(2%)	0.0225(2 1/4%)	0.025(2 1/2%)	0.0275(2 3/4%)
1	1.02000000	1.02250000	1.02500000	1.02750000
2	1.04040000	1.04550625	1.05062500	1.05575625
3	1.06120800	1.06903014	1.07689063	1.08478955
4	1.08243216	1.09308332	1.10381289	1.11462126
5	1.10408080	1.11767769	1.13140821	1.14527334
6	1.12616242	1.14282544	1.15969342	1.17676836
7	1.14868567	1.16853901	1.18868575	1.20912949
8	1.17165938	1.19483114	1.21840290	1.24238055
9	1.19509257	1.22171484	1.24886297	1.27654602
10	1.21899442	1.24920343	1.28008454	1.31165103
11	1.24337431	1.27731050	1.31208666	1.34772144
12	1.26824179	1.30604999	1.34488882	1.38478378
13	1.29360663	1.33543611	1.37851104	1.42286533
14	1.31947876	1.36548343	1.41297382	1.46199413
15	1.34586834	1.39620680	1.44829817	1.50219896
16	1.37278571	1.42762146	1.48450562	1.54350944
17	1.40024142	1.45974294	1.52161826	1.58595595
18	1.42824625	1.49258716	1.55965872	1.62956973
19	1.45681117	1.52617037	1.59865019	1.67438290
20	1.48594740	1.56050920	1.63861644	1.72042843
21	1.51566634	1.59562066	1.67958185	1.76774021
22	1.54597967	1.63152212	1.72157140	1.81635307
23	1.57689926	1.66823137	1.76461068	1.86630278
24	1.60843725	1.70576658	1.80872595	1.91762610
25	1.64060599	1.74414632	1.85394410	1.97036082
26	1.67341811	1.78338962	1.90029270	2.02454575
27	1.70688648	1.82351588	1.94780002	2.08022075
28	1.74102421	1.86454499	1.99649602	2.13742682
29	1.77584469	1.90649725	2.04640739	2.19620606
30	1.81136158	1.94939344	2.09756758	2.25660173
31	1.84758882	1.99325479	2.15000677	2.31865828
32	1.88454059	2.03810303	2.20375694	2.38242138
33	1.92223140	2.08396034	2.25885086	2.44793797
34	1.96067603	2.13084945	2.31532213	2.51525626
35	1.99988955	2.17879356	2.37320519	2.58442581
36	2.03988734	2.22781642	2.43253532	2.65549752
37	2.08068509	2.27794229	2.49334870	2.72852370
38	2.12229879	2.32919599	2.55568242	2.80355810
39	2.16474477	2.38160290	2.61957448	2.88065595
40	2.20803966	2.43518897	2.68506384	2.95987399
41	2.25220046	2.48998072	2.75219043	3.04127052
42	2.29724447	2.54600528	2.82099520	3.12490546
43	2.34318936	2.60329040	2.89152008	3.21084036
44	2.39005214	2.66186444	2.96380808	3.29913847
45	2.43785421	2.72175639	3.03790328	3.38986478
46	2.48661129	2.78299590	3.11385086	3.48308606
47	2.53634352	2.84561331	3.19169713	3.57887093
48	2.58707039	2.90963961	3.27148956	3.67728988
49	2.63881179	2.97510650	3.35327680	3.77841535
50	2.69158803	3.04204640	3.43710872	3.88232177

AMOUNT AT COMPOUND INTEREST $(1 + i)^n$ (Continued)

Periods n	0.02(2%)	0.0225(2 1/4%)	0.025(2 1/2%)	0.0275(2 3/4%)
51	2.74541979	3.11049244	3.52303644	3.98908562
52	2.80032819	3.18047852	3.61111235	4.09878547
53	2.85633475	3.25203929	3.70139016	4.21150208
54	2.91346144	3.32521017	3.79392491	4.32721838
55	2.97173067	3.40002740	3.88877303	4.44631964
56	3.03116529	3.47652802	3.98599236	4.56859343
57	3.09178859	3.55474990	4.08564217	4.69422975
58	3.15362436	3.63473177	4.18778322	4.82332107
59	3.21669685	3.71651324	4.29247780	4.95596239
60	3.28103079	3.80013479	4.39978975	5.09225136
61	3.34665140	3.88563782	4.50978449	5.23228827
62	3.41358443	3.97306467	4.62252910	5.37617620
63	3.48185612	4.06245862	4.73809233	5.52402105
64	3.55149324	4.15386394	4.85654464	5.67593162
65	3.62252311	4.24732588	4.97795826	5.83201974
66	3.69497357	4.34289071	5.10240721	5.99240029
67	3.76887304	4.44060576	5.22996739	6.15719130
68	3.84425050	4.54051939	5.36071658	6.32651406
69	3.92113551	4.64268107	5.49473449	6.50049319
70	3.99955822	4.74714140	5.63210286	6.67925676
71	4.07954939	4.85395208	5.77290543	6.86293632
72	4.16114038	4.96316600	5.91722806	7.05166706
73	4.24436318	5.07483723	6.06515876	7.24558791
74	4.32925045	5.18902107	6.21678773	7.44484158
75	4.41583546	5.30577405	6.37220743	7.64957472
76	4.50415216	5.42515396	6.53151261	7.85993802
77	4.59423521	5.54721993	6.69480043	8.07608632
78	4.68611991	5.67203237	6.86217044	8.29817869
79	4.77984231	5.79965310	7.03372470	8.52637861
80	4.87543916	5.93014530	7.20956782	8.76085402
81	4.97294794	6.06357357	7.38980701	9.00177751
82	5.07240690	6.20000397	7.57455219	9.24932639
83	5.17385504	6.33950406	7.76391599	9.50368286
84	5.27733214	6.48214290	7.95801389	9.76503414
85	5.38287878	6.62799112	8.15695424	10.03357258
86	5.49053636	6.77712092	8.36088834	10.30949583
87	5.60034708	6.92960614	8.56991055	10.59300696
88	5.71235402	7.08552228	8.78415832	10.88421465
89	5.82660110	7.24494653	9.00376228	11.18363331
90	5.94313313	7.40795782	9.22885633	11.49118322
91	6.06199579	7.57463688	9.45957774	11.80719076
92	6.18323570	7.74506621	9.69606718	12.13188851
93	6.30690042	7.91933020	9.93846886	12.46551544
94	6.43303843	8.09751512	10.18693058	12.80831711
95	6.56169920	8.27970921	10.44160385	13.16054584
96	6.69293318	8.46600267	10.70264395	13.52246085
97	6.82679184	8.65648773	10.97021004	13.89432852
98	6.96332768	8.85125871	11.24446530	14.27642255
99	7.10359423	9.05041203	11.52557693	14.66902417
100	7.24464612	9.25404630	11.81371635	15.07242234

AMOUNT AT COMPOUND INTEREST $(1 + i)^n$ (Continued)

Periods	Rate i			
n	0.03(3%)	0.0325(3 1/4%)	0.035(3 1/2%)	0.0375(3 3/4%)
1	1.03000000	1.03250000	1.03500000	1.03750000
2	1.06090000	1.06605625	1.07122500	1.07640625
3	1.09272700	1.10070308	1.10871788	1.11677148
4	1.12550881	1.13647593	1.14752300	1.15865042
5	1.15927407	1.17341140	1.18768631	1.20209981
6	1.19405230	1.21154727	1.22925533	1.24717855
7	1.22987387	1.25092255	1.27227926	1.29394774
8	1.26677008	1.29157754	1.31680904	1.34247078
9	1.30477318	1.33355381	1.36289735	1.39281344
10	1.34391638	1.37689430	1.41059876	1.44504394
11	1.38423387	1.42164337	1.45996972	1.49923309
12	1.42576089	1.46784678	1.51106866	1.55545433
13	1.46853371	1.51555180	1.56395606	1.61378387
14	1.51258972	1.56480723	1.61869452	1.67430076
15	1.55796742	1.61566347	1.67534883	1.73708704
16	1.60470644	1.66817253	1.73398604	1.80222781
17	1.65284763	1.72238814	1.79467555	1.86981135
18	1.70243306	1.77836575	1.85748920	1.93992927
19	1.75350605	1.83616264	1.92250132	2.01267662
20	1.80611123	1.89583792	1.98978886	2.08815200
21	1.86029457	1.95745266	2.05943147	2.16645770
22	1.91610341	2.02106987	2.13151158	2.24769986
23	1.97358651	2.08675464	2.20611448	2.33198860
24	2.03279411	2.15457416	2.28332849	2.41943818
25	2.09377793	2.22459782	2.36324498	2.51016711
26	2.15659127	2.29689725	2.44595856	2.60429838
27	2.22128901	2.37154641	2.53156711	2.70195956
28	2.28792768	2.44862167	2.62017196	2.80328305
29	2.35656551	2.52820188	2.71187798	2.90840616
30	2.42726247	2.61036844	2.80679370	3.01747139
31	2.50008035	2.69520541	2.90503148	3.13062657
32	2.57508276	2.78279959	2.00670759	3.24802507
33	2.65233524	2.87324058	3.11194235	3.36982601
34	2.73190530	2.96662089	3.22086033	3.49619448
35	2.81386245	3.06303607	3.33359045	3.62730178
36	2.89827833	2.16258475	3.45026611	3.76332559
37	2.98522668	3.26536875	3.57102543	3.90445030
38	3.07478348	3.37149323	3.69601132	4.05086719
39	3.16702698	3.48106676	3.82537171	4.20277471
40	3.26203779	3.59420143	3.95925972	4.36037876
41	3.35989893	3.71101298	4.09783381	4.52389296
42	3.46069589	3.83162090	4.24125799	4.69353895
43	3.56451677	3.95614858	4.38970202	4.86954666
44	3.67145227	4.08472341	4.54334160	5.05215466
45	3.78159584	4.21747692	4.70235855	5.24161046
46	3.89504372	4.35454492	4.86694110	5.43817085
47	4.01189503	4.49606763	5.03728404	5.64210226
48	4.13225188	4.64218983	5.21358898	5.85368109
49	4.25621944	4.79306100	5.39606459	6.07319413
50	4.38390602	4.94883548	5.58492686	6.30093891

AMOUNT AT COMPOUND INTEREST $(1 + i)^n$ (Continued)

Periods n	Rate i			
	0.04(4%)	0.0425(4 1/4%)	0.045(4 1/2%)	0.0475(4 3/4%)
1	1.04000000	1.04250000	1.04500000	1.04750000
2	1.08160000	1.08680625	1.09202500	1.09725625
3	1.12486490	1.13299552	1.14116613	1.14937592
4	1.16985856	1.18114783	1.19251860	1.20397128
5	1.21665290	1.23134661	1.24618194	1.26115991
6	1.26531902	1.28367884	1.30226012	1.32106501
7	1.31593178	1.33823519	1.36086183	1.38381560
8	1.36856905	1.39511018	1.42210061	1.44954684
9	1.42331181	1.45440237	1.48609514	1.51840031
10	1.48024428	1.51621447	1.55296942	1.59052433
11	1.53945406	1.58065358	1.62285305	1.66607423
12	1.60103222	1.64783136	1.69588143	1.74521276
13	1.66507351	1.71786419	1.77219610	1.82811037
14	1.73167645	1.79087342	1.85194492	1.91494561
15	1.80094351	1.86698554	1.93528244	2.00590552
16	1.87298125	1.94633243	2.02237015	2.10118604
17	1.94790050	2.02905156	2.11337681	2.20099237
18	2.02581652	2.11528625	2.20847877	2.30553951
19	2.10684918	2.20518591	2.30786031	2.41505264
20	2.19112314	2.29890631	2.41171402	2.52976764
21	2.27876807	2.39660983	2.52024116	2.64993160
22	2.36991879	2.49846575	2.63365201	2.77580335
23	2.46471554	2.60465054	2.75216635	2.90765401
24	2.56330416	2.71534819	2.87601383	2.04576758
25	2.66583633	2.83075049	3.00543446	3.19044154
26	2.77246978	2.95105739	3.14067901	3.34198751
27	2.88336858	3.07647732	3.28200956	3.50073192
28	2.99870332	3.20722761	3.42969999	3.66701668
29	3.11865145	3.34353478	3.58403649	3.84119998
30	3.24339751	3.48563501	3.74531813	4.02365698
31	3.37313341	3.63377450	3.91385745	4.21478068
32	3.50805875	3.78820992	4.08998104	4.41498276
33	3.64838110	3.94920884	4.27403018	4.62469445
34	3.79431634	4.11705021	4.46636154	4.84436743
35	3.94608899	4.29202485	4.66734781	5.07447488
36	4.10393255	4.47443590	4.87737846	5.31551244
37	4.26808986	4.66459943	5.09686049	5.56799928
38	4.43881345	4.86284491	5.32621921	5.83247925
39	4.61636599	5.06951581	5.56589908	6.10952201
40	4.80102063	5.28497024	5.81636454	6.39972431
41	4.99306145	5.50958147	6.07810094	6.70371121
42	5.19278391	5.74373868	6.35161548	7.02213750
43	5.40049527	5.98784758	6.63743818	7.35568903
44	5.61651508	6.24233110	6.93612290	7.70508426
45	5.84117568	6.50763017	7.24824843	8.07107576
46	6.07482271	6.78420445	7.57441961	8.45445186
47	6.31781562	7.07253314	7.91526849	8.85603832
48	6.57052824	7.37311580	8.27145557	9.27670014
49	6.83334937	7.68647322	8.64367107	9.71734340
50	7.10668335	8.01314834	9.03263627	10.17891721

AMOUNT AT COMPOUND INTEREST $(1 + i)^n$ (Continued)

Periods n	Rate i			
	0.05(5%)	0.0525(5 1/4%)	0.055(5 1/2%)	0.0575(5 3/4%)
1	1.05000000	1.05250000	1.05500000	1.05750000
2	1.10250000	1.10775625	1.11302500	1.11830625
3	1.15762500	1.16591345	1.17424138	1.18260886
4	1.21550625	1.22712391	1.23882465	1.25060887
5	1.27628156	1.29154791	1.30696001	1.32251888
6	1.34009564	1.35935418	1.37884281	1.39856371
7	1.40710042	1.43072027	1.45467916	1.47898113
8	1.47745544	1.50583309	1.53468651	1.56402254
9	1.55132822	1.58488933	1.61909427	1.65395384
10	1.62889463	1.66809602	1.70814446	1.74905618
11	1.71033936	1.75567106	1.80209240	1.84962692
12	1.79585633	1.84784379	1.90120749	1.95598046
13	1.88564914	1.94485559	2.00577390	2.06844934
14	1.97993160	2.04696050	2.11609146	2.18738518
15	2.07892818	2.15442593	2.23247649	2.31315982
16	2.18287459	2.26753329	2.35526270	2.44616651
17	2.29201832	2.38657879	2.48480215	2.58682109
18	2.40661923	2.51187418	2.62146627	2.73556330
19	2.52695020	2.64374757	2.76564691	2.89285819
20	2.65329771	2.78254432	2.91775749	3.05919754
21	2.78596259	2.92862789	3.07823415	3.23510140
22	2.92526072	2.08238086	3.24753703	3.42111973
23	3.07152376	3.24420585	3.42615157	3.61783411
24	3.22509994	3.41452666	3.61458990	3.82585957
25	3.38635494	3.59378931	3.81339235	4.04584650
26	3.55567269	3.78246325	4.02312893	4.27848267
27	3.73345632	3.98104257	4.24440102	4.52449542
28	3.92012914	4.19004731	4.47784307	4.78465391
29	4.11613560	4.41002479	4.72412444	5.05977151
30	4.32194238	4.64155109	4.98395129	5.35070837
31	4.53803949	4.88523252	5.25806861	5.65837410
32	4.76494147	5.14170723	5.54726238	5.98373061
33	5.00318854	5.41164686	5.85236181	6.32779512
34	5.25334797	5.69575832	6.17424171	6.69164334
35	5.51601537	5.99478563	6.51382501	7.07641284
36	5.79181614	6.30951188	6.87208538	7.48330657
37	6.08140694	6.64076125	7.25005008	7.91359670
38	6.38547729	6.98940122	7.64880283	8.36862851
39	6.70475115	7.35634478	8.06948699	8.84982465
40	7.03998871	7.74255288	8.51330877	9.35868957
41	7.39198815	8.14903691	8.98154076	9.89681422
42	7.76158756	8.57686135	9.47552550	10.46588104
43	8.14966693	9.02714657	9.99667940	11.06766920
44	8.55715028	9.50107176	10.54649677	11.70406018
45	8.98500779	9.99987803	11.12655409	12.37704364
46	9.43425818	10.52487163	11.73851456	13.08872365
47	9.90597109	11.07742739	12.38413287	13.84132526
48	10.40126965	11.65899232	13.06526017	14.63720146
49	10.92133313	12.27108942	13.78384948	15.47884054
50	11.46739979	12.91532162	14.54196120	16.36887387

AMOUNT AT COMPOUND INTEREST $(1 + i)^n$ (Continued)

	Rate i			
Periods n	0.06(6%)	0.0625(6 1/4%)	0.065(6 1/2%)	0.0675(6 3/4%)
1	1.06000000	1.06250000	1.06500000	1.06750000
2	1.12360000	1.12890625	1.13422500	1.13955625
3	1.19101600	1.19946289	1.20794963	1.21647630
4	1.26247696	1.27442932	1.28646635	1.29858845
5	1.33822558	1.35408115	1.37008666	1.38624317
6	1.41851911	1.43871123	1.45914230	1.47981458
7	1.50363026	1.52863068	1.55398655	1.57970207
8	1.59384807	1.62417009	1.65499567	1.68633195
9	1.68947896	1.72568073	1.76257039	1.80015936
10	1.79084770	1.83353577	1.87713747	1.92167012
11	1.89829856	1.94813176	1.99915140	2.05138285
12	2.01219647	2.06988999	2.12909624	2.18985119
13	2.13292826	2.19925812	2.26748750	2.33766615
14	2.26090396	2.33671175	2.41487418	2.49545861
15	2.39655819	2.48275623	2.57184101	2.66390207
16	2.54035168	2.63792850	2.73901067	2.84371546
17	2.69277279	2.80279903	2.91704637	3.03566625
18	2.85433915	2.97797397	3.10665438	3.24057373
19	3.02559950	3.16409734	3.30858691	3.45931245
20	3.20713547	3.36185342	3.52364506	3.69281604
21	3.39956360	3.57196926	3.75268199	3.94208113
22	3.60353742	3.79521734	3.99660632	4.20817160
23	3.81974966	4.03241843	4.25638573	4.49222319
24	4.04893464	4.28444458	4.53305081	4.79544825
25	4.29187072	4.55222236	4.82769911	5.11914101
26	4.54938296	4.83673626	5.14149955	5.46468303
27	4.82234594	5.13903228	5.47569702	5.83354913
28	5.11168670	5.46022180	5.83161733	6.22731370
29	5.41838790	5.80148566	6.21067245	6.64765737
30	5.74349117	6.16407851	6.61436616	7.90637424
31	6.08810064	6.54933342	7.04429996	7.57537950
32	6.45338668	6.95866676	7.50217946	8.08671762
33	6.84058988	7.39358343	7.98982113	8.63257106
34	7.25102528	7.85568239	8.50915950	9.21526961
35	7.68608679	8.34666254	9.06225487	9.83730031
36	8.14725200	8.86832895	9.65130143	10.50131808
37	8.63608712	9.42259951	10.27863603	11.21015705
38	9.15425235	10.01151198	10.94674737	11.96684265
39	9.70350749	10.63723148	11.65828595	12.77460453
40	10.28571794	11.30205845	12.41607453	13.63689033
41	10.90286101	12.00843710	13.22311938	14.55738043
42	11.55703267	12.75896442	14.08262214	15.54000361
43	12.25045463	13.55639970	14.99799258	16.58895385
44	12.98548191	14.40367468	15.97286209	17.70870824
45	13.76461083	15.30390434	17.01109813	18.90404604
46	14.59048748	16.26039837	18.11681951	20.18006915
47	15.46591673	17.27667326	19.29441278	21.54222382
48	16.39387173	18.35646534	20.54854961	22.99632392
49	17.37750403	19.50374443	21.88420533	24.54857579
50	18.42015427	20.72272845	23.30667868	26.20560466

AMOUNT AT COMPOUND INTEREST $(1 + i)^n$ (Continued)

Periods		Rate i		
n	0.07(7%)	0.0725(7 1/4%)	0.075(7 1/2%)	0.0775(7 3/4%)
1	1.07000000	1.07250000	1.07500000	1.07750000
2	1.14490000	1.15025625	1.15562500	1.16100625
3	1.22504300	1.23364983	1.24229687	1.25098423
4	1.31079601	1.32308944	1.33546914	1.34793551
5	1.40255173	1.41901343	1.43562933	1.45240051
6	1.50073035	1.52189190	1.54330153	1.56496155
7	1.60578148	1.63222906	1.65904914	1.68624608
8	1.71818618	1.75056567	1.78347783	1.81693015
9	1.83845921	1.87748168	1.91723866	1.95774223
10	1.96715136	2.01359910	2.06103156	2.10946726
11	2.10485195	2.15958504	2.21560893	2.27295097
12	2.25219159	2.31615495	2.38177960	2.44910467
13	2.40984500	2.48407618	2.56041307	2.63891028
14	2.57853415	2.66417171	2.75244405	2.84342583
15	2.75903154	2.85732416	2.95887735	3.06379133
16	2.95216375	3.06448016	3.18079315	3.30123516
17	3.15881521	3.28665497	3.41935264	3.55708088
18	3.37993228	3.52493745	3.67580409	3.83275465
19	3.61652754	3.78049542	3.95148940	4.12979313
20	3.86968446	4.05458134	4.24785110	4.44985210
21	4.14056237	4.34853849	4.56643993	4.79471564
22	4.43040174	4.66380753	4.90892293	5.16630610
23	4.74052986	5.00193357	5.27709215	5.56669482
24	5.07236695	5.36457375	5.67287406	5.99811367
25	5.42743264	5.75350535	6.09833961	6.46296748
26	5.80735292	6.17063449	6.55571508	6.96384746
27	6.21386763	6.61800549	7.04739371	7.50354564
28	6.64883836	7.09781089	7.57594824	8.08507043
29	7.11425705	7.61240218	8.14414436	8.71166339
30	7.61225504	8.16430134	8.75495519	9.38681730
31	8.14511290	8.75621318	9.41157683	10.11429564
32	8.71527080	9.39103864	10.11744509	10.89815355
33	9.32533975	10.07188894	10.87625347	11.74276045
34	9.97811354	10.80210089	11.69197248	12.65282439
35	10.67658148	11.58525320	12.56887042	13.63341828
36	11.42394219	12.42518406	13.51153570	14.69000819
37	12.22361814	13.32600990	14.52490088	15.82848383
38	13.07927141	14.29214562	15.61426844	17.05519132
39	13.99482041	15.32832618	16.78533858	18.37696865
40	14.97445784	16.43962983	18.04423897	19.80118372
41	16.02266989	17.63150299	19.39755689	21.33577546
42	17.14425678	18.90978696	20.85237366	22.98929806
43	18.34435475	20.28074651	22.41630168	24.77096866
44	19.62845959	21.75110063	24.09752431	26.69071873
45	21.00245176	23.32805543	25.90483863	28.75924943
46	22.47262338	25.01933945	27.84770153	30.98809126
47	24.04570702	26.83324156	29.93627915	33.38966833
48	25.72890651	28.77865157	32.18150008	35.97736763
49	27.52992997	30.86510381	34.59511259	38.76561362
50	29.45702506	33.10282384	37.18974603	41.76994868

AMOUNT AT COMPOUND INTEREST $(1 + i)^n$ (Continued)

Periods n	0.08(8%)	0.0825(8 1/4%)	0.085(8 1/2%)	0.0875(8 3/4%)
			Rate i	
1	1.08000000	1.08250000	1.08500000	1.08750000
2	1.16640000	1.17180625	1.17722500	1.18265625
3	1.25971200	1.26848027	1.27728912	1.28613867
4	1.36048896	1.37312989	1.38585870	1.39867581
5	1.46932808	1.48641310	1.50365669	1.52105994
6	1.58687432	1.60904218	1.63146751	1.65415268
7	1.71382427	1.74178816	1.77014225	1.79889104
8	1.85093021	1.88548569	1.92060434	1.95629401
9	1.99900463	2.04103826	2.08385571	2.12746974
10	2.15892500	2.20942391	2.26098344	2.31362334
11	2.33163900	2.39170139	2.45316703	2.51606538
12	2.51817012	2.58901675	2.66168623	2.73622110
13	2.71962373	2.80261063	2.88792956	2.97564045
14	2.93719362	3.03382601	3.13340357	3.23600898
15	3.17216911	3.28411666	3.39974288	3.51915977
16	3.42594264	3.55505628	3.68872102	3.82708625
17	3.70001805	3.84834842	4.00226231	4.16195630
18	3.99601950	4.16583717	4.34245461	4.52612747
19	4.31570106	4.50951873	4.71156325	4.92216363
20	4.66095714	4.88155403	5.11204612	5.35285295
21	5.03383372	5.28428224	5.54657005	5.82122758
22	5.43654041	5.72023552	6.01802850	6.33058499
23	5.87146365	6.19215495	6.52956092	6.88451118
24	6.34118074	6.70300774	7.08457360	7.48690591
25	6.84847520	7.25600587	7.68676236	8.14201017
26	7.39635321	7.85462636	8.34013716	8.85443606
27	7.98806147	8.50263303	9.04904881	9.62919922
28	8.62710639	9.20410026	9.81821796	10.47175415
29	9.31727490	9.96343853	10.65276649	11.38803264
30	10.06265689	10.78542221	11.55825164	12.38448549
31	10.86766944	11.67521954	12.54070303	13.46812797
32	11.73708300	12.63842515	13.60666279	14.64658917
33	12.67604964	13.68109523	14.76322913	15.92816573
34	13.69013361	14.80978558	16.01810360	17.32188023
35	14.78534429	16.03159290	17.37964241	18.83754475
36	15.96817184	17.35419931	18.85691201	20.48582991
37	17.24562558	18.78592075	20.45974953	22.27834003
38	18.62527563	20.33575921	22.19882824	24.22769478
39	20.11529768	22.01345935	24.08572865	26.34761807
40	21.72452150	23.82956975	26.13301558	28.65303466
41	23.46248322	25.79550925	28.35432190	31.16017519
42	25.33948187	27.92363876	30.76443927	33.88669052
43	27.36664042	30.22733896	33.37941660	36.85177594
44	29.55597166	32.72109442	36.21666702	40.07630633
45	31.92044939	35.42058471	39.29508371	43.58298314
46	34.47408534	38.34278295	42.63516583	47.39649416
47	37.23201217	41.50606255	46.25915492	51.54368740
48	40.21057314	44.93031271	50.19118309	56.05376005
49	43.42741899	48.63706351	54.45743365	60.95846405
50	46.90161251	52.64962124	59.08631551	66.29232966

AMOUNT AT COMPOUND INTEREST $(1 + i)^n$ (Continued)

Periods	Rate i			
n	0.09(9%)	0.0925(9 1/4%)	0.095(9 1/2%)	0.0975(9 3/4%)
1	1.09000000	1.09250000	1.09500000	1.09750000
2	1.18810000	1.19355625	1.19902500	1.20450625
3	1.29502900	1.30396020	1.31293237	1.32194561
4	1.41158161	1.42457652	1.43766095	1.45083531
5	1.53862395	1.55634985	1.57423874	1.59229175
6	1.67710011	1.70031221	1.72379142	1.74754019
7	1.82803912	1.85759109	1.88755161	1.91792536
8	1.99256264	2.02941827	2.06686901	2.10492309
9	2.17189328	2.21713946	2.26322156	2.31015309
10	2.36736367	2.42222486	2.47822761	2.53539301
11	2.58042641	2.64628066	2.71365924	2.78259383
12	2.81266478	2.89106162	2.97145686	3.05389673
13	3.06580461	3.15848482	3.25374527	3.35165166
14	3.34172703	3.45064466	3.56285107	3.67843770
15	3.64248246	3.76982929	3.90132192	4.03708537
16	3.97030588	4.11853850	4.27194750	4.43070120
17	4.32763341	4.49950331	4.67778251	4.86269456
18	4.71712042	4.91570737	5.12217185	5.33680728
19	5.14166125	5.37041030	5.60877818	5.85714599
20	5.60441077	5.86717325	6.14161210	6.42821773
21	6.10880774	6.40988678	6.72506525	7.05496896
22	6.65860043	7.00280131	7.36394645	7.74282843
23	7.25787447	7.65056043	8.06352137	8.49775420
24	7.91108317	8.35823727	8.82955590	9.32628524
25	8.62308066	9.13137421	9.66836371	10.23559805
26	9.39915792	9.97602633	10.58685826	11.23356886
27	10.24508213	10.89880877	11.59260979	12.32884182
28	11.16713952	11.90694858	12.69390772	13.53090390
29	12.17218208	13.00834132	13.89982896	14.85016703
30	13.26767847	14.21161289	15.22031271	16.29805832
31	14.46176953	15.52618708	16.66624241	17.88711900
32	15.76332879	16.96235939	18.24953544	19.63111310
33	17.18202838	18.53137763	19.98324131	21.54514663
34	18.72841093	20.24553006	21.88164924	23.64579843
35	20.41396792	22.11824159	23.96040591	25.95126378
36	22.25122503	24.16417894	26.23664448	28.48151199
37	24.25383528	26.39936549	28.72912570	31.25845941
38	26.43668046	28.84130680	31.45839264	34.30615921
39	28.81598170	31.50912768	34.44693994	37.65100973
40	31.40942005	34.42372199	37.71939924	41.32198318
41	34.23626786	37.60791628	41.30274216	45.35087654
42	37.31753197	41.08664853	45.22650267	49.77258700
43	40.67610984	44.88716352	49.52302042	54.62541423
44	44.33695973	49.03922615	54.22770736	59.95139212
45	48.32728610	53.57535456	59.37933956	65.79665285
46	52.67674185	58.53107486	65.02037682	72.21182650
47	57.41764862	63.94519929	71.19731262	79.25247959
48	62.58523700	69.86013022	77.96105732	86.97959635
49	68.21790833	76.32219227	85.36735777	95.46010699
50	74.35752008	83.38199505	93.47725675	104.76746742

AMOUNT AT COMPOUND INTEREST $(1 + i)^n$ (Continued)

Periods n	Rate i			
	0.10(10%)	0.105(10 1/2%)	0.11(11%)	0.115(11 1/2%)
1	1.10000000	1.10500000	1.11000000	1.11500000
2	1.21000000	1.22102500	1.23210000	1.24322500
3	1.33100000	1.34923262	1.36763100	1.38619587
4	1.46410000	1.49090205	1.51807041	1.54560840
5	1.61051000	1.64744677	1.68505816	1.72335337
6	1.77156100	1.82042868	1.87041455	1.92153900
7	1.94871710	2.01157369	2.07616015	2.14251599
8	2.14358881	2.22278892	2.30453777	2.38890533
9	2.35794769	2.45618176	2.55803692	2.66362944
10	2.59374246	2.71408085	2.83942099	2.96994683
11	2.85311671	2.99905934	3.15175729	3.31149071
12	3.13842838	3.31396057	3.49845060	3.69231214
13	3.45227121	3.66192643	3.88328016	4.11692804
14	3.79749834	4.04642870	4.31044098	4.59037476
15	4.17724817	4.47130371	4.78458949	5.11826786
16	4.59497299	4.94079060	5.31089433	5.70686867
17	5.05447028	5.45957362	5.89509271	6.36315856
18	5.55991731	6.03282885	6.54355291	7.09492180
19	6.11590904	6.66627588	7.26334373	7.91083780
20	6.72749995	7.36623484	8.06231154	8.82058415
21	7.40024994	8.13968950	8.94916581	9.83495133
22	8.14027494	8.99435690	9.93357404	10.96597073
23	8.95430243	9.93876437	11.02626719	12.22705737
24	9.84973268	10.98233463	12.23915658	13.63316896
25	10.83470594	12.13547977	13.58546380	15.20098340
26	11.91817654	13.40970514	15.07986482	16.94909649
27	13.10999419	14.81772418	16.73864995	18.89824258
28	14.42099361	16.37358522	18.57990145	21.07154048
29	15.86309297	18.09281167	20.62369061	23.49476763
30	17.44940227	19.99255690	22.89229657	26.19666591
31	19.19434250	22.09177537	25.41044919	29.20928249
32	21.11377675	24.41141178	28.20559861	32.56834998
33	23.22515442	26.97461002	31.30821445	36.31371022
34	25.54766986	29.80694407	34.75211804	40.48978690
35	28.10243685	32.93667320	38.57485103	45.14611239
36	30.91268053	36.39502389	42.81808464	50.33791532
37	34.00394859	40.21650140	47.52807395	56.12677558
38	37.40434344	44.43923404	52.75616209	62.58135477
39	41.14477779	49.10535362	58.55933991	69.77821057
40	45.25925557	54.26141575	65.00086731	77.80270479
41	49.78518112	59.95886440	72.15096271	86.75001584
42	54.76369924	66.25454516	80.08756861	96.72626766
43	60.24006916	73.21127240	88.89720115	107.84978844
44	66.26407608	80.89845601	98.67589328	120.25251411
45	72.89048369	89.39279389	109.53024154	134.08155323
46	80.17953205	98.77903724	121.57856811	149.50093186
47	88.19748526	109.15083616	134.95221060	166.69353902
48	97.01723378	120.61167395	149.79695377	185.86329601
49	106.71895716	133.27589972	166.27461868	207.23757505
50	117.39085288	147.26986919	184.56482674	231.06989618

AMOUNT AT COMPOUND INTEREST $(1 + i)^n$ (Continued)

Periods		Rate i		
n	0.12(12%)	0.125(12 1/2%)	0.13(13%)	0.135(13 1/2%)
1	1.12000000	1.12500000	1.13000000	1.13500000
2	1.25440000	1.26562500	1.27690000	1.28822500
3	1.40492800	1.42382812	1.44289700	1.46213537
4	1.57351936	1.60180664	1.63047361	1.65952365
5	1.76234168	1.80203247	1.84243518	1.88355934
6	1.97382269	2.02728653	2.08195175	2.13783985
7	2.21068141	2.28069735	2.35260548	2.42644824
8	2.47596318	2.56578451	2.65844419	2.75401875
9	2.77307876	2.88650758	3.00404194	3.12581128
10	3.10584821	3.24732103	3.39456739	3.54779580
11	3.47854999	3.65323615	3.83586115	4.02674823
12	3.89597599	4.10989067	4.33452310	4.57035924
13	4.36349311	4.62362701	4.89801110	5.18735774
14	4.88711229	5.20158038	5.53475255	5.88765104
15	5.47356576	5.85177793	6.25427038	6.68248393
16	6.13039365	6.58325017	7.06732553	7.58461926
17	6.86604089	7.40615644	7.98607785	8.60854286
18	7.68996580	8.33192600	9.02426797	9.77069614
19	8.61276169	9.37341675	10.19742280	11.08974012
20	9.64629309	10.54509384	11.52308776	12.58685504
21	10.80384826	11.86323057	13.02108917	14.28608047
22	12.10031006	13.34613439	14.71383077	16.21470134
23	13.55234726	15.01440119	16.62662877	18.40368602
24	15.17862893	16.89120134	18.78809051	20.88818363
25	17.00006441	19.00260151	21.23054227	23.70808842
26	19.04007214	21.37792670	23.99051277	26.90868035
27	21.32488079	24.05016754	27.10927943	30.54135220
28	23.88386649	27.05643848	30.63348575	34.66443475
29	26.74993047	30.43849329	34.61583890	39.34413344
30	29.95992212	34.24330495	39.11589796	44.65559145
31	33.55511278	38.52371807	44.20096469	50.68409630
32	37.58172631	43.33918283	49.94709010	57.52644930
33	42.09153347	48.75658068	56.44021181	65.29251996
34	47.14251748	54.85115327	63.77743935	74.10701015
35	52.79961958	61.70754742	72.06850647	84.11145652
36	59.13557393	69.42099085	81.43741231	95.46650315
37	66.23184280	78.09861471	92.02427591	108.35448108
38	74.17966394	87.86094155	103.98743178	122.98233602
39	83.08122361	98.84355924	117.50579791	139.58495138
40	93.05097044	111.19900415	132.78155163	158.42891982
41	104.21708689	125.09887966	150.04315335	179.81682400
42	116.72313732	140.73623962	169.54876328	204.09209523
43	130.72991380	158.32826958	191.59010251	231.64452809
44	146.41750346	178.11930327	216.49681583	262.91653938
45	163.98760387	200.38421618	244.64140189	298.41027220
46	183.66611634	225.43224320	276.44478414	338.69565895
47	205.70605030	253.61127360	312.38260608	384.41957291
48	230.39077633	285.31268280	352.99234487	436.31621525
49	258.03766949	320.97676816	398.88134970	495.21890431
50	289.00218983	361.09886417	450.73592516	562.07345639

AMOUNT AT COMPOUND INTEREST $(1 + i)^n$ (Continued)

Rate i

Periods n	0.14 (14%)	0.145 (14 1/2%)	0.15 (15%)	0.155 (15 1/2%)
1	1.14000000	1.14500000	1.15000000	1.15500000
2	1.29960000	1.31102500	1.32250000	1.33402500
3	1.48154400	1.50112362	1.52087500	1.54079887
4	1.68896016	1.71878655	1.74900625	1.77962270
5	1.92541458	1.96801060	2.01135719	2.05546422
6	2.19497262	2.25337214	2.31306077	2.37406117
7	2.50226879	2.58011110	2.66001988	2.74204066
8	2.85258642	2.95422721	3.05902286	3.16705696
9	3.25194852	3.38259015	3.51787629	3.65795078
10	3.70722131	3.87306572	4.04555774	4.22493316
11	4.22623230	4.43466025	4.65239140	4.87979780
12	4.81790482	5.07768599	5.35025011	5.63616645
13	5.49241149	5.81395046	6.15278762	6.50977225
14	6.26134910	6.65697328	7.07570576	7.51878695
15	7.13793798	7.62223440	8.13706163	8.68419893
16	8.13724930	8.72745839	9.35762087	10.03024977
17	9.27646420	9.99293985	10.76126400	11.58493848
18	10.57516918	11.44191613	12.37545361	13.38060394
19	12.05569287	13.10099397	14.23177165	15.45459756
20	13.74348987	15.00063810	16.36653739	17.85006018
21	15.66757845	17.17573062	18.82151800	20.61681950
22	17.86103944	19.66621156	21.64474570	23.81242653
23	20.36158496	22.51781224	24.89145756	27.50335264
24	23.21220685	25.78289502	28.62517619	31.76637230
25	26.46191581	29.52141479	32.91895262	36.69016000
26	30.16658403	33.80201994	37.85679551	42.37713481
27	34.38990579	38.70331283	43.53531484	48.94559070
28	39.20449260	44.31529319	50.06561207	56.53215726
29	44.69312156	50.74101070	57.57545388	65.29464163
30	50.95015858	58.09845725	66.21177196	75.41531109
31	58.08318078	66.52273355	76.14353775	87.10468431
32	66.21482609	76.16852992	87.56506841	100.60591037
33	75.48490175	87.21296676	100.69982867	116.19982648
34	86.05278799	99.85884694	115.80480298	134.21079959
35	98.10017831	114.33837974	133.17552342	155.01347352
36	111.83420328	130.91744481	153.15185194	179.04056192
37	127.49099173	149.90047430	176.12462973	206.79184901
38	145.33973058	171.63604308	202.54332419	238.84458561
39	165.68729286	196.52326932	232.92482281	275.86549638
40	188.88351386	225.01914337	267.86354623	318.62464832
41	215.32720580	257.64691916	308.04307817	368.01146881
42	245.47301461	295.00572244	354.24953990	425.05324647
43	279.83923665	337.78155220	407.38697088	490.93649968
44	319.01672979	386.75987726	468.49501651	567.03165713
45	363.67907196	442.84005947	538.76926899	654.92156398
46	414.59414203	507.05186809	619.58465934	756.43440640
47	472.63732191	580.57438896	712.52235824	873.68173939
48	538.80654698	664.75767536	819.40071197	1009.10240900
49	614.23946356	761.14753829	942.31081877	1165.51328239
50	700.23298846	871.51393134	1083.65744158	1346.16784116

AMOUNT AT COMPOUND INTEREST $(1 + i)^n$ (Continued)

Periods		Rate i		
n	0.16(16%)	0.165(16 1/2%)	0.17(17%)	0.175(17 1/2%)
1	1.16000000	1.16500000	1.17000000	1.17500000
2	1.34560000	1.35722500	1.36890000	1.38062500
3	1.56089600	1.58116712	1.60161300	1.62223437
4	1.81063936	1.84205970	1.87388721	1.90612539
5	2.10034166	2.14599955	2.19244804	2.23969733
6	2.43639632	2.50008948	2.56516420	2.63164437
7	2.82621973	2.91260424	3.00124212	3.09218213
8	3.27841489	3.39318394	3.51145328	3.63331400
9	3.80296127	3.95305929	4.10840033	4.26914396
10	4.41143508	4.60531407	4.80682839	5.01624415
11	5.11726469	5.36519090	5.62398922	5.89408687
12	5.93602704	6.25044739	6.58006738	6.92555208
13	6.88579137	7.28177121	7.69867884	8.13752369
14	7.98751799	8.48326346	9.00745424	9.56159034
15	9.26552087	9.88300194	10.53872146	11.23486864
16	10.74800420	11.51369726	12.33030411	13.20097066
17	12.46768488	13.41345730	14.42645581	15.51114052
18	14.46251446	15.62667776	16.87895329	18.22559011
19	16.77651677	18.20507959	19.74837535	21.41506838
20	19.46075945	21.20891772	23.10559916	25.16270535
21	22.57448097	24.70838914	27.03355102	29.56617879
22	26.18639792	28.78527335	31.62925470	34.74026008
23	30.37622159	33.53484345	37.00622799	40.81980559
24	35.23641704	39.06809262	43.29728675	47.96327157
25	40.87424377	45.51432791	50.65782550	56.35684409
26	47.41412277	53.02419201	59.26965584	66.21929181
27	55.00038241	61.77318369	69.34549733	77.80766787
28	63.80044360	71.96575900	81.13423187	91.42400975
29	74.00851458	83.84010924	94.92705129	107.42321146
30	85.84987691	97.67372726	111.06465001	126.22227346
31	99.58585721	113.78989226	129.94564051	148.31117132
32	115.51959437	132.56522448	152.03639940	174.26562630
33	134.00272947	154.43848652	177.88258730	204.76211090
34	155.44316618	179.92083680	208.12262714	240.59548031
35	180.31407277	209.60777487	243.50347375	282.69968936
36	209.16432441	244.19305773	284.89906429	332.17213500
37	242.63061632	284.48491225	333.33190522	390.30225862
38	281.45151493	331.42492277	389.99832910	458.60515388
39	326.48375732	386.11003503	456.29804505	538.86105581
40	378.72115849	449.81819081	533.86871271	633.16174058
41	439.31654385	524.03819230	624.62639387	743.96504518
42	509.60719087	610.50449402	730.81288083	874.15892808
43	591.14434141	711.23773554	855.05107057	1027.13674050
44	685.72743603	828.59196190	1000.40975257	1206.88567009
45	795.44382580	965.30963562	1170.47941051	1418.09066235
46	922.71483793	1124.58572549	1369.46091029	1666.25652826
47	1070.34921199	1310.14237020	1602.26926504	1957.85142071
48	1241.60508591	1526.31586128	1874.65504010	2300.47541933
49	1440.26189966	1778.15797839	2193.34639691	2703.05861771
50	1670.70380360	2071.55404483	2566.21528439	3176.09387581

AMOUNT AT COMPOUND INTEREST $(1 + i)^n$ (Continued)

Periods n	Rate i 0.18(18%)	0.185(18 1/2%)	0.19(19%)	0.195(19 1/2%)	0.20(20%)
1	1.18000000	1.18500000	1.19000000	1.19500000	1.20000000
2	1.39240000	1.40422500	1.41610000	1.42802500	1.44000000
3	1.64303200	1.66400662	1.68515900	1.70648987	1.72800000
4	1.93877776	1.97184785	2.00533921	2.03925540	2.07360000
5	2.28775776	2.33663970	2.38635366	2.43691020	2.48832000
6	2.69955415	2.76891805	2.83976086	2.91210769	2.98598400
7	3.18547390	3.28116789	3.37931542	3.47996869	3.58318080
8	3.75885920	3.88818395	4.02138535	4.15856259	4.29981696
9	4.43545386	4.60749798	4.78544856	4.96948229	5.15978035
10	5.23383555	5.45988510	5.69468379	5.93853134	6.19173642
11	6.17592595	6.46996385	6.77667371	7.09654495	7.43008371
12	7.28759263	7.66690716	8.06424172	8.48037122	8.91610045
13	8.59935930	9.08528498	9.59644764	10.13404361	10.69932054
14	10.14724397	10.76606270	11.41977269	12.11018211	12.83918465
15	11.97374789	12.75778430	13.58952950	14.47166762	15.40702157
16	14.12902251	15.11797440	16.17154011	17.29364281	18.48842589
17	16.67224656	17.91749966	19.24413273	20.66590315	22.18611107
18	19.67325094	21.22903760	22.90051795	24.69575427	26.62333328
19	23.21443611	25.15640955	27.25161636	29.51142635	31.94799994
20	27.39303460	29.81034532	32.42942347	35.26615449	38.33759992
21	32.32378083	35.32525921	38.59101393	42.14305461	46.00511991
22	38.14206138	41.86043216	45.92330658	50.36095026	55.20614389
23	45.00763243	49.60461211	54.64873482	60.18133557	66.24737267
24	53.10900627	58.78146535	65.03199444	71.91669600	79.49684720
25	62.66862740	69.65603644	77.38807338	85.94045172	95.39621664
26	73.94898033	82.54240318	92.09180733	102.69883981	114.47545997
27	87.25979679	97.81274777	109.58925072	122.72511357	137.37055197
28	102.96656021	115.90810611	130.41120836	146.65651072	164.84466236
29	121.50054105	137.35110574	155.18933794	175.25453031	197.81359483
30	143.37063844	162.76106030	184.67531215	209.42916372	237.37631380
31	169.17735336	192.87185646	219.76362146	250.26785064	284.85157656
32	199.62927696	228.55314990	261.51870954	299.07008152	341.82189187
33	235.56254681	270.83548263	311.20726435	357.38874741	410.18627025
34	277.96380524	320.94004692	370.33664458	427.07955316	492.22352430
35	327.99729018	380.31395560	440.70060705	510.36006602	590.66822915
36	387.03680242	450.67203738	524.43372239	609.88027890	708.80187499
37	456.70342665	534.04636430	624.07612965	728.80693328	850.56224998
38	538.91004369	632.84494170	742.65059428	870.92428527	1020.67469998
39	635.91385155	749.92125591	883.75420719	1040.75452090	1224.80963997
40	750.37834483	888.65668825	1051.66750656	1243.70165248	1469.77156797
41	885.44644690	1053.05817558	1251.48433281	1486.22347471	1763.72588156
42	1044.82680734	1247.87393806	1489.26635604	1776.03705228	2116.47105788
43	1232.89563266	1478.73061660	1772.22696369	2122.36427748	2539.76526945
44	1454.81684654	1752.29578067	2108.95008679	2536.22531159	3047.71832334
45	1716.68387891	2076.47050010	2509.65060328	3030.78924734	3657.26198801
46	2025.68697712	2460.61754262	2986.48421790	3621.79315058	4388.71438561
47	2390.31063300	2915.83178800	3553.91621930	4328.04281494	5266.45726273
48	2820.56654694	3455.26066878	4229.16030097	5172.01116385	6319.74871528
49	3328.26852539	4094.48389250	5032.70075815	6180.55334080	7583.69845834
50	3927.35685996	4851.96341262	5988.91390220	7385.76124226	9100.43815000

PRESENT VALUE $1/(1 + i)^{n}$ *

The following table gives the value of unit amount due in n years at rate of interest i, compounded annually, $1/(1 + i)^{n} = v^{n}$

Periods	Rate i				
n	0.0025(1/4%)	0.004167(5/12%)	0.005(1/2%)	0.005833(7/12%)	0.0075(3/4%)
1	0.99750623	0.99585062	0.99502488	0.99420050	0.99255583
2	0.99501869	0.99171846	0.99007450	0.98843463	0.98516708
3	0.99253734	0.98760345	0.98514876	0.98270220	0.97783333
4	0.99006219	0.98350551	0.98024752	0.97700301	0.97055417
5	0.98759321	0.97942457	0.97537067	0.97133688	0.96332920
6	0.98513038	0.97536057	0.97051808	0.96570361	0.95615802
7	0.98267370	0.97131343	0.96568963	0.96010301	0.94904022
8	0.98022314	0.96728308	0.96088520	0.95453489	0.94197540
9	0.97777869	0.96326946	0.95610468	0.94899906	0.93496318
10	0.97534034	0.95927249	0.95134794	0.94349534	0.92800315
11	0.97290807	0.95529211	0.94661487	0.93802354	0.92109494
12	0.97048187	0.95132824	0.94190534	0.93258347	0.91423815
13	0.96806171	0.94738082	0.93721924	0.92717495	0.90743241
14	0.96564759	0.94344978	0.93255646	0.92179779	0.90067733
15	0.96323949	0.93953505	0.92791688	0.91645182	0.89397254
16	0.96083740	0.93563657	0.92330037	0.91113686	0.88731766
17	0.95844130	0.93175426	0.91870684	0.90585272	0.88071231
18	0.95605117	0.92788806	0.91413616	0.90059922	0.87415614
19	0.95366700	0.92403790	0.90958822	0.89537619	0.86764878
20	0.95128878	0.92020372	0.90506290	0.89018346	0.86118985
21	0.94891649	0.91638544	0.90056010	0.88502084	0.85477901
22	0.94655011	0.91258301	0.89607971	0.87988815	0.84841589
23	0.94418964	0.90879636	0.89162160	0.87478524	0.84210014
24	0.94183505	0.90502542	0.88718567	0.86971192	0.83583140
25	0.93948634	0.90127013	0.88277181	0.86466802	0.82960933
26	0.93714348	0.89753042	0.87837991	0.85965338	0.82343358
27	0.93480646	0.89380623	0.87400986	0.85466782	0.81730380
28	0.93247527	0.89009749	0.86966155	0.84971117	0.81121966
29	0.93014990	0.88640414	0.86533488	0.84478327	0.80518080
30	0.92783032	0.88272611	0.86102973	0.83988394	0.79918690
31	0.92551653	0.87906335	0.85674600	0.83501303	0.79323762
32	0.92320851	0.87541578	0.85248358	0.83017037	0.78733262
33	0.92090624	0.87178335	0.84824237	0.82535580	0.78147158
34	0.91860972	0.86816599	0.84402226	0.82056914	0.77565418
35	0.91631892	0.86456365	0.83982314	0.81581025	0.76988008
36	0.91403384	0.86097624	0.83564492	0.81107896	0.76414896
37	0.91175445	0.85740373	0.83148748	0.80637510	0.75846051
38	0.90948075	0.85384604	0.82735073	0.80169853	0.75281440
39	0.90721272	0.85030311	0.82323455	0.79704907	0.74721032
40	0.90495034	0.84677488	0.81913886	0.79242659	0.74164796
41	0.90269361	0.84326129	0.81506354	0.78783091	0.73612701
42	0.90044250	0.83976228	0.81100850	0.78326188	0.73064716
43	0.89819701	0.83627779	0.80697363	0.77871935	0.72520809
44	0.89595712	0.83280776	0.80295884	0.77420316	0.71980952
45	0.89372281	0.82935212	0.79896402	0.76971317	0.71445114
46	0.89149407	0.82591083	0.79498907	0.76524922	0.70913264
47	0.88927090	0.82248381	0.79103390	0.76081115	0.70385374
48	0.88705326	0.81907102	0.78709841	0.75639883	0.69861414
49	0.88484116	0.81567238	0.78318250	0.75201209	0.69341353
50	0.88263457	0.81228785	0.77928607	0.74765079	0.68825165

*$a_{n\rceil i}$ may be constructed from these tables by use of the formula $\dfrac{1 - (1 + i)^{-n}}{i}$.
See page 573.

$a_{n\rceil i}$ may be constructed from these Tables by use of the formula $a_{n\rceil i} = \dfrac{i}{1 - v^{n}} = n\rceil_{i} + i$.

PRESENT VALUE $1/(1 + i)^n$ (Continued)

Periods			Rate i		
n	0.0025(1/4%)	0.004167(5/12%)	0.005(1/2%)	0.005833(7/12%)	0.0075(3/4%)
51	0.88043349	0.80891736	0.77540902	0.74331479	0.68312819
52	0.87823790	0.80556086	0.77155127	0.73900393	0.67804286
53	0.87604778	0.80221828	0.76771270	0.73471808	0.67299540
54	0.87386312	0.79888957	0.76389324	0.73045708	0.66798551
55	0.87168391	0.79557468	0.76009277	0.72622079	0.66301291
56	0.86951013	0.79227354	0.75631122	0.72200907	0.65807733
57	0.86734178	0.78898610	0.75254847	0.71782178	0.65317849
58	0.86517883	0.78571230	0.74880445	0.71365877	0.64831612
59	0.86302128	0.78245208	0.74507906	0.70951990	0.64348995
60	0.86086911	0.77920539	0.74137220	0.70540504	0.63869970
61	0.85872230	0.77597217	0.73768378	0.70131404	0.63394511
62	0.85658085	0.77275237	0.73401371	0.69724677	0.62922592
63	0.85444474	0.76954593	0.73036190	0.69320308	0.62454185
64	0.85231395	0.76635279	0.72672826	0.68918285	0.61989266
65	0.85018848	0.76317291	0.72311269	0.68518593	0.61527807
66	0.84806831	0.76000621	0.71951512	0.68121219	0.61069784
67	0.84595343	0.75685266	0.71593544	0.67726150	0.60615170
68	0.84384382	0.75371219	0.71237357	0.67333372	0.60163940
69	0.84173947	0.75058476	0.70882943	0.66942872	0.59716070
70	0.83964037	0.74747030	0.70530291	0.66554637	0.59271533
71	0.83754650	0.74436876	0.70179394	0.66168653	0.58830306
72	0.83545786	0.74128009	0.69830243	0.65784908	0.58392363
73	0.83337442	0.73820424	0.69482829	0.65403388	0.57957681
74	0.83129618	0.73514115	0.69137143	0.65024081	0.57526234
75	0.82922312	0.73209078	0.68793177	0.64646973	0.57097999
76	0.82715523	0.72905306	0.68450923	0.64272053	0.56672952
77	0.82509250	0.72602794	0.68110371	0.63899306	0.56251069
78	0.82303491	0.72301537	0.67771513	0.63528723	0.55832326
79	0.82098246	0.72001531	0.67434342	0.63160288	0.55416701
80	0.81893512	0.71702770	0.67098847	0.62793989	0.55004170
81	0.81689289	0.71405248	0.66765022	0.62429816	0.54594710
82	0.81485575	0.71108960	0.66432858	0.62067754	0.54188297
83	0.81282369	0.70813902	0.66102346	0.61707792	0.53784911
84	0.81079670	0.70520069	0.65773479	0.61349917	0.53384527
85	0.80877476	0.70227454	0.65446248	0.60994118	0.52987123
86	0.80675787	0.69936054	0.65120644	0.60640382	0.52592678
87	0.80474600	0.69645863	0.64796661	0.60288698	0.52201169
88	0.80273915	0.69356876	0.64474290	0.59939054	0.51812575
89	0.80073731	0.69069088	0.64153522	0.59591437	0.51426873
90	0.79874046	0.68782495	0.63834350	0.59245836	0.51044043
91	0.79674859	0.68497090	0.63516766	0.58902240	0.50664063
92	0.79476168	0.68212870	0.63200763	0.58560636	0.50286911
93	0.79277973	0.67929829	0.62886331	0.58221014	0.49912567
94	0.79080273	0.67647962	0.62573464	0.57883361	0.79541009
95	0.78883065	0.67367265	0.62262153	0.57547666	0.49172217
96	0.78686349	0.67087733	0.61952391	0.57213918	0.48806171
97	0.78490124	0.66809361	0.61644170	0.56882106	0.48442850
98	0.78294388	0.66532143	0.61337483	0.56552218	0.48082233
99	0.78099140	0.66256076	0.61032321	0.56224243	0.47724301
100	0.77904379	0.65981155	0.60728678	0.55898171	0.47369033

PRESENT VALUE $1/(1 + i)^n$ (Continued)

Periods			Rate i		
n	0.01(1%)	0.001125(1 1/8%)	0.0125(1 1/4%)	0.0150 (1½%)	0.0175(1 3/4%)
1	0.99009901	0.98887515	0.98765432	0.98522167	0.98280098
2	0.98029605	0.97787407	0.97546106	0.97066175	0.96589777
3	0.97059015	0.96699537	0.96341833	0.95631699	0.94928528
4	0.96098034	0.95623770	0.95152428	0.94218423	0.93295851
5	0.95146569	0.94559970	0.93977706	0.92826033	0.91691254
6	0.94204524	0.93508005	0.92817488	0.91454219	0.90114254
7	0.93271805	0.92467743	0.91671593	0.90102679	0.88564378
8	0.92348322	0.91439054	0.90539845	0.88771112	0.87041157
9	0.91433982	0.90421808	0.89422069	0.87459224	0.85544135
10	0.90528695	0.89415880	0.88318093	0.86166723	0.84072860
11	0.89632372	0.88421142	0.87227746	0.84893323	0.82626889
12	0.88744923	0.87437470	0.86150860	0.83638742	0.81205788
13	0.87866260	0.86464742	0.85087269	0.82402702	0.79809128
14	0.86996297	0.85502835	0.84036809	0.81184928	0.78436490
15	0.86134947	0.84551629	0.82999318	0.79985150	0.77087459
16	0.85282126	0.83611005	0.81974635	0.78803104	0.75761631
17	0.84437749	0.82680846	0.80962602	0.77638526	0.74458605
18	0.83601731	0.81761034	0.79963064	0.76491159	0.73177990
19	0.82773992	0.80851455	0.78975866	0.75360747	0.71919401
20	0.81954447	0.79951995	0.78000855	0.74247042	0.70682458
21	0.81143017	0.79062542	0.77037881	0.73149795	0.69466789
22	0.80339621	0.78182983	0.76086796	0.72068763	0.68272028
23	0.79544179	0.77313210	0.75147453	0.71003708	0.67097817
24	0.78756613	0.76453112	0.74219707	0.69954392	0.65943800
25	0.77976844	0.75602583	0.73303414	0.68920583	0.64809632
26	0.77204796	0.74761516	0.72398434	0.67092052	0.63694970
27	0.76440392	0.73929806	0.71504626	0.66898574	0.62599479
28	0.75683557	0.73107348	0.70621853	0.65909925	0.61522829
29	0.74934215	0.72294040	0.69749978	0.64935887	0.60464697
30	0.74192292	0.71489780	0.68888867	0.63976243	0.59424764
31	0.73457715	0.70694467	0.68038387	0.63030781	0.58402716
32	0.72730411	0.69908002	0.67198407	0.62099292	0.57398247
33	0.72010307	0.69130287	0.66368797	0.61181568	0.56411053
34	0.71297334	0.68361223	0.65549429	0.60277407	0.55440839
35	0.70591420	0.67600715	0.64740177	0.59386608	0.54487311
36	0.69892495	0.66848667	0.63940916	0.58508974	0.53550183
37	0.69200490	0.66104986	0.63151522	0.57644309	0.52629172
38	0.68515337	0.65369578	0.62371873	0.56792423	0.51724002
39	0.67836967	0.64642352	0.61601850	0.55953126	0.50834400
40	0.67165314	0.63923216	0.60841334	0.55126232	0.49960098
41	0.66500311	0.63212080	0.60090206	0.54311559	0.49100834
42	0.65841892	0.62508855	0.59348352	0.53508925	0.48256348
43	0.65189992	0.61813454	0.58615656	0.52718153	0.47426386
44	0.64544546	0.61125789	0.57892006	0.51939067	0.46610699
45	0.63905492	0.60445774	0.57177290	0.51171494	0.45809040
46	0.63272764	0.59773324	0.56471397	0.50415265	0.45021170
47	0.62646301	0.59108355	0.55774219	0.49670212	0.44246850
48	0.62026041	0.58450784	0.55085649	0.48936170	0.43485848
49	0.61411921	0.57800528	0.54405579	0.48212975	0.42737934
50	0.60803882	0.57157506	0.53733905	0.47500468	0.42002883

PRESENT VALUE $1/(1 + i)^n$ (Continued)

Periods	Rate *i*				
n	0.01(1%)	0.001125(1 1/8%)	0.0125(1 1/4%)	0.0150 (1½%)	0.0175(1 3/4%)
51	0.60201864	0.56521637	0.53070524	**0.46798491**	0.41280475
52	0.59605806	0.55892843	0.52415332	**0.46106887**	0.40570492
53	0.59015649	0.55271044	0.51768229	0.45425505	0.39872719
54	0.58431336	0.54656162	0.51129115	0.44754192	0.39186947
55	0.57852808	0.54048120	0.50497892	0.44092800	0.38512970
56	0.57280008	0.53446843	0.49874461	0.43441182	0.37850585
57	0.56712879	0.52852256	0.49258727	0.42799194	0.37199592
58	0.56151365	0.52264282	0.48650594	0.42166694	0.36559796
59	0.55595411	0.51682850	0.48049970	0.41543541	0.35931003
60	0.55044962	0.51107887	0.47456760	0.40929597	0.35313025
61	0.54499962	0.50539319	0.46870874	0.40324726	0.34705676
62	0.53960358	0.49977077	0.46292222	0.39728794	0.34108772
63	0.53426097	0.49421090	0.45720713	0.39141669	0.33522135
64	0.52897126	0.48871288	0.45156259	0.38563221	0.32945587
65	0.52373392	0.48327602	0.44598775	0.37993321	0.32378956
66	0.51854844	0.47789965	0.44048173	0.37431843	0.31822069
67	0.51341429	0.47258309	0.43504368	0.36878663	0.31274761
68	0.50833099	0.46732568	0.42967277	0.36333658	0.30736866
69	0.50329801	0.46212675	0.42436817	0.35796708	0.30208222
70	0.49831486	0.45698566	0.41912905	0.35267692	0.29688670
71	0.49338105	0.45190177	0.41395462	0.34746495	0.29178054
72	0.48849609	0.44687443	0.40884407	0.34233000	0.28676221
73	0.48365949	0.44190302	0.40379661	0.33727093	0.28183018
74	0.47887078	0.43698692	0.39881147	0.33228663	0.27698298
75	0.47412949	0.43212551	0.39388787	0.32737599	0.27221914
76	0.46943514	0.42731818	0.38902506	0.32253793	0.26753724
77	0.46478726	0.42256433	0.38422228	0.31777136	0.26293586
78	0.46018541	0.41786337	0.37947879	0.31307523	0.25841362
79	0.45562912	0.41321470	0.37479387	0.30844850	0.25396916
80	0.45111794	0.40861775	0.37016679	0.30389015	0.24960114
81	0.44665142	0.40407194	0.36559683	0.29939916	0.24530825
82	0.44222913	0.39957670	0.36108329	0.29497454	0.24108919
83	0.43785063	0.39513148	0.35662547	0.29061531	0.23694269
84	0.43351547	0.39073570	0.35222268	0.28632050	0.23286751
85	0.42922324	0.38638882	0.34787426	0.28208917	0.22886242
86	0.42497350	0.38209031	0.34357951	0.27792036	0.22492621
87	0.42076585	0.37783961	0.33933779	0.27381316	0.22105770
88	0.41659985	0.37363621	0.33514843	0.26976666	0.21725572
89	0.41247510	0.36947956	0.33101080	0.26577996	0.21351914
90	0.40839119	0.36536916	0.32692425	0.26185218	0.20984682
91	0.40434771	0.36130448	0.32288814	0.25798245	0.20623766
92	0.40034427	0.35728503	0.31890187	0.25416990	0.20269057
93	0.39638046	0.35331029	0.31496481	0.25041369	0.19920450
94	0.39245590	0.34937976	0.31107636	0.24671300	0.19577837
95	0.38857020	0.34549297	0.30723591	0.24306699	0.19241118
96	0.38472297	0.34164941	0.30344287	0.23947487	0.18910190
97	0.38091383	0.33784861	0.29969666	0.23593583	0.18584953
98	0.37714241	0.33409010	0.29599670	0.23244909	0.18265310
99	0.37340832	0.33037340	0.29234242	0.22901389	0.17951165
100	0.36971121	0.32669805	0.28873326	0.22562944	0.17642422

PRESENT VALUE $1/(1 + i)^n$ (Continued)

Periods	Rate i			
n	0.02(2%)	0.0225(2 1/4%)	0.025(2 1/2%)	0.0275(2 3/4%)
1	0.98039216	0.97799511	0.97560976	0.97323601
2	0.96116878	0.95647444	0.95181440	0.94718833
3	0.94232233	0.93542732	0.92859941	0.92183779
4	0.92384543	0.91484335	0.90595064	0.89716573
5	0.90573081	0.89471232	0.88385429	0.87315400
6	0.88797138	0.87502427	0.86229687	0.84978491
7	0.87056018	0.85576946	0.84126524	0.82704128
8	0.85349037	0.83693835	0.82074657	0.80490635
9	0.83675527	0.81852161	0.80072836	0.78336385
10	0.82034830	0.80051013	0.78119840	0.76239791
11	0.80426304	0.78289499	0.76214478	0.74199310
12	0.78849318	0.76566748	0.74355589	0.72213440
13	0.77303253	0.74881905	0.72542038	0.70280720
14	0.75787502	0.73234137	0.70772720	0.68399728
15	0.74301473	0.71622628	0.69046556	0.66569078
16	0.72844581	0.70046580	0.67362493	0.64787424
17	0.71416256	0.68505212	0.65719506	0.63053454
18	0.70015937	0.66997763	0.64115691	0.61365892
19	0.68643076	0.65523484	0.62552772	0.59723496
20	0.67297133	0.64081647	0.61027094	0.58125057
21	0.65977582	0.62671538	0.59538629	0.56569398
22	0.64683904	0.61292457	0.58086467	0.55055375
23	0.63415592	0.59943724	0.56669724	0.53581874
24	0.62172149	0.58624668	0.55287535	0.52147809
25	0.60953087	0.57334639	0.53939059	0.50752126
26	0.59757928	0.56072997	0.52623472	0.49393796
27	0.58586204	0.54839117	0.51339973	0.48071821
28	0.57437455	0.53632388	0.50087778	0.46785227
29	0.56311231	0.52452213	0.48866125	0.45533068
30	0.55207089	0.51298008	0.47674269	0.44314421
31	0.54124597	0.50169201	0.46511481	0.43128391
32	0.53063330	0.49065233	0.45377055	0.41974103
33	0.52022873	0.47985558	0.44270298	0.40850708
34	0.51002817	0.46929641	0.43190534	0.39757380
35	0.50002761	0.45896960	0.42137107	0.38693314
36	0.49022315	0.44887002	0.41109372	0.37657727
37	0.48061093	0.43899268	0.40106705	0.36649856
38	0.47118719	0.42933270	0.39128492	0.35668959
39	0.46194822	0.41988528	0.38174139	0.34714316
40	0.45289042	0.41064575	0.37243062	0.33785222
41	0.44401021	0.40160954	0.36334695	0.32880995
42	0.43530413	0.39277216	0.35448483	0.32000968
43	0.42676875	0.38412925	0.34583886	0.31144495
44	0.41840074	0.37567653	0.33740376	0.30310944
45	0.41019680	0.36740981	0.32917440	0.29499702
46	0.40215373	0.35932500	0.32114576	0.28710172
47	0.39426836	0.35141809	0.31331294	0.27941773
48	0.38653761	0.34368518	0.30567116	0.27193940
49	0.37895844	0.33612242	0.29821576	0.26466122
50	0.37152788	0.32872608	0.29094221	0.25757783

PRESENT VALUE $1/(1 + i)^n$ (Continued)

Periods	Rate i			
n	0.02(2%)	0.0225(2 1/4%)	0.025(2 1/2%)	0.0275(2 3/4%)
51	0.36424302	0.32149250	0.28384606	0.25068402
52	0.35710100	0.31441810	0.27692298	0.24397471
53	0.35009902	0.30749936	0.27016876	0.23744497
54	0.34323433	0.30073287	0.26357928	0.23109000
55	0.33650425	0.29411528	0.25715052	0.22490511
56	0.32990613	0.28764330	0.25087855	0.21888575
57	0.32343738	0.28131374	0.24475956	0.21302749
58	0.31709547	0.27512347	0.23878982	0.20732603
59	0.31087791	0.26906940	0.23296568	0.20177716
60	0.30478227	0.26314856	0.22728359	0.19637679
61	0.29880614	0.25735801	0.22174009	0.19112097
62	0.29294720	0.25169487	0.21633179	0.18600581
63	0.28720314	0.24615635	0.21105541	0.18102755
64	0.28157170	0.24073971	0.20590771	0.17618253
65	0.27605069	0.23544226	0.20088557	0.17146718
66	0.27063793	0.23026138	0.19598593	0.16687804
67	0.26533130	0.22519450	0.19120578	0.16241172
68	0.26012873	0.22023912	0.18654223	0.15806493
69	0.25502817	0.21539278	0.18199241	0.15383448
70	0.25002761	0.21065309	0.17755358	0.14971726
71	0.24512511	0.20601769	0.17322300	0.14571023
72	0.24031874	0.20148429	0.16899805	0.14181044
73	0.23560661	0.19705065	0.16487615	0.13801503
74	0.23098687	0.19271458	0.16085478	0.13432119
75	0.22645771	0.18847391	0.15693149	0.13072622
76	0.22201737	0.18432657	0.15310389	0.12722747
77	0.21766408	0.18027048	0.14936965	0.12382235
78	0.21339616	0.17630365	0.14572649	0.12050837
79	0.20921192	0.17242411	0.14217218	0.11728309
80	0.20510973	0.16862993	0.13870457	0.11414412
81	0.20108797	0.16491925	0.13532153	0.11108917
82	0.19714507	0.16129022	0.13202101	0.10811598
83	0.19327948	0.15774105	0.12880098	0.10522237
84	0.18948968	0.15426997	0.12565949	0.10240620
85	0.18577420	0.15087528	0.12259463	0.09966540
86	0.18213157	0.14755528	0.11960452	0.09699795
87	0.17856036	0.14430835	0.11668733	0.09440190
88	0.17505918	0.14113286	0.11384130	0.09187533
89	0.17162665	0.13802724	0.11106468	0.08941638
90	0.16826142	0.13498997	0.10835579	0.08702324
91	0.16496217	0.13201953	0.10571296	0.08469415
92	0.16172762	0.12911445	0.10313460	0.08242740
93	0.15855649	0.12627331	0.10061912	0.08022131
94	0.15544754	0.12349468	0.09816500	0.07807427
95	0.15239955	0.12077719	0.09577073	0.07598469
96	0.14941132	0.11811950	0.09343486	0.07395104
97	0.14648169	0.11552029	0.09115596	0.07197181
98	0.14360950	0.11297828	0.08893264	0.07004556
99	0.14079363	0.11049221	0.08676355	0.06817086
100	0.13803297	0.10806084	0.08464737	0.06634634

PRESENT VALUE $1/(1 + i)^n$ (Continued)

Periods		Rate i		
n	0.03(3%)	0.0325(3 1/4%)	0.035(3 1/2%)	0.0375(3 3/4%)
1	0.97087379	0.96852300	0.96618357	0.96385542
2	0.94259591	0.93803681	0.93351070	0.92901727
3	0.91514166	0.90851022	0.90194271	0.89543834
4	0.88848705	0.87991305	0.87144223	0.86307310
5	0.86260878	0.85221603	0.84197317	0.83187768
6	0.83748426	0.82539083	0.81350064	0.80180981
7	0.81309151	0.79941000	0.78599096	0.77282874
8	0.78940923	0.77424698	0.75941156	0.74489517
9	0.76641673	0.74987601	0.73373097	0.71797125
10	0.74409391	0.72627216	0.70891881	0.69202048
11	0.72242128	0.70341129	0.68494571	0.66700769
12	0.70137988	0.68127002	0.66178330	0.64289898
13	0.68095134	0.65982568	0.63940415	0.61966167
14	0.66111781	0.63905635	0.61778179	0.59726426
15	0.64186195	0.61894078	0.59689062	0.57567639
16	0.62316694	0.59945838	0.57670591	0.55486881
17	0.60501645	0.58058923	0.55720378	0.53481331
18	0.58739461	0.56231402	0.53836114	0.51548271
19	0.57028603	0.54461407	0.52015569	0.49685080
20	0.55367575	0.52747125	0.50256588	0.47889234
21	0.53754928	0.51086804	0.48557090	0.46158298
22	0.52189250	0.49478745	0.46915063	0.44489926
23	0.50669175	0.47921302	0.45328563	0.42881856
24	0.49193374	0.46412884	0.43795713	0.41331910
25	0.47760557	0.44951945	0.42314699	0.39837985
26	0.46369473	0.43536993	0.40883767	0.38398058
27	0.45018906	0.42166579	0.39501224	0.37010176
28	0.43707675	0.40839302	0.38165434	0.35672459
29	0.42434636	0.39553803	0.36874815	0.34389093
30	0.41198676	0.38308768	0.35627841	0.33140331
31	0.39998715	0.37102923	0.34423035	0.31942487
32	0.38833703	0.35935035	0.33258971	0.30787940
33	0.37702625	0.34803908	0.32134271	0.29675123
34	0.36604490	0.33708385	0.31047605	0.28602528
35	0.35538340	0.32647346	0.29997686	0.27568702
36	0.35503243	0.31619706	0.28983272	0.26572242
37	0.33498294	0.30624413	0.28003161	0.25611800
38	0.32522615	0.29660448	0.27056194	0.24686072
39	0.31575355	0.28726826	0.26141250	0.23793805
40	0.30655684	0.27822592	0.25257247	0.22933788
41	0.29762800	0.26946820	0.24403137	0.22104855
42	0.28895922	0.26098615	0.23577910	0.21305885
43	0.28054294	0.25277109	0.22780590	0.20535793
44	0.27237178	0.24481462	0.22010231	0.19793535
45	0.26443862	0.23710859	0.21265924	0 19078106
46	0.25673653	0.22964512	0.20546787	0.18388536
47	0.24925876	0.22241658	0.19851968	0.17723890
48	0.24199880	0.21541558	0.19180645	0.17083268
49	0.23495029	0.20863494	0.18532024	0.16465800
50	0.22810708	0.20206774	0.17905337	0.15870651

PRESENT VALUE $1/(1 + i)^n$ (Continued)

Periods n	0.04(4%)	0.0425(4 1/4%)	0.045(4 1/2%)	0.0475(4 3/4%)
		Rate i		
1	0.96153846	0.95923261	0.95693780	0.95465894
2	0.92455621	0.92012721	0.91572995	0.91136414
3	0.88899636	0.88261603	0.87629660	0.87003737
4	0.85480419	0.84663408	0.83856134	0.83058460
5	0.82192711	0.81211902	0.80245105	0.79292086
6	0.79031453	0.77901105	0.76789574	0.75696502
7	0.75991781	0.74725281	0.73482846	0.72263964
8	0.73069021	0.71678926	0.70318513	0.68987077
9	0.70258674	0.68756764	0.67290443	0.65858785
10	0.67556417	0.65953730	0.64392768	0.62872349
11	0.64958093	0.63264969	0.61619874	0.60021335
12	0.62459705	0.60685822	0.58966386	0.57299604
13	0.60057409	0.58211819	0.56427164	0.54701293
14	0.57747508	0.55838676	0.53997286	0.52220804
15	0.55526450	0.53562279	0.51672044	0.49852797
16	0.53390818	0.51378685	0.49446932	0.47592169
17	0.51337325	0.49284110	0.47317639	0.45434051
18	0.49362812	0.47274926	0.45280037	0.43373796
19	0.47464242	0.45347650	0.43330179	0.41406965
20	0.45638695	0.43498945	0.41464286	0.39529322
21	0.43883360	0.41725607	0.39678743	0.37736823
22	0.41295539	0.40024563	0.37970089	0.36025607
23	0.40572633	0.38392866	0.36335013	0.34391987
24	0.39012147	0.36827689	0.34770347	0.32832446
25	0.37511680	0.35326321	0.33273060	0.31343624
26	0.36068923	0.33886159	0.31840248	0.29922314
27	0.34681657	0.32504709	0.30469137	0.28565455
28	0.33347747	0.31179577	0.29157069	0.27270124
29	0.32065141	0.29908467	0.27901502	0.26033531
30	0.30831867	0.28689177	0.26700002	0.24853013
31	0.29646026	0.27519594	0.25550241	0.23726027
32	0.28505794	0.26397692	0.24449991	0.22650145
33	0.27409417	0.25321527	0.23397101	0.21623050
34	0.26355209	0.24289235	0.22389589	0.20642530
35	0.25341547	0.23299026	0.21425444	0.19706473
36	0.24366872	0.22349186	0.20502817	0.18812862
37	0.23429685	0.21438068	0.19619921	0.17959772
38	0.22528543	0.20564094	0.18775044	0.17134367
39	0.21662061	0.19725750	0.17966549	0.16367893
40	0.20828904	0.18921582	0.17192870	0.17145367
41	0.20027793	0.18150199	0.16452507	0.14917110
42	0.19257493	0.17410263	0.15744026	0.14240678
43	0.18516820	0.16700492	0.15066054	0.13594919
44	0.17804635	0.16019657	0.14417276	0.12978443
45	0.17119841	0.15366577	0.13796437	0.12389922
46	0.16461386	0.14740122	0.13202332	0.11828088
47	0.15828256	0.14139206	0.12633810	0.11291731
48	0.15219476	0.13562787	0.12089771	0.10779695
49	0.14634112	0.13009868	0.11569158	0.10290878
50	0.14071262	0.12479489	0.11070965	0.09824228

PRESENT VALUE $1/(1 + i)^n$ (Continued)

Periods	Rate i			
n	0.05(5%)	0.0525(5 1/4%)	0.055(5 1/2%)	0.0575(5 3/4%)
1	0.95238095	0.95011876	0.94786730	0.94562648
2	0.90702948	0.90272567	0.89845242	0.89420944
3	0.86383760	0.85769660	0.85161366	0.84558812
4	0.82270247	0.81491363	0.80721674	0.79961051
5	0.78352617	0.77426473	0.76513434	0.75613287
6	0.74621540	0.73564345	0.72524583	0.71501927
7	0.71068133	0.69894865	0.68743681	0.67614115
8	0.67683936	0.66408423	0.65159887	0.63937697
9	0.64460892	0.63095888	0.61762926	0.60461180
10	0.61391325	0.59948588	0.58543058	0.57173692
11	0.58467929	0.56958278	0.55491050	0.54064957
12	0.55683742	0.54117129	0.52598152	0.51125255
13	0.53032135	0.51417699	0.49856068	0.48345395
14	0.50506795	0.48852921	0.47256937	0.45716685
15	0.48101710	0.46416077	0.44793305	0.43230908
16	0.45811152	0.44100786	0.42458109	0.40880291
17	0.43629669	0.41900984	0.40244653	0.38657486
18	0.41552065	0.39810911	0.38146590	0.36555542
19	0.39573396	0.37825094	0.36157906	0.34567889
20	0.37688948	0.35938331	0.34272896	0.32688311
21	0.35894236	0.34145683	0.32486158	0.30910932
22	0.34184987	0.32442454	0.30792567	0.29230196
23	0.32557131	0.30824185	0.29187267	0.27640847
24	0.31006791	0.29286636	0.27665656	0.26137917
25	0.29530277	0.27825783	0.26223370	0.24716706
26	0.28124073	0.26437798	0.24856275	0.23372772
27	0.26784832	0.25119048	0.23560450	0.22101912
28	0.25509364	0.23866079	0.22332181	0.20900153
29	0.24294632	0.22675609	0.21167944	0.19763738
30	0.23137745	0.21544522	0.20064402	0.18689114
31	0.22035947	0.20469855	0.19018390	0.17672921
32	0.20986617	0.19448793	0.18026910	0.16711982
33	0.19987254	0.18478663	0.17087119	0.15803293
34	0.19035480	0.17556925	0.16196321	0.14944012
35	0.18129029	0.16681164	0.15341963	0.14131454
36	0.17265741	0.15849087	0.14551624	0.13363077
37	0.16443563	0.15058515	0.13793008	0.12636479
38	0.15660536	0.14307377	0.13073941	0.11949389
39	0.14914797	0.13593708	0.12392362	0.11299659
40	0.14204568	0.12915637	0.11746314	0.10685257
41	0.13528160	0.12271389	0.11133947	0.10104262
42	0.12883962	0.11659277	0.10553504	0.09554857
43	0.12270440	0.11077698	0.10003322	0.09035326
44	0.11686133	0.10525128	0.09481822	0.08544044
45	0.11129651	0.10000122	0.08987509	0.08079474
46	0.10599668	0.09501304	0.08518965	0.07640164
47	0.10094921	0.09027367	0.08074849	0.07224742
48	0.09614211	0.08577071	0.07653885	0.06831907
49	0.09156391	0.08149236	0.07254867	0.06460432
50	0.08720373	0.07742742	0.06876652	0.06109156

PRESENT VALUE $1/(1 + i)^n$ (Continued)

Periods	Rate i			
n	0.06(6%)	0.0625(6 1/4%)	0.065(6 1/2%)	0.0675(6 3/4%)
1	0.94339623	0.94117647	0.93896714	0.93676815
2	0.88999644	0.88581315	0.88165928	0.87753457
3	0.83961928	0.83370649	0.82784909	0.82204643
4	0.79209366	0.78466493	0.77732309	0.77006692
5	0.74725817	0.73850817	0.72988084	0.72137416
6	0.70496054	0.69506652	0.68533412	0.67576034
7	0.66505711	0.65418025	0.64350621	0.63303076
8	0.62741237	0.61569906	0.60423119	0.59300305
9	0.59189846	0.57948147	0.56735323	0.55550637
10	0.55839478	0.54539432	0.53272604	0.52038068
11	0.52678753	0.51331230	0.50021224	0.48747605
12	0.49696936	0.48311746	0.46968285	0.45665203
13	0.46883902	0.45469879	0.44101676	0.42777708
14	0.44230096	0.42795180	0.41410025	0.40072794
15	0.41726506	0.40277817	0.38882652	0.37538917
16	0.39364628	0.37908533	0.36509533	0.35165262
17	0.37136442	0.35678619	0.34281251	0.32941698
18	0.35034379	0.33579877	0.32188969	0.30858733
19	0.33051301	0.31604590	0.30224384	0.28907478
20	0.31180473	0.29745497	0.28379703	0.27079605
21	0.29415540	0.27995762	0.26647608	0.25367312
22	0.27750510	0.26348952	0.25021228	0.23763289
23	0.26179726	0.24799014	0.23494111	0.22260693
24	0.24697855	0.23340248	0.22060198	0.20853108
25	0.23299863	0.21967292	0.20713801	0.19534527
26	0.21981003	0.20675099	0.19449579	0.18299323
27	0.20736795	0.19458917	0.18262515	0.17142223
28	0.19563014	0.18314274	0.17147902	0.16058289
29	0.18455674	0.17236964	0.16101316	0.15042893
30	0.17411013	0.16223025	0.15118607	0.14091703
31	0.16425484	0.15268729	0.14195875	0.13200659
32	0.15495740	0.14370569	0.13329460	0.12365957
33	0.14618622	0.13525241	0.12515925	0.11584034
34	0.13791153	0.12729639	0.11752042	0.10851554
35	0.13010522	0.11980837	0.11034781	0.10165391
36	0.12274077	0.11276081	0.10361297	0.09522614
37	0.11579318	0.10612783	0.09728917	0.08920482
38	0.10923885	0.09988501	0.09135134	0.08356423
39	0.10305552	0.09400942	0.08577590	0.07828031
40	0.09722219	0.08847946	0.08054075	0.07333050
41	0.09171905	0.08327478	0.07562512	0.06869368
42	0.08652740	0.07837627	0.07100950	0.06435005
43	0.08162962	0.07376590	0.06667559	0.06028108
44	0.07700908	0.06942673	0.06260619	0.05646939
45	0.07265007	0.06534280	0.05878515	0.05289873
46	0.06853781	0.06149911	0.05519733	0.04955384
47	0.06465831	0.05788151	0.05182848	0.04642046
48	0.06099840	0.05447672	0.04866524	0.04348521
49	0.05754566	0.05127221	0.04569506	0.04073556
50	0.05428836	0.04825619	0.04290616	0.03815978

PRESENT VALUE $1/(1 + i)^n$ (Continued)

Rate i

Periods n	0.07(7%)	0.0725(7 1/4%)	0.075(7 1/2%)	0.0775(7 3/4%)
1	0.93457944	0.93240093	0.93023256	0.92807425
2	0.87343873	0.86937150	0.86533261	0.86132181
3	0.81629788	0.81060280	0.80496057	0.79937059
4	0.76289521	0.75580680	0.74880053	0.74187525
5	0.71298618	0.70471497	0.69655863	0.68851532
6	0.66634222	0.65707689	0.64796152	0.63899333
7	0.62274974	0.61265911	0.60275490	0.59303326
8	0.58200910	0.57124392	0.56070223	0.55037889
9	0.54393374	0.53262837	0.52158347	0.51079247
10	0.50834929	0.49662319	0.48519393	0.47405334
11	0.47509280	0.46305192	0.45134319	0.43995670
12	0.44401196	0.43175004	0.41985413	0.40831248
13	0.41496445	0.40256414	0.39056198	0.37894430
14	0.38781724	0.37535118	0.36331347	0.35168844
15	0.36244602	0.34997779	0.33796602	0.32639299
16	0.33873460	0.32631962	0.31438699	0.30291692
17	0.31657439	0.30426072	0.29245302	0.28112940
18	0.29586392	0.28369298	0.27204932	0.26090895
19	0.27650833	0.26451560	0.25306913	0.24214288
20	0.25841900	0.24663459	0.23541315	0.22472657
21	0.24151309	0.22996232	0.21898897	0.20856294
22	0.22571317	0.21441708	0.20371067	0.19356190
23	0.21094688	0.19992269	0.18949830	0.17963981
24	0.19714662	0.18640810	0.17627749	0.16671908
25	0.18424918	0.17380709	0.16397906	0.15472769
26	0.17219549	0.16205789	0.15253866	0.14359878
27	0.16093037	0.15110293	0.14189643	0.13327033
28	0.15040221	0.14088851	0.13199668	0.12368476
29	0.14056282	0.13136458	0.12278761	0.11478864
30	0.13136712	0.12248446	0.11422103	0.10653238
31	0.12277301	0.11420462	0.10625212	0.09886996
32	0.11474113	0.10648449	0.09883918	0.09175866
33	0.10723470	0.09928624	0.09194343	0.08515885
34	0.10021934	0.09257458	0.08552877	0.07903374
35	0.09366294	0.08631663	0.07956164	0.07334918
36	0.08753546	0.08048171	0.07401083	0.06807348
37	0.08180884	0.07504122	0.06884729	0.06317724
38	0.07645686	0.06996850	0.06404399	0.05863317
39	0.07145501	0.06523870	0.05957580	0.05441594
40	0.06678038	0.06082862	0.05541935	0.05050203
41	0.06241157	0.05671666	0.05155288	0.04686963
42	0.05832857	0.05288267	0.04795617	0.04349850
43	0.05451268	0.04930785	0.04461039	0.04036984
44	0.05094643	0.04597468	0.04149804	0.03746621
45	0.04761349	0.04286684	0.03860283	0.03477142
46	0.04449859	0.03996908	0.03590961	0.03227046
47	0.04158747	0.03726721	0.03340428	0.02994938
48	0.03886679	0.03474798	0.03107375	0.02779525
49	0.03632410	0.03239905	0.02890582	0.02579606
50	0.03394776	0.03020890	0.02688913	0.02394066

PRESENT VALUE $1/(1 + i)^n$ (Continued)

Periods		Rate i		
n	0.08(8%)	0.0825(8 1/4%)	0.085(8 1/2%)	0.0875(8 3/4%)
1	0.92592593	0.92378753	0.92165899	0.91954023
2	0.85733882	0.85338340	0.84945529	0.84555423
3	0.79383224	0.78834494	0.78290810	0.77752114
4	0.73502985	0.72826322	0.72157428	0.71496196
5	0.68058320	0.67276048	0.66504542	0.65743629
6	0.63016963	0.62148775	0.61294509	0.60453912
7	0.58349040	0.57412263	0.56492635	0.55589804
8	0.54026888	0.53036732	0.52066945	0.51117061
9	0.50024897	0.48994672	0.47987968	0.47004194
10	0.46319349	0.45260667	0.44228542	0.43222247
11	0.42888286	0.41811240	0.40763633	0.39744595
12	0.39711376	0.38624702	0.37570168	0.36546754
13	0.36769792	0.35681018	0.34626883	0.33606211
14	0.34046104	0.32961679	0.31914178	0.30902263
15	0.31524170	0.30449588	0.29413989	0.28415874
16	0.29189047	0.28128950	0.27109667	0.26129539
17	0.27026895	0.25985173	0.24985869	0.24027162
18	0.25024903	0.24004779	0.23028450	0.22093942
19	0.23171206	0.22175315	0.21224378	0.20316269
20	0.21454821	0.20485280	0.19561639	0.18681627
21	0.19865575	0.18924046	0.18029160	0.17178507
22	0.18394051	0.17481798	0.16616738	0.15796328
23	0.17031528	0.16149467	0.15314965	0.14525360
24	0.15769934	0.14918676	0.14115176	0.13356652
25	0.14601790	0.13781687	0.13009378	0.12281979
26	0.13520176	0.12731350	0.11990210	0.11293774
27	0.12518682	0.11761063	0.11050885	0.10385080
28	0.11591372	0.10864723	0.10185148	0.09549498
29	0.10732752	0.10036696	0.09387233	0.08781148
30	0.09937733	0.09271774	0.08651828	0.08074619
31	0.09201605	0.08565149	0.07974035	0.07424937
32	0.08520005	0.07912378	0.07349341	0.06827528
33	0.07888893	0.07309356	0.06773586	0.06278187
34	0.07304531	0.06752292	0.06242936	0.05773045
35	0.06763454	0.06237683	0.05753858	0.05308547
36	0.06262458	0.05762294	0.05303095	0.04881423
37	0.05798572	0.05323135	0.04887645	0.04488665
38	0.05369048	0.04917446	0.04504742	0.04127508
39	0.04971341	0.04542675	0.04151836	0.03795410
40	0.04603093	0.04196467	0.03826577	0.03490032
41	0.04262123	0.03876644	0.03526799	0.03209225
42	0.03946411	0.03581195	0.03250506	0.02951011
43	0.03654084	0.03308263	0.02995858	0.02713573
44	0.03383411	0.03056132	0.02761160	0.02495240
45	0.03132788	0.02823217	0.02544848	0.02294474
46	0.02900730	0.02608053	0.02345482	0.02109861
47	0.02685861	0.02409287	0.02161734	0.01940102
48	0.02486908	0.02225669	0.01992382	0.01784002
49	0.02302693	0.02056045	0.01836297	0.01640461
50	0.02132123	0.01899349	0.01692439	0.01508470

PRESENT VALUE $1/(1 + i)^n$ (Continued)

| Periods | Rate i | | | |
n	0.09(9%)	0.0925(9 1/4%)	0.095(9 1/2%)	0.0975(9 3/4%)
1	0.91743119	0.91533181	0.91324201	0.91116173
2	0.84167999	0.83783232	0.83401097	0.83021570
3	0.77218348	0.76689457	0.76165385	0.75646077
4	0.70842521	0.70196299	0.69557429	0.68925811
5	0.64993139	0.64252906	0.63522767	0.62802561
6	0.59626733	0.58812728	0.58011659	0.57223290
7	0.54703424	0.53833161	0.52978684	0.52139672
8	0.50186628	0.49275204	0.48382360	0.47507674
9	0.46042778	0.45103162	0.44184803	0.43287175
10	0.42241081	0.41284359	0.40351419	0.39441617
11	0.38753285	0.37788887	0.36850611	0.35937692
12	0.35553473	0.34589370	0.33653626	0.32745050
13	0.32617865	0.31660751	0.30733813	0.29836036
14	0.29924647	0.28980092	0.28067410	0.27185454
15	0.27453804	0.26526400	0.25632337	0.24770346
16	0.25186976	0.24280458	0.23408527	0.22569791
17	0.23107318	0.22224675	0.21377651	0.20564730
18	0.21199374	0.20342952	0.19522969	0.18737795
19	0.19448967	0.18620551	0.17829195	0.17073162
20	0.17843089	0.17043983	0.16282370	0.15556411
21	0.16369806	0.15600900	0.14869744	0.14174407
22	0.15018171	0.14280000	0.13579675	0.12915177
23	0.13778139	0.13070938	0.12401530	0.11767815
24	0.12640494	0.11964245	0.11325598	0.10722383
25	0.11596784	0.10951254	0.10343012	0.09769825
26	0.10639251	0.10024031	0.09445673	0.08901891
27	0.09760781	0.09175315	0.08626185	0.08111062
28	0.08954845	0.08398457	0.07877795	0.07390489
29	0.08215454	0.07687375	0.07194333	0.06733931
30	0.07537114	0.07036499	0.06570167	0.06135700
31	0.06914783	0.06440731	0.06000153	0.05590615
32	0.06343838	0.05895406	0.05479592	0.05093955
33	0.05820035	0.05396253	0.05004193	0.04641417
34	0.05339481	0.04939362	0.04570039	0.04229081
35	0.04898607	0.04521155	0.04173552	0.03853377
36	0.04494135	0.04138357	0.03811463	0.03511050
37	0.04123059	0.03787970	0.03480788	0.03199134
38	0.03782623	0.03467249	0.03178802	0.02914928
39	0.03470296	0.03173684	0.02903015	0.02655971
40	0.03183758	0.02904973	0.02651156	0.02420019
41	0.02920879	0.02659015	0.02421147	0.02205029
42	0.02679706	0.02433881	0.02211093	0.02009138
43	0.02458446	0.02227808	0.02019263	0.01830650
44	0.02255455	0.02039184	0.01844076	0.01668018
45	0.02069224	0.01866530	0.01684087	0.01519834
46	0.01898371	0.01708494	0.01537979	0.01384815
47	0.01741625	0.01563839	0.01404547	0.01261790
48	0.01597821	0.01431432	0.01282692	0.01149695
49	0.01465891	0.01310235	0.01171408	0.01047558
50	0.01344854	0.01199300	0.01069779	0.00954495

PRESENT VALUE $1/(1 + i)^n$ (Continued)

Periods n	Rate i			
	0.10(10%)	0.105(10 1/2%)	0.11(11%)	0.115(11 1/2%)
1	0.90909091	0.90497738	0.90090090	0.89686099
2	0.82644628	0.81898405	0.81162243	0.80435963
3	0.75131480	0.74116204	0.73119138	0.72139877
4	0.68301346	0.67073487	0.65873097	0.64699441
5	0.62092132	0.60699989	0.59345133	0.58026405
6	0.56447393	0.54932116	0.53464084	0.52041619
7	0.51315812	0.49712323	0.48165841	0.46674097
8	0.46650738	0.44988527	0.43392650	0.41860177
9	0.42409762	0.40713599	0.39092477	0.37542760
10	0.38554329	0.36844886	0.35218448	0.33670636
11	0.35049390	0.33343788	0.31728331	0.30197880
12	0.31863082	0.30175374	0.28584082	0.27083301
13	0.28966438	0.27308031	0.25751426	0.24289956
14	0.26333125	0.24713150	0.23199482	0.21784714
15	0.23939205	0.22364842	0.20900435	0.19537860
16	0.21762914	0.20239676	0.18829220	0.17522744
17	0.19784467	0.18316449	0.16963262	0.15715466
18	0.17985879	0.16575972	0.15282218	0.14094588
19	0.16350799	0.15000879	0.13767764	0.12640886
20	0.14864363	0.13575456	0.12403391	0.11337118
21	0.13513057	0.12285481	0.11174226	0.10167818
22	0.12284597	0.11118082	0.10066870	0.09119120
23	0.11167816	0.10061613	0.09069252	0.08178583
24	0.10152560	0.09105532	0.08170498	0.07335052
25	0.09229600	0.08240301	0.07360809	0.06578522
26	0.08390545	0.07457286	0.06631359	0.05900020
27	0.07627768	0.06748675	0.05974197	0.05291497
28	0.06934335	0.06107398	0.05382160	0.04745738
29	0.06303941	0.05527057	0.04848793	0.04256267
30	0.05730855	0.05001861	0.04368282	0.03817280
31	0.05209868	0.04526571	0.03935389	0.03423569
32	0.04736244	0.04096445	0.03545395	0.03070466
33	0.04305676	0.03707190	0.03194050	0.02753781
34	0.03914251	0.03354923	0.02877522	0.02469759
35	0.03558410	0.03036129	0.02592363	0.02215030
36	0.03234918	0.02747628	0.02335462	0.01986574
37	0.02940835	0.02486542	0.02104020	0.01781681
38	0.02673486	0.02250264	0.01895513	0.01597920
39	0.02430442	0.02036438	0.01707670	0.01433112
40	0.02209493	0.01842930	0.01538441	0.01285302
41	0.02008630	0.01667810	0.01385983	0.01152738
42	0.01826027	0.01509330	0.01248633	0.01033845
43	0.01660025	0.01365910	0.01124895	0.00927216
44	0.01509113	0.01236118	0.01013419	0.00831583
45	0.01371921	0.01118658	0.00912990	0.00745815
46	0.01247201	0.01012361	0.00822513	0.00668892
47	0.01133819	0.00916163	0.00741005	0.00599903
48	0.01030745	0.00829107	0.00667570	0.00538030
49	0.00937041	0.00750323	0.00601415	0.00482538
50	0.00851855	0.00679026	0.00541815	0.00432769

PRESENT VALUE $1/(1 + i)^n$ (Continued)

Periods		Rate i		
n	0.12(12%)	0.125(12 1/2%)	0.13(13%)	0.135(13 1/2%)
1	0.89285714	0.88888889	0.88495575	0.88105727
2	0.79719388	0.79012346	0.78314668	0.77626191
3	0.71178025	0.70233196	0.69305016	0.68393120
4	0.63551808	0.62429508	0.61331873	0.60258255
5	0.56742686	0.55492896	0.54275994	0.53090974
6	0.50663112	0.49327018	0.48031853	0.46776188
7	0.45234922	0.43846239	0.42506064	0.41212501
8	0.40388323	0.38974434	0.37615986	0.36310573
9	0.36061002	0.34643942	0.33288483	0.31991695
10	0.32197324	0.30794615	0.29458835	0.28186515
11	0.28747610	0.27372991	0.26069765	0.24833934
12	0.25667509	0.24331547	0.23070589	0.21880118
13	0.22917419	0.21628042	0.20416450	0.19277637
14	0.20461981	0.19224926	0.18067655	0.16984702
15	0.18269626	0.17088823	0.15989075	0.14964495
16	0.16312166	0.15190065	0.14149624	0.13184577
17	0.14564434	0.13502280	0.12521791	0.11616368
18	0.13003959	0.12002027	0.11081231	0.10234685
19	0.11610678	0.10668468	0.09806399	0.09017344
20	0.10366677	0.09483083	0.08678229	0.07944796
21	0.09255961	0.08429407	0.07679849	0.06999821
22	0.08264251	0.07492806	0.06796327	0.06167243
23	0.07378796	0.06660272	0.06014448	0.05433694
24	0.06588210	0.05920242	0.05322521	0.04787396
25	0.05882331	0.05262437	0.04710195	0.04217970
26	0.05252081	0.04677722	0.04168314	0.03716273
27	0.04689358	0.04157975	0.03688774	0.03274249
28	0.04186927	0.03695978	0.03264402	0.02884801
29	0.03738327	0.03285314	0.02888851	0.02541675
30	0.03337792	0.02920279	0.02556505	0.02239361
31	0.02980172	0.02595803	0.02262394	0.01973005
32	0.02660868	0.02307381	0.02002119	0.01738331
33	0.02375775	0.02051005	0.01771786	0.01531569
34	0.02121227	0.01823116	0.01567953	0.01349400
35	0.01893953	0.01620547	0.01387569	0.01188899
36	0.01691029	0.01440486	0.01227937	0.01047488
37	0.01509848	0.01280432	0.01086670	0.00922897
38	0.01348078	0.01138162	0.00961655	0.00813125
39	0.01203641	0.01011700	0.00851022	0.00716410
40	0.01074680	0.00899289	0.00753117	0.00631198
41	0.00959536	0.00799368	0.00666475	0.00556121
42	0.00856728	0.00710549	0.00589801	0.00489975
43	0.00764936	0.00631599	0.00521948	0.00431696
44	0.00682978	0.00561421	0.00461901	0.00380349
45	0.00609802	0.00499041	0.00408762	0.00335109
46	0.00544466	0.00443592	0.00361736	0.00295250
47	0.00486131	0.00394304	0.00320120	0.00260132
48	0.00434045	0.00350493	0.00283292	0.00229192
49	0.00387540	0.00311549	0.00250701	0.00201931
50	0.00346018	0.00276932	0.00221859	0.00177913

PRESENT VALUE $1/(1 + i)^n$ (Continued)

Periods n	Rate i			
	0.14(14%)	0.145(14 1/2%)	0.15(15%)	0.155(15 1/2%)
1	0.87719298	0.87336245	0.86956522	0.86580087
2	0.76946753	0.76276196	0.75614367	0.74961114
3	0.67497152	0.66616765	0.65751623	0.64901397
4	0.59208028	0.58180581	0.57175325	0.56191686
5	0.51936866	0.50812734	0.49717674	0.48650810
6	0.45558655	0.44377934	0.43232760	0.42121914
7	0.39963732	0.38758021	0.37593704	0.36469189
8	0.35055905	0.33849800	0.32690177	0.31575056
9	0.30750794	0.29563144	0.28426241	0.27337711
10	0.26974381	0.25819340	0.24718471	0.23669014
11	0.23661738	0.22549642	0.21494322	0.20492652
12	0.20755910	0.19694010	0.18690715	0.17742556
13	0.18206939	0.17200009	0.16252796	0.15361521
14	0.15970999	0.15021842	0.14132866	0.13300018
15	0.14009648	0.13119513	0.12289449	0.11515167
16	0.12289165	0.11458090	0.10686477	0.09969841
17	0.10779969	0.10007065	0.09292589	0.08631897
18	0.09456113	0.08739795	0.08080512	0.07473504
19	0.08294836	0.07633009	0.07026532	0.06470566
20	0.07276172	0.06666383	0.06110028	0.05602222
21	0.06382607	0.05822169	0.05313068	0.04850409
22	0.05598778	0.05084863	0.04620059	0.04199488
23	0.04911209	0.04440929	0.04017443	0.03635920
24	0.04308078	0.03878540	0.03493428	0.03147983
25	0.03779016	0.03387372	0.03037764	0.02725526
26	0.03314926	0.02958403	0.02641534	0.02359763
27	0.02907830	0.02583758	0.02296986	0.02043085
28	0.02550728	0.02256557	0.01997379	0.01768905
29	0.02237481	0.01970792	0.01736851	0.01531519
30	0.01962702	0.01721216	0.01510305	0.01325991
31	0.01721669	0.01503246	0.01313309	0.01148044
32	0.01510236	0.01312878	0.01142008	0.00993977
33	0.01324768	0.01146618	0.00993050	0.00860586
34	0.01162077	0.01001414	0.00863522	0.00745097
35	0.01019366	0.00874597	0.00750889	0.00645105
36	0.00894181	0.00763840	0.00652947	0.00558533
37	0.00784369	0.00667109	0.00567780	0.00483578
38	0.00688043	0.00582628	0.00493722	0.00418682
39	0.00603547	0.00508846	0.00429323	0.00362495
40	0.00529427	0.00444407	0.00373324	0.00313849
41	0.00464410	0.00388128	0.00324630	0.00271731
42	0.00407377	0.00338976	0.00282287	0.00235265
43	0.00357348	0.00296049	0.00245467	0.00203692
44	0.00313463	0.00258558	0.00213449	0.00176357
45	0.00274968	0.00225815	0.00185608	0.00152690
46	0.00241200	0.00197218	0.00161398	0.00132199
47	0.00211579	0.00172243	0.00140346	0.00114458
48	0.00185595	0.00150431	0.00122040	0.00099098
49	0.00162803	0.00131381	0.00106122	0.00085799
50	0.00142810	0.00114743	0.00092280	0.00074285

PRESENT VALUE $1/(1 + i)^n$ (Continued)

	Rate i			
Periods				
n	0.16(16%)	0.165(16 1/2%)	0.17(17%)	0.175(17 1/2%)
1	0.86206897	0.85836910	0.85470085	0.85106383
2	0.74316290	0.73679751	0.73051355	0.72430964
3	0.64065767	0.63244421	0.62437056	0.61643374
4	0.55229110	0.54287057	0.53365005	0.52462446
5	0.47611302	0.46598332	0.45611115	0.44648890
6	0.41044225	0.39998568	0.38983859	0.37999055
7	0.35382953	0.34333535	0.33319538	0.32339622
8	0.30502546	0.29470846	0.28478237	0.27523082
9	0.26295298	0.25296863	0.24340374	0.23423900
10	0.22668360	0.21714046	0.20803738	0.19935234
11	0.19541690	0.18638666	0.17780973	0.16966156
12	0.16846284	0.15998855	0.15197413	0.14439282
13	0.14522659	0.13732923	0.12989242	0.12288751
14	0.12519534	0.11787916	0.11101916	0.10458511
15	0.10792701	0.10118383	0.09488817	0.08900861
16	0.09304053	0.08685307	0.08110100	0.07575201
17	0.08020735	0.07455199	0.06931709	0.06446979
18	0.06914427	0.06399313	0.05924538	0.05486791
19	0.05960713	0.05492972	0.05063708	0.04669609
20	0.05138546	0.04714998	0.04327955	0.03974135
21	0.04429781	0.04047208	0.03699107	0.03382243
22	0.03818776	0.03473999	0.03161630	0.02878505
23	0.03292049	0.02981973	0.02702248	0.02449791
24	0.02837973	0.02559634	0.02309614	0.02084929
25	0.02446528	0.02197110	0.01974029	0.01774407
26	0.02109076	0.01885932	0.01687204	0.01510134
27	0.01818169	0.01618825	0.01442055	0.01285220
28	0.01567387	0.01389550	0.01232525	0.01093805
29	0.01351196	0.01192747	0.01053440	0.00930898
30	0.01164824	0.01023817	0.00900376	0.00792253
31	0.01004159	0.00878813	0.00769553	0.00674258
32	0.00865654	0.00754346	0.00657737	0.00573837
33	0.00746253	0.00647507	0.00562169	0.00488372
34	0.00643322	0.00555800	0.00480486	0.00415635
35	0.00554588	0.00477082	0.00410672	0.00353732
36	0.00478093	0.00409512	0.00351002	0.00301049
37	0.00412149	0.00351512	0.00300001	0.00256212
38	0.00355301	0.00201727	0.00256411	0.00218052
39	0.00306294	0.00258994	0.00219155	0.00185577
40	0.00264047	0.00222312	0.00187312	0.00157938
41	0.00227626	0.00190826	0.00160096	0.00134415
42	0.00196230	0.00163799	0.00136834	0.00114396
43	0.00169163	0.00140600	0.00116952	0.00097358
44	0.00145831	0.00120687	0.00099959	0.00082858
45	0.00125716	0.00103594	0.00085435	0.00070517
46	0.00109376	0.00088922	0.00073021	0.00060015
47	0.00093427	0.00076328	0.00062411	0.00051076
48	0.00080541	0.00065517	0.00053343	0.00043469
49	0.00069432	0.00056238	0.00045592	0.00036995
50	0.00059855	0.00048273	0.00038968	0.00031485

PRESENT VALUE $1/(1 + i)^n$ (Continued)

Periods	Rate i				
n	0.18(18%)	0.185(18 1/2%)	0.19(19%)	0.195(19 1/2%)	0.20(20%)
1	0.84745763	0.84388186	0.84033613	0.83682008	0.83333333
2	0.71818443	0.71213659	0.70616482	0.70026785	0.69444444
3	0.60863087	0.60095915	0.59341581	0.58599820	0.57870370
4	0.51578888	0.50713852	0.49866875	0.49037507	0.48225309
5	0.43710922	0.42796500	0.41904937	0.41035570	0.40187757
6	0.37043154	0.36115189	0.35214233	0.34339389	0.33489798
7	0.31392503	0.30476953	0.29591792	0.28735891	0.27908165
8	0.26603816	0.25718948	0.24867052	0.24046770	0.23256804
9	0.22545607	0.21703753	0.20896683	0.20122820	0.19380670
10	0.19106447	0.18315404	0.17560238	0.16839180	0.16150558
11	0.16191904	0.15456037	0.14756502	0.14091364	0.13458799
12	0.13721953	0.13043069	0.12400422	0.11791937	0.11215665
13	0.11628773	0.11006809	0.10420523	0.09867729	0.09346388
14	0.09854893	0.09288447	0.08756742	0.08257514	0.07788657
15	0.08351604	0.07838352	0.07358606	0.06910054	0.06490547
16	0.07077630	0.06614643	0.06183703	0.05782472	0.05408789
17	0.05997992	0.05581977	0.05196389	0.04838888	0.04507324
18	0.05083044	0.04710529	0.04366713	0.04049279	0.03756104
19	0.04307664	0.03975130	0.03669507	0.03388518	0.03130086
20	0.03650563	0.03354540	0.03083619	0.02835580	0.02608405
21	0.03093698	0.02830836	0.02591277	0.02372870	0.02173671
22	0.02621778	0.02388891	0.02177544	0.01985665	0.01811393
23	0.02221845	0.02015942	0.01829869	0.01661645	0.01509494
24	0.01882920	0.01701217	0.01537705	0.01390498	0.01257912
25	0.01595695	0.01435626	0.01292189	0.01163596	0.01048260
26	0.01352284	0.01211499	0.01085873	0.00973721	0.00873550
27	0.01146003	0.01022362	0.00912498	0.00814829	0.00727958
28	0.00971189	0.00862752	0.00766805	0.00681865	0.00606632
29	0.00823042	0.00728061	0.00644374	0.00570599	0.00505526
30	0.00697493	0.00614398	0.00541491	0.00477488	0.00421272
31	0.00591096	0.00518479	0.00455034	0.00399572	0.00351060
32	0.00500929	0.00437535	0.00382382	0.00334370	0.00292550
33	0.00424516	0.00369228	0.00321329	0.00279807	0.00243792
34	0.00359759	0.00311585	0.00270025	0.00234148	0.00203160
35	0.00304881	0.00262941	0.00226911	0.00195940	0.00169300
36	0.00258373	0.00221891	0.00190682	0.00163967	0.00141083
37	0.00218960	0.00187250	0.00160237	0.00137211	0.00117569
38	0.00185560	0.00158017	0.00134653	0.00114821	0.00097974
39	0.00157254	0.00133347	0.00113154	0.00096084	0.00081645
40	0.00133266	0.00112529	0.00095087	0.00080405	0.00068038
41	0.00112937	0.00094962	0.00079905	0.00067285	0.00056698
42	0.00095710	0.00080136	0.00067147	0.00056305	0.00047248
43	0.00081110	0.00067626	0.00056426	0.00047117	0.00039374
44	0.00068737	0.00057068	0.00047417	0.00039429	0.00032811
45	0.00058252	0.00048159	0.00039846	0.00032995	0.00027343
46	0.00049366	0.00040640	0.00033484	0.00027611	0.00022786
47	0.00041836	0.00034296	0.00028138	0.00023105	0.00018988
48	0.00035454	0.00028941	0.00023645	0.00019335	0.00015823
49	0.00030046	0.00024423	0.00019870	0.00016180	0.00013186
50	0.00025462	0.00020610	0.00016698	0.00013540	0.00010988

COMPOUND AMOUNT OF 1 FOR FRACTIONAL PERIODS

$$(1 + i)^{1/p}$$

p	i = ¼%	5/12%	1/2%	7/12%	3/4%
2	1.0012492	1.0020812	1.0024969	1.0029124	1.0037430
3	1.0008326	1.0013870	1.0016639	1.0019407	1.0024938
4	1.0006244	1.0010400	1.0012477	1.0014552	1.0018697
6	1.0004162	1.0006932	1.0008316	1.0009699	1.0012461
12	1.0002089	1.0003466	1.0004157	1.0004848	1.0006229
13	1.0001921	1.0003199	1.0003837	1.0004475	1.0005749
26	1.0000960	1.0001599	1.0001919	1.0002237	1.0002874
52	1.0000480	1.0000800	1.0000959	1.0001119	1.0001437
365	1.0000068	1.0000114	1.0000137	1.0000159	1.0000205

p	1%	1 1/8%	1 1/4%	1 1/2%	1 3/4%
2	1.0049876	1.0056093	1.0062306	1.0074721	1.0087121
3	1.0033223	1.0037360	1.0041494	1.0049752	1.0057996
4	1.0024907	1.0028008	1.0031105	1.0037291	1.0043466
6	1.0016598	1.0018663	1.0020726	1.0024845	1.0028956
12	1.0008295	1.0009327	1.0010357	1.0012415	1.0014468
13	1.0007657	1.0008609	1.0009560	1.0011459	1.0013354
26	1.0003828	1.0004304	1.0004779	1.0005728	1.0006675
52	1.0001914	1.0002152	1.0002389	1.0002864	1.0003337
365	1.0000273	1.0000307	1.0000340	1.0000408	1.0000475

p	2%	2 1/4%	2 1/2%	2 3/4%	3%
2	1.0099505	1.0111874	1.0124228	1.0136568	1.01488916
3	1.0066227	1.0074444	1.0082648	1.0090839	1.00990163
4	1.0049629	1.0055782	1.0061922	1.0068052	1.00741707
6	1.0033059	1.0037153	1.0041239	1.0045317	1.00493862
12	1.0016516	1.0018559	1.0020598	1.0022633	1.00246627
13	1.0015244	1.0017130	1.0019012	1.0020890	1.00227634
26	1.0007619	1.0008562	1.0009502	1.0010440	1.00113752
52	1.0003809	1.0004280	1.0004750	1.0005218	1.00056860
365	1.0000543	1.0000610	1.0000676	1.0000743	1.00008099

p	3 1/4%	3 1/2%	3 3/4%	4%	4 1/4%
2	1.01612007	1.01734950	1.01857744	1.01980390	1.02102889
3	1.01071805	1.01153314	1.01234693	1.01315940	1.01397058
4	1.00802781	1.00863745	1.00924598	1.00985341	1.01045974
6	1.00534474	1.00575004	1.00615452	1.00655820	1.00696106
12	1.00266881	1.00287090	1.00307254	1.00327374	1.00347450
13	1.00246326	1.00264977	1.00283586	1.00302153	1.00320680
26	1.00123087	1.00132401	1.00141692	1.00150963	1.00160212
52	1.00061525	1.00066178	1.00070821	1.00075453	1.00080074
365	1.00008763	1.00009425	1.00010087	1.00010746	1.00011404

p	4 1/2%	4 3/4%	5%	5 1/4%	5 1/2%
2	1.02225242	1.02347447	1.02469508	1.02591423	1.02713193
3	1.01478046	1.01558905	1.01639636	1.01720238	1.01800713
4	1.01106499	1.01166915	1.01227223	1.01287424	1.01347517
6	1.00736312	1.00776438	1.00816485	1.00856452	1.00896339
12	1.00367481	1.00387468	1.00407412	1.00427313	1.00447170
13	1.00339165	1.00357610	1.00376014	1.00394378	1.00412701
26	1.00169439	1.00178645	1.00187831	1.00196995	1.00206138
52	1.00084684	1.00089283	1.00093871	1.00098449	1.00103016
365	1.00012060	1.00012715	1.00013368	1.00014020	1.00014670

COMPOUND AMOUNT OF 1 FOR FRACTIONAL PERIODS
$$(1 + i)^{1/p} \text{ (Continued)}$$

p	5 3/4%	6%	6 1/4%	6 1/2%	6 3/4%
2	1.02834819	1.02956301	1.03077641	1.03198837	1.03319892
3	1.01881061	1.01961282	1.02041378	1.02121347	1.02201192
4	1.01407504	1.01467385	1.01527159	1.01586828	1.01646393
6	1.00936149	1.00975879	1.01015532	1.01055107	1.01094605
12	1.00466984	1.00486755	1.00506483	1.00526169	1.00545813
13	1.00430985	1.00449228	1.00467432	1.00485597	1.00503722
26	1.00215261	1.00224363	1.00233444	1.00242504	1.00251545
52	1.00107572	1.00112118	1.00116654	1.00121179	1.00125693
365	1.00015318	1.00015965	1.00016611	1.00017255	1.00017897

p	7%	7 1/4%	7 1/2%	7 3/4%	8%
2	1.03440804	1.03561576	1.03682207	1.03802697	1.03923048
3	1.02280912	1.02360508	1.02439981	1.02519330	1.02598557
4	1.01705853	1.01765208	1.01824460	1.01883609	1.01942655
6	1.01134026	1.01173370	1.01212638	1.01251830	1.01290946
12	1.00565415	1.00584974	1.00604492	1.00623968	1.00643403
13	1.00521808	1.00539365	1.00557863	1.00575833	1.00593764
26	1.00260564	1.00269564	1.00278544	1.00287503	1.00296443
52	1.00130197	1.00134691	1.00139175	1.00143648	1.00148112
365	1.00018538	1.00019178	1.00019816	1.00020452	1.00021087

p	8 1/4%	8 1/2%	8 3/4%	9%	9 1/4%
2	1.04043260	1.04163333	1.04283268	1.04403065	1.04522725
3	1.02677661	1.02756644	1.02835506	1.02914247	1.02992867
4	1.02001598	1.02060440	1.02119179	1.02177818	1.02236356
6	1.01329986	1.01368952	1.01407843	1.01446659	1.01485402
12	1.00662797	1.00682149	1.00701461	1.00720732	1.00739963
13	1.00611657	1.00629512	1.00647328	1.00665107	1.00682849
26	1.00305362	1.00314262	1.00323142	1.00332003	1.00340844
52	1.00152565	1.00157008	1.00161441	1.00165864	1.00170277
365	1.00021721	1.00022353	1.00022984	1.00023613	1.00024241

p	9 1/2%	9 3/4%	10%	10 1/4%	10 1/2%
2	1.04642248	1.04761634	1.04880885	1.05000000	1.05118980
3	1.03071368	1.03149749	1.03228012	1.03306155	1.03384181
4	1.02294793	1.02353131	1.02411369	1.02469508	1.02527548
6	1.01524070	1.01562665	1.01601187	1.01639636	1.01678012
12	1.00759153	1.00778304	1.00797414	1.00816485	1.00835516
13	1.00700553	1.00718220	1.00735849	1.00753442	1.00770998
26	1.00349665	1.00358467	1.00367250	1.00376014	1.00384759
52	1.00174680	1.00179073	1.00183457	1.00187831	1.00192195
365	1.00024867	1.00025492	1.00026116	1.00026738	1.00027359

p	10 3/4%	11%	11 1/4%	11 1/2%	11 3/4%
2	1.05237826	1.05356538	1.05475116	1.05593560	1.05711873
3	1.03462089	1.03539881	1.03617555	1.03695113	1.03772555
4	1.02585489	1.02643333	1.02701079	1.02758727	1.02816279
6	1.01716316	1.01754548	1.01792708	1.01830797	1.01868815
12	1.00854507	1.00873459	1.00892373	1.00911247	1.00930082
13	1.00788517	1.00806000	1.00823447	1.00840857	1.00858231
26	1.00393485	1.00402191	1.00410879	1.00419548	1.00428199
52	1.00196549	1.00200894	1.00205229	1.00209555	1.00213871
365	1.00027978	1.00028596	1.00029212	1.00029828	1.00030441

COMPOUND AMOUNT OF 1 FOR FRACTIONAL PERIODS

$(1 + i)^{1/p}$ (Continued)

p	12%	12 1/4%	12 1/2%	12 3/4%	13%
2	1.05830052	1.05948101	1.06066017	1.06183803	1.06301458
3	1.03849882	1.03927094	1.04004191	1.04081174	1.04158044
4	1.02873734	1.02931094	1.02988357	1.03045525	1.03102598
6	1.01906762	1.01944639	1.01982445	1.02020181	1.02057848
12	1.00948879	1.00967638	1.00986358	1.01005040	1.01023684
13	1.00875570	1.00892873	1.00910140	1.00927372	1.00944569
26	1.00436831	1.00445444	1.00454039	1.00462616	1.00471174
52	1.00218177	1.00222475	1.00226763	1.00231041	1.00235310
365	1.00031054	1.00031665	1.00032275	1.00032883	1.00033490

p	13 1/4%	13 1/2%	13 3/4%	14%	14 1/4%
2	1.06418983	1.06536379	1.06653645	1.06770783	1.06887792
3	1.04234800	1.04311443	1.04387974	1.04464393	1.04540700
4	1.03159577	1.03216461	1.03273252	1.03329948	1.03386552
6	1.02095445	1.02132974	1.02170433	1.02207824	1.02245146
12	1.01042291	1.01060860	1.01079391	1.01097885	1.01116342
13	1.00961730	1.00978857	1.00995949	1.01013006	1.01030029
26	1.00479715	1.00488237	1.00496741	1.00505227	1.00513695
52	1.00239570	1.00243821	1.00248063	1.00252295	1.00256519
365	1.00034096	1.00034700	1.00035303	1.00035905	1.00036505

p	14 1/2%	14 3/4%	15%	15 1/4%	15 1/2%
2	1.07004673	1.07121426	1.07238053	1.07354553	1.07470926
3	1.04616896	1.04692981	1.04768955	1.04844820	1.04920575
4	1.03443063	1.03499481	1.03555808	1.03612042	1.03668185
6	1.02282401	1.02319588	1.02356707	1.02393760	1.02430745
12	1.01134762	1.01153145	1.01171492	1.01189802	1.01208075
13	1.01047017	1.01063972	1.01080892	1.01097778	1.01114630
26	1.00522146	1.00530578	1.00538993	1.00547391	1.00555771
52	1.00260733	1.00264938	1.00269134	1.00273322	1.00277500
365	1.00037104	1.00037702	1.00038298	1.00038893	1.00039487

p	15 3/4%	16%	16 1/4%	16 1/2%	16 3/4%
2	1.07587174	1.07703296	1.07819293	1.07935166	1.08050914
3	1.04996221	1.05071757	1.05147186	1.05222506	1.05297719
4	1.03724237	1.03780199	1.03836069	1.03891850	1.03947542
6	1.02467663	1.02504516	1.02541302	1.02578022	1.02614677
12	1.01226313	1.01244514	1.01262679	1.01280809	1.01298903
13	1.01131449	1.01148235	1.01164986	1.01181705	1.01198391
26	1.00564133	1.00572479	1.00580807	1.00589117	1.00597411
52	1.00281670	1.00285831	1.00289983	1.00294126	1.00298261
365	1.00040080	1.00040671	1.00041261	1.00041850	1.00042438

p	17%	17 1/4%	17 1/2%	17 3/4%	18%
2	1.08166538	1.08282039	1.08397417	1.08512672	1.08627805
3	1.05372824	1.05447823	1.05522715	1.05597501	1.05672181
4	1.04003143	1.04058656	1.04114080	1.04169416	1.04224664
6	1.02651266	1.02687790	1.02724250	1.02760644	1.02796975
12	1.01316961	1.01334984	1.01352972	1.01370925	1.01388843
13	1.01215044	1.01231663	1.01248251	1.01264805	1.01281328
26	1.00605687	1.00613947	1.00622190	1.00630416	1.00638625
52	1.00302387	1.00306504	1.00310612	1.00314713	1.00318804
365	1.00043024	1.00043609	1.00044193	1.00044775	1.00045357

COMPOUND AMOUNT OF 1 FOR FRACTIONAL PERIODS

$$(1 + i)^{1/p} \text{ (Continued)}$$

p	18 1/4%	18 1/2%	18 3/4%	19%
2	1.08742816	1.08857705	1.08972474	1.09087121
3	1.05746755	1.05821225	1.05895590	1.05969850
4	1.04279823	1.04334896	1.04389881	1.04444780
6	1.02833241	1.02869444	1.02905583	1.02941658
12	1.01406726	1.01424575	1.01442389	1.01460169
13	1.01297817	1.01314275	1.01330701	1.01347095
26	1.00646817	1.00654993	1.00663152	1.00671294
52	1.00322887	1.00326962	1.00331028	1.00335086
365	1.00045937	1.00046516	1.00047093	1.00047670

p	19 1/4%	19 1/2%	19 3/4%	20%
2	1.09201648	1.09316056	1.09430343	1.09544512
3	1.06044007	1.06118060	1.06192010	1.06265857
4	1.04499593	1.04554319	1.04608959	1.04663514
6	1.02977671	1.03013620	1.03049507	1.03085332
12	1.01477914	1.01495626	1.01513303	1.01530947
13	1.01363457	1.01379788	1.01396087	1.01412354
26	1.00679421	1.00687530	1.00695624	1.00703701
52	1.00339135	1.00343176	1.00347209	1.00351234
365	1.00048245	1.00048819	1.00049392	1.00049964

MATHEMATICAL SYMBOLS AND ABBREVIATIONS

Symbols and Abbreviations of Commercial Arithmetic

#	Number (if written before a numeral); pounds (weight), lb. (if written after a numeral.)	Apr.	April	Dr.	Debit, debtor, doctor
		a/s	Account sales		
		Aug.	August	E	East
		av.	Average	ea.	Each
		avoir.	Avoirdupois	e.g.	(exempli gratia) for example
		bal.	Balance		
		bbl. or	Barrel	etc.	And so forth
@	At, as "@ 5¢ per C," for "at 5 cents per hundred."	brl.		ex.	Example, exercise, express
		bk.	Bank, book		
		bl.	Bale	exch.	Exchange
		B/L	Bill of lading	exp.	Expense
%	Per cent; per hundred.	bu.	Bushel	F	Fahrenheit
		bx.	Box	Feb.	February
¢	Cents (placed after figures)	C	(centum) hundred	f.o.b.	Free on board
				Fri.	Friday
$	Dollars, (prefixed before figures).	cd.	Cord	frt.	Freight
		cg.	Centigram	ft. or f.	Foot
		ch.	Chain	gal.	Gallon
£	Pounds (British currency)	chg.	Charge	gi.	Gill
		c.i.f.	Carriage and insurance free.	gr.	Grain
√	Check mark			gro.	Gross
&	And, as in "Smith, Jones & Co."	ck.	Check	gr. gro.	Great gross
		cm.	Centimeter	guar.	Guarantee
		cml.	Commercial	hf.	Half
c/o	Care of	Co.	Company, county	hhd.	Hogshead
A	Acre			hr.	Hour
a/c	Account	c.o.d.	Cash on delivery	i.e.	(id est) that is
acct.	Account	coll.	Collection	in.	Inch, inches
ad val	(ad valorem), according to value	com.	Commission	ins.	Insurance
		cr.	Credit, creditor, crate	*inst.*	(instant) the present month
A.M.	(ante meridiem)	cs.	Case	int.	Interest
or	in the morning,	c. or	Cent	inv.	Invoice
a.m.	between midnight and the following noon. 12:00 A.M. is noon, better 12:00 M, 12:01 A.M. is one minute after midnight.	ct.		inv'y	Inventory
		cu.	Cubic	Jan.	January
		cwt.	Hundredweight	kg.	Keg, kilogram
		d	Pence (British currency)	km.	Kilometer
				lb. lbs.	Pound, pounds
		da.	Day	lp	List price
		Dec.	December	ltd.	Limited
		dept.	Department	L.S.	(locus sigillis) place for the seal
		dft.	Draft		
amt.	Amount	disc.	Discount		
ans.	Answer	dm.	Decimeter	M	(mille) thousand; meridiem as in 12:00 M
ap	Apothecaries' weight or measure	do.	Ditto		
		doz.	Dozen		
		dr.	Dram	m.	Mill, meter

MATHEMATICAL SYMBOLS AND ABBREVIATIONS (Continued)

Symbols and Abbreviations of Commercial Arithmetic

Mar.	March	P.M.	(post meridiem)	Sat.	Saturday
mdse.	Merchandise	*or*	in the after-	sec.	Second
mi.	Mile	p.m.	noon, between	sec'y	Secretary
min.	Minute		noon and the	Sept.	September
mm.	Millimeter		following mid-	set.	Settlement
mo.	Month		night. 12:00	sig.	Signed, signa-
Mon.	Monday		P.M. is mid-		ture
mortg.	Mortgage		night, 12:01	sq.	Square
N, NE,	North, North-		P.M. is one	stk.	Stock
NW,	east, North-		minute after	Sun.	Sunday
etc.	west, etc.		noon.	T.	Ton
no. *or*	Number	pp.	Pages	temp.	Temperature
numb.		pr.	Pair	Thu.	Thursday
Nov.	November	*prox.*	(proximo) in the	treas.	Treasurer,
Oct.	October		following		treasury
O.K.	Correct		month	Tues.	Tuesday
oz.	Ounce	pt.	Pint, point	*ult.*	(ultimo) in the
p.	Page	pwt.	Pennyweight		last month
par.	Paragraph	(*or*		*via*	By way of
pay't	Payment	dwt.)		viz.	(videlicet)
pc.	Piece	qr.	Quire		namely
pd.	Paid	qt.	Quart	vol.	Volume
per	By, by the, as in	rd.	Rod, road	W	West
	"per C," "per	rec'd	Received	Wed.	Wednesday
	M," "per doz."	rec't	Receipt	wk.	Week
pfd.	Preferred	rm.	Ream	wt.	Weight
pk.	Peck, pecks	S, SE,	South, South-	yd.	Yard
pkg.	Package	SW,	east, South-	yr.	Year
		etc.	west, etc.		

Symbols Belonging to Plane Geometry

In blackboard presentation combined with oral discussion a variety of informal abbreviations is acceptable. But in written reports it is best to use only standard abbreviations, preferably those which are found on a typewriter. Avoid characters not sufficiently distinctive as to remain legible and unambiguous when written hurriedly. When used as nouns, the plural may be indicated by adding "s"; when used as relations the copula "is" and preposition "to" may be deleted.

A°	*Angle* associated with the point or vector A. Use "rt°" for "right angle," and "st°" for "straight angle." Avoid ∠ which resembles symbol for "less than." Use "arc" rather than "⌒" to avoid confusion with bar for "line segment."
∠	Angle
∡	Angles

MATHEMATICAL SYMBOLS AND ABBREVIATIONS (Continued)

⊙	Circle. ⊙ A(B) designates the circle with center A passing through B. ⊙ (AB) has AB as diameter, and ⊙ (ABC) circumscribes △ABC. ⊙A, r has center A, radius r.
Ⓢ	Circles.
A:B(S)	Collinear. The line AB passes through the point S. Use $\overline{AB}$(S) for "S lies between A and B."
≅	Congruent. (Same shape and same size).
A:B(S,r)	Point of division. "S divides AB in the ratio AS:BS = r." Use (S, −) for internal division, and (S, +) for external division.
=	Equal, equivalent. The quantity measured may be indicated in parenthesis at the right of the statement, as "(area)," "(vol.)," "(angle)." Avoid pictogram ≏.
$\overline{\wedge}$	Perspective. See ABC:DEF(S) below.
$\underline{\wedge}$	Projective. See ABC::DEF below.
a/b	Fraction (with numerator a, denominator b). Same meaning as quotient "a ÷ b" (with dividend a, divisor b) and ratio a:b (with antecedent a, consequent b).
$\dot{\sim}$	Homothetic (Similar and perspective). "ABC $\dot{\sim}$ DEF" indicates that corresponding lines, such as BC and EF, are parallel. Use "$\dot{\sim}$ (S, r)" for "the homothecy with center S and ratio r."
AB	Line, segment, vector. When further distinctions are desired, use $\overline{AB}$ (or *AB*) for the length of the line segment (distance between A and B), use $\overrightarrow{AB}$ for the vector (displacement from A toward B), and use A:B for the infinite line (determined by the two points).
‖	Parallel.
▱	Parallelogram (vertices are named in counterclockwise order).
⊥	Perpendicular.
ABC::DEF	Projective (related by a sequence of perspectivities). Same meaning as pictogram "$\underline{\wedge}$."
ABC:DEF(S)	Perspective. The lines A:D and B:E and C:F are concurrent at the point S (center of perspectivity). Same meaning as pictogram "$\overline{\wedge}$."
QED	End of proof.
QEF	End of construction.
Ɍ	Cross ratio, anharmonic ratio Ɍ(AC, BD) = AB · CD/ AD · CB. Ɍ = −1 means "harmonic" and may be used for collinear points (range), concurrent lines (pencil), or cyclic quadrangle. Ɍ(CA, BD) = 1/Ɍ(AC, BD) = Ɍ(AC, DB). Also Ɍ(AB, CD) = 1 − Ɍ(AC, BD).
∼	Similar. △ABC ∼ △DEF means that A corresponds to D, B to E, and C to F, respectively.
☐	Square. Use "rect" for "rectangle," "quad" for

MATHEMATICAL SYMBOLS AND ABBREVIATIONS (Continued)

	"quadrilateral" (or quadrangle), and "trap" for "trapezoid" rather than pictograms.
ABC $\backsim$ DEF(r = 1)	Displaced by translation. (The triangles are congruent and similarly placed).
$\triangle$	Triangle. Use "isos" for "isosceles triangle" (naming vertex opposite base first).
$\overset{\cdot}{\mathrm{B}}$	Vertex. In using triliteral symbol ABC, A is on the initial side, B is the vertex, C is on the terminal side. The vertex may be marked with a caret "ABC" or by superscript position "A$^\mathrm{B}$C."

General Mathematical Symbols and Abbreviations

"Bold-face" or gothic type—To indicate vectors corresponding italic type indicates magnitude of the vector. In manuscript and at the blackboard, bold-faced type is variously indicated by wavy underscoring, or enclosure in a circle, or even by wavy overscoring. Some persons use German type.

Half-spaces—In writing numbers with many recorded digits, half-spaces (rather than commas or other marks) may well be used to separate convenient groups of digits. Thus $\pi = 3.14159\ 26536 -$.

Superscripts—To indicate: **1.** powers, as in x^2, $(a - x)^n$, etc. In modern practice $a^0 = 1$ always by definition (except for $a = 0$). Also in ∞', ∞^2, etc., indicating number of degrees of freedom. Wherever the context restricts the value of a to non-negative (real) values and n to positive integers, $a^{1/n}$ means the non-negative (real) nth root of a. For complex numbers, x^y is defined as $e^{y\,(\log x)}$, where the principal value of $\log x$ is to be taken. In tables 0.0^5314 may be used to indicate 0.00000314. Note special use of $\sin^n x$ for $(\sin x)^n$ except for $n = -1$, also for $\cos^n x$, etc. **2.** symbolic powers, or order of iteration, as in T^n or in D^n $(= d^n/dx^n)$, or in inverse functions as in $\sin^{-1}$, $\cos^{-1}$, $\sinh^{-1}$, etc. **3.** order of differentiation, as in y' ("y prime"), y'' ("y second," or "y double prime"), $\cdots$, $y^{(N)}$, $\cdots$ **4.** feet and inches, as in $3'4''$. **5.** degrees, minutes, seconds, as in $34°5'17''$. Do not omit ° for common angles. Write $0°$, $30°$, $45°$, $60°$, etc., not 0, 30, 45, 60, etc. Do not use superscript, ^{r}, for radians. Write $180° = \pi$ rad, but write $\cos (\pi/3)$ for $\cos 60°$. **6.** days, hours, minutes, seconds, as in $10^\mathrm{d}3^\mathrm{h}27^\mathrm{m}5.3^\mathrm{s}$. **7.** degrees of temperature as in $104°$. Where C (for Centigrade) or F (for Fahrenheit) is given, recent usage approves the omission of the °, thus $100\mathrm{C} = 212\mathrm{F}$, and $-40\mathrm{C} = -40\mathrm{F}$. **8.** For use with integral sign $\int$, and with vertical bar $|$, see these symbols. **9.** Vertex, as in $A^\mathrm{B}C$.

Dot-accents—To indicate derivatives with respect to time, (Newton's notation), as in $\dot{x}$ for x-component of velocity, and $\ddot{x}$ for x-component of acceleration.

Subscripts—To indicate: **1.** position in a sequence, set, or matrix, as in a_1, a_2, a_3, $\cdots a_n$, $\cdots$, or $a_0x^n + a_1x^{n-1} + \cdots + a_rx^{n-r} + \cdots a_n$ or in $\begin{pmatrix} a_{11}a_{12}a_{13} \\ a_{21}a_{22}a_{23} \end{pmatrix}$. **2.** general distinguishing mark. Two subscripts may be written adjacently without commas as a_{11} and to be read "a sub one one," not "a sub eleven." A subscript is sometimes enclosed in parentheses as in $F_{(0)1}$ where such distinction seems demanded. For special uses see associated symbols.

MATHEMATICAL SYMBOLS AND ABBREVIATIONS (Continued)

Juxtaposition—To indicate: **1.** the algebraic product, as in $2bxy$.   **2.** the logical product as in AB where A and B are given classes, and in symbolic logic. Also written with centrally placed dot as $A \cdot B$.   **3.** the group product, as in ST (the result of performing first S, then T, or in aH, the co-set consisting for given a of all operations ah, where h is in H.   **4.** general operational or functional combination as in dy/dx, $\sin x$, $\log x$, $\max y$, $\lim x_n$, etc.   **5.** sequence of points or other elements determining a geometric figure, as line AB, parallelogram $ABCD$, angle ABC, etc.   **6.** sum of products (in tensor notation) when index appears as subscript for one factor and superscript for another.   Thus $a_i x^i$ means $\Sigma a_i x^i$, in tensor notation.

( )—Parentheses ("round brackets") to indicate: **1.** aggregation, as in $(a + b) \cdot (a - b) = a^2 - b^2$.   **2.** argument of function, as in $f(x)$, $g(x,y)$, etc.   **3.** sequence or set, as in $a = (a_i)$, $x = (x_{ij})$, (x,y,z), etc.   **4.** matrix, as in $\begin{pmatrix} a_{11}a_{12}a_{13} \\ a_{21}a_{22}a_{23} \end{pmatrix}$ also written as $\begin{Vmatrix} a_{11}a_{12}a_{13} \\ a_{21}a_{22}a_{23} \end{Vmatrix}$.   **5.** permutation (or substitution) in group theory as in $\begin{pmatrix} a_1 a_2 a_3 \\ b_1 b_2 b_3 \end{pmatrix}$ where a_i is replaced by $b_i (i = 1,2,3)$.   **6.** binomial coefficient, as in $\binom{n}{r} = n!/[r!(n - r)!]$.   This is also designated by $C_{n,r}$ or $_nC_r$.   For n,r, positive integers, $\binom{-n}{r} = (-1)^r \binom{n + r - 1}{r}$, $\binom{n}{-r} = 0$, by definition.   **7.** cycle or cylic permutation (in group theory) as in (a_1, a_2, a_3) for $\begin{pmatrix} a_1 a_2 a_3 \\ a_2 a_3 a_1 \end{pmatrix}$.   **8.** greatest common divisor, as in $(30,42) = 6$, $(7,5) = 1$.   **9.** inner product as in $(ab) = \Sigma_i a_i b_i$.   **10.** segment or open interval, as in (a,b), for system of values of x, where $a < x < b$.

Superscript ( )—To indicate: **1.** general index as distinguished from exponent.   **2.** index of order of derivative as in y, y', $\cdots$, $y^{(n)}$, $\cdots$.   **3.** "factorial," as in $x^{(r)} = x(x - 1) \cdots (x - r + 1)$.   By definition $x^{(-r)} = 1/[(x + 1) \cdot (x + 2) \cdots (x + r)]$.

[ ]—Brackets ("square brackets"), to indicate: **1.** aggregation.   **2.** argument of function as with ( ).   **3.** greatest integer in, as $[2] = 2$, $[-7/3] = -3$.   **4.** inner product (for coefficients in normal equations in the method of least squares), as in $[aa]$, $[XY]$, etc.   **5.** outer product of vectors.   Other notations are $V\,ab$ and $a \times b$.   **6.** divided difference (in formal interpolation). $[x_i] = y_i$, $[x_i, x_{i+1}] = (y_{i+1} - y_i)/(x_{i+1} - x_i)$, $\cdots$ $[x_i, x_{i+1}, \cdots, x_{i+r}] = ([x_{i+1}, \cdots, x_{i+r}] - [x_i, \cdots, x_{i+r-1}])/(x_{i+r} - x_i)$.   **7.** range of points (in projective geometry) as in $[P]$.   **8.** base (basis) of Abelian group, as in $[a,b, \cdots, k]$.   **9.** module or ideal, as $[2] = [0, \pm2, \pm4, \cdots, \pm 2n, \cdots]$.   **10.** Christoffel symbol, as in $\begin{bmatrix} mn \\ p \end{bmatrix} = \frac{1}{2}\left(\frac{\partial g_{pm}}{\partial x^n} + \frac{\partial g_{pn}}{\partial x^m} = \frac{\partial g_{mn}}{\partial x^p} \right)$.   **11.** closed interval, as in $[a,b]$ for system of values of x where $a \leqq x \leqq b$.

Subscript note.   The use of adjacent subscripts, rather than of indices placed directly below is recommended on account of its availability for running text, and its economy of space and of expense in type setting.   Thus use $\sum_i$ rather than $\sum\limits_i$, $\int_a^b$ rather than $\int\limits_a^b$, etc.

MATHEMATICAL SYMBOLS AND ABBREVIATIONS (Continued)

{ }—Braces ("curly brackets") to indicate: **1.**: aggregation, as in $\{(x - a)$ $(x - b)\}^2$. **2.** class of (in theory of aggregates), where the general element only is mentioned, as in $\{a_i\} = [a_1, a_2, a_3]$, $(i = 1,2,3)$. **3.** Christoffel symbol, as in $\left\{ \begin{matrix} m\ n \\ p \end{matrix} \right\} = g^{rp} \left[\begin{matrix} m\ n \\ p \end{matrix} \right]$. **4.** the members in a uniquely determined set, as in $\{x_1, x_2, \cdots x_n\}$.

< >—Angle brackets to indicate: **1.** aggregation. **2.** closed interval as with [ ]. **3.** Angle between as in $A \cdot B = AB \cos <A, B>$. Use sparingly because of ambiguity with signs of inequality.

| |—Vertical bars, to indicate: **1.** absolute value (modulus of complex number). as $|a + ib|^2 = a^2 + b^2$. **2.** magnitude of (for vectors) as $a = |a|$. **3.** determinant, as in $\begin{vmatrix} a & b \\ c & d \end{vmatrix} = ad - bc$. The use of the notation $|a_{ij}|$ for the determinant of the matrix (a_{ij}), is common but is ambiguous. The notation det (a_{ij}) may be used for this determinant.

‖ ‖—Double bars, to indicate: **1.** matrix as in $\begin{Vmatrix} a_{11}a_{12}a_{13} \\ a_{21}a_{22}a_{23} \end{Vmatrix}$ or in $\|a_{ij}\|$. **2.** generalized length (for metrical spaces), as in $\|f\|^2 = \int f^2(x)dx$. **3.** To indicate the length of a vector, as in $\|X\|$.

(], [).—For intervals, as $(a,b]$, for system of values of x for which $a < x \leq b$, and $[a,b)$, for system of values of x for which $a \leq x < b$. Similarly $(a,b >$, and $< a,b)$ are sometimes used for these respectively.

⟨ ⟩—Brackets ("bent brackets"), to indicate an ordered set of objects, as in $\langle x, y, z \rangle$.

⊢—Is deducible from.

⊨—Is valid, or is a tautology (in logic), as in $\models A$ (A is valid).

∪—(is) the union, or sum or join (of), as in $A \cup B$.

∩—(is) the intersection, or product (of), as in $A \cap B$.

⊃—**1.** contains (or containing) as proper sub-class. **2.** implies (or implying).

⊇—contains (or containing) as sub-class. (Some writers use, ⊃, for this.)

⊂—(is) contained as proper sub-class within.

⊆—(is) contained as sub-class within. (Some writers use, ⊂, for this.)

≡—**1.** (is) identical with. $\equiv_x$ indicates (is) identical with for all values of x for which both members are defined. **2.** (is) congruent to (with respect to indicated modulus) as in $a \equiv b$ (mod m). **3.** (is) equivalent to (in formal logic).

=—(is) equal (to).

∧—and (in logic).

∨—or (in logic), as in $p \vee q$ (p or q), and/or

⊻—exclusive or, as in $p \veebar q$ (p or q, but not both).

<—(is) less than.

>—(is greater than. Use "less than" preferably as in "$a < x < b$" rather than "$b > x > a$" since former corresponds to order of real numbers on x-axis.

≦ or ≤—(is) less than or equal to. Sometimes read (in the case of real numbers) as "(is) not greater than."

≧ or ≥—(is) greater than or equal to. Sometimes read (in the case of real numbers) as "(is) not less than."

MATHEMATICAL SYMBOLS AND ABBREVIATIONS (Continued)

$\not\equiv$—**1.** (is) not identically equal (to). (Not "identically unequal to"), is unequal to for at least one value. **2.** (is) not congruent (to).

$\neq$—(is) not equal (to).

$\lesseqgtr$—**1.** (is) not equal (to), (for real quantities). **2.** (Sometimes when explained by context) less than or greater than respectively.

$\sim$—**1.** (is) formally, asymptotically, or approximately equal to. (The context should make the meaning specific.) Do not use $\doteq$ for "approximately equal to." **2.** (is) similar (to). **3.** not (in some works on formal logic). **4.** used to indicate the equivalence of two matrices.

Use "iff" for "if and only if." Alternately "$^{(n)}$ as" (read "as" may be used for "necessary and sufficient."

$\rightarrow$—**1.** approaches (as a limit), as in $\lim\limits_{x\to a} f(x) = b$, $f(x) \to b$, as $x \to a$, etc. (Do not use $\doteq$). Not usually employed with long expressions. **2.** leads to, validates, implies (in logic). **3.** corresponds to. **4.** "if . . . , then . . . " relation (in logic).

$\leftrightarrow$—**1.** mutually implies (in logic). **2.** in one-to-one correspondence with, corresponds reciprocally to. **3.** if and only if, also iff.

$\downarrow$—decreases monotonically to a limit.

$\uparrow$—increases monotonically to a limit.

Superscript $\rightarrow$—directed line as $\overrightarrow{AB}$.

$|$—Vertical bar, to indicate: **1.** value at, as in $f(x)|_a = f(a)$, or $f(x)|_{x=a} = f(a)$. **2.** value between as in $f(x)|_a^b = f(b) - f(a)$. **3.** is a divisor of, divides (in number theory) as $3|6$, $3/\underline{6}$ for "3 divides 6" or use solidus $6/3$ to indicate that this quotient is an integer, or $(x - a)|(x^2 - a^2)$. **4.** inner product (with parentheses) as $(a|b) = \Sigma_i a_i b_i$.

\ or /—Stroke, mark of cancellation as in $3x = \not{6}^{\,2}$, $x + 3 = \not{7}^{\,4}$.

/—Solidus, or oblique rule, to indicate: **1.** actual or symbolic division, as in $3/7$, $(x - a)/(x - b)$, d/dx, dy/dx, d^2y/dx^2. Do not write ambiguously $a - b/c - d$, but $(a - b)/(c - d)$ or $a - (b/c) - d$, as may be intended. Do not write a/bc but $(a/b)c$ or $a/(bc)$ as intended. Write a proportion as $a/b = c/d$ not $a:b::c:d$. Where A, B, C, D designate displayed expressions, write the proportion as $\dfrac{A}{B} = \dfrac{C}{D}$. In commercial typing in place of $8\tfrac{5}{12}$, it is usual to write 8-5/12. The solidus form a/b, adapted to running text should be used where conveniently possible, rather than the displayed form $\dfrac{a}{b}$. **2.** quotient or factor group (in group theory) as G/H, (where H is a normal subgroup of G). **3.** per, as in ft/sec. **4.** discount symbol, as in Cash 6, 4/5, 2/30, n/90 indicating 6% discount for immediate payment, 4% discount if paid within 5 days, 2% discount if paid within 30 days, no discount thereafter, but face amount of bill is due (net) not later than the 90th day. **5.** shilling, (in British currency) as 3/6d, or 10/ $-$.

Superscript ‾‾—Vinculum. This may be regarded as obsolescent for general use as a mark of aggregation due to its unsuitability for monotype setting. In conjunction with the radical sign it is widely used, but may often be avoided. There is little logical or historical basis for using $\sqrt{2}$ rather than

MATHEMATICAL SYMBOLS AND ABBREVIATIONS (Continued)

$\sqrt{\ }2$. For a longer expression, one may write $\sqrt{(x^2 + a^2)}$ rather than $\sqrt{x^2 + a^2}$. Instead of $\sqrt{x - a}\,(x - b)$, one might write $(x - b)\sqrt{(x - a)}$. In geometry, the vinculum may be used for line segments as in $\overline{AB}$.

Superscript $\overline{\ \ \ }$—Bar. To indicate: **1.** complex conjugate of, as $\bar{z}$. This is somewhat inconvenient for "upper extended" letters and capitals as, $\bar{b}, \bar{h}, \bar{X}$, etc. Also indicated by *conj*, as *conj* $(x + iy) = x - iy$ or by use of a "star" as in z^*. **2.** arithmetic mean value of, as in $\bar{x}, = \sum_i x_i/n$. **3.** closure of (in topology), as in $\bar{E}$ (the closure of E). **4.** "least upper," as in $\overline{\lim}$, and $\bar{B}$ for least upper limit and least upper bound, respectively. See "sup." **5.** repeating decimal, as in $1.\overline{14} = 1.141414 \cdots$.

Subscript $\underline{\ \ \ \ }$—To indicate: **1.** italics (in manuscript). **2.** "greatest lower," as in $\underline{\lim}$, and $\underline{B}$, for greatest lower limit, and greatest lower bound respectively. See "inf."

$\overline{\ \ \ }$ —horizontal rule, sign of division, as in $\dfrac{x - a}{x + a}$. Ordinarily the solidus form, adapted to running text, is preferred, as in $(x - a)/(x + a)$. When numerator and denominator are both complicated, the displayed form using horizontal rule may be avoided by writing "A/B, where $A = \cdots$, and $B = \cdots$."

$-$ (centrally placed)—Minus sign. To indicate: **1.** subtraction as in $7 - 2 = 5$, $a^2 - b^2 = (a - b)(a + b)$. **2.** overestimate, as in $3.5-$. **3.** approach through negative values as in $-\infty$ and -0. **4.** region where variable indicated by context is negative (in graphs). **5.** logical difference (in theory of classes). **6.** in $(-)^n$, the sign expressed by $(-1)^n$.

(on line)—**1.** decimal point. In the decimal representation of a number between 0 and 1, the cipher, 0, should (except in tables) appear before the decimal point. Thus 0.314 not .314. Notation by powers of 10, ("scientific notation") is recommended, especially when recording approximate values; thus to four significant figures, 3.140×10^9 and 3.140×10^{-6}. **2.** (sometimes used in quoting bond prices) as in 95.17 for $95^{17}\!/\!_{32}$. **3.** (sometimes used in recording mental age) as in 12.3 for 12 yr. 3 mo. **4.** (in symbolic logic) as mark of punctuation separating terms, also as, "and."

$:$—Colon. To indicate: **1.** hours, in recording time, as in 4:10 p.m. **2.** ratio (an obsolescent form) as in $a:b$. The form a/b is preferred. **3.** (in symbolic logic) as mark of punctuation separating groups of terms, as in $p \cdot p \supset q :\supset :q$. **4.** Indicates infinite line $A:B$, collinearity $A:B(S)$, and perspectivity $A:B$. **5.** such that (in logic). $\cdot$ (centrally placed)—**1.** mark of algebraic multiplication, particularly where mere juxtaposition would be ambiguous, as in $\overline{AB} \cdot \overline{CD}$. **2.** (for vectors), the mark of inner or dot multiplication as in $a \cdot b = ab \cos < ab$. Other notations are (ab) and $S\,ab$.

. (placed above line)—to indicate repeating decimal, used in pairs, as in $1.7\dot{3}\dot{5} = 1.735735735 \cdots$.

$\cdots$ (preferably centrally placed)—"three dots" meaning "and so forth," or "and so forth up to." Particularly when the reader knows what has been omitted, as in the sequence of natural integers, etc. as in $1, 2 \cdots, n, \cdots$; or $a_0, a_1, \cdots, a_n, \cdots$, or $1, \cdots, m$.

MATHEMATICAL SYMBOLS AND ABBREVIATIONS (Continued)

∴—hence, therefore.   Inverted ∵ since.

∷, ∷∶, ∷∷, etc.—(in symbolic logic), marks of punctuation stronger than ·
and ∶

„—ditto.

∘ (centrally placed)—indicates (in classes or sets) the composite of functions, as
in $g{\circ}f$.

$+$ plus sign.   To indicate: **1.** addition, as in $2 + 3$, $a + b$, 10^{a+1}.   **2.** under-
estimate, as in $3.5+$.   **3.** continued fraction as in $a_0 + \dfrac{1}{a_1+} \dfrac{1}{a_2+} \cdots$ for

$a_0 + \cfrac{1}{a_1 + \cfrac{1}{a_2+}}.$ **4.** approach through positive values as in $+\infty$, and in $+0$

5. region where variable indicated by the context is positive, (in graphs).
6. logical addition (in theory of classes).   **7.** " . . or . . or both," (in
formal logic).   Note: In writing series indicate sign before and after dots of

omission, as $a_0 + a_1 + \cdots + a_n$, or $1 - \dfrac{1}{2} + \dfrac{1}{3} + \cdots + (-1)^{n-1}\dfrac{1}{n}.$

8. in abstract group theory a group or co-set may be expressed as the sum
of its elements.

$\oplus$—denoting a logical operation of summation between elements of a set,
such as the sum of vectors.

$\pm$—**1.** "plus or minus."   The repeated appearance of $\pm$ as in $\pm a \pm b \pm c$ is
ambiguous.   In many cases the sign $\pm$ before a term which appears repeat-
edly is intended to indicate the systematic use of the positive determination
or of the negative determination throughout.   Thus one may write
$(a \pm b)^3 = a^3 \pm 3a^2b + 3ab^2 \pm b^3$.   Where the context restricts the value
of a to non-negative (real) values, $\sqrt{a}$ means the non-negative (real) square
root of a.   Hence when both signs are desired, write $\pm$ before the radical.
For roots of a quadratic equation $ax^2 + bx + c = 0$, use $\pm$ as in
$\dfrac{-b \pm \sqrt{b^2 - 4ac}}{2a}.$ **2.** (in theory of observation), "with a probable error of."
As in 17.2 ± 0.5 cm.

$\mp$—"minus or plus respectively."   Used in context where $\pm$ has appeared
previously, as in $a^3 \pm b^3 = (a \pm b)(a^2 \mp ab + b^2)$.   Here upper signs are
to be taken throughout, or else lower signs.   The notation $\pm a \mp b \pm c$ is
ambiguous, meaning perhaps one of the four values $\pm(a - b) \pm c$, or one of
the two values $\pm(a - b + c)$.

$\times$—**1.** times, (sign of algebraic multiplication).   Used chiefly in arithmetic,
as in $2 \times 2 = 4$, 7.3×10^4.   **2.** (for vectors) the sign of outer or cross
multiplication.   **3.** (for classes) the Cartesian product.   Thus $A \times B$ is the
class of all ordered pairs (a,b) where a is an element of A, and b of B.

$\otimes$—denoting a logical operation of multiplication between elements of a set,
such as the product of vectors.

$\div$—sign of division.   Used chiefly in arithmetic.   Should be replaced by
solidus, /, where convenient.

$\sqrt{}\sqrt[n]{}$—square root of, nth root of.   (See discussion under "superscript," and
under "vinculum").   By custom, for a positive, $\sqrt{(-a)}$ means usually
$i\sqrt{a}$, rather than $-i\sqrt{a}$, but the latter unambiguous forms are preferred.

!—"factorial," as in $3! = 1 \cdot 2 \cdot 3 = 6$. $0! = 1$, (by definition).   The ele-

MATHEMATICAL SYMBOLS AND ABBREVIATIONS (Continued)

mentary arithmetic definition of factorial n, may be replaced in favor of the definition as a special case of the Gamma function $\Gamma(x)$. For $-1 < n$,

$n! = \Gamma(n + 1), = \int_0^\infty x^n e^{-x} dx$. For n a large natural number, Stirling's

asymptotic formula (extended) yields $n! \sim \sqrt{2n\pi}\,(n/e)^n \left(1 + \dfrac{1}{12n} + \right.$

$\dfrac{1}{288n^2} - \dfrac{139}{51840n^3} - \cdots \left.\right)$. Note: Do not use the obsolescent form $\lfloor n$ for $n!$

$\int, \displaystyle\int_a^b, \int_a^x, \iint, \int_c$ —Integral signs. (use preferably bold-face type)

$\displaystyle\int_a^b \int_c^d f(x,y)\,dx\,dy$ denotes $\displaystyle\int_a^b \left(\int_c^d f(x,y)\,dx\right) dy, = \int_a^b dy \int_c^d dx f(x,y)$.

$\oint$—curvilinear integral over closed path free from singularities. (Use preferably bold-face type.)

§—section, or article.

❡ or ¶—paragraph.

$\propto$—varies as. Instead of $y \propto x$ one may write $y = kx$, k being the constant factor of proportionality.

∇—nabla—To indicate: **1.** linear vector operator $\left(\dfrac{\partial}{\partial x}, \dfrac{\partial}{\partial y}, \dfrac{\partial}{\partial z}\right)$ as used also in divergence, gradient, and curl (or rotation). **2.** backward difference (in interpolation theory) $\nabla a_n = a_n - a_{n-1}$.

∇^2—Laplace operator. Sometimes written Δ.

$\boxdot$—Four dimensional differential operator of D'Alembert and Poincare [= point carré].

$^\circ, ', '', ''', \cdots, (N) \cdots,$ (superscript)—superscript numbers. See "superscripts."

∞—infinity. Use $+\infty$ or $-\infty$ respectively, where direction of approach along real numbers is to be indicated. Otherwise use ∞ rather than $\pm\infty$. Note: "$n \to \infty$," may be read "as n increases without bound." Lim $f(x) = \infty$ means "Lim $1/f(x) = 0$," so that whenever one variable "becomes infinite" the meaning is that its reciprocal "becomes zero."

$\in$—(is) a member (of), as in $x \in A$. Several objects can be denoted as members in a set A by $x_1, x_2, \cdots x_n \in A$.

$\notin$—(is) not a member (of).

$\mathcal{P}$—denotes a power set, as in $\mathcal{P}(A)$ which denotes the set of all subsets of a set A.

$\aleph$—Aleph (initial Hebrew letter) transfinite cardinal number, in particular that of all real numbers. $\aleph_0$ (aleph null) first transfinite cardinal. Use of Hebrew letters for transfinite numerals is recommended: "aleph" (omit the null) for the cardinal of the set of integers; ℶ "beth" for the cardinal of the continuum (number of points on a line); and ℷ "gimel" for the cardinal of functions of a real variable.

$\mathfrak{F}$—the Farey series. $\mathfrak{F}_n$ denotes the Farey series of order n.

α—Alpha. To indicate: **1.** (in analytic geometry of 3 dimensions), direction angle with X-axis. **2.** angular acceleration. **3.** (in statistics) $\alpha_0 = 1$, $\alpha_1 = 0$, $\alpha_2 = 1$, $\alpha_3 = \mu_3/\sigma^3$, $\alpha_4 = \mu_4/\sigma^4 = \mu_4/\mu_2^2$. **4.** (in mathematical astronomy), right ascension (also indicated by R.A.) **5.** angle of triangle

MATHEMATICAL SYMBOLS AND ABBREVIATIONS (Continued)

at A, opposite side a.   **6.** root of algebraic equation as in $a(x - \alpha)(x - \beta)$ $(x - \gamma) = 0$.

B—(Greek Beta)—$B(m,n) = \Gamma(m)\Gamma(n)/\Gamma(m + n)$, (Eulerian Beta-function).

β—Beta.   To indicate: **1.** (in analytic geometry of 3 dimensions), direction angle with Y-axis.   **2.** (in statistics), $\beta_1 = \alpha_3{}^2 = \mu_3{}^2/\mu_2{}^3$, $\beta_2 = \alpha_4 = \mu_4/\mu_2{}^2$. **3.** angle of triangle at B, opposite side b.   **4.** root of algebraic equation. See α.

Γ—$\Gamma(x)$ Gamma-function.   See "!"   Among numerous definitions equivalent for positive real values of x, are the two following: (i) $\Gamma(x) = \lim_{n \to \infty}$ $\dfrac{1 \cdot 2 \cdots n}{x(x + 1) \cdots (x + n - 1)} n^{x-1}$, $x > 0$.   (ii) $\Gamma(x) = \displaystyle\int_0^\infty e^{-t} t^{x-1} dt$, $R(x) > 0$.

γ—Gamma.   To indicate: **1.** (in analytic geometry of 3 dimensions) direction angle with Z-axis.   **2.** Euler or Mascheroni constant.   (Also indicated by C.) $\gamma = \lim_{n \to \infty} \left(\dfrac{1}{1} + \dfrac{1}{2} + \cdots + \dfrac{1}{n} - \log n \right) = 0.57721 \quad 56649 \quad 01532$ $86060 \quad 65120 \cdots$ **3.** angle of triangle at C, opposite side c.   **4.** radius of geodesic curvature.   **5.** universal constant of gravitation $= 6.670 \times 10^{-8}$ cm^3/(gm. sec^2).   **6.** root of algebraic equation, see α.

Δ—Delta.   To indicate: **1.** triangle (in plane geometry).   (For right triangle, write rtΔ, not $\angle$).   Also area of triangle.   **2.** increment, as in Δx, Δf, $f(x + \Delta x)$, etc.   **3.** forward difference (interpolation theory). $\Delta a_n = a_{n+1} - a_n$.   **4.** Laplacian operator $\dfrac{\partial^2}{\partial x^2} + \dfrac{\partial^2}{\partial y^2}$, or $\dfrac{\partial^2}{\partial x^2} + \dfrac{\partial^2}{\partial y^2} + \dfrac{\partial^2}{\partial z^2}$, also designated by ∇^2.   **5.** selected square root of the discriminant of a given polynomial, as in $\Delta^2 = b^2 - 4ac$ for the polynomial $ax^2 + bx + c$.   **6.** triangular number, (of form $(n^2 - n)/2$).   **7.** Legendre's radical, $\Delta(\varphi)^2 = 1 - k^2 \sin^2 \varphi$.

δ—Delta.   To indicate: **1.** positive constant dependent upon ϵ that may be chosen initially as near to zero as desired.   (In theory of limits, of continuity, etc.)   **2.** variation of.   **3.** (in interpolational theory) central difference $\delta y_{c+i+\frac{1}{2}} = y_{c+i+1} - y_{c+i}$.   **4.** (in mathematical astronomy) apparent declination.   **5.** number of double points, or nodes (Plücker number). **6.** (in statistics) deviation.   **7.** force of interest, $e^\delta = 1 + i$, (in mathematics of finance).   **8.** Kronecker Delta, $\delta_{ij} = 0$ for $i \neq j$, $= 1$ for $i = j$. In tensor notation, also $\delta_i{}^j$.   One has $\delta_{ij} = \begin{pmatrix} o \\ i - j \end{pmatrix}$ or $C_{0, i-i}$.   **9.** unit elongation (in strength of materials).

∂—curly d.   To indicate: **1.** partial differentiation as in $\partial f(x,y)/\partial x$.   **2.** The Jacobian operator, as in $\partial(u,v,w)/\partial(x,y,z)$.   This is variously represented, sometimes as $J\left(\dfrac{u,v,w}{x,y,z}\right)$ etc.   **3.** a specified square root of the discriminant D.   (also sometimes as Δ.)

ϵ—Epsilon.   To indicate: **1.** positive constant, that may be chosen initially independently as near to zero as desired.   (In theory of limits, of continuity etc.)   **2.** primitive root of unity.   **3.** (is) member of, (relation of element to containing class).   **4.** eccentricity of conic section, usually better designated by e.   **5.** (in mathematical astronomy) obliquity of ecliptic. **6.** an ϵ-number is a transfinite ordinal or a certain limiting type.   Note: Do not use ϵ or ε for Napierian base except in engineering.   See e.

MATHEMATICAL SYMBOLS AND ABBREVIATIONS (Continued)

ͻ—(Inverted Epsilon). Such that.

∉—(is not a member of.)

ζ—Zeta. To indicate: **1.** Riemann Zeta-function $\zeta(s) = \Sigma_{n=1}^{\infty} n^{-s}$ (for $s > 1$). **2.** (in statistics) a test of linearity. $\zeta = \eta^2 - r^2$.

η—Eta. To indicate: **1.** general variable or unknown constant, analogous to y as in case of moving system of coordinates, etc. Used in ordered set (ξ,η,ζ). **2.** a confocal coordinate. See ξ. **3.** (in statistics), correlation ratio. **4.** order-type of the aggregate of all rational numbers.

Θ—Theta. To indicate: **1.** Theta-function. See ϑ. **2.** absolute temperature (where t is used for time).

θ—Theta. To indicate: **1.** general angular displacement (in trigonometry and analytic geometry). **2.** (in plane polar coordinates $(r \text{ cis } \theta)$) angle from initial ray to radius vector, $x = r \cos \theta$, $y = r \sin \theta$. **3.** (in cylindrical coordinates $(r\ \theta\ z)$) angle from initial radial half-plane to radial half-plane containing radius vector. **4.** (in spherical coordinates (r,θ,φ)) co-latitude (measured from zenith) and (in astronomy) zenith distance. This notation is traditional in mathematical physics. In texts on analytic geometry, usage varies, θ being employed frequently for the longitude. See φ. **5.** Theta-function. See ϑ. **6.** (in formal theory of operations) a displacement operator. **7.** ordinary temperature (when t is used for time).

ϑ—Theta-function. Definitions and notations vary widely. For elliptic Theta-functions the notation given here is that followed by Whittaker and Watson. Here $\vartheta_i(o,q)$ designates the value of $\vartheta_i(o,q)$, ϑ_i', the value of $d\vartheta_i(z,q)/dz$. $(i = 1,2,3,4)$. These are defined by $\vartheta_1(z,q) = 2q^{\frac{1}{4}} \sin Z - 2q^{\frac{9}{4}} \sin 3z + 2q^{\frac{25}{4}}$ $\sin 5z - \cdots$ $\vartheta_2(z,q) = 2q^{\frac{1}{4}} \sin z + 2q^{\frac{9}{4}} \sin 3z + 2q^{\frac{25}{4}} \sin 5z + \cdots$ $\vartheta_3(z,q)$ $= 1 + 2q \cos 2z + 2q^4 \cos 4z + 2q^9 \cos 6z + \cdots$ $\vartheta_4(z,q) = 1 - 2q \cos$ $2z + 2q^4 \cos 4z - 2q^9 \cos 6z + \cdots$.

ι—Iota, number of inflexions (a Plücker number).

ͻ—inverted Iota, (in formal logic) the unique element fulfilling description stated.

κ—Kappa, number of cusps. (A Plücker number).

Λ—Lambda, sometimes used for null-class.

λ—Lambda. To indicate: **1.** general linear parameter (e.g., in a pencil), as in $F + \lambda G$. **2.** running index, as in $x_\lambda (\lambda = 1, 2, \cdots)$. **3.** longitude (in mathematical astronomy). **4.** characteristic value (as in λ_i) in theory of linear differential equations of second order, linear integral equations, etc. **5.** order-type of the aggregate of all real numbers. **6.** In solid analytic geometry (λ, μ, ν) are direction cosines.

μ—Mu. To indicate: **1.** running index, usually used with λ, as in $x_\lambda y_\mu$. **2.** general linear parameter, when used with λ, as in $\lambda F + \mu G$. **3.** (in statistics) moment, about the arithmetic mean, as in $\mu_k = \Sigma_i f_i (x_i - \bar{x})^k$, $\mu_2 = \sigma^2 =$ variance. **4.** μ_x, force of mortality $= -d(\log_e l_x)/dx$. **5.** (in number theory) inversion function of Moebius and Mertens. **6.** Various physical constants such as permeability, reduced mass. **7.** Integrating factor which converts integrable expression into exact differential form.

ν—Nu. To indicate: **1.** running index, usually with λ and μ. **2.** (in statistics) moment about arbitrary origin A (in "short method") as in $\nu_k = \Sigma_i f_i (x_i - A)^k$. **3.** Frequency.

ξ—Xi. To indicate: **1.** general variable, or unknown constant analogous to

MATHEMATICAL SYMBOLS AND ABBREVIATIONS (Continued)

x, as in moving systems of coordinates, etc. **2.** a confocal coordinate as in

(i) confocal ellipses and hyperbolas, $\dfrac{x^2}{a^2 - \lambda} + \dfrac{y^2}{b^2 - \lambda} = 1$, $-\infty < \xi < b^2 <$

$\eta < a^2$. (ii) confocal ellipsoids and hyperboloids of revolution, $\dfrac{x^2}{a^2 - \lambda} +$

$\dfrac{y^2 + z^2}{b^2 - \lambda} = 1$, $-\infty < \xi < b^2 < \eta < a^2$. (iii) confocal parabolas, $y^2 + 2\lambda$.

$(x - \lambda) = 0$, $-\infty < \xi < 0 < \eta < +\infty$. (iv) confocal paraboloids of revolution, $y^2 + z^2 + 2\lambda(x - \lambda) = 0$, $-\infty < \xi < 0 < \eta < +\infty$. (v) confocal

ellipsoids and hyperboloids, $\dfrac{x^2}{a^2 - \lambda} + \dfrac{y^2}{b^2 - \lambda} + \dfrac{z^2}{c^2 - \lambda} = 1$, $-\infty < \xi <$

$c^2 < \eta < b^2 < \zeta < a^2$. (vi) confocal paraboloids, $\dfrac{x^2}{a^2 - \lambda} + \dfrac{y^2}{b^2 - \lambda} = 2z - \lambda$,

$-\infty < \xi < b^2 < \eta < a^2 < \zeta < +\infty$. (ξ, η, ζ), Xi, eta, zeta, are used as alternates for rectangular coordinates (x, y, z).

Π, $\Pi_i \Pi_{i=m}^{n}$, $\Pi_{(R)}$ or $\underset{(R)}{\Pi}$—**1.** product of terms with index i, or j, etc. ranging from

m to n, or over R. Do not use $\underset{i}{\Pi}$, $\underset{i=m}{\overset{n}{\Pi}}$, etc. (Bold-faced type preferred.)

2. (in some formal logical treatments) "for every."

Π_{ij}, Π_{ijk}, $\cdots$ —$\Pi_i \Pi_j$, $\Pi_i \Pi_j \Pi_k$, etc.

π—Pi. **1.** the ratio of the length of circumference of a circle, to the diameter. $\pi = 3.14159\ 26535\ 89793\ 23846 \cdots$ **2.** general notation for plane, projectivity, projective, period, etc.

ρ—Rho. **1.** radius of geodesic curvature. **2.** proportionality factor, as in $\rho X_i = \Sigma_j a_{ij} x_j$.

$\sum$, $\sum_i$, $\sum_{i=m}^{n}$, $\sum_{(R)}$ or $\underset{(R)}{\sum}$—Sigma. **1.** summation, sum of terms of index i,

or j, etc., ranging from m to n, or over range R. Do not use $\underset{i}{\sum}$, $\underset{i=m}{\overset{n}{\sum}}$, etc.

(bold-faced type preferred). **2.** (on some formal logical treatments) "for at least one." **3.** (in number theory) $\Sigma_{d/n}$ summation extended over all divisors of n. **4.** (in mathematical astronomy) Σ-pt is the intersection of the meridian with the equator.

Σ_{ij}, Σ_{ijk} $\cdots$ —$\Sigma_i \Sigma_j$, $\Sigma_i \Sigma_j \Sigma_k$, etc.

σ—Sigma. To indicate: **1.** radius of torsion. **2.** (in statistics) standard deviation $\sigma^2 N = \Sigma_i (x_i - \bar{x})^2 f_i$. **3.** (in number theory), $\sigma_k(n) =$ sum of kth powers of divisors of n. **4.** any one of several analogous Sigma-functions. The simplest elliptic Sigma-function $\sigma(x)$ is related to the Weierstrassian $\wp$ function by $\wp u = -d^2 \log \sigma u / du^2$. One has $\sigma u = u \left\{ 1 - \dfrac{g_2}{2} \dfrac{u^4}{5!} \right.$

$\left. - 6g_3 \dfrac{u^6}{7!} - \dfrac{9}{4}g_2^2 \dfrac{u^8}{9!} - 18g_2 g_3 \dfrac{u^{10}}{11!} - \cdots \right\}$ **5.** proportionality factor, usually used with ρ.

τ—Tau. To indicate: **1.** number of bitangents (a Plücker number). **2.** time (when t is used for temperature). **3.** torsion (of curve in space).

Υ—Upsilon. (In mathematical astronomy) vernal equinox.

ϕ—Phi. **1.** Used to indicate the Golden Ratio or Section, $\phi = 1.61803\ 39887$ $49894 \cdots$. **2.** Used to denote Euler's function, where $\phi(m)$ is the number

MATHEMATICAL SYMBOLS AND ABBREVIATIONS (Continued)

of positive integers not greater than and prime to m. **3.** The null (or empty) set containing no elements.

φ—Phi. To indicate: **1.** general functional symbol, especially for polynomials. **2.** (in spherical coordinates, (r,θ,φ), longitude from x to y in right-handed system. In some astronomical work the z-axis points to the zenith, θ is the zenith-distance, and φ is the latitude. In some works on analytic geometry the roles of θ and φ are interchanged, although the system given is traditional mathematical physics. $x = r \sin \theta \cos \varphi$, $y = r \sin \theta \sin \varphi$, $z = r \cos \theta$. **3.** (in geocentric coordinates, (r,φ,λ), φ = latitude (not co-latitude as with spherical coordinates). **4.** (in plane polar coordinates (r,φ).) Used chiefly as specialized case of spherical coordinates $(r,\pi/2,\varphi)$. See θ. **5.** inclination of plane curve, $\tan \varphi = dy/dx = m$. **6.** (in number theory.) Euler's function or indicatrix. $\varphi(n)$ is the number of positive integers not exceeding n and prime to n. **7.** $\varphi_i(x)$, characteristic function, see λ_i. **8.** argument in Legendre's elliptic integrals. $E(k,\varphi) = \int_0^\varphi \Delta(\varphi)d\varphi$, $F(k,\varphi) = \int_0^\varphi d\varphi/\Delta(\varphi)$. **9.** the normal probability function of Laplace and Gauss in the form $\varphi(t) = \dfrac{1}{\sqrt{2\pi}}e^{\frac{-t^2}{2}}$. **10.** $\varphi_n(x)$, sometimes used for Bernoulli polynomial. See $B_n(x)$.

χ—Chi. (In statistical theory) χ^2 is a measure of goodness of fit, devised by Karl Pearson. $\chi^2 = \Sigma(f_i - Np_i)^2/(Np_i)$ for N items, with p_i the probability of appearances and f_i the frequency for items in an ith class.

ψ—Psi. To indicate: **1.** general functional symbol (usually with φ). **2.** angle from radius vector to tangent of plane curve. **3.** (with geocentric coordinates in mathematical astronomy), co-latitude. See φ.

Ω—Omega. To indicate: **1.** a certain annihilator in the theory of binary concomitants. **2.** (with subscript) transfinite ordinals of certain minimal type. **3.** (in geometry of the triangle) Ω,Ω', the Brocard points.

ω—Omega. To indicate: **1.** angular velocity. **2.** first transfinite ordinal, order-type of the aggregate of all natural numbers. **3.** imaginary cube root of unity, related to i, by $\omega = (-1 + i\sqrt{3})/2$. **4.** ω_1, ω_2, ω_3, half-periods of Weierstrassian $\wp$-function. **5.** (in geometry of the triangle) Brocard angle. $\cot \omega = \cot A + \cot B + \cot C$.

A—**1.** A vertex, and the associated angle of $\triangle ABC$. See α. **2.** A_{ij}, algebraic complement of a_{ij} in determinant, D. $A_{ij} = dD/da_{ij}$. **3.** (in astronomy) azimuth. **4.** (in astronomy) astronomical unit, mean geocentric distance to the sun. **5.** acres. **6.** area.

Å—ångstrom.

$\mathbf{V}_x$—For every x.

AM—arithmetic mean. See also superscript $^{-}$.

Ans.—answer.

AP—arithmetic progression.

Ax—axiom.

a—**1.** (in elementary algebra) initial term in arithmetic or geometric progression. **2.** (with subscript) coefficient in Fourier series, $(a_0/2) + \Sigma_{n=1}^{\infty}(a_n \cos nx + b_n \sin nx)$. **3.** (with two indices) element in matrix or determinant, as in $\begin{pmatrix} a_{11} & a_{12} & a_{13} \\ a_{21} & a_{22} & a_{23} \end{pmatrix}$ or $\begin{vmatrix} a_{11} & a_{12} \\ a_{21} & a_{22} \end{vmatrix}$. **4.** (in elementary geometry) apothegm. **5.** (in

MATHEMATICAL SYMBOLS AND ABBREVIATIONS (Continued)

geometry or triangle) first side-line, also length of first side of the triangle.
6. (in elementary analytic geometry) x-intercept.   **7.** (in elementary analytic geometry) semi-major axis of ellipse or semi-transverse axis of hyperbola, etc.   Thus latus rectum of central conic is $2p = 2b^2/a$, eccentricity $e = c/a$.   For central conics and quadrics the a is sometimes associated with x, as in $(x^2/a^2) + (y^2/b^2) = 1$, even when a may be less than b, or as in $-(x^2/a^2) + (y^2/b^2) = 1$, where a is the semi-conjugate axis.

abs—absolute value of.

acc—acceleration.

am—amplitude function. $\varphi = \operatorname{am} u$, where $u = F = \int_0^\varphi d\varphi/\Delta(\varphi)$.

amp—amplitude of vibration.

antilog—antilogarithm.

approx—approximate(ly).

arc (in "arc sin" etc.)—inverse.   Also written $\sin^{-1}$ etc.   Do not use "arc" for inverse of hyperbolic functions.   Write $\sinh^{-1}$, etc.

arg—argument.   Angle in polar coordinates $r \operatorname{cis} \theta$, and in complex number. $re^{i\theta}$ for r and θ real.   Better than "arc" and more legible than superscript -1 to indicate inverse hyperbolic functions, though "$\sinh^{-1} x$" is often used.

av—average.

B—**1.** (With subscripts) Bernoulli numbers and polynomials.   To indicate what usage among many is being followed in any given case, authors would do well to list the values of the first few Bernoulli numbers as for example, $B_1 = \frac{1}{2}$, $B_2 = \frac{1}{6}$, $B_3 = 0$, $B_4 = -\frac{1}{30}$, etc.   The Bernoulli polynomials, are defined as $B_n(x) = \Sigma_{r=0}^n \binom{n}{r} B_r x^{n-r}$, and satisfy $B_n(x + 1) - B_n(x) = nx^{n-1}$ with the choice of notation for Bernoulli numbers given above.   (Also designated by $\varphi_n(x)$.)   See page 613 for a second definition of Bernoulli numbers. **2.** bound (general symbol). $\bar{B}$, $\underline{B}$ designate least upper, and greatest lower bound respectively.   Preferred notations are "sup" and "inf" respectively. **3.** a vertex and the associated angle of $\triangle ABC$.   See β.   **4.** (in elementary solid geometry), area of base of a solid.

b—**1.** (in elementary geometry) length of base of plane figure. b, b', parallel bases of trapezoid.   **2.** (in elementary analytic geometry) y-intercept. **3.** (in elementary analytic geometry) semi-axis.   See a.   **4.** (in geometry of the triangle) second side-line, also length of second side of the triangle.

bei(z)—Thomson-Bessel   function, $\operatorname{bei}(z) = \dfrac{(\frac{1}{2}z)^2}{(2!)^2} - \dfrac{(\frac{1}{2}z)^6}{(6!)^2} + \dfrac{(\frac{1}{2}z)^{10}}{(10!)^2} - \cdots$

ber$(z) \pm i \operatorname{bei}(z) = J_0(zi\sqrt{\ } \pm i) = I_0(z\sqrt{\ } \pm i)$.

ber(z)—Thomson-Bessel function.   (See bei(z).) $\operatorname{ber}(z) = 1 - \dfrac{(\frac{1}{2}z)^4}{(4!)^2} + \dfrac{(\frac{1}{2}z)^8}{(8!)^2} -$ $\cdots$.

(B)-space—A Banach space.

B_m^s—An s-dimensional Betti group modulo m (m prime).

B_0^s—An s-dimensional Betti group relative to the group of integers.

C—**1.** arbitrary constant of integration.   **2.** (in elementary geometry) circumference of circle; also, circle.   **3.** general symbol for curve.   **4.** (with subscripts) combination, as in $C_{n,r}$ or $_nC_r$, the number of combinations of n things taken r at a time (without repetitions).   The form $_nC_r$ or even ^nC_r is

MATHEMATICAL SYMBOLS AND ABBREVIATIONS (Continued)

widely used but the notation $C_{n,r}$ or $C(n,r)$ or $\binom{n}{r}$ is to be preferred. **5.** Roman numeral for "hundred." **6.** Euler or Mascheroni constant. Also designated by γ. (See γ.) **7.** (chiefly as subscript) contour of integration. **8.** Centigrade, degree Centigrade, as $-52C$.

C_I—(in topology) class of spaces satisfying first axiom of countability, or property of satisfying first axiom of countability.

C_{II}—Same as above for second axiom of countability.

$\underline{C}$—(underlined) the set of complex numbers.

$\underset{\sim}{C}$—(wavy underline) indicates congruence of two n-square matrices.

Ci—cosine integral function, $Ci(x) = \int_{\infty}^{x} (\cos u/u)du$.

c—**1.** (in geometry of triangle) third side-line, also length of third side of triangle. **2.** (in elementary analytic geometry), z-intercept. **3.** (in elementary analytic geometry) semi-axis. (See a.)

cis—$\operatorname{cis} \theta = \cos \theta + i \sin \theta = e^{i\theta} = exp(i\theta)$. Used to distinguish polar coordinates $r \operatorname{cis} \theta$ from rectangular coordinates. Using Gaussian coordinates, $r \operatorname{cis} \theta = x + iy$. In de Moivres' formula $\operatorname{cis}^n \theta = \operatorname{cis} n\theta$.

cn—cosine amplitude function. (Jacobian elliptic function.)

colog—cologarithm, = log of reciprocal = negative of log (especially with base 10).

conj—(complex) conjugate (of). See superscript —.

cos—cosine = sine of the complementary angle.

$\cos^{-1}$—inverse cosine (of). Also written arc cos. $\theta = \cos^{-1} x$ means $\cos \theta = x$. Arc cos x (with capital A) indicates principal value, $0 < \theta < \pi$.

cosh—hyperbolic cosine (of). Do not write Cos nor $\mathfrak{Cof}$ (in German letters).

$\cosh^{-1}$—inverse hyperbolic cosine of. Also written as arg cosh.

covers—coversed sine or coversine.

csc—cosecant (of). Reciprocal of sine.

$\csc^{-1}$—inverse cosecant (of). Also written arc csc.

ctn also cot—cotangent (of). Reciprocal of tangent.

ctn^{-1}—inverse cotangent (of). Also written as $\cot^{-1}$, arc cot, or arc ctn.

ctnh—hyperbolic cotangent (of). Also written as coth.

ctnh^{-1}—inverse hyperbolic cotangent of. Also written as arg coth or arg ctnh.

cu—cubic. In arithmetic "cubic feet" is written "cu ft" but "ft³" is better.

cum—cumulative.

D—**1.** differential operator, as in $Dy = y'$, $d_x f(x,y) = \partial f/\partial x$. **2.** Roman numeral for "five hundred." **3.** general symbol for denominator, or for determinant. **4.** discriminant of binary form, or of polynomial. **5.** (in statistical theory), (with subscripts 0, 1, $\cdots$, 10), decile marks. **6.** $D(a_1, a_1, \cdots, a_n)$ sometimes designates the Vandermonde determinant.

$$\begin{vmatrix} 1a_1 & \cdots & a_1^{n-1} \\ \cdots & \cdots & \cdots \\ 1a_n & \cdots & a_n^{n-1} \end{vmatrix}$$

Def—definition.

Dem—demonstration, proof.

d—**1.** (in elementary algebra), common difference in arithmetic progression. **2.** differential operator, as in d^2y/dx^2. **3.** (in elementary geometry) diameter. **4.** (as superscript) days, as in $2^d3^h17^m$. **5.** (British currency) pence.

MATHEMATICAL SYMBOLS AND ABBREVIATIONS (Continued)

deg—degree, degrees. In navigation use 3 digits measured clockwise from north, so that 090 is due east. In trigonometry use cis θ to indicate direction measured counterclockwise from the positive x-axis, so that cis 90 is the direction of the positive y-axis.

det—determinant of, as in det (a_{ii}).

div—divergence of, also indicated by $\nabla \cdot$ (with nabla and dot).

dn—dn(z), a Jacobian elliptic function.

∃—(there) exists.

∃|—there exist uniquely.

E—**1.** E, F, G fundamental differential quantities of first order for surfaces. **2.** $E(k, \varphi)$, Legendre's normal elliptic integral, of the second kind, $E = E(k, \varphi)$ $\int_0^{\varphi} \Delta(\varphi) d\varphi$. **3.** east. **4.** (in Euler's polyhedral formula) number of edges of polyhedron. **5.** displacement operator, $E(f(x)) = f(x + 1)$. **6.** (in mathematical astronomy) equation of time.

Ei—exponential integral function $Ei(x) = \int_{-\infty}^{x} \frac{e^v dv}{v}$.

Eq—equation.

Ex—exercise.

e—**1.** base of natural (or Napierian) logarithms. In place of e^A one may write exp A. $e = 2.71828\ 18284\ 59045\ 23536 \cdots$ $\log_{10} e = M = 0.43429\ 44819$ $03251\ 82765 \cdots$ $\log_e 10 = 1/M = 2.30258\ 50929\ 94045\ 68402$. In some engineering work, where e is used otherwise, the base of natural logarithms is designated by ϵ. **2.** eccentricity of a conic. **3.** $e_1 = \wp(\omega_1)$, $e_2 = \wp(\omega_2)$, $e_3 = \wp(\omega_3)$, for Weierstrassian elliptic functions. **4.** (in mathematical astronomy) eccentricity of earth's orbit. **5.** (in elementary solid geometry) length of lateral edge (of right pyramid, prism, etc.).

eq—equivalent to.

erf—error function, $\text{erf}(x) = \dfrac{2}{\sqrt{\pi}} \int_0^x e^{-v^2} dv$.

erfc—complementary function to error function, $\text{erfc}(x) = 1 - \text{erf}(x) = \dfrac{2}{\sqrt{\pi}} \int_x^{\infty} e^{-v^2} dv$.

exp—exponential function of, as in $\exp(a^2 + b^2)$ for $e^{a^2+b^2}$. One could also write this "e^u where $u = a^2 + b^2$."

exsec—Exsecant

F—Force.

F—**1.** general symbol for function or functional. **2.** the second fundamental differential quantity of first order for surfaces. See E. **3.** (in Euler's polyhedral formula) number of faces of polyhedron. **4.** $F(k, \varphi)$, Legendre's normal elliptic integral of the first kind, $F = F(k, \varphi) \int_0^{\varphi} d\varphi / \Delta(\varphi)$. See Δ and E. φ is here the amplitude of F, $\varphi = \text{am } F$. **5.** $F(a, b; c : x)$, hypergeometric function. **6.** Fahrenheit, degree Fahrenheit, as in 70F. **7.** falsity (in logic).

FS—Fourier series.

Fig.—figure.

Fr—frontier set of.

f—**1.** general symbol for function or functional. **2.** f_i, frequency of X_i in

MATHEMATICAL SYMBOLS AND ABBREVIATIONS (Continued)

univariate table. **3.** frequency of vibration. **4.** feet as in f/s, feet per second. Preferable ft/sec.

ft—feet. See also f and $'$.

G—**1.** general symbol for group. **2.** the third fundamental differential quantity of first order for surfaces. **3.** $G(x_1, \cdots, x_n; \xi_1, \cdots, \xi_n)$ Green's function for two points in n-space. **4.** (constant) linear group of points on an algebraic curve. See g. **5.** gravitational constant.

G.C.T.—Greenwich civil time.

GCD—greatest common divisor.

GCS—greatest common subgroup.

GF—Galois field, as in $GF(p^n)$.

GM—geometric mean.

GP—geometric progression.

g—**1.** general function symbol, used with f. **2.** (terrestrial) gravitational attraction. **3.** (variable) linear group of points on an algebraic curve. See G. **4.** g_i, frequency of y_i in bivariate table. **5.** general coefficient in tensor, as in $g_{ij}^{k} x^i y^i z_k$.

gd—Gudermannian. $e^u = \tan\left(\dfrac{\pi}{4} + \dfrac{1}{2}\,\text{gd u}\right)$. If $\theta = \text{gd u}$ then

$$\begin{aligned}
\sin\theta &= \tanh u, & \cos\theta &= \operatorname{sech} u \\
\tan\theta &= \sinh u, & \cot\theta &= \operatorname{csch} u \\
\sec\theta &= \cosh u, & \csc\theta &= \coth u
\end{aligned}$$

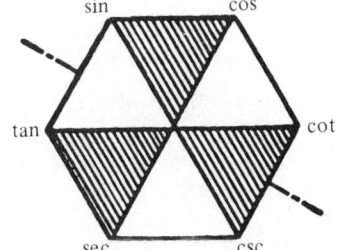

and corresponds to flipping the trigonometric hexagon on an axis perpendicular to cos-sec diagonal. Every vertex of the hexagon is the product of its adjacent vertices, (exhibiting 6 products, and 12 quotients, such as tan/sec = sin) opposite vertices are reciprocals, and in each shaded sector the Pythagorean identity holds. These identities also hold for hyperbolic functions except that Pythagorean sum is at right (so that $\tanh^2 + \operatorname{sech}^2 = 1$).

grad—gradient of. Also written ∇.

H—**1.** general symbol for subgroup, as in G/H, particularly for normal (or self-conjugate) subgroup. **2.** Hessian, as $H(f) = \det\dfrac{\partial^2 f}{\partial x_i \partial x_j}$. **3.** $H_n(x)$, nth Hermite polynomial, $H_n(x) = e^{x^2} D^n e^{-x^2}$. **4.** $H(P_1, P_3; P_2, P_4)$ is the proposition that P_1 and P_3 separate harmonically P_2 and P_4. **5.** orthocenter of triangle where altitudes meet. **6.** $H(q_1, \cdots, q_n, t, p_1, \cdots, p_n)$ Hamiltonian function (in mathematical physics). **7.** mean curvature of surface, $H = EG - F^2$. **8.** (in mathematical astronomy) hour-angle. Also designated by t. **9.** Hilbert space, also $\mathfrak{H}$.

$\mathfrak{H}$—Hilbert space.

HCF—highest common factor.

MATHEMATICAL SYMBOLS AND ABBREVIATIONS (Continued)

HM—harmonic mean.

HP—(in elementary algebra) harmonic progression.

Hyp.—hypothesis.

h—**1.** (in interpolation theory), distance, between uniformly spaced ordinates. **2.** class interval, in x. **3.** increment of x. Also Δx. **4.** (as superscript) hours as in $8^h 15^m$. **5.** (terminal) hyperbolic, as in $\sinh$, $\tanh^{-1}$, etc. **6.** altitude ("height").

hav—haversine (of). hav $x = (\text{vers } x)/2 = (1 - \cos x)/2$.

I—**1.** general symbol for interval, and for definite integral. **2.** Roman numeral for "one." Write IV not IIII, IX not VIIII. **3.** $I(\ )$, imaginary part of, also designated by $\Im(\ )$, or $\text{Im}(\ )$. **4.** $I_n(z)$, the Bessel function "of imaginary argument," $I_n(z) = \sum_{m=0}^{\infty} \dfrac{(\frac{1}{2})z^{n+2m}}{m!\Gamma(n+m+1)}$. **5.** (in geometry of triangle) in center where angle bisectors meet. **6.** sometimes used for the identity as an operation in a group.

$\Im$—(Black letter) imaginary part of. See I.

Im—imaginary part of. See I.

i—**1.** running index, as in a_i, $i = 1, \cdots, n$. **2.** one of the two imaginary square roots of -1. (In electrical engineering, when it is used for the current, j is used for this imaginary unit.)

i—i, j, k, unit vectors in a right-handed rectangular system. $i \times j = k$, $j \times k = i$, $k \times i = j$.

inf.—("infimum") greatest lower bound.

J—**1.** Jacobian as in $J\left(\dfrac{u,v,w}{x,y,z,}\right)$, also designated by $\partial(u,v,w)/\partial(x,y,z)$. **2.** $J_n(z)$, Bessel coefficient of order n. **3.** Jacobian curve. **4.** Jacobian group of points in a linear series of groups of points on an algebraic curve.

j—**1.** running index, with i. **2.** (sometimes in electrical engineering) $\sqrt{(-1)}$. *See i.*

j—a unit vector. See i.

K—**1.** specific curvature of surface. **2.** kernel of integral equation, as in $u(x) = f(x) + \lambda \int_a^b \bar{K}(x,t)u(t)dt$. K_n, the nth iterated kernel is then defined recursively by $K_1 \equiv K$, $K_n(x,y) = \int_a^b K_{n-1}(x,t)K(t,y)dt$. Also designated by $K^{(n)}$. **3.** K, iK', periods for Jacobian elliptic functions. **4.** Symmedian (Lemoine) center of triangle. **5.** $K_n(z)$, the Bessel function ("second solution") $\lim_{\nu \to n} \dfrac{(-1)^n}{2}\left[\dfrac{I_{-\nu}(z) - I_\nu(z)}{\nu - n}\right]$

k—**1.** proportionality factor for variation. Do not use $y \propto x$. **2.** running index, used with h. **3.** k,k', modulus and complementary modulus respectively of Jacobian elliptic functions. **4.** class interval, in y. **5.** increment in y. Also Δy.

k—a unit vector. Sèe i.

kei, ker—Bessel functions defined as real for real z and satisfying, $\text{ker}(z) + i\,\text{kei}(z) = K_0(z\sqrt{\pm i})$.

L—**1.** general symbol for linear function. **2.** general symbol for linear system, or linear space. **3.** limit, as in $L_{n \to \infty} e^{-n} = 0$. See "lim." **4.** Roman nu-

MATHEMATICAL SYMBOLS AND ABBREVIATIONS (Continued)

meral for "fifty." **5.** length. Also designated by l. **6.** first fundamental differential quantity of second order for surfaces. **7.** Lexis ratio, $\sigma/\sqrt{pq/s}$, for sets of s objects each. **8.** $L_n(x)$, nth Laguerre polynomial, $L_n(x)e^{-x}n! = D^n(e^{-x}x^n)$.

LCD—lowest common denominator.

LCM—lowest (or least) common multiple.

l—**1.** running index. **2.** (in elementary algebra) last term (of arithmetic or geometric progression). **3.** $l = \cos \alpha$, directional cosine, (with x-axis). **4.** length. Also designated by L.

lat.—latitude.

li—logarithmic integral or integral logarithm function, $li(x) = \int_0^x du\,/\log u$.

lim—limit ( ), $\overline{\lim}$, least upper limit, $\underline{\lim}$, greatest lower limit.

ln—(Sometimes) natural logarithm of.

log—logarithm (of). In theoretical work, the natural base, e, is understood; in numerical computation with tables, the base 10 is understood unless otherwise specified. Some writers use "ln" for natural logarithm of. Where ambiguity is otherwise likely, indicate the base, thus $\log_b x$, $\log_{10} x$, $\log_b x$.

long—longitude.

M—**1.** Roman numeral, thousand. **2.** arithmetic mean. Also designated by superscript bar, as X, or by AM. **3.** centroid (in geometry of triangle) where medians meet. **4.** second fundamental differential quantity of second order for surfaces.

M.D.—mean deviation.

Md—median.

Mm—mid-mean, arithmetic mean of data in range Q_1 to Q_3.

Mo—mode.

m—**1.** general symbol for natural number, or integer, usually used with n. **2.** slope of line, dy/dx. **3.** $m = \cos \beta$, directional cosine (with y-axis). **4.** m_a, m_b, m_c, median lines, lengths of medians of triangle. **5.** (as subscript) meridian measurement. **6.** class of an algebraic plane curve (a Plücker number). **7.** (superscript) minutes, as in $10^d13^h5^m$. **8.** meters.

max—maximum (of).

meas—measure (of).

mi—miles.

min—**1.** minimum (of). **2.** minutes. **3.** mi. n. = nautical miles (at equator each minute of longitude corresponds to one nautical mile).

mod—**1.** modulus (of), as in $\mod(re^{i\theta}) = r$. **2.** modulo as in $7 \equiv -3 (\mod 5)$.

N—**1.** third fundamental differential quantity of second order for surfaces. **2.** north. **3.** total frequency in a statistical distribution.

n—**1.** general symbol for natural number or integer. **2.** $n = \cos \gamma$, directional cosine (with z-axis). **3.** order or degree of plane algebraic curve (a Plücker number). **4.** (in elementary algebra) number of terms in finite progression. **5.** (sometimes) total frequency. See N. **6.** outward normal to surface, as in $\cos (\theta, n)$.

O—**1.** origin of coordinates. **2.** circumcenter of triangle where the perpendicular bisectors of the sides meet. **3.** of comparable order with, as $\sum_{n=0}^N n = O(N)^2$.

o—of inferior order to, as $\log n = o(n)$.

MATHEMATICAL SYMBOLS AND ABBREVIATIONS (Continued)

ord—order.

P—**1.** general symbol for polynomial, in particular the interpolational polynomial. **2.** product moment. Also expressed by p. **3.** general symbol for point. The common notation indicating the coordinate system used as $P(x,y,z)$, $P(r,\theta,\varphi)$, etc., is not recommended. **4.** general probability distribution function, in particular any one of Pearson's standard types, or Poisson's forms. **5.** $P_n(x)$, Legendre polynomial, $2^n n! P_n(x) = D^n(x^2 - 1)^n$. **6.** total force due to pressure. **7.** function, as in $P dx + Q dy$, and in $y' + P(x)y = Q(x)$. **8.** $P_{n,r}$ or $_nP_r$, or $P(n,r)$, number of permutations of n distinct things taken r at a time (without repetitions), $n!/(n - r)!$. **9.** general potential due to finite number of particles. In Newtonian case $P = \Sigma_i m_i / r_i$. See U and W. **10.** horizontal parallax. **11.** north celestial pole.

PE—probable error. See $\pm$.

$P(E)$—Probability of E.

$P(E \wedge F)$—Probability of both E and F.

$P(E \backslash F)$—Probability of E, given F.

$P(E \veebar F)$—Probability of E or F, but not both.

$P(E \vee F)$—Probability of E or F or both.

Post.—postulate.

Prob.—**1.** problem. **2.** probability.

Prop.—proposition.

PS—power series.

Pt.—point.

$\wp$—Weierstrassian elliptic function.

p—**1.** general symbol for prime number. **2.** semi-latus rectum. **3.** probability ratio. **4.** genus (or deficiency) of a plane algebraic curve (a Plücker number). **5.** perpendicular distance from origin to given line or plane.
6. p_n, numerator of nth convergent of continued fraction $a_0 + \dfrac{1}{a_1 +} \dfrac{1}{a_2 +}$
$\cdots$ $(p_{-1} = 0,\ p_0 = 1)$, $p_1 = a_0$, $p_{n+1} = a_n p_n + p_{n-1}$. **7.** p_{12}, p_{13}, p_{14}, p_{23}, p_{24}, p_{34}, line coordinates (point system). **8.** sometimes "per," as in "*rpm*," revolutions per minute. This use is not recommended. **9.** perimeter. Use s for semiperimeter. **10.** $p(n)$, total number of partitions of n. **11.** p_i, impulse component. **12.** the genus of an orientable surface.

p—page. pp—pages.

pos.—positive.

Q—**1.** general symbol for quadratic form or quadratic manifold. **2.** Q_1, Q_3 first and third quartile marks. (Q_2 is the median, Md.) **3.** function, as in $P dx + Q dy$, and in $y' + P(x)y = Q(x)$. **4.** $Q(P_1, P_2, P_3; P_4, P_5, P_6)$, quadrangular set of six points.

Q—(underlined) the set of rational numbers.

Q^+—(underlined) the set of positive rational numbers.

QD—quartile deviation.

Q.E.D.—("Quod erat demonstrandum") which was to be proved.

Q.E.F.—("Quod erat faciendum") which was to be constructed.

q—**1.** complementary probability. $q = 1 - p$. **2.** q_n, denominator of nth convergent of continued fraction, $a_0 + \dfrac{1}{a_1 +} \dfrac{1}{a_2 +} \cdots$ $(q_0 = 0)$, $q_1 = 1$, $q_{n+1} = a_n q_n + q_{n-1}$. **3.** q_{12}, q_{13}, q_{14}, q_{23}, q_{24}, q_{34}, line coordinates (plane sys-

MATHEMATICAL SYMBOLS AND ABBREVIATIONS (Continued)

tem). **4.** q_1, q_2, quartile distances from the median. **5.** q_i, force component. **6.** the number of cross-caps on a non-orientable surface.

R—**1.** general symbol for remainder. $R_n(x)$, remainder after n terms in power-series in x. **2.** radius, in particular circumradius of triangle. **3.** real part of. Also indicated by **IR** (Black letter), and Re. **4.** general symbol for range of variable, as in $\int_{(R)}$.

R—(underlined) the set of real numbers.

R^+—(underlined) the set of positive real numbers.

$\Re$ —(Black letter) real value of. See R.

R. A.—right ascension. Also designated by α.

R_m^s—An s-dimensional Betti number modulo m (m prime).

R_0^s—An s-dimensional Betti number relative to the group of integers.

Re—real value of. See R.

RMS—root-mean-square. $\sqrt{(\Sigma_{i=1}^n x^2/n)}$.

r—**1.** general running index, as in rth term. **2.** radius (see R), in particular in radius of triangle. **3.** coefficient of linear correlation, correlation coefficient. **4.** (in elementary algebra) common ratio between successive terms in a geometric progression. **5.** distance, in polar and in spherical coordinates; projected distances in cylindrical coordinates. **6.** (sometimes) revolutions, as in $r.p.m.$ (revolutions per minute). **7.** (sometimes) (superscript) radians, as in $2\pi^{(r)}$. (This usage is not recommended.) **8.** the number of boundary curves on a surface.

rad—**1.** radius. **2.** radians. Where no units are indicated angles are measured in radians, sin 30 means "sine of 30 radians," not sin 30°. Do not write sin a^r or sin $a^{(r)}$ for sin a (where a is measured in radians), since superscript r is sometimes interpreted as "revolutions."

rot—rotation or curl of vector. Also designated by $\nabla \times$ (nabla and cross).

S—**1.** general symbol for space, as S_n, space of n dimension. See L. **2.** general symbol for sum, as in S_n, sum of first n terms of given sequence or series. See s. **3.** south. **4.** standard error of estimate. **5.** radius of spherical curvature of curve. **6.** a set (any collection of distinguishable objects).

∂S—Boundary of a set S.

Si—1st sine-integral function $\mathrm{Si}(x) = \int_0^x (\sin u/u)du$. See si.

S.T.—sidereal time.

s.—**1.** general running index. Used with r. **2.** general symbol for sum, as in s_n sum of first n terms of sequence or series. See S. **3.** (in elementary algebra), sum of arithmetic or of geometric progression. **4.** $s_k(n)$, sum of kth powers of first n natural numbers. **5.** s_k, sum of the kth powers of the roots of an algebraic equation. **6.** arc length. **7.** slant height. **8.** (usually as superscript) seconds. **9.** semi-interquartile range. **10.** semi-perimeter of triangle, $s = (a + b + c)/2$. **11.** (sometimes) number of individuals in sample. **12.** root-mean-square deviation about arbitrarily assumed origin, (in "short method").

sec—secant (of). Reciprocal of cosine.

$\sec^{-1}$—inverse secant (of). Also designated by arc sec.

sech—hyperbolic secant (of). Do not use Sec or $\mathfrak{Sec}$ (in German letters).

sech^{-1}—inverse hyperbolic secant of. Also written as arg sech.

MATHEMATICAL SYMBOLS AND ABBREVIATIONS (Continued)

si—2nd sine-integral function, $\beta_i(x) = \int_{\infty}^{x} (\sin u/u)du$.   See Si.

sgn—(signum) sign (of), more generally for z complex, sgn $z = z/|z|$.

Use $\sigma_1 = \begin{pmatrix} + & + \\ - & - \end{pmatrix}$ for the signum of the sine (in the corresponding quadrant).

Use $\sigma_2 = \begin{pmatrix} - & + \\ - & + \end{pmatrix}$ for the signum of the cosine.

and $\sigma_3 = \begin{pmatrix} - & + \\ + & - \end{pmatrix}$ for the signum of the tangent.

Thus $d(\text{arc sin } x)/dx = \sigma_2/\sqrt{1 - x^2}$;
$\qquad d(\text{arc cos } x)/dx = -\sigma_1/\sqrt{1 - x^2}$
and $\sigma_1/\sigma_2 = \sigma_1\sigma_2 = \sigma_3$.

sin—sine (of).   Do not use Sin.   In general triangle sin $A = a/d$ where d is circumdiameter.   Identity $d = a/\sin A = b/\sin B = c/\sin C$ is the "law of sines."

sin⁻¹—inverse sine (of).   Also designated arc sin.

sinh—hyperbolic sine (of).

sinh⁻¹—inverse hyperbolic sine of—also written as arg sinh.

sk—skewness of frequency distribution.

sn—(Jacobian elliptic function), sine amplitude.

sq—square.

sup—(supremum) least upper bound.   Sometimes designated by L.U.B., or l.u.b.

T—**1.** total time, (as in time of flight of projectile).   **2.** clock time.   **3.** general symbol for transformation, T^n, nth iterate of T.   **4.** tons.   **5.** (in logic), true or truth.   **6.** absolute temperature.

Th—theorem.

t—**1.** general variable or parameter.   **2.** time.   (In navigation) use 4 digits 0230 for 2:30 a.m., and 1430 for 2:30 p.m.   See τ.   See "dot accent."   **3.** ordinary temperature.   See T, τ, θ.

tan—tangent (of).

tan⁻¹—inverse tangent (of).   Also designated by arc tan.

tanh—hyperbolic tangent (of).   Do not use Tan or 𝔗an (in German letters).

tanh⁻¹—inverse hyperbolic tangent (of).   Do not use arc tanh.   Also written as arg tanh.

T_0-space—A topological space such that for distinct x and y there is either a neighborhood of x not containing y or a neighborhood of y not containing x.

T_1-space—A topological space such that for distinct x and y there is a neighborhood of x not containing y.

T_2-space—A Hausdorff topological space.

T_3-space—A T_2-space which is regular.

T_4-space—A T_2-space which is normal.

U-general (line surface or volume) potential.   In Newtonian case, $U = \int_{(L)} \frac{\mu dL}{r}$, or $\int_{(S)} \frac{\mu dS}{r}$, or $\int_{(V)} \frac{\mu dV}{r}$.   See P and W.

u—**1.** general variable, especially dependent variable or real part thereof. See w.   **2.** u_n, Lucas' function $u_n = (\alpha^n - \beta^n)/(\alpha - \beta)$, α, β, roots of given quadratic.

V—**1.** Roman numeral, five.   **2.** (in Euler's polyhedral formula) number of

MATHEMATICAL SYMBOLS AND ABBREVIATIONS (Continued)

vertices. **3.** general harmonic function. **4.** volume. **5.** coefficient of variation.

v—(linear) velocity.

v—**1.** general variable, especial dependent variable, used with u, or coefficient of pure imaginary part thereof. See w. **2.** v_n, Lucas' function $\alpha^n + \beta^n$, α, β, roots of given quadratic. See u_n. **3.** speed.

vers—versed sine or versine.

W—**1.** west. **2.** general potential of double layer. In Newtonian case,

$$W = \int_{(S)} v \frac{\partial}{\partial n}\left(\frac{1}{r}\right) dS, = -\int_{(S)} \frac{v}{r^2} \cos (r,n) \, dS. \text{ See } P \text{ and } U. \quad \textbf{3. } \text{Wron-}$$

skian,

$$W = \begin{vmatrix} y_1 \ y_1' & \cdots & y_1^{(n-1)} \\ \cdots & \cdots & \cdots \\ y_n \ y_n' & \cdots & y_n^{(n-1)} \end{vmatrix}.$$

4. total weight. Also designated by Wt. **5.** work (or energy). Also designated by Wk.

Wt.—weight. See W.

w—**1.** general symbol for variable, particularly dependent variable. Used with u and v as in $J\left(\dfrac{u,v,w}{x,y,z}\right)$, etc. **2.** dependent complex variable, $w = u + iv$, or $w(z) = u(x,y) + iv(x,y)$ where $z = x + iy$, x,y,u,v, real.

X—**1.** Roman numeral, ten; as in XCIII, etc. **2.** X_i, original numerical data for x-variates, (previous to change of origin or scale). **3.** general symbol for variable point, particularly on x-axis. **4.** function, as in $X dx + Y dy + Z dz$ or $\dfrac{dx}{X} = \dfrac{dy}{Y} = \dfrac{dz}{Z}$.

x—**1.** general symbol for independent variable or unknown. **2.** first rectangular coordinate. In space a right-handed coordinate system such as indicated by

is recommended. The former with OZ directed to the zenith is more common. **3.** real part of independent complex variable $z = x + iy$.

Y—**1.** Y_i, original numerical data for y-variates (previous to change of origin or scale). **2.** function as in $X dx + Y dy + Z dz$, or $\dfrac{dx}{X} = \dfrac{dy}{Y} = \dfrac{dz}{Z}$.

y—**1.** general symbol for dependent (real) variable. **2.** general symbol for second independent variable, r unknown. **3.** second rectangular coordinate. See x. **4.** pure imaginary coefficient, in independent complex variable, $z = x + iy$.

Z—zenith.

$\underline{Z}$—(underlined) the set of integers.

$\underline{Z}^+$—(underlined) the set of positive integers.

Z.T.—zone time.

z—**1.** independent complex variable, $z = x + iy$. **2.** general symbol for third independent variable or unknown. **3.** third rectangular coordinate. See x. **4.** axial coordinate in cylindrical coordinates (r, θ, z). **5.** zenith distance, $(90^\circ - h)$. **6.** Fisher's z statistic.

MATHEMATICAL SYMBOLS AND ABBREVIATIONS (Continued)

Selected Symbols Used in Financial and Actuarial Theory

α—net premium in first policy year.

β—net premium in each policy year after the first.

δ—force of interest (and of discount) $e^\delta = 1 + i$.

ω—terminal recorded age in mortality table, "limiting" age.

A_x—commutation symbol, present value of net single premium for whole life policy on (x), $= M_x/D_x$.

$a_{\overline{n}|i}$—present value of annuity for unit periodic payment, $= (1 - v^n)/i$.

$a_{\overline{n}|i}^{(p)}$—present value of an annuity of 1 per annum at interest rate i, payable p times a year (in installments of $1/p$ each).

a_x—commutation symbol, present value of (ordinary) whole life annuity on (x) of unit annual payment.

$a_x^{(m)}$—present value of whole life annuity on (x), of unit annual payment, payable m times a year.

$n|a_x$—present value of whole life annuity, on (x), deferred n years for unit annual payment.

$a_{x\overline{n}|}$—present value of temporary life annuity, on (x), for n years, for unit annual payment.

$a_{\infty i}$—present value of perpetuity at rate of interest, i.

$a_{\infty i}$—present value of perpetuity due at rate of interest, i.

a_x—commutation symbol present value of whole life annuity due, on (x), of unit annual payment.

$a_{\overline{n}|i}$—present value of an annuity due, for unit periodic payments at interest rate i.

B—book value.

B_k—book value, after k years.

C—**1.** original cost. **2.** capitalized cost.

C_x—commutation symbol, $= v^{x+1}d_x$.

c_x—natural premium at age x, $= C_x/D_x$.

D—total simple discount.

D_b—total bank discount.

D_c—cash discount, where for example, "terms 4/10, 2/30, n/90" designates 4% discount for payment within 10 days, 2% thereafter but within 30 days, payable net in 90 days.

D_t—trade discount.

D_x—commutation symbol, $= v^x l_x$.

d—rate of simple discount, $= 1 - v = (1 + i)^{-1} = i/(1 + i)$.

d_x—number dying between ages x and $x + 1$, according to mortality table (for 100,000 alive at age 10).

E—present value of expectation.

$_nE_x$—present value of an n-year pure endowment to (x), $= v^n l_{x+n}/l_x$.

e_x—curtate expectation of life for (x), $= (l_x + \cdots + l_\omega)/l_x$.

$\overset{o}{e}_x$—complete expectation of life, for (x), $= e_x + \frac{1}{2}$.

F—**1.** net-cost-rate factor. **2.** face value of bond.

I—total interest (ordinary simple).

I'—total interest (exact, simple).

i—rate of interest (effective).

MATHEMATICAL SYMBOLS AND ABBREVIATIONS (Continued)

$j_{(p)}$—nominal rate of interest convertible p times a year corresponding to effective annual rate i, $= p[(1 + i)^{1/p} - 1]$.

k_x—valuation symbol, $= C_x/D_{x+1}$.

$_nk_x$—valuation symbol, $= (M_x - M_{x+n})/D_{x+n}$, $[_1k_x = k_x]$, accumulated cost of insurance.

L—**1.** list price (for trade discount).   **2.** salvage value.

l_x—number living at age x according to mortality table.

N_x—("open bar N"), commutation symbol, $= D_x + D_{x+1} + \cdots + D\omega$.

n—number of conversion periods (for compound interest).

P—principal.

P_b—bank proceeds.

P_x—net annual premium for ordinary whole life policy, on (x), for unit annual payment $= A_x/(1 + a_x)$.

$_rP_x$—net annual premium for r-payment life policy, $= M_x/(\mathsf{N}_x - \mathsf{N}_{x+r})$.

p—**1.** probability of success.   **2.** interest period/payment interval.

p_x—probability of living for another year for a person of age x (according to mortality table).

$_np_x$—probability that a person aged x will live n years, $= l_{x+n}/l_x$.

p_{xy}—the probability that (x) and (y) will survive jointly for one year.

$_np_{xy}$—the probability that (x) and (y) will survive jointly for n years.

q—probability of failure, $= 1 - p$.

q_x—probability of dying within a year for a person of age x (according to mortality table).

$|_nq_x$—probability that (x) will die within n years.

$_n|q_x$—the probability that (x) will die between ages $x + n$ and $x + n + 1$.

R—**1.** periodic payment or "rent."   **2.** replacement cost.   **3.** repair charge (annual).

S—amount.

S—**1.** scrap value.   **2.** amount of sinking fund.   **3.** subscription price. **4.** amount (at simple interest).

s—amount (at compound interest) for unit principal $= (1 + i)^n$.

$s_{\overline{n}|i}$—amount of annuity for unit periodic payment, $= [(1 + i)^n - 1]/i$.

$s_{\infty i}$—amount of perpetuity at interest rate i.

s_∞—amount of perpetuity due.

$s_{\overline{n}|i}$—amount of an annuity due, for unit periodic payments.

$s_{\overline{n}|i}^{(p)}$—amount at end of n years of annuity of 1 per annum at interest rate i, payable p times a year (in installments of $1/p$ each).

u_x—valuation symbol, $= D_x/D_{x+1}$.

$_nu_x$—valuation symbol, $(\mathsf{N}_x - \mathsf{N}_{x+n})/D_{x+n}$, $[_1u_x = u_x]$, accumulated value of individual survivors payments.

V—purchase price (of bond).

$_tV_x$—terminal reserve of tth policy year on policy on (x) of unit annual payment.

v—present value (at compound interest) for unit principal, $= (1 + i)^{-1}$.

W—wearing value, $=$ original cost minus scrap value.

x—age of insured (to nearest year).

(x)—a person aged x (for use with mortality table).

$x]$—where $[x] + t$ indicates a life, now aged $x + t$, who was accepted for insurance t years ago at age x.

INDEX

A

B

C

D

E

F

G

H

I

J

K

L

M

N

O

P

Q

R

S

T

U

V

W

XYZ